ENCYCLOPEDIA OF
BUDDHISM

EDITORIAL BOARD

ENCYCLOPEDIA OF BUDDHISM

Volume One

A-L

Robert E. Buswell, Jr., Editor in Chief

MACMILLAN
REFERENCE
USA™

THOMSON
GALE™

New York • Detroit • San Diego • San Francisco • Cleveland • New Haven, Conn. • Waterville, Maine • London • Munich

THOMSON
GALE

Encyclopedia of Buddhism

Robert E. Buswell, Jr., Editor in Chief

For more information, contact
Macmillan Reference USA
300 Park Avenue South, 9th Floor
New York, NY 10010
Or you can visit our Internet site at
http://www.gale.com

The publisher wishes to thank the Vergleichende Sprachwissenschaft (Institute of Comparative Linguistics) of the University of Frankfurt, and particularly Dr. Jost Gippert, for their kind permission to use the TITUS Cyberbit font in preparing the manuscript for the *Encyclopedia of Buddhism.* This font was specially developed by the institute for use by scholars working on materials in Asian languages and enables the accurate transliteration with diacriticals of texts from those languages. Further information may be found at http://titus.fkidg1.uni-frankfurt.de.

LIBRARY OF CONGRESS CATALOGING-IN-PUBLICATION DATA

Encyclopedia of Buddhism / edited by Robert E. Buswell, Jr.
p. cm.
Includes bibliographical references and index.
ISBN 0-02-865718-7(set hardcover : alk. paper) — ISBN 0-02-865719-5 (Volume 1) — ISBN 0-02-865720-9 (Volume 2)
1. Buddhism—Encyclopedias. I. Buswell, Robert E.
BQ128.E62 2003
294.3'03—dc21

2003009965

This title is also available as an e-book.
ISBN 0-02-865910-4 (set)
Contact your Gale sales representative for ordering information.

Printed in the United States of America
10 9 8 7 6 5 4

CONTENTS

EDITORIAL AND PRODUCTION STAFF

Linda S. Hubbard
Editorial Director

Judith Culligan, Anjanelle Klisz, Oona Schmid, and Drew Silver
Project Editors

Shawn Beall, Mark Mikula, Kate Millson, and Ken Wachsberger
Editorial Support

Judith Culligan
Copy Editor

Amy Unterburger
Proofreader

Lys Ann Shore
Indexer

Barbara Yarrow
Manager, Imaging and Multimedia Content

Robyn Young
Project Manager, Imaging and Multimedia Content

Lezlie Light
Imaging Coordinator

Tracey Rowens
Product Design Manager

Jennifer Wahi
Art Director

GGS, Inc.
Typesetter

Mary Beth Trimper
Manager, Composition

Evi Seoud
Assistant Manager, Composition

Wendy Blurton
Manufacturing Specialist

MACMILLAN REFERENCE USA

Frank Menchaca
Vice President

Hélène Potter
Director, New Product Development

PREFACE

Buddhism is one of the three major world religions, along with Christianity and Islam, and has a history that is several centuries longer than either of its counterparts. Starting in India some twenty-five hundred years ago, Buddhist monks and nuns almost immediately from the inception of the dispensation began to "to wander forth for the welfare and weal of the many, out of compassion for the world," commencing one of the greatest missionary movements in world religious history. Over the next millennium, Buddhism spread from India throughout the Asian continent, from the shores of the Caspian Sea in the west, to the Inner Asian steppes in the north, the Japanese isles in the east, and the Indonesian archipelago in the south. In the modern era, Buddhism has even begun to build a significant presence in the Americas and Europe among both immigrant and local populations, transforming it into a religion with truly global reach. Buddhist terms such as karma, nirvāṇa, saṃsāra, and kōan have entered common parlance and Buddhist ideas have begun to seep deeply into both Western thought and popular culture.

The *Encyclopedia of Buddhism* is one of the first major reference tools to appear in any Western language that seeks to document the range and depth of the Buddhist tradition in its many manifestations. In addition to feature entries on the history and impact of Buddhism in different cultural regions and national traditions, the work also covers major doctrines, texts, people, and schools of the religion, as well as practical aspects of Buddhist meditation, liturgy, and lay training. Although the target audience is the nonspecialist reader, even serious students of the tradition should find much of benefit in the more than four hundred entries.

Even with over 500,000 words at our disposal, the editorial board realized early on that we had nowhere nearly enough space to do justice to the full panoply of Buddhist thought, practice, and culture within each major Asian tradition. In order to accommodate as broad a range of research as possible, we decided at the beginning of the project to abandon our attempt at a comprehensive survey of major topics in each principal Asian tradition and instead build our coverage around broader thematic entries that would cut across cultural boundaries. Thus, rather than separate entries on the Huichang persecution of Buddhism in China or the Chosŏn suppression in Korea, for example, we have instead a single thematic entry on persecutions; we follow a similar approach with such entries as conversion, festivals and calendrical rituals, millenarianism and millenarian movements, languages, and stūpas. We make no pretense to comprehensiveness in every one of these entries; when there are only a handful of entries in the *Encyclopedia* longer than four thousand words, this would have been a pipe dream, at best. Instead, we encouraged our contributors to examine their topics comparatively, presenting representative case studies on the topic, with examples drawn from two or more traditions of Buddhism.

The *Encyclopedia* also aspires to represent the emphasis in the contemporary field of Buddhist studies on the broader cultural, social, institutional, and political contexts of Buddhist thought and practice. There are substantial entries on topics as diverse as economics, education, the family, law, literature, kingship, and politics, to name but a few, all of which trace the role Buddhism has played as one of Asia's most important cultural influences. Buddhist folk religion, in particular, receives among the most extensive coverage of any topic in the encyclopedia. Many entries also explore the continuing relevance of Buddhism in contemporary life in Asia and, indeed, throughout the world.

Moreover, we have sought to cross the intellectual divide that separates texts and images by offering extensive coverage of Buddhist art history and material culture. Although we had no intention of creating an encyclopedia of Buddhist art, we felt it was important to offer our readers some insight into the major artistic traditions of Buddhism. We also include brief entries on a couple of representative sites in each tradition; space did not allow us even to make a pretense of being comprehensive, so we focused on places or images that a student might be most likely to come across in reading about a specific tradition. We have also sought to provide some coverage of Buddhist material culture in such entries as amulets and talismans, medicine, monastic architecture, printing technologies, ritual objects, and robes and clothing.

One of the major goals of the *Encyclopedia* is to better integrate Buddhist studies into research on religion and culture more broadly. When the editorial board was planning the entries, we sought to provide readers with Buddhist viewpoints on such defining issues in religious studies as conversion, evil, hermeneutics, pilgrimage, ritual, sacred space, and worship. We also explore Buddhist perspectives on topics of great currency in the contemporary humanities, such as the body, colonialism, gender, modernity, nationalism, and so on. These entries are intended to help ensure that Buddhist perspectives become mainstreamed in Western humanistic research.

We obviously could not hope to cover the entirety of Buddhism in a two-volume reference. The editorial board selected a few representative monks, texts, and sites for each of the major cultural traditions of the religion, but there are inevitably many desultory lacunae. Much of the specific coverage of people, texts, places, and practices is embedded in the larger survey pieces on Buddhism in India, China, Tibet, and so forth, as well as in relevant thematic articles, and those entries should be the first place a reader looks for information. We also use a comprehensive set of internal cross-references, which are typeset as small caps, to help guide the reader to other relevant entries in the *Encyclopedia.* Listings for monks proved unexpectedly complicated. Monks, especially in East Asia, often have a variety of different names by which they are known to the tradition (ordained name, toponym, cognomen, style, honorific, funerary name, etc.) and Chinese monks, for example, may often be better known in Western literature by the Japanese pronunciation of their names. As a general, but by no means inviolate, rule, we refer to monks by the language of their national origin and their name at ordination. So the entry on the Chinese Chan (Zen) monk often known in Western writings as Rinzai, using the Japanese pronunciation of his Chinese toponym Linji, will be listed here by his ordained name of Yixuan. Some widely known alternate names will be given as blind entries, but please consult the index if someone is difficult to locate. We also follow the transliteration systems most widely employed today for rendering Asian languages: for example, pinyin for Chinese, Wylie for Tibetan, Revised Hepburn for Japanese, McCune-Reischauer for Korean.

For the many buddhas, bodhisattvas, and divinities known to the Buddhist tradition, the reader once again should first consult the major thematic entry on buddhas, etc., for a survey of important figures within each category. We will also have a few independent entries for some, but by no means all, of the most important individual figures. We will typically refer to a buddha like Amitābha, who is known across traditions, according to the Buddhist lingua franca of Sanskrit, not by the Chinese pronunciation Amito or Japanese Amida; similarly, we have a brief entry on the bodhisattva Maitreya, which we use instead of the Korean Mirŭk or Japanese Miroku.

For pan-Buddhist terms common to most Buddhist traditions, we again use the Sanskrit as a lingua franca: thus, dhyāna (trance state), duḥkha (suffering), skandha (aggregate), and śūnyatā (emptiness). But again, many terms are treated primarily in relevant thematic entries, such as samādhi in the entry on meditation. Buddhist terminology that appears in *Webster's Third International Dictionary* we regard as English and leave unitalicized: this includes such technical terms as dhāraṇī, kōan, and tathāgatagarbha. For a convenient listing of a hundred such terms, see Roger Jackson, "Terms of Sanskrit and Pali Origin Acceptable as English Words," *Journal of the International Association of Buddhist Studies* 5 (1982), pp. 141–142.

Buddhist texts are typically cited by their language of provenance, so the reader will find texts of Indian provenance listed via their Sanskrit titles (e.g., *Sukhāvatīvyūha-sūtra, Saṃdhinirmocana-sūtra*), indigenous Chinese sūtras by their Chinese titles (e.g., *Fanwang jing, Renwang jing*), and so forth. Certain scriptures that have widely recognized English titles are however listed under that title, as with *Awakening of Faith, Lotus Sūtra, Nirvāṇa Sūtra,* and *Tibetan Book of the Dead.*

Major Buddhist schools, similarly, are listed according to the language of their origin. In East Asia, for example, different pronunciations of the same Sinitic logograph obscure the fact that Chan, Sŏn, Zen, and Thiền are transliterations of respectively the Chinese, Korean, Japanese, and Vietnamese pronunciations for the school we generally know in the West as Zen. We have therefore given our contributors the daunting task of cutting across national boundaries and treating in single, comprehensive entries such pan-Asian traditions as Madhyamaka, Tantra, and Yogācāra, or such pan-East Asian schools as Huayan, Tiantai, and Chan. These entries are among the most complex in the encyclopedia, since they must not only touch upon the major highlights of different national traditions, but also lay out in broad swathe an overarching account of a school's distinctive approach and contribution to Buddhist thought and practice.

Compiling an *Encyclopedia of Buddhism* may seem a quixotic quest, given the past track records of similar Western-language projects. I was fortunate to have had the help of an outstanding editorial board, which was determined to ensure that this encyclopedia would stand as a definitive reference tool on Buddhism for the next generation—and that it would be finished in our lifetimes. Don Lopez and John Strong both brought their own substantial expertise with editing multi-author references to the project, which proved immensely valuable in planning this encyclopedia and keeping the project moving along according to schedule. My UCLA colleague William Bodiford surveyed Japanese-language Buddhist encyclopedias for the board and constantly pushed us to consider how we could convey in our entries the ways in which Buddhist beliefs were lived out in practice. The board benefited immensely in the initial planning stages from the guidance art historian Maribeth Graybill offered in trying to conceive how to provide a significant place in our coverage for Buddhist art. Eugene Wang did yeoman's service in stepping in later as our art-history specialist on the board. Words cannot do justice to the gratitude I feel for the trenchant advice, ready good humor, and consistently hard work offered by all the board members.

I also benefited immensely from the generous assistance, advice, and support of the faculty, staff, and graduate students affiliated with UCLA's Center for Buddhist Studies, which has spearheaded this project since its inception. I am especially grateful to my faculty colleagues in Buddhist Studies at UCLA, whose presence here gave me both the courage even to consider undertaking such a daunting task and the manpower to finish it: Gregory Schopen, William Bodiford, Jonathan Silk, Robert Brown, and Don McCallum.

The *Encyclopedia* was fortunate to have behind it the support of the capable staff at Macmillan. Publisher Elly Dickason and our first editor Judy Culligan helped guide the editorial board through our initial framing of the encyclopedia and structuring of the entries; we were fortunate to have Judy return as our copyeditor later in the project. Oona Schmid, who joined the project just as we were finalizing our list of entries and sending out invitations to contributors, was an absolutely superlative editor, cheerleader, and colleague. Her implacable enthusiasm for the project was infectious and helped keep both the board and our contributors moving forward even during the most difficult stages of the project. Our next publisher, Hélène Potter, was a stabilizing force during the most severe moments of impermanence. Our last editor, Drew Silver, joined us later in the project, but his assistance was indispensable in taking care of the myriad details involved in bringing the project to completion. Jan Klisz was absolutely superb at moving the volumes through production. All of us on the board looked askance when Macmillan assured us at our first editorial meeting that we would finish this project in three years, but the professionalism of its staff made it happen.

Finally, I would like to express my deepest thanks to the more than 250 colleagues around the world who willingly gave of their time, energy, and knowledge in order to bring the *Encyclopedia of Buddhism* to fruition. I am certain that current and future generations of students will benefit from our contributors' insightful treatments of various aspects of the Buddhist religious tradition. As important as encyclopedia articles are for building a field, they inevitably take a back seat to one's "real" research and writing, and rarely receive the recognition they deserve for tenure or promotion. At very least, our many contributors can be sure that they have accrued much merit—at least in my eyes—through their selfless acts of disseminating the dharma.

ROBERT E. BUSWELL, JR.

List of Articles

Laos
Justin McDaniel

Law and Buddhism
Rebecca French

Lineage
Albert Welter

Local Divinities and Buddhism
Fabio Rambelli

Logic
John Dunne

Longmen
Dorothy Wong

Lotus Sūtra (Saddharmapuṇḍarīka-sūtra)
Jacqueline I. Stone

Madhyamaka School
Karen Lang

Ma gcig lab sgron (Machig Lapdön)
Andrew Quintman

Mahābodhi Temple
Leela Aditi Wood

Mahākāśyapa
Max Deeg

Mahāmaudgalyāyana
Susanne Mrozik

Mahāmudrā
Andrew Quintman

Mahāparinirvāṇa-sūtra
John S. Strong

Mahāprajāpatī Gautamī
Karma Lekshe Tsomo

Mahāsāṃghika School
Paul Harrison

Mahāsiddha
Andrew Quintman

Mahāvastu
John S. Strong

Mahāyāna
Gregory Schopen

Mahāyāna Precepts in Japan
Paul Groner

Mahīśāsaka
Collett Cox

Mainstream Buddhist Schools
Collett Cox

Maitreya
Alan Sponberg

Maṇḍala
Denise Patry Leidy

Mantra
Richard D. McBride II

Māra
Jacob N. Kinnard

Mar pa (Marpa)
Andrew Quintman

Martial Arts
William Powell

Mātṛceṭa
Peter Khoroche

Medicine
Kenneth G. Zysk

Meditation
Luis O. Gómez

Meiji Buddhist Reform
Richard M. Jaffe

Merit and Merit-Making
George J. Tanabe, Jr.

Mijiao (Esoteric) School
Henrik H. Sørensen

Mi la ras pa (Milarepa)
Andrew Quintman

Milindapañha
Peter Masefield

Millenarianism and Millenarian Movements
Thomas DuBois

Mindfulness
Johannes Bronkhorst

Miracles
John Kieschnick

Mizuko Kuyō
George J. Tanabe, Jr.

Modernity and Buddhism
Gustavo Benavides

Mohe Zhiguan
Brook Ziporyn

Monastic Architecture
Nancy Shatzman Steinhardt

Monasticism
Jeffrey Samuels

Monastic Militias
William M. Bodiford

Mongolia
Patricia Berger

Monks
John Kieschnick

Mozhao Chan (Silent Illumination Chan)
Morten Schlütter

Mudrā and Visual Imagery
Denise Patry Leidy

Mūlasarvāstivāda-vinaya
Gregory Schopen

Murakami Senshō
Richard M. Jaffe

Myanmar
Patrick A. Pranke

Myanmar, Buddhist Art in
Paul Strachan

Nāgārjuna
Paul Williams

Nara Buddhism
George J. Tanabe, Jr.

Nāropa
Andrew Quintman

Nationalism and Buddhism
Pori Park

Nenbutsu (Chinese, Nianfo; Korean, Yŏmbul)
James C. Dobbins

Nepal
Todd T. Lewis

Newari, Buddhist Literature in
Todd T. Lewis

Nichiren
Jacqueline I. Stone

Nichiren School
Jacqueline I. Stone

Nine Mountains School of Sŏn
Sungtaek Cho

Nirvāṇa
Luis O. Gómez

Nirvāṇa Sūtra
Mark L. Blum

Nuns
Karma Lekshe Tsomo

Sautrāntika
Collett Cox

Scripture
José Ignacio Cabezón

Self-Immolation
James A. Benn

Sengzhao
Tanya Storch

Sentient Beings
Daniel A. Getz

Sexuality
Hank Glassman

Shingon Buddhism, Japan
Ryūichi Abé

Shinran
James C. Dobbins

Shintō (Honji Suijaku) and Buddhism
Fabio Rambelli

Shōbōgenzō
Carl Bielefeldt

Shōtoku, Prince (Taishi)
William M. Bodiford

Shugendō
Paul L. Swanson

Shwedagon
Paul Strachan

Śikṣānanda
Chi-chiang Huang

Silk Road
Jason Neelis

Sinhala, Buddhist Literature in
Ranjini Obeyesekere

Skandha (Aggregate)
Mathieu Boisvert

Slavery
Jonathan A. Silk

Sōka Gakkai
Jacqueline I. Stone

Sŏkkuram
Junghee Lee

Soteriology
Dan Cozort

Southeast Asia, Buddhist Art in
Robert L. Brown

Space, Sacred
Allan G. Grapard

Sri Lanka
John Clifford Holt

Sri Lanka, Buddhist Art in
Benille Priyanka

Stūpa
A. L. Dallapiccola

Sukhāvatīvyūha-sūtra
Mark L. Blum

Sukhothai
Pattaratorn Chirapravati

Śūnyatā (Emptiness)
Roger R. Jackson

Sūtra
John S. Strong

Sūtra Illustrations
Willa Jane Tanabe

Suvarṇaprabhāsottama-sūtra
Natalie D. Gummer

Suzuki, D. T.
Richard M. Jaffe

Syncretic Sects: Three Teachings
Philip Clart

Tachikawaryū
Nobumi Iyanaga

Taiwan
Charles B. Jones

Taixu
Ding-hwa Hsieh

Takuan Sōhō
William M. Bodiford

Tantra
Ronald M. Davidson
Charles D. Orzech

Tathāgata
John S. Strong

Tathāgatagarbha
William H. Grosnick

Temple System in Japan
Duncan Williams

Thai, Buddhist Literature in
Grant A. Olson

Thailand
Donald K. Swearer

Theravāda
Kate Crosby

Theravāda Art and Architecture
Bonnie Brereton

Thich Nhat Hanh
Christopher S. Queen

Tiantai School
Brook Ziporyn

Tibet
Ronald M. Davidson

Tibetan Book of the Dead
Bryan J. Cuevas

Tominaga Nakamoto
Paul B. Watt

Tsong kha pa
Georges B. J. Dreyfus

Ŭich'ŏn
Chi-chiang Huang

Ŭisang
Patrick R. Uhlmann

United States
Thomas A. Tweed

Upagupta
John S. Strong

Upāli
Susanne Mrozik

Upāya
Roger R. Jackson

Usury
Jamie Hubbard

Vajrayāna
Ronald M. Davidson

Vaṃsa
Stephen C. Berkwitz

Vasubandhu
Dan Lusthaus

Vidyādhara
Patrick A. Pranke

Vietnam
Cuong Tu Nguyen

Vietnamese, Buddhist Influences on Literature in
Cuong Tu Nguyen

Vijñānavāda
Dan Lusthaus

List of Contributors

Ryūichi Abé
Columbia University
Kūkai
Shingon Buddhism, Japan

Juhn Ahn
University of Michigan
Zen, Popular Conceptions of

Carol S. Anderson
Kalamazoo College
Anitya (Impermanence)
Duḥkha (Suffering)
Four Noble Truths

Urs App
University Media Research, Kyoto, Japan
Yixuan

A. W. Barber
University of Calgary
Ingen Ryūki
Pure Land Schools

Martin Baumann
University of Lucerne, Switzerland
Europe

Heinz Bechert
University of Göttingen
Buddha, Life of the

Gustavo Benavides
Villanova University
Economics
Modernity and Buddhism

James A. Benn
Arizona State University
Diet
Self-Immolation

Patricia Berger
University of California, Berkeley
Mongolia

Stephen C. Berkwitz
Southwest Missouri State University
Vaṃsa

Carl Bielefeldt
Stanford University
Dōgen
Japan
Shōbōgenzō

Mark L. Blum
State University of New York, Albany
Daosheng
Death
Gyōnen
Huiyuan
Nirvāṇa Sūtra
Sukhāvatīvyūha-sūtra

William M. Bodiford
University of California, Los Angeles
Anuttarasamyaksaṃbodhi (Complete, Perfect Awakening)
Ganjin
Ippen Chishin
Konjaku monogatari
Monastic Militias
Shōtoku, Prince (Taishi)
Takuan Sōhō

Cynthea J. Bogel
University of Washington
Esoteric Art, East Asia

Mathieu Boisvert
University of Quebec at Montreal
Pratītyasamutpāda (Dependent Origination)
Skandha (Aggregate)

Stephen R. Bokenkamp
Indiana University
Daoism and Buddhism

George D. Bond
Northwestern University
Anagārika Dharmapāla
Arhat
Buddhavacana (Word of the Buddha)

Daniel Boucher
Cornell University
Dharmarakṣa
Paramārtha

Bonnie Brereton
University of Michigan
Theravāda Art and Architecture

Karen L. Brock
Albuquerque, New Mexico
Daitokuji
Hōryūji and Tōdaiji
Japan, Buddhist Art in
Phoenix Hall (at the Byōdōin)
Portraiture

Johannes Bronkhorst
University of Lausanne, Switzerland
Hinduism and Buddhism
Karma (Action)
Mindfulness

Jeffrey Broughton
California State University, Long Beach
Bodhidharma
Fazang
Zongmi

Robert L. Brown
University of California, Los Angeles
Los Angeles County Museum of Art
Buddha Images
Indonesia and the Malay Peninsula
Southeast Asia, Buddhist Art in

Robert E. Buswell, Jr.
University of California, Los Angeles
Doubt
Icchantika

José Ignacio Cabezón
University of California, Santa Barbara
Prayer
Scripture

Jason A. Carbine
University of Chicago
Burmese, Buddhist Literature in

David W. Chappell
Soka University of America
Repentance and Confession

Pattaratorn Chirapravati
California State University, Sacramento
Ayutthaya
Sukhothai

Eunsu Cho
University of Michigan
Fanwang jing (Brahmā's Net Sūtra)
Wŏnch'ŭk
Wŏnhyo

Sungtaek Cho
Korea University
Hyujŏng
Nine Mountains School of Sŏn
Yujŏng

William Chu
University of California, Los Angeles
Deqing
Path
Yinshun
Zhuhong

Bongkil Chung
Florida International University
Wŏnbulgyo

Philip Clart
University of Missouri–Columbia
Folk Religion, China
Syncretic Sects: Three Teachings

Richard S. Cohen
University of California, San Diego
India

Alan Cole
Lewis and Clark College
Family, Buddhism and the

Collett Cox
University of Washington
Abhidharma
Abhidharmakośabhāṣya
Dharmaguptaka
Mahīśāsaka
Mainstream Buddhist Schools
Sarvāstivāda and Mūlasarvāstivāda
Sautrāntika

Dan Cozort
Dickinson College
Soteriology

Kate Crosby
University of London, United Kingdom
Persecutions
Theravāda

Bryan J. Cuevas
Florida State University
Intermediate States
Rebirth
Saṃsāra
Tibetan Book of the Dead

A. L. Dallapiccola
University of Edinburgh, United Kingdom
Stūpa

Jacob P. Dalton
International Dunhuang Project, British Library
Bsam yas (Samye)
Bsam yas Debate
Ḍākinī
Klong chen pa (Longchenpa)
Padmasambhava
Rnying ma (Nyingma)

Ronald M. Davidson
Fairfield University
Initiation
Sa skya Paṇḍita (Sakya Paṇḍita)
Tantra
Tibet
Vajrayāna

Max Deeg
University of Vienna, Austria
Devadatta
Mahākāśyapa

Mahinda Deegalle
Bath Spa University College, United Kingdom
Education

Karen Derris
Harvard University
Dhyāna (Trance State)

James C. Dobbins
Oberlin College
Exoteric-Esoteric (Kenmitsu) Buddhism in Japan
Genshin
Hōnen
Kamakura Buddhism, Japan
Nenbutsu (Chinese, Nianfo; Korean, Yŏmbul)
Rennyo
Shinran

Georges B. J. Dreyfus
Williams College
Dge lugs (Geluk)
Tsong kha pa

Thomas DuBois
National University of Singapore
Millenarianism and Millenarian Movements

Paul Dundas
University of Edinburgh, United Kingdom
Jainism and Buddhism

John Dunne
University of Wisconsin, Madison
Dharmakīrti
Dignāga
Logic

Johan Elverskog
Southern Methodist University
Islam and Buddhism

Sarah Fremerman
Stanford University
Ikkyū

Rebecca French
State University of New York, Buffalo
Law and Buddhism

David L. Gardiner
Colorado College
Ennin
Saichō

Alexander Gardner
University of Michigan
Lama
Oṃ maṇi padme hūṃ

Suzanne Gay
Oberlin College
Provincial Temple System (Kokubunji, Rishōtō)

Rupert Gethin
University of Bristol, United Kingdom
Cosmology
Heavens
Realms of Existence

Daniel A. Getz
Bradley University
Precepts
Pure Land Buddhism
Sentient Beings

Robert M. Gimello
Harvard University
Bodhi (Awakening)
Satori (Awakening)

Hank Glassman
Haverford College
Sexuality

Roger Goepper
Cologne Museum, Germany
Alchi
Himalayas, Buddhist Art in

Luis O. Gómez
University of Michigan
Amitābha
Bodhicitta (Thought of Awakening)
Desire
Faith
Meditation
Nirvāṇa
Psychology
Pure Lands

Allan G. Grapard
University of California, Santa Barbara
Dōkyō
Space, Sacred

Paul Groner
University of Virginia
Mahāyāna Precepts in Japan

William H. Grosnick
La Salle University
Tathāgatagarbha

Natalie D. Gummer
Beloit College
Suvarṇaprabhāsottama-sūtra
Women

Anne Hansen
University of Wisconsin, Milwaukee
Cambodia
Khmer, Buddhist Literature in

Helen Hardacre
Harvard University
Laity

Paul Harrison
University of Canterbury, New Zealand
An Shigao
Buddhānusmṛti (Recollection of the Buddha)
Canon
Mahāsāṃghika School
Pratyutpannasamādhi-sūtra

Jens-Uwe Hartmann
University of Munich, Germany
Āgama/Nikāya
Languages

Richard P. Hayes
University of New Mexico
Language, Buddhist Philosophy of

Maria Heim
California State University, Long Beach
Dāna (Giving)
Evil

Steven Heine
Florida International University
Oxherding Pictures

James W. Heisig
Nanzan Institute for Religion and Culture, Nanzan University, Japan
Christianity and Buddhism

John Clifford Holt
Bowdoin College
Refuges
Sri Lanka

Ding-hwa Hsieh
Truman State University
Awakening of Faith (Dasheng qixin lun)
Taixu
Zonggao

Chi-chiang Huang
Hobart and William Smith Colleges
Dharmadhātu
Śikṣānanda
Ŭich'ŏn

Jamie Hubbard
Smith College
Critical Buddhism (Hihan Bukkyō)
Sanjie Jiao (Three Stages School)
Usury

Nobumi Iyanaga
Tokyo, Japan
Tachikawaryū

Roger R. Jackson
Carleton College
Candrakīrti
Karuṇā (Compassion)
Prajñā (Wisdom)
Śūnyatā (Emptiness)
Upāya

Richard M. Jaffe
Duke University
Clerical Marriage in Japan
Inoue Enryō
Meiji Buddhist Reform
Murakami Senshō
Suzuki, D. T.

Charles B. Jones
The Catholic University of America
Taiwan

John Jorgensen
Griffith University, Australia
Chan School
Hakuin Ekaku

Leslie S. Kawamura
University of Calgary
Bodhisattva(s)
Pāramitā (Perfection)

Hee-Sung Keel
Sogang University, South Korea
Korea

John P. Keenan
Middlebury College
Asaṅga

Richard K. Kent
Franklin and Marshall College
Arhat Images

George A. Keyworth
University of Colorado
Confucianism and Buddhism
Juefan (Huihong)
Poetry and Buddhism

Peter Khoroche
Cambridge, United Kingdom
Āryaśūra
Aśvaghoṣa
Jātakamālā
Mātṛceṭa

John Kieschnick
Institute of History and Philology, Academia Sinica, Taiwan
Biographies of Eminent Monks (Gaoseng zhuan)
Daoxuan
Miracles
Monks

Jongmyung Kim
Youngsan University, South Korea
Chogye School
Korean, Buddhist Influences on Vernacular Literature in

Richard King
Liverpool Hope University College, United Kingdom
Colonialism and Buddhism

Jacob N. Kinnard
College of William and Mary
Divinities
Indra
Māra
Viṣṇu
Worship
Yakṣa

Ria Kloppenborg
Utrecht University, Netherlands
Pratyekabuddha

Karil J. Kucera
St. Olaf College
Bāmiyān
Hells, Images of

Charles Lachman
University of Oregon
Bodhisattva Images
Chan Art

François Lagirarde
Ecole Française d'Extrême-Orient, Bangkok, Thailand
Gavāṃpati

Lewis Lancaster
University of California, Berkeley
Prajñāpāramitā Literature

Karen Lang
University of Virginia
Āryadeva
Madhyamaka School

Junghee Lee
Portland State University
Sŏkkuram

Denise Patry Leidy
Metropolitan Museum of Art, New York
Cave Sanctuaries
Maṇḍala
Mudrā and Visual Imagery

Todd T. Lewis
College of the Holy Cross
Nepal
Newari, Buddhist Literature in

Dan Lusthaus
University of Missouri–Columbia
Faxiang School
Vasubandhu
Vijñānavāda
Yogācāra School

Victor H. Mair
University of Pennsylvania
Bianwen
Bianxiang (Transformation Tableaux)
Chinese, Buddhist Influences on Vernacular Literature in
Entertainment and Performance

John J. Makransky
Boston College
Buddhahood and Buddha Bodies

Eleanor Mannikka
Indiana University of Pennsylvania
Bayon

John C. Maraldo
University of North Florida
History

Peter Masefield
University of Sydney, Australia
Ghosts and Spirits
Milindapañha

Gail Maxwell
Los Angeles County Museum of Art
Buddha, Life of the, in Art
Esoteric Art, South and Southeast Asia
India, Buddhist Art in

Alexander L. Mayer
University of Illinois at Urbana-Champaign
Commentarial Literature
Dreams
Faxian
Xuanzang
Yijing

Richard D. McBride II
The University of Iowa
Dhāraṇī
Mantra
Printing Technologies
Samguk yusa (Memorabilia of the Three Kingdoms)

Justin McDaniel
Harvard University
Laos
Paritta and Rakṣā Texts

John R. McRae
Indiana University
Heart Sūtra
Huineng
Kumārajīva
Ordination
Platform Sūtra of the Sixth Patriarch (Liuzu tan jing)

John N. Miksic
National University of Singapore
Borobudur
Indonesia, Buddhist Art in

Pankaj N. Mohan
University of Sydney, Australia
Kingship

Anne E. Monius
Harvard University
India, South

Robert E. Morrell
Washington University in St. Louis
Japanese, Buddhist Influences on Vernacular Literature in

Anne Nishimura Morse
Museum of Fine Arts, Boston
Ritual Objects

Susanne Mrozik
Western Michigan University
Mahāmaudgalyāyana
Śāriputra
Upāli

A. Charles Muller
Toyo Gakuen University, Japan
Hyesim
Kihwa
Renwang jing (Humane Kings Sūtra)

Jan Nattier
Indiana University
Akṣobhya
Buddha(s)
Central Asia
Conversion
Decline of the Dharma
Dīpaṃkara
Vipaśyin

Jason Neelis
University of Washington
India, Northwest
Silk Road

John Newman
New College of Florida
Kālacakra

Cuong Tu Nguyen
George Mason University
Vietnam
Vietnamese, Buddhist Influences on Literature in

Ranjini Obeyesekere
Princeton University
Sinhala, Buddhist Literature in

Reiko Ohnuma
Dartmouth College
Gender
Jātaka
Viśvantara

Patrick Olivelle
University of Texas at Austin
Hair

Grant A. Olson
Northern Illinois University
Thai, Buddhist Literature in

Charles D. Orzech
University of North Carolina, Greensboro
Tantra

Youngsook Pak
University of London, United Kingdom
Korea, Buddhist Art in

Jin Y. Park
American University
Communism and Buddhism

Pori Park
Arizona State University
Han Yongun
Nationalism and Buddhism

Sung Bae Park
State University of New York at Stony Brook
Chinul

Bhikkhu Pasadika
Philipps University, Marburg, Germany
Ānanda
Rāhula

Richard K. Payne
Institute of Buddhist Studies, Graduate Theological Union, Berkeley, California
Ritual

Linda Penkower
University of Pittsburgh
Zhanran

Mario Poceski
University of Florida
Chengguan
China
Daoyi (Mazu)
Huayan jing
Huayan School

William Powell
University of California, Santa Barbara
Martial Arts

John Powers
Australian National University, Australia
Hermeneutics
Laṅkāvatāra-sūtra
Saṃdhinirmocana-sūtra

Patrick A. Pranke
University of Michigan
Abhijñā (Higher Knowledges)
Myanmar
Satipaṭṭhāna-sutta
Vidyādhara
Vipassanā (Sanskrit, Vipaśyanā)

Charles S. Prebish
The Pennsylvania State University
Councils, Buddhist

Leonard C. D. C. Priestley
University of Toronto
Pudgalavāda

Benille Priyanka
University of California, Los Angeles
Sri Lanka, Buddhist Art in

Christopher S. Queen
Harvard University
Ambedkar, B. R.
Buddhadāsa
Engaged Buddhism
Thich Nhat Hanh

Andrew Quintman
University of Michigan
Bka' brgyud (Kagyu)
Jo khang
Kailāśa (Kailash)
Karma pa
Ma gcig lab sgron (Machig Lapdön)
Mahāmudrā
Mahāsiddha
Mar pa (Marpa)
Mi la ras pa (Milarepa)
Nāropa
Potala

Fabio Rambelli
Sapporo University, Japan
Hachiman
Honji Suijaku
Local Divinities and Buddhism
Shintō (Honji Suijaku) and Buddhism

Ian Reader
Lancaster University, United Kingdom
Folk Religion, Japan

Barbara E. Reed
St. Olaf College
Ethics

Eric Reinders
Emory University
Etiquette
Politics and Buddhism

Marylin Martin Rhie
Smith College
China, Buddhist Art in

Michael R. Rhum
Chicago, Illinois
Amulets and Talismans
Folk Religion, Southeast Asia

David E. Riggs
University of California, Los Angeles
Ryōkan

Brian O. Ruppert
University of Illinois at Urbana-Champaign
Japanese Royal Family and Buddhism

Jewels
Relics And Relics Cults

Richard Salomon
University of Washington
Gāndhārī, Buddhist Literature in

Jeffrey Samuels
Western Kentucky University
Monasticism

K. T. S. Sarao
Chung-Hwa Institute of Buddhist Studies, Taiwan
Anātman/Ātman (No-Self/Self)

Morten Schlütter
Yale University
Kōan
Mozhao Chan (Silent Illumination Chan)

Juliane Schober
Arizona State University
Biography

Gregory Schopen
University of California, Los Angeles
Diamond Sūtra
Mahāyāna
Mūlasarvāstivāda-vinaya
Vinaya

Jonathan A. Silk
University of California, Los Angeles
Buddhist Studies
Slavery

Andrew Skilton
Cardiff University, United Kingdom
Disciples of the Buddha
Sanskrit, Buddhist Literature in
Vimalakīrti

Henrik H. Sørensen
Seminar for Buddhist Studies, Copenhagen, Denmark
Huayan Art
Kyŏnghŏ
Mijiao (Esoteric) School

Gareth Sparham
University of Michigan
Atisha
Bu ston (Bu tön)
Dalai Lama
Panchen Lama
Saṅgha

Alan Sponberg
University of Montana
Kuiji
Maitreya

Cyrus Stearns
Clinton, Washington
Sa skya (Sakya)

Nancy Shatzman Steinhardt
University of Pennsylvania
Monastic Architecture

Jacqueline I. Stone
Princeton University
Daimoku
Lotus Sūtra (Saddharmapuṇḍarīka-sūtra)
Nichiren
Nichiren School
Original Enlightenment (Hongaku)
Sōka Gakkai

Tanya Storch
University of the Pacific
Dao'an
Sengzhao
Zhao lun

Paul Strachan
Gerona, Spain
Ananda Temple
Myanmar, Buddhist Art in
Shwedagon

John S. Strong
Bates College
Ālayavijñāna
Aśoka
Buddhacarita
Buddhaghosa
Hīnayāna
Lalitavistara
Mahāparinirvāṇa-sūtra
Mahāvastu
Sūtra
Tathāgata
Upagupta

Paul L. Swanson
Nanzan Institute for Religion and Culture, Nanzan University, Japan
Shugendō

Donald K. Swearer
Swarthmore College
Consecration
Thailand

George J. Tanabe, Jr.
University of Hawaii
Abortion
Chanting and Liturgy
Kōben
Merit and Merit-Making
Mizuko Kuyō
Nara Buddhism

Willa Jane Tanabe
University of Hawaii
Robes and Clothing
Sūtra Illustrations

Joel Tatelman
Social Sciences and Humanities Research Council of Canada
Anāthapiṇḍada
Avadāna
Avadānaśataka
Divyāvadāna

Stephen F. Teiser
Princeton University
Folk Religion: An Overview
Ghost Festival
Hells

Thanissaro Bhikkhu (Geoffrey DeGraff)
Metta Forest Monastery, Valley Center, California
Wilderness Monks

Kyoko Tokuno
University of Washington
Apocrypha
Catalogues of Scriptures

Kevin Trainor
University of Vermont
Pilgrimage

Karma Lekshe Tsomo
University of San Diego
Mahāprajāpatī Gautamī
Nuns
Prātimokṣa

Thomas A. Tweed
University of North Carolina
United States

Patrick R. Uhlmann
University of California, Los Angeles
Ŭisang

Oskar von Hinüber
University of Freiburg, Germany
Dhammapada
Pāli, Buddhist Literature in

Mariko Namba Walter
Harvard University
Ancestors

Jonathan S. Walters
Whitman College
Festivals and Calendrical Rituals

Eugene Y. Wang
Harvard University
Pure Land Art

Paul B. Watt
DePauw University
Jiun Onkō
Tominaga Nakamoto

Christian K. Wedemeyer
University of Copenhagen, Denmark
Bon

Albert Welter
University of Winnipeg
Lineage
Yanshou
Zanning

Roderick Whitfield
University of London, United Kingdom
Central Asia, Buddhist Art in
Dunhuang
Famensi
Reliquary

Charles Willemen
Academy of Sciences, Belgium
Dharma and Dharmas

Duncan Williams
University of California, Irvine
Parish (Danka, Terauke) System in Japan
Temple System in Japan

Paul Williams
University of Bristol, United Kingdom
Bhāvaviveka
Bodhicaryāvatāra
Nāgārjuna
Śāntideva

Liz Wilson
Miami University of Ohio
Ascetic Practices
Body, Perspectives on the

Dorothy Wong
University of Virginia
Longmen
Yun'gang

Leela Aditi Wood
University of Michigan
Ajaṇṭā
Bodh Gayā
Jātaka, Illustrations of
Mahabodhi Temple
Sāñcī

Dale S. Wright
Occidental College
Philosophy

Nobuyoshi Yamabe
Kyushu Ryukoku Junior College, Japan
Consciousness, Theories of

Michael Zimmermann
University of Hamburg, Germany
War

Brook Ziporyn
Northwestern University
Mohe Zhiguan
Tiantai School
Zhili
Zhiyi

Kenneth G. Zysk
University of Copenhagen, Denmark
Medicine

Synoptic Outline of Entries

This outline provides a general overview of the conceptual structure of the *Encyclopedia of Buddhism*. The outline is organized under twenty-four major categories, a few of which are subcategorized. The entries are listed alphabetically within each category or subcategory. For ease of reference, one entry may be listed under several categories.

Art History

Ajaṇṭā
Arhat Images
Bāmiyān
Bayon
Bianxiang (Transformation Tableaux)
Bodh Gayā
Bodhisattva Images
Borobudur
Buddha Images
Buddha, Life of the, in Art
Cave Sanctuaries
Central Asia, Buddhist Art in
Chan Art
China, Buddhist Art in
Daitokuji
Dunhuang
Esoteric Art, East Asia
Esoteric Art, South and Southeast Asia
Famensi
Hells, Images of
Himalayas, Buddhist Art in
Hōryūji and Tōdaiji
Huayan Art
India, Buddhist Art in
Indonesia, Buddhist Art in
Japan, Buddhist Art in
Jātaka, Illustrations of
Jewels
Jo khang
Kailāśa (Kailash)
Korea, Buddhist Art in
Longmen
Mahābodhi Temple
Maṇḍala
Monastic Architecture
Mudrā and Visual Imagery
Myanmar, Buddhist Art in
Oxherding Pictures
Phoenix Hall (at the Byōdōin)
Portraiture
Potala
Pure Land Art
Reliquary
Sāñcī
Shwedagon
Sŏkkuram
Southeast Asia, Buddhist Art in
Sri Lanka, Buddhist Art in
Stūpa
Sūtra Illustrations
Theravāda Art and Architecture
Yun'gang

Biographies

Ambedkar, B. R.
Anagārika Dharmapāla
Ānanda
Anāthapiṇḍada
An Shigao
Arhat
Āryadeva
Āryaśūra
Asaṅga
Aśoka
Aśvaghoṣa
Atisha
Bhāvaviveka
Biographies of Eminent Monks (Gaoseng zhuan)
Biography
Bodhidharma
Buddhadāsa
Buddhaghosa
Buddha, Life of the
Bu ston (Bu tön)
Candrakīrti
Chengguan
Chinul
Dalai Lama
Dao'an
Daosheng
Daoxuan
Daoyi (Mazu)
Deqing
Devadatta
Dharmakīrti
Dharmarakṣa
Dignāga
Disciples of the Buddha
Dōgen
Dōkyō
Ennin
Faxian
Fazang
Ganjin
Gavāṃpati
Genshin
Gyōnen
Hakuin Ekaku
Han Yongun
Hōnen
Huineng
Huiyuan
Hyesim
Hyujŏng
Ikkyū
Ingen Ryūki
Inoue Enryō
Ippen Chishin
Jiun Onkō

Japan, Buddhist Art in
Japanese, Buddhist Influences on Vernacular Literature in
Japanese Royal Family and Buddhism
Jiun Onkō
Kamakura Buddhism, Japan
Kōan
Kōben
Konjaku Monogatari
Kūkai
Laity
Local Divinities and Buddhism
Lotus Sūtra (Saddharmapuṇḍarīka-sūtra)
Mahāyāna Precepts in Japan
Meiji Buddhist Reform
Mizuko Kuyō
Murakami Senshō
Nara Buddhism
Nichiren
Nichiren School
Original Enlightenment (Hongaku)
Parish (Danka, Terauke) System in Japan
Phoenix Hall (at the Byōdōin)
Provincial Temple System (Kokubunji, Rishōtō)
Pure Land Buddhism
Pure Land Schools
Rennyo
Ryōkan
Saichō
Satori (Awakening)
Shingon Buddhism, Japan
Shinran
Shintō (Honji Suijaku) and Buddhism
Shōbōgenzō
Shōtoku, Prince (Taishi)
Shugendō
Sōka Gakkai
Suzuki, D. T.
Tachikawaryū
Takuan Sōhō
Tantra
Tiantai School
Tominaga Nakamoto
Vajrayāna
Zen, Popular Conceptions of

Korea

Chan Art
Chan School
Chinul
Chogye School
Confucianism and Buddhism
Esoteric Art, East Asia
Han Yongun
Huayan Art
Huayan School
Hyesim
Hyujŏng
Kihwa
Kōan
Korea
Korea, Buddhist Art in
Korean, Buddhist Influences on Vernacular Literature in
Kyŏnghŏ
Nine Mountains School of Sŏn
Samguk Yusa (Memorabilia of the Three Kingdoms)
Sŏkkuram
Tiantai School
Ŭich'ŏn
Ŭisang
Wŏnbulgyo
Wŏnch'ŭk
Wŏnhyo
Yujŏng

Southeast Asia

Amulets and Talismans
Ananda Temple
Ancestors
Ayutthaya
Bayon
Borobudur
Buddhadāsa
Burmese, Buddhist Literature in
Cambodia
Communism and Buddhism
Esoteric Art, South and Southeast Asia
Folk Religion, Southeast Asia
Hinduism and Buddhism
Indonesia and the Malay peninsula
Islam and Buddhism
Khmer, Buddhist Literature in
Laos
Local Divinities and Buddhism
Myanmar
Myanmar, Buddhist Art in
Pāli, Buddhist Literature in
Paritta and Rakṣā Texts
Shwedagon
Southeast Asia, Buddhist Art in
Sukhothai
Thai, Buddhist Literature in
Thailand
Theravāda
Theravāda Art and Architecture
Thich Nhat Hanh
Upagupta
Vietnam
Vietnamese, Buddhist Influences on Literature in

Sri Lanka

Anagārika Dharmapāla
Buddhaghosa
Esoteric Art, South and Southeast Asia
Hinduism and Buddhism
Pāli, Buddhist Literature in
Paritta and Rakṣā Texts
Sinhala, Buddhist Literature in
Sri Lanka
Sri Lanka, Buddhist Art in
Theravāda
Theravāda Art and Architecture
Vaṃsa

Tibet and Mongolia

Atisha
Bka' brgyud (Kagyu)
Bon
Bsam yas (Samye)
Bsam yas Debate
Bu ston (Bu tön)
Communism and Buddhism
Ḍākinī
Dalai Lama
Dge lugs (Geluk)
Engaged Buddhism
Islam and Buddhism
Jo khang
Kailāśa (Kailash)
Karma pa
Klong chen pa (Longchenpa)
Lama
Ma gcig lab sgron (Machig Labdrön)
Mahāmudrā
Mahāsiddha
Maṇḍala
Mar pa (Marpa)
Mi la ras pa (Milarepa)
Mongolia
Nāropa
Oṃ Maṇi Padme Hūṃ
Padmasambhava
Panchen Lama
Potala
Rnying ma (Nyingma)
Sa skya (Sakya)
Sa skya Paṇḍita (Sakya Paṇḍita)
Tantra
Tibet
Tibetan Book of the Dead
Tsong kha pa
Vajrayāna
Vidyādhara

Disciples of the Buddha

Ānanda
Anāthapiṇḍada
Arhat
Disciples of the Buddha
Gavāṃpati
Mahākāśyapa
Mahāmaudgalyāyana
Mahāprajāpatī Gautamī
Ordination
Rāhula
Saṅgha
Śāriputra
Upagupta
Upāli

Divinities, Ghosts, and Spirits

Ancestors
Ḍākinī
Death
Divinities
Ghost Festival
Ghosts and Spirits
Hachiman
Heavens
Hells
Hells, Images of
Honji Suijaku
Indra
Intermediate States
Local Divinities and Buddhism
Māra
Viṣṇu
Yakṣa

Doctrines and Doctrinal Study

Abhidharma
Ālayavijñāna
Anātman/Ātman (No-Self/Self)
Anitya (Impermanence)
Anuttarasamyaksaṃbodhi (Complete, Perfect Awakening)
Ascetic Practices
Bodhi (Awakening)
Bodhicitta (Thought of Awakening)
Body, Perspectives on the
Bsam yas Debate
Buddha-nature
Buddhavacana (Word of the Buddha)
Buddhist Studies
Consciousness, Theories of
Critical Buddhism (Hihan Bukkyō)
Dāna (Giving)
Death
Decline of the Dharma
Desire
Dhāraṇī
Dharma and Dharmas
Dharmadhātu
Dhyāna (Trance State)
Doubt
Duḥkha (Suffering)
Ethics
Evil
Faith
Four Noble Truths
Hermeneutics
Hīnayāna
Icchantika
Initiation
Intermediate States
Karma (Action)
Karuṇā (Compassion)
Language, Buddhist Philosophy of
Logic
Mindfulness
Nirvāṇa
Original Enlightenment (Hongaku)
Pāramitā (Perfection)
Path
Philosophy
Prajñā (Wisdom)
Pratītyasamutpāda (Dependent Origination)
Psychology
Rebirth
Saṃsāra
Skandha (Aggregate)
Śūnyatā (Emptiness)
Tathāgatagarbha
Upāya
Vipassanā (Sanskrit, Vipaśyanā)

Folk Religions and Popular Practices

Amulets and Talismans
Ancestors
Arhat
Arhat Images
Ascetic Practices
Bianwen
Bianxiang (Transformation Tableaux)
Chanting and Liturgy
Cosmology
Ḍākinī
Daoism and Buddhism
Dāna (Giving)
Death
Dhāraṇī
Diet
Entertainment and Performance
Evil
Faith
Family, Buddhism and the
Festivals and Calendrical Rituals
Folk Religion: An Overview
Folk Religion, China
Folk Religion, Japan
Folk Religion, Southeast Asia
Gavāṃpati
Ghost Festival
Ghosts and Spirits
Hachiman
Heart Sūtra
Heavens
Hells
Hells, Images of
Hinduism and Buddhism
Honji Suijaku
Indra
Initiation
Intermediate States
Karma (Action)
Laity
Local Divinities and Buddhism
Martial Arts
Merit and Merit-Making
Pilgrimage
Rebirth
Self-Immolation
Sentient Beings
Tibetan Book of the Dead
Upagupta
Vimalakīrti
Viṣṇu
Viśvantara

Humanities, Thematic Entries

Abortion
Body, Perspectives on the
Colonialism and Buddhism
Death
Desire
Education
Entertainment and Performance
Ethics
Evil
Family, Buddhism and the
Gender
Hermeneutics
Languages
Lineage
Mizuko Kuyō
Modernity and Buddhism
Nationalism and Buddhism
Persecutions
Philosophy
Psychology
Ritual
Sexuality
Slavery
Space, Sacred
War
Women

Literary Genres and Collections

Abhidharma
Āgama/Nikāya
Apocrypha
Avadāna
Bianwen
Biographies of Eminent Monks (Gaoseng zhuan)
Biography
Canon
Catalogues of Scriptures
Commentarial Literature
Hermeneutics
Konjaku Monogatari
Languages
Poetry and Buddhism
Prajñāpāramitā Literature
Samguk Yusa (Memorabilia of the Three Kingdoms)
Scripture

Literature, Indigenous; Buddhist Influences on

Bianwen
Burmese, Buddhist Literature in

Sūtra
Tantra
Vinaya
Vaṃsa

Jātaka, Avadāna and Story Literature
Avadāna
Avadānaśataka
Bodhicaryāvatāra
Buddhacarita
Divyāvadāna
Lalitavistara
Jātaka
Jātakamālā
Konjaku Monogatari
Mahāvastu
Samguk Yusa (Memorabilia of the Three Kingdoms)
Vaṃsa

Sūtra
Āgama/Nikāya
Diamond Sūtra
Fanwang jing (Brahmā's Net Sūtra)
Heart Sūtra
Huayan jing
Laṅkāvatāra-sūtra
Lotus Sūtra (Saddharmapuṇḍarīka-sūtra)
Mahāparinirvāṇa-sūtra
Nirvāṇa Sūtra
Prajñāpāramitā Literature
Pratyutpannasamādhi-sūtra
Renwang jing (Humane Kings Sūtra)
Saṃdhinirmocana-sūtra
Satipaṭṭhāna-sutta
Scripture
Sukhāvatīvyūha-sūtra
Sūtra
Sūtra Illustrations
Suvarṇaprabhāsottama-sūtra

Tantra
Kālacakra
Tantra

Vinaya
Law and Buddhism
Mūlasarvāstivāda-vinaya
Prātimokṣa
Vinaya

Sexuality and Gender Issues
Abortion
Ḍākinī
Gender
Hair
Laity
Mizuko Kuyō
Monks
Nuns
Saṅgha
Sexuality
Women

Social, Economic, and Political Issues
Colonialism and Buddhism
Communism and Buddhism
Conversion
Councils, Buddhist
Dalai Lama
Death
Decline of the Dharma
Diet
Economics
Education
Engaged Buddhism
Entertainment and Performance
Ethics
Etiquette
Family, Buddhism and the
Festivals and Calendrical Rituals
Folk Religion: An Overview
Folk Religion, China
Folk Religion, Japan
Folk Religion, Southeast Asia
Gender
Ghost Festival
Ghosts and Spirits
Hair
History
Honji Suijaku
Japanese Royal Family and Buddhism
Jewels
Kingship
Laity
Law and Buddhism
Martial Arts
Medicine
Merit and Merit-Making
Millenarianism and Millenarian Movements
Mizuko Kuyō
Modernity and Buddhism
Monastic Militias
Nationalism and Buddhism
Persecutions
Politics and Buddhism
Provincial Temple System (Kokubunji, Rishōtō)
Self-Immolation
Shintō (Honji Suijaku) and Buddhism
Silk Road
Slavery
Usury
Vinaya
War

MAPS

THE DIFFUSION OF BUDDHISM

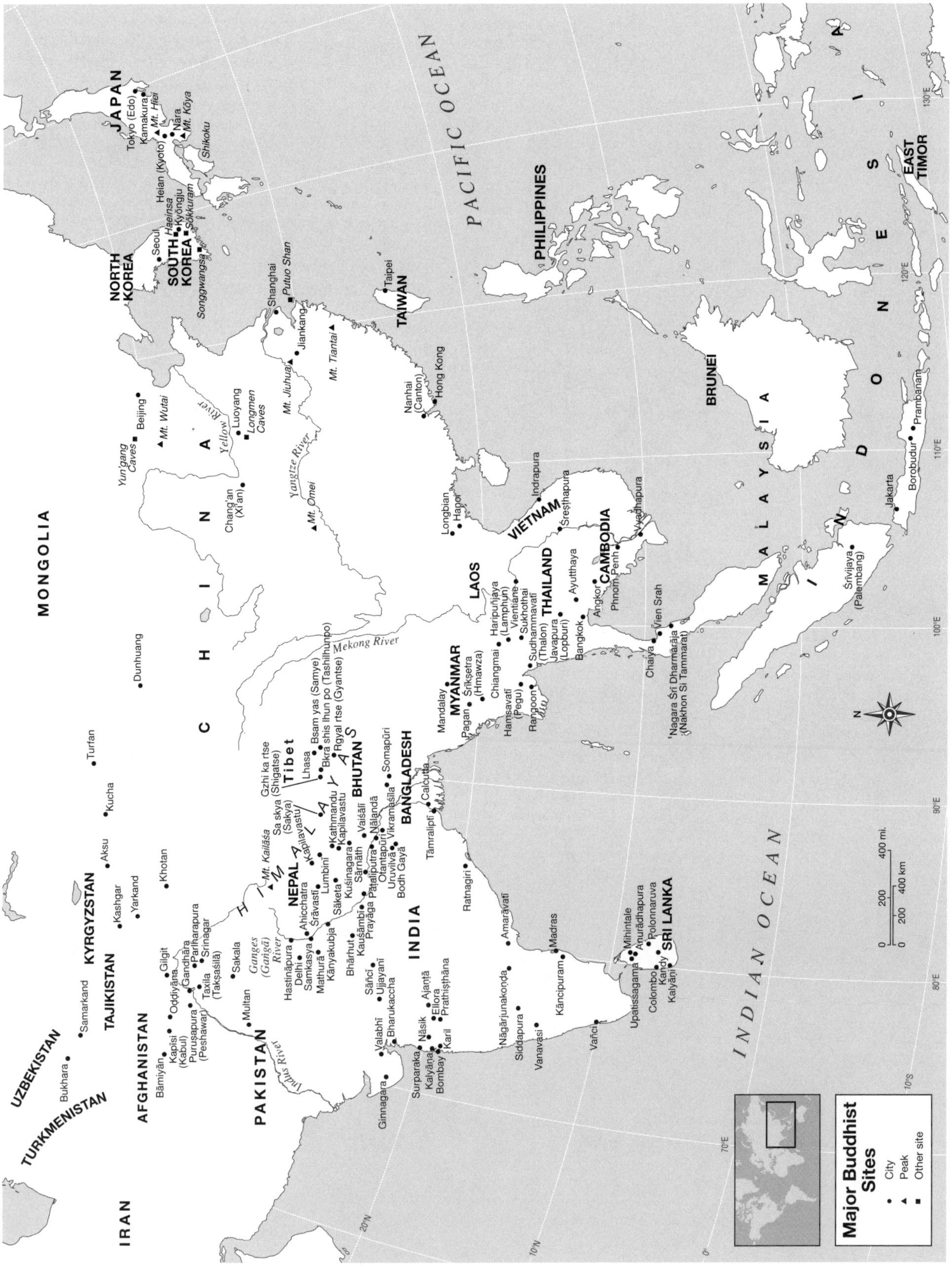

Map of the Indian subcontinent and East and Southeast Asia, with major Buddhist sites identified. XNR Productions, Inc. Reproduced by permission of the Gale Group.

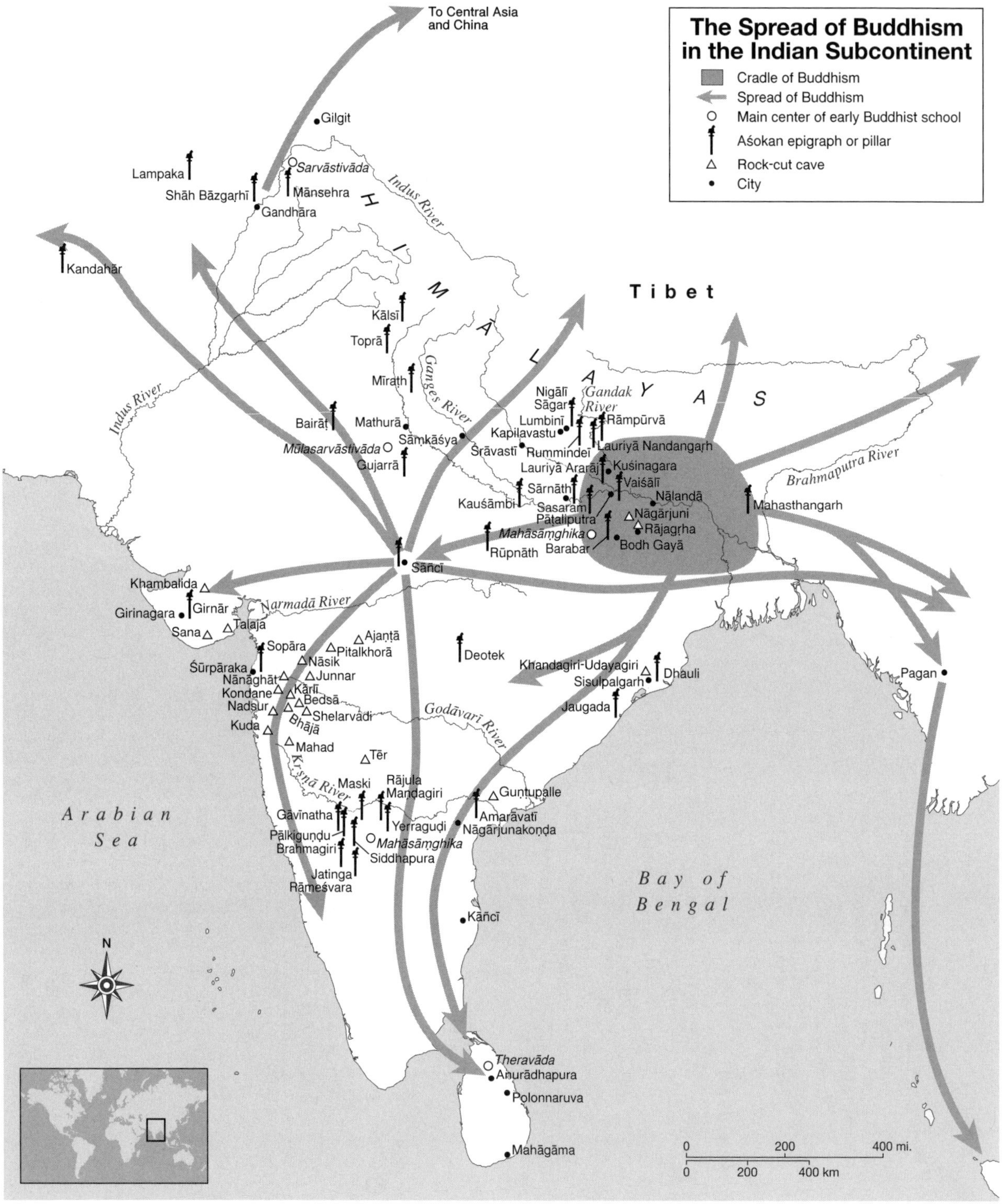

Map of the Indian subcontinent, with arrows showing the spread of Buddhism. XNR Productions, Inc. Reproduced by permission of the Gale Group.

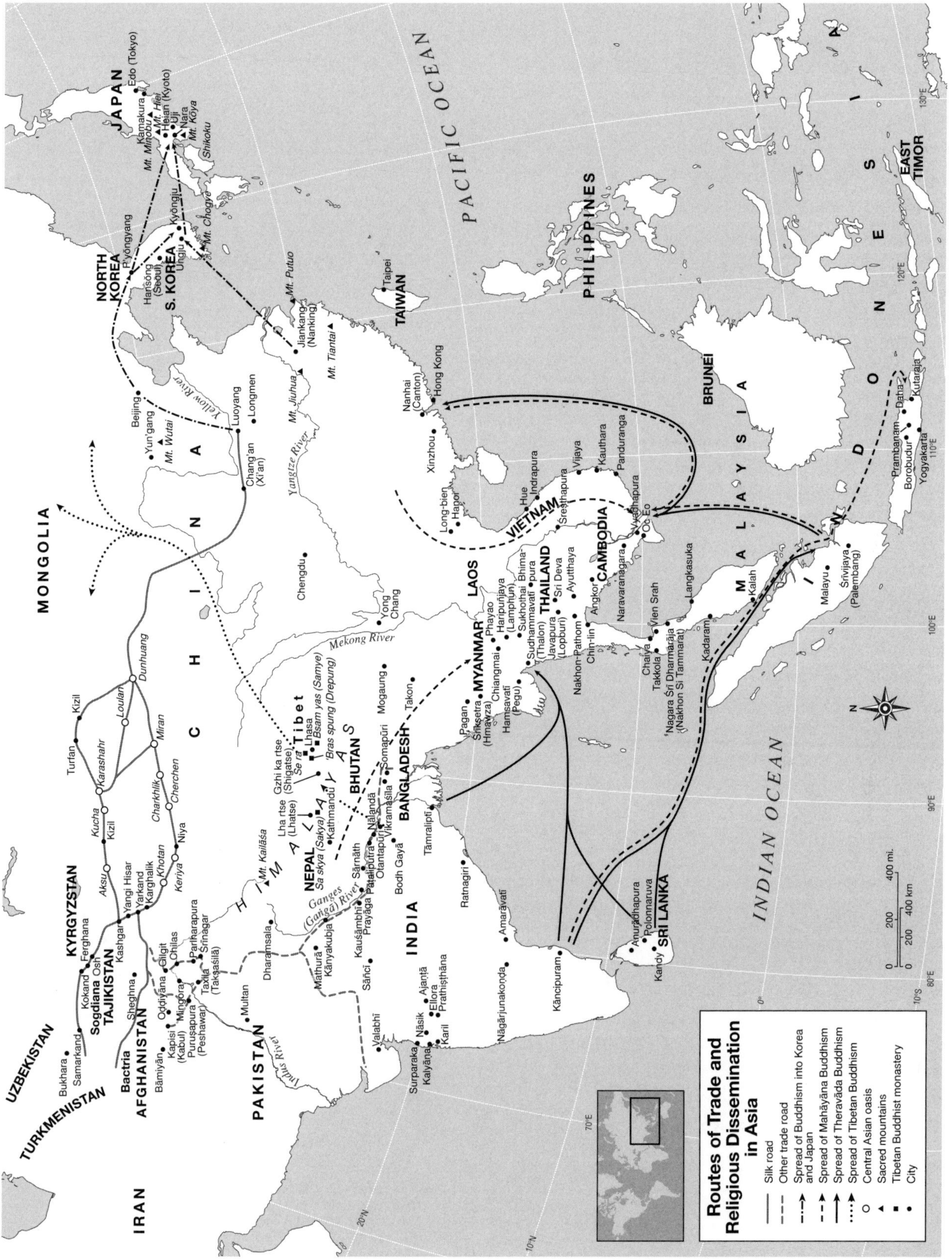

Map of trade routes and religious dissemination of Buddhism in Asia. XNR Productions, Inc. Reproduced by permission of the Gale Group.

A

ABHIDHARMA

In the centuries after the death of the Buddha, with the advent of settled monastic communities, there emerged new forms of religious praxis and modes of transmitting and interpreting the teaching. In this more organized setting, Buddhist practitioners began to reexamine received traditions and to develop new methods of organization that would make explicit their underlying significance and facilitate their faithful transmission. Although begun as a pragmatic method of elaborating the received teachings, this scholastic enterprise soon led to new doctrinal and textual developments and became the focus of a new form of scholarly monastic life. The products of this scholarship became revered tradition in their own right, eventually eclipsing the dialogues of the Buddha and of his disciples as the arbiter of the true teaching and determining both the exegetical method and the salient issues that became the focus of later Indian Buddhist doctrinal investigations.

Abhidharma, its meaning and origins

This scholastic enterprise was called *abhidharma* (Pāli: *abhidhamma*), a multivalent term used to refer to the new techniques of doctrinal interpretation, to the body of texts that this interpretation yielded, and finally to the crucial discriminating insight that was honed through doctrinal interpretation and employed in religious praxis. Traditional sources offer two explanations for the term *abhidharma*: "with regard to (*abhi*) the teaching (dharma)" or the "highest or further (*abhi*) teaching (dharma)." The subject of *abhidharma* analysis was, of course, the teaching (dharma) as embodied in the dialogues of the Buddha and his disciples. However, *abhidharma* did not merely restate or recapitulate the teaching of the sūtras, but reorganized their content and explicated their implicit meaning through commentary. In *abhidharma,* the specific content of the various individual sūtras was abstracted and reconstituted in accordance with new analytical criteria, thereby allowing one to discern their true message. This true message, as set down in *abhidharma* texts, consists of the discrimination of the various events and components (*dharma*) that combine to form all of experience. This discrimination in turn enables one to distinguish those defiling factors that ensnare one in the process of REBIRTH from those liberating factors that lead to enlightenment. And finally, when the defiling and liberating factors are clearly distinguished, the proper PATH of practice becomes clear. Hence, *abhidharma* was no mere scholastic commentary, but rather soteriological exegesis that was essential for the effective practice of the path.

Traditional sources do not offer a uniform account of the origins of the *abhidharma* method or of the *abhidharma* corpus of texts. Several traditional accounts attribute the composition of *abhidharma* texts to a first council supposedly held immediately after the death of the Buddha, at which his teachings were arranged and orally recited in three sections: the dialogues (sūtra); the disciplinary monastic codes (VINAYA); and the taxonomic lists of factors (*mātṛkā* or *abhidharma*). Implicitly, therefore, these traditional sources attribute authorship of the *abhidharma* to the Buddha himself. This question of the authorship and, by implication, the authenticity and authority of the *abhidharma* continued to be a controversial issue within subsequent, independent *abhidharma* treatises. Although many MAINSTREAM BUDDHIST SCHOOLS accepted the authority of *abhidharma* texts and included them within their canons as the word of the Buddha, several schools rejected the authority of *abhidharma* and claimed that *abhidharma* treatises were composed by fallible, human teachers.

Independent *abhidharma* treatises were composed over a period of at least seven hundred years (ca. third or second centuries B.C.E. to fifth century C.E.). The appearance and eventual proliferation of these independent *abhidharma* treatises coincides with the emergence of separate schools within the early Buddhist community. Doctrinal differences among various groups, which were, in part, the natural result of differing lineages of textual transmission, were refined in scholastic debates and amplified by the composition of independent *abhidharma* exegetical works. Scholarly opinion on the sources for the genre of independent *abhidharma* treatises is divided between two hypotheses, each of which finds support in structural characteristics of *abhidharma* texts. The first hypothesis emphasizes the practice of formulating matrices or taxonomic lists (*mātṛkā*) of all topics found in the traditional teaching, which are then arranged according to both numeric and qualitative criteria. The second hypothesis stresses the doctrinal discussions (*dharmakathā*) in catechetical style that attempt to clarify complex or obscure points of doctrine. These two structural characteristics suggest a typical process by which independent *abhidharma* treatises were composed: A matrix outline served to record or possibly direct discussions in which points of doctrine were then elaborated through a pedagogical question and answer technique.

Regardless of which hypothesis more accurately represents the origin of independent *abhidharma* treatises, this dual exegetical method reflects a persistent tendency in the Buddhist tradition, from the earliest period onward, toward analytical presentation through taxonomic categories and toward discursive elaboration through catechesis. The need to memorize the teaching obviously promoted the use of categorizing lists as a mnemonic device, and certain sūtras describe this taxonomic method as a way of encapsulating the essentials of the teaching and averting dissension. Other sūtras proceed much like oral commentaries, in which a brief doctrinal statement by the Buddha is analyzed in full through a process of interrogation and exposition. Both of these methods, amply attested in the sūtra collection, were successively expanded in subsequent independent scholastic treatises, some of which were not included within the sectarian, canonical *abhidharma* collections. For example, the collection of miscellaneous texts (*khuddakapiṭaka*) of the canon of the THERAVĀDA school includes two texts utilizing these methods that were not recognized to be canonical "*abhidharma*" texts. The *Paṭisambhidāmagga* (*Path of Discrimination*) contains brief discussions of doctrinal points structured according to a topical list (*mātikā*), and the *Niddesa* (*Exposition*) consists of commentary on the early verse collection, the *Suttanipāta.* In fact, a clear-cut point of origin for the *abhidharma* as an independent section of the textual canon only reflects the perspective of the later tradition that designates, after a long forgotten evolution, certain texts as "*abhidharma*" in contrast to sūtras or other possibly earlier expository works that share similar characteristics.

Abhidharma texts

Traditional accounts of early Indian Buddhist schools suggest that while certain schools may have shared some textual collections, many transmitted their own independent *abhidharma* treatises. XUANZANG (ca. 600–664 C.E.), the Chinese Buddhist pilgrim who visited India in the seventh century C.E., is reported to have collected numerous texts of as many as seven mainstream Buddhist schools. These almost certainly included canonical *abhidharma* texts representing various schools. However, only two complete canonical collections, representing the Theravāda and Sarvāstivāda schools, and several texts of undetermined sectarian affiliation are preserved. Even though each of the Theravāda and Sarvāstivāda *abhidharma* collections contains seven texts, the individual texts of the two collections cannot be neatly identified with one another. However, a close examination of certain texts from each collection and a comparison with other extant *abhidharma* materials reveals similarities in the underlying taxonomic lists, in exegetical structure, and in the topics discussed. These similarities suggest either contact among the groups who composed and transmitted these texts, or a common ground of doctrinal exegesis and even textual material predating the emergence of the separate schools.

The Theravāda canonical *abhidharma* collection, the only one extant in an Indian language (Pāli), contains seven texts:

1. *Vibhaṅga* (*Analysis*);
2. *Puggalapaññatti* (*Designation of Persons*);
3. *Dhātukathā* (*Discussion of Elements*);
4. *Dhammasaṅgaṇi* (*Enumeration of Factors*);

5. *Yamaka* (*Pairs*);
6. *Paṭṭhāna* (*Foundational Conditions*); and
7. *Kathāvatthu* (*Points of Discussion*).

The Sarvāstivāda canonical *abhidharma* collection, also including seven texts, is extant only in Chinese translation:

1. *Saṅgītiparyāya* (*Discourse on the Saṅgīti*);
2. *Dharmaskandha* (*Aggregation of Factors*);
3. *Prajñaptiśāstra* (*Treatise on Designations*);
4. *Dhātukāya* (*Collection on the Elements*);
5. *Vijñānakāya* (*Collection on Perceptual Consciousness*);
6. *Prakaraṇapāda* (*Exposition*); and
7. *Jñānaprasthāna* (*Foundations of Knowledge*).

Certain other early *abhidharma* texts extant in Chinese translation probably represent the *abhidharma* canonical texts of yet other schools: for example, the **Śāriputrābhidharmaśāstra* (T. 1548), which may have been affiliated with a Vibhajyavāda school, or the **Saṃmatīyaśāstra* (T. 1649) affiliated by its title with the Saṃmatīya school, associated with the Vātsīputrīyas.

In the absence of historical evidence for the accurate dating of the extant *abhidharma* treatises, scholars have tentatively proposed relative chronologies based primarily upon internal formal criteria that presuppose a growing complexity of structural organization and of exegetical method. It is assumed that *abhidharma* texts of the earliest period bear the closest similarities to the sūtras, and are often structured as commentaries on entire sūtras or on sūtra sections arranged according to taxonomic lists. The *Vibhaṅga* and *Puggalapaññatti* of the Theravādins and the *Saṅgītiparyāya* and *Dharmaskandha* of the Sarvāstivādins exemplify these characteristics. The next set of *abhidharma* texts exhibits emancipation from the confines of commentary upon individual sūtras, by adopting a more abstract stance that subsumes doctrinal material from a variety of sources under an abstract analytical framework of often newly created categories. This middle period would include the five remaining canonical texts within the Theravāda and the Sarvāstivāda *abhidharma* canonical collections. The catechetical style of commentarial exegesis, evident even in the earliest *abhidharma* texts, becomes more structured and formulaic in texts of the middle period. The final products in this process of abstraction are the truly independent treatises that display marked creativity in technical terminology and doctrinal elaboration. Some of the texts, in particular the *Kathāvatthu* of the Theravādins and the *Vijñānakāya* of the Sarvāstivādins, display an awareness of differences in doctrinal interpretation and factional alignments, although they do not adopt the developed polemical stance typical of many subsequent *abhidharma* works.

The composition of *abhidharma* treatises did not end with the canonical collections, but continued with commentaries on previous *abhidharma* works and with independent summary digests or exegetical manuals. Within the Theravāda tradition, several fifth-century C.E. commentators compiled new works based upon earlier commentaries dating from the first several centuries C.E. They also composed independent summaries of *abhidhamma* analysis, prominent among which are the *Visuddhimagga* (*Path of Purification*) by BUDDHAGHOSA and the *Abhidhammāvatāra* (*Introduction to Abhidhamma*) by Buddhadatta. The *Abhidhammatthasaṅgaha* (*Collection of Abhidhamma Matters*) composed by Anuruddha in the twelfth century C.E. became thereafter the most frequently used summary of *abhidhamma* teaching within the Theravāda tradition.

The first five centuries C.E. were also a creative period of efflorescence for the *abhidharma* of the Sarvāstivādins. In texts of this period, summary exposition combines with exhaustive doctrinal analysis and polemical debate. The teaching is reorganized in accordance with an abstract and more logical structure, which is then interwoven with the earlier taxonomic lists. Preeminent among these texts for both their breadth and their influence upon later scholastic compositions are the voluminous, doctrinal compendia, called *vibhāṣā*, which are represented by three different recensions extant in Chinese translation, the last and best known of which is called the *Mahāvibhāṣā* (*Great Exegesis*). Composed over several centuries from the second century C.E. onward, these ostensibly simple commentaries on an earlier canonical *abhidharma* text, the *Jñānaprasthāna*, exhaustively enumerate the positions of contending groups on each doctrinal point, often explicitly attributing these views to specific schools or masters. Instead of arguing for a single, orthodox viewpoint, the *vibhāṣā* compendia display an encyclopedic intention that is often content with comprehensiveness in cataloguing the full spectrum of differing sectarian positions. The *vibhāṣā* compendia are repositories of several centuries of scholastic activity representing multiple branches of the Sarvāstivāda school, which was spread throughout greater northwestern India. However, they came to be particularly associated by tradition with the Sarvāstivādins of Kashmir who, thereby, acquired the appellation, Sarvāstivāda-Vaibhāṣika.

Three other texts composed during the same period that are associated with the northwestern region of Gandhāra display a markedly different structure and purpose: the **Abhidharmahṛdayaśāstra* (*Heart of Abhidharma*) by Dharmaśreṣṭhin; the **Abhidharmahṛdayaśāstra* (*Heart of Abhidharma*) by Upaśānta; and the **Miśrakābhidharmahṛdayaśāstra* (*Heart of Abhidharma with Miscellaneous Additions*) by Dharmatrāta. Composed in verse with an accompanying prose auto-commentary, these texts function as summary digests of all aspects of the teaching presented according to a logical and nonrepetitive structure. In contrast to the earlier numerically guided taxonomic lists well-suited as mnemonic aids, these texts adopt a new method of organization, attempting to subsume the prior taxonomic lists and all discussion of specific doctrinal points under general topical sections. This new organizational structure was to become paradigmatic for the texts of the final period of Sarvāstivāda *abhidharma*.

This final period in the development of Sarvāstivāda *abhidharma* treatises includes texts that are the products of single authors and that adopt a polemical style of exposition displaying a fully developed sectarian self-consciousness. They also employ increasingly sophisticated methods of argumentation in order to establish the position of their own school and to refute at length the views of others. Despite this polemical approach, they nonetheless purport to serve as well-organized expository treatises or pedagogical digests for the entirety of Buddhist teaching. The *Abhidharmakośa* (*Treasury of Abhidharma*), including both verses (*kārikā*) and an auto-commentary (*bhāṣya*), by VASUBANDHU became the most important text from this period, central to the subsequent traditions of *abhidharma* studies in Tibet and East Asia. Adopting both the verse-commentary structure and the topical organization of the **Abhidharmahṛdaya*, the *Abhidharmakośa* presents a detailed account of Sarvāstivāda *abhidharma* teaching with frequent criticism of Sarvāstivāda positions in its auto-commentary. The *Abhidharmakośa* provoked a response from certain Kashmiri Sarvāstivāda masters who attempted to refute non-Sarvāstivāda views presented in Vasubandhu's work and to reestablish their own interpretation of orthodox Kashmiri Sarvāstivāda positions. These works, the **Nyāyānusāraśāstra* (*Conformance to Correct Principle*) and **Abhidharmasamayapradīpikā* (*Illumination of the Collection of Abhidharma*) by Saṅghabhadra and the *Abhidharmadīpa* (*Illumination of Abhidharma*) by an unknown author who refers to himself as the Dīpakāra (author of the *Dīpa*) were the final works of the Sarvāstivāda *abhidharma* tradition that have survived.

Abhidharma exegesis

Abhidharma exegesis evolved over a long period as both the agent and the product of a nascent and then increasingly disparate Buddhist sectarian self-consciousness. Given the voluminous nature of even the surviving literature that provides a record of this long doctrinal history, any outline of *abhidharma* method must be content with sketching the most general contours and touching on a few representative examples. Nonetheless, scanning the history of *abhidharma*, one discerns a general course of development that in the end resulted in a complex interpretative edifice radically different from the sūtras upon which it was believed to be based.

In its earliest stage, that is, as elaborative commentary, *abhidharma* was guided by the intention simply to clarify the content of the sūtras. Taxonomic lists were used as a mnemonic device facilitating oral preservation and transmission; catechetical investigation was employed in a teaching environment of oral commentary guided by the pedagogical technique of question and answer. Over time, the taxonomic lists grew in complexity as the simpler lists presented in the sūtra teachings were combined in new ways, and additional categories of qualitative analysis were created to specify modes of interaction among discrete aspects of the sūtra teaching. The initially terse catechetical investigation was expanded with discursive exposition and new methods of interpretation and argumentation, which were demanded by an increasingly polemical environment. These developments coincided with a move from oral to written methods of textual transmission and with the challenge presented by other Buddhist and non-Buddhist groups. In its final stage, *abhidharma* texts became complex philosophical treatises employing sophisticated methods of argumentation, whose purpose was the analysis and elaboration of doctrinal issues for their own sake. The very sūtras from which *abhidharma* arose were now subordinated as mere statements in need of analysis that only the *abhidharma* could provide. No longer serving as the starting point for *abhidharma* exegesis, the sūtras were invoked only as a supplemental authority to buttress independent reasoned investigations or to corroborate doctrinal points actually far removed from their scriptural antecedents.

Abstract analysis, which is the guiding principle of *abhidharma* exegesis, also became the salient characteristic of its doctrinal interpretation. The analytical tendency, evident in lists present even in the sūtras, expanded in *abhidharma* to encompass all of experience. In very simple terms, *abhidharma* attempts an exhaustive and systematic accounting of every possible type of experience in terms of its ultimate constituents. *Abhidharma* views experience with a critical analytical eye, breaking down the gross objects of ordinary perception into their constituent factors or dharmas and clarifying the causal interaction among these discrete factors. This analysis was not, however, motivated by simple abstract interest, but rather by a soteriological purpose at the very core of Buddhist religious praxis. Analysis determines the requisite factors of which each event consists, distinguishing those factors that lead to suffering and rebirth from those that contribute to their termination. This very process of analysis was identified with the insight that functions in religious praxis to cut off ensnaring factors and to cultivate those leading to liberation.

Abhidharma analysis focused on refining these lists of factors and on investigating the problems that arise in using them to explain experience. Simple enumerations of factors found in the earlier sūtras include the lists of five aggregates (skandha), twelve sense-spheres (*āyatana*), and eighteen elements (*dhātu*) that were used to describe animate beings, or the lists of practices and qualities that were to be incorporated into the set of thirty-seven limbs of enlightenment, whose cultivation results in the attainment of enlightenment. These earlier analytical lists were preserved in *abhidharma* treatises and integrated into comprehensive and complex intersecting classifications that aimed to clarify both the unique identity of each factor and all possible modes of conditioning interaction among them. The *abhidharma* treatises of various schools proposed differing lists of factors containing as many as seventy-five, eighty-one, or one hundred discrete categories. For example, the Sarvāstivādins adopted a system of seventy-five basic categories of factors distinguished according to their intrinsic nature (*svabhāva*), which were then grouped in five distinct classes. The first four classes (material form [*rūpa*]—eleven; mind [*citta*]—one; mental factors [*caitta*]—forty-six; and factors dissociated from material form and mind [*cittaviprayuktasaṃskāra*]—fourteen) comprise all conditioned factors (*saṃskṛta*), that is, factors that participate in causal interaction and are subject to arising and passing away. The fifth class comprises three unconditioned factors (*asaṃskṛta*), which neither arise nor pass away.

Through *abhidharma* analysis, all experiential events were explained as arising from the interaction of a certain number of these factors. Particular occurrences of individual factors were further characterized in accordance with additional specific criteria or sets of qualities including their moral quality as virtuous, unvirtuous, or indeterminate, their locus of occurrence as connected to the realm of desire, the realm of form, the formless realm, or not connected to any realm, their connection to animate experience as characteristic of SENTIENT BEINGS or not, and their conditioning efficacy as resulting from certain types of causes or leading to certain types of effects. To give an example, a particular instance of a mental factor, such as conception (*saṃjñā*), can be virtuous in moral quality, characteristic of sentient beings, connected to the realm of desire, and so on. In other circumstance, another occurrence of the same factor of conception, while still characteristic of sentient beings, can be unvirtuous and connected to the realm of form. Although the specific character of each instance of conception differs as virtuous, or unvirtuous, and so on, all such instances, regardless of their particular qualities, share the same intrinsic nature as conception and can, therefore, be placed within the same fundamental category. Thus, the taxonomic schema of seventy-five factors represents seventy-five categories of intrinsic nature, each of which occurs phenomenally or experientially in innumerable instances. Through this disciplined exercise of exhaustive analysis in terms of constituent factors, experience can be seen as it actually is, the factors causing further suffering can be discarded, and those contributing toward liberation can be isolated and cultivated.

This exhaustive *abhidharma* analysis of experience occasioned a number of doctrinal controversies that served to demarcate different schools. Many of these controversies were directed by fundamental disagreements that could be termed ontological, specifically concerning the way in which the different factors constituting experience exist and the dynamics of their interaction or conditioning. Such ontological concerns motivated the early lists of factors in the sūtras, which were used to support the fundamental Buddhist teaching of no-self (anātman) by demonstrating that no perduring, unchanging, independent self (ātman) could be found. In *abhidharma* treatises the focus of ontological concern shifted from gross objects, such as the self, to the factors or dharmas of which these objects were understood to consist.

Perhaps the most distinctive ontology was proposed by the Sarvāstivādins, "those who claim *sarvam asti*," or "everything exists." Beginning from the fundamental Buddhist teaching of ANITYA (IMPERMANENCE), they suggested that the constituent factors of experience exist as discrete and real entities, arising and passing away within the span of a single moment. But such a view of experience as an array of strictly momentary factors would seem to make continuity and indeed any conditioning interaction among the discrete factors impossible. Factors of one moment, whose existence is limited to that moment, could never condition the arising of subsequent factors that do not yet exist; and factors of the subsequent moment must then arise without a cause since their prior causes no longer exist. To safeguard both the Buddhist teaching of impermanence and the conditioning process that is essential to account for ordinary experience, the Sarvāstivādins suggested a novel reinterpretation of existence. Each factor, they claimed, is characterized by both an intrinsic nature, which exists unchanged in the past, present, and future, and an activity or causal efficacy, which arises and passes away due to the influence of conditions within the span of the present moment. Only those factors that are defined by both intrinsic nature and the possibility of activity exist as real entities (*dravya*); the composite objects of ordinary experience that lack intrinsic nature exist only as mental constructs or provisional designations (*prajñapti*). This model, the Sarvāstivādins claimed, preserves the Buddhist doctrine of impermanence, since each factor's activity arises and passes away, and yet also explains continuity and the process of conditioning, since factors exist as intrinsic nature in the past, present, and future. Such past (or future) existent factors can then, through various special types of causal efficacy, serve as conditions in the arising of subsequent factors. The Sarvāstivāda ontological model became the subject of heated debate and was rejected by other schools (e.g., the Theravāda and the Dārṣṭāntika) who claimed that factors exist only in the present, and not in the past and future. According to the Dārṣṭāntikas, intrinsic nature cannot be distinguished from a factor's activity. Instead, a factor's very existence is its activity, and experience is nothing other than an uninterrupted conditioning process. The fragmentation of this conditioning process into discrete factors possessed of individual intrinsic nature and unique efficacy is nothing but a mental fabrication.

These ontological investigations generated complex theories of conditioning and intricate typologies of causes and conditions. There is evidence for several rival classifications of individual causes and conditions, each of which accounts for a specific mode of conditioning interaction among specific categories of factors: For example, the Theravādins proposed a set of twenty-four conditions; the Sarvāstivādins, two separate sets of four conditions and six causes. Besides establishing different typologies of causes and conditions, the schools also disagreed on the causal modality exercised by these specific types. The Sarvāstivādins acknowledged that certain of these causes and conditions arise prior to their effects, while others, which exert a supportive conditioning efficacy, arise simultaneously with their effects. The Dārṣṭāntikas, however, allowed only successive causation; a cause must always precede its effect. In these debates about causality, the nature of animate or personal conditioning—that is, efficacious action, or KARMA—and the theory of dependent origination intended to account for animate conditioning were, naturally, central issues because of their fundamental role in all Buddhist teaching and practice.

The investigation of these doctrinal controversies, which came to occupy an ever greater position in later *abhidharma* treatises, required the development of more formal methods of argumentation that employed both supporting scriptural citations and reasoned investigations. In the earliest examples of such arguments, reasoned investigations did not yet possess the power of independent proof and were considered valid only in conjunction with supportive scriptural citations. This reliance upon scriptural citations spurred the development of a systematic HERMENEUTICS that would mediate conflicting positions by judging the authenticity and authority of corroborating scriptural passages and determining the correct mode of their interpretation. In general, the interpretative principles applied were inclusive and harmonizing; any statement deemed in conformity with the teaching of the Buddha or with his enlightenment experience was accepted as genuine. Hierarchies were created that incorporated divergent scriptural passages by valuing them differently. And finally, contradictory passages in the sūtras or within *abhidharma* texts were said to represent the variant perspectives from which the Buddhist teaching could be presented. Notable for its parallel with later Buddhist ontology and epistemology was the hermeneutic technique whereby certain passages or texts were judged to have explicit meaning (*nītārtha*) expressing absolute truth or reality, while others were judged to have implicit meaning (*neyārtha*) expressing mere conventional truth. And for the *abhidharma* texts, the sūtras were merely implicit and in need of further interpretation that could be provided only by the explicit *abhidharma* treatises. In *abhidharma* texts of the later period, reasoned investigations were deemed sufficient, and the supporting scriptural references became decontextualized commonplaces, cited simply to validate the use of key terms in an *abhidharma* context. Reasoned investigations began to be appraised by independent non-scriptural criteria, such as internal consistency, and the absence of logical faults, such as fallacious causal justification. The doctrinal analysis and methods of argumentation developed within *abhidharma* treatises defined the course for later Indian Buddhist scholasticism, which refined and expanded its *abhidharma* heritage through the addition of new doctrinal perspectives, increasingly sophisticated techniques of argument, and a wider context of both intra- and extra-Buddhist debate.

See also: **Abhidharmakośabhāṣya; Anātman/Ātman (No-Self/Self); Canon; Commentarial Literature; Councils, Buddhist; Dharma and Dharmas; Psychology; Sarvāstivāda and Mūlasarvāstivāda**

Bibliography

Bareau, André. "Les Sectes bouddhiques du Petit Véhicule et leurs Abhidharmapiṭaka." *Bulletin de l'École Française d'Extrême-Orient* 50 (1952): 1–11.

Cox, Collett. "The Unbroken Treatise: Scripture and Argument in Early Buddhist Scholasticism." In *Innovation in Religious Traditions: Essays in the Interpretation of Religious Change*, ed. Michael A. Williams, Collett Cox, and Martin S. Jaffee. Berlin and New York: de Gruyter, 1992.

Cox, Collett. *Disputed Dharmas: Early Buddhist Theories on Existence.* Tokyo: International Institute for Buddhist Studies, 1995.

Cox, Collett. "Kaśmīra: Vaibhāṣika Orthodoxy (Chapter 3)." In *Sarvāstivāda Buddhist Scholasticism*, by Charles Willemen, Bart Dessein, and Collett Cox. Leiden, Netherlands: Brill. 1997.

Frauwallner, Erich. *Studies in Abhidharma Literature and the Origins of Buddhist Philosophical Systems*, tr. Sophie Francis Kidd. Albany: State University of New York Press, 1995.

Gethin, Rupert. "The Mātikās: Memorization, Mindfulness, and the List." In *In the Mirror of Memory: Reflections on Mindfulness and Remembrance in Indian and Tibetan Buddhism*, ed. Janet Gyatso. Albany: State University of New York Press, 1992.

Hirakawa Akira. *A History of Indian Buddhism: From Śākyamuni to Early Mahāyāna*, tr. Paul Groner. Honolulu: University of Hawaii Press, 1990.

Nyanatiloka Mahāthera. *Guide through the Abhidhamma Piṭaka* (1938). Kandy, Sri Lanka: Buddhist Publication Society, 1971.

Potter, Karl; with Buswell, Robert E.; Jaini, Padmanabh S.; and Reat, Noble Ross; eds. *Abhidharma Buddhism to 150* A.D., Vol. 7: *Encyclopedia of Indian Philosophies.* Delhi: Motilal Banarsidass, 1996.

Watanabe Fumimaro. *Philosophy and Its Development in the Nikāyas and Abhidhamma.* Delhi: Motilal Banarsidass, 1983.

COLLETT COX

ABHIDHARMAKOŚABHĀṢYA

The *Abhidharmakośa* (*Treasury of Abhidharma*) was composed by the fourth- or fifth-century Indian Buddhist master, VASUBANDHU. No scholarly consensus exists concerning whether or not Vasubandhu, the author of the *Abhidharmakośa*, should be identified with Vasubandhu, the author of numerous MAHĀYĀNA and YOGĀCĀRA SCHOOL treatises. According to traditional biographical accounts, Vasubandhu composed the verses of the *Abhidharmakośa*, or *kārikā*, as a digest of orthodox Kashmiri Sarvāstivāda-Vaibhāṣika *abhidharma* doctrine. However, in his prose auto-commentary, the *bhāṣya*, Vasubandhu frequently criticized Sarvāstivāda doctrinal positions and presented his own divergent interpretations.

Typical of the later *abhidharma* genre of polemical, summary digests, the *Abhidharmakośa* attempts to present the entirety of *abhidharma* doctrinal teaching according to a logical format, while also recording variant, sectarian interpretations and often lengthy arguments on specific points. For his organizational structure and much of his content, Vasubandhu relied upon earlier *abhidharma* treatises: notably, for content, upon the massive scholastic compendia (*vibhāṣā*) of Kashmir, and for structure and tenor of interpretation, upon the *Abhidharmahṛdaya* (*Heart of Abhidharma*) texts of Gandhāra. The *Abhidharmakośa* is divided into nine chapters (*nirdeśa*):

1. Elements (*dhātu*)
2. Faculties (*indriya*)

3. Worlds (*loka*)
4. Action (karma)
5. Contaminants (*anuśaya*)
6. Path of Religious Praxis and Religious Persons (*mārgapudgala*)
7. Knowledge (jñāna)
8. Meditative States (*samāpatti*)
9. Person (*pudgala*)

The ninth chapter contains a refutation of the theory of the existence of the person and may represent a separate treatise by Vasubandhu, appended to the remainder of the *Abhidharmakośa.* The *Abhidharmakośa* became the most influential early Indian Buddhist *Abhidharma* text within the later scholastic traditions of Tibet and East Asia, where it served as a textbook within monastic curricula and generated numerous commentaries.

See also: **Abhidharma; Dharma and Dharmas; Sarvāstivāda and Mūlasarvāstivāda**

Bibliography

La Vallée Poussin, Louis de, trans. *L'Abhidharmakośa de Vasubandhu,* 6 vols. Paris: Paul Geuthner, 1923–1931. English trans. Leo M. Pruden, *Abhidharmakośabhāṣyam,* Vols. 1–4. Berkeley, CA: Asian Humanities Press, 1988–1990.

COLLETT COX

ABHIJÑĀ (HIGHER KNOWLEDGES)

Abhijñā (Pāli, *abhiññā*; higher knowledge) refers to a stereotyped set of typically six spiritual powers ascribed to buddhas and their chief disciples. The first five are mundane and attainable through the perfection of concentration (samādhi) in meditative trance (dhyāna; Pāli, *jhāna*). As earthly attainments, they are deemed available to non-Buddhist sages. In contrast, the sixth higher knowledge is supramundane and exclusively Buddhist, and attainable only through insight (*vipaśyanā;* Pāli, *vipassanā*) into the Buddhist truths.

The five mundane *abhijñās* include:

- The divine eye (*divyacakṣus*; Pāli, *dibbacakkhu*), or the ability to see the demise and rebirth of beings according to their good and evil deeds;
- The divine ear (*divyaśrota*; Pāli, *dibbasota*), the ability to hear heavenly and earthly sounds far and near;
- Knowledge of other minds (*cetaḥparyāyajñāna*; Pāli, *cetopariyañāṇa*), the ability to know the thoughts and mental states of others;
- Recollection of previous habitations (*pūrvanivāsānusmṛti*; Pāli *pubbenivāsānusati*), the ability to remember one's former existences from one to thousands of rebirths, through the evolution and destruction of many world systems;
- Various supernatural powers (*ṛddhi*; Pāli, *iddhi*), such as the ability to create mind-made bodies, project replicas of oneself, become invisible, pass through solid objects, move through the earth, walk on water, fly through the air, touch the sun and moon, and ascend to the highest heaven.

In the MAHĀPARINIRVĀṆA-SŪTRA (Pāli, *Mahāparinibbāna-sutta*; *Great Discourse on the Parinirvāṇa*), the Buddha tells his disciple ĀNANDA that one who perfects the four bases of supernatural power (*ṛddhipāda*; Pāli, *iddhipāda*) can live for an entire eon, or for the remaining portion of an eon should he so desire.

The sixth and only supramundane *abhijñā* is the most important. Called "knowledge of the extinction of the passions" (*āśravakṣaya*; Pāli, *āsavakkhaya*), it is equivalent to arhatship. The passions extinguished through this knowledge are sensuality (kāma), becoming (*bhava*), ignorance (avidyā; Pāli, *avijjā*), and views (*dṛṣṭi*; Pāli, *diṭṭhi*).

Historically, the six *abhijñās* can be seen as an elaboration of an earlier Buddhist paradigm of human perfection called the "three knowledges" (*traividya*; Pāli, *tevijjā*). Comprised of the recollection of former habitations, the divine eye, and knowledge of the extinction of the passions, the three knowledges form the content of the Buddha's awakening in early canonical depictions of his enlightenment experience.

Although mastery of the six *abhijñās* is an attribute of all perfect buddhas, the early Buddhist tradition was ambivalent toward the display of supernatural powers by members of the monastic order. In the *Kevaddha-sutta* (*Discourse to Kevaddha*), the Buddha disparages as vulgar those monks who would reveal such powers to the laity, and in the VINAYA or monastic code, he makes it an offense for them to do so. Despite these strictures, wonder-working saints were lionized in the literatures of all Buddhist schools, and they became the focus of numerous ARHAT cults, such as those devoted to the worship of the disciples UPAGUPTA and MAHĀKĀŚYAPA. The MAHĀYĀNA tradition elaborated upon the *abhijñās* and *ṛddhis* of early Buddhism in its depictions of the attainments of celestial bodhisattvas and cosmic buddhas. In Buddhist TANTRA, these same powers became the model for a host of magical abilities called *siddhis* possessed by tantric masters and displayed as signs of their spiritual perfection.

See also: **Dhyāna (Trance State); Meditation; Vipassanā (Sanskrit, Vipaśyanā)**

Bibliography

Buddhaghosa. *The Path of Purification (Visuddhimagga)*, tr. Bhikkhu Nyanamoli. Berkeley, CA: Shambhala, 1964.

Katz, Nathan. *Buddhist Images of Human Perfection: The Arahant of the Sutta Pitaka Compared with the Bodhisattva and the Mahasiddha.* Delhi: Motilal Banarsidass, 1982.

Ray, Reginald A. *Buddhist Saints in India: A Study in Buddhist Values and Orientations.* New York: Oxford University Press, 1994.

PATRICK A. PRANKE

ABORTION

Abortion is the deliberate termination of pregnancy by mechanical or pharmaceutical means that result in the death of an unborn fetus. Since the death of the fetus is willfully caused, abortion is the subject of heated controversy. Just as Christians are divided in their opinions about abortion, Buddhists likewise present a range of views from unequivocal condemnation to active support. Between the extremes are various attempts to justify abortion without completely affirming it, or to question it without totally rejecting it. There are also those who remain silent on the issue.

Early Buddhist teachings and practices

Early Buddhist texts describe the formation of the fetus in great detail. At conception the fetus is in a liquid state and takes on flesh at the end of two weeks. Hands, feet, and a head appear by the fifth week, and the embryo is mature after three months. In physical terms, life begins with conception, but since the new fetus takes shape around a state of being that has already had previous lives, it represents a continuation of life and not just the beginning of new life. Most texts deny that the transmigrating state of being is a permanent soul, but they also define different kinds of INTERMEDIATE STATES that provides the karmic transition from one bodily life to the next. The exact nature of this intermediate state is the subject of debate, but the belief that there is some kind of vital continuity between one incarnation and the next means that the beginning of life does not take place at conception but precedes it. Each conception, however, is not taken lightly and the termination of bodily life at any stage is generally regarded as killing.

Abortion is therefore not supported in early Buddhist teachings. It violates the first precept against the taking of life and goes against other teachings that condemn acts causing harm to others. Rituals performed for the fetus affirm its life and request protection for it and its mother. Monks who performed an abortion or helped a woman obtain abortion drugs were subject to punishment, including expulsion from the order. A monk could also be punished for reciting magical spells to prevent birth, or even for advising a woman to get an abortion.

Traditional methods of performing abortions were crude and often not very effective. Medicines were used, but they could harm the mother or fail to produce the desired result. Abortionists used heating and scorching, as well as heavy manipulation, including trampling, of the womb, to terminate a pregnancy. Since intention is an important consideration in determining the seriousness of an offense, early texts discuss the different levels of infraction involved in cases in which death occurs to the mother or the fetus or both. The most serious crime is committed when the fetus alone dies as the intended victim.

Modern views and practices

With the development of safer and more effective means of abortion through modern medical practices, the abortion rate in Buddhist countries has risen. According to a survey done in 1981, it was estimated that there were thirty-seven abortions for every one thousand women of childbearing age in Thailand, a country in which over 90 percent of the population is Buddhist. The same survey estimated that there were sixty-five to ninety abortions among Japanese women of childbearing age. The United States rate was 22.6, according to this survey.

These statistics show that early Buddhist proscriptions against abortion have not prevented its practice. Aware of Buddhist teachings against abortion, modern

Buddhists have adopted a variety of strategies for relating theory with practice. In Thailand, for example, one approach makes the distinction between the ordained clergy, who are forbidden to be involved with abortion, and lay followers, who are allowed to have abortions without any religious or moral sanction. Some monks argue that while abortion is morally wrong in terms of Buddhist teachings, the decision for or against it is a matter of individual judgment. Other Thai Buddhists invoke the teaching on UPĀYA (SKILLFUL MEANS) by which an act can be justified if the intent behind it is pure. If pregnancy threatens the health or life of the mother, then its termination through abortion can be justified because the intention is to save the mother.

Modern Japanese Buddhists likewise have developed means for dealing with the problem of carrying out abortions in the face of the precept against killing. Using the modern term *mizuko*, literally "water child," for the fetus, William R. LaFleur in his influential book, *Liquid Life* (1992), explains the strategy of obscuring the point at which life begins and seeing fetal development as a continuum of liquid slowing becoming solid. This watery ambiguity disallows a fixed definition of the precise point at which life begins, and termination of the process through abortion likewise obscures any judgment that killing has taken place. LaFleur argues that fetal life is not so much terminated as returned to its origins, where it is put on hold and can await another occasion for its birth. While there is as yet little evidence to indicate the extent to which ordinary Japanese share this liquid life theory, it is not without its influence.

Another modern development among Japanese Buddhists for dealing with abortion is MIZUKO KUYŌ, or rite for aborted fetuses. Popular in the 1970s and 1980s, the rite has been criticized by Jōdo Shinshū (True Pure Land School) and other Buddhists as being a moneymaking scheme that takes advantage of people's superstitious fears that the souls of the aborted fetuses will curse them. Others defend *mizuko kuyō* as a legitimate Buddhist ritual that can help people deal with their feelings of sadness and guilt. That some people feel guilt over abortion indicates that they feel that in some way a wrong has been committed.

Abortion is widely practiced in Buddhist countries, and the Buddhist responses vary from condemnation to justification. As indicated by studies showing that the majority of Japanese women having abortions do not feel guilt, the most popular response is toleration and acceptance of the act despite teachings that reject it, and many Buddhists remain silent, voicing no moral judgment one way or the other.

See also: **Precepts**

Bibliography

Hardacre, Helen. *Marketing the Menacing Fetus in Japan.* Berkeley: University of California Press, 1997.

Keown, Damien, ed. *Buddhism and Abortion.* Honolulu: University of Hawaii Press, 1999.

LaFleur, William R. *Liquid Life: Abortion and Buddhism in Japan.* Princeton, NJ: Princeton University Press, 1992.

GEORGE J. TANABE, JR.

ĀGAMA/NIKĀYA

The terms *Āgama* and *Nikāya* denote the subdivisions of the Sūtrapiṭaka (Pāli, Suttapiṭaka; Basket of Discourses) within the CANON. *Āgama* has the basic meaning of (received) tradition, canonical text, and (scriptural) authority, while *Nikāya* means both collection and group. *Nikāya* also denotes an ordination lineage that allows the joint performance of legal acts of the Buddhist order (SAṄGHA), a meaning that will not be explored in this entry.

It is not known when monks started to gather individual discourses of the Buddha into structured collections. According to tradition, the Buddha's discourses were already collected by the time of the first council, held shortly after the Buddha's death in order to establish and confirm the discourses as "authentic" words of the Buddha (*buddhavacana*). Scholars, however, see the texts as continuously growing in number and size from an unknown nucleus, thereby undergoing various changes in language and content. For at least the first century, and probably for two or three centuries, after the Buddha's death, the texts were passed down solely by word of mouth, and the preservation and intact transmission of steadily growing collections necessitated the introduction of ordering principles. The preserved collections reveal traces of an earlier structure that classified the texts into three, four, nine, or even twelve sections (*aṅga*), but this organizing structure was superseded by the Tripiṭaka scheme of arranging texts into the three (*tri*) baskets (*piṭaka*) of discipline (VINAYA), discourses (sūtras), and systematized teachings (ABHIDHARMA). All Buddhist schools whose literature has been preserved divided the Sūtrapiṭaka further into sections called Āgama or Nikāya. Neither term is school-specific; the notion that the THERAVĀDA school used the term *Nikāya* while other schools used *Āgama* is justified neither by Pāli nor by Sanskrit sources.

There are either four or five Āgamas and Nikāyas considered canonical by the various MAINSTREAM BUDDHIST SCHOOLS: the Dīrghāgama (Pāli, Dīghanikāya; Collection of Long Discourses); the Madhyamāgama (Pāli, Majjhimanikāya; Collection of Discourses of Middle Length); the Saṃyuktāgama (Pāli, Saṃyuttanikāya; Connected Discourses); the Ekottar(ik)āgama (Pāli, Aṅguttaranikāya; Discourses Increasing by One); and the Kṣudrakāgama (Pāli, Khuddhakanikāya; Collection of Small Texts). Some schools do not accept a Kṣudraka section as part of the Sūtrapiṭaka; others classify it as a separate piṭaka. The sequence of the five (or four) sections varies, but if included, the Kṣudraka always comes last. The names refer to the ordering principle of each section: the Dīrgha (long) contains the longest discourses; the Madhyama (middle) contains those of medium-length; and the Saṃyukta (connected) contains shorter sūtras connected by their themes. The Ekottarika (Growing by one) or Aṅguttara (Increasing number of items) comprise discourses arranged in ascending order according to numbered sets of terms, from sūtras treating one term up to those dealing with groups of ten or more. The contents of the Kṣudraka (small texts) vary significantly from version to version: Most of the works that seem to form its nucleus are composed in verse and apparently belong to the oldest strata of the canon. Some of them, such as the DHAMMAPADA, rank among the best known Buddhist texts.

It is not known how many versions of the Sūtrapiṭaka were once transmitted by the various schools in India. Equally unknown is the number of languages and dialects used for this purpose. At present, only the Pāli Suttapiṭaka of the Theravāda school is completely preserved. Four Āgamas are available in Chinese translation: the Dīrgha, the Madhyama, the Saṃyukta, with three translations, two of them incomplete, and the Ekottarika. These were translated from the collections of different schools: The Dīrghāgama probably belongs to the DHARMAGUPTAKA, the Madhyamāgama and Saṃyuktāgama to the (Mūla)Sarvāstivādins, and the Ekottarikāgama to the MAHĀSĀṂGHIKA SCHOOL.

In the early twentieth century, numerous fragments of Sanskrit sūtra manuscripts were found in Central Asia, enabling scholars to recover at least a small part of the Sūtrapiṭaka of the (Mūla)Sarvāstivādins. Later, fragments of the Ekottarikāgama of the same school came to light among the Gilgit finds. Recent manuscript finds from Afghanistan and Pakistan also contain many sūtra fragments from the scriptures of at least two schools, the (Mūla)Sarvāstivādins and probably the Mahāsāṃghikas. Most notable among them is a manuscript of the Dīrghāgama of the (Mūla)Sarvāstivādins. Unlike colophons of vinaya texts, those of single sūtras or sūtra collections never mention schools, and this often renders a definite school ascription difficult. School affiliation of Āgama texts may have been less important than modern scholars tend to believe.

The different versions of the Sūtrapiṭaka are by no means unanimous with regard to the number and type of sūtras included in each section. To give one example: The Dīghanikāya of the Theravāda school contains thirty-four texts, while the Dīrghāgama in Chinese translation contains only thirty. In the incompletely preserved Dīrghāgama of the (Mūla)Sarvāstivādins, however, forty-seven texts are so far attested. Only twenty of them have a corresponding text in the Chinese Dīrghāgama, and only twenty-four correspond to texts in the Pāli version. For eight of them, a parallel text is found in the Majjhimanikāya of the Pāli; at least four have no parallel at all. The agreement between the different versions of a sūtra varies significantly. Versions may be close in some passages and loose in others. Often a considerable part of a sūtra consists of formulaic passages, and the wording of these formulas is version specific. Further differences may be found in the sequence of passages, in the names of places and persons, and also in doctrine. All this indicates a common origin, followed by a long period of separate transmissions with independent redactional changes.

There are many examples of text duplicates in two sections of the same Sūtrapiṭaka. For example, the *Satipaṭṭhāna-sutta* (*Foundation of Mindfulness*) of the Pāli canon is contained in both the Dīgha- and the Majjhimanikāya. This may be an indication of a separate transmission for each Āgama/Nikāya in earlier times, another indication being terms like Dīghabhāṇaka (reciter of the Dīgha section) to refer to the respective specialist during the phase of oral transmission in the Pāli tradition. At least in the case of the Mūlasarvāstivādins, many sūtras are also duplicated in their Vinaya.

When growth and redactional changes of the various collections came to an end, they began to form what can best be described as part of a canon of the respective schools. However, very little is known about the use or ritual and educational functions of the collections during early times. Because of their status as scriptural authority, quotations from the sūtras are numerous in the COMMENTARIAL LITERATURE of the various schools. Certain sūtras also continued to be transmitted individually or in fixed selections designed for specific religious purposes, and it appears that such texts played a much more important role in the life of Buddhists than the complete collections. Not all the sūtras were collected as Āgamas/Nikāyas; the MAHĀYĀNA sūtras, for instance, never came to be included in such a classification scheme.

See also: **Buddhavacana (Word of the Buddha); Pāli, Buddhist Literature in; Sanskrit, Buddhist Literature in; Scripture**

Bibliography

Hinüber, Oskar von. *A Handbook of Pāli Literature.* Berlin and New York: de Gruyter, 1996.

Lamotte, Étienne. *History of Indian Buddhism: From the Origins to the Saka Era* (1958), tr. Sara Webb-Boin. Louvain-la-Neuve, Belgium: Université catholique de Louvain, Institut orientaliste, 1988.

Mayeda, Egaku. "Japanese Studies on the School of the Chinese Āgamas." In *Zur Schulzugehörigkeit von Werken der Hīnayāna-Literatur,* 2 vols., ed. Heinz Bechert. Göttingen, Germany: Vandenhoeck and Ruprecht, 1985–1987.

Mizuno, Kōgen. *Buddhist Sūtras: Origin, Development, Transmission.* Tokyo: Kōsei, 1982.

JENS-UWE HARTMANN

AJAṆṬĀ

Carved into a precipitous gorge in northern Maharashtra, Ajaṇṭā's thirty Buddhist cave monasteries were excavated in two phases. The three finished Śātavāhana caves (ca. first century C.E.) typify contemporaneous and earlier Western Indic cave monasteries. Ajaṇṭā's other caves all date to the Vākāṭaka emperor Hariṣena's reign (ca. 460–480 C.E.). The Śātavāhana and Vākāṭaka excavations reveal differences in donorship, layout, and design.

Containing numerous and generally terse Prakrit inscriptions, the earlier caves evidence a collective and socially eclectic pattern of patronage. Most of the Sanskrit Vākāṭaka donative inscriptions are later intrusions into abandoned caves. Of the four *programmatic* inscriptions, three are lengthy eulogies in verse. They record that individual members of the ruling elites donated one or more caves in their entirety, giving them to the Buddha as his residence rather than to the three jewels or the SAṄGHA as theretofore.

Differences in site layout and cave design reflect these changes. Both phases manifest two architectural types based on structural wooden prototypes. Ajaṇṭā's worship halls share apsidal plans, caitya windows, barrel-vaulted roofs, and monumental STŪPAS, while differing in the nature and amount of their painting and sculpture. Repeated buddha figures and joyous worshipers throng the Vākāṭaka stūpa halls. Most significant is the hieratically scaled buddha who, as it were, emerges from each central stūpa. Framed within an architectural structure, these active buddhas transform the later stūpa halls into *gandhakuṭīs,* the Buddha's personal residences.

Early vihāras (residential caves) typically take the form of large flat-roofed quadrangular rooms without pillars. Doorways leading to cells punctuate their sparsely decorated interior walls. The Vākāṭaka donors added internal pillars, a colonnaded porch, and rich decorations in relief and paint onto this basic plan. A rear cell located immediately opposite the main doorway was expanded into an ornate pillared antechamber with a large internal cell. Tenanted by a monolithic statue of the Buddha preaching from a cosmic throne, this cell is (1) the *gandhakuṭī* where the Buddha resides as the spiritual and administrative head of his monks, and (2) the shrine where he is worshiped.

These innovations speak to differences in Buddhist practice and belief. Vihāras with shrines signal a departure from the earlier centralization of public worship, when the only shrines were stūpa halls. In the early phase, the most potent manifestation of the Buddha's living presence was the central stūpa that embodied his body relics (*śarīra*); at Vākāṭaka Ajaṇṭā, the most potent manifestation was the monumental Buddha image dwelling in his *gandhakuṭī.* Profuse ornamentation transformed relatively austere monasteries into richly jeweled cave palaces atop a cosmic mountain, appropriate residences for the Vākāṭaka Buddha, who, as the Emperor of Ascetics, was the prime cosmic being. The belief in and practice of the bodhisattva PATH evidenced in caves 17 and 26 simultaneously reveal his imitable and human aspects. Vākāṭaka Ajaṇṭā's fabled narratives participated in these changes. Characterized by an idealized naturalism that represents beings in action, the Ajaṇṭā style "cosmologizes" landscapes and beings. It thus expresses the simultaneously transcendental and imitable nature of the Buddha performing his wondrous deeds.

See also: **Jātaka, Illustrations of; Relics and Relics Cults**

Bibliography

Dehejia, Vidya. *Discourse in Early Buddhist Art: Visual Narratives of India.* New Delhi: Munshiram Manoharlal, 1997.

Kramrisch, Stella. "Ajaṇṭā." In *Exploring India's Sacred Art: Selected Writings of Stella Kramrisch,* ed. Barbara Stoler Miller. Philadelphia: University of Pennsylvania Press, 1983.

Parimoo, Ratan, et al., eds. *The Art of Ajaṇṭā: New Perspectives.* New Delhi: Books and Books, 1991.

Schlingloff, Dieter. *Studies in the Ajaṇṭā Paintings: Identifications and Interpretations.* Delhi: Ajaṇṭā Publications, 1987.

Schlingloff, Dieter. *Guide to the Ajaṇṭā Paintings: Narrative Wall Paintings.* New Delhi: Munsiram Manoharlal, 1999.

Spink, Walter. "Ajaṇṭā's Chronology: Cave 1's Patronage." In *Chhavi II: Rai Krishnadasa Felicitation Volume.* Benares, India: Bharat Kala Bhavan, 1981.

Spink, Walter. "The Achievement of Ajaṇṭā." In *The Age of the Vākāṭakas,* ed. A. M. Shastri. New Delhi: Harman, 1992.

Spink, Walter. "The Archaeology of Ajaṇṭā." *Ars Orientalis* 21 (1992): 67–94.

Spink, Walter. "Before the Fall: Pride and Piety at Ajaṇṭā." In *The Powers of Art: Patronage in Indian Culture,* ed. Barbara Stoler Miller. Delhi: Oxford University Press, 1992.

Yazdani, Ghulam. *Ajaṇṭā: The Color and Monochrome Reproductions of the Ajaṇṭā Frescoes Based on Photography,* 4 vols. London: Oxford University Press, 1930.

LEELA ADITI WOOD

AKṢOBHYA

One of a large number of so-called celestial buddhas known to MAHĀYĀNA Buddhists in India during the first millennium, Akṣobhya was believed to inhabit a paradise-like world system far to the east, known as Abhirati (extreme delight). Bodhisattvas reborn there could make rapid progress toward buddhahood, while śrāvakas could achieve arhatship within a single life. Belief in Akṣobhya appears to have emerged in India around the beginning of the first millennium C.E. and spread widely in Buddhist communities before being eclipsed by the growing popularity of AMITĀBHA. Today Akṣobhya is known mainly as one of the five directional buddhas who appear in tantric ritual texts.

Bibliography

Chang, Garma C. C., ed. *The Dharma-Door of Praising Tathāgata Akṣobhya's Merits* (partial translation of the *Akṣobhyavyūha*). In *A Treasury of Mahāyāna Sūtras: Selections from the Mahāratnakūṭa Sūtra,* tr. Buddhist Association of the United States. University Park and London: Pennsylvania State University Press, 1983.

Dantinne, Jean, trans. *La splendeur de l'inébranlable (Akṣobhyavyūha).* Louvain-la-Neuve, Belgium: Institut Orientaliste, 1983.

Nattier, Jan. "The Realm of Akṣobhya: A Missing Piece in the History of Pure Land Buddhism." *Journal of the International Association of Buddhist Studies* 23, no. 1 (2000): 71–102.

JAN NATTIER

ĀLAYAVIJÑĀNA

The *ālayavijñāna* (storehouse consciousness) is the most fundamental of the eight consciousnesses recognized in the VIJÑĀNAVĀDA school of thought. It is said to contain all the "seeds" for the "consciousness-moments" or "consciousness-events" that people generally call reality.

See also: **Consciousness, Theories of; Psychology**

JOHN S. STRONG

ALCHI

The small village of Alchi (A lci), located about seventy kilometers west of Leh in Ladakh on an alluvial terrace on the left bank of the river Indus, has as its center an ancient religious area (*chos 'khor*). Alchi's religious area is composed of a large STŪPA, a three-storied temple (*Gsum brtsegs*), a congregation hall (*'dus khang*), two small chapels, and a later building, the so-called New Temple (*Lha khang gsar ma*). The site's thick white-washed walls of mud and stone follow the Tibetan tradition of architecture; the wooden facades and the beams and pillars of the interior structures are clearly Kashmiri in style.

The congregation hall, which dates to the late eleventh or early twelfth century, is the oldest building in the complex; the hall includes a Sarvavid-Vairocana sculpture at its back end and rich wall paintings that are mainly variants of the Vajradhātu-maṇḍala based on the Tibetan translation of the *Sarvatathāgata-Tattvasaṃgraha* (*Symposium of Truth of All Buddhas*). The three-storied temple, with three colossal clay sculptures of bodhisattvas in the niches, has similar maṇḍalas in its murals. The temple also houses representations of Tārā and Avalokiteśvara, along with many tathāgatas and secular figures. A series of images of priests in the second upper story ends with 'Bri-gung-pa (1143–1217), which leads to a date of around 1200 C.E. The stylistic elegance and sophistication of the murals has its roots in Kashmir. The so-called Great Stūpa is in fact a chapel in *pañcāyatana* form housing a stūpa and decorated with "thousands" of buddhas and a group of priests. Tibetan inscriptions in all three buildings give the names, though no dates, of the founders, who apparently belonged to the ruling families of the Ladakhi kingdom. The murals in the smaller New Temple show a different iconographic tradition and clearly belong to a slightly later Tibetan style.

See also: **Cave Sanctuaries; Himalayas, Buddhist Art in; India, Buddhist Art in; Monastic Architecture**

Bibliography

Goepper, Roger. *Alchi: Ladakh's Hidden Buddhist Sanctuary: The Sumtsek.* London: Serindia, 1996.

Pal, Pratapaditya (text), and Fournier, Lionel (photographs). *A Buddhist Paradise: The Murals of Alchi, Western Himalayas.* Vaduz, Liechtenstein: Ravi Kumar, 1982.

ROGER GOEPPER

AMBEDKAR, B. R.

Bhimrao Ramji Ambedkar (1891–1956), leader of India's Dalits (untouchables) and principal draftsman of India's constitution, led millions of his followers to Buddhist conversion. After earning doctoral degrees from Columbia University in New York and the London School of Economics, Ambedkar passed the English bar and launched a campaign of legal and moral challenges to the Hindu caste system. In *The Buddha and His Dhamma* (1957) and other writings, Ambedkar combined elements of Buddhist ethics, American pragmatism, and Protestant "social gospel" theology to formulate a socially and politically engaged Buddhism that he called "New Vehicle" (*Navayāna*) Buddhism.

See also: **Engaged Buddhism**

Bibliography

Ambedkar, Bhimrao Ramji. *The Buddha and His Dhamma.* Bombay: R. R. Bhole, 1957.

Queen, Christopher S. "Dr. Ambedkar and the Hermeneutics of Buddhist Liberation." In *Engaged Buddhism: Buddhist Liberation Movements in Asia,* ed. Christopher S. Queen and Sallie B. King. Albany: State University of New York Press, 1996.

Sangharakshita. *Ambedkar and Buddhism.* Glasgow, UK: Windhorse, 1986.

CHRISTOPHER S. QUEEN

AMITĀBHA

Amitābha (Sanskrit, limitless light) is one of the so-called celestial or mythic buddhas who inhabit their own buddha-field and intervene as a saving force in our world. According to the *Larger* SUKHĀVATĪVYŪHA-SŪTRA, in a previous life Amitābha was the monk Dharmākara, who vowed that as part of his mission as a BODHISATTVA he would purify and adorn a world, transforming it into the most pure and beautiful buddha-field. Once he attained full awakening and accomplished the goals of his vows, Dharmākara became the Buddha Amitābha. He now resides in the world he purified, known as Sukhāvatī (blissful). From this world he will come to ours, surrounded by many bodhisattvas, to welcome the dead and to lead them to REBIRTH in his pure buddha-field.

The figure of Amitābha is not known in the earliest strata of Indian Buddhist literature, but around the beginning of the common era he appears as the Buddha of the West in descriptions of the buddhas of the five directions. The cult of Amitābha most likely developed as part of the early MAHĀYĀNA practice of invoking and worshiping "all the buddhas" and imagining some of these as inhabiting distant, "purified" worlds, usually associated with one of the cardinal directions. The myth of his vows and pure land may have developed in close proximity to, or in competition with, similar beliefs associated with other buddhas like AKṢOBHYA (another one of the early buddhas of the five directions, whose eastern pure land is known as Abhirati).

Although Amitābha shares many of the qualities associated with other buddhas of the Mahāyāna, he is generally linked to the soft radiance of the setting sun, which suffuses, without burning or blinding, all corners of the universe (in East Asia he is also linked to moonlight). The emphasis on his luminous qualities (or those of his halo), which occupies an important role in East Asian iconography, does not displace or contradict the association of Amitābha with a religion of voice and sound; his grace is secured or confirmed by calling out his name, or, rather, invoking his name with the ritual expression of surrender: "I pay homage to Amitābha Buddha." Even in texts that emphasize imagery of light, such as the *Dazhidu lun* (*Treatise on the Great Perfection of Wisdom*), he is still the epitome of the power of the vow and the holy name.

Amitābha is represented in *dhyānamudrā,* perhaps suggesting the five hundred kalpas of meditation that led Dharmākara to his own enlightenment. An equally characteristic posture is *abhayamudrā* (MUDRĀ of protection from fear and danger), which normally shows the buddha standing.

In its more generalized forms, however, FAITH in Amitābha continues to this day to include a variety of practices and objects of devotion. A common belief, for instance, is the belief that his pure land, Sukhāvatī, is blessed by the presence of the two bodhisattvas Avalokiteśvara and Mahāsthāmaprāpta. Faith in the saving power of these bodhisattvas, especially Avalokiteśvara, was often linked with the invocation of the sacred name of Amitābha, the recitation of which could bring the bodhisattva Avalokiteśvara to the believer's rescue. The overlapping of various beliefs and practices, like the crisscrossing of saviors and sacred images, is perhaps the most common context for the appearance of Amitābha—it is the case in China, Korea, and Vietnam, and in Japanese Buddhism outside the exclusive Buddhism of the Kamakura reformers.

The perception of Amitābha as one among many saviors, or the association between faith in him and the wonder-working powers of Avalokiteśvara, are common themes throughout Buddhist Asia. It is no accident that the PANCHEN LAMA of Tibet is seen as an incarnation of Amitābha, whereas his more powerful counterpart in Lhasa, the DALAI LAMA, is regarded as the reincarnation of the Bodhisattva Avalokiteśvara.

See also: **Nenbutsu (Chinese, Nianfo; Korean, Yŏmbul); Pure Lands**

Bibliography

Foard, James; Michael Solomon; and Richard K. Payne, eds. *The Pure Land Tradition: History and Development.* Berkeley: Regents of the University of California, 1996.

Gómez, Luis O. "Buddhism as a Religion of Hope: Observations on the 'Logic' of a Doctrine and Its Foundational Myth." *Eastern Buddhist* New Series 32, no. 1 (Spring 1999/2000): 1–21.

Gómez, Luis O., trans. and ed. *The Land of Bliss: The Paradise of the Buddha of Measureless Light: Sanskrit and Chinese Versions of the Sukhāvatīvyūha Sūtras* (1996), 3rd printing, corrected edition. Honolulu: University of Hawaii Press, 2000.

Tsukinowa, Kenryū; Ikemoto, Jūshin; and Tsumoto, Ryōgaku. "Amita." In *Encyclopaedia of Buddhism,* Vol. 1, Fasc. 3., ed. G. P. Malalasekera. Colombo, Sri Lanka: Government Press of Ceylon, 1964.

Zürcher, E. "Amitābha." In *The Encyclopedia of Religion,* Vol. 1., ed. Mircea Eliade. New York: Macmillan, 1987.

LUIS O. GÓMEZ

AMULETS AND TALISMANS

Amulets are small, mystically charged objects carried upon the person that provide the bearer with good fortune or protection from harm. Amulets are carried by members of many Buddhist cultures, most prominently in the THERAVĀDA countries of mainland Southeast Asia (Burma [Myanmar], Thailand, Laos, and Cambodia). These amulets are almost always explicitly Buddhist in form. They often take the form of small Buddha images or representations of holy people. They can also be representations of sacred objects, such as *cetiyas. Cetiyas* (Sanskrit, *caitya*) are reliquary monuments, such as STŪPAS. The sale of Buddhist amulets can be an effective means of raising funds.

Amulets are usually either stamped medallions or molded clay statuettes—similar to votive tablets—that are small enough to be worn on a chain around the neck. Stamped medallions, usually of bronze, are a relatively modern but very popular type. They are often issued in honor of a particularly holy monk and bear the monk's portrait on the obverse. The reverse can bear representations of renowned stūpas or apotropaic texts and designs, such as magical number squares. Amulets can also be short sacred passages (usually gāthā) written on paper, cloth, or metal. In Southeast Asia, texts on base or precious metal are wound into tight little tubes. Texts on paper are similarly rolled up and put into a small container. Texts on cloth can be carried folded up and put into a breast pocket; it would be sacrilegious to carry them in a lower pocket. These amulets are especially popular in Cambodia. Texts or magical diagrams can also be written on larger pieces of cloth or paper and carried folded up in other types of containers, such as cloth pouches or lockets made of wood, brass, or silver. This type of amulet is used in Tibet and China.

Amulets derive their power from the blessings of monks with reputations for being exceptionally holy and mystically powerful. The amulets can be seen as small objects in which the power of the sacred is crystallized, as with holy relics. Once crystallized, this power can be used by ordinary people who are not themselves holy or powerful. This power comes from both the words—Pāli or Sanskrit blessings—and the personal power of the monks who chant them. The right words must be spoken by the right person for the transfer of power to be effective. Individual monks acquire this power after years of meditation; it is demonstrated by their ability to perform miracles. The ideal monk is an ascetic hermit who spends his days in meditation and who has been ordained since he was a boy.

While amulets are most commonly worn for generalized protection, they often have very specific protective properties. A given amulet, for instance, may protect against puncture wounds (such as those from bullets or knives), but not against crushing wounds (such as those from truncheons). It is not unusual to see men, and to a lesser extent women, wearing several amulets. Special metal neck chains are made for this purpose. Thriving amulet markets can be found near some large urban Buddhist monasteries. The value of an amulet is a function of the power of its initial blessing (which derives from the holiness of the monk who blessed it), its age and rarity, and any history of demonstrated efficacy that is attached to it. An amulet is more valuable if it is known, for example, to have saved someone from a terrible car wreck.

See also: **Merit and Merit-Making; Relics and Relic Cults**

Bibliography

Tambiah, Stanley Jeyaraja. *The Buddhist Saints of the Forest and the Cult of Amulets: A Study in Charisma, Hagiography, Sectarianism, and Millennial Buddhism.* Cambridge, UK: Cambridge University Press, 1984.

MICHAEL R. RHUM

ANAGĀRIKA DHARMAPĀLA

Anagārika Dharmapāla (1864–1933) was the leading figure in the Sri Lankan Buddhist renaissance that sought to restore Buddhism during the late colonial period. Born Don David Hēvāvitarana into an elite Sinhala Buddhist family, he met Colonel Henry Olcott and Madame Elena Petrovna Blavatsky and joined their newly formed Buddhist Theosophical Society in 1884 in Sri Lanka (then Ceylon). Seeing the depressed condition of Buddhism in both Sri Lanka and India, Dharmapāla took it as his mission to revive Buddhism. In his work he sought to enable Buddhists to address the twofold task of recovering their identity and finding ways to respond to modernity. Creating a new role for himself in Buddhism, he became an *anagārika* (homeless one), who was neither a monk nor a layperson, and he took the name Dharmapāla (protector of the dharma).

A tireless activist, Dharmapāla worked in India, where he founded the Maha Bodhi Society and sought to restore the Buddhist shrine of the sacred bodhi tree at the site of the Buddha's enlightenment in BODH GAYĀ. Through his writings and his brilliant oratory, he critiqued the colonial and Christian suppression of Buddhism and Buddhists. Relying on Buddhist texts such as the *Mahāvaṃsa,* he linked Buddhism and Sinhala nationalism and challenged Sinhala Buddhists to reclaim their true identity and abandon their attachment to colonial values. Dharmapāla popularized a reformed Buddhism that was characterized by a lay orientation, a this-worldly asceticism, an activist and moralist focus, and a strong social consciousness. Dharmapāla traveled widely in Asia preaching these ideas, and he introduced the West to his reformist vision when he represented Buddhism at the World Parliament of Religions in Chicago in 1893.

Bibliography

Bond, George D. *The Buddhist Revival in Sri Lanka: Religious Tradition, Reinterpretation, and Response.* Columbia: University of South Carolina Press, 1988.

Gombrich, Richard, and Obeysekere, Gananath. *Buddhism Transformed: Religious Change in Sri Lanka.* Princeton, NJ: Princeton University Press, 1988.

GEORGE D. BOND

ĀNANDA

Ānanda was a close relative of the Buddha. The Buddha ordained Ānanda, and as the Buddha grew old, he chose Ānanda to serve as his attendant. Thus, Ānanda became the Buddha's constant companion for the twenty-five years preceding the Buddha's death. The canonical texts are replete with examples of Ānanda's dedicated care for the Buddha's comfort, health, and safety. In an extreme situation, Ānanda was even prepared to risk his life to save that of his master. Ānanda is depicted in the scriptures as extremely amicable toward both ordained or laypersons. He was known as a brilliant organizer who essentially served as the Buddha's personal secretary, as he would be called in present terms. Ānanda was instrumental in the creation of the Buddhist order of NUNS, a move that the Buddha did not initially favor. Ānanda, however, asked the Buddha if women were capable of realizing supreme enlightenment like men, whereupon the Buddha answered in the affirmative.

Ānanda was the key figure in the transmission of the BUDDHAVACANA (WORD OF THE BUDDHA). He served as an indispensable authority at the First Council, which was held to codify the Buddha's legacy soon after his death. Ānanda is reported to have recited the texts of the discourses (sūtras); in the line that opens all sūtras—"Thus have I heard"—the *I* refers to Ānanda. The Buddha's declaration that Ānanda was foremost among the erudite and upright is a monument to his talents, moral strength, and determination. Ānanda was said to have lived an extraordinarily long life. He later came to be revered as the second Indian patriarch of the CHAN SCHOOL.

See also: **Councils, Buddhist; Disciples of the Buddha**

Bibliography

Malalasekera, G. P. "1. Ānanda." *Dictionary of Pāli Proper Names,* Vol. 1. London: Indian Text Series, 1937–1938.

Wang, Bangwei. "The Indian Origin of the Chinese Chan School's Patriarch Tradition." In *Dharmadūta: Mélanges offerts au Vénérable Thich Huyên-Vi,* ed. Bhikkhu Tampalawela Dhammaratana and Bhikkhu Pāsādika. Paris: Éditions You-Feng, 1997.

BHIKKHU PĀSĀDIKA

ANANDA TEMPLE

The most uplifting of Pagan temples, the Ananda was built by King Kyanzittha in the mid-eleventh century. The Ananda Temple represents the maturity of the early period style at Pagan. Based on a single story elevation, it is a balanced and harmonious design with its central spire rising from a square base and terraces. The true effect is best seen from the west side, where nineteenth-century donors did not add covered walkways. The plan is a Greek cross: a two hundred-foot central square with four prayer halls that project out at the cardinal points. Facing these prayer halls, the four cardinal shrines are set in giant arched niches cut into the block. These contain colossal standing buddhas. Only the south image is original early period; the others are Konbaung replacements from the late eighteenth and early nineteenth centuries, as are the splendid carved wood doors at the entrance to the outer ambulatory. These images are dramatically lit by concealed shafts that connect to skylights contained in the external pediments. Fragments of the original paintings have been recovered in the halls; the remainder, which would have covered all the walls and vaults, were whitewashed by misguided do-gooders during an earlier period. There is a double ambulatory running around the main block over which the exterior terraces climb. These terraces contain glazed plaque scenes of the JĀTAKAS. Around the base are more glazed plaques depicting the attack and defeat of the army of MĀRA (the personification of evil who tried to tempt the Buddha just before his enlightenment). Inside, the outer ambulatory contains ninety relief scenes from the life of the Buddha. This was a time when people were converting to the new faith and these scenes were intended to teach the story of the Buddha's life. The stone carving is vigorous and at times dynamic. As with the entire building there is an energy and excitement to these scenes. The Ananda is a monument to the establishment of THERAVĀDA as the state religion of Myanmar (Burma). There is none of the grand complacency of the colossal late temples; the place vibrates with the force of a newfound faith.

See also: **Monastic Architecture; Myanmar; Myanmar, Buddhist Art in; Southeast Asia, Buddhist Art in**

Bibliography

Duroiselle, Charles. *The Ananda Temple at Pagan.* Delhi: Manager of Publications, Archaeological Survey of India, 1937.

Luce, G. H. *Old Burma—Early Pagan.* 3 vols. Locust Valley, NY: J. J. Augustin, 1969–1970.

Strachan, Paul. *Pagan: Art and Architecture of Old Burma.* Whiting Bay, Arran, Scotland: Kiscadale Publications, 1989.

PAUL STRACHAN

ANĀTHAPIṆḌADA

Sudatta, usually called Anāthapiṇḍada (Pāli, Anāthapiṇḍika; Giver of Alms to the Destitute), the wealthy merchant of Śrāvastī and donor of the famous Jetavana Monastery in India, was perhaps the Buddhist order's most important patron. An ardent and learned lay disciple (*upāsaka*), he was particularly devoted to the Buddha and to his disciple ŚĀRIPUTRA. Anāthapiṇḍada died listening to the dharma.

See also: **Disciples of the Buddha**

Bibliography

Dennis, Mark, and Dennis, Joseph, trans. "Anāthapiṇḍada, Pūrṇa, and Kotikarna in the *Mahāsaṃghika Vinaya.*" In *The Glorious Deeds of Pūrṇa,* ed. Joel Tatelman. Richmond, UK: Curzon, 2000.

Johnston, E. H., trans. *The Buddhacarita, or, Acts of the Buddha.* Delhi: Motilal Banarsidass, 1935–1937.

Malalasekera, G. P. "Anāthapindika." In *Dictionary of Pāli Proper Names.* London: J. Murray, 1937–1938. Reprint, London: Pāli Text Society, 1974.

Nyanaponika, Thera, and Hecker, Hellmuth. *Great Disciples of the Buddha: Their Lives, Their Works, Their Legacy,* ed. Bhikkhu Bodhi. Boston: Wisdom, 1997.

JOEL TATELMAN

ANĀTMAN/ĀTMAN (NO-SELF/SELF)

The Vedic Sanskrit term *ātman* (Pāli, attā), literally meaning breath or spirit, is often translated into English as self, soul, or ego. Etymologically, anātman (Pāli, anattā) consists of the negative prefix *an* plus *ātman* (i.e., without ātman) and is translated as no-self, no-soul, or no-ego. These two terms have been employed in the religious and philosophical writing of India to refer to an essential substratum within human beings. The idea of ātman was fully developed by the Upaniṣadic and Vedāntic thinkers who suggested that there does exist in one's personality, a permanent, unchanging, immutable, omnipotent, and intelligent ātman, which is free from sorrow and leaves the body at death. The *Chāndogya Upaniṣad,* for instance, states that the ātman is "without decay, death, grief." Similarly, the *Bhagavadgītā* calls the ātman "eternal . . . unborn . . . undying . . . immutable, primordial . . . all-pervading." Some Upaniṣads hold that the ātman can be separated from the body like the sword from its scabbard and can travel at will away from the body, especially in sleep. But Buddhism maintains that since everything is conditioned, and thus subject to ANITYA (IMPERMANENCE), the question of ātman as a self-subsisting entity does not arise. The religion points out that anything that is impermanent is inevitably DUḤKHA (SUFFERING) and out of our control (anātman), and thus cannot constitute an ultimate self.

According to Buddhism, beings and inanimate objects of the world are constructed (*saṃskṛta*), as distinguished from NIRVĀṆA, which is unconstituted (*asaṃskṛta*). The constituted elements are made up of the five SKANDHA (AGGREGATE) or building blocks of existence: the physical body (*rūpa*), physical sensation (*vedanā*), sensory perception (*saṃjñā, saññā*), habitual tendencies (saṃskāra, *saṃkhāra*), and consciousness (*vijñāna, viññāna*). The last four of these skandhas are also collectively known as *nāma* (name), which denotes the nonmaterial or mental constituents of a being. *Rūpa* represents materiality alone, and inanimate objects therefore are included in the term *rūpa.* A living being composed of five skandhas is in a continuous state of flux, each preceding group of skandhas giving rise to a subsequent group of skandhas. This process is going on momentarily and unceasingly in the present existence as it will go on also in the future until the eradication of avidyā (ignorance) and the attainment of nirvāṇa. Thus, Buddhist analysis of the nature of the person centers on the realization that what appears to be an individual is, in fact, an ever-changing combination of the five skandhas. These aggregates combine in various configurations to form what is experienced as a person, just as a chariot is built of various parts. But just as the chariot as an entity disappears when its constituent elements are pulled apart, so does the person disappear with the dissolution of the skandhas. Thus, what we experience to be a person is not a thing but a process; there is no human being, there is only becoming. When asked who it is, in the absence of a self, that has feeling or other sensations, the Buddha's answer was that this question is wrongly framed: The question is not "who feels," but "with what as condition does feeling occur?" The answer is contact, demonstrating again the conditioned nature of all experience and the absence of any permanent substratum of being.

Just as the human being is analyzed into its component parts, so too is the external world with which one interacts. This interaction is one of consciousness (*vijñāna*) established through cognitive faculties (*indriya*) and their objects. These faculties and their objects, called spheres (*āyatana*), include both sense and sense-object, the meeting of which two is necessary for consciousness. These three factors that together comprise cognition—the sense-faculty, the sense-object, and the resultant consciousness—are classified under the name *dhātu* (element). The human personality, including the external world with which it interacts, is thus divided into skandha, *āyatana,* and *dhātu.* The generic name for all three of them is dharma, which in this context is translated as "elements of existence." The universe is made up of a bundle of elements or forces (saṃskāras) and is in a continuous flux or flow (*santāna*). Every dharma, though appearing only for a single instant (*kṣaṇa*), is a "dependently originating element," that is, it depends for its origin on what had gone before it. Thus, existence becomes "dependent existence," where there is no destruction of one thing and no creation of another. Falling within this scheme, the individual is entirely phenomenal, governed by the laws of causality and lacking any extraphenomenal self within him or her.

In the absence of an ātman, one may ask how Buddhism accounts for the existence of human beings, their identity, continuity, and ultimately their religious goals. At the level of "conventional truth" (*saṃvṛtisatya*), Buddhism accepts that in the daily transactional world, humans can be named and recognized as more or less stable persons. However, at the level of the "ultimate truth" (*paramārthasatya*), this unity and stability of personhood is only a sense-based construction of our productive imagination. What the Buddha encouraged is not the annihilation of the feeling of self, but the elimination of the belief in a permanent and eternal "ghost in the machine." Thus, the human being in Buddhism is a concrete, living, striving creature, and his or her personality is something that changes, evolves, and grows. It is the concrete human, not the transcendental self, that ultimately achieves perfection by constant effort and creative will.

The Buddhist doctrine of REBIRTH is different from the theory of reincarnation, which implies the transmigration of an ātman and its invariable material rebirth. As the process of one life span is possible without a permanent entity passing from one thought-moment to another, so too is a series of life-processes possible without anything transmigrating from one existence to another. An individual during the course of his or her existence is always accumulating fresh KARMA (ACTION) affecting every moment of the individual's life. At DEATH, the change is only comparatively deeper. The corporeal bond, which held the individual together, falls away and his or her new body, determined by karma, becomes one fitted to that new sphere in which the individual is reborn. The last thought-moment of this life perishes, conditioning another thought-moment in a subsequent life. The new being is neither absolutely the same, since it has changed, nor totally different, being the same stream (*santāna*) of karmic energy. There is merely a continuity of a particular life-flux; just that and nothing more. Buddhists employ various similes to explain this idea that nothing transmigrates from one life to another. For example, rebirth is said to be like the transmission of a flame from one thing to another: The first flame is not identical to the last flame, but they are clearly related. The flame of life is continuous, although there is an apparent break at so-called death. As pointed out in the MILINDAPAÑHA (*Milinda's Questions*), "It is not the same mind and body that is born into the next existence, but with this mind and body . . . one does a deed . . . and by reason of this deed another mind and body is born into the next existence." The first moment of the new life is called consciousness (*vijñāna*); its antecedents are the saṃskāras, the prenatal forces. There is a "descent" of the consciousness into the womb of the mother preparatory to rebirth, but this descent is only an expression to denote the simultaneity of death and rebirth. In this way, the elements that constitute the empirical individual are constantly changing but they will never totally disappear till the causes and conditions that hold them together and impel them to rebirth, the craving (*tṛṣṇā*; Pāli, *taṇhā*), strong attachment (*upādāna*) and the desire for reexistence (*bhava*), are finally extinguished.

See also: **Consciousness, Theories of; Dharma and Dharmas; Intermediate States**

Bibliography

Collins, Steven. *Selfless Persons: Imagery and Thought in Theravāda Buddhism.* Cambridge, UK: Cambridge University Press, 1982.

Conze, Edward. *Buddhist Thought in India: Three Phases of Buddhist Philosophy.* London: Allen and Unwin, 1962.

de Silva, Lynn A. *The Problem of the Self in Buddhism and Christianity.* Colombo, Sri Lanka: Study Centre for Religion and Society, 1975.

Hick, John. *Death and Eternal Life.* London: Macmillan, 1976.

Kalupahana, D. J. *The Principles of Buddhist Psychology.* Albany: State University of New York Press, 1987.

Murti, T. R. V. *The Central Philosophy of Buddhism: A Study of the Mādhyamika System,* 2nd edition. London: Allen and Unwin, 1960.

Pérez-Remón, Joaquín. *Self and Non-Self in Early Buddhism.* The Hague, Netherlands: Mouton, 1980.

Rahula, Walpola. *What the Buddha Taught,* revised edition. Bedford, UK: Fraser Gallery, 1967.

K. T. S. SARAO

ANCESTORS

The meaning of *ancestor* differs among different cultures, depending on their kinship system and their beliefs regarding the deceased. *Ancestor* could refer to the originator of an ancestral lineage or the soul of a dead person who is memorialized in a family shrine. The Sanskrit word for ancestor, *preta,* is related to the Vedic term *pitaraḥ* (fathers). According to an ABHIDHARMA commentary, *Mahāvibhāṣā* (Chinese, *Dapiposha lun*; *Great Exegesis*), Yama, the first mortal who died and became the king of the netherworld, is called *preta-rāja* (king of the dead) or *pitṛ-rāja* (king of fathers). Thus, in ancient India, the words *preta* and *pitaraḥ* were almost interchangeable in their use. This reflects the patrilineal kinship system of ancient India and the ancestral rites that were performed and maintained through the male line.

In Asia, various forms of ancestor worship were incorporated into Buddhist rites. Ancestral rites and ceremonies are particularly prominent in East Asia, where MAHĀYĀNA Buddhism and Confucianism predominated and interacted. Southeast Asian societies, where THERAVĀDA Buddhism flourished, observe similar Buddhist rites for ancestors, but the continuity of a family lineage is not the main motive of their rites. In general, ancestor worship entails belief in the protective power of the deceased members of a particular family, lineage, or a tribal group. It is also based on the desire to overcome fear of the corpse and elevate the newly deceased to the level of respected ancestors, which continue to interact with the living.

Buddhist ideas of soul and afterlife

According to Buddhist scriptures, questions regarding existence in the afterlife constitute one of the fourteen issues on which the Buddha did not elaborate because such matters cannot be proven by experience or logic. Buddhist teachings denied any unchangeable or permanent entity, such as a soul, since all phenomena are seen as subject to ANITYA (IMPERMANENCE). The Buddha is said to have instructed his disciples not to deal with funerals, unless they were for family members. The Buddha's funeral is said to have been performed according to the ancient Indian customs for the funeral of a cakravartin (wheel-turning emperor or king, who rules the world), and no Buddhist funerals for the dead were established at that time. Buddhist ideas of no-self (anātman) were the opposite of Brahmanical beliefs concerning the continuity of the self. Later, however, some Buddhist schools modified the idea of no-self by, for example, positing the ĀLAYAVIJÑĀNA (storehouse consciousness) as that which undergoes rebirth. One widely accepted theory is the Sarvāstivāda school's stance on KARMA (ACTION) as the continuing force that sets in motion a new existence after death. Whatever philosophical terms the Buddhist scholars used, continuity of the individual after death was more or less assumed. These ideas, such as karma, provided the theoretical background for ancestral rites for the Buddhists.

Buddhist ancestral rites developed and incorporated non-Buddhist beliefs and practices from Hinduism, Confucianism, Daoism, and Shintō, as well as from the popular folk beliefs of the people in Asia. In almost all Asian cultures, indigenous spirit cults play a major role in ancestor worship and veneration: for example, the *phi* spirit of Thai people, the *nat* of the Burmese, the *tama* of the Japanese, and the *po* and *gui* of the Chinese. These potentially dangerous spirits can become ancestors through Buddhist pacification rituals and memorial rites.

The Ghost Festival and merit transfer

The most widespread Buddhist ancestral festival is the GHOST FESTIVAL, or *yulanpen* (Japanese, Obon), which was recorded in Chinese Buddhist sources as early as the fifth century. During the Ghost Festival, ancestors are invited back to this world for a feast, which is prepared by the family members. This festival is based on the Buddhist legend of MAHĀMAUDGALYĀYANA, one of the ten leading disciples of the Buddha. Mahāmaudgalyāyana is well known for liberating his mother from hell. His mother was unable to eat since all the food she tried to eat changed into fire before she put it into her mouth. Mahāmaudgalyāyana's offerings to the community of monks saved her from hell, and she was reborn in an upper heaven. This *yulanpen* festival unites the Buddhist components of hungry ghosts and salvation with Chinese indigenous belief in pacifying dead spirits. In China, imitation paper money and miniature furniture and houses are burned to enrich the dead in the netherworld. With proper family offerings, these spirits can be transformed into protective ancestors.

This legend of *yulanpen* is based on Chinese Buddhist scriptures, but the idea of food offerings for ancestors also existed in pre-Buddhist India. An example of this is the main feature of the śrāddha feast, where sacred rice balls, or *piṇḍa,* were offered to ancestors. In these Indian rites, a feast is provided for the Brahmans, and the merit of this act is transferred to the ancestors. This kind of direct and indirect ritual feeding of ancestors has been incorporated into Buddhist ancestral rites such as *yulanpen* and other rites to feed hungry ghosts.

In *yulanpen* and related rites, an altar outside the main chapel was set up with food for the hungry ghosts, and various sūtras were recited in order to feed them and provide prayers for the pretas' possible future enlightenment. This kind of ritual act of *pūjanā* or, as Lynn deSilva calls it, "spiritual nourishment" (p. 155) was made for various revered objects such as the "three jewels" of the Buddha, dharma, and saṅgha, as well as for parents, teachers, elders, and the souls of the dead. The objects of offering were primarily food but also included incense (fragrance), clothes, bedding for monks, flowers, lights (candles and other bright lights), music, and right actions. In these offering ceremonies, the Buddha is symbolically invited into the ceremonial place and given praise and offerings. Confessional prayers are recited and certain MANTRA (e.g., *nenbutsu,* DHĀRAṆĪ, or DAIMOKU, depending on which Buddhist school one belongs to) are chanted in front of the Buddha. The merit accrued from these offerings and sūtra recitations is transferred to the dead.

In Sri Lanka, the deceased who did not reach the proper afterworld are feared by the living. Various sicknesses and disasters are alleged to be caused by these floating spirits of the dead. In order to pacify such ghosts, Buddhist monks are called upon to perform the *pirit* rites and to distribute magic threads and water to those afflicted. These floating spirits are eventually transformed into benevolent ancestors by the power of the *pirit* rites. Thai and Burmese Buddhists observe the same rite, but it is called the *paritta* ritual (Spiro, pp. 247–250). In Thailand, *bun khaw saak* (merit-making with puffed rice) and *org phansa* (end of Lent) are held annually in *wats* (monasteries), and offerings are made to the ancestors collectively (Tambiah, p. 190). The merit of such acts is transferred to the deceased, yet Stanley Tambiah is reluctant to call these ceremonies ancestral worship since they do not involve systematized or formalized interaction between the deceased and the living. Nevertheless, he notes that the Buddhist monks act as mediators between death and rebirth, and they eliminate the dangers and pollution of death. In Korea, Buddhist monks do not widely deal with death rituals or rites of feeding deceased spirits and ancestors, unlike Thai or Japanese monks, even though Koreans have similar beliefs in spirits as those of other East Asian people. Shamans (Korean, *mudang*) largely deal with these ancestral rites.

Intermediate states and memorial rites

The timing interval of memorial rites for the dead varies. In Sri Lanka, the rites (*pūjanās*) are to be held on the seventh day, three months, and one year after the death day. These memorial rites are called *mataka dānēs,* and monks are invited for the memorial feasts. The ABHIDHARMAKOŚABHĀṢYA and other Buddhist texts describe the judgments said to be undergone by the dead in the INTERMEDIATE STATES (Sanskrit, *antarābhava*; Chinese, *zhongyou*) every seven days after death, up to the forty-ninth day. The forty-ninth day is the final date when the realm of REBIRTH—whether in the hells, the heavens, or other realms—will be decided. Thus it marks the end of first mourning period for the living. In China, memorial rites for the deceased assume the form of Ten Buddha Rites (Chinese, *shifoshi*), which include seven weekly rites held every seven days up to the forty-ninth day, and on the hundredth day, one year, and the third year anniversaries—in total, ten memorial rites.

In Japan, three to five more rites were added, including rites held on the seventh, thirteenth, and thirty-third anniversaries. Observing ancestral rites is a major part of Japanese Buddhist practice, and death related rituals and services, such as funerals and memorial rites, have become the major source of monastic financing. According to folklorist Yanagida Kunio, the deceased souls, which are called *hotoke* (buddha) or spirits (Japanese, *shōrei*) are purified through these memorial rites. Once pacified, they become *kami* (deities) after the thirty-third anniversary memorial rite. These deified ancestors eventually lose their individual personalities as time passes and converge into the collective group of divine ancestors, which resides in the ancestral tablets (Japanese, *ihai*) and in ancestral family tombs. In Japan, *ihai* tablets are the most significant object in a Buddhist altar. They are enshrined in Japanese homes, with the exception

A Zen (Chan school) priest paying respect at his parents' gravesite in the cemetery of the Kōtokoji in Tokyo, 1992. © Don Farber 2003. All rights reserved. Reproduced by permission.

of those of Jōdo Shinshū, one of the major lineages of Pure Land adherents. The ancestral tablet is Chinese Confucian in origin but was popularized by Buddhist monks during the fifteenth and sixteenth centuries (Fujii, 1988, p. 20).

Family tombs are also important objects of ancestral worship in Japan. Early tombs are modeled on the STŪPAS in India, where relics of the Buddha are enshrined. Japanese ancestral tombs are visited by family members to commemorate their ancestors during the Obon ancestral festival. Unlike the Chinese and Japanese, Thai and Burmese Buddhists do not show much interest in building and maintaining elaborate graves because tombs are not regarded as ancestral residences.

Founder worship in Japan

Another characteristic of Japanese Buddhism in relation to ancestor worship is worship of the founders of various Buddhist schools and sects, many of which were established during the Kamakura period (1185–1333). Those most frequently worshipped include KŪKAI (774–835) of the Shingon Tantric school; Eisai (1141–1215) of Rinzai Zen; DŌGEN (1200–1253) of Sōtō Zen; HŌNEN (1133–1212) of the Pure Land sect or Jōdoshū; SHINRAN (1173–1263) of Jōdo Shinshū; and NICHIREN (1222–1282) of the Nichiren school. These founders are worshipped and revered as divine "fathers" of their respective lineages. The followers of these founders are considered the "children" of the father-founders, using a family analogy. The blood lineage (Japanese, *kechimyaku*) is interpreted in a spiritual sense as the bond connecting the founder and the followers through various rites. This founder worship is the basis of salvific and devotional Japanese Buddhism, since schools and lineages were formed and developed upon the basis of the revelatory experience of these founders. Several annual rites are performed to commemorate the birth, death, and other major life events of the founders or prominent monks who contributed to the different schools of Buddhism in Japan. The stūpas, which contain the remains of founders and prominent monks, are usually constructed within a monastery complex of the headquarters of a particular lineage or sect. Furthermore, statues of the founders and prominent monks are made and placed near the central objects of worship, usually Buddha figures or MAṆḌALAS.

Conclusion

Although Śākyamuni Buddha did not affirm the existence of an unchanging soul, Buddhism, in its development over many centuries in different parts of Asia, provides a rich theoretical and ritual basis for ancestral rites. One aspect of this basis is the idea of repeated birth in the lower six realms of existence: the realms of the hells, hungry ghosts, animals, humans, demigods (asura), or heavenly deities, depending upon one's karma from past lives. This idea of karma, of ancient Indian origin, was inherited by Buddhists and is understood as the continuing individual process that undergoes the cycle of rebirth. The concept of PRATĪTYASAMUTPĀDA (DEPENDENT ORIGINATION) also contributed to ancestor worship, as the theory was understood, especially by the laypeople, to mean that past, present, and future lives are connected. Moreover, the idea of NIRVĀṆA, which is often explained with the analogy of extinguishing a candle, evolved into the idea of dharmakāya or dharma body, which is not affected by the death of the physical body of the Buddha (Sanskrit, nirmāṇakāya). The Buddha's funeral and the subsequent development of relic worship gave further impetus to the worship of ancestors.

The main concept underlying Buddhist ancestral rituals is the transfer of merit, which is practiced in almost all Buddhist countries. In the rituals of merit transfer, giving offerings to the Buddha is regarded as the same thing as offering to ancestors. The unity of the living and the dead or the bond between descendants and ancestors is assured and affirmed by participating in and observing the Buddhist ancestral rites. In Southeast Asia, ancestor worship is not as evident as in East Asia, but the continual transfer of merit though offerings to monks and the saṅgha provides the opportunity to commemorate and nourish ancestral spirits.

See also: **Cosmology; Death; Lineage; Merit and Merit-Making**

Bibliography

Ahern, Emily M. *The Cult of the Dead in a Chinese Village.* Stanford, CA: Stanford University Press, 1973.

deSilva, Lynn A. *Buddhism: Beliefs and Practices in Sri Lanka.* Colombo, Sri Lanka: de Silva, 1974.

Freedman, Maurice. *Lineage Organization in Southeastern China.* London: University of London, Athlone Press, 1958.

Fujii Masao. "Soshi shinkō no keisei to tenkai" (The formation and development of founder worship in Japan). *Taishō daigaku daigaku-in kenkyū ronshū* 6 (1982): 23–39.

Fujii Masao. *Sosen saiki* (Ancestral rites). Bukkyō minzogu-gaku taikei, Vol. 4. Tokyo: Meicho shuppan, 1988.

Gombrich, Richard Francis, and Obeyesekere, Gananath. *Buddhism Transformed: Religious Change in Sri Lanka.* Princeton, NJ: Princeton University Press, 1988.

Holt, John C. "Assisting the Dead by Venerating the Living: Merit Transfer in the Early Buddhist Tradition." *Numen* 28, no. 1 (1981): 1–28.

Jordan, David K. *Gods, Ghosts, and Ancestors: The Folk Religion of a Taiwanese Village.* Berkeley: University of California Press, 1972.

Lee, Kwang Kyu. "The Concept of Ancestors and Ancestor Worship in Korea." *Asian Folklore Studies* 43 (1984): 199–214.

Smith, Robert J. *Ancestor Worship in Contemporary Japan.* Stanford, CA: Stanford University Press, 1974.

Spiro, Melford E. *Buddhism and Society: A Great Tradition and Its Burmese Vicissitudes.* New York: Harper, 1970.

Takeda Chōshū. *Sosen sūhai* (Ancestor worship). Kyoto: Heirakuji Shoten, 1971.

Tamamura Taijō. *Sōshiki Bukkyō* (Funeral Buddhism). Tokyo: Daihorinkaku, 1964.

Tambiah, Stanley J. *Buddhism and the Spirit Cults in North-East Thailand.* Cambridge, UK: Cambridge University Press, 1970.

Teiser, Stephen. *The Ghost Festival in Medieval China.* Princeton, NJ: Princeton University Press, 1988.

Yanagida Kunio. *Senzo no hanashi.* Tokyo: Tsukuma shobō, 1946. English translation by Fanny Hagin Mayer and Ishiwara Yasuyo. *About Our Ancestors: The Japanese Family System.* Tokyo: Bunshōdō, 1970.

MARIKO NAMBA WALTER

ANITYA (IMPERMANENCE)

Impermanence, as the Sanskrit word *anitya* or Pāli word *anicca* are generally translated, is one of the three characteristics of the phenomenal world, or the world in which human beings live. The other two characteristics are DUḤKHA (SUFFERING) and no-self (anātman). The concept of impermanence is fundamental to all Buddhist schools: Everything that exists in this world is impermanent. No element of physical matter or any concept remains unchanged, including the SKANDHA (AGGREGATE) that make up individual persons. Things in the world change in two ways. First, they change throughout time. Second, everything in this world is influenced by other elements of the world, and thus all existence is contingent upon something else. Because of this state of interdependence, everything that exists in this world is subject to change and is thus impermanent. Impermanence is the cause of suffering, because humans attempt to hold on to things that are constantly changing, on the mistaken assumption that those things are permanent.

NIRVĀṆA is the only thing that lies beyond the reach of change, because it exists beyond the conceptual dualism of existence or nonexistence. Traditionally, Buddhist texts explain that because nirvāṇa is not dependent upon other elements in the world, it is described as "uncreated" and "transcendent." In short, nirvāṇa is not subject to change and is therefore not impermanent. For one who pursues the path toward enlightenment, the goal is to recognize the truth of impermanence by learning how not to depend upon the notion that things exist permanently in the world. According to the THERAVĀDA school of Buddhism, the first step in knowing the nature of reality is recognizing that neither the self nor the world exist permanently. Impermanence is woven throughout all of Buddhism, from its texts to artistic representations of Buddhist concepts.

See also: **Anātman/Ātman (No-Self/Self); Bodhi (Awakening); Four Noble Truths; Path; Pratītyasamutpāda (Dependent Origination)**

Bibliography

Conze, Edward. *Buddhist Thought in India: Three Phases of Buddhist Philosophy.* Ann Arbor: University of Michigan Press, 1962.

Karunadasa, Y. "The Buddhist Critique of Sassatāvada and Ucchedavāda: The Key to a Proper Understanding of the Origin and Doctrines of Early Buddhism." *Middle Way* 74, no. 2 (1999): 69–79.

CAROL S. ANDERSON

AN SHIGAO

An Shigao is the Chinese name of a Parthian Buddhist translator active in the Chinese capital Luoyang circa 148 to 180 C.E. Tradition represents him as a prince who renounced his throne to propagate the dharma in distant lands, becoming a hostage at the Han court, but little is known about his life. Scholars disagree over whether he was a layman or a monk, a follower of the MAHĀYĀNA or not. What is certain is that he was the first significant translator of Buddhist texts into Chinese. Fewer than twenty genuine works of his are thought to have survived. They include sūtras on such important topics as the FOUR NOBLE TRUTHS, PRATĪTYASAMUTPĀDA (DEPENDENT ORIGINATION), the SKANDHA (AGGREGATE), and MINDFULNESS of breathing and other techniques of self-cultivation, as well as several treatises on similar subjects (one of them an early version of Saṅgharakṣa's *Yogācārabhūmi*). Two works are in fact anthologies of short sūtras, while two other longer sūtras (*Daśottara, Arthavistara*) are compendia of terms, thus providing Chinese Buddhists with a comprehensive treatment of their new religion's ideas and vocabulary. All the translations are of mainstream (Śrāvakayāna) literature, most apparently affiliated with the Sarvāstivāda school. The first propagator of ABHIDHARMA and meditation texts in China, An Shigao also pioneered the field of Chinese Buddhist translations, and may have established the translation committee as the standard approach. While his archaic renditions were soon superseded by his successors, some of the terms he used (like the transcriptions *fo* for Buddha or *pusa* for bodhisattva) have stood the test of time and are still current in East Asia today.

See also: **Mainstream Buddhist Schools**

Bibliography

Forte, Antonino. *The Hostage An Shigao and His Offspring.* Kyoto, Japan: Italian School of East Asian Studies, 1995.

Zürcher, Erik. *The Buddhist Conquest of China: The Spread and Adaptation of Buddhism in Early Medieval China.* Leiden, Netherlands: Brill, 1959.

Zürcher, Erik. "A New Look at the Earliest Chinese Buddhist Texts." In *From Benares to Beijing: Essays on Buddhism and Chinese Religion in Honour of Prof. Jan Yün-hua,* ed. Koichi Shinohara and Gregory Schopen. Oakville, ON: Mosaic, 1991.

PAUL HARRISON

ANUTTARASAMYAKSAṂBODHI (COMPLETE, PERFECT AWAKENING)

Anuttarasamyaksaṃbodhi is a Sanskrit term for unsurpassed (*anuttara*), complete and perfect (*samyak*) awakening (*saṃbodhi*). Buddhist texts frequently use this term to describe the awakened wisdom acquired by buddhas and tathāgatas and to indicate that the content of that awakening transcends all conceptions and cannot be compared to the knowledge or wisdom of any other being, whether human or divine.

See also: **Bodhi (Awakening)**

WILLIAM M. BODIFORD

APOCRYPHA

The term *apocrypha* has been used in Western scholarship to refer to Buddhist literature that developed in various parts of Asia in imitation of received texts from the Buddhist homeland of India. Texts included under the rubric of apocrypha share some common characteristics, but they are by no means uniform in their literary style or content. Apocrypha may be characterized collectively as a genre of indigenous religious literature that claimed to be of Indian Buddhist pedigree or affiliation and that came to acquire varying degrees of legitimacy and credence with reference to the corpus of shared scripture. Some apocrypha, especially in East Asian Buddhism, purported to be the BUDDHAVACANA (WORD OF THE BUDDHA) (that is, sūtra) or the word of other notable and anonymous exegetes of Indian Buddhism (śāstra). Others claimed to convey the insights of enlightened beings from India or of those who received such insights through a proper line of transmission, as in the case of Tibetan "treasure texts" (*gter ma*) that were hidden and discovered by qualified persons. Still others were modeled after canonical narrative literature, as in the case of apocryphal JĀTAKA (birth stories of the Buddha) from Southeast Asia. Thus, what separates apocrypha from other types of indigenous Buddhist literature was their claimed or implied Indian attribution and authorship. The production of apocryphal texts is related to the nature of the Buddhist CANON within each tradition. The Chinese and Tibetan canons remained open in order to allow the introduction of new scriptures that continued to be brought from India over several centuries, a circumstance that no doubt inspired religious innovation and encouraged the creation of new religious texts, such as apocrypha. The Pāli canon of South and Southeast Asia, on the other hand, was fixed at a relatively early stage in its history, making it more difficult to add new materials.

The above general characterization offers a clue as to the function and purpose of apocrypha: They adapted Indian material to the existing local contexts—be they religious, sociocultural, or even political—thereby bridging the conceptual gulf that otherwise might have rendered the assimilation of Buddhism more difficult, if not impossible. The perceived authority inherent in the received texts of the tradition was tacitly recognized and adopted to make the foreign religion more comprehensible to contemporary people in the new lands into which Buddhism was being introduced. Indeed history shows that some apocryphal texts played seminal roles in the development of local Buddhist cultures as they became an integral part of the textual tradition both inside and outside the normative canon. But not all apocrypha were purely or even primarily aimed at promoting Buddhist causes. Some Chinese apocrypha, for example, were all about legitimating local religious customs and practices by presenting them in the guise of the teaching of the Buddha. These examples illustrate that the authority of SCRIPTURE spurred literary production beyond the confines of Buddhism proper and provided a form in which a region's popular religious dimensions could be expressed in texts.

Of the known corpus of apocrypha, the most "egregious" case may be East Asian Buddhist apocrypha that assumed the highest order of Indian pedigree, by claiming to be the genuine word of the Buddha himself. Naturally their claims to authenticity did not go unnoticed among either conservative or liberal factions within the Buddhist community. During the medieval period these texts became objects of contempt as well as, contrarily, materials of significant utility and force in the ongoing sinification of Buddhism. Thus Chinese Buddhist apocrypha epitomize the complexity of issues surrounding the history, identity, and function of Buddhist apocrypha as a broader genre of Buddhist literature.

Chinese Buddhist apocrypha

Chinese Buddhist apocrypha began to be written almost contemporaneously with the inception of Buddhist translation activities in the mid-second century C.E. According to records in Buddhist CATALOGUES OF SCRIPTURES, the number of apocrypha grew steadily every generation, through at least the eighth century. Most cataloguers were vehement critics of apocrypha, as can be gauged from their description of them as either "spurious" or "suspected" scriptures, or from statements that condemned these scriptures as eroding the integrity of the Buddhist textual transmission in China. Despite the concerted, collective efforts of the cataloguers and, at times, the imperial court to root out these indigenous scriptures, it was not until the compilation of the first printed Buddhist canon, the Northern Song edition (971–983), that new textual creation waned and eventually all but ceased. The production of apocrypha in China was thus a phenomenon of the manuscript period, when handwritten texts of local origin could gain acceptance as scripture and even be included in the canon, the result being an enigmatic category of scripture that is at once inauthentic and yet canonical.

Modern scholarship's discovery of such "canonical apocrypha" testifies to the complexity and difficulty of textual adjudication as well as to the authors' sophisticated level of comprehension and assimilation of Buddhist materials. It was never easy for traditional bibliographical cataloguers to determine scriptural authenticity. Success in ferreting out apocryphal texts—especially when the texts in question were composed by authors with extensive knowledge of Buddhist doctrines and practice and with substantial literary skill—required extensive exposure to a wide range of Buddhist literature. In addition, the task was at times deliberately compromised—as in the case of the *Lidai sanbaoji* (*Record of the Three Treasures throughout Successive Dynasties*; 597)—for no other reason than the polemical need to purge from the canon any elements that might subject Buddhism to criticism from religious and ideological rivals, such as Daoists and Confucians. The *Lidai sanbaoji* added many false author and translator attributions to apocrypha in order to authenticate those texts as genuine scripture; and once its arbitrary attributions were accepted in a state-commissioned catalogue, the *Da-Zhou kanding zhongjing mulu* (*Catalogue of Scriptures, Authorized by the Great Zhou Dynasty*; 695), the Chinese tradition accepted the vast majority of those texts as canonical. The *Kaiyuan shijiao lu* (*Record of Śākyamuni's Teachings, Compiled during the Kaiyuan Era*; 730)—recognized as the best of all traditional catalogues—was critical of both these predecessors, but even it was unable to eliminate all these past inaccuracies due in part to the weight of tradition. Canonical apocrypha are therefore ideal examples of the clash of motivations and compromises reached in the process of creating a religious tradition. These apocrypha thus added new dimensions to the evolving Buddhist religion in China due in part to their privileged canonical status, but also, more importantly, because of their responsiveness to Chinese religious and cultural needs.

There are some 450 titles of Chinese apocryphal texts listed in the traditional bibliographical catalogues. In actuality, however, the cumulative number of apocrypha composed in China is closer to 550 when we take into account both other literary evidence, as well as texts not listed in the catalogues but subsequently discovered among Buddhist text and manuscript collections in China and Japan. Approximately one-third of this total output is extant today—a figure that is surprisingly large, given the persistent censorship to which apocrypha were subjected throughout the medieval period. This survival rate is testimony to their effectiveness as *indigenous* Buddhist scripture and attests to the continued reception given to these texts by the Chinese, even such knowledgeable exegetes as ZHIYI (538–597), the systematizer of the TIANTAI SCHOOL of Chinese Buddhism. The vitality of the phenomenon of apocrypha in China also catalyzed the creation of new scriptures in other parts of East Asia, though to nowhere near the same extent as in China proper.

The extant corpus of apocrypha includes both canonical apocrypha as well as texts preserved as citations in Chinese exegetical works. Apocrypha were also found in the two substantial medieval manuscript collections discovered in modern times. The first is the DUNHUANG cache of Central Asia discovered at the turn of the twentieth century, which included manuscripts dating from the fifth to eleventh centuries. The second is the Nanatsu-dera manuscript canon in Nagoya, Japan, which was compiled during the twelfth century based on earlier manuscript editions of the Buddhist canon. It was discovered in 1990 to have included apocrypha of both Chinese and Japanese origin. The most astonishing historical finding in this canon was the *Piluo sanmei jing* (*The Scripture on the Absorption of Piluo*), an apocryphon attested in the bibliographical catalogue compiled by the renowned monk-scholar DAO'AN (312–385), but previously unknown. The Japanese manuscript is the only extant copy of this extremely early Chinese apocryphon. Other findings are no less valuable in ascertaining the overall history of apocrypha: Both the Dunhuang and Nanatsu-dera manuscripts included many titles with no known record in the catalogues, evidence indicating that indigenous scriptural creation was even more prolific than had previously been recognized. Moreover, scholars have suggested or identified convincingly some of the Nanatsu-dera apocrypha as Japanese compilations based on Indian texts or Chinese apocryphal materials. Thus the apocrypha extant in Japan serve as witness to the currency and impact of this contested, but obviously useful, material.

Texts and contents

The extant corpus of apocryphal literature defies simple description, as each text has its own unique doctrinal or practical orientation, motive, and literary style and technique. Some of the canonical apocrypha skillfully synthesized orthodox Buddhist material from India without any apparent indication of their native pedigree; others, however, propagated popular beliefs and practices typical of local culture while including negligible Buddhist elements, save for the inclusion of the word *sūtra* (*jing*) in the title. The majority falls somewhere between the two extremes, by promoting Buddhist beliefs and practices as the means of accruing worldly and spiritual merit. A few scholars have attempted to make typological classifications of all extant apocrypha, but these remain problematic until the corpus is thoroughly studied and understood in its religious and sociocultural contexts. What follows therefore is a selected review of some of the raison d'être of apocrypha, which are reflected in the ways in which Buddhist teachings are framed and presented.

We will begin with two examples of apocrypha that assembled MAHĀYĀNA doctrine in ways that would support a theory or practice that had no exact counterpart in Indian Buddhism. First, the AWAKENING OF FAITH (DASHENG QIXIN LUN) reconstructed Buddhist orthodoxy by synthesizing three major strands of Indian doctrine—ŚŪNYATĀ (EMPTINESS), ĀLAYAVIJÑĀNA (storehouse consciousness), and TATHĀGATAGARBHA (womb/embryo of buddhas)—in order to posit an ontology of mind in which the mind could simultaneously be inherently enlightened and yet subject to ignorance. After its appearance in the sixth century, the *Awakening of Faith* became perhaps the most prominent example of the impact apocrypha had on the development of Chinese Buddhist ideology, as it became the catalyst for the development of the sectarian doctrines of such indigenous schools as Tiantai, Huayan, and Chan. The text is also a prime example of the ways in which an indigenous author selectively appropriated and ingeniously synthesized Indian materials in order better to suit a Chinese religious context. Second, the *Jin'gang sanmei jing* (*The Scripture of Adamantine Absorption*, or *Vajrasamādhi-sūtra*) is an eclectic amalgam of a wide range of Mahāyāna doctrine, which sought to provide a foundation for a comprehensive system of meditative practice and to assert the soteriological efficacy of that system. The scripture is also one of the oldest works associated with the CHAN SCHOOL in China and Korea, and is thus historically significant. Unlike other apocrypha discussed elsewhere in this entry, one study suggests that this sūtra is actually a Korean composition from the seventh century (Buswell 1989). This scripture, along with Japanese apocrypha mentioned earlier, is thus a barometer of the organic relationship that pertained between Buddhism in China and the rest of East Asia and demonstrates the pervasive impetus for indigenous scriptural creation throughout the region.

Other apocrypha incorporated local references and inferences in order to better relate certain Buddhist values and stances to the surrounding milieu. PRECEPTS are the bedrock of Buddhist soteriology and figure prominently as a theme among apocrypha, as, for example, in the FANWANG JING (BRAHMĀ'S NET SŪTRA). This scripture reformulated the Mahāyāna bodhisattva precepts in part by correlating them with the Confucian notion of filial piety (*xiao*), a conspicuous maneuver that betrays both the Chinese pedigree of the text as well as its motive to reconcile two vastly different value systems. It also addressed problems arising from secular control over Buddhist institutions and membership—a blending of religious instruction and secular concerns that was not atypical of apocrypha, as we will see again below.

Other apocrypha that have precepts as a prominent theme specifically targeted the LAITY; such texts include the *Piluo sanmei jing* (*The Scripture of the Absorption of Piluo*), *Tiwei jing* (*The Scripture of Tiwei*), and *Chingjing faxing jing* (*The Scripture of Pure Religious Cultivation*). These apocrypha taught basic lay moral guidelines, such as the five precepts, the ten wholesome actions, and the importance of DĀNA (GIVING), all set within a doctrinal framework of KARMA (ACTION) and REBIRTH. These lay precepts are at times presented as the sufficient cause for attaining buddhahood, a radically simplified PATH that is no doubt intended to encourage the participation of the laity in Buddhist practice. These precepts are also often presented as being superior to the five constant virtues (*wuchang*) of Confucianism, or to any of the tangible and invisible elements of the ancient Chinese worldview, including the cosmological network of yin and yang, the five material elements, and the five viscera of Daoist internal medicine. The idea of filial piety is most conspicuous in the *Fumu enzhong jing* (*The Scripture on Profound Gratitude toward Parents*), which is based on the Confucian teaching of "twenty-four [exemplary types of] filial piety" (*ershihsi xiao*). The text highlights the deeds of an unfilial son and exhorts him to requite his parents' love and sacrifice by making offerings to the three JEWELS (the Buddha, the dharma, and the SAṄGHA). The scripture has been one of the most popular apocrypha since the medieval period.

The law of karma and rebirth mentioned above is a ubiquitous theme or backdrop of apocrypha. The text commonly known as the *Shiwang jing* (*The Scripture on the Ten Kings*) illustrated the alien Buddhist law to a Chinese audience by depicting the afterlife in purgatory. After death, a person must pass sequentially through ten hell halls, each presided over by a judge; the individual's postmortem fate depended on the judges' review of his or her deeds while on earth. This bureaucratization of hell was an innovation that mirrored the Chinese sociopolitical structure. This scripture's pervasive influence can be gauged from the many paintings, stone carvings, and sculptures of the ten kings—typically garbed in the traditional attire and headgear of Chinese officials—that were found in medieval East Asian Buddhist sites.

Given that apocryphal scriptures were products of specific times and places, it is no surprise that they also criticized not only the contemporary state of religion but also society as a whole, and even the state and its policies toward Buddhism. Such criticisms were often framed within the eschatological notion of the DECLINE OF THE DHARMA, which was adapted from Indian sources. The RENWANG JING (HUMANE KINGS SŪTRA) described corruption in all segments of society, natural calamities and epidemics, state control and persecution of Buddhism, and the neglect of precepts by Buddhist adherents. The suggested solution to this crisis was the perfection of wisdom (*prajñāpāramitā*), whose efficacy would restore order in religion and society and even protect the state from extinction. The scripture was popular in medieval East Asia, especially among the ruling class, not least because of its assertion of state protection. The *Shouluo biqiu jing* (*The Scripture of Bhikṣu Shouluo*) offered a different solution to eschatological crisis: It prophesized the advent of a savior, Lunar-Radiant Youth, during a time of utter disorder and corruption. Such a messianic message is of course not without precedent in Indian Buddhism—the cult of the future buddha MAITREYA is the ubiquitous example—but the suggestion of a savior in the present world might easily be construed as politically subversive, and as a direct challenge to the authority of the secular regime. This scripture is one of those lost apocrypha that was discovered among the Dunhuang manuscript cache some fourteen hundred years after the first recorded evidence of its composition.

The preceding coverage has touched upon only a small part of the story of Buddhist apocrypha. Even this brief treatment should make clear, however, that apocrypha occupy a crucial place in the history of Buddhism as a vehicle of innovation and adaptation, which bridged the differences between the imported texts of the received Buddhist tradition and indigenous religion, society and culture. As such, they also offer substantial material for cross-cultural and comparative studies of scripture and canon in different religious traditions.

See also: **Daoism and Buddhism; Millenarianism and Millenarian Movements**

Bibliography

Buswell, Robert E., Jr. *The Formation of Ch'an Ideology in China and Korea: The Vajrasamādhi-Sūtra, a Buddhist Apocryphon.* Princeton, NJ: Princeton University Press, 1989.

Buswell, Robert E., Jr., ed. *Chinese Buddhist Apocrypha.* Honolulu: University of Hawaii Press, 1990.

Jaini, Padmanabh S., and Horner, I. B. *Apocryphal Birth Stories (Paññāsa-Jātaka),* 2 vols. London: Pali Text Society, 1985.

Kapstein, Matthew T. *The Tibetan Assimilation of Buddhism: Conversion, Contestation, and Memory.* Oxford: Oxford University Press, 2000.

Makita, Tairyō. *Gikyō kenkyū* (Studies on Suspect Scriptures). Kyoto: Kyoto Daigaku Jinmon Kagaku Kenkyūsho, 1976.

Makita, Tairyō, and Ochiai, Toshinori, eds. *Chūgoku senjutsu kyōten* (Scriptures Composed in China); *Chūgoku Nihon senjutsu kyōten: kanyaku kyōten* (Scriptures Composed in China and Japan, Scriptures Translated into Chinese [Extractions]); and *Chūgoku Nihon senjutsu kyōten: senjutsusho* (Scriptures and Commentaries Composed in China and Japan). Nanatsu-dera koitsu kyōten kenkyū sōsho (The Long Hidden Scriptures of Nanatsu-dera, Research Series), Vols. 1–5. Tokyo: Daitō Shuppansha, 1994–2000.

Mochizuki, Shinkō. *Bukkyo kyōten seiritsushi ron* (Study on the Development of Buddhist Scriptures). Kyoto: Hōzō-kan, 1946.

Orzech, Charles D. *Politics and Transcendent Wisdom: The Scripture for Humane Kings in the Creation of Chinese Buddhism.* University Park: Pennsylvania State University Press, 1998.

Teiser, Stephen F. *The Scripture on the Ten Kings and the Making of Purgatory in Medieval Chinese Buddhism.* Honolulu: University of Hawaii Press, 1994.

Tsukamoto, Zenryū. *Tsukamoto Zenryū chosakushū,* Vol. 2: *Hokuchō bukkyōshi kenkyū* (Collected Works of Tsukamoto Zenryū, Vol. 2: Studies on the Buddhist History of Northern Dynasties). Tokyo: Daitō Shuppansha, 1974.

Yabuki, Keiki. *Meisha yoin: kaisetsu* (Echoes of the Singing Sands: Explanations). Tokyo: Iwanami Shoten, 1933.

Zürcher, Erik. "Prince Moonlight: Messianism and Eschatology in Early Medieval Chinese Buddhism." *T'oung-pao* 68 (1982), 1–59.

KYOKO TOKUNO

ARHAT

The arhat (Sanskrit) or *arahant* (Pāli) is a being who has attained the state of enlightenment that is the goal of THERAVĀDA and other MAINSTREAM BUDDHIST SCHOOLS. The arhat is fully human yet has reached a transcendent state of wisdom and liberation that the texts describe as being almost identical with that of the Buddha. In this way, the arhat fulfills a dual role as both an ideal for imitation and an object of veneration.

As an ideal of imitation, the arhat represents the completion of the gradual PATH that leads from the stage of an ordinary person, characterized by ignorance, to that of an enlightened person endowed with wisdom. Theravāda texts describe this path as having two levels: the mundane or worldly, and the supramundane. Theravāda held that the path was open to all beings who could master the attainments required, and it subdivided the path into four stages that must be completed over many lifetimes. These four stages are termed the four paths (*mārga*) or the four noble persons (*ārya-pudgala*), and comprise (1) the path of stream-attainment (*srotāpanna mārga*), (2) the path of once-returning (*sakṛdāgāmi mārga*), (3) the path of nonreturning (*anāgāmi mārga*), and (4) the path of the arhat. The division of the path into these stages extending over many lifetimes served to make the ideal of arhatship more viable for ordinary people.

The Buddhist CANON contains many sūtras that spell out in detail the nature of the perfections that must be accomplished at each of the stages of the path in order to progress toward arhatship. The perfection of moral conduct (*śīla*) constitutes the first requirement of the path. In the *Visuddhimagga (Path to Purification)*, BUDDHAGHOSA (fifth century C.E.) explains that a person on the path must fulfill the PRECEPTS, living by compassion and nonviolence, living without stealing and depending on the charity of others, practicing chastity, speaking truth, and following all of the major and minor precepts. Having made progress in *sīla,* the aspiring arhat moves to perfect the restraint of sense faculties. Controlling the senses rather than allowing the senses to control him or her, the aspirant experiences a state of peace. The next stage involves the development of samādhi, or concentration, and here the chief obstacles to be overcome are the five hindrances (*nīvaraṇa*), which include sensual desire, ill will, sloth and torpor, excitement and flurry, and DOUBT.

Closely related to this formulation of the states to be conquered is the list of mental fetters (*saṃyojana*) that must be abandoned in order to progress from the stage of stream-enterer to that of arhat. A person attains the fruit of stream-entry by eliminating the first three fetters: mistaken belief in a self, doubt, and trust in mere rites and RITUALS. To progress to the stage of the once-returner, a person must reduce lust, ill will, and delusion. The third noble person, the nonreturner, completes the destruction of the first five fetters by completely destroying sensual desire and ill will. To become an arhat one must proceed to eliminate the five remaining fetters, called higher fetters: desire for material existence, desire for immaterial existence, conceit, restlessness, and ignorance.

Having eliminated these negative states, the arhat-to-be enters the successive *jhānas* (Sanskrit, dhyāna) or trance states of samādhi, and attains the mental factors ending in pure MINDFULNESS and equanimity. The *Dīghanikāya* contrasts persons who have reached this stage with ordinary persons by stating that those who attain this level are as happy as prisoners who have been set free or as people who have found their way out of the wilderness to safety (D.1.72f.). To move beyond this stage, the potential arhat perfects the six ABHIJÑĀ (HIGHER KNOWLEDGES). The first three of these comprise what can be called miraculous powers: the ability to do the miraculous deeds traditionally attributed to Indian holy persons, such as becoming invisible, flying through the air, walking on water, and other physical and psychic powers. The three remaining *abhijñā* comprise the three knowledges: knowledge of one's previous lives, the "divine eye" (*divyacakṣu*) that allows one to see others' past lives, and knowledge of the destruction of the cankers. Having reached this stage, the arhat is described throughout the Pāli canon as "one who has destroyed the cankers, who has done what was to be done, who has laid down the burden . . . and is liberated."

The detailed and somewhat formulaic canonical descriptions of the arhat's path serve both to present the path as an imitable goal and to emphasize how distant this goal is from the ordinary person. Theravāda supplemented these normative descriptions of the path to arhatship with hagiographical accounts of the great arhats who had completed this path. The difficulty of the path implied that the figures who had completed it were greatly to be venerated. The canonical and commentarial stories of the great arhats describe them as performing meritorious deeds in their previous lives, which led to their having opportunities to hear and follow the dharma. Through hearing the dharma and practicing the path, these arhats reached the perfection of wisdom and compassion. Theravādin accounts praise these arhats for attaining various forms of perfection in relation to the world. Free from the snares of desire, the arhats were not attached to the material world. For example, the female arhat, Subhā, who had overcome all attachments and was living as a nun in the forest, plucked out her eye and gave it to a pursuer who said that he was attracted to her because of her deerlike eyes. The stories of other arhats stress their perfection of qualities such as equanimity, nonattachment, and peace. Great arhats like Mahākassapa (Sanskrit, MAHĀKĀŚYAPA) and Aññā-Koṇḍoñña were revered for their ability to teach the dharma, and other arhats were remembered for serving as advisers and counselors to the people. Veneration of these great arhats by ordinary persons at the lower levels of the path both leads to and is in itself imitation of the arhats' path to development.

Although the arhat plays a primary role in Theravāda Buddhism, the ideal is also found in some MAHĀYĀNA texts that mention a group of sixteen (or sometimes eighteen) great arhats. Mahāyāna sūtras teach that the Buddha requested these sixteen arhats to remain in the world to teach the dharma until the next Buddha, MAITREYA, appears.

See also: **Arhat Images; Bodhi (Awakening); Disciples of the Buddha**

Bibliography

Bond, George D. "The Arahant: Sainthood in Theravada Buddhism." In *Sainthood: Its Manifestations in World Religions,* ed. Richard Kieckhefer and George D. Bond. Berkeley: University of California Press, 1988.

Horner, I. B. *The Early Buddhist Theory of Man Perfected.* London: Williams and Norgate, 1936.

Tambiah, S. J. "The Buddhist Arahant: Classical Paradigm and Modern Thai Manifestations." In *Saints and Virtues,* ed. John S. Hawley. Berkeley: University of California Press, 1987.

GEORGE D. BOND

ARHAT IMAGES

The depiction of arhats (Chinese, *luohan*; Japanese, *rakan*; Korean, *nahan*) in painting and sculpture is a time-honored one in East Asian Buddhist art. Literally meaning "one worthy of honor," arhats are senior disciples of the Buddha who attained awakening through his teaching. After the sūtra about sixteen "great" arhats, *Da aluohan Nandimiduoluo suo shuo fazhuji* (*Record of the Abiding Law as Spoken by the Great Arhat Nandimitra,* T.2030), was translated into Chinese in the mid-seventh century, worship centered on this select group, which eventually expanded from sixteen to eighteen and then to five hundred in number. These select arhats, said to reside in remote mountain fastnesses and believed to possess miraculous powers, had been given the charge to protect the buddhadharma until the buddha of the future, MAITREYA, makes his appearance, and this kalpa (or cycle) of existence comes to an end. From the late ninth century onward, arhats inspired a fervent cultic worship in Central Asia and throughout East Asia.

One clue that suggests why such worship was so enduring may be found in the *Record of the Abiding Law.* There the believer is instructed to show devotion to the arhats by supporting the monastic order. The sūtra states that such devotional actions call forth the arhats, although they disguise their "transcendent natures," to mingle amidst human beings, bestowing upon pious donors "the reward of that fruit that surpasses all others" (i.e., the attainment of buddhahood). Another factor that contributed to the flourishing of arhat worship in China was the probable

An arhat, or enlightened disciple, with a fly whisk. (Chinese painting by Guanxiu, 832–912.) The Art Archive/Private Collection Paris/Dagli Orti. Reproduced by permission.

association of the miracle-working arhats named in the sūtra and subsequently depicted in paintings and sculpture with the fabled but indigenous Daoist immortals, who were also thought to reside in remote realms and possess supernatural powers; indeed, the Sanskrit term *arhat* was first translated into Chinese by borrowing terms from the Daoist lexicon that refer to such immortals.

The beginnings of the depiction of the sixteen arhats named in the *Record of the Abiding Law* are obscure; the available visual evidence consists of mere fragments or later copies of paintings. Textual sources, however, indicate that by the latter half of the ninth century, as the arhats' cultic worship became well-established, painters of note, such as Guanxiu (832–912) and Zhang Xuan (tenth century), depicted the theme, apparently in the form of iconic portraits. By this time there appear to have been two approaches to depicting arhats: either as monks with Chinese facial features or as distinctly exotic, even grotesque beings. Guanxiu, a Chan priest and accomplished poet who was said to have derived inspiration for his painting from prayer-induced visions, was heralded by later historians as having been the first to portray the arhats, in the words of Huang Xiufu (late tenth/early eleventh century), as foreign in appearance, "having bushy eyebrows and huge eyes, slack-jawed and big-nosed," and in a landscape setting, "leaning against a pine or a boulder." Such characteristics can be seen in a set of sixteen hanging scrolls in the Imperial Household Agency, Tokyo, that is generally thought to best preserve Guanxiu's powerful conception. Guanxiu's radical vision was perpetuated in sets of arhat paintings produced throughout the medieval period in China and Japan.

By the latter half of the twelfth century the mode of representing arhats in the guise of more familiar, sinicized monks, albeit sometimes performing miraculous feats, included their placement in much more elaborate landscape settings and the suggestion of narrative implications far beyond the content of the *Record of the Abiding Law.* Skilled at conjuring up such dramatic renditions in ink and color on silk, professional Buddhist painters in cities like Ningbo in Zhejiang province created large sets of hanging scrolls that depicted what had now become the five hundred arhats. One of the most significant sets to survive from a Ningbo workshop is that produced in 1178 by Lin Tinggui and Zhou Jichang.

Arhats, because of their ascetic devotion to the dharma, became a favored subject of adherents to the CHAN SCHOOL. Whereas resplendent sets of paintings, like the one mentioned above, were hung in temple halls for public worship, renderings in ink monochrome and often with exceptionally delicate lineation, known as *baimiao* or plain line drawing, were enjoyed by monks and lay worshippers in more intimate and scholarly exchanges. From the twelfth century onward in China, but especially at times when the Chan school was revitalized by the presence and activity of prominent clerics, depictions of arhats in this more scholarly mode of painting reappeared with new vigor and subtle invention.

As a complement to painted images, sculpted representations of arhats occupied temple halls as well. Few early examples survive, however. Offering a glimpse of what must have been a vibrant tradition are five magnificent ceramic sculptures of arhats, slightly larger than lifesize and featuring a three-color glaze, that were found in a cave in Hebei province early in the twentieth century. From a presumed set of sixteen, they are thought to date to the late eleventh or early twelfth century. Sinicized portrayals, they reflect the characterization of the arhats as familiar monks; nevertheless, because of the talent of the nameless artisans who created them, they are imbued with a meditative authority befitting the arhats' mission to remain ever steadfast in protecting the dharma.

See also: **Arhat; Chan Art; Daoism and Buddhism**

Bibliography

De Visser, Marinus W. *The Arhats in China and Japan.* Berlin: Oesterheld, 1923.

Fong, Wen. *The Lohans and a Bridge to Heaven.* Washington, DC: Smithsonian Institution, Freer Gallery of Art, 1958.

Kent, Richard K. "Depictions of the Guardians of the Law: Lohan Painting in China." In *Latter Days of the Law: Images of Chinese Buddhism 850–1850,* ed. Marsha Weidner. Lawrence: Spenser Museum of Art, University of Kansas; Honolulu: University of Hawaii Press, 1994.

Smithies, Richard, "The Search for the Lohans of I-chou (Yixian)." *Oriental Art* 30, no. 3 (1984): 260–274.

Watanabe, Masako. "Guanxiu and Exotic Imagery in Rakan Paintings." *Orientations* 31, no. 4 (2000): 34–42.

RICHARD K. KENT

ĀRYADEVA

Āryadeva (ca. 170–270 C.E.) in his major work, *Catuḥśataka (Four Hundred Verses)*, defends the MADHYAMAKA SCHOOL against Buddhist and Brāhmaṇical opponents. The commentary of CANDRAKĪRTI (ca. 600–650 C.E.) on this text identifies Āryadeva as a Sinhala king's son who renounced the throne, traveled to South India, and became NĀGĀRJUNA's main disciple.

Bibliography

Lang, Karen. *Āryadeva's Catuḥśataka: On the Bodhisattva's Cultivation of Merit and Knowledge.* Copenhagen, Denmark: Akademisk Forlag, 1986.

Sonam, Ruth. *Yogic Deeds of Bodhisattvas: Gyel-tsap on Āryadeva's Four Hundred.* Ithaca, NY: Snow Lion, 1994.

Tillemans, Tom J. F. *Materials for the Study of Āryadeva, Dharmāpala, and Candrakīrti,* 2 vols. Vienna: Arbeitskreis für Tibetische und Buddhistische Studien Universität Wien, 1990.

KAREN LANG

ĀRYAŚŪRA

Āryaśūra was a fourth-century C.E. Sanskrit poet. His famous work, the JĀTAKAMĀLĀ (*Garland of Jātakas*), contains thirty-four stories about the noble deeds of the Buddha in previous incarnations, exemplifying in particular the PĀRAMITĀ (PERFECTION) of generosity, morality, and patience. Written in prose interspersed with verse, it is one of the Buddhist masterpieces of classical Sanskrit literature.

See also: **Jātaka; Sanskrit, Buddhist Literature in**

Bibliography

Khoroche, Peter, trans. *Once the Buddha Was a Monkey: Ārya Śūra's Jātakamālā.* Chicago: University of Chicago Press, 1989.

PETER KHOROCHE

ASAṄGA

Asaṅga (ca. 320–ca. 390) is regarded as the founder of the Yogācāra tradition of MAHĀYĀNA philosophy. His biography reports that he was born in Puruṣapura, India, and converted to Mahāyāna from the HĪNAYĀNA, later convincing his brother VASUBANDHU to make the same move. Together they systematized the teachings of Yogācāra, authoring the main Yogācāra commentaries and treatises. Asaṅga's many works include *Abhidharmasamuccaya* (*A Compendium of Abhidharma*), which presents and defines technical terms and usages, and the *Xīanyang shengjiao lun,* extant only in Chinese translation, a text that summarizes the truly compendious *Yogācārabhūmi* (*Stages of Yogic Practice*), with which he is also connected as author/editor. Other commentaries are attributed to him on important Yogācāra and some Prajñāpāramitā and Madhyamaka works as well. By far his principal work is the *Mahāyānasaṃgraha* (*Summary of the Great Vehicle*), in which he presents the tenets of Yogācāra in clear and systematic fashion, moving step by step, first explaining the basic notion of the storehouse consciousness and its functional relationship to the mental activities of sensing, perceiving, and thinking, then outlining the structure of consciousness in its three patterns of the other-dependent (dependent arising applied to the very structure of consciousness), the imagined, and the perfected, which is the other-dependent emptied of clinging to the imagined. He then sketches how the mind constructs its world; he develops a critical philosophy of mind that, in place of ABHIDHARMA's naive realism, can understand understanding, reject its imagined pattern, and—having attained the perfected state of ŚŪNYATĀ (EMPTINESS)—engage in other-dependent thinking and action. Asaṅga thereby reaffirms the conventional value of theory, which had appeared to be disallowed by earlier Madhyamaka dialectic. He treats the practices conducive to awakening (perfections, stages, discipline, concentration, and nonimaginative wisdom) and finally turns to the abandonment of delusion and the realization of buddhahood as the three bodies of awakening. Asaṅga's work is a compendium of critical Yogācāra understanding of the mind.

See also: **Consciousness, Theories of; Madhyamaka School; Yogācāra School**

Bibliography

Keenan, John P., trans. *The Summary of the Great Vehicle by Bodhisattva Asaṅga (Translated from the Chinese of Paramārtha).* Berkeley, CA: Numata Center for Buddhist Translation and Research, 1992.

Lamotte, Étienne, ed. and trans. *La Somme du Grand Véhicule d'Asaṅga* (*Mahāyānasaṃgraha*), Vol. 1: *Version tibétaine et chinoise* (*Hiuan-tsang*); Vol. 2: *Traduction et commentaire.* Louvain-la-Neuve, Belgium, 1938–39. Reprint, 1973.

Rahula, Walpola, ed. and trans. *Le compendium de la superdoctrine* (*Abhidharmasamuccaya*) *d'Asaṅga.* Paris: École Française d'Extrême-Orient, 1971. Reprint, 1980.

JOHN P. KEENAN

ASCETIC PRACTICES

Buddhism arose in India at a time when a number of non-Vedic ascetic movements were gaining adherents. These Śramaṇic traditions offered a variety of psychosomatic disciplines by which practitioners could experience states transcending those of conditioned existence. Accounts of the Buddha's quest for awakening depict the BODHISATTVA engaging in ascetic disciplines common to many Śramaṇic groups of his time. The bodhisattva reportedly lived in the wilderness, practiced breath-control, gave little care to his manner of dress, and fasted for long periods, strictly controlling his intake of food. But these accounts are not entirely consistent. Most indicate that the bodhisattva practiced asceticism for a period of six years; others (namely the *Sutta Nipāta* 446, and the *Aṅguttara Nik-*

āya 4:88) state that the period of ascetic practice was seven years in duration. All accounts depict the bodhisattva practicing a regimen characterized by abstemious self-control, but details differ. Some say that he went unclothed in the manner of some Śramaṇic groups, that he wore only animal skins or bark clothing, and that he subsisted on fruits and roots. Some indicate that his meals consisted only of a single grain of rice, or a single jujube fruit.

The most critical discrepancy in these accounts of the bodhisattva's experiments in asceticism is the fact that where early sources such as the *Sutta Nipāta* praise asceticism, later accounts describe the bodhisattva reaching a point where he rejects asceticism and discovers the Middle Way. Later accounts link this discovery of a PATH between the extremes of self-indulgence and self-mortification to the achievement of BODHI (AWAKENING). The bodhisattva, according to these accounts, had reached such a point of emaciation that he could feel his spinal cord by touching his abdomen (e.g., *Majjhima Nikāya* 1:80, 1: 246). Fainting from hunger and near to death, the bodhisattva had to rethink his methodology. A critical juncture in his ascetic regimen occurred when he accepted an offering of rice boiled in milk and was rejected by his ascetic companions as a hedonist.

To understand why later accounts repudiate asceticism as a path to awakening and link the practice of the Middle Way to the achievement of awakening, it is necessary to consider the history of Buddhist engagement with rival religious groups and how polemics shaped the development of Buddhism in India. As Buddhism spread from its initial heartland, it became important that Buddhists take a stand on asceticism so as to clearly differentiate themselves from other non-Vedic Śramaṇic groups. Rivalry with Jains was particularly intense, as Buddhists competed for support from more or less the same segment of the lay population that Jain monastics relied upon for their financial support. Hajime Nakamura (*Gōtama Buddha*, pp. 63ff.) suggests that antiascetic sentiments began to be expressed as Buddhists responded to critical remarks made by Jains to the effect that Buddhist monastics were lazy and self-indulgent. Nakamura argues that the biographical tradition of the Buddha's discovery of the Middle Way after practicing extreme asceticism was developed in this polemical context. Other scholars have focused on internal developments within Buddhism and seen evidence of a historical shift away from early asceticism. Reginald Ray, for example, argues in *Buddhist Saints in India* (pp. 295–317) that ascetic practices were the central focus of Buddhism in early days, but later were marginalized with the growth of settled MONASTICISM.

Historical issues aside, there are other reasons for ambivalence within Buddhist traditions with regard to asceticism. On the one hand, ascetic practices are central to developing an attitude of being content with little, an important aspect of the salutary detachment that Buddhists seek to inculcate. But on the other hand, asceticism can be practiced for a variety of unwholesome, self-aggrandizing reasons. Because of concerns about possible misuse, ascetic practices have been regarded as optional rather than mandatory aspects of the path.

Lists of ascetic practices differ. In THERAVĀDA contexts, the classical list of ascetic practices (*dhutaṅga*) includes thirteen items: wearing patchwork robes recycled from cast-off cloth, wearing no more than three robes, going for alms, not omitting any house while going for alms, eating at one sitting, eating only from the alms bowl, refusing all further food, living in the forest, living under a tree, living in the open air, living in a cemetery, being satisfied with any humble dwelling, and sleeping in the sitting position (without ever lying down). MAHĀYĀNA texts mention twelve ascetic practices (called *dhūtaguṇa*). They are the same as the Theravāda list except they omit two rules about eating and add a rule about wearing garments of felt or wool.

Several of the thirteen *dhutaṅga* are virtual emblems of the SAṄGHA in Theravāda countries. For example, at the end of Theravāda ordination ceremonies, members of the saṅgha are instructed in the four ascetic customs known as the four resorts (Pāli, *nissaya*): begging for alms, wearing robes made from cast-off rags, dwelling at the foot of a tree, and using fermented cow urine as medicine (as opposed to more palatable medicines like molasses and honey). These four practices, often mentioned in canonical texts, undoubtedly go back to the beginnings of Buddhism in India.

Studies of contemporary saints in Buddhist Asia (such as those by Carrithers, Tambiah, and Tiyavanich) suggest that those who follow ascetic practices enjoy tremendous prestige. Bank presidents residing in Bangkok travel hundreds of miles and endure all kinds of hardships to visit and make offerings to WILDERNESS MONKS of the Thai forest traditions. There is no denying that the Buddhist emphasis on moderation militates against extreme asceticism. But it is equally clear from ethnographic and textual studies that ascetic practices are deeply woven into the fabric of Buddhism.

See also: **Diet; Robes and Clothing; Self-Immolation**

Bibliography

Cakraborti, Haripada. *Asceticism in Ancient India.* Calcutta: Punthi Pustak, 1973.

Carrithers, Michael. *The Forest Monks of Sri Lanka: An Anthropological and Historical Study.* Delhi: Oxford Press, 1983.

Dantinne, Jean. *Les qualities de l'ascete (Dhutaguṇa).* Brussels: Thanh-Long, 1991.

Gombrich, Richard. *Theravāda Buddhism: A Social History from Ancient Benares to Modern Colombo.* New York: Routledge, 1988.

Nakamura, Hajime. *Gōtama Buddha.* Tokyo: Buddhist Books International, 1977.

Ray, Reginald. *Buddhist Saints in India: A Study in Buddhist Values and Orientations.* New York: Oxford University Press, 1994.

Tambiah, Stanley. *The Buddhist Saints of the Forest and the Cult of Amulets: A Study in Charisma, Hagiography, Sectarianism, and Millennial Buddhism.* Cambridge, UK: Cambridge University Press, 1984.

Tiyavanich, Kamala. *Forest Recollections: Wandering Monks in Twentieth-Century Thailand.* Honolulu: University of Hawaii Press, 1997.

Liz Wilson

AŚOKA

Aśoka (ca. 300–232 B.C.E.; r. 268–232 B.C.E.), the third ruler of the Indian Mauryan empire, became a model of KINGSHIP for Buddhists everywhere. He is known today for the edicts he had inscribed on pillars and rock faces throughout his kingdom, and through the legends told about him in various Buddhist sources.

In one of his edicts, Aśoka expresses regret for the suffering that was inflicted on the people of Kaliṅga (present-day Orissa) during his conquest of that territory. Henceforth, he proclaims, he will renounce war and dedicate himself to the propagation of dharma. Just what he meant by this statement has been a subject of debate. Some have understood the word *dharma* here to mean the Buddha's teaching, and so have read Aśoka's change of heart in Kaliṅga as a conversion experience. In a few subsequent inscriptions, it is true, Aśoka does refer specifically to Buddhist sites (such as the Buddha's birthplace, which he visited in person) and to Buddhist texts, but, in general, for him, the propagation of dharma seems to have implied an active moral polity of social concern, religious tolerance, and the observance of common ethical precepts. In one edict, for instance, he orders fruit and shade trees to be planted and wells to be dug along the roads for the benefit of travelers. In others, he establishes medical facilities for humans and animals; he commissions officers to help the poor and the elderly; and he enjoins obedience to parents, respect for elders, and generosity toward and tolerance of priests and ascetics of all sects.

Throughout the ages, however, Aśoka was best known to Buddhists not through his edicts but through the legends that were told about him. These give no doubt about his conversion to Buddhism and his specific support of the monastic community. In Sanskrit and Pāli sources, Aśoka's kingship is said to be the karmic result of an offering he made to the Buddha in a past life. In this life, it is his encounter with an enlightened Buddhist novice that changes him from being a cruel and ruthless monarch into an exemplary righteous king (*dharmarāja*), a universal monarch (*cakravartin*). As such, he undertakes a series of great acts of merit: He redistributes the relics of the Buddha into eighty-four thousand stūpas built all over his kingdom; he establishes various Buddhist sites of PILGRIMAGE; he becomes a supporter of charismatic saints such as UPAGUPTA and Piṇḍola; he fervently worships the bodhi tree at BODH GAYĀ; and he gives away (and then redeems) his kingship and all of his possessions to the SAṄGHA. In addition, in the Sri Lankan *vaṃsas* (chronicles), he is said to purify the teaching by convening the Third Buddhist Council, following which he sends missionary-monks, including his own son Mahinda, to various lands within his empire and beyond (e.g., Sri Lanka).

These stories helped define notions of Buddhist kingship throughout Asia, and gave specificity to the mythic model of the wheel-turning, dharma-upholding cakravartin. From Sri Lanka to Japan, monarchs were inspired by the image of Aśoka as a propagator of the religion, distributor of wealth, sponsor of great festivals, builder of monasteries, and guarantor of peace and prosperity. In particular, the legend of his construction of eighty-four thousand stūpas motivated several Chinese and Japanese emperors to imitate it with their own schemes of relic and wealth distribution, which served to unify their countries and ritually reassert their sovereignty.

See also: **Councils, Buddhist; India; Sri Lanka**

Bibliography

Barua, B. M. *Asoka and His Inscriptions,* 2 vols. Calcutta: New Age, 1946.

Li Rongxi, trans. *The Biographical Scripture of King Asoka.* Berkeley, CA: Numata Center for Buddhist Translation and Research, 1993.

Nikam, N. A., and McKeon, Richard, eds. and trans. *The Edicts of Asoka.* Chicago: University of Chicago Press, 1966.

Strong, John S. *The Legend of King Aśoka.* Princeton, NJ: Princeton University Press, 1983.

Thapar, Romila. *Aśoka and the Decline of the Mauryas.* Oxford: Oxford University Press, 1961.

JOHN S. STRONG

AŚVAGHOṢA

Aśvaghoṣa (ca. 100 C.E.) was a Sanskrit poet and dramatist. As is the case with nearly all the writers of ancient India, legend and fictional anecdote take the place of biographical fact, but the association of Aśvaghoṣa with the Kushan king Kaniṣka is at least chronologically possible.

Aśvaghoṣa is the author of two long poems, among the earliest extant in Sanskrit: BUDDHACARITA (*Acts of the Buddha*) and *Saundarananda,* about the conversion of the Buddha's half-brother Nanda. Fewer than half of the twenty-eight cantos of the *Buddhacarita* survive complete in the original Sanskrit, bringing the story only as far as the Buddha's enlightenment, but Tibetan and Chinese translations preserve the entire work. Only fragments survive of Aśvaghoṣa's nine-act play, *Śāriputraprakaraṇa* (*The Matter* [or *Drama*] *of Śāriputra*), about the conversion of ŚĀRIPUTRA and MAHĀMAUDGALYĀYANA, later to become two of the Buddha's main disciples. Of the other works attributed to Aśvaghoṣa, only the fragments of another drama are likely to be his.

The profound knowledge of brahmanical lore displayed in his writing supports the Chinese tradition that he was born a brahman and only later converted to Buddhism. Conversion is the main theme of two of his works and also figures prominently in the third. His avowed purpose in writing was to win converts to the Buddha's teaching by the charm of his art and the intensity of his conviction. Aśvaghoṣa's fame as a writer and the legend of his life contributed to his renown in East Asia and resulted in a number of works, such as the AWAKENING OF FAITH (DASHENG QIXIN LUN), being falsely attributed to him.

See also: **Sanskrit, Buddhist Literature in**

Bibliography

Johnston, E. H., ed. and trans. *The Saundarananda of Aśvaghoṣa,* 2 vols. London: Oxford University Press, 1928 and 1932.

Johnston, E. H., ed. and trans. *The Buddhacarita or, Acts of the Buddha.* Delhi: Motilal Banarsidass, 1993.

Lüders, Heinrich. "Das Śāriputraprakaraṇa, ein Drama des Aśvaghoṣa." In *Philologica Indica.* Göttingen, Germany: Vandenhoeck & Ruprecht, 1940.

PETER KHOROCHE

ATISHA

Atisha (982–1054) was born to the ruler of a minor kingdom in Northeast India. He studied under the best Buddhist teachers of his time, including Jetāri (whose name is also written Jitāri) and Bodhibhadra. After some years of married life he entered the Buddhist order, where he was given the name Dīpaṃkaraśrījñāna (Light of Wisdom). Atisha, the name by which he is better known, is an *apabhraṃśa* (proto-Bengali) form of the common Buddhist Sanskrit term *atiśaya,* which means "surpassing intention or kindness." In Tibet, Atisha is more commonly known as Jo bo rje (pronounced Jowojay), which conveys the idea of holiness and leadership.

According to later hagiographical accounts, after becoming a monk, Atisha studied in the four great monastic universities of the Pāla dynasty (eighth to twelfth centuries): Nālandā, Otantapūri, Vikramaśīla, and Somapūri. He then traveled to Suvarṇadvīpa (perhaps Sumatra in present-day Indonesia), where he met his most important teacher, Dharmakīrtiśrī, a Cittamātra (Mind Only) philosopher who taught Atisha MAHĀYĀNA altruism (*bodhicitta*). Atisha returned to India when he was middle-aged, and the Pāla king Nayapāla appointed him abbot of Vikramaśīla, where he launched a program of monastic renewal.

At the end of the tenth century, the king of Mnga' ris (Ngari) in far western Tibet, Ye shes 'od (Yeshay ö), sent a group of twenty-one Tibetans to India, among them the great translator Rin chen bzang po (958–1055). Ye shes 'od was a descendant of the original Tibetan royal line that had ended in central Tibet in about 840, a date that marks the end of the first spread of Buddhism (*snga dar*) in Tibet. Rin chen bzang po's return to Mnga' ris after his travels in India is the traditional date for the beginning of the second spread (*sphyi dar*) of Buddhism.

According to hagiographical accounts, late in his life Ye shes 'od told his son Byang chub 'od (Changchub ö, 984–1078) to invite Atisha, then the foremost Indian Buddhist scholar, to help further the spread of Buddhism in Tibet. Atisha accepted the invitation and arrived in Mnga' ris in 1042. He never returned to India, traveling and teaching extensively before his death in central Tibet in 1054.

In western Tibet Atisha collaborated with Rin chen bzang po on Tibetan translations of PRAJÑĀPĀRAMITĀ LITERATURE. Atisha later collaborated in central Tibet with Nag mtsho tshul khrims rgyal ba (Nagtso Tsultrim gyalwa) on Tibetan translations of many fundamental texts of the Madhayamaka (Middle Way). Of his many Tibetan disciples the most important is 'Brom ston rgyal ba'i byung gnas (Dromtön Chökyi jungnay, 1008–1064), who founded Rva sgreng (Reting), the first monastery of the Bka' gdams (Kadam) sect. The Bka' gdams, which evolved into the DGE LUG (GELUK) or Yellow Hat sect, is the Tibetan sect with which the name of Atisha is most closely associated.

Among Atisha's best known works is his *Byang chub sgron me* (*Lamp for the Path*), taught soon after arriving in Tibet. In it he classifies practitioners of Buddhism into three types (those of lesser, middling, and superior capacities), and he stresses the importance of a qualified guru, the need for a solid foundation of morality, the central place of Mahāyāna altruism, and an understanding of ultimate reality. He also sets forth the practice of TANTRA as a powerful technique for quickly reaching enlightenment. Atisha's works influenced all the later Tibetan Buddhist sects (BKA' BRGYUD, SA SKYA, and Dge lugs). Some later Dge lugs writers, influenced by TSONG KHA PA's *Lam rim chen mo* (*Stages of the Path to Enlightenment,* written in 1403) projected onto the historical Atisha a mythical perfect guru who became for them the symbol of their exclusive form of monasticism and scholastic learning.

See also: **Tibet**

Bibliography

Chattopadhyaya, Alaka. *Atiśa and Tibet.* Calcutta: Indian Studies Past and Present, 1967.

Eimer, Helmut. *Rnam thar rgyas pa: Materialien zu eine Biographie der Atiśa* (*Dīpaṁkaraśrījñāna*). Wiesbaden, Germany: Harrassowitz, 1979.

Sherburne, Richard, trans. *The Complete Works of Atiśa Śrī Dīpaṁkara Jñāna.* New Delhi: Aditya Prakashan, 2000.

GARETH SPARHAM

AVADĀNA

As a genre of Buddhist literature, the Sanskrit term *avadāna* (Pāli, *apadāna*; Chinese, *piyu*; Tibetan, *rtogs par brjod pa's sde*) denotes a narrative of an individual's religiously significant deeds. Often these narratives constitute full-fledged religious biographies, sometimes of eminent monastics, sometimes of ordinary lay disciples. The *avadānas* portray, frequently with thematic and narrative complexity, concrete human actions that embody the truths propounded in the doctrine (dharma) and the discipline (VINAYA).

Avadānas range from formulaic tales that simply dramatize the workings of KARMA (ACTION) and the efficacy of FAITH and devotion, to fantastical adventure stories, to the sophisticated art of virtuosi poets. Like modern novels and short stories, *avadānas* offer something for every taste. The *avadāna* literature draws on diverse sources: actual lives, the biography of the Buddha and tales of his former births (JĀTAKA), biographical accounts in the canonical literature, and the vast, pan-Indian store of secular story-literature. Indian Buddhists composed *avadānas* from about the second century B.C.E. to the thirteenth century C.E. Thereafter, Buddhists elsewhere in Asia continued the tradition. In India and beyond, *avadāna* stories also inspired narrative painting.

Structurally, *avadānas,* like *jātakas* (which came to be considered a subcategory of *avadāna*), consist of a story of the present (*pratyutpannavastu*), a story of the past (*atītavastu*), and a juncture (*samavadhāna*) in which the narrator, always the Buddha or another enlightened saint, identifies characters in the past as former births of characters in the present. For the story of the past, some *avadānas* substitute a prediction (*vyākaraṇa*) of the protagonist's spiritual destiny.

The earliest *avadānas,* like the *Apadāna* and the *Sthavīrāvadāna* (ca. second century B.C.E.), are autobiographical narratives in verse attributed to the Buddha's immediate disciples. In contrast, biographical anthologies from the first to the fourth centuries C.E., such as the AVADĀNAŚATAKA (*A Hundred Glorious Deeds*), *Karmaśataka* (*A Hundred Karma Tales*), and DIVYĀVADĀNA (*Heavenly Exploits*), are in mixed prose and verse and feature a much wider range of characters. The *Avadānaśataka* stories are brief and formulaic, those of the *Karmaśataka* less so, and those of the *Divyāvadāna* the most complex and diverse. The sixth- to eighth-century Pāli commentaries (*aṭṭhakathā*) and several collections preserved only in Chinese contain many *avadāna* and *avadāna*-type stories.

Just as Hindu poets retold stories of heroes from the epics and Purāṇas, Buddhist poets retold the lives of their own heroes. The second-century Kumāralāta, in his *Kalpanāmaṇḍitikā Dṛṣṭāntapaṅkti* (*A Collection of Parables Ornamented by the Imagination*), first adapted the prose-and-verse format to the demands of belles lettres. His successors from the fourth to the eighth centuries, ĀRYAŚŪRA, Haribhaṭṭa, and Gopadatta, composed ornate poetry (*kāvya*) in the form of *bodhisattvāvadānamālās* (garlands of *avadānas* concerning the Buddha's previous births). Similarly, the eleventh-century Hindu poet Kṣemendra drew on the MŪLASARVĀSTIVĀDA VINAYA to compose the *Bodhisattvāvadāna-kalpalatā*, which became important in Nepal and Tibet.

The mostly unpublished verse *avadānamālās* (garlands of *avadānas*), which constitute a later subgenre, are anonymous works, composed in the style of Hindu Purāṇas, that display MAHĀYĀNA influences. Several of these retell stories from earlier sources, some in a distinctively Nepalese idiom.

As scholars increasingly recognize narrative as a mode of knowing distinct from, but in no way inferior to, philosophical discourse, they can look forward to learning much from a literary genre that has played an essential role in Buddhist self-understanding for more than two thousand years.

See also: **Sanskrit, Buddhist Literature in**

Bibliography

Burlingame, Eugene Watson, trans. *Buddhist Legends,* 3 vols. Cambridge, MA: Harvard University Press, 1921; London: Pāli Text Society, 1979.

Chavannes, Edouard, trans. *Cinq cents contes et apologues extraits du Tripitaka chinois,* 4 vols. Paris: Ernest Leroux, 1910–1935.

Cutler, Sally Mellick. "The Pāli *Apadāna* Collection." *Journal of the Pāli Text Society* 20 (1994): 1–42.

Feer, Léon, trans. *Avadāna-çataka: Cent légendes bouddhiques.* Paris: Ernest Leroux, 1891.

Handurukande, Ratna, ed. and trans. *Five Buddhist Legends in the Campū Style.* Bonn, Germany: Indica et Tibetica Verlag, 1984.

Hofinger, Marcel, ed. and trans. *Le Congrès du Lac Anavatapta: Vies de Saints Bouddhiques, Extrait du Vinaya des Mūlasarvāstivādin Bhaiṣajyavastu.* Vol. 1: *Légendes des Anciens* (*Sthavirāvadāna*). Vol. 2: *Légendes du Bouddha* (*Buddhāvadāna*). Louvain-la-Neuve, Belgium: Institut Orientaliste and Peeters Press, 1982–1990.

Iwamoto, Yutaka. *Bukkyō setsuwa kenkyū josetsu* (An Introduction to the Study of Buddhist Legends). Tokyo: Kaimei Shoin, 1978.

Jones, J. J., trans. *The Mahāvastu,* 3 vols. London: Pāli Text Society, 1949–1956.

Jones, John Garrett. *Tales and Teachings of the Buddha: The Jātaka Stories in Relation to the Pāli Canon.* London: Allen and Unwin, 1979.

Lamotte, Étienne. *History of Indian Buddhism,* tr. Sara Webb-Boin. Louvain-la-Neuve, Belgium: Institut Orientaliste and Peeters Press, 1988.

Nakamura, Hajime. *Indian Buddhism: A Survey with Bibliographical Notes.* Delhi: Motilal Banarsidass, 1987.

Pruitt, William, trans. *The Commentary on the Verses of the Therīs.* Oxford: Pāli Text Society, 1998.

Ray, Reginald A. *Buddhist Saints in India: A Study in Buddhist Values and Orientations.* New York: Oxford University Press, 1994.

Strong, John S. "The Buddhist Avadānists and the Elder Upagupta." *Mélanges chinois et bouddhiques* 22 (1985): 862–881.

Strong, John S. *The Legend and Cult of Upagupta: Sanskrit Buddhism in North India and Southeast Asia.* Princeton, NJ: Princeton University Press, 1992.

Takahata, Kanga, ed. *Ratnamālāvadāna: A Garland of Precious Gems or, a Collection of Edifying Tales, Belonging to the Mahāyāna.* Tokyo: Toyo Bunko Oriental Library, 1954.

Tatelman, Joel. "The Trials of Yaśodharā and the Birth of Rāhula: A Synopsis of *Bhadrakalpāvadāna* II–IX." *Buddhist Studies Review* 15, no. 2 (1998): 1–42.

Tatelman, Joel, trans. "The Trials of Yaśodharā: The Legend of the Buddha's Wife in the *Bhadrakalpāvadāna.*" *Buddhist Literature* 1 (1999): 176–261.

Tatelman, Joel, trans. *The Glorious Deeds of Pūrṇa.* Richmond, UK: Curzon, 2000.

Willemen, Charles, trans. *The Storehouse of Sundry Valuables.* Berkeley, CA: Numata Center for Buddhist Translation and Research, 1994.

Winternitz, Maurice. *A History of Indian Literature,* 2 vols., tr. S. Ketkar and H. Kohn. Calcutta: University of Calcutta Press, 1927; New Delhi: Oriental Books Reprint Corporation, 1977.

JOEL TATELMAN

AVADĀNAŚATAKA

The *Avadānaśataka* (*A Hundred Glorious Deeds*) is an anthology of one hundred biographical stories in Sanskrit from the first to second centuries C.E. The stories are thematically organized into ten "books" that portray the truth of the doctrine of KARMA (ACTION) and the power of religious DĀNA (GIVING), FAITH, and devotion. An earlier version is preserved in Chinese (*Taishō* no. 200).

See also: **Avadāna; Divyāvadāna; Jātaka**

Bibliography

Bagchi, P. C. "A Note on the Avadānaśataka and Its Chinese Translation." *Visvabharati Annals* 1 (1945): 56–61.

Fa Chow, trans. "Chuan Tsi Pai Yuan King and the Avadānaśataka." *Visvabharati Annals* 1 (1945): 35–55.

Feer, Léon, trans. *Avadana-çataka: Cent légendes bouddhiques.* Paris: Ernest Leroux, 1891. Reprint, Amsterdam: APA-Oriental Press, 1979.

Strong, John S. "The Transforming Gift: An Analysis of Devotional Acts of Offering in Buddhist Avadāna Literature." *History of Religions* 18 (1979): 221–237.

JOEL TATELMAN

AVALOKITEŚVARA. *See* **Bodhisattva(s)**

AVATAṂSAKA-SŪTRA. *See* **Huayan Jing**

AWAKENING OF FAITH (DASHENG QIXIN LUN)

The *Dasheng qixin lun* (*Treatise on the Awakening of Faith According to the Mahāyāna*) is a Chinese apocryphal composition believed to have been written during the sixth century. The text is important for its appropriation of the TATHĀGATAGARBHA, the doctrine of Buddha-nature, into the central teaching of Chinese Buddhist schools such as Huayan and Chan. The *Dasheng qixin lun* explains how ordinary, deluded beings can attain enlightenment without renouncing this worldly life. The text was reputed to have been written in Sanskrit by AŚVAGHOṢA (Chinese, Maming; first century C.E.) and then translated into Chinese in 550 by the Indian dharma master PARAMĀRTHA (Chinese, Zhendi; 499–569). However, no Sanskrit version of this text exists, and most scholars accept its indigenous Chinese provenance.

The *Dasheng qixin lun* is divided into five parts. In part one, the author explains his motives for writing the treatise. In part two, he outlines the significance of his discussion. In part three, he focuses on two aspects of mind to explicate the relationship between enlightenment and ignorance, nirvāṇa and saṃsāra, or the absolute and the phenomenal. In part four, he enumerates five practices that aid the believer in the awakening and growth of faith, with an emphasis on calmness and insight meditation. In part five, he describes the benefits that result from cultivating the five practices. The content of the *Dasheng qixin lun* is often summarized as "One Mind, Two Aspects, Three Greatnesses, Four Faiths, and Five Practices."

The composition of the *Dasheng qixin lun* represents a process of Sinicization of Indian Buddhism. The text seeks to synthesize tathāgatagarbha and *yogācāra* philosophies of mind by positing that one mind has two aspects: the absolute aspect, which is the equivalent of the tathāgatagarbha, and the phenomenal aspect, which refers to the ĀLAYAVIJÑĀNA (storehouse consciousness). Since the tathāgatagarbha is the underlying ontological matrix upon which the phenomenal aspect of mind is grounded, the latter always has the potential to be transformed into the absolute mind. Ignorance is simply the manifestation of one's defiled modes of consciousness, which do not have distinct characteristics of their own and are not separate from the mind's true essence. To attain enlightenment, one needs only to free oneself from deluded thoughts and cultivate faith in one's inherently pure mind. Enlightenment is accordingly conceptualized as a process in which one fully actualizes one's initial awakening into one's true nature through religious cultivation and meditative practice.

The *Dasheng qixin lun* has exerted a profound impact on the development of East Asian Buddhism; numerous Buddhist exegetes in China, Korea, and Japan have written commentaries on it and have incorporated its thesis into their systems of thought. The terminology and hermeneutic of the *Dasheng qixin lun* represent a Chinese shift away from the apophasis of the Madhyamaka teaching of ŚŪNYATĀ (EMPTINESS) to the kataphasis of the doctrine of immanent Buddha-nature. Its use of the paradigm of *ti* (essence) and *yong* (function) in analyzing the relationship between the abstract and the phenomenal realms also plays an influential role in the Huayan teachings of *lishi wuai* (unimpeded interpenetration between principle and phenomena) and *shishi wuai* (unimpeded interpenetration of all phenomena). Most importantly, through its explicit linkage of tathāgatagarbha and *ālayavijñāna,* the *Dasheng qixin lun* succeeds in adapting the tathāgatagarbha doctrine to the indigenous Chinese milieu. It assures the Mahāyāna ideal of universal salvation and affirms the sanctity of life in this world. Its assumption of the inherent purity and enlightenment in the minds of all sentient beings also provides an ontological basis for the Chan school's doctrine of "seeing one's nature and attaining Buddhahood" (*jianxing chengfo*).

See also: **Apocrypha; Chan School; China; Huayan School**

Bibliography

Buswell, Robert E., Jr. *The Formation of Ch'an Ideology in China and Korea: The Vajrasamādhi-sūtra, a Buddhist Apocryphon.* Princeton, NJ: Princeton University Press, 1989.

Buswell, Robert E., Jr., ed. *Chinese Buddhist Apocrypha.* Honolulu: University of Hawaii Press, 1990.

Gregory, Peter N. *Tsung-mi and the Sinification of Buddhism.* Princeton, NJ: Princeton University Press, 1991.

Hakeda, Yoshito S., trans. and ed. *The Awakening of Faith, Attributed to Aśvaghoṣa.* New York: Columbia University Press, 1967.

DING-HWA HSIEH

AYUTTHAYA

Ayutthaya was a kingdom in what is now Thailand. It was ruled by thirty-six kings between 1350 and 1767. The art of Ayutthaya is typically divided into four phases associated with its major political eras: 1350 to 1488, 1488 to 1628, 1629 to 1733, and 1733 to 1767. The city was destroyed by the Burmese in 1767.

The two most important monasteries of the early periods were Mahathat (erected in 1384 by King Boromaraja I) and Ratchaburana (erected in 1424 by Boromaraja II). Like monasteries in the earlier kingdom of SUKHOTHAI, the alignment of the *wihan* (assembly hall), *prang* (tower shaped in Khmer fashion), and *ubosot* or *bot* (congregation and ordination hall) followed a single east-west axis. Smaller *prangs* and *wihans* were enclosed around the central tower within a rectangular gallery, where a row of buddha images was placed. The main *prangs* were generally marked halfway up by niches facing each cardinal direction, in each of which was placed a buddha image; each prang was crowned by a metal finial in the shape of a *vajra* (pronged ritual instrument). Relics, buddha images, and votive tablets were deposited in the *prangs*' relic chambers. For instance, exquisite gold royal regalia and vessels were found in the deposit of Wat Ratchaburana. Wat Chai Wattabaram, built by King Prasat Thong in 1630, is an example of the later phase of *prang* structure.

The Sri Lankan bell-shaped *chedi* popular in Sukhothai was used extensively in Ayutthaya. Notable Ayutthayan features are a higher base, rows of small columns around the railing on the top, and an elongated finial. A good example of this type is Wat Phra Sisanphet, erected in 1491 by King Ramathibodi II.

The only surviving complete late Ayutthayan monastery is Wat Naphramen, built in the middle of the sixteenth century. Its *ubosot* is rectangular, with thick walls, slit windows, and tall octagonal pillars crowned by lotus capitals. The ceiling is decorated with gold star clusters. The main image placed at the end of the hall is the only remaining large-scale seated and bejeweled bronze Buddha. The base of the *ubosot,* curved into a boat shape in early Ayutthaya, became straighter in the later phases.

See also: **Monastic Architecture; Southeast Asia, Buddhist Art in; Thailand**

Bibliography

Boisselier, Jean, and Beurdeley, Jean-Michel. *The Heritage of Thai Sculpture.* Bangkok, Thailand: Asia Books, 1987.

Woodward, Hiram W., Jr. *The Sacred Sculpture of Thailand: The Alexander B. Griswold Collection, The Walters Art Gallery.* Bangkok, Thailand: River Books, 1997.

PATTARATORN CHIRAPRAVATI

B

BĀMIYĀN

Located 240 miles northwest of Kabul in present-day Afghanistan, Bāmiyān was a point of intersection on the major thoroughfares of antiquity. References to Bāmiyān as a religious center can be found in the writings of the Chinese pilgrim to India XUANZANG (ca. 600–664 C.E.). The site ultimately fell into disuse after its annihilation by Genghis Khan in 1222, an act of revenge for his son's death during the siege of the citadel Shahr-i-Zohak, which sits high above the Bāmiyān valley. In the eighteenth century, Buddhist images at the site were used for artillery practice by the Mogul emperor Aurangzeb, and in the nineteenth century Bāmiyān was explored by British archaeologists. The most extensive research done at Bāmiyān was under the auspices of the French.

The trading post of Bāmiyān sits in a lush valley beneath the mountains of the Hindu Kush, with a precipitous mountain at its back and an escarpment suitable for carving at its face. This escarpment came to be covered with innumerable grottos carved from the living rock, comprising Buddhist assembly halls, meditation caves, and icon niches. All told they cover at least one mile. Until 2001, there stood within carved niches a monumental fifty-three-meter buddha image at the western end, and a smaller thirty-five-meter buddha at the eastern end. Originally covered with brilliant pigments and gold, these buddha figures left a lasting impression on Xuanzang, as well as on the thirteenth-century Arab geographer Yakut. Both remarked upon the great buddha images of Bāmiyān as being without compare elsewhere in the world.

There is debate as to the iconographic identity of the two images. It is generally argued that the smaller buddha figure represented the historical Buddha, Śākyamuni, largely because that is how the image is referenced in most of the chronicles of the times. The larger buddha is thought to have represented the universal buddha Vairocana. Written accounts of this statue as wearing a crown support this possible iconographic identification. This statue, like its smaller counterpart, displayed the drapery patterning that originated in Gandhāra. Constructed no later than the sixth century C.E., both images were first carved out of the living rock, then completed using an additive technique employing wooden dowels to attach additional pieces, covered by clay and stucco, and lastly painted. The interior of the image niches were also covered with painted depictions reflecting the syncretic beliefs of the rulers of Bāmiyān at the time. Both statues were missing their faces as early as the eighteenth century, with at least one scholar arguing that the faces were once covered by metal plates, which were easily removed.

The colossal buddhas of Bāmiyān survived the vicissitudes of the various political changes in the region until March 2001. After issuing an edict against images and idolatry, the reigning Islamic fundamentalist Taliban regime in Afghanistan—after spurning attempts by international organizations to buy or preserve the statues—proceeded to destroy them. Two days of artillery barrages were required to successfully destroy what Aurangzeb had left behind. The niches that protected the buddha images still remain, their outlines forever an echo of what were once the most awe-inspiring BUDDHA IMAGES in all of Asia.

See also: **Huayan Art; Persecutions**

Bibliography

Baker, P. H. B., and Allchin, F. R. *Shahr-i Zohak and the History of the Bāmiyān Valley, Afghanistan.* Oxford: B.A.R., 1991.

Beal, Samuel, trans. *Si-yu-ki: Buddhist Records of the Western World, Chinese Accounts of India,* Vol. 1. Calcutta: Susil Gupta, 1957.

Flood, Finbarr Barry. "Between Cult and Culture: Bāmiyān, Islamic Iconoclasm, and the Museum." *Art Bulletin* 84, no. 4 (2002): 641–659.

Godard, André, et al. *Les antiquités bouddhiques de Bāmiyān: Memoires de la délégation archéologique Française en Afghanistan,* Vol. 2. Paris: Éditions Van Oest, 1928.

Klimburg-Salter, Deborah E. *The Kingdom of Bāmiyān: Buddhist Art and Culture of the Hindu Kush.* Naples and Rome: Istituto universitario orientale, Dipartimento di studi asiatici, 1989.

Rowland, Benjamin. *The Art of Central Asia.* New York: Crown, 1974.

KARIL J. KUCERA

BAYON

The Bayon is a twelfth-century royal Khmer (Cambodian) temple. One of Southeast Asia's most famous monuments, the Bayon is a densely crowded sandstone temple constructed under King Jayavarman VII (r. 1181–ca. 1220) at Angkor Thom in northwest Cambodia. This pyramid temple, a MAHĀYĀNA site, marked the end of an ancient royal Khmer tradition dominated by Hindu gods.

Axial entrances on all four sides cross through a rectangular outer and inner gallery carved with bas-reliefs that glorify the king's history. On the upper elevation a series of connected structures leads to the massive, round central tower. Its dark interior once housed a large, nāga-protected buddha. At its consecration, Jayavarman was symbolically joined to this buddha and imbued with a divine cast in the process. And at his death, the king's ashes would have been placed underneath this image, creating a certain conceptual kinship between the Bayon and a STŪPA with its internal relics.

The well-known guardian faces on the Bayon's fifty-two towers wear characteristic choker necklaces and originally stared straight ahead. But when many had their eyes recut to gaze downward, Avalokiteśvara became their most likely new identity. These recut eyes were one of several changes during construction that drastically altered the temple's configuration and meaning.

Although Buddhist, the Bayon followed tradition in its merging of regional or ancestral gods with Buddhist and Hindu deities. VIṢṆU is found almost exclusively on the western side of the temple, Śiva more often on the south, and Buddhist imagery on the north and east. The Bayon was the last major Khmer monument to embrace the tradition that gave it birth, destined to wither and die in less than one hundred years.

See also: **Cambodia; Hinduism and Buddhism; Local Divinities and Buddhism; Southeast Asia, Buddhist Art in**

Bibliography

Dufour, Henri. *Le Bayon d'Angkor Thom,* 2 vols. Paris: Commission archeologique de l'Indochine, 1910–1914.

Dumarçay, Jacques, and Groslier, Bernard-Philippe. *Le Bayon.* Paris: École Française d'Extrême-Orient, 1967 and 1973.

ELEANOR MANNIKKA

BHĀVAVIVEKA

Bhāvaviveka was a MADHYAMAKA SCHOOL philosopher who lived from perhaps 500 to 570 C.E. His name may have been Bhavya or Bhāviveka, and he may have come from South India. Bhāvaviveka's attack on the interpretation of Madhyamaka by Buddhapālita (c. 500 C.E.) led later Tibetans to refer to him as the founder of the Svātantrika-Madhyamaka. Bhāvaviveka's works include the *Prajñāpradīpa* (*Lamp of Wisdom*) on NĀGĀRJUNA, and the *Madhyamakahṛdayakārikā* (*Verses on the essence of Madhyamaka*) with *Tarkajvālā* (*Blaze of Reasoning,* an autocommentary), an early encyclopedia of Indian philosophy.

Bibliography

Eckel, Malcolm D. *To See the Buddha: A Philosopher's Quest for the Meaning of Emptiness.* Princeton, NJ: Princeton University Press, 1992.

Iida, S. *Reason and Emptiness: A Study of Logic and Mysticism.* Tokyo: Hokuseido Press, 1980.

Lopez, Donald S., Jr. *A Study of Svātantrika.* Ithaca, NY: Snow Lion, 1987.

Ruegg, David S. *The Literature of the Madhyamaka School of Philosophy in India.* Wiesbaden, Germany: Harrassowitz, 1981.

PAUL WILLIAMS

BIANWEN

Until the early twentieth century, with the discovery of a cache of important manuscripts at DUNHUANG, Gansu Province, in the far northwest of China, *bianwen* (transformation texts) were completely unknown to scholars. Once literary historians became aware of them, however, they soon realized that these texts, which date to the Tang (618–907) and Five Dynasties (907–960) periods, filled a crucial gap in scholarly understanding of the development of Chinese popular literature. They are the earliest substantial specimens of vernacular writing in China, and they represent the earliest examples of prosimetric narratives in Chinese. That is to say, they are the first Chinese texts that alternate sung, declaimed, or intoned verse and spoken prose to advance a narrative. As such, they had an enormous impact upon virtually all later performing arts (including full-scale operatic drama) and vernacular fiction in China. They also provide vital evidence for the sources of many popular tales of later times, and they embody first-hand data about storytelling in medieval China. Although the *bianwen* are not, as was once thought, promptbooks used in performance, they bear the marks of derivation from oral literature.

The *wen* in *bianwen* means text; the *bian* component, however, caused tremendous confusion during the first half-century of research on the genre. After intensive investigation involving comparisons with texts written in Sanskrit, Tibetan, and other languages, it has become clear that *bian* in *bianwen* refers to transformational manifestations evoked by spiritually powerful individuals (comparable to the Sanskrit terms *nirmāṇa* and *ṛddhi.*) The oral precedents of *bianwen* utilized picture scrolls as illustrative devices to enhance the performance, and *bianwen* are closely connected to the artistic genre known as BIANXIANG (TRANSFORMATION TABLEAUX). The earliest *bianwen* describe Buddhist subjects, but wholly secular themes, both historical and contemporary in nature, were soon added.

See also: **Chinese, Buddhist Influences on Vernacular Literature in; Entertainment and Performance**

Bibliography

Mair, Victor H. *T'ang Transformation Texts: A Study of the Buddhist Contribution to the Rise of Vernacular Fiction and Drama in China.* Cambridge, MA: Council of East Asian Studies, Harvard University, 1989.

Pai, Hua-wen. "What Is '*pien-wen*'?" tr. Victor H. Mair. *Harvard Journal of Asiatic Studies* 44, no. 2 (1984): 493–514.

VICTOR H. MAIR

BIANXIANG (TRANSFORMATION TABLEAUX)

It is commonly assumed that *bianxiang* (transformation tableaux) are the matching illustrations for BIANWEN (transformation texts), a genre of popular Buddhist narratives that was discovered at DUNHUANG. There are, indeed, many similarities. For example, *bianxiang* are also associated with the cave temples of Dunhuang, both genres flourished during the medieval period, both were intended for the portrayal of Buddhist themes, and, above all, the *bian* of both genre names means "transformation" or "transformational manifestation." There are, however, significant differences. Whereas *bianwen* sometimes dealt with secular subjects, *bianxiang* are exclusively religious in nature. Furthermore, while *bianwen* are folkish in nature, *bianxiang* are often the products of high culture. Finally, whereas evidence for *bianwen* is restricted almost exclusively to the manuscripts from Dunhuang, evidence (largely textual) for *bianxiang* is related to localities spread over the length and breadth of China.

Bianxiang are also frequently confused with MAṆḌALA. Here, too, there are similarities and differences, but the situation is more complex than with *bianwen,* despite the fact that *bianxiang* and maṇḍala are both artistic genres, since *bianxiang* may share features of maṇḍala and vice versa. Basically, whereas *bianxiang* connotes a narrative moment, event, place, or sequence of moments, events, or places pictorially or sculpturally represented, a maṇḍala is an object or icon, usually having a circular arrangement, intended to serve as the focus of worship or meditation.

The chief subjects of *bianxiang* are paradise scenes (especially the Western Pure Land), depictions of the contents of famous sūtras (particularly the LOTUS SŪTRA), incidents from the life of the Buddha (especially his NIRVĀṆA), deeds of various BODHISATTVAS (particularly Avalokiteśvara) and ARHATS (e.g., ŚĀRIPUTRA), and so forth. *Bianxiang* were favored by the adherents of the CHAN SCHOOL, and the tradition of painting *bianxiang* was transmitted to Japan, where it became an integral part of Buddhist popular culture. Vivid records of the commissioning and actual painting of *bianxiang* have been preserved, and they afford valuable insights into the motivation and organization of Buddhist devotees in medieval China.

See also: **Hells, Images of; Pure Land Art; Sūtra Illustrations**

Bibliography

Mair, Victor H. "Records of Transformation Tableaux (*pien-hsiang*)." *T'oung Pao* 72, no. 3 (1986): 3–43.

Wu Hung. "What Is *Bianxiang*?—On the Relationship between Dunhuang Art and Dunhuang Literature." *Harvard Journal of Asiatic Studies* 52, no. 1 (1992): 111–192.

VICTOR H. MAIR

BIOGRAPHIES OF EMINENT MONKS (GAOSENG ZHUAN)

"Biographies of Eminent Monks" is a genre of Chinese Buddhist writing consisting primarily of four biographical collections, all compiled by monks: (1) *Biographies of Eminent Monks* (*Gaoseng zhuan*), completed around 530 by Huijiao (497–554); (2) *Further Biographies of Eminent Monks* (*Xu gaoseng zhuan*), first draft completed in approximately 650 by DAOXUAN (596–667) with later additions in the 660s; (3) *Biographies of Eminent Monks [Compiled] during the Song Dynasty* (*Song gaoseng zhuan*), completed in 982 by ZANNING (919–1001); and (4) *Biographies of Eminent Monks [Compiled] during the Ming Dynasty* (*Ming gaoseng zhuan*), completed in 1617 by Ruxing (d.u.). Although there is some overlap in time between collections, in general each picks up where the last left off. Daoxuan, for example, wrote mostly on monks who lived after Huijiao's collection was completed.

Of the four books, Huijiao's has been the most influential and the most admired for its style. It has been one of the most widely read historical works by any Chinese monk.

Huijiao's *Biographies of Eminent Monks* established the format for the later versions. He divided the 275 biographies contained in his collection into ten categories: (1) "Translators"; (2) "Exegetes"; (3) "Divine Wonders," devoted to wonder-workers; (4) "Practitioners of Meditation"; (5) "Elucidators of the Regulations," devoted to scholars of the VINAYA or monastic rules; (6) "Those who Sacrificed Themselves," for monks who sacrificed their bodies in acts of charity or devotion; (7) "Chanters of Scriptures"; (8) "Benefactors," for monks who solicited funds for Buddhist construction and other enterprises; (9) "Hymnodists," devoted to monks skilled in intoning liturgy; and (10) "Proselytizers." At the end of each section, Huijiao appended a treatise in which he discusses the theme of the section. In his treatise on translators, Huijiao gives a brief history of the transmission of Buddhist scriptures and discusses the difficulties of translating Indian texts into Chinese. An introduction to the book lists previous collections of monastic biographies, and explains how Huijiao distinguished his work from them.

Subsequent works followed Huijiao's format with some changes. Most notably, Daoxuan combined the sections for hymnodists and proselytizers, and then added a section for "Protectors of the Dharma," devoted to monks who defended Buddhism from its enemies at court and elsewhere.

The compilers of the collections followed Chinese historiographical custom in the composition of their biographies. In general, they relied on previous sources, directly quoting them without attribution. Major sources included the texts of stele inscriptions, usually composed soon after a monk's death by a local literatus at the request of the monk's followers. The compilers also drew on other literary accounts, including prefaces to works written by the monk in question, and collections of miracle stories; they occasionally based biographies on oral traditions concerning particular monks. In most cases, the original sources for the biographies are lost, but occasionally it is possible to reconstruct the sources for biographies in the later collections. As the title suggests, criterion for inclusion was based on a monk's "eminence," or rank. With a few exceptions, only monks regarded by the compilers as admirable are accorded biographies.

See also: **Biography; History**

Bibliography

Kieschnick, John. *The Eminent Monk: Buddhist Ideals in Medieval Chinese Hagiography.* Honolulu: University of Hawaii Press, 1997.

Wright, Arthur F. "Biography and Hagiography: Hui-chiao's *Lives of Eminent Monks.*" In *Studies in Chinese Buddhism,* ed. Robert M. Somers. New Haven, CT: Yale University Press, 1990.

JOHN KIESCHNICK

BIOGRAPHY

Many religious traditions develop elaborate narratives about the life of the founding figure. Such sacred biographies often include accounts of mythic events and miracles that underscore the virtues and attainments of the founder. These narratives give shape to the history and legitimate the social institutions of emergent religious traditions. Buddhism has elaborated and embellished its biographical emphasis to create a sacred biography not only of the Buddha's final life but also of his earlier lives, the lives of his disciples, the lives of other enlightened beings, and ultimately the lives of all SENTIENT BEINGS who witness the Buddha's teaching. Biography may be understood as a core concept of the Buddhist tradition; it is a cultural idiom that continues to engender religious meaning in practice, doctrine, and belief. The importance of the Buddha's biography lies in the ways in which it has shaped the tradition in the centuries following his death (Reynolds). Indeed, Buddhist concern with life stories has generated biographical genres and modes of religious behavior that are articulated in oral narratives, classical and vernacular texts, visual art, and ritual, as well as in the cultural histories of Buddhist polities in much of Asia. The remainder of this entry describes some of the ways in which sacred biography has shaped the development of Buddhism in diverse cultural contexts.

Each of the major branches of Buddhism offers a different version of the life of the Buddha; these biographies are informed by doctrines specific to each school or lineage. Themes in the biographies of Gautama may illustrate not only his unique spiritual achievements, but also characteristics attributed to buddhas in general. In addition, biographical themes in the life or lives of the Buddha are often incorporated into the biographical narratives of other remarkable individuals, such as ARHATS, BODHISATTVAS, or eminent monks.

There are differing versions of the Buddha's biography, and scholars cannot identify a single or "original" source in Buddhist literature. After his death, accounts of the Buddha's life and teaching were transmitted orally for several centuries. Gradually, the Buddha's message became codified and committed to written texts that eventually came to be known as the Buddhist CANON. Numerous passages in the Buddhist sūtras and VINAYA refer to events and episodes of the Buddha's life, and there are many texts throughout the Buddhist tradition that describe mythic events and sacred qualities of the Buddha. The biographies that eventually emerged were initially not systematized or even organized in temporal sequence. It took some five centuries for the Buddha's biographical accounts to become standardized and formalized.

The Buddha's final life

Certain mythic episodes are salient in many accounts of the Buddha's life, despite the diversity in the stories that make up the Buddha's biography. According to these accounts, Siddhārtha's conception was immaculate, as a white elephant entered his mother's womb. His birth was painless, and, taking his first strides, he announced that this was his final and culminating life. Brahmin astrologers whom his father had consulted prophesied that the child would become either a world conqueror (cakravartin) who rules over a social and political universe, or a buddha who transcends ordinary reality through spiritual enlightenment. Raised in luxury and tutored in the seclusion of the palace, Siddhārtha eventually married Yaśodharā and fathered a son, RĀHULA. Curious about life outside the palace, Siddhārtha encountered the inescapable human condition of old age, sickness, and death. This insight led him to discover that human existence is conditioned by suffering. Having fulfilled his obligations as a householder, he resolved to leave his indulgent life and renounce society. He became a wandering mendicant and apprenticed himself to several gurus. Eventually, he realized that extreme asceticism does not lead to enlightenment, and he determined to follow a middle path between indulgence and asceticism. Like other buddhas before him, he resolved to meditate under a bodhi tree until he achieved NIRVĀṆA. While he was seated in meditation, MĀRA, the Evil One, challenged him in vain with the promise of unlimited power, with attacks by his mighty army, and, finally, with his sensuous daughters. Rebuffing each offer, Gautama gained three knowledges (*traividya*; Pāli, *tevijjā*) on his path to enlightenment: He remembered all his past lives, he came to understand that the nature of one's existence is the result of past action, and finally, he gained complete knowledge of his liberation. The Buddha hesitated to preach, however, until the intervention of a god (deva) persuaded him to teach the dharma and to reveal his model for practice and the path to nirvāṇa for others to follow.

In the course of a ministry that lasted more than forty years, the Buddha established the monastic order (SAṄGHA) and preached to a growing early Buddhist community. A prominent lay supporter, King Bimbisāra, donated land to establish the first permanent residence for monks. When the Buddha passed away and left the cycle of REBIRTH (SAṂSĀRA), he was given the funerary rites of a world conqueror, and his relics were enshrined throughout the Buddhist world. His disciples convened the first Buddhist Council shortly after his death to compile his teachings, and the Buddhist tradition began to take shape in the transition from the founder's charismatic life to the emerging institutional history and doctrinal developments. For instance, AŚOKA's cult of relics helped promote the institutionalization of the Theravāda monastic lineage. Doctrinal interpretations of the bodies of the Buddha that are specific to the major branches of the tradition also correspond to their respective interpretations of the Buddha's sacred biography.

The story of the Buddha's culminating life in saṃsāra illustrates central beliefs and doctrines of Buddhism, including Gautama's model for and path to enlightenment, his message, and the establishment of Buddhist institutions. The story also legitimates the veneration of the Buddha's relics and the STŪPAS that enshrine them, as well as the veneration of icons and images that embody his biography. These sacred objects are closely associated with the Buddha's biography and establish his presence in rituals. They remind Buddhists of the Buddha's enlightenment and of his absence from the cycle of rebirth.

The *jātaka* tradition

Central motifs of the sacred biography, especially the Buddha's remembrance of past lives in visions that culminated in his enlightenment, eventually developed into an elaborate genre of tales called JĀTAKA, which are stories of the Buddha's former lives. In the Pāli tradition, *jātaka* attained semicanonical status in compilations containing up to 550 such stories that recount the perfection of virtues by the buddha-to-be. These tales about the Buddha's past lives as a king, ascetic, monkey, or elephant do not follow a systematized sequence, but they do share a similar narrative structure. Generally, each story opens with a frame in the narrative present, namely the final life of Gautama Buddha, and identifies the place and occasion for the story about a past rebirth about to be recounted. The account then unfolds events in a former rebirth of the Buddha and concludes by explaining the outcome according to universal laws of Buddhist causality. The story of the former life becomes the dramatic stage upon which the consequences of moral action are illustrated. *Jātaka* stories generally conclude by returning to the time of the Buddha's final life and identifying companions of the Buddha with dramatis personae in the story just recounted.

Perhaps the best-known *jātaka* in the THERAVĀDA world is the *Vessantara Jātaka,* in which the buddha-to-be, in his life as Prince Vessantara (Sanskrit, VIŚVANTARA), perfects the virtue of generosity (*dāna*). Vessantara gives away everything a king or householder might value: his prosperity, power, home, and even his family, only to have it all restored at the conclusion of the tale.

Jātaka tales figure prominently in a variety of ways in Buddhist cultures; they appear in temple paintings, children's stories, movie billboards and, most recently, comic books. They offer abundant material for religious education. Central motifs in the biographies of the Buddha elucidate moral principles, values, and ethics, and certain well-known *jātaka* tales serve a didactic purpose in teaching younger generations about the tradition. *Jātakas* are salient across Buddhist communities and the themes they recount readily resonate with other aspects of religious knowledge and practice. As such, recounting certain *jātaka* stories in public sermons or even representing them in paintings can serve as commentary on current social and political issues. Stories about the Buddha's former lives are also a form of entertainment. In Burma, for example, these stories have traditionally been the subject of popular theatrical performances that continue through the night.

Cultural contexts of the biographical genre

In visual art, biographical references can be found in Buddhist architecture, in sculptures and icons of the Buddha, and in the visual narratives of paintings and stone carvings. Paintings of *jātaka* stories can be seen along walkways in monastery grounds and along the staircases leading to pilgrimage sites. *Jātaka* paintings also often decorate the inner spaces of Buddhist temples. Certain hand gestures (MUDRĀ) or poses displayed in BUDDHA IMAGES refer to particular moments in his life, such as when he touched the earth as witness to his meritorious deeds at the time of his enlightenment or when he reclined at the moment of his departure from the cycle of rebirth. At BOROBUDUR in Java, a magnificent MAHĀYĀNA Buddhist stūpa from the seventh to the ninth century C.E., carved stone plates along the meditation path depict *jātaka* scenes that have been "read" by scholars in much the same way one would read a textual narrative. Whatever the initial motivation for the creation of visual portrayals of events from the Buddha's biographies, such images serve as objects of meditation, contemplation, and ritual reminders of the Buddha.

Many Buddhist rituals invoke salient idioms from the Buddha's biography. For example, Burmese Buddhists, especially the Shan people, celebrate a boy's temporary initiation as a novice with a ritual reenactment of Siddhārtha's splendorous life and departure from the palace. In Thailand, stories of the Buddha's life as Vessantara are chanted on ritual occasions and at the behest of devout lay patrons. Images of the Buddha are consecrated through an eye-opening ceremony, and a deferential protocol of behavior is required in front of consecrated images; one behaves as if one were in the Buddha's presence. Lastly, pilgrimages are undertaken to sites that commemorate episodes of the Buddha's life, as well as places that contain relics of the Buddha, such as BODH GAYĀ in northeast India, the site of the Buddha's enlightenment.

Biographies of the Buddha also give voice to local interpretations, and the Buddhist biographical genre includes numerous apocryphal *jātaka* stories. Countless stories about the Buddha's many lives enrich the biographical idiom in local Buddhist traditions, chronicles, myths, and religious sites, thereby linking persons and places with the Buddha's pristine early community. One way this occurs is through relating universal biographical themes to particular local features. For example, the colossal Burmese Mahāmuni was constructed, according to local myth, in the Buddha's likeness, and it is said to have been enlivened by him during a visit to the region now known as Arakan. Stories like this serve to legitimate not only the particular image, but, more significantly, all of its royal patrons and protectors through Burmese dynastic history. The Mahāmuni complex further links the geographical and cultural periphery of lower Burma to central Buddhist concepts in the Buddha's biography (Schober). In the Theravāda tradition, apocryphal stories, local traditions, and peripheral locations are thus brought together to construct and perpetuate biographical extensions of the Buddha's lives.

In the traditions of Mahāyāna and VAJRAYĀNA Buddhism, we find many life stories of other buddhas, bodhisattvas, and embodiments of enlightenment from the past, present, and even future. Such an expansion of the biographical genre made it possible to integrate preexisting religious and cultural values into Buddhist belief systems. In China, for example, Buddhist BIOGRAPHIES OF EMINENT MONKS (GAOSENG ZHUAN) are informed by biographical conventions borrowed from the indigenous Confucian tradition. Like their counterparts in other branches of Buddhism, biographies of eminent Chinese monks take up familiar themes (Kieschnick). Asceticism, miracle working, healing, and scholarship commonly figure in biographies of eminent monks to underscore how their lives emulate and perpetuate extraordinary events in the biography of the Buddha. Such stories emphasize links between teachers and their disciples in order to construct a lineage that, at least in principle, is believed to establish a historical connection to the idealized time of the Buddha. Biographies of famous monks also commonly recount miracles associated with relics or they describe extraordinary practices with which charismatic monks have been credited.

In this way, Buddhist sacred biography is a genre that seeks to demonstrate that the accomplishments that eminent monks achieve in later periods share features in common with the words and acts of the founder of Buddhism. Buddhist sacred biography thus locates the Buddha's life story with specific Buddhist communities. By linking the universal with geographic peripheries and particular cultures, Buddhist biography engages the religious imagination of Buddhists and contributes to the continuing vitality of the tradition.

See also: **Buddha, Life of the, in Art; Jātaka, Illustrations of**

Bibliography

Kieschnick, John. *The Eminent Monk: Buddhist Ideals in Medieval Chinese Hagiography.* Honolulu: University of Hawaii Press, 1997.

Reynolds, Frank E. "The Many Lives of the Buddha." In *The Biographical Process: Studies in the History and Psychology of Religion,* ed. Frank E. Reynolds and Donald Capps. The Hague, Netherlands: Mouton, 1976.

Schober, Juliane, ed. *Sacred Biography in the Buddhist Traditions of South and Southeast Asia.* Honolulu: University of Hawaii Press, 1997.

JULIANE SCHOBER

BKA' BRGYUD (KAGYU)

Bka' brgyud (pronounced Kagyu) may be translated as "oral lineage" or "lineage of the Buddha's word." Many traditions of Tibetan Buddhism use the term *bka' brgyud* to describe the successive oral transmission, and therefore authenticity, of their teachings. The name *Bka' brgyud*, however, most commonly refers to the Mar pa Bka' brgyud (the oral lineage of Mar pa), a stream of tantric Buddhist instructions and meditation practices initially brought to Tibet from India by the Tibetan translator MAR PA (MARPA) in the eleventh century. Although the Bka' brgyud subsequently developed into a complex structure of autonomous subsects and branch schools, later Western writings tended to describe it as one of four sects of Tibetan Buddhism, to be distinguished from the RNYING MA (NYINGMA), SA SKYA (SAKYA), and DGE LUGS (GELUK). Another Tibetan typology of tantric traditions enumerates the Mar pa Bka' brgyud as one of eight streams of tantric instruction, the so-called *sgrub brgyud shing rta chen po brgyad* (eight great chariot-like lineages of achievement), which includes traditions such as the Rnying ma, the Bka' gdams of Atisha, and the Gcod instructions of MA GCIG LAB SGRON (MACIG LAPDON). Some Tibetan historians have referred to the lineage stemming from Mar pa with the near homonym Dkar brgyud (pronounced Kargyu), which means "white lineage," describing the white cotton robes worn by mendicant yogins of this tradition, and stressing their commitment to intensive meditation practice.

Each of the various Bka' brgyud subsects trace their lineage back to the primordial tantric buddha Vajradhara, who is considered an incontrovertible source of authentic Buddhist instruction. According to traditional accounts, the Indian MAHĀSIDDHA (great adept) Tilopa (988–1069) received visionary instructions from Vajradhara, later passing them on to his principal disciple, the Bengali scholar and adept NĀROPA (1016–1100). The latter transmitted his chief instructions (codified as the *Nā ro chos drug*, or the *Six Doctrines of Nāropa*) to Mar pa. Mar pa returned to Tibet, where he translated, arranged, and disseminated these practices, together with those of the meditational system of MAHĀMUDRĀ, most famously to his yogin disciple MI LA RAS PA (Milarepa; 1028/40–1111/23). These early figures—the buddha Vajradhara, the Indians Tilopa and Nāropa, and their Tibetan successors Mar pa and Mi la ras pa—form the earliest common segment of the Bka' brgyud lineage, a line of individuals largely removed from an institutionalized monastic setting. One of Mi la ras pa's foremost disciples, the physician-monk Sgam po pa Bsod nams rin chen (1079–1153), merged the instructions he received from this lineage with the monasticism and systematic exegetical approach he learned during his earlier training under masters of the Bka' gdams sect. Sgam po pa, therefore, appears to have spearheaded the true institutionalization of the Bka' brgyud, founding an important monastery and retreat center near his homeland in the southern Tibetan region of Dwags po. For this reason, the many subsequent branches of the Bka' brgyud are also collectively known as the Dwags po Bka' brgyud.

The Bka' brgyud later split into numerous divisions, known in Tibetan as the *four major* and *eight minor* Bka' brgyud subsects (*Bka' brgyud che bzhi chung brgyad*), where the terms *major* and *minor* carry neither quantitative nor qualitative overtones, but rather indicate a relative proximity to the master Sgam po pa and his nephew Dwags po Sgom tshul (1116–1169). The four major Bka' brgyud subsects follow from the direct disciples of these two masters. These include:

1. The Karma Bka' brgyud, also known as the Karma Kaṁ tshang, which is directed by the Karma pa hierarchs and originated with the first Karma pa Dus gsum mkhyen pa (1110–1193). This sect held great political power in Tibet from the late fifteenth to early seventeenth centuries and continues to be one of the most active among the four, especially in Eastern Tibet and in exile.
2. The Tshal pa Bka' brgyud, which originated with Zhang tshal pa Brtson grus grags pa (1123–1193).
3. The 'Ba' rom Bka' brgyud, which originated with 'Ba' rom Dar ma dbang phyug (1127–1199) and forged early ties with the Tangut and Mongol Courts.
4. The Phag gru Bka' brgyud, which originated with the great master Phag mo gru pa Rdo rje rgyal po (1110–1170), who established a seat at Gdan sa thil Monastery in Central Tibet. This monastery, together with an ancestral home in nearby Rtses thang, became the center of the powerful ruling Phag mo gru family during the fourteenth and fifteenth centuries.

The incipience of the eight lesser Bka' brgyud subsects is traced back to the disciples of Phag mo gru pa Rdo rje rgyal po. These include:

1. The 'Bri gung Bka' brgyud, which originated with 'Bri gung 'Jigs rten mgon po (1143–1217) and held great political influence during the thirteenth century.

2. The Stag lung Bka' brgyud, which originated with Stag lung thang pa Bkra shis dpal (1142–1210).
3. The Gling ras Bka' brgyud, which originated with Gling rje ras pa Padma rdo rje (1128–1288) and later became the 'Brug pa Bka' brgyud under his disciple Gtsang pa rgya ras Ye shes rdo rje (1161–1211). The latter subsect rose to prominence under royal patronage in Bhutan.
4. The G.ya' bzang Bka' brgyud, which originated with Zwa ra ba Skal ldan ye shes seng ge (d. 1207).
5. The Khro phu Bka' brgyud, which originated with Rgya tsha (1118–1195), Kun ldan ras pa (1148–1217), and their nephew Khro phu lotsāva Byams pa dpal (1173–1228).
6. The Shug gseb Bka' brgyud, which originated with Gyer sgom Tshul khrims seng ge (1144–1204).
7. The Yel pa Bka' brgyud, which originated with Ye shes brtsegs pa (d.u.).
8. The Smar tshang Bka' brgyud, which originated with Smar pa grub thob Shes rab seng ge (d.u.).

Many of these subsects have since died out as independent institutional systems. A few, such as the Karma Bka' brgyud, 'Bri gung Bka' brgyud, and 'Brug pa Bka' brgyud, continue to play an important role in the religious lives of Tibetan Buddhists inside Tibet, across the Himalayan regions, and in Europe and the Americas since the Tibetan exile during the latter half of the twentieth century.

See also: Tibet

Bibliography

Guenther, Herbert V., trans. *The Life and Teaching of Nāropa.* Boston and London: Shambhala, 1986.

Gyaltsen, Khenpo Könchok, trans. *The Great Kagyu Masters: The Golden Lineage Treasury.* Ithaca, NY: Snow Lion, 1990.

Lhalungpa, Lobsang P., trans. *The Life of Milarepa.* New York: Dutton, 1977. Reprint, Boston: Shambhala, 1984.

Richardson, Hugh. "The Karma-pa Sect: A Historical Note." *Journal of the Royal Asiatic Society* (1958): 139–164 and (1959): 1–18. Reprinted in *High Peaks, Pure Earth: Collected Writings on Tibetan History and Culture,* ed. Michael Aris. London: Serindia, 1998.

Smith, E. Gene. "Golden Rosaries of the Bka' brgyud Schools." In *Dkar brgyud gser 'phreng: A Golden Rosary of Lives of Eminent Gurus,* compiled by Mon-rtse-pa Kun-dga'-dpal-ldan and ed. Kun-dga'-brug-dpal. Leh, India: Sonam W. Tashigang, 1970. Reprinted in *Among Tibetan Texts,* ed. Kurtis R. Schaefer. Boston: Wisdom, 2001.

Torricelli, Fabrizio, and, Naga, Sangye T., trans. *The Life of the Mahasiddha Tilopa.* Dharamsala, India: Library of Tibetan Works and Archives, 1995.

Trungpa, Chögyam, and the Nalanda Translation Committee, trans. *The Rain of Wisdom.* Boston: Shambhala, 1980.

Trungpa, Chögyam, and the Nalanda Translation Committee, trans. *The Life of Marpa the Translator.* Boston: Shambhala, 1986.

ANDREW QUINTMAN

BODH GAYĀ

The Buddha attained complete and perfect enlightenment while seated on the diamond throne (*vajrāsana*) under the bodhi tree at Bodh Gayā. Also called the seat of enlightenment (*bodhimaṇḍa*), this throne is said to be located at the earth's navel, the only place on earth that rests directly on the primordial layer of golden earth supporting the cosmos. Only there can the earth support a buddha undergoing full enlightenment without breaking apart. The *bodhimaṇḍa* numbers among the numerous invariables in all buddhas' biographies, which have only three distinguishing features. These are the genus of their bodhi trees, and the places of their births and deaths. Hence, individual buddhas are identified with and by their particular bodhi trees, Śākyamuni's being the pipal tree (*ficus religiosa*).

The enlightenment is further ritualized and solemnized by its being embedded in an elaborate sequence of actions, beginning with Siddhārtha's decision to abandon physical austerities and to follow the middle way. Despite the site's extent, the ground is thick with sacred traces of the Buddha performing these actions. According to the Chinese pilgrims FAXIAN (ca. 337–418 C.E.) and XUANZANG (ca. 600–664 C.E.), individuals hailing from different places and eras erected STŪPAS, pillars, railings, temples, and monasteries to memorialize deeds and places. An example is the jewel-walk, one of the seven spots where the Buddha spent one week of his seven-week experience of enlightenment.

Though the emperor AŚOKA probably established Bodh Gayā and the bodhi tree as Buddhism's most sacred Buddhist PILGRIMAGE site and object, the earliest extant remains and inscriptions are Śuṅgan (second to first century B.C.E.). Recording three Śuṅgan noblewomen's donations to the King's Temple, its railing and the jewel-walk posts, these inscriptions inaugurate an ongoing domestic and foreign tradition of donations and repairs. Early inscriptions also record Sri Lankan, Burmese, and Chinese pilgrimage. For example, Sri Lankan donative activity began with King Meghavarman's building of the Mahābodhi Monastery (ca. fourth century C.E.) to house Sinhalese monks. Beginning in the eleventh century, the kings of Burma sent several expeditions to repair the temple.

Muslim invaders vandalized Bodh Gayā, probably before the last Burmese repair in 1295. The site remained desolate until the seventeenth century, when a Mahant settled there. Gaining ownership of the site, he salvaged its archaeological remains to build a Śaivate monastery near the MAHĀBODHI TEMPLE. The nineteenth century saw the resurgence of foreign Buddhist pilgrimage and Burmese reparative expeditions. The latter inspired British interest, resulting in colonial excavation and rebuilding in the 1880s. In 1891 ANAGĀRIKA DHARMAPĀLA founded the Mahābodhi Society in Sri Lanka to reestablish Buddhist ownership of the site. A lengthy legal battle ended victoriously in 1949. Today, Bodh Gayā is a thriving center of international Buddhism, attracting millions of Buddhist pilgrims every year from all over the world. Continuing a long-standing tradition, Buddhist sects throughout Asia (Sri Lanka, Burma [Myanmar], Thailand, Vietnam, China, Japan, Tibet, Nepal, and Bhutan) have established flourishing missions and built and repaired monasteries and temples there.

See also: **Bodhi (Awakening)**

Bibliography

Ahir, D. C. *Buddha Gayā through the Ages.* Delhi: Sri Satguru, 1994.

Barua, Benimadhab. *Gayā and Buddha-Gayā,* Vol. 1: *Early History of the Holy Land* (1931). Varanasi, India: Bhartiya, 1975.

Barua, Dipak Kumar. *Buddha Gayā Temple: Its History.* Buddha Gaya, India: Buddha Gaya Temple Management Committee, 1975. Second revised edition, 1981.

Beal, Samuel, trans. *Si-yu-ki: Buddhist Records of the Western World, Translated from the Chinese of Hiuen Tsiang (A.D. 629).* London: Trubner, 1884. Reprint, Delhi: Oriental Books Reprint Corp., 1969.

Bhattacharyya, Tarapada. *The Bodhgayā Temple.* Calcutta: Firma K. L. Mukhopadhyah, 1966.

Legge, James, trans. *A Record of Buddhistic Kingdoms, Being an Account by the Chinese Monk Fa-Hsien of His Travels in India and Ceylon (A.D. 399–414) in Search of the Buddhist Books of Discipline.* Oxford: Clarendon, 1886. Reprint, New York: Paragon, 1965.

Leoshko, Janice, ed. *Bodhgayā: The Site of Enlightenment.* Bombay: Marg, 1988.

LEELA ADITI WOOD

BODHI (AWAKENING)

The Sanskrit and Pāli word *bodhi* derives from the Indic root √*budh* (to awaken, to know). It was rendered into Chinese either by way of transliteration, as *puti* (Japanese, *bodai*; Korean, *pori*), or by way of translation. The most common among the many Chinese translations are *jue* (Japanese, *kaku*; Korean, *kak*; "to be aware") and *dao* (Japanese, *dō*; Korean, *to*; "the way"). The standard Tibetan translation is *byang chub* (purified and perfected). Those who are attentive to the more literal meaning of the Indic original tend to translate *bodhi* into English as "awakening," and this is to be recommended. However, it has long been conventional to translate it as "enlightenment," despite the risks of multiple misrepresentation attendant upon the use of so heavily freighted an English word.

General characterizations of bodhi

In the most general terms, *bodhi* designates the attainment of that ultimate knowledge by virtue of which a being achieves full liberation (*vimokṣa, vimukti*) or NIRVĀṆA. Sometimes the term is understood to refer to the manifold process of awakening by which one comes variously and eventually to know the truth of things "as they truly are" (*yathābhūtaṃ*), thereby enabling liberation from DUḤKHA (SUFFERING) and REBIRTH for both self and others. At other times *bodhi* is taken to refer to the all-at-once culmination of that process. In the latter sense, the term *bodhi* may be said to belong to the large category of names for things or events so ultimate as to be essentially ineffable, even inconceivable. However, in the former more processive sense, either as a single term standing alone or as an element in any number of compounds (*bodhicitta, bodhisattva, abhisaṃbodhi, bodhicaryā*, etc.), *bodhi* is a subject of extensive exposition throughout which it is made clear that the term belongs more to the traditional categories of PATH (mārga), practice (*caryā, pratipatti*), or cause (*hetu*) than to the category of fruition or transcendent effect (*phala*). Thus, despite a common tendency in scholarship to regard *bodhi* as a synonym for *nirvāṇa, vimokṣa,* and so on, it is best to treat *bodhi* as analytically distinct in meaning from the various terms for the result or consequence of practice.

Although the term *bodhi* often refers to the liberating knowledge specifically of BUDDHAS (awakened ones), it is not reserved for that use alone; *bodhi* is also ascribed to other and lesser kinds of liberated beings, like the ARHAT. When the full awakening of a buddha is particularly or exclusively intended, it is common to use the superlative form, ANUTTARASAMYAKSAṂBODHI (COMPLETE, PERFECT AWAKENING). In East Asian Buddhist discourse, particularly in the CHAN SCHOOL (Japanese, Zen), one encounters other terms (e.g., Chinese, *wu;* Japanese, *satori*) that are also translated as "awakening" or "enlightenment." These other terms are perhaps related in meaning to *bodhi,* but they were very seldom used actually to translate the Indic word, are not admitted to be precisely synonymous with it, and in their common usages notably lack its sense of ultimacy or finality. They refer rather to certain moments or transient phases of the processes of realization arising in the course of contemplative practice. As such they are the focus of much dispute over their purportedly "sudden" or "gradual" occurrence.

Traditional accounts of bodhi found in or derived from South Asian sources are often connected to accounts of Śākyamuni's own liberating knowledge, attained in his thirty-fifth year, in the final watch of his first night "beneath the bodhi tree." He is said then to have achieved, in a climax to eons of cultivation extending through innumerable past lives, the ultimate knowledge (*vidyā*) or ABHIJÑĀ (HIGHER KNOWLEDGES)—that is, knowledge of the extinction of the residual impurities (*āsravakṣayajñāna;* literally, "oozings" or "cankers") of sensual desire (kāma), becoming (*bhava*), views (*dṛṣṭi*), and ignorance (avidyā). This extinguishing or purgative knowledge arises precisely in the immediate verification of the FOUR NOBLE TRUTHS—that is, in the intuitive confirmation (*abhisamaya*) of the truth of *duḥkha* (suffering), the truth of the origin (*samudaya*) of suffering in craving (*tṛṣṇā*) and ignorance (avidyā), the truth of the cessation (*nirodha*) of suffering, and the truth of the path (mārga) leading to the cessation of suffering. To the limited and questionable extent that one can conceive of bodhi as an experience, these knowings or extinctions are, so to speak, the content or object of Śākyamuni's experience of awakening, and the four noble truths are what it was that he awakened to. We may note in this classical account of bodhi the convergence of two modes of soteriological discourse—a discourse of purgation or purification signaled by the use of terms like eradication (*kṣaya*) and canker (*āsrava*), and a discourse of veridical cognition, exemplified by such terms as knowledge (*vidyā*) and *abhijñā.* Bodhi is thus shown to be, at once, a cleansing and a gnosis, an understanding that purifies and a purification that illuminates.

The more systematic or scholastic traditions of Buddhism commonly expound bodhi in terms of its constituent factors (*bodhipakṣa, bodhipakṣikadharma*). These, of course, are components of awakening in the sense of an extended process or path rather than in the sense of a single, unitary culmination of a path. There are thirty-seven such factors, grouped in seven somewhat overlapping categories. The four "foundations of MINDFULNESS" (*smṛtyupasthāna*) are mindfulness or analytical meditative awareness of the body (*kāya*), of feelings (*vedanā*), of consciousness (*vijñāna*), and of mind-objects (dharma). The four "correct eliminations" (*samyakprahāṇa*) or "correct exertions" (*samyakpradhāna*) are the striving to eliminate evil that has already arisen, to prevent future evil, to produce future good, and to increase good that has already arisen. The four "bases of meditative power" (*ṛddhipāda*) are aspiration (*chanda*), strength (*vīrya*), composure of mind (*citta*), and scrutiny (*mīmāṃsā*). The five "faculties" (*indriya*) are FAITH (śraddhā), energy (*vīrya*), mindfulness (*smṛti*), concentration (samādhi), and PRAJÑĀ (WISDOM). The five "powers" (*bala*) are five different degrees of the five faculties ranging from the lowest degree sufficient to be simply a follower of the Buddha, through the higher degrees necessary to achieve the higher degrees of sainthood: status as a stream winner (*śrotāpanna*), a once-returner (*sakṛdāgāmin*), a nonreturner (*anāgāmin*), and an arhat. The seven "limbs of awakening" (*bodhyaṅga*) are memory (*smṛti*), investigation of teaching (*dharmapravicaya*), energy (*vīrya*), rapture (*prīti*), serenity (*praśrabdhi*), concentration (samādhi), and equanimity (*upekṣā*). The final eight factors are the components of the noble eightfold path.

So manifold and complex a characterization of bodhi, as a process comprising multiple parts, serves to underscore the fact that awakening is clearly not an end divorced from its means, nor a realization separate from practice; rather it is the sum and the perfection of practice. This fact is often explicitly acknowledged in Buddhism—in assertions of the unity of realization and practice or in the variously formulated insistence that practice is essential to realization. Such claims must be kept in mind as cautions against the temptation to conceive of bodhi as a wholly autonomous, self-generated, and entirely transcendent "experience." Indeed, it could serve even as warrant for banning the very use of modern, largely Western notions of "experience" (pure experience, religious experience, mystical experience, etc.) from all discussions of bodhi or analogous terms. To speak of "the experience of awakening," rather than of, say, the performance or the cultivation of awakening, is to risk reifying the process and, worse still, isolating it from the rest of Buddhism.

Bodhi in the Mahāyāna

The characterizations of awakening sketched above are common to the whole of Buddhism. Among notions of bodhi that are especially emphasized in MAHĀYĀNA one must note its conception as an object of noble aspiration. The ideal Mahāyāna practitioner, the BODHISATTVA, is essentially defined as one who aspires to bodhi, one who dedicates himself to the enactment of bodhi for himself but also and especially for all beings. This is the sense of the word operative in the term *bodhicittotpada,* the arousal of BODHICITTA (THOUGHT OF AWAKENING), a locution rich in conative significance that conveys the affective dimension, the emotive power, of liberating knowledge, as well as its necessary association with the virtue of KARUṆĀ (COMPASSION).

Also characteristic of Mahāyāna is a recurrent concern with identifying the source of the capacity for awakening. Is it natural or inculcated? In sixth-century China there appeared a text entitled the AWAKENING OF FAITH (DASHENG QIXIN LUN) that was attributed to AŚVAGHOṢA but was probably a Chinese contribution to the evolving tradition of TATHĀGATAGARBHA (matrix or embryo of buddhahood) thought. This text coined the term "original awakening" (*benjue*), contrasting that with "incipient awakening" (*shijue*). The former refers to an innate potential awakening, a natural purity of mind (*cittaprakṛtiviśuddhi*) or underlying radiance of mind (*prabhāsvaratvaṃ cittasya*), which enables practice and so engenders the actualization of awakening. The latter refers to the process of actualization itself, by which one advances from the nonawakened state, through seeming and partial awakening, to final awakening. Drawing upon a usage of linguistics, we might speak of the pair as awakening in the mode of competence and awakening in the mode of performance. The notion of a natural enlightenment that abides as a potency in the very sentience of SENTIENT BEINGS (later called buddha-nature) and issues in the gradual enactment of actual awakening stood in contrast to alternative views found in certain traditions of the YOGĀCĀRA SCHOOL of Buddhism, according to which awakening is the outcome of the radical transformation of a mind (*āśrayaparāvṛtti*) that is naturally or inveterately defiled. This notion proved very fruitful throughout East Asian Buddhism but fostered in the Japanese Tendai (Chinese, Tiantai) school an especially powerful and enduring doctrine of ORIGINAL ENLIGHTENMENT (HONGAKU) that left its mark on nearly all of medieval and early modern Japanese Buddhism. It also had profound ethical implications insofar as the notion of original or natural awakening was commonly invoked, or was said to be invoked, for antinomian or laxist purposes on the grounds that one's originally awakened condition rendered effortful practice otiose.

Comparable to the idea of original awakening, but even stronger and bolder, is the startling claim resonant in much of Chinese, Korean, and Japanese Buddhism that awakening is not merely potentially present in the mundane sentient condition but actually identical with the worst of that condition. This seemingly paradoxical assertion is classically conveyed in the aphorism, "the afflictions (*kleśa*) are identical with awakening." In conventional theory, bodhi is the eradication of the *kleśa* (affective hindrances like anger, lust, greed, etc.); the assertion that the *kleśa* and bodhi are one and the same would therefore seem, at least at first glance, to be not only heterodox but also perverse and self-contradictory. It appears to stand the conventional view of awakening on its head. However, justification for so seemingly outrageous a claim is to be found in the doctrine of ŚŪNYATĀ (EMPTINESS), according to which any sentient event or condition, being necessarily empty (*śūnya*) of self-nature or own being (*svabhāva*), mysteriously incorporates all other sentient events or conditions. Hell entails buddhahood; evil entails good; and vice versa. Thus, even an impulse of lust or hatred harbors the aspiration for awakening, and awakening is not a condition or process that depends upon or consists in the complete extinction of imperfection.

The sudden/gradual issue

The concept of original awakening was also central to Chan discourse about "sudden" (Chinese, *dun*; Japanese, *ton*) and "gradual" (Chinese, *jian*; Japanese, *zen*) awakening. Here the term for awakening is the Chinese word *wu* (read in Japanese as *satori* or *go*), and, as noted above, *wu* is to be distinguished from *bodhi,* although it is not wholly unrelated. The terms sudden awakening (*dunwu*) and gradual awakening (*jianwu*) were, of course, instruments of polemic. Certain Chan traditions criticized others for being gradualist in their understanding and practice of awakening while claiming themselves to be subitist. The former, of course, is a term of disparagement, the latter a term of strong approbation. No school ever itself claimed to be gradualist; all laid claim to sudden awakening. In the eighth century the so-called Southern Chan school, derived from the teachings of the sixth patriarch HUINENG (ca. 638–713), claimed to offer sudden or all-at-once awakening while alleging that the so-called Northern School, derived from the teachings of Shenxiu (ca. 606–706), espoused a gradual or step-by-step, and thus ultimately bogus, awakening. The Northern School, which was actually as subitist as any, died out as a distinct Chan lineage, whereas the Southern School flourished to the point that all post-eighth-century Chan derives from the Southern School and so adheres *de rigueur* to the position that true awakening comes suddenly or all at once. In effect this is simply a variation on the theme of original awakening, for the asserted suddenness or all-at-once character of awakening is really just a function of its being, as it were, always and already present in one's very nature as a sentient being. It need not be formed but only acknowledged, and acknowledgement is always all at once. It must be noted, however, that only in the most extreme and eccentric traditions of Chan did the claim of "sudden awakening" ever imply the actual rejection of effortful practice. Instead, such gradual practice was typically held to be necessary, but necessary chiefly as the sequel to a quickening moment of sudden awakening, functioning to extend what was glimpsed in sudden awakening so as to make it permanent, habitual, and mature.

Bodhi as "enlightenment"

It was noted above that the most common English rendering of *bodhi* (or *wu* or *satori*) is "enlightenment." There are grounds for such a translation. Some of the earliest usages of the word *enlightenment* show it to have meant something like spiritual illumination, and spiritual illumination is not so far from "awakening." However, the term *enlightenment* is also commonly employed in the West to designate an age in European intellectual and cultural history, roughly the eighteenth century, the dominant voices of which were those of philosophers like Voltaire, Condorcet, and Diderot, who all declared the supremacy of reason over faith, and the triumph of science and rational ethics over religion. Such thinkers were harshly dismissive of the kinds of piety, faith, asceticism, and mystical insight that we saw above to be among the components or factors of bodhi. To be sure, the awakening of the Buddha was not a suspension or an abrogation of reason, but neither was it simply an exercise of what Voltaire would have meant by *reason*. Better then to use the more literal rendering of "awakening," which also has the advantage of conveying the concrete imagery of calm alertness and clear vision that the Buddhist traditions have always had in mind when speaking of bodhi.

Bibliography

Gethin, Rupert M. L. *The Buddhist Path to Awakening: A Study of the Bodhi-Pakkhiyā Dhammā,* 2nd edition. Oxford: Oneworld, 2001.

Gregory, Peter N., ed. *Sudden and Gradual: Approaches to Enlightenment in Chinese Thought.* Honolulu: University of Hawaii Press, 1987.

Ruegg, David S. *Buddha-nature, Mind, and the Problem of Gradualism in Comparative Perspective: On the Transmission and Reception of Buddhism in India and Tibet.* London: School of Oriental and African Studies, 1989.

Stone, Jacqueline I. *Original Enlightenment and the Transformation of Medieval Japanese Buddhism.* Honolulu: University of Hawaii Press, 1999.

ROBERT M. GIMELLO

BODHICARYĀVATĀRA

Bodhicaryāvatāra (*Introduction to the Conduct That Leads to Enlightenment*; *Byang chub sems dpa'i spyod pa la 'jug pa*) is, with CANDRAKĪRTI's seventh-century *Madhyamakāvatāra* (*Introduction to Madhyamaka*), the most important text integrating Madhyamaka philosophy into the bodhisattva path. The text is structured around meditation on the altruistic "awakening mind" or BODHICITTA (THOUGHT OF AWAKENING) and its development through PĀRAMITĀ (PERFECTION). The longest chapter is on PRAJÑĀ (WISDOM) and treats philosophical analysis. Written by ŚĀNTIDEVA (ca. 685–763), the poem was popular in late Indian Buddhism and has been enormously important in Tibet.

See also: **Bodhisattva(s); Madhyamaka School**

Bibliography

Brassard, Francis. *The Concept of Bodhicitta in Śāntideva's Bodhicaryāvatāra.* Albany: State University of New York Press, 2000.

Crosby, Kate, and Skilton, Andrew, trans. *Śāntideva: The Bodhicaryāvatāra.* Oxford: Oxford University Press, 1995.

Gyatso, Geshe Kelsang. *Meaningful to Behold*, tr. Tenzin Norbu. London: Wisdom, 1986.

Wallace, Visna A., and Wallace, B. Allan, trans. *A Guide to the Bodhisattva Way of Life (Bodhicaryāvatāra).* New York: Snow Lion, 1997.

Williams, Paul. *Altruism and Reality: Studies in the Philosophy of the Bodhicaryāvatāra.* Richmond, UK: Curzon, 1998.

PAUL WILLIAMS

BODHICITTA (THOUGHT OF AWAKENING)

The English phrase "thought of awakening" is a mechanical rendering of the Indic term *bodhicitta.* The original term is a compound noun signifying "thought directed at or focused on awakening," "a resolution to seek and/or attain awakening," or "the mind that is (virtually or intrinsically) awakening (itself)." The concept is known in non-Mahāyāna sources (e.g., *Abhidharmadīpa,* pp. 185–186, 192) and occurs in transitional texts such as the MAHĀVASTU, but gains its doctrinal and ritual importance in MAHĀYĀNA and tantric traditions.

Technical definitions

In its most common denotation the term *bodhicitta* refers to the resolution to attain BODHI (AWAKENING) in order to liberate all living beings, which defines and motivates the BODHISATTVA's vow. However, even this simple definition entails several layers of meaning and practice. The resolution to attain awakening can be seen as a state of mind or a mental process, but it is also the solemn promise (the vow as verbal act) embodied or expressed in particular ritual utterances, acts, and gestures (recitation of the vows, dedication of merit, etc.). *Bodhicitta* is also the motivating thought and sentiment behind the spiritual practice or career (*caryā*) of the bodhisattva; as such, it is the defining moment and the moving force behind the course of action that follows and enacts the initial resolution (the first appearance of the thought, known as *bodhicittotpāda*). As moving force and motivation it is also the mental representation of the goal (awakening) and the essential spirit of the practice (a usage sometimes rendered in English as "an awakened attitude"). Finally, the culmination of the intention of the vow and of the subsequent effort in the PATH—that is, awakening itself—may also be regarded as technically *bodhicitta.* As a further extension of this usage, the term *bodhicitta* may also refer to the fundamental source or ground for the resolution, namely, innate enlightenment.

In a narrow psychological sense, *bodhicitta* is the first conscious formulation of an aspiration: to seek full awakening (buddhahood) in order to lead all SENTIENT BEINGS to liberation from DUḤKHA (SUFFERING). Conceived as a wish, as an intention that arises or occurs in the mind, the *bodhicitta* is a sort of decision; but in the traditional Buddhist view of mental culture, feelings and wishes can be fostered or cultivated. Accordingly, the *bodhicitta* is generally believed to require mental culture and self-cultivation, perhaps as an integral part of the purpose it embodies. The continued cultivation of the intention, the practice or exercise of the thought of awakening, helps develop a series of mental states and behavioral changes that gradually approximate the object of the wish: full awakening as a compassionate buddha or bodhisattva.

Ritual uses and meanings

This practice of the thought of awakening begins with a RITUAL enactment, usually as part of the so-called sevenfold supreme worship (*saptavidhā-anuttarapūjā*), which includes, among other things, the rituals of taking the bodhisattva vows and the dedication of merit. Some Indian authors (e.g., ĀRYAŚŪRA and Candragomin) composed their own ritual for the production and adoption of the *bodhicitta.* In these liturgical settings the *bodhicitta* appears prominently as the focus of the ritual of the bodhisattva vow, which in many Mahāyāna liturgies replaced or incorporated earlier rituals for the adoption of the PRECEPTS or rituals preparatory for meditation sessions. Such rituals proliferated in East Asia and Tibet.

Although the model for many Tibetan liturgies was arguably a reworking of ritual elements in the *Śikṣāsamuccaya* and the BODHICARYĀVATĀRA of ŚĀNTIDEVA (ca. seventh century C.E.), the tradition combined a variety of sources in developing a theology and a liturgy of the thought of awakening. The *Thar pa rin po che'i rgyan* of Sgam po pa (1079–1153 C.E.) distinguishes the ritual based on Śāntideva's teachings from the rituals from the lineage of Dharmakīrti Suvarṇadvīpin of Vijayanagara (fl. ca. 1000 C.E.)—presumably received through ATISHA (982–1054 C.E.).

Most Mahāyāna traditions consecrate the initial thought as the impetus and hence the most important moment in the bodhisattva's career: the breaking forth of an idea, the aspiration to the good, and a rare and valuable event. This event, in both its internal, psychological form and its ritual, public form is called "giving rise to the thought of awakening," or, "causing the (first) appearance of a thought directed at awakening" ([*prathama*]-*bodhicittotpāda*). In its most literal and concrete sense, this is the moment when a bodhisattva encounters, or creates the conditions for, the appearance of the earnest wish to attain awakening for the benefit of all sentient beings. In Śāntideva's explanation, the vow as expression of *bodhicitta* is closely associated with the adoption of the precepts of the bodhisattva (*bodhisattvasaṃvara*), which are seen as the means for preserving and cultivating the initial resolution. This close link is recognized in many other ritual plans; for instance, the repentance rites (*wuhui*, "five ways to repent") of the TIANTAI SCHOOL follow an ascending hierarchy that is somehow parallel to the sevenfold act of worship but begins with confession (*canhui*) and culminates with the resolution (*fayuan*) to seek awakening for the sake of all living beings.

Indian Mahāyāna scholastic accounts assume for the most part that a concerted and conscious effort to cultivate the *bodhicitta* by setting out on the path (called *prasthānacitta*) is necessary for awakening. Nonetheless, the ritual expression of the vow (called "the thought of the vow," *praṇidhicitta*), and the adoption of the bodhisattva precepts (*saṃvara*) in the presence of a spiritual mentor (*kalyāṇamitra*), or before all the buddhas of the universe, is sometimes seen as a guarantee of eventual awakening. Some authors (notably Śāntideva in his *Bodhicaryāvatāra*) conceive of *bodhicitta* as a force so potent that it appears to be external to the person's own will, effort, or attention. In this conception, once a person has given rise to the resolution, the *bodhicitta* is, as it were, awakening itself, present, in manifest or latent form, in that person's mental processes.

Thought of awakening as awakened thought

We may speak of a historical process whereby the abstract notion or the psychological reality of a resolution became an autonomous spiritual force. The process is already suggested in Mahāyāna sūtras that glorify the *bodhicitta* as both the sine qua non of Mahāyāna practice and the essence or substance of awakening: It is a hidden treasure, like a panacea or powerful medicinal herb (see, for example, the "Maitreyavimokṣa" chapter of the *Gaṇḍavyūha-sūtra*). What may have been a hyperbolic celebration of the *bodhicitta*, however, soon took the form of a reification or deification of this mental state or sequence of mental states. The thought of awakening is present even if one lacks all virtue, like a jewel hidden in a dung heap; one who gives rise to the thought will be venerated by gods and humans (*Bodhicaryāvatāra*). And, in a metaphor chosen as the title for one of the fourteenth Dalai Lama's commentaries, the thought of awakening is like a flash of lightning in the dark night of human delusion. What is more, sūtras and śāstras alike agree that the thought of awakening protects from all dangers the person who conceives of it.

Insofar as the *bodhicitta* is also the starting point for Mahāyāna practice proper, it is a precondition and a basis for the virtues of a buddha (the *buddhadharmas*), and hence, impels, as it were, all the positive faculties and states generated in the path. The thought of awakening hence manifests itself throughout the path, in all stages of the bodhisattva's development (*Mahāyānasūtrālaṃkāra*, chap. 4, following the *Akṣayamatinirdeśa*). The *First Bhāvanākrama* of Kamalaśīla states that the foundation (*mūla*) for these virtues, and for the omniscience of a full buddha, is KARUṆĀ (COMPASSION), but, referring to the *Vairocanābhisaṃbodhi*, adds that *bodhicitta* is the generating and impelling cause (*hetu*) of buddhahood.

Furthermore, insofar as *bodhicitta* is the mind of awakening, it is a beginning that is an end in itself. To paraphrase Kamalaśīla's *Second Bhāvanākrama*, there are two types of *bodhicitta*, the conventional one of ritual and process, and the absolute one that is both the innate potency to become awakened and the mind that has attained the ultimate goal, awakening itself. The distinction between these two aspects or levels of *bodhicitta* is perhaps an attempt to account for the difference between the ritual and conventional enactment of a resolution, the spirit of commitment, the magnetic force of an ideal representation, and a sacred presence (awakening itself). Psychologically the idea may reflect a desire to understand how conviction and good intent can exist next to lack of conviction and a desire for what is not virtuous—in short how an ideal can be both a clear and heartfelt conviction and a distant goal.

The distinction between a provisional or conventional thought of awakening (*saṃvṛtibodhicitta*) and one that is or embodies the ultimate goal (*paramārthabodhicitta*) plays a central role in tantric conceptions of the "physiology" and "psychology" of ritual and meditation, in India and beyond. For it serves as a link between ritual convention and timeless truth, and between disparate branches of the tradition—

linking, for instance, the sūtra or pāramitā aspects of the path with the tantric stages, on the ground that all stages manifest some aspect of *bodhicitta.* This is arguably the most important function of *bodhicitta* as an explanatory or apologetic category in path theory and is highlighted in classic *lam rim* literature (for a contemporary presentation, see Gyatso).

The thought as icon

The thought of awakening is also a pivotal concept in Mahāyāna ethical speculation: In some ways *bodhicitta* is shorthand for the instinct of empathy and the cultivation of compassion as foundations for Buddhist involvement with SAṂSĀRA. It epitomizes important dimensions of intentionality, as attitude toward others and attitudes toward self, as well as intention as the direction in which transformative behavior moves.

A term so laden with meanings almost fits naturally as the core around which one could build further ritual tropes, as one can see in relatively early tantras like the *Mahāvairocana-sūtra.* The *Guhyasamāja-tantra* devotes its second chapter to *bodhicitta,* describing it as the solid core (*sāra, vajra*) of the body, speech, and mind of all the buddhas. Since this ultimate reality is, not surprisingly, the emptiness of all things, the text implicitly builds a bridge between the ethical and ritual life of the practitioner's body, speech, and mind, and both the reality and its sacred embodiment in all buddhas.

Bodhicitta is also a force that empowers the practitioner, and therefore plays an important role in some tantric rites of initiation or CONSECRATION (abhiṣeka). A common homology imagines *bodhicitta* as masculine potency—UPĀYA and the seed of awakening—and prajñā as the feminine "lotus-vessel" that receives the *bodhicitta.* Thus, *bodhicitta* becomes *bindu* (the "droplets" of awakening) and hence the semen that stands for the generative power of awakening. Because *bodhicitta* as *bindu* or semen represents the male potency of awakened saints, it is not uncommon for a female participant (a *yoginī* present symbolically or in person) to be seen as *vidyā* or prajñā, whereas *bodhicitta* stands for *upāya.* Classical Indian physiology assumed that females also have semen, hence the disciple receiving initiation ingested, symbolically or literally, the sexual fluids of both the guru (male) and the *yoginī* (female) as a way to give rise to the thought of awakening—thus generated, as it were, from the union of mother and father.

Summary interpretations

The above tapestry shows how the concept of *bodhicitta* ties together liturgy, systematic theories of awakening and the path, and the foundations of Buddhist ethics. It is a concept as important for the history of Mahāyāna ritual as those of the vow (*praṇidhāna*) and the dedication of merit (*puṇyapariṇāmanā*). A social history of the concept would include its function as a secure solid ground outside social and sectarian differences: It is, as it were, a thin, but steely thread that links the specifics of ritual and theology with the idea of a timeless and ineffable liberating reality. As a source of authority, *bodhicitta* is both an inner drive and an untainted reality beyond individual differences.

Theologically, *bodhicitta* is, in part, a functional equivalent to the family of concepts encompassed by Hindu notions of *prasāda* and Western concepts of grace: *Bodhicitta* stands for the mystery of the presence of the holy in an imperfect human being who is in need of liberation and imagines it, despite the unlikelihood of the presence of even the mere idea of perfection in such an imperfect being.

See also: **Original Enlightenment (Hongaku)**

Bibliography

Brassard, Francis. *The Concept of Bodhicitta in Śāntideva's Bodhicaryāvatāra.* Albany: State University of New York Press, 2000.

Bstan 'dzin rgya mtsho (Tenzin Gyatso, Dalai Lama XIV). *A Flash of Lightning in the Dark of Night: A Guide to the Bodhisattva's Way of Life,* tr. the Padmakara Translation Group. Boston and London: Shambhala, 1994.

Gyatso, Geshe Kelsang. *Essence of Vajrayāna: The Highest Yoga Tantra Practice of Heruka Body Maṇḍala.* London: Tharpa, 1997.

Khunu Rinpoche. *Vast as the Heavens, Deep as the Sea: Verses in Praise of Bodhicitta,* tr. G. Sparham. Somerville, MA: Wisdom, 1999.

Kong sprul Blo gros mtha' yas (Lodro Thaye Kongtrul, Jamgon Kongtrul). *The Light of Wisdom: The Root Text, Lamrim yeshe nyingpo by Padmasambhava . . . Commentary on the Light of Wisdom by Jamgon Kongtrul the Great.* Boston: Shambhala, 1999.

Nanayakkara, S. K. "Bodhicitta." In *Encyclopaedia of Buddhism,* Vol. 3, Fasc. 2, ed. G. P. Malalasekera, 1972.

LUIS O. GÓMEZ

BODHIDHARMA

Within the CHAN SCHOOL or tradition, Bodhidharma (ca. early fifth century) is considered the first patriarch of China, who brought Chan teachings from India to China, and the twenty-eighth patriarch in the transmission of the torch of enlightenment down from Śākyamuni Buddha. Bodhidharma is the subject of countless portraits, where he is represented as an Indian wearing a full beard with rings in his ears and a monk's robe, frequently engaged in the nine years of cross-legged sitting which he was loath to interrupt, even when a prospective disciple cut off his own arm to prove his sincerity. Modern scholars have come to doubt many of the elements in this legendary picture.

Of the ten texts attributed to Bodhidharma, the most authentic is probably an unnamed compilation one can provisionally call the *Bodhidharma Anthology*. This anthology opens with a biography and an exposition of his teaching, both composed by Tanlin, a sixth-century specialist in the *Srīmālādevīsiṃhanāda-sūtra* (Chinese, *Shengman shizi hou jing; Sūtra of Queen Śrīmālā*). Tanlin's biography presents Bodhidharma as the third son of a South Indian king. Of Bodhidharma's route to China, Tanlin says, "He subsequently crossed distant mountains and seas, traveling about propagating the teaching in North China." This more historically feasible Bodhidharma came to North China via Central Asia.

Tanlin explains Bodhidharma's teaching as "entrance by principle and entrance by practice" (*liru* and *xingru*). "Entrance by principle" involves awakening to the realization that all SENTIENT BEINGS are identical to the true nature (*dharmatā*)—if one abides in "wall examining" (*biguan*) without dabbling in the scriptures, one will "tally with principle." "Wall examining" has been the subject of countless exegeses, from the most imaginative and metaphorical (be like a wall painting of a bodhisattva gazing down upon the suffering of saṃsāra) to the suggestion that it refers to the physical posture of cross-legged sitting in front of a wall. Later Tibetan translations gloss it as "abiding in brightness" (*lham mer gnas*), a tantric interpretation that also invites scrutiny.

"Entrance by practice" is fourfold: having patience in the face of suffering; being aware that the conditions for good things will eventually run out; seeking for nothing; and being in accord with intrinsic purity. The anthology also includes three *Records* (again the title is provisional) consisting of lecture materials, dialogues,

Bodhidharma (ca. early fifth century), the first Chan patriarch of China. (Japanese wood sculpture, Edo period, 1600–1868). © Reunion des Musées Nationaux/Art Resource, NY. Reproduced by permission.

and sayings. *Record I* has a saying attributed to Bodhidharma: "When one does not understand, the person pursues dharmas; when one understands, dharmas pursue the person." Later Chan did not appropriate this saying for its Bodhidharma story.

Two other early sources of information on Bodhidharma deserve mention. The first is a sixth-century non-Buddhist source, the *Luoyang qielan ji* (*Record of the Buddhist Edifices of Luoyang*), which twice mentions an Iranian-speaking Bodhidharma from Central Asia. The second is the seventh-century *Xu gaoseng zhuan* (*Further Biographies of Eminent Monks*) by DAOXUAN (596–667). It contains a Bodhidharma entry (a slightly reworked version of Tanlin's piece), an entry on Bodhidharma's successor, Huike, and a critique of Bodhidharma's style of meditation. Here, Bodhidharma is said to have (1) come to China by the southern sea route, and (2) handed down a powerful mystery text, the LAṄKĀVATĀRA-SŪTRA (*Discourse of the Descent into Lanka*), to Huike. Holders of this sūtra were thought to be capable of uncanny feats, such as sitting cross-legged all night in a snowbank. The later Chan picture of Bodhidharma incorporates both Daoxuan's southern sea route and his sacramental transmission of the *Laṅkāvatāra*. By the early eighth century, the first Chan histories had assembled these key elements as the Bodhidharma story, drawing principally upon Daoxuan's work.

See also: **China**

Bibliography

Broughton, Jeffrey L. *The Bodhidharma Anthology: The Earliest Records of Zen.* Berkeley: University of California Press, 1999.

Faure, Bernard. "Bodhidharma as Textual and Religious Paradigm." *History of Religions* 25, no. 3 (1986): 187–198.

Faure, Bernard. *Le traité de Bodhidharma: Première anthologie du bouddhisme Chan.* Paris: Le Mail, 1986.

Yanagida Seizan, ed. and trans. *Daruma no goroku.* Zen no goroku 1. Tokyo: Chikuma shobō, 1969.

JEFFREY BROUGHTON

BODHISATTVA(S)

The term *bodhisattva* (Pāli, *bodhisatta*; Tibetan, *byang chub sems pa*; Chinese, *pusa*; Korean, *posal,* Japanese, *bosatsu*) refers to a *sattva* (person) on a Buddhist mārga (PATH) in pursuit of BODHI (AWAKENING) or one whose nature is awakening. In the Mahāyāna tradition, a bodhisattva is a practitioner who, by habituating himself in the practice of the PĀRAMITĀ (PERFECTION), aspires to become a buddha in the future by seeking ANUTTARASAMYAKSAṂBODHI (COMPLETE, PERFECT AWAKENING) through PRAJÑĀ (WISDOM) and by benefiting all sentient beings through KARUṆĀ (COMPASSION). A bodhisattva is one who courageously seeks enlightenment through totally and fully benefiting others (*parārtha*), as well as himself (*svārtha*). A bodhisattva is also termed a *mahāsattva* or "Great Being" because he is a Mahāyāna practitioner who seeks *anuttarasamyaksaṃbodhi* and who is equipped with the necessities for enlightenment—*puṇyasambhāra* (accumulation of merits) and *jñānasambhāra* (accumulation of wisdom)—and the quality of *upāya-kauśalya* (skillful means); that is, he knows how to act appropriately in any situation.

According to the *Bodhisattvabhūmi,* the *bodhisattvayāna* (spiritual path of a bodhisattva) is considered to be superior to both the *śrāvakayāna* (spiritual path of the disciples) and the *pratyekabuddhayāna* (spiritual path of a self-awakened buddha) because a bodhisattva is destined to attain enlightenment by removing the *kleśajñeyāvaraṇa* (emotional and intellectual afflictions), whereas those on the other two spiritual paths aspire for NIRVĀṆA, that is, extinction of emotional afflictions only.

The bodhisattva is known by different appellations; for example, in *Mahāyāna-sūtrālaṃkāra* XIX: 73–74, the following fifteen names are given as synonyms for *bodhisattva*:

1. *mahāsattva* (great being)
2. *dhīmat* (wise)
3. *uttamadyuti* (most splendid)
4. *jinaputra* (Buddha's son)
5. *jinādhāra* (holding to the Buddha)
6. *vijetṛ* (conqueror)
7. *jināṅkura* (Buddha's offspring)
8. *vikrānta* (bold)
9. *paramāścarya* (most marvelous)
10. *sārthavāha* (caravan leader)
11. *mahāyaśas* (of great glory)
12. *kṛpālu* (compassionate)
13. *mahāpuṇya* (greatly meritorious)
14. *īśvara* (lord)
15. *dhārmika* (righteous).

Bodhisattvas are of ten classes:

1. *gotrastha* (one who has not reached purity yet)
2. *avatīrṇa* (one who investigates the arising of the enlightenment mind)
3. *aśuddhāśaya* (one who has not reached a pure intention)
4. *śuddhāśaya* (one who has reached a pure intention)
5. *aparipakva* (one who has not matured in the highest state)
6. *paripakva* (one who has matured in the highest state)
7. *aniyatipatita* (one who although matured has not yet entered contemplation)
8. *niyatipatita* (one who has entered contemplation)
9. *ekajātipratibaddha* (one who is about to enter the supreme enlightenment)

10. *caramabhavika* (one who has entered supreme enlightenment in this life).

Regarding the bodhisattva's practice, different texts use different categories to discuss the process. For example, the *Daśabhūmika-sūtra* refers to the *daśabhūmi* (ten spiritual stages) of a bodhisattva, while the *Bodhisattvabhūmi* makes reference to twelve vihāra (abodes), adding two vihāra to the list of ten *bhūmis*: *gotravihāra* (abode of the bodhisattva family) and *adhimukticaryāvihāra* (abode of firm resolution), the latter of which continues throughout the next ten abodes. The last ten of the vihāras essentially correspond to the ten bodhisattva stages of the *Daśabhūmika-sūtra,* although each has a name different from the names of the stages. In each of the ten stages of the *Daśabhūmika-sūtra,* a distinct pāramitā is practiced so that the bodhisattva gradually elevates himself to the final goal of enlightenment. The stages of practice according to the *Daśabhūmika-sūtra,* with their corresponding pāramitās, are as follows:

1. *pramudita-bhūmi* (joyful stage): *dānapāramitā* (perfection of charity)
2. *vimala-bhūmi* (free of defilements stage): *śīlapāramitā* (perfection of ethical behavior)
3. *prabhākarī-bhūmi* (light-giving stage): *dhyānapāramitā* (perfection of contemplation)
4. *arcīṣmatī-bhūmi* (glowing wisdom stage): *kṣāntipāramitā* (perfection of patience)
5. *sudurjayā-bhūmi* (mastery of utmost difficulty stage): *vīryapāramitā* (perfection of energy)
6. *abhimukhī-bhūmi* (wisdom beyond definition of impure or pure stage): *prajñāpāramitā* (perfection of wisdom)
7. *dūrāṅgamā-bhūmi* (proceeding afar stage [in which a bodhisattva gets beyond self to help others]): *upāyakauśalyapāramitā* (perfection of utilizing one's expertise)
8. *acala-bhūmi* (calm and unperturbed stage): *praṇidhānapāramitā* (perfection of making vows to save all sentient beings)
9. *sadhumati-bhūmi* (good thought stage): *balapāramitā* (perfection of power to guide sentient beings)
10. *dharmamagha-bhūmi* (rain cloud of dharma stage): *jñānapāramitā* (perfection of all-inclusive wisdom)

However, the numbers of stages of a bodhisattva are inconsistent from sūtra to sūtra and from commentary to commentary. One finds fifty-two stages in the *Pusa yingluo benye jing* (Taishō no. 1485), fifty-one in the RENWANG JING (HUMANE KINGS SŪTRA, Taishō no. 245), forty in both the FANWANG JING (BRAHMĀ'S NET SŪTRA, Taishō no. 1484) and the *Avataṃsaka-sūtra* (HUAYAN JING, Taishō no. 278), fifty-seven in the *Śūrangama[samādhi]-sutra* (Taishō no. 642), fifty-four in the *Cheng weishi lun* (Taishō no. 1591), four in the *Mahāyānasaṃgraha* (*She dasheng lun,* Taishō no. 1594), and both thirteen and seven stages in the *Bodhisattvabhūmi* (*Pusa dichi jing,* Taishō no. 1581).

There are other classifications of bodhisattvas, such as those who enter enlightenment quickly and those who enter gradually; those who are householders and those who are not, each divided into nine classes; those who are extremely compassionate, such as Avalokiteśvara; and those who are extremely wise, such as Mañjuśrī. MAITREYA bodhisattva is considered to be the future buddha who is prophesized to appear in this world. Śākyamuni himself is understood to have been a bodhisattva in his past lives and is so called in the accounts of his previous births (JĀTAKA).

In order to distinguish him from the śrāvakas and PRATYEKABUDDHAS, who benefit only themselves, a Mahāyāna bodhisattva is characterized as one who makes vows to benefit all sentient beings, as well as himself. In the Pure Land tradition, for example, according to the *Larger* SUKHĀVATĪVYŪHA-SŪTRA, the Bodhisattva Mahāsattva Dharmākara makes forty-eight vows and becomes the Buddha of Infinite Light and Life (AMITĀBHA or Amitāyus), who resides in the Western Quarter and functions as a salvific buddha.

Among the well-known bodhisattvas, Avalokiteśvara and Maitreya are probably the most popular in East Asia. In the East Asian Buddhist tradition, Avalokiteśvara, better known by the Chinese name Guanyin (Korean, Kwanseŭm; Japanese, Kannon), is worshiped by both clergy and laity as a mother figure, a savior, and a mentor, who responds to the pain and suffering of sentient beings. In Tibet, Tenzin Gyatso, the fourteenth DALAI LAMA, is considered to be a reincarnation of Avalokiteśvara.

Maitreya (Pāli, Metteyya) bodhisattva, who is said to dwell in Tuṣita heaven, is known as the "future buddha" because he will appear in this world to reestablish Buddhism after all vestiges of the current dispensation of Śākyamuni Buddha have vanished. Tradition holds that ASAṄGA went to Tuṣita to study

An image of the bodhisattva Avalokiteśvara being worshiped by the donor of the painting. (Chinese painting from the caves of Dunhuang, tenth century.) The Art Archive/Musée Guimet Paris/Dagli Orti. Reproduced by permission.

under Maitreya, where he received five treatises from him that became the basis for establishing the YOGĀCĀRA SCHOOL. Worship of Maitreya as the future buddha has also contributed to MILLENARIANISM AND MILLENARIAN MOVEMENTS in several Buddhist traditions.

Mañjuśrī and Samantabhadra are bodhisattvas who are often depicted in a triad together with the primordial Buddha Vairocana. Samantabhadra stands on Vairocana's right side and Mañjuśrī on his left. Samantabhadra is also often shown seated on the back of a white elephant, holding a wish-fulfilling jewel, a lotus flower, or a scripture, exemplifying his role as the guardian of the teaching and practice of the Buddha. Mañjuśrī, by contrast, represents wisdom, and is depicted wielding a flaming sword that cuts through the veil of ignorance.

Buddhist scholars and savants of India, such as NĀGĀRJUNA and VASUBANDHU, have been referred to as bodhisattvas; in China, DAO'AN, for example, is known as Yinshou *pusa*. In more modern times, founders of new Buddhist movements in China, Taiwan, Japan, and the United States are considered by followers to be bodhisattvas and, in some cases, even buddhas.

See also: **Bodhisattva Images; Mudrā and Visual Imagery**

Bibliography

Dayal, Har. *The Bodhisattva Doctrine in Buddhist Sanskrit Literature.* London: Kegan Paul, Trench, Trubner, 1932.

Dutt, Nalinaksha, ed. *Bodhisattva-bhūmiḥ.* Patna, India: K. P. Jayaswal Research Institute, 1978.

Hardacre, Helen, and Sponberg, Alan, eds. *Maitreya, the Future Buddha.* Cambridge, UK: Cambridge University Press, 1988.

Kawamura, Leslie S., ed. *The Bodhisattva Doctrine in Buddhism.* Waterloo, ON: Wilfrid Laurier University Press, 1981.

Ogihara Unrai, ed. *Bodhisattva-bhūmi: A Statement of Whole Course of the Bodhisattva.* Tokyo: Sankibo Buddhist Book Store, 1971.

Yü Chün-fang. *Kuan-yin: The Chinese Transformation of Avalokiteśvara.* New York: Columbia University Press, 2001.

LESLIE S. KAWAMURA

BODHISATTVA IMAGES

Although they play a fairly limited role in early Buddhism, BODHISATTVAS came to occupy a position of preeminence in later Buddhist literature. Moreover, visual representations of bodhisattvas comprise one of the largest and most important categories of imagery in Buddhist art. Despite this popularity, however, depictions of bodhisattvas, as with anthropomorphic depictions of BUDDHAS, apparently did not first appear until at least several centuries after the lifetime of the historical Buddha, Śākyamuni. Various explanations have been proposed to account for the relatively late emergence of the cult of images in Buddhism, but the textual and archaeological record remains inconclusive on several important fronts, such as the contentious question of when—and why—the earliest images of buddhas and bodhisattvas were created. While many aspects of the origin of the bodhisattva in the context of Buddhist art thus remain unresolved, the subsequent evolution and transmission of images of bodhisattvas are easier to chart.

Early representations

Judged on the basis of surviving stone sculpture from India, which constitutes the largest block of early evidence, the iconography of buddhas and of bodhisattvas differs in several key respects. A second-century triad from Gandhāra illustrates the typical characteristics of the two figural types. The central Buddha is depicted as an ascetic, with a simple coiffure, the plain robes customarily worn by a monk, and no other sort of adornment; the flanking bodhisattvas, by contrast, are depicted as very much of this world, with elaborate hairstyles and headdresses, rich robes, and the sorts of jeweled necklaces, bracelets, and earrings typically reserved for royalty. More than merely a reflection of stylistic preferences, these differences have long been interpreted as carrying deeper meaning. The simplicity of the Buddha's presentation, for example, can be seen as indicative of his status as one who has renounced the material world, while the ornamentation of the bodhisattva invokes analogies between earthly and spiritual power, and between material and spiritual abundance.

It should be noted that there are several other images, such as a red sandstone sculpture from Mathurā, that seem to contradict this general categorization: Although the standing figure exhibits the lack of adornment associated with images of the Buddha, the inscription labels it very clearly as a bodhisattva. In fact, such representations are reflections of a popular early motif that emphasized Śākyamuni's status as a bodhisattva, both in previous lives and just prior to becoming a buddha. This tradition, however, was certainly overshadowed by more typical imagery of the so-called *mahāsattvas,* or "Great Beings," as the well-known bodhisattvas generally associated with MAHĀYĀNA Buddhism were often called. It is this later ideal of powerful, transcendent figures dedicated to alleviating suffering in the human realm that underlies the development of the complex and multifaceted iconography of bodhisattvas that permeates the Buddhist world.

While there are, then, certain general characteristics shared by almost all bodhisattvas, there are also many specific individual traits that serve to distinguish one from another. Often these take the forms of particular attributes, such as the vase carried by MAITREYA, the thunderbolt (Sanskrit, *vajra*) held by Vajrapāṇi, or the sword and book frequently given to Mañjuśrī, while in other instances a bodhisattva might be paired with a specific animal mount, as are Samantabhadra and his elephant. In practice, however, this kind of straightforward iconographical identification is often made more difficult by the fact that many traits evolve over time, of course, or are transformed in different geographical regions; furthermore, some bodhisattvas can assume multiple physical forms, each with its own distinguishing characteristics. A closer look at some of the traditions of representation of Avalokiteśvara, undoubtedly the single most popular bodhisattva in the pantheon, will help to illustrate the nature and scope of these complexities.

The Bodhisattva of Compassion

The Bodhisattva Avalokiteśvara (Perceiver of the Sounds of the World) appears frequently in Indian Buddhist literature and art, and in both arenas assumes a multiplicity of forms and plays a variety of roles. In some sūtras, the Avalokiteśvara is merely a background figure, so to speak, and pictorially and sculpturally he is often portrayed as a subordinate attendant to the Buddha; over time, however, he was increasingly represented in both mediums as the focus of attention. What remains constant, and thus serves as a unifying element in the majority of literary and artistic depictions, is an emphasis on Avalokiteśvara as the embodiment of infinite KARUṆĀ (COMPASSION). One concrete expression of this emphasis can be seen in the many literary accounts detailing how the bodhisattva can save someone from the perils of the world. Iconographically, this theme is reflected by such features as the multiple limbs and heads with which Avalokiteśvara is often endowed (underscoring this special ability to help those in distress), and by the image of AMITĀBHA Buddha usually found in his headdress (alluding to the Western Paradise where Avalokiteśvara may help one be reborn).

The popularity of Avalokiteśvara spread to China (where he is known as Guanyin) and other parts of East Asia (Japan, Kannon; Korea, Kwanseŭm), and grew to such an extent that it essentially overshadowed that of all other bodhisattvas. Initially this was brought about in part by the widespread appeal of the LOTUS SŪTRA (SADDHARMAPUṆḌARĪKA-SŪTRA), several early translations of which were made into Chinese, in which Guanyin figures prominently; in fact, chapter 25, which details some thirty-three different manifestations of Guanyin, was often published and circulated as an independent text. Many well-known depictions of Guanyin are based on imagery from the *Lotus Sūtra,* and it is perhaps the elasticity of form described

The Bodhisattva Avalokiteśvara—the Bodhisattva of Compassion—shown with a thousand arms, symbolizing his ability to help those in distress. (Chinese wood sculpture.) © Reunion des Musées Nationaux/Art Resource, NY. Reproduced by permission.

in the sūtra that made it possible for different branches of Buddhism to be associated with different characteristic representations of the bodhisattva. Thus, to give just two examples: While PURE LAND BUDDHISM favored images of Guanyin leading souls to paradise, the CHAN SCHOOL preferred the so-called Water-Moon Guanyin and its allusions to the illusory nature of the phenomenal world.

Of all the developments associated with representations of Avalokiteśvara, none has received as much scholarly attention as the gender transformation that Guanyin underwent in China. While it is true that bodhisattvas are theoretically beyond such dualities as male and female, early depictions of Guanyin often exhibit decidedly male characteristics (such as the mustache common in both Indian and Chinese portrayals), while the *Lotus Sūtra* also lists various specifically female forms that Guanyin is capable of assuming. Whether influenced by these literary descriptions, or because compassion was perceived as a more feminine emotional trait, or in response to the cosmological tendency in traditional China to create yin/yang pairings of complementary forces such as wisdom and compassion, whatever complex combination of factors was at play, the outcome was that Guanyin emerged in China as the goddess of mercy and compassion, and retained that status throughout later East Asian artistic traditions.

Meanings beyond the text

Images of Avalokiteśvara, despite their great variety and multiplicity, share a common emphasis on the virtue of karuṇā, and exhibit remarkable continuity over time and location. To a great extent, this is due to a close correlation between text and image; indeed, the primary meanings for most representations of bodhisattvas derive from sūtras and other literary sources. There are, however, many instances where bodhisattva imagery exhibits different patterns of development, and derives meaning from other arenas. The Bodhisattva Kṣitigarbha, for example, who may have evolved from pre-Buddhist Indian earth gods, rarely appears in either art or literature in India. In China, by contrast, as the Bodhisattva Dizang, Kṣitigarbha is frequently depicted in illustrations of scenes of hell (though his popularity drops off remarkably after the thirteenth century), while in Japan, where he is known as Jizō, he has long been popularized as the protector of children. Lastly, as Chijang *posal,* he was one of the most important bodhisattvas in Korean Buddhism during the Chosŏn period (1392–1910), and most traditional Korean monastic complexes had a special Kṣitigarbha Hall where paintings of Chijang and the Kings of Hell were the focus of ritual offerings on behalf of the deceased during the mourning period for the dead. Each of these instances demonstrates the frequently localized meanings of a given theme that can evolve apart from canonical textual sources.

On an even more particularized level, bodhisattva imagery has often been linked to historical individuals, a phenomenon that certainly can alter visual meaning in a number of ways. For example, BODHIDHARMA, the reputed transmitter of Chan Buddhism from India to China, is claimed in Chan tradition as an incarnation of Avalokiteśvara. This may account for both the somewhat surprising frequency with which Avalokiteśvara is depicted in images connected with Chan, as well as the structural similarities between such images as "Bodhidharma on a Reed" and the "White-robed Guanyin" or "Guanyin with Willows"—similarities that are clearly intended to appropriate the aura of the bodhisattva for the Chan patriarch. (In a similar vein, the DALAI LAMA of Tibetan Buddhism is also viewed as an incarnation of Avalokiteśvara, and here, too, the identification certainly serves to reinforce claims of spiritual authority.) There are also well-attested examples that link secular, rather than religious, leaders with bodhisattvas. In China, the infamous Empress Wu Zetian (d. 706) of the Tang dynasty, for example, went to great lengths to encourage belief in the idea that she was an incarnation of the Bodhisattva Maitreya, and it has been claimed that various Buddhist images that she sponsored actually bear her own likeness. In the Qing dynasty, the Qianlong emperor (r. 1736–1795) had himself portrayed on multiple occasions as the Bodhisattva Mañjuśrī, enshrined at the center of a complex MAṆḌALA, while in the late nineteenth century the empress dowager Zixi cast herself as Guanyin in elaborate living tableaux that were preserved in photographs. Whatever religious motivations may lie behind such acts, the ends they served can justifiably be described as more political than religious.

In short, if many images of bodhisattvas, whether painted or sculpted, are informed by sincere attempts to convey the spiritual powers associated with these Great Beings whose superhuman exploits were made famous by Mahāyāna sūtras, there are other images that attempt to borrow these connotations for different purposes. At the same time, there are also cases in which representations of bodhisattvas are so far removed from the context of Buddhism that they are essentially depleted of religious meaning altogether. For example, while it is difficult to determine whether the elegant *blanc-de-chine* ceramic images of Guanyin first popularized in the seventeenth century were originally admired and sought out primarily for their formal and aesthetic qualities, that certainly became the case for the avid collectors, mainly foreign, who started to amass them in the early twentieth century. In the end, even a bodhisattva is powerless in the face of commodification.

See also: **Buddha, Life of the, in Art; Hells, Images of; Mudrā and Visual Imagery; Sūtra Illustrations**

Bibliography

Czuma, Stanislaw J. *Kushan Sculpture: Images from Early India.* Cleveland, OH: Cleveland Museum of Art, 1985.

Huntington, Susan L. *The Art of Ancient India: Buddhist, Hindu, Jain.* New York: Weatherhill, 1985.

Hurvitz, Leon, trans. *Scripture of the Lotus Blossom of the Fine Dharma.* New York: Columbia University Press, 1976.

Murase, Miyeko. "Kuan-yin as Savior of Men: Illustration of the Twenty-fifth Chapter of the *Lotus Sūtra* in Chinese Painting." *Artibus Asiae* 37, nos. 1–2 (1971): 39–74.

Schopen, Gregory. "Monks and the Relic Cult in the *Mahāparinibbāna-sutta.*" In *Bones, Stones, and Buddhist Monks: Collected Papers on the Archaeology, Epigraphy, and Texts of Monastic Buddhism in India.* Honolulu: University of Hawaii Press, 1997.

Seckel, Dietrich. *Buddhist Art of East Asia,* tr. Ulrich Mammitzsch. Bellingham: Center for East Asian Studies, Western Washington University, 1989.

Whitfield, Roderick, and Farrer, Anne. *Caves of the Thousand Buddhas: Chinese Art from the Silk Route.* London: British Museum, 1990.

Yü, Chün-fang. *Kuan-yin: The Chinese Transformation of Avalokiteśvara.* New York: Columbia University Press, 2001.

CHARLES LACHMAN

BODY, PERSPECTIVES ON THE

The path to NIRVĀṆA or awakening, for Buddhists, involves the entire human being as a psychophysical complex. Although known to distinguish physical processes from psychic processes for the purpose of analysis, Buddhists do not ascribe to the notion (articulated by other religious traditions originating in India) that within every person there exists an eternal nonphysical self that may be said to "have" or "occupy" a body. For Buddhists, physical processes are dependent upon mental processes and vice versa. Thus, Buddhist traditions utilize the body as an object of contemplation and as a locus of transformation.

Buddhist scriptures and meditation manuals present a wide variety of meditations that focus on the body. Many involve mindful awareness of everyday activity: MINDFULNESS of breathing; mindfulness of modes of deportment, such as standing and sitting; and mindfulness of routine activities, such as walking, eating, and resting. Others meditations are analytic in nature. The body may be broken down into its four material elements: earth or solidity, water or fluidity, fire or heat, and air or movement. Such analytic exercises are particularly helpful for overcoming the illusion of an enduring "self" (ātman; Pāli, *attan*). In the *Majjhimanikāya* (*Group Discourses of Middle Length;* III. 90–1), the analysis of the body into its four material elements is compared to the quartering of an ox; once the ox is so divided, the generic concept of "flesh" diminishes recognition of the individuality of the ox.

Although members of other religious communities in ancient India also practiced such meditations on the physical elements of earth, water, fire, and air in the body, Indian Buddhists developed a uniquely Buddhist form of meditation on the body, which is praised in Buddhist scripture as the sine qua non of salvation. Called "mindfulness of the body," this contemplative technique entails breaking the body down into its thirty-two constituent parts, including internal organs such as the heart, the liver, the spleen, and the kidneys. The anatomical analysis in this cultivation of mindfulness of the body is so detailed that some scholars credit members of the early Buddhist monastic order (SAṄGHA) with a decisive role in the development of ancient Indian anatomical theory. Kenneth Zysk has argued that concern with ritual impurity limited the extent to which other (namely Brahmanical or proto-Hindu) religious specialists could serve as healers and carry out empirical studies based on dissection. Restrictions concerning the handling of bodily wastes from persons of different social classes and the disposal of dead bodies limited what Brahmanical caregivers could offer in the way of medical care and empirical research. With their relative, but certainly not absolute, indifference to Brahmanical purity strictures, members of the Buddhist saṅgha acquired a great deal of empirical knowledge of bodily processes and led the way in medical advances.

The ambiguity of the body

If Zysk is correct in asserting that Buddhist monastic communities in India were less hindered by constraints concerning the handling of bodily wastes and dead bodies, this is not to say that members of the Buddhist saṅgha regarded the body as intrinsically valuable, nor that their conceptions of the body were untouched by concerns about bodily purity and pollution. Cultivating distaste for the body by noting with disgust the discharges from various apertures of the body constitutes an initial stage of psychophysical training practiced by monastics of virtually all Buddhist denominations. With its orifices producing mucus, earwax, sweat, excrement, and the like, the body is conventionally imagined as a rot-filled pustule, a boil with many openings leaking pus. For MONKS and NUNS who are afflicted by sensual desire and who view bodily pleasures like eating, bathing, self-adornment, and sexual activity as inherently pleasing, developing a sense of aversion toward the body by visualizing it as a foul pustule or by contemplating corpses in various stages of putrefaction is recommended as an antidote to sensuality.

And if the generic human body is comparable to a leaky bag of filth, the female body is regarded as even more disgusting. This perception is perhaps due to the fact that it has an additional aperture lacking in males, an aperture prone to emitting periodic quantities of blood (Faure, p. 57). In any case, literary representations of meditations of the loathsomeness of the body tend to be overwhelmingly androcentric. Such narratives, embedded in hagiographies of various denominations, are filled with scenes of dying and diseased women observed by male spectators. Female spectators who appear in such narratives are depicted in ways that conform to the andocentric orientation of the genre. Male bodies almost never function as objects of contemplation for women in these narratives. Instead, women contemplating the foulness of the body observe their own aging bodies or those of other women. While Buddhist discourse holds all bodies to be impermanent and subject to disease, such hagiographies suggest there is nothing so effective as a female body to make this basic truth concrete.

As unsettling as many of these accounts may be, one should not assume that Buddhists are phobic about the body. The aversion such accounts induce is not an end in itself but a remedy for pleasure-seeking. Ultimately the outlook meditators seek is neither attraction nor revulsion but indifference. Contemplation of the foulness of the body is sometimes described as a "bitter medicine" that may be terminated once greed for bodily pleasures has been overcome. After having served its purpose as a counteractive practice, disgust for the body should ideally give way to a more neutral attitude. Moreover, in comparison with the bodies of nonhumans, the human body is a blessing. Buddhists across Asia recognize that human birth is rare, and many Buddhists regard human embodiment as an essential prerequisite for achieving awakening. Although human bodies may be of a gross material nature compared to those of divine beings dwelling in heavenly realms, humans enjoy occasions for awakening that gods and goddesses lack by virtue of the very sublime material conditions in which they live. Rebirth as a god or goddess is a worthy goal for LAITY, who may not be in immediate pursuit of awakening, but it holds little charm for those monks and nuns who do not wish to defer their awakening by hundreds of years. For them, embodiment as a human being is a valuable opportunity not to be wasted.

Thus, much depends on the perspective when evaluating the status of the human body for Buddhists. If treated as an intrinsically valuable thing, the body can obstruct the experience of awakening, preventing one from seeing things as they really are. But when used instrumentally as a locus of meditation and insight, the body has immense value, more precious than a wish-fulfilling jewel. Hence the Buddha is reported to have affirmed in the *Saṃyuttanikāya* (*Connected Discourses*; 1.62) that the body, with its attendant psychic processes, is the locus of salvation, the path to a transcendent, deathless condition.

Subtle bodies, salvific bodies

Thus the body may present the face of a friend or a foe, depending on what goals one wishes to achieve in life and how well one invests the body's resources in achieving those goals. Monastic training, like a regimen of physical training, develops capacities unknown to those without self-discipline. If one dedicates oneself to the disciplined cultivation of Buddhist virtues (i.e., salutary physical, moral, and cognitive states), those virtues will be instantiated in the form and appearance of one's body. Buddhist texts promote the goal of bodily transformation, promising sweet-smelling, beautiful, and healthy bodies to those who cultivate virtue, even while teaching that in their natural condition all bodies are smelly, impermanent havens of disease and death. Given this emphasis on bodily transformation through the cultivation of virtue, it should come as no surprise that Buddhists advocate contact with and contemplation of the bodies of buddhas and saints such as ARHATS and BODHISATTVAS. Contact with such beings is salutary not just because such beings are virtuous and helpful, but because their discipline has transformed them to the point where their bodies exude medicinal effects. Like walking apothecaries, Buddhist saints are said to heal disease upon contact with the afflicted just as their words heal the disease (*duḥkha*) that according to Buddhists afflicts all unawakened beings.

Accounts of the salutary effects of seeing buddhas, arhats, and bodhisattvas—or even formulating the aspiration to have such experiences—are commonplace in many genres of Buddhist literature. Seeing their radiant skin, bright eyes, and decorous deportment engenders serenity and joy; the sight is said to be at once tranquilizing and stimulating. This Buddhist emphasis on the benefits of seeing the body of the Buddha or other religious virtuosi can in part be explained by the South Asian milieu in which Buddhism arose. Many South Asian religious traditions promote the practice of participatory seeing (*darśana*) whereby the observer participates in the sacrality of the observed by visual contact. If one cannot gaze upon the bodies of Buddhist saints, one can nevertheless recollect the features of the body of the Buddha. The contemplative practice of recollecting the extraordinary features of the body of the Buddha, with its thirty-two major and eighty minor distinguishing marks, is common to all Buddhist traditions. The Buddha is also embodied in his teachings (dharma). While some Buddhists insist that this body of teaching is the only proper object of reverence and that adoration of the physical form is misguided, Kevin Trainor notes that textual passages warning against attachment to the Buddha's physical form are outnumbered by passages advocating such devotion.

The gift of the body

In accordance with the principle that the body has no intrinsic value, but gains value through the manner in which it is used, Buddhists extol the practice of offering one's body to others out of compassion. Tales of the former lives of the Buddha narrate many occasions in which the Buddha-to-be offered his flesh to starving animals at the expense of his life. Whereas THERAVĀDA Buddhists regard such altruistic practices as praiseworthy but not necessarily to be imitated, MAHĀYĀNA Buddhists regard self-sacrifice as an essential component of the Buddhist path.

In addition to offering their bodies as food for starving beings, followers of the bodhisattva path also gain merit by burning the body as an act of religious devotion. The locus classicus for the practice of SELF-IMMOLATION is an incident narrated in the LOTUS SŪTRA (SADDHARMAPUṆḌARĪKA-SŪTRA). In a previous life, the bodhisattva Bhaiṣajyarāja ingested copious amounts of flammable substances and then set fire to his body as an offering to the buddhas. The burning of the entire body or parts of the body, such as an arm or a finger, is highly celebrated in Chinese Buddhist texts composed from the fifth through the tenth centuries. The practice continues today in symbolic form in Chinese Buddhist monastic ordinations: The ordinand's eagerness to make such an offering is signaled by the burning of several places on the head with cones of incense. In preparing the body for immolation, Chinese Buddhists reportedly followed special grain-free diets that drew on Daoist traditions associated with the pursuit of immortality. James Benn has demonstrated that these grain-free diets were also used by Buddhist adepts in preparation for self-mummification, whereby the deceased adept's body would serve an iconic function as an object of worship.

Self-immolation has also been developed in interesting ways in Southeast Asia. During the Vietnam War, Vietnamese monks and nuns used self-immolation as a means of political protest. They attracted considerable attention to their cause by performing public self-immolations in protest against the Diem regime, which had imposed restrictive measures on the practice of Buddhism and the activities of Buddhist monks and nuns.

When its sacrifice for the sake of others is advocated, the body is clearly an essential element of religious practice. However, even putting such heroic measures aside, one cannot embark on the bodhisattva path without regarding the body as an essential means of fulfilling one's bodhisattva vows. One of the central vows of the bodhisattva is a statement that one is eager to undergo billions of repeated embodiments in the cycle of REBIRTH (saṃsāra) in order to help others achieve awakening.

In contrast to the Mahāyānist emphasis on postponing final awakening for eons and eons, Buddhist tantra (VAJRAYĀNA) stresses speed of attainment, promising the achievement of buddhahood in one lifetime. The body is said to contain the seeds of buddhahood, the prerequisites for achieving full awakening in this lifetime. Hence the human body as a focus of practice is central to Vajrayāna Buddhism. Practitioners regard the body as a microcosm of the universe, with all its gods, goddesses, and other powerful beings. Such beings are invoked and their powers harnessed for the goal of full awakening by touching various parts of the body using special hand gestures and by chanting MANTRAS or sacred utterances.

See also: **Anātman/Ātman (No-Self/Self); Buddhahood and Buddha Bodies; Gender; Sexuality**

Bibliography

Collins, Steven. "The Body in Theravāda Buddhist Monasticism." In *Religion and the Body,* ed. Sara Coakley. New York: Cambridge University Press, 1997.

Das, Veena. "Paradigms of Body Symbolism: An Analysis of Selected Themes in Hindu Culture." In *Indian Religion,* ed. Richard Burghart and Audrey Canthe. London: Curzon, 1985.

Dissanayake, Wimal. "Self and Body in Theravāda Buddhism." In *Self as Body in Asian Theory and Practice,* ed. Thomas P. Kasulis with Roger T. Ames and Wimal Dissanayake. Albany: State University of New York Press, 1993.

Faure, Bernard. *The Red Thread: Buddhist Approaches to Sexuality.* Princeton, NJ: Princeton University Press, 1998.

Pye, Michael. "Perceptions of the Body in Japanese Religion." In *Religion and the Body,* ed. Sara Coakley. New York: Cambridge University Press, 1997.

Trainor, Kevin. *Relics, Ritual, and Representation in Buddhism: Rematerializing the Sri Lankan Theravāda Tradition.* Cambridge, UK: Cambridge University Press, 1997.

Wijayaratna, Mohan. *Buddhist Monastic Life According to the Texts of the Theravāda Tradition,* tr. Claude Grangier and Steven Collins. New York: Cambridge University Press, 1990.

Williams, Paul. "Some Mahāyāna Buddhist Perspectives on the Body." In *Religion and the Body,* ed. Sara Coakley. New York: Cambridge University Press, 1997.

Zysk, Kenneth. *Asceticism and Healing in Ancient India: Medicine in the Buddhist Monastery.* New York: Oxford University Press, 1991.

LIZ WILSON

BON

Bon (pronounced *pön*) is often characterized as the indigenous, pre-Buddhist religion of Tibet. While not entirely untrue, such a description is misleading. There are clearly indigenous Tibetan elements in historical Bon, and some of these elements likely predate the arrival of Buddhism in Tibet. But because there was no effective Tibetan literary language before the introduction of Buddhism, there is scant evidence from which to reconstruct pre-Buddhist Bon. Moreover, because the Bon that is known from later sources (and exists to this day alongside Tibetan Buddhism) is a highly syncretic religious complex, deeply conditioned by its encounter with Indian (and probably other) forms of Buddhism, it cannot rightly be considered either indigenous or pre-Buddhist.

Historical Bon itself claims to be a direct descendant of—indeed identical with—a religion known as *Bon* that existed during the centuries before the introduction of Buddhism to Tibet in the eighth century. The few extant sources from the royal dynastic period in Tibet do suggest the existence during this period of a religious formation that may have been known as Bon, whose priests were called *bon po,* and perhaps also *gshen.* As reconstructed from these sources, this early- or proto-Bon seems to have included a strong belief in an afterlife and to have involved a system of funerary rites, animal sacrifices, and royal consecration ceremonies as primary foci. It thus bears little resemblance to later Bon.

There seems to have been some friction between proto-Bon and Buddhism in the dynastic period. Later sources from both traditions tell of Buddhist PERSECUTIONS of Bon, which the Buddhist king Khri srong lde btsan (pronounced Trisong Detsen; r. 755–797 C.E.) is said to have formally proscribed around 785. Buddhists tell of a subsequent Bon persecution of Buddhism. Both accounts share many similar features (banishing of priests, hiding of books for later recovery, etc.), so the historicity of many of the details is open to doubt, although nearly contemporaneous documents preserved in DUNHUANG do indicate some tension between the traditions.

Later Bon considers its "founder" to have been the teacher Gshen rab mi bo (pronounced Shenrap Miwo), from the semimythical land of 'Ol mo lung ring. As in the MAHĀYĀNA account of Śākyamuni Buddha, Gshen rab is said to have been an enlightened being who emanated in this world as the preordained teacher of the present world-age. Yet, unlike Śākyamuni, accounts of whom emphasize early renunciation of his kingdom and married life, Gshen rab is said to have remained a layman until late in life, working to propagate Bon as a prince, together with his many wives and offspring.

The documented historical period of Bon begins with the "rediscovery" of many allegedly ancient Bon scriptures by Gshen chen klu dga' (pronounced Shenchen Lugah, 996–1035) around 1017; these texts make up a substantial part of the current Bon CANON. Gshen chen klu dga' was a native of west-central Gtsang province, and the majority of early Bon institutions were centered in that area. He and his disciples created the scriptural and institutional base for Bon during the next four centuries. In 1405 Shes rab rgyal mtshan (pronounced Shayrap Gyeltsen, 1356–1415) founded the monastery of Sman ri (pronounced Menree), which was to become the most important Bon center until the twentieth century. The eminent scholar of Bon, Per Kværne, has suggested that the Bon canon was fixed in this period, likely no later than 1450.

Bon was reputedly persecuted again under the rule of the fifth DALAI LAMA (1617–1682) and during the succeeding two centuries, during which time Bon monasteries were closed, destroyed, or converted, though some scholars downplay the extent of this persecution. The canon was subjected to further revision in the mid-eighteenth century by Kun grol grags pa (pronounced Kundrol Takpa, 1700–?), who prepared a detailed catalogue of its scriptures. Subsequently, in the nineteenth century, Bon experienced something of a resurgence. The primarily Buddhist Non-sectarian (*ris med*) Movement, in which the Bon teacher Shar rdza bkra shis rgyal mtshan (pronounced Shardza Tashi Gyeltsen, 1858–1935) collaborated, expressed collegial respect for Bon and vice versa. The importance of the great perfection (*rdzogs chen*) and rediscovered treasure (*gter ma*) teachings in both the Non-sectarian Movement and Bon provided the foundation for mutual recognition and cross-fertilization. From this time until the present, there have been some who speak of Bon as the "fifth school" of Tibetan Buddhism, in addition to the RNYING MA (NYINGMA), SA SKYA (SAKYA), BKA' BRGYUD (KAGYU), and DGE LUGS (GELUK).

There are in fact many similarities between Bon and the Tibetan Buddhist traditions, which make such an identification—while ultimately untenable—not entirely unreasonable. In fact, the basic teachings of Bon are virtually identical to those found in Tibetan Buddhism. Both traditions commonly refer to the ideal, enlightened being by the term *sangs rgyas* (Sanskrit, buddha) and to enlightenment itself by the term *byang chub* (Sanskrit, BODHI [AWAKENING]). In addition to these exact correspondences, one also sometimes finds the use of alternative, but functionally equivalent, terms. For instance, the term *bon* is contrasted with *chos* (dharma), a key word in Buddhist thought. Yet, *bon* occurs in Bon literature in exactly the same contexts as *chos* does in Buddhism; Bon texts speak, for example, of a "bon body" (*bon sku*), which is essentially the same as the Buddhist "dharma body" (*chos sku*), both serving as the first of a triad that includes the beatific body (*longs sku*) and the emanation body (*sprul sku*). The structure of their canons is also similar. Like the Buddhists, the Bonpos divide their sacred scriptures into two classes—one containing scriptures of revealed word (in the case of Bon, those attributed to Gshen rab), the other the writings of later saints. In both traditions, the collection of revealed scriptures is known as the *Bka' 'gyur* (pronounced *kanjur*). The Buddhists refer to their collection of commentaries as the *Bstan 'gyur* (pronounced *tanjur*), while the Bonpos call theirs the *Brten 'gyur* (a homonym).

Although Bon appears in many respects to be a completely "buddhicized" tradition in its forms, doctrines, and practices, many old indigenous traditions remain in the core of Bon, especially with regard to COSMOLOGY, sacred narratives, and pantheon. Thus, though the Bon revealed in the sources available to scholars cannot be considered the indigenous, pre-Buddhist religion of Tibet, these distinctively Bon elements do provide a glimpse of what may have been some of the ancient religious forms of pre-Buddhist Tibet.

See also: **Tibet**

Bibliography

Karmay, Samten Gyaltsen, ed. and trans. *The Treasury of Good Sayings: A Tibetan History of Bon.* London: Oxford University Press, 1972.

Karmay, Samten Gyaltsen. *The Arrow and the Spindle: Studies in History, Myths, Rituals, and Beliefs in Tibet.* Kathmandu, Nepal: Mandala Book Point, 1998.

Kværne, Per. "The Canon of the Tibetan Bonpos." *Indo-Iranian Journal* 16 (1974): nr. 1, 18–56; nr. 2, 96–144.

Kværne, Per. "Śākyamuni in the Bon Religion." *Temenos* 25 (1989): 33–40.

Kværne, Per. "The Bon Religion of Tibet: A Survey of Research." In *The Buddhist Forum,* Vol. 3, ed. Tadeusz Skorupski and Ulrich Pagel. New Delhi: Heritage, 1995.

Kværne, Per. *The Bon Religion of Tibet: The Iconography of a Living Tradition.* London: Serindia, 1995. Reprint, Boston: Shambhala, 2001.

Martin, Dan. *Unearthing Bon Treasures: Life and Contested Legacy of a Tibetan Scripture Revealer, with a General Bibliography of Bon.* Leiden, Netherlands: Brill, 2001.

Snellgrove, David, ed. and trans. *The Nine Ways of Bon: Excerpts from the gZi-brjid.* London: Oxford University Press, 1967. Reprint, Boulder, CO: Prajñā Press, 1980.

CHRISTIAN K. WEDEMEYER

BOROBUDUR

Borobudur is a monumental structure that was erected in the Kedu plain in south central Java, on the foundation of an older shrine of unknown form. Construction began about 790 C.E., and alterations continued to be made until approximately 850 C.E. From above, Borobudur resembles a MAṆḌALA, in that it consists of a large STŪPA (burial mound) surrounded by three round terraces, on each of which are more stūpas (108 in all); farther from the central stūpa are four square terraces. In profile, the monument resembles a mountain, since the transition from each terrace is marked by a staircase rising to the next.

Reliefs (1,350 panels) illustrate texts, such as JĀTAKA and AVADĀNA tales, the *Mahākarmavibhaṅga,* the LALITAVISTARA, the *Gaṇḍavyūha,* and the *Bhadracari.* Niches atop the walls of the galleries contain BUDDHA IMAGES. These images exhibit different hand positions according to their location on the monument. These hand positions, or mudrā, symbolize the conquest of illusion, charity, meditation, dispelling of fear, and teaching. The seventy-two stūpas on the round terraces, which are hollow, contain images whose hand positions symbolize the Buddha's first sermon in Deer Park at Benares.

This combination of stūpa, mountain, and maṇḍala was never replicated elsewhere, but its influence is visible in Cambodia and through that intermediary in Thailand and Burma (Myanmar). No inscriptions survive to tell us what the monument signified to the Javanese, but the ten relief series suggest that it may have functioned to enable selected individuals to pass symbolically through the ten stages on the PATH to becoming a BODHISATTVA. The form of Buddhism followed by the builders of Borobudur emphasized the role of bodhisattvas, but was less esoteric than later expressions in Java and Sumatra wherein such deities as Vajrasattva and Trailokyavijaya were emphasized. The bodhisattvas Mañjuśrī and Samantabhadra play key roles in the texts narrated on Borobudur. These deities were also popular in East Asia at this time.

The monument's construction coincides with a period during which a dynasty known as the Śailendra (mountain lord) dominated central Java politically. Around 830 C.E. a Buddhist queen married a Hindu king of the Sañjaya line. The great Hindu monument of Loro Jonggrang at Prambanam was constructed between about 830 and 856. Narrative reliefs depicting the *Ramāyana* and Kṛṣṇa texts on Loro Jonggrang may have been motivated by the desire to present a Hindu response to Borobudur.

See also: **Huayan Art; Indonesia, Buddhist Art in**

Bibliography

Gómez, Luis, and Woodward, Hiram W., Jr., eds. *Barabudur: History and Significance of a Buddhist Monument.* Berkeley, CA: Asian Humanities Press, 1981.

Miksic, John N. *Borobudur: Golden Tales of the Buddhas.* Berkeley, CA: Periplus Editions, 1990.

JOHN N. MIKSIC

BSAM YAS (SAMYE)

Founded around 779 C.E., Bsam yas (Samye) was Tibet's first monastery. Although a few temples of worship had been built earlier in Tibet, Bsam yas was the first fully functioning monastery. Upon its completion, the first seven Tibetan Buddhist monks were ordained by Śāntarakṣita, the famous abbot of the Indian monastery Vikramaśīla. Soon after, the famous BSAM YAS DEBATE was held, ostensibly to decide which form of Buddhism Tibetans would follow, that of India or that of China.

Bsam yas was built during the reign of King Khri srong lde btsan (r. 755–797), the second of the three great Buddhist kings of Tibet's early imperial period. This king had invited Śāntarakṣita to Tibet to assist him in establishing Buddhism as the state religion. According to traditional accounts, when the king began work on his new monastery, local spirits who were opposed to the foreign religion created obstacles so numerous that not even the building's foundation could be laid. Śāntarakṣita, whose strengths lay in monastic learning and not in battling demonic forces, could not help. The king was forced to find someone trained in the arts of Buddhist tantra. Śāntarakṣita recommended the renowned master, PADMASAMBHAVA, from the kingdom of Uḍḍiyāna in northwestern India. Upon Padmasambhava's arrival, the great *tāntrika* quickly subdued the troublesome spirits, forcing them to take vows to forever protect Buddhism in Tibet.

Bsam yas played a central role in Khri srong lde btsan's lifelong project to make Buddhism the state religion of Tibet. At the time of its construction, the Tibetan empire was at the height of its power. In 763, Tibetans even occupied the Chinese capital of Chang'an, where they installed a puppet emperor for a brief time. Bsam yas was built as a symbol of Tibet's newfound international prestige, and the central cathedral's three stories were designed in the traditional architectural styles of India, China, and Tibet, respectively.

Bsam yas's universalism was further reflected in the layout of the whole monastic complex—a cosmogram of the Indian world system. According to this system, the central axis of Mount Sumeru is surrounded by four continents, one in each of the cardinal directions. Similarly at Bsam yas, around the central cathedral were built four buildings, their shapes corresponding to those of the continents.

The monastery was also built to represent a three-dimensional MAṆḌALA in a design modeled on the great Indian Buddhist monastery of Otantapūri, located in today's Bihar. The particular maṇḍala represented by Bsam yas seems to have been that of the Buddha Vairocana. Recent scholarship has suggested that the Tibetan imperial cult may have given special prominence to this deity, and that this close association was also reflected in the arrangement of Bsam yas. According to early sources, a statue of Vairocana was originally positioned on the second floor as the central image; another Vairocana statue, this in his four-faced Sarvavid form, was installed on the top floor.

The same layout can still be observed. Bsam yas was severely damaged a number of times by fires (seventeenth century), earthquakes and more fires (nineteenth century), and Chinese invaders (twentieth century), but the restorations seem to have remained largely faithful to its original plan. The central cathedral was rebuilt in 1989 following the most recent desecrations, and renovations continued throughout the 1990s on other parts of the complex.

See also: **Tibet**

Bibliography

Chan, Victor. *Tibet Handbook: A Pilgrimage Guide.* Chico, CA: Moon, 1994.

Kapstein, Matthew. *The Tibetan Assimilation of Buddhism: Conversion, Contestation, and Memory.* New York: Oxford University Press, 2001.

Snellgrove, David, and Richardson, Hugh. *A Cultural History of Tibet* (1968). Boston: Shambala, 1995.

JACOB P. DALTON

BSAM YAS DEBATE

Among Western scholars, the Bsam yas Debate has generated more speculation than any other single event in Tibetan history. Around 797 C.E., a philosophical debate is said to have taken place at BSAM YAS (SAMYE), the first Buddhist monastery in Tibet. The debate was held in order to decide, in effect, which form of Buddhism would be adopted by the Tibetan royal court—that of the Chinese CHAN SCHOOL or Indian Buddhism. The debate was presided over by the Tibetan king, Khri srong lde btsan (r. 755–797), and the two sides were represented by the Chinese master *Huashang* Moheyan (Sanskrit, Mahāyāna) and the Indian scholar Kamalaśīla, respectively. According to Tibetan sources, the Indian side was declared the winner; Moheyan and his disciples were banished from the country, and Indian Buddhism was established as the state religion. The alleged victory for the Indian side has strongly shaped Tibetans' understanding of their own religious heritage.

The philosophical issue at stake was how enlightenment should be attained—immediately or after a period of extensive training. Thus, according to the famous history (*Chos 'byung*) composed by BU STON (BU TÖN) rin chen grub (1290–1364), Moheyan opened the debate by explaining that just as clouds, be they white or black, obscure the sky, so do all activities, be they virtuous or nonvirtuous, perpetuate REBIRTH in SAṂSĀRA. Therefore, he concluded, the cessation of all mental activity leads immediately to the highest liberation. Kamalaśīla responded to this philosophical quietism by explaining the stages of analytic meditation. He stressed that even nonconceptual wisdom results from a specific process of gradual analysis. Moheyan was soundly defeated, and some of his disciples were so humiliated that they committed suicide.

Bu ston's account, which is largely representative of the normative Tibetan historical tradition, is clearly a biased one. He frames his narrative with a prophecy made by Śāntarakṣita, the Indian master who helped to establish Bsam yas and ordained the first nine Buddhist monks in Tibet. Here, shortly before his death, Śāntarakṣita predicts a controversy between two Buddhist groups and instructs that his disciple, Kamalaśīla of Nālandā, should be summoned to resolve the dispute. Bu ston's account then closes with a story vilifying Moheyan, in which the Chinese master sends some "Chinese butchers" to murder Kamalaśīla by squeezing his kidneys.

This Tibetan version of events has been complicated by the discovery of a Chinese work titled the *Dunwu dasheng zhengli jue* (*Verification of the Greater Vehicle of Sudden Awakening*). The text was unearthed from the caves at DUNHUANG, a region once frequented by Moheyan. A translation was first published by Paul Demiéville in his 1952 article, *Le concile de Lhasa*. The Chinese work purports to be a word-for-word record of the debate written by Wangxi, a direct disciple of Moheyan. Its version of events differs radically from those of the various Tibetan sources; in this version, Moheyan wins the debate. This discovery has led some scholars to doubt the very existence of the debate, suggesting that instead it should be viewed as indicative of an ongoing controversy through a series of only indirect encounters between Chinese and Indian factions at the Tibetan royal court. That said, it remains that all available sources agree that a debate of some kind did take place.

It is unclear whether Kamalaśīla knew about the Chinese text when, apparently at the Tibetan king's request, he composed his three famous treatises summarizing the debate's central themes, each called a *Bhāvanākrama* (*Stages of Meditation*). The Indian and Chinese works address many of the same topics, but part ways on a number of important points. The Chinese work, for example, gives considerable attention to the doctrine of TATHAGATAGARBHA (buddhanature), while Kamalaśīla does not even mention it. Similarly, the Chinese work remains silent on a number of issues that are crucial to Kamalaśīla's argument—the need to develop compassion and the stages of meditation are two examples. Both texts, it seems, reflect their authors' concerns with developments in their own countries more than with each other. It is unclear whether all three of Kamalaśīla's works were composed in Tibet.

Indeed, the teachings of Moheyan should be understood within the context of eighth-century Chinese Chan, itself a milieu of highly charged polemics. According to other Dunhuang documents, Moheyan belonged to the lineage of the Northern school of Chan. This school had already come under attack earlier in the eighth century by Shenhui (684–758) of the so-called Southern school, and its lineage continued to be contested from many sides throughout Moheyan's lifetime. Such a polarizing environment certainly would have influenced Moheyan, and the fragments of his teachings found at Dunhuang support the common view of him as extreme in his advocacy of immediate enlightenment.

In addition to its doctrinal ramifications, the Bsam yas Debate certainly had a strong political component. The nature of these more political concerns can be detected in yet another work that discusses the debate. The *Sba bzhed* (*Testimony of Ba*) is an early Tibetan account of the relevant period, purportedly written by a minister to Khri srong lde btsan. Several editions of the work exist, and all agree that the Indian side won. A close reading of the various *Sba bzhed* editions suggests that a central issue driving the debate may have been the Tibetan court's adoption of the Indian Buddhist cosmological framework. This framework, with its "lawlike operation of karma," may have offered eighth-century Tibetans an attractive foundation for political governance. According to this reading, it was the antinomian aspect of the popular Chinese teachings that threatened the new political order.

All such interpretations of the Bsam yas Debate remain, however, just that—interpretations. All we can say for certain is that the debate has served a number of different ends. In the later Tibetan tradition, the debate was used as evidence for India's importance as the only authentic source for Buddhist teachings. The debate also served as a weapon in polemical disputes between opposing Tibetan Buddhist groups. Perhaps the most well-known example of this trend appears in the writings of SA SKYA PAṆḌITA (SAKYA PAṆḌITA, 1182–1251). There, the author equates the Moheyan side with the Tibetan tradition of *Rdzogs chen* by criticizing the "Self-Sufficient White Remedy" (*dkar po chig thub*) doctrine of the BKA' BRGYUD (KAGYU) pa for being like the "*Rdzogs chen* of the Chinese tradition" (*rgya nag lugs kyi rdzogs chen*). Possible links between Chinese Chan and early Tibetan *Rdzogs chen* remain unclear, but the two teachings appear to bear some similarities, and these were certainly what caught the attention of later Tibetan polemicists.

See also: **Bodhi (Awakening); Tibet**

Bibliography

Demiéville, Paul. *Le concile de Lhasa: une controverse sur le quiétisme entre bouddhistes de l'Inde et de la Chine au VIIIe siècle de l'ère chrétienne.* Paris: Imprimerie Nationale de France, 1952.

Gómez, Luis O. "Indian Materials on the Doctrine of Sudden Enlightenment." In *Early Ch'an in China and Tibet,* ed. Whalen Lai and Lewis Lancaster. Berkeley, CA: Asian Humanities Press, 1983.

Gómez, Luis O. "The Direct and Gradual Approaches of Zen Master Mahāyāna: Fragments of the Teachings of Mo-ho-yen." In *Studies in Ch'an and Hua-Yen,* ed. Robert M. Grimello and Peter N. Gregory. Honolulu: University of Hawaii Press, 1983.

Jackson, David. "Sa skya pandita the 'Polemicist': Ancient Debates and Modern Interpretations." *Journal of the International Association of Buddhist Studies* 13, no. 2 (1990): 17–116.

Kapstein, Matthew. *The Tibetan Assimilation of Buddhism: Conversion, Contestation, and Memory.* New York: Oxford University Press, 2001.

Obermiller, Eugéne. *History of Buddhism (Chos-hbyung) by Buston,* 2 vols. Heidelberg, Germany: Harrassowitz, Leipzig, 1931, 1932.

Wangdu, Pasang, and Diemberger, Hildegard. *Dba' bzhed: The Royal Narrative Concerning the Bringing of the Buddha's Doctrine to Tibet.* Vienna: Verlag der osterreichischen akademie der wissenschaften, 2000.

JACOB P. DALTON

BUDDHA(S)

The term *buddha,* literally "awakened one," is one of many Indian epithets applied to the founder of the Buddhist religion. A buddha is defined, first and foremost, as one who has undergone the profoundly transformative experience known as NIRVĀṆA and who, as a result, will never be subject to the cycle of birth and death again. Women and men who experienced this same awakening by following in the footsteps of the Buddha were referred to as ARHATS or "worthy ones," an epithet also applied to the Buddha himself. These disciples, however, were not themselves referred to as buddhas, for that term was reserved for those rare individuals who experienced BODHI (AWAKENING) on their own in a world with no knowledge of Buddhism. Moreover, to attain awakening without the help of a teacher was not in itself sufficient to be classified as a buddha, for those who did so but did not teach others how to replicate that experience were known instead as PRATYEKABUDDHAS, a term variously explained as "individually enlightened" or "enlightened through (an understanding of) causation." In addition to attaining nirvāṇa without assistance from others, the classical definition of a buddha includes teaching others what one has found. A buddha is, in sum, not only the discoverer of a timeless truth, but the founder of a religious community.

It is possible—though far from certain—that the earliest Buddhist tradition knew of only one such figure, the so-called historical Buddha, Siddhārtha Gautama, also known as Śākyamuni (sage of the Śākya clan). But the notion that other buddhas had preceded him appeared at an early date, and may well have been assumed by Śākyamuni himself. Over the next four to five centuries Buddhists came to believe that other such buddhas would also appear in the distant future; some even claimed that buddhas were living at the present time, though in worlds unimaginably distant from our own. While the belief in past and future buddhas came to be accepted by all Buddhist schools, the idea of the simultaneous existence of multiple buddhas appears to have gained general currency only in MAHĀYĀNA circles.

Buddhas of the past

The earliest datable evidence for a belief in the existence of buddhas prior to Śākyamuni comes from the time of King AŚOKA (ca. 300–232 B.C.E.), who claimed in one of his inscriptions to have enlarged the memorial mound (STŪPA) of a previous buddha named

Konākamana (Pāli, Konāgamana; Sanskrit, Konākamuni or Kanakamuni). No names of other buddhas are mentioned, and there is no way to determine whether Aśoka viewed Konākamana as belonging to a larger lineage scheme. Within a century or so after Aśoka's time, however—and possibly much earlier, depending on what dates are assigned to materials in the Pāli canon—other names had been added to the list as well.

Seven buddhas. A wide range of literary, artistic, and epigraphical sources refers to "seven buddhas of the past," a list including Śākyamuni and six prior buddhas: Vipaśyin, Śikhin, Viśvabhū, Krakucchanda, Kanakamuni, and Kāśyapa. A *terminus ante quem* for the emergence of this tradition is again supplied by an inscription, in this case on a stūpa railing at Bhārhut in north-central India (ca. second century B.C.E.), where Śākyamuni's predecessors (with the exception of Śikhin, where the railing has been damaged) are mentioned by name. The same six buddhas, together with Śākyamuni, are prominently featured on the gateways to the great stūpa at SĀÑCĪ (ca. first century B.C.E.). Subsequently, they appear, both in artistic works and in inscriptions, at a host of other Buddhist sites.

The widespread agreement on both the number and sequence of these previous buddhas in surviving sources—including canonical scriptures preserved in Pāli and Chinese that can be attributed to several distinct ordination lineages (*nikāyas*)—suggests that the list of seven was formulated at an early date. More specifically, it points to the likelihood that this list had been standardized prior to the first major schism in Buddhist history, the split between the self-proclaimed "Elders" (Sthaviras) and "Majorityists" (Mahāsāṃghikas, or Great Assembly), which took place between a century and a century and a half after the Buddha's death.

The most detailed discussion of Śākyamuni's predecessors in early (i.e., non-Mahāyāna) canonical literature is found in the Pāli *Mahāpadāna-suttanta* (*Dīghanikāya, sutta* no. 14) and in other recensions of the same text preserved in Chinese translation (*Taishō* 1[1], 2, 3, 4, and 125[48.45]). Here the lives of the seven buddhas, from Vipaśyin (Pāli, Vipassī) to Śākyamuni himself, are related in virtually identical terms, from a penultimate existence in the Tuṣita heaven, to a miraculous birth, to the experience of nirvāṇa and a subsequent preaching career. Only in minor details—such as the names of their parents, their life spans, and the caste into which they were born—can these biographies be distinguished.

Implicit in this replication of a single paradigmatic pattern is the assumption that all buddhas-to-be (Sanskrit, BODHISATTVA) must carry out an identical series of practices, after which they will teach a dharma identical to that of their predecessors. In subsequent centuries this would lead to the idea that by replicating the deeds of Śākyamuni and his predecessors in every detail, other Buddhists, too, could strive to become buddhas rather than arhats.

Not all the members of this list of seven, despite their parallel life stories, appear to have played equally significant roles in cultic practice. If we divide the list into subgroups of "archaic" buddhas said to have lived many eons ago (Vipaśyin, Śikhin, and Viśvabhū), and "ancient" buddhas described as preceding Śākyamuni in the present eon (Krakucchanda, Kanakamuni, and Kāśyapa), a clear pattern can be discerned. While the ancient buddhas are all associated with known geographical locations, the towns where the archaic buddhas are said to have lived have no clear historical referent. When the Chinese monk FAXIAN (ca. 337–ca. 418) visited India at the beginning of the fifth century C.E., for example, he was taken to three towns in northeast India (all within range of the city of Śrāvastī), where the ancient buddhas were said to have lived, and he was shown stūpas said to contain their remains. No comparable pilgrimage sites connected with the three archaic buddhas are mentioned, either in Faxian's report or in those of subsequent Chinese visitors. Based on surviving images and inscriptions, as well as on further data found in the travel accounts of Faxian and later Chinese pilgrims, J. Ph. Vogel has suggested that the buddha Kāśyapa may have been an especially popular object of veneration.

Twenty-five buddhas. An expanded version of the list of seven, totaling twenty-five buddhas in all, is attested in the Pāli *Buddhavaṃsa,* though it appears to be little known outside the THERAVĀDA tradition. This list extends still further into the past to begin with the buddha DĪPAṂKARA, in whose presence the future Śākyamuni made his initial vow to attain buddhahood. Although the story of Dīpaṃkara is not included in the Pāli collection of JĀTAKA tales recounting Śākyamuni's former lives, it does appear in the *Nidānakathā,* an introduction to that collection that is generally assigned to the fifth century C.E. and quotes directly from earlier sources such as the *Buddhavaṃsa* and the *Cariyāpiṭaka.* The story is frequently depicted in art from the Gandhāra region, though it is virtually absent from other Buddhist sites, suggesting that it may have originated at the northwestern fringes of the Indian cultural sphere.

Though no occurrence of the list of twenty-five buddhas of the past has yet been identified in Mahāyāna scriptures, the first buddha in this series, Dīpaṃkara, plays a significant role in these texts. Since Śākyamuni Buddha was portrayed as having made his initial vow to become a buddha in the presence of Dīpaṃkara, this motif became quite common in the writings of advocates of the bodhisattva path in subsequent centuries.

Buddhas of the future

The earliest lists of multiple buddhas referred only to Śākyamuni and his predecessors. Around the turn of the millennium, however, a shorter list of five—consisting of four buddhas of the past (the ancient buddhas Krakucchanda, Kanakamuni, Kāśyapa, together with Śākyamuni) along with one buddha of the future (MAITREYA; Pāli, Metteyya)—was compiled. The weight of this tradition is still anchored firmly in the past, but the door was now open to speculation on other buddhas who might also appear in the future. Besides introducing a buddha-of-the-future for the first time, this list was also innovative in its optimism about the nature of the present age, for these five figures were labeled buddhas of the *bhadrakalpa* (fortunate eon).

The list of five buddhas remained standard in the Theravāda tradition, but a longer list of one thousand buddhas of the *bhadrakalpa* frequently appears in Mahāyāna scriptures. An intermediary list, consisting of five hundred buddhas of the *bhadrakalpa,* appears to have circulated mainly in Central Asia. In all of these systems Maitreya holds pride of place as the next buddha to appear in our world. Like all buddhas-to-be, he is said to be spending his penultimate life in the Tuṣita heaven, from which he surveys our world to determine the right time and place to be born.

Estimates varied as to the amount of time that would elapse between our own age and the coming of Maitreya. One of the most common figures was 5.6 billion years; other traditions offered a figure of 560 million. While many Buddhists worked to acquire merit in order to be born here on earth in that distant era when Maitreya would at last attain buddhahood, others strove to be reborn more immediately in his presence in the Tuṣita heaven. Still others strove for visionary encounters with Maitreya, through which they could see him in his heavenly realm even before departing from this life.

Buddhas of the present

All of the traditions discussed above share the assumption that only one buddha can appear in the world at any given time. Each buddha is portrayed as having discovered a truth about reality (i.e., an understanding of the dharma) that had, prior to his time, been utterly lost. Since a buddha can appear, therefore, only in a world without any knowledge of Buddhism, only one such figure can exist at a time.

This restriction applies, however, only if one posits the existence of just one world system, and around the turn of the millennium some Buddhists began to articulate a new view of the universe that consisted not of one, but of hundreds or thousands of such worlds. This made possible, for the first time, the idea that other buddhas might currently be living and teaching, albeit in worlds unimaginably distant from our own. Scriptures reflecting this perspective speak of other world systems located "throughout the ten directions"—that is, in the four cardinal directions, the four intermediate directions, the zenith, and the nadir.

Many Indian texts refer simply to these buddhas of the ten directions in the aggregate, but occasionally particular figures are named, some of whom appear to have gained a strong following in India. By far the most prominent are the buddha AKṢOBHYA, said to dwell in a world known as Abhirati (extreme delight) far to the east, and the buddha AMITĀBHA (also known as Amitāyus), dwelling in the land of Sukhāvatī (blissful) in the distant west. These two figures, together with others currently presiding over comparably glorious realms, have come to be known in English-language studies as *celestial buddhas.*

The term *celestial buddha* has no precise equivalent in Sanskrit (nor for that matter in Chinese or Tibetan), yet it can serve as a convenient label for those buddhas who are presently living and teaching in worlds other than our own and into whose lands believers may aspire to be reborn. Conditions in these lands are portrayed as idyllic, comparable in many respects to Buddhist heavens; indeed, this comparison is made explicit in scriptures describing the worlds of celestial buddhas, such as the *Akṣobhyavyūha* and the larger SUKHĀVATĪVYŪHA-SŪTRA. Yet these realms are not heavens in the strict sense, but "amputated" world systems, shorn only of the lower realms (*durgati*) of hell-beings, animals, and ghosts.

In addition to inhabiting such glorious places—said to be the by-product of their activities as bodhisattvas, and in some cases (most notably in the

The buddha Amitābha, a celestial buddha who resides in the Western paradise of Sukhāvatī. (Vietnamese sculpture, eighteenth or nineteenth century.) © Reunion des Musées Nationaux/Art Resource, NY. Reproduced by permission.

Sukhāvatīvyūha) described as resulting from specific "world-designing" vows—celestial buddhas, like the archaic buddhas of our own world, are described as having immensely long life spans. Yet the factors that elicited these seemingly parallel circumstances are not the same. In the case of the archaic buddhas, their long life spans are the corollary of their being placed at a point in the cycle of evolution-and-devolution where human life spans in general stretch to between sixty thousand and eighty thousand years; the same is true of the future buddha Maitreya, who is scheduled to appear in our world when the maximum life span of eighty thousand years has again arrived (Nattier 1991). In the case of celestial buddhas, on the other hand, their long life spans are necessitated by their role as the presiding buddhas in other realms to which believers from other worlds might aspire to be reborn. Such an aspiration for rebirth makes sense, of course, only if the believer is confident that the buddha in question will still be alive when he or she arrives.

Celestial buddhas are not, however, described as immortal; the *Akṣobhyavyūha* makes much of Akṣobhya's eventual *parinirvāṇa* and autocremation, while early translations of the *Sukhāvatīvyūha* make it clear that Avalokiteśvara will succeed to the position of reigning buddha of Sukhāvatī after Amitābha has passed away. Thus the lives of these buddhas—while far more glorious in circumstances and far longer in duration—still echo the pattern set by Śākyamuni.

Other developments would subsequently take place, such as the claim that Śākyamuni Buddha had already attained nirvāṇa prior to his appearance in this world and the concomitant assumption that his life span was immeasurably, though not infinitely, long, and the even grander claim that all buddhas who appear in this or any other world are merely manifestations of an eternal dharma-body. Throughout most of the history of Buddhism in India, however, buddhas continued to be viewed as human beings who had achieved awakening as Śākyamuni did, even as the list of their qualities and their attainments grew ever more glorious.

See also: **Buddhahood and Buddha Bodies; Lotus Sūtra (Saddharmapuṇḍarīka-sūtra); Pure Lands**

Bibliography

Gómez, Luis O. *The Land of Bliss: The Paradise of the Buddha of Measureless Light.* Honolulu: University of Hawaii Press, 1996.

Harrison, Paul M. *The Samādhi of Direct Encounter with the Buddhas of the Present: An Annotated English Translation of the Tibetan Version of the Pratyutpanna-Buddha-Saṃmukhāvasthita-Samādhi-Sūtra.* Tokyo: International Institute for Buddhist Studies, 1990.

Nattier, Jan. *Once upon a Future Time: Studies in a Buddhist Prophecy of Decline.* Fremont, CA: Asian Humanities Press, 1991.

Nattier, Jan. "The Realm of Akṣobhya: A Missing Piece in the History of Pure Land Buddhism." *Journal of the International Association of Buddhist Studies* 23, no. 1 (2000): 71–102.

Norman, K. R. "The Pratyeka-Buddha in Buddhism and Jainism." In *Buddhist Studies Ancient and Modern: Collected Papers on South Asia,* no. 4, ed. Philip Denwood and Alexander Piatigorsky. London: Centre of South Asian Studies, University of London, 1983.

Sponberg, Alan, and Hardacre, Helen, eds. *Maitreya: The Future Buddha.* Cambridge, UK: Cambridge University Press, 1988.

Vogel, J. Ph. "The Past Buddhas and Kāśyapa in Indian Art and Epigraphy." In *Asiatica: Festschrift Friedrich Weller,* ed. Johannes Schubert and Ulrich Schneider. Leipzig, Germany: Harrassowitz, 1954.

JAN NATTIER

BUDDHACARITA

The *Buddhacarita* (*Acts of the Buddha*) by AŚVAGHOṢA is a second-century C.E. biography recounting in ornate verse the life of the Buddha from his birth to the distribution of his relics. The epic poem comprises twenty-eight chapters, only fourteen of which are extant in the original Sanskrit. The remainder are preserved in Tibetan and Chinese translations.

See also: **Buddha, Life of the; Sanskrit, Buddhist Literature in**

Bibliography

Beal, Samuel, trans. *The Fo-sho-hing-tsan-king: A Life of Buddha,* by Aśvaghosha Bodhisattva. Reprint edition, Delhi: Motilal Banarsidass, 1964.

Johnston, E. H., trans. "The Buddha's Mission and Last Journey (*Buddhacarita,* xv to xxviii)." *Acta Orientalia* 15 (1937): 26–32, 85–111, 231–292.

Johnston, E. H., trans. *The Buddhacarita, or, Acts of the Buddha.* Reprint edition, Delhi: Motilal Banarsidass, 1972.

JOHN S. STRONG

BUDDHADĀSA

Buddhadāsa (Ngeaum Panich, 1906–1993), a Thai Buddhist monk and scholar, was a prolific commentator on the Pāli literature of the THERAVĀDA school and an influential preceptor of ENGAGED BUDDHISM. Ordained at the age of twenty-one, Buddhadāsa became widely known for his critical intellect, his interest in meditation, and his gifts as a teacher. He founded Suan Mōkh (Garden of Liberation), an important monastery and international center for engaged Buddhist thought and training in Thailand. In his voluminous writings, Buddhadāsa developed the ideas of dhammic socialism, spiritual politics, fellowship of restraint (*saṅgamaniyama*), and interfaith dialogue based on Buddhist principles of selflessness, interdependence, and nonattachment.

Bibliography

Jackson, Peter A. *Buddhadāsa: A Buddhist Thinker for the Modern World.* Bangkok, Thailand: Siam Society, 1988.

Santikaro, Bhikkhu. "Buddhadāsa Bhikkhu: Life and Society through the Natural Eyes of Voidness." In *Engaged Buddhism: Buddhist Liberation Movements in Asia,* ed. Christopher S. Queen and Sallie B. King. Albany: State University of New York Press, 1996.

Swearer, Donald K., ed. *Me and Mine: Selected Essays of Bhikkhu Buddhadāsa.* Albany: State University of New York Press, 1989.

CHRISTOPHER S. QUEEN

BUDDHAGHOSA

The most famous and prolific of the Pāli commentators and exegetes, Buddhaghosa was active at the beginning of the fifth century C.E. According to the *Mahāvaṃsa* (*Great Chronicle*), he was an Indian brahmin of considerable scholarly genius who hailed from the kingdom of Magadha. He was converted to Buddhism by a monk named Revata and went to Sri Lanka at his teacher's instigation to study the Sinhalese commentaries at the Mahāvihāra Monastery. The monks there tested him by asking him to explicate two dharma verses. The result was the *Visuddhimagga* (*Path of Purity*), a work that remains the greatest compendium of THERAVĀDA thought ever written and that has had a lasting impact on the tradition. In three parts, the *Visuddhimagga* thoroughly and systematically treats all aspects of the topics of morality, meditation, and wisdom.

Buddhaghosa subsequently went on to write commentaries on many works of the Pāli CANON. Chief among them are separate commentaries on the *Vinayapiṭaka* (*Book of the Discipline*); on the *Dīgha, Majjhima, Saṃyutta,* and *Aṅguttara nikāyas* (the books of long, middle, kindred, and gradual sayings); and on the books of the ABHIDHARMA. In these works, which contain both exegeses of words and contextual excursi, Buddhaghosa succeeded in more or less defining the ways scholars have read the Theravāda canonical texts ever since. Buddhaghosa's life story may also be found, greatly embellished, in a late Pāli chronicle known as the *Buddhaghosuppatti* (*The Development of the Career of Buddhaghosa*).

Bibliography

Gray, James, ed. and trans. *Buddhaghosuppatti or the Historical Romance of the Rise and Career of Buddhaghosa.* London: Luzac, 1892. Reprinted, 1999.

Law, Bimala Churn. *Buddhaghosa.* Bombay: Bombay Branch of the Royal Asiatic Society, 1946.

JOHN S. STRONG

BUDDHAHOOD AND BUDDHA BODIES

The term *buddhahood* (*buddhatva*) refers to the unique attainment of buddhas that distinguishes them from all other kinds of holy being. Buddhahood constitutes the fullest possible realization of ultimate reality and total freedom from all that obscures it, together with all qualities that flow from such a realization. Buddhahood is described in two closely related ways: in terms of its distinctive characteristics, and in terms of buddha "bodies."

Characteristics of buddhahood

Early Buddhist texts ascribe qualities to Śākyamuni Buddha that distinguish him from other ARHATS (those who have realized NIRVĀṆA) and that render him the supreme teacher of the world. He was said to possess ten unmatched powers of penetrating awareness, four peerless forms of fearlessness, and supreme compassion for all beings. His body was endowed with thirty-two marks of a great person (*mahāpuruṣa*), the fruit of immeasurable virtue from previous lives (*Dīghanikāya* 3.142–179). As the outflow of his enlightenment he also possessed supernormal powers (*ṛddhis*) superior to those of others; these included the power to project multiple physical forms of diverse kinds (*nirmāṇas*), to control physical phenomena, to know others' minds and capacities, to perceive directly over great distances and time, and to know and skillfully communicate the freedom of nirvāṇa (*Majjhimanikāya* 1.69–73; Makransky, pp. 26–27). Śākyamuni's enlightened qualities exemplify those possessed by all prior buddhas and by all buddhas to come, qualities that enable each buddha to reintroduce the dharma to the world in each age.

Buddha bodies (*kāyas*)

The Indic term *kāya* refers to the physical body of a living being. It therefore carries the secondary meaning of a collection or aggregate of parts. In Buddhist texts over time, *kāya* came to include a third meaning—base or substratum, since one's body is the base of many qualities. The term also came to connote the embodiment of ultimate truth in enlightened knowledge and activity.

Buddha embodied in dharma and in forms. For early Buddhist traditions, Śākyamuni's body with thirty-two special marks constituted his primary physical expression of enlightenment. But his power to manifest himself to others extended beyond the confines of his physical body, since he created a "mind-made" body (*manomayakāya*) to teach his deceased mother in a heaven, and occasionally projected copies of his body, or created diverse forms, to carry out enlightened activities (*nirmāṇa*). All such manifest forms were referred to as *rūpakāya,* the embodiment (*kāya*) of the Buddha in forms (*rūpa*).

Of special importance was the dharma, the truths that the Buddha had realized and taught, encapsulated in the FOUR NOBLE TRUTHS, the very source of the charismatic power expressed through his physical body and teaching. Metaphorically, the dharma itself was understood as his essential being, his very body. So the *Dīghanikāya* (*Group of Long Discourses*) says that the Buddha instructed his disciples, when asked their family lineage, to reply, "I am a true son of the Buddha, born of his mouth, born of dharma, created by the dharma, an heir of the dharma. Why? Because buddhas are those whose body is dharma (dharmakāya), (3.84).

After the Buddha's physical death, the distinction between his dharma body (dharmakāya) and his form body (*rūpakāya*) grounded two legacies of communal practice (Reynolds 1977, p. 376). "Body of dharma" (dharmakāya) referred especially to the corpus of teachings the Buddha bequeathed to his monastic SAṄGHA, whose institutional life centered on the recitation, study, and practice of them. On the other hand, the relics from the cremation of the Buddha's physical body (*rūpakāya*) were placed in reliquary mounds (STŪPAS) at which laity (and monks and nuns as well) practiced ritual forms of reverence for the Buddha modeled on forms of devotion shown to him during his lifetime.

In THERAVĀDA and Sarvāstivāda traditions, dharmakāya also referred to the Buddha's supramundane realizations, his powers of awareness, fearlessness, compassion, and skillful means, as noted above. Here dharmakāya refers to the Buddha's "body of dharma(s)," where *dharmas* are pure qualities of enlightened mind (Makransky, p. 27).

The power of Buddha's nirvāṇa in the world. Scholastics of those schools maintained that the Buddha's final nirvāṇa at his physical death was an unconditioned attainment, a total passing away from the conditioned world of beings. Yet many practices of Buddhist communities seem to have functioned to mediate the power of the Buddha's nirvāṇa to the world long after he was physically gone. Stūpas containing relics of the Buddha, when ritually consecrated, "came alive" for devotees with the presence of the Buddha, representing the Buddha not only as the field of merit for offerings, but as a continuing source of salvific power for the world. Thus, many stories tell of Buddhist devotees who witnessed miraculous events or had spontaneous visions of the Buddha at stūpas. The distribution of the Buddha's relics among many stūpas over time cosmologized the Buddha, ritually rendering the power of his dharmakāya (his attainment of nirvāṇa) pervasively present to the world through his *rūpakāya* (physical embodiment) in many stūpas (Strong, p. 119). Statues and paintings of the Buddha had similar ritual functions, while also serving as support for meditative practices that vividly brought to mind the qualities of the Buddha while visualizing his physical form (*buddhānusmṛti*). Accomplished meditators were said to have visions and dreams of the Buddha, and to experience the Buddha's qualities and powers as vividly present in their world. All such ritual and yogic practices functioned to render the salvific power of his nirvāṇa, even after he was physically gone, a continuing presence in the saṃsāric world.

Several schools deriving from Mahāsāṃghika tradition appear to have given doctrinal expression to these patterns of understanding. They asserted that the Buddha was wholly supramundane, that his salvific power was all-pervasive, and that his body that had perished at the age of eighty was just a mind-made (*manomaya*) or illusory creation (*nirmāṇa*), not his real body. Rather, his real body was pure and limitless, its life endless. Theravāda and Sarvāstivāda scholastics had claimed that the Buddha's final nirvāṇa had destroyed the sole creative cause of his saṃsāric experience (defiled karma), resulting in a final nirvāṇa beyond creation or conditionality. But the Mahāsāṃghikas, by asserting that the Buddha's *rūpakāya* was pure and limitless, seemed to be saying that his long BODHISATTVA practice of prior lives had not only destroyed the impure causes of his SAṂSĀRA, but functioned as pure creative cause for his nirvāṇic attainment to embody itself limitlessly for beings. Along similar lines, the LOTUS SŪTRA (SADDHARMAPUṆḌARĪKA-SŪTRA), an early MAHĀYĀNA scripture, declared the Buddha's life and salvific activity to span innumerable eons, beyond his apparent physical death.

Pure buddha fields and celestial buddhas. This understanding of a buddha's nirvāṇa as not just the cessation of defilement but also the manifestation of vast salvific power was developed in a wide range of Mahāyāna scriptures of early centuries C.E. The centrality of bodhisattvas in Mahāyāna sūtras, each of whom vows to become a buddha, supported a new Buddhist cosmology of multiple buddhas simultaneously active throughout the universe. Each such buddha wields enlightened power within his own field of salvific activity for the beings karmically connected to him. On the path to buddhahood, therefore, bodhisattvas vow to "purify" their fields, by collecting immeasurable amounts of merit and wisdom (as pure creative causes for their buddha fields), by training other bodhisattvas in similar practices, and by transferring their merit to other beings so they may be reborn in such fields (Williams, pp. 224–227). The purest such fields are heavenly domains of buddhas of infinite radiance, power, and incalculable life span, such as AMITĀBHA or AKṢOBHYA, buddhas whose pure fields (or PURE LANDS) consist of jeweled palaces and radiant natural scenes, where all conditions are perfect for communicating and realizing enlightenment. Those born near such a celestial buddha, either by the power of their own practice or by faith in the power of such a buddha, make quick progress to enlightenment. Late fourth-century C.E. Mahāyāna treatises, such as the *Mahāyānasūtrālaṃkāra* (*Ornament of Mahāyāna Scriptures*) and *Abhisamayālaṃkāra* (*Ornament of Realization*), created a new vocabulary for such celestial buddhas, referring to them as sambhogakāya, the perfect embodiment (*kāya*) of buddhahood for supreme communal enjoyment (*sambhoga*) of dharma (Nagao, pp. 107–112).

The unrestricted nirvāṇa of the buddhas and the three buddha kāyas. These Mahāyāna understandings developed within a nexus of other developing doctrines. *Prajñāpāramitā* (Perfection of Wisdom) sūtras and early Madhyamaka treatises declared all phenomena to be empty of substantial independent existence (*svabhāvaśūnya*), hence illusory. When bodhisattvas attain direct knowledge of that truth, they realize that all things in their intrinsic emptiness have always been in nirvāṇic peace, that saṃsāra is undivided from nirvāṇa. Through such wisdom, the bodhisattva learns to embody the freedom and power of nirvāṇa while continuing to act skillfully within saṃsāra for the sake of others. When this bodhisattva path of wisdom and skillful means is fully accomplished, its simultaneous participation in saṃsāra and nirvāṇa becomes the essential realization of buddhahood. This is referred to in Yogācāra and later Madhyamaka treatises as a buddha's "unrestricted nirvāṇa" (*apratiṣṭhita* nirvāṇa); it is unrestricted because it is bound neither to saṃsāra nor to a merely quiescent nirvāṇa, but possessed of limitless and spontaneous activity, all-pervasive and eternal, radiating its power to beings throughout all existence, drawing them toward enlightenment (Makransky, pp. 85–87).

In the Perfection of Wisdom sūtras, the term *dharmatā* (literally "thinghood") refers to the real nature of things, undivided in their emptiness yet diverse in their appearance. In treatises that formalized the concept of the buddhas' unrestricted nirvāṇa, the *dharmatā* of all things as the limitless field of the buddhas' enlightened knowledge and power came to be referred to as dharmakāya, now meaning the buddhas' "embodiment of *dharmatā*" (of ultimate reality; Makransky, pp. 34–37, 199–201). Dharmakāya, as the nondual awareness of the emptiness of all things, is undifferentiated among buddhas, yet serves as the basis for diverse manifestations. It is therefore also etymologized as the undivided basis (*kāya*) of all the buddha qualities (dharmas). A synonym for it in such treatises was *svabhāvikakāya,* meaning the buddhas' embodiment (*kāya*) of the intrinsic nature (*svabhāva*) of things.

The celestial sambhogakāya buddhas, then, represent the primary manifestation of dharmakāya, perfectly embodying the nonduality of appearance (*rūpa*) and emptiness (dharma). For this reason, the sensory phenomena of sambhogakāya pure fields—gentle breezes, flowing rivers, even the birds—continually disclose the nirvāṇic nature of things to the bodhisattva assemblies arrayed there.

But formulators of the buddhas' unrestricted nirvāṇa, as noted above, understood the dharmakāya's salvific activity to radiate to beings of all realms, not just to those in pure buddha fields. Such all-pervasive buddha activity is carried out by innumerable manifestations within the empty, illusory worlds of beings. In Yogācāra and later Madhyamaka treatises, the limitlessly diverse ways that buddhahood was said to manifest in Mahāyāna scriptures came to be classified under the term *nirmāṇakāya,* meaning buddhahood embodied in diverse, illusory manifestations (*nirmāṇa*). As such, nirmāṇakāya encompasses three broad categories. First, since the world itself in its empty, illusory nature is undivided from nirvāṇa, any aspect of the world has the potential to disclose the essence of buddhahood (to function as nirmāṇakāya) when a person's mind becomes pure enough to notice. Second, buddhas and advanced bodhisattvas have great power to project illusory replicas and visionary forms to beings (*nirmāṇas*) to help guide them toward enlightenment. Such illusory projections further support the disclosure of all things as illusory appearances of empty reality. Third, all sorts of beings who serve to communicate the buddhas' truths function as agents of buddha activity, hence as nirmāṇakāya, from supreme human paradigms like Śākyamuni to the innumerable bodhisattvas of Mahāyāna scriptures who carry out much of the Buddha's teaching and salvific activity, and who appear in all walks of life and as all types of beings.

Thus developed the basic Mahāyāna doctrine of three buddha *kāyas*—dharmakāya, sambhogakāya, and nirmāṇakāya—which informed the buddhalogies that developed throughout Asia, contributing to the Huayan, Tiantai, Zhenyan, Chan, and Jingtu traditions of China, thence Korea and Japan, and to all Tibetan Buddhist traditions. Some scholars, seeking to analyze the relationship between transcendental and phenomenal aspects of buddhahood, divided the three *kāyas* into four. So XUANZANG in seventh-century China distinguished two aspects of sambhogakāya, while Haribhadra in eighth-century India divided dharmakāya in two by reference to conditioned and unconditioned aspects (Makransky, pp. 216–218).

In Indian Yogācāra and later Madhyamaka treatises, the three *kāya* doctrine was associated with a developmental model of path: Buddhahood is to be attained by the radical transformation of all aspects of a person's defiled consciousness into buddha *kāyas* and wisdoms. Mahāyāna texts whose central teaching was buddha nature (TATHĀGATAGARBHA), on the other hand, emphasized a discovery model of path: Buddha *kāyas* manifest automatically as the mind is purified, for the very essence of mind (buddha nature) is already replete with their qualities (Nagao, pp. 115–117).

Tantric Buddhist traditions of India, East Asia, and Tibet drew upon both such models. The teaching of buddha nature undergirds the "three mysteries" uncovered by tantric praxis, through which the practitioner discovers that his or her body, speech, and mind are undivided from those of the buddhas, which are one with the three *kāyas.* Tantric traditions have also drawn upon Yogācāra and Madhyamaka models of transformation to construct homologies expressed in MAṆḌALAS. Indian and Tibetan praxis of highest yoga tantras engages four energy centers in the body, which frame correspondences between the fourfold aspects of the unenlightened person, the fourfold aspects of path that ultimately transforms them, and four resultant buddha *kāyas,* all of which take visual expression in the four directions of the maṇḍala. Within such a system, a fourth *kāya* representing highest tantric attainment is added to the prior three *kāyas,* and is designated by terms such as *sahajakāya,* "embodiment of co-presence (of nirvāṇa and saṃsāra)," or *mahāsukhakāya,* "embodiment of great bliss" (the tantrically embodied bliss of nondual wisdom and means; Snellgrove, p. 251).

Japanese PURE LAND BUDDHISM (Jōdoshū, Jōdo Shinshū) has emphasized the transcendental power of buddhahood embodied in the sambhogakāya Amitābha. Because this is the period of the DECLINE OF THE DHARMA (*mappō*), it is argued, people are no longer able to accomplish the path through their own power but must rely upon the buddha Amitābha, whose power to take the devotee into his pure field at death is received in faith through recitation of his name (NENBUTSU [CHINESE, NIANFO; KOREAN, YŎMBUL]). Zen traditions, on the other hand, based upon the doctrine of buddha nature, have emphasized the immanence and immediacy of enlightenment. Through Zen practice, it is said, buddhahood complete with all *kāyas* is to be discovered intimately within one's present mind, body, and world. So the Japanese eighteenth-century Zen teacher HAKUIN EKAKU wrote, "This very place, the pure lotus land; this very body, the buddha body."

See also: **Buddhānusmṛti (Recollection of the Buddha); Relics and Relics Cults**

Bibliography

Griffiths, Paul J. *On Being Buddha: The Classical Doctrine of Buddhahood.* Albany: State University of New York Press, 1994.

La Vallée Poussin, Louis de, trans. and ed. *Vijñaptimātratāsiddhi: La Siddhi de Hiuan-tsang.* Paris: Geuthner, 1928–1948.

Makransky, John J. *Buddhahood Embodied: Sources of Controversy in India and Tibet.* Albany: State University of New York Press, 1997.

Nagao, Gadjin. "On the Theory of Buddha-Body (*Buddhakāya*)." In *Mādhyamika and Yogācāra: A Study of Mahāyāna Philosophies, Collected Papers of G. M. Nagao,* tr. and ed. Leslie S. Kawamura. Albany: State University of New York Press, 1991.

Reynolds, Frank. "The Several Bodies of Buddha: Reflections on a Neglected Aspect of Theravāda Tradition." *History of Religions* 16, no. 4 (1977): 374–389.

Reynolds, Frank E., and Hallisey, Charles. "The Buddha." In *Buddhism and Asian History,* ed. Joseph M. Kitagawa and Mark D. Cummings. New York: Macmillan, 1989.

Sharf, Robert H. *Coming to Terms with Chinese Buddhism.* Honolulu: University of Hawaii Press, 2002.

Snellgrove, David. *Indo-Tibetan Buddhism.* Boston: Shambhala, 1987.

Strong, John S. *The Legend of King Aśoka: A Study and Translation of the Aśokavadāna.* Princeton, NJ: Princeton University Press, 1983.

Williams, Paul M. *Mahāyāna Buddhism: The Doctrinal Foundations.* New York: Routledge, 1989.

JOHN J. MAKRANSKY

BUDDHA IMAGES

Buddha images—whether they are Indian, Thai, Chinese, or Japanese—are usually readily recognizable. The date an image was created rarely confuses its identification as Buddhist because the iconography of the Buddha image has remained constant almost from the earliest invention of the image type, even though the style of the figure has varied depending on date and geographical location. The term *iconography* refers to the forms or characteristics of an image, whereas *style* refers to the ways in which these forms or characteristics are crafted or made.

The iconography of the Buddha image includes representing the Buddha as a MONK, wearing a monk's robe, and with his hair shaved. A monk wears two or three simple items of clothing, including an untailored and unsewn undercloth (*antaravāsaka*), a rectangular cloth worn like a skirt that reaches to the ankles and is folded under at the waist or belted with a piece of cloth. An upper garment (*uttarāsaṅga*), a second rectangular cloth held behind the back and thrown over the shoulders like a shawl, is worn over the undercloth. There are two ways to wear it, either covering both shoulders or under the right armpit. A third cloth, which is rarely worn, except in cold climates, is sometimes folded and placed over the left shoulder during special ceremonial occasions. The actual monk's robes are dyed in shades of yellow. This simple attire can usually be discerned on Buddha images, although artists tended to arrange the cloth in various decorative ways, such as producing a perfectly symmetrical fall of the robe on both sides of the body, or fashioning the folds in rhythmic patterns.

Monks shave the HAIR on their heads and faces, and the Buddha performed the tonsure on himself when he left his palace and courtly life for that of a wandering mendicant. With a stroke of his sword he removed his long topknot, and some texts note that the remaining hair formed small curls that turned toward the right. Indian artists by the second century C.E. depicted the Buddha's hair as small ringlets over the head, which came to be called snail-shell curls. In some artistic traditions, these curls developed into rows of small bumps.

The Buddha, however, was not simply a monk; he was born a great man (*mahāpuruṣa*) and was identified as such by certain bodily signs (*lakṣaṇa*). Some of these, such as his sweet voice, could not be produced in art, but others, such as his cranial protuberance, could be depicted. The extent to which the artists attempted to reproduce the *lakṣaṇa* varied according to place and time, but the cranial bump became standard for most images.

There are, of course, many different buddhas, but the Buddha of our historic period, Śākyamuni, was a human being, and it is overwhelmingly Śākyamuni who is represented in the earliest images in India. Thus, he consistently has two arms, unlike images of Hindu deities from the same period, who often have multiple arms. Also associated with Śākyamuni Buddha are certain hand positions (mudrā) and postures. One popular early type depicted the Buddha seated with his legs crossed and his right hand held up with the palm out. Although artistic depictions of these gestures and postures developed over time and came to be associated with certain narrative events, they are highly restricted in number and reappear again and again.

Thus, the shared iconography—the monk's robe, shaved hair, certain bodily marks, and limited hand positions and body postures—have made it possible for the Buddha image, no matter the style, to be identifiable across time and geography.

Two of the most intriguing, yet controversial, questions regarding Buddha images are when they were first made and why. The earliest images were produced in two locations in South Asia: Mathurā, a city sixty miles south of Delhi, and Gandhāra, a region centered on Taxila in present-day Pakistan. The first Buddha image is usually believed to have been created around the first century C.E. The Buddha image types produced in these two regions were radically different in style. Although the iconographic parameters outlined above were generally followed in both places, the Gandhāra images are related to Western classical (Roman and Hellenistic) art, whereas the Mathurā images are related to the north Indian style seen in earlier anthropomorphic sculptures of various local or pan-Indian deities, such as YAKṢAS.

The early Mathurā type, such as the nine-foot-tall Buddha dedicated by the monk Bala, is a monumental image that stands with knees locked, staring straight ahead, his left arm akimbo with a fist on his hip. The robe is thin and transparent, revealing the body. The Gandhāra type, on the other hand, wears all three garments, completely masking the body underneath, the emphasis being on the pattern of the heavy, deep folds of fabric.

It is clear to scholars today, however, that the earliest images were probably not as sophisticated and well-defined as those described above, and some scholars have begun to identify groups and individual images that suggest an earlier development. While these images vary considerably, they share a modest size and nascent iconography that includes the *uttarāsaṅga* worn not as a covering robe but, like a layman, as a bunched shawl.

Also at issue is the interplay of the development of the Buddha image with that of images of other anthropomorphic deities of the same period—both Hindu and Jain. All three religions were practiced in Mathurā, and some of the earliest images developed there. Of the three religious groups, the Jains probably produced the first anthropomorphic icons at Mathurā; these are tiny figures of their naked Jinas on stone reliefs dated to as early as the second century B.C.E. It seems reasonable to expect that the three religions interacted and competed at Mathurā, with their anthropomorphic images developing together. Indeed, images from Mathurā shared the same style, whether Jain, Buddhist, or Hindu.

Given such evidence, it is likely that the first small, rather indifferent, Buddha figures were created around the first century B.C.E. It is unlikely that such figures were the focus initially of worship or an icon cult, although by around 100 C.E., when the Bala and Gandhāra Buddha images were created, such cults were certainly in place.

Still, assuming the Buddha lived in the fifth century B.C.E., it is of interest that no anthropomorphic images of the Buddha existed until some four hundred years after his death. This early period was not without Buddhist art, however. Although the famous King AŚOKA of the third century B.C.E. was predisposed to Buddhism, the only artwork from his reign that might be labeled *Buddhist* is the single lion capital with a wheel (cakra) from Sārnāth. But from the mid-second and first centuries B.C.E., there is an explosion of Buddhist art associated with stūpas, including those at Bhārhut and SĀÑCĪ. At these and other sites, extensive narrative reliefs depicting the Buddha's life stories and past lives (JĀTAKA) were carved in stone. However, even though the Buddha as a human being could be shown in such *jātaka* scenes, he is not represented in any reliefs of this period. The absence of the Buddha in anthropomorphic form is called *aniconic* in art historical literature. How to interpret this absence is at the center of extensive scholarly debate, but the initial absence accentuates the importance of Buddha images created later.

The early Buddhist sites in India clearly show that the STŪPA (and thus the relic enshrined therein) was the focus of worship. Other symbolic forms, such as the tree or the wheel, were also worshiped. There were extensive narrative reliefs associated with these sites, particularly with stūpas. Eventually, anthropomorphic images began to be used in depictions of the Buddha's life stories. It appears that interest in the anthropomorphic images lay more in their narrative function, and not in their function as icons. The popularization of an icon cult may have been an innovation of a few clerics, most particularly the monk Bala and his associates, who placed enormous Mathurā Buddha images at several sites in northern India. Very quickly, however, the Buddha image became widespread in South Asia.

A single image, without any narrative context, is difficult to "read." Certain places and periods had favorite image types, and the different Buddhist schools, such as THERAVĀDA and MAHĀYĀNA, used and interpreted Buddha images in different ways. Nevertheless, the actual images themselves remain iconographically consistent.

For example, the favorite form that the Buddha image takes, whether standing or seated, what arm positions are shown, and how the robe is worn, have been shown to be determined not so much by religious concerns but by artistic traditions. Various regions and periods favor certain dominant types of Buddha images, with a limited number of secondary forms. Theravāda Buddha images are extremely limited in their iconography. Almost all seated images in Sri Lanka, for example, are in meditation. Mahāyāna Buddhism uses the different hand gestures of seated Buddha images to construct systems of five, six, and seven image MAṆḌALA. However, the fact that an image might be in earth-touching gesture, for example, is not itself sufficient to tell us whether it is Śākyamuni at the moment of calling the earth to witness or rather the Mahāyāna Buddha AKṢOBHYA. There is no difference artistically. This issue calls into question whether we can even speak of Mahāyāna art, at least in terms of Buddha images. Rather it is context, not iconography,

Statue of the Buddha at the eighth-century grotto shrine of Sŏkkuram near Pulguksa, South Korea. © Carmen Redondo/Corbis. Reproduced by permission.

that defines the image. Likewise, the Buddha images reflect no difference in the way the different bodies of the Buddha (the trikāya) are represented. It is only when we move to the VAJRAYĀNA Buddhist systems, such as those of Nepal and Tibet, with new definitions of the Buddha and his body, that the art becomes clearly differentiated.

See also: **Bodhisattva Images; Buddha, Life of the, in Art; Jainism and Buddhism; Mudrā and Visual Imagery; Robes and Clothing**

Bibliography

Coomaraswamy, Ananda Kentish. *The Origin of the Buddha Image.* New Delhi: Munshiram Manoharlal, 1972.

Dehejia, Vidya. "Aniconism and the Multivalence of Emblems." *Ars Orientalis* 21 (1991): 45–66.

Ghose, Rajeshwari, with Puay-peng Ho and Yeung Chun-tong. *In the Footsteps of the Buddha: An Iconic Journey from India to China.* Hong Kong: University Museum and Art Gallery, University of Hong Kong, 1998.

Griswold, A. B. "Prolegomena to the Study of the Buddha's Dress in Chinese Sculpture, Part I." *Artibus Asiae* 26 (1963): 85–131.

Huntington, Susan L. "Aniconism and the Multivalence of Emblems: Another Look." *Ars Orientalis* 22 (1992): 111–156.

Huntington, Susan L., and Huntington, John C. *Leaves from the Bodhi Tree: The Art of Pala India (8th–12th Centuries) and Its International Legacy.* Seattle, WA: Dayton Art Institute, 1989.

Lohuizen-de Leeuw, Johanna Engelberta van. "New Evidence with Regard to the Origin of the Buddha Image." In *South Asian Archaeology 1979: Papers from the Fifth International Conference of the Association of South Asian Archaeologists in Western Europe Held in the Museum für Indische Kunst der Staalichen Museen Preussischer Kulturbesitz Berlin,* ed. Herbert Härtel. Berlin: D. Reimer, 1981.

Lyons, Islay, and Ingholt, Harald. *Gandharan Art in Pakistan.* New York: Pantheon Books, 1957.

Menzies, Jackie, ed. *Buddha: Radiant Awakening.* Sydney, Australia: Art Gallery of New South Wales, 2001.

Pal, Pratapaditya, ed. *Light of Asia: Buddha Śākyamuni in Asian Art.* Los Angeles: Los Angeles County Museum of Art, 1984.

Quintanilla, Sonya. "Ayagapatas: Characteristics, Symbolism, and Chronology." *Artibus Asiae* 60 (1990): 79–137.

Schopen, Gregory. "On Monks, Nuns, and 'Vulgar' Practices: The Introduction of the Image Cult into Indian Buddhism." *Artibus Asiae* 49 1/2 (1988–1989): 153–168.

Snellgrove, David L., ed. *The Image of the Buddha.* Tokyo: Kodansha International, 1978.

Zwalf, W., ed. *Buddhism: Art and Faith.* London: British Museum, 1985.

ROBERT L. BROWN

BUDDHA, LIFE OF THE

The term *buddha* (literally, "awakened") refers to a fully enlightened being who has attained perfect knowledge and full liberation from REBIRTH. *Buddha* is not a proper name but a general term that may be applied to all enlightened beings. Therefore, the historical Buddha may be designated using this term from the time of his enlightenment (bodhi) only. Before that moment, he was a BODHISATTVA, one who was on the way of obtaining full enlightenment. At the same time, the term *buddha* is used as an honorary title for the founder of the Buddhist religion, the only buddha living in the current historical period.

The dates of the historical Buddha

There is no reliable information concerning the dates of the historical Buddha's life that has been unanimously accepted by Buddhist tradition and by scholars. Traditional dates of the *parinirvāṇa* (the decease of the Buddha) range widely from 2420 B.C.E. to 290 B.C.E. The dates proposed by scholars who contributed to a 1988 symposium in Göttingen, Germany, on *The Dating of the Historical Buddha,* vary from 486 B.C.E. (the so-called corrected long chronology) to 261 B.C.E. The THERAVĀDA tradition calculates the death of the Buddha to have occurred in 544 or 543 B.C.E., 218 years before the consecration of King AŚOKA (ca. 300–232 B.C.E.) as calculated by this tradition. Taking into account the obvious error in this chronology, which was discovered when exact dates for King Aśoka became known, most Western and Indian scholars calculate 487 or 486 B.C.E. as the date of the Buddha's death. However, early Buddhist texts from mainland India belonging to the *Mūlasarvāstivāda* tradition, as well as two references in the earliest historiographic work of the Theravāda tradition (the *Dīpavaṃsa* or *The Chronicle of the Island* [of Sri Lanka]) date this event to one hundred years before the rule of King Aśoka, or 368 B.C.E. (the so-called short chronology). In addition, later Tibetan and East Asian Buddhist texts provide a considerable variety of earlier dates.

The lists of the so-called patriarchs are of great importance for a reliable calculation of the dates of the historical Buddha. All early Buddhist traditions list only five patriarchs, not enough for an interval of 218 years between the Buddha's *parinirvāṇa* and King Aśoka. In Indian tradition, information about the succession of teachers was much more reliably handed down than any dates. For this and many other reasons, including the state of development of Indian society at the time of the Buddha, we may conclude that the Buddha passed away at a later date than that handed down by Theravāda tradition, including its variant, the corrected long chronology. Although the available information does not allow scholars to arrive at an exact dating, it is safe to suppose that the Buddha passed away some time between 420 B.C.E. and 350 B.C.E. at the age of approximately eighty years.

Sources for the biography of the historical Buddha

On the basis of the available sources it is possible to reconstruct a fairly reliable biography of the man who was to become the Buddha. The sources are the canonical texts of the Theravāda, the SARVĀSTIVĀDA AND

MŪLASARVĀSTIVĀDA, and the DHARMAGUPTAKA traditions. Only the Theravāda texts are fully extant in the original Indian version in Pāli; the texts of the other traditions are fully extant only from Chinese or Tibetan translations and partially from incomplete Sanskrit texts. These texts do not provide coherent biographies of the historical Buddha, but they do offer considerable autobiographical and biographical information that was handed down during the first three to five centuries after the death of the Buddha. Oral tradition of the Buddha's teaching in various local dialects was responsible for minor differences in these traditions and for the insertion of mythic lore, which shall not be considered in the following summary of the Buddha's biography.

The life of the future Buddha

Before his departure from home. The historical Buddha was born into the Śākya family, which belonged to the kṣatriya (noble) caste, considered by Buddhists to be the highest caste. He was later known by the honorary title Śākyamuni, which means "sage of the Śākya clan." The Śākyas were not kings, but they formed a class of nobles within a republican system of government that held regular meetings of the members of the leading families. The future Buddha belonged to the Gautama clan, so he was later on known as Gautama Buddha. His individual name was Siddhārtha (Pāli, Siddhattha), his father's name was Śuddhodana (Pāli, Suddhodana), and his mother's name was Māyā. Detailed information on Māyā is mainly derived from later literature. The family resided in Kapilavastu (Pāli, Kapilavatthu) at the foot of the Himalayas near the present-day Indian-Nepalese border. The future Buddha is said to have been born in Lumbinī, also near the Indian-Nepalese border. In 248 B.C.E., Aśoka placed a pillar with an inscription commemorating the birth of Śākyamuni Buddha (the so-called Rummindeī inscription) in Lumbinī. Therefore, it is certain that during the time of Aśoka this place was identified as the birthplace of the Buddha. Lumbinī is considered to be one of the four main Buddhist pilgrimage sites on the Indian subcontinent.

Because Māyā died shortly after Siddhārtha was born, the future Buddha was raised by MAHĀPRAJĀPATĪ GAUTAMĪ (Pāli, Mahāpajāpatī Gotamī), the younger sister of his mother and second wife of Śuddhodana. The autobiographical passages of the early texts describe in much detail the luxurious conditions of the bodhisattva's life in his home. Siddhārtha was married to Yaśodharā (Pāli, Yasodharā), who is also called Rāhulamātā (mother of Rāhula) in the early texts. RĀHULA was their only son. The bodhisattva Siddhārtha was not satisfied with his sumptuous life because he realized that, like all beings, he was subject to old age, disease, and death. This perception caused him, at the age of twenty-nine, to abandon his home, don monk's robes, shave his head, and go forth to live as a homeless ascetic. Early texts explicitly state that he did this "though his parents did not consent and wept full of affliction." The legend that Gautama left his home in secret is of later origin.

A noteworthy account of an early contemplative experience of the bodhisattva before he left his home is reported in the *Mahāsaccaka-sutta* of the *Majjhimanikāya* in the Pāli scriptures. Here, the Buddha is said to have reported that he had already experienced the first DHYĀNA (TRANCE STATE) as a youth when he sat under a rose apple tree while his father conducted a ceremony.

Ascetic life and austerities. After he left home, Gautama visited the leading yoga masters of the period: Ārāḍa Kālāma (Pāli, Āḷāra Kālāma) and Udraka Rāmaputra (Pāli, Uddaka Rāmaputta). When Gautama did not attain salvation under their direction, he went to a site near the river Nairañjanā (Pāli, Nerañjarā) and engaged in extreme ASCETIC PRACTICES (Sanskrit, *duṣkaracaryā*; Pāli, *dukkarakārikā*) for six years, hoping to reach his goal in this way. Five other ascetics joined him as followers. However, when he finally understood that this extreme austerity would not lead to salvation, that it was fruitless, he ended these efforts, ate a substantial meal, took a bath in the river, and sat down under a tree of the botanical species *ficus religiosa,* which Buddhists thereafter called the *bodhi tree.* It was here, seven years after he had left home, that he obtained BODHI (AWAKENING), perfect enlightenment, and thereby became a *samyaksambuddha,* or "fully enlightened one."

The period of teaching and dissemination. After enlightenment, the Buddha remained in meditation for several days. In the beginning he was hesitant to preach the way to liberation that he had discovered (his dharma) because he doubted that others would understand it. However, he finally decided to preach, and he set out toward the city of Benares (Vārāṇasī). On the way, he met Upaka, a follower of the Ājīvika group of ascetics, but Upaka did not take the Buddha's words seriously and went his own way. The Buddha then reached Ṛṣipatana (in other texts called Ṛṣivadana; Pāli, Isipatana) near Benares, and here he delivered his first sermon, the famous *Dharmacakrapravartana-sūtra* (Pāli, *Dhammacakkappavattana-sutta*), the discourse at Benares by which the wheel of the dharma was "Set into Motion." In this sermon, the Buddha explained the middle way between the extremes of luxury and asceticism, the FOUR NOBLE TRUTHS (the truth of suffering, the truth of the origin of suffering, the truth of the extinction of suffering, and the truth of the eightfold PATH leading to the extinction of suffering), as well as the impersonality of all beings. The site where the Buddha delivered this sermon is now known as Sārnāth, and it is one of the most important Buddhist places of PILGRIMAGE.

The Buddha accepted his first disciples on this occasion and thereby established the SAṄGHA, the Buddhist monastic community. He continued teaching his doctrine for the next forty-five years. The Buddha's itinerary extended from his hometown Kapilavastu and Śrāvastī in the north, to Vārāṇasī (Benares), Rājagṛha (Rājgir), Vaiśālī (Besarh), Kauśāmbi (Kosam), Nālandā, and several other places in the Ganges basin. Later commentarial texts provide exact information about the places where the Buddha took up residence during the rainy season of each particular year of his teaching period, but it is doubtful that the dates provided in these texts are reliable.

A number of important events occurred during this period, including the conversion of ŚĀRIPUTRA (Pāli, Sāriputta) and MAHĀMAUDGALYĀYANA (Pāli, Mahāmogallāna), who became the Buddha's two chief disciples; the ordination of MAHĀKĀŚYAPA (Pāli, Mahākassapa), who was to become the convener of the First Buddhist Council (*saṅgīti* or *saṅgāyanā*) in Rājagṛha after the Buddha's demise; and the visit of the Buddha to his home town, where he met his father Śuddhodana and his foster mother Mahāprajāpatī Gautamī, and where his son Rāhula and several other members of the Śākya family joined the saṅgha. Among them was UPĀLI, who was considered the most proficient monk in questions of monastic discipline and who acted as expert in this capacity during the First Buddhist Council. ĀNANDA, a member of the Śākya clan and a cousin of the Buddha, accompanied the Buddha during the last decades of his life. He was instrumental in persuading the Buddha to admit women into the saṅgha, thus establishing the *Bhikṣuṇī Saṅgha.*

Among the important lay followers of the Buddha was Bimbisāra, the king of Magadha. The Buddha was five years older than Bimbisāra, and Bimbisāra is reported to have become a follower of the Buddha fifteen years after his accession to the throne. Bimbisāra dedicated the Veṇuvana (Pāli, Veḷuvana) grove near his residence at Rājagṛha to the Buddhist saṅgha; it become the first *ārāma* (place of permanent residence for monks). Until he was imprisoned by his son, Bimbisāra did whatever he could to promote the Buddhist community.

The Buddha's adversary was his cousin DEVADATTA, who was ordained when the Buddha visited Kapilavastu. However, Devadatta later attempted to take the Buddha's place and provoked a schism in the saṅgha. Devadatta was supported by Ajātaśatru, King Bimbisāra's son. Devadatta and Ajātaśatru even tried to kill the Buddha, but they failed. Ajātaśatru then dethroned his father and imprisoned him with the order that he should be starved to death. Traditional Buddhist chronology dates the beginning of Ajātaśatru's reign to the eighth year before the Buddha's death. It seems that Ajātaśatru, most probably for political reasons, supported the Buddha during his last years; the Buddha's public support was too great to oppose.

The last days of the Buddha. Although the chronological order of the events described in the preceding paragraphs remains uncertain, there is reliable information about the last days in the life of the historical Buddha. This information is handed down in the MAHĀPARINIRVĀṆA-SŪTRA (Pāli, *Mahāparinibbān-sutta*), which is available in several versions that differ only on minor points. The account begins with the visit of King Ajātaśatru's minister, Varṣākāra (Pāli, Vassakāra), on the mountain Gṛdhrakūṭa (Pāli, Gijjhakūṭa). Varṣākāra had been sent by the king in order to ask the Buddha if a campaign against the Vṛji (Pāli, Vajjī) confederation would be successful. The Buddha responded by explaining the seven conditions necessary for the prosperity of a state, which he had earlier taught to the Vṛjians. After Varṣākāra's departure, the Buddha explained to the monks the analogous conditions of prosperity of the saṅgha.

After he delivered a sermon in Pāṭaliputra (modern Patna) and crossed the river Ganges, the Buddha traveled toward Vaiśālī, where he converted the courtesan Āmrapālī (Pāli, Ambapālī). At that time, the Buddha also met leading members of the Licchavi confederation, but different texts vary in their versions of this event. Afterwards, the Buddha visited Veṇugrāmaka (Pāli, Belugāma or Beluvagāmaka), where he spent the rainy season with Ānanda. There the Buddha fell ill and was near death, but he recovered. At that time Ānanda asked the Buddha if there were additional instructions that the Buddha had not yet revealed to his disciples. The Buddha declared that he had completely and openly explained his dharma.

From Vaiśālī the Buddha traveled in the direction of Kuśinagara (Pāli, Kusināra). In Pāvā he accepted a meal from the smith Cunda, which caused a diarrhea that led to his death. The Buddha reached Kuśinagara (Pāli, Kusināra), where he admonished his disciples to continue their endeavor toward the final goal without cessation, and he passed away.

Early legendary expansions

The preceding paragraphs reduce the record of the Buddha's life to its historical essence. This account relies on comparative studies of the ancient texts; these include studies of the various early traditions of the *Mahāparinirvāṇa-sūtra,* the *Mahāvadāna-sūtra,* and other texts by Ernst Waldschmidt and André Bareau, as well as similar investigations made by other scholars. The existing texts include a multitude of legendary stories that crept in and, step by step, changed the original character of the biography of the Buddha. These compilations were written down in their final form centuries after the Buddha's death and only after a long period of oral transmission.

Although there is no coherent biographical text of the life of the Buddha in the early canonical works, later texts provide full biographies, and such works are available from various Buddhist traditions. In these works, the Buddha's biography is extended by a multitude of myths and legendary accounts. All these accounts begin by describing former existences of the Buddha; most begin with the story of the former buddha DĪPAṂKARA, who existed many kalpas (world periods) ago. When the ascetic Sumedha met Dīpaṃkara, Sumedha took the vow to become a buddha himself in a future age and he received Dīpaṃkara's confirmation by a prophecy (*vyākaraṇa*). He thereby became a bodhisattva who was eventually to be reborn as the historical Gautama Buddha. During the subsequent kalpas, Dīpaṃkara confirmed the bodhisattva's vow and received confirmation from the buddhas of these kalpas. Finally, he was reborn in the Tuṣita heaven, where he decided to descend to the human world.

In the human world, the bodhisattva was reincarnated as the son of Māyā, the wife of King Śuddhodana. Several miracles are associated with the bodhisattva's conception and birth. For example, the conception took place even though Māyā had not had sexual relations with Śuddhodana. This myth parallels the Christian belief in the supernatural conception of Jesus. There was an earthquake on the day of the conception because a *mahāsattva* (great being) was to come into human existence. The brahmins at the court of Śuddhodana predicted that Māyā's son would become either a buddha or a universal monarch (*cakravartin*), and several other miracles were observed at that time. The bodhisattva is said to have entered into the womb of Māyā through the right side of her chest in the shape of a white elephant.

Māyā decided to visit her parents in the village of Devaḍaha. Before arriving there, she gave birth to the bodhisattva in the grove of Lumbinī. On the same day, the bodhisattva's future wife and his horse Kanthaka were also born. The king named the prince Siddhārtha, which means "he whose aims are fulfilled." The traditional biographies report that the bodhisattva lived in great luxury, and his palaces and other aspects of his life are described in detail. The bodhisattva made Yaśodharā his first wife, but he is said to have had a number of other wives as well.

Knowing the prophecy that the prince Siddhārtha would become either a buddha or a cakravartin, his father did everything he could to keep the prince from seeing signs of old age, sickness, or death. However, during visits to the park Siddhārtha witnessed a very old man, a sick man, a corpse, and finally an ascetic. After this he received news of the birth of his son Rāhula.

Then one night he witnessed his consorts splayed in disgusting array, and he decided to leave the worldly life. He ordered his charioteer Channa to saddle his horse Kanthaka, he entered his wife's room for a last look at her and at their son, and then he took his leave from the world (*pravrajyā*). This story of the four sights definitely does not belong to the earliest traditions of the life of the historical Buddha, but it became a constituent of all biographies of the Buddha at an early date. Originally it was derived from the legendary biography of a former buddha that is narrated in the *Mahāvadāna-sūtra* in the form of a sermon of the Buddha.

At the time of his departure from his home, the bodhisattva was twenty-nine years old. After following the instructions of several teachers mentioned earlier, and after undergoing extreme ascetic practices, the bodhisattva obtained full enlightenment (*samyak-sambodhi*) under the bodhi tree at BODH GAYĀ.

MĀRA, the evil one, is said to have tried to prevent the Buddha from teaching his doctrine to humankind. But the Buddha had become invincible by the power of his perfections, and he successfully repelled Māra. From the moment the Buddha decided to teach the dharma, he was the *Samyaksambuddha,* the "Fully Enlightened Buddha" of the current world period.

The records of the Buddha's first sermon at Benares are certainly based on historical reminiscences. Some of the many events that are narrated in the various biographies of the Buddha do, in fact, have a historical background, especially those events that occurred during his period of teaching. However, all these stories were greatly exaggerated and many stories were invented in the later period. Among them, the JĀTAKA and AVADĀNA stories are important. These stories claim to be narratives of the Buddha's former existences, before he was reborn in his last existence. Such stories are already found in later parts of the canonical collections of Buddhist scriptures, but many new stories of this kind were invented up till the medieval period. Similarly, the Buddha's supernatural powers are also described in early canonical texts, but many additional supernatural faculties are described in later texts.

While some features are more or less common to all biographies of the Buddha, there are many differences in the details. Complete biographies of the Buddha seem to have been compiled no earlier than the second century C.E., as Étienne Lamotte points out in *Histoire du bouddhisme indien: Des origines à l'ère śaka* (pp. 725–736). The most famous biography of the Buddha is the BUDDHACARITA, which was composed by the poet AŚVAGHOṢA, a brahmin who was converted to Buddhism. This work was widely read in Buddhist countries and transcended sectarian doctrinal differences. A Buddha biography from the *Mūlasarvāstivāda* tradition, probably the most widespread of the so-called schools (*nikāya*) of Buddhism in medieval India, has come down to us in a Tibetan translation. This text was translated into English by W. W. Rockhill in 1884. Another famous biography of the Buddha composed in mainland India is the LALITAVISTARA. It professes to be a work of the Sarvāstivāda school of HĪNAYĀNA Buddhism, but in fact shows strong influence of early MAHĀYĀNA Buddhism. This is also true of the MAHĀVASTU which, though a work of the MAHĀSĀṂGHIKA SCHOOL of mainstream Buddhism, shows many characteristics of "Mahāyāna-in-the-making" or "semi-Mahāyāna." Several other Indian texts of this genre have survived in Chinese translations only.

The Theravāda tradition of Buddhism includes short biographies of the Buddha in late canonical texts that may have been composed in India and brought to the Island of Sri Lanka in the first or second century C.E., at the latest. The earliest available comprehensive biography of the Buddha in this tradition, however, is the *Jātakanidāna* (ca. fifth or sixth century C.E.). It forms the introduction of the commentary on the *jātaka* stories. Descriptions of the life of the Buddha in East Asian and in Central Asian traditions are greatly influenced by the legendary accounts as handed down in the later Indian tradition because they are largely based on translations of Sanskrit texts composed in mainland India.

Buddhas of earlier ages

As mentioned earlier, a buddha is not a unique being; there were and will be buddhas in the past and in the future. However, there is only one buddha in the world at any time. The texts describe the biographies of many buddhas who lived in earlier periods. The mythical biographies of six buddhas of antiquity are described in a sermon preached by the historical Buddha. This sermon is found in all parallel versions of the early *Mahāvadāna-sūtra* (Pāli, *Mahāpadāna-suttanta*). Later Mahāyāna texts and Theravāda literature have increased the number of buddhas of antiquity more and more.

The cult of the relics of the Buddha

When the historical Buddha passed away, his funeral rites were performed in accordance with traditional practice. The cremation was carried out by the Mallas, who lived in Kuśinagara. The bones left after the cremation were divided because King Ajātaśatru and other influential personalities claimed a share of the relics. The relics were enshrined in several STŪPAS, and soon the cult of stūpas developed into an important feature of Buddhism. It is believed that relics of the Buddha were later further divided and distributed to many sacred places. Besides the corporeal relics, material objects used by the Buddha, including his alms bowl, were venerated as relics and deposited in stūpas.

Buddhas of the future

Though the dharma as taught by the Buddha is eternal and immutable, the tradition of the dharma and the process by which it was handed down in the world is subject to the universal law of impermanence. After a certain period, the dharma will disappear from this world, and it will not be known until it is rediscovered by the next buddha. Thus, to be a buddha is not only a personal quality of a particular being, but rather a task to be fulfilled by any bodhisattva in one of the innumerable kalpas. As with the buddhas of the past, there are similarities in the various biographies of the buddhas who are expected to appear in future ages. These biographies are largely modeled on the main features of the life and legend of the historical Buddha. The next Buddha to appear in the world is MAITREYA. Throughout the centuries, many texts dealing with prophecies concerning the coming of Maitreya were composed.

Types of Buddhas

The historical Buddha, the founder of the Buddhist religious tradition, was a *samyaksambuddha* (Pāli, *sammāsambuddha*); that is, he has reached NIRVĀṆA by his own efforts without receiving instruction from anyone else. The Buddha was fully enlightened and thus was able to preach the dharma to others. There is another type of buddha: the PRATYEKABUDDHA (Pāli, *paccekabuddha*), who obtains nirvāṇa by his own efforts but is not able to teach the way to salvation to other beings.

In the Mahāyāna tradition, buddhas are supernatural beings who have descended to the human world out of compassion. There are several classes of transcendental buddhas and transcendental bodhisattvas. They are brought into relation with particular buddha fields (*buddhakṣetra*), which they are supposed to rule. These buddhas and bodhisattvas (e.g., AKṢOBHYA, AMITĀBHA or Amitāyus, Avalokiteśvara, Bhaiṣajyaguru, Mañjuśrī, etc.) became the main object of veneration in Mahāyāna Buddhism. In the later development of Mahāyāna, the concept of *Ādi-buddha,* representing ultimate reality, was developed. It is to be found particularly in the texts of the KĀLACAKRA system.

Epithets of the Buddha

Buddhist literature offers several synonyms for the term *buddha,* as well as epithets mainly or exclusively used to refer to buddhas. An ancient term for a buddha is TATHĀGATA (thus come/gone one). As R. O. Franke pointed out, this term refers to an old messianic expectation that an enlightened being would appear in this world (pp. xiv–xxix). Some epithets relate to particular qualities of buddhas, such as *samyaksambuddha* (a perfect enlightened one); other terms relate to the buddhas' intellectual or moral qualities, for example *sarvajña* (omniscient). The most famous list of epithets for the Buddha is found in the ancient sūtras announcing the coming of a *tathāgata.* The epithets listed there are *bhagavat* (elevated), arhat (holy), *samyaksambuddha* (fully enlightened), *vidyācaraṇasaṃpanna* (endowed with knowledge and good moral conduct), *sugata* (who has gone the right way), *lokavid* (who knows the world), *anuttara* (who cannot be surpassed), *puruṣadamyasārathi* (the charioteer of men that need to be tamed), and *śāstā devamanuṣyānām* (the teacher of gods and men). The *Mahāvyutpatti,* a classical Buddhist lexicographical work, lists as many as eighty epithets for the Buddha.

See also: **Buddha, Life of the, in Art; Pāramitā (Perfection)**

Bibliography

Bareau, André. *Recherches sur la biographie du Buddha,* 3 vols. Paris: Presses de l'École Française d'Extrême-Orient, 1971–1995.

Bechert, Heinz, ed. *Die Sprache der ältesten buddhistischen Überlieferung: The Language of the Earliest Buddhist Tradition.* Göttingen, Germany: Vandenhoeck and Ruprecht, 1980.

Bechert, Heinz, ed. *The Dating of the Historical Buddha.* Vols. 1–3. Göttingen, Germany: Vandenhoeck and Ruprecht, 1991–1997.

Carrithers, Michael. *The Buddha,* 12th edition. Oxford: Oxford University Press, 1996.

Dutoit, Julius. *Die duṣkaracaryā des Bodhisattva in der buddhistischen Tradition.* Strassburg, Germany: Trübner, 1905.

Ebert, Jorinda. *Parinirvāṇa: Untersuchungen zur ikonographischen Entwicklung von den Anfängen bis nach China.* Wiesbaden, Germany: Steiner, 1985.

Edwardes, Michael. *A Life of the Buddha, from a Burmese Manuscript.* London: Folio Society, 1959.

Foucaux, P. E., trans. *Le Lalitavistara,* 2 vols. Paris: Musée Guimet, 1884–1892.

Foucher, A. *La vie du Bouddha d'après les textes et les monuments de l'Inde.* Paris: Maisonneuve, 1949. Available in English as *The Life of the Buddha According to the Ancient Texts and Monuments of India,* tr. Simone Brangier Boas. Middletown, CT: Wesleyan University Press, 1963.

Franke, R. O. *Dīghanikāya: Das Buch der langen Texte des buddhistischen Kanons.* Göttingen, Germany: Vandenhoeck and Ruprecht, 1913.

Frauwallner, Erich. "The Historical Data We Possess on the Person and Doctrine of the Buddha." *East and West* 7 (1956): 309–312. Reprinted in Frauwallner, Erich. *Kleine Schriften,* ed. G. Oberhammer and E. Steinkellner. Wiesbaden, Germany: Steiner, 1982.

Hirakawa, Akira. *A History of Indian Buddhism*, tr. Paul Groner. Honolulu: University of Hawaii Press, 1990.

Johnston, E. H., ed. and trans. [Aśvaghoṣa]. *The Buddhacarita or Acts of the Buddha*, 2 vols. Lahore: University of the Panjab, 1935–1936. Reprint in 1 vol., Delhi: Motilal Barnassidass, 1972.

Jones, J. J., trans. *The Mahāvastu*, 3 vols. London: Luzac, 1949–1956.

Klimkeit, Hans-Joachim. *Der Buddha: Leben und Lehre*. Stuttgart: Kohlhammer, 1990.

Krom, Nicolaas Johannes, ed. *The Life of Buddha on the Stūpa of Barabudur According to the Lalitavistara Text*. The Hague, Netherlands: Nijhoff, 1926.

Lamotte, Étienne. "The Buddha, His Teachings, and His Sangha." In *The World of Buddhism: Buddhist Monks and Nuns in Society and Culture*, ed. Heinz Bechert and Richard Gombrich. London: Thames and Hudson, 1984.

Lamotte, Étienne. *Histoire du bouddhisme indien: Des origines à l'ère śaka*. Louvain, Belgium: Publications Universitaires, 1958. Available in English as *History of Indian Buddhism: From the Origins to the Saka Era*, tr. Sara Webb-Boin. Louvain-la-Neuve, Belgium: Institut Orientaliste, 1988.

Mukherjee, Biswadeb. *Die Überlieferung von Devadatta, dem Widersacher des Buddha in den kanonischen Schriften*. München: Kitzinger, 1966.

Nakamura, Hajime. *Gotama Buddha*. Los Angeles and Tokyo: Buddhist Books International, 1977.

Nakamura, Hajime. *Indian Buddhism: A Survey with Bibliographical Notes*. Tokyo: Kansai University, 1980.

Ñāṇamoli, Bhikkhu, ed. and trans. *The Life of the Buddha, as It Appears in the Pali Canon*. Kandy, Sri Lanka: Buddhist Publication Society, 1972.

Narada Maha Thera. *The Buddha and His Teachings*, 2nd edition. Singapore: Stamford Press, n.d.

Oldenberg, Hermann. *Buddha: Sein Leben, Seine Lehre, Seine Gemeinde*, 13th edition. Stuttgart: Cotta, 1959. Available in English as *Buddha: His Life, His Doctrine, His Order*, tr. William Hoey. Delhi: Indological Book House, 1971.

Rockhill, William Woodville. *The Life of the Buddha and the Early History of His Order, Derived from Tibetan Works*. London: Kegan Paul, 1884.

Saddhatissa, Hammalawa. *The Life of the Buddha*. London: Allen and Unwin, 1976.

Schumann, Hans Wolfgang. *Der historische Buddha*. Köln, Germany: Diederichs, 1982.

Silva-Vigier, Anil de. *The Life of the Buddha Retold from Ancient Sources: Illustrated with 160 Works of Asian Art*. London: Phaidon, 1955.

Snellgrove, David L. *The Image of the Buddha*. New Delhi: Vikas/UNESCO, 1978.

Thomas, Edward J. *The Life of Buddha as Legend and History*, 6th edition. London: Routledge and Kegan Paul, 1960.

Waldschmidt, Ernst. *Die Überlieferung vom Lebensende des Buddha: Eine vergleichende Analyse des Mahāparinirvāṇasūtra und seiner Textentsprechungen*, 2 vols. Göttingen, Germany: Vandenhoeck and Ruprecht, 1944–1948.

Waldschmidt, Ernst. *Die Legende vom Leben des Buddha*. Berlin: Wegweiser, 1929. Reprint, Graz, Austria: Verlag für Sammler, 1982.

Wieger, Léon. *Bouddhisme chinois*. Vol. 2: *Les vies chinoises du Buddha*. Paris: Cathasia, 1913.

Windisch, Ernst. *Māra und Buddha*. Leipzig, Germany: Hirzel, 1895.

Zafiropulo, Ghiorgo. *L'illumination du Buddha: Essais de chronologie relative et de stratigraphie textuelle*. Innsbruck, Austria: Institut für Sprachwissenschaft, 1993.

HEINZ BECHERT

BUDDHA, LIFE OF THE, IN ART

Because no single account of the Buddha's life survives, many Indian texts, most notably the LALITAVISTARA and the BUDDHACARITA, have been used to inspire artists seeking to represent important events from the Buddha's biography. Narrations were also composed in China and ancient Tibet. The number of events that are codified as important varies from four to 108. Events that could be associated with particular sites in northeast India usually formed the core of the lists; for example, the Buddha's birth in Lumbinī, his enlightenment in BODH GAYĀ, his first sermon in Sārnāth, and his death in Kuśinagara. The Buddha's previous lives are extensively presented as instructive examples or parables, so the JĀTAKAS (birth stories) also inspired countless artworks portraying the "life" of the Buddha. Different Buddhist traditions and different countries chose from among these stories the ones that spoke to their particular needs. The life of the Buddha as narrated in art also became a model for characterizing the lives of other Buddhist teachers and deities. The transcendent buddhas of the MAHĀYĀNA and VAJRAYĀNA traditions, for example, are characterized as concrete manifestations of Śākyamuni by depicting them with attributes and gestures linked to particular events in the Buddha's life.

It can be argued that since texts refer to the Buddha's life to teach particular doctrines, they put their own spin on the events. The same could be said about the visual arts because choices must be made about

A representation of the birth of the Buddha. (From a painting at Yongjusa in Suwŏn, South Korea.) © Leonard de Selva/Corbis. Reproduced by permission.

which events to emphasize and how to interpret their meaning. However, the visual images that are used by all schools and regions to narrate the Buddha's life seem to provide a more resonant level of clarity to the Buddha's teachings than could be achieved with texts alone.

From the dream of Queen Māyā to the great renunciation

The Buddha's mother, Queen Māyā (sometimes Mahāmāyā, "Great Illusion"), dreamt that a silvery-white elephant, holding a white lotus flower in its trunk, entered her right side. Brahmanic priests asked to interpret the dream foretold the birth of a son who would become either a great monarch or a sage. This miracle is portrayed only on early Indian STŪPA reliefs in which Māyā reclines with a small elephant floating above her. The symbolism of the elephant probably resonated with early patrons as the pan-Indian symbol of supreme royalty and of the life-giving rain from thunderclouds.

Māyā gave birth to the future Buddha at Lumbinī, a village in southern Nepal. She entered a grove of trees, reached up to grasp a branch, and the prince emerged from her right side. This miraculous birth is often depicted on aniconic reliefs that include no image of the baby. Māyā is shown as a nearly nude Indian fertility spirit called a *śālabhañjikā*, a *yakṣī* who stands in a dance posture holding the branch of a tree. Beginning in the second century C.E. in the Gandhāra region in present-day Pakistan, a tiny child is shown emerging from her side. In artworks from China and Japan, Māyā is shown as a fully clothed dancer with a baby diving out of her long right sleeve.

The Buddha cuts his hair as he renounces the world. (Tibetan painting, eighteenth century.) The Art Archive/Musée Guimet Paris/Dagli Orti (A). Reproduced by permission.

After the child is born, he is bathed by two streams of water. In Indian depictions, the water comes either from jars held by gods or from the trunks of elephants. In Southeast Asia, the water flows from the mouths of mythical serpents called nāgas. In the Himalayas and East Asia, dragons take over this role. The art of each region uses whichever local creature represents the power of water to confer royal status (the abhiṣeka ritual) and to purify. In Japan there is an annual lustration ceremony of the baby Buddha called Kanbutsu.

The Buddha's life as the prince Siddhārtha Gautama is depicted as one of sheltered dalliance and a time of training in the skills needed to rule a kingdom. When he was about twenty-nine years old, after he has had a son appropriately named Rāhula (fetter), Siddhārtha is motivated to leave the palace to seek an understanding of the suffering he sees in the world. This event, which is frequently depicted in the art of South and Southeast Asia, is called the "great renunciation" because it represents the enormous sacrifice of his princely lifestyle. Siddhārtha rides out on a horse whose hooves are supported by demigods (YAKṢAS) so that the horse makes no noise to wake Siddhārtha's family. In aniconic representations the horse has no rider, but a parasol above the horse indicates Siddhārtha's presence. In South and Southeast Asia the fact that the Buddha was born to be a prince and renounced this privileged life is of great importance because by this act he denied both caste and royal obligations, and affirmed the value of seeking enlightenment.

From the search for truth to enlightenment

Siddhārtha practiced yogic austerities almost to the point of death in his supreme effort to gain higher states of consciousness. Artists in the Gandhāra region sculpted an image of this emaciated figure in what would be called today a superrealistic style. Every bone, vein, and hollowed surface of his body is shown in glaring detail. The CHAN SCHOOL of East Asia also celebrates this stage of the Buddha's life in paintings of a scruffy figure emerging from the mountains and in sculptures of an emaciated, bearded figure in deep thought, although not in a traditional meditation posture. The THERAVĀDA and Chan view of the Buddha's life honors the extremes in his search for truth as he pushed his body and mind to their farthest limits.

When starvation did not reveal the truth to Siddhārtha, he took nourishment offered by a girl named Sujātā—an event sometimes shown in Indian reliefs and Southeast Asian paintings, and he vowed to sit beneath a fig tree in meditation until he became enlightened. Images of the Buddha Śākyamuni seated in a meditation posture, which appear throughout Buddhist Asia, refer to this vow.

While meditating beneath the bodhi tree, the name it acquired after his enlightenment, Siddhārtha was assaulted by MĀRA, the Buddhist god of death and desire. Called the Māravijaya, or conquest of Māra, this event is a common subject of sculptures and paintings in all parts of Buddhist Asia. Māra, often riding an elephant, leads both his armies of demons and his beautiful daughters in an effort to distract Siddhārtha from his vow. The Buddha is often shown seated in meditation in the midst of these figures with his right hand reaching down to touch the earth (*bhūmisparśamudrā*) as he asks the earth to bear witness to his perfection and utter commitment to becoming a buddha, an awakened or enlightened one immune to death or desire. Māra is thus defeated. The earth-touching gesture alone also refers to the defeat of Māra and signifies the moment when Siddhārtha Gautama becomes the Buddha. On aniconic monuments, the Buddha's

Buddha Śākyamuni and Scenes from the Life of Buddha, copper sculpture with traces of gilding, Nepal, twelfth century. Los Angeles County Museum of Art, Gift of Mr. and Mrs. Michael Phillips. Reproduced by permission. The center of this image shows the Buddha in the *bhūmisparśa-mudrā* at the moment of his enlightenment beneath the bodhi tree. Beginning below the Buddha's left knee, counterclockwise, the events represented are: birth and first seven steps at Lumbinī; miracle at Sankisya; first sermon at Sārnāth; monkey offering honey; the Buddha's *parinirvāṇa* surrounded by disciples; Buddha preaching to his mother; miracle at Śrāvastī; taming the mad elephant; and the emaciated Buddha during his search for truth.

enlightenment is represented by an empty seat beneath a tree.

After the Buddha was enlightened, he remained in meditation for seven weeks. During this time a torrential rain occurred and the serpent king (*nāgarāja*) named Mucalinda protected the Buddha from the storm by lifting him above the waters and spreading his seven hoods out over the Buddha's head. Images of this event are common in Cambodia where the nāga is especially revered and seen to be the protector of the Cambodian king. During the Khmer empire in the early thirteenth century, a cult was introduced around this image, possibly to honor King Jayavarman VII (r. ca. 1181–1219) as both a living buddha and as the protector of his kingdom. After this king's reign ended, there was an iconoclastic reaction in Cambodia to Jayavarman's use of the images to have himself worshiped as a god.

From the first sermon to the *parinirvāṇa*

The Buddha delivered his first sermon at the Deer Park in Sārnāth. Images showing him with the "turning the Wheel of the Dharma" gesture (*dharmacakra-mudrā*) refer to this event. The importance of this gesture is that the Buddha is setting in motion the FOUR NOBLE TRUTHS and revealing the middle path by which anyone can transcend the sufferings of living in the world. This image further represents all of the Buddha's teachings as expounded by the various miracles and doctrines, and is therefore used in art throughout Asia. A wheel alone can also symbolize the *dharmacakra* and the first sermon, especially if it is surrounded by two deer to indicate the context of the teaching. This symbol is commonly sculpted on Mahāyāna and Vajrayāna monasteries or temples, as well as on early aniconic monuments.

The Buddha taught and performed miracles for more than forty years after his enlightenment. Any standing Buddha image, often displaying the protection (*abhaya*) and giving (*varada*) gestures, can be viewed as representing this stage in Śākyamuni's life. The walking Buddha image in Thailand represents the impact of this part of the Buddha's life especially well. The aniconic version of the Buddha's ministry is equally eloquent: footprints to represent the Buddha's continued presence in this world. The great miracle at Śrāvastī, when the Buddha multiplied himself before a congregation to demonstrate that his potential exists everywhere, is a frequent subject in South Asian and Chinese arts, especially in painting, where it may simply be shown as a whole mural of identical buddhas.

When he was approaching nearly eighty years old, the Buddha Śākyamuni traveled to a city called Kuśinagara and died. In the texts this event is called his *parinirvāṇa,* the Buddha's complete or final achievement of NIRVĀṆA. The primary symbol of the Buddha's *parinirvāṇa* is the STŪPA, the commemorative monument to his death; as the stūpa form evolved into the *mchod rten* (*chorten*), *dagoba,* and the pagoda, it retained this symbolism. Images of the Buddha's *parinirvāṇa* show him reclining on his right side with his head resting on his right hand. Depictions of this "posture" vary in size, from tiny to colossal: Huge sculptures of the *parinirvāṇa* can be found in India, Sri Lanka, and many sites in East and Southeast Asia. A colossal image was erected at the archaeological site of ancient Kuśinagara in the twentieth century. The meaning of the stūpa and the reclining Buddha encompasses the promise that any human being can achieve nirvāṇa like the Buddha if they follow his last teaching: "work toward enlightenment with diligence."

See also: **Buddha, Life of the; Central Asia, Buddhist Art in; China, Buddhist Art in; Dunhuang; India, Buddhist Art in; Indonesia, Buddhist Art in; Jātaka, Illustrations of; Mudrā and Visual Imagery; Sāñcī; Southeast Asia, Buddhist Art in; Sri Lanka, Buddhist Art in; Theravāda Art and Architecture**

Bibliography

Cummings, Mary. *The Lives of the Buddha in the Art and Literature of Asia.* Ann Arbor: University of Michigan Press, 1982.

Dehejia, Vidya. "On Modes of Visual Narration in Early Buddhist Art." *Art Bulletin* 71 (1990): 374–392.

Dehejia, Vidya. "Aniconism and the Multivalence of Emblems." *Ars Orientalis* 21 (1991): 45–66.

Dehejia, Vidya. *Discourse in Early Buddhist Art: Visual Narratives of India.* New Delhi: Munshiram Manoharlal, 1997.

Ghose, Rajeshwari, ed. *In the Footsteps of the Buddha: An Iconic Journey from India to China* (exhibition catalogue). Hong Kong: University Museum and Art Gallery, University of Hong Kong, 1998.

Huntington, Susan L. "Early Buddhist Art and the Theory of Aniconism." *Art Journal* 49, no. 4 (1990): 401–408.

Huntington, Susan L. "Aniconism and the Multivalence of Emblems." *Ars Orientalis* 22 (1992): 111–156.

Karetzky, Patricia E. *Early Buddhist Narrative Art: Illustrations of the Life of the Buddha from Central Asia to China, Korea and Japan.* Lanham, MD: University Press of America, 2000.

Pal, Pratapaditya. *Light of Asia: Buddha Śākyamuni in Asian Art.* Seattle and London: University of Washington Press, 1984.

GAIL MAXWELL

BUDDHA-NATURE. *See* Tathāgatagarbha

BUDDHĀNUSMṚTI (RECOLLECTION OF THE BUDDHA)

Buddhānusmṛti (recollection of the Buddha) is the first of a set of up to ten *anusmṛtis* (acts of recollection or calling to mind) that are used for both meditative and liturgical purposes. The full set of ten *anusmṛtis* comprises Buddha, dharma, saṅgha, morality, liberality, deities, respiration, death, parts of the body, and peace. Buddhist practitioners focus their minds on these subjects by reciting a set text or formula listing their salient qualities. The recollection of the Buddha was the most important *anusmṛti,* eventually becoming an independent practice.

Initially the relevant formula comprised the so-called ten epithets or titles of the Buddha, in that practitioners were instructed to recall that the Buddha was indeed worthy, correctly and fully awakened, perfected in knowledge and conduct, blessed, knower of the world, supreme, trainer of humans amenable to training, teacher of gods and humankind, Buddha, and lord. This credal rehearsal of the Buddha's qualities was held by authorities like BUDDHAGHOSA (fifth century C.E.) to purify the mind of defilements and prepare it for advanced meditation. However, other benefits were also ascribed to the practice, so that *buddhānusmṛti* was, for example, thought useful for apotropaic purposes, for warding off fear and danger, as well as for generating merit.

At some stage *buddhānusmṛti* was augmented to include the calling to mind not only of the Buddha's virtues but also his physical appearance. Iconography probably influenced this process, which by the second century C.E. had given rise to the Mahāyānist *pratyutpannasamādhi,* a full-fledged visualization of the spiritual and physical qualities of any buddha of the present age, not just Gautama. This meditation incorporated the earlier form of *buddhānusmṛti,* whose text remained the nucleus of the mental operations required, even though its recitation was eventually shortened to the invocation of the buddha's name. In Chinese Buddhism, consequently, *buddhānusmṛti* is known as *nianfo,* in which the element *nian* refers both to thinking about the buddha (*fo*) and reciting him, or rather his name. *Nianfo* came primarily to refer to invocation of the name of AMITĀBHA, on account of the importance of that buddha's cult in East Asia. The words *Namu amituo fo* (hail to the Buddha Amitābha) have accordingly become a prime liturgical and ritual formula for Chinese Buddhists, who have used them in communal worship, in personal devotions, even as a Buddhist greeting when answering the telephone. Similar developments have occurred in Korea and Japan. Even Buddhists who are not devotees of Amitābha have been deeply influenced by this practice, one example of this being the invocation of the DAIMOKU, or the sacred title of the LOTUS SŪTRA (SADDHARMAPUṆḌARĪKA-SŪTRA), by followers of the NICHIREN SCHOOL.

The persistence of *buddhānusmṛti* and its derivatives testifies to the central importance in Buddhism of the relationship between those who seek salvation and the awakened teacher who shows them the PATH, and it reflects the belief that focusing the mind on the qualities of the awakened one helps aspirants to liberation move closer toward realizing those qualities themselves. The latter notion is explicitly developed in MAHĀYĀNA Buddhism, and even more so in VAJRAYĀNA, where it informs the tantric practice of "deity yoga."

See also: **Buddha(s); Chanting and Liturgy; Nenbutsu (Chinese, Nianfo; Korean, Yŏmbul)**

Bibliography

Conze, Edward. *Buddhist Meditation.* Allen and Unwin: London, 1956.

Harrison, Paul. "Commemoration and Identification in Buddhanusmrti." In *In the Mirror of Memory: Reflections on Mindfulness and Remembrance in Indian and Tibetan Buddhism,* ed. Janet Gyatso. Albany: State University of New York Press, 1992.

PAUL HARRISON

BUDDHAVACANA (WORD OF THE BUDDHA)

The term *buddhavacana* (word of the Buddha) is the designation used by Buddhists to describe the contents of the Buddhist CANON, the Tripiṭaka. By designating the Tripiṭaka the "word of the Buddha," Buddhism identifies its scriptures with the dharma of the Buddha and thereby makes an important claim about the authority and authenticity of the canon. While employing this term to support the authority of the scriptures, however, Buddhists have explained the meaning of *buddhavacana* in two different ways. One explanation holds that the Tripiṭaka is literally the word of the Buddha, spoken by him and committed to memory by his immediate disciples at the First Council just after his death. This literal interpretation maintains that the Tripiṭaka contains all the teachings that the Buddha gave from his first words after his enlightenment to his last teachings before his *parinirvāṇa*.

Another explanation, however, suggests a more liberal interpretation of the meaning of the "word of the Buddha." The roots of this interpretation go back to the *Mahāpadesa-sutta* of the Pāli canon (*Dīghanikāya*, 123f.), which sets out a procedure and criteria for determining which teachings should be accepted as the "word of the Buddha." This sūtra explains that if one receives a teaching from a variety of sources, including the Buddha, a SAṄGHA gathering, or a wise teacher, then one should test it by comparing it with an established core of teachings (*sutta* and vinaya). If the teaching in question proves consistent with the authoritative core of teachings then it can be declared to be the "word of the Buddha." This second explanation makes the wisdom of the Buddha, rather than the historical career of the Buddha, the basis for the authority of the canon.

See also: **Councils, Buddhist; Hermeneutics; Scripture**

Bibliography

Bond, George D. *The Word of the Buddha: The Tipiṭaka and Its Interpretation in Theravada Buddhism.* Colombo, Sri Lanka: Gunasena, 1982.

Lamotte, Étienne. "La critique d'authenticite dans le bouddhisme." *India Antique* (1947): 216–232. Leyden, Netherlands: Brill, 1947. English translation by Sara Boin-Webb, "The Assessment of Textual Authenticity in Buddhism." *Buddhist Studies Review* 1, no. 1 (1983): 4–15.

GEORGE D. BOND

BUDDHIST STUDIES

Buddhist studies as an umbrella term for the disinterested or nonapologetic inquiry into any aspect of Buddhism or Buddhist traditions generally refers to the modern, academic study of Buddhism in all forms. This approach became possible only with the development in post-Enlightenment Europe of the notion of a comparative study of religions; as a product of this tradition, Buddhist studies has always assumed an outsider's perspective, even when the scholars carrying out such studies are themselves Buddhists. The field is therefore an inherently etic, rather than emic, enterprise. This is what separates Buddhist studies, also sometimes referred to as *Buddhology*, from the practice of Buddhism, or from what some today call *Buddhist theology*.

Major trends

Several major trends may be noticed in the modern study of Buddhism, among which is a tendency to emphasize scriptures, doctrine, and history, with relatively less attention devoted to areas such as RITUAL and material culture. These trends may be attributed to a combination of individual and social-historical factors. Until recently most Westerners who studied Buddhism were first trained in the Western classics, and many were Christian missionaries, or at least deeply familiar with Christian history and thought. Thus, their attempts to locate in Buddhism features parallel to those they recognized in Christianity led them to concentrate their attentions in particular directions. The geographical regions of Buddhism that have received scholarly attention may also be closely mapped against political history: Colonialism and other aspects of Western expansion into Asia, including missionary activity, account for English scholarly interest in India and Ceylon, French interest in Southeast Asia, and German and Russian interest in Central Asia, and therefore for the comparative emphasis placed on those regions by scholars from those countries. Likewise, Japanese interest in Chinese Buddhism may be correlated not only to geographic proximity and to the fact that Japanese Buddhism traces its roots directly to China, but also to the period of Japanese military occupation of China before and during World War II, although these same factors apply in the case of Korea, which has nevertheless received considerably less Japanese scholarly attention.

In this light, it is no surprise that, for example, serious studies of Japanese Buddhism by Western scholars were a rarity until the post–World War II era, since the country itself was for most intents and purposes inaccessible to outsiders. Likewise, the tremendous flowering of studies of Tibetan Buddhism since the early 1960s is a direct result of the Chinese invasion of Tibet in 1950, and the subsequent escape to India and beyond of the DALAI LAMA and tens of thousands of other refugees in 1959, thus bringing the literary and living resources of the Tibetan Buddhist tradition into significant contact with outsiders for the first time. Among the most pronounced recent trends in contemporary Buddhist studies is a reduced emphasis on philological or textual studies and a greater stress directed toward cultural or theory-oriented work.

Traditional approaches

Of course, Buddhists and non-Buddhists alike have examined and reflected upon the tradition from a variety of perspectives from a very early period. Traditional Buddhist histories attest to a long-standing and keen interest by Buddhists in their own history: Such histories include the Ceylonese *Dīpavaṃsa* (*Chronicle of the Island*) and *Mahāvaṃsa* (*Great Chronicle*) and other histories in Pāli; similar Southeast Asian works, often in vernacular languages; Tibetan works, including the famous histories (*Chos 'byung*) of BU STON and Tāranātha, as well as many other, often local, histories; and numerous Chinese, Korean, and Japanese works. While such histories tend to concern themselves with such matters as the relations between the Buddhist monastic communities and political rulers, a different although sometimes related genre of literature, the doxography or classification of tenets, attempts instead to provide a "history" of Buddhist doctrine. Perhaps the oldest clear example of such a text is Bhāvaviveka's *Tarkajvālā* (*Blaze of Reasoning*), but the genre reaches its full glory in the Tibetan *grub mtha'* and Chinese *panjiao* doxographical literatures. Such texts, however useful, are not histories as such, since their views on the developments of thought or what we would call intellectual history are polemical and not chronological; nor are they disinterested catalogues of doctrines or teachings, since they invariably seek to establish the ultimate primacy of the positions held by their authors. From the non-Buddhist perspective, texts such as Arabic "universal histories" and the accounts of early Christian missionaries have also noticed and described Buddhism since medieval times.

Most scholars of Buddhism concentrate on the study of Buddhism in one particular cultural area, be it India, China, Tibet, or the like. There are good reasons why this is so. Since Buddhism is so fully integrated into the cultural matrix of every land in which it is found, to study the Buddhism of a certain region requires not only a command of the relevant language or languages of a culture area, but also a knowledge of its history, literature, and so on. Although less common today, when many Buddhist scholars consider themselves first and foremost students of Buddhism, in earlier generations those who studied Indian Buddhism were primarily Indologists, as those who studied Chinese Buddhism were Sinologists. While familiarity with the wide range of cultural facts about India and China, respectively, allowed such scholars to approach Buddhism within its cultural context, there is also much to be learned by examining Buddhism across cultural boundaries, laying emphasis upon its translocal unity rather than on, or in addition to, its local particularity. The latter approach tends to locate the study of Buddhism nearer to religious studies, the history of religions, or comparative religion than it does to area studies.

To a great extent, modern Buddhist studies has emphasized the investigation of ancient texts and their doctrinal contents, with significantly less effort having been put into tracing the place of Buddhism within its broader social context, or into observation of the activities of contemporary Buddhists. The latter lack of emphasis may be seen even in the case of scholars who reside for long periods in Buddhist environments. Thus the great Hungarian scholar Alexander Csoma de Kőrös (1784–1842), who spent several years of intense study in Tibet, produced a number of extremely valuable studies concerning the mountain of Buddhist literature that he read there, but he recorded virtually nothing of what he must have observed of Buddhist monastic or lay life. This is an imbalance that still remains to be redressed sufficiently.

Focus on India

Until recently, India, the land of Buddhism's birth, was the prime focus of the majority of scholarly attention paid to Buddhism. This tendency may be attributed directly to the widespread idea that the essence of a tradition is to be discovered in its origins, with subsequent developments demonstrating little more than the decay of a once pristine core. This idea in turn is fundamentally based on the evangelical Protestant anti-Catholicism of the nineteenth century, as can be seen clearly, for instance, in the case of the great pioneer of Indian and Buddhist studies, F. Max Müller (1823–1900). This Protestant view may also be seen in the priority given to studies of the earliest Buddhist scriptures. It can hardly be a coincidence that so many of those European scholars who first began to pay attention to the later, especially philosophical, literature of Buddhism were Belgian and French Catholics, rather than English or German Protestants. Japanese scholars, for different historical reasons, were traditionally more concerned with aspects of the later phases of Buddhism, until influenced by Protestant agendas beginning in the late 1800s. In particular, the significant attention they and other scholars from traditionally Buddhist cultures have given to doctrine may be explained at least in part as a result of their research having evolved from a fusion of traditional sectarian scholarship with modern Western-influenced methodologies.

The rigorous study of Indian Buddhism began with the investigation of its literature in Pāli and Sanskrit. Among the most important early publications on Pāli were Viggo Fausbøll's 1855 edition of the DHAMMAPADA (*Words of the Doctrine*) and from 1877 the JĀTAKA (*Birth Stories of the Buddha*), and Robert Caesar Childer's 1875 *A Dictionary of the Pāli Language.* The accessibility of these texts tended to significantly influence the ways in which the most ancient Buddhist tradition was imaginatively reconstructed, and still does even today. In 1881 T. W. Rhys Davids (1843–1922) founded the Pāli Text Society in London, and it is to this society that we owe almost all publications of Pāli literature in the West, and most of the published translations of that literature. Recognition must also be given to the philological contributions of Danish scholars, chief among them the massive project of the *Critical Pāli Dictionary* begun in 1924 and ongoing.

Given its historically heavy bias toward textuality, among the most significant landmarks in the history of Buddhist studies must be counted the editions and translations of Buddhist scriptures and related materials. The publication in Japan between 1924 and 1935 of the Taishō edition of the Chinese Buddhist CANON marks a watershed. For the first time, scholars attempted to apply notions of textual criticism to the vast corpus of Chinese Buddhist canonical literature, and to organize its presentation in a scientific fashion; this edition is the standard one in use today. Likewise, the Japanese photo-reprint edition of a complete Tibetan Buddhist canon (the Peking Bka' 'gyur [Kanjur] and Bstan 'gyur [Tanjur]) in the early 1960s for the first time made these treasures widely available to scholars.

Owing to the disappearance of Buddhism from India in roughly the thirteenth century, none of what may have been the Sanskrit canonical collections of Buddhist literature has survived in its entirety, and its treatment has correspondingly been less systematic and comprehensive. The study of this literature began in 1837, when the British government resident in Nepal, Brian Houghton Hodgson (1800–1894), sent eighty-eight Buddhist Sanskrit manuscripts to Paris. These immediately came under the scrutiny of Eugène Burnouf (1801–1852), who in the fifty-one years of his life produced an astonishing body of work, the value of which persists to the present day. He was one of the first Europeans to study the Pāli language carefully, which prepared him well for his work on the Sanskrit materials. Burnouf's *Introduction à l'histoire du Buddhisme Indien* (1844) made extensive use of these texts, as did his copiously annotated translation of the LOTUS SŪTRA (SADDHARMAPUṆḌARĪKA-SŪTRA), published in 1852. These works, along with Hendrik Kern's history of Indian Buddhism (1882–1884) and Émile Senart's (1847–1928) study of the life of the Buddha (1873–1875), were among the first careful scientific investigations of Buddhism carried out on the basis of a good knowledge of relevant sources.

Burnouf, who was perhaps not incidentally Müller's teacher, may be seen as the father of a Franco-Belgian school of Buddhist scholarship, for just as the regions that were studied may be roughly mapped against a political background, so too may we notice national or regional traditions of scholarship on Buddhism. To this Franco-Belgian school belong, among others, the Indologists Léon Feer (1830–1902), Senart, Sylvain Lévi (1863–1935), Louis de la Vallée Poussin (1869–1938), Alfred Foucher (1865–1952), and Étienne Lamotte (1904–1983), as well as the Sinologists Edouard Chavannes (1865–1918), Paul Pelliot (1878–1945), and Paul Demiéville (1894–1979). Most of these individuals in fact contributed significantly to more than one field, while nevertheless standing firmly in the philological rather than the more recent cultural studies camp. Feer, for example, edited, translated, and studied texts in Pāli, Sanskrit, and Tibetan, as well as other languages, while Lévi contributed to Indian, Chinese, Tibetan, and Central Asian studies.

At almost the same time that Davids and Burnouf were engaged in their textual studies, archaeological investigations of Buddhist sites by Alexander Cunningham (1814–1893), James Burgess (1832–1917), and James Fergusson (1808–1886), among others, were being carried out across India. In the north in particular, efforts to trace the locations central to the Buddha's life were guided by the archaeologists' reading of the recently translated travel account of XUANZANG (ca. 600–664), a Chinese monk who visited India in the seventh century. This way of using non-Indian materials is typical: Until comparatively recently, texts in Chinese and Tibetan were studied much less for their own sake than for the light they might shine on India, and in fact the majority of texts in Chinese and Tibetan to which attention was been paid by scholars were translations into those languages of texts of Indian origin, rather than native works. It is only since the 1980s that significant interest has been directed both at indigenous works and at the ways in which translations work not as calques of foreign texts but as localized adaptations of those works.

Despite this archaeological research, strictly historical studies of Indian Buddhism have been significantly less common than doctrinal investigations, one exception being studies devoted to AŚOKA. From the time of James Prinsep's initial decipherment in 1834, the inscriptions of the emperor Aśoka have fascinated researchers. Subsequently, scholars such as Georg Bühler (1837–1898), J. F. Fleet (1847–1917), Sten Konow (1867–1948), and Heinrich Lüders (1869–1943) paid careful attention to these and other more strictly Buddhist Indian inscriptions, although it was not until quite recently that attempts have been made to comprehensively collect these materials. In a number of innovative studies since about 1975, Gregory Schopen has revived interest in these vital sources. Inscriptional studies of Southeast Asian sources were carried out mostly by French scholars, while it is to Japanese scholars that we owed most of our materials on Chinese Buddhist inscriptions until very recently, when Chinese scholars themselves have taken up the task of their collection and study.

In significant respects, the directions taken by Buddhist studies have been steered by chance factors. Early interest in Pāli scriptures was not due only to the idea that they reflect the oldest, and thus the most original and pure, state of Buddhism, or to the fact that by virtue of being written in an Indo-European language they seemed linguistically less foreign to Europeans than texts in Chinese or Tibetan. It was also essential that the texts themselves be physically accessible, something that was possible primarily due to the European colonial presence in Sri Lanka and Southeast Asia. Correspondingly, it was Hodgson's gifts to Burnouf, and the existence of other manuscript collections in European libraries, along with the fact that Müller was encouraged in this direction by his Japanese students, especially Takakusu Junjirō (1866–1945), that facilitated and inspired early studies of MAHĀYĀNA scriptures. The influences on research priorities, particularly of Japanese ways of understanding Buddhist traditions, deserve to be further investigated. Great assistance was rendered to the investigation of Indian Mahāyāna literature by Franklin Edgerton's publication in 1953 of a dictionary and grammar of Buddhist Sanskrit; its importance can be judged by the fact that the dictionary is used even by scholars of Japanese and Chinese Buddhism.

Occasional chance discoveries of manuscript materials have also had an important impact on research agendas. The so-called Gilgit manuscripts, discovered from a stūpa in what is now Pakistan and published by Nalinaksha Dutt between 1939 and 1959, the Sanskrit materials discovered largely by German expeditions in Central Asia (and published primarily in the series *Sanskrithandschriften aus den Tufanfunden*), and the DUNHUANG manuscripts, mostly in Chinese and Tibetan, kept centrally in London, Paris, and Beijing, along with more recent finds in Afghanistan and in Japanese monasteries, have permitted scholars to uncover aspects of Buddhist thought and practice that had remained entirely unknown, had become obscured in later traditions, or had even been intentionally suppressed. The Dunhuang collections in particular, along with the wall paintings adorning the caves at the site, have proven so important that an entire field of Dunhuang studies has sprung up around their investigation. In addition to the *Lotus Sūtra*, so imporant in East Asian Buddhism and the recipient of much scholarly attention since the days of Burnouf, the PRAJÑĀPĀRAMITĀ LITERATURE has also been much studied, most notably by Edward Conze (1904–1979).

Although Western philosophers and historians of philosophy have rarely shown interest in Buddhist thought, this is one of the most active areas in Buddhist studies. The foremost scholar of Indian Buddhist thought was without a doubt la Vallée Poussin, who, in addition to producing significant editions of Pāli texts, edited, translated, and studied Madhyamaka texts such as CANDRAKĪRTI's *Prasannapadā* (*Clear-Worded Commentary*) and *Madhyamakāvatāra* (*Introduction to the Madhyamaka*) and Prajñākaramati's *Bodhcaryāvatāra-pañjikā* (*Commentary on Śāntideva's Introduction to the Practice of the Bodhisattva*), and texts of the logicians such as DHARMAKĪRTI's *Nyāyabindu* (*Drop of Logic*). La Vallée Poussin also translated with copious annotation VASUBANDHU's ABHIDHARMAKOŚABHĀṢYA (*Treasury of Abhidharma*) and Xuanzang's Yogācāra compendium, the *Vijñaptimātratāsiddhi* (*Establishment of the Doctrine of Mere Cognition*). In this way he almost single-handedly provided the basis for much of the subsequent study of Buddhist thought. Others who contributed importantly to this project include Lévi, who published a number of important Sanskrit texts, including some central to the YOGĀCĀRA SCHOOL, his Japanese student Susumu Yamaguchi (1895–1976), Gadjin Nagao, and Lamotte. Philosophical investigations of the Yogācāra and Madhyamaka traditions continue to occupy many scholars, among whom D. S.

Ruegg and Lambert Schmidthausen have produced outstanding work. Considerable attention has also been given to the later Indian logical tradition since the days of Theodore Stcherbatsky (1866–1942) in the pre–World War II period. Thanks to the efforts of Erich Frauwallner (1898–1974), especially in the decade after the war, Vienna became the center of such studies, carried on now by Ernst Steinkellner and his students and colleagues, including many young Japanese researchers.

Tantric Buddhism, whether that of India, Tibet, China, or Japan, has received comparatively little attention from scholars, no doubt due, in part, to the extreme difficulty of the subject. Its potentially titillating aspects have, predictably, attracted many who are more concerned with seeing in these traditions either esoteric truths or licentiousness, rather than properly understanding them as highly developed forms of the practical application of the complex philosophical systems developed out of the Madhyamaka and Yogācāra systems. Numerous publications purport to address the topic of TANTRA, particularly in Tibetan Buddhism, but the utility of most of these works is open to serious doubt.

Tibetan Buddhism

For a long time, Tibetan Buddhist studies concentrated almost exclusively on making available Indian literature that had been translated and transmitted in Tibetan, despite the fact that among the very earliest scholars in the field were Isaak Jakob Schmidt (1779–1847), Anton von Schiefner (1817–1879), and W. P. Wassiljew (1818–1900), Russians familiar with the living monastic traditions of Mongolia in which were preserved the tradition of Tibetan Buddhist scholarship. Studies such as those of Stcherbatsky and his pupil Eugène Obermiller (1901–1935) on Madhyamaka philosophy and logic as well as historiography, while deeply indebted to Tibetan scholarship, nevertheless kept their prime focus on India, and the same may be said to some extent of the work of the Japanese pioneers of Tibetan studies, although Teramoto Enga (1872–1940), Kawaguchi Ekai (1866–1945), Aoki Bunkyō (1886–1956), and Tada Tōkan (1890–1967) all also spent time studying in Tibet itself. Especially since the massive Russian collections have never been widely accessible, the Japanese collections of Tibetan literature accumulated by these travelers, including both Tibetan translations of canonical materials and native works, were the most important resources available until the last quarter of the twentieth century.

Although some scholars, such as Giuseppe Tucci (1894–1984), had indeed studied Tibetan Buddhism itself, rather than merely seeing in Tibetan translations an otherwise unavailable source of Indian materials, it was the flow of Tibetans fleeing Tibet in 1959 that was decisive for the development of the study of indigenous Tibetan traditions, especially since many of the refugees were highly educated native scholars who were eager to share their knowledge with researchers in England, the United States, and Japan. When the Tibetans fled, moreover, they brought with them libraries of theretofore inaccessible textual materials that, thanks almost single-handedly to the efforts of E. Gene Smith of the U.S. Library of Congress, were reprinted and distributed around the world, making possible for the first time widespread access to the treasures of the Tibetan Buddhist literary tradition. A secondary factor in the development of Tibetan Buddhist studies has been the tremendous religious growth of Tibetan Buddhism itself in the West, made possible primarily by the presence of these refugee Tibetans, and the high profile of the DALAI LAMA on the world stage. Since this has contributed to a general interest in Tibet, one side effect has been an increasing interest in the academic study of Tibetan Buddhism. The same may be said for Zen Buddhism, in which the popularity of the religious practices has had the additional result of inspiring further scholarship on the tradition.

Chinese Buddhism

What was true for Tibetan Buddhist studies also applies to many studies of Chinese Buddhist materials, namely that they were often engaged in with the goal of supplementing the study of Indian Buddhism, rather than for their own sake. This was the case with such works as the comparative catalogues correlating Chinese translations with their Pāli counterparts, or catalogues of Chinese translations of Indian texts. Yet significant investigations of Chinese Buddhism also have a long history. The combined efforts of scholars such as Tang Yongtong (1894–1964), Tsukamoto Zenryū (1898–1980), Demiéville, and Erik Zürcher have allowed us to begin to understand the overall trends of Buddhism in China, and the development of a true Chinese Buddhism, while recent studies by Antonino Forte, Michel Strickmann (1942–1994), and Victor Mair, among others, have opened up new avenues of inquiry into topics such as relations between the Buddhist monastic establishment and the state, esoteric traditions, and the role of Buddhism in the evolution of Chinese vernacular literature.

The CHAN SCHOOL of Buddhism, usually known in the West by the Japanese pronunciation *Zen,* has elicited much attention, although relatively little of this interest has translated into critical scholarship. Japanese scholars belonging to both the Rinzai and Sōtō schools have, of course, always been keenly interested in their own traditions, but it was the discovery early in the twentieth century in the Dunhuang manuscript collections of theretofore completely unknown Chan texts that shattered traditional mythologies, motivating a series of studies by scholars such as Hu Shih (1891–1962), Yabuki Keiki (1879–1939), and the famous D. T. SUZUKI (1870–1966), as a result of which it became more and more difficult to accept as fact the Zen tradition's own stories about itself. A more recent generation of scholars, prominent among them young Americans, was inspired and taught by Yanagida Seizan, Iriya Yoshitaka (1910–1998), and others, and continues to contribute to a radical rethinking of all aspects of the Chan school.

Japanese Buddhist studies

Most research on Japanese Buddhism until quite recently has been limited to sectarian histories and doctrinal studies, although historians have also taken note of Buddhism as a social force in Japanese history. Traditional Japanese scholarship produced superb works of synthesis, including those concerning works of Indian origin in Chinese translation. Many of these have been of tremendous assistance to modern scholarship, as is the case with Saeki Kyokuga's 1887 annotated edition of the encyclopedic *Abhidharmakośa*; La Vallée Poussin's debt to this work can be seen on every page of his outstanding multivolume French translation (*L'Abhidharmakośa de Vasubandhu,* 1923–1931).

The bulk of Japanese scholarly attention, however, has been devoted to the background of contemporary Japanese schools, both proximately within Japan and more remotely in their Chinese antecedents. Thus scholars of Kegon, the Japanese branch of the HUAYAN SCHOOL, have studied the HUAYAN JING in Chinese translation, works of the Huayan patriarchs, and the works of Japanese Kegon scholars, while Tendai scholars have studied the *Lotus Sūtra,* and works of ZHIYI (538–597) and later TIANTAI SCHOOL masters, and of SAICHŌ (767–822) and his successors. In the course of such studies, generally little attention is given to other schools or to contextual data. While the value of such works, including for the study of Chinese Buddhism, should not be underestimated, by the same token its limitations must be recognized. Despite excellent Japanese scholarship on Indian and Tibetan Buddhism beginning in the late nineteenth century, it was only well into the twentieth century that Japanese scholars began to apply anything like the same approaches to their own traditions, and even today most Japanese scholarship on Japanese Buddhism would be better classified as theology (*shūgaku*) than Buddhist studies.

Among the most important research materials resulting from this modern traditional scholarship are the editions of canonical works of the various sects; some of these works, such as the *Dainippon Bukkyō Zensho* (1912–1922), cross over lineage boundaries, while others, such as the collected works of great founders such as DŌGEN (1200–1253), KŪKAI (774–835), SHINRAN (1173–1263), and so forth, do not. This said, it is hard for those not familiar with the Japanese language to appreciate how truly vast and comprehensive is Japanese scholarship on Buddhism, much of which is not limited at all to the Buddhism of Japan. Momentous projects, such as Ono Genmyō's multivolume annotated bibliography of almost all Buddhist literature then known (*Bussho kaisetsu daijiten,* 1932–1935), or Mochizuki Shinkō's almost simultaneous publication of a massive encyclopedia of Buddhism (*Bukkyō daijiten,* 1932–1936), remain basic and essential research tools for the study of Buddhism, despite the advances the intervening years of study have brought. Japanese dictionaries of Buddhist technical vocabulary too, beginning with that of Oda Tokunō (*Bukkyō daijiten,* 1917) and including notably the more recent work of Nakamura Hajime (*Bukkyōgo daijiten,* 1981), have no good parallels in works in other languages.

Buddhist studies in other traditionally Buddhist countries has been less active. Certainly Sri Lankan scholars have devoted considerable attention to multiple aspects of THERAVĀDA Buddhism, particularly in Sri Lanka itself. The same might be said to some extent of scholars in other Southeast Asian countries, not to mention the studies of Korean Buddhism undertaken by Korean scholars, and very recently of Tibetan Buddhism by Tibetans. That much of this work is published in little-known languages, however, limits its broader influence.

Anthropological studies

Somewhat unexpectedly, perhaps, the area of the Buddhist world that has received the most attention from anthropologists has been Southeast Asia, including Sri Lanka. These studies consider not only MONASTICISM, but the status of Buddhist institutions in lay society, Buddhism and politics, and other issues. The living traditions of Chinese Buddhism received some attention from Japanese scholars, especially during the period of Japanese occupation, while the meticulous studies of Johannes Prip-Møller (*Chinese Buddhist Monasteries,* 1937) and the later investigations of Holmes Welch (especially *The Practice of Chinese Buddhism: 1900–1950,* 1967) have recorded a world that has now almost entirely disappeared. Surprisingly little work has been done on the contemporary Buddhism of Japan, despite the ease of access to monasteries and lay Buddhist centers, or on Tibet, although attention paid to the latter has increased recently. Despite considerable interest in the Buddhist monastic codes (VINAYA) from the earliest days of Buddhist studies through the recent work of Hirakawa Akira (1915–2002) and Schopen, little has been done to compare these classical prescriptive codes with actual Buddhist monastic practices.

Buddhist art

The study of Buddhist art deserves its own treatment, in part because, unfortunately, it has yet to find its rightful place in the mostly text-based field of Buddhist studies. It remains true that most art historians are not sufficiently familiar with Buddhist literature or thought, and that most Buddhist scholars have, at best, only a passing familiarity with the tools and methods of art historians, although some pioneering art historians, such as Foucher, were thoroughly familiar with literary sources as well, and some textualists, such as Dieter Schlingloff, work comfortably with art historical materials. Nevertheless, it is impossible to understand Buddhism in any cultural context without an appreciation of its varieties of artistic expression. Beginning with the first modern encounters with Buddhist arts, however, scholars have attempted to understand their meaning and role. A great deal of attention has been given to the sculpture of the Gandharan region, most notably because of its obvious strong Greek influence, to Chinese monumental sculpture, Southeast Asian sculpture, Japanese sculpture and painting, and to Tibetan painting and bronze images. Studies remarkable for their depth and breadth include the Japanese multivolume examinations of the YUN'GANG and LONGMEN cave complexes, Tucci's monumental study of Tibetan art (*Tibetan Painted Scrolls,* 1949), and Dutch studies of the BOROBUDUR monument in Java.

Fields such as the study of Buddhist music and dance have been almost entirely ignored, despite their obvious centrality in Buddhist WORSHIP and the daily life of both monastic and lay Buddhism in all cultural contexts. Likewise, it is only recently that Buddhist ritual has drawn the attention of investigators.

Thematic studies have occupied an important place in Buddhist studies. Chief among the topics of discussion for many years were the character of the Buddha, the date at which he lived, and the meaning of NIRVĀṆA. More recently, issues such as the meaning of ŚŪNYATĀ (EMPTINESS) in the MADHYAMAKA SCHOOL, the status of experience and enlightenment in Chan, and, self-reflexively, how Buddhist studies itself should be carried out, have attracted considerable attention. It is likely that in the years to come, such more conceptual and theoretical studies, as well as comparative investigations, will become more common.

See also: **Languages**

Bibliography

Beal, Samuel. *The Romantic Legend of Śākya Buddha.* London: Trübner, 1875.

Beal, Samuel. *Si-yu-ki: Buddhist Records of the Western World.* London: Kegan Paul, Trench, Trübner, 1906.

Burgess, James. *Report on the Buddhist Cave Temples and Their Inscriptions: Archaeological Survey of Western India 4.* London: Trübner, 1883.

Burnouf, Eugène. *Introduction à l'histoire du Buddhisme Indien.* Paris: Imprimerie Royal, 1844.

Burnouf, Eugène. *Le Lotus de la Bonne Loi.* Paris: Imprimerie Nationale, 1852.

Cunningham, Alexander. *The Bhilsa Topes: Or, Buddhist Monuments of Central India: Comprising a Brief Historical Sketch of the Rise, Progress, and Decline of Buddhism; with an Account of the Opening and Examination of the Various Groups of Topes around Bhilsa.* Bombay: Smith, Taylor; London: Smith, Elder, 1852.

Edgerton, Franklin. *Buddhist Hybrid Sanskrit Grammar and Dictionary.* New Haven, CT: Yale University Press, 1953.

Griffiths, Paul J. "Recent Work on Classical Indian Buddhism." *Critical Review of Books in Religion* 6 (1993): 41–75.

Jong, J. W. de. *A Brief History of Buddhist Studies in Europe and America.* Tokyo: Kosei, 1997.

Kern, Hendrik. *Geschiedenis van het Buddhisme in Indie.* Haarlem: H. D. Theenk Willink, 1882–1884.

La Vallée Poussin, Louis de. *Bouddhisme: Opinions sur l'histoire de la dogmatique.* Paris: Gabriel Beauchesne, 1909.

La Vallée Poussin, Louis de. *L'Abhidharmakośa de Vasubandhu.* Paris: Geuthner, 1923–1931. Reprint, Brussels: Institut Belge des hautes Études Chinoises, 1971.

Lamotte, Étienne Paul Marie. *Histoire du bouddhisme Indien, des origines à l'ére śaka* (1958). Reprint, Louvain, Belgium: Université de Louvain, Institut Orientaliste, 1976. English translation, *History of Indian Buddhism: From the Origins to the Saka Era*, tr. Sara Webb-Boin. Louvain-la-Neuve, Belgium: Université de Louvain, 1988.

Lamotte, Étienne Paul Marie. *Le Traité de la grande Vertu de Sagesse.* Louvain, Belgium: Université de Louvain, 1944–1980.

Lopez, Donald S., Jr., ed. *Curators of the Buddha: The Study of Buddhism under Colonialism.* Chicago: University of Chicago Press, 1995.

McRae, John R. "Chinese Religions: The State of the Field." Part 2: "Living Religious Traditions: Buddhism." *Journal of Asian Studies* 54, no. 2 (1995): 354–371.

Müller, F. Max. *Buddhist Texts from Japan. Anecdota Oxoniensia, Texts, Documents, and Extracts, Chiefly from Manuscripts in the Bodleian and Other Oxford Libraries.* Aryan series, Vol. 1, Part 1. Oxford: Clarendon Press, 1881.

Nagao, Gadjin. "Reflections on Tibetan Studies in Japan." *Acta Asiatica* 29 (1975): 107–128.

Obermiller, Eugène (Evgenni Eugen'evich). *History of Buddhism. (Chos 'byung)* by Bu-ston: Part 1: *The Jewelry of Scripture.* Part 1: *The History of Buddhism in India and Tibet.* Heidelberg, Germany: Harrassowitz, 1931–1932.

Prip-Møller, Johannes. *Chinese Buddhist Monasteries: Their Plan and Its Function as a Setting for Buddhist Monastic Life.* Copenhagen, Denmark: Gads Forlag; London: Oxford University Press, 1937.

Strickmann, Michel. "A Survey of Tibetan Buddhist Studies." *Eastern Buddhist* 10, no. 1 (1977): 128–149.

Sueki, Yasuhiro. *Bibliographical Sources for Buddhist Studies: From the Viewpoint of Buddhist Philology.* Tokyo: International Institute for Buddhist Studies, 1998–2001.

Takakusu Junjirō. *A Record of the Buddhist Religion as Practised in India and the Malay Archipelago (A.D. 671–695) by I-Tsing.* Oxford: Clarendon Press, 1896.

Welch, Holmes. *The Practice of Chinese Buddhism: 1900–1950.* Cambridge, MA: Harvard University Press, 1967.

JONATHAN A. SILK

BURMA. *See* Myanmar

BURMESE, BUDDHIST LITERATURE IN

Belonging to the Sino-Tibetan family of languages, Burmese constitutes the primary language of the largest ethnic group in Myanmar (Burma). Burmese comprises two distinct styles, each with its own set of linguistic particles to mark the syntactical relations between words. Generally speaking, colloquial Burmese is used when people meet and talk; literary Burmese is used for published materials. And yet, colloquial Burmese sometimes appears in printed form, as in books that contain dialogue. Likewise, literary Burmese may be used in some spoken contexts, such as when news is read on the radio.

For purposes of this survey, the discussion of Burmese Buddhist literature will be divided into two parts: The first part distills developments in Burmese Buddhist literature from the twelfth century up to and extending into the nineteenth century; the second part focuses on relevant developments from the nineteenth century onwards.

Twelfth to nineteenth centuries

Inscriptions or *kyok*ᶜ *cā* (stone-writings) make up the only form of extant Burmese writing prior to the mid-fifteenth century, and they continue to be an important form of writing throughout Myanmar's pre-British colonial period (the British completed their military conquest of Myanmar in 1885; Myanmar gained independence in 1948). The earliest Burmese inscriptions come from Pagan, a major city-state in central Myanmar that reached the zenith of its political and cultural development in the twelfth and thirteenth centuries. The inscriptions, primarily in prose, often record the meritorious deeds of kings and other laypeople, in particular the construction and donation of monastic and other religious buildings. The inscriptions also sometimes record Buddhist laws set down by kings. The earliest Buddhist law inscription, an edict on theft, dates to 1249.

The sixteenth through the nineteenth centuries witnessed the development of a large body of legal materials composed in manuscript form in Burmese, Pāli, and other languages (e.g., Mon). These legal materials attempt to encode, legislate, and offer precedents for Buddhist practice. Common to the legal literature were *rājasat*ᶜ, which were laws set down by kings, and *dhammasat*ᶜ, which were law texts written, for example, by monks.

Historical and biographical materials, such as *rājavaṅ*ᶜ (historical accounts of the lineages of kings), are yet another type of Burmese literature with Buddhist elements in pre-nineteenth-century Myanmar. These materials recount the exploits and intrigues of rulers and others, their lines of descent, and their acts of

Buddhist patronage. *Rājavaṅ*ʿ have been written since the fifteenth century. However, the first *rājavaṅ*ʿ to attempt to offer a continuous history of Myanmar was Ū" Kalā"'s *Mahārājavaṅ*ʿ *krī"* (*Great Chronicle*), which appeared around 1724 (Herbert and Milner, p. 13).

Burmese Buddhist poetic literature appears in the historical record from about 1450 onwards. Among the poetic forms are *pyui*', lengthy and embellished translations of Pāli texts that deal with an event or series of events in the Buddha's life or previous lives (*jātakas*). A famous example of *pyui*'-type poetry is the *Kui" khan" pyui*' (the *pyui*' in nine sections), which was authored by a monk in 1523 and based on a *jātaka* tale about a king who wanted an heir.

Finally, Burmese commentaries such as *nissayas* have been composed since the mid-fifteenth century. *Nissayas* were used to communicate in Burmese the inflections, syntax, and meanings of Pāli texts and passages. *Nissayas* and other commentaries continue to play a prominent role in the teaching and transmitting of Pāli texts and ideas up through and extending beyond the nineteenth century.

Nineteenth to twenty-first centuries

Despite, and partly due to, the political and economic challenges that have confronted Myanmar since the nineteenth century (e.g., colonial conquest, military rule, prolonged economic stagnation), the country has witnessed an efflorescence of Burmese Buddhist literature. As with the various types of Buddhist literature mentioned above, contemporary literature exhibits strong continuities with the conceptual and textual world of the THERAVĀDA Pāli canon, as well as with the Buddhist literary traditions of South and Southeast Asia.

In the contemporary period, there are four types of Burmese Buddhist literature that overlap with and extend several of the pre-nineteenth-century types. By no means exhaustive of available contemporary Burmese literature, the four highlight the range of literature readily accessible to those wishing to investigate Buddhist culture and practice in Myanmar. They are: (1) historical and biographical literature, (2) commentarial literature, (3) legal literature, and (4) devotional and meditational literature. Each type of material has been and continues to be used pedagogically, ritually, ethically, and politically.

Contemporary historical and biographical literature addresses the development and spread of Buddhism. Topics include the building of pagodas and other religious monuments, the activities of Buddhist-minded leaders, and the lives of various monks and laypeople. Overall, contemporary Burmese Buddhist histories and biographies participate in a predominant tradition of South and Southeast Asian religio-historical writing, which includes the *vaṃsa* literature of Sri Lanka and the *tamnān* literature of Thailand, as well as components of the *kyok*ʿ *cā* and *rājavaṅ*ʿ literatures of Myanmar. An example of contemporary Burmese historical writing is Mahādhamma Saṅkraṃ's *Sāsanālaṅkāra cā tam*ʿ" (*Ornaments of the Dispensation*), written in 1831 and considered by many Burmese to be an authoritative discussion of the history of Buddhism in Myanmar. Phui" Kyā"'s *Kyoṅ*ʿ" *to*ʿ *rā Rvhe kyaṅ*ʿ *Cha rā to*ʿ *bhu rā" krī" theruppatti* (*Life of the Kyauntawya Shwegyin Sayadaw*, 1925) offers a short but informative biography of a monk who became abbot at the Kyauntawya Monastery in Yangon (Rangoon), the capital of Myanmar.

Commentarial materials fall into at least two broad categories. One category consists of materials written in the *nissaya* style of word-by-word translation. Such writings appear in a large number of contexts, including, for example, monastic cremation volumes like *Bhaddanta Indācāra ʾAntimakharī"* (*Reverend Indacara's Final Journey*, 1993), which includes *nissaya* passages that explain the Pāli notion of *saṃvega* (religious emotion).

A second category of commentary consists of treatises on portions of the Pāli canon and other Buddhist texts. An example of a commentarial treatise is Arhaṅʿ Janakābhivaṃsa's *Kuiy*ʿ *kyaṅ*ʿ ' *ʾabhidammā*, which typifies the exposition of *abhidhamma* (metaphysics) prevalent in contemporary Myanmar. Since its first publication in 1933, Janakābhivaṃsa's text has seen several editions and an English translation by U Ko Lay, *Abhidhamma in Daily Life* (1999).

Contemporary legal materials include *vinicchaya* literature, which concerns rulings given by learned monks. These rulings are promulgated within different monasteries and monastic courts. Whether a given *vinicchaya* is accepted by civil authorities, monks, and laypeople as legally valid is by no means a certainty; however, when a monastic court has been appointed by the state, and the civil and monastic authorities in question agree upon a decision, the chances for general acceptance increase.

A representative example of *vinicchaya* literature hails from 1981, when a body of monks made a ruling on rebirth theory, which was published as a massive tome, complete with documentary photographs, titled

Lū se lū phrac' vādānuvāda vinicchaya (*Court Decision on Transmigration*). *Vinicchaya* literature, as well as the contexts in which it is produced and deployed, could be profitably studied in light of Burmese Buddhist legal sources (e.g., *rājasat's*, *dhammasat's*) and culture dating to precolonial Myanmar.

Devotional and meditative literature includes handbooks focused on different aspects of daily practice associated with the Buddha and his teachings. Such handbooks help explain the meaning and dynamics of devotional and meditative activity. Examples include Ū" Taṅ' Cui"'s *Pu tī" cip' naññ'"* (*Method of Reciting Stanzas*, 1999) and Muigh'" Ññhaṅ'" Cha rā to''s *Vipassanā 'a lup pe" cañ' tarā" krī"* (*Way of Vipassanā Practice*, 1958). The latter volume discusses the intricacies of VIPASSANĀ (SANSKRIT, VIPAŚYANĀ; insight) MEDITATION, which has become popular in South and Southeast Asia, as well as in the West.

In closing, it should be emphasized that there are several kinds of material that fall outside the types discussed here. These materials include novels, such as Gurunanda's *Samavati e* tac' bhava saṃsarā* (*The Life of Samavati*, 1991), which draws its story about a queen from the fifth-century philosopher BUDDHAGHOSA's commentary on the DHAMMAPADA (a work of verse in the Pāli canon). Clearly, a vast literature awaits those willing to engage the complexities of Burmese and the Burmese Buddhist world.

See also: **Myanmar; Myanmar, Buddhist Art in; Pāli, Buddhist Literature in**

Bibliography

Bhe Moṅ' Taṅ', Ū". *Mran'mā cā pe samuiṅ'"* (*History of Burmese Literature*). Yangon, Myanmar: Sudhammavatī, 1955.

Chulalongkonmahawitthayalai, et al. *Comparative Studies on Literature and History of Thailand and Myanmar.* Bangkok, Thailand: Institute of Asian Studies, Chulalongkorn University, 1997.

Herbert, Patricia, and Milner, Anthony, eds. *South-East Asia: Languages and Literatures, a Select Guide.* Honolulu: University of Hawaii Press, 1989.

Hla Pe. *Burma: Literature, Historiography, Scholarship, Language, Life, and Buddhism.* Pasir Panjang, Singapore: Institute of Southeast Asian Studies, 1985.

Houtman, Gustaaf. "The Biography of Modern Burmese Buddhist Meditation Master U Ba Khin: Life before the Cradle and past the Grave." In *Sacred Biography in the Buddhist Traditions of South and Southeast Asia*, ed. Juliane Schober. Honolulu: University of Hawaii Press, 1997.

Huxley, Andrew. "Studying Theravāda Legal Literature." *Journal of the International Association of Buddhist Studies* 20, no. 1 (1997): 63–91.

Janakābhivaṃsa, Arhaṅ'. *Abhidhamma in Daily Life*, tr. and ed. U Ko Lay. Yangon, Myanmar: Aung Thein Nyunt, 1999.

Khin Maung Nyunt. *An Outline History of Myanmar Literature: Pagan Period to Kon-baung Period.* Revised edition. Yangon, Myanmar: Cā pe Biman', 1999.

Kratz, E. Ulrich, ed. *Southeast Asian Languages and Literatures: A Bibliographical Guide to Burmese, Cambodian, Indonesian, Javanese, Malay, Minangkabau, Thai, and Vietnamese.* London and New York: I. B. Tauris, 1996.

Smyth, David, ed. *The Canon in Southeast Asian Literatures: Literatures of Burma, Cambodia, Laos, Malaysia, the Philippines, Thailand, and Vietnam.* Richmond, UK: Curzon, 2000.

JASON A. CARBINE

BU STON (BU TÖN)

Bu ston rin chen grub (pronounced Bu tön rinchendrub, 1290–1364) was the most illustrious member of Zhwa lu Monastery in Gtsang (Tsang), located in west central Tibet. He was also the Tibetan scholar most active in collating and editing the Tibetan Buddhist CANON, the *Bka' 'gyur* and *Bstan 'gyur*. The *Bka' 'gyur* (*Kanjur*) is the collection of Tibetan translations of works attributed to the Buddha. The *Bstan 'gyur* (*Tanjur*) is the collection of Tibetan translations of important Buddhist commentaries and other related materials. The formation of the *Bka' 'gyur* and *Bstan 'gyur* began with the collecting of manuscripts and translations of Buddhist texts into Tibetan in the early ninth century. The process culminated in the early fourteenth century when, according to the *Blue Annals* (a translation of Gzhon nu dpal's *Deb ther sngon po*), manuscripts scattered over many monasteries and temples in Tibet were gathered together in Snar thang (Narthang) Monastery.

Bu ston then took the Snar thang version of the canon to Zhwa lu, where he checked the translations against Indian originals, added other works, and produced a *Bka' 'gyur* and an authoritative version of the *Bstan 'gyur*. The *Bka' 'gyur* and *Bstan 'gyur* that Bu ston edited is the origin of the majority of the extant Tibetan canons. The categories under which he grouped the various texts are the most widely used and admired. He gives a detailed description of his work in his *Chos 'byung* (*History of Buddhism*), partially translated into English by the Russian scholar Eugène Obermiller in the 1930s.

Bu ston was a conservative editor. As D. S. Ruegg says in *The Life of Bu ston Rinpoche* (1966), "Bu ston . . . follows an objective criterion of authenticity which can be accepted by any editor" (p. 28). In practice this led Bu ston to exclude some tantras accepted as authentic by the Rnying ma (Nyingma), or Old School, of Tibetan Buddhism on the grounds that no original Indian version could be located.

Bu ston's collected works (*gsung 'bum*) include more than two hundred titles in seventeen volumes. Besides his work on the canon, Bu ston composed important commentaries on the yoga set of tantras and on the Kālacakra *Tantra.* He also wrote a well-known commentary on the Perfection of Wisdom sūtras called *Lung gi nye ma,* as well as a commentary on the *Abhidharmasamuccaya* of Asaṅga. Even before Bu ston, Zhwa lu Monastery was known for its expertise in these two areas, and a Zhwa lu school of Tibetan Buddhism is mentioned in earlier histories. After Bu ston, the Zhwa lu school went into decline and was largely eclipsed by the Sa skya (Sakya), Bka' brgyud (Kagyu), and Dge lugs (Geluk) sects, but the tradition of studying Bu ston's works continued. It became so widespread that the study of Bu ston's works (*bu lugs*) became a minor tradition in itself.

Bu ston's views were highly influential in his day (for example, Tsong kha pa's *Sngags rim chen mo*—partially translated into English by Jeffrey Hopkins as *Tantra in Tibet*—draws heavily on Bu ston's work on the yoga tantras) and remain so today. Bu ston's works are still the central texts for study in a number of Tibetan monasteries.

See also: Tibet

Bibliography

Eimer, Helmut, ed. *Transmission of the Tibetan Canon: Papers Presented at a Panel of the 7th Seminar of the International Association for Tibetan Studies, Graz 1995.* Vienna: Verlag der Österreichischen Akademie der Wissenschaften, 1997.

Obermiller, Eugène, trans. *History of Buddhism.* Heidelberg, Germany: Harrassowitz, 1931–1932.

Ruegg, David Seyfort, trans. *The Life of Bu ston Rinpoche.* Rome: Istituto Italiano per il Medio ed Estreme Oriente, 1966.

Gareth Sparham

C

CAMBODIA

Cambodia in the twenty-first century understands itself as a THERAVĀDA Buddhist nation. While this self-conscious identification as a Theravāda nation is fairly recent, the history and development of Buddhism in the region that constitutes present-day Cambodia extend back nearly two millennia. During this time numerous transformations occurred that led scholars to suppose that the Khmer Buddhism of today is markedly different from Khmer Buddhism even two centuries ago, before the rise of modern Buddhist institutions in Cambodia. Certain major continuities are also evident in the past two millennia: the intertwining of Buddhist, brahmanist, and spirit practices and understandings; the close ties between religion and political power; and the important role of Buddhist ideas in the articulation of social and ethical values.

The region known today as Cambodia was inhabited two thousand years ago by Khmer-speaking peoples who appear to have congregated in small chiefdoms referred to as Funan by the Chinese. Archeological evidence suggests that Indian merchants, explorers, and monks imported Buddhism into this region at least as early as the second century C.E. The exact manner of the importation of Buddhism, along with other Indian ideas, into Southeast Asia, a process called Indianization, is not fully understood. A consensus has emerged among many historians, however, that Indians probably never established a political and economic process akin to modern colonization by Europeans in Southeast Asia; nor is there thought to have been a large-scale movement of Indian emigrants to Southeast Asia. Rather, many aspects of the language, arts, and literature, as well as philosophical, religious, and political thought of Indians, were adopted, assimilated, and transformed by Southeast Asians during the first centuries C.E., possibly through a combination of economic, diplomatic, and religious contacts both with India and Indians directly, and also through the cultural medium of other Southeast Asian courts and traders.

Buddhist and brahmanic practices coexisted and became intertwined with local animist traditions and spirit beliefs in the Khmer regions from the second century onward. Buddhist missionaries and pilgrims were active during this period, which may have contributed to the introduction of Buddhism into Southeast Asian courts. Chinese histories indicate that at least one Buddhist from Funan, a monk named Nāgasena, traveled to China in the sixth century. Chinese monks traveling to India by sea stopped en route to visit many sites in present-day Southeast Asia. While no indigenous Buddhist texts from this early period remain, items discovered by archeologists at the site of Oc-Eo (a port city during the Funan era) include Buddha images associated with the MAHĀYĀNA tradition. Chinese records from the period describe Buddhist, Śaivite, and spirit cults and practices among the Khmer, with the central court rituals seemingly concerned with devotion to Śiva, especially through the worship of Śiva-lingam.

Epigraphic evidence for the Buddhist presence begins to appear in the seventh century, during the period referred to as pre-Angkor, when the Khmer regions were apparently dominated by a group of chiefdoms or kingdoms referred to in Chinese records as Chenla. It is difficult to characterize the nature of religious life during this period. Recent historiography on the pre-Angkor period resists the tendency of older scholarship to overinterpret limited epigraphic evidence or conflate European or Indian models of

KINGSHIP and society onto the Khmer context. Inscriptions from the period, predominantly in Khmer and Sanskrit, suggest that the pre-Angkorian rulers were for the most part devotees of Śiva or VIṢṆU, but this does not mean that an Indian-like "Hinduism" was in existence. Drawing on persuasive linguistic evidence, the historian Michael Vickery has pointed to the practice among pre-Angkor Khmer of attributing Indian names to their own indigenous deities. Most pre-Angkor rulers appear to have tolerated and to varying degrees supported Buddhism in their courts, but to what extent Buddhism was known beyond the courts is difficult to gauge. Iconography and historical records from the period suggest that Buddhist influences were being felt from India, China, Sri Lanka, and other parts of Southeast Asia, such as Dvāravatī and Champa, with more than one form of Buddhism in evidence. Numerous Avalokiteśvara figures, as well as a reference to "Lokeśvara" (Avalokiteśvara) appearing in an inscription dated 791 from the Siemreap area of present-day Cambodia, indicate the presence of Mahāyāna ideas. Yet some early Pāli inscriptions have also been found along with Sri Lankan and Dvāravatī style Buddha images showing Theravāda influence.

By the end of the pre-Angkor period, kings were expanding their territories and centralizing political and economic authority, while at the same time seeking to align themselves with deities perceived to hold universal power. The Khmer political concept of a close association between king and deity, known in Sanskrit inscriptions as the *devarāja* cult, must have grown out of indigenous traditions linking rulers and local deities of the earth. It developed more fully during the Angkor period, from the ninth through thirteenth centuries, starting with the kingship of Jayavarman II (r. 802–854). Inscriptions speak of Jayavarman's patronage of a *devarāja* cult that associated him with Śiva, either as "god-king" or as a devotee of Śiva, "king of the gods." While the exact relationship between king and deity denoted by this phrase remains controversial among scholars, there is no doubt that the power of kings and deities were closely interwoven in a cult that became a model for the later Angkorian kings. From readings of inscriptions, Angkorian art, and other historical accounts, scholars have surmised that the considerable political and economic influence wielded by Angkorian kings was inseparable from their associations with fertility and agriculture, their superior moral status, and their roles as protectors and propagators of religious devotion, associations that were carried into the later Buddhist kingships. This range of powers was embodied in their building projects, typically of reservoirs, images, and mountain temples, such as Angkor Wat, the fabulous temple built by Sūryavarman II (r. 1113–ca. 1150) and dedicated to Viṣṇu.

During the Angkorian period, a fuller picture of Buddhism emerges. While most of the earlier Angkorian kings were Śaivite or devotees of the combined Śiva-Viṣṇu deity Harihara, Mahāyāna Buddhism was also becoming increasingly intertwined with kingship. Yaśovarman, regarded as the founder of Angkor (889–900), built three hermitages outside of his capital dedicated to Śiva, Viṣṇu, and the Buddha. Rājendravarman II (r. ca. 944–ca. 968), Jayavarman V (r. ca. 968–ca. 1001), Sūryavarman I (r. 1001–1050), and Jayavarman VI (r. 1080–1107) were all patrons of Mahāyāna Buddhism, though their reigns too remained syncretic. Mahāyāna Buddhism came to the forefront, however, during the reign of Jayavarman VII (r. 1181–ca. 1218), considered to be the "last great Angkorian king." The complex reasons for Jayavarman VII's promotion of Buddhism over other Angkorian cults, historian David Chandler suggests, may have stemmed from an apparent estrangement from the Angkor court as well as a period spent in Champa, where Mahāyāna Buddhism was influential. After repelling several bloody Cham invasions, Jayavarman VII responded to the suffering in the aftermath of war with public works intended to embody his compassion: roads, rest houses, hospitals, and reservoirs. His temples Ta Prohm and Preah Kan, built to honor his parents in combination with the goddess of wisdom, Prajñāpāramitā, and the bodhisattva Lokeśvara (symbolizing compassion), contained inscriptions enumerating the thousands of people connected with each temple complex. The BAYON temple in the center of his capital contained a central image of the Buddha, with four-faced images of the bodhisattva Lokeśvara on its towers and exteriors. This image has sometimes been interpreted as a likeness of the king as well, possibly representing a Buddhistic extension of the *devarāja* concept to linking of king and BODHISATTVA. Following Jayavarman, Buddhism and kingship have remained closely intertwined in Cambodia.

During the eleventh through thirteenth centuries, the same period that Islamization was occurring in maritime Southeast Asia, Theravāda Buddhism rose to prominence throughout mainland Southeast Asia. Scholars are unable to wholly account for the spread of Theravāda Buddhist ideologies and practices during

A view of Angkor Wat, the great twelfth-century Buddhist–Hindu temple complex in Cambodia. © Chris Lisle/Corbis. Reproduced by permission.

this period, but historiography in general is moving away from a clear-cut demarcation between Mahāyāna and Theravāda Buddhism in Southeast Asia, as well as the idea that one form of Buddhism simply and rapidly supplanted the other. More likely, given the syncretic traditions in Southeast Asia, different Buddhist ideas and practices became intermingled, just as Buddhism itself became interwoven with spirit worship. Theravāda Buddhism had coexisted with other forms of Buddhism for centuries but became gradually more influential as the Theravāda kingdoms of Pagan and SUKHOTHAI (in present-day Myanmar and Thailand) developed into larger regional powers. As the dominant influence of Angkor waned, increasing contact with these kingdoms may have contributed to the spread and authority of Theravāda ideas in the Khmer regions. A Khmer prince, possibly a son of Jayavarman VII, is supposed to have been among a group of Southeast Asian monks who traveled to Sri Lanka for study at the end of the twelfth century; he was ordained in the Mahāvihāra (also known in Southeast Asia as "Sinhalese") order, a lineage they carried back to Pagan. In post-Angkorian Cambodia, it has been suggested, a backlash against the extravagant Mahāyāna expressions of Jayavarman VII led to a "Hindu revival," and Theravādins may have used this as an opportunity to assert their own interpretations and practices. During the course of the next two centuries, Theravāda Buddhism became assimilated into all levels of Khmer society and synthesized in court and villages with older brahmanic and spirit practices, such as agricultural fertility rites and the worship of *neak ta* (local spirits).

The post-Angkorian or "middle period," dated by Ashley Thompson from the end of Angkorian influence (the thirteenth through fourteenth centuries) until the mid-nineteenth century, was until recently perceived as one of decline by scholars fixated on the disappearance of the great civilization of Angkor. Recent scholarship tends to view the middle period in terms of multiple shifts: The population and agricultural centers of the kingdom shifted geographically south; cultural influences moved from, as well as to, the Thais; religious devotion continued to be syncretistic but with an emphasis on Theravāda forms and ideas, as reflected in the wooden Theravāda vihāras built adjacent to Angkorian brahmanic stone temples and the shift in iconography from images of Indian deities to images of the Buddha; Pāli replaced Sanskrit as the language of inscriptions and literature; Khmer also came increasingly to be used, and much of the classical Khmer literature was composed during this time. Theravāda ideas of kingship, MERIT AND MERIT-MAKING, and KARMA (ACTION); a growing emphasis on the biography of the Buddha; and a COSMOLOGY and ethical orientation expressed in ideas about birth, REBIRTH, and moral development in the three-tiered world of the Trai Bhum are reflected in the art, epigraphy, and literature of the period. At Nogor Vatt, for instance, a sixteenth-century inscription translated by Thompson refers to the merit produced by a royal couple, the king's subsequent rebirth in Tuṣita heaven, and his resolve to become an ARHAT at the time of the Buddha MAITREYA. Buddhist iconography from the period focused on the depiction of the Buddha, and vernacular literary compositions such as the Rāmkerti transformed its hero into a Buddhist bodhisattva.

The eighteenth and much of the nineteenth centuries in Cambodia were a period of almost continual warfare and unrest, with the Khmer trying to repel invasions from both their Siamese and Vietnamese neighbors. Historical sources from the period suggest that the Buddhist material culture that had been developed during the middle period was widely damaged or destroyed as a result of warfare and social chaos. Beginning in 1848, when Ang Duong (r. 1848–1860) was installed on the Khmer throne by the Siamese, a renovation of Khmer Buddhism was initiated that would last for at least a century. During the rest of the nineteenth century, Khmer Buddhists rebuilt damaged monasteries and monk-scholars traveled to Bangkok to copy lost manuscripts and study Pāli.

The two most prominent Khmer monks of the nineteenth century were Samtec Sangharāj Dīen (1823–1913), who became the saṅgha head in 1857, and Samtec Sugandhādhipatī Pān (1824–1894), the monk who is attributed with the importation of the Thammayutnikāi to Cambodia. Both were educated and ordained in Bangkok, which served as the regional center for Buddhist education during this period. Dīen was captured as a prisoner of war by the Siamese army as a young boy and sent to Bangkok as a slave, where he served in the entourage of Prince Ang Duong. He was ordained as a novice at the age of eleven and by the time he ordained as a monk in 1844, had already won attention for his intellectual pursuits. In 1849 Ang Duong requested that Dīen be sent to Cambodia to head up the restoration of Buddhism in the kingdom, which he undertook until his death in 1913. He resided at Vatt Uṇṇalom in Phnom Penh, the chief Mahānikāi temple. Pān was born in 1824 in Battambang (a Khmer province under Siamese control until 1907) and was ordained as a novice there. In 1837 he went to Bangkok to study Pāli, and eventually ended up as a student at Wat Bovoranives under Mongkut. The date of his return to Cambodia and the founding of the Thammayut sect in Cambodia has been attributed both to the reigns of Ang Duong and Norodom (r. 1860–1904), either in 1854 or 1864. Under Norodom, Pān constructed the seat of the Thammayut order at Vatt Bodum Vaddey in Phnom Penh. In the 1880s he sent a delegation of Khmer monks to Ceylon to obtain relics and a Bo tree to plant in the new monastery. He died in 1894, with the title of "Samtec Sugandhādhipatī," the chief of the Thammayut order and the second highest monastic rank in the kingdom.

The new Khmer Buddhism that began to emerge in this period was probably unlike the older Buddhism it replaced. François Bizot has argued that in spite of the presence of Pāli inscriptions and literature, Theravāda Pāli scholarship was in fact not well established in Cambodia before the nineteenth century, that canonical Tipiṭaka texts were not widely used, and that tantric teachings were more prominent in Cambodia than in other Theravāda areas of Southeast Asia. If this theory is correct, traces of this older Khmer Buddhism were increasingly destroyed after the mid-nineteenth century, and new ideas of Theravāda orthodoxy took its place. This newly emerging Buddhism had Siamese, Khmer, and French sources and influences.

Although the Thammayutnikāi imported from Siam and patronized by the royal family never took wide hold outside of urban areas, its reformist ideas influenced young Khmer monks in the more traditional Mahānikāi order in Cambodia. These young monks, led in particular by Chuon Nath (1883–1969) and Huot Tath (1891–1975), pushed for a series of innovations in the Khmer saṅgha beginning in the early twentieth century: the use of print for sacred texts (rather than traditional methods of inscribing manuscripts); a higher degree of competence in Pāli and Sanskrit studies among monks; a vision of orthodoxy based on understanding of VINAYA texts for both bhikkhu and laypersons; and modernization in pedagogical methods for Buddhist studies. These reforms were not uniformly accepted within the Khmer saṅgha. Early attempts by Nath to introduce print were met with resistance from established saṅgha officials and led to increasing factionalism between modernists and traditionalists within the Mahānikāi that continued into the 1970s. The reformist efforts led by modernist monks did, however, coincide with both the pedagogical ideologies and political interests of French colonial administrators who backed Nath and Tath in an effort to reinvigorate Buddhist education within the protectorate. The French administration took on the role of saṅgha patron in part to foster European models of scientific education but also, fearing Siamese influence, to stem the flow of Khmer Buddhist literati to Bangkok. The modernist agenda also countered the influence of cosmologically oriented Buddhism in the provinces, where French rule in the late nineteenth century was plagued by peasant insurrections connected with predictions of a Buddhist *dhammik* (righteous ruler) who would usher in the epoch of the Buddha Maitreya.

By 1930, when the Buddhist Institute was established under the directorship of French curator Susanne Karpelès, most of the modern Buddhist institutions in Cambodia were in place. For the next forty-five years, the Buddhist Institute led the development of modern Buddhism in Cambodia, issuing frequent publications of critical editions of texts in Khmer and Pāli, as well as scholarly and popular studies related to Buddhism and Khmer literature and history, many of which appeared in its important publication, *Kambujasuriyā.* Besides its prominent role in articulating a modern Khmer expression of Buddhism, the Buddhist Institute became a site for imagining Khmer nationalism, and monks were among the most prominent dissidents against the French colonial regime. The institute also helped give rise to the development of the Communist Party in Cambodia. Mean (Son Ngoc Minh) and Sok (Tou Samouth), later leaders of Khmer communism, were both recruited by Karpelès for Buddhist education. In spite of this early connection between Buddhism and the Communist Party, once the Khmer Rouge took power in April 1975, they quickly sought to eradicate Buddhism in Democratic Kampuchea. Many monks were executed or forced to disrobe, Buddhist monasteries were destroyed or appropriated for other purposes, and Buddhist text collections were discarded. Nearly two million people died as a result of Khmer Rouge policies enacted between 1975 and 1979.

Since the Vietnamese invasion of 1979 that brought an end to the Khmer Rouge regime, Buddhism has slowly reemerged in Cambodia, in some ways resembling pre-1970 Buddhism and in other ways quite altered. The subsequent governments of Cambodia since 1979 have gradually lifted initial restrictions on Buddhist participation and expression, pre-1970 saṅgha organization has been restored and many temples (*vatt*) have been rebuilt, often from contributions from Khmer living in other countries. New research by anthropologist John Marston suggests that older strains of Khmer Buddhist thought, such as millenarianism and tensions between modernists (*smāy*) and traditionalists (*purāṇ*), have reemerged in this new period. Political leaders continue to situate themselves as patrons of the saṅgha in order to gain legitimacy. On the other hand, the loss of so many monks, intellectuals, and texts, as well as an entire generation of young laypeople raised without any religious education at all, is seen by contemporary Buddhist leaders as a major obstacle to the rebuilding process and an irreparable break with the past. In addition, the traumatic experience of so much of the population has in some cases ushered in new kinds of cynicism and questioning of basic Buddhist truths, such as the efficacy of the law of karma (action). At the same time, other Khmer

The promenade at Angkor Wat, 1997. AP/Wide World Photos. Reproduced by permission.

identify even more strongly with Buddhism. Many seek to remember the dead through merit-making ceremonies or to ease traumatic memories through meditation practice. New global Buddhist ideas in the form of ENGAGED BUDDHISM (such as Buddhist-led care for AIDS patients), human rights education, and conflict mediation techniques, taught through the medium of Buddhist concepts, are also reaching contemporary Khmer Buddhists. One of the best-known monks of the post-Khmer Rouge period, Mahā Ghosananda, a student of Gandhian ideas, began leading peace marches across Cambodia in 1989. These marches, known as *dhammayātrā* (dharma pilgrimages), have crossed war zones and called attention to injustices in contemporary society.

See also: **Communism and Buddhism; Khmer, Buddhist Literature in; Southeast Asia, Buddhist Art in**

Bibliography

Ang Choulean. *Les êtres surnaturels dans la religion populaire khmère.* Paris: Cedoreck, 1986.

Bhattacharya, Kamaleswar. "The Religions of Ancient Cambodia." In *Sculpture of Angkor and Ancient Cambodia: Millennium of Glory,* ed. Helen Ibbitson Jessup and Thierry Zephir. Washington, DC: National Gallery of Art, 1997.

Bizot, François. *Le Figuier à cinq branches.* Paris: École française de l'Extrême-Orient, 1981.

Buddhist Institute. *Biography of Samdech Preah Sanghareach Chuon-Nath, the Chief of Mahanikaya Order.* Phnom Penh, Cambodia: Buddhist Institute, 1970.

Bunchan Mul. "The Umbrella War of 1942." In *Peasants and Politics in Kampuchea, 1942–1981,* ed. Ben Kiernan and Chanthou Boua. London: Zed Press; Armonk, NY: Sharpe, 1982.

Chandler, David. *A History of Cambodia,* 3rd edition. Boulder, CO: Westview Press, 2000.

Chau-Seng. *L'Organisation Buddhique au Cambodge.* Phnom Penh, Cambodia: Université Buddhique Preah Sihanouk Raj, 1961.

Coedès, George. *The Indianized States of Southeast Asia,* ed. Walter F. Vella and tr. Susan Brown Cowing. Honolulu: University Press of Hawaii, 1968.

Forest, Alain. *Le culte des genies protecteurs au Cambodge: analyse et traduction d'un corpus de texts sur les neak ta.* Paris: Editions L'Harmattan, 1992.

Harris, Ian. "Buddhism in Extremis: The Case of Cambodia." In *Buddhism and Politics in Twentieth-Century Asia,* ed. Ian Harris. London: Pinter, 1999.

Keyes, Charles F. "Communist Revolution and the Buddhist Past in Cambodia." In *Asian Visions of Authority: Religion and the Modern States of East and Southeast Asia,* ed. Charles F. Keyes, Laurel Kendall, and Helen Hardacre. Honolulu: University of Hawaii Press, 1994.

Khin Sok. *Le Cambodge entre le Siam et le Viêtnam (de 1775 à 1860).* Paris: École Française d'Extrême-Orient, 1991.

Kiernan, Ben. *How Pol Pot Came to Power.* London: Verso, 1985.

Leclère, Adhémard. *Le bouddhisme au Cambodge.* Paris: E. Leroux, 1899.

Mabbett, Ian. "A Survey of the Background to the Variety of Political Traditions in South-east Asia." In *Patterns of Kingship and Authority in Traditional Asia,* ed. Ian Mabbett. London: Croom Helm, 1985.

Mabbett, Ian, and Chandler, David. *The Khmers.* Oxford: Blackwell Press, 1995.

Osborne, Milton E. *The French Presence in Cochinchina and Cambodia: Rule and Response (1859–1905).* Ithaca, NY: Cornell University Press, 1969.

Porée-Maspero, Eveline. *Étude sur les rites agraires des Cambodgiens,* Vols. 1–3. Paris: Mouton, 1962.

Reid, Anthony, ed. *Southeast Asia in the Early Modern Era: Trade, Power, and Belief.* Ithaca, NY: Cornell University Press, 1993.

Tarling, Nicholas. *The Cambridge History of Southeast Asia,* Vol. 1: From Early Times to ca. 1800. Cambridge, UK: Cambridge University Press, 1992.

Thompson, Ashley. "Changing Perspectives: Cambodia after Angkor." In *Sculpture of Angkor and Ancient Cambodia: Millennium of Glory,* ed. Helen Ibbitson Jessup and Thierry Zephir. Washington, DC: National Gallery of Art, 1997.

Thompson, Ashley. "Introductory Remarks between the Lines: Writing Histories of Middle Cambodia." In *Other Pasts: Women, Gender, and History in Early Modern Southeast Asia,* ed. Barbara Watson Andaya. Manoa: University of Hawaii Press, 2000.

Vickery, Michael. *Society, Economics, and Politics in Pre-Angkor Cambodia: The 7th–8th Centuries.* Tokyo: Centre for East Asian Cultural Studies for Unesco, Toyo Bunko, 1998.

Yang Sam. *Khmer Buddhism and Politics 1954–1984.* Newington, CT: Khmer Studies Institute, 1987.

ANNE HANSEN

CAMBODIA, BUDDHIST ART IN.

See **Southeast Asia, Buddhist Art in**

CANDRAKĪRTI

Candrakīrti (ca. 600–650 C.E.) is best known as a Madhyamaka-school Indian philosopher and commentator. Little is known of his life, though later Tibetan biographies associate him with the north Indian monastic university of Nālandā. His two major works are the *Madhyamakāvatāra* (*Introduction to Madhyamaka*) and *Prasannapadā* (*Clear Words*).

The *Madhyamakāvatāra* is a versified introduction to Madhyamaka thought, organized into ten chapters that correspond to the ten perfections (pāramitā) mastered by Mahāyāna BODHISATTVAS. The sixth chapter, corresponding to the perfection of wisdom, is the longest and most important. In it, Candrakīrti refutes a variety of Buddhist and non-Buddhist views, and explores the meaning of such basic Buddhist ontological categories as the two truths, no-self, and emptiness.

The *Prasannapadā* is a prose commentary on the *Madhyamakakārikā* (*Verses on the Middle Way*; second century C.E.), Nāgārjuna's foundational MADHYAMAKA SCHOOL text. In his commentary, Candrakīrti brilliantly adumbrates Nāgārjuna's critique of philosophical categories, and insists, contrary to his predecessor Bhāvaviveka (ca. 490–570 C.E.) that the Mādhyamika philosopher must avoid syllogistic reasoning, and must defeat opponents solely through drawing out the absurd consequences of their own statements. This methodological approach was later known as Prāsaṅgika (consequentialist) Madhyamaka, in contradistinction to the approach that favored using formal inference to establish Madhyamaka views independently, the Svātantrika.

Candrakīrti was influential among later Indian Mādhyamikas, but achieved his greatest fame in Tibet, where he came to be regarded by many as the Madhyamaka commentator par excellence. He was particularly important for the founder of the DGE LUGS (GELUK) tradition, TSONG KHA PA (1357–1419), who placed his work at the center of monastic education on Madhyamaka, and made him a thinker whose views are discussed and debated by Tibetan scholars to this day.

Bibliography

Huntington, C. W., and Wangchen, Geshé Namgyal. *The Emptiness of Emptiness: An Introduction to Early Indian Mādhyamika.* Honolulu: University of Hawaii Press, 1989.

Sprung, Mervyn; Murti, T. R. V.; and Vyas, U. S., trans. *Lucid Exposition of the Middle Way: The Essential Chapters from the Prasannapadā of Candrakīrti.* Boulder, CO: Prajñā Press, 1979.

ROGER R. JACKSON

CANON

There is no such thing as *the* Buddhist canon. In fact, the concepts of canon and canonicity are especially problematic in Buddhism, given the wide geographical spread and great historical variety of the religion, together with the absence of any central authority. If the term *canon* is defined loosely as a more or less bounded set of texts accorded preeminent authority and sanctity, then each Buddhist school or tradition to evolve developed its own canon in the process. While agreeing on the centrality of the notion of BUDDHAVACANA (WORD OF THE BUDDHA) as capable of leading others to awakening, Buddhists may and do differ over what actually constitutes this *buddhavacana.*

In view of the perennial possibility of disagreement and misunderstanding, Buddhists formulated explicit guidelines for authenticating religious teachings as true *buddhavacana* and interpreting them correctly. These guidelines include the four great authorities (*mahāpadeśa*), which directed that teachings were to be accepted as authentic if they were heard from (1) the Buddha himself; (2) a SAṄGHA of elders; (3) a group of elder monks specializing in the transmission of dharma (i.e., sūtra), VINAYA or *mātṛkās* (the matrices or mnemonic lists that became the ABHIDHARMA); or (4) a single elder specializing therein. But teachings heard from any of these authorities could only be accepted if they conformed with existing scriptural tradition (i.e., with the sūtra and vinaya), and also, according to a variant formulation, if they did not contradict the nature of things (*dharmatā*). Another set of principles, not subscribed to by all Buddhist groups, held that in receiving and interpreting teachings one should follow the four refuges or reliances (*pratiśaraṇa*), relying on the dharma taught in preference to the person teaching it, the meaning (or spirit) of it rather than the letter, sūtras of definitive or explicit meaning (*nītārtha*) rather than implicit meaning requiring interpretation (*neyārtha*), and direct understanding (jñāna) rather than discursive knowledge (*vijñāna*).

Even while emphasizing seniority and tradition, these interpretative principles place a higher premium on content and its realization than they do on form and obedience to it. Truth (dharma) emerges as the primary value, ever the same whether buddhas arise to preach it or not, independent of particular formulations by particular people, so that eventually the statement "All that the Buddha has said is well said" is turned around: Whatever is well said (i.e., true) is the word of the Buddha. Canonicity is therefore defined in functional terms: If a teaching is meaningful, if it is in line with the dharma, and if it tends to eliminate the defilements and lead to liberation, then any product of inspiration (*pratibhāna*) may be accepted as the word of the Buddha. Under such conditions, innovations inevitably crept in, some of them rejected as not being the true word of the Buddha, but some of them finding acceptance, especially if they accorded in spirit with existing belief. It was in this way that the Mahāyāna sūtras eventually came to be accepted by some Buddhists as *buddhavacana,* as did the Buddhist tantras after them. Thus Buddhism functioned from early on with what is almost a contradiction in terms, an "open canon," in which commonly accepted principles of authenticity take the place of a rigidly defined and bounded set of texts in a given linguistic form. The latter would have been well-nigh impossible in any case because Buddhism functioned in a situation of regional and linguistic diversity, with Buddhists living in autonomous self-governing communities.

Form, content, and transmission

Agreement in such circumstances was by consensus, despite occasional attempts by kings and emperors to enforce orthodoxy. Several so-called councils (*saṃgīti,* group recitations) are supposed to have been held as the fledgling saṅgha tried to maintain unity on what was to be accepted as the true word of the Buddha or the correct interpretation of the rules of discipline. The first council at Rājagṛha took place after the death of the Buddha. At this council, the disciple ĀNANDA recited the sūtras (discourses delivered by the Buddha, or others accorded equivalent authority), and UPĀLI recited the vinaya (rules of discipline for renunciants). The community accepted their recounting of these two bodies of texts, with only some monks dissenting.

Yet even this account of a saṅgha relatively united as to what the Buddha had taught may oversimplify history. Later councils (at Vaiśālī, Pāṭaliputra, etc.) were occasions for more serious disagreements, which led to the formation of the different *nikāyas* by sects or schools each recognizing the validity of its own ordination lineage only. In India it appears that each *nikāya* came to transmit its own set of sacred texts, initially dividing them into sūtra and vinaya. In some schools, the sūtra and vinaya were supplemented from about the second century B.C.E. onwards by the *abhidharma,* an even more variable set of texts (seven for the Sarvāstivādins, a different seven for the Theravādins, and so on), which systematized the teachings in terms of the particular categories they fell under. Some schools rejected this third category, but for most the notion of the canon as consisting of the three baskets (*tripiṭaka*) of sūtra, vinaya, and *abhidharma* became standard. The *tripiṭaka* of one school, as far as scholars know, was never the same as that of the next, although the loss of the literature of most schools makes it difficult to be certain about the extent of difference. Nevertheless, there are certain commonalities. For example, the *sūtra-piṭakas* were divided into sections (*nikāyas, āgamas*) according to such criteria as length, subject, or numerical category (there was also a miscellaneous category, for texts that did not fit any of these). The vinayas were divided into rules for men and rules for women, these being ordered according to the seriousness of the offense, with other sections devoted to particular aspects of community life (ordination, official acts, property, etc.). The resulting collections of texts, which are referred to as *canons,* were therefore quite varied, extensive, and structurally complex.

One of the primary functions of the Buddhist order was to preserve and transmit all this literature, at first orally, then in writing, from generation to generation, even though Buddhists have always had a keen sense of the fragility of this enterprise. They believe that this effort is bound to fail in the end, due to human weakness, so that the work of a buddha will need to be done over and over again. Different groups of renunciants took responsibility for the transmission of different sections of their school's canon, committing them to memory, although occasionally people with prodigious mental powers mastered the whole canon. One consequence of this "division of labor" is that the same text can occur in two or more different places in a given canon. Oral transmission also led to extreme redundancy and repetition, the same formulas and blocks of text recurring in many different contexts.

From about the first century B.C.E. onward the texts began to be committed to writing, on palm leaf, birch bark, and other materials. This was only partially successful in preserving the texts for posterity, and most have been lost. The only canon to survive in its entirety is that of the Theravādins, written in the Pāli language. It shows that some schools kept their scriptures in ancient tongues, but in the extant fragments of other schools' canons it is apparent that a continuous process of Sanskritization was under way. The use of various Indian languages is another sign of the absence of any central authority. In one sense all Buddhist scriptures, even those in Pāli, are translations; it is not known what language(s) the Buddha himself spoke, but he is supposed to have sanctioned his followers' use of their own dialects for transmitting his teachings. The Buddhist canon is thus thoroughly multilingual. Parts of the canons of many Indian schools are extant in Chinese or Tibetan translation, as well as in Sanskrit fragments displaying different degrees of regularization from earlier Prakritic or Middle Indic dialect forms to classical Sanskrit. Thus the vinayas of six schools have survived, as well as parts of the *sūtra-piṭakas* of the Sarvāstivādins, the DHARMAGUPTAKAS, and the MAHĀSĀṂGHIKAS. *Abhidharma* texts from various schools, in particular the Theravādins and the Sarvāstivādins, also survive. But while manuscripts continue to be found, the greater part of the Indian Buddhist canons has no doubt vanished forever. Buddhist teachings, which emphasize the inevitability of transformation and loss, have themselves succumbed to it.

Even when it was fully extant, it is unlikely that many Buddhists ever knew their canon in its entirety, as a Muslim might know the Qur'an or a Christian the Bible. The Buddhist scriptures are simply too extensive, so that most members of the order would have been familiar with and used only a small number of them, a functional partial canon as opposed to an ideal complete one. Scholars also believe that Buddhists belonging to different mainstream or Śrāvakayāna schools would have accepted much of what the other groups transmitted as canonical, agreeing on the broad principles, and differing only on particular points of doctrine, and, more importantly, on points of monastic discipline. Some of the most heated disputes in the history of the order were over the vinaya. With the advent of the MAHĀYĀNA, with its prodigious outpouring of new scriptures, the scope for disagreement increased, and the bounds of the Buddhist canon became less distinct. The Mahāyāna canon was even more open than the mainstream one, and followers of that path are in most cases unlikely to have known more than a tiny fraction of the literature it generated. The same is true of tantric Buddhism, with its many classes of tantras, ritual and soteriological texts, which outnumbered even the Mahāyāna sūtras.

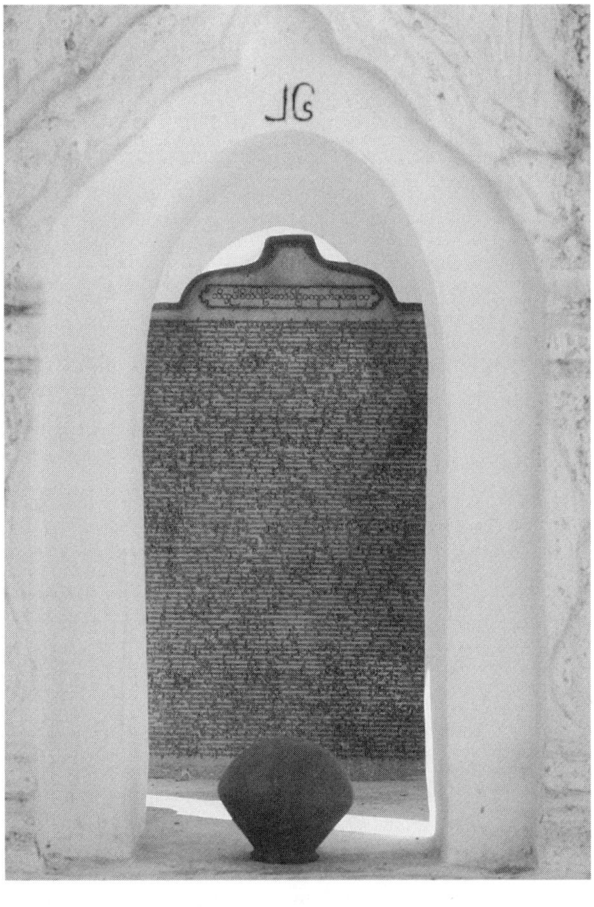

A stone tablet carved with a sacred text in Pāli, one of 729, each housed in its own miniature pagoda at a site in Mandalay, Myanmar (Burma). © Christine Kolisch/Corbis. Reproduced by permission.

Buddhist canons outside India

The complexity of this picture increased still further when Buddhism spread beyond the greater Indian cultural area. Although the Pāli canon of the Theravādins eventually established itself as the standard in Sri Lanka and Southeast Asia, in Central Asia and China different schools coexisted, and the Mahāyāna orientation was dominant. The Chinese translated scriptures belonging to these different schools and to this new movement with great zeal, the result being that the Chinese Buddhist canon took on a rather different shape. At first the work of bibliographers and cataloguers, later the product of imperial decree, authorized and funded by the court, the Chinese Buddhist canon (Dazangjing, literally "Great Storehouse Scripture") was a far more comprehensive collection. It eventually included Chinese translations of texts from the *tripiṭakas* of different Indian schools and of huge quantities of the Mahāyāna sūtras and Buddhist tantras produced in India from approximately the first century C.E. onward, as well as commentaries and treatises, texts written in China, biographies of monks and nuns, lexicographical works, and even the catalogues of Buddhist scriptures themselves. The sheer number and diversity of texts made the use of the tripartite structure of the *tripiṭaka* unfeasible. What is more, the Chinese retained different translations of the same text, often produced many centuries apart, affording modern scholars an excellent view of how texts and translation techniques developed over time.

Thus the Chinese Buddhist canon, which became the standard in Korea and Japan as well, is vast. It has appeared in numerous editions, many of them made with imperial patronage, although the one most often consulted by scholars today is the *Taishō shinshū daizōkyō* (*New Edition of the Buddhist Canon Made during the Taishō Reign*), published in Japan from 1924 to 1934 in one hundred volumes, each of which runs to about a thousand pages (eighty-five volumes of texts containing 2,920 works, twelve volumes of iconography, and three of catalogues). Yet, immense as it is, the *Taishō* is not the only edition; many others have survived as well, and thus "the Chinese Buddhist canon" is itself an abstraction of many highly variable collections. This proliferation of editions was in part due to state involvement, as each successive set of rulers sought to legitimate themselves politically as patrons of religion, or aspired for reasons of piety to the merit that the propagation of the *buddhadharma* generates.

These ideological considerations were instrumental in stimulating the invention and spread of PRINTING TECHNOLOGIES in East Asia, long before they were known in the West. Thus the world's oldest printed works are Buddhist texts, and from the tenth century onward the earlier manuscript copies of the Chinese Buddhist canon were replaced by printed editions, first using carved wooden blocks, then movable metal type. The production of these editions required resources that in those days only states could muster, although in recent times wealthy religious and commercial organizations have also become involved.

The same is true of Tibet, where in the fourteenth century the efforts of cataloguers trying to make sense of the sheer diversity of Buddhist texts combined with the interests of political authorities, intent on their own kind of order, to produce the first of many editions of the Tibetan canon, the Old Snar thang. Unlike the Chinese, the Tibetans were generally disinclined to preserve multiple translations of the same text, but their canon (upon which the Mongolian canon is also based) is equally vast. It has two major divisions, the *Bka' 'gyur* (the Word Translated; i.e., *buddhavacana*) and the *Bstan 'gyur* (the Teachings Translated; i.e., commentaries and other treatises). The *Bka' 'gyur* includes the three subdivisions of vinaya (that of the Mūlasarvāstivāda school), sūtra (predominantly Mahāyāna sūtras, in their various categories), and TANTRA (also arranged in various classes). The *Bstan 'gyur* also reflects these categories. The arrangement of all these texts differs according to edition, and sometimes one edition carries works not found in another.

As is the case with the Chinese canon, the Tibetan translations preserve much that is lost in Sanskrit. Some of the most prestigious editions (Peking, Sde dge, Snar thang, etc.) have been mass-produced woodblock prints; others have been manuscript productions, written by hand on expensive papers with ink made of precious metals and enclosed between ornate covers studded with jewels. The resources expended on this activity have been enormous, and the results are objects of great beauty. For Tibetans, as for other Buddhists, the sanctity of the canon derives from the sanctity of the liberating truth it contains and of the person who uttered it, and therefore the scriptures too are the focus of worship and veneration. They are not like any other books, but embody a special power, and must therefore be treated with reverence and respect, in a way similar, but not identical, to the way in which Jews approach the Torah, Christians the Bible, and Muslims the Qur'an.

Canon and canonicity are therefore never the same from one religion to the next, even if common themes can be found. Furthermore, the Buddhist canon turns out to be a large family of collections of texts in different languages and from different places, all sharing descent from a common set of forebears—the divergent oral reports of what the Buddha had taught, which were circulating among his disciples at his death some time in the fifth century B.C.E. Not unitary in content or linguistic expression even at the beginning, it is unimaginably diverse in both respects two and a half millennia later, as it continues to grow with editions and translations into English and other modern languages. At the same time, the Buddhist canon is unified by a common concern with setting out the path to salvation. Just as the waters of the ocean, however vast, have the same taste of salt at any point, so too all

A Tibetan book, printed from hand-carved woodblocks. © Tiziana and Gianni Baldizzone/Corbis. Reproduced by permission.

the many teachings of the Buddha have a single taste everywhere, that of liberation. And as to the path by which liberation is attained, Buddhists are fond of quoting the verse (*Udānavarga* 28.1):

> Not doing any evil, accomplishing what is good,
>
> Purifying one's own mind: this is the teaching of the Buddha.

See also: **Āgama/Nikāya; Apocrypha; Catalogues of Scriptures; Councils, Buddhist; Languages; Scripture**

Bibliography

Davidson, Ronald M. "An Introduction to the Standards of Scriptural Authenticity in Indian Buddhism." In *Chinese Buddhist Apocrypha,* ed. Robert E. Buswell, Jr. Honolulu: University of Hawaii Press, 1990.

Grönbold, Günter. *Der buddhistische Kanon: Eine Bibliographie.* Wiesbaden, Germany: Harrassowitz, 1984.

Harrison, Paul. "A Brief History of the Tibetan Bka' 'gyur." In *Tibetan Literature: Studies in Genre,* ed. Roger Jackson and José Cabezón. New York: Snow Lion, 1996.

Lamotte, Étienne. "La critique d'authenticité dans le bouddhisme." In *India Antiqua* (1947): 213–222. Leiden, Netherlands: Brill, 1947. English translation by Sara Boin-Webb, "The Assessment of Textual Authenticity in Buddhism." *Buddhist Studies Review* 1, no. 1 (1983): 4–15.

Lamotte, Étienne. "La critique d'interprétation dans le bouddhisme." *Annuaire de l'Institut de Philologie et d'Histoire Orientales et Slaves* 9 (1949): 341–361. English translation by Sara Boin-Webb, "The Assessment of Textual Interpretation in Buddhism." In *Buddhist Hermeneutics,* ed. Donald S. Lopez, Jr. Honolulu: University of Hawaii Press, 1988.

Lancaster, Lewis. "Buddhist Literature: Canonization." In *The Encyclopedia of Religion,* ed. Mircea Eliade, Vol. 2. New York: Macmillan, 1986.

Norman, K. R. *Pāli Literature: Including the Canonical Literature in Prakrit and Sanskrit of All the Hīnayāna Schools of Buddhism.* Wiesbaden, Germany: Harrassowitz, 1983.

Pagel, Ulrich. "Buddhism." In *Sacred Writings,* ed. Jean Holm. London and New York: Pinter, 1994.

Ray, Reginald. "Buddhism: Sacred Text Written and Realized." In *The Holy Book in Comparative Perspective,* ed. Frederick M. Denny and Rodney L. Taylor. Columbia: University of South Carolina Press, 1985.

von Hinüber, Oskar. *A Handbook of Pāli Literature.* Berlin: de Gruyter, 1996.

PAUL HARRISON

CATALOGUES OF SCRIPTURES

Catalogues of scriptures (*jinglu*) are bibliographical records of Chinese Buddhist literature of Indian, Central Asian, and indigenous provenance. Their beginnings can be traced with reasonable certainty to the mid-third century C.E., a century after the translation of Buddhist literature began in China. Compilation of catalogues in China continued throughout subsequent centuries, generating a total of approximately eighty catalogues by the end of the eighteenth century, though only one-third of them are extant today. Catalogues were also compiled in Korea and Japan whenever recensions of the Sinitic Buddhist CANON were introduced and domestic editions compiled. Most Chinese catalogues were private undertakings by a single individual, usually a monk, although a few are official, state-sponsored compilations made by a group of learned monks appointed for the task. Buddhist catalogues were a natural outgrowth of the Chinese secular bibliographical tradition that was in place by the first century C.E., and their compilation is a quintessentially East Asian phenomenon, there being nothing equivalent to them in Indian Buddhist literature. The catalogues offer indispensable source material for reconstructions of Buddhist history in not only East Asia but India as well.

Some 80 percent of the catalogues date from the Tang dynasty (618–907) or earlier, from the period when the substantial part of the translations of Buddhist scriptures into Chinese was accomplished. The primary goal of this group of catalogues was the verification of textual history and authenticity, and the determination of canonicity—a function of the conditions of the time when new translations were continually being added to a still-fluid Buddhist canon, and texts of indeterminate history or questionable identity proliferated. The fact that texts were disseminated at this time through hand-copying was a factor in this proliferation, for anyone with the means and inclination could, and often did, write new manuscripts and portray them as authentic Buddhist SCRIPTURE. Thus the catalogues of this period were both prescriptive and proscriptive in function, in that they classified texts to be either included in or excluded from the canon. In a real sense, they held the key to the fate of texts and, by extension, the formation of the Buddhist canon in China. By contrast, post-Tang catalogues were essentially descriptive and were indexes to the printed canons, merely listing their established and fixed entries.

The *Chu sanzang jiji* (*A Compilation of Notices on the Translation of the Tripiṭaka,* ca. 515) by Sengyou (445–518) is not only the earliest extant catalogue, but also preserves part of an even earlier catalogue by the renowned monk-scholar DAO'AN (312–385). The value of this catalogue also derives from the fact that it set the standard for cataloguing methods by employing a minute typological classification based on textual and doctrinal characteristics. Most of the cumulative list of divisions and categories of Buddhist literature that appear in medieval catalogues originated in the work of Sengyou: new or old translations; anonymous and variant translations; spurious scriptures; abridged scriptures; extant and nonextant translations; MAHĀYĀNA and HĪNAYĀNA literature in the three divisions of scripture, discipline, and treatise; translator known or unknown. Indigenous compilations, such as prefaces to scriptures, histories of Buddhism, biographies of monks and translators, and Buddhist catalogues themselves were also included to illustrate the proper transmission of Buddhism and its literature.

The *Lidai sanbao ji* (*Record of the Three Treasures throughout Successive Dynasties,* 597) by Fei Changfang (d.u.) introduced a chronological catalogue of translations arranged according to the dates and dynasties of translators, an innovation that was adopted in subsequent catalogues. Unfortunately, Fei also altered or fabricated numerous translator and author attributions to minimize the number of scriptures of questionable pedigree, as a way of ensuring the credibility of the Buddhist textual transmission. This catalogue was a case where criteria for textual authenticity were compromised for polemical reasons. A state-commissioned catalogue, the *Da-Zhou kanding zhongjing mulu* (*Catalogue of Scriptures, Authorized by the Great Zhou,* 695), kept many of Fei's arbitrary attributions and helped create an enigmatic category of scriptures that were both inauthentic and yet canonical.

The *Kaiyuan shijiao lu* (*Record of Śākyamuni's Teachings, Compiled during the Kaiyuan Era,* 730) by Zhisheng (d.u.) was the most critical and thorough catalogue in its evaluation of textual histories and represented the culmination of the art of Buddhist cataloguing that had begun nearly half a millennium earlier. Its influence is evident in the contents and organization of East Asian printed canons, all the way up to the modern standard edition, the *Taishō shinshū daizōkyō* (1924–1934). However, even this catalogue, with all its critical apparatus, accepted some of the problematic attributions that originated in the *Lidai sanbao ji*. Thus, despite the wealth of invaluable historical material they contain, not all catalogues, or the attributions included therein, are uniformly dependable. Their data must be used cautiously, by thoroughly cross-referencing information found in the different extant catalogues.

See also: **Apocrypha; Printing Technologies**

Bibliography

Hayashiya Tomojirō. *Kyōroku kenkyū* (*Studies on Buddhist Catalogues*). Tokyo: Iwanami Shoten, 1941.

Kawaguchi Gishō. *Chūgoku Bukkyo ni okeru kyōroku kenkyū* (*Studies on Buddhist Catalogues in Chinese Buddhism*). Kyoto: Hōzōkan, 2000.

Tokuno, Kyoko. "The Evaluation of Indigenous Scriptures in Chinese Buddhist Bibliographical Catalogues." In *Chinese Buddhist Apocrypha*, ed. Robert E. Buswell, Jr. Honolulu: University of Hawaii Press, 1990.

KYOKO TOKUNO

CAVE SANCTUARIES

Cave sanctuaries are manmade structures built into natural or excavated caves in the side of a mountain, canyon wall or cliff. Found in India and Afghanistan, at various sites along the SILK ROAD in CENTRAL ASIA, and in China, cave sanctuaries range from single chambers to enormous monastic compounds that include halls for worship and teaching, living quarters for monks and travelers, and spaces such as kitchens and libraries. As way stations for travelers, these sites played an important role in the development and dissemination of Buddhism.

The genesis of cave sanctuaries is unclear. They may have their roots in the ancient Indic tradition of asceticism, whose adherents had long made use of such natural structures in pursuit of their renunciatory lifestyles. The earliest rock-cut caves in India were excavated in the third century B.C.E. during the rule of AŚOKA at sites such as Lomas Rishi and Sudama in Bihar province. It should be noted that an inscription on the entrance to the Lomas Rishi cave states that it was dedicated for the use of the Ājīvākas, a prominent ascetic group. Both Lomas Rishi and Sudama were simple structures consisting of an inner circular chamber housing a STŪPA, and a rectangular outer hall, presumably a place where devotees could congregate for lectures and other forms of teaching.

Located about 105 miles south of Bombay, the caitya or worship hall at Bhājā is more complicated. Extending about sixty feet into the mountainside and approximately twenty-nine feet high, it consists of an apsidal chamber bracketed by tall columns on both sides. The wooden ribs appended to the ceilings of the central and side aisles have no structural purpose but reflect the use of prototypes of wood, bamboo, and thatch in the construction of the earliest cave sanctuaries. The columns help to define the path for traditional circumambulation (*pradakṣiṇa*) of the stūpa placed at the rear of the chamber. Vihāra 19 at the same site consists of two large inner chambers that were used communally and smaller individual quarters. Each cell contains a raised rock-cut bed with a pillow and a small niche in the wall used for holding a lantern.

The caitya hall at Karli was built between 50 and 75 C.E. It is 124 feet long, 46.5 feet wide, and 45 feet high, and contains thirty-six columns capped with couples seated on kneeling elephants. The façade was elaborately carved with a large horseshoe-shaped arch that defined the primary window.

Twenty major sites and numerous minor sites patronized by individual travelers and wealthy artistic and commercial guilds were constructed in western India from 100 B.C.E. to 200 C.E. However, the region is best known for AJAṆṬĀ, a group of twenty-six caves built by the ruling elite on both sides of the Waghora River in the late fifth century C.E. Ajaṇṭā is renowned for its delicate but powerful sculptures, such as those seen on the façade of cave 19, and its extraordinarily beautiful wall paintings, many of which record events from the past lives (JĀTAKA) of the historical Buddha, Śākyamuni. Representations of bodhisattvas, worship images in the residential halls, and the addition of seated buddhas at the front of the stūpas in the caitya halls illustrate contemporaneous changes in Buddhist thought. Other important centers in western India are found at Aurangabad and in some structures at Ellora. MAṆḌALA-like compositions, female deities, and the depiction of bodhisattvas with multiple heads in the sixth- and seventh-century caves at Aurangabad reflect further changes in the religion.

Noted for its (now destroyed) colossi, BĀMIYĀN (mid-sixth to seventh century C.E.) in Afghanistan is the most extensive Buddhist site in that country. One of the enormous standing buddhas was about 183 feet high, while the other measured about 127 feet. The famous seventh-century Chinese pilgrim XUANZANG (ca. 600–664) records a third colossus, representing a

The interior of cave 19, one of the twenty-six caves of Ajaṇṭā, constructed in the late fifth century, at Maharashtra, India. The pillars and the stūpa with the figure of the Buddha in relief were carved from the living rock. © Lindsay Hebberd/Corbis. Reproduced by permission.

buddha in final transcendence, or *parinirvāṇa,* as part of the original construction. Bāmiyān and the neighboring sites of Kakrak and Foladi are also noted for a distinctive school of painting that combined Indian, Sassanian Persian, and other elements.

From the fourth to the eighth century, over two hundred caves were constructed at the Central Asian site of Kizil near the city of Kucha in what is now the Xinjiang Uighur autonomous region of China. Kizil and related sites such as Kumtura (about a hundred caves) and Kizilgara (forty-six caves) were patronized by the rulers of Kucha, a prominent oasis kingdom on the northern branch of the Silk Road. Many of the caves have a unique structure consisting of a front chamber linked to a back chamber by two small arcades. Sculptures and paintings in shades of gold, blue, and green cover the wall. Preaching scenes or encapsulated representations of *jātaka* stories are standard. Some of the earliest representations of the transcendent Buddha Vairocana are also found at these sites. Caves found farther east in the Turfan area include those at Toyok and Bezeklik. Both have suffered substantial depredations.

China has the largest numbers of cave sanctuaries in Asia, and several of the most famous are found in Gansu, a province in the northwest with links to the Silk Road that played a seminal role in the introduction of Buddhism to China. Dating from the fourth to the fourteenth century, the nearly five-hundred decorated caves at Mogao and those at related sites near the city of DUNHUANG provide invaluable information for the development of Chinese Buddhist art. Some of the earliest caves have a pillar in the center thought to derive from the stūpas in early Indian construction. Later chambers are open or have low-lying platforms at the back. Early imagery includes sculptures of buddhas and bodhisattvas and paintings of past-lives stories. Representations of paradises and illustrations based on prominent texts are found in caves dating from the sixth to the eighth century, while those excavated in the thirteenth and fourteenth centuries contain seminal imagery for later Tibetan art. Comparable developments are found in the Yulin grottoes, the Western Thousand Buddha Caves (*Xiqianfodong*), and the Eastern Thousand Buddha Caves (*Dongqianfodong*) in the same region. The Binglinsi caves near Lanzhou and the Maijishan caves near Tianshui, which also contain both paintings and sculptures, are among the larger sites in Gansu.

The fifty-three caves at YUN'GANG in Shansi province are renowned for the five colossal sculptures that dominate caves 16 through 20. Built in the late fifth century under the patronage of the Northern Wei (386–534) rulers, the Yun'gang caves share the iconography found in contemporaneous structures at Dunhuang, but they contain no paintings, only sculptures.

LONGMEN near Luoyang in Hebei province was begun in the early sixth century. Longmen houses over two thousand caves, some large, some small, as well as thirty-six hundred inscriptions. About one-third of the caves were constructed during the Northern Wei and the rest during the Tang dynasty (618–907). The Fengxiansi, which was begun under the rule of the Tang emperor Gaozong (r. 649–683) and finished around 675, is the most famous at the site. Four guardians, two bodhisattvas, and two monks attend a fifty-foot-high seated buddha. The figures are noted for elegant and

The late-seventh-century Fengxiansi at Longmen, Henan Province, China. The seated Buddha is fifty-five feet high. © Robert D. Fiala, Concordia University, Seward, Nebraska. Reproduced by permission.

careful carving. Other centers, many of which were begun after the dissolution of the Northern Wei empire in the mid-sixth century, include Gongxian and Xiangtangshan in Hebei, Tianlongshan in Shansi, and other sites in Shandong. Numerous smaller excavations, often consisting of a single cave, are also known at many sites in northern China. A few sites are also found in the south.

Although not common after the tenth century, cave sanctuary construction flourished in the southwestern province of Sichuan during the Tang and Song (960–1279) dynasties. Several centers are found near Dazu. The Sichuan caves contain distinctive imagery including scenes of daily life, Chan OXHERDING PICTURES, and icons common in later esoteric traditions.

Carefully assembled with cut-stone panels, SŎKKURAM, located on top of Mount T'oham on the eastern outskirts of Kyŏngju, is a Korean response to Indian cave sanctuaries. In contrast to India and China, there were no natural caves in Korea, or at least none suitable, and Sŏkkuram was entirely manmade. Constructed between 751 and 774, Sŏkkuram has a round main hall that opens to a rectangular anteroom. A large free-standing buddha seated in the center of the main hall is attended by bodhisattvas, guardians, and other figures carved on the walls in high relief.

See also: **Monastic Architecture**

Bibliography

Caswell, James, O. *Written and Unwritten: A New History of the Buddhist Caves at Yungang.* Vancouver: University of British Columbia Press, 1988.

Chūgoku Sekkutsu (The Grotto Art of China). A series in Japanese and Chinese on major Chinese sites. Beijing: Wenwu Chubansha; Tokyo: Heibonsha, 1980–.

Dehejia, Vidya. *Early Buddhist Rock Temples: A Chronology.* Ithaca, NY: Cornell University Press, 1972.

Howard, Angela Falco. *Summit of Treasures: Buddhist Cave Art of Dazu, China.* Trumbull, CT: Weatherhill, 2001.

Mitra, Debala. *Buddhist Monuments.* Calcutta: Sahitay Samsad, 1971.

DENISE PATRY LEIDY

CELIBACY. *See* Sexuality

CENTRAL ASIA

Unlike most regions of the world, there is no universally accepted definition of what constitutes "Central Asia." The region will be defined in this entry as constituting the network of oasis towns comprising the ancient SILK ROAD, stretching from Afghanistan to DUNHUANG. The grasslands inhabited by nomadic peoples to the north, and the Tibetan highlands to the south—together commonly referred to as *Inner Asia*—have separate histories and will be treated elsewhere in entries on TIBET and MONGOLIA.

A natural dividing point between western and eastern Central Asia is Kashgar, the westernmost city in the Tarim basin. Located at the western edge of what is today the People's Republic of China, this city serves as a logical boundary for discussions of this region in both ancient and modern times.

Western Central Asia

The earliest evidence of a Buddhist presence in this region dates from the time of King AŚOKA (mid-third century B.C.E.), who left inscriptions in Greek and Aramaic at Qandahar and Laghman (both in modern Afghanistan). Though not specifically Buddhist in content—Aśoka's explicit discussions of Buddhism are restricted to a relatively small area in and around the territory of ancient Magadha—they do provide concrete evidence that Afghanistan had come under the control of a Buddhist ruler.

In the territory of Gandhāra (northern Pakistan and eastern Afghanistan) and Bactria (northern Afghanistan and southern Uzbekistan), Buddhist temple complexes excavated at Airtam, Kara-tepe, Fayaz-tepe, and Dalverzin-tepe (in some cases accompanied by inscriptions by their donors) offer testimony to the importance of Buddhism in the region during the Kushan period (ca. late first to third centuries C.E.) and possibly before (Rhie). Even farther to the west, excavations in the Merv oasis (the easternmost part of ancient Parthia in modern Turkmenistan) have yielded archaeological remains of Buddhist temples, as well as Buddhist scriptures in Sanskrit dating from the fourth to the sixth centuries, including a VINAYA text belonging to the Sarvāstivāda school (Utz). Monasteries excavated at Adzhina-tepe and other sites in southern Tadjikistan provide evidence of the survival of Buddhism in the region down to at least the eighth century (Stavisky).

Afghanistan has also been the site of two spectacular manuscript finds in recent years (though the precise spots of the discoveries are not known): the British Library collection, dating from the first century C.E. (Salomon 1999 and 2000), and the Schøyen Collection, containing texts from the second to seventh centuries C.E. (Braarvig et al. 2000 and 2002). The British Library manuscripts include both canonical scriptures (possibly associated with the DHARMAGUPTAKA school) and local compositions; the Schøyen collection includes a number of well-known MAHĀYĀNA scriptures. The fact that all of these texts are written in Prakrit or Sanskrit rather than translated into local vernaculars (with the exception of a fragmentary text in Bactrian, whose precise nature is uncertain) is typical of those few Buddhist texts found throughout the region, where Buddhists seem to have been content to read and transmit their scriptures in the "church languages" of India (Nattier).

In contrast to the territories of Gandhāra, Bactria, and eastern Parthia, where Buddhism flourished for many centuries, in the territory of ancient Sogdiana (northern Uzbekistan) Buddhist motifs appear only as minor elements in non-Buddhist artistic productions, confirming the reports of Chinese travelers that attest to almost no Buddhist presence in the region. Though several figures of Sogdian ancestry played key roles as missionaries and translators during the formative period of Chinese Buddhism (if the Chinese ethnikon *Kang* does indeed correspond to *Sogdian,* about which there is some controversy), and though one Buddhist site may now have been identified in Sogdiana (Stavisky), at present it appears that Sogdian Buddhism was essentially an expatriate phenomenon. Other parts of western Central Asia, such as Ferghana and Khwarezm, seem to have had little or no Buddhist population at all.

Buddhists in Gandhāra appear to have flourished during the first century C.E. under the patronage of the Sakas (referred to in Indian sources as Śakas), an Iranian-speaking people whose sponsorship of Buddhist donations is well attested in inscriptions, and who are mentioned in the British Library fragments by name. Under the Kushan (Sanskrit, Kuṣāṇa) dynasty (ca. late first to third centuries C.E.) Buddhism continued to receive significant support as well. Legends of the conversion of the Kushan ruler Kanishka (Sanskrit,

Kaniṣka) to Buddhism, however, are probably no more than that, for no inscription describes him as a Buddhist (or even as making a donation to a Buddhist community) and the justly famous images of the Buddha on his coins comprise a distinct minority in a vast sea of Iranian, Greek, and Indian deities. Recent archaeological findings, which point to a drop in trade between Bactria and Sogdiana during the Kushan period, suggest that, rather than providing a conduit for the transmission of Buddhism to East Asia, the Kushans may instead have erected a barrier on their eastern frontier (Naymark). If this is the case, it would explain the silence of Chinese sources concerning Kanishka and his successors, and it would suggest that it may have been their Saka predecessors rather than the Kushans themselves who facilitated the initial diffusion of Buddhism to eastern Central Asia and China.

It has sometimes been suggested that the invasion of the Hephthalite Huns (late fifth to early sixth centuries C.E.) dealt a serious blow to Buddhism in western Central Asia, but accounts by Chinese travelers, such as Songyun (early sixth century) and XUANZANG (ca. 600–664), report that Buddhism continued to prosper despite the damage done during the Hephthalite conquest. Xuanzang singles out the Lokottaravāda branch of the MAHĀSĀṂGHIKA SCHOOL as being particularly influential at BĀMIYĀN, where two colossal Buddha statues (fifty-three and thirty-five meters in height), destroyed by the Taliban in 2001, may have expressed the distinct buddhological views of this school.

A more significant threat to the fate of Buddhism in the region was the long-term expansion of Islam. Beginning in the seventh century, western Central Asia began to experience significant Arab incursions, and by the end of the tenth century, Buddhism had largely disappeared even in Gandhāra itself (Stavisky).

Eastern Central Asia

A Buddhist presence in northern China is documented in historical and literary sources beginning in the middle of the first century C.E., and on this basis scholars have inferred that Buddhists must have passed through eastern Central Asia—that is, the territory of the Tarim basin (modern Xinjiang in the People's Republic of China)—no later than the beginning of the first millennium C.E. Despite the proximity of this area, which would later host several flourishing Buddhist city-states, records of the initial phase of Buddhist teaching and translation activity in China do not mention the presence of missionaries from eastern Central Asia (nor for that matter from India itself), but instead from western Central Asian territories such as Parthia, Sogdiana, and the Kushan realm (Zürcher).

The earliest evidence of a Buddhist presence in the Tarim basin—aside from a manuscript of the *Dharmapada* (in Gāndhārī language and Kharoṣṭhī script) found near Khotan, which has been assigned to the second century C.E. but may have been imported from elsewhere—dates from approximately two centuries later. A cache of civil documents written in the Gāndhārī language and the Kharoṣṭhī script from the kingdom known to the Chinese as Shanshan (centered at Miran, in the southeastern part of this region) has been dated to the early third century C.E., and it attests to the existence of an incipient Buddhist SAṄGHA, though apparently without any full-time and celibate clergy.

By the fourth century C.E. a significant Buddhist presence had been established in the Tokharian-speaking city-states of Kucha and Agni on the northeastern route, where the Sarvāstivāda school was especially prominent. Buddhism flourished under royal patronage and numerous monasteries and convents were founded. A substantial number of texts in Sanskrit were imported and subsequently copied locally, most of them of Sarvāstivāda affiliation. In contrast to the standard practice in western Central Asia, however, Buddhists in the Tarim basin began to translate scriptures into their own vernacular languages around the beginning of the sixth century C.E. The Tokharians appear to have been the first to make this move, and texts in both Agnean (Tokharian A) and Kuchean (Tokharian B) dating to around 500 to 700 C.E. have been discovered. This local literature continues to be mainly Sarvāstivāda in content; among cultic figures, the future Buddha MAITREYA appears to have been an object of special interest.

Despite the conversion to the Mahāyāna of KUMĀRAJĪVA (350–409/413 C.E., a native of Kucha and later a famous translator of Buddhist texts into Chinese), few followed his lead, and non-Mahāyāna teachings remained the norm in Kucha and Agni until at least the seventh century. In the kingdom of Khotan (in the southwestern Tarim basin), by contrast, Mahāyāna traditions found an early and fervent following. The ascendancy of the Mahāyāna is reported already in FAXIAN's travel report (early fifth century) and *The Book of Zambasta*, an anthology of Buddhist texts recast in Khotanese poetry (early eighth century), which makes it clear that Mahāyāna Buddhism was preferred.

With the fall of the Uygur kingdom in Mongolia in 842 C.E., Turkic-speaking peoples began to pour into the Tokharian territories of the northeast (though some non-Uygur Turks had preceded them). Initially they adopted local Sarvāstivāda traditions, sometimes in combination with Manichaean traditions brought with them from Mongolia. With the growth of Chinese influence, however, the Uygurs increasingly drew on Chinese Mahāyāna scriptures and practices. Most of later Uygur literature—including such famous works as the SUVARṆAPRABHĀSOTTAMA-SŪTRA, the LOTUS SŪTRA (SADDHARMAPUṆḌARĪKA-SŪTRA), and the *Vimalakīrtinirdeśa*—is translated from the Chinese (Elverskog).

Buddhism continued to flourish in eastern Central Asia down to the beginning of the eleventh century, when the Muslim conquest of Khotan in 1004 signaled the beginning of the end of Buddhist dominance in the region. These territories are today populated almost entirely by Turkic-speaking Muslims, who have little knowledge of the flourishing Buddhist cultures that preceded them.

See also: **Central Asia, Buddhist Art in; Gāndhārī, Buddhist Literature in; Islam and Buddhism; Mainstream Buddhist Schools; Persecutions; Sarvāstivāda and Mūlasarvāstivāda**

Bibliography

Braarvig, Jens; Hartmann, Jens-Uwe; Kazunobu Matsuda; and Sander, Lore; eds. *Buddhist Manuscripts in the Schøyen Collection,* Vol. 1. Oslo, Norway: Hermes, 2000.

Braarvig, Jens; Harrison, Paul; Hartmann, Jens-Uwe; Kazunobu Matsuda; and Sander, Lore; eds. *Buddhist Manuscripts in the Schøyen Collection,* Vol. 2. Oslo, Norway: Hermes, 2002.

Elverskog, Johan. *Uygur Buddhist Literature.* Turnhout, Belgium: Brepols, 1997.

McRae, John R., and Nattier, Jan, eds. *Buddhism across Boundaries: Chinese Buddhism and the Western Regions.* Honolulu: University of Hawaii Press, 2004.

Mémoires de la Delegation Archeologique Française en Afghanistan. Paris: De Boccard, 1928 (and subsequent volumes in the series).

Nattier, Jan. "Church Language and Vernacular Language in Central Asian Buddhism." *Numen* 37, no. 2 (1990): 195–219.

Naymark, Aleksandr. "Sogdiana, Its Christians and Byzantium: A Study of Artistic and Cultural Connections in Late Antiquity and Early Middle Ages." Ph.D. diss. Indiana University, 2001.

Rhie, Marylin Martin. *Early Buddhist Art of China and Central Asia.* Leiden, Netherlands: Brill, 1999.

Rosenfield, John. *Dynastic Arts of the Kushans.* Berkeley: University of California Press, 1967.

Salomon, Richard. *Ancient Buddhist Scrolls from Gandhāra: The British Library Kharoṣṭhī Fragments.* Seattle: University of Washington Press, 1999.

Salomon, Richard. *A Gāndhārī Version of the Rhinoceros Sūtra: British Library Kharoṣṭhī Fragment 5B.* Seattle: University of Washington Press, 2000.

Sims-Williams, Nicholas. *New Light on Ancient Afghanistan: The Decipherment of Bactrian.* London: School of Oriental and African Studies, University of London, 1997.

Stavisky, Boris. "The Fate of Buddhism in Middle Asia." *Silk Road Art and Archaeology* 3 (1993–1994): 113–142.

Utz, David. "Arsak, Parthian Buddhists, and 'Iranian' Buddhism." In *Buddhism across Boundaries: Chinese Buddhism and the Western Regions,* ed. John R. McRae and Jan Nattier. Honolulu: University of Hawaii Press, 2004.

Zürcher, Erik. "Han Buddhism and the Western Region." In *Thought and Law in Qin and Han China: Studies Dedicated to Anthony Hulsewé on the Occasion of His Eightieth Birthday,* ed. W. L. Idema and E. Zürcher. Leiden, Netherlands: Brill, 1990.

JAN NATTIER

CENTRAL ASIA, BUDDHIST ART IN

More than half a million years ago, plate movements of the earth's crust, by thrusting up the Himalayas and the Tibetan plateau, prevented monsoons from reaching the interior and desertified the area to the north; yet glacial melt streams from the Kunlun mountains and the Tianshan range created extensive fertile oases along the edges of the Taklamakan desert. In *De la Grèce à la Chine* (1948), René Grousset memorably described the SILK ROAD as a chaplet or rosary of oasis towns strung around this great desert. Even today, the Keriya river supports well-spaced pastoral households over 250 kilometers into the desert, but at one time, the ease of growing fruit and grains led to the existence of settled and prosperous kingdoms, where Buddhism flourished from the third century C.E. onward. Side-by-side with translations of the scriptures, the arts of architecture, sculpture, and painting had their own contribution to make to this exchange of ideas.

Architecture

The practice of Buddhism by communities of monks required places remote enough for undisturbed meditation, yet close enough to centers of population whose devotional activities could support them. Cells for the monks, undecorated save perhaps for a single image of the Buddha in meditation, and larger shrines for images of the Buddha and narratives of his life and teachings, could easily be hollowed out of the soft rocks and gravel or sand conglomerates of the region: At some sites hundreds of caves survive, often with a great deal of their painted imagery (Kizil and other sites near Kucha, Toyuq, Bezeklik, and DUNHUANG). The architecture ultimately derives from India, but at Dunhuang, the early caves and individual niches show features typical of Chinese wooden architecture, such as the transverse front chamber with simulated gable ceiling.

Architectural monuments include great stūpas (Rawak, Endere) and monastic buildings (Keriya, Tumshuk, Miran, Gaochang, Beiting). Architectural style, particularly of CAVE SANCTUARIES, depends on the topography and characteristics of the natural materials at each site. The basic plan consisted of an anterior cell with the main image centrally placed opposite the entrance, and a smaller rear chamber, lower in height, with entrances on either side of the main image, allowing circumambulation (*pradakṣiṇa*) around it.

Wall paintings

Both cave sanctuaries and constructed buildings were decorated with wall paintings, a great many of which have survived, although many have been removed from their original sites to museums in London, Paris, New Delhi, Saint Petersburg, and Seoul. Mineral pigments were used.

Two Buddhist sanctuaries along the Keriya River were excavated in the mid-1990s. The two buildings were constructed of wooden pillars with reed and clay walls, with a central chamber two meters square, surrounded by a 1.5-meter wide corridor. Although the walls had collapsed to a height of some twenty to ninety centimeters, the scattering of painted fragments and of fallen timbers enabled one sanctuary to be reconstructed almost in its entirety. In the lower register were mural paintings of life-size standing buddhas in Indian style, three on each side (except on the entrance wall), each buddha with two small buddhas in the upper corners, while in the upper part of each wall was a series of smaller panels, each with two smaller seated buddhas in gray or orange robes, one above the other.

Sculptures

Except at Dunhuang, few sculptures remain in situ; archaeological explorers removed many of them early in the twentieth century. Throughout the region, the stucco images are intimately related to the mural decoration: Aureoles and nimbi are regularly painted on the walls behind them, and share the same style. Often, it is these painted features alone that survive, clearly indicating whether the lost image was seated or standing.

Two Adoring Bodhisattvas. A wall painting at Kizil, China. (Central Asian/Chinese, seventh century.) Freer Gallery of Art Library. Reproduced by permission.

Rawak stūpa, some sixty kilometers north of Khotan, still stands in a rectangular enclosure whose corners are oriented to the cardinal directions and whose walls were lined with large and small clay sculptures attached to a wooden armature. Once the form had been built up in clay, the surface was smoothed and coated with a final thin layer of gypsum plaster, and painted, using the same pigments employed for the mural paintings. Aurel Stein in 1900 and 1901 and Emil Trinkler in 1930 both made partial excavations of the site, but because of the fragility of the unbaked clay sculptures, some remain buried beneath the sands.

In the whole region of the Taklamakan, clay stucco was the most common form of sculpture. Major elements of the imagery were often produced with the aid of molds, some of which have survived: They range from decorative details and miniature BUDDHA IMAGES to heads and individual body parts, such as hands and feet, and even whole figures of up to about a quarter or a third life-size, such as a complete seated buddha excavated near Khotan. From Tumshuk, near Kucha, come three almost complete tableaux, each about eighty centimeters in height and sixty centimeters wide, illustrating crucial episodes in individual JĀTAKA stories, evidently composed using a number of such molds.

A folding carved wooden shrine depicting Amitābha Buddha with the eight great bodhisattvas. (Central Asian, ca. 850–950.) The Nelson-Atkins Museum of Art, Kansas City, Missouri. Reproduced by permission.

Small wooden images dating from the fifth century C.E. onward have been found at sites such as Toyuq and Gaochang. These images furnished a means for the dissemination of iconography and style, and include both single images and narrative scenes. Several examples exist in triptych form, in which hinged panels with smaller narrative scenes flank the central image; when closed, they are fastened by means of a clasp, protecting the images within and presenting a tall smooth exterior.

Kucha

Kucha, on the northern route, is surrounded by Buddhist monuments. The cave temples of Kizil, some sixty kilometers to the west, are lavishly decorated with wall paintings. The sixth-century C.E. dating proposed by Albert von Le Coq and Ernst Waldschmidt is slow to be discarded in favor of Su Bai's dating, supported by carbon-14 tests at the site, which suggest a third-century C.E. start.

Shrines at Kizil have an entrance leading directly into a barrel-vaulted longitudinal chamber, with the main image in a niche directly opposite. Large preaching scenes appear on the lateral walls below a balcony of heavenly figures, while the vault, springing from a corbel, depicts individual preaching scenes or *jātaka* stories in a diamond lattice. For purposes of *pradakṣiṇa* or ritual circumambulation of the main image, a lower vaulted passage leads to a narrow rear chamber in which the Buddha's *parinirvāṇa* is depicted in mural paintings or in sculptured form. The final element in the iconographical program is a half-circular lunette over the entrance, often portraying MAITREYA, the buddha of the future, sometimes with twin niches beneath for smaller stucco or clay sculptures. The largest caves at Kizil, with a colossal central image, had up to five successive balconies with sculptures instead of paintings on the lateral walls.

Sites along the southern route include Niya, Miran, Endere, and Loulan; those along the north include Karashahr, Gaochang, Bezeklik, and Toyuq. The two routes rejoined near the Chinese border west of Dunhuang, where at least one of the fifth-century Northern Wei caves (cave 257) displays a narrative depicted with iconography and style similar to the same narrative at Kizil (cave 224), the only major difference being the placing of the story on the crown of the vault in Kizil, and at waist level on the side walls in Dunhuang. On this occasion at least, the same craftsmen must have worked at both sites, changing the placement to suit the local architectural schema.

At the Chinese end of the Silk Road, the huge natural cave (no. 169) at Binglingsi, on the Yellow River near Lanzhou, bears a date of 420 C.E. The larger than life-size clay sculptures modeled on wooden armatures are closely related in style to contemporary stone sculptures at Mathurā, showing how rapid was the transmission of both iconography and style, with the necessary adaptation to local materials.

See also: **Bāmiyān; Central Asia; China; China, Buddhist Art in; Monastic Architecture**

Bibliography

Baumer, Christoph. *Southern Silk Road: In the Footsteps of Sir Aurel Stein and Sven Hedin.* Bangkok, Thailand: Orchid Press, 2000.

Debaine-Francfort, Corinne; Idriss, Abduressul; et al. *Keriya, mémoires d'un fleuve: archéologie et civilisation des oasis du Taklamakan.* Suilly-la-Tour: Editions Findakly; Paris: Electricité de France, 2001.

Giès, Jacques, and Cohen, Monique. *Sérinde, terre de Bouddha: dix siècles d'art sur la route de la soie.* Paris: Réunion des Musées Nationaux, 1995.

Gropp, Gerd. *Archäologische Funde aus Khotan Chinesisch-Ostturkestan: die Trinkler-Sammlung im Übersee-Museum.* Bremen, Germany: Röver, 1974.

Härtel, Herbert, and Yaldiz, Marianne. *Along the Ancient Silk Routes: Central Asian Art from the West Berlin State Museums.* New York: Metropolitan Museum of Art, 1982.

Howard, Angela Falco. "In Support of a New Chronology for the Kizil Mural Paintings." *Archives of Asian Art* 44 (1991): 68–83.

Maillard, Monique; Jera Bezard, Robert; and Gaulier, Simone. *Buddhism in Afghanistan and Central Asia.* Leiden, Netherlands: Brill, 1976.

Muséum d'Histoire Naturelle de Paris. *La route de la soie.* Paris: Arthaud, 1985.

Nara Prefectural Museum of Art. *The Silk Road and the World of Xuanzang.* Tokyo: Asahi Shimbun, 1999.

Whitfield, Roderick; Agnew, Neville; and Whitfield, Susan. *Cave Temples of Mogao: Art and History on the Silk Road.* Los Angeles: Getty Conservation Trust, 2000.

RODERICK WHITFIELD

CEYLON. *See* **Sri Lanka**

CHAN ART

From the point of view of art history, the CHAN SCHOOL (Japanese, Zen; Korean, Sŏn), more than any other form of Buddhism, has long been associated with distinctive modes of visual representation. Looking at Japan, for instance, such disparate forms as architecture, ceramics, tea ceremony, gardens, sculpture, and painting have been viewed as elements of a broad and unified Zen aesthetic that cuts across traditional boundaries. Since there is no category or concept of "Chan art" in surviving texts from the Tang (618–907) or Song (960–1279) dynasties, however, when the Chan school achieved its peak popularity, the historical origins of this aesthetic in China remain murky, at best. Indeed, in light of this lack of sources, scholars have had to develop their own criteria and definitions. A closer look at how these conceptions have evolved, particularly with regard to painting, may help illuminate the larger question (and problem) of how to define Chan art.

Western interest in art forms connected with Chan Buddhism was a natural outgrowth of the broader interest in Chan and Zen that began in the early 1900s and blossomed over the course of the century. One of the first scholars to identify Chan art (especially Chan painting) as a specific subcategory of Buddhist art was the eminent British Asianist Arthur Waley, whose *Introduction to the Study of Chinese Painting* (1923) contained a chapter titled "Zen Buddhism and Its Relation

Bodhidharma, putative fifth-century founder of Chan Buddhism, depicted during a legendary meditation in a cave, painted by a Japanese Zen monk Fugai Ekun (1568–1654) who himself lived in caves. (Japanese, seventeenth century.) Freer Gallery of Art Library. Reproduced by permission.

to Art" that proved to be enormously influential. (Waley, as was typical at the time, uses the Japanese term *Zen* rather than *Chan,* even when he is writing about China.) In particular, Waley's focus on the notion of painting as a vehicle for the expression of religious ideals provided a model approach that continues to be employed in many discussions of Chan art, even if some historians of art and religion have challenged some of its underlying assumptions.

Following Waley's example, it became common to define Chan art primarily in terms of subject matter, focusing on images (such as representations of BODHIDHARMA, the putative founder of Chan in China) that derive from Chan history and literature. Such works often carry additional meanings relating to Chan doctrine or ideology, as well. For example, the great many surviving paintings that depict the early Chan patriarchs might be interpreted as a pictorial counterpart to the concern with issues of lineage and transmission that figures so prominently in early Chan textual sources. In a similar vein, images of monks carrying hoes or chopping bamboo have frequently been related to the premium that Chan is said to place on the value of manual labor. While these kinds of explanatory strategies are relatively straightforward, most attempts to define Chan art also introduce other important issues concerning Chan ideals that merit further scrutiny—in particular, iconoclasm and self-expression.

Art and iconoclasm

One of the most distinctive attributes of Chan, as characterized in popular accounts, is its emphasis on eccentric and iconoclastic behavior, and images that celebrate these qualities are among the most commonly cited examples of Chan art. This repertoire would include portraits of such Tang dynasty figures as Hanshan and Shide—the wild poet of Cold Mountain and his impish sidekick—and the monk Bird's Nest, who took up residence in a tree, as well as other subjects equally noted for their unconventional appearance and frequently outlandish conduct.

In several well-known instances, the notion of iconoclastic behavior is not merely figurative. One painting, attributed to the thirteenth-century painter Liang Kai and executed in monochrome ink in an abbreviated manner, purportedly shows the sixth Chan patriarch HUINENG (638–713) tearing up sūtras with apparent gusto and evident glee. Another work, by the early fourteenth-century painter Yintuoluo, depicts "The Monk from Danxia Burning a Wooden Image of the Buddha." In most situations, one would expect such acts of desecration to be met with shock and disapproval, but what is noteworthy in this context is that ripping up a sacred text and burning a religious statue are presented not as acts of blasphemy but rather as manifestations of spiritual nonattachment. The philosophical basis for this view is cleverly demonstrated by the literary accounts of the incident depicted in Yintuoluo's painting.

> Once, the monk from Danxia was staying at the Huilin Monastery. The weather was very cold, so the Master took a wooden statue of the Buddha and made a fire with it. When someone criticized him for doing so, the Master said: "I burned it in order to extract the sacred relics it contained." The man said: "But how can you extract the sacred relics from an ordinary piece of wood?" The Master replied: "Well, if it is nothing more than a piece of wood, then why scold me for burning it?" (Fontein and Hickman, pp. 36–37)

Another Japanese depiction of Bodhidharma. (Japanese scroll painting, late sixteenth century.) © Copyright The British Museum. Reproduced by permission.

Quite apart from the obviously intentional humor of the anecdote (and of its pictorial representation), this inversion of sacred and profane is clearly meant to demonstrate in a graphic way the Chan school's avowed independence from words and images.

Art and expression

In the examples cited thus far, Chan art is essentially defined as a function of representation: Subject matter (or, more precisely, the correlation between pictorial content and Chan doctrine) is given precedence over style and authorship. A somewhat different, though complementary, approach, postulates that there are levels of meaning that can be generated by

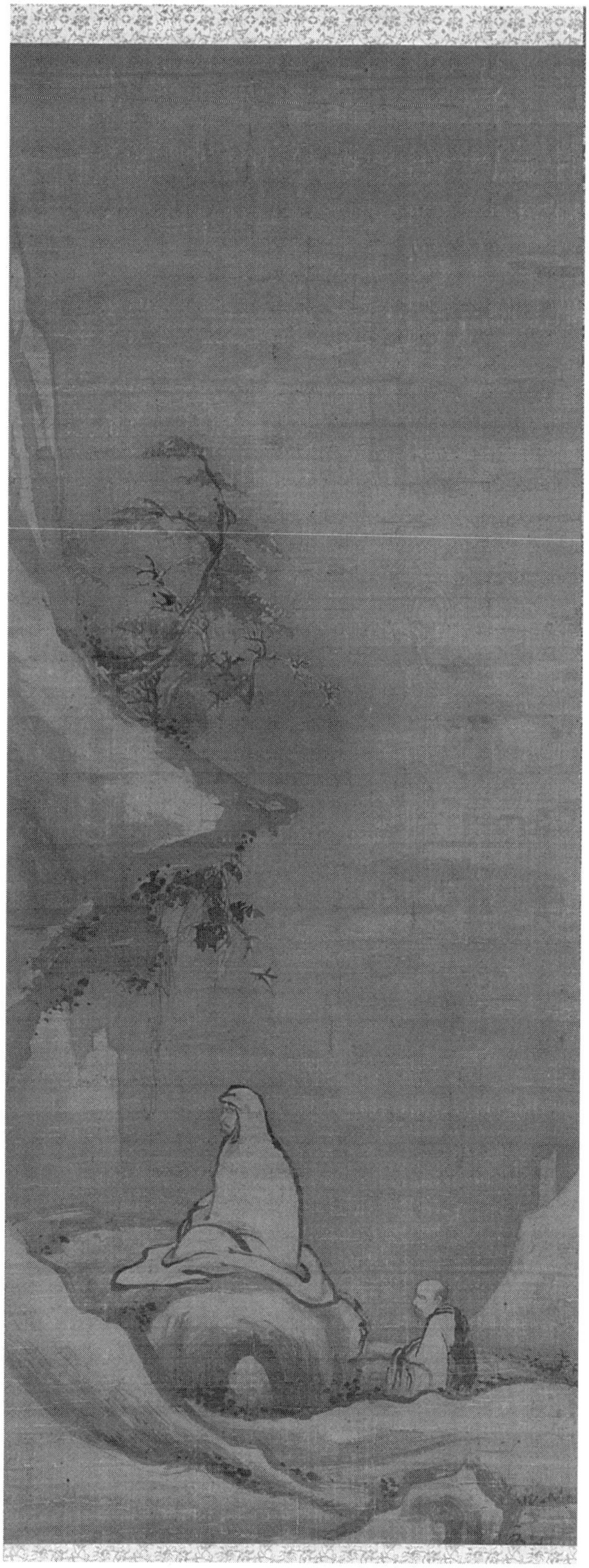

Bodhidharma Meditating Facing a Cliff, China, late Song dynasty (960–1270). Hanging scroll, ink on silk, 116.2 x 46.35 cm. © The Cleveland Museum of Art, 2003. John L. Severance Fund, 1972.41. Reproduced by permission.

artistic practice as well as by artistic product—levels of meaning, that is, that are a function of the creative act itself. From this perspective, an explicit connection would be drawn between the so-called splashed ink (*pomo*) mode of painting, characterized by rough and seemingly improvisational brushwork, and the emphasis on intuition, immediacy, and sudden enlightenment commonly associated with orthodox Chan teachings. In other words, the meaning of such works is located in the manner of execution, and does not depend on nor arise from any particular subject matter or iconography.

Some writers go even further, suggesting that there are artworks that embody Chan content (or essence) in a way that transcends issues of subject matter, style, and function altogether. According to this account, a new kind of painting developed in China during the twelfth and thirteenth centuries in the Chan monasteries clustered around the West Lake in Hangzhou. Executed by monk-painters, such works came to be seen both as a form of religious practice and as a record of the painter's spiritual achievement. As the well-known art historian Michael Sullivan describes it, "In seeking a technique with which to express the intensity of his intuition, the Chan painter turned to the brush and . . . proceeded to record his own moments of truth" (p. 148). From this point of view, in short, the unique and ineffable quality of Chan painting is nothing less than the embodiment of the enlightened mind of the painter.

The artist who is most often used to exemplify this ideal is the thirteenth-century Chinese monk Fachang, better known as Muqi, whose *Six Persimmons* is undoubtedly the most frequently reproduced and best-known example of Chan painting. Although this small, sketchy, monochrome painting might not seem like much at first glance, it has been repeatedly hailed as the greatest Chan painting of all time. Appropriately enough, it was Waley who first rhapsodized about the work, declaring *Six Persimmons* to be endowed with "a stupendous calm" (p. 231). For Waley, as for later commentators, this quality stands as a manifestation of the painter's spiritual achievement, as a living expression of the painter's original mind (Pallis, p. 44). Put bluntly: *Six Persimmons* is a great Chan painting, the argument goes, because Muqi was profoundly awakened.

Ultimately, this idea of the work of art as the physical embodiment of the spiritual realization of its maker lies behind the claims that a somewhat unlikely activity such as archery, say, can be a form of Chan art. That is, if the absence or presence of Chan essence in a painting depends upon the painter's own achievement, it then follows that virtually any activity or product, so to speak, will be similarly endowed. From there it is only a small step to the countless books and web sites that make Zen art forms (in some cases facetiously, to be sure) of everything from photography, writing, and psychoanalysis, to smoking, ice resurfacing, and procrastination.

Chan art as anti-art?

If Chan art from Waley onward has been characterized as diverging from other forms of Buddhist art both in terms of what it represents and how it represents it, it has also been portrayed as functioning differently from the norm. In comparison to traditional Buddhist art, which emphasizes the replication of set iconographical subjects and styles that conform to a canonical ideal, the Chan emphasis on iconoclasm—both figurative and literal—constitutes a kind of anti-Buddhist art. As one scholar puts it, "In (Chan/) Zen Buddhism, cult images in the traditional sense play as little a part as classic Mahāyāna sūtras. After all, (Chan/) Zen is looking for 'independence from holy scriptures' and 'a special transmission outside traditional doctrines.'" Thus, while cult images and icons are worshiped by other Buddhists, the Chan practitioner "ridicules the popular worship of relics" (Brinker 1996, pp. 38–39). Like claims about the Chan school itself, in short, Chan painting is presented here as unfettered by orthodox tradition.

A serious challenge to the basic assumptions of such interpretations has been offered by T. Griffith Foulk and Robert H. Sharf (1993/1994) in a detailed study of portraits of Chan abbots (a large and important subset of Chan-associated images). As they show quite convincingly, such portraits played an important role in Chan funerary and memorial rituals, and they conclude that "the portrait of the abbot, like the living abbot on his high seat, is thus properly viewed as a religious icon—it is a manifestation of buddhahood and a focus for ritual worship. As such, the portrait is functionally equivalent to the mummified remains of the abbot, to the relics of the Buddha, or to a stupa, in that it denotes the Buddha's presence in his very absence" (p. 210).

Their assertion—that Chan painting here functions very much like orthodox Buddhist painting does elsewhere—parallels several studies of Chan institutional history, which similarly conclude that Chan monasticism, contrary to popular perception, did not radically differ from supposed mainstream practices. That is, regardless of lineage or school affiliation, all Buddhist monks in the Song period took part in similar practices and rituals (e.g., studying and chanting sūtras, engaging in seated meditation) that were essentially part of the very structure of the monastic institution as a whole, and thus did not vary much between designated Chan monasteries and other establishments (Foulk, pp. 220–221).

From the perspective of art history, the relative lack of differentiation in terms of day-to-day activities and procedures between Chan monks and non-Chan monks suggests the likelihood of comparable continuity with regard to the images employed in support of those same activities. It suggests, that is, that Chan painting and Buddhist art, far from constituting inverse categories, should instead be understood as largely coextensive. If the popular conception of Chan and Zen doctrine as irrational and free from orthodox strictures is essentially a modern misreading (Sharf), so, too, must the prevailing definitions of Chan art as unfettered embodiments of the enlightened mind be seen as the result of the same false premises. There is little question that Chan visual culture served particular rhetorical and ideological claims, but we must also recognize that Chan art served the same sorts of iconic, ritual, and social functions as orthodox Buddhist art traditions.

See also: **China, Buddhist Art in; Japan, Buddhist Art in; Korea, Buddhist Art in; Zen, Popular Conceptions of**

Bibliography

Brinker, Helmut. *Zen in the Art of Painting,* tr. George Campbell. New York: Arkana, 1987.

Brinker, Helmut. *Zen: Masters of Meditation in Images and Writings,* tr. Andreas Leisinger. Zurich, Switzerland: Artibus Asiae, 1996.

Fontein, Jan, and Hickman, Money. *Zen Painting and Calligraphy: An Exhibition of Works of Art Lent by Temples, Private Collectors, and Public and Private Museums in Japan, Organized in Collaboration with the Agency for Cultural Affairs of the Japanese Government.* Boston: Museum of Fine Arts, 1970.

Foulk, T. Griffith. "Sung Controversies Concerning the 'Separate Transmission' of Ch'an." In *Buddhism in the Sung,* ed. Peter N. Gregory and Daniel A. Getz, Jr. Honolulu: University of Hawaii Press, 1999.

Foulk, T. Griffith, and Sharf, Robert H. "On the Ritual Use of Ch'an Portraiture in Medieval China." *Cahiers d'Extreme-Asie* 7 (1993/1994): 149–219.

Hisamatsu Shin'ichi. "On Zen Art." *Eastern Buddhist* new series 1, no. 2 (1966): 21–33.

Munsterberg, Hugo. *Zen and Oriental Art.* Rutland, VT: Tuttle, 1965.

Pallis, Tim. "Nanrei Sohaku Kabori and His Teaching of Shikan One: A Remembrance." *FAS Society Journal* (Summer 1992): 37–45.

Seckel, Dietrich. *Buddhist Art of East Asia,* tr. Ulrich Mammitzsch. Bellingham: Center for East Asian Studies, Western Washington University, 1989.

Sharf, Robert H. "The Zen of Japanese Nationalism." In *Curators of the Buddha: The Study of Buddhism under Colonialism,* ed. Donald S. Lopez, Jr. Chicago: University of Chicago Press, 1995.

Sullivan, Michael. *The Arts of China,* 3rd edition. Berkeley: University of California Press, 1984.

Waley, Arthur. *An Introduction to the Study of Chinese Painting.* London: Ernest Benn, 1923.

Weidner, Marsha, ed. *Latter Days of the Law: Images of Chinese Buddhism 850–1850.* Lawrence, KS: Spencer Museum of Art, 1994.

CHARLES LACHMAN

CHAN SCHOOL

The doctrinal assumptions of the Chan school are that all beings possess a potential to become a buddha, and that potential can be realized through MEDITATION or through the removal of obstructing preconceptions and attachments. Dissatisfied with existing meditation practices and complex philosophies, Chan proposed a direct "seeing" of one's inherent buddhahood, accomplished through such means as challenging repartee, intensive meditation, and puzzling *gong'an* (Japanese KŌAN; Korean, *kongan*). Such techniques made the role of the teacher paramount. To symbolize that the Chan teacher was the true, legitimate heir to the Buddha, Chan claimed for its teachers an unbroken lineal succession to the enlightened mind of the Buddha via the Indian monk BODHIDHARMA (ca. early fifth century C.E.).

Meditators and ascetics from the late sixth century, hoping to replicate the enlightenment of Śākyamuni Buddha, sought a distinctive MAHĀYĀNA meditation practice and list of precepts appropriate for BODHISATTVAS. They coalesced into several lineages of monks united in attempts to create genealogies from Bodhidharma. The pupils of Hongren (601–674) obtained a following among the metropolitan elite of Tang China, which resulted in contests for lineage legitimacy. These were ignited around 730 by Shenhui (684–758), who accused his rivals of teaching gradual enlightenment, not suitable for Mahāyāna adherents. His propaganda prompted a redefinition of Chan. Shenhui's own lineage, which he claimed derived from Hongren via HUINENG (638–713), whom he titled the Sixth Patriarch, became known as the Southern Lineage (*nanzong*). Shenhui combined Buddhist genealogies with a Chinese imperial mourning lineage (*zong*) to forge a link between himself, Huineng, and the Buddha via Bodhidharma. This linkage was refined later into a unilinear genealogy of twenty-eight Indian and six Chinese patriarchs (*zu*). The term *Chanzong,* in the sense of a Chan lineage, was first used in the 780s and soon became the main identifier for the traditions called *Chan* (Korean, *Sŏn*; Japanese, *Zen*; Vietnamese, *Thiền*).

The word *chan* was originally part of the term *channa,* a Chinese transcription of the Sanskrit term DHYĀNA (TRANCE STATE), but even the earliest Chan texts devalued the four dhyānas, samādhi, and other meditative states as mere elimination of sensation, a tranquility easily disturbed after withdrawing from those states. Shenhui redefined *chan* as *prajñāpāramitā* (the perfection of wisdom). The PLATFORM SŪTRA OF THE SIXTH PATRIARCH (LIUZU TAN JING), a text from the 780s attributed to Huineng, defined *chan* as the buddha-nature or the ability to "internally see the fundamental nature and not be confused." Eventually *chan* was equated with the essence of Buddhism. Huineng, who had his own sūtra, was seen as a buddha-incarnate, implying thereby that only the Chan lineage transmitted the true, verifiable understanding of the Buddha himself.

Doctrinal and behavioral bases

The doctrinal foundation of Chan was a mixture of TATHĀGATAGARBHA (buddha-nature) ideas and prajñāpāramitā analysis. The earliest texts mention a pure, original buddha-nature (*foxing*) inherent in everyone, which becomes obscured by mental pollutants or ignorance. As a result of ambiguities in Chinese translations concerning the tathāgatagarbha, disputes arose over whether meditation was needed to "see the (buddha-)nature" (*jianxing*) by removing the pollution, or whether detachment from habitual conceptualization allowed this buddha-identity to emerge naturally. This issue was related to whether the realization was a gradual buildup to a breakthrough of "becoming buddha" (*chengfo*) or an instantaneous all-at-once enlightenment (*wu*) or "being buddha" (*jifo*). After Shenhui, Chan lineages favored the latter, although some accused Shenhui of intellectualizing the process. It was agreed, as in the *Platform Sūtra*, that samādhi (*ting*) and prajñā (*hui*) are indivisible, an idea reinforced by the NIRVĀṆA SŪTRA, which stated that "because the samādhi and prajñā of the buddhas are equal, they clearly see the buddha-nature."

The search for ethical conduct or precepts suitable to Mahāyāna in sixth- and seventh-century China was not meant to replace the VINAYA precepts of mainstream Buddhism, but to supplement them. Some thought bodhisattva precepts to be the true spirit of Buddhism. The *Nirvāṇa Sūtra* attracted Chan's interest by stating that only recipients of the bodhisattva precepts could see the buddha-nature. The bodhisattva precepts advocated intention rather than formal observance, such that KARUṆĀ (COMPASSION) could override a basic Vinaya precept like that against lying. They therefore inspired Chan. The *Platform Sūtra* preached the "formless precepts" and the nonexistence of transgression in the (pure) mind. One's own (buddha-) nature is thus the nature of the precepts.

Chan tradition claims that the first monastic code of conduct for Chan was issued by Huaihai (749–814) on Mount Baizhang. His reputed saying, "A day without work is a day without food," encapsulated three themes: the antiformalism derived from the bodhisattva precepts; the preexisting Chinese monastic custom of monks doing physical labor despite Vinaya prohibitions; and agrarian self-sufficiency. Although a distinctive Chan canon or "pure rules" (Chinese, *qinggui*) may have only appeared in the eleventh century, general procedures for the operation of the monastery on Mount Baizhang probably took form over hundreds of years, giving Chan a sense of institutional independence as an order within the SAṄGHA. This development did not make Chan a separate sect or denomination, for its clergy still obeyed the Vinaya and precepts, and their practices overlapped with those of other schools. They often inhabited the same monastery with non-Chan clergy. Yet as early as the 850s, the visiting Japanese Tendai (Chinese, Tiantai) monk, Enchin, characterized them as maintaining "this mind is the buddha as their theme, the mind with no attachments as their practice, and the dharmas are empty as their meaning. They transmit the robe and bowl from the time of the Buddha, which things are passed from master to disciple" as symbols of the confirmation of enlightenment.

Developments in China

As Chan gained a larger following, it developed a specialized literature and branch lineages that tended to use differing techniques and contrasting styles. The subtlety, ambiguity, and lack of set forms in Chan teachings required an audience with a sophisticated grasp of Buddhism for it to be understood. Despite their rhetoric, Chan monks were well educated in Buddhist scriptures, as required for the state certification of monks that was commonly imposed in East Asia. They encouraged a liberal or meditative interpretation of the scriptures, despising scholastic literalism.

The earliest Chan texts were mostly treatises (*lun*) on topics such as expedient means and the mind, commentaries on popular sūtras, hagiographical collections, hymns, and apocryphal sūtras. These forms all merged in the *Platform Sūtra* of the 780s, which incorporated a pseudo-hagiography of Huineng, sermons, a genealogy, dialogues, and verses of transmission. Initially controversial, it became the principal Chan scripture during the Song dynasty (960–1279).

The figure of Huineng became a crux, for two lineages from him, via DAOYI (MAZU; 709–788) and Shitou Xiqian (700–791), led to two branches that subsumed or superseded all other lineages. Daoyi taught the immanence of "this mind is the buddha," in which enlightenment could occur amid everyday happenings, and so "the ordinary mind is the Way." Daoyi's heirs spread across China and even into Korea. The Mazu style, later dubbed patriarchal Chan (*zushi Chan*) to contrast with the intellectual TATHĀGATA Chan (*rulai Chan*) of Shenhui, was distinguished by shouts and blows, sharp repartee, and the use of everyday events as opportunities for enlightenment. This was epitomized by Linji YIXUAN (d. 866), an heir to the style, who demanded a critical attitude, even toward Buddhism and his own teachings, and self-confidence to act upon that attitude: "If you meet the Buddha, kill him." For Yixuan, enlightenment was an urgent necessity of the current moment.

Xiqian's branch tended to eremitic austerity and poetic expression of sophisticated doctrine. This branch, including the Caodong house of Dongshan Liangjie (807–869) and Caoshan Benji (840–901), expressed stages of understanding and enlightenment in diagrams, often circles, to illustrate the dialectical progress toward complete enlightenment in a return to the source, the untrammeled mind. These evolved into the popular OXHERDING PICTURES. An intellectual codification of Chan practice was even introduced into the radical, iconoclastic Linji house, with formulations such as the four selections of the person and environment or the three phrases.

Systematization

As Chan grew from a small, minority movement in the seventh century into a popular and major part of the Buddhist establishment by the twelfth century, it took on more Chinese features, and had to accommodate itself more to the state and the needs of a broad and diverse audience. Chan consequently developed a characteristically Chinese Buddhist literature and it coalesced into several distinct branches with their own techniques, styles, and literatures.

Chan teachers' words were written down as early as the seventh and eighth centuries. Shenhui's dialogues used colloquial language, which may have influenced the forerunners of the "recorded sayings" texts attributed to Daoyi, Huangbo Xiyun (d. 850), and Zhaozhou Congshen (778–987). Covertly recorded by pupils and recompiled to include verses and brief biographies, these sermons and dialogues in colloquial Chinese depict mundane happenings. They differ from Buddhist commentaries and treatises in literary Chinese, and were less structured. These discourse records (Chinese, *yulu*) constitute the bulk of Chan literature, especially from the Song dynasty onward.

The intellectualization of Chan dates back to Guifeng ZONGMI (780–841) of the Shenhui lineage, which systematically characterized and ranked the Chan lineages, and correlated them with doctrinal formulations. Zongmi wrote many sūtra commentaries and incorporated Huayan philosophy into Chan.

In reaction to the increasing popularity and immense wealth of the Buddhist order, which included Chan, Emperor Wu (r. 841–846) launched the xenophobic Huichang persecution of Buddhism on economic and rationalist grounds. Clergy were laicized and monasteries confiscated. The differing reactions to the persecution, and the geographic dispersion of some Chan groups, induced self-reflection; concerns about succession within specific monasteries reinvigorated interest in genealogy. As membership had grown, the lineages (*zong*) subdivided into houses (*jia*) descended from Huineng. From the late ninth century, masters issued certificates of inheritance, occupation of a monastery by a lineage gained significance, styles of teaching diverged, and the split of China into ten states in the early tenth century promoted regional differences. Monks began to ask teachers about their "house style" (*jiafeng*) around this time. Fayan Wenyi (885–958) identified five houses—Caodong, Linji, Yunmen, Guiyang, and Fayan—and described them in terms of the verbal jousts or *wenda* (questions and answers) between masters and pupils. He attacked their sectarianism and lack of doctrine as all style and no substance.

The Fayan house, versed in Huayan philosophy, led Chan in the tenth and eleventh centuries, producing some of the most important Chan scholars. Yongming YANSHOU (904–975) harmonized Chan and doctrine (*jiao*), and melded Chan with *nianfo* (recollection of a buddha's name). Daoyuan (n.d.) compiled the *Jingde chuandeng lu* (*Records of the Transmission of the Lamplight [of enlightenment compiled during the] Jingde Reign*, 1104), a genealogically arranged set of brief hagiographies primarily concerned with recording the words of enlightenment occasions (*jiyu*).

The Fayan house was not alone in its influence, however. The momentarily popular Yunmen house also contributed to the *gong'an* evolution through the sayings of its founder, Yunmen Wenyan (864–949), as it picked out earlier enlightenment exchanges (*nian'gu*), commented on them (*zhuyu*; Japanese, *jakugo*), and provided substitute answers to questions and dialogues (*daiyu, bieyu*). Eventually the Fayan, Yunmen, and Linji houses combined to create the *gong'an*, originally meaning legal precedents. From the enlightenment dialogues in *chuandeng lu*, Yunmen and Linji monks selected cases, to which they appended verses. These juxtapositions of colloquial dialogues and literary poems morphed into collections like the *Biyan lu* (*Blue Cliff Record*) by Keqin (1063–1135). He and Wuzu Fayan (1024–1104), who made famous the Zhaozhou *wu* (Japanese, *mu*; English, no) *gong'an*, promoted each *gong'an* as a singular aid to an instantaneous enlightenment. Fayan advised practitioners to concentrate on the *wu* word only, and not think of the entire dialogue on the buddha-nature. ZONGGAO (1089–1163), who took up the *wu* topic, supposedly burnt his master's *Biyan lu* anthology because students were infatuated with its literary qualities. This was a period when "lettered Chan" (*wenzi Chan*), and indulgence in Chan literature, was popular. Led by Huihong (1071–1128), a poet of the Huanglong faction of the Linji house, this type of Chan was denigrated by Zonggao as mere bookishness. He said Huihong's *gong'an* ignored daily life and were only random poetical cases. Zonggao, in contrast, directed attention to one word only, *wu*, or Wenyan's "dried shit-stick," in order to assist the many lay followers by simplifying contemplation practice.

Concentration on *wu* would lead to a breakthrough. This single word was called a *huatou* (key word or critical phrase) and "examining the key word" (*kanhua*) was touted as a shortcut method. It had to be experienced, like the sword of the barbarian enemy, as an immediate problem of life and death. This contemplation became mainstream Chan practice in China, Japan, Korea, and Vietnam, for it could be used even during everyday activities.

Zonggao attacked MOZHAO CHAN (SILENT ILLUMINATION CHAN) as the heresy of quietism, which lacks self-doubt. The barb was aimed at Hongzhi Chengjue (1091–1157) of the Caodong house, and at meeting the demands for a patriotic Buddhism after the loss of North China to the Jürchens in 1126. Asserting that the mundane law is the same as the Buddha Law, Zonggao maintained that one had to be active, not pacifist and quietist. This patriotic Chan resulted in the building of the "Five Mountain and Ten Monasteries" network, wherein the state appointed Chan abbots, whose sermons and rituals were for the salvation of the state and sentient beings.

Modern Chan

Having long been part of the Buddhist establishment, Chan became less distinguishable from Buddhism in general after the Song dynasty. While it maintained the distinctively Chan technique of *kanhua*, it also adopted elements of the Pure Land devotions, and fought the rising tide of syncretism.

The state Chan and *gong'an* practice extended into the Yuan dynasty (1279–1368), which codified the *qinggui* (pure rules) in 1336. The *qinggui* and the preceding Song-dynasty codes evidence increasing monastic bureaucracy, hierarchy, and prayers for emperors. The 1336 code essentially remained the rule book for Chan thereafter, and the Ming dynasty (1368–1644) mandated it as the code for all monks, Chan or not. Gaofeng Yuanmiao (1238–1295) clarified the technique of DOUBT in *kanhua*, stating that one first needed a basis in FAITH, then furious determination, and finally intense doubt. His pupil Zhongfeng Mingben (1263–1323) combined *kanhua* and Yanshou's *nianfo Chan*, and ZHUHONG (1532–1612) developed it. By the late Ming, disputes between the Caodong and Linji houses discredited Chan monks, so lay Chan adherents rose to prominence in the succeeding Manchu Qing dynasty (1644–1912). While many followed the ways of Zhuhong and DEQING (1546–1623), laymen like Qian Qianyi (1582–1684) claimed that Chan had been so formalized that "today's Chan is not Chan, but simply *gong'an* . . . blows and shouts . . . theories of expedient means."

In the twentieth century, monastic Chan was revived by Xuyun (ca. 1840–1959) and other reformers, but was largely confined to the large monasteries of Jiangsu and Zhejiang. Linji Chan membership was generally nominal, lineage outranked doctrine. Since the 1980s, there has been a resurgence of interest in Chan, mostly an intellectual curiosity about this most Chinese form of Buddhism.

Monastic routine. Descriptions of monastic routine in the first half of the twentieth century show that sitting in meditation and concentration on *huatou* were the norm. Although prayers for rain, funeral ceremonies, and anniversaries of Chan and monastic founders played a part, meditation was still the prime practice in major Chan monasteries. With the exception of administrators and service-providers, the other monks lived, meditated, and slept in the *chantang* (Japanese, *zendō*; meditation hall), also called *sengtang* (monks' hall). Contemplatives sat on meditation benches lining the walls, and exercised between meditation sessions by circumambulating in the vacant center, which contained only an image of Bodhidharma or MAHĀKĀŚYAPA. During intensive meditation periods, monks typically meditated nine hours per day, slept five hours, rising at 3:00 A.M. and retiring at 10:00 P.M. The monks could consult the abbot or instructor regarding their meditation practice. Summer was for pilgrimage, consultations with other teachers, or relaxation. Similar routines are maintained in Korea, Japan, and Vietnam.

Internationalization

The use of Chinese script, the firm establishment of Buddhism for several centuries, and a desire to reform Buddhism were preconditions for the acceptance of Chan Buddhism. Consequently, importation was made with the assistance of elites. All traditions later attempted to antedate the earliest transmission to create an aura of antiquity and further national pride.

Korea (Sŏn). After scholastic and devotional Buddhism were firmly established in Korea, monks traveling to China from the Korean state of Silla began to encounter Chan in the early to mid-eighth century. Chan attracted Korean attention once the exploits of Musang (684–762), a scion of the royal house of Silla, who became a famous Chan master in Sichuan, were reported in Korea. Musang had been an early teacher of Mazu Daoyi, and a considerable number of Silla monks, including Toŭi (d. 825), came to study with Daoyi and his pupils. However, once they returned to Korea, their teachings met strong resistance from the established forms of Buddhism.

Therefore, after earlier abortive attempts to introduce Chan, when Toŭi returned in 821 with Mazu Chan, he experienced much opposition, and took Chan into the mountains and away from the court. Eight lineage founders studied under Daoyi's heirs; only one under Caodong. Most had studied teachings of the HUAYAN SCHOOL (Korean, Hwaŏm), the dominant doctrinal tradition in Silla Korea, but were dissatisfied with its abstruse and impractical scholasticism. These lineages were collectively called *kusan* (the NINE MOUNTAINS SCHOOL OF SŎN) from 1084.

The Five Houses were imported early in the Koryŏ dynasty (918–1392), and King Kwangjong (r. 950–975) introduced the Fayan house (Korean, Pŏban) by sending thirty-six monks to study with the Chan monk Yanshou in China. The monk ŬICH'ŎN (1055–1101) founded the Tiantai (Korean, Ch'ŏnt'ae) school to overcome the rivalry of Sŏn and Hwaŏm deeming that iconoclastic Sŏn needed doctrinal foundations. Many Pŏban monks joined Ŭich'ŏn, and this, plus corruption in the saṅgha, weakened Sŏn.

Consequently, CHINUL (1158–1210) was moved to revitalize Sŏn by combining it with Hwaŏm philosophy to provide a doctrinal base, inspired by the ideas of Zongmi. Unable to make a pilgrimage to the mainland to study with Chinese masters, Chinul was successively enlightened by his own reading of the *Platform Sūtra,* a commentary on the *Huayan jing* by Li Tongxuan (635–730), and by reading the works of Zonggao on *hwadu* (Chinese, *huatou*). *Hwadu* was for able students; lesser lights could adopt Zongmi's sudden enlightenment followed by gradual cultivation to remove residual habits. Subsequently, *hwadu* practice predominated, and the Linji style prevailed among the sixteen generations of successors at Chinul's monastery on Chogyesan, something reinforced once the Mongols forcibly reopened communications with China. Koryŏ monks, particularly T'aego Pou (1301–1382) and Naong Hyegŭn (1320–1376), who wanted to improve *hwadu* practice, sought confirmation of their enlightenment within the lineage of Wuzu Fayan (1024–1104). They attempted to unite the *kusan* under the name of the Chogye order. They also tried to enforce monastic disciple through the state, but the saṅgha's corruption and the weakness of Koryŏ allowed the rise of the anti-Buddhist Chosŏn dynasty (1392–1910) and a fundamentalist neo-Confucianism.

Initially the new Chosŏn rulers did not persecute Buddhism, which had several able Sŏn monk defenders. Restrictions increased, and King Sejong (r. 1419–1450) forcibly combined the Chogye, Ch'ŏnt'ae, and another school into the Sŏnjong. Under later kings the repression was so severe that the Sŏn lineage may have been severed. All current lineages allegedly revert to Pyŏkkye Chŏngsim (late fifteenth century), who had been compulsorily laicized. His master is unknown. The result was controversy over whether later Sŏn was descended from Pou via Chŏngsim, or went back to Chinul. The main descendant of Chŏngsim, HYUJŎNG (1520–1604), revived Sŏn's fortunes by leading a monk army against the invading Japanese in 1592.

The revival was temporary, for soon the state herded the monks into the mountains or conscripted them into labor service. Zonggao's ideas provided the best defense against intolerant neo-Confucianism, allowing Sŏn practice to dominate elite Chosŏn dynasty Buddhism, but at the cost of infiltration by Confucian values. Sŏn practice retreated increasingly into "lettered Chan" and ritual, or Pure Land devotions. However, Chinul's ideas continued to have support, and several important teachers tried to revive Sŏn.

The Japanese annexation of Korea (1910–1945) brought clashes between a pro-Japanese Sōtō Zen clique and a traditionalist Korean Linji (Imje) faction, and between modernizers like HAN YONGUN (1879–1944), who advocated married clergy, and conservative celibate monks who founded the Sŏn Academy in 1921. The Chogye order, founded in 1941, included pro-Japanese married clergy, as well as nationalistic celibates, which led the non-celibates to form the breakaway T'aego order in 1970. This also invoked the old dispute over the founding patriarch of Sŏn, Chinul or Pou, a controversy raised even later by the former head of the Chogye order, T'oe'ong Sŏngch'ŏl (1912–1993), who championed Pou and rejected Chinul's emblematic soteriology of sudden enlightenment followed by gradual cultivation. For Sŏngch'ŏl, once one has seen the nature and become buddha, gradual cultivation is superfluous. In North Korea, all Sŏn clerics are married and retired from the regular workforce, being subservient to the state.

Japan (Zen). The Japanese Hossō (Yogācāra) and Tendai (Tiantai) schools, without understanding the new meaning of *chan,* imported Chan cultivation as a subordinate component of their practice from the 660s. In the mid-twelfth century, communication was reopened with Song dynasty China, and Chan's importation was justified in terms of the powers of ascetic meditation and "natural wisdom." Myōan Eisai (1141–1215) introduced Linji (Japanese, Rinzai) as part of Tendai, while Dainichi Nōnin (ca. 1189) attempted to establish an independent Zen assembly without sanction of a Chinese master, based on "natural wisdom" or ORIGINAL ENLIGHTENMENT (HONGAKU). For this Nōnin was attacked by Eisai and DŌGEN Kigen (1200–1253). But Eisai was attacked in turn by Tendai prelates, and he retaliated by asserting that Zen was the essence of Buddhism, and his pupils founded independent Zen monasteries. The Japanese saying, "Rinzai (for) shoguns, Sōtō (for) peasants," reflects the social classes each school aimed at.

Sōtō. The Sōtō (Chinese, Caodong) school believed that as one is already buddha, anybody can allow that status to emerge by a "quietist" sitting in meditation, without striving to become buddha. Dōgen, venerated as the founder of Sōtō, introduced the Caodong Chan of Ruqing (1163–1228), but the practice soon became more complex and added *kōan* to its repertoire.

Dōgen emphasized independence by ascetic meditation in the mountains away from the capitals, bodhisattva-precepts ordinations apart from the Tendai monopoly, and thorough Chan monastic routines. Receiving transmission in a Caodong lineage from China, he advocated sitting in meditation only (*shikantaza*) as the sole way to enlightenment, and he misread the *Nirvāṇa Sūtra* to say "all being is enlightenment." He attacked Zonggao, despised the memorization of *kōan* and dialectical formulae, and even disparaged the notion of a Zen school (*Zenshū*). He claimed that the only transmission of the "Storehouse of the Eye of the True Dharma" (*shōbōgenzō*) came via Shitou Xiqian, so he, Dōgen, had brought the only true Buddhism to Japan. Yet his own magnum opus, the *Shōbōgenzō,* a masterpiece in Japanese and Chinese, was ignored and not rehabilitated until the 1700s. The Sōtō lineages derived from Dōgen, however, spread rapidly throughout rural Japan, the powers of meditation and the precepts converting warriors and villagers alike. Catering to their clients' needs, Sōtō created country-wide networks of over ten thousand monasteries. In doing so, much of Dōgen's "pure Zen" was shed for the joint practice of Zen and esoteric Buddhism. The arrival of the Chinese Ōbaku monks in the 1650s stimulated the revival of monastic rules and Dōgen's teachings. Scholarship on Dōgen Zen and disputes over its interpretation continue today, with a CRITICAL BUDDHISM scholarship even denying that Zen and tathāgatagarbha thought are Buddhist.

Rinzai. Rinzai (Chinese, Linji) used the *kōan* as the primary means to attain enlightenment. Being more active in the use of blows, shouts, and witty exchanges, this "opportunist" Zen targeted the warrior class. Rinzai was restricted to the capitals and mixed with Tendai and Shingon until Song-dynasty Chan was implanted by Chinese monks fleeing the Mongols in the thirteenth century. Attracted by their Chinese culture and their disciplined Zen, the warrior rulers invited them to Kamakura. These monks brought the Chan of Zonggao and the Song as a whole package: language, *kōan,* discipline, and architecture. They also introduced neo-Confucianism and the arts, and inspired the imitation of the Five Mountains network (*gozan*) of Song China. The Gozan network, which was ranked in three tiers, was state-controlled and located in Kamakura and then Kyoto, with provincial branches later. The warrior elite and emperors patronized Rinzai, especially the Nanzen Monastery, making Yishan Yining (1247–1317) and Musō Sōseki (1275–1351) abbots there. The main role of the Gozan was cultural, as centers for the arts. These centers were gradually secularized, weakening Zen practice; wars in the 1460s ended their influence, although a Nanzenji monk introduced Zen to the Ryūkyū Kingdom in the 1450s.

The Gozan were superseded by the Daitokuji and Myōshinji lineages, which gained merchant supporters. These monasteries had been built with the aid of Shūhō Myōchō (Daitō kokushi, 1282–1337). Rinzai assisted the Tokugawa state control of Buddhism and the spread of neo-Confucianism, actions that weakened it. But monks like Takuan Sōhō (1573–1645), the last prominent member of the Daitokuji lineage, explained neo-Confucianism in terms of Zen and sword-fighting as the removal of ego, ideas suitable to the samurai. The Ōbaku influx stimulated a revival of the Myōshinji lineage, with Bankei Yōtaku (1622–1693) teaching that *kōan* are too artificial. However, Mujaku Dōchū (1653–1744) saw the Ōbaku as rivals, railed against them, and pioneered Rinzai scholarship. HAKUIN EKAKU (1686–1768), the restorer of Rinzai, reacted against Yōtaku and championed *kanna* (Chinese, *kanhua*) Zen. Modern Rinzai largely derives from him.

Ōbaku. This Ming-dynasty form of Chan was introduced by Chinese monks fleeing Mount Huangbo in Fujian before the Manchu invasion in 1647. Although a Linji lineage, Rinzai and China's Linji had diverged over the centuries, so when the monks arrived in the 1650s, the Japanese objected to the Ōbaku (Chinese, Huangbo) use of *nianfo* (Japanese, *nenbutsu*; recollection of the Buddha's name) in Chan. Many Japanese were, however, fascinated by the new import, and Ōbaku long retained its Chinese style in food, language, architecture, ritual, and dress. Abbots of Manpukuji, Ōbaku's monastic headquarters, were always to be Chinese, but the last Chinese abbot died in 1784, and was succeeded by a Japanese abbot. Ōbaku took over some monasteries in the Myōshinji lineage, so there was intense rivalry between them. Ōbaku directed more attention to study of the sūtras and discourse records (*goroku*), and away from decontextualized *kōan* as in the *Hekigan roku* (Chinese, *Biyan lu*; *Blue Cliff Record*). They invented their own *kōan*, thinking the Japanese use of *kōan* courses that encouraged rote memorization a form of "lettered Zen" of set poetic replies and textbook manuals.

In 1872 the government permitted monks to marry, and so the majority of Zen priests after World War II were married, resulting in the inheritance by sons of small temples from their Zen priest fathers. To maintain the temple, they spend most of their time at funeral services or chanting sūtras.

Vietnam (Thiền). Chan probably gained a minor following among the ethnic Vietnamese elites beginning in the ninth century, although tradition asserts it arrived in 580 C.E. with Vinītaruci (d. 594), an Indian monk who allegedly studied under Sengcan (d. 606). Another tradition maintains that Chan arrived in 820 with Wuyan Tong (d. 826), a supposed pupil of Huaihai. During the Lý dynasty (1009–1225), Confucianism came to dominate, so court elites, such as the monk Thông Biện (d. 1134), fabricated lineages back to China. The Mongol invasions inspired the Trần-dynasty (1225–1407) emperor Nhân-Tông (r. 1279–1293), who defeated the invaders, to become a monk and found the short-lived Trúc Lâm lineage. The Ming conquest (1413–1428) and Lê dynasty (1414–1788) imposed a Confucian anti-Buddhist policy, and so Chinese Linji monks who fled the Manchu conquest in the 1660s, headed for the mid-coast of Vietnam, where the Nguyễn warlords held sway. This Linji (Vietnamese, Lâm Tế), combined Chan and Pure Land practice. The stronghold of Thiền Buddhism, as the Chan tradition became known, remained in the cities of central Vietnam, and the saṅgha was nominally Lâm Tế. Thiền had a following only among the intellectual, urban elites, and since the unification of Buddhism in 1963, Thiền has been subsumed into a syncretic Buddhism.

Conclusion

Chan is the most Confucian form of Buddhism, and it has been in constant rivalry with neo-Confucianism. It is also elitist, given the strict requirements for practice and the requirements to read literary Chinese, even though some popularizers, writing in the colloquial vernacular, contributed to the development of national languages. However, there was often a gap between ideal and practice, for the tradition also had to meet the needs of clients, who wanted easier practices, funeral rites, and the transfer of merit. This was a constant tension, as was the need for the confirmation of enlightenment, which led to many genealogical disputes and inventions.

See also: **China; Confucianism and Buddhism; Japan; Korea; Lineage; Poetry and Buddhism; Syncretic Sects: Three Teachings; Vietnam; Zen, Popular Conceptions of**

Bibliography

Baroni, Helen J. *Ōbaku Zen: The Emergence of the Third Sect of Zen in Tokugawa Japan.* Honolulu: University of Hawaii Press, 2000.

Bodiford, William M. *Sōtō Zen in Medieval Japan.* Honolulu: University of Hawaii Press, 1993.

Buswell, Robert E., Jr., trans. *The Korean Approach to Zen: The Collected Works of Chinul.* Honolulu: University of Hawaii Press, 1983. Reprinted as *Tracing Back the Radiance: Chinul's Korean Way of Zen.* Honolulu: University of Hawaii Press, 1991.

Buswell, Robert E., Jr. *The Zen Monastic Experience: Buddhist Practices in Contemporary Korea.* Princeton, NJ: Princeton University Press, 1992.

Chang, Chung-Yuan, trans. *Original Teachings of Ch'an Buddhism: Selected from the Transmission of the Lamp.* New York: Vintage, 1971.

Collcutt, Martin. *Five Mountains: The Rinzai Zen Monastic Institution in Medieval Japan.* Cambridge, MA: Harvard University Press, 1981.

Dumoulin, Heinrich. *Zen Buddhism: A History,* Vol. 1: *India and China,* tr. James W. Heisig and Paul Knitter. New York: Macmillan, 1988.

Dumoulin, Heinrich. *Zen Buddhism: A History,* Vol. 2: *Japan,* tr. James W. Heisig and Paul Knitter. New York: Macmillan, 1990.

Faure, Bernard. *The Rhetoric of Immediacy: A Cultural Critique of Chan/Zen Buddhism.* Princeton, NJ: Princeton University Press, 1991.

Faure, Bernard. *Chan Insights and Oversights: An Epistemological Critique of the Chan Tradition.* Princeton, NJ: Princeton University Press, 1993.

Faure, Bernard. *The Will to Orthodoxy: A Critical Genealogy of Northern Chan Buddhism,* tr. Phyllis Brooks. Stanford, CA: Stanford University Press, 1997.

Gimello, Robert M., and Gregory, Peter N., eds. *Studies in Ch'an and Hua-yan.* Honolulu: University of Hawaii Press, 1983.

Gregory, Peter N., ed. *Traditions of Meditation in Chinese Buddhism.* Honolulu: University of Hawaii Press, 1986.

Hsu, Sung-peng. *A Buddhist Leader in Ming China: The Life and Thought of Han-shan Te-ch'ing, 1546–1623.* University Park: Pennsylvania State University Press, 1979.

Hubbard, Jamie, and Swanson, Paul L., eds. *Pruning the Bodhi Tree: The Storm over Critical Buddhism.* Honolulu: University of Hawaii Press, 1997.

Keel, Hee-Sung. *Chinul: The Founder of the Korean Sŏn Tradition.* Berkeley, CA: Berkeley Buddhist Studies Series, 1984.

Korean Buddhist Research Institute, comp. *Sŏn Thought in Korean Buddhism.* Seoul: Dongguk University Press, 1998.

LaFleur, William R., ed. *Dōgen Studies.* Honolulu: University of Hawaii Press, 1985.

Lai, Whalen, and Lancaster, Lewis R., eds. *Early Ch'an in China and Tibet.* Berkeley, CA: Berkeley Buddhist Studies Series, 1983.

McRae, John R. *The Northern School and the Formation of Early Ch'an Buddhism.* Honolulu: University of Hawaii Press, 1986.

Nguyen Cuong Tu. *Zen in Medieval Vietnam: A Study and Translation of the Thiền Uyển Tập.* Honolulu: University of Hawaii Press, 1997.

Smith, Bardwell L., ed. *Unsui: A Diary of Zen Monastic Life,* text by Eshin Nishimura, drawings by Giei Sato. Honolulu: University Press of Hawaii, 1973.

Thich Thien-An. *Buddhism and Zen in Vietnam,* ed. Carol Smith. Los Angeles: College of Oriental Studies, 1975.

Welch, Holmes. *The Practice of Chinese Buddhism.* Cambridge, MA: Harvard University Press, 1967.

Yampolsky, Philip B., trans. and ed. *The Platform Sutra of the Sixth Patriarch.* New York and London: Columbia University Press, 1967.

Yampolsky, Philip B., trans. *The Zen Master Hakuin: Selected Writings.* New York and London: Columbia University Press, 1971.

Yu, Chun-fang. *The Renewal of Buddhism in China: Chu-hung and the Late Ming Synthesis.* New York and London: Columbia University Press, 1981.

JOHN JORGENSEN

CHANTING AND LITURGY

Chanting and RITUAL are the liturgical means of transforming doctrinal and moral ideals into experience. The types, uses, and meanings of chants and rituals are vast, ranging from those performed by individuals as everyday custom, to elaborate temple ceremonies for large groups. There are appropriate rituals for serious ascetics seeking enlightenment, as well as for casual believers seeking worldly benefits such as health, wealth, and a good spouse. Defined by scriptures and sectarian traditions, chanting and ritual are carried out as prescribed actions, but they are also the means by which practitioners express their own concerns. The repeated performances of certain chants and rituals are part of the everyday fabric of Buddhist cultures, and give members their religious identities.

Repetition also invites people to lose or forget the doctrinal meanings of chants and rituals. Chanting produces liturgical rhythms valued for their audible or musical effects rather than their textual messages. Since chants consist of words, they have linguistic meaning, but chanting often produces sounds that cannot be recognized as a regular spoken language. The HEART SŪTRA (*Prajñāpāramitāhṛdaya-sūtra*), for example, is popular in East Asia as a Chinese text about emptiness, a fundamental MAHĀYĀNA teaching, but when it is chanted in Japan, each Chinese character is given a Japanese pronunciation without any change in the Chinese grammatical word order of the text. The audible result is neither Japanese nor Chinese, but a ritual language unto itself. Many Japanese laypersons who have memorized the *Heart Sūtra* as a chant do not know what it means, but they are untroubled by the question of meaning since the value of the chant lies in its phonetics rather than its philosophy. This is the case for other Chinese Buddhist texts chanted with Japanese pronunciations.

Chanting in this sense supersedes reading. Chanting only the first Chinese character on each page of an entire scripture is believed to be equal to reading every character. Understood as a consummation rather than a subversion of reading, chanting first characters is based on the idea that single words or phrases can evoke the virtue and power that all of the words combined are trying to explain. Reading for meaning is a useful step for grasping the truth of a text, but it is a means, not the final objective. All Buddhist traditions emphasize the supreme value of experiencing the truth of a text, and chanting aims at that objective. Chanting the *Heart Sūtra* without

A monk beats a drum as other monks pray at the Ivolginski Datsan Temple in Buryatiya, Siberia, 2002. © Oleg Nikishin/Getty Images. Reproduced by permission.

understanding its discursive meaning is not a violation of the text, but the fulfillment of it.

Just as single words can epitomize entire pages, so can the title of a scripture embrace its totality. Chanting sūtra titles is a common practice, and in Japan, for example, the basic practice of NICHIREN SCHOOL Buddhism is chanting the phrase *Namu Myōhō-renge-kyō* (Homage to the *Lotus Sūtra*). While Nichiren Buddhists chant the text of the LOTUS SŪTRA (SADDHARMAPUṆḌARĪKA-SŪTRA) as well, chanting the Japanese title, *Myōhō-renge-kyō,* is a necessary and sufficient means for relating the truth of the sūtra to the individual believer and his or her concerns. Chanted repeatedly, the title itself bears the power of the entire scripture, and is regarded by some Nichiren traditions as the main object of worship. The popular Sanskrit mantra, OṂ MAṆI PADME HŪṂ (Praise be the jewel lotus) and its Tibetan version, not only evokes the bodhisattva of compassion, Avalokiteśvara, but also epitomizes all of the Buddhist teachings.

In a similar manner, chanting the name of a deity evokes all of its power. One of the most popular practices in East Asia is chanting the name of the Buddha of the Western Paradise (Sanskrit, AMITĀBHA; Japanese, Amida; Chinese, Amituo). Pure Land Buddhist traditions are built on recitations of Amitābha's name, and countless Japanese Buddhists over the centuries have chanted the phrase *Namu Amida Butsu* (Homage to Amitābha Buddha) in hopes that they will be reborn into Amitābha's pure land. This practice is known as the *nenbutsu* in Japan, *nianfo* in China, and *yŏmbul* in Korea.

All of these terms conflate recitation with MINDFULNESS. *Nenbutsu,* for instance, means to be mindful of a buddha, and does not signify chanting. The term, however, is used synonymously with chanting because a proper state of mindfulness is essential to it. In addition to the formulaic words or phrases, which are also known as MANTRA, it is the quality of mind that distinguishes chanting from other oral functions such as speaking and singing. The effectiveness of mantras in bringing about intended effects depends on the chanter's state of mind, as well as the power of the words and the format of articulation.

Chanting is a form of sacred music, and its ritual format often includes instrumental accompaniment.

Bells, gongs, drums, horns, and other instruments are used to provide rhythm and emphasis. In East Asia a common accoutrement is a hollowed-out piece of wood that is hit with a padded stick to produce resonant thumps setting the pace. Round in shape, it is covered with fish scales and is called the "wooden fish" because fish do not close their eyes even when they sleep. In shape and sound, the instrument makes a point about mindfulness.

Chanting and ritual give shape to abstract doctrines, moral values, individual concerns, and communal identity. They provide structures through which important transactions take place. Clerical and lay participants sing praises, submit petitions, make confessions, request absolutions, present dedications, give offerings, receive blessings, and transfer the merit of the ritual to others, often the deceased. Nearly all Buddhists seek their highest spiritual—and often worldly—aspirations through ritual means. A few traditions, such as Jōdo Shinshū in Japan, deny that chanting and ritual are mechanisms for salvation, but even in this case, believers fervently chant the *nenbutsu* not as a ritual means for gaining REBIRTH in the pure land but as an expression of gratitude for having already been saved by the grace of Amitābha.

See also: **Buddhānusmṛti (Recollection of the Buddha); Entertainment and Performance; Etiquette; Language, Buddhist Philosophy of; Meditation; Merit and Merit-Making; Mudrā and Visual Imagery; Nenbutsu (Chinese, Nianfo; Korean, Yŏmbul)**

Bibliography

Kalupahana, David, ed. *Buddhist Thought and Ritual.* St. Paul, MN: Paragon House, 1991.

Lopez, Donald S., ed. *Buddhism in Practice.* Princeton, NJ: Princeton University Press, 1995.

Nhat Hahn, Thich, comp. *Plum Village Chanting and Recitation Book.* Berkeley, CA: Parallax, 2000.

Wong, Deborah Anne. *Sounding the Center: History and Aesthetics in Thai Buddhist Performance.* Chicago: University of Chicago Press, 2001.

GEORGE J. TANABE, JR.

CHENGGUAN

Chengguan (738–839) is the reputed fourth patriarch of the HUAYAN SCHOOL of Chinese Buddhism. Revered for his erudite and prolific scholarship, he was among the most influential monks of his time. Although not a direct student of the third Huayan patriarch FAZANG (643–712), Chengguan was recognized as Fazang's spiritual successor on the basis of his exceptional learning and prominence, which made him the Huayan tradition's leading figure among his contemporaries. During his formative years, Chengguan became proficient in the scriptures of Buddhism and the doctrines of other Chinese schools, including the CHAN SCHOOL (especially the Niutou and Northern schools), the TIANTAI SCHOOL, and Sanlun. His writings also reveal mastery of the Confucian classics and the works of early Daoist philosophers, especially Laozi and Zhuangzi.

During his long and highly successful monastic career, Chengguan was associated with seven Tang Chinese emperors, and his supporters and admirers included numerous influential officials and literati. The imperial court recognized his achievements by granting him the honorific titles of national teacher and grand recorder of the clergy. Chengguan's magnum opus is the massive *Huayan jing suishu yanyi chao* (in ninety fascicles), which contains his commentary and subcommentary to the eighty-fascicle translation of the HUAYAN JING (*Flower Garland Scripture*). He also wrote other exegetical works, including a commentary on Prajña's forty-fascicle translation of the *Huayan jing*, and a few shorter tracts. Chengguan's key contribution to the development of Huayan doctrine is the theory of four realms of reality (DHARMADHĀTU)—the realms of: (1) individual phenomena (*shi fajie*); (2) principle (*li fajie*); (3) nonobstruction between principle and phenomena (*lishi wuai fajie*); and (4) nonobstruction among phenomena (*shishi wuai fajie*).

Bibliography

Gregory, Peter N. "Ch'eng-kuan and Hua-yen." In *Tsung-mi and the Sinification of Buddhism.* Princeton, NJ: Princeton University Press, 1991.

MARIO POCESKI

CHINA

During its long history in China, which spans nearly twenty centuries, Buddhism developed flourishing traditions, exerted far-reaching influence on intellectual and religious life, and left its mark on virtually all aspects of Chinese society and culture. The transmission of Buddhism into China involved the wholesale introduction of (at first) alien complexes of ideas and institutions that opened new horizons of intellectual inquiry and spiritual exploration, thereby enlarging the contours of Chinese civilization and enriching its contents. Through their mutual encounter, both Buddhism and Chinese traditions were profoundly transformed, with Buddhism adding new elements to Chinese civilization while at the same time undergoing dramatic changes in the process of its adaptation to China's social ethos and cultural milieu.

Historical overview: First century to tenth century

Buddhism first entered China around the beginning of the common era, during the Eastern Han dynasty (25–220 C.E.). The first Buddhist missionaries arrived through the empire's northwestern frontier, accompanying merchant caravans that traversed the network of trade routes known as the SILK ROAD, which linked China with CENTRAL ASIA and Persia, with additional links to West and South Asia. By that time Buddhism had already establish a strong presence within the Central Asian kingdoms that controlled most of the trade along the Silk Road. Early literary evidence of Buddhism's entry into China links the foreign religion with the Han monarchy and its ruling elites. Such connection is explicit in the well-known story about Emperor Ming's (r. 58–75 C.E.) dream about a golden deity, identified by his advisers as the Buddha. That supposedly precipitated the emperor's sending of a western-bound expedition that brought back to China the first Buddhist text (and two missionaries, according to a later version of the story). Taking into consideration the court-oriented outlook of traditional Chinese historiography, such focus on the emperor's role in the arrival of Buddhism should not come as a surprise. However, in light of the prevalent patterns of economic and cultural interaction between China and the outside world during this period, it seems probable that Buddhism had already entered China prior to Emperor Ming's reign.

Most of the early Buddhist monks who entered China were associated with the MAHĀYĀNA tradition, which was increasing in popularity even while it was still undergoing creative doctrinal development. The foreign missionaries—most of whom were Kushans, Khotanese, Sogdians, and other Central Asians—entered a powerful country with evolved social and political institutions, long-established intellectual and religious traditions, and a profound sense of cultural superiority. In the course of the initial contacts, some members of the Chinese elites found the new religion to be inimical to the prevalent social ethos. The institution of MONASTICISM, with its stress on ascetic renunciation, which included celibacy and mendicancy, was alien to the Chinese and went against the Confucian-inspired mores adopted by the state and the ruling aristocracy.

In response to the initial spread of the alien religion, some Chinese officials articulated a set of critiques that highlighted perceived areas of conflict between Buddhism and the prevalent Confucian ideology. The principal object of the criticisms was the monastic order (SAṄGHA). Buddhist monks were accused of not being filial because their adoption of a celibate lifestyle meant they were unable to produce heirs and thereby secure the continuation of their families' lineages. Additional criticisms were leveled on economic and political grounds. Monks and monasteries were accused of being unproductive and placing an unwarranted economic burden on the state and the people, while the traditional Buddhist emphasis on independence from the secular authorities was perceived as undermining the traditional authority of the emperor and subverting the established sociopolitical system. From a doctrinal point of view, Buddhism was perceived as being overtly concerned with individual salvation and transcendence of the mundane realm, which went counter to the pragmatic Confucian emphasis on human affairs and sociopolitical efficacy. Finally, Buddhism met disapproval on account of its foreign origin, which in the eyes of its detractors made it unsuitable for the Chinese.

Despite these misgivings, by the fall of the Han dynasty in 220 Buddhism had managed to gain a foothold in China. Its growth sharply accelerated during the period of disunion (311–589), the so-called Six Dynasties period, which constitutes the second phase of Buddhist history in China. It was an age of political fragmentation as non-Chinese tribes established empires that ruled the north, while the south was governed by a series of native dynasties. Ironically, the unstable situation encouraged the spread of Buddhism. In the eyes of many educated Chinese the collapse of the old imperial order brought discredit to the prevailing Confucian ideology, which created an intellectual vacuum and a renewed sense of openness to new ideas. Buddhism was also attractive to the non-Chinese rulers in the north, who were eager to use its universalistic teachings in their search for political legitimacy. Another contributing factor was the growing interest in religious and philosophical Daoism. Many upper-class Chinese who were familiar with Daoist texts and teachings were drawn to Buddhism's sophisticated doctrines, colorful rituals, and vast array of practices, including MEDITATION. Buddhist teachings and practices bore reassuring (if often superficial) resemblance to those of Daoism, while they also provided original avenues for spiritual growth and inspiring answers to questions about ultimate values. The growth of Buddhism was further enhanced by the adaptability of the Mahāyāna traditions that were imported into China. The favorable reception of Buddhism was greatly aided by its capacity to be responsive to native cultural norms, sociopolitical demands, and spiritual predilections, while at the same time retaining fidelity to basic religious principles.

During the period of division, Buddhism in the north was characterized by close connections between the clergy and the state, and by interest in thaumaturgy, asceticism, devotional practice, and meditation. In contrast, the south saw the emergence of so-called gentry Buddhism. Some southern elites (a group that included refuges from the north) who were interested in metaphysical speculation were especially attracted to the Buddhist doctrine of ŚŪNYATĀ (EMPTINESS), which was often conflated with Daoist ideas about the nature of reality. The southern socio-religious milieu was characterized by close connections between literati-officials and Buddhist monks, many of whom shared the same cultured aristocratic background. Despite two anti-Buddhist PERSECUTIONS during the 452–466 and 547–578 periods, by the sixth century Buddhism had established strong roots throughout the whole territory of China, and had permeated the societies and cultures of both the northern and the southern dynasties. Moreover, Chinese Buddhism was exported to other parts of East Asia that were coming under China's cultural influence, above all Korea and Japan.

The reunification of the empire under the Sui dynasty (589–618) is often designated as the starting point for the next phase in the evolution of Chinese Buddhism. Under the pro-Buddhist Sui regime, and especially during the succeeding Tang dynasty (618–907), Chinese Buddhism reached great heights of intellectual creativity, religious vitality, institutional vigor, and monastic prosperity. Throughout the Sui-Tang period, Buddhism was widely accepted and practiced by members of all social classes, from poor peasants to aristocrats and the royal family. A number of Tang emperors offered lavish patronage to Buddhism, although such support was usually accompanied by efforts to control the religion and harness its power and prestige for political ends. By this time, the early rapprochements between Buddhism and the Chinese state evolved into a close relationship between the two. Despite the earlier efforts on the part of monastic leaders to secure a semblance of independence for the monastic community, Buddhism became firmly integrated into the sociopolitical establishment. With their prayers and rituals the clergy accrued merit and provided supernatural protection for the dynasty and the state. Buddhism also provided the rulers with an additional source of legitimacy, which was used in an especially skillful manner by Empress Wu Zetian (r. 684–705), the only female monarch in Chinese history and one of the greatest patrons of Buddhism. In exchange, the state offered political patronage and financial support to the Buddhist church, and bestowed on the clergy various benefits such as exemption from taxation, corvée labor, and military service. The state also asserted its right to control key aspects of religious life, including bestowal of monastic ordinations, building of monasteries, and entry of new texts into the Buddhist canon.

During the Sui-Tang period Buddhism was by far the most powerful and creative religious and intellectual tradition in the empire, eclipsing both Confucianism and Daoism (even though the other two traditions also flourished during this period). The main schools of Chinese Buddhism, such as Tiantai, Huanyan, and Chan, were also formed during this era, thereby giving rise to uniquely Sinitic systems of Buddhist philosophy and methods of praxis. The strength of Buddhism and the durability of its institutions were severely tested during the Huichang era of Emperor Wuzong (r. 841/842–845), who initiated the most devastating anti-Buddhist persecution. The emperor ordered destruction of virtually all monasteries in the empire and mass return to lay life of the clergy. The onset of the persecutions was influenced by a number of complex factors, including the influence of the emperor's Daoist advisers, economic considerations, dismay over monastic corruption, and latent anti-Buddhist sentiments among pro-Confucian officials. Even though the persecution was short-lived and Buddhism quickly rebounded, many scholars see the persecution as a turning point and the beginning of the extremely protracted decline of Buddhism in China.

Historical overview: Eleventh century to present

Late imperial China—covering the period from the Song (960–1279) until the end of the Qing dynasty

(1644–1911)—can be taken to correspond to a fourth phase in the history of Chinese Buddhism. The history of Buddhism during this era is usually told as a narrative of decline, punctuated with occasional efforts to revive the great tradition's ancient glories. Some historians have argued that such a negative characterization of post-Tang Buddhism does not do justice to the religious vitality and institutional strength of Song Buddhism. It is undeniable that under the Song, Buddhism exerted strong influence and attracted a large following among members of all social classes. The religion continued to enjoy state patronage and the monastic vocation attracted many individuals. Buddhist influence on Chinese culture was also pervasive, as can be observed in the literature and visual arts of the period. At the same time, there were signs of creeping decline, especially in terms of intellectual creativity, notwithstanding new developments in Tiantai scholasticism and Chan literature and praxis. The intellectual decline is evident in the lack of compelling Buddhist responses to the serious challenge posed by the Song Confucian revival. The shift of the Chinese elite's interest away from Buddhism and toward Confucianism was further boosted by the acceptance of neo-Confucianism, as formulated by its great systematizer Zhu Xi (1130–1200), as official state orthodoxy during the fourteenth century. For the rest of the imperial period Buddhism managed to survive, albeit in diminished capacity and often on the margins. For the most part Buddhism after this point assumed a conservative stance, as there was no emergence of major new traditions or significant paradigm shifts.

The beginning of the last phase in the history of Chinese Buddhism coincides with China's entry into the modern period. During the final decades of the imperial era, China's inability to adequately respond to the challenges of modernity—rudely brought to its doorstep by the increasing encroachment of the colonial powers on Chinese territory in the nineteenth century—led to erosion and eventually disintegration of its age-old social and political institutions. After the republican revolution of 1912, efforts at creating a strong and stable modern state ended in failure. The bleak situation was exacerbated by China's moribund economy and rampant corruption. During this tumultuous period, the adverse sociopolitical circumstances affected Buddhist institutions, and traditional beliefs and practices were rejected by many educated Chinese as outdated superstitions. In the face of the new predicament, Buddhism still managed to stage a minor revival. In some quarters, the revitalization took the form of renewed interest in traditional intellectual and religious activities, such as philosophical reflection on Buddhist doctrines and the practice of Chan meditation. Others, however, tried to reconstitute the Buddhist tradition along modern lines. The progressive agenda of the reformers included establishment of educational institutions where the clergy received modern education. In addition, efforts were made to internationalize Chinese Buddhism by establishing connections with Buddhist traditions in other countries.

With the communist victory in the civil war and the establishment of the People's Republic in 1949, Buddhism had to contend with a governing ideology that had little sympathy for traditional religious beliefs and practices. During the 1950s the new regime was mainly concerned with controlling Buddhism by instituting policies that restricted the activities of the clergy and imposed state supervision over Buddhist organizations. The situation rapidly deteriorated during the 1960s and reached its lowest point with the violent suppression of Buddhism (along with other religions) during the worst excesses of the Cultural Revolution. At the time it seemed that the twenty centuries of Buddhist history in China might be coming to an end. With the institution of more liberal policies during the late 1970s, however, Buddhism began to stage a slow comeback. The modest resurgence of Buddhism in China involves restoration of temples and monasteries, ordination of clergy, revival of traditional beliefs and practices, and increased interest in academic study of Buddhism as a part of traditional Chinese culture. Chinese Buddhism is also thriving in TAIWAN, as well as among immigrant Chinese communities throughout Asia and in the West.

Texts and literary activities

During the early phases of Buddhism in China, one of the primary concerns for both the foreign missionaries and the native followers was to produce reliable translations of Buddhist sacred texts. The task of translating the scriptures and other canonical texts was daunting because of the sheer size of the Buddhist canon (which was constantly expanding as new texts were introduced) and because of the lack of bilingual expertise among the foreign missionaries and the native clergy, which was exacerbated by the Chinese aversion to learning foreign languages. During the early period many of the translations were small private undertakings, typically led by a foreign monk who was aided by Chinese assistants. The early translations often display a tendency to render Buddhist ideas by recourse to concepts from native Chinese thought. A case in point is the putative method of "matching the meaning" (*geyi*), which involved pairing of key Buddhist terms with Chinese expressions primarily derived from Daoist sources. While this hermeneutical strategy facilitated the wider diffusion of Buddhist texts and ideas among educated Chinese, it was criticized by eminent monks such as DAO'AN (312–385) as an obstacle to the proper understanding of Buddhism.

The situation changed during the fifth century, in large part because of the translation activities of KUMĀRAJĪVA (350–409/413), arguably the most famous and influential translator in the history of Chinese Buddhism. Born in Kucha, Kumārajīva arrived in the capital of Chang'an in 401. With the generous support of the court, which facilitated the formation of a translation bureau, Kumārajīva and his assistants produced a large number of readable translations of key Mahāyāna scriptures and other exegetical works. As a testimony to the success of Kumārajīva's efforts, most of his translations remained the standard versions throughout the history of Buddhism in East Asia. Kumārajīva also taught a number of talented disciples about the fine points of Mahāyāna doctrines, especially the Madhyamaka philosophy of NĀGĀRJUNA (ca. second century C.E.).

A number of influential translators followed in Kumārajīva's footsteps, including PARAMĀRTHA (499–569), whose translations of Yogācāra texts served as a catalyst for the huge Chinese interest in the doctrines of this Indian school of Mahāyāna philosophy. One of the last great translators was the famous Tang monk XUANZANG (ca. 600–664). After returning from his celebrated PILGRIMAGE to India, where for many years he studied at the main centers of Buddhist learning, Xuanzang spent the last two decades of his life translating the numerous manuscripts he brought back to China. His work was undertaken under imperial auspices, and his numerous assistants included leading Buddhist scholars. Despite their superior styling and greater philological accuracy, Xuanzang's translations did not achieve the same widespread acceptance as Kumārajīva's translations.

In addition to the translations of canonical texts from Sanskrit and other Indic languages, there was also a large body of apocryphal texts composed in China whose origins were concealed by presenting them as translations of Indian texts. The Chinese APOCRYPHA included both popular religious tracts as well as texts that contained sophisticated explorations of doctrinal themes. Works that belong to the first category included apocryphal scriptures that dealt with popular religious topics, such as moral principles, eschatological and messianic beliefs, cultic practices, and preternatural powers. They often crossed the porous lines separating Buddhism from popular beliefs, and because of that they were sometimes criticized by members of the monastic elite. On the other end of the spectrum, there were apocryphal texts dealing with doctrinal issues, which exemplified Chinese appropriations of Mahāyāna teachings that resonated with native intellectual concerns and ways of thinking. Even though the problematic provenance of these texts was frequently noted by medieval Buddhist cataloguers, a good number of them achieved wide acclaim and became part of the CANON.

Besides texts translated from foreign languages, the Chinese Buddhist canon also came to include a large number of texts composed by Chinese authors. These texts are written in a number of genres and cover a wide range of perspectives on diverse aspects of Buddhist beliefs, doctrines, practices, and institutions. They include exegetical works (especially commentaries on important scriptures), encyclopedias, collections of biographies of eminent monks, texts dealing with monastic regulations and practices, meditation and ritual manuals, historical works, and systematic expositions of Sinitic doctrinal systems (such as Huayan and Tiantai). A large part of the canon includes texts produced by the main schools of Chinese Buddhism. An example of that type are the Chan school's records of sayings (*yulu*) and *gong'an* (Japanese, KŌAN) collections. In addition, there are a large number of extracanonical works—such as collections of miracle tales—that deal with popular Buddhist beliefs and practices. Buddhist themes and ideas can also be found in secular literary works, such as the poems of major Chinese poets, including Wang Wei (701–761) and Bo Juyi (772–846) during the Tang, and Su Shi (1037–1101) during the Song period.

Schools and traditions

The study of Chinese Buddhism in terms of specific "schools" (*zong*), an approach that has commonly been adopted by scholars working in the field, is complicated by the multivalent connotations of the Chinese term *zong*. In the Buddhist context the term *zong* can mean a specific doctrine (or an interpretation of it), an essential purport or teaching of a canonical text, an exegetical tradition, or a religious group bound together by shared ideals and adherence to a common set of principles. When the term is used in the last sense, it does not denote separate sects, as defined in typologies formulated by sociologists of religion. The distinct schools of Chinese Buddhism lacked institutional independence. They primarily represented distinct doctrinal or exegetical orientations, or loosely-organized religious groups that were subsumed within the mainstream monastic order. It is also important to note that as a rule these schools involved only a small segment of the monastic elite, and local manifestations of Buddhist religiosity among ordinary people mostly had little direct connection with them.

During the early period, the intellectual and religious agendas of Chinese Buddhism were largely shaped by texts and teachings that originated in India. During the fourth and fifth centuries the most influential school of Mahāyāna was the Madhyamaka (Middle Way), whose teachings of śūnyatā attracted the attention of Chinese scholiasts. The interest in Madhyamaka philosophy was stimulated by the arrival of Kumārajīva, and it culminated with the formation of the Sanlun (Three Treatises) school by Jizang (549–623), which is usually described as a Chinese version of Madhyamaka. Notwithstanding these developments, the sixth century was the beginning of a general move within Chinese Buddhism away from the relentless apophasis of Madhyamaka doctrine toward increased interest in teachings that presented more positive depictions of the nature of reality and the quest for salvation, especially as articulated by the Yogācāra and TATHĀGATAGARBHA traditions. The strong interest in YOGĀCĀRA SCHOOL teachings about the nature of consciousness and the stages of spiritual practice eventually led to the development of the Shelun school (based on the *Mahāyānasaṃgraha* of ASAṄGA) and the Dilun school (based on VASUBANDHU's commentary on the *Daśabhūmikasūtropadśa*). Both of them were primarily exegetical traditions, centered around small groups of elite scholarly monks who were bound by shared religious and intellectual interests.

The tathāgatagarbha, together with the closely related Buddha-nature doctrine, originally occupied a marginal position in Indian Buddhism. Although these theories did not give rise to any new Chinese schools, they became key doctrinal tenets and articles of belief for the new Buddhist traditions that emerged during the Sui-Tang period. This new Buddhism is principally associated with the teachings of the Tiantai, Huayan, Chan, and Pure Land schools. Each of them was a unique Sinitic tradition that had no direct counterpart in Indian Buddhism, and their emergence is viewed as the culmination of the Sinification of Buddhist doctrines and practices. Tiantai and Huayan were especially renowned for their scriptural exegesis and creation of sophisticated systems of Buddhist doctrine that represent the highest intellectual achievements of Chinese Buddhism. On the other hand, Chan and Pure Land offered compelling soteriological frameworks and methods of spiritual practice. In the case of Chan the main practice was meditation, while the Pure Land tradition emphasized faith and devotional practices. Chan and Pure Land came to dominate the religious landscape of Chinese Buddhism from the late Tang onward, with Chan being more popular among the monastic elites and their educated followers, and Pure Land enjoying a greater following among the masses.

Interactions with other religious traditions

The history of Chinese religions is usually discussed in terms of the "three teachings": Confucianism, Daoism, and Buddhism. China's religious history during the last two millennia was to a large extent shaped by the complex patterns of interaction among these three main traditions and popular religion. The history of Buddhism in China was significantly influenced by its contacts with the indigenous traditions, which were also profoundly transformed through their encounter with Buddhism.

The initial arrival of Buddhism into China during the Han dynasty coincided with the emergence of religious Daoism. During the early period the acceptance of Buddhism was helped by the putative similarities between its beliefs and practices and those of Daoism. With the increased popularity and influence of Buddhism, from the late fourth century onward Daoism absorbed various elements from Buddhism. In the literary arena, that included large-scale adoption of Buddhist terminology and style of writing. The Daoist canon itself was modeled on the Buddhist canon, following the same threefold division. In addition, numerous Buddhist ideas—about merit, ethical conduct, salvation, compassion, rebirth, retribution, and the like—were absorbed into Daoism. The Buddhist influence also extended into the institutions of the Daoist church, and Daoist monasteries and temples were to a large extent modeled on their Buddhist counterparts.

During the medieval period, intellectual and religious life in China was characterized by an ecumenical spirit and broad acceptance of a pluralistic outlook. The prevalent view was that the three traditions were complimentary rather than antithetical. Buddhism and

Daoism were primarily concerned with the spiritual world and centered on the private sphere, whereas Confucianism was responsible for the social realm and focused on managing the affairs of the state. Even though open-mindedness and acceptance of religious pluralism remained the norm throughout most of Chinese history, such accommodating attitudes did not go uncontested. In addition to the Confucian criticisms of Buddhism, which repeatedly entered public discourse throughout Chinese history, there were occasional debates with Daoists that were in part motivated by the ongoing competition for official patronage waged by the two religions.

More conspicuous expressions of exclusivist sentiments came with the emergence of neo-Confucianism during the Song period. The stance of leading Confucian thinkers toward Buddhism was often marked by open hostility. Notwithstanding their criticism of Buddhist doctrines and institutions, neo-Confucian thinkers drew heavily on Buddhist concepts and ideas. As they were trying to recapture intellectual space that for centuries had been dominated by the Buddhists, the leaders of the Song Confucian revival remade their tradition in large part by their creative responses to the encounter with Buddhism.

Throughout its history Chinese Buddhism also interacted with the plethora of religious beliefs and practices usually assigned to the category of popular religion. Buddhist teachings about KARMA (ACTION) and REBIRTH, beliefs about other realms of existence, and basic ethical principles became part and parcel of popular religion. In addition, Buddhist deities—such as Guanyin, the bodhisattva of compassion—were appropriated by popular religion as objects of cultic worship. The influence went both ways, as popular deities were worshiped in Buddhist monasteries and Buddhist monks performed rituals that catered to common beliefs and customs, such as worship of ANCESTORS.

See also: **Chan School; China, Buddhist Art in; Confucianism and Buddhism; Daoism and Buddhism; Huayan School; Pure Land Schools; Syncretic Sects: Three Teachings; Taiwan; Tiantai School**

Bibliography

Buswell, Robert E., ed. *Chinese Buddhist Apocrypha.* Honolulu: University of Hawaii Press, 1990.

Ch'en, Kenneth. *Buddhism in China: A Historical Survey.* Princeton, NJ: Princeton University Press, 1964.

Ch'en, Kenneth. *The Chinese Transformation of Buddhism.* Princeton, NJ: Princeton University Press, 1973.

Gernet, Jacques. *Buddhism in Chinese Society: An Economic History from the Fifth to the Tenth Centuries,* tr. Franciscus Verellen. New York: Columbia University Press, 1995.

Gimello, Robert. "Apophatic and Kataphatic Discourse in Mahāyāna: A Chinese view." *Philosophy East and West* 26, no. 2 (1976): 117–136.

Gregory, Peter N. *Tsung-mi and the Sinification of Buddhism.* Princeton, NJ: Princeton University Press, 1991.

Gregory, Peter N., and Getz, Daniel A., Jr., eds. *Buddhism in the Sung.* Honolulu: University of Hawaii Press, 1999.

Teiser, Stephen F. *The Scripture of the Ten Kings and the Making of Purgatory in Medieval Chinese Buddhism.* Honolulu: University of Hawaii Press, 1994.

Weinstein, Stanley. *Buddhism under the T'ang.* Cambridge, UK: Cambridge University Press, 1987.

Welch, Holmes. *The Practice of Chinese Buddhism: 1900–1950.* Cambridge, MA: Harvard University Press, 1975.

Wright, Arthur F. *Buddhism in Chinese History.* Stanford, CA: Stanford University Press, 1959.

Zürcher, Erik. *The Buddhist Conquest of China: The Spread and Adaptation of Buddhism in Early Medieval China,* 2 vols. Leiden, Netherlands: Brill, 1959.

MARIO POCESKI

CHINA, BUDDHIST ART IN

In the Asian Buddhist world, China is second only to India for its importance in the development and preservation of Buddhism and Buddhist art. China became the great reservoir and innovator of East Asian Buddhism and its art, and inspired important schools of Buddhism and Buddhist art in Korea and Japan, as well as other regions. The range of Chinese Buddhist art is vast, stretching for nearly two thousand years from the Later Han dynasty (25 B.C.E.–220 C.E.) well into the Qing dynasty (1644–1911). Often its sources reach directly to India and its contiguous regions, to Central Asia, and even Tibet in the later centuries; there is also a complex interrelationship with the latter two regions. New interpretations and styles formed quickly in China, offering an evolving and stimulating development frequently reflecting the schools of Buddhist thought that emerged in China, as well as imagery with popular connotations. Behind the brief survey presented in this entry, one must keep in mind the incredible richness of the repertoire and of the innumerable innovative interpretations offered by China in all the arts of painting, sculpture, architecture, cave temple art, and decorative and ritual arts throughout this long period of growth, fluorescence, and development that created one of the world's truly magnificent Buddhist art cycles.

Later Han (25 B.C.E.–220 C.E.), Three Kingdoms (220–265/280 C.E.), and Western Jin (265/280–317 C.E.)

Reliable written documents indicate the presence in China of Buddhist temples as early as the mid-first century C.E., during the Later Han dynasty. By the end of the second century, records concerning the military officer Zerong describe his construction in Pengcheng (northern Jiangsu) of a large storied pavilion "with piled up metal plates on top" and a gilded buddha image inside. Such a multistoried structure topped by plates (*chattra*) also appears in a rare Later Han tomb tile from Sichuan. These examples point to the existence of the Chinese-style pagoda or STŪPA and the presence of gilded buddha imagery by the late Later Han period in China. Though the first major Buddhist translation activity occurred in Luoyang during the second half of the second century with the foreign monks AN SHIGAO and Lokakṣema, we have yet to see any Buddhist art from that center for this period, with the exception of the stone fragments of a curb encircling a well that bear an inscription mentioning "the saṅgha of the four quarters" in Kharoṣṭhī script, another indication of the undoubtedly potent foreign influences in this early phase of Buddhist activity in China.

However, within the last several decades a few remains have been presented as probable late Later Han Buddhist imagery, most notably the splendid gilt-bronze seated Buddha with flame shoulders in Harvard University's Sackler Museum and a selection of stone reliefs at the site of Kongwangshan in eastern Jiangsu. The Harvard Buddha, of quite large size, has long been cited as a major early sculpture of Gandhāran form, but has been shown to stylistically relate to Chinese tomb art dating to the second half of the second century and to sculpture from the site of Khalchayan (ca. first century B.C.E. to first century C.E.) excavated in southern Uzbekistan in ancient northern Bactria. This image, probably the earliest known Buddha image from China, appears to have its stylistic sources more decisively in the Bactrian rather than the Gandhāran region. The Kongwangshan site consists of a hill with its boulders carved with a variety of sculptures in the late Later Han style. Among the images are Xiwangmu (Queen Mother of the West), dancing figures in foreign dress (Kushan style), a seated and standing buddha, a *parinirvāṇa* scene, and a scene from a JĀTAKA of the sacrifice of the bodhisattva to the starving tigress. Though simple, the images are iconographically accurate and testify to Buddhist activity that was somehow integrated with images of other popular beliefs—a typical phenomenon in Late Han.

From the Three Kingdoms and Western Jin periods, a clear distinction emerged between images that strictly follow orthodox Buddhist iconography and those of popular, mostly funerary, art that incorporate Buddhist elements, often with unorthodox changes. The latter are various and found in a wide area of distribution. They include, for example, small seated buddhas on ceramic vessels (some the elaborate *hunping* funerary urns) and bronze mirrors (possibly as auspicious talismans) in the south; buddhas on money trees and clay tomb bricks in Sichuan; a standing bodhisattva on a belt buckle from a tomb dated 262 from Wuchang in Hebei; and reliefs in tombs such as at Yinan in Shandong. On the other hand, the famous gilt-bronze standing bodhisattva in the Fujii Yūrinkan, probably a MAITREYA, is of mainstream, orthodox imagery, stylistically related to contemporary sculptures from Swat, Toprak Kala, and Miran. This bodhisattva is said to have come from near Chang'an (present-day Xi'an), where the great monk DHARMARAKṢA was active with translating and teaching in the last half of the third century.

By the end of the Western Jin Buddhism was reaching a point of viability in China, albeit with the major support of foreign monks and the foreign communities engaged in trade along the SILK ROAD. Unfortunately, just as the fall of the Han dynasty in the early third century occasioned turmoil and mass migration within China, so too, at the end of the Western Jin, northern China collapsed into chaos from famines and a series of disastrous invasions and warfare by northern minorities. These events threw the country into hardship for several decades and virtually transformed the demographics of China as the aristocratic families of the north fled south or to the Gansu region to escape the devastation.

Eastern Jin (317–420) in the south and the Sixteen Kingdoms (317–439) in the north

The Eastern Jin provided some continuity to this volatile, fluid, disruptive period. Most of our knowledge of Buddhist art from the Eastern Jin comes from written records, which speak of miraculous images, King AŚOKA images, colossal buddhas (the oldest, ca. 370s, being that in DAO'AN's (312–385) monastery at

Xiangyang in Henan), wondrous sculptures made by Daikui, the famous VIMALAKĪRTI wall painting by Gu Kaizhi, and so on. We can speculate on the appearance of some of these recorded masterpieces of Eastern Jin Buddhist art from later replicas. One of the most interesting is the case of the inscribed King Aśoka buddhas found in Chengdu that date from the mid-sixth century but clearly replicate an older, probably fourth century, model. Also, the Vimalakīrti relief in cave 3 at LONGMEN, from the early sixth century, may follow the fourth-century Gu Kaizhi prototype. Other clues come from the invaluable sources of the Korean Koguryŏ tomb paintings, such as those at tomb 3 at Anak, dated to around 357, and the tomb at Tŏkhŭngri, dated to 408 or 409, and others that have early examples of Buddhist subjects.

Most extant remains, however, probably come from the North and from Gansu, both areas dominated by a series of successive small kingdoms, known as the Sixteen Kingdoms, of the five minority nationalities. This period in North China is one of the most difficult to access, but it is becoming evident that it is prolific in Buddhist art remains, generally confirming and complementing the important strides made in Buddhism under the Chinese masters Dao'an and HUIYUAN (334–416) and the overwhelming achievement of the translations of KUMĀRAJĪVA (350–409/413 C.E.) in the early fifth century. Most images are from small bronze buddha altars, which, in the few surviving complete examples consist of a *dhyānāsana* buddha on a lion throne, a *mandorla*, a canopy, and a four-footed stand. The identity of these small buddhas, most in meditation, is not certain, but at least one (datable to 426, now in the Metropolitan Museum of Art, New York) names the buddha as Maitreya. The earliest identifiable Guanyin appears around 400 (Asian Art Museum of San Francisco) and there are early bronze reliefs of such LOTUS SŪTRA (SADDHARMAPUṆḌARĪKA-SŪTRA) themes as Śākyamuni and Prabhūtaratna that appear as early as the early fifth century. The Buddhist-Daoist stele of Wei Wenlang from Yaoxian (north of Chang'an), though not without controversy, probably dates to 424 and may be the oldest known stone stele with Buddhist imagery. A gilt-bronze pendant-legged seated buddha, dated (Liu) Song 423, confirms this iconographic form as a Maitreya by an inscription on the back of its *mandorla*, which itself is the earliest known version in bronze of the elaborate flame-bordered *mandorlas* seen in fully developed form in numerous bronze sculptures under the Tuoba (Northern) Wei later in the century. It is becoming clear that many iconographic types and stylistic features that were previously thought to be Northern Wei were actually formulated earlier, in the late fourth and early fifth centuries in the south, around Chang'an and in Gansu.

The Gansu Buddhist materials are probably the most significant discoveries of the last forty years in Chinese Buddhist art. Though there is currently no consensus on the precise dating of all of the early sculptures, paintings, cave temples, and stone stūpas from Gansu, the Amitāyus niche in cave 169 at Binglingsi is dated with certainty to 420 during the time of the Eastern Qin in southern Gansu. Most of the superb painted clay sculptures positioned randomly around this large natural cave, as well as the surviving wall paintings, which stylistically relate to paintings in cave GK20 at Kumtura in Kucha, date to this time or earlier. Similarly, the earliest caves at Maijishan (caves 78 and 74, each with three magnificent large, seated clay buddhas), where the famous monk Gaoxuan stayed for a number of years in about 415, are probably early fifth century.

From the central area of Gansu, then known as Liangzhou, the cave temples at Tiantishan, southeast of Wuwei, and Jintasi near Zhangye, have spectacularly rare remains, the former mainly paintings and the latter mainly sculpture, both from the period of Northern Liang under Juqu Mengxun (r. 401–433). Juqu Mengxun is known from literary records to have opened caves now believed to be those at Tiantishan, and to have made a colossal buddha on behalf of his mother, the earliest colossal stone (probably cave) image in China. The early caves at both sites contain the earliest use of the central pillar cave temple form in China.

From the western end of Gansu, there are early caves at Wenshushan near Jiuchuan and three early caves at DUNHUANG (caves 268, 272, 275). Cave 272 includes a Maitreya Buddha, and cave 275 has a colossal cross-ankled Maitreya Bodhisattva. Wall paintings in cave 272 show celestial listeners and the thousand buddhas. In cave 275 *jātakas* and scenes from the Buddha's life are portrayed along the side walls of the long chamber. A rare group of stone stūpas was discovered from Jiuchuan and Dunhuang, most dating from the early decades of the fifth century under the Northern Liang. The stūpas are carved with sūtra texts, trigrams with trigram figures from the *Yijing* (*Book of Changes*), and the seven buddhas of the past along with Maitreya Bodhisattva. Two other stone stūpas have been found in Gaochang (Turfan), where the Northern Liang fled after the Northern Wei onslaught in 439 and where

Northern Liang survived as the last of the Sixteen Kingdoms up to the 460s.

Northern Wei (386–534), Eastern Wei (534–550), Western Wei (535–557), Northern Qi (550–577), and Northern Zhou (557–581) in the north; (Liu) Song (420–479), Southern Qi (479–502), Liang (502–557) and Chen (557–589) in the south; unified China under the Sui (581/589–618)

After 439, emphasis shifted to the Northern Wei, which developed its Buddhist art rapidly after the harsh Buddhist persecution of 444 to 452. Besides numerous stone relief images (steles) and magnificent gilt-bronze sculptures, the most stupendous achievements occurred at the cave site of YUN'GANG near the capital of Pingcheng (Datong) from the 460s through the 480s. The so-called five Tanyao caves, with their five colossal images carved from living rock, in some sense surpass in concept even the colossi of BĀMIYĀN and Kucha, both of which probably had several grand colossal buddha images by this time. Yun'gang presents a single coherent group of five colossi, the identity of which, however, is still being debated by scholars. Work continued at Yun'gang with the fully embellished twin caves 7 and 8, datable to around the 470s, and the twin caves 5 and 6, dating from around the 480s, the latter with a huge central pillar and fully assimilated new style of loose, flared "Chinese" robe design for the buddha images. This stylistic change, distinct from Liangzhou or Central Asian inspired styles, probably came to the north from South China. Caves 7 and 8 appear to be related to the sculptural traditions of the northern Silk Road, especially that of Tumshuk.

Though work continued at Yun'gang into the fifth century, after the Northern Wei moved its capital to Luoyang in 494, attention turned to the new imperial cave temple site at Longmen, which became the pièce de résistance from the latter years of the Northern Wei. It is by way of the groundbreaking studies of both Yun'gang and Longmen by Seiichi Mizuno and Toshio Nagahiro and the ongoing studies of the Dunhuang Research Institute for the Dunhuang caves that we have access to and understanding of these enormous cave temple sites that represent the truly glorious heritage of Chinese Buddhist art.

The multiple tiers and niches of the oldest cave at Longmen, the Guyangtong, have many individual dedications and show primary focus on Maitreya. Cave 3, on the other hand, which dates to around 515, is an imperial cave with a single plan completely executed to produce a coherent and spectacular scheme, probably centered around the buddhas of the three times (past, present, and future) as the main icons. The large impressive sculptures are massive heavy shapes beneath spreading robes of shallow parallel step pleats and elaborately curving hems that flare to the sides or cascade over the pedestal as seen in the Śākyamuni Buddha on the rear wall. The abstract carving of the faces lends a strongly iconic air to the powerful imagery. Other caves followed at Longmen and also at Gongxian near Luoyang, but the Northern Wei collapsed around 534 or 535 and its territory was divided between east and west for a short time before changing hands again to the Northern Qi in the northeast and Northern Zhou in the northwest. For Buddhist art, however, this period remains one of continued fluorescence.

Luoyang was a city of magnificent temples and pagodas under the Northern Wei, and, as far as we can tell from literary records, the same was true of the capital (Nanking) of the Liang under Emperor Wu (r. 502–549) in the south. We can surmise some of the Liang achievements because they are probably reflected in the Buddhist art of important finds from Chengdu in Sichuan. The hoard of sculptures from the Wanfosi contained many complete steles, some of which have reliefs of Pure Land imagery that are invaluable for documenting the developments of this form of Buddhist art, which appears to have begun as early as the early fifth century.

The Xiangtangshan caves in Henan and Hebei testify to major cave temple activity under the Northern Qi. Besides the magnificent central pillar caves at North Xiangtangshan, a large relief of AMITĀBHA's Western Pure Land from the southern site shows a simple setting of pavilions, a lotus pond with reborn figures, and images of the Buddha and his attendant bodhisattvas portrayed in the smooth, abstract, minimalist style of the Northern Qi. The stone sculptures from the Xiudesi in Hebei, some with dated inscriptions, the popular *siwei* (contemplative) bodhisattva, and the spectacular hoard unearthed in Qingzhou in Shandong, many still possessing gilding and original paint, amplify the corpus of Northern Qi Buddhist art and reveal the wide range and subtle stylistic variations in the sculptural repertoire.

Stone stelae, which rose to prominence during the first half of the sixth century and which were frequently donated by special groups or religious societies, gave way in mid-century to new innovations, such as perforating elements of the stele, and to the independent stone image, some of great size. Images from the Northern Zhou tended to be laden with jewelry in bodhisattva figures and to have a sense of natural mass and movement, contrary to the Northern Qi's hermetic, aloof, and pristinely pure abstract imagery, which was possibly inspired by the styles of the Gupta Sārnāth school of India. Regional distinctions in imagery were particularly pronounced during this period and they continued into the Sui dynasty.

Dunhuang, with its semiautonomous status at the far reaches of northwest China, saw continued activity throughout the Northern Wei and into the Northern Zhou, and the site generally developed its own traditions in the second half of the fifth century to around the end of the Northern Wei. By the time of cave 285 in the Western Wei, however, artists at Dunhuang had adopted Chinese style drapery and also incorporated some Central Asian iconographic features. Maijishan was also active throughout this period, with caves of painted clay imagery, wall paintings, and some important stone steles, including a rare example that depicts the Buddha's life in narrative scenes. The Tianlongshan caves in Shanxi, opened in the Eastern Wei, continued with the production of remarkably beautiful sculptures in the Northern Qi and Sui.

Following the Buddhist persecution by the Northern Zhou in the late 570s and the unification of China under the Sui, Buddhist art gained momentum under imperially sponsored restorations and construction projects. New cave sites in Shandong at Tuoshan and Yunmenshan emerged, and Dunhuang entered one of it most flourishing periods, beginning a wave of production that carried on into the Tang period and beyond. The TIANTAI SCHOOL was strong in China and the *Lotus Sūtra* is reflected in the paintings of caves 419 and 420 at Dunhuang. The regional variations encountered in the mid-sixth century continued into the Sui with certain developments: Early Sui images became more grandiose and monumentalized; during the late Sui images began to loosen toward a slightly more naturalistic impression, as seen in the painting of Mañjuśrī Bodhisattva, depicted with superbly confident line drawing, in cave 276 at Dunhuang. The great period of the abstract icon came to an end in the Sui. Very few large pagodas or stūpas survive from this period, the most striking being the monumental twelve-sided, fifteen-story, parabolically-shaped brick pagoda at Songshan in Henan, dated to around 520, and a stone square-image pagoda with four entrances (*simenta*), dated 611, at the ancient Shentongsi in Shandong.

Avalokiteśvara as the guide of beings to the halls of paradise. (Chinese painting from cave 17 at Dunhuang, tenth century.) © Copyright The British Museum. Reproduced by permission.

Tang dynasty (618–907) and the Five Dynasties (907–960)

Although the collapse of the Sui in 617 and the formative decades of the Tang brought an initial hiatus in the production of Buddhist art, the eventual long-lasting cohesion helped to engender unprecedented developments in Buddhism and its arts in China. Except for Dunhuang, where the opening of new cave chapels continued at a more or less constant rate, it was not until around the 640s that Buddhist art began to appear with prominence in central China, mostly in the capital at Chang'an and at Longmen near Luoyang.

With the return of the monk-pilgrim XUANZANG (ca. 600–664) from his astonishing travels to India from 628 to 645, the emperor sponsored the building of the Great Wild Goose Pagoda in the capital to house the manuscripts he brought back. Austere, grand, and monumental, this Tang brick pagoda still remains a beloved landmark overlooking the city. Activity at the Longmen caves dominated the latter part of the seventh century with the most spectacular work being cave 19 (672–675) with its colossal image of Vairocana, the mystical/cosmic buddha of the HUAYAN SCHOOL, the branch of Buddhism in China founded on the study of the HUAYAN JING (*Avataṃsaka-sūtra*) and brilliantly expounded by Huayan masters, such as Zhiyan (602–668) and FAZANG (643–712), in the seventh century. Cave 19 may have been a conscious reflection of the grandeur of the Tang empire, which reached a new dimension with its conquests throughout the century into Central Asia.

PURE LAND BUDDHISM flowered in the seventh century under Shandao and found expression in depictions of AMITĀBHA's Pure Land, Sukhāvatī, many of which survive in wall paintings at Dunhuang, beginning with the earliest complete representation in cave 220, dated 642, and evolving throughout the Tang into masterworks of huge scale and detailed imagery. These paintings particularly followed the *Guan Wuliangshou jing* (*Sūtra on the Meditation of Amitāyus*) that incorporates the sixteen meditations of Queen Vaidehī, as seen in the early eighth-century wall painting in cave 217 at Dunhuang. By the time of cave 148, dated to around 775, a vast panoramic vision is presented in the *boneless* technique of using planes of color without line. These color washes create a fluid, shimmering, ethereal effect on the broad, tilted plane that conjures vast space, reflecting developments in Chinese landscape painting that evolved during the Tang period.

During the mid-seventh to early eighth centuries, elements of esoteric Buddhism appeared in, for example, figures of the eleven-headed Guanyin, but it would not be until the second half of the eighth century, with the teaching of the Indian monk Amoghavajra, that the full panoply of tantric MAṆḌALA imagery would become well established. A group of marble images dating from around 775 from the site of the Anguosi in Chang'an offers the best surviving early examples of these esoteric teachings, which became especially influential at Wutaishan and later in Shingon Buddhism (of the yoga tantra type), which was introduced by KŪKAI (774–835) to Japan following his study in China from 804 to 806.

Sculpture from the first half of the eighth century reached a high degree of naturalism, tempered by abstract patterning. The Tang caves at Tianlongshan, such as caves 21, 14, 6, 18, and 17 (in chronological sequence), have the most splendid array of stone sculptures from the first half of the eighth century. The seated buddha from cave 21 (possibly the cave of the 707 stele describing the donation made by General Xun [of Korean descent] and his wife) is a marvel of powerful muscular body, with subtly defined limbs and torso. The body is draped with a robe whose rib folds form patterns of lines that help to clarify the articulate parts of the body in an independent yet complementary manner. The moon-shaped face is tense and the features carved into strongly modeled eyes and a dramatically curled mouth. The styles of the Tianlongshan imagery of this time derive from artistic modes of contemporary art of Kashmir, Afghanistan, and Central Asia, probably stimulated by renewed contact over the Silk Road during the seventh century and first half of the eighth century.

By the late eighth to ninth centuries the style of sculpture became more mannered and consciously antinatural while still retaining naturalistic elements that had evolved since the early Tang. Images became otherworldly in defiance of weight and normality of proportioning. At Dunhuang this development appears in the images of cave 159 and in central China in the stucco sculptures of the main shrine hall of the Foguangsi Monastery at Wutaishan, where the images reach a height of manneristic naturalism, combining naturalistic qualities with mannered distortions. The Foguangsi shrine hall was built in 857 after the third and most devastating of the Buddhist persecutions in China from around 845 to 847. It remains today as the oldest large wooden temple structure in China. The main hall of the nearby Nanchansi was built earlier, before 782, but it is only a three-bay hall, whereas the Foguangsi hall is a seven-bay structure. Foguangsi's monumental Tang style timber construction has strong simple bracketing, bold powerful lines in the façade, and a rare early method of construction. In the words of Liang Sicheng, an early pioneer of architectural studies in China, the structural parts "give the building an overwhelming dignity that is not found in later structures."

As the Tang empire declined during the late ninth century, Buddhist art diminished in general, except for areas such as Sichuan and Dunhuang, both of which saw major productions at this time. Dunhuang, which had been under Tibetan occupation from the 780s to 840s, flourished under the local control of the Zhang and then the Cao family well into the tenth century. Many of the silk paintings found by Aurel Stein in the "library" room of cave 17 and taken to the British Museum date to this period. The earliest Chan paintings appeared during the late ninth to early tenth centuries. The CHAN SCHOOL had become one of the major movements of Buddhism in China from the seventh century. The Luohan paintings by Guanxiu are the earliest works related to what came to be known as a Chan interpretation. In some paintings Guanxiu used a broken-ink technique that, along with the individualistic styles of Shike of the tenth century, was destined to make a lasting impact on Chinese painting.

During the Five Dynasties, a formality appeared in the sculptures at Dunhuang, and wall paintings tend to repeat in minute detail the depictions of various sūtras, a development that had become popular during the later years of the Tang. In the numerous large caves of this time the effect is astounding for its detail. In cave 61, for example, there are large female donor figures of the Cao family, and the entire back wall is occupied by a mythical "map" of Wutaishan as a sacred place. At this point, a real geographic place in China was treated as an icon itself, thus merging the concept of Pure Land with sacred spaces on earth. In general, the art of the Five Dynasties period prolonged the styles of Tang into its final, more formalized stage.

Avalokiteśvara, the bodhisattva of compassion, seated in a posture of royal ease. (Chinese wood sculpture, Liao dynasty, 907–1125.) The Nelson-Atkins Museum of Art, Kansas City, Missouri. Reproduced by permission.

Northern Song (960–1127), Liao (907–1125), Xixia (late tenth–1223), Jin (1115–1234), Southern Song (1127–1279), and Dali in Yunnan (937–1253)

Though a culturally high period in China, the eleventh to the thirteenth centuries were not without fragmentation. In the South, at the Yanxiadong during the mid-tenth century in Hangzhou there is an early example of the group of sixteen (or eighteen) Luohans with Guanyin, a theme that came to pervade this period. Guanyin is sometimes shown garbed in a robe covering the head and body, a depiction that came to be known as the "white-robed" Guanyin. Various forms of Guanyin had been growing in popularity since the sixth century, but the blossoming and expanding of these forms became a major factor in Chinese Buddhist art of this period. For example, the independent kingdom of Wuyue in the South produced a distinctive bodhisattva portrayal with prominent jewel-encrusted ornamentation and a stiff and quiet body with a gentle face. Throughout the Song period Dazu in Sichuan developed into a major site of impressive reliefs that connote a great maṇḍala for PILGRIMAGE based in large part on the plans of the founding monk, who consciously incorporated local popular, as well as esoteric, themes into the Buddhist tableaux. In addition, Maijishan in Gansu produced numerous stucco images at this time.

The Xixia kingdom in the northwest emerged as a major state from the late tenth century until its defeat by Genghis Khan's troops in 1223. In addition to Buddhist art in a variant of the Song mode, from the late twelfth century the Xixia produced a major body of art in Tibetan style, especially paintings, probably introduced by the BKA' BRGYUD (KAGYU) and possibly also by SA SKYA (SAKYA) lamas who came to the Xixia court from central Tibet. Many of these remains, which are also recognized as a major branch of early central Tibetan style painting, now reside in the Khara Khoto collection in the Hermitage Museum in Saint Petersburg, Russia. Dunhuang is dominated by the Xixia, which not only did extensive renovation of the site, but also opened important new caves, as it also did at Yulin, where esoteric Tibetan style imagery exists side by side with Song style imagery.

Much of the Buddhist art during the Northern Song period survives in the Shanxi, Hebei, and Manchuria regions; most of it was produced under the Khitan Liao. Great temples such as the Duluosi of 984 in northern Hebei, the Fengguosi in Manchuria, and the

The bodhisattva Avalokiteśvara. (Chinese hanging scroll painting, Song or Yuan dynasty, thirteenth–fourteenth century.) The Nelson-Atkins Museum of Art, Kansas City, Missouri. Reproduced by permission.

Upper and Lower Huayansi in Datong (northern Shanxi), as well as numerous brick pagodas throughout the area, express the activity of the Liao. Ensembles tended to center on Guanyin and on esoteric imagery of the Five Tathāgathas. The tallest and oldest wooden pagoda survives in Yingxianin Shanxi; built during the mid-eleventh century, it is a marvel of timber construction, with each story containing a central altar with large stucco statues. Dozens of magnificent remains of statues of Guanyin, mostly in polychrome and gilded wood and portraying the bodhisattva as seated in a rocky grotto in a pose of royal ease, testify to the continuing and dominant focus on Guanyin. The Luohans also rose to great prominence in this period, an early set being the famous ceramic statues from Yizhou in Hebei, datable to the early eleventh century. These sculptures all exemplify the naturalistic trends of the Song period, expressed in the realism of the face and hands and the heavy, naturally folded drapery, without recourse to abstract patterns. The Song image represents a truly humanistic interpretation of the most popular Buddhist images, those indicative of compassion (Guanyin) and exemplary teachers (Luohans), in large part spurred by the active Chan and Huayan thought of this time.

These trends continued into the Southern Song period. Cycles of Luohans, many portrayed in paintings following the Li Gonglin model, using rich color and a landscape setting, as well as refined depictions of Amitābha and his bodhisattvas, are masterful works by academic painters or by the ateliers of professional Buddhist painters in the South, especially centered in Ningpo. The Dali kingdom in Yunnan saw a flourishing Buddhist culture at this time that also produced exquisite art. However, the most innovative Buddhist art comes from the contributions of Chan painters, especially the paintings of Liangkai and Muqi during the first half of the thirteenth century. Both of these masters had the ability to not only offer a fresh interpretation of Chan themes, many of which were new to the Buddhist art repertoire, but also to express these themes in such a way that the very manner of execution becomes a Buddhist statement. The depth of understanding raised Buddhist art to its highest level, where the way in which the subject is painted is as much an expression of Buddhist thought as is the Chan content of the painting. The work of Liangkai and Muqi established a Chan painting tradition that was carried on by others into the late thirteenth and fourteenth centuries, though never with such resounding success as by these two masters.

Yuan (1234–1368), Ming (1368–1644), and Qing (1644–1911) dynasties

Buddhist art in the Yuan dynasty followed several streams. Besides Chan painting, which includes Chan legendary characters, portraits of Chan masters, Guanyin, nature themes, calligraphy, and so on, there was the academic style of colorful paintings, especially on the subject of Luohans, of which there are many wonderful sets. In sculpture, powerful, heavy images of Guanyin seated on craggy rocks—a theme popular from the eleventh century and probably representing

Guanyin from the *Gaṇḍavyūha* of the *Huayan jing*—continues as a major icon in the Yuan and early Ming dynasties, which produced especially powerful examples with robes full of movement. Other trends evolved in sculpture, especially those with a Nepalese-Tibetan cast, such as the styles brought to China by Anige, the Nepalese artist introduced to Kublai Khan by Phags pha, the influential Sa skya hierarch at the Yuan court. The impact of Tibetan Buddhist art on China was strong during the Yuan (Mongol ruled) period and can be seen in the sculptures of the Feilaifeng in Hangzhou, in the magnificent cycle of esoteric paintings of Śākya lineage in cave 465 at Dunhuang, and at the Buddhist sanctuary at Wutaishan, where the enormous Indo-Tibetan style pagoda at the Tayuansi dominates the valley.

The Ming dynasty produced some impressive sculptures, such as the colossal one thousand-armed Guanyin, and the one thousand-armed Wenshu and Puxian bodhisattvas at the Zhongshansi in Taiyuan (Shanxi). Many gorgeous paintings and wall paintings, often of extraordinarily intense color and skillful drawing, such as those at the Fahaisi near Beijing and still surviving in many temples of Qinghai province, document the flourishing painting schools and active temple building and decorating, especially during the early Ming. Paintings, sculptures, and superb huge *kesi* woven tapestries made during the Yongle era (1403–1425) were often sent to Tibet as gifts, where they influenced Tibetan Buddhist art forms during the fifteenth century. From this time on, China and Tibet have a particularly close interrelation in Buddhist art. This is notable during the reign of the Qing dynasty Qianlong emperor in the eighteenth century. With the building of the Yonghegong in Beijing, a center for the DGE LUGS (GELUK), the order of the DALAI LAMAS, the influences of Tibetan Buddhism were further solidified. Many of the monasteries around Beijing, the Chinese capital since the Yuan, have imagery that is strongly Tibetan in character and iconography, including the many forms of Buddhist icons common to Tibetan tantric Buddhist practice, such as those similar to the splendid seventeenth-century sculpture of Paramaśukha Cakrasaṃvara. This final productive phase of Buddhist art in China was wedded to Tibetan Buddhist traditions, but there were also occasional masterworks of Buddhist art produced by the leading painters of the time and some sculptural styles following older traditions, especially in the south.

Since the 1960s the Chinese continue to discover, document, and study major segments of their Buddhist art, and specialized studies by Western scholars probe new directions, such as the role of patron-donors; the interaction with popular art and with Daoist art; the beginnings of specific imagery, such as Pure Land imagery; the incorporation of data from local records; iconographic, religious, and interpretive issues; sources of the art; regional distinctions; problems of chronologies and dating; the relationships with Central Asian art; and the impact of Chinese Buddhist art on that of surrounding areas, particularly Korea and Japan. All of these diverse and complex studies are ongoing and will surely open up new understandings of the vast and deep subject of Chinese Buddhist art.

See also: **Arhat Images; Bodhisattva Images; Buddha Images; Cave Sanctuaries; Chan Art; Huayan Art; Monastic Architecture; Pure Land Art**

Bibliography

Bunker, Emma C. "Early Chinese Representations of Vimalakīrti." *Artibus Asiae* 30 (1968): 28–52.

Chūgoku sekkutsu (Chinese Stone Caves), 9 vols. Tokyo: Heibonsha, 1980–1990.

Gridley, Marilyn L. *Chinese Buddhist Sculpture under the Liao.* New Delhi: International Academy of Indian Culture and Aditya Prakashan, 1993.

Howard, Angela Falco. "Royal Patronage of Buddhist Art in Tenth Century Wu Yüeh." *Bulletin of the Museum of Far Eastern Antiquities, Stockholm* 57 (1985): 1–60.

Howard, Angela Falco. *The Imagery of the Cosmological Buddha.* Leiden, Netherlands: Brill, 1986.

Howard, Angela Falco. *Summit of Treasures: Buddhist Cave Art of Dazu, China.* Trumbull, CT: Weatherhill, 2001.

Matsubara, Saburō. *Chūgoku Bukkyō chōkoku shiron* (A History of Chinese Buddhist Sculpture), 4 vols. Tokyo: Yoshikawa Kōbunkan, 1995.

Mizuno, Seiichi, and Nagahiro, Toshio. *Ryūmon Sekkutsu no Kenkyū* (Study of the Buddhist Cave Temples at Lung-men). Tokyo: Zauho Press, 1941.

Mizuno, Seiichi, and Nagahiro, Toshio. *Yün-kang,* 16 vols. Kyoto: Jimbunkagaku kenkyusho, 1952–1956.

Piotrovski, Mikhail, ed. *Lost Empire of the Silk Road: Buddhist Art from Khara Khoto (X–XIII Century).* Milan, Italy: Thyssen-Bornemisza Foundation, 1993.

Rhie, Marylin M. "A T'ang Period Stele Inscription and Cave XXI at T'ien-lung shan." *Archives of Asian Art* 28 (1974–1975): 6–33.

Rhie, Marylin M. *Interrelationships between the Buddhist Art of China and the Art of India and Central Asia from 618–755 A.D.* Naples, Italy: Istituto Universitario Orientale (Supplementum to *Annali* 48), 1988.

Rhie, Marylin M. *Early Buddhist Art of China and Central Asia.* Leiden, Netherlands: Brill, Vol. 1: 1999; Vol. 2: 2002.

Sekino, Tei. *Ryōkin jidai no kenchiku to sono butsuzō (Architecture of the Liao and Jin Dynasties and Their Buddhist Images)*, 3 vols. Tokyo: Tōhō bunka gakuin Tōkyō kenkyūjo, 1934–1944.

Siren, Osvald. *Chinese Sculpture from the Fifth to the Fourteen Century,* 4 vols. London: Ernest Benn, 1925.

Soper, Alexander C. *Literary Evidence for Early Buddhist Art in China.* Ascona, Italy: Artibus Asiae, 1959.

Soper, Alexander C. "South Chinese Influence on the Buddhist Art of the Six Dynasties Period." *Bulletin of the Museum of Far Eastern Antiquities, Stockholm* 32 (1960): 47–112.

Soper, Alexander C. "Imperial Cave-Chapels of the Northern Dynasties: Donors, Beneficiaries, Dates." *Artibus Asiae* 208 (1966): 241–270.

Steinhardt, Nancy Shatzman. *Liao Architecture.* Honolulu: University of Hawaii Press, 1997.

Su Bai. *Zhongguo shiku si yanjiu (Research on Chinese Stone Cave Temples).* Beijing: Wenwu chubanshe, 1996.

Tokiwa, Daij, and Sekino, Tadashi. *Shina bunka shiseki,* 12 vols. Tokyo: Hōzōkan, 1940.

Wang, Eugene. "What Do Trigrams Have to Do with Buddhas? The Northern Liang Stūpas as a Hybrid Spatial Model." *Journal of Anthropology and Aesthetics* 35 (Spring 1999): 70–91.

Weidner, Marsha, ed. *Latter Days of the Law: Images of Chinese Buddhism, 850–1850.* Lawrence, KS: Spencer Museum of Art, 1994.

Whitfield, Roderick. *Dunhuang, Caves of the Singing Sands: Buddhist Art from the Silk Road,* 2 vols. London: Textile and Art Publications, 1995.

Wong, Dorothy C. "Four Sichuan Buddhist Steles and the Beginnings of Pure Land Imagery in China." *Archives of Asian Art* 51 (1998–1999): 56–79.

Wu Hung. "Buddhist Elements in Early Chinese Art (2nd and 3rd centuries A.D.)." *Artibus Asiae* 47, nos. 3–4 (1986): 263–352.

Zhongquo meishu juanji (Collection of Chinese Art), 60 vols. Shanghai, China: Renmin meishu chubanshe and Shanghai renmin meishu chubanshe, 1987–1989.

MARYLIN MARTIN RHIE

CHINESE, BUDDHIST INFLUENCES ON VERNACULAR LITERATURE IN

Until the progressive May Fourth Movement of 1919, the preferred medium for writing in China for the previous three millennia had always been one or another form of Literary Sinitic, also called Classical Chinese. From at least the Han period (206 B.C.E.–220 C.E.), and perhaps from its very inception, Literary Sinitic was an artificial language separated from everyday speech by an enormous gulf. Consequently, command of the highly allusive literary language was possible only for a small proportion of the population, roughly 2 percent, who could afford to devote years of study to it.

With the advent of Buddhism in China during the last century of the Han dynasty, a demotic style of writing that was closer to speech—here referred to as Vernacular Sinitic—gradually began to emerge. The same characters were used to write both Literary and Vernacular Sinitic, but the morphemes, and especially the words, grammar, and syntax differed radically between these two kinds of Sinitic writing.

Buddhism and language

The question of exactly how a foreign religion like Buddhism could have had such an enormous impact on linguistic usage in China is extraordinarily complex. Some of the factors involved are: (1) a conscious desire on the part of Buddhist teachers and missionaries (starting with the Buddha himself) to speak directly to the common people in their own language; (2) the maintenance of relatively egalitarian social values among Buddhists in contrast to a strongly hierarchal Confucian order; (3) an emphasis on hymnody, storytelling, drama, lecture, and other types of oral presentation; and (4) the perpetuation of sophisticated Indian scholarship on linguistics, which highlighted the importance of grammar and phonology as reflected in actual speech, in contrast to Chinese language studies, which focused almost exclusively on the characters as the perfect vehicle for the essentially mute book language. Probably of overriding importance, however, was the nature of the process of translating texts written in Sanskrit and other Indian and Central Asian languages into Chinese. This usually involved teams of Chinese and foreign monks who knew each other's language only imperfectly. Their discussions on various renderings, conducted orally, resulted in bits of vernacular seeping into what was otherwise a basically Literary Sinitic medium. This vernacular coloration, coupled with the massive borrowing of Indic words (it is estimated that approximately thirty-five thousand new names and terms entered Chinese through the agency of Buddhism) and even grammatical usages and syntactic structures, led to the creation of a peculiar written style that may be referred to as Buddhist Hybrid Sinitic or Buddhist Hybrid Chinese.

As people from various walks of life, both inside and outside of the Buddhist establishment, became familiar with the notion that it was possible to write down elements of spoken language, the length of the written vernacular grew from occasional words to a stray sentence or two, and then to a few sentences or even a whole paragraph. Eventually, entire texts written in heavily vernacularized Literary Sinitic came to be composed. In this manner, Vernacular Sinitic was born in China.

Dunhuang manuscripts

The first sizable collection of texts consisting of more than a few words or lines that are conspicuously vernacular were recovered in the early twentieth century from the famous cave library of manuscripts at DUNHUANG, located at the far western end of the northwestern province of Gansu. Sealed up during the early part of the eleventh century, the cave yielded more than forty thousand manuscripts that are currently preserved mainly in Paris, London, and Beijing, although there are smaller collections in St. Petersburg (Russia), Japan, Finland, and elsewhere. Most of the manuscripts are sūtras that were already well known, but there are also several hundred uniquely important documents and texts that provide detailed information about daily monastic and lay life. In particular, the Dunhuang manuscripts include about 150 texts dating to the eighth through tenth centuries (primarily from the later part of that period) that represent the earliest group of vernacular narratives in China.

For the first half century of research on the Dunhuang manuscripts, the entire corpus of vernacular narratives was referred to as BIANWEN (transformation texts), and this loose usage still continues to find acceptance in many quarters, largely out of sheer habit. Technically speaking, *bianwen* are characterized by, among other features, the prosimetric form (alternating between spoken and sung portions), vernacular language, the special verse-introductory formula "*X chu, ruowei chen shuo?*" ([This is the] place [where X happens], how does it go?), and a close relationship to pictures. *Bianwen* were originally restricted to religious themes, but they were later also used to describe secular subjects, such as heroes from the past and the present. Another significant aspect of *bianwen* is that they were copied by lay students and derive from a tradition of oral storytelling with pictures, whose most outstanding practitioners were women from secular society.

To be distinguished from *bianwen* are other Dunhuang vernacular genres called *jiangjing wen* (sūtra lecture texts, elaborate exegeses of specific scriptures), *yazuo wen* (seat-settling texts, prologues for the sūtra lecture texts), *yinyuan* (circumstances, stories illustrating karmic consequences), and *yuanqi* (causal origins, tales illustrating the effects of karma). These vernacular prosimetric genres, which were strictly religious in nature, were used for particular services and were characterized by specific pre-verse formulas. Unlike *bianwen*, with its lay background, *jiangjing wen*, *yazuo wen*, *yinyuan*, and *yuanqi* seem to have been produced and used by monks of varying status.

Like *bianwen*, these vernacular genres were preserved only at Dunhuang. Although intensive research has demonstrated that such types of literature must have been current elsewhere in China, no printed or manuscript evidence survives to document them. How did it happen that material proof for such popular genres survived only in a remote, peripheral region? The answer is simple. No one was interested in preserving anything written in the vernacular. In other words, vernacular manuscripts were not considered worth preserving and should, by all rights, have been left to disintegrate, which, outside of Dunhuang, is precisely what happened. In addition, Dunhuang's remoteness from the mainstream traditions of central China probably contributed to the chances for preservation of the written vernacular. Until recently, it was considered by proper Confucian literati to be almost immoral to write in the vernacular, and they certainly would not have taken pains to preserve vernacular texts for future generations. However, since the Dunhuang cave monasteries were so thoroughly Buddhist and located on the frontier, the keepers of the libraries there deemed even *bianwen*, *jiangjing wen*, *yazuo wen*, *yinyuan*, and *yuanqi* to be worthy of protection. The dry climate of the desert region also played a key role in the preservation of the Dunhuang manuscripts. Finally, by sheer chance, the Dunhuang manuscripts were placed in a side cave in the early years of the eleventh century, where they were sealed up, plastered over with wall-paintings, and forgotten for ten centuries. When they were rediscovered at the beginning of the twentieth century, it was as though a time capsule had been opened, preserving unchanged a marvelous slice of life, thought, and art from Tang (618–907) and Five Dynasties (907–960) China.

Manifestations in Chan, fiction, and drama

Not long after Tang lay Buddhists and the monks who preached to them decided there was nothing wrong in trying to write down their stories and sermons more or less as they had spoken them, adherents of the Chan school of Buddhism began to use the vernacular when recording the *yulu* (dialogues) of their masters. Around the same time, a few eccentric lay Buddhists who went by such names as Han Shan (Cold Mountain) and Wang Fanzhi (Brahmacārin [Devotee] Wang) also liberally sprinkled their verse with vernacularisms.

Once Buddhists had shown the way and it became obvious that writing more or less the way one spoke was possible, then secular vernacular writing similarly became feasible. Imperceptibly, there arose what modern scholars have come to call the *koine,* a sort of proto-Mandarin that served as a lingua franca to bridge the gap of unintelligibility among the numerous Sinitic *fangyan* (topolects or so-called dialects). The consequences of this phenomena for the development of subsequent Chinese popular literature were profound. This was particularly true of fiction and drama, where many of the same linguistic and stylistic conventions that had been employed by Buddhists for their vernacular stories and lectures persisted in popular literature.

Thus, with the Buddhist sanctioning of the written vernacular, a sequence of revolutionary developments occurred that radically transformed Chinese literature for all time. Moreover, hand in hand with vernacularization came other Buddhist-inspired developments in Chinese literature. Aside from Buddhist topics, such as the Tang monk Xuanzang's (ca. 600–664) pilgrimage to India that was immortalized in the Ming-dynasty (1368–1655) novel *Xiyou ji* (*Journey to the West*), the very notion that fiction was something fabricated out of whole cloth, something created by the mind of the author, can be traced to Buddhist sources. Prior to the advent of Buddhism, there was no full-blown fiction (in the sense that it was something "made up") in China. Instead, there were only short anecdotes, tales based on historical events, and what were known in the Six Dynasties (222–589) period as *zhiguai* (accounts of abnormalities). Even the latter were thought to be based squarely on events that had really happened. Hence the role of the author was merely to record some extraordinary incident. During the Tang dynasty, there arose a genre called *chuanqi* (chronicles of the strange). Like *zhiguai, chuanqi* were written in Literary Sinitic and maintained the pretense that they were relating an incident or series of incidents that had actually transpired. However, *chuanqi* are much more inventive and elaborate than *zhiguai.* This sort of fertile fictionalizing was fostered by ontological presuppositions, such as māyā (illusion) and Śūnyatā (Emptiness), brought to China with Buddhism.

Similar developments occurred in drama, where, along with increasing vernacularization, came Indian practices that were transmitted via Buddhism. Among these are the introduction of himself directly to the audience by a character upon entry to the stage, face painting, fixed puppetlike gestures and postures, and so forth. Such resemblances to Indian theater are particularly pronounced in southern Chinese drama.

Another type of Indian fiction and drama that can be found in China is dramatic narrative or narrational drama. In India, there was a seamless continuum of oral and performing arts that ranged from storytelling to puppet plays and the human theater. The vast majority of genres in this tradition subscribed to the notion that a succession of narrative moments or loci was being related by the bard or portrayed by actors. Furthermore, most Indian oral and performance genres that have dramatic narrative as their organizing principle consist of a combination of singing and speaking. All of these attributes, in fact, apply to the Chinese vernacular tradition of oral performance. Thus vernacularization is by no means an isolated instance of Buddhism's impact upon Chinese fiction and drama, although it may well be the single most distinctive characteristic.

While the Buddhist tradition of vernacular, prosimetric narrative became secularized in fiction and drama, the religious expression of this literary form also continued in such genres as *baojuan* (precious scrolls). Late Ming and Qing accounts reveal that "precious scrolls" were very popular as a form of entertainment and instruction.

Ultimate impact

Despite the enthusiastic favor the written vernacular found with the bulk of the populace, who through it were increasingly empowered with literacy, to the end of the empire in 1911, the mainstream Confucian literati never accepted anything other than Literary Sinitic as a legitimate medium for writing. To them the vernacular was crude and vulgar, beneath the dignity of a gentleman to contemplate. But merchants, storytellers, craftsmen, physicians, and individuals from many other walks of life paid no heed to this opinion and proceeded to forge a fully functional written vernacular on the foundations that had been laid by the Buddhists of medieval China. In the end, they created a national language called *guoyu,* a term that can ultimately be traced back to the Sanskrit expression *deśa-bhāṣā* (language of a country).

Although there are a few examples of vernacular elements in non-Buddhist texts from before the Tang period, they are extremely rare. A careful examination of the trajectory of the early written vernacular in China reveals that it is unmistakably and overwhelmingly related to Buddhist contexts. In other words, it is safe to say that Buddhism legitimized the writing of the vernacular language in China.

See also: **Apocrypha; Buddhavacana (Word of the Buddha); Entertainment and Performance; Languages; Poetry and Buddhism**

Bibliography

Chavannes, Édouard, trans. *Cinq cents contes et apologues: Extraits du Tripitaka Chinois.* Paris: Ernest Leroux, 1910–1911.

Idema, Wilt, and Haft, Lloyd. "Popular Literature: *Ci* and *Bianwen*." In *A Guide to Chinese Literature.* Ann Arbor: Center for Chinese Studies, University of Michigan, 1997.

Jan, Yün-hua. "Buddhist Literature." In *The Indiana Companion to Traditional Chinese Literature,* ed. William H. Nienhauser, Jr. Bloomington: Indiana University Press, 1986.

Liu, Ts'un-yan. *Buddhist and Taoist Influences on Chinese Novels.* Vol. 1: *The Authorship of the Feng Shen Yen I.* Wiesbaden, Germany: Harrassowitz, 1962.

Mair, Victor H., trans. and ed. *Tun-huang Popular Narratives.* Cambridge, UK: Cambridge University Press, 1983.

Mair, Victor H. "The Narrative Revolution in Chinese Literature: Ontological Presuppositions." *CLEAR* (*Chinese Language: Essays, Articles, Reviews*) 5, no. 1 (1983): 1–27.

Mair, Victor H., ed. *A Partial Bibliography for the Study of Indian Influence on Chinese Popular Literature. Sino-Platonic Papers* 3. Philadelphia: Department of Oriental Studies, University of Pennsylvania, 1987.

Mair, Victor H. "Buddhism and the Rise of the Written Vernacular in East Asia: The Making of National Languages." *Journal of Asian Studies* 53, no. 3 (1994): 707–751.

Mair, Victor H., ed. *The Columbia Anthology of Traditional Chinese Literature.* New York: Columbia University Press, 1994.

Mair, Victor H., ed. *The Shorter Columbia Anthology to Traditional Chinese Literature.* New York: Columbia University Press, 2000.

Mair, Victor H. "Buddhism in *The Literary Mind and Ornate Rhetoric*." In *A Chinese Literary Mind: Culture, Creativity, and Rhetoric in Wenxin Diaolong,* ed. Zong-qi Cai. Stanford, CA: Stanford University Press, 2001.

Mair, Victor H., and Wagner, Marsha. "Tun-huang wen-hsüeh [Literature]." In *The Indiana Companion to Traditional Chinese Literature,* ed. William H. Nienhauser, Jr. Bloomington: Indiana University Press, 1986.

Overmyer, Daniel L. *Precious Volumes: An Introduction to Chinese Sectarian Scriptures from the Sixteenth and Seventeenth Centuries.* Cambridge, MA: Harvard University Asia Center, 1999.

Schmid, Neil. "Tun-huang Literature." In *The Columbia History of Chinese Literature,* ed. Victor H. Mair. New York: Columbia University Press, 2001.

Schmidt-Glintzer, Helwig, and Mair, Victor H. "Buddhist Literature." In *The Columbia History of Chinese Literature,* ed. Victor H. Mair. New York: Columbia University Press, 2001.

Waley, Arthur, trans. *Ballads and Stories from Tun-huang: An Anthology.* New York: Macmillan, 1960.

Zürcher, E. "Late Han Vernacular Elements in the Earliest Buddhist Translations." *Journal of the Chinese Language Teachers Association* 12, no. 3 (1977): 177–203.

VICTOR H. MAIR

CHINUL

Chinul ("Puril Pojo *kuksa*"; 1158–1210), founder of the CHOGYE SCHOOL of the Sŏn (Chinese, Chan; Japanese, Zen) school, is one of the preeminent figures in the history of Korean Buddhism. His work contains three related but distinct accomplishments. First, he helped initiate the practice of *kongan* (Chinese, *gong'an*; Japanese, KŌAN) meditation within the Korean Sŏn tradition. Second, he attempted to reconcile the longstanding conflict between the Sŏn schools, which focused on meditation practice, and the doctrinal or Kyo schools, which focused on scriptural study. Third, he formulated a theory of enlightenment that sought to bridge the sudden-gradual debate that had long troubled the Korean Buddhist world. Often termed "sudden enlightenment and gradual cultivation," Chinul's theory posited an initial sudden enlightenment experience that ongoing practice would deepen and enrich.

Three separate enlightenment experiences define Chinul's spiritual journey. He became a monk at the age of eight, and at twenty-five passed an examination meant to select clergy for high administrative service. Instead of taking a post, he left the capital and went south, eventually settling at the monastery of Ch'ŏngwŏnsa. There, he read the PLATFORM SŪTRA OF THE SIXTH PATRIARCH (LIUZU TAN JING), which triggered the first of his enlightenment experiences. In 1185, at the age of twenty-eight, he moved to the monastery of Pomunsa and read the *Huayan lun* (*Treatise on the*

Huayan Jing), by Li Tongxuan (635–730), an eighth-century Huayan theorist. It spurred him to intensify his meditation practice until he achieved his second enlightenment experience. In 1198, at the age of forty, he moved to Sangmuju Hermitage on Mount Chiri, where he read the *Dahui shuzhuang* (*Recorded Sayings of Dahui*), the words of Dahui ZONGGAO (1089–1163), an influential Chinese Chan thinker of the twelfth century. This triggered his third and most important enlightenment experience, which led to his descent from Mount Chiri. He moved to the monastery of Songgwangsa, where he meditated, lectured, and wrote for an audience of monks and laypeople until his death in 1210.

Chinul's written work shows the influence of the three texts mentioned above, and exhibits his original contributions. *Wŏndon sŏngbullon* (*The Complete and Sudden Attainment of Buddhahood*) formulates what Chinul called the "perfect and sudden approach by means of faith and understanding." The clearest single statement of his theory of sudden enlightenment and gradual cultivation, however, is found in his treatise *Pŏpchip pyŏrhaengnok chŏryo pyŏngip sagi* (*Excerpts from the Dharma Collection and Special Practice Record*), published in 1209, just before his death, which draws heavily on the thought of ZONGMI (780–841).

Arguably, Chinul's most influential work is a posthumously published text called *Kanhwa kyŏrŭiron* (*Resolving Doubts about Observing the Hwadu*), which advocates Dahui's so-called shortcut approach of *kongan* or *hwadu* ("critical phrase") meditation. It contains a discussion contrasting what Chinul called "live" and "dead" words in the "investigation" of *hwadu*. Chinul warns against dead words, meaning the intellectual investigation of the meaning of the *hwadu*, in favor of live words, by which he means full participation in the word on a nonintellectual and nondualistic basis.

The book's legacy has been controversial because its theory of the live word and exclusive advocacy of the "shortcut" or *hwadu* method seem to contradict Chinul's own earlier attempts at synthesizing doctrinal and meditative practice. This apparent reversal had a profound impact on the subsequent history of Korean Sŏn. Chinul's immediate successor, HYESIM (1178–1234), abandoned attempts to reconcile Sŏn practice with scriptural study in favor of an exclusive focus on *hwadu* meditation—a focus that continues in Korean Sŏn to this day.

See also: **Chan School; Nine Mountains School of Sŏn**

Bibliography

Buswell, Robert E., Jr., trans. *The Korean Approach to Zen: The Collected Works of Chinul.* Honolulu: University of Hawaii Press, 1983. Reprinted as *Tracing Back the Radiance: Chinul's Korean Way of Zen.* Honolulu: University of Hawaii Press, 1991.

Han'guk Pulgyo chŏnsŏ (*Collected Works of Korean Buddhism*), Vol. 4. Seoul: Dongguk University Press, 1982.

Kang, Kun Ki. *Moguja Chinul Yŏn'gu* (*A Study of Chinul*). Seoul: Puch'ŏnim Sesang, 2001.

Keel, Hee-Sung. *Moguja Chinul: Founder of the Korean Sŏn Tradition.* Berkeley, CA: Berkeley Buddhist Studies Series, 1984.

Shim, Jae Ryong. *Korean Buddhism: Tradition and Transformation.* Seoul: Jimoondang, 1999.

Yi, Chongik, *Kangoku Bukkyō no kenkyū* (*A Study of Korean Buddhism*). Tokyo: Kokusho Kankōkai, 1980.

SUNG BAE PARK

CHOGYE SCHOOL

The Chogye school, which is unique to Korea, constitutes the mainstream of Buddhism in contemporary Korea. There have been two distinct Chogye schools known in Korean history. One school traces its origins to the NINE MOUNTAINS SCHOOL OF SŎN (*Kusan Sŏnmun*) that was active until the mid-Koryŏ period (918–1392). These Sŏn schools united into one main school after the twelfth century, thus establishing the Chogye school. However, this institution came to a close in 1424 as a result of the anti-Buddhist policies of the Chosŏn government, which favored Confucianism. The second Chogye school emerged during the Japanese colonial period (1910–1945). The Korean ecclesiastical order began to use the name *Chogye* in 1941, but it was not until 1962 that the Chogye School of Korean Buddhism (*Taehan Pulgyo Chogyejong*) was officially established.

Both continuity and discontinuity are apparent in the history and ideology of the two Chogye schools. Contemporary scholarship does not distinguish between the two, however, and scholars have developed a variety of ideas concerning the origins and the lineage of the Chogye school. It is certain that the first Chogye school was directly related to the CHAN SCHOOL. *Chogye* is the Korean pronunciation for the Chinese word *Caoqi*, the name of the mountain of residence of HUINENG (638–713), the sixth patriarch of Chinese Chan school; thus, the name Chogye reflects the fundamental Chan influence on Korean Buddhism. However, the Chogye school in contemporary Korea is not exclusively a Sŏn school. Although it professes to be a Sŏn school, it embraces various schools of Buddhist doctrine (*kyo*) as well as Pure Land beliefs into its system of thought, making the Korean approach to Chan quite different from its counterparts in China and Japan.

One of the lingering issues surrounding the Chogye school in contemporary Korea is its dharma lineage. The constitution of the school stipulates that Toŭi (d. 825) was the founder of the school, CHINUL (1158–1210) its reviver, and T'aego Pou (1301–1382) its harmonizer. In addition, Korean Buddhist scholars have developed many different theories regarding Chogye lineage. These theories, however, are not always based on historical fact, but are a product of ideologically motivated attempts to connect Korean Buddhism to the "orthodox" lineage of the Chinese Linji Chan tradition. Although most Korean Buddhist specialists believe that Chinul was not the founder of the Chogye school, it is evident that during the Koryŏ period the movement was led by his dharma successors, and the Chogye school of contemporary Korea adopted the thought of Chinul as its theoretical support.

The origins of the Chogye school, its founder, historical development, and dharma lineage need to be further clarified with the understanding that there were two distinct Chogye schools throughout Korean history. This is an extremely important issue because the search to understand the exact identity of the school itself will, by extension, describe that of Korean Buddhism and history.

See also: **Colonialism and Buddhism; Korea**

Bibliography

Buswell, Robert E., Jr. *The Zen Monastic Experience: Buddhist Practice in Contemporary Korea.* Princeton, NJ: Princeton University Press, 1992.

Keel, Hee-Sung. "Han'guk Pulgyo ŭi chŏngch'esŏng t'amgu: Chogyejong ŭi yŏksa wa sasang ŭl chungsim ŭro hayŏ" (The Chogye School and the Search for Identity of Korean Buddhism). *Han'guk chonggyo yŏn'gu (Journal of Korean Religions)* 2 (2000): 159–193.

Lee, Peter H., ed. *Sourcebook of Korean Civilization,* Vol. 1. New York: Columbia University Press, 1993.

Pak, Hae-Dang. "Chogyejong ŭi pŏpt'ong sŏl e taehan kŏmt'o" (A Critical Research on the Dharma Lineages of the Chogye School). *Ch'orhak SaSang (A Journal of Philosophical Ideas)* 11 (2000): 43–62.

JONGMYUNG KIM

CH'ŎNT'AE SCHOOL.

See **Tiantai School**

CHRISTIANITY AND BUDDHISM

From their beginnings Buddhism and Christianity reached out beyond the region of their birth. It was inevitable that their paths would cross, but for the first fifteen hundred years these encounters were of little significance to either faith. A brief period of enthusiasm by Christian missionaries for Buddhist teachings followed, only to be extinguished by a posture of confrontation that lasted for nearly four hundred years. It was not until the twentieth century that full and meaningful contact between the two religions developed.

Antiquity

The greatest missionary effort of Buddhism was concentrated between the third century B.C.E. and the eighth century C.E., by the end of which it had reached virtually all of Asia. Buddhist history records no Constantine or Holy Roman Empire to elevate the religion to the stature of a multinational force; Buddhism participated in no colonial exploits such as those that transported Christianity around the globe from the sixteenth to the nineteenth centuries. Emblematic figures, such as the Greek king Menander who converted to Buddhism in the second century B.C.E., Emperor AŚOKA who established a Buddhist kingdom in third-century B.C.E. India, and Prince SHŌTOKU who proclaimed a Buddhist-inspired constitution in seventh-century Japan, were able to secure ascendancy for Buddhism at a local level, but had no imperial designs on neighboring countries, let alone on the West.

The Christian mission was a different story. Already from its earliest years it turned east to establish communities in predominantly Zoroastrian Persia and in India. The Gnostic Christian Mani is said to have traveled from Persia to India in the third century, declaring the Buddha a special messenger of God alongside Moses and Jesus. Despite certain doctrinal coincidences—especially in the case of Gnosticism—speculation concerning the influence of Buddhism on the Essenes, the early Christians, and the gospels is without historical foundation. Indeed, aside from a brief report in the writings of Clement of Alexandria (200 C.E.), based largely on Greek historians, there is no extended record of Buddhist beliefs in Christian literature until the Middle Ages.

During the third and fourth centuries Christianity spread to the major urban centers of Asia, and in the fifth century to China. These small Christian communities barely brushed shoulders with the Buddhist faith, but even this contact came to an end with the outbreak of PERSECUTIONS in the late Tang dynasty against all foreign religions. From the tenth to the sixteenth centuries, barbarian invasions in Europe and the advance of Islam would erect more formidable barriers between the West and Asia, further limiting the possibility of Buddhist–Christian interaction.

Late Middle Ages and Renaissance

Travelers from Europe in the thirteenth century, such as Giovanni de Piano Carpini and William of Ruysbroeck, were the first to send back to Europe reports of Buddhism as a religion whose scriptures, doctrine, saints, monastic life, meditation practices, and rituals were comparable to those of Christianity. Records of the voyages of Marco Polo from 1274 to 1295 include expressions of admiration for the religion and mention Buddha as a saintly figure lacking only the grace of baptism. During the next fifty years Christian monks like Giovanni de Montecorino (in 1289), Odorico da Pordenone (from 1318 to 1330), and Giovanni Marignolli (from 1338 to 1353) traveled more widely and confirmed the unity of the Buddhist faith around Asia.

Mention should also be made of the legend of Barlaam and Josaphat, a story of uncertain authorship but popularized through an eleventh-century Greek translation. It tells of Josaphat, an Indian prince, converting to Christianity under the guidance of the monk Barlaam. So beloved did the story become that the two saints were eventually accepted into the Roman martyrology. Only around the middle of the nineteenth century was the hoax uncovered: Josaphat was a recasting of the Prince Siddhārtha based on the first-century biography of the Buddha. The saints were not removed from the liturgical calendar, however, until the middle of the twentieth century.

Many of the first Catholic missionaries to arrive in Asia in the sixteenth century sent home idyllic accounts of Buddhism. Among them was Francis Xavier, whose direct contact with Buddhist monks and scholars in Japan from 1549 to 1551 opened the way for successors to study Buddhism in greater depth. Relying on their reports, the French orientalist Guillaume Postel in 1552 ventured to call Buddhism "the greatest religion in the world." Reading his words, missionaries in Goa on the coast of India concluded that the Gospel must have been preached in these lands already, though its truth dimmed over the centuries by the darkness of sin.

This was one side of the picture. When Vasco da Gama and the Portuguese colonizers came to Ceylon, now Sri Lanka, in 1505, they confiscated Buddhist properties across the land, with the full cooperation of the Christian missionaries. During the seventeenth and eighteenth centuries the Dutch continued the suppression. Elsewhere, when Matteo Ricci entered China in 1583 he quickly forsook his interest in Buddhism for Confucianism, rejecting the former as an inferior religion and its monks as the dregs of Chinese society. His contemporaries Michele Ruggeri and Alessandro Valignano—as indeed did the majority of missionaries in China for centuries to come—concurred.

In THERAVĀDA lands, the missionaries were often more positive. In seventeenth-century Thailand a number of French priests actually lived in Buddhist monasteries. The century before, in Burma, several missionaries had written tracts favorable to Buddhism. In Cambodia there are records of a similarly positive approach, though it is Giovanni Maria Leria who is better remembered for his bitter hatred of the religion, rejecting Buddhism as a deliberate wile of the devil to transform all that is beautiful in Christianity. His views were to become the norm that held throughout most of the eighteenth and nineteenth centuries. An exception is Paul Ambrose Bigandet, bishop of Rangoon from 1854 to 1856, who mediated an exchange of letters between the DALAI LAMA and Pope Clement XII in which the latter recognized Buddhism as "leading to the happiness of eternal life."

The modern age

It is only with the arrival of Sanskrit studies in Europe in the late eighteenth century and the subsequent availability of Buddhist texts that one can speak of a proper encounter in the West with Buddhism. Esteem for its tenets and practices grew apace, and the end of the century saw the first examples of Westerners converting to Buddhism and even entering the monastic life. Buddhist associations were formed in Germany, England, and later in the United States. Monks accompanying emigrants from several Asian lands to the Americas gave additional strength to the presence of Buddhism in the West.

The World Parliament of Religions held in Chicago in 1893 symbolized the change in attitude that had taken place in the Christian world, though not without opposition from the established churches. These initiatives prompted favorable responses from several quarters of the Buddhist world of Asia.

While all of this was taking place, the continued role of Christianity in the colonizing of Asia was provoking a backlash from Buddhists. In Sri Lanka, now under British rule, Methodist missionaries had begun to study Buddhism in the 1840s as a tool for conversion. In the following decades the Buddhists fought back, supported by European Theosophists who helped them to organize along Western lines. The outbreak of riots, followed by a nationalistic fervor that spilled over into the twentieth century, exacerbated tensions. It was not until the 1960s that steps toward dialogue and cooperation could be made.

Similar confrontations were taking place in Japan. When the country opened its doors to the outside world in 1854 after two hundred years of seclusion, Japan's Buddhist establishment began to fear its own demise and took steps to oppress the Christian missions during the 1890s. Subsequent generations abandoned this approach and began the long journey to a more creative coexistence and dialogue with Christianity.

The world missionary conference at Edinburgh in 1910 was the first public forum in the Christian world to recommend a constructive approach to the religions of Asia. Formal declarations at the Second Vatican Council in Rome (1965) and at the Uppsala assembly of the World Council of Churches (1968) paved the way for more direct rapprochement. Concerted efforts to organize Buddhist–Christian dialogue through worldwide associations and journals began in earnest and reached a groundswell in the 1980s. The Society for Buddhist–Christian Studies, based in the United States and with active membership both in Asia and throughout Europe, lent academic respectability to the dialogue. Christian institutes devoted to dialogue at the scholarly level already existed in several lands of East Asia and in 1981 organized themselves into a network based in Japan and known as Inter-Religio. An exchange of Buddhist and Christian monastics, initiated in 1979, continues in the twenty-first century. Christian theological centers throughout the West, and increasingly in Asia, are deepening their commitment to the encounter with Buddhism, and there are clear signs that the Buddhist world has begun to respond in kind.

See also: Entries on specific countries; **Colonialism and Buddhism**

Bibliography

de Lubac, Henri. *Recontre du bouddhisme et de l'occident.* Paris: Éditions Montaigne, 1952.

Thelle, Notto R. *Buddhism and Christianity in Japan: From Conflict to Dialogue, 1854–1899.* Honolulu: University of Hawaii Press, 1987.

von Brück, Michael, and Lai, Whalen. *Christianity and Buddhism: A Multicultural History of Their Dialogue,* tr. Phyllis Jestice. Maryknoll, NY: Orbis Books, 2001.

Zago, Marcello. *Buddhismo e cristianesimo in dialogo: Situazione, rapporti, convergenze.* Rome: Città Nuova, 1985.

JAMES W. HEISIG

CLERICAL MARRIAGE IN JAPAN

Temple wives and families have existed covertly for much of Japanese Buddhist history. Since at least the time of SHINRAN (1173–1262), the founder of the True Pure Land denomination (Jōdo Shinshū), clerical followers of Shinran have openly married and, frequently, passed on their temples from father to son. Shin temple wives, known as *bōmori* (temple caretakers), traditionally have played an important role in ministering to parishioners, caring for the temple, and raising the temple children. The ambiguous term *jizoku,* referring to both the wife and the children of a temple abbot, was officially coined in a 1919 Pure Land (Jōdo) denomination regulation guaranteeing the right of succession to the registered child of the abbot (*jūshoku*) in the case of his death.

Clerical marriage became open and temple families general among all denominations of Japanese Buddhism following the state's decriminalization of clerical marriage in 1872. Although bitterly resisted for decades by the leaders of many non-Shin denominations, proponents of the practice advocated allowing clerical marriage and temple families as the best way to create a vigorous Buddhism capable of competing with the family-centered Protestantism, with its married ministers, that was making headway in Japan in the late nineteenth century. Despite opposition from many Buddhist leaders, clerical marriage proved popular, spreading to the majority of clerics in most denominations of monastic Buddhism by the late 1930s.

Today, all denominations of Japanese Buddhism have granted de facto legitimacy to clerical marriage and temple families. Most temples are inherited by either the biological or adoptive son of the abbot, and temple wives play a vital—although still frequently unacknowledged—part in managing the temple, serving parishioners, raising the temple family, and participating in the religious activities of the temple.

See also: **Meiji Buddhist Reform**

Bibliography

Jaffe, Richard M. *Neither Monk nor Layman: Clerical Marriage in Modern Japanese Buddhism.* Princeton, NJ: Princeton University Press, 2001.

Kawahashi, Noriko. "Jizoku (Priests' Wives) in Sōtō Zen Buddhism: An Ambiguous Category." *Japanese Journal of Religious Studies* 22/1–2 (1995): 161–183.

Uan Dōnin. "A Refutation of Clerical Marriage," tr. Richard M. Jaffe. In *Religions of Asia in Practice: An Anthology,* ed. Donald Lopez, Jr. Princeton, NJ: Princeton University Press, 1999.

RICHARD M. JAFFE

COLONIALISM AND BUDDHISM

If colonialism is defined specifically as the enforced occupation of a region or control of a population, subsequently maintained through either direct coercion or cultural and ideological hegemony, then Buddhist societies and cultures have been both subject to, and agents of, colonialism throughout the centuries. A good example of the association of Buddhism with colonial expansionism can be found, for instance, in the development of certain forms of Buddhist nationalism in Japan in the modern era. During the period of the Meiji Restoration in Japan (1868–1912), Japan became an increasingly powerful presence in East Asia as a result of its victories in the Sino-Japanese (1895) and Russo-Japanese (1904–1905) wars and its emergence on the world stage as a modern nation-state. As an imperial power Japan also annexed Korea (1910) and invaded Manchuria (1931), eventually losing control of these regions after its defeat in World War II.

Buddhism as a justification for colonialism

During the late nineteenth and early twentieth centuries a number of Buddhist figures, such as Kimura Shigeyuki and Mitsui Koshi, upheld the Japanese nation not only as the culmination of Buddhist cultural development, but also as a legitimating factor in Japanese imperial policies. In this context Buddhist nationalist movements and key figures such as the Zen teacher Sōen Shaku (1859–1919) often justified Japanese military expansionism in terms of the missionary spread of Buddhist teachings and the "upholding of humanity and civilization" (Sōen; see Sharf). According to Tanaka Chigaku (1861–1939), a lay Buddhist follower inspired by NICHIREN, the Buddhist teaching reached its fulfillment in the particular form of the Japanese nation. This, he argued, created a duty on the part of Japan to spread its own (MAHĀYĀNA) form of the Buddha's teachings to the rest of the world, with the explicit aim of transforming the world into a "vast Buddhist country." In 1914 Chigaku founded the "National Pillar Society," a nationalist movement concerned with a spiritual and moral regeneration of Japan, and attracted a number of followers, including Ishihara Kanji (1893–1981), the military mastermind behind the invasion of Manchuria in 1931.

Modern Japanese examples of the commingling of Buddhist tradition and culture with ultranationalist and colonialist motivations are striking but not unique in Buddhist history, especially when the line between national or ethnic allegiance and Buddhist affiliation becomes blurred. In the *Mahāvaṃsa* (*Great Chronicle*), a Sinhalese Buddhist chronicle emerging from the Mahāvihāra Buddhist sect of Anurādhapura, the story of King Duṭṭhagāmaṇī's conquests in Sri Lanka, the slaughter of his opponents, and the colonization of the entire island are all justified on the grounds that the non-Buddhists are in fact "not human." This justification and account of the island's history is, of course, all but impossible to reconcile with the Buddha's own emphasis upon compassion and nonviolence. The *Mahāvaṃsa,* however, has played a significant role in underpinning the modern historical consciousness of the Sinhalese people and the rise of some of the more aggressive forms of Sinhalese Buddhist nationalism (Sinhalatva) in the twentieth century.

The colonization of Buddhist societies

On a broader historical scale, however, Buddhist societies have generally been subject to, rather than an explicit motivating force behind, colonial expansionism. The Chinese invasion of Tibet in 1950, for instance, has resulted in an aggressively pursued policy designed to suppress Tibetan Buddhist culture and institutions in line with the antireligious stance of the Chinese Communist regime. One consequence of this, of course, has been the Tibetan Buddhist diaspora to India and the West in the late twentieth century, most notably that of the DALAI LAMA, often referred to as "the spiritual leader of the Tibetan people," and currently living in exile in Dharamsala in northern India. From the point of view of the ruling Communist Party of China the colonization of Tibet is little more than a reoccupation of Chinese lands that has afforded the liberation of the Tibetan people "from serfdom." It is clear, however, that the history of Tibet, partly for reasons of geographical isolation, but also because of its long Buddhist history, represents a highly distinctive culture and polity and has many affinities with South Asian culture and traditions.

The sixteenth to twentieth centuries witnessed the colonization of large parts of the globe by Europeans on a scale that was historically unprecedented. European colonialism has left an indelible mark upon the ways in which Asian Buddhists experience "modernity" and their own sense of cultural, national, and religious identity.

On May 27, 1498, the Portuguese explorer Vasco da Gama arrived on the southwest coast of India. This was a turning point in the history of Asia and Europe. There had, of course, been interaction between Asia and Europe since long before the common era (e.g., along the SILK ROAD), but not to the extent that was precipitated by da Gama's arrival. Portugal, sanctioned by the Vatican to expand the Christian empire to the East, established an early monopoly in the exploration of Asian territories and the plundering of Asian resources. Gradually, however, there was wider European involvement in the exploration and colonization of the Asian world. The spread of the Protestant Reformation throughout Europe allowed for a challenge to the Portuguese monopoly, based as it was upon papal sanction. In the 1590s, for instance, the Dutch took control of much of Ceylon (now Sri Lanka) and Indonesia. The British were excluded from Indonesia and so concentrated on consolidating their interests on the Indian mainland and in Ceylon and Burma. The French established a few bases on the subcontinent (such as in Pondicherry on the southeast coast of India) but turned the main focus of their attention to Indochina (mainly Cambodia, Laos, and Vietnam).

In broad terms, there were two main waves of Western influence upon Asian Buddhism during the colonial period. First, the effect of widespread Christian missionary activity by Europeans, and then later the impact of Western secular models of nationalism and scientific rationalist philosophies. Both waves precipitated a complex series of responses, leading to the rise of Buddhist nationalism and what some scholars have called "Protestant Buddhism" (Gombrich and Obeyesekere) or "Buddhist modernism" (Bechert) and the development of a variety of syntheses between traditional Buddhist values and contemporary ideologies such as Marxism, free-market capitalism, and scientific empiricism.

In the latter half of the twentieth century, the independence gained by many former colonies in South and Southeast Asia left a political vacuum into which stepped a variety of indigenous interest groups and political movements. Some of these movements involve implicit (and sometimes explicit) appeal to Buddhist traditions and values in the formulation of their stances. One feature of this has been the rise of Buddhist forms of nationalist politics of varying ideological shades. "Buddhist socialism," for instance, developed as a political force in states such as Cambodia and Burma. Despite some misgivings by the sizable ethnic minority groups, Burma, under the leadership of U Nu, recognized Buddhism as the country's official state religion in 1961. A military coup under General Ne Win quickly ensued in 1962, however, leading to the establishment of a more radical left-wing military regime and the disestablishment of Buddhism. Burma (renamed Myanmar) remains under military rule, although this has not prevented the development of pro-democracy movements, focused mainly upon the inspirational figure of Aung San Suu Kyi, winner of the 1991 Nobel Prize for peace and herself inspired by Buddhist principles in her campaign for democratic elections. Similarly, in Sri Lanka (Ceylon), Buddhist nationalist movements have played a significant role in postindependence politics. The Sri Lankan example serves as an illustration of the impact of European colonialism upon indigenous Buddhist traditions and institutions.

In the sixteenth and seventeenth centuries the Dutch controlled much of Ceylon and Indonesia. Economic inducements were offered to local "heathens" to convert to Christianity, and this effort was combined with vigorous missionary polemics against the "idolatrous" and superstitious practices of the Buddhists. In 1711 the Dutch issued a proclamation in Ceylon that explicitly forbade Christian involvement in "the ceremonies of heathenism," with the penalty of a public flogging and a year's imprisonment for those found engaging in such practices. In 1795 the British first appeared on the coast and by 1815 they had annexed the whole island.

Three factors have been crucial in the colonial transformation of indigenous Asian subjectivities: the reconfiguration of politics and civil society under colonial rule, the transformation of modes of educating the population, and the role of the printing press in the dissemination of ideas among the indigenous population. In the case of Ceylon, the key factor was the introduction of the Colebrooke-Cameron Reforms of the 1830s, which sought to unify the political economy of the island, promote laissez-faire capitalism, and establish a national educational framework to be delivered through the medium of the English language. These changes led to the development of a new middle class within Sinhalese society that was educated in English and empowered by the new social, economic, and political reforms. This was to have a profound effect upon the Sinhalese population's appreciation of its Buddhist heritage (Scott; Gombrich and Obeyesekere). Similar processes were underway throughout the colonized regions of southeast Asia at this time.

The first printing press was introduced to Ceylon by the Dutch in 1736 and was immediately put to use in the printing of local vernacular translations of Christian texts and, later, classical European literature. In a speech to the Methodist Missionary Society Committee, on October 3, 1831, D. J. Gogerly outlined the importance of the printing press as a vehicle for undermining the authority of indigenous Buddhist traditions. Gogerly stated that "at present, it is by means of the Press [that] our principal attacks must be made upon this wretched system. . . . We must direct our efforts to pull down the stronghold of Satan." Gogerly was a missionary in Ceylon for forty-four years and also worked as a translator of the Pāli Buddhist scriptures into English. It was not until 1862, however, that, as a result of a gift from the king of Siam (now Thailand), Sinhalese Buddhists themselves gained access to a printing press and were thus able to disseminate their own materials and literature to the native population.

The establishment of a uniform educational system by the European colonizers tended to promote European Christian forms of education and literacy, either through the direct medium of European languages or by the study of European and Christian literature in vernacular translations. The curriculum and agenda in this context usually involved the teaching of Euro-Christian values alongside mathematics, science, and a Eurocentric version of history. The overall effect of taking the burden of educating the population away from the Buddhist monastic communities, where it constituted one of the traditional roles of the bhikkhus, was to undermine the status of the SAṄGHA within society. Later the number of Christian missionary schools declined and secular government schools increased in number. Beginning in the mid-nineteenth century, however, a reformist spirit developed within Buddhist circles, partly in response to the criticisms of Christian missionary groups, which sought to reform the saṅgha. In Ceylon, with the help of the American Colonel Henry Steel Olcott and his Buddhist Theosophical Society (founded in 1880), three higher education institutes and some two hundred Buddhist high schools were set up to protect and preserve the study of the Buddhist tradition.

Orientalism and the rise of "Protestant Buddhism"

Many of the westernized middle-class groups that emerged in Southeast Asia as a result of European colonial reforms first encountered their own Buddhist traditions through the mediating lenses of European textbooks, literature, and translations of Buddhist sacred texts. This reflects an important factor in understanding the way in which Buddhism develops and is presented in the modern era, namely the role of "BUDDHIST STUDIES" as a Western academic enterprise and the enormous authority accorded to Western scholars and texts in representing Buddhism during the colonial era (King; Lopez). Western interest in understanding Asian civilizations precipitated a "discovery" and translation of Buddhist sacred texts into modern European languages. Western scholars, however, generally replicated a series of basic Christian assumptions in their approach to Buddhism (Almond; King). There was a strong tendency to emphasize Buddhist sacred texts as the key feature in determining the nature of Buddhism as a religious tradition. This approach tended to ignore Buddhist traditions as changing historical phenomena and also underplayed the role of ritual practices and local networks and beliefs in the preservation and renewal of Buddhist forms of life. Buddhist sacred literature has traditionally been revered in Asian societies, but this reverence rarely led to a depreciation of local practices and beliefs that were not found in the ancient canonical literature. Buddhism as a living tradition tended to be either ignored or denigrated by Orientalist scholars as a corruption of the original teachings.

This attitude had a profound effect upon the emerging middle-class elites of Asian societies in the nineteenth century. This was the case even for nations that were not subject to European colonization such as

Japan (Sharf) and Thailand, illustrating perhaps that modernist reformism is not simply a by-product of European colonialism. In a Southeast Asian context, "Protestant" influence can be seen most clearly in the views of reformist leaders such as ANAGĀRIKA DHARMAPĀLA (born David Hewavitarane, 1864–1933) in Sri Lanka and Sayadaw U Ottama (d. 1921) in Burma. Both emphasized the need for a "Buddhist Reformation" in order to overcome what they saw as the decadence of the "superstitious ritualism" of folk or "village" Buddhism. This also involved a call for the saṅgha to become more socially reformist and service-oriented with regard to the needs of lay society. The trends can be seen to involve a number of "Protestant" elements. First, there is the desire to return to the purity of the Buddha's original teachings, bereft of popular superstitions. Second, there is an emphasis on bringing an understanding of Buddhist sacred literature directly to the people as the basis for understanding the Buddha's message. Finally, there is also an emphasis upon "this-worldly asceticism" to be manifested through acts of social service and in some cases political activism by the monks.

Although Western influence is evident in all of these trends one should be careful not to read such reformist projects merely as mirrored responses to a European Christian agenda. This would be to erase the indigenous aspects of such responses. "Protestant Buddhism," if one can call it that, not only reflected the impact of European ideas upon Asian Buddhists, but also represented indigenous protestations against European colonialism and the claim that Western civilization was morally and spiritually superior to Buddhism. The promotion of a socially oriented ethic, while clearly a response to centuries of Christian missionary criticism of Buddhism as a world-denying tradition, was firmly grounded in Buddhist notions of compassionate service to all. A key shift that began during this period (and which provided the intellectual foundation for what has since become known as "ENGAGED BUDDHISM") was the rearticulation of traditional Buddhist goals, such as NIRVĀṆA, in socio-political and often explicitly anticolonial terms. In Burma, for instance, the monk and political activist U Ottama explicitly linked the attainment of liberation to freedom from social, economic, and colonial oppression. In the 1940s this link was rearticulated by Aung San (father of Aung San Suu Kyi) in the notion of a "mundane liberation" (*lokanibbāṇa*) of the Burmese people from British colonial rule (Houtman). The latter half of the twentieth century saw the end of European imperialism and the establishment of independent states in the former Asian colonies. In this context the process of understanding the effects that centuries of European colonial influence had upon Buddhist civilization and its significance has only just begun.

See also: **Christianity and Buddhism; Communism and Buddhism; Modernity and Buddhism; Nationalism and Buddhism**

Bibliography

Almond, Philip. *The British Discovery of Buddhism.* Cambridge, UK: Cambridge University Press, 1988.

Bechert, Heinz. "The Buddhist Revival in East and West." In *The World of Buddhism: Buddhist Monks and Nuns in Society and Culture,* ed. Heinz Bechert and Richard Gombrich. London: Thames and Hudson, 1984.

Gombrich, Richard, and Obeyesekere, Gananath. *Buddhism Transformed: Religious Change in Sri Lanka.* Princeton, NJ: Princeton University Press, 1988.

Houtman, Gustaaf. *Mental Culture in Burmese Crisis Politics: Aung San Suu Kyi and the National League of Democracy.* Tokyo: Institute for the Study of Languages and Cultures of Asia and Africa, 1999.

King, Richard. *Orientalism and Religion: Postcolonial Theory, India, and "the Mystic East."* London and New York: Routledge, 1999.

Ling, Trevor. *Buddhism, Imperialism, and War: Burma and Thailand in Modern History.* London: Allen and Unwin, 1979.

Lopez, Donald S., Jr., ed. *Curators of the Buddha: The Study of Buddhism under Colonialism.* Chicago: Chicago University Press, 1995.

Scott, David. *Refashioning Futures: Criticism after Postcoloniality.* Princeton, NJ: Princeton University Press, 1999.

Sharf, Robert. "The Zen of Japanese Nationalism." In *Curators of the Buddha: The Study of Buddhism under Colonialism,* ed. Donald S. Lopez, Jr. Chicago: Chicago University Press, 1995.

Sōen (Soyen), Shaku. *Sermons of a Buddhist Abbot: Addresses on Religious Subjects,* tr. D. T. Suzuki. New York: Weiser, 1971 (originally published 1906).

Tambiah, Stanley. *World Conqueror and World Renouncer: A Study of Buddhism and Polity in Thailand against a Historical Background.* Cambridge, UK: Cambridge University Press, 1976.

RICHARD KING

COMMENTARIAL LITERATURE

Buddhist commentarial writing spans a period of more than two thousand years. Its rich production, of which only a fragment has survived the vicissitudes of history, closely mirrors all facets of the doctrinal and many aspects of the cultural and social development of the religion.

One may, in the widest possible sense, conceive of all Buddhist scriptures as commentarial: The sūtra discourses comment on the Buddha's insights and the PATH, the ABHIDHARMA literature comments on the teachings given in the discourses, and the MAHĀYĀNA literature comments on the meaning of ŚŪNYATA (EMPTINESS) underlying the teachings. Commentaries elaborate on meaning (*artha*), meaning that demands special attention. The writing of commentaries belongs, alongside other modes of practice, among the ways of preserving and spreading the dharma. In terms of cultural history, the significance of commentarial literature consists in its capacity to reflect general cultural and religious trends and to serve as a venue for developing interpretative skills and working out fundamental intellectual issues.

ZANNING (919–1001), a representative of the Chinese tradition, explains the significance of Buddhist commentaries in his *Song gaoseng zhuan* (*Song Biographies of Eminent Monks*): "perfecting the way—this is dharma; carrying the dharma—this is sūtra; explaining sūtra—this is commentary" (T.2061:50.735b). Commentaries by definition are situated downstream of the flow of tradition and thus are never able to supersede scripture. Yet given the priority of meaning (*artha*) before wording (*vacana*), commentaries are expected to reiterate and bring to light the meaning that is hidden within scripture.

Indian commentaries

The teachings of the dharma, from the very beginning, called for commentary. Thus one not only learns that the Buddha was frequently called upon to elaborate on teachings he had given, but equally that the Buddha considered some of his disciples, such as ŚĀRIPUTRA, to be equally capable of stating the teachings clearly. But this stage is still one of oral exegesis. Only with the establishment of the Buddhist CANON (tripiṭaka) did monks begin to write commentaries. In the course of interpreting the teachings, schools of interpretation arose. The two major extant strains of South Asian commentarial writing are the THERAVĀDA commentaries, written in Pāli, and the SARVĀSTIVĀDA AND MŪLASARVĀSTIVĀDA commentaries in Sanskrit. The latter have been translated into Chinese. In addition, a few commentaries from other schools are extant.

At the beginning of the fifth century, BUDDHAGHOSA—on the basis of earlier Sinhala commentaries—composed a series of commentarial works on the Pāli canon. Among them were two commentaries on the VINAYA: *Samantapāsādikā* (*The All-Pleasing*) and *Kaṅkhāvitaraṇī* (*Overcoming Doubt*). The *Samantapāsādikā* was translated into Chinese by Saṅghabhadra in 489 as the *Shanjianlü pibosha* (T.1462). The *Kaṅkhāvitaraṇī* is a commentary on the *Patimokkha* (Sanskrit, PRĀTIMOKṢA). As was the case with the vinaya, once the *Suttapiṭaka* had been established, a number of commentaries on its texts came to be written. Of particular importance are Buddhaghosa's commentaries on the *nikāyas* (*Sumaṅgalavilāsinī, Papañcasūdanī, Sāratthappakāsinī, Manorathapūranī, Paramāṭṭhajotikā*), and on the *abhidhamma* (*Aṭṭhasālinī, Saṃmohavinodanī, Pañcappakaraṇāṭṭhakathā*).

In the case of the Sarvāstivāda, its writings are for the most part preserved only in Chinese. Its single most important treatise is Katyāyanīputra's *Jñanaprasthāna* (*Foundations of Knowledge*, composed around 50 B.C.E.), to which are related the six treatises (*pādaśāstra*): *Dharmaskandha, Saṃgītiparyāya, Dhātukāya, Prakaraṇa, Vijñānakāya*, and *Prajñapti*. The major exegetical collection, the *Mahāvibhāṣā* (*Great Exegesis*), compiled at a council held by Kaṇiṣka, is also related to the *Jñanaprasthāna*. Six of the seven treatises of this abhidharma *piṭaka* were translated by XUANZANG (ca. 600–664).

Chinese commentaries

Though it is difficult to define beginnings, scholars know that Zhi Qian (fl. 223–253) and Kang Senghui (?–280) were already composing commentaries during the third century C.E. But commentaries probably gained importance only around the time of DAO'AN (312–385). From the biographical literature, one can glean indications of a thriving early commentarial literature, but it is almost completely lost. Examples of this earliest phase are Chen Hui's (ca. 200 C.E.) *Yin chi ru jing*; Dao'an's *Ren ben yu sheng jing zhu*; SENGZHAO's (374–414) *Zhu Weimo jing*; and FAXIAN's (ca. 337–418) *Fanwang jing pusa jie shu*.

Around the beginning of the fifth century, a new type of commentary emerged. Dao'an and DAOSHENG (ca. 360–434) played major roles in this transition. Fayao's (ca. 420–477) NIRVĀṆA SŪTRA and Zhu Fa-chong's (ca. 268) LOTUS SŪTRA commentaries (both lost), and Zhu Daosheng's extant *Lotus* commentary are the earliest examples of this new type of commentary. Two extensive commentaries from the first half of the sixth century are also extant: one (in seventy-one fascicles) on the *Nirvāṇa Sūtra* (*Da ban niepan jing ji jie,* 509) collected by Baoliang, the other (in eight fascicles) on the *Lotus* (*Fahua jing yiji,* 529) collected by Fayun (467–529). Both of these commentaries played important roles in the formation of the Sinitic Buddhist schools, and both reveal an important feature of this type of literature, namely, their explicit or implicit referencing of earlier exegesis.

The third phase of Chinese Buddhist commentarial writing began with the masters of the Sui dynasty (589–618) and was followed by a long series of extremely prolific masters of the Tang dynasty (618–907), who developed their doctrinal positions in the context of systematic exegetic efforts, eventually setting the stage for the emergence of schools of exegesis such as Tiantai, Huayan, and Faxiang. Noteworthy representatives of that phase are the Dilun master Jingying Huiyuan (523–596); the Sanlun master Jizang (549–623); the Tiantai masters ZHIYI (538–597), Guanding (561–632), and ZHANRAN (711–782); the Faxiang masters WŎNCH'ŬK (613–696, from Korea), KUIJI (632–682), Huizhao (?–714), and Zhizhou (679–723); the Huayan masters Zhiyan (628–668), WŎNHYO (617–686, from Korea), FAZANG (643–712), CHENGGUAN (738–840), and the lay Li Tongxuan (?–730); and the esoteric master Yixing (683–727).

The major exegetes commonly wrote commentaries on a broad set of scriptures. Thus one and the same scripture is marked by a long series of commentarial treatments. The *Lotus Sūtra,* the DIAMOND SŪTRA, and the HEART SŪTRA, respectively, are the scriptures most often commentated on in China. There are about eighty extant Chinese commentaries on each of these sūtras. Besides these, the HUAYAN JING, *Vimalakīrti, Wuliangshou, Amituo, Yuanjue, Nirvāṇa, Laṅkāvatāra,* and *Fanwang jing* also drew much exegetic attention. Among the treatises, the AWAKENING OF FAITH (DASHENG QIXIN LUN) was most often commentated on. The extant commentaries serve as the most important sources for information on the formation and development of Chinese Buddhist thought.

Exegesis, the plurality of transmissions, and the commentarial context

The development of Chinese Buddhist commentarial literature was influenced by the fact that the transmission of scriptures was far from systematic. At almost any period a broad set of scriptures of diverse provenance was available that reflected various stages of the development of Buddhist doctrine. This plurality was born from translations in the third and fourth centuries of dhyāna, *prajñāpāramitā,* and tathāgatagarbha scriptures, in the early fifth century by a series of Madhyamaka and Sarvāstivāda abhidharma works, and in the sixth and seventh centuries by the systematic Yogācāra and abhidharma transmission of Xuanzang. This situation necessitated the creation of a method that allowed the systematic integration of all available teachings under a common roof (*panjiao*). The premises of this method were that all scriptures could be assigned to different stages in the Buddha's teaching career, that they all address different audiences according to their respective maturity, and that they make the ultimate meaning explicit to varying degrees. In terms of commentarial practice this translated into a set of rules of interpretation. Foremost among these rules was the fourfold prop (*catuḥpratisaraṇa*) of Buddhist HERMENEUTICS, which emphasized meaning (*artha*) before wording (*vacana*), complete meaning (*nīta*) before incomplete meaning (*neya*), and true insight (prajñā) before cognition and reasoning (*vijñāna*).

Some Chinese commentators indicate that their commentaries were based on lectures, and written commentaries were often composed by disciples on the basis of lecture notes, so that one can assume that the two major contexts of commentary writing are lecturing and translating. There is evidence from DUNHUANG showing the homiletic context of scriptural interpretation, and this background does not seem to have ever been completely lost. In the context of translating from Indian or Central Asian languages into Chinese, translation and interpretation could not be separated because translators usually offered explanations of the scripture being translated, and the explanations often crept into the text itself. Thus, for example, the writings of Sengzhao on PRAJÑĀPĀRAMITĀ LITERATURE were based on his cooperation with KUMĀRAJĪVA (344–409/413), or the commentaries of Kuiji were created in the context of the translation academy of Xuanzang.

Types of commentaries

The oldest type of Chinese commentary, the *zhu* (only three of which are extant), may derive from an oral context. The *zhu* is a straightforward line-by-line exegesis that weaves glosses into the main text. These commentaries are prefaced by introductions that interpret the title and explain the setting of the discourse and the reasons for the commentary. This simple type of commentary was superseded by the *shu* commentary, which flourished between the sixth and mid-ninth centuries. The *shu* embodies the best of the monastic and scholastic tradition, exhibiting all signs of a flourishing exegetic culture and displaying a level of sophistication probably unsuited for the nonexpert laity.

Two major features characterize *shu* commentary, namely, its method of segmenting the scripture (*kepan*) and its topical introductions. The topical introductions discuss the scope of the commentary and the issues at stake for the Buddhist commentator. The introductions comprise two major groups of topics: dogmatic (the aim of the teaching, the meaning of the title, the work's basic thought, the intended audience of the teaching, its relationship to other teachings) and historical (the transmissions of the work and the history of its promulgation, including places and conventions, history of its translation, and its miraculous power).

This type of commentarial introduction reflects not only on Chinese exegesis, but on major issues of Buddhist exegesis. Accordingly, VASUBANDHU (fourth century C.E.), a major representative of Indian exegesis, summarized in his *Vyākhyāyukti* (*Practice of Exegesis*; extant only in Tibetan) the commentarial task: state the aim of the teaching (*prayojana*), state its overall meaning (*piṇḍa*) and its detailed meaning (*padārtha*), state its internal consequence (*anusaṃdhika*), refute objections (*codyaparihāra*) with regard to wording (*śabda*) and meaning (*artha*), in order to show its perfection (*yukti*). Chinese commentators classify Vasubandhu's first two tasks as independent introductory topics; the other three are incorporated into the main body of exegesis.

Vasubandhu presumes that the word of the Buddha is perfect, that all scriptures are the Buddha's word, that only perfect words need and deserve commentary, and that a person cannot understand scripture unless he or she understands the purpose of a certain teaching. In particular, one must understand a scripture in terms of the audience it is meant to address, especially if the audience is not deemed to be mature enough to comprehend the scripture's deeper meanings. This latter assumption was a fundamental element in determining the liberty a commentator might take in interpreting scripture.

Segmental analysis

Chinese scholastic commentary is also characterized by segmental analysis (*kepan*), by which the author assigns to scripture a chain of exegetic terms. The most obvious aspect of this approach, which gained importance after the fifth century, consists in the segmenting of scripture into (1) introduction (*xu*), which gives the setting of the discourse (location, participants, occasion); (2) main body (*zhengzong*), which consists in the discourse proper, and (3) eulogy (*liutong*), which describes the joy of the listeners and the promise of the spread of the dharma. This triple partition of sūtra may have derived from the *Fodi jing lun* (T.1530.26:291c). Although segmental analysis is related by tradition to Dao'an, the oldest extant example of its application can be found in Fayun's *Lotus Sūtra* commentary (*Fahua jing yiji*, T.1715.33:574c).

Beneath this first tripartite level, scholastic commentaries have further layers of segmentation, which consist of a sequence of exegetic terms (often several hundred) assigned to designated passages of scripture. One group of exegetic terms specifically marks off parts of scripture as phases of dialogue between the speaker and the interlocutor. Since most sūtras are in the form of dialogues between the Buddha and his disciples, it is possible that the first step a commentator might have taken was to segment the sequence of speech acts. Indeed, in some of the older commentaries of the early Tang period, the exegetic chain is built around a dialogic baseline. Knowing that an exegetic chain may include several hundred terms, the modern reader may wonder how any reader could be expected to keep track of the commentary's expository structure. In order to remedy this situation, graphic charts displaying the exegetic structure were developed. Although it may seem otherwise, most *kepan* and their accompanying charts are probably rooted in the homiletic situation, and are not a product of a culture dominated by writing. In fact, the *kepan* structures point back to the earliest stage of Buddhist exegesis, where they may have served as mnemonic aids for oral interpretation.

After the Tang period, *kepan*-style exegesis yielded to other methods, and scholastic introduction in general was replaced by newer, simpler forms. The genre of commentarial literature as a whole from the Song dynasty (960–1279) onward shows a process of simplification, a transformation that probably resulted, in part, from the advent of new PRINTING TECHNOLOGIES.

This simplification process was also part of a major transformation of the social context of exegesis. Whereas before the Song, commentators were mainly monks, from the Song onward a substantial body of commentaries were written by lay Buddhists. In addition, the CHAN SCHOOL and its rhetoric of immediate insight without reliance on words found support in the fundamental notion of the ineffability of the ultimate meaning of the dharma, which may have substantially impeded the further development of formal scriptural exegesis. Despite these factors, and though many assume that the genre of Buddhist exegesis passed its zenith centuries ago, commentaries on Buddhist teachings are still being written.

See also: **Canon; China; India; Scripture**

Bibliography

Gómez, Luis O. "Exegesis and Hermeneutics." In "Buddhist Literature," in *Encyclopedia of Religion,* Vol. 2, ed. Mircea Eliade. New York: Macmillan, 1987.

Kim Young-ho. *Tao-sheng's Commentary on the Lotus Sūtra: A Study and Translation.* Albany: State University of New York Press, 1990.

Lamotte, Étienne. "Assessment of Textual Interpretation in Buddhism." In *Buddhist Hermeneutics,* ed. Donald S. Lopez, Jr. Honolulu: University of Hawaii Press, 1988.

Maraldo, John C. "Hermeneutics and Historicity in the Study of Buddhism." *Eastern Buddhist* 19, no. 1 (1986): 17–43.

ALEXANDER L. MAYER

COMMUNISM AND BUDDHISM

Buddhism faced one of its greatest challenges during the twentieth century when the majority of Asian nations, which were traditionally Buddhist, became involved with communism. Mongolia was the first Asian country to become communist (1924), followed by North Korea (1948), China (1949), Tibet (1951), Vietnam (1975), Cambodia (1975), and Laos (1975).

Initial encounter

At the early stages of the Buddhist–communist encounter, coexistence did not seem impossible. Those who hoped for peaceful coexistence speculated on the similarities between communism and Buddhism: Neither Buddhists nor communists believe in a creator deity, and both Buddhism and communism are based on a vision of universal egalitarianism. In fact, the Buddhist community (SAṄGHA) was even compared with a communist society.

The seeming compatibility, however, was overshadowed by a number of conflicting ideologies. Communism is based on materialism, whereas in Buddhism primacy of the material world is rejected in favor of NIRVĀṆA. To communists, environments determine a human being's consciousness, whereas Buddhism emphasizes the individual practitioner's capacity to overcome human limitations through spiritual cultivation. In addition, Buddhism holds nonviolence and compassion as the core of its teaching, whereas communism foregrounds conflict between different social classes and endorses the use of violence in support of the proletarian revolution and the communist agenda.

Despite these differences, communism and Buddhism managed a coexistence for a brief period. In its early stages, communism gained support because it was recognized as the antithesis of foreign dominance in Asian nations at the final stage of imperialist history. People in Mongolia supported communists in their efforts to free the nation from Chinese dominance. North Korean communism gained power as a buffer against Japanese colonialists and American capitalist imperialism. Chinese communism set itself up as a defense against the threat created by the invasion of the Western powers at the beginning of the twentieth century. Vietnamese communists claimed to be nationalists fighting for the independence of Vietnam from the imperialist French and capitalist Americans. Because the Buddhist tradition had existed in Asia for more than fifteen hundred years, it could be seen by communists as a confirmation of national identity, while communism was seen as a means of defending a nation against foreign invasion. Thus, a coalition between Buddhism and communism seemed possible.

Conflict

Buddhists soon faced reality. Once communist groups won the wars and communist nation-states began to take shape, Buddhists were forced to realize that the basic antagonism of Marxism toward all religion could not be challenged. Religion in Marxist philosophy is "the opium of the people." Communists view religion as a fantasy and superstition that deludes people about their social condition. According to communism, religion is a tool used by the bourgeoisie to exploit the proletariat and thus delay the proletarian revolution.

Only a few years after Asian nations fell to communism, the initial tolerance toward Buddhism was replaced by extreme antagonism. Communist parties launched severe PERSECUTIONS of Buddhists and instigated an irreparable dismantling of Buddhist traditions. By the late 1930s more than fifteen thousand monks in the Mongolian People's Republic were declared enemies of the state and deported to Siberian

Chinese vice-premier Chen Yi enters Lhasa in 1956 to attend ceremonies marking the incorporation of Tibet into the Chinese state. He is accompanied by the Dalai Lama and the Panchen Lama. The Dalai Lama went into exile in 1959. © Bettmann/Corbis. Reproduced by permission.

labor camps, where they soon perished from starvation and overwork. During the late 1940s communists in North Korea conducted a systematic removal of religion from society, followed by the complete eradication of all religious practice during the 1960s and 1970s. Immediately after the establishment of the communist government in China, opportunities for religious practice were reduced and ordination was restricted. At the outset of the Cultural Revolution in the mid-1960s, Buddhist practice all but disappeared from China. In Vietnam, repression of religion began with the victory of the communists in April 1975, after which communists destroyed or confiscated Buddhist pagodas and Buddhist office buildings. By 1982 there were only about twenty-three hundred monks left in Cambodia, a drastic decrease from the sixty thousand monks in Cambodia in 1975 when the nation first became communist. The situation in Tibet is unique in that the communists were not Tibetans but Chinese who claimed Tibet as their territory. Before the Chinese invasion, there were more than six thousand monasteries in Tibet; fewer than twenty monasteries survived persecution by Chinese communists. The spiritual and political leader of Tibet, the fourteenth DALAI LAMA, was exiled to India in 1959.

Since the communist persecutions began, Buddhists have generally held fast to the Buddhist teaching against injuring others. Vietnamese monks performed SELF-IMMOLATION as a protest against communist persecution, and for half a century the Dalai Lama has appealed to the world to stop the suffering of the Tibetan people and the destruction of Tibetan Buddhism, but Buddhists have refused to resort to violence to settle the tragedy brought upon Buddhism and Buddhist followers. The Buddhist message of nonviolent protest has brought awareness to the world of the importance of the peaceful resolution of conflicts and the urgency of human rights issues. Through their faithfulness to Buddhist teachings and their belief in human values in

A Chinese police officer watches as Buddhist monks celebrate the Tibetan New Year at a Tibetan Buddhist temple in Beijing, 1999. © AFP/Corbis. Reproduced by permission.

a time of suffering, Buddhist monks and nuns in persecuted nations were able to demonstrate the value of religion in human societies.

In the 1990s communist governments began to show relative tolerance toward Buddhism, and religious practices began to resurface as Buddhist monasteries were renovated and Buddhist objects were recognized as national treasures. In Tibet, despite increasing tolerance toward Buddhism, the Chinese continue to refuse to allow the Dalai Lama to be repatriated. In countries where Buddhism faces a revival it still has obstacles to overcome. After decades of persecution and restrictions on ordination, a new generation of Buddhist young people has not emerged to succeed aging monks and nuns. How the Buddhist revival will fill the gap and make up for the lost decades remains unclear.

See also: **Modernity and Buddhism; Nationalism and Buddhism**

Bibliography

Benz, Ernst. *Buddhism or Communism: Which Holds the Future of Asia?,* tr. Richard Winston and Clara Winston. Garden City, NY: Doubleday, 1965.

Bstan 'dzin rgya mtsho (Dalai Lama XIV). *Freedom in Exile: The Autobiography of the Dalai Lama.* New York and San Francisco: Harper, 1990.

Harris, Ian. "Buddhism *in Extremis*: The Case of Cambodia." In *Buddhism and Politics in Twentieth-Century Asia,* ed. Ian Harris. London and New York: Pinter, 1999.

Ling, Trevor. *Buddha, Marx, and God: Some Aspects of Religion in the Modern World.* New York: St. Martin's Press, 1979.

Nhat Hanh, Thich. *Vietnam: Lotus in a Sea of Fire.* New York: Hill and Wang, 1967.

Queen, Christopher S., and King, Sallie B., eds. *Engaged Buddhism: Buddhist Liberation Movements in Asia.* Albany: State University of New York Press, 1996.

Schecter, Jerrold L. *The New Face of Buddhism: Buddhism and Political Power in Southeast Asia.* New York: Coward-McCann, 1967.

Schwartz, Ronald D. "Renewal and Resistance: Tibetan Buddhism in the Modern Era." In *Buddhism and Politics in Twentieth-Century Asia,* ed. Ian Harris. London and New York: Pinter, 1999.

Sin Pŏpt'a. *Pukhan Pulgyŏ yon'gu. A Study of Buddhism in North Korea in the Late Twentieth Century.* Seoul: Minjoksa, 2000.

Stuart-Fox, Martin. "Lao: From Buddhist Kingdom to Marxist State." In *Buddhism and Politics in Twentieth-Century Asia,* ed. Ian Harris. London and New York: Pinter, 1999.

Welch, Holmes. *Buddhism under Mao.* Cambridge, MA: Harvard University Press, 1972.

JIN Y. PARK

COMPASSION. *See* Karuṇā (Compassion)

CONCENTRATION. *See* Meditation

CONFESSION. *See* Repentance and Confession

CONFUCIANISM AND BUDDHISM

Chinese religions are traditionally divided into the three teachings of Confucianism (*Rujiao*), Daoism (*Daojiao*), and Buddhism (*Fojiao*). Because Chinese cultural patterns (*wen*) were disseminated, primarily in the form of writing, throughout East Asia, these three teachings spread to Korea, Japan, and parts of Southeast Asia. Confucians (*ru*) were scholars who took as their principal task the administration and maintenance of an ordered society, which they hoped to achieve by remaining active participants in it (*zaijia*). Buddhists lived as monks and nuns in monastic communities (SAṄGHA), renouncing the world (*chujia*) behind walls and gates to free themselves and others from the bondage of the cycle of life and death (SAṂSĀRA). Over the course of two millennia of close interaction in China, Confucians and Buddhists clashed on issues ranging from bowing to the emperor and one's parents to the foreign ancestry and routines of the Buddhist faith. Even so, indigenous Chinese Buddhist doctrines and practices stimulated developments within the late-imperial Confucian renaissance known in Western scholarship as neo-Confucianism.

Historical and cultural considerations

The history of interaction between Confucianism and Buddhism in China is the history of Chinese Buddhism in the public and social sphere. Because Confucian teachings were initially transmitted to Korea and Japan principally by Buddhist monks, successful, separate, and local Confucian traditions did not develop in Japan or Korea until the neo-Confucian era; the relationship between Buddhism and Confucianism that developed in China is representative of wider trends throughout the East Asian region.

Confucianism became a religious and philosophical tradition (*ruxue*) with the establishment of the five classics (*wujing*) as the basis for official education in 136 B.C.E. The five classics include the *Shijing* (*Classic of Poetry*), the *Shujing* (*Classic of History*), the *Yijing* (*Classic of Changes*), the *Liji* (*Record of Rites*), and the *Chunqiu zuozhuan* (*Zuo Commentary to the Annals of the Spring and Autumn Period*). In addition to these books, the sayings of Confucius (Kong Qiu, 551–479 B.C.E.), called the *Lunyu* (*Analects*), and the teachings of Mencius (Mengzi, Meng Ke, ca. 371–289 B.C.E.) and Xunzi (Xun Qing, d. 215 B.C.E.), among other classical commentaries, as well as state-promoting ritual manuals and cosmological treaties, were sponsored by early Confucians (*rujia*).

Scholars and the clergy: The question of Buddhist patronage

During the Han dynasty (206 B.C.E.–220 C.E.), Buddhism remained essentially an elusive, foreign creed, practiced primarily among the many Central Asian merchant communities that grew in Chinese trade centers. Buddhism did not pose an institutional threat to the burgeoning Confucian orthodox tradition of statecraft or to the emergent Huang-Lao proto-Daoist religious groups. During the interval between the fall of the Han and establishment of the Sui dynasty (581–618), however, piecemeal Buddhist doctrines and practices—especially teachings about DHYĀNA (TRANCE STATE) and ŚŪNYATĀ (EMPTINESS) as explained in the PRAJÑĀPĀRAMITĀ LITERATURE—were of great interest to both non-Chinese rulers in the north and southern aristocrats. Serindian monks and their Chinese counterparts in the north and south after 310 C.E. began to trade verses of poetry with aristocrats to communicate Buddhist theories in a Chinese context. The outcome of these exchanges between Confucian-trained aristocrats, Buddhist monks, and Daoist adepts is known as "dark learning" (*xuanxue*). "Pure talk" (*qingtan*) exchanges that included discussions about poetry and comparisons between MAHĀYĀNA Buddhist thought and the *Laozi* and *Zhuangzi*—two Chinese classical texts that later became associated with Daoism—resulted from this interaction.

Because Confucianism at this time comprised a diffuse category of aristocratic pursuits and interests (at least in part because the failings of Confucian statecraft were considered responsible for the downfall of the Han) rather than an exclusive set of doctrines and precepts, Buddhism began to surface as a formidable religious institution. During the early decades of the fifth century, full translations of Indian Buddhist monastic codes (VINAYA) were completed; the vinaya regulated the lives of monks and nuns in Chinese monasteries in ways that were more consistent with Indian societal norms. This development prompted Emperor Wudi (r. 424–451) of the Northern Wei dynasty (386–534) to initiate the first anti-Buddhist PERSECUTIONS at the request of both his Daoist and Confucian ministers Kou Qianzhi (d. 448) and Cui Hao (381–450). Both advisers wished to transform the state into a more sinified society, and saw members of the recently disciplined saṅgha as world-renouncing and discourteous to the emperor and secular worthies. Emperor Wudi of the Northern Zhou (557–581) also accepted this rationale and instigated anti-Buddhist persecutions that resulted in the widespread defrocking of monks and nuns and the confiscation of monastic property. These policies indicate that by 446 the institutional footprint of the Buddhist church was broad enough to challenge indigenous Chinese power blocks.

With the establishment of Sui hegemony over north and south China by 589, the Buddhist church became both an instrument of state promotion through its Buddhist relic (*śarīra*) distribution campaigns, and the object of censure by Confucians and Daoists critical of Buddhist economic and social influence throughout China. During the early decades of the Tang dynasty (618–907), Confucian and Daoist advisors submitted memorials to the throne condemning the Buddhist church for myriads of reasons, including claims of illegal ordinations, religious arrogance, commercial activities, and tax evasion, which led emperor Gaozu (r. 618–627) in 626 to proclaim Confucianism and Daoism the two pillars of the state. Prior to Empress Wu Zhao's (r. 690–705) foundation of the short-lived Zhou dynasty and the An Lushan rebellion (755–763), the Tang court and its Confucian administrators adopted a policy of tepid tolerance toward Buddhism and allowed it to expand. Emperor Taizong (r. 627–650) famously sponsored XUANZANG's (ca. 600–664) translation projects after his return from India with hundreds of Sanskrit manuscripts.

Empress Wu Zhao forever changed the world of Confucians and Buddhists in China. Her rise to power conflicted with traditional Confucian ideology favoring male rulers, which prompted her to institute sweeping reforms in the Confucian official examination system. Wu Zhao employed an open examination system for officials in order to counter the power of the ingrained aristocratic families who were hostile to her. Thus, the examination system originally set up during the Han, and institutionalized during the Sui, became a vehicle to promote scholars who did not necessarily hail from aristocratic or influential families. When the Tang ruling house was reestablished under emperor Xuanzong (r. 713–755), the cultivation of belles lettres—defined as refined knowledge of the classics and the composition of poetry (*shih*)—remained the basis for receiving the highest honors in the palace examinations as "presented scholars" (*jinshi*). Confucian learning during Xuanzong's reign was memorialized in the writings of Wang Wei (701–761), Li Bai (701–762), and Du Fu (712–770)—three of China's greatest poets—while bureaucrats implemented imperial decrees designed to restrain the institutional power of Buddhist monasteries, which had been extravagantly patronized by Wu Zhao. In 725 Xuanzong traveled to sacred Mount Tai to perform the Confucian state rites of *feng* and *shan*, and during his reign he received Indian esoteric Buddhists at court and helped to establish a small esoteric Buddhist institution in China.

The most significant anti-Buddhist persecution in China occurred during the Huichang era (841–845). Emperor Wuzong took note of memorials to the throne by Confucian stalwarts like Han Yu (768–824)—who, after witnessing a procession of a finger-joint relic of the Buddha in 819, wrote the polemical *Lun fogu biao* (*Memorial on the Buddha's Bone*)—and adopted policies to suppress the influence of Buddhism throughout Chinese society. Wuzong ordered the seizure of monastic properties, expelled monks and nuns from monasteries, and prohibited youths from taking tonsure. By 845 Wuzong's policies had led to the defrocking of 260,000 nuns and monks and the destruction of more than 4,600 monasteries and 40,000 shrines. Wuzong's antiforeign decrees also effectively eradicated Zoroastrianism, Nestorian Christianity, and Manichaeism from China in an attempt to address the threat that the Uighurs and Tibetans posed from the northwest and west.

Han Yu's memorial, however, epitomized the antiforeign sentiment from a Confucian standpoint by suggesting that Buddhism was a barbarian cult, and that the Buddha himself was a barbarian—meaning someone who does not know the proper relationship between ruler and minister, father and son, or who does not wear ancient Chinese garb. Hence, if the Buddha were to arrive in China the emperor would merely give him an audience, a banquet, and award him a suit of clothes, after which he would be escorted under guard to the border. Han Yu thought that Buddhism threatened the Confucian administration of Chinese society by inciting people to publicly worship the Buddha bone.

Confucian and Chinese patriarchs

During the Song dynasty (960–1279) Confucian scholars and Buddhist monks were both bitter enemies and close allies. The early Song court supported new Buddhist translation projects, awarded exceptional patronage to followers of the CHAN SCHOOL, and facilitated debates between Confucian officials about fiscal, educational, and social policies. After the An Lushan rebellion, patronage for Buddhism and its institutions fell to a new southern gentry class, formed through the massive population shift southward as people fled the war-torn north. Between 742 and 1200, the population of north China grew by 58 percent, while it doubled or tripled in the south. Most of the new southern gentry were not connected to the elite families that provided the pool of civil-service applicants between the Han and Tang dynasties. Therefore, the Song imperial examinations provided the basis for a much more loyal and dynamic Confucian-educated bureaucracy than ever before. On the borders of Song territory, non-Chinese states threatened the Confucian world order, and the gentry literati (*wenren*) produced by the examination system responded in two ways: the "learning of culture" and neo-Confucianism.

Adherents of the learning of culture approach, including the poet and scholar Su Shi (1036–1101), argued that Chinese (Confucian) culture endured through literature, including the cultivation of poetry and prose. To Su Shi, Buddhist doctrines did not clash with Confucian principles, and Buddhist monks, especially from the Chan lineage, could appreciate the value of cultural patterns and transmit them too. Those who supported neo-Confucianism, however, vehemently condemned the renunciant lifestyle and popular appeal of Buddhism. Initially, Zhou Dunyi (1017–1073) and the Cheng brothers—Cheng Yi (1033–1107) and Cheng Hao (1032–1085)—and later Zhu Xi (1130–1200) advocated studying the path of ancient Confucian sages, in particular Mencius, in order to rectify one's character, become a moral leader of society, and follow the principle, rather than the manifested phenomena (*ji*), of the ancients. Zhu Xi, in particular, encouraged followers to study the "four books" in addition to the traditional five classics: the *Analects*, the teachings of Mencius, *Daoxue* (*Great Learning*), and *Zhongyong* (*Doctrine of the Mean*). Later followers sometimes included the *Xiaojing* (*Classic of Filial Piety*) instead of Mencius. Neo-Confucians contended that they transmitted the knowledge and foundation for dynastic and social legitimacy (*zhengtong*), which had been ignored since the time of Mencius. Even though neo-Confucian notions of transmission and self-cultivation were directly borrowed from the Chan school, Chan Buddhists became the principal focus of neo-Confucian indignation.

Gentry and popular Buddhism

It was not until 1313 that the neo-Confucian approach to official education outlined in the Cheng-Zhu school was adopted as the state orthodoxy. During subsequent dynasties, tensions grew between Cheng-Zhu trained officials and Buddhist monks and nuns. Without learning of culture supporters, the Chinese saṅgha, which was now dominated by members of the Chan lineage, became more focused on obtaining patronage from local gentry than from the state. During the Ming dynasty (1368–1644), the Confucian official Wang Yangming (1472–1529) turned to Chan Buddhist practices and teachings to create a Confucian meditation practice known as quiet sitting (*jingzuo*). Monasteries received largesse from local gentry and became centers of learning and culture at a time when the state could no longer support local Confucian academies. Buddhism during the Ming and Qing (1644–1911) dynasties became an integral part of the three teachings triad of institutionalized Chinese religions. This occurred despite the increasing divide between Confucian officials and Buddhists, and Buddhist rhetoric to the contrary, which was influenced by foreign imperial houses importing Tibetan and Mongolian Buddhist traditions into the Chinese capital of Beijing.

See also: **China; Daoism and Buddhism; Syncretic Sects: Three Teachings**

Bibliography

Bol, Peter K. *"This Culture of Ours": Intellectual Transitions in T'ang and Sung China.* Stanford, CA: Stanford University Press, 1992.

Brook, Timothy. *Praying for Power: Buddhism and the Formation of Gentry Society in Late-Ming China.* Cambridge, MA: Harvard University Press, 1993.

Gernet, Jacques. *Buddhism in Chinese Society: An Economic History from the Fifth to the Tenth Centuries,* tr. Franciscus Verellen. New York: Columbia University Press, 1995.

Zürcher, E. *The Buddhist Conquest of China: The Spread and Adaptation of Buddhism in Early Medieval China.* Leiden, Netherlands: Brill, 1959. Reprint, 1972.

GEORGE A. KEYWORTH

CONSCIOUSNESS, THEORIES OF

The English word *consciousness* usually translates the Sanskrit word *vijñāna* (Pāli, *viññāna*), although in some contexts *vijñāna* comes closer to the concept of *subconsciousness.* In Buddhism in general (except in the Yogācāra tradition), *vijñāna* is considered to be synonymous with two other Sanskrit words—*citta* and *manas*—that roughly correspond to the English word *mind.* Buddhism denies the existence of a substantial and everlasting soul (ātman), but unlike materialistic traditions, Buddhism never negates the existence of consciousness (or mind). From a Buddhist point of view, consciousness is differentiated from the soul in that the former is an ever-changing, momentary, and impermanent element. Consciousness, however, is considered to continue like a stream and is thought to be somehow transmitted from one life to the next, thus enabling karmic causality over lifetimes. This continuity of consciousness represents, in a sense, the personal identity. Consciousness also keeps the body alive and distinguishes animate beings from inanimate elements. Therefore, consciousness is one of the key factors of Buddhism.

When the word *consciousness* is used, it appears to refer mainly to the cognitive function directed to its object. Thus, this word is defined in the *Saṃyuttanikāya* (*Kindred Sayings*) III:87 as: "Because it recognizes [something], it is called *consciousness.*"

More specifically, six types of consciousness are enumerated in Buddhist texts: visual consciousness, auditory consciousness, olfactory consciousness, gustatory consciousness, tactile consciousness, and mental consciousness. These six consciousnesses must be supported by the corresponding, unimpaired sense faculties (eye, ear, nose, tongue, body, and mind) in order to recognize their respective objects (color/form, sound, smell, taste, tactile sensation, and concepts). When these three elements (sense faculty, object, and consciousness) come together ("contact," *sparśa*), cognition comes about.

The word *consciousness,* however, often appears without specification regarding sense faculty or object, as, for example in the list of the five SKANDHA (AGGREGATE): body/matter (*rūpa*), sensation (*vedanā*), ideation (*saṃjñā*), volition (saṃskāra), and consciousness (*vijñāna*). This type of bare "consciousness" is also found in several other important contexts.

Rebirth and the theory of dependent origination

The notion of consciousness plays a cardinal role in the context of REBIRTH, within the large framework of PRATĪTYASAMUTPĀDA (DEPENDENT ORIGINATION). In those early scriptures that propound very simple forms of Buddhist causation there are two basic patterns: one centering on consciousness and psycho-physical existence (*nāmarūpa*), and the other centering on desire (*tṛṣṇā*) and appropriation (*upadhi, upādāna*). According to the scriptures that put forth the first pattern, as long as the consciousness has objects (*ālambana*) to be conceived and to be attached to, it stays in the realm of SAṂSĀRA, and the psycho-physical existence will enter the womb (i.e., one will be reborn in the next life without being liberated from saṃsāra). Scriptural admonitions to guard the "doors" of one's sense faculties so that one does not grasp at cognitive objects would be closely related to this idea of consciousness.

Since several expressions meaning *desire* also appear in the context of consciousness attached to its objects, these two patterns are in fact closely related. Eventually these two patterns were combined into more developed systems of dependent origination, consisting of ten or twelve items. Even the full-fledged system of the twelve causal links basically consists of two portions: the first (one through seven; ignorance through sensation) centering on consciousness, and the second (eight through twelve; desire through old age and death) centering on desire. (Later Sarvāstivāda and Yogācāra interpretations of dependent origination, though differing greatly from each other, also support this division.) Therefore, the full-fledged theory of dependent origination is in a way an elaboration of the simpler causation theories described above. In this system also, the third item, consciousness, is usually understood as the consciousness at the moment of conception, and thus it retains its nature as described in the very early texts.

According to Yogācāra tradition, at the time of one's death, a powerful attachment to one's own existence arises and makes one's consciousness grasp the next life. Furthermore, according to both the Sarvāstivāda and Yogācāra schools, the consciousness in the INTERMEDIATE STATE sees the parents making love. If the being is about to be reborn as a boy, he is attached to the mother and hates the father. If the being is about to be reborn as a girl, she is attached to the father and hates the mother. Driven by this perverted thought, the being enters the womb, and the consciousness merges with the united semen and "blood," after which the semen-blood combination becomes a sentient embryo. Even when a being is about to be reborn in a hell, it misconceives the hell as something desirable, and driven by its attachment to the "desirable place," it hastens to the hell. Thus, in these cases also, the basic structure of consciousness attached to some object and bound to the realm of saṃsāra resembles the structure of consciousness found in the less developed stage of Buddhist causation theory.

The ālayavijñāna theory and the theory of the eight consciousnesses

In the YOGĀCĀRA SCHOOL, consciousness that merges with the semen-blood combination is understood as the *storehouse consciousness* (ĀLAYAVIJÑĀNA). According to this school, the storehouse consciousness, the deepest layer of one's subconsciousness, maintains all the residue of past KARMA (ACTION) as "seeds," which will give rise to their fruits in the future. This theory enabled the Yogācāra school to explain the problems of reincarnation and karmic retribution without resorting to the concept of substantial soul.

The storehouse consciousness is also linked to the idealistic theory propounded by Yogācāra. Buddhism had an idealistic tendency from the early stages of its history, and the state of the external world was linked to the collective karma/desire of SENTIENT BEINGS. An interesting example is found in a Buddhist cosmogonical legend, which states that as the desire of sentient beings became more gross, the surrounding world became less and less attractive. On the basis of meditative experiences, the Yogācāra tradition elaborated this tendency into a sophisticated philosophical system in which the world that people experience is actually a projection of their own consciousness. The seeds kept in the storehouse consciousness are considered to be the source of this projected world.

Another important function of the storehouse consciousness is the physiological maintenance of the body. Since the early stages of Buddhism, consciousness was considered to be the element that distinguishes animate beings from inanimate matter. Unless consciousness appropriates (i.e., maintains) the body, the body becomes a senseless corpse. Since, however, the stream of consciousnesses on the surface level is sometimes interrupted (as in the states of dreamless sleep, fainting, or deep absorption), it was difficult to explain how the body is maintained during those unconscious periods. Because the storehouse consciousness continues to operate even when the surface consciousnesses do not arise, the introduction of the storehouse consciousness solves the problem of physiological maintenance of the body.

In addition to the storehouse consciousness, the Yogācāra school introduced another subconscious layer of mind, namely the *defiled mind* (*kliṣṭamanas*). This is a subconscious ego-consciousness that is always operative in the depths of the mind. According to the Yogācāra system, the defiled mind is always directed to the storehouse consciousness and mistakes the latter for a substantial self. By introducing the concept of defiled mind, the Yogācāra school pointed out that the subconscious ego-mind is hiding behind the scene even when one is trying to do good things on the conscious level. Thus, from this point of view, the minds of deluded, ordinary sentient beings are always defiled, regardless of the moral nature of the surface consciousnesses. Thus, in addition to the conventional six types of consciousness, the Yogācāra school introduced two subconscious layers of mind—defiled mind and storehouse consciousness—and constructed a system of eight types of consciousness. These eight consciousnesses are linked to *citta,* manas, and *vijñāna* in the following way: The storehouse consciousness corresponds to *citta,* the defiled mind to manas, and the conventional six consciousnesses to *vijñāna.*

Simultaneous versus successive operations of plural consciousnesses

Since the Yogācāra model of eight consciousnesses means that two layers of unconscious mind are always operating behind the conventional six consciousnesses, it naturally presupposes the simultaneous operations of different types of consciousness. This position, however, was not uncontroversial among Buddhist traditions. Since the stream of consciousness represents a personal identity in Buddhism, there was a strong opinion that more than one stream of consciousness could not exist simultaneously in any sentient being at a given moment. According to this position, strongly advocated by the Sarvāstivāda school, when one feels, for example, that one is seeing something and listening to something at the same time, the visual consciousness and the auditory consciousness are in fact operating in rapid succession and not simultaneously.

It is recorded that some schools belonging to the Mahāsāṃghika lineage did not share this opinion, but it seems to have been widely accepted by other schools. The SAUTRĀNTIKA (Those Who Follow Sūtras) tradition, which, according to the common view, was an offshoot of the Sarvāstivāda school, was considered to have shared the Sarvāstivāda opinion on this matter, but this has been questioned recently by some scholars.

Sautrāntika theories of consciousness

The exact identity of the tradition called "Sautrāntika" is one of the biggest problems in current Buddhist scholarship. Sautrāntika is commonly believed to have been preceded by a tradition called Dārṣṭāntika (Those Who Resort to Similes). However, the exact relationship between these two traditions is a matter of dispute.

Generally speaking, both Dārṣṭāntika and Sautrāntika seem to have had nominalistic tendencies; thus they challenged the realistic system of Sarvāstivāda on many points. For example, in both the Sarvāstivāda and Yogācāra schools, consciousness(es) are considered to be associated with various psychological factors (*caitta*), such as lust and hatred, which are themselves distinct elements. The Dārṣṭāntika tradition, on the other hand, treats psychological factors as something not distinct from the consciousness itself. The Dārṣṭāntika and Sautrāntika traditions also tend not to admit a causal relationship between two simultaneous elements. In order for a cause to bring about a result, the cause must be at least one moment prior to the result. Thus, the cognitive object, which is considered to be a cause of consciousness, must precede the cognition of that object. In addition, what one perceives is the cognitive image of an object within one's consciousness; one cannot directly perceive the object itself. The existence of the external object, however, is inferred from its cognitive image.

Theory of consciousness in Buddhist epistemology

The Dārṣṭāntika and Sautrāntika traditions are considered to have exerted a strong influence over Buddhist epistemologists such as DIGNĀGA (ca. 480–540) and DHARMAKĪRTI (ca. 600–660). At the same time, Dignāga also clearly inherited the idealistic system of Yogācāra, as is shown in the theory of *cognition cognizing itself* (*svasaṃvitti*) in the *Pramāṇasamuccaya* (verses 1.8cd–12).

Further, one of Dignāga's important contributions (*Pramāṇasamuccaya [Collected Writings on the Means of Cognition]*, verses 1.2–8ab) was the redefinition of *perception* (*pratyakṣa*) and its strict differentiation from *inference* (*anumāna*). He maintained that the cognition of the five sense consciousnesses (from visual through tactile) are always perception, and that the mental consciousness operates in both perception and inference. This distinction between the five sense consciousnesses and the mental consciousness is in line with the theories of Sarvāstivāda and Yogācāra.

Relationship with the tathāgatagarbha theory

Another development in the theory of consciousness is the association of the storehouse consciousness with the TATHĀGATAGARBHA (embryo of tathāgata, or buddha-nature) theory. The storehouse consciousness was originally conceived as the root of the deluded mind and the defiled world, and thus is itself defiled. It was to be transformed into pure wisdom when one attains awakening, but the storehouse consciousness before the transformation was not considered to be a pure element in the original Yogācāra system. However, some lines of the Yogācāra tradition, most notably the position presented in the LAṄKĀVATĀRA-SŪTRA (*Discourse on the Occasion of the [Buddha's] Entry into Laṅka*) came to associate, and even identify, the storehouse consciousness with the tathāgatagarbha, the pure element latent in deluded, ordinary beings. Since some Indian masters who transmitted the Yogācāra doctrine to China, most notably PARAMĀRTHA (499–569), were heavily influenced by these lines of thought, the exact relationship between the storehouse consciousness and the tathāgatagarbha became an important issue in Chinese Buddhism.

See also: **Anātman/Ātman (No-Self/Self); Philosophy; Psychology; Sarvāstivāda and Mūlasarvāstivāda**

Bibliography

Aramaki, Noritoshi. "On the Formation of a Short Prose Pratītyasamutpāda Sūtra." In *Buddhism and Its Relation to Other Religions: Essays in Honour of Dr. Shozen Kumoi on His Seventieth Birthday,* ed. Kumoi Shozen Hakushi Koki Kinenkai. Kyoto: Heirakuji Shoten, 1985.

Hattori, Masaaki, ed. and trans. *Dignāga, on Perception, Being the Pratyakṣapariccheda of Dignāga's Pramāṇasamuccaya from the Sanskrit Fragments and the Tibetan Versions.* Cambridge, MA: Harvard University Press, 1968.

Kritzer, Robert. *Rebirth and Causation in the Yogācāra Abhidharma.* Vienna: Arbeitskreis für Tibetische und Buddhistische Studien, Universität Wien, 1999.

Schmithausen, Lambert. *Ālayavijñāna: On the Origin and the Early Development of a Central Concept of Yogācāra Philosophy.* Tokyo: International Institute for Buddhist Studies, 1987.

NOBUYOSHI YAMABE

CONSECRATION

Consecration has been broadly defined as "an act or ritual that invests objects, places, or people with religious significance, often by way of power and holiness" (Bowker, p. 234). In terms of Buddhism, consecration has been characterized as a ritual that transmutes an image or a STŪPA from a mundane object into the nature of a Buddha (Bentor 1997). Consecrated objects include not only images and stūpas, but representational paintings, books, and other objects. *Abhiṣeka,* the Sanskrit term ordinarily translated as "consecration," expands this signification to include KINGSHIP (*rājābhiṣeka*) and designates the act or ritual specifically as one of sprinkling or anointing with sacred water. This entry deals with the ritual techniques for sanctifying objects that figure specifically in Buddhist devotional practice, in particular images and stūpa-enshrined relics, to the exclusion of sacred places such as monasteries and revered personages such as monks and kings. Furthermore, even though water lustration features prominently in consecration rituals, this essay broadens the meaning of *abhiṣeka* beyond the act of anointing to include various techniques and devices by which these objects are sacralized, making them powerful and auspicious both for what they symbolize or represent and what they become via the act of consecration. For example, a consecrated BUDDHA IMAGE simultaneously both *represents* and *is* the living presence of the Buddha, while an unconsecrated image merely symbolizes the Blessed One.

An image of the Buddha or a Buddhist saint becomes an *icon* in the sense that it partakes of the substance of that which it represents by means of a consecration ritual. By contrast, a bodily relic of the Buddha (*śarīradhātu*) by its inherent nature partakes of the Buddha's very substance. Consequently, a stūpa becomes an icon when it enshrines a relic, and a relic may be placed inside a Buddha image for the same purpose. A bodily relic so employed serves as one of the means by which Buddha images and stūpas are consecrated. The Chinese practice of venerating the mummified body of an eminent monk can be seen as the ultimate expression of such iconization, the complete fusion of an image of a saint and relic-body.

As different signs or material artifacts of use and association—footprint, bodhi tree, alms bowl, image, and even book—came to signify the presence of the absent ("*parinirvāṇized*") Buddha, so various ritual techniques evolved for instilling them with the presence and power of the Buddha. Not surprisingly, the primary signs were associated with the most important venues of devotional practice, namely, stūpa enshrined relics and Buddha images. Throughout Buddhist Asia from India to Japan, stūpas, pagodas, and image halls became major features of that part of the monastic complex referred to as the "Buddha's dwelling place" (*buddhavāsa*), complementing the "monk's dwelling place" (*saṅghāvāsa*). As these terms suggest, the monastery served and continues to serve not only as a place where monks pursue the paths of meditation and study but participate in devotional practices as ritual functionaries. One of the ritual acts performed by monks that is central to venerating the Buddha (*buddhapūja*) includes consecrating icons.

Making the Buddha present

Not surprisingly, all consecration rituals throughout Asia are not the same. They reflect different Buddhist traditions as well as the particular cultures in which they flourished. Although no one ritual fits all cases, there are commonalities. Preeminently, Buddha images and relics as well as other material artifacts associated with the Buddha make the Buddha available to a particular time and place. In doing so they serve as the Buddha's functional equivalent or double, especially in ritual contexts.

The *Kosalabimbavaṇṇanā* (*The Laudatory Account of the Kosala Image*), a thirteenth-century Pāli Sinhalese text, describes how the image functions as the Buddha's double. Like the better known Mahāyāna version of the story associated with King Udayāna, the Buddha's absence becomes the occasion for the construction of an image of the Blessed One. In the Pāli rendition, King Pasenadi of Kosala pays the Buddha a visit only to find him away on a journey. When the Buddha returns the following day, the king laments how disappointed he was not to see the Buddha and requests that an image in the likeness of the tathāgata be made for the benefit of the whole world. The Blessed One acquiesces, adding that whoever builds an image of whatever size and material accrues an immeasurable, incalculable benefit. Returning to his residence, King Pasenadi (Sanskrit, Prasenajit) orders a Buddha image made of sandalwood displaying the thirty-two marks of a Great Person (Sanskrit, *mahāpuruṣa*; Pāli, *mahāpurisa*) inlaid with gold and clothed in yellow robes. After its completion he invites the Buddha to see the image housed in a bejeweled shrine. As the Buddha enters the shrine, the statue behaves as if it were animated, rising to greet the Fully Enlightened One who states that after his *parinirvāṇa* the image will perpetuate his teaching (dharma) for five thousand years. The story stipulates that presencing the Buddha through material relics, in this case an image, provides the locus for the expression of religious sentiment and the opportunity to make merit through ritual offerings. Furthermore, in materializing the Buddha and the dharma—a key feature of consecration ritual—such representations ensure the perpetuation of the religion (*sāsana*).

Consecration as transformation

Phenomenologically, consecration rituals transform images, caitya, and other material signs of the Buddha into Buddha surrogates. As recounted in the MAHĀPARINIRVĀṆA-SUTRA, at the Buddha's cremation his body is transmuted into corporeal relics, not by water as in an abhiṣeka rite, but via fire. The *parinirvāṇed* body assumes a new, dispersed form in bodily relics, objectified artifacts of the Buddha's charisma. Regarding Buddha images, the *Kosalabimbavaṇṇanā* and other textual accounts ascribe qualities of the living Buddha to the icon, including animation. "Opening the eyes of the Buddha," the pan-Buddhist term for image consecration rituals, conveys a similar meaning. A mere object, in this case an anthropomorphic representation rather than a crystalline relic, becomes a buddha. In East Asia eye-opening rituals were also believed to enliven portraits of charismatic monks as well as empower ancestral tablets (Japanese, *ihai*) enshrined in monasteries and home altars.

In Southeast Asia such transformation involves a mimetic ritual process informed, as Bernard Faure suggests in his study of the flesh icons of mummified Chan monks, by the "logic of metonymy and synecdoche in which the shadow or trace becomes as real as the body" (p. 170). The northern Thai consecration ritual begins at sunset and concludes at sunrise, mirroring the three watches of the night of the bodhisattva's achievement of buddhahood. During the course of the evening, monks recite the story of the future Buddha's renunciation of worldly goals, his years as a wandering ascetic, MĀRA's temptations, and his final awakening. In Cambodia and northern Thailand reenactments of episodes from the Buddha's biography, in particular Sujātā's offering of milk and honey rice gruel, highlight the performative nature of the ritual. At sunrise monks chant the auspicious verses attributed to the Buddha upon his awakening: "Through many a birth I wandered in saṃsāra, seeing, but not finding the builder of the house. Sorrowful is birth again and again. O house-builder! You are seen. You shall build no house again. All your rafters are broken; your ridgepole is shattered. My mind has attained the unconditioned; the end of craving is achieved."

The physical space in which the consecration ritual is conducted also mimetically replicates the Buddha's biography. Throughout the ceremony the main image being consecrated is placed on a bed of grass under a bodhi tree sapling in a monastery's image hall. The area is designated as the *bodhimaṇḍa*, the throne of enlightenment that miraculously grew from a grass mat, the *dāna* gift provided the future Buddha by Sottiya, the forester. An auspicious cord extends from the previously consecrated temple image around the *bodhimaṇḍa*, thereby forging a conduit to the first Buddha image authenticated by the Buddha himself. Other ritual paraphernalia symbolize specific episodes in the story of the bodhisattva's enlightenment quest, as well as the tathāgata Buddhas of the current age.

During the ceremony the heads of the images placed within the *bodhimaṇḍa* are shrouded by a white cloth and their eyes covered with beeswax. They have been sequestered, much as the future Buddha left his palace and sought the solitude of the forest. At sunrise, monks chant the *gāthā* (verse) of awakening and the head and eye coverings of the images are removed, symbolizing that with the opening of the eyes, the images have been infused with the qualities of Buddhahood: "The Buddha filled with boundless compassion practiced the thirty perfections for many eons, finally reaching enlightenment. I pay homage to that Buddha. May all these qualities be invested in this image. May the Buddha's boundless omniscience be invested in this image until the *śāsanā* ceases to exist." In different Buddhist cultures the act of opening the eyes of the image takes different forms. Eyes may be symbolically or literally painted on the image or the eye lightly scratched with a needle; regardless of its form, however, it is by opening an image's eyes that it becomes a living cult icon.

The ritual process that transforms mere image to iconic Buddha substitute imprints the Buddha's story on the image. Narratives play an equally important role in the transformation of other material artifacts into representations of the Buddha and Buddhist saints. Stūpa enshrined relics dot the map of the Buddha's itinerary throughout greater Asia: The generous distribution of HAIR relics, predictions of the future discovery of bone relics by righteous monarchs, and footprints embedded in stone and earth witness to the continuing presence of the Buddha. Stories associated with these events figure prominently not only in the creation of sacred sites but in annual reconsecration and renewal ceremonies.

That a corporeal relic may be inserted into a Buddha image and images may be enshrined in a stūpa together with relics points to the belief that both serve as living Buddha icons. As further evidence of this belief, image consecration rituals in northern Thailand may include the insertion of a set of internal organs made from silver into the image. When a cavity in the back of the sandalwood image brought to Japan by the Japanese Buddhist pilgrim Chōnen (938–1016) and enshrined at Seiryōji in Kyoto was opened up in 1954, it was found to contain a similar set of internal organs made from silk.

Buddhahood requires extraordinary mental and physical attainments. Consequently, instilling these miraculous qualities into the image figures prominently in consecration rituals. In northern Thailand, the Buddha image consecration *sutta* infusing mental and spiritual perfections (*pārami*) into the image is recited, monks reputed to have achieved higher states of mental awareness and power are said to "pour" (*phae*) them into the consecrated images while seated in meditation around the *bodhimaṇḍa.* In the Tibetan tradition *sādhana* meditation techniques are at the core of the consecration (*rab gnas*) of images and stūpas. Elaborate visualization procedures involve several stages: dissolving the object to be consecrated into emptiness; visualizing the chosen Buddha (*yi dam*) out of emptiness; inviting this Buddha and its visualized form into the image; transforming them into nonduality; and finally transforming nondual emptiness into the original appearance of the image. (Bentor 1997).

Consecration as dharmicization

On the night of his enlightenment, the Buddha perceived the cause of suffering and the path to its cessation. This awakening resulted in penetrating the illusions that obscure understanding the nature of things (dharma) as ANITYA (IMPERMANENCE) and causally co-arising and interdependent (PRATĪTYASAMUTPĀDA). In short, the terms *buddha* and *dharma* are mutually inclusive; buddhahood necessitates dharmicization. Consequently, stūpas, images, and other signs of the Buddha, such as the bodhi tree, represent the dharma as well, recalling the statement attributed to the Buddha, "Whoever sees me, sees the dharma." Consecration rituals, therefore, not only Buddhacize objects, they also dharmicize them.

Dharmicization as a function of consecration rituals takes several different forms. Copies of sūtras and other texts may be placed in larger than life-size images or stūpas during consecration rituals. This practice contributed to the "cult of the book" as a material relic of the Buddha, especially in the Mahāyāna tradition. Evidence for the practice of magically infusing the formula of dependent origination ("Those dharmas which arise from a cause/the tathāgata has declared their cause/and that which is their cessation/thus the great renunciant has taught") into images ad stūpas exists from the second century C.E. and continues to the present as a pan-Buddhist practice. In the Tibetan tradition, ATISHA (982–1054) refers to the mantric use of this formula in consecration rituals, and it is currently employed in conjunction with mirror divination in Chinese and Korean Buddha image consecrations. Other Buddhist traditions employ signature sūtras as a central feature of image consecration. In the Japanese NICHIREN SCHOOL it is believed that placing the LOTUS SŪTRA (SADDHARMAPUṆḌARĪKA-SŪTRA) before an image during its consecration guarantees that it will become a Buddha of pure and perfect teaching (Stone).

In Southeast Asia elaborate techniques developed for dharmacizing Buddha images and stūpas. In northern Thailand the construction of a Buddha image or a stūpa included attaching dharmic *yantras* (diagrams) to it, and in Cambodia implanting dharmic marks (Sanskrit, *lakṣaṇa*; Pāli, *lakkhaṇa*) plays a central role in the consecration of a Buddha image. The officiating monk touches various parts of the body of the image while chanting Pāli phrases (DHĀRAṆĪ), thereby creating a dharmic body of doctrinal concepts corresponding to the bodily parts of the image. This transmutation enables a representation made from wood or bronze, already rendered living by the opening of the eyes, to become a cult icon worthy of veneration (Bizot).

Consecration as empowerment

The cult of relics, images, portraits, mummified remains, and other representations of the Buddha and Buddhist saints reflect a thaumaturgical belief that the miraculous powers associated with extraordinary spiritual attainment can be objectified in material form. Thus, consecration rituals incarnate the Buddha and ARHATs not primarily as idealized spiritual mentors and personifications of the dharma but as wonder-workers, protectors, and grantors of boons. Consecration rituals, therefore, infuse into these icons a variety of powers associated especially with the mental and physical attributes acquired through ascetic practices, especially meditation.

Since from the outset the Buddha was venerated not only as a teacher but as a miracle worker, representations of the Blessed One can be seen in similar terms. The cult of the power of relics and images should not be understood as a later, degenerate form of Buddhist piety but as one of the ingredients of Buddhist belief and practice from its earliest days. Consecration rituals, in this regard, can be seen as a practical means by which this aspect of Buddhism spread and flourished throughout Buddhist Asia.

In Cambodia the consecration ritual infuses not only the Buddha's supernal qualities associated with his awakening into the image but various protective powers, including the power of gods and spirits, the souls of ancestors, and tutelary deities. During the 1989 consecration of the repaired stūpa atop Doi Suthep mountain overlooking the northern Thai city of Chiang Mai, the powers of the protective spirits of the mountain, the spirits of wonder-working ascetics who dwell on the mountain, and Chiang Mai's renowned kings were invoked, as well as the power of the Buddha relics enshrined there.

Annual rituals reconsecrating images and relic-enshrined stūpas are often accompanied by stories bearing witness to their miraculous powers. Relics radiating brilliant rays appear before awed onlookers, or valued images reputed to have previously disappeared or been stolen may suddenly reappear in order to be lustrated and otherwise venerated by the faithful. Moreover, consecration rituals are not only occasions to enliven and empower new or repaired images. Devotees may bring previously consecrated home shrine images, AMULETS AND TALISMANS, and other representations of the Buddha and Buddhist saints to be reconsecrated time and again, thereby increasing their perceived protective power and their real economic value.

Buddhist consecration rituals embody the complexity of the religion's rich cultural tapestry. In particular, they open a window to a more nuanced understanding of Buddhist devotionalism where images, relics, and other material representations of the Buddha and Buddhist saints occupy a central place.

See also: **Initiation; Relics and Relics Cults; Reliquary; Space, Sacred**

Bibliography

Bentor, Yael. *Consecration of Images and Stūpas in Indo-Tibetan Tantric Buddhism.* Leiden, Netherlands: Brill, 1996.

Bentor, Yael. "The Horseback Consecration Ritual." In *Religions of Tibet in Practice,* ed. Donald S. Lopez, Jr. Princeton, NJ: Princeton University Press, 1997.

Bizot, François. "La consecration des statues et le culte des morts." In *Recherches nouvelles sur le Cambodge,* ed. François Bizot. Paris: École Francaise d'Extreme-Orient, 1994.

Bowker, John, ed. *Oxford Dictionary of World Religions.* Oxford and New York: Oxford University Press, 1997.

Faure, Bernard. *The Rhetoric of Immediacy: A Cultural Critique of Chan/Zen Buddhism.* Princeton, NJ: Princeton University Press, 1991.

Gombrich, Richard. "The Consecration of a Buddha Image." *Journal of Asian Studies* 26, no. 1 (1966): 23–36.

Ruelius, Hans. "Netrapratisthapana-eine Singhalesische Zeremonie zur Weihe von Kultbildern." In *Buddhism in Ceylon and Studies in Religious Syncretism in Buddhist Countries,* ed. Heinz Bechert. Götttingen, Germany: Vandenhoeck und Ruprecht, 1978.

Stone, Jacqueline. "Opening the Eyes of Wooden and Painted Images." In *The Writings of Nichiren Daishonin.* Tokyo: Sōka Gakkai, 1999.

Swearer, Donald K. "Hypostasizing the Buddha: Buddha Image Consecration in Northern Thailand." *History of Religions* 34, no. 3 (1995): 263–280.

Swearer, Donald K. *Becoming the Buddha.* Princeton, NJ: Princeton University Press, 2004.

Thompson, Laurence G. "Consecration Magic in Chinese Religion." *Journal of Chinese Religions* 19 (1991): 1–12.

DONALD K. SWEARER

CONVERSION

In most times and places allegiance to Buddhism has not been an exclusive affair. Buddhist devotees have felt comfortable worshipping various local deities, as well as earning merit by making offerings to non-Buddhist mendicants (in India), embracing Confucian as well as Buddhist values (in China), or visiting Shintō shrines as well as Buddhist temples (in Japan). The inscriptions of the Indian king AŚOKA (ca. mid-third century B.C.E.)—the earliest surviving written Buddhist records—portray him both as affirming his own Buddhist identity and as supporting other religious groups. The English word *conversion,* usually understood to mean the complete abandonment of one religion and exclusive adherence to another, has little relevance in such a setting.

The closest analogue to the Western notion of individual conversion is the act of becoming a lay brother (*upāsaka*) or lay sister (*upāsikā*), portrayed in early scriptures as a formal act of affiliation involving "taking refuge" in the three jewels (buddha, dharma, and SAṄGHA) and vowing to uphold the five lay PRECEPTS. Similar rituals are still performed today in many Buddhist societies, ranging from Sri Lanka to Taiwan. An alternative analogue might be found in the experience of becoming a stream-enterer (Pāli, *sotāpanna*), at which point one is said to attain a firsthand conviction of the truth of the Buddha's teachings. This generally takes place, however, only after a prolonged period of practice, demonstrating once again the lack of fit between the idea of conversion and Buddhist maps of the PATH.

Most commonly, adherence to Buddhism has not been the result of individual acts of faith but of a choice made by a ruler (e.g., in Sri Lanka in the third century B.C.E. or in Japan and Tibet in the seventh century C.E.) in the course of political consolidation and imposed upon the population at large. Such top-down or societal conversion (Horton) has been the standard mode of transmission of Buddhism outside India, with the notable exceptions of China and the West. Such exclusive state sponsorship has often been temporary, with a return to the norm of accommodating other local religious practices once a new political equilibrium has been achieved.

Examples of conversion in the exclusivist sense are easiest to find in Buddhist societies that have been significantly affected by a Western colonial or missionary presence, such as Sri Lanka (where the public conversion to Buddhism by Colonel Henry Steel Olcott under British colonial rule in the late nineteenth century has left a lasting legacy) or South Korea (where the growth of Protestant Christianity in recent decades has led to a strong polarization between Buddhists and Christians). Some Buddhist-based "new religions" in Japan, above all the SŌKA GAKKAI, also require their followers to renounce all other religious beliefs and practices.

Ironically, the Western notion of conversion appears to be falling out of favor among new adherents of Buddhism in the West, who often describe themselves as "taking up the practice of Buddhism" rather than "converting to the Buddhist religion." This reluctance to use the term *conversion* reflects not only the traditional absence of a sharp boundary between Buddhist and non-Buddhist practices in Asian societies, but also the profound changes currently taking place in the very notion of what constitutes "religion" in the modern West.

See also: **Colonialism and Buddhism; Local Divinities and Buddhism; Ordination**

Bibliography

Adikaram, E. W. *Early History of Buddhism in Ceylon.* Colombo, Sri Lanka: M. D. Gunasena, 1953.

Beltz, Johannes. *Mahar, Bouddhiste, et Dalit: conversion religieuse et emancipation sociopolitique dans l'Inde des castes.* Bern, Switzerland: Lang, 2001.

Gregory, Peter N. "Describing the Elephant: Buddhism in America." *Religion in American Culture* 11, no. 2 (2001): 233–263.

Hammond, Phillip E., and Machacek, David W. *Sōka Gakkai in America: Accommodation and Conversion.* Oxford: Oxford University Press, 1999.

Horton, Robin. "African Conversion." *Africa* 41, no. 2 (1971): 85–108.

Kapstein, Matthew. *The Tibetan Assimilation of Buddhism: Conversion, Contestation, and Memory.* New York: Oxford University Press, 2000.

Nattier, Jan. "Who Is a Buddhist? Charting the Landscape of Buddhist America." In *The Faces of Buddhism in America,* ed. Charles S. Prebish and Kenneth K. Tanaka. Berkeley: University of California Press, 1998.

Prothero, Stephen. *The White Buddhist: The Asian Odyssey of Henry Steel Olcott.* Bloomington: Indiana University Press, 1996.

Thapar, Romila. *Asoka and the Decline of the Mauryas,* 2nd edition. Delhi: Oxford University Press, 1973.

Zürcher, Erik. *The Buddhist Conquest of China: The Spread and Adaptation of Buddhism in Early Medieval China.* Leiden, Netherlands: Brill, 1959.

JAN NATTIER

COSMOLOGY

Although the earliest Buddhist texts of the MAINSTREAM BUDDHIST SCHOOLS—the *nikāyas* or *āgamas* (fourth to third century B.C.E.)—do not set out a systematic cosmology, many of the ideas and details of the developed cosmology of the later traditions are, in fact, present in these texts. Some of these have been borrowed and adapted from the common pool of early Indian cosmological notions indicated in, for example, the Vedic texts (1500 to 500 B.C.E.). The early ideas and details are elaborated in the later texts of systematic Buddhist thought, the ABHIDHARMA (third to second century B.C.E.), and presented as a coherent and consistent whole, with some variation, in the exegetical *abhidharma* commentaries and manuals that date from the early centuries C.E. Three principal *abhidharma* traditions are known to contemporary Buddhism and scholarship, those of the THERAVĀDA, the Sarvāstivāda, and the Yogācāra. The Theravāda or "southern" tradition has shaped the outlook of Buddhism in Sri Lanka and Southeast Asia. The Sarvāstivāda or "northern" tradition fed into the *abhidharma* system of the MAHĀYĀNA school of thought known as "yoga practice" (*yogācāra*) or "ideas only" (*vijñaptimātra*), and their perspective on many points has passed into the traditions of East Asian and Tibetan Buddhism. The elaborate cosmology presented by these *abhidharma* systems is substantially the same, differing only on points of detail. This traditional cosmology remains of relevance to the worldview of ordinary Buddhists in traditional Buddhist societies.

Along with many of the details, the four basic principles of the developed *abhidharma* Buddhist cosmology are assumed by the *nikāya* and *āgama* texts:

1. The universe has no specific creator; the sufficient cause for its existence is to be found in the Buddhist cycle of causal conditioning known as PRATĪTYASAMUTPĀDA (DEPENDENT ORIGINATION).
2. There is no definite limit to the universe, either spatially or temporally.
3. The universe comprises various realms of existence that constitute a hierarchy.
4. All beings are continually reborn in the various realms in accordance with their past KARMA (ACTION); the only escape from this endless round of REBIRTH, known as SAṂSĀRA, is the knowledge that constitutes the attainment of NIRVĀṆA.

Levels of existence

The *abhidharma* systems agree that saṃsāra embraces thirty-one principal levels of existence, although they record slight variations in the lists of these levels. Any being may be born into any one of these levels. In fact, during the course of their wandering through saṃsāra it is perhaps likely that all beings have at some time or another been born in most of these levels of existence. The most basic division of the thirty-one levels is threefold: the realm of sensuality (*kāmadhātu, -loka*) at the bottom of the hierarchy; the realm of pure form or subtle materiality (*rūpadhātu, -loka*) in the middle; and the formless realm (*arūpadhātu, -loka*) at the top.

The realm of sensuality is inhabited by beings endowed with the five physical senses and with minds that are in one way or another generally occupied with the objects of the senses. The sensual realm is further divided into unhappy destinies and happy destinies. Unhappy destinies comprise various unpleasant forms of existence consisting of a number of HELLS, hungry ghosts (preta), animals, and jealous gods (asura, which are, according to some, a separate level, but to others, a class of being subsumed under the category of either hungry ghosts or gods). Rebirth in these realms is as a result of unwholesome (*akuśala*) actions of body, speech, and thought (e.g., killing, taking what is not given, sexual misconduct, idle chatter, covetousness, ill will, wrong view, and untrue, harsh, or divisive speech). The happy destinies of the sensual realm comprise various increasingly pleasant forms of existence consisting of human existence and existence as a divinity or god (deva) in one of the six heavens of the sense world. Rebirth in these realms is a result of wholesome (*kuśala*) actions of body, speech, and thought, which are opposed to unwholesome kinds of action.

Above the relatively gross world of the senses is the subtler world of "pure form." This consists of further heavenly realms (reckoned as sixteen, seventeen, or eighteen in number) occupied by higher gods called *brahmās,* who have consciousness but only two senses—sight and hearing. Beings are reborn in these realms as a result of mastering increasingly subtle meditative states known as the four DHYĀNA (TRANCE STATE). These are attained by stilling the mind until it becomes completely concentrated and absorbed in an object of meditation, temporarily recovering its natural brightness and purity. The five highest realms of the form world are known as the *pure abodes,* and these are occupied by divinities who are all either *nonreturners* (spiritually advanced beings of great wisdom who are in their last birth and who will reach enlightenment before they die) or beings who have already gained enlightenment. All the beings of the pure abodes are thus in their last life before their final liberation from the round of rebirth through the attainment of NIRVĀṆA.

The subtlest and most refined levels of the universe are the four that comprise "the formless realm." At this level of the universe the body with its senses is completely absent, and existence is characterized by pure and rarified forms of consciousness, once again corresponding to higher meditative attainments.

World systems

The lower levels of the universe, that is, the realms of sensuality, arrange themselves into various distinct world discs (*cakravāḍa*). At the center of a *cakravāḍa* is the great world mountain, Sumeru or Meru. This is surrounded by seven concentric rings of mountains and seas. Beyond these mountains and seas, in the four cardinal directions, are four great continents lying in the great ocean. The southern continent, Jambudvīpa (the continent of the rose-apple tree), is inhabited by ordinary human beings; the southern part, below the towering range of mountains called the abode of snows (*himālaya*), is effectively India, the known world and the land where buddhas arise. At the outer rim of this world disc is a ring of iron mountains holding in the ocean. In the spaces between world discs and below are various hells; in some sources these are given as eight hot hells and eight cold hells. An early text describes how in the hell of Hot Embers, for example, beings are made to climb up and down trees bristling with long, red hot thorns, never dying until at last their bad karma is exhausted (*Majjhimanikāya* iii, 185).

On the slopes of Mount Sumeru itself and rising above its peak are the six HEAVENS inhabited by the gods of the sense world. The lowest of these is that of the Gods of the Four Kings of Heaven, who guard the four directions. On the peak of Mount Sumeru is the heaven of the Thirty-Three Gods, which is ruled by its king, INDRA or Śakra (Pāli, Sakka), while in the shadow of Mount Sumeru dwell the jealous gods called asuras, who were expelled from the heaven of the Thirty-Three by Indra. Above the peak is the Heaven of the Contented Gods or Tuṣita, where buddhas-to-be, like the future MAITREYA, are reborn and await the time to take birth. The highest of the six heavens of the sense world is that of the Gods who have Power over the Creations of Others, and it is in a remote part of this heaven that MĀRA, the Evil One, lives, wielding his considerable resources in order to prevent the sensual world from losing its hold on its beings. The six heavens of the sense world are inhabited by gods and goddesses who, like human beings, reproduce through sexual union, though some say that in the higher heavens this union takes the form of an embrace, the holding of hands, a smile, or a mere look. The young gods and goddesses are not born from the womb, but arise instantly in the form of a five-year-old child in the lap of the gods (*Abhidharmakośa* iii, 69–70).

Above these sense-world heavens is the Brahmā World, a world of subtle and refined mind and body. Strictly, *brahmās* are neither male nor female, although it seems that in appearance they resemble men. The fourteenth-century Thai Buddhist cosmology, the *Three Worlds According to King Ruang,* describes how their faces are smooth and very beautiful, a thousand times brighter than the moon and sun, and with only one hand they can illuminate ten thousand world systems (Reynolds and Reynolds, p. 251). A Great Brahmā of even the lower *brahmā* heavens may rule over a thousand world systems, while *brahmās* of the higher levels are said to rule over a hundred thousand. Yet it would be wrong to conclude that there is any one or final overarching Great Brahmā—God the Creator. It may be that beings come to take a particular Great Brahmā as creator of the world, and a Great Brahmā may himself even form the idea that he is creator, but this is just the result of delusion on the part of both parties. In fact the universe recedes upwards with one class of Great Brahmā being surpassed by a further, higher class of Great Brahmā. Thus the world comprises "its gods, its Māra and Brahmā, this generation with its ascetics and brahmins, with its princes and peoples" (*Dīghanikāya* i, 62).

The overall number of world systems that constitute the universe in its entirety cannot be specified. The *nikāya/āgama* texts sometimes talk in terms of the thousandfold world system, the twice-thousandfold world system, and the thrice-thousandfold world system or *trichilicosm.* According to north Indian traditions, the last of these embraces a total of one billion world systems, while the southern traditions say a trillion. But even such a vast number cannot define the full extent of the universe; there is no spatial limit to the extent of world systems.

Cycles of time

The temporal limits of the universe are equally elusive. World systems as a whole are not static; they themselves go through vast cycles of expansion and contraction across vast eons of time. World systems contract in great clusters of a billion at a time. Most frequently this contraction is brought about by the destructive force of fire, but periodically it is brought about by water and wind. This fire starts in the lower realms of the sense-sphere and, having burnt up these, it invades the form realms; but having burnt up the realms corresponding to the first dhyāna, it stops. The realms corresponding to the second, third, and fourth dhyānas and the four formless realms are thus spared destruction. But when the destruction is wreaked by water, the three realms corresponding to the second dhyāna are included in the general destruction. The destruction by wind invades and destroys even the realms corresponding to the third dhyāna. Only the subtle realms corresponding to the fourth dhyāna and the four formless meditations are never subject to this universal destruction.

The length of time it takes for the universe to complete one full cycle of expansion and contraction is known as a *mahākalpa* (great eon). A *mahākalpa* is made up of four intermediate eons consisting of the period of contraction, the period when the world remains contracted, the period of expansion, and the period when the world remains expanded. The length of a great eon is not specified in human years but only by reference to similes:

> Suppose there was a great mountain of rock, seven miles across and seven miles high, a solid mass without any cracks. At the end of every hundred years a man might brush it just once with a fine Benares cloth. That great mountain of rock would decay and come to an end sooner than even the eon. So long is an eon. And of eons of this length not just one has passed, not just a hundred, not just a thousand, not just a hundred thousand. (*Saṃyuttanikāya* ii, 181–182)

The Buddha is said to have declared that saṃsāra's—that is, our—beginning was inconceivable and that its starting point could not be indicated; the mother's milk drunk by each of us in the course of our long journey through saṃsāra is greater by far than the water in the four great oceans (*Saṃyuttanikāya* ii, 180–181).

Within this shifting and unstable world of time and space that is saṃsāra, beings try to make themselves at ease. The life spans of beings vary. In general, beings who inhabit the lower realms of existence live shorter, more precarious, lives, while the gods live longer; at the highest realms, gods live vast expanses of time—up to eighty-four thousand eons. Yet the happiness that beings find or achieve cannot be true happiness, not permanently lasting, but merely a relatively longer or shorter temporary respite. Beings in the lowest hell realms experience virtually continuous pain and suffering until the results of the actions that brought them there are exhausted. In contrast, beings in the higher *brahmā* worlds experience an existence entirely free of all overt suffering; but while their lives may endure for inconceivable lengths of time in human terms, they must eventually come to an end once again when the results of the actions that brought them there are exhausted.

A Tibetan *thang ka* (scroll painting) depicting the Wheel of Life. © Earl and Nazima Kowall/Corbis. Reproduced by permission.

Cosmology and psychology

An important principle of the Buddhist cosmological vision lies in the equivalence of cosmology and PSYCHOLOGY, the way in which the various realms of existence relate rather closely to certain commonly (and not so commonly) experienced states of mind. Buddhist cosmology is at once a map of different realms of existence and a description of all possible experiences. This can be appreciated by considering more fully the Buddhist understanding of the nature of karma. Essentially the world we live in is our own creation: We have created it by our own karma, by our deeds, words, and thoughts motivated either by greed, hatred, and delusion or by nonattachment, friendliness, and wisdom. The cosmos is thus a reflection of our actions, which are in turn the products of our hearts and minds. For in this fathom-long body with its mind and consciousness, said the Buddha, lies the world, its arising, its ceasing, and the way leading to its ceasing (*Saṃyuttanikāya* i, 62).

Essentially the states of mind that give rise to unwholesome actions—strong greed, hatred, and delusion—lead to rebirth in the unhappy destinies or realms of misfortune. A life dominated by the mean spiritedness of greed leads to rebirth as a hungry ghost, a class of being tormented by unsatisfied hunger; a life dominated by the mental hell of hatred and anger leads to rebirth in one of the hell realms where one suffers terrible pain; while a life dominated by willful ignorance of the consequences of one's behavior leads to rebirth as an animal, a brute existence ruled by the need to eat and reproduce. On the other hand, the generous, friendly, and wise impulses that give rise to wholesome actions lead to rebirth in the happy realms as a human being or in one of the six realms of the gods immediately above the human realm, where beings enjoy increasingly happy and carefree lives. By developing states of deep peace and contentment through the practice of calm meditation, and by developing profound wisdom through insight meditation, one is reborn as a *brahmā* in a realm of pure form or formlessness, which is a reflection of those meditations.

In short, if one lives like an animal, one is liable to reborn as an animal; if one lives like a human being, one will be reborn as a human being; if one lives like a god, one will be reborn as a god. But just as in day-to-day experience one fails to find any physical or mental condition that is reliable and unchangeable, that can give permanent satisfaction and happiness, so, even if one is reborn in the condition of a *brahmā* living eighty-four thousand eons, the calm and peaceful condition of one's existence is not ultimately lasting or secure. Just as ordinary happiness is in this sense DUḤKHA (SUFFERING) or unsatisfactory, so too are the lives of the *brahmās*, even though they experience no physical or mental pain.

Nirvāṇa and buddhas

The only escape from this endless round is the direct understanding of the FOUR NOBLE TRUTHS—suffering, its cause, its cessation, and the PATH leading to its cessation—and the attainment of nirvāṇa. Significantly nirvāṇa is not included in the thirty-one realms of rebirth, since these define the conditioned world of space and time, and nirvāṇa is precisely not a place where one can be reborn and where one can exist for a period of time. Nirvāṇa is the unconditioned, the deathless, beyond space and time, known directly at the moment of enlightenment. Some beings may find the path to nirvāṇa by their own efforts and become a PRATYEKABUDDHA (solitary buddha), but most must await the appearance in the world of a *samyaksaṃbuddha* (perfectly and fully awakened one), like Gautama, the buddha of the current age. Such buddhas tread the ancient path of all buddhas, and can show others the way to release. Yet they appear in the world only rarely, though views on precisely how rarely vary. According to the Theravāda, some eons like our present are auspicious (*bhadda*) with a total of five buddhas, of whom Gautama (Pāli, Gotama) was the fourth and Maitreya (Pāli, Metteyya) will be the fifth. Other eons may have no buddhas at all.

A buddha's sphere of influence is known as his *buddha-field* (*buddhakṣetra*) and is not confined to the particular world system into which he is born. The Theravāda sources (e.g., *Visuddhimagga* xiii, 31) distinguish his (1) *field of birth,* which extends to the ten thousand world systems that tremble when he is conceived, born, gains enlightenment, teaches, and attains final nirvāṇa; (2) *field of authority,* which extends to the hundred billion world systems throughout which the utterance of the great protective discourses (*mahāparitta*) is efficacious; and (3) *field of experience,* which potentially extends to infinite numbers of world systems.

Mahāyāna perspectives

The basic cosmology outlined above with some variation is assumed by the Mahāyāna sūtras, as well as the authors of the systematic treatises of Indian Mahāyāna Buddhist thought. However, the Mahāyāna cosmological vision increasingly expands its attention beyond "our" world system and our buddha to include other buddhas and their spheres of influence. Early Buddhist writings and the non-Mahāyāna schools such as the Theravāda and Sarvāstivāda emphasize the impossibility of the appearance in the world of two buddhas at the same time (for how could there be two "bests"?).

But this raises the question of what precisely constitutes the world. Mahāyāna writings tend to respond by suggesting that while it is true that there can be only one buddha at a time in a single trichilicosm (set of a billion world systems), since there are innumerable trichilicosms, there can in fact be innumerable buddhas at the same time in these different trichilicosms. Thus Mahāyāna writings tend to focus on the universe as made up of innumerable clusters of world systems, and each of these sets of world systems has its own series of buddhas. Since these sets of world systems are not absolutely closed off from each other, we even now in our part of the universe—called the Saha world—have access to the living buddhas of other parts. A cluster of vast numbers of world systems constitutes in effect the buddha-field or potential sphere of influence of a buddha. It is this buddha-field that a bodhisattva seeks to purify through his wisdom and compassion on the long road to buddhahood. The notion of a purified buddha-field is related in the development of Mahāyāna thought to the notion of a buddha's pure land, such as Sukhāvatī—the Realm of Bliss of the buddha AMITĀBHA/Amitāyus, where the conditions for attaining enlightenment are particularly propitious if one can but be reborn there. But the question persists whether such PURE LANDS are to be found in some far flung part of the cosmos or are here now, if we had but the heart to know it.

The Mahāyāna notion of buddha-fields with their buddhas and bodhisattvas finds expression in the HUAYAN JING in a wondrous cosmic vision of a universe constituted by innumerable world systems, each with its buddha, floating in the countless oceans of a cosmic lotus, of which again the numbers are countless. This vision ends in the conception of a multiverse of worlds within worlds where the buddha, or buddhas, are immanent.

See also: **Divinities; Realms of Existence**

Bibliography

Boyd, James W. *Satan and Māra: Christian and Buddhist Symbols of Evil.* Leiden, Netherlands: Brill, 1975.

Cleary, T., trans. *The Flower Ornament Scripture: A Translation of the Avatamsaka Sutra,* 3 vols. Boston: Shambala, 1984–1987.

Gethin, Rupert. "Meditation and Cosmology: From the Aggañña Suttå to the Mahāyāna." *History of Religions* 36 (1997): 183–219.

Gombrich, Richard F. "Ancient Indian Cosmology." In *Ancient Cosmologies,* ed. Carmen Blacker and Michael Loewe. London: Allen and Unwin, 1975.

Gombrich, Richard F. *Precept and Practice: Traditional Buddhism in the Rural Highlands of Ceylon.* Oxford: Oxford University Press, 1971. Second edition: *Buddhist Precept and Practice: Traditional Buddhism in the Rural Highlands of Ceylon.* Delhi: Motilal Banarsidass, 1991.

Kirfel, Willibald. *Die Kosmographie der Inder.* Bonn and Leipzig, Germany: Schroeder, 1920.

Kloetzli, Randy. *Buddhist Cosmology: From Single World System to Pure Land.* Delhi: Motilal Banarsidass, 1983.

Kongtrul, Jamgön Lodrö Tayé. *Myriad Worlds: Buddhist Cosmology in Abhidharma, Kalacakra, and Dzog-chen.* Ithaca, NY: Snow Lion, 1995.

Ling, Trevor O. *Buddhism and the Mythology of Evil: A Study in Theravāda Buddhism.* London: Allen and Unwin, 1962. Reprint, Oxford: Oneworld, 1997.

Mārasinghe, M. M. J. *Gods in Early Buddhism: A Study in Their Social and Mythological Milieu as Depicted in the Nikāyas of the Pāli Canon.* Vidyalankara: University of Sri Lanka, 1974.

Masson, Joseph. *La Religion populaire dans le canon bouddhique pali.* Louvain, Belgium: Bureaux du Muséon, 1942.

Reynolds, Frank E., and Reynolds, Mani B., trans. *Three Worlds According to King Ruang: A Thai Buddhist Cosmology.* Berkeley: University of California, 1982.

Sadakata, Akira. *Buddhist Cosmology: Philosophy and Origin.* Tokyo: Kosei, 1997.

Tambiah, Stanley J. *Buddhism and the Spirit Cults in North-East Thailand.* Cambridge, UK: Cambridge University Press, 1970.

RUPERT GETHIN

COUNCILS, BUDDHIST

Before the Buddha died, his statements to the monks that they might abolish all the lesser and minor disciplinary precepts and work out their own salvation with diligence provided ample bewilderment to the members of the early SAṄGHA. Because these statements were open to ecclesiastic interpretation, the early community decided to hold periodic councils designed to encourage tacit agreement with regard to matters of doctrine and discipline. In so doing, it was hoped that uniformity would be affirmed and sectarianism discouraged.

Whether the early councils were truly historical events has long been a matter of contention in Buddhist communities. While most Asian Buddhists believe that the first council was a historical event, its historicity is questioned by virtually all Buddhist scholars. They argue that while it was not unlikely that a small group of Buddha's intimate disciples gathered after his death, a council held in the grand style described in the scriptures is almost certainly a fiction. On the other hand, almost all scholars agree that the second and following councils were historical events. Of special importance is the Vaiśālī or second council, which paved the way for the first great schism in early Buddhism.

The first council was said to have been held in Rājagṛha, India, in the year of the Buddha's death, generally thought to have occurred in the fourth or fifth century B.C.E. Fearful that the community would dissolve through uncertainty over the founder's teachings, the saṅgha held a council to preclude that possibility. MAHĀKĀŚYAPA, one of the Buddha's chief disciples, was appointed president of the council and selected five hundred ARHAT monks as participants. Another disciple, UPĀLI, recited the disciplinary rules known as the *Vinayapiṭaka* (*Basket of Discipline*), while ĀNANDA recited the Buddha's discourses, establishing the *Sūtrapiṭaka*. Functionally, this important event established authority for the group in the absence of its leader.

The Vaiśālī council, deemed the second Indian Buddhist council in all accounts, occurred about one hundred years after the Buddha's death. It was convened to resolve a dispute over supposedly illicit monastic behavior, such as accepting gold and silver. To resolve the conflict, a council of seven hundred monks met in Vaiśālī. Revata was appointed president of the council, and Sarvagāmin was questioned on ten points of possibly inappropriate monastic behavior. Each point was rejected by Sarvagāmin, the offending practices outlawed, and concord reestablished, although significant disagreements had obviously begun to appear in the still-unified Buddhist community. It has been postulated that Buddhist sectarianism began shortly after the Vaiśālī council, with the Mahāsāṃghika school and Sthavīras emerging as individual sects following a non-canonical council held shortly after the Vaiśālī event.

Another council was held in Pāṭaliputra around 250 B.C.E. during the reign of King AŚOKA. Aśoka convened the council under Moggaliputta Tissa with the intention of establishing the orthodoxy of the dharma. A thousand monks were assembled, and, under Tissa's guidance, various viewpoints were considered and either sanctioned or rejected, with the proponents of rejected views being expelled from the city. This council is mentioned only in the Pāli records, and for this reason it is often referred to as the third THERAVĀDA council.

A Theravāda council was held under King Vaṭṭagāmaṇī of Sri Lanka in 25 B.C.E., following a famine and in the midst of schismatic unrest in the Buddhist community. Vaṭṭagāmaṇī convened the conference in the capital city of Anurādhapura at the monastery known as Mahāvihāra. The meeting committed the Pāli Buddhist scriptures to writing, thus "closing" the three baskets of scriptures in the Theravāda tradition.

Around 100 C.E. another council was held under the Kushan king Kanishka, probably in Gandhāra. A great scholar named Vasumitra presided, assisted by the learned AŚVAGHOṢA. In addition to compiling a new Vinaya, they prepared a commentary called the *Mahāvibhāṣā* (*Great Exegesis*) on the ABHIDHARMA text *Jñānaprasthāna* (*Foundation of Knowledge*), which became the standard reference work for all Sarvāstivāda abhidharma issues.

Almost seven centuries later, around 792, a council was held in Lhasa, Tibet, under King Khri srong lde btsan. It was convened at the recently completed monastery BSAM YAS (SAMYE) in order to resolve differences between Chinese and Indian notions of practice and enlightenment. Tibetan sources claim that the Chinese position was defeated, continuing an Indian basis for the development of Tibetan Buddhism.

In modern times, a council was held in Rangoon, Burma (Myanmar), in 1871; this council is sometimes referred to as the fifth Theravāda council. Convened during the reign of King Mindon Min, this council was charged with revising the Pāli texts. The revised texts were inscribed on 729 marble tablets, and enshrined in stūpas to ensure their survival.

Finally, a council considered to be the sixth Theravāda council was held in Rangoon in 1954 to recite and confirm the whole Pāli canon. This council was scheduled to coincide with the celebration of the 2,500th anniversary of the Buddha's death. The prime minister of Burma, U Nu, delivered the opening address to the approximately twenty-five hundred monks in attendance. The council was a national festival in Burma, and helped established solidarity for Theravāda Buddhists throughout the world.

See also: **Bsam yas Debate; India; Mahāsāṃghika School; Mainstream Buddhist Schools; Pudgalavāda; Sarvāstivāda and Mūlasarvāstivāda**

Bibliography

Bareau, André. *Les premiers conciles bouddhiques.* Paris: Presses Universitaires de France, 1955.

Bareau, André. *Les sectes Bouddhiques du Petit Véhicule.* Saigon, Vietnam: École Française d'Extrême Orient, 1955.

Prebish, Charles. "A Review of Scholarship on the Buddhist Councils." *Journal of Asian Studies* 33, no. 2 (1974): 239–254.

CHARLES S. PREBISH

CRITICAL BUDDHISM (HIHAN BUKKYŌ)

The term *critical Buddhism* (*hihan Bukkyō*) refers to Hakamaya Noriaki (1943–) and Matsumoto Shirō's (1950–) critique of Buddha-nature (TATHĀGATAGARBHA) and ORIGINAL ENLIGHTENMENT (HONGAKU) as not Buddhist. Theological and apologetic in nature, yet using the traditional textual and philological methods of academic scholarship (both scholars are specialists in Indian and Tibetan Buddhist studies), critical Buddhism asserts that Buddha-nature and similar doctrines are examples of Hindu-like thinking of a substantial self (ātman), which Buddhism opposes with the doctrines of no-self and causality (*pratītya-samutpāda*). Critical Buddhism further asserts that these monistic doctrines deny language and thinking in favor of an ineffable and nonconceptual mysticism contrary to the discriminating awareness (prajñā) and selfless compassion that constitutes Buddhist awakening.

Critical Buddhism is therefore critical in at least two senses: It is critical of certain widely held Buddhist doctrines, and it asserts that the critical discrimination of reality and the judicious use of reason and language to teach that reality are the hallmarks of buddhahood.

A third aspect of critical Buddhism is a fierce critique of Buddhist schools, thinkers, and social programs that, based on the triumphalism inherent in a doctrine of ineffable truth, support the status quo and perpetuate social injustice. Hakamaya and Matsumoto are especially concerned with the role of Buddhist doctrine in various forms of Japanese nationalism and, as ordained Zen monks teaching at Zen universities, single out their own Sōtō Zen teachings for particular criticism, raising questions about how the founder DŌGEN (1200–1253) has been interpreted within the Sōtō school and about the proper role of theology within academic as well as sectarian practice. They have also written about HŌNEN (1133–1212), SHINRAN (1173–1263), Myōe (1173–1232), the Kyoto School, and others, as well as critiquing the ideal of objective academic scholarship in the study of Buddhism.

See also: **Chan School; Hinduism and Buddhism; Modernity and Buddhism**

Bibliography

Bodiford, William. "Zen and the Art of Religious Prejudice: Efforts to Reform a Tradition of Social Discrimination." *Japanese Journal of Religious Studies* 23 (1996): 1–28.

Heine, Steven. "After the Storm: Matsumoto Shirō's Transition from 'Critical Buddhism' to 'Critical Theology.'" *Japanese Journal of Religious Studies* 28 (2001): 133–146.

Hubbard, Jamie, and Swanson, Paul, eds. *Pruning the Bodhi Tree: The Storm over Critical Buddhism.* Honolulu: University of Hawaii Press, 1997.

JAMIE HUBBARD

D

DAIMOKU

The term *daimoku,* literally "title," refers specifically to the title of the *Lotus Sūtra* (*Myōhō-renge-kyō* in Japanese pronunciation) or to its invocation, usually in the form "Namu Myōhō-renge-kyō." The *daimoku* was chanted in various liturgical and devotional settings in Japan's Heian period (794–1185) and was later given a doctrinal foundation by Nichiren (1222–1282). It is the central practice of the NICHIREN SCHOOL.

See also: **Chanting and Liturgy; Lotus Sūtra (Saddharmapuṇḍarīka-sūtra)**

Bibliography

Dolce, Lucia Dora. "Esoteric Patterns in Nichiren's Interpretation of the Lotus Sutra." Ph.D. diss. University of Leiden, 2002.

Stone, Jacqueline I. "Chanting the August Title of the *Lotus Sūtra*: *Daimoku* Practices in Classical and Medieval Japan." In *Re-Visioning "Kamakura" Buddhism,* ed. Richard K. Payne. Honolulu: University of Hawaii Press, 1999.

JACQUELINE I. STONE

DAITOKUJI

Daitokuji, founded in 1326 as a Rinzai Zen monastery by Shūhō Myōchō (Daitō Kokushi, 1282–1338), occupies a vast forested precinct at Murasakino in northwest Kyoto. Built initially with imperial patronage, Daitokuji rose to the head of the Gozan (Five Mountains) system. After its destruction by fire and war in the 1450s to the 1460s, patrons from the warrior and merchant classes funded Daitokuji's renewal under the leadership of IKKYŪ Sōjun (1394–1481). After demotion from the Gozan ranks in 1486, Daitokuji became independent.

Daitokuji consists of the main complex (*garan*) of gates and communal structures aligned on a north-south axis, surrounded by semi-independent subtemples (*tatchū*) spreading out in all directions. Each subtemple includes an abbot's quarters, which served as a mortuary site (*bodaisho*) for both patrons and abbots who are jointly commemorated on the central altars and in mortuary precincts. Many of these abbots' quarters are surrounded by dry landscape gardens, with interior spaces graced by paintings produced by the finest painting workshops of the sixteenth and later centuries. Subtemple storehouses contain an extraordinary inventory of paintings, calligraphies, books, documents, and other objects, many of them imported from China and Korea. Today most of the twenty-three remaining subtemples are closed to the general public except during designated openings.

Perhaps even more than Zen, Daitokuji owes its continuing reputation and patronage to the world of tea (*chanoyu*) in the lineage of Sen no Rikyū (1522–1591). In 1589 Rikyū rebuilt Daitokuji's Sanmon Gate, and designated the Jūkōin subtemple as his family mortuary site.

See also: **Japan, Buddhist Art in; Monastic Architecture**

Bibliography

Covell, Jon Carter, and Yamada Sōbin. *Zen at Daitokuji.* Tokyo: Kodansha, 1974.

Kraft, Kenneth L. *Eloquent Zen: Daitō and Early Japanese Zen.* Honolulu: University of Hawaii Press, 1992.

Levine, Gregory P. "Switching Sites and Identities: The Founder's Statue at the Zen Buddhist Temple Kōrin'in." *Art Bulletin* 83, no. 1 (2000): 72–104.

KAREN L. BROCK

ḌĀKINĪ

The term *ḍākinī* is already seen in the fourth to fifth centuries B.C.E. in the works of the Sanskrit grammarian, Pāṇini. There, the term refers to a type of flesh-eating female deity that appears in the retinue of the goddess, Kālī. Over the following centuries, *ḍākinīs* continued to be a part of the Indian pantheon, though only as relatively minor figures. In the eighth century C.E., however, as Buddhist TANTRA was taking shape, *ḍākinīs* began to acquire a greater importance. Initially it seems that the term was used to refer to human women who gathered around sacred sites and rituals. Portrayed as typically low caste—prostitutes, washerwomen, and the like—these women would serve as consorts for the male tantric practitioners. These socially liminal women were held to have a mysterious and dangerous power, and before long *ḍākinīs* were cast as enlightened beings in their own right, Vajrayoginī, Vajravārāhī, and Ekajāti being some better known examples.

The *Yogaratnamālā* (*Garland of Jewel-like Yogas*), an Indian commentary on the *Hevajra Tantra*, derives the term *ḍākinī* from the Sanskrit root, *dai*, meaning "to fly." The accuracy of this derivation has been debated by Western scholars, but it was clearly accepted by Tibetans when they chose to translate the term as *mkha' 'gro* (sky dancer). The *ḍākinī* thus described is often understood as able to move freely through the space of reality, the DHARMADHĀTU.

In Tibet, *ḍākinī* can refer either to a living woman Buddhist teacher or to a spirit of ambivalent nature. Regarding the latter type, the idea has persisted that *ḍākinīs* are attracted by Buddhist practitioners, drawn in swarms to powerful meditators like mosquitoes to blood. Tibetans further distinguish two kinds of *ḍākinīs*: gnostic (*ye shes*) and flesh-eating (*sha za*), also called "otherworldly" and "worldly"—the former being helpful for one's progress along the Buddhist PATH, and the latter harmful. Telling one type from the other is famously difficult, so that, just as was the case in eighth-century India, *ḍākinīs* in Tibet continued to hold a dangerous power. The Buddhist practitioner's difficulty in judging them is made worse by a tendency for each type to blur into the other, so that a gnostic *ḍākinī* can suddenly become dangerous, and a flesh-eating *ḍākinī* can provide assistance. Ultimately, the meditator is advised not to fall victim to either dualistic conceptualization of these gossamer beings.

The *ḍākinī*'s enigmatic nature has helped it to serve a mercurial role in Tibetan Buddhism, slipping easily between the human realm and those of the buddhas. For followers of the RNYING MA (NYINGMA) school, this role has placed *ḍākinīs* at the center of the "treasure" (*gter ma*) revelation process. A *ḍākinī* often guides the treasure revealer to the discovery site, and then the treasure teachings themselves are typically received in the condensed language of the *ḍākinīs* (*mkha' 'gro skad*). Like the *ḍākinī* herself, the symbolic syllables (*mkha' 'gro brda yig*) of her language are polyvalent, their significance difficult to determine. The process for decoding these encrypted teachings is a mysterious one, involving the revealer opening his body's cakras to allow the treasury of the Buddhist teachings to flow forth unimpeded. Thus the *ḍākinī*'s language suggests a shimmering field of possibilities rather than a single determinate meaning.

See also: **Women**

Bibliography

Dowman, Keith. *Sky Dancer: The Secret Life and Songs of the Lady Yeshe Tshogye.* London: Routledge and Kegan Paul, 1984.

Gyatso, Janet. *Apparitions of the Self: The Secret Autobiographies of a Tibetan Visionary.* Princeton, NJ: Princeton University Press, 1998.

Klein, Anne. *Meeting the Great Bliss Queen: Buddhists, Feminists, and the Art of the Self.* Boston: Beacon, 1995.

Snellgrove, David. *Indo-Tibetan Buddhism: Indian Buddhists and Their Tibetan Successors.* Boston: Shambala, 1987.

JACOB P. DALTON

DALAI LAMA

The position of Dalai Lama, dating in its present form from the mid-seventeenth century, is a uniquely Tibetan institution, embodying the most important secular and religious presence in Tibet. *Dalai* is the

Mongolian translation of the Tibetan name *Rgya mtsho* (pronounced "Gyatso"), which means "ocean," and *bla ma* (pronounced "LAMA"), a general Tibetan name for a respected religious teacher.

The name *Dalai Lama* was first used by Altan Khan, a Tumed Mongolian chieftain, for his teacher Bsod nams (Sonam) rgya mtsho (1543–1588). Bsod nams rgya mtsho and his followers then gave the name posthumously to Dge 'dun (Gendun) rgya mtsho (1476–1542) and Dge 'dun grub (Gendun Drup, 1391–1474), a student of the great scholar TSONG KHA PA (1357–1419), saying that each later Dalai Lama was the reincarnation of the earlier. The followers of Tsong kha pa, later called the DGE LUGS (GELUK) or Yellow Hat sect, probably saw the prestige that was gained through the system of reincarnation by older sects like the Karma BKA' BRGYUD (KAGYU), and borrowed the idea of reincarnation from them.

The fourth Dalai Lama was the grandson of Altan Khan. He was soon followed by the "Great Fifth" Dalai Lama, Ngag dbang (Ngawang) rgya mtsho (1617–1682). The Great Fifth Dalai Lama and his teacher, Blo bzang chos kyi rgyal mtshan (Lobsang Chökyi Gyaltsen, 1567–1662), forged a coalition between the Dge lug, the RNYING MA (NYINGMA) sect, parts of the Tibetan aristocracy, and the most powerful of the competing Mongolian factions to overcome the Karma Bka' brgyud and their Gtsang (Tsang) patrons of west central Tibet.

Fifth and sixth Dalai Lamas

The coalition created a new government called the Tuṣita Palace (Dga' ldan pho brang) based in Lhasa. The Dalai Lamas headed this government and lived, after its completion, in the colossal POTALA palace started by the Great Fifth Dalai Lama in 1645 on the ruins of a palace built by the early Tibetan emperor Srong btsan sgam po (Songtsen Gampo). After his death, the Great Fifth's prime minister (some say natural son) Sangs rgyas (Sangyay) rgya mtsho finished the palace that came to symbolize and dominate Tibet in 1695. After the founding of the Dga' ldan pho brang government and the building of the Potala, the Dalai Lamas were not just head lamas of 'Bras spung (Drepung), the largest of the Dge lugs pa monasteries; they were heads of the government of Tibet as well.

For his help in spiritual and political matters, the fifth Dalai Lama gave the name Pan chen bla ma (PANCHEN LAMA) to his teacher Blo bzang chos kyi rgyal mtshan, abbot of Bkra shis lhun po (Tashi Lunpo), the largest Dge lugs pa monastery in Gtsang. From this period comes the theory of the Dalai Lamas as emanations of Avalokiteśvara, here conceived as the BODHISATTVA of compassion, and Panchen Lamas as emanations of AMITĀBHA. In tantric Buddhism there are five buddha families, each headed by a buddha. The head of Avalokiteśvara's buddha family is Amitābha, reflecting the esteem the Dalai Lama had for his teacher. The association of Dalai Lamas with Avalokiteśvara reflects the great importance the bodhisattva Avalokiteśvara has throughout Tibet and the ubiquitous presence of his mantra, OṂ MAṆI PADME HŪṂ.

The sixth Dalai Lama (1683–1706) was in many respects a tragic figure. Sangs rgyas rgya mtsho concealed the death of the Great Fifth Dalai Lama until completing the construction of the Potala in order to forestall the difficulties inherent in an interregnum period. Sangs rgyas rgya mtsho prevented the new incarnation, Tshe dbyangs (Tseyang) rgya mtsho, from contact with the outside world, and he set up an elaborate subterfuge to make the people think the fifth Dalai Lama was in a long retreat. As he grew up, Tshe dbyangs rgya mtsho rebelled against the life of the celibate monk expected of a Dalai Lama, and he took to frequenting Lhasa taverns disguised as an ordinary layman. He had affairs with young women whom he met there, and expressed his longing to be with them obliquely in his poems, which are widely known and sung even today throughout Tibet.

Though beloved by ordinary Tibetans, Tshe dbyangs rgya mtsho offended the Quoshot Mongol leader Lhasang Khan, who was shocked by what he saw as Tshe dbyangs rgya mtsho's immoral behavior. Lhasang Khan killed the prime minister, captured Tshe dbyangs rgya mtsho, and took him to the 'A mdo region of eastern Tibet, where he died at the age of twenty-four in 1706. Lhasang Khan set up his own relative as an alternative sixth Dalai Lama, a move that alienated Tibetans.

After the death of Tshe dbyangs rgya mtsho, Tibetans opposed to Lhasang Khan's candidate turned to the Dzungars, a powerful western Mongolian tribe with deep devotion to the Dalai Lamas. This alarmed the Manchu-Chinese emperor Kangxi, who saw the Dzungars as a threat to Manchu interests. Manchu troops invaded Tibet and the seventh Dalai Lama, Skal bzang (Kelsang) rgya mtsho (1708–1757), was finally installed in Lhasa, after much negotiation, as Dalai Lama in 1720, with Manchu backing. Apart from replacing the post of prime minister with a council of ministers call the Bka' shag (Kashag), Skal bzang rgya mtsho devoted himself to Buddhist studies and gained some fame as a writer of religious books. The Bka' shag met in Lhasa and was answerable only to the Dalai Lamas or, when the Chinese presence was powerful, to the Chinese representatives (*ambans*).

For nearly 150 years from the death of Skal bzang rgya mtsho until the twelfth Dalai Lama 'Phrin las (Trinlay) rgya mtsho, effective political power was in the hands of regents appointed from among the powerful Dge lugs pa lamas, monks, and nobility. The eighth Dalai Lama, 'Jam dpal (Jampel) rgya mtsho (1758–1804), remained detached from political affairs. The ninth through the twelfth Dalai Lamas all died young: the ninth—Lung rtogs (Lungtok) rgya mtsho (1805–1815); the tenth—Tshul khrims (Tsultrim) rgya mtsho (1816–1837); the eleventh—Mkhas grub (Khedrub) rgya mtsho (born 1855 and died within a year of birth); and the twelfth—'Phrin las rgya mtsho (1856–1875).

The procedure for choosing Dalai Lamas evolved over time. Dreams of respected religious figures and visions of oracles have always been important. Since the time of the third Dalai Lama, Bsod nams rgya mtsho, in the sixteenth century, visions appearing on the surface of a sacred lake near Chos 'khas rgyal (Chökhar Gyal) in south central Tibet have been considered significant. In the case of the seventh Dalai Lama, lines from Tshe dbyangs rgya mtsho's poem—"I will not fly far. I will come back from Li thang"—were considered an important clue by those charged with locating the place of rebirth. Such seemingly innocuous statements, or in some cases actual letters detailing a birthplace, remain an important part of the selection process, as does the ability of the child candidate to differentiate items belonging to the earlier Dalai Lama when they are placed alongside similar items.

The influence of China on the selection of Dalai Lamas stems from the turbulent years after the death of the sixth Dalai Lama and the Manchu intervention in the early eighteenth century. The Manchu general Fu Kang'an delivered a golden urn from the Manchu emperor to be used for the selections of high lamas. The Manchu representatives (*ambans*), who remained in Tibet after the Chinese army returned to Tibet, witnessed the procedure of choosing a name from the golden urn. From this period also comes the schism between the Dalai and Panchen Lamas, as the Manchus exploited the traditional rivalry between central Tibet and western Gtsang to counterbalance the power of the Dge lugs pa sect. The Manchus backed the Gtsang-based Panchen Lamas strongly.

Thirteenth and fourteenth Dalai Lamas

The thirteenth Dalai Lama, Thub bstan (Tubten) rgya mtsho (1876–1933), who, like the fifth, is called the "Great," overcame entrenched Dge lugs pa monastic power and reasserted the authority of the Dalai Lama as a political institution. After surviving an attempted assassination, Thub bstan rgya mtsho introduced reforms, first in the large Dge lugs pa monasteries and then in the government ministries led by members of the Bka' shag. According to Melvyn Goldstein in *A History of Modern Tibet* (1989), the thirteenth Dalai Lama attempted two reforms of Tibetan society in particular that would have better prepared Tibet for the difficulties of the modern world: modernization of the army and introduction of a democratically elected assembly. He failed in both reform efforts because of entrenched conservatism and vested interests.

The thirteenth Dalai Lama skillfully governed Tibet during the time of the "Great Game," the rivalry for control of the Central Asian regions that lay between the empires of czarist Russia and British India. Fearful of Russian influence, the viceroy of British India, Lord Minto, sent out an army under Colonel Francis Edward Younghusband that invaded Tibet in 1904. The Dalai Lama fled to Mongolia and then to China. When the Chinese invaded Tibet five years later the Dalai Lama in turn fled to British India, making his way to Darjeeling. He was hosted there by Sir Charles Bell, a British political officer, whose book *A Portrait of the Dalai Lama: The Life and Times of the Great Thirteenth* (1946) introduced the Dalai Lama to the English-speaking world.

Before his death in 1933 the Great Thirteenth Dalai Lama wrote a letter, now viewed as his political testament, in which he foresaw great change and suffering for the Tibetan people if they did not adapt quickly to the modern world. Unfortunately the leaders of Tibet during the regency period were unable to rise to this difficult task, and the fourteenth Dalai Lama, Bstan 'dzin rgya mtsho (Tenzin Gyatso), was destined to perform the nearly impossible task of leading a people clinging to a country disintegrating before their eyes into an uncertain future.

Born Hla mo don grub (Lhamo Dhundup) to an ordinary farming family in 1935, the fourteenth Dalai

Lama was given the name Bstan 'dzin rgya mtsho when he became a monk. *Bstan 'dzin* means "holder of the Buddha's doctrine." Out of respect, Tibetans call him Sku 'dun (pronounced "Kundun"), which means literally "the presence before us." The regent, Rva streng (Reting) rin po che, guided a search party to the northeastern region of Tibet after a sign given after death by the thirteenth Dalai Lama, whose body had miraculously turned to face in that direction. A house like the future fourteenth Dalai Lama's had also appeared on the surface of the sacred lake. When special marks were observed on Hla mo don grub's body and he was able to distinguish items belonging to the thirteenth Dalai Lama from among similar items, Rva streng rin po che declared him the reincarnation. After payment of a large ransom to the local Chinese warlord, Rva streng had the young boy brought to Lhasa, where he was enthroned in 1940 at the age of five.

The fourteenth Dalai Lama divided his early years between the Potala and the Nor bu gling kha summer palace, studying Buddhism under the supervision of learned Dge lugs pa monks. This changed abruptly in 1950 when, at the age of fifteen, a political crisis forced the Tibetan government to ask him to assume both political and spiritual authority.

In China, decades of civil war and instability ended with the dominance of the Chinese Communist Party led by Mao Zedong. Mao immediately declared Tibet an integral part of the Chinese motherland and China's Red Army marched in, easily defeating the badly equipped Tibetans in 1950 at Chamdo, on the traditional border between central and eastern Tibet. In desperation, Tibet's political leaders invested the young Dalai Lama with full political authority. In 1951 China forced a totally defeated Tibet to sign the Seventeen Point Agreement in which it was declared that Tibet had always been a part of China.

The fourteenth Dalai Lama finished his traditional studies in 1959. Soon after, when the Chinese army suppressed a Tibetan uprising in Lhasa protesting tightening Chinese control, the Dalai Lama fled as a refugee to India. He was eventually followed by about 100,000 of his people.

In India, as Thubten Samphel says in *The Dalai Lamas of Tibet* (2000), "the Fourteenth Dalai Lama has managed to transform a medieval Central Asian institution into a positive force recognized globally" (p. 68). He reorganized the Tibetan government in exile along more democratic lines and spearheaded attempts to introduce modern education to Tibetan children. In his

The fourteenth Dalai Lama, Bstan 'dzin rgya mtsho (Tenzin Gyatso), travels widely to promote his ideas for peace and reconciliation in Tibet and the world. Here he is seen speaking in California in 2001. © David McNew/Getty Images. Reproduced by permission.

campaign against the Chinese presence in Tibet, the fourteenth Dalai Lama has preached accommodation and nonviolence. In 1987, in an address to the U.S. Congress, he unveiled a five-point peace plan that envisions Tibet as a neutral zone of peace. The next year, in Strasbourg, France, he announced his willingness to accept that Tibet is a part of China if there were a strong devolution of power that would allow Tibet to be self-governing and to retain its distinctive identity. For these efforts he received the Nobel Prize for peace in 1989.

The religious beliefs of the fourteenth Dalai Lama are summed up in a verse of the eighth-century Indian saint ŚĀNTIDEVA that he often quotes: "As long as space endures, as long as suffering remains, may I too remain, to dispel the misery of the world." The fourteenth Dalai Lama travels widely, giving explanations of Buddhist teaching and exchanging ideas with scientists and leaders of other faiths.

See also: **Communism and Buddhism; Tibet**

Bibliography

Bell, Charles. *A Portrait of the Dalai Lama: The Life and Times of the Great Thirteenth.* London: Collins, 1946.

Bstan 'dzin rgya mtsho (Dalai Lama XIV). *My Land and My People.* New York: McGraw Hill, 1962.

Goldstein, Melvyn. *A History of Modern Tibet, 1913–1951: Demise of the Lamaist State.* Berkeley: University of California Press, 1989.

Samphel, Thubten, and Tendar. *The Dalai Lamas of Tibet.* New Delhi: Lustre Press, 2000.

GARETH SPARHAM

DĀNA (GIVING)

It is difficult to overstate the centrality of generosity and gift giving (*dāna*) in Buddhism. *Dāna* is a supreme virtue perfected by BODHISATTVAS, a key practice of providing economic support to monks and nuns and the Buddhist establishment, and a means of generating religious merit.

Dāna is first in the lists of the PĀRAMITĀ (PERFECTION) that a bodhisattva cultivates through the many eons of lives that culminate in buddhahood. Giving in this context is not only an instance of renunciation of material possessions, it also illustrates the bodhisattva's infinite compassion and regard for others in need. One of the best-known stories in the Buddhist world is the tale of Siddhārtha Gautama's penultimate life in which he completes the final perfection of generosity as the bodhisattva Vessantara (Sanskrit, VIŚVANTARA). Vessantara's extraordinary perfection is the gift of his children and wife to a greedy brahman, a gift so magnificent that it causes the earth to quake. Other celebrated acts of the bodhisattva's generosity include occasions described in the JĀTAKA literature in which he offers up his limbs, his eyes, and even his life to those in hunger or in need.

In addition to being a moral ideal of a bodhisattva, *dāna* is also a practice with considerable social and economic significance in Buddhist cultures. Basic to the Indian traditions in which Buddhism first developed is the distinction between householder and renouncer. *Dāna,* a term broadly employed in South Asian religions, should be understood within the context of the relationship of complete economic dependency of monks and nuns on royal gifts and the alms of lay householders. The LAITY give food and other requisites to monks and nuns through daily ritualized alms rounds or through the making of offerings at monasteries. Although monks and nuns are not expected to reciprocate these gifts, they can offer the gift of the Teaching (*dharmadāna*), which is often exalted as the highest gift.

Laypeople are motivated to give *dāna* in part because it provides them with religious merit. *Dāna,* when given joyfully and graciously, generates karmic merit that results in worldly benefits in this life, as well as a fortunate rebirth in the next life. Important factors determining the merit one earns by making a gift are the motivations of the donor, the propriety and suitability of the gift, and the worthiness of the recipient. The logic of this last variable ensures that laypeople will want to give to the worthiest "field of merit," ideally a learned and pious monk, to earn the most merit from the gift. While some traditions within Buddhism, particularly within the MAHĀYĀNA, extol giving without discrimination to the poor and needy, there is in *dāna* ideology a general preference for ensuring support for esteemed monks and nuns.

While texts on lay morality stress the generosity of the laity, donative inscriptions across the Buddhist world record gifts given by pious monks and nuns, as well laypeople, to building and supporting Buddhist institutions. Gifts of kings, such as those of King AŚOKA (third century B.C.E.), of almshouses and monasteries to Buddhist communities, record the importance of royal patronage in the establishment, development, and preservation of Buddhism.

See also: **Ethics; Merit and Merit-Making**

Bibliography

Cone, Margaret, and Gombrich, Richard F., trans. *The Perfect Generosity of Prince Vessantara: A Buddhist Epic.* Oxford: Clarendon Press, 1977.

Endo, Toshiichi. *Dāna: The Development of Its Concept and Practice.* Colombo, Sri Lanka: Gunasena, 1987.

Schopen, Gregory. *Bones, Stones, and Buddhist Monks: Collected Papers on the Archaeology, Epigraphy, and Texts of Monastic Buddhism in India.* Honolulu: University of Hawaii Press, 1997.

Sizemore, Russell, F., and Swearer, Donald K., eds. *Ethics, Wealth, and Salvation: A Study in Buddhist Social Ethics.* Columbia: University of South Carolina Press, 1990.

MARIA HEIM

DAO'AN

Dao'an (312–385 C.E.) is a pivotal figure in all main developments within Chinese Buddhism during its period of adaptation within early medieval Chinese society. His life coincided with the brutal political situation in the country following the collapse of the Han dynasty in 220. Until age fifty-three, he migrated through many parts of northern China, where he built up several Buddhist communities that were later forced to disperse due to calamities of the time. Around 365, he settled in Xiangyang (Hubei), where he headed a distinguished Buddhist community of more than three hundred members for about fifteen years. In 379, Fu Jian (357–387) of the Former Qin dynasty destroyed Xiangyang, forcing Dao'an to move to Chang'an, where he died six years later while serving as the main leader of the local SAṄGHA and adviser to the emperor.

Dao'an's rich contributions can be divided into several categories. First, he changed the rules for translating Buddhist texts into Chinese when he demanded that the *geyi* (matching the meaning) system of translation be abolished and proper Chinese Buddhist terminology be developed. Second, his influential commentaries explained the DHYĀNA (TRANCE STATE) techniques, specifically in translations attributed to AN SHIGAO (late second or early third century C.E.). Third, Dao'an systematized the Chinese tripiṭaka. In 374 he published *Zongli zhongjing mulu* (*Comprehensive Systematic Catalogue of Scriptures*), in which he divided translations made by known translators from the anonyms, successfully establishing new criteria of authenticity for the Chinese Buddhist CANON. The criteria were applied to Buddhist texts in Chinese by later scholars including Sengyou (445–518), Fajing (fl. late sixth century), DAOXUAN (596–667), and Zhisheng (fl. early eighth century). Fourth, Dao'an developed the VINAYA literature and monastic practice within China. In the absence of complete translations of the *Vinaya-piṭaka*, he designed his own strict rules for monks, including the practice of changing their surnames to Shi (from the Chinese transliteration Shijiamouni for the Sanskrit Śākyamuni). Due to Dao'an's untiring advocacy, the *Sarvāstivāda-vinaya* was finally translated into Chinese by KUMĀRAJĪVA (350–409/413). Fifth, he developed a form of *prajñāpāramitā* philosophy, specifically the doctrine of the *wuben* (essential non-beingness), which served as a precursor to the Chinese reception of ŚŪNYATA (EMPTINESS) expounded during the second century C.E. by NĀGĀRJUNA.

In addition to these scholarly achievements, Dao'an established good communications between the saṅgha and secular governments. Despite the political hardships he endured, he was able to organize sponsorship from several political leaders; his friendship with Fu Jian and Emperor Xiaowu (r. 373–397) of the Jin dynasty are particularly notable. Dao'an's advocacy built the worship of the future Buddha MAITREYA into one of the most important East Asian Buddhist cults. His outstanding disciples, who influenced development of Chinese Buddhism in the next generation, included HUIYUAN (334–416), the vaunt-courier in the PURE LAND SCHOOLS, and Zhu Fatai, the leader of Buddhism in Yangzhou.

See also: **Catalogues of Scriptures; China; Commentarial Literature**

Bibliography

Ch'en, Kenneth. *Buddhism in China: A Historical Survey.* Princeton, NJ: Princeton University Press, 1964.

Link, Arthur. "Biography of Tao-an." *T'oung Pao* 46 (1958): 1–48.

T'ang, Yung-t'ung. *Han Wei liang Jin Nanbeichao fojiaoshi* (*History of Buddhism during Han, Wei, two Jin, and Southern and Northern Dynasties*). Shanghai: Shang Wushuguan, 1938.

Ui Hakuju. *Shaku Dōan Kenkyū* (*Research on Shi Dao'an*). Tokyo: Iwanami Shoten, 1956.

Zürcher, Erik. *The Buddhist Conquest of China: The Spread and Adaptation of Buddhism in Early Medieval China.* Leiden, Netherlands: Brill, 1959.

TANYA STORCH

DAOISM AND BUDDHISM

Modern scholars use the term *Daoism* to denote a wide variety of Chinese social groups and attitudes. Almost any activity engaged in by the elite that was not associated with governance has been labeled *Daoist.* In this entry, the term will be restricted to the Daoist religion, here defined as the collection of cognate and loosely organized Chinese religious organizations, first attested during the first century C.E., that "practiced the Dao" (Way) and traced their understandings to revelations emanating from the Dao at various times in human history. The most important among these revelations was that of the deified Laozi, who brought new understandings of the text historically ascribed to him, the *Daode jing* (*The Way and Its Power*), to Zhang Daoling, the first Celestial Master and founder of Zhengyi (Correct Unity) Daoism, in 142 C.E. Likewise, the term *Daoist* will refer to those—generally priests, but also a few lay practitioners—who devoted their lives to Daoist practice.

These are necessarily vague definitions, for Daoism was never a single *ism,* since its organization, doctrines, practices, and even history were constantly being reimagined; nor did it require, except in its earliest stages, strict adherence to a creed. In the process of its unstructured development, Daoist practice came to incorporate a wide spectrum of beliefs, attitudes, and goals, all allegedly finding their source in the Dao. In fact, the endurance of the religion in Chinese society stemmed from its permeable belief system and relative lack of organizational structure. These features softened the religion's outlines and allowed for strategies of eclecticism and co-option that assured the spread of Daoism, though Daoists were few, throughout two millennia of Chinese history.

As the Chinese struggled to understand the Buddhist religion, they naturally did so on their own terms, most often through recourse to indigenous traditions of practice and worship. Buddhist sūtras had to be translated into Chinese, and Buddhist doctrine had to be explained in native terms. Daoism either informed or recorded native understandings by adapting Buddhist doctrine and practice to its own uses. As a result, literally everywhere one looks in the record of Chinese Buddhism—RITUAL, iconography, monastic economy, PHILOSOPHY, and even translation and the creation of sūtras—one finds elements that might be elucidated by reference to Daoist parallels. While successive dynasties, and some Buddhists as well, sought to clarify the boundaries between the two religions, beyond the walls of the monastery this attempt proved less than successful.

Proponents of the Daoist religion brought further political pressures on Buddhism. Often, Daoist organizations defined themselves with respect to devotees of popular sects and Buddhists, whose practices did not accord with theirs. By redefining the doctrines and practices of other religions in their own terms, such Daoist groups would attempt to supplant them. In the case of Buddhism, the goal was to replace the foreign religion with a "more authentic" Chinese version. Several imperial moves to repress the Buddhist religion are directly traceable to this attempted co-option.

The interplay of Buddhism and Daoism can thus be characterized as a complex dance of appropriation and accommodation, interspersed with periods of suspicion and antipathy. This entry will present in diachronic perspective a few of the highlights of this diverse history.

First to sixth centuries C.E.

The earliest interactions between the two religious complexes reveal Chinese attempts to naturalize the foreign religion. The putative use of "Daoist" terms to translate early Buddhist scriptures has perhaps been overemphasized, since the Daoism of the first to the third centuries could claim little unique religious terminology beyond that found in the *Daode jing,* the *Zhuangzi,* and other widely used texts. It is nonetheless significant that both religions drew upon a common fund of Chinese terms, with their established connotations, to express their central concepts. For example, Buddhist *vihāra,* or monasteries, and Daoist meditation chambers were both called *jingshe,* a term that originally designated a pure chamber used in preparation for ancestral sacrifice and that later referred to a Confucian study hall.

Several of the earliest mentions of Buddhism in Chinese historical texts record that the Han emperor Huan (r. 147–167) performed joint sacrifices to the deified Laozi, the Yellow Emperor, and the Buddha. Around the same time, the notion arose that Laozi, who was reputed to have disappeared in the west after composing his *Daode jing,* had become the Buddha. This legend was repeated, and greatly expanded, in Daoist sources, including a circular distributed among Zhengyi groups in northern China in 255, to show the superiority of Daoist practices over those crafted specifically for unruly barbarians. Around 300, a scripture was produced, the *Huahu jing* (*Scripture of [Laozi's] Conversion of the Barbarians*). This text, with later accretions, continued to play a role in religious controversy into the fourteenth century. Versions of the legend were also taken up in early Buddhist apologetic treatises and indigenously composed sūtras, where it was argued that Laozi and other venerated figures of Chinese history were in fact disciples of the Buddha.

By the latter half of the fourth century, Daoist scriptural traditions originating in the south reveal the extent to which Buddhism had come to transform Chinese worldviews. The Shangqing (Upper Purity) scriptures revealed to Yang Xi (ca. 330–386) show vague traces of Buddhist concepts, such as REBIRTH.

Several hagiographies granted to Yang mention the practice of Buddhism, though these are clearly regarded as only one way to approach the proper study of transcendence found in Daoist scriptures. In addition, Yang's transcripts include a series of oral instructions from celestial beings that borrow heavily from the early Chinese Buddhist *Sishier zhang jing* (*Scripture in Forty-two Sections*). Descriptive flourishes in Shangqing depictions of deities and heavenly locales also betray new emphases introduced with Buddhism.

The Lingbao (Numinous Treasure) scriptures, compiled during the late fourth and early fifth centuries, represent an attempt at religious synthesis that encompassed both Buddhism and early forms of Daoism. Lingbao cosmology, soteriology, attitudes toward scripture, ecclesiastical organization, and ritual practice all were adapted from the Buddhism that is attested to in the works of such early translators as Zhi Qian (fl. 220–250) and Kang Senghui (d. 280). Most strikingly, the Lingbao scriptures contain reworked passages from the works of these translators, as well as passages drawn from earlier Daoist texts, all purportedly revealed in their original form, in earlier world-systems. In this way, the Lingbao scriptures were portrayed as replacing all earlier sources of religious knowledge, and they were so represented to the emperors of the Liu-Song dynasty (420–479).

Scholars have yet to fully explore what this remarkable synthesis can reveal of the Buddhist practice of this period. What is clear is that the idea of SAṂSĀRA, with its various postmortem destinies and salvation through transfer of merit, was already widely accepted among the Chinese populace. The Lingbao scriptures did not, however, hold NIRVĀṆA as a goal. Rather, salvific practice was aimed at securing either REBIRTH into the heavens or into a favorable earthly destination, such as the family of a "prince or marquis." This acceptance of nearly all aspects of Buddhist soteriology except nirvāṇa was to characterize Daoism from this time forward. In the competition for ritual patronage, Daoists would claim that Buddhism was the "religion of death," while their practices were dedicated to "life." Insofar as the ritual practice of Daoism took its initial form in these early Lingbao texts, such attitudes toward Buddhism became a feature of future interactions between the two religions.

Sixth to tenth centuries

One might construct a history of the vicissitudes of the two religions on the basis of imperial patronage, beginning with Liang Wudi's (r. 502–549) suppression of Daoism, through Zhou Wudi's (r. 560–578) attempt to ban Buddhism, the Sui emperors' support of Buddhism, and the favoritism toward Daoism shown by the early Tang emperors, who held that they were descended from Laozi. This account, however, would misrepresent the intense interactions between Buddhism and Daoism during this period. While Buddhists composed new sūtras that foretold the apocalyptic DECLINE OF THE DHARMA, provided charms for personal protection, accommodated Chinese filial practice or announced the potential utility of Buddhism as a support for the state, Daoists produced a number of lengthy scriptures, such as the *Yebao yinyuan jing* (*Scripture on Karmic Retribution and Conditions*) and the *Benji jing* (*Scripture on the Origin Point*), that exposed similar Daoist concerns while also elaborating Daoist versions of key Buddhist concepts. These doctrinal developments were catalogued in *Daojiao yishu* (*Pivot of the Dao*), which contains sections on "the three vehicles," the *fashen* (dharmakāya), and Dao-nature, which can be compared to Buddha-nature.

In terms of both doctrine and practice, the Tang dynasty saw further efforts to harmonize the "Three Religions"—Buddhism, Daoism, and Confucianism. Imperial patronage and efforts at control resulted in doctrinal and organizational systematization for both Buddhism and Daoism. Daoists created initiation grades based on the canonical organization of their scriptural traditions and constructed monasteries throughout the kingdom, leading to the emergence of a fully-formed monastic Daoism. Monasteries were the sites of large-scale ritual performances, such as the Buddhist Ullambana ritual and the Daoist Retreat of the Yellow Registers, based on a procedure found in the early Lingbao scriptures. Both of these rites were designed to secure the release of the dead from the HELLS and guide them into more fortunate paths of rebirth or ascension into the heavens. In this and other respects, one begins to see, at least among the elite classes for whom there is a written record, the beginnings of competition between Buddhist and Daoist priests to provide ritual services that were often quite similar in aim and content.

Eleventh to fourteenth centuries

With the better documentation provided by the widespread use of printing and the spread of literacy, an extremely lively religious scene becomes apparent. Daoism's shift from court to local centers, noticed by modern scholars, is perhaps merely the result of increased documentation revealing what had been occurring beneath the surface all along. While elite practitioners continued to be enamored of distinctive practices leading to personal transcendence, as found in Chan or Daoist Inner Alchemy, it now becomes apparent how thoroughly Buddhism and Daoism had blended at the local level. In both Buddhist and Daoist contexts, there are examples of minor Buddhist deities cast in the role of protector deities in local cults; rites of "universal salvation" whereby the dead were rescued from the hells and brought into the ritual space for transfer; and ritual masters who embodied deities and caused child-mediums to become possessed by disease-demons, so that these might be interrogated and expelled. This latter practice derives from Tantric rituals, with their warrior deities and therapeutic aims.

Just as local gods were added to the Daoist pantheon, new modes of scriptural production and lay association were incorporated into Daoism and began to play a central role in the development of Chinese religious life. An example is the cult of the god Wenchang, a local deity from Sichuan later recognized officially as the god of literature. A book detailing his epiphanies and support of the "Three Religions" of Confucianism, Daoism, and Buddhism was revealed by spirit-writing in 1181.

One of the several influential schools of Daoism begun during this period was Quanzhen (Way of Complete Perfection), founded by Wang Zhe (1112–1170). Quanzhen, which is the dominant form of officially-recognized Daoism in modern China, teaches celibacy, asceticism, strict monasticism, moral instruction, and self perfection through inner alchemy. In many ways, Quanzhen self-consciously modeled itself on Chan Buddhism. Quanzhen masters gained the patronage of the Mongol Yuan rulers and, during the mid-thirteenth century, were accused by Buddhists of occupying monasteries, running them as Daoist institutions, and spreading a version of the *Huahu jing.* The literary legacy of Quanzhen Daoism is vast and includes volumes of didactic verse and dialogic records similar to Chan *yulu.*

Another influential school was the Qingwei (Pure Tenuity) school of ritual practice, which incorporated Tantric rites, MUDRĀ, and MAṆḌALA practice into traditional Daoist cosmogenic transformation rituals. These ritual innovations have been preserved by Zhengyi practitioners into the twenty-first century.

Fifteenth century to the present

The ethnically Han emperors of the Ming dynasty (1368–1644) tended to favor Daoism, but strove to bring all public religious expression under strict regulation. They gave official approval to the Zhengyi school over Quanzhen, which had dominated the previous period, and they patronized the printing of the Daoist canon in 1445 and a supplement in 1598. These remain major resources upon which scholars and practicing Daoists alike rely. Nonetheless, such official oversight tends to purge from the official records much that is vital to understanding the growth of the religion.

Elite neo-Confucians of this period adapted both Buddhist and Daoist thought to their own ends. In some cases, such as that of Lin Zhao'en (1517–1598), a self-styled "Master of the Three Teachings," attempts were made to popularize these beliefs. Lin's "Three in One Teaching," influential throughout southeastern China for about 150 years, was meant to eliminate all other denominations under a Confucianism supported by the subsidiary doctrines of Buddhism and Daoism.

More problematic from the state's point of view was the proliferation of lay, scripturally-based, sectarian groups such as the White Lotus Society. Such groups, unlike the Wenchang cult, cannot be categorized as other than eclectic. These societies based their practice of scriptural recitation and meditation on scriptures that innovated freely with beliefs and practices extracted from the canonical writings of both Buddhism and Daoism, overlain with "Confucian" moral concerns that by this time had become the property of both religions. Sectarian scriptures and personalized fortunes in verse form were often produced through spirit-writing sessions conducted in Daoist and, to a lesser extent, Buddhist temples. Such new religious groups, patronized even by officials and their wives, provided an alternative to institutionalized religion.

Qing dynasty (1644–1911) efforts at control were no more successful than those of preceding dynasties. While Tibetan Buddhism was the religion of the Qing emperors, recognition was given, as it is in China today, to the two Daoist schools Zhengyi and Quanzhen. But the tendencies toward simplification and syncretism of the preceding centuries precluded categorical taming of the vibrant religious scene. For instance, while modern Quanzhen venerates Wang Changyue (d. 1680), the officially-recognized first abbot of the Baiyun guan in Beijing, another influential patriarch of the school, Min Yide (1758–1836), is perhaps better representative of the times, and certainly better remembered today. While fulfilling his father's wishes and serving as an official in Yunnan, Min supposedly met the mysterious Man of the Way of Chicken-foot Mountain, who bestowed upon him the inner alchemical practices of the Heart School of West India through two scriptures. One of these concerns the methods of salvation propounded by the three sages—Confucius, Laozi, and Śākyamuni—while the other was a DHĀRAṆĪ text spoken by the Buddha. In addition, Min received a Northern Dipper meditation text containing mantras to be pronounced in imitation of Sanskrit.

In contemporary China, Taiwan, and other Chinese communities, there are continued official attempts to distinguish Daoism from Buddhism through the creation of governing organizations, the registration of priests, and local oversight—all familiar in the history of Chinese religion. Nonetheless, the most prominent characteristic of Chinese religion as it is practiced and imagined remains its eclectic, all-embracing character.

See also: **Apocrypha; Confucianism and Buddhism; Syncretic Sects: Three Teachings**

Bibliography

Andersen, Poul. "Taoist Talismans and the History of the Tianxin Tradition." *Acta Orientalia* 57 (1996): 141–152.

Berling, Judith A. *The Syncretic Religion of Lin Chao-en.* New York: Columbia University Press, 1980.

Bokenkamp, Stephen R. "The Yao Boduo Stele as Evidence for the Dao-Buddhism of the Early Lingbao Scriptures." *Cahiers d'Extrême-Asie* 9 (1996–1997): 54–67.

Bokenkamp, Stephen R. *Early Daoist Scriptures.* Berkeley: University of California Press, 1997.

Bokenkamp, Stephen R. "Lu Xiujing, Buddhism, and the First Daoist Canon." In *Culture and Power in the Reconstitution of the Chinese Realm, 200–600,* ed. Scott Pearce, Audrey Spiro, and Patricia Ebrey. Cambridge, MA: Harvard University Press, 2001.

Boltz, Judith M. *A Survey of Taoist Literature: Tenth to Seventeenth Centuries.* Berkeley, CA: Institute of East Asian Studies, 1987.

Davis, Edward L. *Society and the Supernatural in Song China.* Honolulu: University of Hawaii Press, 2001.

Dean, Kenneth. *Taoist Ritual and Popular Cults of Southeast China.* Princeton, NJ: Princeton University Press, 1993.

Kohn, Livia. *Laughing at the Tao: Debates among Buddhists and Taoists in Medieval China.* Princeton, NJ: Princeton University Press, 1995.

Kohn, Livia, ed. *Daoism Handbook.* Leiden, Netherlands: Brill, 2000.

Lopez, Donald S., Jr., ed. *Religions of China in Practice.* Princeton, NJ: Princeton University Press, 1996.

Robinet, Isabelle. *Taoism: Growth of a Religion,* tr. Phyllis Brooks. Stanford, CA: Stanford University Press, 1997.

Schipper, Kristofer M. "Purity and Strangers: Shifting Boundaries in Medieval Taoism." *T'oung Pao* 80 (1984): 61–81.

Schipper, Kristofer M. *The Taoist Body,* tr. Karen C. Duval. Berkeley: University of California Press, 1994.

Yoshioka Yoshitoyo. *Dōkyō to bukkyō* (*Daoism and Buddhism*), 3 vols. Tokyo: Kokusho Kankōkai, 1959, 1970, 1976.

Zürcher, Erik. "Buddhist Influence on Early Taoism." *T'oung Pao* 66 (1980): 84–147.

Zürcher, Erik. "Prince Moonlight." *T'oung Pao* 68 (1982): 1–75.

STEPHEN R. BOKENKAMP

DAOSHENG

Daosheng (355–434) was an influential Chinese scholar-monk. He was popular as a lecturer with the educated classes and famous for advancing the theory of a "sudden" experience of enlightenment. Ordained at a young age, Daosheng gave his first Buddhist lecture at fifteen. In 397 he traveled to Lushan where he studied for seven years under HUIYUAN (334–416) and Saṅghadeva. Daosheng then journeyed to Chang'an with three other disciples of Huiyuan to learn and assist KUMĀRAJĪVA (350–409/413), probably helping in Kumārajīva's translations of the *Vimalakīrti-sūtra* and the LOTUS SŪTRA (SADDHARMAPUṆḌARĪKA-SŪTRA). Of his many monographs only his commentary on the *Lotus Sūtra* is extant; but Daosheng's opinions are often quoted in other works, allowing scholars to reconstruct his core ideas.

Daosheng was severely criticized for his stubborn refusal to accept the accuracy of the first translation of the Mahāyāna NIRVĀṆA SŪTRA because of its claim that all sentient beings possess the buddha-nature except for the evil ICCHANTIKA. After returning to Lushan in 430, he was exonerated and praised for his insight when a new, expanded translation of this sūtra that had removed the *icchantika* exclusion was brought to him.

Daosheng was perhaps the first person in China to see the mārga (PATH) implications of the buddha-nature doctrine famously extolled in the *Nirvāṇa Sūtra.* This sūtra preaches the positive aspects of NIRVĀṆA as pure, eternal, personal, and so on, and Daosheng linked this with the buddha-nature concept to affirm a pure, blissful "true self" that can only be realized suddenly. If the buddha-nature is indivisible, he argued, then it is realized completely or not at all. He advocated a gradual path of training to prepare one for this sudden flash of insight, thereby completing the path in that moment of epiphany. This led to heightened interest in the *Nirvāṇa Sūtra* and serious debate in China and Tibet over sudden versus gradual conceptions of the path.

See also: **Bodhi (Awakening); Tathāgatagarbha**

Bibliography

Kim, Young-ho. *Tao-sheng's Commentary on the Lotus Sūtra: A Study and Translation.* Albany: State University of New York Press, 1990.

Liu, Ming-Wood. "The Early Development of the Buddha-Nature Doctrine in China." *Journal of Chinese Philosophy* 16 (1989): 1–36.

MARK L. BLUM

DAOXUAN

Daoxuan (596–667) was one of the most versatile and prolific Chinese monks of the medieval period. Son of a prominent official, he became a monk at an early age and soon earned a reputation for erudition and industry. Although sources disagree on Daoxuan's place of origin, he lived for most of his adult life in or near the Tang capital at Chang'an, where he worked for a brief period at the translation center of the great translator XUANZANG (ca. 600–664) and served as abbot of Ximing Monastery. Daoxuan's writings include a catalog of Buddhist texts, various historical works, numerous works on the monastic regulations, and records of his visionary encounters with divine beings.

Daoxuan's most influential historical works are a large compilation of accounts of monks titled *Xu gaoseng zhuan* (*Further Biographies of Eminent Monks*) and *Guang hongming ji* (*Expanded Collection of the Propagation of Light*), a collection of documents by more than 130 authors relating for the most part to debates between Buddhists and their detractors at court. Daoxuan's most important work on the monastic regulations, *Sifenlü shanfan buque xingshichao* (*Notes on Conduct: Abridgements and Emendations to the Four-Part Regulations*), attempts to provide a handbook for monastic practice based on the *Dharmaguptakavinaya* (Chinese, *Sifen lü*).

Various legends circulated about Daoxuan's life, the most famous of which were that a spirit placed a tooth of the Buddha in his protection and that he was the reincarnation of the sixth-century monk Sengyou.

See also: **Biographies of Eminent Monks (Gaoseng zhuan); History; Vinaya**

Bibliography

Shinohara, Koichi. "Changing Roles of Miraculous Images in Medieval Chinese Buddhism: A Study of the Miraculous Images Section of Daxuan's *Ji-shenzhou Sanbao Gantonglu.*" In *Images, Miracles, and Authority in Asian Religious Traditions,* ed. Richard Davis. Boulder, CO: Westview Press, 1998.

Shinohara, Koichi. "The Kaṣāya Robe of the Past Buddha Kāśyapa in the Miraculous Instruction Given to the Vinaya Master Daoxuan (596–667)." *Chung-hwa Buddhist Journal* 13 (2000): 299–367.

JOHN KIESCHNICK

DAOYI (MAZU)

Mazu Daoyi (709–788) is one of the main figures in the history of the CHAN SCHOOL. The appearance of Mazu and his disciples represented a key point in the historical development of Chan, as the fragmented schools of early Chan were replaced by a new orthodoxy identified with his Hongzhou school. Because of his great influence on the subsequent growth of Chan, Mazu is widely recognized as the leading Chan teacher during the tradition's putative "golden age" during the eighth and ninth centuries.

Born in the western province of Sichuan in a local gentry family, Mazu entered religious life as a teenager. His early teachers were noted Chan monks in his native province. During the mid-730s he traveled to Hunan, where he studied with Huairang (677–744), an obscure disciple of the "Sixth Patriarch" HUINENG (638–713). Mazu then went on to establish monastic communities in southeast China. After his move to Hongzhou (the provincial capital of Jiangsi), during the final two decades of his life, Mazu emerged as a highly popular religious teacher who attracted a large number of eminent monastic and lay disciples.

Mazu did not leave any written records. His *Mazu yulu* (*Mazu's Discourse Record*), which was compiled during the eleventh century and contains diverse materials with varied provenances, is still widely read and recognized as a principal text of the Chan canon. Among his best-known teachings, succinctly expressed as popular Chan adages, are "Mind is Buddha" and "Ordinary mind is the Way."

Bibliography

Cheng-chien Bhikshu, trans. *Sun-Face Buddha: The Teachings of Ma-tsu and the Hung-chou School of Ch'an.* Berkeley, CA: Asian Humanities Press, 1993.

MARIO POCESKI

DEATH

As in all religions, death is an event of monumental importance for Buddhism. From one point of view death may appear as a nonissue in Buddhism because the assumption of transmigration guarantees that death is not final. Death nevertheless reminds the Buddhist that human life is the best existence from which to pursue liberation, but it is relatively short; moreover, as an unusual reward of meritorious KARMA (ACTION), human life cannot be taken for granted as one's next REBIRTH and may not come again for a long time. Death also reminds the Buddhist that repeated rebirths do not guarantee progress toward realizing NIRVĀṆA; in fact each existence in SAṂSĀRA is difficult to control and so permeated by DUḤKHA (SUFFERING) in one form or another that it is exceedingly difficult to cease producing karma and escape. Belief in transmigration thus does not remove the sense of insecurity that accompanies death, and for that reason the goal of nirvāṇa is often described as "deathless" (*amṛta*) because it eliminates all such anxieties. The journey of the prince Siddhārtha outside the palace walls in the biographies of the Buddha similarly show the centrality of death as a religious problem: It is after seeing a corpse that Siddhārtha grows morose and troubled, setting up the next and final encounter with a mendicant who not only shows him the possibility of pursuing a spiritual life, but explains his own motivation as seeking "that most blessed state in which extinction is unknown."

Considering the complexity of the impact death has on Buddhism, it may be helpful to approach the matter in four thematic ways: (1) in doctrine, (2) in praxis, (3) in memorializing the death of the Buddha, and (4) in funerary culture.

Doctrinal death and mythical roots

Philosophical associations with death abound in the various credos that Buddhism has produced over the centuries. In the early tradition, the FOUR NOBLE TRUTHS define humankind's central problem as *duḥkha* and indicate how it can be overcome. But the tradition also analyzes *duḥkha* itself as fourfold: birth, aging, disease, and death. Similarly, the last of the twelve "limbs" in the PRATĪTYASAMUTPĀDA (DEPENDENT ORIGINATION) formula is "aging and death," indicating the inevitable dissolution of all sentient life. Even the "three characteristics" of all conditioned existence—ANITYA (IMPERMANENCE), *duḥkha,* and anātman (nonsubstantiality)—imply the centrality of death because the deepest resonance of this truth is not the desire for permanent sources of happiness, but a permanent source of our own existence.

Death itself is described in various ways throughout the canon. The DHAMMAPADA and *Suttanipāta* frame it poetically ("just as ripe fruit falls quickly from the tree" or "like a cow being led to slaughter"), but the later *nikāyas* and ABHIDHARMA literature are more analytical. Here death is explained as the cessation of the continuity of the five SKANDHA (AGGREGATES), the crumbling of the body, and the ending of the *āyus* (life span) or *jīvitendriya* (faculty of living). Generally the *jīvitendriya* is the force that sustains human life through the continuous changes to the five aggregates, and is held to be of predetermined length. This is death in "due time," and it is contrasted with "untimely" death caused by encountering unexpected circumstances, such as being murdered, being eaten by a wild animal, succumbing to illness, and so on. In the THERAVĀDA commentarial tradition, final moments of consciousness are described in some detail, when past karmic deeds or signs of such "settle" on the individual, and then a vision of one's future destiny occurs, such as the appearance of fire signifying hell, a mother's womb indicating rebirth in the human realm, or pleasure groves and divine palaces for a future in a heavenly realm. Then comes a momentary "death awareness" (*cuticitta*) followed immediately by "rebirth linking consciousness" (*paṭisandhiviññāṇa*) signifying the next life. The relationship between these two is said to be one of neither identity nor otherness; likened to an echo it is caused by previous events but not identical to them.

As the skandhas are formed from a collectivity of causes and conditions that are temporary in nature, the skandhas themselves are impermanent, constantly arising and ceasing. Death from the point of view of this "momentariness" doctrine is in fact something that recurs moment after moment. In this and the "end of a lifetime" notions of death, how the karmic identity continues is a key question. The dissolution of the self never means the dissolution of karma.

Some schools speak of four stages of life: birth, the period between birth and death, death, and the period between death and rebirth. According to the ABHIDHARMAKOŚABHĀṢYA and Yogācāra literature, one explanation of this process is that in the presence of a life span the *jīvitendriya* holds onto bodily warmth and consciousness symbiotically and unceasingly until the "due time." At that point all three—life, warmth, and consciousness—abandon the body and death ensues, described as akin to throwing off a piece of wood, whereupon karma forces the three to seek another body. Here it would seem that the physical body is something other than these three animating functions and that only in combination is a finite lifetime produced. Another doctrine posits the *antarābhava,* an INTERMEDIATE STATE between death and the next life wherein one is transformed into an entity called a *gandharva,* originally a semidivine being associated with fertility and the god Soma in pre-Buddhist Indian myths. Possessing subtle versions of all five aggregates reflective of one's next birth, for most people in this state some perception is possible but willpower is limited to finding an appropriate womb to descend into, and the common view gives the *gandharva* forty-nine days to accomplish this task. Advanced practitioners known as *nonreturners,* however, can attain nirvāṇa from this state. This conception was readily accepted into the MAHĀYĀNA, where it gave rise to a variety of beliefs and practices designed to help the recently deceased alter their destined rebirth.

The gods Yama and MĀRA reflect another mythical aspect of the Buddhist concept of death. Son of a *gandharva,* Yama is depicted in the *Ṛg Veda* as the first mortal; deciding to remain among the dead, Yama becomes the lord of that realm. In the *Atharva Veda* he acquires a messenger, Mṛtyu, who later appears in the KĀLACAKRA as death lurking within the body of sentient beings. Otherwise, King Yama's role is generally restricted to the unseen world of the dead, where he becomes the judge before whom the deceased must stand to receive karmic sentencing to determine their status in the next birth. Yama is thus a negative symbol of saṃsāra itself, and he can be seen holding the six-realm wheel of life in the VAJRAYĀNA, which also includes a deity, Yamāntaka, who represents his defeat. If Buddhists fear Yama in the next world, they fear Ma ¯ra, also called the "king of death" (*Suttanipāta*), in this one. From his attempts to dissuade the bodhisattva from attaining enlightenment via the enticement of lust and the fear of attack, Māra symbolizes personal death, the death of Buddhism as a religion, and the evils of destruction and uncontrolled desire. Derived from a verb meaning to die or kill (*mṛ*), there are various forms of Māra, residing within the aggregates, in the *kleśas* (defilements), in one of the heavens of the desire-realm (*kāmaloka*), and so on. Although in one sense Māra is death itself, he is most commonly depicted as a deity who is resentful of the dharma and devoted to hindering the spiritual progress of the practitioner.

Death as a theme of praxis

Meditations on death run throughout the Buddhist tradition. This comes from the fact that the Buddha identified death as the ultimate and therefore most potentially instructive form of *duḥkha.* Death as a theme in focused RITUAL or MEDITATION is similarly called the key to the "gate of deathlessness." From very early there have been two famous forms of death-praxis, known as *death-mindfulness* (*maraṇasmṛti*) and *meditation on pollution* (*aśubhabhāvanā*). These are mentioned in various places in the Pāli canon, but their fullest descriptions are found in the *Visuddhimagga* by BUDDHAGHOSA.

Mindfulness of death is aimed at fostering existential acceptance of the reality of death and allowing that realization to influence one's life fully. The Buddha was appalled at how common it was for people to go through life as if they were not going to die, and this form of meditation uses eight topics for the practitioner to contemplate:

1. death as executioner,
2. death as ruinous of all forms of happiness and success,
3. death as inevitable for everyone regardless of their power,
4. death as coming about by an infinite number of causes,
5. death as close at hand,
6. death as signless, or coming without warning signs,
7. death as the end of a life span that is in fact short,
8. death as a constant in life.

This practice aims at liberating individuals from natural attachments to their own existence, and thus leads to mindfulness of the three marks of existence: *anitya, duḥkha,* and anātman.

Meditation on pollution is similarly aimed at deepening one's acceptance of the reality of death, but in this practice the point is driven home by actually going to look at decaying human corpses. As described in the *Suttanipāta* (202–203), when the practitioner sees the corpse, he "sees the body as it (really) is" and thinks, "As is this (body of mine), so is that (corpse); as is that, so is this." Statements like this express one strain in Buddhist thought that regards the body as essentially foul and not the locale of one's identity. But despite one's proximity to corpses in various degrees of decay—a remarkably bold concept considering the contagious nature of pollution in Hinduism—Buddhaghosa tells us that ultimately the meditator comes away from this exercise feeling not angst but joy because now that he has accepted the reality of death, he knows he is on the path to defeat it. In Thailand this meditation is often performed at morgues.

Belief that one's state of mind at the moment of death not only passively reflects but can actively influence what happens after death led to the corresponding belief that the true purpose of all praxis is preparation for that final moment. For example, the *Dantabhūmi-sutta* points to this final "act of time" (*kālakriyā*) as something "tamed" or "untamed."

In East Asia, a variation of death-mindfulness is the use of death as an existential KŌAN in the CHAN SCHOOL. This is apparent in the charismatic Chinese teacher YANSHOU (904–975), who believed that suicide "reciprocated the kindness of the dharma" if done with the proper state of mind. He saw this as a way to actualize the perfection of giving (*dānapāramitā*) and thereby attain enlightenment. Yanshou reflects Buddhist ambivalence about suicide, manifesting the principle that one's life is only a tool that can be manipulated or even given away when necessary. Death also shows up prominently in the rhetoric of Japanese Zen during the Tokugawa period (1603–1868). Suzuki Shōsan (1579–1655), for example, was motivated to pursue Zen practice by an obsession with death, and he felt grateful to death for having deepened his practice. The great Rinzai teacher HAKUIN EKAKU (1686–1768) is famous for teaching the imperative of an explosive spiritual breakthrough he called the "great death." In a similar vein, Shidō Bunan (1603–1676) wrote:

> Die while alive, and be completely dead,
>
> Then do whatever you will, all is good.

About which the modern Zen master Shibayama Zenkei (1894–1974) comments, "The aim of Zen training is to die while alive, that is, to actually become the self of no-mind, and no-form, and then to revive as the True Self of no-mind and no-form" (p. 46). In this form of spiritual death, one's known identity is dissolved, rather abruptly according to Hakuin, yielding a new, more genuine self untainted by discursive, judgmental thinking and totally free to think and act as one pleases.

Memorializing the death of the Buddha

The *Mahāparinibbāna-sutta* (DN 2:140–142) describes in some detail the circumstances of the Buddha's passing, how he viewed his upcoming death, and how his body was treated afterward. Despite his admonition against attaching value to his corpse—"What is there in seeing this wretched body? Whoever sees dharma, sees me."—the Buddha instructed his attendant ĀNANDA to give him a funeral like a "king of kings," explained as wrapping the body in five hundred layers of cloth, placing it inside an iron vessel, and then burning it on a funeral pyre. He also authorized the building of one STŪPA at a crossroads to house his remains, extolling the welfare it would bring believers who visited and paid their respects. But even this bow to relic worship was not enough: There was such a clamoring for his *śarīra* (relics) by the eight kings of the region that all were given portions after the cremation, leading initially to the construction of eight stūpas containing them, with two more later erected that enshrined the bowl used to collect the relics and the ashes from the pyre. The sūtra also promises rebirth in heaven for anyone who makes PILGRIMAGE "with hearts of reverence" to four sites memorializing the Buddha's historical presence—where he was born, achieved enlightenment, delivered his first sermon, and passed away.

The sūtra is probably only canonizing pilgrimage routes that began immediately after the Buddha's death. Stūpa worship increased during the third century B.C.E. under King AŚOKA, who is said to have opened up the original ten stūpas and distributed the relics therein among eighty-four thousand new stūpas built throughout the land. Images of the Buddha also served as public memorials to the founder after his death, though they appear in mass quantities somewhat later. Their similarity to stūpas in this regard can be seen in the fact that both often contain relics, symbols of their animation. Stūpas and images thus became symbols of the corporeal presence of the Buddha and his enlightened followers; at times they evolved into mausoleums of architectural sophistication, as at the great stūpa complex at SĀÑCĪ in central India where the relics of ŚĀRIPUTRA and MAHĀMAUDGALYĀYANA are said to be enshrined and where BUDDHA IMAGES from Mathurā were brought in. Relics for the consecrations of stūpas and images were exported to other Buddhist nations such as Sri Lanka and China, allowing a physical "presence" of the Buddha in death over an expanded area that could not have taken place while he was alive.

One oddity within the *Mahāparinibbāna-sutta* is how the narrative deals with the paradox of a buddha dying when he himself professed his ability to continue living until the end of the kalpa. The Tathāgata relates to ĀNANDA how Māra has repeatedly appeared before him and requested that he relent and die on the spot, but he has consistently found excuses to put him off. This time, however, he has decided to go ahead and let his time run out. Almost akin to a pronouncement of suicide, the sūtra reads, "And now, Ānanda, the Tathāgata has today at Chāpāla's shrine consciously and deliberately rejected the rest of his allotted time" (5:37). Ānanda swiftly responds by beseeching the Buddha three times to remain in the world, living until the end of the kalpa, but each time the Buddha refuses. He then describes no less than sixteen previous occasions when he remarked to Ānanda how much he liked a particular place and could remain there for the duration of the kalpa, hinting that Ānanda should ask him to do so. But each time Ānanda did not understand, and the Buddha now explains that without such an outside request, he is powerless to alter his historical fate. To beseech the Buddha now as he approaches death is too late: "The time for making such a request is past." Ānanda's dim-wittedness is thus made the scapegoat for humankind having to suffer century upon century without a buddha.

Funerary culture

Putting aside the death of the founder, which has unique historical significance, it may be useful in considering the various ways in which the living relate to the dead in Buddhist cultures throughout Asia to divide such expression into the care and treatment of the *uncommon dead*, the *common dead*, and the *unknown dead*. Under the rubric of uncommon dead, would be saints, kings, and lesser religious and political leaders who are typically memorialized in ways that manifest their power and influence. Relations between the common dead and the living is typically dominated by familial concerns regarding how kinfolk can assist the recently deceased in their postmortem "journey," and the flip side of this relationship, which is how the dead can either enhance or disrupt the lives of the living depending on how appropriately such assistance is rendered. The unknown dead appear most commonly in pious efforts to help all beings born in the lower realms of hell and what are usually referred to as *hungry ghosts*. In all cases, the care and treatment of corpses naturally reflect different attitudes about the expected relationship between the deceased and those left behind.

Two universal principles are often evident in all three categories of funerary culture. First is that in every society in Asia that may be considered traditionally Buddhist, indigenous belief structures regarding the dead that were operative before the assimilation of Buddhism persist and form an integral part of that assimilation. This has resulted in a hybridization of funerary practices under the guise of Buddhist rituals and rhetoric. Within each nation there is considerable diversity in how the dead are treated, and these differences in local culture expose any notion of ethnic homogeneity as political myth. This is particularly true in the care and treatment of the common dead, where the Buddhist input into that amalgam varies widely. There has been easy acceptance of the doctrine of transmigration in Tibet, for example. By contrast, in China deep traditions of family obligations beyond the grave have meant less than full acceptance of the presumption that each rebirth places the individual into a new family wherein the previous family is completely forgotten. It was thus normative in China to use the surname of the Buddha upon taking the tonsure, signifying a public shift of filial affiliation to the SAṄGHA.

Monks are intimately connected with funerary culture in all Buddhist countries, usually in ways that combine Buddhist and non-Buddhist beliefs about death, and it has been common for monasteries to derive significant revenue from related activities such as cremation, burial, and services for the family. While cremation has been the norm in India since before the birth of Buddhism, this was not so for the rest of Asia, and although there is no scriptural demand for cremation in Buddhism, its adoption on the continent came with the dissemination of Buddhist culture. Thus did the arrival of Buddhism bring cremation as a common approach to the care and treatment of the dead in much of the Buddhist world. But burial has remained the norm in Mongolia, and in Tibet the body is brought to a mountaintop, broken up, and fed to birds. In China cremation appears to have been wide-

The funeral and cremation of a revered Korean monk. © Nathan Benn/Corbis. Reproduced by permission.

spread only during the Song and Yuan dynasties and the period since the Communist revolution in 1949; here resistance stems from the ancient belief that the dead emerge in the afterlife with a kind of ethereal body that needs to be fully intact to function properly.

The second principle is that when we speak of how the dead are viewed by the living, we should recognize that they are merely one part of another reality wherein are also found a host of supernatural entities such as celestial beings, spirits, fairies, gods of one sort of another, Māra, Yama, future and past buddhas, bodhisattvas, and so forth. This other world is not separate from ours but for the most part is hidden to us. We can glimpse traces of it, however, through unorthodox states of mind experienced in meditative trance, dreams, portents, miraculous manifestations, and occasional encounters with individuals from that realm.

The *Mahāparinibbāna-sutta* defines four types of uncommon dead by identifying who deserves to be memorialized by means of building sacred stūpas over their graves: buddhas, PRATYEKABUDDHAS, śrāvakas, and righteous wheel-turning kings (cakravartin). The sūtra states that these four groups are worthy of memorial stūpas because when a believer looks upon their grave-mound and thinks "This is the stūpa of . . . ," the heart of that person will be made calm and happy, and when that believer dies this personal experience will result in rebirth in a heavenly realm. The sūtra thus canonizes the belief that stūpas built to mark the graves of sacred historical persons will be embodied with the power to transform believing pilgrims who make contact with those stūpas such that their karmic status will be so purified that rebirth in heaven is assured. This is just one example of the fact that belief in the religious power of material expressions of the uncommon dead begins very early in Buddhism. In Mahāyāna countries, cremated remains of eminent monks were often inspected to find relics in the form of jewels or shining bone nuggets, confirming their status as bodhisattvas and prompting burial under stūpas. In China there are numerous stories of the cremated bones of saints found linked in a chain.

Many have pointed to the presence of relics in stūpas and other funerary paraphernalia as the basis of their power, and indeed relics have played a prominent role in sanctifying not only stūpas, but monasteries, shrines, statues, and so forth. The extreme form of sanctifying the corporeal remains of a saint is to display the mummified body on an altar. This tradition was not uncommon in Mahāyāna countries, reflecting the belief that an "attained" individual leaves behind a "diamond-like" body that remains erect. This view is of a piece with the early belief that buddhas were inevitably marked with thirty-two major and eighty minor physical abnormalities, such as long ears and tongues or webbed hands and feet, stemming from the principle that spiritual achievement brought corporeal manifestations, much like the stigmata in Europe. Numerous mummified monks can still be viewed in China and Japan today, and in 2002 a deceased *rin po che* (teacher) in Mongolia was discovered in this form. We know that the drinking of lacquer, a poison that ended the saint's life but also stiffened his joints, preceded some of these mummified deaths.

But a tomb does not need a relic to be considered sacred. In Japan, where the relics of famous monks are frequently kept on the altars of monasteries, the uncommon dead typically have multiple tombs with or without something material of the individual interred therein. For example, the fact that the body of Oda Nobunaga (1534–1582), the general who reunited the country after a hundred years of war, was never recovered did not impede the establishment of at least sixteen "empty" burial sites to honor him. While such gravesite mimes are not universal, the stūpa or pagoda, its architectural variant, did become a universal burial marker for the uncommon dead throughout Buddhist Asia. Typically these house relics of the deceased in the form of *śarīra,* bone fragments remaining after cremation. As with the Buddha, such burial edifices frequently have become both the objects of pilgrimage and centers for monastic communities.

The burial sites of the uncommon dead may also serve as focal points of sectarian identity. When this occurs, other expressions of collective identity, such as larger mausoleums and the pilgrimage routes, typically accompany it. In Japan, this pattern is particularly striking, having led to the custom of interring the common dead at the burial sites of saints, such as KŪKAI and SHINRAN, both founders of their major denominations. The recent dead are thereby thought to be purified by their proximity to the sacred dead, improving their karmic status for achieving rebirth in Tuṣita Heaven or AMITĀBHA's Pure Land. Since family members in Japan often want the remains of their loved ones to be kept nearby yet also desire to help them after death, what is left of the body (ashes and bits of bone after cremation, whole bones when the flesh has disappeared after an earth burial) may be divided and two graves created—one at a local cemetery, and another at the site of the saint. The Honganji branch of Shinran's denomination has been selling spots for interment at the grave of Shinran since at least the sixteenth century, a policy that has created both revenue and a deep sense of fealty among the branch's nonclergy members.

It should also be noted that rebirth in the Pure Land of Amitābha has slowly grown into a kind of normative objective of postmortem ritual for most of the Mahāyāna world, from Tibet to Japan, since the seventh century, cutting across a range of schools, beliefs, and sectarian identities. The rhetoric of attaining the Pure Land promises nonbacksliding status and swift progress to buddhahood, yet it also includes the imperative to postpone buddhahood in order to return to saṃsāra to help others attain a similar postmortem peace.

One of the important principles guiding relations between the dead and their deceased kin or intimates is that of merit transfer (*parivaṭṭa, pariṇāma*), a fundamental theme in funerary rituals devoted to raising the recently deceased to the Pure Land, for example. Adopted from earlier Brahmanic rites for the dead called *śrāddha* that elevated the status of the recently deceased from unstable ghost (preta) to divinity (deva), Buddhism similarly began with tales of ghosts who are incapable of initiating action to improve their situation. In the Theravāda text *Petavatthu,* the ghost of a deceased person may appear to someone in his or her family requesting that offerings be made to the saṅgha with the merit ritually transferred to the ghost. If the ghost is morally capable of appreciating the goodness of the act, he or she can be transformed into a deity, just as in Brahmanism.

In the Mahāyāna, the practice of merit transfer is greatly expanded, but it shares with Theravāda a presumption that the efficacy depends upon the ability of the deceased to perceive religious messages ritually sent to him or her and to appreciate their meaning. It is widely believed in Mahāyāna countries that in the intermediate state one has the potential to refuse the saṃsāric body offered and, if one can steer clear of distractions, awaken to the truth and proceed directly to nirvāṇa. The so-called TIBETAN BOOK OF THE DEAD is meant to guide the dead when confronted with different choices as to what path to follow in that realm. Kinfolk and close friends gather repeatedly to

The funeral procession of a Tibetan monk in Darjeeling, India, 1989. © Don Farber 2003. All rights reserved. Reproduced by permission.

chant sūtras and make donations to the saṅgha, producing a store of merit that is ritually transferred to the deceased.

Care of the unknown or nonkin dead typically occurs on an individual basis, such as when a pilgrim dies on the road, but there is also a famous institutional example in the Chinese GHOST FESTIVAL. Here Chinese notions of ravenous ghosts and Indian concepts of preta fused into the hungry ghost image—beings in the preta realm that are obsessed with hunger as they try to fill a large belly with a tiny mouth; the hungry ghost can never get enough to feel satisfied. Based on the indigenous *Yulanpen jing,* a ritual tradition began in the medieval period for a yearly festival to transfer merit to all beings in the preta realm by making donations to the saṅgha. This festival is still practiced throughout East Asia, and is particularly vibrant in Japan.

See also: **Abortion; Ancestors; Buddha, Life of the; Cosmology; Ghosts and Spirits; Hells; Mahāparinirvāṇa-sūtra; Merit and Merit-Making; Rebirth; Relics and Relics Cults**

Bibliography

Ashikaga, Ensho. "The Festival for the Spirits of the Dead in Japan." *Western Folklore* 9, no. 3 (1950): 217–228.

Benard, Elisabeth. "The Tibetan Tantric View of Death and Afterlife." In *Death and Afterlife: Perspectives of World Religions,* ed. Hiroshi Obayashi. New York and London: Greenwood Press, 1992.

Blum, Mark. "Stand by Your Founder: Honganji's Struggle with Funereal Orthodoxy." *Japanese Journal of Religious Studies* 27, nos. 3–4 (2000): 180–212.

Bond, George. "Theravāda Buddhism's Meditations on Death and the Symbolism of Initiatory Death." *History of Religions* 19 (1980): 237–258.

Bowker, John. "Buddhism." In *The Meanings of Death.* New York and Cambridge: Cambridge University Press, 1991.

Cuevas, Brian. "Predecessors and Prototypes: Towards a Conceptual History of the Buddhist Antarābhava." *Numen* 43 (1996): 263–302.

Ebrey, Patricia. "Cremation in Sung China." *American Historical Review* 95, no. 2 (1990): 406–428.

Gielen, Uwe P. "A Death on the Roof of the World: The Perspective of Tibetan Buddhism." In *Death and Bereavement across Cultures,* ed. Colin M. Parkes, Pittu Laungani, and Bill Young. London and New York: Routledge, 1997.

Holck, Frederick, ed. *Death and Eastern Thought: Understanding Death in Eastern Religions and Philosophies.* Nashville, TN: Abingdon Press, 1974.

Holt, John C. "Assisting the Dead by Venerating the Living: Merit Transfer in the Early Buddhist Tradition." *Numen* 28, no. 1 (1981): 1–28.

Keyes, Charles. "From Death to Birth: Ritual Process and Buddhist Meanings in Northern Thailand." *Folk* (Copenhagen) 29 (1987): 181–190.

King, Winston. "Practicing Dying: The Samurai-Zen Death Techniques of Suzuki Shosan." In *Religious Encounters with Death: Insights from the History and Anthropology of Religions,* ed. Frank Reynolds and Earl Waugh. University Park: Pennsylvania State University Press, 1976.

Klein, Anne C. "Buddhism." In *How Different Religions View Death and Afterlife,* 2nd edition, ed. Christopher Jay Johnson and Marsha McGee. Philadelphia: Charles Press, 1991.

Ñāṇamoki Bhikkhu, trans. *The Path of Purification by Bhadantācariya Buddhaghosa.* Kandy, Sri Lanka: Buddhist Publication Society, 1975.

Reynolds, Frank E. "Death as Threat, Death as Achievement: Buddhist Perspectives with Particular Reference to the Theravāda Tradition." In *Death and Afterlife: Perspectives of World Religions,* ed. Hiroshi Obayashi. New York and London: Greenwood Press, 1992.

Shibayama Zenkei. *A Flower Does Not Talk,* tr. Sumiko Kudo. Rutland, VT: Charles E. Tuttle, 1970.

Tambiah, S. J. *Buddhism and the Spirit Cults in Northeast Thailand.* Cambridge, UK: Cambridge University Press, 1970.

Teiser, Stephen. *The Ghost Festival in Medieval China.* Princeton, NJ: Princeton University Press, 1987.

Thurman, Robert, trans. *The Tibetan Book of the Dead.* New York: Bantam, 1994.

Wayman, Alex. "Studies in Yama and Māra." *Indo-Iranian Journal* 3, nos. 1–2 (1959): 44–131.

Wayman, Alex. "The Religious Meaning of Concrete Death in Buddhism." In *Sens de la mort dans le Christianisme et les autres religions,* ed. Mariasusai Dhavamony. Rome: Gregorian University Press, 1982.

Welter, Albert. "Life, Death and Enlightenment: Buddhist Ethics in a Chinese Context." In *Life Ethics in World Religions,* ed. Dawne C. McCance. Atlanta, GA: Scholars Press, 1998.

Wijesekera, N. D. "Beliefs and Ceremonial Associated with Death in Ceylon." *Journal of the Royal Asiatic Society* (Ceylon Branch) New Series 8, no. 2 (1963): 225–244.

Yetts, W. Perceval, "Notes on the Disposal of Buddhist Dead in China." *Journal, Royal Asiatic Society* (1911): 699–725.

MARK L. BLUM

DECLINE OF THE DHARMA

The first of the "three marks of existence"—ANITYA (IMPERMANENCE), anātman (no-self), and DUḤKHA (SUFFERING)—holds that all conditioned (that is, causally produced) phenomena are transitory. With striking consistency, most Buddhists over the centuries have believed this to imply that Buddhism itself—as a historically constructed religious tradition flowing from the life and teachings of a particular individual—must also have a finite duration. While the truth about the nature of reality (dharma) propounded by Śākyamuni and other buddhas before him is considered to be unchanging, particular expressions of that truth, and the human communities that embody them, are viewed as conditioned, and thus impermanent, phenomena. According to this widely held understanding, each buddha discovers the same truth about reality as that realized by his predecessors, and then he teaches it to a community of followers. After a certain period of time, however (commonly ranging from five hundred to five thousand years), this truth will be forgotten, thus necessitating its rediscovery by another buddha in the future.

In addition to this general assumption of transitoriness, Indian Buddhists have shared with their Jain and Hindu counterparts the idea that the present age is part of a cycle of decline. The entire cosmos, and with it the moral and spiritual capacity of human beings, is viewed as being on a downward cycle, with each succeeding generation being less spiritually adept than the last. In this context it is not surprising that Buddhists have anticipated a gradual erosion both in the quality and quantity of the transmitted teachings and in the karmic character of their practitioners. Such expectations have been recorded in a wide range of prophecies of the decline and eventual disappearance of Buddhism found in Buddhist canonical texts.

Timetables of decline

The earliest tradition offering a specific figure for the duration of the dharma predicts that Buddhism will endure for only five hundred years. This prophecy, found in the VINAYA texts of several different ordination lineages (*nikāya*) and dating from perhaps a century or so after the Buddha's death, is generally intertwined with the claim that Buddhism would have survived for a full one thousand years were it not for the fateful decision made by Śākyamuni to ordain women as well as men. As a direct result of the presence of NUNS within the monastic community, the life span of the Buddhist teachings will be cut in half.

Early in the first millennium C.E., however, as the Buddhist community became aware that this initial figure of five hundred years had already passed, new traditions extending the life span of the dharma beyond this limit began to emerge. A 1,000-year timetable seems to have been especially popular in Sarvāstivāda circles, appearing in a wide variety of literary genres (including sūtras, VINAYA texts, and AVADĀNA tales, as well as in scholastic works) associated with this lineage. The figure of 1,000 years also appears in several MAHĀYĀNA texts, including the *Bhadrakalpika-sūtra* and a commentary on the larger *Prajñāpāramitā-sūtra* (*Perfection of Wisdom Sūtra*) preserved only in Chinese (*Da zhidu lun*).

With the passage of time even this extended number proved insufficient, however, and still longer timetables were proposed. Later Mahāyāna scriptures offer figures of 1,500 years, 2,000 years, and 2,500 years, of which the latter became especially influential in East Asia. In THERAVĀDA circles a still longer timetable of 5,000 years was adopted; this timetable has been known since at least the fifth century C.E., when it appeared in BUDDHAGHOSA's commentary on the *Aṅguttaranikāya.* The figure of 5,000 years has also become standard in Tibetan Buddhism, drawn perhaps from the *Byams pa'i mdo* (**Maitreya-sūtra*), which survives in two Tibetan translations. A slightly different figure of 5,104 years is also used by Tibetan Buddhists, calculated on the basis of an apocalyptic prophecy found in the *Kālacakra Tantra.*

According to all of these traditions, after the requisite time has elapsed Buddhism will completely disappear from this world. Only at the time of the next buddha, MAITREYA (commonly calculated at 5.6 billion, or sometimes 560 million, years from now), will the truth discovered by Śākyamuni and prior buddhas be made available again. In East Asia, however, calculations of the life span of the Buddhist religion took a different turn, based on the development of a system of three periods in the history of the dharma. According to this system, the third period in the life span of the dharma was generally described as lasting for 10,000 years—a number that implies "infinity" in East Asia. As a result, for East Asian Buddhists the life span of the dharma has been radically extended, even as this final period is described as one of decadence and decline.

The periodization of decline

Texts predicting that the Buddhist religion will last only five hundred years do not subdivide this figure into smaller periods. With the advent of longer timetables, however, Buddhists began to identify discrete stages or periods within the overall process of decline. A wide range of periodization systems can be found in Indian Buddhist texts, ranging from two 500-year periods (in the *Mahāvibhāṣā*) to a 1,000-year period followed by a 500-year period (in the *Karuṇāpuṇḍarīka-sūtra*) to five 500-year periods (in the Chinese translation of the *Candragarbha-sūtra*). Clearly there was no consensus among Indian Buddhists on the total duration of the dharma or its periodization once the initial agreement on a 500-year life span had been left behind.

Amid this great variety, however, a twofold periodization scheme came to be widely influential in Indian Mahāyāna circles. According to this system (which seems to have been formulated early in the first millennium C.E.), after the Buddha's death there would first be a period of the true dharma (*saddharma*), followed by a period of the "semblance" or "reflection" of the true dharma (*saddharma-pratirūpaka*). During the first period, the Buddhist teachings are still available in their full form, and liberation can still be attained; during the second, at least some elements of the Buddhist repertoire remain available, but conditions for spiritual practice are far less propitious. The term *saddharma-pratirūpaka* has sometimes been wrongly translated into English as "counterfeit dharma," a concept that does appear elsewhere in Buddhist literature, though not in the context of this two-period scheme. It is quite clear, however, that Buddhist writers viewed the period of the "reflected dharma" as a time when access to genuine Buddhist teachings was still available, albeit in a diluted and rapidly disappearing form.

The distinction between *saddharma* and *saddharma-pratirūpaka* appears to have been most useful as a conceptual bridge between the older system of five hundred years and longer systems, and as the expected duration of the dharma moved beyond 1,500 years to still longer figures, this twofold periodization system seems to have gone out of use. Though references to the *saddharma* and the *saddharma-pratirūpaka* continued to appear occasionally in other Mahāyāna texts (for example, in the LOTUS SŪTRA, where they play a prominent role), longer periodization schemes for the duration of the dharma that were formulated in India, including the 5,000-year system now used in the Theravāda world and the comparable 5,000-year system employed in Tibet, generally proceed without reference to these terms.

In East Asia, however, these expressions played a central role in calculations of the duration of the dharma. The concepts of *saddharma* and *saddharma-pratirūpaka* appeared in China by the third century C.E., where they were translated as *zhengfa* (correct dharma) and *xiangfa* (image [or semblance] dharma), respectively, by DHARMARAKṢA (Zhu Fahu, fl. 265–309 C.E.). Combining these neatly parallel Chinese terms with a third expression, *moshi* (final age; used to translate the Sanskrit *paścimakāla,* "latter time"), subsequent generations of Chinese thinkers constructed a three-part periodization scheme consisting of the "correct dharma" (*zhengfa*), "semblance dharma" (*xiangfa*), and "final dharma" (*mofa*). This third and final period, which is unknown in Indian sources, was understood as a period when Buddhism is still known, but human spiritual capacity is at an all-time low. In China this third and final period was commonly calculated as having begun in 552 C.E.; in Japanese sources (drawing on different translated scriptures) the more common date for the onset of *mofa* (Japanese, *mappō*) is 1052. In both cases, however, it was expected to endure for the foreseeable future, a period regularly described as lasting "10,000 years and more."

Causes of decline

On one level, the decline and eventual disappearance of the dharma is viewed in Buddhist sources as automatic, simply resulting from the principle of the transitoriness of all conditioned things. On another level, however, Buddhists have sought to identify specific factors that may contribute to—or conversely, that may inhibit—the ongoing process of decline.

As noted above, the earliest tradition points to the presence of women in the monastic order as the critical factor in Buddhism's early demise. Other explanations soon appeared, however, many of which point to internal causes—that is, the conduct of members of the Buddhist community themselves—as bringing about the disappearance of Buddhism. These include lack of respect toward various elements of the Buddhist tradition, lack of diligence in meditation practice, and carelessness in the transmission of the teachings. Other accounts point to sectarian divisions or the appearance of false teachings as the cause of decline. Finally, excessive monastic association with secular society also regularly appears as a contributing cause.

Other accounts, however, link the decline of the dharma to forces impinging on the Buddhist community from without. Modern secondary sources have often blamed declining Buddhist fortunes on PERSECUTIONS or foreign invasions, but when Buddhist scriptures point to external causes it is generally not persecution or conquest but excessive patronage of the Buddhist community that is blamed for its decadence and decline.

Responses to the idea of decline

Though most Buddhists before the modern period have shared the idea that Buddhism is in the process of decline, responses to this idea have varied widely. In Sri Lanka, for example, the steady decline of the dharma spelled out in the writings of Buddhaghosa is associated with an emphasis on the importance of preserving the written teachings, and it also harmonizes well with the widespread assumption that it is no longer possible to attain arhatship in this day and age. In Tibet, by contrast, where the dharma is also expected to last for 5,000 years, there is far greater optimism about the possibilities for practice and attainment in the present age, due in part to the assumption that tantric practice offers a short-cut to enlightenment.

In East Asia the concept of *mofa* effectively overshadowed worries about the eventual disappearance of Buddhism, leading instead to a focus on the challenge of practicing Buddhism during this prolonged and decadent final age. In China concern with *mofa* appears to have peaked in the sixth and seventh centuries C.E., when it inspired such figures as Daochuo (562–645) and Shandao (613–681) to emphasize the necessity of relying on the Buddha AMITĀBHA in this difficult time. Xinxing (540–594), founder of the SANJIE JIAO (THREE STAGES SCHOOL), by contrast, held that even greater efforts were needed in order to make progress in such a decadent age. After the seventh century, attention to *mofa* appears to have receded in China, and it is of relatively little importance (except as a rhetorical flourish used in critiques of the monastic saṅgha) in most of East Asia today.

In Japan, however, *mappō* has remained a central and governing concept, above all for members of PURE LAND SCHOOLS and the NICHIREN SCHOOL. Zen Buddhists, by contrast, have often dismissed the relevance of the idea, claiming that what could be accomplished in Śākyamuni Buddha's time is equally accessible today. Though agreeing on little else, Pure Land and Nichiren Buddhists share the idea that the age of *map-*

pō constitutes a new dispensation requiring an easier and more universal religious practice.

See also: **Dharma and Dharmas**

Bibliography

Chappell, David W. "Early Forebodings of the Death of Buddhism." *Numen* 27 (1980): 122–153.

Durt, Hubert. *Problems of Chronology and Eschatology: Four Lectures on the Essay on Buddhism by Tominaga Nakamoto (1715–1746).* Kyoto: Scuola di Studi sull'Asia Orientale, 1994.

Hubbard, Jamie. *Absolute Delusion, Perfect Buddhahood: The Rise and Fall of a Chinese Heresy.* Honolulu: University of Hawaii Press, 2001.

Nattier, Jan. *Once upon a Future Time: Studies in a Buddhist Prophecy of Decline.* Berkeley, CA: Asian Humanities Press, 1991.

Stone, Jacqueline I. "Seeking Enlightenment in the Last Age: Mappō Thought in Kamakura Buddhism." *Eastern Buddhist* 18, no. 1 (1985): 28–56 and 18, no. 2 (1985): 35–64.

JAN NATTIER

DEQING

Hanshan Deqing, or Deqing Chengyin (1546–1623), is one of the so-called Four Eminent Monks of the Ming Dynasty, whose prolific works influenced and reflected the syncretistic trends of his days in Chinese Buddhism. Of patriarchal stature later in both the Chan and PURE LAND SCHOOLS, he advocated the combined practice of "recitation of the Buddha's name" and the "investigation of the critical phrase" (*kan huatou*) for the greater part of his missionary career. Later in his life, he grew singularly devout to Pure Land, noticeably after he founded the Fayun Chan Monastery in 1617 with the intent of re-creating the paradigmatic Pure Land community of the first patriarch HUIYUAN (334–416).

Deqing's extensive learning in Confucianism and Daoism made him a vocal and celebrated figure among literati and officials. Though the imperial favor long granted to him was interrupted when he was (possibly falsely) charged with illicitly establishing monasteries, and as a result was removed from the government-appointed abbotship of the Haiyin Monastery in 1596, his monastic status was returned to him by 1615, earning him a heightened reputation. During exile, he was invited to serve as abbot at the fabled Caoxi site of the Sixth Patriarch of the Chan school, HUINENG, where he revitalized many of its purportedly "original" institutional traditions.

Deqing was well known in both his lectures and written works for his simultaneously harmonizing and polemical treatment of the Three Religions (Buddhism, Confucianism, and Daoism). His syncretistic agenda extended to the doctrinal reconciliation of most of the viable Buddhist schools of his days. An anthology of his works was compiled under the title *Hanshan dashi mengyou ji* (*Complete Works of the Great Master Hanshan [Written] while Roaming in a Dream*).

See also: **Chan School; Confucianism and Buddhism; Daoism and Buddhism; Syncretic Sects: Three Teachings**

Bibliography

Hsu, Sung-peng. *A Buddhist Leader in Ming China: The Life and Thought of Han-shan Te-ch'ing.* University Park: Pennsylvania State University Press, 1979.

Wu, Pei-yi. "Spiritual Autobiography of Te-ch'ing." In *The Unfolding of Neo-Confucianism,* ed. William de Bary and the Conference on Seventeenth-Century Chinese Thought. New York and London: Columbia University Press, 1975.

WILLIAM CHU

DESIRE

In contemporary Western discourse, the complex and culture-bound term *desire* is sometimes used as an approximate equivalent for Buddhist concepts that denote different aspects of appetition, in preference to older, and more common, renderings of Asian concepts such as the passions, lust, sensual pleasure, and craving. Terms in the latter family of words have been preferred perhaps because of their association with Western notions of asceticism and abstinence.

In religious traditions with ascetic leanings the disappointments of love are seen as signs that attachment is inherently painful. But even the trite aphorism that "love always brings pain" may be seen as only a vague reference to the set of complex problems one faces when considering the psychological and philosophical relationship between satisfaction and dissatisfaction, longing and disappointment, attachment and love soured or lost.

Attempts to understand and control the longing that leads to disappointment and pain form an important dimension of ascetic and philosophical ideals in the West among the Stoics and their Christian heirs, and in several strands of Indian religious thought. Among these strands, the principle of the primacy of desire takes a particularly important place among Buddhist traditions, where it assumes the position of a canonical creed: Desire is the root of REBIRTH and suffering. In its strongest form the doctrine may state that "the world is lead by thirst (*taṇhā*), the world is dragged around by thirst; everything is under the power of this single factor, thirst" (*Suttanipāta* 1. 7. 3 *Taṇhāsutta,* vol. 1, p. 39).

The "burden" of the SKANDHAS (AGGREGATES) is defined as craving, an unquenchable "thirst that leads to repeated birth, is tied to delight and passion, desires now this now that. This is the thirst of sense desire, the thirst for existence, the thirst for cessation" (*Suttanipāta,* 3. 1. 3 *Bhārasutta,* vol. 1, p. 26).

The juxtaposition of formulas of this kind suggests that the central concept is not "desire" in its normal, restricted sense, but "desire" in the broad sense of the drive or impulse that makes us want to achieve or possess, including the drive to live on and the wish to stop the pain of living. Although the dominant theme in Buddhist traditions has been desire as sense desire, it is often presented in complementary contraposition to displeasure (hatred, animosity, disgust), and indifferent ignorance (cognitive stupor or blindness). These three modes of thinking, feeling, and acting may be summarized in the three terms: desire, disgust, and unawareness—a triad known as the "three poisons" or the fundamental *kleśas* (defiling afflictions). These three summarize or epitomize the factors that lead to suffering and REBIRTH.

Thirst is therefore a superordinate term that includes and signifies primarily passionate desire, but that also includes the drive to hate or repel, and the wish not to know (the drive to remain unaware). It is willful desire and passionate desire and delight, but it is also the mental act of holding on to that which is wanted (*upayūpādānā cetaso*) and the complex process of claiming possession, dwelling on something, and being inclined or predisposed to something (*adhiṭṭhānābhinivesānusayā; Suttanipāta,* 3.1. 3.1 *Bhārasutta,* vol. 1, p. 26).

As the tradition shifts emphasis to either one of the fundamental *kleśas,* its understanding of desire changes in important ways. Desire as concupiscence is associated with the ascetic leanings of the monastic tradition; an emphasis on the noxious effects of disgust and displeasure is associated with the bodhisattva's compassion and toleration for the vicissitudes of SAṂSĀRA; and, more consciously in the development of the tradition, an understanding of desire as unawareness is associated with the idea that insight liberates from craving and suffering. Thus, the famous lines from the MAHĀVASTU, "desire I know your root, you arise from conceptual representation," is quoted by the MADHYAMAKA SCHOOL as proof that the royal road to vanquishing suffering and craving is seeing through the emptiness of the constructions that underlie the objects of desire.

This particular turn in the Buddhist understanding of desire is characteristic of MAHĀYĀNA and is also expressed in more radical and paradoxical statements, such as the idea that awakening is nothing but the *kleśas* themselves. Such notions may be seen as leading naturally into the doctrinal rethinking of the body and desire in the tantric tradition, where earlier ascetic concerns with the body and the passions are transformed into new ways of turning the profane human being into the sacred body of a buddha.

See also: **Path; Pratītyasamutpāda (Dependent Origination); Psychology**

Bibliography

Olson, Carl. *Indian Philosophers and Postmodern Thinkers: Dialogues on the Margins of Culture.* New York: Oxford University Press, 2002.

LUIS O. GÓMEZ

DEVADATTA

Devadatta is the paradigmatically wicked and evil personality in Buddhist tradition and literature. One scholar, Reginald Ray, calls him a "condemned saint," pointing out the somewhat contradictory description of his personality in the canonical literature. There are various major and minor legends about Devadatta's actions against the Buddha and the Buddhist community. He seems to fill the role of the scapegoat in Buddhist literature; all bad action condemned by Buddhist moral and monastic rules is heaped upon him. The three most serious acts leading to Devadatta's fall into hell, described by the Buddhist commentary

Mahāprajñāpāramitā-śāstra (Chinese, *Dazhidu lun*; English, *The Great Perfection of Wisdom Treatise*) attributed to NĀGĀRJUNA (ca. second century C.E.), are causing the first schism of the Buddhist order, wounding the Buddha, and killing a Buddhist nun named Utpalavarṇā.

Devadatta is the cousin of the Buddha and is said to have been his rival before the Buddha's enlightenment. Devadatta kills an elephant presented to the buddha-to-be and is beaten by the Buddha in an archery contest. Devadatta is also reported to have entered the Buddhist order with other members of the Śākya clan, where he soon achieved magical power that he used to gain the support of Ajātaśatru, the crown prince of Magadha, who finally, as a parallel crime to Devadatta's attacks on the Buddha, killed his father, Bimbisāra, and put himself on the throne of Magadha. Devadatta tried several times to assassinate the Buddha by releasing a drunken elephant to attack him, by throwing a rock at him from atop Vultures' Peak (Gṛdhrakūṭa), and by trying to scratch him with his poisoned fingernails.

The historical core of the legends surrounding Devadatta is his attempt to split the Buddhist order (*saṅghabheda*). He first tried to persuade the Buddha to transfer the leadership of the order to him under the pretext of introducing five stricter, more ascetic, rules for monks (*dhūtaguṇa*; ASCETIC PRACTICES), but the Buddha refused. Devadatta succeeded in attracting a group of followers, but they were eventually led back to the Buddha's order by the Buddha's main disciples, MAHĀMAUDGALYĀYANA and ŚĀRIPUTRA.

In Mahāyāna texts such as the LOTUS SŪTRA (SADDHARMAPUṆḌARĪKA-SŪTRA), however, Devadatta is rehabilitated insofar as the Buddha prophesies that Devadatta will become a Buddha in the far future, despite his misdeeds, because he has accumulated good KARMA (ACTION) in a past existence. In their descriptions of Buddhist India, the Chinese pilgrims FAXIAN (ca. 337–418), XUANZANG (ca. 600–664), and YIJING (635–713) refer to a monastic order of Devadatta's that may have existed from the lifetime of the Buddha to the early seventh century. A careful comparison of the traditions and their contradictions, however, seems to indicate that this saṅgha of Devadatta was a recent religious group in India during the first centuries C.E. As such it refers to the earlier schismatic order ascribed to Devadatta that attempted to gain legitimation as a religious group connected to, but still separated from, the Buddhist tradition.

See also: **Disciples of the Buddha**

Bibliography

Deeg, Max. "The Saṅgha of Devadatta: Fiction and History of a Heresy in the Buddhist Tradition." *Journal of the International College for Advanced Buddhist Studies* 2 (1999): 183–218.

Mukherjee, Biswadeb. *Die Überlieferung von Devadatta, dem Widersacher des Buddha, in den kanonischen Schriften.* Munich: J. Kitzinger, 1966.

Ray, Reginald A. *Buddhist Saints in India: A Study in Buddhist Values and Orientations.* New York: Oxford University Press, 1994.

MAX DEEG

DGE LUGS (GELUK)

Although the place of the scholar TSONG KHA PA (1357–1419) in the formulation of the main ideas and practices of the Dge lugs (pronounced *Geluk*) tradition is clear, his role in the creation of a separate tradition is less obvious. What is clear is that Tsong kha pa, who had received his training mostly from SA SKYA (SAKYA) scholars, stressed the importance of separate monastic institutions. It is also known that he was exceptionally charismatic and made an enormous impression on his contemporaries in Tibet, where he had a large following of powerful families and highly gifted students, including Rgyal tshab (1364–1432) and Mkhas grub (1385–1438). These institutional facts, along with the power of Tsong kha pa's ideas, explain the development of the Dge lugs as a tradition claiming to represent the apex of Tibetan Buddhism. This claim is reflected in the highly loaded name (*Dge lugs pa* means "the virtuous ones") that adherents later chose to call themselves.

The beginnings were, however, quite different. During the first decades of the fifteenth century, Tsong kha pa's followers were known as *Dga' ldan pa* (the ones from the monastery of Dga' ldan) and seem to have been just one group within a tradition in which sectarian affiliations were fluid. This situation changed during the later decades of the fifteenth century. The details of this process cannot be described here, but a few relevant events must be kept in mind: the rapid increase in the size of the three monasteries around Lhasa; the creation of other large monasteries, such as Bkra shis lhun po, founded in 1445 by Dge 'dun grub (1391–1474); the move to Lhasa by Dge 'dun grub's reincarnation, Dge 'dun rgya mtsho (1475–1542), who was recognized posthumously as the Second DALAI LAMA; and Dge 'dun rgya mtsho's construction of a large estate at 'Bras pung, the Dga' ldan pho brang, which became the seat of the Dalai Lamas. Equally relevant is the development of sectarian differences, as reflected in the acerbic critiques of Tsong kha pa by other Sa skya thinkers such as Rong ston (1367–1449) and Stag tshang (1405–d.u.).

This process was further strengthened by the political climate of the times, particularly the rise of political tensions between the groups vying for power in Tibet: the Ring pung family supported by the bka' brgyud and the Sa skya, and forces from Central Tibet supported by the Dge lugs. The next century and a half saw a veritable civil war between these two groups, which ended only in 1642 with the victory of the forces of Central Tibet supported by a Mongolian tribe, the Gushri Khan's Qoshot, and the installation of the Fifth Dalai Lama (1617–1682) as the ruler of Tibet.

The rise of the Dalai Lamas as the leaders of the Dge lugs school cannot be explored here. It is important, however, to note that originally the Dga' ldan tradition was not directed by reincarnated lamas. Its head, the Holder of the Throne of Dga' ldan, was chosen from among senior scholars, the first being Rgyal tshab and the second Mkhas grub. Gradually, however, the power of the head of the tradition was eclipsed by reincarnated lamas, who became the de facto leaders of the Dge lugs. The victory of the Fifth Dalai Lama also seems to have involved a power struggle among reincarnated lamas whose dark reflections can be seen in the myths surrounding the controversial deity, Rdo rje shugs ldan. There, the Fifth Dalai Lama's government is depicted as being responsible for the death of Gragspa Rgyal mtsham, one of the main Dge lugs lamas of that time.

The victory of the Dalai Lamas marked a decisive turn for the Dge lugs, which henceforth became the dominant tradition. Its great monasteries, particularly the three monastic seats around Lhasa, became the undisputed centers of learning in Tibet, drawing scholars from all parts of the Tibetan religious world. Even non–Dge lugs scholars would go there to receive training. The rule of the Dalai Lamas' government also ensured that the Dge lugs school could avail itself of the resources of the state. In this way, it maintained its hegemony more or less unchallenged until the invasion of Tibet by the People's Republic of China in 1950. The consequences of this tragic situation have yet to emerge, but it is likely that the Dge lugs tradition will not find it easy to maintain its dominant position.

See also: **Panchen Lama; Tibet**

Bibliography

Cabezón, José Ignacio. "The Regulations of a Monastery." In *Religions of Tibet in Practice,* ed. Donald S. Lopez, Jr. Princeton, NJ: Princeton University Press, 1997.

Dreyfus, Georges B. J. "The Shuk-den Affair: The History and Nature of a Quarrel." *Journal of the International Association of Buddhist Studies* 21, no. 2 (1998): 227–270.

Dreyfus, Georges B. J. *The Sound of Two Hands Clapping: The Education of a Tibetan Buddhist Monk.* Berkeley: University of California Press, 2002.

Ellingson, T. "Tibetan Monastic Constitutions: The bCa Yig." In *Reflections on Tibetan Culture: Essays in Memory of Turrell V. Wylie,* ed. Lawrence Epstein and Richard F. Sherburne. Lewiston, NY: Edwin Mellen Press, 1990.

Gyatso, Lobsang. *Memoirs of a Tibetan Lama,* tr. Gareth Sparham. Ithaca, NY: Snow Lion, 1998.

Tarab Tulku. *A Brief History of Tibetan Academic Degrees in Buddhist Philosophy.* Copenhagen, Denmark: Nordic Institute of Asian Studies, 2000.

GEORGES B. J. DREYFUS

DHAMMAPADA

The *Dhammapada* (*Words of the Doctrine*) is one of the most popular texts of the THERAVĀDA canon. It is embedded in the fifth part of the Suttapiṭaka as the second text of the *Khuddakanikāya* (*Group of Small Texts*). The content of the 423 mostly gnomic verses is often only very loosely connected to Buddhism. The verses are divided into twenty-six *vaggas* (sections), such as "on the world," "on the Buddha," or "on thirst." Consequently, many parallels are also found in non-Buddhist texts, such as the *Mahābhārata.* Moreover, numerous parallel collections exist in Buddhist literature, including the *Dharmapada* in Gāndhārī of the DHARMAGUPTAKA school from Central Asia, the "Patna" *Dharmapada* of the Sāmmatīya school, and the *Udānavarga* of the (Mūla)Sarvāstivāda school.

The history of these collections and their interrelation is obscured by constant contamination and mutual borrowing of verses. The linguistic features of some verses indicate that the beginnings might reach back to a very early period. Most likely material has been added over a long span of time. There is a voluminous commentary on the *Dhammapada* explaining the wording of individual verses and adding stories on the supposed occasion on which the Buddha is thought to have uttered a verse. The *Dhammapada* was the first Pāli text ever critically edited in Europe, by the Danish scholar Viggo Fausbøll (1821–1908) in 1855.

See also: **Gāndhārī, Buddhist Literature in; Pāli, Buddhist Literature in**

Bibliography

Burlingame, Eugene Watson, trans. *Buddhist Legends,* 3 vols. Cambridge, MA: Harvard University Press, 1921.

Carter, John Ross, and Paliwadana, Mahinda, trans. and eds. *The Dhammapada: A New English Translation.* New York: Oxford University Press, 1987.

Hinüber, Oskar von, and Norman, K. R., eds. *Dhammapada.* Oxford: Pāli Text Society, 1994.

Norman, K. R., trans. *The Word of the Doctrine.* Oxford: Pāli Text Society, 2000.

Osier, Jean-Pierre. *Les stances de la loi.* Paris: Garnier-Flammarion, 1997.

OSKAR VON HINÜBER

DHĀRAṆĪ

The term *dhāraṇī* refers to spells, incantations, or mnemonic codes, and literally means "to hold," "to support," or "to maintain." Originating in Vedic religion, dhāraṇī often consist of incomprehensible combinations of syllables in Sanskrit. Buddhist dhāraṇī may be long or short and are usually untranslatable. Dhāraṇī comprise a large portion of the Buddhist CANON of scripture and most of the important Mahāyāna sūtras conclude with or include sections on dhāraṇī, for example the HEART SŪTRA and the LOTUS SŪTRA (SADDHARMAPUṆḌARĪKA-SŪTRA). Various types of dhāraṇī are mentioned in Buddhist literature, for example, mantra-dhāraṇī, by which a BODHISATTVA acquires charms to allay plagues, and mnemonic dhāraṇī, by which a bodhisattva's memory and perception are enhanced to remember sūtras or salient points of doctrine. In some texts the word *dhāraṇī* also appears in compounds with the word *mantra.*

During the twentieth century Western scholars tried to assert a precise distinction between dhāraṇī and mantra by following the strict denotations of the terms. Strictly speaking, dhāraṇī should refer to memory aids to hold, support, or protect something in the mind, while mantra refer to syllabic formula, spells, and incantations. However, in Buddhist hagiography monk-thaumaturges do not make these distinctions, and in Buddhist commentarial literature, monk-scholars classify dhāraṇī into various types but always make provision for spell-type dhāraṇī. Also, dhāraṇī collections contain many spells and procedures for their intended use by laypersons.

The sounds of dhāraṇī are powerful of themselves and generate merit by merely reciting them. They also function by means of the doctrine of the "transference of merit." By chanting dhāraṇī one obtains merit for oneself by drawing upon the inexhaustible stores of merit possessed by buddhas, bodhisattvas, and gods for use in this world, usually for protection and to counteract problems understood to be the fruits of one's own karma, but this power may also be used to work other kinds of miracles. Since dhāraṇī were later popular among tantric masters, dhāraṇī texts are often, perhaps misleadingly, classified as proto-tantric.

See also: **Language, Buddhist Philosophy of; Mantra; Merit and Merit-Making**

Bibliography

Chou Yi-liang. "Tantrisim in China." *Harvard Journal of Asiatic Studies* 8 (March 1945): 241–332.

Lamotte, Étienne. "Obtenir les portes de Souvenance et de Concentration." In *Le traité de la grande vertu de sagesse de Nāgārjuna (Mahāprajñāpāramitāśāstra),* Vol. 4, pp. 1854–1869. Louvain, Belgium: Institut orientaliste, Université de Louvain, 1966–1976.

RICHARD D. MCBRIDE II

DHARMA AND DHARMAS

Sanskrit uses the term *dharma* in a variety of contexts requiring a variety of translations. *Dharma* derives from the root √*dhṛ*° (to hold, to maintain) and is related to the Latin *forma.* From its root meaning as "that which is established" comes such translations as law, duty, justice, religion, nature, and essential quality. Its oldest form, *dharman,* is found in the pre-Buddhist *Ṛgveda,* which dates to at least three thousand years ago. Thus, the Buddha must have known and used the term even before his enlightenment. At present, *dharma* is used generically for "religion," indicating religious beliefs and practices. THERAVĀDA Buddhism uses the Pāli variant *dhamma*; Gāndhārī Prākrit, as attested in the *Dharmapada* from Khotan (second century C.E., probably of DHARMAGUPTAKA affiliation) uses either *dhama* or *dharma*. Gāndhārī, the language(s) of the Gandhāran cultural area, including Gandhāra, Bactria, and Khotan, was the language used by the Buddhist schools in that area, such as Sarvāstivāda, Mahāsāṃghika, Dharmaguptaka, and so on. It is also the language from which most Chinese translations before the time of KUMĀRAJĪVA (350–409/413) derive. It is the Buddhist literature of the Gandhāra region that was introduced to China during the first century B.C.E. through at least the fourth century C.E. The Chinese phonetic transliteration attests to the word *dhama*, but in canonical literature the term is almost always translated as *fa* (Japanese *hō*; Korean *pŏp*). The common Chinese meaning of *fa* is law, plan, or method, but it is now vested with the full range of Buddhist meanings as well.

The Buddhist interpretation of dharma

The traditional meaning of *dharma* can be understood as uniform norm, universal and moral order, or natural law; it also includes one's social duty and proper conduct. The Buddha understood this universal order in terms of PRATĪTYASAMUTPĀDA (DEPENDENT ORIGINATION), an eternal law governing all elements in this conditioned world. This dharma, which was rediscovered by the Buddha, was the subject matter of his teaching; hence, *dharma* also means teaching or doctrine.

The twelve links in the chain of dependent origination are explained in the sūtras of both the Pāli *nikāyas* (divisions of the scriptural texts) and the Chinese *āgamas* ("transmission" of Buddha's word), as well as in many scholastic texts. Two links are said to be in the past: ignorance (avidyā), which produces formations (saṃskāra). The meaning of *formations* comes close to KARMA (ACTION). Eight links are in the present: consciousness (*vijñāna*), producing name-and-form (*nāmarūpa*), a quasi-person, which leads to the six sensory faculties (*ṣaḍāyatana*), which lead to contact (*sparśa*) between the six sensory faculties, their objects, and the resulting six consciousnesses. This leads to feeling or experiencing (*vedanā*), which leads to craving (*tṛṣṇā*), which brings grasping (*upādāna*), which leads to becoming or existence (*bhava*). Two links are in the future: birth (*jāti*) and old age and death (*jarāmaraṇa*). This process explains the natural law that is the dharma. The PATH toward deliverance from this process governing birth, death, and rebirth can be found in the FOUR NOBLE TRUTHS.

The word *dharma* is also used for the corpus of discourses, the scriptural texts, that expound the Buddha's teaching. The practice of dharma is found in the VINAYA, the monastic instructions. The practical application of dharma, involving the rules and regulations and their sanctions, is contained in the PRĀTIMOKṢA. Each of these rules is also called *dharma*. Dharma and vinaya together constitute the teachings of the Buddha; what in the West is called *Buddhism*, the Buddhists themselves call the *Dharmavinaya*.

The Buddha, who had realized enlightenment not far from the capital of Magadha, preached his first sermon, the *Dharmacakrapravartana-sūtra* (*Turning the Wheel of Dharma*), in Sārnāth in the Deer Park, some distance from the banks of the Ganges in Vārāṇasī or Benares. This sermon explains the path to salvation via the four noble truths. The Buddha's diagnosis sees everything as DUḤKHA (SUFFERING), which has a cause (*samudaya*), namely craving, which can be extinguished (*nirodha*) through the noble eightfold path (mārga):

1. Right view
2. Right intention
3. Right speech
4. Right action
5. Right livelihood
6. Right effort
7. Right mindfulness
8. Right concentration

In the sequence of the eightfold path one distinguishes the monastic practice of cultivating PRAJÑĀ (WISDOM), morality (*śīla*), and concentration (samādhi). Steps one and two of the path correspond to wisdom. *Prajñā* is commonly translated as wisdom, even though this is the meaning that it received in a Mahāsāṃghika milieu in northwestern India as a reaction against the Sarvāstivāda. The Sarvāstivāda sees *prajñā* as an analytical knowledge of factors, or dharmas. Steps three to five of the path correspond to morality, which purifies one's conduct. Concentration corresponds to steps seven and eight. All three practices are associated with step six. Dharma, the doctrine, may also be understood as the truth about the phenomenal world, and how to

A golden dharma wheel between two deer, representing the Buddha preaching the first sermon at the Deer Park, Sārnāth. Sculpture at the Jo khang temple, Lhasa, Tibet. © Brian Vikander/CORBIS. Reproduced by permission.

do away with its defilements. Thus, dharma also means knowledge, freeing one from phenomenal existence. The whole process of dependent origination begins with ignorance or nescience (avidyā). Dharma also means morality because it contains a code of moral conduct, and it means duty because one has a duty to comply with it while striving for NIRVĀṆA. These interpretations of dharma join the age-old understanding of the term as natural law and social duty, but this time given a Buddhist interpretation.

Dharma is also the second of the three JEWELS OR REFUGES (triratna)—Buddha, dharma, SAṄGHA. Taking this triple refuge is nowadays an essential criterion for being considered a Buddhist. The dharma is the truth and protector. The Buddha is the teacher of the dharma and becomes its personification. The disciples were advised to take the dharma as their guide after the Buddha's death. The dharma is the essence of the Buddha. Upon discovering the dharma, Śākyamuni attained buddhahood. The saṅgha, the monastic order, puts dharma into practice in daily life.

MAHĀYĀNA Buddhism explains buddhahood by distinguishing two, three, or four aspects or bodies (*kāya*). The two bodies are the law-body (dharmakāya), which is the dharma, the essence of a buddha, and the material body (*rūpakāya*), the physical aspect. The law-body is a personification of the truth of the universal law. Better known is the three-body breakdown, which includes the body of enjoyment (sambhogakāya) or the reward-body, the body that enjoys the reward for previous meritorious conduct. It is the ideal buddha-body in the realm of the real (DHARMADHĀTU). An example would be AMITĀBHA, who made forty-eight vows while he was the bodhisattva Dharmākara, and he gained buddhahood in the Western Paradise of Sukhāvatī after a long period of practice. The transformation-body (nirmāṇakāya) appears as a person during his or her earthly existence, and belongs to a specific time and place; Śākyamuni, the historical Buddha, is an example of transformation-body.

The *Tripiṭaka*, the "three baskets" of the canon that contain the teaching, are also regarded as the teaching, the dharma. The first basket, the sūtras, is traditionally divided into either nine or twelve parts, based on literary form. The *Sūtrapiṭaka* is now divided into *nikāyas* or *āgamas*. The second of the three baskets contains the vinaya. With the phase of scholastic or ABHIDHARMA Buddhism during the last centuries B.C.E. and the first centuries C.E., *abhidharma* was added as a third basket, but not all schools agreed with this classification. Even within the Sarvāstivāda there was a difference of opinion. One branch, the Vaibhāṣikas, who were active in Kashmir from the third till the middle of the seventh century C.E. and were long considered to be the orthodoxy, said that the *Abhidharmapiṭaka* was the Buddha's word. The earlier and very diverse western Sarvāstivāda groups in the Gandhāra area did not agree and considered only the sūtras to be definitive truth. These groups were called SAUTRĀNTIKA, as opposed to Vaibhāṣika, and they did not have an *Abhidharmapiṭaka,* only *abhidharma* works.

Dharmas, or factors

The factors or constituents of the dharma, the teachings, are also called dharma(s). Such dharmas are psychophysical factors, which flow according to the natural process of dependent origination. Dharma theory explains how the human being is a flux or continuum (*santāna*), without any permanent factor or soul (ātman). Existing reality is called the "realm of the real" (*dharmadhātu*). Buddhism concerns itself with the phenomenal, by which existence is recognized. This phenomenal world is in constant change. Buddhism sees all phenomena as formations (saṃskāra), formative forces or volitions that are formed (*saṃskṛta*) by causes and conditions. Formation has an active and a passive meaning. Factors (dharmas) are formed, but sometimes at least one unformed or uncompounded factor, NIRVĀṆA, is recognized. The Sarvāstivāda, which had a tremendous influence in northwestern India and in East Asia, distinguish three unformed or uncompounded (*asaṃskṛta*) factors. Everything that is an obvious object of consciousness is a factor. A person, just like the whole of existence, is a flux, a series of impermanent factors, but sentient life has a sentient element: mind (manas) or consciousness. A human being is a flow of material and immaterial factors set in motion by karma and controlled by the law of dependent origination. Dharma theory explains how existence functions in the context of a human continuum. It explains its ultimate factors and it contains the possibility of stopping this continuum.

Originally Buddhism used a threefold classification of factors: (1) five SKANDHA (AGGREGATE), (2) twelve bases or sense fields (*āyatana*), and (3) eighteen elements (*dhātu*). During the last centuries B.C.E., the dharma theory developed considerably in *abhidharma* Buddhism. The most influential dharma theory was that of the diverse Sarvāstivāda schools. Other schools either adopted most of the Sarvāstivāda dharma theory (as did the Mahīśāsaka), introduced minor changes (Dharmaguptaka), were influenced by it (Buddhaghosa in fifth-century Theravāda), reacted to it (Mahāsāṃghika, Madhyamaka), or built on it (Vijñānavāda). The Vaibhāṣikas in Kashmir inherited a fivefold classification from their Gandhāran brethren, who, after about 200 C.E., came to be called Sautrāntikas. Even among the western Sarvāstivādins there was no general agreement about the number of factors.

Nevertheless, the Sarvāstivāda branch that was most influential in Central and East Asia, in the Gandhāran part of northwestern India, and in Kashmir after the demise of the Vaibhāṣikas, was the branch that ultimately based its classification on such texts as the *Abhidharmahṛdaya* (*Heart of Scholasticism*) and on the *Aṣṭagrantha* (*Eight Compositions*), both probably from the first century B.C.E. This branch used a fivefold classification as found in the *Pañcavastuka* (*Five Things*), which was translated in China during the second century C.E. and advocated a Buddhist version of the five elements or modes that were popular at the time. The *Aṣṭagrantha* was revised and renamed *Jñānaprasthāna* (*Course of Knowledge*) at the end of the second century C.E. and became the central text or corpus (*śarīra*) for the Vaibhāṣikas. The *Abhidharmahṛdaya* was commented on in the *Miśrakābhidharmahṛdaya* (*Sundry Heart of Scholasticism*), and this text was the basis of Vasubandhu's ABHIDHARMAKOŚABHĀṢYA (*Storehouse of Abhidharma*), which dates to the early fifth century. The influence of the *Abhidharmakośabhāṣya,* or *Kośa,* was and is considerable. When a Tibetan text was written to instruct Khubilai's Mongol crown prince in Buddhism late in the thirteenth century, the manual was based on the *Kośa.* However, the old classification in five aggregates was never forgotten. When Skandhila, a Gandhāran living in "orthodox" Kashmir during the fifth century, composed his *Abhidharmāvatāra* (*Introduction to Scholasticism*), he classified the factors on the basis of the five aggregates or skandhas, but added the three unformed factors.

The original threefold classification of dharmas

The earliest division of the factors was into five skandha, twelve bases or sense fields (*āyatana*), and eighteen elements (*dhātu*). The five aggregates (*skandha* means literally "bundles") divide sentient life into five psychophysical elements:

1. Form or matter (*rūpa*)
2. Feeling (*vedanā*)
3. Notions or perceptions (*saṃjñā*)
4. Formations (saṃskāra), also called volitions or formative forces
5. Consciousness (*vijñāna*)

Aggregates two through five may be called *name* (*nāma*). *Name-and-form* is a synonym for the five aggregates, which are fundamentally impermanent. They have nothing one might consider to be a "self," and they bring suffering, being inevitably subject to change. The first five DISCIPLES OF THE BUDDHA became ARHATS (saints) upon understanding the teaching of the egolessness of the aggregates. Matter has mass; it obstructs. It incorporates the four great elements: earth (hardness), water (moisture), fire (heat), air (motion). Feelings may be physical or mental, and are classified as either pleasant, unpleasant, or neutral. Notions are concepts, which are formed; one may have the concepts of color and form, for example, when seeing a green leaf. Formations are the mind in action, in which volition (*cetanā*) is central. Consciousness is the cognitive function.

The twelve bases (*āyatana*) refer to the process of cognition. *Āyatana* means "a place of entry," namely the six sense organs or faculties (*indriya*), the six internal bases. Alternatively, *āyatana* can refer to that which enters, namely the six objects (*viṣaya*) of cognition, the six external bases. The twelve *āyatana* are: the six bases of eye, ear, nose, tongue, body, and mind; and the six objects of color or form, sound, smell, taste, palpables, and mental or immaterial objects (the factors).

The eighteen elements are distinguished in relation to the flow of life in the three realms of existence: the realm of sensuality (*kāmadhatu*), the realm of subtle matter (*rūpadhātu*), and the immaterial realm (*ārūpadhātu*). The first twelve constitute the above twelve bases (*āyatana*), to which are added the six corresponding consciousnesses: visual consciousness through to mental consciousness.

Sarvāstivāda dharma theory

Many Sarvāstivāda texts elaborate on dharma theory. Besides the texts already mentioned, one may add the *Dharmaskandha* (*Aggregate of Factors*) and the *Prakaraṇa* (*Treatise*). Existence is described in four categories of formed factors, totaling seventy-two factors, and one category of three unformed or unconditioned factors, thus giving seventy-five dharmas in all. The five categories are:

1. Matter (*rūpa*)
2. Thought (*citta*)
3. Thought-concomitants or mentals (*caitta*) associated with thought, arising in association with pure consciousness or mind
4. Formations dissociated from thought (*cittaviprayukta*)
5. Unformed factors (*asaṃskṛta*)

Form or matter contains eleven factors: the first five faculties and their objects, plus unmanifested form (*avijñaptirūpa*). When mental action is made manifest in physical or vocal action, it is described by the term *intimation* (*vijñapti*). When it is not externalized or made manifest, the material aspect is nonintimated, and thus unmanifested. One might understand *avijñaptirūpa* as the moral character of a person or a force of habit. It is a potential form, preserved in the physical body. Not all branches of the Sarvāstivāda school distinguished this material factor, but it appears in the *Śāriputrābhidharma,* which is said to be of Dharmaguptaka affiliation.

The second category—thought—is just the one factor of mind, or pure consciousness. In the classification of the eighteen elements, it includes the six consciousnesses, plus the mind element. It is the consciousness aggregate and also the internal mind faculty. The third category is the forty-six thought-concomitants, which are factors associated with thought. Not all adherents of the Sarvāstivāda school agreed with the existence of these factors. For example, Dharmatrāta (second century C.E.), a Dārṣṭāntika (probably a Sautrāntika who followed the long vinaya), says that these factors are only subdivisions of volition, and he denies their separate existence. Buddhadeva (first century C.E.) says that they are none other than thought itself. But the *Kośa* enumerates forty-six thought-concomitants.

Ten mental factors accompany every thought; these are the factors "of large extent" (*mahābhūmika*), that is, basic or general. They are:

1. Feeling (*vedanā*)
2. Notion (*saṃjñā*)

3. Volition (*cetanā*)
4. Contact (*sparśa*)
5. Attention (*manaskāra*)
6. DESIRE (*chanda*)
7. Inclination or aspiration (*adhimokṣa*)
8. MINDFULNESS (*smṛti*)
9. Concentration (samādhi)
10. Comprehension (*mati,* prajñā)

Ten factors accompany every wholesome thought; these are the wholesome factors of large extent (*kuśalamahābhūmika*). They are:

1. FAITH (śraddhā)
2. Diligence (*apramāda*)
3. Repose (*praśrabdhi*)
4. Equanimity (*upekṣa*)
5. Shame, with reference to oneself (*hrī*)
6. Aversion, with reference to other people's bad actions (*apatrāpya*)
7. Noncovetousness (*alobha*)
8. Nonmalevolence (*adveṣa*)
9. Nonviolence (*ahiṃsā*)
10. Strenuousness (*vīrya*)

Six factors accompany every defiled thought; these are the defiled factors of large extent (*kleśamahābhūmika*). They are:

1. Confusion (*moha*)
2. Negligence (*apramāda*)
3. Mental dullness (*kausīdya*)
4. Nonbelief (*āśraddhya*)
5. Sloth (*styāna*)
6. Frivolity (*auddhatya*)

Two factors accompany every unwholesome thought; these are called unwholesome factors of large extent (*akuśalamahābhūmika*). They are:

1. Shamelessness (*āhrīkya*)
2. Lack of modesty (*anapatrāpya*)

Ten defiled factors of limited extent (*upakleśaparīttabhūmika*), which may occur at various times, are:

1. Anger (*krodha*)
2. Hypocrisy (*mrakṣa*)
3. Stinginess (*mātsarya*)
4. Envy (*īrṣyā*)
5. Ill-motivated rivalry (*pradāsa*)
6. The causing of harm (*vihiṃsā*)
7. Enmity (*upanāha*)
8. Deceit (māyā)
9. Trickery (*śāṭhya*)
10. Arrogance (*mada*)

Eight undetermined (*aniyata*) factors have variant moral implications and may accompany either a wholesome, unwholesome, or indeterminate thought. They are:

1. Initial thought (*vitarka*)
2. Discursive thought (*vicāra*)
3. Drowsiness (*middha*)
4. Remorse (*kaukṛtya*)
5. Greed (*rāga*)
6. Hatred (*pratigha*)
7. Pride (*māna*)
8. DOUBT (*vicikitsā*) about the teaching

Fourteen factors are neither material nor mental and are dissociated from thought (*cittaviprayukta*). They are:

1. Acquisition (*prāpti*), a force that controls the collection of elements in an individual life-continuum, which links an acquired object with its owner
2. Dispossession (*aprāpti*), which separates an acquired object from its owner
3. Homogeneity (*sabhāgatā*)
4. Nonperception (*āsaṃjñika*), a force that leads one to the attainment of nonperception
5. Attainment of nonperception (*asaṃjñisamāpatti*), which is produced by the effort to enter trance after having stopped perceptions

6. Attainment of cessation (of notions and feeling, *nirodhasamāpatti*), the highest state of trance
7. Life force (*jīvitendriya*)
8. Birth or origination (*jāti*)
9. Duration (*sthiti*)
10. Old age or decay (*jarā*)
11. Impermanence or extinction (*anityatā*)

The last three factors are the characteristics of a conditioned factor:

12. Force imparting meaning to letters (*vyañjanakāya*)
13. Force imparting meaning to words (*nāmakāya*)
14. Force imparting meaning to phrases (*pādakāya*)

Finally, there are three unformed factors. They are:

1. Space (*ākāśa*)
2. Extinction through discernment (*pratisaṃkhyānirodha*), namely through comprehension of the truths and separation from impure factors
3. Extinction not through discernment (*apratisaṃkhyānirodha*), owing to a lack of a productive cause

Some Sautrāntikas asserted that these factors are not real. They count forty-three factors. All factors exist in all three time periods of past, present, future. This belief explains the term *Sarvāstivāda,* which means "the teaching that all exists." The Mahīśāsakas, who split from the Sarvāstivāda, supported the Sarvāstivāda in this thesis.

A general classification of all factors could be: (1) impure (*sāsrava*) factors, chiefly influenced by ignorance, and (2) pure (*anāsrava*) factors, tending toward appeasement under the influence of wisdom.

Theravāda *dhamma* theory

The Theravāda *dhamma* theory is outlined in the school's *Abhidhammapiṭaka,* primarily in the *Dhammasaṅgaṇi* (*Enumeration of Dhammas*) and in the *Dhātukathā* (*Discussion of Elements*). The ethical classification of *dhammas* as wholesome, unwholesome, and neutral (*avyākata*) is central. The last category has four divisions:

1. Resultant consciousness or thinking (*vipākacitta*)
2. Functional consciousness (*kriyācitta*)
3. Matter
4. The unconditioned factor *nibbāna* (nirvāṇa)

Some factors are not found in the traditional threefold classification. For example, matter contains the faculty "femininity" (*itthindriya*). The final Theravāda *dhamma* theory is found in manuals dating from the fifth century on. Knowing that they belong to the Sthaviravāda group, it is not surprising that there is Sarvāstivāda (Sautrāntika) influence. Buddhadatta, a fifth-century contemporary of Skandhila, makes a fourfold classification in his *Abhidhammāvatāra* (*Introduction to Scholasticism*): form, thought, mentals, *nibbāna.* BUDDHAGHOSA, in the fifth century, defines factors as "those which maintain their own specific nature," while Buddhadatta says factors possess specific and general characteristics. Theravāda typically uses a classification of 170 factors and four categories, but there are other classifications, such as eighty-one conditioned factors (matter 28, thought 1, mental 52) and one unconditioned factor, nibbāna.

Analysis of dharmas in the Madhyamaka school

The MAHĀSĀṂGHIKA SCHOOL, rival of the Sarvāstivāda ever since the first schism, multiplied the number of unconditioned factors, even adding dependent origination itself to the list. One Mahāsāṃghika subschool, the Prajñaptivāda, taught that conditioned factors are only denominations (*prajñapti*) and the twelve bases are the products of the aggregates, the only real entities. Another subschool, the Lokottaravāda, held that only the unconditioned factors are real. The ideas of the Mahāyāna MADHYAMAKA SCHOOL may have started within the Mahāsāṃghika milieu in northwestern India, in opposition to the dominant Sarvāstivāda school. The Madhyamaka school itself was organized in southern India (Āndhra) around 200 C.E., at the same time that the Vaibhāṣikas were organizing in Kashmir to the north. The Madhyamaka school rejected the reality of any factor and claimed that all conceptual thinking was empty (*śūnya*). The real is devoid of thought-construction (*vikalpa*) and can be realized only through nondual wisdom (prajñā). NĀGĀRJUNA (ca. second century C.E.) interpreted the law of dependent origination to mean relativity or ŚŪNYATĀ (EMPTINESS). According to Nāgārjuna, nothing is real when taken separately. He was not interested in delineating the number of factors or in constructing any classification schemata, but he was interested in the inherent nature of factors (*dharmatā*). Existence is only valid from a conventional (*saṃvṛti*) point of view, but it is not valid when viewed from the standpoint of absolute (*paramārtha*) truth.

Vijñānavāda dharma theory

The Vijñānavāda or YOGĀCĀRA SCHOOL agrees with Madhyamaka that all is empty, but posits that consciousness is real. Vijñānavāda postulates a kind of subconscious, called the *storehouse consciousness* (ĀLAYAVIJÑĀNA). Phenomenal existence is the illusory projection of that storehouse consciousness. Every factor stored in the *ālayavijñāna* is a seed (*bīja*), a Sautrāntika term. One should do away with tainted seeds and develop untainted seeds. The school also distinguishes a consciousness called mind (manas), which clings to the idea of self. In East Asia this school is called the FAXIANG SCHOOL (Sanskrit, *dharmākāra*) or "characteristics of dharmas." *Dharma* here refers to the hundred factors this school distinguishes, elaborating on the Sarvāstivāda classification. What became the East Asian variety of Yogācāra was first taught in Nālandā by Dharmapāla (439–507) and taken to China by XUANZANG in 645. It claims that the specific nature of a factor is distinct from its specific mode. Their one hundred factors are:

1. Eight thought factors, namely the eight consciousnesses
2. Fifty-one associated mental factors (5 universal, 5 limited, 11 wholesome, 6 defiled, 20 secondary defilements, and 4 indeterminate)
3. Eleven matter factors
4. Twenty-four dissociated factors
5. Six unconditioned factors

Most important is the eighth consciousness, the storehouse consciousness, which stores the seeds of all potential manifestations.

See also: **Āgama/Nikāya; Anātman/Ātman (No-Self/Self); Buddhahood and Buddha Bodies; Consciousness, Theories of; Cosmology; Psychology; Sarvāstivāda and Mūlasarvāstivāda**

Bibliography

Chatterjee, Ashok Kumar. *The Yogācāra Idealism,* 2nd edition, 2nd reprint. Delhi: Motilal Banarsidass, 1999.

Frauwallner, Erich. *Studies in Abhidharma Literature and the Origins of Buddhist Philosophical Systems,* tr. Sophie F. Kidd. New York: State University of New York Press, 1995.

Hirakawa, Akira. "The Meaning of 'Dharma' and 'Abhidharma'." In *Indianisme et Bouddhisme: Mélanges offerts a Mgr. Étienne Lamotte.* Louvain, Belgium: Institut Orientaliste de Louvain, Peeters Press, 1980.

Lamotte, Étienne. *History of Indian Buddhism: From the Origins to the Śaka Era,* tr. Sara Webb-Boin. Louvain, Belgium: Peeters Press, 1988.

La Vallée Poussin, Louis de. *Abhidharmakośabhāṣyam,* 4 vols., tr. Leo M. Pruden. Berkeley, CA: Asian Humanities Press, 1991.

Masuda, Jiryo. "Origin and Doctrines of Early Indian Buddhist Schools." *Asia Major* 2 (1925): 1–78.

Mizuno, Kogen. *Essentials of Buddhism: Basic Terminology and Concepts of Buddhist Philosophy and Practice.* Tokyo: Kosei, 1996.

Ñyāṇatiloka Mahathera. *Guide through the Abhidhamma Piṭaka.* Kandy, Sri Lanka: Buddhist Publication Society, 1983.

Potter, Karl H., ed. *Encyclopedia of Indian Philosophies,* Vol. 7: *Abhidharma Buddhism to 150 A.D.* Delhi: Motilal Banarsidass, 1998.

Potter, Karl H., ed. *Encyclopedia of Indian Philosophies,* Vol. 8: *Buddhist Philosophy from 100 to 350 A.D.* Delhi: Motilal Banarsidass, 1999.

Rhys Davids, Caroline A. F. *A Buddhist Manual of Psychological Ethics: Dhammasaṅgaṇi,* 3rd edition. Oxford: Pāli Text Society, 1997.

Skorupski, Tadeusz. "Buddhist Dharma and Dharmas." In *The Encyclopedia of Religion,* ed. Mircea Eliade. New York: Macmillan, 1987.

Stcherbatsky, Theodore. *The Central Conception of Buddhism and the Meaning of the Word 'Dharma,'* 2nd Indian reprint. Delhi: Motilal Banarsidass, 1974.

Takakusu Junjiro. *The Essentials of Buddhist Philosophy,* 3rd edition, 3rd reprint. Delhi: Motilal Banarsidass, 1998.

CHARLES WILLEMEN

DHARMADHĀTU

Dharmadhātu, composed of dharma (law, principle, or reality) and *dhātu* (realm or element), is translated literally as "realm of reality." It generally refers to all things that can be perceived with the sense faculties. It also refers to the physical universe, of which time, space, and all living beings are constituent elements. In the HUAYAN SCHOOL of Buddhism, *dharmadhātu* is identified with the "Thusness" (reality) of the Buddha. The fourfold *dharmadhātu* outlined in the Huayan school consists of (1) the world of phenomena, (2) the world of principle, (3) the world of principle and phenomena united in harmony, and (4) the world of all phenomena interwoven or identified in perfect harmony.

See also: **Huayan Jing**

CHI-CHIANG HUANG

DHARMAGUPTAKA

The term *Dharmaguptaka* means "those affiliated with the teacher Dharmagupta." The Dharmaguptaka mainstream Indian Buddhist school, a subschool of the Sthavira branch, is attested by inscriptions in the northwestern region of the Indian subcontinent. The Dharmaguptakas possessed their own monastic disciplinary code (VINAYA) and shared many doctrinal views attributed to the Vibhajyavādins.

See also: **Mainstream Buddhist Schools**

COLLETT COX

DHARMAKĪRTI

The Indian thinker Dharmakīrti (ca. 600–670 C.E.), whose biographical details remain obscure, responded to the works of his predecessor DIGNĀGA (ca. 480–540 C.E.) to establish the basic theories of Buddhist LOGIC. In doing so, Dharmakīrti sought to explain how we can obtain completely certain, indubitable knowledge.

The *Pramāṇavārttika* (*Commentary on Reliable Knowledge*), Dharmakīrti's best-known work, ostensibly comments on Dignāga's *Pramāṇasamuccaya* (*Compendium on Reliable Knowledge*), but Dharmakīrti actually revises Dignāga's theories in order to close gaps that prevent certainty. Concerning perception, Dignāga appeared to allow that a raw sense-datum—the uninterpreted phenomenal content of a perception—could never be erroneous, even in the case of perceptual illusion. Seeing that this renders all perception fallible, Dharmakīrti maintains that a reliable perception must involve a strict and regular causal relation between the perception and its object. This emphasis on causality reflects Dharmakīrti's innovative application of *telic efficacy* (*arthakriyā*) as the criterion for reality and, by extension, for all reliable knowledge. In brief, only causally efficient entities are real, and if knowledge is reliable, it must direct one to an object that has the causal capacity to accomplish one's goal. An important corollary is the claim that, to be causally efficient, a real thing can exist for only an instant.

Another crucial innovation comes in response to Dignāga's theory of inference, according to which the inductive process of determining the relation between evidence (such as smoke) and what it indicates (such as fire) is apparently fallible. Seeking certainty, Dharmakīrti argues for a "relation in essence" between evidence and what it proves. Inference thereby becomes immune to doubt, but at the cost of an inflexible appeal to definitions (smoke, for example, is by definition that which comes from fire).

Dharmakīrti's epistemic and logical theories were eventually adopted by most Indian Buddhist thinkers, and among Tibetan Buddhists, the *Pramāṇavārttika* is still the subject of extensive study and debate. In particular, the monastic curriculum of the DGE LUGS (GELUK) school places considerable emphasis on Dharmakīrti's Buddhist logic.

See also: **Yogācāra School**

Bibliography

Dreyfus, Georges B. *Recognizing Reality: Dharmakīrti's Philosophy and Its Tibetan Interpretations.* Albany: State University of New York Press, 1997.

Tillemans, Tom J. F. *Scripture, Logic, Language: Essays on Dharmakīrti and His Tibetan Successors.* Boston: Wisdom, 1999.

JOHN DUNNE

DHARMARAKṢA

Dharmarakṣa (Chinese, Zhu Fahu; ca. 233–310 C.E.) was one of the most prolific translators of Indian Buddhist texts into Chinese. According to traditional biographies, Dharmarakṣa was a descendant of the Yuezhi, a Central Asian people whose precise ethnicity and native language are still debated. He was born at DUNHUANG, a military colony and mercantile hub in the westernmost reach of the Chinese empire. Although his family is said to have lived at Dunhuang for generations, Dharmarakṣa is the first mention of

Buddhism in this region. He became a novice monk at an early age, studying with an Indian teacher while developing his skills in Chinese. His translation career began in 266 and continued for more than forty years, resulting in the translation of over 150 Buddhist texts into Chinese. He was assisted in his endeavors by a considerable number of Indian, Central Asian, and Chinese collaborators—some monks, some laymen—the most prominent of whom was Nie Chengyuan, a Chinese *upāsaka* with whom Dharmarakṣa worked in the northern Chinese city of Chang'an.

Dharmarakṣa translated a number of mainstream Buddhist works, but his most notable contributions are his translations of Mahāyāna texts, including such large and well-known sūtras as the LOTUS SŪTRA (SADDHARMAPUṆḌARĪKA-SŪTRA), the *Guangzan jing* (*Pañcaviṃśatisāhasrikāprajñāpāramitā-sūtra*; *Perfection of Wisdom in 25,000 Lines*), and the *Xianjie jing* (*Bhadrakalpika-sūtra*; *Scripture on the Fortunate Aeon*). Dharmarakṣa died at the age of seventy-eight amidst the social and political chaos that marked northern China at the beginning of the fourth century. His translations laid the foundation for the textual exegesis and doctrinal developments of the fourth century, epitomized in the work of the monk DAO'AN (312–385). In the early fifth century, many of Dharmarakṣa's translations were superseded by the retranslations of the Kuchean monk KUMĀRAJĪVA (350–409/413).

See also: **China; Mahāyāna; Prajñāpāramitā Literature**

Bibliography

Boucher, Daniel. "Gāndhārī and the Early Chinese Buddhist Translations Reconsidered: The Case of the Saddharmapuṇḍarīkasūtra." *Journal of the American Oriental Society* 118.4 (1998): 471–506.

Tsukamoto Zenryū. *A History of Early Chinese Buddhism. From Its Introduction to the Death of Hui-yüan*, Vol. 1, tr. Leon Hurvitz. Tokyo: Kodansha International Ltd., 1985.

DANIEL BOUCHER

DHYĀNA (TRANCE STATE)

Dhyāna (Pāli, *jhāna*) is a trance state experienced through particular meditative practices. According to traditional Buddhist thought, there are eight trance states. These are divided into two categories: The first four dhyānas are part of the realm of form, and the final four are part of the formless realm. The division between the form and formless dhyānas is not absolute; the higher formless dhyānas (trance states five through eight) are themselves considered a division of the fourth dhyāna belonging to the realm of form. Thus, the eight dhyānas form a continuous hierarchical structure.

The practice of mental concentration (*śamatha*; Pāli, *samatha*) is the condition for the meditative experience of these trance states. As mental concentration increases, the practitioner gains entry to increasingly higher levels of absorption. This progression is a process of stilling or calming mental states and achieving the joy of tranquility and peace. In the fourth dhyāna all sensations are extinguished, resulting in a state of equanimity. The attainment of the fourth dhyāna gives access to the four formless dhyānas, the states of infinite space, infinite consciousness, nothingness, and neither-perception-nor-nonperception. The fourth dhyāna, characterized by equanimity and one-pointedness, also gives rise to a set of supernatural powers, including the power to know one's former lifetimes.

The experience of trance states is not viewed as an end in itself, but rather a means to the final goal of NIRVĀṆA. The levels of dhyāna are categorized as conditioned and impermanent and thus ultimately unsatisfactory. The experience of absorptions are temporary; they last only for as long as the mind remains concentrated. When concentration ends, the unwholesome qualities of the mind return and the blissful feelings experienced in the first four dhyānas cease. For these reasons, the experience of trance states is to be joined to the cultivation of PRAJÑĀ (WISDOM; Pāli, *paññā*). The mental transformation accomplished through the experience of the dhyānas prepares the mind for training in wisdom and the specific practices of the cultivation of insight, *vipaśyanā* (Pāli, *vipassanā*). Concentration can also be pursued together with insight as each absorption is experienced and then transcended when it is analyzed as impermanent.

There is a parallel between dhyāna as interiorized meditative states and as cosmological heavenly realms. The first four dhyānas correspond to the seventeen HEAVENS of the realm of form, resting above the lower heavens of the realms of desire. The four higher dhyānas correspond to the four levels of the formless heavens, the uppermost realm of the cosmos. Dhyānas can therefore be experienced for temporary periods through meditative concentration or for longer durations through REBIRTH into one of the form or formless heavenly realms.

Dhyāna is also defined in relation to a ninth realm higher than either the meditative or cosmological levels of absorptions. This state of the cessation of perception and sensation is attained by those who join perfected concentration and insight.

See also: **Cosmology; Meditation; Psychology; Vipassanā (Sanskrit, Vipaśyanā)**

Bibliography

Buddhaghosa, Bhadantācariya. *The Path of Purification,* tr. Bhikkhu Nanamoli. Berkeley, CA: Shambhala, 1976.

Nyanaponika, Thera. *The Heart of Buddhist Meditation.* New York: Samuel Weiser, 1975.

Payutto, Phra Prayudh. *Buddhadhamma: Natural Laws and Values for Life,* tr. Grant A. Olson. Albany: State University of New York Press, 1995.

KAREN DERRIS

DIAMOND SŪTRA

Judged by almost any conventional standard the text known as the *Diamond Sūtra* (Sanskrit, *Vajracchedikā-prajñāpāramitā-sūtra*) was, and remained, an important MAHĀYĀNA sūtra across wide geographic boundaries and over a very long time. The date of its composition in Sanskrit is uncertain. Arguments have been made for the second and fourth centuries of the common era. It was first translated into Chinese at the very beginning of the fifth century, but both VASUBANDHU and ASAṄGA, two learned Indian monks who probably lived in the fourth or fifth centuries, had already written authoritative commentaries on it, and this would seem to require that it was already an important text in their day, and had therefore been in circulation for some time. Whereas for many Mahāyāna sūtras only very recent eighteenth- and nineteenth-century Sanskrit manuscripts survive, for the *Diamond Sūtra* we have at least three much earlier manuscripts that date from the fifth to the seventh centuries and come from widely separated places. The existence of such early manuscript remains may also testify to the text's importance, and certainly reveals, when compared with later versions and translations, how the text developed and changed its shape over time.

Once translated into Chinese in the fifth century, the *Diamond Sūtra* was then translated again at least five more times by some of the brightest luminaries of Chinese Buddhist scholasticism, and perhaps eighty or more commentaries were written on it in Chinese. The *Diamond Sūtra,* and several Indian commentaries on it, were also translated into Tibetan, and further translations, paraphrases, and developments of it survive, in whole or in part, in a wide range of Central Asian languages—Khotanese, Sogdian, Uigur, and so on. The *Diamond Sūtra* was, obviously, the focus everywhere of an enormous amount of attention in learned Buddhist circles.

The *Diamond Sūtra,* however, was not of interest only to the learned. In the practice oriented and at least rhetorically anti-intellectual schools of Chinese Chan, for example, it was also assigned an important place. In the carefully constructed religious biography of the famous, if largely legendary, sixth patriarch HUINENG, the *Diamond Sūtra* appears as the pivot of his religious life: Huineng was supposed to have been an illiterate woodcutter when he heard it being recited and it transformed his life. In fact, the recitation and copying of the *Diamond Sūtra* was in itself in many places, and at many times, a widespread religious practice undertaken for a variety of less elevated, but no less crucial purposes. Tales of the "miraculous" power of the recitation and copying of the *Diamond Sūtra* are preserved not just in Chinese and Japanese collections of "miracle tales," but also in Tibetan and Mongolian. This clearly was a text that worked on many levels, and for a variety of different kinds of Buddhists.

The *Diamond Sūtra* is, of course, not its real name, but an abbreviation based largely on early attempts to translate its title into English. In Sanskrit it is called the *Vajracchedikā-prajñāpāramitā.* Bearing in mind that *vajra* is an almost untranslatable Sanskrit term referring to a kind of divine and dreadful weapon, like a discus or thunderbolt, and only by secondary association applied to the hard, cutting properties of a diamond, the title might be translated as "The Perfection of Wisdom [text] that Cuts like a Thunderbolt." This title would seem to suggest several things. First the *Vajracchedikā* is classified by its title as a perfection of wisdom text, and this claim has, by and large, been accepted by modern scholarship, even though its relationship to this larger group of texts remains problematic. Almost from the beginnings of modern BUDDHIST STUDIES it was described as a succinct summary of the perfection of wisdom, but the *Vajracchedikā* makes no mention of several seemingly definitional perfection of wisdom ideas like ŚŪNYATĀ (EMPTINESS) and UPĀYA (skill in means).

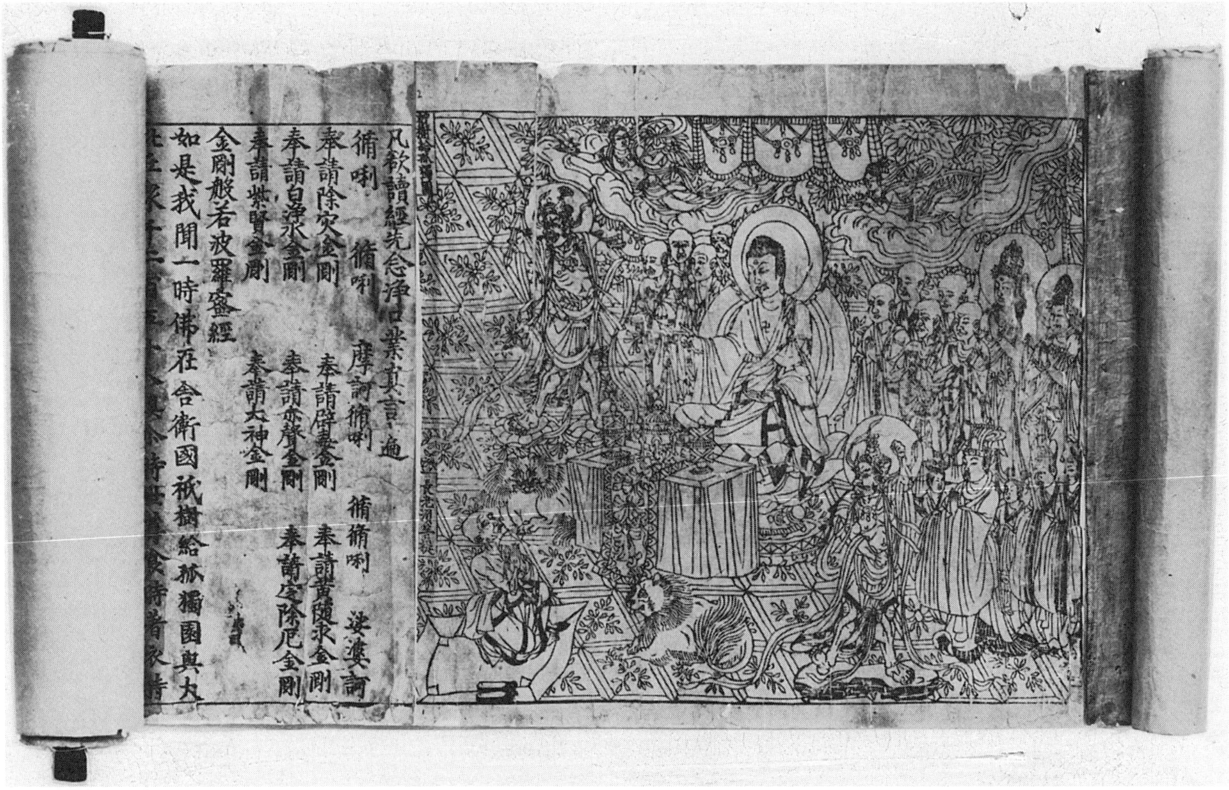

A scroll printed in 868 C.E., found at Dunhuang, containing the Chinese text of the *Diamond Sūtra*. The Granger Collection, New York. Reproduced by permission.

This is puzzling. Equally puzzling, and hence the enormous number of commentaries written on it, is what the text means. But the second thing the original title might suggest is that any search for meaning in this text may be fundamentally misdirected. According to its original title, the "wisdom" it refers to does not explain or describe. It cuts or shatters. This in turn might suggest that a religious text of this sort was not meant to convey ideas or doctrine, but was rather designed to affect, rearrange, or shatter established ways of seeing oneself, the world, and conventional religious practices. At one point in the text the monk Subhūti is described as bursting into tears of amazement and wonder at what the Buddha was reported to have said. This response, a rather unmonkish reaction, is apparently the anticipated response to the "message" of the text, and it is virtually certain that large numbers of those who have tried to more systematically analyze it have also been reduced to tears.

See also: **Chan School; Prajñāpāramitā Literature**

Bibliography

Conze, Edward, trans. *Buddhist Wisdom Books.* London: Allen and Unwin, 1958.

Müller, F. Max, ed. *The Sacred Books of the East,* Vol. 49: Buddhist Mahāyāna Texts, Part 2: xii–xix; 110–144. London: Oxford University Press, 1894.

Schopen, Gregory. "The Manuscript of the Vajracchedikā Found at Gilgit: An Annotated Transcription and Translation." In *Studies in the Literature of the Great Vehicle,* ed. Luis O. Gómez and Jonathan A. Silk. Ann Arbor: University of Michigan Press, 1989.

GREGORY SCHOPEN

DIET

The correct obtaining, preparation, and consumption of food have been always been important to the SAṄGHA. The Buddha's own religious career prior to his enlightenment, when at one point he subsisted on a single grain of rice per day, showed that liberation is not possible through extreme fasting. But equally to be avoided is attachment to the sensual pleasure of eating. Thus, food should be seen as necessary to sustain the body but as fundamentally repulsive, somewhat like unpleasant-tasting medicine. There are meditations that focus on the repulsiveness of food, and food obtained on the begging round is often deliberately mixed together to form an unappetizing paste.

The saṅgha was intended to be dependent on the LAITY for its food, and the VINAYA stresses that monks and nuns were to eat only what was given. They were not to produce their own food, nor even to consume food that they found. The daily begging round ensured that the saṅgha was always made aware of its responsibilities to lay donors, as well as offering ample opportunities for laypeople to make merit from DĀNA (GIVING).

The vinaya and later East Asian monastic regulations also have numerous rules about how food is to be consumed in the monastery. According to the vinaya, monks and nuns should not eat solid food after noon, although in East Asia monks do take supplementary meals.

Despite the first precept against killing, a keen awareness of compassion toward animals and insects, and the consistent denigration of occupations such as butcher, hunter, or fisherman, a vegetarian diet was not required of the early saṅgha in India. In southern Asia and Tibet, meat given to monks is permitted, unless the animal was killed specifically for them. Mahāyāna sūtras such as the NIRVĀṆA SŪTRA and the LAṄKĀVATĀRA-SŪTRA spoke out strongly against meat eating. These texts, in combination with the precepts of the apocryphal FANWANG JING (BRAHMĀ'S NET SŪTRA), decisively affected the monastic diet in China and Korea. Monks and nuns in those countries are strictly vegetarian. In Japan monks are extremely unlikely to be vegetarian, although there is still a tradition of Buddhist vegetarian cuisine based on Chinese recipes. In addition to meat, Chinese and Korean Buddhists also avoid the "five pungent herbs" (garlic, onions, ginger, Chinese chives, and leeks), which are thought to overstimulate the emotions and interfere with meditation.

In Chinese and Korean monasteries, everyday meals consist mostly of rice and vegetables. On festive days glutinous rice or noodles may be served in place of white rice, and the monks may receive other treats of cakes or candies. Vegetarian feasts sponsored by lay donors also feature more variety of dishes. In Japan certain temples have become associated with special types of food served on festive days. At Sanpōji in Kyoto, for example, once a year daikon (white radishes) are boiled in large vats and given to parishioners. It is said that they prevent paralysis. Steamed rice with citrus peel, a favorite dish of NICHIREN (1222–1282), is also served.

A young monk prays before his meal in Mandalay, Myanmar (Burma). © Owen Franken/Corbis. Reproduced by permission.

See also: **Ascetic Practices; Merit and Merit-Making**

Bibliography

Buswell, Robert E. *The Zen Monastic Experience: Buddhist Practice in Contemporary Korea.* Princeton, NJ: Princeton University Press, 1992.

Chapple, Christopher Key. *Nonviolence to Animals, Earth, and Self in Asian Traditions.* Albany: State University of New York Press, 1993.

Mather, Richard. "The Bonze's Begging Bowl: Eating Practices in Buddhist Monasteries in Medieval India and China." *Journal of the American Oriental Society* 101, no. 4 (1981): 417–424.

Ruegg, David Seyfort. "Ahiṃsā and Vegetarianism in the History of Buddhism." In *Buddhist Studies in Honour of Walpola Rahula.* London: Gordon Fraser, 1980.

Welch, Holmes. *The Practice of Chinese Buddhism.* Cambridge, MA: Harvard University Press, 1967.

JAMES A. BENN

DIGNĀGA

An Indian proponent of the YOGĀCĀRA SCHOOL about whose life little is known, Dignāga (ca. 480–540 C.E.) is renowned as the initial formulator of Buddhist LOGIC. In his most important work, *Pramāṇasamuccaya* (*Compendium on Reliable Knowledge*), Dignāga examines perception, language, and inferential reasoning. Dignāga maintains that perception is a preconceptual bare apprehension of real things, and that perception is therefore devoid of all conceptual activity. Language, in contrast, involves concepts, but concepts are actually fictions created through a process of "exclusion" or *apoha.* In other words, the concept *blue* appears to correspond to some real sameness that all blue things share (their *blueness*), but in fact, that sameness is a fiction constructed through excluding everything that is irrelevant. This position allows Dignāga to deny that concepts (such as *self*) correspond directly to real things in the world.

Dignāga's views on perception and language were highly influential for subsequent Buddhists, but his greatest influence lay in his analysis of inferential reasoning. Unlike previous Indian thinkers, Dignāga keenly distinguished between the reasoning used in debate and the underlying rational structure of all inferences. Focusing on the relation between inferential evidence (such as smoke) and that which it is meant to prove (such as fire), he presented a systematic taxonomy of the cases where that relation holds or fails. This analysis supports his famed formulation of the three aspects of all valid evidence.

Although an important innovator in the history of Buddhist philosophy, Dignāga was soon superseded by DHARMAKĪRTI (ca. 600–670 C.E.), whose presentation of Buddhist logic was adopted by subsequent Buddhist thinkers in India and Tibet.

Bibliography

Hattori, Masaaki. *Dignāga, On Perception.* Cambridge, MA: Harvard University Press, 1968.

Hayes, Richard P. *Dignāga on the Interpretation of Signs.* Dordrecht, Netherlands: Kluwer, 1988.

JOHN DUNNE

DĪPAṂKARA

The earliest lists of past buddhas consist only of six previous buddhas plus Śākyamuni, but in subsequent centuries the list was expanded to twenty-five, beginning with a buddha known as Dīpaṃkara (Lightmaker). According to relatively late Pāli works, such as the *Buddhavaṃsa* and the *Nidānakathā,* it was in the presence of Dīpaṃkara that the future Śākyamuni first made his vow to become a buddha.

Dīpaṃkara's complete absence from the Pāli sutta literature makes it virtually certain that traditions concerning this buddha did not gain general currency until several centuries after Śākyamuni Buddha's death. The distribution of artistic images of Dīpaṃkara—which abound in Gandhāra, but are virtually absent from other sites—points to the likelihood that the story of Dīpaṃkara was first formulated on the far fringes of northwest India. It may also be significant that the story of Dīpaṃkara related in the MAHĀVASTU (i.193ff)—a work ascribed to the Lokottaravāda branch of the MAHĀSĀṂGHIKA SCHOOL, known to have flourished in what is today Afghanistan—is rich in narrative detail, while the account found in such THERAVĀDA sources as the *Buddhavaṃsa* (and based on it, the *Nidānakathā*) is more formulaic. Dīpaṃkara himself eventually became the subject of JĀTAKA tales relating his previous lives, preserved in medieval Theravāda texts (Derris) and in early Chinese translations (Chavannes, story no. 73).

The story of Dīpaṃkara's prediction of the future Śākyamuni's eventual attainment of buddhahood came to play an especially important role in MAHĀYĀNA circles, where aspiring BODHISATTVAS interpreted the story as an indication that they too must be reborn during the time of a living buddha and receive a prediction (*vyākaraṇa*) in his presence.

See also: **Buddha(s); Buddha Images; India, Northwest**

Bibliography

Chavannes, Edouard, trans. *Cinq cents contes et apologues extraits du tripiṭaka chinois,* 4 vols. Paris: Ernest Leroux, 1910.

Derris, Karen. "Virtue and Relationship in the Theravādin Biographies." Ph.D. diss. Harvard University, 2000.

Soper, Alexander. "Dīpaṃkara." In *Literary Evidence for Early Buddhist Art in China.* Ascona, Switzerland: Artibus Asiae, 1959.

JAN NATTIER

DISCIPLES OF THE BUDDHA

The disciples of the Buddha form a diverse category of human, nonhuman, and divine figures. This entry will restrict its discussion to those presented by the Indian Buddhist tradition as personal disciples of the historical Buddha. Even so, the discussion will be selective.

Traditionally, discipleship is classified in two categories: (1) specialists, who relinquish most of their social privileges and duties and become full-time practitioners of the Buddha's teachings, who observe a number of regulatory rules (VINAYA), and who are usually described as MONKS and NUNS (bhikṣu and *bhikṣuṇī*); and (2) people who express faith in the Buddha, offer material support, and receive simplified teachings that emphasize generosity, and who are described as laymen and laywomen (*upāsaka* and *upāsikā*). These two categories of discipleship were open only to human beings (there is a special question in the monastic ordination intended to exclude disguised serpent deities). Nevertheless, the interaction of the Buddha with DIVINITIES is a prominent feature of his biography and an important factor in the development of the community of disciples. Key disciples of all kinds also appear as coprotagonists in stories of former lives of the Buddha (JĀTAKA), thus extending their relationship into previous lives and the distant past.

The Buddha is depicted recruiting followers from all classes of society: brahmins, kṣatriyas (warrior class), and members of the lower classes, including untouchables. He eventually admitted women as personal disciples, and he freely interacted with and taught divine beings, including Śakra (see "The Questions of Sakka" in Davids and Davids, pp. 299–321). The Buddha also interacted with practitioners of other religious traditions, in some cases acquiring them as disciples, in others failing to convert them to his following. The Buddha is also depicted in some accounts of the period after his enlightenment as visiting the heavens of Buddhist COSMOLOGY and teaching there, most famously to his mother (indicating the significance of the child–mother relationship in Buddhist culture). In most of the countries of South and Southeast Asia there are also local traditions that the Buddha magically visited, often leaving an indelible footprint as evidence of his presence, and thus initiating the transmission of Buddhism in each region through a tradition beginning with personal discipleship. Throughout history and into the modern period, many monastic traditions regard themselves as the continuing manifestation of a lineage that springs from one of the personal disciples of the Buddha.

Our knowledge of the Buddha's disciples is primarily derived from scriptural sources, and the growth of the initial body of disciples is documented in the first part of an important VINAYA text of the THERAVĀDA tradition called the *Mahāvagga*. This text includes a fascinating account of the first of the Buddha's personal disciples. In the early weeks of his post-enlightened life, the Buddha is portrayed passing the time seated beneath various trees in the vicinity of BODH GAYĀ and gradually interacting with other beings, interactions through which his following is initiated and grows. Curiously, these interactions are not always positive or fruitful, and the text indicates that the creation of a community of disciples was not a foregone conclusion.

Significantly, the Buddha is first approached by what is described as an arrogant brahmin. They exchange greetings and in response to a question the Buddha explains the nature of true spiritual excellence. No outcome to the encounter is recorded, perhaps reflecting the ambiguous relationship that existed between the Buddhist community and the highest-ranking class in brahmanical society. The second encounter occurs during a great storm, when the king of the serpent deities, Mucalinda, reverentially winds his body around the Buddha to protect him. When the storm is over the serpent takes the form of a young man and worships the Buddha, but the Buddha does not teach him. The third encounter involves two passing merchants, Tapussa and Bhallika, who offer the Buddha food. The Buddha accepts this offering, and the merchants take refuge in him and are thus recognized as his first disciples. Significantly, they receive no teaching from him and continue with their trade. It is clear from both textual and archaeological sources that the early Buddhist community benefited enormously from recruitment among the merchant class and was spread geographically along the major trade routes of ancient India and beyond.

At this point in the account the Buddha undergoes a crisis of indecision. Reflecting on the difficulty with which he himself had achieved BODHI (AWAKENING), he thinks that it would be impossible to teach other people to do the same. He is, however, importuned by a deity called Sahampati, who convinces him through argument that some people "with little dust in their eyes" would be capable of responding to the advice the Buddha could offer, and thus the Buddha decides to teach. He begins a process of reflection on who might be suited to become a disciple. He considers previous teachers, who turn out to be dead, and finally fixes on his fellow ascetics with whom he had lived immediately before his enlightenment. He sets out for Benares, where they still reside, and en route meets with an Ājīvaka practitioner called Upaka, who recognizes a spiritual quality in the Buddha, but given the opportunity to follow him merely says "Maybe!" and walks on. The Buddha acquires full-time disciples only after residing for some time with his five former fellow ascetics. Ājñātakauṇḍinya (Pāli, Aññātakoṇḍañña), Vāṣpa (Vappa), Bhadrika (Bhaddiya), Mahānāman (Mahānāma), and Aśvajit (Assaji) are eventually won over by the Buddha's presence and by his verbal teachings and, in the order just given, become his first five ordained disciples.

This development is followed by a quick expansion that begins with the conversion of a local playboy called Yaśa (Yasa), who becomes a monk. Soon Yaśa's parents become lay followers, suggesting a pattern of family discipleship that was doubtless followed in other families where a child entered the order. Subsequently, fifty-four friends and associates of Yaśa became bhikṣus.

At this point the Buddha requires that his full-time disciples, now numbered at sixty, wander at will around the region and share his teachings. The result of this is an expansion of the monastic community that stretches the Buddha's capacity to function as personal teacher for every recruit. Soon the Buddha allows existing disciples to ordain new recruits, and thus the circle of personal discipleship of the Buddha was understood to have been limited by geographical distance. There is no indication of how long it took to go from zero disciples to the formation of a self-sustaining community, though it must have taken many months or even years.

Although the community expanded outside the immediate control of the Buddha, he nevertheless continued to acquire personal disciples throughout his life, and the records describe the Buddha's personal interactions with numerous individuals. Foremost among these are ĀNANDA, ŚĀRIPUTRA (Sāriputta), and MAHĀMAUDGALYĀYANA (Moggallāna). Ānanda was a cousin of the Buddha and became his close companion or attendant for around thirty years. Ānanda's familiarity with the Buddha's life meant that at the first Buddhist council after the Buddha's death, Ānanda was asked to recite all the discourses that he had ever heard the Buddha give. Thus, most sūtras, or discourses, begin with the phrase "*evaṃ mayā śrutaṃ*" (Thus have I heard). The monk UPĀLI, a former barber who shaved all the ordinands' heads, performed a similar role for the vinaya. Ānanda did not become an ARHAT during the Buddha's life and is therefore occasionally portrayed as having behaved less than perfectly. He is also depicted as the advocate of female ordination into the monastic order, a development that the Buddha apparently says will reduce the community's duration, and it is through Ānanda's encouragement that the Buddha finally ordains his aunt and foster mother MAHĀPRAJĀPATĪ GAUTAMĪ (Mahapajāpatī). It was Mahāprajāpatī who raised Siddhārtha, the Buddha-to-be, after the early death of his mother, but she was not content with the role of lay disciple. She therefore became the first *bhikṣunī,* and was recognized by the Buddha as the female disciple of longest standing. Other female disciples also achieved personal renown, including Dhammadinna, whom the Buddha described as foremost in preaching.

The Buddha's most eminent disciples, however, were Śāriputra and Mahāmaudgalyāyana. These two were childhood friends who left home to pursue the religious life, at first together, but eventually separating on the agreement that the first to find the true way would seek out the other. After meeting Assaji and being converted by him, Śāriputra found Mahāmaudgalyāyana and together they were ordained by the Buddha, who appointed them his chief disciples. Mahāmaudgalyāyana was renowned for his meditative attainments, Śāriputra for his wisdom and analytical abilities.

The Buddha also identified those possessed of greatest meditative attainments and wisdom among his nuns, Kṣemā (Khemā) and Utpalavarṇā (Uppalavaṇṇā), and his laywomen, Kubjottarā (Khujjuttarā) and Uttarā (Uttarā). Among his male lay followers he identified the foremost in generosity as ANĀTHAPIṆḌADA (Anāthapiṇḍika) and the chief of dharma teachers as Citra (Citta) (Woodward, pp. 79–80). Many other disciples are singled out by the Buddha for other forms of personal excellence (Woodward, pp. 16–25), and moving samples of poetry composed by these and other of his disciples, both male and female, are recorded in two Pāli texts called the *Theragāthā* and *Therīgāthā* (Norman). The monk MAHĀKĀŚYAPA (Mahākassapa) was recognized as the foremost practitioner of asceticism; he later took control of funeral arrangements immediately after the Buddha's death. Other important disciples include UPAGUPTA, who was especially revered among the Buddhists of Southeast Asia and became the focus of cult and ritual there, and Anāthapiṇḍada (Anāthapiṇḍika), whose name means "feeder of the destitute." Anāthapiṇḍada, a banker and perhaps the most famous lay disciple,

LEFT: The bodhisattva Samantabhadra and his śakti (female partner/creative power), from a nineteenth-century Tibetan *thang ka*. © *Archivo Iconografico, S.A./Corbis. Reproduced by permission.*

BELOW: A Buddhist temple in the Thai style, the Wat Buddhapadīpa, at Wimbledon, London. © *Tim Page/Corbis. Reproduced by permission.*

TOP: Pusading Monastery in the Wutai Mountains of Shanxi province, China. © *Dean Conger/Corbis. Reproduced by permission.*

BOTTOM: Entrances to cave sanctuaries excavated from the early sixth through the eighth century C.E. in the cliffs on the riverbank at Longmen. This site contains over two thousand such caves. © *Robert D. Fiala, Concordia University, Seward, Nebraska. Reproduced by permission.*

TOP: The recumbent Buddha entering parinirvāṇa, from an eighteenth-century Tibetan *thang ka. The Art Archive/Musée Guimet Paris/Dagli Orti (A). Reproduced by permission.*

BOTTOM: Prince Siddhārtha encounters a corpse on an outing beyond the palace walls, a decisive episode in the life of the Buddha. Chinese, 1818, hand-colored woodblock print. *The British Library. Reproduced by permission.*

Hell, as represented by the Pure Land school. This scene was copied from a thirteenth-century original in the Seishū Raigō temple. Japanese, eighteenth century, ink and color on paper scroll. *Copyright The British Museum. Reproduced by permission.*

A carved panel depicting an unidentified bodhisattva, from a portable shrine. Kashmir, eighth century C.E., painted wood and ivory. *Copyright The British Museum. Reproduced by permission.*

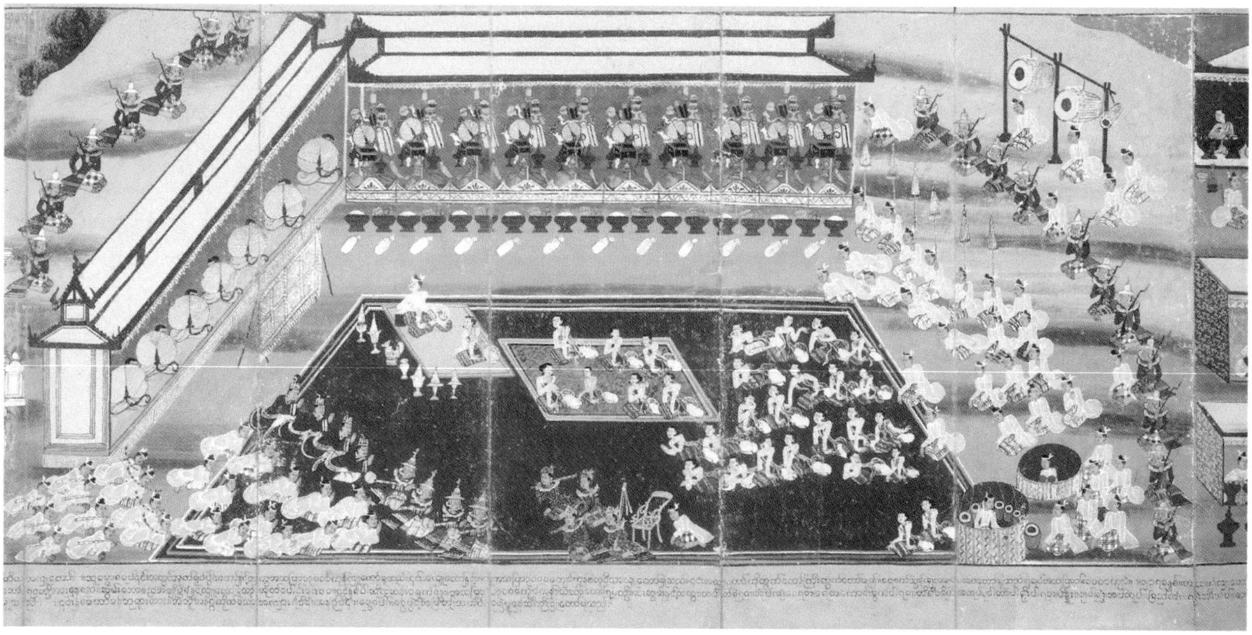

TOP: King Mindon of Burma (r. 1853–1878) making donations to the Buddhist monks. This image is from an illustrated book the king had made to record his donations in detail, including their cost, and to testify to his merit. Burmese, mid-nineteenth century, painting on paper. *The British Library. Reproduced by permission.*

BOTTOM: Jātaka tales of the Buddha's last ten births, adapted from traditional Thai manuscript illustrations by a Thai artist for a British patron, Captain Low. Thai, ca. 1820, painting on paper. *The British Library. Reproduced by permission.*

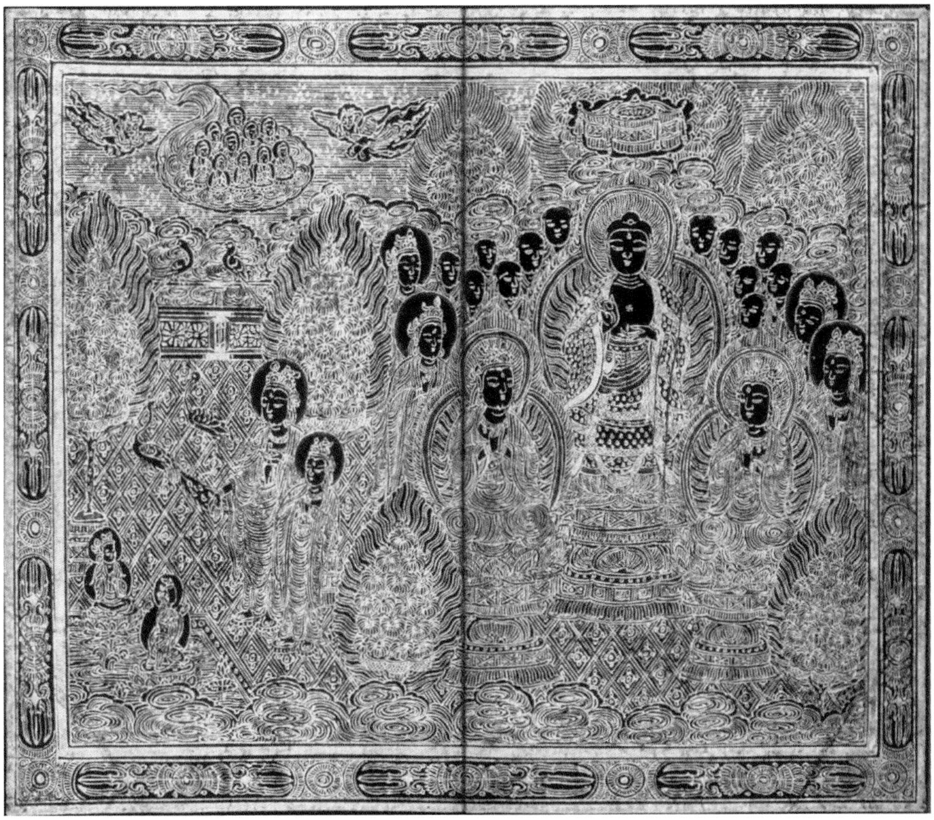

Top: Illustration from the *Amitābha Sūtra.* The image depicts Śākyamuni preaching to bodhisattvas, monks, divinities, and other buddhas. The calligraphy, of Kumārajīva's Chinese translation of the text, was done by a Korean monk for the sake of his deceased mother. Korean, Koryŏ dynasty (918–1392), 1341, gold and silver paint on blue paper. *Copyright The British Museum. Reproduced by permission.*

Bottom: A realistic sculpture of a lay Buddhist, probably a prosperous merchant. Japanese, ca. 1700, lacquered and painted wood. *Copyright The British Museum. Reproduced by permission.*

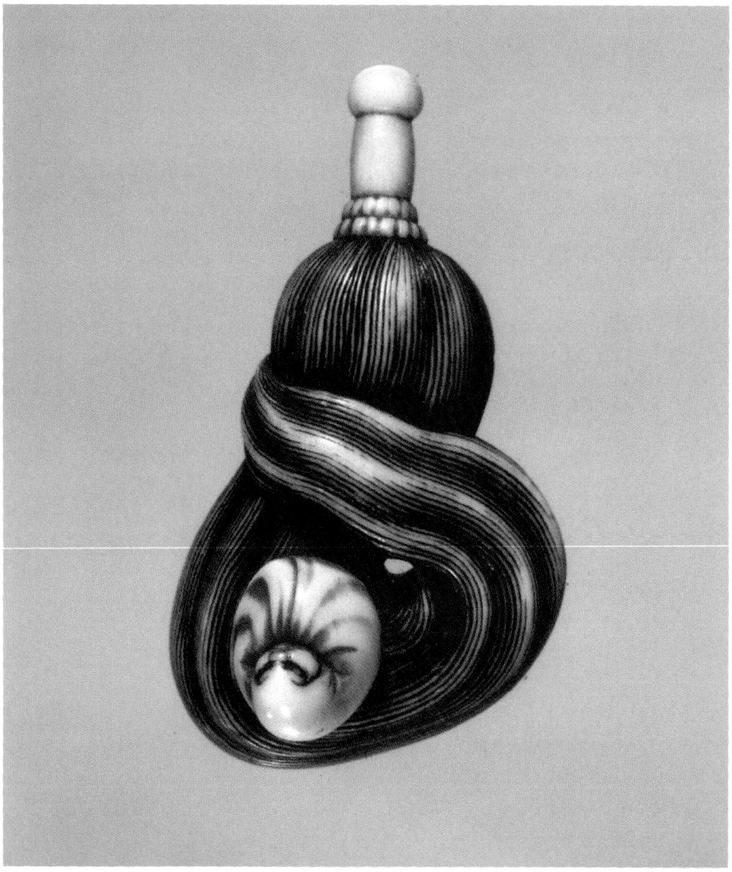

Left: Netsuke, the devices used to attach pouches or other objects to the belt of a Japanese robe, were often elaborately carved. This one represents Bodhidharma, semilegendary first patriarch of the Chan school of Buddhism, during his nine-year-long seated meditation. He is shown sitting—his legs having fallen off—on a flyswatter. Japanese, nineteenth century, carved ivory. *Copyright The British Museum. Reproduced by permission.*

Below: The Chinese recension of the *Lotus Sūtra* (*Saddharmapuṇḍarīka-sūtra*). The borders are ornamented with gold and silver foil, and the entire scroll is sprinkled with gold dust. Japanese, Kamakura period (1185–1333), ca. 1240–1280, block printing on paper scroll. *The British Library. Reproduced by permission.*

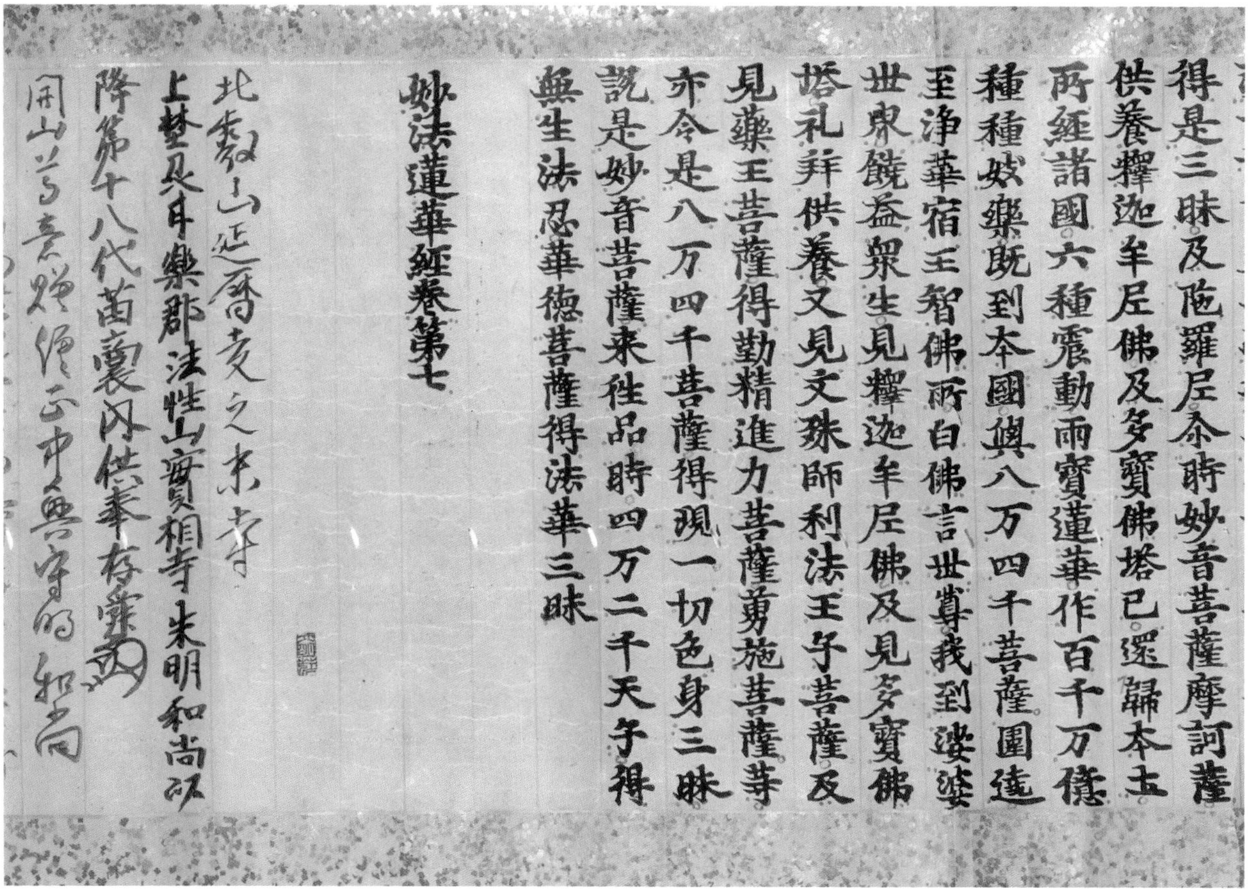

bought for the Buddha at fabulous expense the famous Jetavana (Jeta's Grove) at Śrāvastī, where he had a monastery built. Texts tell of Anāthapiṇḍada's deathbed grief when he realized that the Buddha had reserved his higher teaching exclusively for his monastic followers (Horner, pp. 309ff.).

Also important was the turncoat monk and disciple, DEVADATTA, first cousin of the Buddha, who is remembered for his conspiracies to murder the Buddha and split the SAṄGHA. These are regarded as the most heinous crimes a monk can commit in relation to the saṅgha. Devadatta also attempted unsuccessfully to introduce extra requirements into the vinaya, including vegetarianism and four of the permitted asceticisms, which included wearing only rag robes and eating only begged food. Bizarrely, the Chinese pilgrim FAXIAN reported in the early fifth century C.E. that in the Buddhist homeland Devadatta still had a significant following who worshiped not Śākyamuni but the three buddhas previous to him.

Also important were the Buddha's royal disciples: Prasenajit (Pasenadi), king of Kośala, who is credited with commissioning the first Buddha image; Bimbisāra, king of Magadha; and Bimbisāra's son Ajātaśatru (Ajātasattu), who after initially conspiring with Devadatta, became a devout disciple of the Buddha (see *Sāmaññaphala-sutta* in Davids, 1899, pp. 65ff.).

In later layers of Buddhist canonical literature a number of these disciples continue to appear as protagonists. Of particular importance is the promotion to chief interlocutor in the PRAJÑĀPĀRAMITĀ LITERATURE of Subhūti, a monk and disciple noted in the *āgamas* and *nikāyas* as chief of those who dwell in the forest and, presumably thereby, also the one most worthy of offerings. Other MAHĀYĀNA sūtras and VAJRAYĀNA tantras present a host of new and presumably fictive disciples.

See also: **Buddha, Life of the; Councils, Buddhist**

Bibliography

Davids, Thomas W. Rhys, trans. *Dialogues of the Buddha,* Part 1. London: Luzac, 1899.

Davids, Thomas W. Rhys, and Davids, Caroline A. F. Rhys, trans. *Dialogues of the Buddha,* Part 2. London: Luzac, 1910.

Davids, Thomas W. Rhys, and Oldenberg, Hermann. *Vinaya Texts,* Part 1. Oxford: Sacred Books of the East, 1885.

Horner, Isaline B., trans. *The Middle Length Sayings* III. London: Pāli Text Society, 1977.

Norman, Kenneth R., trans. *The Elders' Verses* I and II. London: Pāli Text Society, 1969 and 1971.

Nyānaponika Thera, and Hecker, Hellmuth. *Great Disciples of the Buddha: Their Lives, Their Works, Their Legacy.* Boston: Wisdom, 1997.

Ray, Reginald. *Buddhist Saints in India: A Study in Buddhist Values and Orientations.* New York: Oxford University Press, 1994.

Woodward, F. L., trans. *Gradual Sayings.* London: Pāli Text Society, 1932.

ANDREW SKILTON

DIVINITIES

From its very origins, Buddhism has recognized a wide range of divinities (*devas,* a term frequently translated as "gods"), while taking pains to emphasize that the Buddha himself is not divine, but human (*Aṅguttaranikāya,* 2.37–9). The various divinities are powerful superhuman beings who influence the world in manifold ways. Although many of these divinities have Vedic (Hindu) origins, in the early Buddhist tradition they are not considered immortal, but rather are trapped in SAṂSĀRA and thus, like all SENTIENT BEINGS, are subject to the law of KARMA (ACTION) and therefore DEATH and REBIRTH.

In the early texts of the Pāli canon, divinities inhabit several different realms. In the lower realm of desire (*kāmadhātu*), above the human realm, live the various deities and spirits, who frequently do battle with a group of jealous and mischievous deities, the *asuras* (similar to the Greek Titans). The various divinities include the four divine kings; the thirty-three gods residing in the *trāyastriṃśa* heaven, divinities incorporated from the Vedas and presided over by Śakra (INDRA); MĀRA and Yama, the gods of illusion and death; and BODHISATTVAS in their penultimate lives, including, currently, MAITREYA (Pāli, Metteya). Above the sense realm, in the realm of pure form (*rūpadhātu*), abide the pure divinities, most significantly the Great Brahmā and his ministers, and, at the very top, the *anāgāmins* (nonreturners), who live out their penultimate existence before enlightenment in this realm.

One of the most important divinities is Māra, the god of death, lust, greed, false views, delusion, and illusion. Māra is a common presence in early Buddhist texts, distracting the Buddha and, after his enlightenment, questioning his very status as an enlightened being. Although Māra is "defeated" by the Buddha, he continues to cause trouble, and he figures prominently in later texts, iconography, and local traditions throughout the Buddhist world.

Especially active in the world are the nāgas, yakṣas, *piśācas,* and *gandharvas,* divinities generally thought to have been incorporated into Buddhism from non-Vedic, indigenous traditions. Nāgas (female, *nāginī*) are snakelike beings who in early texts typically live at the base of trees and are associated with both chaos and fertility. Likewise, YAKṢAS (Pāli, *yakkha*) are indigenous Indian tree spirits, wild, demonic, and sexually prolific beings who live in solitary places and are hostile toward people, particularly monks and nuns, whose meditation they disturb by making loud noises. Frequently, both nāgas and yakṣas are converted to Buddhism and "tamed," becoming active, positive forces in the world and protectors of Buddhism; for instance, when the Buddha-to-be was meditating just prior to his enlightenment, it was a nāga who sheltered him from the elements.

The range of divinities in the Buddhist world is staggering when local traditions are taken into account. In Burma (Myanmar), such divinities are known collectively as *nats,* in Thailand as *phi,* in Sri Lanka as *yakas;* they are extremely important in popular Buddhist practice and frequently associated with kingship, since all serve as guardians of Buddhism. In Burma, for instance, there are thirty-seven official *nats* (although in practice there are many more), regarded as invisible, magical personal forces who inhabit trees, and in most villages there are small shrines in trees thought to be inhabited. These shrines, brightly decorated with colored cloth and tinsel, are tended and worshiped to ensure that the *nats* protect the village and provide prosperity, fertility, and other benefits. In Thailand, the various forms of *phi* include *phi dong,* which are the guardian spirits of the forest, the *phi puya tayai* (ancestral spirits), and the truly horrific *phi mae mai* (widow ghosts), who kill human men in their search for husbands.

In Sri Lanka, Hindu gods are frequently worshiped by Buddhists. Thus the god Kataragama, a local variant of the god Skanda, is typically regarded as a bodhisattva. Kataragama is extremely popular, to the point that the divinity's main shrine, in the southeastern corner of the island, is probably the most popular religious site in the entire country. Buddhists (as well as Hindus, Muslims, and Christians) go to Kataragama for special requests—protection, fertility, financial success, even vengeance—and repay his favors by performing a variety of penances, including body piercing, walking on hot coals, and hanging from hooks.

As the MAHĀYĀNA schools developed in both India and in East Asia, so did the pantheon of divine figures, and with this expansion the very conception of divinity also expanded. Bodhisattvas such as Mañjuśrī, Avalokiteśvara, and Maitreya become extremely important, using their skillful means actively to spread wisdom and to save beings in peril. Likewise, as the conception of the Buddha and buddhahood became more complex, the so-called celestial Buddhas (*pañcatathāgātas*) emerge, a group of five manifestations of the Buddha's divine qualities. In the PURE LAND SCHOOLS, the cosmos is imagined as an infinite collection of world systems, each of which is a Buddha field where a fully enlightened being resides; these become divinities, with whom especially accomplished devotees can continuously interact.

Avalokiteśvara in particular becomes extremely popular in East Asia, where he is known as Guanyin in China, Kannon in Japan, and Kwanŭm in Korea; in the case of Guanyin, the divinity is manifested as a female figure. The female divinity Tārā—perhaps originally a local divinity herself—also emerges as a divine savior who protects and nurtures her devotees; she is popular throughout the Mahāyāna and VAJRAYĀNA world, particularly in Nepal and Tibet. The perfection of wisdom texts (*prajñāpāramitā* sūtras) become personified in the figure of Prajñāpāramitā, wisdom incarnate, the divine "mother" of all enlightened beings.

With the rise of the Vajrayāna, the divine pantheon expands to a seemingly limitless degree, with a vast range of buddha families, bodhisattvas, goddesses, yogins, and all manner of fierce divinities. MAṆḌALAS frequently depict these buddha families and their associated divinities. Meditations and rituals focused on such divinities are too numerous to mention and are frequently intended to bring the divinity to life. In the practice of deity yoga, for instance, the meditator can bring the divinity to life in him or herself by realizing the inseparability of the self and the divinity.

In sum, the Buddhist understanding of divinities must be seen as fluid and expansive. Divine beings multiply markedly as the tradition develops. New divinities are introduced at both the local and pan-Buddhist level, and the characteristics of the various divinities also shift, with new qualities—both abstract (passive) and concrete (active)—constantly being introduced. The Buddha himself took on increasingly complex divine characteristics as the tradition developed in India and beyond, which, in turn, frequently became manifest as individual divinities, a process that continues into the present day. Consistent with the early literature that lays out Buddhism's basic cosmological view, though, in a relative sense, such beings are very real and very active in the world; in an absolute sense, however, they are ultimately only creations of our minds, useful as symbols and metaphors for the enlightenment process, but, like everything else, empty.

See also: **Cosmology; Folk Religion: An Overview; Ghosts and Spirits; Kūkai; Local Divinities and Buddhism; Viṣṇu**

Bibliography

Asher, Frederick M. *The Art of Eastern India, 300–800 A.D.* Minneapolis: University of Minnesota Press, 1980.

Bhattacharyya, Benoytosh. *The Indian Buddhist Iconography.* Calcutta: Firm K. L. Mukhopadhyay, 1959.

Getty, Alice. *The Gods of Northern Buddhism: Their History and Iconography.* New York: Dover, 1988.

Kinnard, Jacob N. *Imaging Wisdom: Seeing and Knowing in the Art of Indian Buddhism.* Richmond, UK: Curzon Press, 1999.

JACOB N. KINNARD

DIVYĀVADĀNA

The fourth-century C.E. Sanskrit *Divyāvadāna* (*Heavenly Exploits*) contains thirty-eight biographical narratives that celebrate the lives of paradigmatic figures in Buddhist history, authenticate local dharma traditions, and dramatize the importance of moral discipline, KARMA (ACTION), DĀNA (GIVING), and the power of faith and devotion. Many of the narratives also demonstrate the central role of storytelling, a dimension of Buddhist tradition that has only recently attracted the careful scholarly attention long accorded doctrine, history, and philosophy.

These narratives derive largely from the MŪLASARVĀSTIVĀDA VINAYA (twenty-one stories) and the vinayas of other Buddhist monastic schools (nine stories), but also adapt canonical sūtras (chapters 3, 17, 34). Two chapters (36, 38) reproduce the work of classical Sanskrit poets.

Among other subjects, the *Divyāvadāna* portrays the adventures of wealthy merchants who become Buddhist monks (chapters 1, 2, 8, 35), recounts the family and religious lives of Indian kings (chapters 3, 26–29, 37), and describes the origins of the "Wheel of Life," well known in the West from Tibetan paintings (chapter 21). Readers also find the conversion of MĀRA, the Buddhist "Satan" (chapter 26), and the love story of Sudhana and Manoharā (chapters 30, 31), and learn both what happens when a man offers his daughter to the Buddha (chapter 36) and when an outcaste woman falls in love with an eminent monk (chapter 33). The *Divyāvadāna* also includes stories about women who studied Buddhist scripture in their own homes and others who, out of love or jealousy, cast spells, blinded their own sons, or committed mass murder.

In the *Divyāvadāna,* as in other *avadānas,* scholars find a meeting of scriptural, literary, doctrinal, and social themes that informed Indian Buddhism—in short, an indispensable window on the ancient tradition.

See also: **Avadāna; Avadānaśataka**

Bibliography

Strong, John S., trans. *The Legend of King Aśoka.* Princeton, NJ: Princeton University Press, 1983.

Tatelman, Joel, trans. *The Glorious Deeds of Pūrṇa.* Richmond, UK: Curzon, 2000.

Winternitz, Maurice. *A History of Indian Literature,* 2 vols., tr. S. Ketkar and H. Kohn. Calcutta: University of Calcutta Press, 1927; New Delhi: Oriental Books Reprint Corporation, 1977.

JOEL TATELMAN

DOCTRINE. *See* **Abhidharma; Dharma and Dharmas**

DŌGEN

Dōgen (1200–1253), an early Japanese Zen figure, is regarded as the founder of the Japanese Sōtō school of Chan Buddhism (Japanese, Zen). Born to an aristocratic family, Dōgen entered the Buddhist order as a child. After studying Tiantai Buddhism (Japanese, Tendai), he became a follower of Myōzen (1184–1225), who was a disciple of Eisai (1141–1215), a prominent Japanese exponent of Zen. In 1223 Dōgen accompanied Myōzen to China, where he stayed at the Jingde

Monastery on Mount Tiantong. There, he received dharma transmission from the abbot, Tiandong Rujing (1163–1228), in the Caodong (Japanese, Sōtō) LINEAGE. Returning to Japan in 1227, Dōgen established Kōshōji, a monastery near the capital of Heian-kyō (modern Kyoto), making it one of the first Japanese institutions to introduce the Song-dynasty style of Chan monastic practice. Dōgen soon attracted a following, including monks of the so-called Daruma school, who would become the leaders of the early Sōtō community. In 1242 Dōgen left the capital area for Echizen (modern Fukui prefecture), where he founded Eiheiji (originally named Daibutsuji), the monastery that subsequently became the headquarters of one faction of the Sōtō school. Except for a brief trip to the new military capital at Kamakura in 1247, he spent his remaining years at Eiheiji, returning to Heian-kyō only in the last days of his final illness.

Dōgen was a prolific author who composed essays on Zen practice such as the *Fukan zazengi* (*Universal Promotion of the Principles of Seated Meditation*) and *Gakudō yōjinshū* (*Admonitions on the Study of the Way*); treatises on Zen monastic rules, later collected under the title *Eihei shingi* (*Eihei Rules of Purity*); a record of his study with Rujing entitled *Hōkyōki* (*Record of the Hōkyō Era*); and Japanese verse collected as *Sanshō dōei* (*Songs of the Way from Mount Sanshō*). Dōgen's teachings were collected in a ten-volume work entitled *Eihei kōroku* (*The Extended Record of Eihei*).

Among his writings, Dōgen is best known for SHŌBŌGENZŌ (*Treasury of the Eye of the True Dharma*), a collection of vernacular essays composed over many years. Modern editions contain approximately ninety-five texts, but the work has come down in several redactions, and the original form of the collection remains uncertain. Though there is some variation in genre, the majority of the essays develop their themes through comments on passages from the literature recording the teachings of the Chinese Chan masters, from which the collection takes its name. Though seemingly little studied for several centuries after their composition, the texts of the *Shōbōgenzō* became a primary source for the development of Sōtō Zen doctrine during the seventeenth and eighteenth centuries, and the *Shōbōgenzō* has been the object of many commentaries from that time up to the present. In the twentieth century, the work became highly regarded as a classic of Japanese Buddhist thought and was much studied by scholars of philosophy, religion, intellectual history, language, and literature. The texts of the *Shōbōgenzō* have been translated several times into modern Japanese, as well as into English and other Western languages.

See also: **Chan School; Japan; Tiantai School**

Bibliography

Bielefeldt, Carl. *Dōgen's Manuals of Zen Meditation.* Berkeley: University of California Press, 1998.

Bodiford, William. *Sōtō Zen in Medieval Japan.* Honolulu: University of Hawaii Press, 1993.

CARL BIELEFELDT

DŌKYŌ

Dōkyō (Yuge zenji, d. 772) was a powerful monk of the Hossō (Yogācāra) school who attempted to establish a Buddhist theocracy in Japan. Dōkyō is said to have spent several years performing austerities on the Katsuragi mountain range, an early seat of what would later be known as mountain religion (SHUGENDŌ). The earliest record of his presence in Buddhist circles of the Nara capital is dated 749, when he participated in a sūtra copying ceremony.

Royal instability led to a growth in the power of Buddhist institutions and monks through the mid-eighth century. Emperor Shōmu (r. 724–749) and his consort Kōmyō established Tōdaiji, which still stands today as a massive symbol of court patronage of Buddhism. When her father retired, Empress Kōken (Ae no Himemiko, 719–770) ascended the throne in 749 and attended the massive inauguration of Tōdaiji. Buddhist cultural and political power seemed to rule, and it is almost a foregone conclusion that Dōkyō witnessed these events.

Empress Kōken, however, was not married, and the absence of a male heir is probably what caused her to abdicate in 758 in favor of the imperial prince Ōi, who ascended the throne under the name Junnin. Three years later, the retired empress fell ill and Dōkyō performed rites for her recovery, marking the second time Dōkyō's name appears in historical records. He would have engaged in "secret rites of heavenly constellations" (*sukuyō hihō*), about which there are no details, although it is clear that the aristocracy's interest in this aspect of esoteric Buddhism began to rise around that time. His ministrations were deemed successful, and the retired empress came to regard Dōkyō as her personal healer (*zenji*), as well as her spiritual adviser, and she increasingly relied on him for political direction. Rumors began to spread, however, that her relationship with Dōkyō was inappropriate. When Emperor Junnin remonstrated her, it is said that the retired empress took umbrage and granted ever more support to Dōkyō. At the same time she began to plot to remove Junnin from the throne. In 763 she appointed Dōkyō to the position of monarchal vice-rector (*shōsōzu*), a decision that caused deep resentment on the part of the chancellor at the time, Fujiwara no Nakamaro (706–764). Nakamaro attempted to place a favorite as the next in line to the throne, but he was thwarted by Dōkyō, who had him exiled. Nakamaro was assassinated in 764. Empress Kōken immediately appointed Dōkyō to the new position of Buddhist minister of state (*daijin zenji*), and she deposed Junnin, who was exiled to Awaji Island and assassinated the following year. In late 763 the empress reascended the throne, this time under the name Shōtoku, and she gave Dōkyō ever more power.

In 765 she appointed Dōkyō to the highest office, naming him Buddhist chancellor of state (*dajōdaijin zenji*), and in 766 she appointed him to a new position that must have ruffled many a feather: Buddhist hegemon (*hō-ō*) or dharma king. The following year, offices for this new position were created, and Dōkyō was granted military powers. Soon court members were required to pay respects to him on the first day of the year, when—for the first time in history—the government performed Buddhist rites of penance within the compounds of the imperial palace. In 768 it was revealed that the main deity of the Usa shrine in Kyushu (Yahata, also known as HACHIMAN) had uttered an oracle saying that Dōkyō should be the next emperor. Shocked by this claim, courtiers who were faithful to the imperial lineage sent a trusted member, Wake no Kiyomaro (733–799), to Usa to confirm the oracle. Even though Kiyomaro would have been promised riches by Dōkyō if the outcome was in his favor, Kiyomaro is said to have received there an oracle to the effect that Dōkyō was an impostor.

A few months after the "revelation," Empress Shōtoku passed away, and, in a series of political moves that are not altogether clear, the Fujiwara house reasserted its dominance in the political world and over the Hossō monks. Dōkyō was exiled to northeastern Japan, where he died in 772 in what some say must have been an ignominious fashion. He was stripped of all titles that had been granted by his paramour, the only woman to have served twice as empress. The Hachiman deity was then given the title of Great Bodhisattva, and became the object of a long-lasting cult.

See also: **Hōryūji and Tōdaiji; Yogācāra School**

Bibliography

Bender, Ross. "The Hachiman Cult and the Dōkyō Incident." *Monumenta Nipponica* (Tokyo) 34, no. 2 (1979): 125–153.

Weinstein, Stanley. "Aristocratic Buddhism." In *The Cambridge History of Japan*, Vol. 2: *Heian Japan*, ed. Donald H. Shively and William H. McCullough. Cambridge, UK: Cambridge University Press, 1999.

ALLAN G. GRAPARD

DOUBT

Doubt (Sanskrit, *vicikitṣā*; Chinese, *yi*) serves in different Buddhist traditions as either a hindrance to spiritual development or a catalyst for contemplative insight. In the MAINSTREAM BUDDHIST SCHOOLS of South Asia, doubt refers to skepticism about claims made within the tradition regarding such cardinal teachings as conditionality, the constituents of spiritual cultivation, or the Buddha, dharma, and saṅgha. Thus, doubt obstructs confidence in and tacit acceptance of the religion's teachings, and it hinders the development of PRAJÑĀ (WISDOM).

Doubt was the fifth of the five hindrances (*nivāraṇa*) to DHYĀNA (TRANCE STATE)—along with sensual desire, ill-will, sloth and torpor, and restlessness and worry—and it had no constructive role to play in Indian Buddhist meditation. Doubt was rather an obstacle to overcome through prajñā, sustained thought (*vicāra*), and the investigation of dharmas (*dharmapravicaya*). Doubt could be temporarily allayed on the second stage of dhyāna and overcome permanently at the first stage of sanctity (i.e., stream-entry).

By the time East Asian Buddhists fully appraised doubt, this debilitating skepticism had been transformed into a principal force driving the meditator toward enlightenment. In the KŌAN meditation of the CHAN SCHOOL, for example, the "sensation of doubt" (Chinese, *yiqing*) became the principal catalyst to contemplation by provoking a profound existential quandary. Doubt generated through inquiry into the keyword or critical phrase (Chinese, *huatou*) of the kōan grows to take in all perplexities and uncertainties that one confronts in everyday life. Doubt eventually creates such tremendous pressure in the mind of the meditator that it "explodes" (Chinese, *po*), destroying in the process the conventional point of view that constitutes the ego, and freeing the mind to experience the multivalent levels of selfless interrelationships that characterize enlightenment in the Chan school.

See also: **Meditation; Path; Psychology**

Bibliography

Buswell, Robert E., Jr. "The Short-Cut Approach of *K'an-hua* Meditation: The Evolution of a Practical Subitism in Chinese Ch'an Buddhism." In *Sudden and Gradual: Approaches to Enlightenment in Chinese Thought,* ed. Peter N. Gregory. Honolulu: University of Hawaii Press, 1987.

Buswell, Robert E., Jr. "The Transformation of Doubt (*Yiqing*) in Chinese Buddhist Meditation." In *Love and Emotions in Traditional Chinese Literature,* ed. Halvor Eifring. Leiden, Netherlands: Brill, 2003.

Jayatilleke, Kulatissa Nanda. *Early Buddhist Theory of Knowledge.* London: Allen and Unwin, 1963.

Nyanaponika Thera, trans. and comp. "The Five Mental Hindrances and Their Conquest: Selected Texts from the Pāli Canon and the Commentaries." *Wheel Series* 26 (1947). Reprint, Kandy, Sri Lanka: Buddhist Publication Society, 1961.

ROBERT E. BUSWELL, JR.

DREAMS

In Buddhism, as in most ancient cultures, it was widely assumed that the images seen in dreams conveyed important knowledge. Thus, dreams not only play a major role in descriptions of the life of Buddha and in the biographies of eminent representatives of the Buddhist traditions, but dreams became the basis of cults, of the construction of monasteries, and of the diagnosis of disease.

Dreams in Śākyamuni's biography

Within the Buddhist tradition, records about Śākyamuni abound with accounts of dreams, and it is also reported that the Buddha was familiar with the interpretation of dreams. The Buddha's birth is marked by a dream: It is reported that he descended from Tuṣita heaven in the form of a white elephant and entered the womb of his sleeping mother, Mahāmāyā, who saw the event in a dream. When Gautama's wife Yaśodharā became aware that she was pregnant, Gautama's foster mother Mahāprajāpatī and his father Śuddhodana experienced dreams. After Gautama had been instructed by the celestial ones to pursue a life of homelessness, he appeared to his father in a dream in which he departed from the palace with his hair shorn. Then, when Gautama's father tried to bind him to the world, the celestial ones caused Śuddhodana to experience seven dreams about his son's departure. At the same time, Yaśodharā had twenty dreams concerning the departure of her husband. That same night, Gautama himself dreamed a five-part dream that confirmed his decision to leave. While the prince was readying himself to escape, Yaśodharā dreamed a three-part dream in which the moon fell to the earth, her teeth fell out, and she lost her right arm.

The Buddha's death is also marked by a series of dreams. Tradition relates that the Buddha's disciple Subhadra dreamed of the Buddha's NIRVĀṆA a short time before the event. Both ĀNANDA and the king Ajātaśatru also had important dreams on the night of the Buddha's nirvāṇa.

The dogmatic classification of dreams

Given the Buddhist concern with questions about the nature of existence and the traditional belief that dreams reveal the nature of the mind, and given the Buddhist proclivity for analysis and classification, it is not surprising that Buddhist literature includes attempts to classify dreams. One such classification can be found in the *Vibhāṣā* (second century C.E.; T1545: 27.193c), where it is said that dreams are: (1) guided from outside and induced by higher beings such as gods, seers, sages, or by spells or drugs; (2) based on past events, so that one sees in a dream what one previously perceived or thought about, or what one did as a habitual action; (3) based on events that will come to pass, so that if something favorable or unfavorable is going to occur, one will see signs of it beforehand in a dream; (4) based on discrimination, so that if one is longing for, striving after, or sorrowing about something, one will see this in a dream; and (5) based on illness, so that if the elements are out of balance, one may see in one's dream the nature of a certain element that is present in excess.

Although this classification attempts to account for both ordinary and extraordinary dreams, it is the prognostic dream that played the greatest role in narratives like biography and pseudo-biography. But it was in scholastic contexts that the dogmatic implications of the dream state found the most attention. What is it that makes dreams dreams? The *Vibhāṣā* (T1545:27.

193b) asserts that it is the mind and its concomitant dharmas, which during sleep take on the shape of the mind's respective objects, and which, on the basis of remembrance, can be related to others after waking. It is clear that this definition of dreams can easily be extended to nondream states of mind. Accordingly, the *Vibhāṣā* points to the role of volitional activity, and emphasizes that its range of influence is restricted to this realm of desire (*kāmadhātu*).

Dreams as images of the mind

All beings dream except for the Buddha, the awakened one, who clearly must be liberated from both the seductive and the haunting images of dreaming. This point serves as the focus of the use of the dream image in the MAHĀYĀNA tradition, where dreams are no more than phantasmagorical visions, visitations within the confused karmic consciousness. While dreaming, one sees that which does not actually exist, or at least is other than perceived by the dreamer. Accordingly, the Yogācāra treatise *Cheng weishi lun* (*Vijñaptimātratāsiddhi-śāstra* [*Establishing the Exclusivity of Vijñāna*]; T1585: 31.46b) states that "all dharmas arise within the mind as if deceptive images, a flurry of sparks, a dream image, a reflection in a mirror, shadows, an echo, the moon in water, magical beings generated through transformation. Though they seem to, they do not actually possess [substantial] existence." Similar formulations are found in many scriptures, emphasizing that the relationship of the dream to the waking state is like that of the waking state to an awakened state. But it is important to understand, as VASUBANDHU argued in the fourth century C.E., that the thing glimpsed in a dream, while it does not in fact fulfill the function it appears to fulfill in the dream, is nevertheless definite in respect to space and time. The dream thus serves as an emblem of the ordinary waking state of mind.

Dreams as paths to liberation

But "if it is so that on awaking from a dream one recognizes everything purely as projection, why does one then not also recognize on awaking that the actual material realm is nothing more than cognition?" In answering this question, Vasubandhu emphasizes that only after awaking can one recall the dream as a dream. In analogy, only when one has truly awakened can one recognize, or recall, that whatever one perceived previously as the waking state had been more like a dream than a true state of wakefulness. Although dreams usually represent an obstacle to liberation, dreaming itself can become the site of liberation. Since the dream is considered to be of the same nature as the waking state's projection of the world, the wakeful dreamer can dream himself or herself into the border between phenomena and emptiness. Thus, the difference between the dream and the waking state is actively erased, and the dream is assigned a privileged status.

See also: **Bodhi (Awakening); Kōben; Meditation**

Bibliography

Bodiford, William M. "Chidō's Dreams of Buddhism." In *Religions of Japan in Practice,* ed. George J. Tanabe, Jr. Princeton, NJ: Princeton University Press, 1999.

Brown, Carolyn T., ed. *Psycho-Sinology: The Universe of Dreams in Chinese Culture.* Washington, DC: Asia Program, Woodrow Wilson International Center for Scholars; Lanham, MD: Distrib. University Press of America, 1988.

Eggert, Marion. *Rede vom Traum. Traumauffassungen der Literatenschicht im späten kaiserlichen China.* Stuttgart: Franz Steiner Verlag, 1993.

Tanabe, George J., Jr. *Myōe the Dreamkeeper: Fantasy and Knowledge in Early Kamakura Buddhism.* Cambridge, MA: Harvard University Press, 1993.

ALEXANDER L. MAYER

DUḤKHA (SUFFERING)

Suffering is a basic characteristic of all life in this world, and is the first of the FOUR NOBLE TRUTHS taught by the Buddha and recorded in the various Buddhist canons. Along with ANITYA (IMPERMANENCE) and anātman (no-self), suffering is one of three fundamental characteristics of life in this world.

Duḥkha (Pāli: *dukkha*) is most often translated as "suffering," although the word encompasses a wide range of things that cause pain. It is commonly defined in Buddhist texts as birth, old age, disease, and death; as sorrow and grief, mental and physical distress, and unrest; as association with things not liked and separation from desired things; and as not getting what one wants (as in, for example, the *Saṃyutta-nikāya* [*Book of Kindred Sayings*], volume 5, verse 410 ff.). Buddhist texts summarize what suffering is by referring to a group called the "five aggregates of grasping." The five aggregates of grasping refer to the five things that people cling to in order to think of themselves as independent and enduring beings: the physical body, feelings, perceptions, impulses, and consciousness.

Holding on to each of these five things produces suffering because there is no permanent existence in the world. If a person clings to things whose nature is impermanence, with the hope that those things will remain stable and unchanging, then that person will continually suffer when faced with the inevitability of change. According to Buddhist teachings, suffering is an inescapable characteristic of all life and cannot be alleviated except through enlightenment.

See also: **Anātman/Ātman (No-Self/Self); Path; Pratītyasamutpāda (Dependent Origination); Psychology; Skandha (Aggregate)**

Bibliography

Anderson, Carol S. *Pain and Its Ending: The Four Noble Truths in the Theravāda Buddhist Canon.* Richmond, UK: Curzon, 1999.

Strong, John. *The Experience of Buddhism: Sources and Interpretations,* 2nd edition. Belmont, CA: Wadsworth Press, 2002.

CAROL S. ANDERSON

DUNHUANG

Dunhuang, on the far western border of the Han empire, was founded as a garrison commandery in 111 B.C.E. Some twenty-five kilometers southeast of the town, a long range of barren rocky hills meets a group of high sand dunes. A small stream, running from south to north, has cut the gravel conglomerate to form a cliff one and a half kilometers long, and irrigates a grove of trees and a few fields. Here, from the fourth to the fourteenth centuries, there was almost continuous cutting and decoration of CAVE SANCTUARIES, most of which have survived intact. Now a World Heritage site, Dunhuang was thrust into international prominence at the beginning of the twentieth century with the discovery of a sealed library and the removal to several institutions worldwide (British Museum in London, Musée Guimet in Paris, National Museum in New Delhi, State Hermitage Museum in Saint Petersburg, etc.) of thousands of Buddhist manuscripts and hundreds of paintings on silk and hemp cloth.

During the millennium of activity at the site, however, it would seem that the caves at Dunhuang served a number of very different purposes, whether Buddhist or secular, official or private, and that they represent the hopes and fears of many individuals, be they rich or poor, local residents or passing travelers. Traditionally, the first caves were opened in 366 by the Buddhist monks Yuezun and Faliang for the purpose of meditation. The lonely situation of the site, then known as Miaoyan or the Wonderful Cliff, perhaps implying that it possessed a reputation as a sacred site even in its pre-Buddhist phase, was admirably suited to the scriptural requirement that places of meditation be located well away from centers of population.

The earliest caves extant today, near the middle of the cliff and high above ground level, date from the fifth century. Elements of style and iconography originating somewhat earlier in Kizil, on the northern edge of the Taklamakan desert, blend with typically Chinese architectural features in these early caves. In most there is a square central pillar, with the main image facing the entrance. The walls and ceilings were coated with clay plaster on which were depicted both narrative scenes from the previous lives of Śākyamuni and the legends of his historical life, and the three thousand buddhas of the Bhadrakalpa in serried rows of seated figures.

Dunhuang was not only the gateway to the Western Regions beyond Chinese territory, but it was a site of such magnificence that its fame spread rapidly throughout the region and the Chinese empire, especially after the unification under the Sui dynasty (589–618).

See also: **Bianwen; Bianxiang (Transformation Tableaux); China, Buddhist Art in; Silk Road**

Bibliography

Dunhuang Research Academy, ed. *Chūgoku Sekkutsu: Tonkō Bakkōkutsu* (*Chinese Cave Temples: The Mogao Caves at Dunhuang*), 5 vols. Tokyo and Beijing: Heibonsha and Wenwu Press, 1982.

Dunhuang Research Academy, ed. *Dunhuang shiku yishu* (*The Art of the Dunhuang Caves*), 20 vols. Nanjing, China: Jiangsu Fine Arts Press, 1994.

Dunhuang Research Academy, ed. *Dunhuang shiku quanji* (*Complete Collection of the Dunhuang Caves*), 28 vols. Hong Kong: Commercial Press, 1999.

Giès, Jacques, ed. *The Arts of Central Asia: The Pelliot Collection in the Musée Guimet,* tr. Hero Friesen. London: Serindia, 1996.

Wang, Eugene Y. *Shape of the Visual: Imagining Topography in Medieval Chinese Buddhist Art.* Seattle: University of Washington Press, 2004.

Whitfield, Roderick. *The Art of Central Asia: The Stein Collection at the British Museum,* 3 vols. Tokyo: Kodansha International, 1982–1985.

Whitfield, Roderick. *Dunhuang: Caves of the Singing Sands.* London: Textile and Art Publications, 1996.

Whitfield, Roderick; Whitfield, Susan; and Agnew, Neville. *Cave Temples of Mogao: Art and History on the Silk Road.* Los Angeles: Getty Publications, 2000.

RODERICK WHITFIELD

E

ECONOMICS

Before trying to determine whether it is possible to identify a specifically Buddhist approach to the economic realm, one must keep in mind that religions and the economic sphere interact at various levels. At the most elementary level, religions open up a space, both symbolic and physical, within which economic activities can take place. In the Buddhist world this has involved establishing through RITUAL means a space protected by Buddhist DIVINITIES or by the supernatural beings with whom these divinities coexist. Besides creating a space for agriculture, these ritual resources, generally labeled as "magic," have to be mobilized in order to ensure the fertility of the land. Practices that mobilize the ritual or magical component of religion can be found not just in agricultural societies, but also in industrial societies, such as that of Japan, the "common religion" of Japan being concerned above all with worldly benefits (*genze riyaku*), whose pursuit involves the mobilization of Buddhist doctrines, images, rituals, and sacred scriptures, such as the LOTUS SŪTRA (SADDHARMAPUṆḌARĪKA-SŪTRA).

Need, work, and religion

From the time of the *nikāyas* to the present, Buddhists have been concerned with the reality of the economic sphere, especially with the reality of work. This concern can already be seen in the *Agañña-sutta* of the *Dīghanikāya,* in which the Buddha tells a story about the emergence of social order, political authority, and kingship. According to the *Agañña-sutta,* the greed of the primordial beings causes a process of coarsening and differentiation to take place, a process that results in the appearance of matter, food, unequally endowed bodies, stratification, sex, work, authority, and priests. As the story unfolds, a peculiar interaction between labor and the avoidance of labor develops. Gathering the primordial rice twice a day constitutes work of sorts, so much so that in order to avoid this labor, a being that is given to laziness engages in the work of storing foodstuffs. However, once rice for two meals is gathered there is no way to stop the process, and so the work of gathering increases. Laziness leads to work, work causes the scarcity of rice, laziness and work beget private property, theft, authority, and religion. We find moreover the recognition that in order to avoid chaos it is necessary to have kings, and in order to have kings and people who, by meditating, "put aside evil and unwholesome things," it is necessary to produce the surplus that will feed them. Work is therefore both curse and blessing, for without the disturbance brought about by work, it would not have been necessary to have kings and priests; whereas in order to support them, it is necessary to work even more.

Although in the *Agañña-sutta* we encounter a story of greed that causes an increase in materiality, sex, and rice, in stories collected in Laos, Thailand, and Cambodia we find that rice appears as the result of meritorious acts, then grows as long as Buddhism spreads. Despite the differences, the two myths involve a process of degeneration, both in terms of the length of the lives of the buddhas and the size of the grains of rice. In general, the two myths betray unease toward economic transactions; in fact, according to the Southeast Asian myth, storage and above all exchange—in other words, economic activities—lead to the disappearance of the personified rice. Eventually, the rice returns, only this time, instead of one variety of rice, there are many varieties. Desirable as the varieties of rice are, however, variety is difference, a loss of primordial unity, a unity that will be restored only when MAITREYA, the future buddha, appears. When Maitreya returns, economic transactions will disappear, being replaced by abundance and leisure. Oneness will return as well: The body from which the rice emerged will recover its original form and the varieties of rice will be reunited.

It would be worthwhile to investigate the reasons for the Buddhist concern with explaining the mechanisms that give rise to the economic sphere. The causes may be found in the social changes that took place around the middle of the first millennium B.C.E. These involved the disappearance of the old tribal order, within which the Buddha himself was born, and its replacement by political centralization, taxation, professional armies, and urbanization. The economic and technological counterpart of these developments involved, between 600 and 500 B.C.E., the use of plow agriculture, the widespread cultivation of rice, and the introduction of coins. Cities were important in the spread of Buddhism as well. This is significant for two reasons. First, cities follow the abstract logic of commercial exchange and labor specialization, unlike the countryside, which is regulated by the rhythms of agriculture and thus by the seasons. On the other hand, given the morbidity that accompanies urbanization, a morbidity that would have been exacerbated by the conditions of the eastern Gangetic plain, the urban concentration of wealth and people must have led also to the sense of malaise articulated in the first two of the FOUR NOBLE TRUTHS (suffering and its origin).

Money and abstraction

The widespread use of money in north India since around 500 B.C.E. is also significant because of the connections between money and abstraction, as well as the affinities between money and asceticism. Because money dissolves qualitative differences into quantitative differences, it contributes to the flattening of reality, even while opening it up to analysis. Inasmuch as it serves as the common denominator of aspects of reality that otherwise would be seen as having nothing in common with one another, money contributes to a process of abstraction. It is through money that the qualitative differences among tasks and skills can be dissolved into quantity and can be bought and sold as commodities. Therefore, in a society in which certain forms of labor that are considered degrading are assigned to degraded people, this process of commodification can be considered liberating. In this respect, the economy of salvation underlying a community of religious virtuosi that is open in principle to everybody, as the Buddhist SAṄGHA claimed to be, can be regarded as the counterpart of the economy of more tangible goods.

Money, which is normally understood as that which makes possible the satisfaction of desire, is the condensation of deferred satisfaction if the money is not spent. But, generally, satisfaction is deferred for the sake of a greater satisfaction, and this fact makes it possible to understand the connection between money and sacrifice, on the one hand, and among ASCETIC PRACTICES, money, and capital accumulation, on the other. Early Buddhism can be understood, therefore, both as a commentary and critique on the process of deferral and on the new approach to labor. In this context, the behavior of the followers of the Buddha can be seen as the distillation of the new way of life. It is true that monks and nuns explicitly distanced themselves from the economy, but this happened only to a certain extent, and they engaged in elaborate ruses in order to participate in the economy without having to handle coins. In any case, the very existence of the community of mendicants allowed the new economy to show its strength, for it must be remembered that a degree of abundance is a prerequisite for asceticism. Indeed, increased production was required in order to support not just isolated renouncers, but groups that were sedentary for part of the year.

Money, asceticism, and accumulation

How can one understand, from an economic point of view, the coexistence of this economic growth, however unequal, and the most important prohibitions to which monks were subject, namely the ones against handling money and working? We can assume that these prohibitions rendered visible the autonomy of the economic realm, as well as the relatively new reality of money as the embodiment of labor. Indeed, while isolating the monks from the money economy, the Pāli canon shows a high regard for merchants. It is significant that the first to offer food to the Buddha after the enlightenment were two merchants, both of whom are said to have attained enlightenment without having become monks. The Buddha reciprocated by mentioning a list of constellations and divinities that would protect merchants who undertook long journeys. This exchange seems to suggest the exchanges that were established between monks and their wealthy supporters: While the latter provided the monks the material goods without which they could not survive, the former reciprocated through their command of supernatural means. Among the early supporters of the saṅgha were the *gahapati*, land-based controllers of property, who straddled the divide between the rural and the urban, and also between the castes. Networks were, in fact, crucial in the spread of Buddhism, and merchant groups can be seen as constituting networks that compensated for the disappearance of the democratic tribal political structures, which were being absorbed by the large political entities then emerging in northeastern India.

In terms of the affinity between asceticism and accumulation mentioned earlier one can say that the Buddha's misgivings about ritual, magical practices, and materiality in general led necessarily to the rejection of the expenditures associated with ritual activities, a rejection that freed capital for investment. An example of this rejection of ritual and its replacement by an internalized religion can be found in the *Sigālaka-sutta* of the *Dīghanikāya*. When the Buddha sees Sigālaka engaging in ritual behavior, he tells him that instead of doing that he should abandon the four defilements, avoid doing evil from the four causes, and avoid following the six ways of wasting one's substance. Avoiding these fourteen evil ways involves essentially having an internalized approach to religion, as well as living a disciplined life, away from material and moral dissipation. We see this approach to religion in nineteenth-century Thailand, where King Mongkut sought to reform the saṅgha by purifying it from superstitious practices and promoting scriptural learning, thus becoming a proponent of a "protestant" approach to Buddhism. We find the same protestant ethos in the Vietnamese Hoa Hao movement's rejection of wasteful ritual and concomitant internalization of religion, as well as in the contemporary Thammakai movement, a Buddhist sect popular among the Thai middle class.

Entrepreneurship, worldly and otherworldly

Both as centers of entrepreneurship and innovation as well as of ritual expenditure Buddhist monasteries have functioned as loci of economic activity. In Tibet and in China, pawnshops, mutual financing associations, auctions, and the sale of lottery tickets originated or had close connections with monasteries. In addition, during the Tang dynasty (618–907) Buddhist monasteries engaged in oil production for cooking and for votive lamps, and in running water-powered stone rolling-mills. More directly related to economic expansion was the role of monasteries in bringing new land into cultivation, as well as in causing deforestation. Equally significant has been the role of Buddhist monasteries in the emergence of an autonomous economic domain, as well as the domain of the corporation, which were caused by the separation between the wealth of the institution and that of the individual. What the monasteries have had in common is their function as spaces for giving and receiving, DĀNA (GIVING), a function that has been held in high regard throughout the history of Buddhism. Ultimately, *dāna* consists in giving oneself, as AŚOKA did during the great quinquennial festival, and as Emperor Wu of the Liang dynasty (502–557) in China did on more than one occasion, having to be rescued at great expense to the imperial treasury. In many cases, however, instead of functioning as the vehicle for the surrender of oneself, *dāna* served as conspicuous waste, a process whereby wealth and position could be both demonstrated and solidified. The consequences of this giving were most damaging in China, as the use of corvée labor to build extravagant monasteries inflicted misery on peasants. Analogous developments took place in Southeast Asia. In Cambodia, beginning around 800 C.E., rulers ordered the building of increasingly larger ceremonial complexes in Angkor; these originally served as centers for the management of irrigation until they reached its saturation point in the thirteenth century. In Myanmar (Burma) the construction of temples was initiated by both rulers and ordinary people, but the effects were similar: Vast amounts of wealth were diverted from productive to sumptuary uses, and the tax-exempt status of ever increasing religious property had negative economic consequences, as ritual expenditures inhibited the accumulation of capital necessary for development.

Even when it did not reach the excesses of medieval China, Cambodia, or Myanmar, the ideology of *dāna* has generally had important economic consequences, as consumption by monks has hampered the process of internal differentiation and of capital accumulation. On the other hand, because of the fact that in a collective celebration merit is shared but prestige is not, the richest families, being able to contribute the most, accumulate the most prestige. This means that even though, from the point of view of MERIT AND MERIT-MAKING, we encounter a nonzero-sum game situation, in the context of prestige the monastery as recipient of *dāna* legitimizes social differences, and renders them more visible. This can be seen among Thai peasants, among whom the two highest forms of merit-making—financing the construction of a monastery or becoming a monk—are open only to the rich. In fact, among Thai peasants, it was believed that the *dāna* of a rich person generated greater merit. Likewise, we find in Thai-Lao villages the belief that with good acts one moves up in the social hierarchy, either in a future life or in this one. The economic consequences of this belief is that poor Thai peasants spend a relatively larger portion of their income on merit-making.

The main consequence of *dāna* has been the accumulation of monastic wealth, a fact that has led to attempts at purifying the saṅgha. This can be seen in Myanmar, where since the eleventh century donations to the saṅgha have led to periods of monastic wealth and laxity, which have led eventually to reform of the order; the resulting community was deemed worthy of donations, until the wealth and laxness of the monks brought about a new reform. In any case, monks have sought to keep monastic wealth within their families, passing it mainly from uncle to nephew, in some cases through the manipulation of the rule of pupillary succession.

Giving and freedom from the degradation of need

In the context of giving and receiving it has been pointed out that living according to the PRECEPTS is not a possibility open to laypeople. In fact, in order for monks to live in the proper manner, laypeople have to break the precepts—for example, they must kill in order to feed the monks meat, and they must work, an activity forbidden to the monks. Does this mean, as S. J. Tambiah maintains, that the work of laypeople, insofar as it frees the monks for higher pursuits, is virtuous and deserving of merit, even though in principle it is polluting? Or is it rather that by accepting that which they, in theory, have not demanded, the monks allow the donors to live vicariously a life beyond necessity, while at the same time consuming and thus neutralizing the pollution inherent in all work? Going back to what was said about early Buddhism being a meditation on the process of deferral and on the new approach to labor, we can say that it is also in relation to labor that Buddhism seems to function as the means of transcending the degradation of being subject to need.

Another way of transcending that degradation requires functioning in the world in a manner that avoids engaging in a zero-sum game. This is achieved through the practice of merit transfer, that is, the practice of generating merit for the sake of somebody else. Rather than diminishing the merit, transfer multiplies it; in fact, anyone can partake of this merit without diminishing it in any way; instead, one's desire to partake of the merit generated by somebody else functions as a multiplier.

Having examined a range of Buddhist attitudes toward the economic realm, what seems to be specific to Buddhism in this regard is the extent to which it is concerned with the processes that underlie need and desire, production and work, giving and taking, hierarchy and equality, and coming into being and dissolution.

See also: **Usury**

Bibliography

Chakravarti, Uma. *The Social Dimensions of Early Buddhism.* Delhi and New York: Oxford University Press, 1987.

Gernet, Jacques. *Buddhism in Chinese Society: An Economic History from the Fifth to the Tenth Centuries* (1956). New York: Columbia University Press, 1995.

Gunawardana, R. A. L. H. *Robe and Plough: Monasticism and Economic Interest in Early Medieval Sri Lanka.* Tucson: University of Arizona Press, 1978.

Harvey, Peter. *An Introduction to Buddhist Ethics: Foundations, Values, and Issues.* New York and Cambridge, UK: Cambridge University Press, 2000.

Reader, Ian, and Tanabe, George J., Jr. *Practically Religious: Worldly Benefits and the Common Religion of Japan.* Honolulu: University of Hawaii Press, 1998.

Schopen, Gregory. *Bones, Stones, and Buddhist Monks: Collected Papers on the Archaeology, Epigraphy, and Texts of Monastic Buddhism in India.* Honolulu: University of Hawaii Press, 1997.

Sizemore, Russell F., and Swearer, Donald K., eds. *Ethics, Wealth, and Salvation: A Study in Buddhist Social Ethics.* Columbia: University of South Carolina Press, 1990.

Spiro, Melford E. *Buddhism and Society. A Great Tradition and Its Burmese Vicissitudes.* New York: Harper, 1970.

Tambiah, S. J. *Buddhism and the Spirit Cults in Northeast Thailand.* New York and Cambridge, UK: Cambridge University Press, 1970.

Tambiah, S. J. *World Conqueror and World Renouncer. A Study of Buddhism in Thailand against a Historical Background.* New York and Cambridge, UK: Cambridge University Press, 1976.

GUSTAVO BENAVIDES

EDUCATION

For centuries, Buddhist monasteries throughout Asia played a prominent role in disseminating both religious and secular education. In fact, two of the most important contributions Buddhism made to premodern society was the establishment of educational facilities and the improvement of literacy. The high literacy rates of two modern THERAVĀDA Buddhist states—Sri Lanka and Thailand—suggest the efficiency of these nations' traditional educational infrastructures and the positive attitudes of their societies toward learning, writing, memorizing, and preserving traditional sources of knowledge.

In all the traditions of Buddhism in Asia, Buddhist monasteries have served as educational institutions, disseminating both religious and secular education. This entry, however, examines the educational practices of only one of those traditions—the Theravāda tradition of South and Southeast Asia.

In all Theravāda countries, Buddhist preaching halls have historically functioned as sites for disseminating education related to religious matters, morality, good conduct, and healthy habits. Within traditional Buddhist education, "preaching the doctrine" (*dhammadesanā*) developed the act of teaching, while "listening to the doctrine" (*dhammasavana*) functioned as a form of learning. In this context, "doctrinal discussion" (*dhammasākacchā*) paved the way for those seeking clarification on what they heard in the sermons. *Dhammasākacchā* led to evaluation and analysis of the Buddha's teachings in a more intellectual fashion that included monastic debates, scholastic disputes, and exegetical treatises. These Buddhist learning strategies strengthened critical awareness within Buddhist learners.

Monastic education was largely restricted to the male population, and women had limited access. In addition, traditional Buddhist schools were not operated on a regular basis, and until modern times it was rare for a large class to be taught by a single teacher. Traditionally, teachers met with students individually, and helped them complete set tasks. Lecturing was rare; rather, teachers focused on what students had

A Tibetan monk studying at Rnam gyal (Namgyal) Monastery, in Dharamsala, India, 1997. © Don Farber 2003. All rights reserved. Reproduced by permission.

misunderstood or what they had failed to comprehend on their own. In this traditional Buddhist education system, students had ample opportunity for self-learning through the use of COMMENTARIAL LITERATURE, glossaries, and other learning resources.

Not surprisingly, the traditional monastic curriculum focused on Buddhist themes and was heavily religious in nature, but it covered other subjects as well. In Sri Lanka, a twelfth-century royal decree banned the study of "poetry, drama, and such other base subjects." However, monastic educational institutions—the Pirivenas—continued to provide a well-rounded education. The curriculum of the fifteenth-century Pirivena included a mastery of several languages (Sinhala, Pāli, Sanskrit, Prākrit, and Tamil), plus the study of the Pāli canon, MAHĀYĀNA philosophical texts, Indian philosophy, mathematics, architecture, astronomy, medicine, and astrology. Language learning was always a significant component of Buddhist education for two reasons: Any South and Southeast Asian Buddhist community needed knowledge of Pāli in order to acquire knowledge of Buddhist scriptures, and for the Buddhist missionary, learning languages other than one's own was useful in disseminating Buddhism in various countries.

Although the traditional Buddhist curriculum included training on morals and etiquette, it did not provide the knowledge and skills necessary for the more complex lifestyle of modern times. Though certain subjects, such as medicine and astrology, were covered, monastic education ultimately failed to provide students with a broader education in science and technology, which became a requirement of modern secular society.

See also: **Monasticism**

Bibliography

Education in Ceylon: A Centenary Volume, 3 vols. Colombo, Sri Lanka: Ministry of Education, 1969.

Guruge, Ananda W. P. "Education." In *Encyclopaedia of Buddhism,* vol. 5, ed. W. G. Weeraratne. Colombo, Sri Lanka: Department of Buddhist Affairs, 1991.

Guruge, Ananda W. P. *The Miracle of Instruction: Further Facets of Buddhism.* Singapore: Samadhi Buddhist Society, 1992.

Jayasekera, U. D. *Early History of Education in Ceylon: From Earliest Times up to Mahāsēna.* Colombo, Sri Lanka: Department of Cultural Affairs, 1969.

MAHINDA DEEGALLE

EIGHTFOLD PATH. *See* **Path**

EMPTINESS. *See* **Śūnyatā (Emptiness)**

ENGAGED BUDDHISM

Engaged Buddhism or socially engaged Buddhism is a relatively new Buddhist movement that emphasizes social service and nonviolent activism. Since the mid-twentieth century Buddhist organizations in Asia and the West have drawn upon traditional teachings and practices—such as the PRECEPTS against harming, stealing, and lying; the virtues of kindness and compassion; the principles of selflessness and interdependence; the vow to save all beings; and practices of MEDITATION and skillful means—to protect humans and other beings from injury and suffering. Their concerns include stopping war, promoting human rights, ministering to the victims of disease and disaster, and safeguarding the natural environment.

Two engaged Buddhists have won the Nobel Prize for peace: Bstan 'dzin rgya mtsho (pronounced Tenzin Gyatso), the fourteenth DALAI LAMA of Tibet, was awarded the prize in 1989, and Aung San Suu Kyi, the opposition leader in Burma (Myanmar), won it in 1991. Other leaders of the movement are the Vietnamese monk and poet, THICH NHAT HANH, who coined the term *engaged Buddhism* in the 1960s; the late Indian untouchable activist and statesman, B. R. AMBEDKAR; the Thai activist and writer, Sulak Sivaraksa; the Taiwanese nun who founded hospitals and international relief missions, Ven. Shih Chengyen; and American teachers Robert Aitken, Joanna Macy, Bernard Glassman, John Daido Loori, Joan Halifax, and Paula Green.

Engaged Buddhist organizations have appeared throughout the world. South and Southeast Asia are home to the International Network of Engaged Buddhists, based in Thailand; the Trilokya Bauddha Mahāsaṅgha Sahāyaka Gana, which serves Dalit (low-caste) communities in India; the Dhammayietra peace walk movement in Cambodia, founded by Ven. Mahā Ghosānanda; and the Sarvodaya Shramadana rural development movement, which serves more than eleven thousand villages in Sri Lanka.

East Asia hosts a number of local organizations, such as the Buddhist Coalition for Economic Justice and the environmentalist Chŏngt'o Society in South Korea; international peace organizations, such as the Japan-based, Nichiren-inspired Risshō Kōsekai, Sōka Gakkai International (SGI), and Nipponzan Myōhōji, known for peace walks and "peace pagodas"; and the Buddhist Compassionate Relief Tz'u-chi Association of Taiwan, with its hospitals, rescue teams, and bone-marrow donation program. The West also has its share of engaged Buddhists organizations, including the Buddhist Peace Fellowship and the Zen Peacemaker Community, based in the United States; the Aṅgulimāla Prison Ministry in Britain; the Free Tibet movement, based in New York and Washington, D.C.; and numerous other peace, justice, and service groups in North America, Europe, Australia, and South Africa.

Practitioners and scholars of engaged Buddhism do not agree on its origins. Some argue that social service has appeared in the Buddhist record since the time of the Buddha and King AŚOKA, before the common era, and increasingly since the rise of the BODHISATTVA ethic of MAHĀYĀNA Buddhism in the centuries that followed. Scattered examples of SAṄGHA-based public service and of tension between saṅgha and state have been attested by historians of Asian Buddhism. Others hold that Buddhist activism—particularly collective protest of state corruption, economic injustice, and human rights violations—is unprecedented in Buddhism prior to the twentieth century, and reflects the globalization and hybridization of Asian, European, and American values.

Engaged Buddhism offers new perspectives on traditional teachings. Among these is the belief that human beings can overcome DUḤKHA (SUFFERING). The FOUR NOBLE TRUTHS, an ancient formulation, defines suffering as the psychological discomfort associated with craving for objects or experiences that are impermanent and insubstantial. The cessation of personal suffering is sought by adopting prescribed views, aspirations, actions, speech, vocations, effort, mindfulness, and concentration. The tradition also attributes a person's life circumstances to patterns of motivation and behavior in previous lives, through the universal laws of KARMA (ACTION) and REBIRTH.

Most engaged Buddhists accept these ideas, but stress causes of suffering they believe to be external to the sufferer and collective in nature. The Dalit Buddhists of India believe that caste-group suffering is caused by entrenched social interests that restrict their social mobility, economic opportunity, and political influence. The Buddhists of Southeast Asia, Tibet, and Sri Lanka know that invading armies and local insurgents cause collective suffering—loss of life, livelihood, and homeland. Those afflicted by epidemics and natural disasters recognize the social and natural conditions that cause their sufferings. Thus, for engaged Buddhism, there are true victims who suffer the effects of others' hatred, greed, and delusion, and of impersonal forces beyond their control.

In response to such external causes of suffering, engaged Buddhists typically adopt practices of social service and nonviolent struggle as "skillful means" on the path to liberation. Ambedkar called this *Navayāna* (New Vehicle) Buddhism, alluding to the traditional *yānas* (vehicles) of Buddhist historiography.

See also: **Ethics; Karuṇā (Compassion); Modernity and Buddhism**

Bibliography

Chappell, David W., ed. *Buddhist Peacework: Creating Cultures of Peace.* Somerville, MA: Wisdom, 1999.

Kraft, Kenneth, ed. *Inner Peace, World Peace: Essays on Buddhism and Nonviolence.* Albany: State University of New York Press, 1992.

Queen, Christopher S., ed. *Engaged Buddhism in the West.* Somerville, MA: Wisdom, 2000.

Queen, Christopher S., and King, Sallie B., eds. *Engaged Buddhism: Buddhist Liberation Movements in Asia.* Albany: State University of New York Press, 1996.

Queen, Christopher; Prebish, Charles; and Keown, Damien; eds. *Action Dharma: New Studies in Engaged Buddhism.* London: RoutledgeCurzon, 2003.

Tucker, Mary Evelyn, and Williams, Duncan Ryuken, eds. *Buddhism and Ecology: The Interconnection of Dharma and Deeds.* Cambridge, MA: Harvard University Press, 1997.

CHRISTOPHER S. QUEEN

ENLIGHTENMENT. *See* **Bodhi (Awakening); Original Enlightenment (Hongaku)**

ENNIN

Ennin (794–864), posthumously known as Jikaku Daishi, was a leading monk and abbot in the early years of the Tendai (Chinese, Tiantai) school, who, as a favorite disciple of the founder SAICHŌ (767–822), led the Tendai monastic establishment at Mount Hiei near Kyoto to become a flourishing center for Buddhist study and practice.

Like Saichō, Ennin traveled to Tang dynasty China to study the dharma and returned with knowledge and texts from various traditions. Unlike Saichō, who stayed only a year, Ennin's journey lasted nine years (838–847), and his travel diary records detailed information about China at the time. Unable to get permission to visit the center of Tiantai studies at Mount Tiantai, Ennin instead devoted himself to learning new forms of tantric and Pure Land Buddhist practice, in addition to Tiantai studies, at Mount Wutai and in the capital of Chang'an. His initiation in the *susiddhi* tantric doctrine stimulated the development of a rich new form of practice that consolidated the Tendai *mikkyō* curriculum (*Taimitsu*) on a par with that of the Shingon school's (*Tōmitsu*).

Ennin became the third abbot of Enryakuji on Mount Hiei. His dedication to expanding the monastic complex and its courses of study assured the Tendai school a unique prominence in Japan. While his chief contribution was to strengthen the Tendai tantric Buddhist tradition, the Pure Land recitation practices (*nenbutsu*) that he introduced also helped to lay a foundation for the independent Pure Land movements of the subsequent Kamakura period (1185–1333).

See also: **Original Enlightenment (Hongaku); Tantra; Tiantai School**

Bibliography

Reischauer, Edwin O. *Ennin's Travels in T'ang China.* New York: Ronald Press, 1955.

Reischauer, Edwin O., trans. *Ennin's Diary: The Record of a Pilgrimage to China in Search of the Law.* New York: Ronald Press, 1955.

Saito, Enshi, trans. *Jikaku Daishi Den: The Biography of Jikaku Daishi Ennin.* Tokyo: Sankibō Busshorin, 1992.

DAVID L. GARDINER

ENTERTAINMENT AND PERFORMANCE

As an active missionary religion, Buddhism naturally fostered the attractive presentation of its tenets in the form of tales and dramas. It may well be argued that the Buddha himself encouraged the use of storytelling as a way to capture the attention of an audience and to convince them of whatever principle or precept might be conveyed through a given tale. Such an approach would certainly be sanctioned by the central Buddhist tenet of UPĀYA (skill-in-means or skillful means), whereby a teacher is expected to present his message in a manner that is readily accessible to his auditors, whatever their capacity. Furthermore, the Buddha's own sūtras (ostensibly, as invariably declared in their beginning phrases, all spoken by him) are full of interesting parables and legends. The Buddha also sanctioned the use of the local vernaculars so that the people of various countries and regions would be able to hear his message in their own language. It is clear that the Buddha is represented by the tradition as being intensely concerned about the mode of delivery employed by those who preached his doctrines.

A goodly part of the Buddhist penchant for storytelling and drama may be attributed to the general Indian love of fables and apologues. It is well known that many of the world's best-known tales—including a considerable number of those found in the collections of Aesop and the Grimm brothers—can be traced to Indian sources, such as the *Pañcatantra* (*Five Frameworks*) and the *Kathāsaritsāgara* (*The Ocean of Streams*

Dge lugs monks dance and play special drums during a celebration of Padmasambhava's birthday in Hemis, Ladakh, India, 2001. © Paula Bronstein/Getty Images. Reproduced by permission.

of Stories). The early Buddhists, however, were probably even more partial to memorable narratives than adherents of other Indian religious traditions; witness the mammoth assemblage of JĀTAKAS (birth-stories) and the skillfully elaborated tales of causation in the DIVYĀVADĀNA. Through the very telling of such AVADĀNA and *nidāna* (stories about causation), sophisticated Buddhist concepts are not only made apprehensible and palatable, they become enjoyable and memorable.

The exuberant Indian affection for unforgettable tales also traveled with Buddhism to Central Asia and Southeast Asia. A splendid example of Buddhist tales may be found in *Xianyu jing* (*The Sūtra of the Wise and Foolish*), which consists of hundreds of long and short stories recorded by Buddhist monks from China, who heard them in 445 C.E. in the oasis city of Khotan in eastern Central Asia (Xinjiang). While *The Sūtra of the Wise and Foolish* has not been successfully traced to a single Sanskrit source, it is full of delightfully edifying stories and also exists in a Tibetan recension.

Another noteworthy medieval Buddhist text from Central Asia, but of a quite different nature than *The Sūtra of the Wise and Foolish*, is *Maitreyasamitināṭaka* (*Dance-Drama of the Encounter with* MAITREYA [the Buddha of the Future]). It is one of the few manuscripts written in the extinct language known as Tocharian. Among all the extant fragments, the *Maitreyasamitināṭaka* is by far the longest. Linguistically, Tocharian, which was rediscovered only in the early part of the twentieth century, is extremely important because it is the easternmost representative of the Indo-European family. Also discovered in the early years of the twentieth century was a translation of the *Maitreyasamitināṭaka* written in Old Uyghur, an extinct Turkic language. Thus, there is good primary evidence for a once flourishing tradition of Buddhist dance-drama in Central Asia. Judging from the stage directions in the extant texts, it must have been quite a spectacle.

The tradition of Buddhist drama goes back even earlier than the *Maitreyasamitināṭaka*, which dates to around the eighth century. Indeed, the earliest authenticated Sanskrit dramas are three plays written by Buddhists. Fragmentary manuscripts of these plays have been recovered from the sands of the Turfan basin in Eastern Central Asia. Among these plays is the nine-act *Śāriputraprakaraṇa* (*The Matter of Śāriputra*) by the renowned Mahāyāna scholar and poet AŚVAGHOṢA (ca. 100 C.E.). A full exposition of the elaborate dramaturgical theory embodied in these plays may be found in the *Nāṭyaśāstra* of Bharatamuni, which dates to around the beginning of the common era.

A masked Dge lugs monk dances during the Hemis Festival in Hemis, Ladakh, India, 2001. © Paula Bronstein/Getty Images. Reproduced by permission.

So proficient in thaumaturgy were many Indian and Central Asian Buddhist monks who came to China that some of them relied on their wonder-working skills not only to attract enormous groups of disciples but even to gain favor with the ruler. Perhaps the most famous of these was Fotudeng (d. 349), but many others were noted in historical and anecdotal literature. Buddhist monks were so renowned for their spellbinding powers of narration and prestidigitation that, by the Song dynasty (960–1279), there were various categories of professional storytellers and entertainers who masqueraded as monks. Already in the preceding centuries, the power of Buddhist narrators (of both lay and monastic status) to gather crowds was so great that government recruiters who wished to conscript hundreds of new soldiers would intentionally seek out a storytelling session, rope together those in attendance, and march them off to the front.

The affinity between Buddhism and storytelling also obtained in Japan, where many of the greatest collections of tales (the so-called *setsuwa bungaku* or tale literature), such as *Sangoku denki* (*Stories of Three Kingdoms*; i.e., India, China, and Japan) and *Konjaku monogatari* (*Stories of Yesterday and Today*) were permeated with Buddhist themes and concepts. In certain temples, there were monks (*hōshi*) who specialized in narrating legends with the aid of picture scrolls, and along the roads nuns (*bikuni*), some of whom were nuns in name only, engaged in similar activities. In Tibet, the itinerant *maṇipa* performer, with her *thang ka* (*thanka*) hanging on a wall beside her, likewise used to be a common sight.

Some of the grandest representations of Buddhist performance are to be found in the paradise scenes on the wall-paintings at DUNHUANG in northwestern China. There one can see full orchestras depicted, often with a virtuoso lute player whirling on a small circular rug in the center. It would seem that to the Buddhist, pageantry and performance were as much a part of the celestial realm as they were of the sublunary world.

See also: **Festivals and Calendrical Rituals; Folk Religion: An Overview; Languages**

Bibliography

Idema, Wilt I. "Traditional Dramatic Literature." In *The Columbia History of Chinese Literature,* ed. Victor H. Mair. New York: Columbia University Press, 2001.

Mair, Victor H. "The Buddhist Tradition of Prosimetric Oral Narrative in Chinese Literature." *Oral Tradition* 3, nos. 1–2 (1988): 106–121.

Mair, Victor H. *Painting and Performance: Chinese Picture Recitation and Its Indian Genesis.* Honolulu: University of Hawaii Press, 1988.

Mair, Victor H. "The Contributions of T'ang and Five Dynasties Transformation Texts (*pien-wen*) to Later Chinese Popular Literature." *Sino-Platonic Papers* 12 (August 1989): 1–71.

Mair, Victor H. "The Prosimetric Form in the Chinese Literary Tradition." In *Prosimetrum: Crosscultural Perspectives on Narrative in Prose and Verse,* ed. Joseph Harris and Karl Reichl. Cambridge, UK: Brewer, 1997.

McLaren, Anne E. *Chinese Popular Culture and Ming Chantefables.* Leiden, Netherlands: Brill, 1998.

McLaren, Anne E. "The Oral-Formulaic Tradition." In *The Columbia History of Chinese Literature,* ed. Victor H. Mair. New York: Columbia University Press, 2001.

Pellowski, Anne. *The World of Storytelling* (1977). Revised edition, New York: Wilson, 1990.

VICTOR H. MAIR

ESOTERIC ART, EAST ASIA

This entry considers the esoteric art forms of China, Korea, and Japan. The terms *esoteric art* and *esoteric material culture* are modern designations, whereas terms such as *icon, image,* MAṆḌALA, *ritual implement, painting, symbol,* and *initiation hall*—used in association with esoteric practices—have a long history within the tradition. Esoteric and Tantric Buddhist traditions alike deploy images and objects for efficacious, decorative, and ritual purposes. Esoteric art may refer to painted, sculpted, printed, or textile media representations of esoteric divinities or esoteric symbols, ritual implements and furnishings, and halls or pagodas used for esoteric rites.

The definition of *esoteric art,* like that of *esoteric Buddhism,* may be broad or narrow. Art forms considered here include not only those associated with the systematized Esoteric school of Japanese Shingon and its Chinese inspiration, Zhenyan, but also imagery used in syncretic religious rituals that incorporate esoteric elements. Imagery may be the primary indication of the esoteric content of a rite. Esoteric icons and other types of visual and material representation are recognized as necessary to spiritual and worldly goals, which are understood as interconnected. Esoteric art objects are often crafted of valuable materials and envisaged according to iconographic specifications and stylistic or artistic norms that help render them sacred. In this way, ornamentation, icons, and all types of visual and material goods lend authority and meaning to an esoteric rite. Conversely, esoteric ritual is essential to the perceived efficacy of the image. Esoteric art and ritual are mutually constituting.

Overview of studies and regional histories

There is scant literature on East Asian esoteric art in English, and most of it concerns Japanese Shingon objects. Copious scholarship exists in Japanese on maṇḍala paintings, statues and paintings of Mahāvairocana (Dainichi Nyorai) and the Radiant Kings

(Vidyārāja, Myōō), and esoteric ritual implements. Such scholarship examines artistic and stylistic attributes, iconographic symbolism, textual sources, and the recorded ritual use of the works. Unfortunate consequences of Japanese scholarship include concentrating interest on the Shingon system and its arts at the expense of Japanese Tendai (TIANTAI SCHOOL) or nonesoteric traditions that incorporate esoteric images and doctrine. Seeking cultural parallels, Shingon-based studies tend to focus on Tang Zhenyan examples. Recent exhibitions and studies of later Chinese Buddhist or Daoist art have enriched our view of esoteric art history as they trace the complex history of esoteric Buddhist assimilation in China, and include Chinese esoteric art in the Indo-Tibetan VAJRAYĀNA tradition made during the Yuan (1279–1368) through Qing (1644–1911) dynasties.

The popularity of ferocious manifestations of Avalokiteśvara found in abundance in the Esoteric tradition is evident in artistic remains throughout East Asia. Ten marble statues excavated at the Tang monastery of Anguosi, ancient Chang'an (modern Xi'an), founded in 701, include the Five (alternative opinions give eight) Vidyārāja kings. The latter were introduced to Japan by KŪKAI (774–835) but soon cults devoted to only the central king, Fudō Myōō, prevailed. The canonical set of eight Brilliant Kings, popular from the late Tang in the modern-day provinces of Yunnan (at Jianchuan under the Nanzhao monarchy) and in Sichuan (at Baodingshan), are virtually unknown in Japan and elsewhere in China, indicating significant regional differences in esoteric imagery. The crypt finds at FAMENSI Monastery provide new insights into the contextual history of esoteric material culture. Used in relic processions to the imperial palace, the finely crafted ritual and devotional objects were adorned with esoteric iconography; moreover, they were arranged in patterns or nested sequences intended as maṇḍala.

Esoteric thought had an impact on early Korean Buddhism and its arts but it is difficult to discern in the model generated by sectarian studies. Dhāraṇī sūtras were widely circulated during the Three Kingdoms and sheets printed with esoteric DHĀRAṆĪ may be classified as esoteric material culture. The earliest printed sūtra in the world is a dhāraṇī text dating to 751 found in the Śākyamuni STŪPA at Pulguksa in 1966. Reliefs on seventh- and eighth-century stone stūpas or on gold and gilt-bronze reliquaries found within them provide evidence of cults dedicated to esoteric forms

A vajra bell in gilt bronze. (Japanese, Kamakura period, 1185–1333.) © The Seattle Art Museum, Eugene Fuller Memorial Collection. Reproduced by permission.

of the Healing Buddha (Bhaiṣajyaguru) and the zodiac, and Ursa Major.

Although Tang Esoteric practices were known in Korea, to date neither Mahāvairocana imagery nor maṇḍala examples have been found. Vairocana (Piroch'ana-pul) imagery abounds but it derives from the HUAYAN JING (*Avataṃsaka-sūtra*) and Sŏn (CHAN SCHOOL) texts and is not esoteric. Guardian figures and deities relating to rites for national protection, among them Marīci, Vidyārāja, and Mahāmāyūrī Vidyārāja, were common during the Koryŏ dynasty (918–1392), as were esoteric Avalokiteśvara emanations. The modest Esoteric tradition that had taken root was assimilated, and new Mongolian and Tibetan forms of esotericism replaced them. Huge banner paintings (*kwaebul t'aenghwa*) were made for outdoor rites during the Chosŏn dynasty (1392–1910); these probably derive from Tibetan *thang kas.* The worship halls at Chosŏn monasteries featured paintings and statues of esoteric divinities used in Water and Land or Ten Kings of Hell rites, among others. In China, Water Land rituals (*shuilu dahui*), plenary masses performed with paintings and ritual altar goods, appear to have developed after the Tang dynasty as substitutes for esoteric food distribution rites (*shishi*).

Tantric forms of Tibetan Buddhism flourished in the kingdoms west of China, along the SILK ROAD. Evidence of Vajrayāna or Tantric belief is evident at DUNHUANG as early as the ninth century. Although relatively few caves are Tantric in the strictest sense, six of them were created under the Mongols. The Central Asian Tangut empire of Xixia (1032–1227), positioned at the narrow Gansu passage where the Chinese Silk Road flows westward, worshiped esoteric forms of the Tantric goddess Tārā. Although it was likely made after the Mongol conquest of Xixia in 1227, the style of a Green Tārā on an early thirteenth-century *kesi* tapestry in the Asian Art Museum of San Francisco that was probably hung in a monastery is strongly Tibetan in style.

In the Mongol Yuan dynasty, the *mchod yon* (*choyon*) relationship of lama and patron developed at the Chinese court. The dynasty fell in 1368 but later dynasties maintained the system. During the Ming dynasty (1368–1644) relations with Tibet were revived, especially under the Yongle emperor Zhu Di (1403–1424). During his reign many painted and tapestry *thangkas,* robes, and gilt-bronze images made in the Ming imperial casting and weaving studios were commissioned by the Yongle emperor as gifts to Tibetan and Mongolian monks. Their Tibetan stylistic traits and symbolism were more than an anticipation of the recipients' tastes: The imperial commissions were modeled after earlier gifts made to the Chinese court by Tibetan lamas, and the Ming artists may have been Nepalese or Tibetan as well as Chinese.

The murals created for the Main Hall of Famensi Monastery, west of Beijing (ca. 1439–1444), show imperial taste and Tibetan influence, with esoteric and nonesoteric Buddhist deities in courtly processions in a variety of syncretic figural styles with diverse attributes, such as an elegant eight-armed Sarasvatī (Chinese, Bicai tian) with esoteric implements on the north wall. Representations of the magical northern seven-star dipper (Ursa Major), stars, planets, or the sun and moon often symbolize esoteric concepts in Buddhist and Daoist imagery alike; the origins, however, lie in Chinese cosmological beliefs.

During the Qing dynasty (1644–1911), Tibetan and especially Mongolian lamas were influential at court and were involved in the production of many esoteric works of art. The Qianlong emperor (1736–1795), schooled in Tibetan Buddhism by his parents, had himself depicted as a transformation of various esoteric divinities, such as Mañjuśrī, in paintings that survive today. The State Hermitage Museum in Saint Petersburg, Russia, has many fine Ming and Qing brass statues of esoteric divinities in the Sino-Tibetan style.

From around the ninth century, representations of esoteric divinities are used in a greater range of (non-Esoteric) religious contexts across East Asia. Such syncretism reflects the true nature of Buddhism in practice, where sects or schools are less monolithic than many discussions allow. This admixture is notable in cults that developed around esoteric manifestations of Avalokiteśvara, such as the thousand-armed thousand-eyed Guanyin. At Dunhuang alone there are nearly forty depictions of this deity painted on cave walls and banners, most of which were made during a period of Tibetan occupation beginning around 778 and ending in 848. Many Avalokiteśvara representations are based on the *Nīlakaṇṭha-sūtra* (T. 1060, an unattested Sanskrit text) and its variants, which stress the power of the *Great Compassion Dhāraṇī* and generated numerous commentaries and texts on dhāraṇī recitation as an act of repentance. Repentance rites were performed before paintings and statues of the thousand-armed and thousand-eyed Avalokiteśvara. A late fourteenth-century example is a twenty-seven-foot-tall gilded work, the central of three colossal clay statues in the Great Compassion Hall of the vast Ming monastery of Chongshan, Taiyuan, Shanxi. The repentance ritual became part of Chan praxis in China and Korea and to modern times continues to incorporate esoteric imagery.

Imagery in the Esoteric tradition: Doctrine and practice

The Chinese referred to Buddhism as the "religion of images" (*xiangjiao*). In the Esoteric tradition, the main divinity is understood as both the material form of the divinity (an icon) and as the pure formless divinity (the divinity worshiped). The *Mahāvairocana-sūtra* names three forms by which the main divinity (Japanese, *honzon*; Chinese, *bencun*; Sanskrit, *svayadhidevatā*) is made manifest: a verbal "seed syllable"; a symbol (mudrā, referring not to the hand gesture but to what is usually called the symbol form or *samaya*); or a pictorial representation. Each type is divided into two categories, those with formal qualities and formless main divinity, which are a higher class. These six cross-divide into two groups: characteristic-possessing and characterless *honzon.*

The Japanese Esoteric master Kūkai wrote:

> The dharma is fundamentally unable to be conveyed in words, yet without words it cannot be manifested. The *tathatā* is beyond form but in taking form it is comprehended. . . . Because the Esoteric storehouse is so profound and mysterious it is difficult to manifest with brush and ink. Thus it is revealed to the unenlightened by adopting the form of diagrams and pictures. (*Shōrai mokuroku, Inventory of Imported Items,* 806)

Japanese Esoteric commentaries describe painted and sculpted main icons as formal appearances manifested according to the rules of causation, but without a real body. They are understood as depicting the real buddhas perceived during visualization. In esoteric practice, visuality becomes a definitive feature of the deity. Kūkai's *Hizōki* (*Notes on the Secret Treasury*) discusses the term *honzon* (*KZ*: 2:30) as transmitted to him by his Chinese teacher. It stresses the relationship between the absolute nature of the practitioner's body and that of the main icon. Both the halls for rites and the representational structure of eidetic meditation participate in visual codes and norms. A practitioner will encounter the divinities throughout a highly ordered structure of practices that require him or her to invoke, entertain, and visualize the deity or deity symbols associated with the rite. Non-Esoteric monastery halls are understood as dwelling places of the gods, but Esoteric halls are said to be symbolic embodiments of self-realization: Statues and paintings transform the structure into a localized manifestation of perfection. Yixing's commentary to the *Mahāvairocana-sūtra* explains that a painted or sculpted representation of the main icon is used by novices, and as practice is refined the *honzon* will arise itself entirely from the mind, without "possessing characteristics" (of a form).

Esoteric art forms and types

Thus, the "main icon" in its characteristic-possessing or material form may be understood as one category of esoteric icon, wherein it is the primary image of a hall or the focus of a ritual, but it is also equivalent to the formless and characterless divinity. A main icon may be a sculpted, cloth, or painted representation of a deity. Even if a hall functions in multiple rites and has many icons, there is often a designated main icon. Most Buddhist traditions feature a single buddha, but the esoteric tradition designates main icons from all classes of Buddhist DIVINITIES.

A second possible categorization of esoteric images includes representations of the divinities that are not the primary icon of a hall. "Secret icons" hidden behind closed doors and revealed infrequently are strongly associated with the esoteric tradition and may be a main icon or secondary icon.

The concept of a generative system of bodies, deities, and energies—at once represented and embodied by a maṇḍala—is central to esoteric praxis. Maṇḍalas are a distinct category of representation that, although at the ritual and philosophical center of Esoteric ordination practices, are not understood as a main icon in the manner discussed above. A maṇḍala may be created in two or three dimensions: polychrome paintings or solid-color ground (usually blue or purple) with gold and silver line-paintings are orthodox, but hundreds of individual-deity maṇḍalas and symbol maṇḍalas are known. In China, sculptural and other three-dimensional maṇḍalas form the largest group of extant remains.

Dhāraṇī maṇḍalas and printed or brushed maṇḍalas used as talismans constitute a distinct category, along with other symbolic or representational charms. Many talismanic printed papers were found at the cave complex of Dunhuang, where travelers paused to invoke protection along their journey. Talismanic seals (Chinese, *fuyin*) protect against calamities and grant wishes; texts on the popular esoteric bodhisattva Cintāmaṇicakra found at Dunhuang are impressed with *fuyin.*

A fifth category of esoteric material culture includes RITUAL OBJECTS and goods, such as bells, wands, vases, and vestments. Among all the implements the *vajra* is of the greatest significance. Translated as either "diamond" or "thunderbolt," the *vajra* is forceful and cuts, but cannot be cut itself. A metaphor for wisdom and the dynamic quality of truth, it is juxtaposed with the matrix or womb world (representing compassion) in the Esoteric dual-maṇḍala system. As an implement it is a one-, three-, or five-pronged metal rod similar to the ancient weapon.

Iconographic drawings, depictions of divinities, mudrā, symbols, or other esoteric components form another category and typically function as ritual supports. Drawings are used as the basis for creating paintings or statues, to record complex maṇḍala components, or as study manuals.

Symbolic representations (*samaya*) are, strictly speaking, a type of main divinity, but as icons they may be considered a distinct category. In East Asian

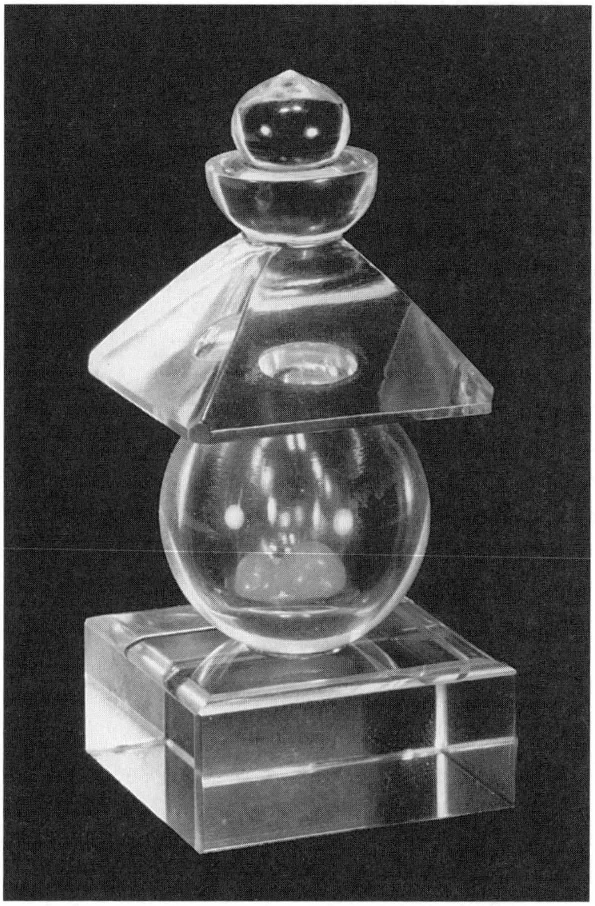

A small crystal reliquary. (Japanese, Kamakura period, 1185–1333.) © The Seattle Art Museum. Reproduced by permission.

esotericism, sexualized bodies or scatological references are the exception and metaphor the norm. Symbols may take the form of a divinity's attribute (e.g., Acala's sword). Stone memorials, reliquaries, and other objects may symbolically represent the five material elements. Seed syllables are invariably comprised of Siddham letters. Iconography (mudrā, posture, color, attributes) might be included here, for such prescriptions constitute a particular kind of symbolic embellishment and art.

Architecture constitutes another distinct category. Halls or structures have specific ritual functions inherent to their layout and decoration. Esoteric pagodas in Japan developed several characteristic shapes, notably the Tahōtō form. An abhiṣeka hall was essential to esoteric practice. The earliest known example in East Asia is the excavated hall of Qinglongsi in modern-day Xi'an. New types of halls with esoteric functions developed at Japanese esoteric monasteries (e.g., the Five Vidyārāja hall, the Five Wisdom Buddha hall) then found a place in Pure Land and other schools' monastic plans.

Another category pertains to Esoteric sectarian history, lineage, and transmission. Included here are keepsakes of the esoteric masters and patriarch images. The Japanese Esoteric master Kūkai was given thirteen items by his Chinese teacher Huiguo during his study in Tang Chang'an, of which eight originally belonged to the great Esoteric masters Vajrabodhi and Amoghavajra. Among them is a twenty-four-centimeter-tall sandalwood portable shrine carved in relief with divinities in the collection of Kongōbuji, Mount Kōya, Japan. Its iconography is not esoteric, nor does it figure in esoteric ceremonies. Nonetheless, the shrine is a significant example of esoteric material culture because it constitutes a form of sectarian patriarchal history.

A tenth and final category is both large and amorphous. It includes paintings, statues, or ritual implements that derive from systematized esoteric traditions found in a Buddhist or other religious context that assimilated esoteric practices and imagery but is not of completely esoteric origin. Examples might include the *vajra* or representations of esoteric emanations of Avalokiteśvara. Found only in Japan are shrine *mandara* paintings, topographies of indigenous *kami* (Shintō) sites and associated gods that typically include one or more esoteric Buddhist deities as avatars of the indigenous gods. In China such assimilated imagery would include, among hundreds of possible examples, images of the Dipper (Ursa Major) Mother.

The categories noted above are not absolute but heuristic. In some cases they differ from modern scholarly views. Modern art-history studies favor works deemed aesthetically superior, regardless of function. For example, an icon with great reputed efficacy but seen as aesthetically inferior may be of lesser interest. Iconographic drawings may be lauded for their drafting and artistic expression, but do not occupy the same status in the esoteric tradition because they are not icons but ritual supports. This is not to imply that visual impact and materials were insignificant. To the contrary, artistic styles associated with a workshop or individual Buddhist craftsman; sumptuous materials such as gems, gold, pigments, or jade; superb construction; and embellishment of objects or sacred spaces were understood as means of devotion. At Famensi the priest who made the silver outer relic container in 871 dedicated it as "a precious box for Śākyamuni Buddha's true body." The innermost container was made of jade, the material treasured above all others in Tang China.

See also: **China, Buddhist Art in; Japan, Buddhist Art in; Korea, Buddhist Art in; Mijiao (Esoteric) School; Shingon Buddhism, Japan; Tantra**

Bibliography

Bogel, Cynthea J. "Canonizing Kannon: The Ninth-Century Esoteric Buddhist Altar at Kanshinji." *Art Bulletin* (March 2002): 30–64.

Daigoji ten (exhibition catalogue). Tokyo: Daigoji Monastery and Nihon Keizai Shinbun, 2001.

Fahai si bihua. Zhongguo luyou chuban she (Fahai monastery wall paintings). Beijing: China Travel and Tourism Press, 1993.

Fomen mibao da Tang yizhen: Shanxi fufeng Famen si digong (Buddhist secret treasures . . . from the Famensi pagoda excavation), Vol. 10. Taipei: Guangfu shuju giye gufen youxi'an gongsi, 1994.

Goepper, Roger. "Some Thoughts on the Icon in Esoteric Buddhism of East Asia." *Studia Sino-Mongolica* (Festchrift H. Frankel), *Münchener Ostasiatiche Studien* 25 (1982): 245–254.

Goepper, Roger. *Aizen-myōō, the Esoteric King of Lust: An Iconological Study.* Zurich: Artibus Asiae and Museum Rietberg, 1993.

Honolulu Academy of the Arts. *Sacred Treasures of Mount Kōya: The Art of Japanese Shingon Buddhism.* Honolulu: Honolulu Academy of the Arts, 2002.

Howard, Angela F. "The Eight Brilliant Kings of Wisdom of Southwest China." *RES* 35, *Anthropology and Aesthetics* (Spring 1999): 93–106.

Ishida Hisatoyo. *Esoteric Buddhist Painting,* tr. E. Dale Saunders. Tokyo, New York, and San Francisco: Kodansha, 1987.

Karetzky, Patricia. "New Archaeological Evidence of Tang Esoteric Art." *T'ang Studies* 12 (1994): 11–37.

Karmay, Heather Stoddard. *Early Sino-Tibetan Art.* Warminster, UK: Aris and Philips, 1975.

Lee Junghee. "A Dated *Avataṃsaka-sūtra* Scroll and the Korean Origin of the Vairocana Buddha Image in the Wisdom-Fist *Mudrā.*" *Oriental Art* 45, no. 2 (1999): 15–25.

Linrothe, Robert N. "Peripheral Visions: On Recent Finds of Tangut Buddhist Art." *Monumenta Serica* 43 (1995): 235–262.

Mizuno Keizaburō; Konno Toshifumi; and Suzuki Kakichi, eds. *Mikkyō jiin to butsuzō* (Esoteric Monasteries and Statues). Tokyo: Kodansha, 1993.

Morse, Anne Nishimura, and Morse, Samuel Crowell (curators). *Object as Insight: Japanese Buddhist Art and Ritual.* Katonah, NY: Katonah Museum of Art, 1995.

Nara National Museum. *Mikkyō kogei* (Applied Art of Japanese Esoteric Buddhism, exhibition catalogue). Nara, Japan: Nara National Museum, 1992.

Orzech, Charles Daniel. "Maṇḍalas on the Move: Reflections from Chinese Esoteric Buddhism, ca. 800 C.E." *Journal of the International Association of Buddhist Studies* 19, no. 2 (1996): 209–243.

Saso, Michael. *Tantric Art and Meditation: The Tendai Tradition.* Honolulu: Tendai Educational Foundation and University of Hawaii Press, 1987.

Sekiguchi Masayuki, ed. *Mikkyō,* Vol. 2: *Zusetsu, Nihon no bukkyō.* Tokyo: Shinchōsha, 1988.

Sørensen, Henrik H. "Typology and Iconography in the Esoteric Buddhist Art of Dunhuang." *Silk Road Art and Archaeology* (Journal of the Institute of Silk Road Studies, Kamakura) 2 (1991–1992): 285–349.

Sperling, Elliot. "The 5th Karma-pa and Some Aspects of the Relationship between Tibet and the Early Ming." In *Tibetan Studies in Honour of Hugh Richardson,* ed. Michael Aris and Aung San Suu Kyi. Warminster, UK: Aris and Philips, 1979.

ten Grotenhuis, Elizabeth. *Japanese Maṇḍalas: Representations of Sacred Geography.* Honolulu: University of Hawaii Press, 1999.

Tokyo National Museum and other National Museums. *Kōbō daishi to Mikkyō bijutsu* (Kōbō Daishi and the Art of Esoteric Buddhism, exhibition catalogue). Tokyo: 1983–1984.

Weidner, Marsha, ed. *Latter Days of the Law: Images of Chinese Buddhism 850–1850.* Lawrence, KS: Spencer Museum of Art, University of Kansas; Honolulu: University of Hawaii Press, 1994.

CYNTHEA J. BOGEL

ESOTERIC ART, SOUTH AND SOUTHEAST ASIA

The Buddhist esoteric arts of India, the Himalayan regions, and Southeast Asia are inspired by the VAJRAYĀNA sect that is sometimes called TANTRA, referring to the texts, called *tantras* (literally, "woven threads"), that the sect uses. These arts are an integral part of the visualized meditation rituals (*sādhana*) that Vajrayāna developed to harness the powers needed to achieve enlightenment in a single lifetime. Vajrayāna arts are called *esoteric* because the intensely complex and mystical quality of the visualized meditations make them mysterious and "secret" to all but the initiated. To fully utilize esoteric art the practitioner must be guided at every step by a qualified teacher; merely following a text will not suffice.

Cakrasaṃvāra and Vajravarahī in Union, Nepal, about 1450, opaque watercolor on cotton hanging scroll (*thang ka*). Los Angeles County Museum of Art, from the Nasli and Alice Heeramaneck Collection, Museum Associates Purchase. Reproduced by permission. This hanging scroll is a visual support for ritual meditation. The practitioner visualizes the two deities in the *yab-yum* posture that signifies the absolute union of compassion and wisdom, "father and mother."

Aesthetically, a few generalizations can be offered about esoteric painting. Because the human form is the yogic "vessel" for following the path, the figure is paramount. Images of symbols are also important as the focus for specific meditations. A MAṆḌALA often combines the use of figures and symbols to striking effect. Composition, depth, and volume are only defined through the juxtaposition of pure contrasting colors and solid defining lines; realistic depictions are not valued. Most of the background and details are idealized and stylized into fluid symmetrical patterns.

Visual supports for ritual meditation

Esoteric Buddhism makes more extensive use of visual imagery and symbols to impart its teachings than any other school of Buddhism. This is because Vajrayāna uses texts so abstruse that their meanings can seemingly be conveyed only through art. Even the name of this path, *vajra,* which literally means "thunderbolt" or "diamond," is expressed in art by a ritual implement that reveals the esoteric truth of the name. The vajra is a scepter with, usually, five prongs joined together at the end; the prongs symbolize the powerful and quick method of practice focused on the five transcendent buddha families, ultimately joined together in the enlightened state. Sometimes a *vajra* may be attached to a bell, which symbolizes PRAJÑĀ (WISDOM). A bell with a *vajra* handle thus represents the perfect balance and necessity of combining method with wisdom to achieve enlightenment.

A wide range of media are used for esoteric arts. Paintings mounted as hanging scrolls (Tibetan, *thang ka*; literally, "something rolled up"), murals on monastery or temple walls, and manuscript illustrations are the most common art forms used as aids for meditation. They are often commissioned as offerings or to commemorate a special event or festival. Sculptures for either altars or niches are cast in metal, carved of wood, or sculpted in clay, usually painted and gilded. Ritual objects and instruments manipulated in meditation rituals or dances (Tibetan, *cham*) are usually cast in metal, but gems and semiprecious stones are also used, along with bones, shells, and rock crystals. More temporary media include woodblock prints, prayer flags, and votive clay images. Offerings, especially initiation maṇḍalas, can be made of almost any material, such as chalk, butter, grains, or sand. The two main forms of sacred architecture in esoteric Buddhism are the STŪPA, called a *mchod rten* (*chorten*) in the Himalayas, and the monastery complex, which includes shrines, dance courtyards, and residences for monks or nuns.

The Buddhist Goddess Vajravarāhī, Central Tibet, fourteenth century, gilded bronze with inlaid gems. Los Angeles County Museum of Art, purchased by the Los Angeles County Museum of Art Board of Trustees in honor of Dr. Pratapaditya Pal, Senior Curator of Indian and Southeast Asian Art, 1970–1995. Reproduced by permission. This *yi dam* or personal deity in a whirling dance posture symbolizes the transcendent wisdom needed to become enlightened.

Transcendent pantheon in esoteric art

The Buddha Śākyamuni is deified, or rather multiplied, as two groups of beings in the esoteric pantheon. His teachings thereby become elaborated in visually concrete systems that are organized by maṇḍalas, mystical diagrams that map out the process of visualized meditations. The first group is comprised of the five transcendent buddhas who parent the five buddha families of deities. The second group encompasses an array of beings, mostly adopted from local traditions, who sponsor specific practices; these are guardians or personal deities called *yi dams* in Tibetan (Sanskrit, *iṣṭadevatā*). Within each sect of Vajrayāna Buddhism, the second group is incorporated into the first group in a way that emphasizes their particular doctrines.

The iconography of this esoteric pantheon is precise. The five transcendent buddhas are identified by color, gesture, and direction in the maṇḍala (east is at the bottom), and each one characterizes a particular aspect of the Buddha Śākyamuni's life:

1. Akṣobhya: "Imperturbable" (*vajra* family), sapphire blue, earth-touching gesture (*bhūmisparśa*-mudrā), east (some sects place Akṣobhya in the center); the Buddha's enlightenment.
2. Ratnasambhava: "Jewel-Born" (jewel family), golden yellow, giving gesture (*varada*-mudrā), south; the Buddha's generosity as shown in his choice to teach and as demonstrated in his previous lives.
3. Amitābha: "Infinite Light" (lotus family), ruby red, meditation gesture (dhyāna-mudrā), west; the Buddha's path of meditation.
4. Amoghasiddhi: "Infallible Success" (karma family), emerald green, protection gesture (*abhaya*-mudrā), north; the Buddha's miraculous powers to protect and save.
5. Vairocana: "Illuminator" (buddha family), diamond white, turning the wheel of the dharma gesture (*dharmacakra*-mudrā), center (some sects place Vairocana in the east); the Buddha's first sermon and all of his teachings.

The colors of *yi dams* are determined by their place within the five families. The talents and weapons they bring to the particular meditation ritual they guide are shown by other attributes. For example, the *yi dam* Vajravarāhī is red because she is related to Amitābha. She carries a ritual chopper with which she cuts through ignorance, because her function is to confer transcendent wisdom. Her consort Cakrasaṃvara is blue because he is related to Akṣobhya, and he carries many weapons because he is charged with providing whatever skillful means, all rooted in compassion, are needed to enable the practitioner to become enlightened.

Regional variations

Indian practitioners and artists of esoteric Buddhism came to the fore after about 500 C.E. They began to make images of many new deities, often displaying ritualized sexual postures (Sanskrit, *yuganaddha* or mahāmudrā). They also increased the depiction and variety of ritual gestures and devices, extended the use of maṇḍalas, and recognized that artistic activity itself could be a form of spiritual practice. The earliest image of a deity holding a *vajra* occurs in the northwestern region of ancient Gandhāra.

The advent of Buddhism in Tibet occurred in the seventh century C.E. Tibetan esoteric arts grew around a seeding of Indian tantric forms among the indigenous shamanic religion called Bon. Particular to Tibet and later Nepal is the extensive use of the posture called *yab-yum*, literally "father-mother" in Tibetan, as a potent visual metaphor for the absolute necessity of joining the goddess's transcendent wisdom with the god's skillful means: They are physically joined in a sexual embrace. The whirling dance posture of mostly nude figures is also characteristic of the Himalayas.

Another Tibetan iconographic form is the lineage painting used to legitimize sects, *tulkus* (*sprul sku*; living incarnations of particular bodhisattvas, such as the Dalai Lama as an incarnation of Avalokiteśvara), and teachers within a genealogy of previous teachers and the transcendent buddha families. Parallel to this development is the wide proliferation of small *mchod rtens* (elongated stūpas) to commemorate, as well as to invoke, the protective powers of teachers, saints, *tulkus*, and sacred scriptures. Huge three-dimensional maṇḍalas, some with interior shrines, are also thought of as *mchod rtens*. Unique to Nepal are the eye-*mchod rtens*, which have an enormous pair of eyes painted on each side of the square base beneath the top spire; these eyes belong either to Vairocana, the Illuminator, or to the primordial buddha principle named Adibuddha.

Ritual objects such as the prayer wheel, the *vajra* (Tibetan, *rdo rje*), the bell, and the *phur pa* (Tibetan, used to "nail" down demons) were extensively developed in the Himalayan regions. The highly sophisticated techniques of making and consecrating these necessary implements spread to Southeast and East Asia.

Esoteric Buddhism in Southeast Asia thrived mainly in Bhutan, Myanmar (Burma), Kampuchea (Cambodia), Malaya, and Indonesian Java. The most important esoteric art forms that remain are the complexes of Angkor Thom in Cambodia and Borobudur in Java, as well as many fine examples of ritual implements and sculptures. Borobudur (about 850 C.E.) elaborates the life of the Buddha Śākyamuni as the ideal path to enlightenment. Each stage is represented on a different level of this enormous three-dimensional maṇḍala, with seventy-two pierced stūpas on the top level, each housing Vairocana as he illuminates the world. This site is both a straightforward and an esoteric commemoration of the Buddha's birth, enlightenment, and death.

See also: **Buddha(s); Esoteric Art, East Asia; Himalayas, Buddhist Art in; Huayan Art; Southeast Asia, Buddhist Art in; Tibet**

Bibliography

Fisher, Robert E. *Art of Tibet.* New York: Thames and Hudson, 1997.

Maxwell, Thomas S. "The Advanced Forms of Buddhism." In *The Gods of Asia: Image, Text, and Meaning.* Delhi: Oxford University Press, 1997.

Mullin, Glenn H., and Weber, Andy. *The Mystical Arts of Tibet.* Atlanta, GA: Longstreet Press, 1996.

Pal, Pratapaditya. *Art of Tibet: A Catalogue of the Los Angeles County Museum of Art Collection.* Los Angeles: Los Angeles County Museum of Art, 1983.

Pal, Pratapaditya. *Art of Nepal: A Catalogue of the Los Angeles County Museum of Art Collection.* Los Angeles: Los Angeles County Museum of Art, 1985.

Pal, Pratapaditya, ed. *On the Path to the Void: Buddhist Art of the Tibetan Realm.* Bombay: Marg, 1996.

Rhie, Marylin M., and Thurman, Robert A. F. *Wisdom and Compassion: The Sacred Art of Tibet,* expanded edition. New York: Abrams, 1996.

Trungpa, Chögyam. *Visual Dharma: The Buddhist Art of Tibet.* Berkeley, CA, and London: Shambhala, 1975.

GAIL MAXWELL

ESOTERIC BUDDHISM.

See **Mijiao (Esoteric) School; Tantra; Vajrayāna**

ETHICS

Buddhist canonical texts have no term that directly translates into the English word *ethics*; the closest term is *śīla* (moral discipline). *Śīla* is one of the threefold disciplines, along with PRAJÑĀ (WISDOM) and mental cultivation (samādhi), which constitute the path leading to the end of suffering. *Śīla* is most closely identified with the widely known five moral PRECEPTS (*pañcaśīla*) of lay Buddhists: not to kill, not to steal, not to lie, not to have inappropriate sex, and not to use intoxicants. The Buddhist tradition has a notion of voluntary and gradualist moral expectations: Lay Buddhists may choose to take the five (in some Buddhist areas fewer) precepts or to take temporarily eight or ten precepts; novices take ten precepts and ordained monks and nuns take over two hundred precepts.

Sources of ethical thinking

In all areas of Buddhism, followers look to the "three treasures" for guidance: the Buddha as teacher, the dharma as the teaching, and the SAṄGHA as the community that transmits the dharma. With these three treasures, Buddhists have rich resources on ethical thinking, especially in the written materials communicating the dharma. The three major divisions of the Buddhist scriptural CANON all contain ethical materials. The sūtras contain moral teachings and ethical reflection; the VINAYA gives moral and behavioral rules for ordained Buddhists, and the ABHIDHARMA literature explores the psychology of morality. In addition to canonical literature, numerous commentaries and treatises of Buddhist schools contain ethical reflections.

The ethical teachings of scripture can be confirmed by one's own reflection. The sūtra's story of the Kālamas is often cited to show the Buddha's emphasis on personal reflection. In this tale the Buddha tells the Kālamas that they should not blindly accept teachings based on tradition, instruction from a respected teacher, or from any other sources without confirming these teachings through their own experience. He helps them see for themselves that actions motivated by greed, hatred, or delusion are unethical, and those motivated by the opposite of greed, hatred, or delusion are ethical.

Ethics as part of the path, and the relationship of ethics to suffering, emptiness, karma, and rebirth

Ethics is a major part of the Buddhist PATH that leads to the end of suffering. The path is sometimes conceived of as a threefold training in which *śīla* provides the foundation for samādhi and prajñā. In the noble eightfold path, *śīla* includes the practices of right action, right speech, and right livelihood. The practice of moral discipline is supportive of the other practices in the path.

THERAVĀDA texts make a distinction between the ordinary path that leads to better REBIRTH and the noble path that leads to NIRVĀṆA. On the ordinary path a person is partly motivated by what is gained through ethical action. On the noble path a person is gradually freed from the false idea of the self and from selfish motivations. An ARHAT who has completed the ordinary path is on the noble path; he or she is beyond ethics and KARMA (ACTION) in the sense that the arhat spontaneously acts morally, and his or her actions no longer have good or bad karmic fruits. The arhat always acts morally without being attached to morality. Many Buddhist scholars (Harvey, Keown, and others) reject the conclusion of anthropological studies in Myanmar (Burma) that there were two separate distinct paths—an ordinary path leading to better rebirths for laypeople and a noble path leading to nirvaṇā for monks (Spiro, King). Instead, they argue that both lay and ordained Buddhists practice the ordinary path with the understanding that the noble path is the eventual long-term goal.

The Buddhist understanding of the nature of reality underscores the importance of ethics. The view that suffering is the nature of lives lived in ignorance emphasizes the need to alleviate suffering in others, as well as in oneself. The view of no-self (anātman) undercuts any clinging to individualistic gain: Since the idea of a separately existing self is false, then one must give up selfishly motivated actions. In MAHĀYĀNA Buddhism the understanding of ŚŪNYATĀ (EMPTINESS) reinforces the idea that there are no independent, separately existing factors of existence. The realization of no-self, emptiness, and interdependence leads to an ethics of consideration for all beings and all things.

According to the Buddhist understanding of the natural law of karma, wholesome actions result in pleasant karmic results and unwholesome actions lead to unpleasant karmic results. But it is not true that an action is good simply because it has pleasant results. Instead, it has pleasant results because the action itself is good. The degree of goodness of an action is dependent on the motive for the action. There is a hierarchy of motives for good actions. As the Chinese monk-scholar YINSHUN (b. 1906) explains it, "Lower people give for the sake of themselves. / Middle people give for their own liberation. / Those who give all for the benefit of others / Are called great people" (p. 228). The karmic result of an action depends not just on the action, but especially on the motive behind the action and on the manner in which it is performed.

The belief in karma and rebirth is important in initially motivating good behavior, in emphasizing its importance, in giving people more empathy for others to whom they were related in previous lives, and in supplying a longer-term perspective for seeing one's ethical development over lifetimes. The rarity of human rebirth makes each human life especially precious as an opportunity for moral and spiritual development.

Ordained and lay Buddhist ethics

For ordained monks and nuns, behavior is guided by the canonical texts in the vinaya. The vinaya contains rules, consequences for violating the rules, and explanations of the origin and interpretation of the rules. Some of the rules are what we would consider ethical guidelines; others are aimed at the smooth operation of the saṅgha and at maintaining the saṅgha's good reputation with lay Buddhists.

For lay Buddhists the foundation for leading a moral life is twofold: the restraints on behavior called for in the five permanent (or eight or ten temporary) precepts, and the encouragement to selfless giving called for in the primary moral virtue of DĀNA (GIVING). Giving is the first Buddhist PĀRAMITĀ (PERFECTION) and by far the most emphasized for lay Buddhists. Other perfections are *śīla* (moral virtue), *kṣānti* (patience), *vīrya* (vigor), DHYĀNA (TRANCE STATE), and prajñā (wisdom). These perfections are discussed in philosophical texts and are embodied by the Bodhisattva in JĀTAKA tales, such as the one about VIŚVANTARA (Pāli, Vessantara), the prince who perfects *dāna* to the point of giving away even his wife and children. Buddhists understand that the precepts and the perfections can be followed at different spiritual levels: Giving done with thought for karmic results is not as good as giving that is performed because it is valued in itself. Giving done selflessly further lessens the false concept of self and thus moves the giver closer to wisdom.

Buddhist texts devote more attention to behavioral norms for ordained members of the saṅgha, but social and political ethics for the rest of society are not ignored. One of the best visions for social relationships is found in the *Sigālovāda-sutta* (*Advice to Sigāla*), in which the Buddha explains the value of mutually supportive and respectful relationships between parents and children, students and teachers, husbands and wives, friends and associates, employers and employees, and householders and renunciants. This particular text lays out the foundations for a harmonious lay community just as the vinaya texts do for a harmonious monastic community.

Buddhist texts that depict conversations between the Buddha and kings often impart political values, such as the Ten Duties of a King, in which the Buddha describes a benevolent monarch whose power is limited by the higher power of the dharma. In South and Southeast Asia, Buddhist ideas of benevolent KINGSHIP had great influence, especially as King AŚOKA became the legendary ideal of Buddhist rulers. In East Asia, Buddhist ideas were usually superseded by Confucian political and social ideals.

Mahāyāna emphases

Mahāyāna Buddhism adds to Buddhist ethics a greater emphasis on the BODHISATTVA as the model for ethical behavior. Bodhisattvas embody the virtues, especially compassion and wisdom, to which all Buddhists should eventually aspire. The bodhisattva masters the perfections through a process of ten stages with the goal of gaining enlightenment for the benefit of all living beings. Bodhisattva vows take several forms, including the vow made by the eighth-century Buddhist saint ŚĀNTIDEVA: "For as long as space endures / And for as long as living beings remain, / Until then may I too abide / To dispel the misery of the world." In East Asian Mahāyāna, an ideal lay Buddhist is the bodhisattva VIMALAKĪRTI, whose wisdom and compassion is shown to outshine even that of monks.

In Theravāda Buddhism there is a strong emphasis on the vinaya, which governs the behavior of the ordained community. In Mahāyāna Buddhism outside India the unifying power of the vinaya has been less significant. East Asians often collapsed vinaya and *śīla* into a single concept (Chinese, *jielü*), thus diluting the distinctiveness of vinaya. In addition, many of the rules seemed irrelevant to a non-Indian cultural environment. In East Asia, the vinaya had to accommodate a very different culture and the already dominant social ethics of Confucianism.

In East Asia some Buddhist schools accepted the teachings of Buddhist morality but believed that it was impossible to follow the precepts correctly in the present age of the DECLINE OF THE DHARMA. The Nichiren and PURE LAND SCHOOLS of Japan have developed this idea most clearly. In these schools the means to enlightenment comes from outside the unenlightened individual. NICHIREN identified the source of that power as the LOTUS SŪTRA (SADDHARMAPUṆḌARĪKA-SŪTRA), which encapsulated the powers of all buddhas and bodhisattvas; the Pure Land leader SHINRAN (1173–1263) identified the source as the compassionate power of AMITĀBHA (Japanese, Amida) Buddha. In these schools, morality has never been seen as a means to an end, but rather as an expression of gratitude, and as empowered by something beyond the individual.

The Chinese CHAN SCHOOL of Buddhism and Tibetan TANTRA sometimes seem to use language that borders on antinomianism. By transcending the dualities of all things, including right and wrong and good and evil, there is the possibility of enlightenment. In fact, the problem is not with the duality of moral precepts, but with the self-centered clinging to moral precepts and the tendency toward self-righteousness.

Comparisons with Western ethics

Western anthropologists studying Theravāda Buddhism in Burma have argued for differing views of morality in monks and laypeople. Melford Spiro identified two forms of Buddhism: *kammatic Buddhism* of laypeople who followed morality in order to gain a better rebirth, and *nibbānic Buddhism* of the monks who followed the path to gain nibbāna (Sanskrit, nirvāṇa). In both cases, the moral precepts are viewed as means to a goal, but to different goals. This understanding of Buddhist ethics places it closest to a Western utilitarian ethics where the goal is the reduction of suffering, and ethics is the means to that goal. In the decades after this anthropological work, other Buddhist scholars have argued from the anthropological data and from textual sources that a utilitarian view of ethics is not appropriate to Buddhism. Damien Keown and others have argued that the best way to understand Buddhist ethics is in terms of Aristotelian virtue ethics. The moral precepts are not to be followed just because they reduce suffering (although they do), but because they are good in themselves. That is, *śīla* is not just a means for gaining wisdom and concentration; *śīla* and wisdom are both part of the final goal of enlightenment and are interdependent. In *The Nature of Buddhist Ethics* (1992) Keown argued that Buddhist ethics are teleological ethics similar to Aristotelian ethics because "the virtues are the means to the gradual realization of the end through the incarnation of the end in the present" (p. 194). In Buddhism, of course, this gradual realization takes place over many lifetimes.

Peter Harvey summed up the field of Buddhist ethics in comparison to Western ethics by acknowledging that "the rich field of Buddhist ethics would be narrowed by wholly collapsing it into any single one of the Kantian, Aristotelian or Utilitarian models, though Buddhism agrees with each in respectively acknowledging the importance of (1) a good motivating will, (2) cultivation of character, and (3) the reduction of suffering in others and oneself" (p. 51).

Contemporary ethical issues

In the contemporary world, Buddhist scholars and leaders have sought to apply Buddhist ethics to moral questions of this age. This is most clearly evident in the ENGAGED BUDDHISM and humanistic Buddhism movements. *Engaged Buddhism* is THICH NHAT HANH's term for bringing Buddhism out of the monastery to deal with pressing social issues. The ideals of engaged Buddhism have been embraced by a wide range of Asian and Western Buddhist leaders and movements. In Chinese Buddhism, humanistic Buddhism (*rensheng fojiao*) was developed by the reformer TAIXU (1890–1947), the scholar Yinshun, the Chan master

Shengyan, and the Taiwanese nun Zhengyan (Cheng Yen) to refer to a form of modern Buddhism involved with current social issues such as education, poverty, pollution, and sickness.

Many current ethical issues are related to the first Buddhist precept: not to harm other beings. The first precept is central to Buddhist discussions of ABORTION, WAR, euthanasia, animal rights, environmentalism, and economic justice. Buddhist writings against war and military violence are some of the best known. Nhat Hanh, the fourteenth DALAI LAMA, Aung San Suu Kyi, and Mahāghosānanda are some of the Buddhist leaders who have argued against violence as a means to resist the oppression in their countries. The Buddhist tradition has nothing quite like a "just war" tradition, only isolated instances where Buddhists have tried to justify violence by claiming their enemies were not truly human. The dominant tradition is pacifist.

Whether violence to one's own body is an acceptable means of protest is disputed. Nhat Hanh considered Vietnamese monks who performed SELF-IMMOLATION during the 1960s and 1970s to be bodhisattvas burning brightly for truth. Others, like the Dalai Lama and Shengyan, have rejected self-immolation, fasting, or other suicidal actions as political means. Early Buddhist scriptures specifically forbid suicide, but this question gets to the heart of the issue of whether bodhisattvas can violate the precepts in order to reduce the suffering of others. In this scenario a bodhisattva violates normative Buddhist ethics with the willingness to take on negative karmic effects in order to benefit other living beings. In one *jātaka* tale the bodhisattva offers his body as a meal to a hungry tigress to prevent her from eating her cubs. There is also a more controversial *jātaka* tale where the Buddha in a previous lifetime (as a bodhisattva) kills a bandit in order to save the lives of five hundred merchants that the bandit is about to kill. The understanding is that the action was motivated by compassion for both the merchants and the bandit, who would suffer terribly from the karmic fruits of these murders. The Dalai Lama, among others, has rejected such violations of Buddhist ethics on the basis that only a fully enlightened being could make such judgments.

See also: **Nichiren School**

Bibliography

Bstan 'dzin rgya mtsho (Tenzin Gyatso, Dalai Lama XIV). *Ethics for a New Millennium.* New York: Riverhead Books, 1999.

Crosby, Kate, and Skilton, Andrew, trans. *Śāntideva: The Bodhicaryāvatāra.* Oxford and New York: Oxford University Press, 1996.

Dharmasiri, Gunapala. *Fundamentals of Buddhist Ethics.* Antioch, CA: Golden Leaves, 1989.

Fu, Charles Wei-hsun, and Wawrytko, Sandra A., eds. *Buddhist Ethics and Modern Society: An International Symposium.* New York: Greenwood Press, 1991.

Harvey, Peter. *An Introduction to Buddhist Ethics: Foundations, Values, and Issues.* Cambridge, UK: Cambridge University Press, 2000.

Journal of Buddhist Ethics. Internet journal available from: jbe.gold.ac.uk/ or jbe.la.psu.edu/.

Katz, Nathan. *Buddhist Images of Human Perfection: The Arahant of the Sutta Piṭaka Compared with the Bodhisattva and Mahāsiddha.* Delhi: Motilal Banarsidass, 1982.

Keown, Damien. *The Nature of Buddhist Ethics.* London: Macmillan, 1992.

Keown, Damien. *Buddhism and Bioethics.* London: Macmillan; New York: St. Martin's Press, 1995.

Keown, Damien, ed. *Contemporary Buddhist Ethics.* London: Curzon, 2000.

Keown, Damien; Prebish, Charles S.; and Husted, W. R.; eds. *Buddhism and Human Rights.* London: Curzon, 1998.

King, Winston L. *In the Hope of Nibbāna: An Essay on Theravāda Buddhist Ethics.* LaSalle, IL: Open Court, 1964.

Kraft, Kenneth, ed. *Inner Peace, World Peace: Essays on Buddhism and Nonviolence.* Albany: State University of New York Press, 1992.

Little, David, and Twiss, Sumner B. *Comparative Religious Ethics: A New Method.* New York: Harper, 1978.

Nakasone, Ronald Y. *Ethics of Enlightenment: Essays and Sermons in Search of a Buddhist Ethic.* Fremont, CA: Dharma Cloud, 1990.

Nhat Hanh, Thich, et al. *For a Future to Be Possible: Commentaries on the Five Wonderful Precepts.* Berkeley, CA: Parallax Press, 1993. Revised edition, 1998.

Prebish, Charles S., ed. *Buddhist Ethics: A Cross-Cultural Approach.* Dubuque, IA: Kendall/Hunt, 1992.

Queen, Christopher S., and King, Sallie B., eds. *Engaged Buddhism: Buddhist Liberation Movements in Asia.* Albany: State University of New York Press, 1996.

Saddhatissa, Hammalawa. *Buddhist Ethics: Essence of Buddhism.* London: Allen and Unwin, 1970.

Sizemore, Russell F., and Swearer, Donald K., eds. *Ethics, Wealth, and Salvation: A Study in Buddhist Social Ethics.* Columbia: University of South Carolina Press, 1990.

Spiro, Melford E. *Buddhism and Society: A Great Tradition and Its Burmese Vicissitudes.* London: Allen and Unwin, 1971.

Wayman, Alex. *Ethics of Tibet: Bodhisattva Section of Tsong-Kha-Pa's Lam Rim Chen Mo.* Albany: State University of New York Press, 1991.

Yin-shun. *The Way to Buddhahood: Instructions from a Modern Chinese Master,* tr. Wing Yeung. Boston: Wisdom, 1998.

BARBARA E. REED

ETIQUETTE

Models of polite behavior appear throughout Buddhist literature, as when disciples of the Buddha bow and circumambulate the Buddha, or when preachers of the dharma are treated with respect. While the Vinaya Piṭaka is the scriptural source of guidance on monastic discipline, there is also a much larger written and oral VINAYA tradition, consisting of commentaries, digests, and ad hoc instructions. Whereas Vinaya texts define the fundamental nature of the SAṄGHA, the term *etiquette* tends to apply to less crucial, and yet more pervasive, rule-governed behavior: posture when standing, the direction of the gaze, sequences of seniority in the dining hall, how to hold chopsticks, terms of polite address, how to bow. In daily life, this attention to detail does not always have a scriptural basis, and etiquette varies widely by region, time period, sect, and even from monastery to monastery.

Etiquette is not only a matter of interpersonal relations, but also governs maintenance of the material objects of Buddhism, such as robes, bowls, icons, and monastery boundaries. Changes in behavior serve to demarcate sacred space, for example, when MONKS in Southeast Asia roll down their robes to cover both arms when they exit the monastery, and roll them up to expose one arm when they return. Walking through doors is also an occasion for RITUAL. In China, the act of entering is governed by a ritual code, and behavior is modified according to one's location inside or outside. One is careful to step over the "bridge" or "saddle" of the doorway, which in some cases can be quite a high step. If the front façade has three large doors, one enters through those on the sides, not by the central door. When entering by the left of the three gates, one should put the left foot in first; if through the right gate, the right foot is first. In some cases, shoes are removed or changed. Stepping into the temple space, the first act should be a bow. The *Jiaojie xinxue biqiu xinghu lüyi* (*Admonitions for Novice Monks on the Behavioral Norms of the Vinaya*), a guide to monastic etiquette by the Tang dynasty monk DAOXUAN (596–667), instructs: "When entering the monastery gate, bow, and then kneel, and recite the customary praises to the Buddha. . . . Gather up your sitting-cloth, join palms and bend the body. Then, with a serious expression, walk slowly on one side of the walkway, looking ahead." When leaving, "perform obeisance according to the correct method: three bows before the Buddha, one bow as you reach the gate, one more bow outside the gate. When there are a few monks, bow once to each in order. When there are many monks, bow to the group three times." When circumambulating an image or sacred site, one should move clockwise with palms together, and with one's right shoulder to the object of reverence, possibly with the right shoulder bared.

The most common Buddhist polite gesture is the *añjali,* also known as the *namaskāra* or *namas te,* (Japanese, *Gasshō*; Thai, *wai*). The palms of the hands are pressed together in front of the body and the head or torso leans forward to a greater or lesser degree. In many cases, the height of the hands indicates the actor's perceived or intended social position vis-à-vis the other person: The hands are held higher when gesturing toward people "higher-up" than oneself. In an *añjali* to a fully ordained monk the hands are usually held at the forehead, compared to in front of the chin when offered to most laity. When an adult offers an *añjali* to return the greeting of a child, the hands are held at heart level.

In some parts of Asia, particular devotion may be shown by placing one's hands on the feet of a monk. As with the spatial distinction of height, the timing of this gesture also matters: The subordinate initiates the gesture.

Conversely, the fact that monks do not bow to laity (not even to the king) is a means of asserting monkhood as an ideal social order outside of the world. Conflicts of etiquette have occurred, such as the persistent debates over monks not bowing to their own parents or to the Chinese emperor. These debates brought Buddhist and Confucian models of etiquette into direct conflict. The virulence of these debates indicates the importance of etiquette, as arguments for and against drew upon fundamental pillars of Buddhist or Confucian doctrine.

Members of the ordained community continue to perform obeisance to each other, however, and Buddhist scriptures encode the orthodox hierarchy: All nuns, no matter how senior, bow to all monks, no matter how junior. Novices bow to the fully ordained, and juniors bow to seniors. Seniority is measured in "dharma years," that is, the number of Lenten seasons since full ordination.

When the many particular rules have been internalized, the intended result is a dignified demeanor (*īryāpatha*; Chinese, *weiyi*), a kind of self-possession of the body and its robes. Buddhist monastic guides reveal an elaborate regime of bodily control, especially a mindful control of the hands; there are rules against flapping the arms around, standing with arms akimbo, carelessly scratching or blowing one's nose when in the presence of superiors, tickling people, and so on. Etiquette should also be controlled at meal times; the PRĀTIMOKṢA (the list of monastic precepts, a set of vows assumed as part of the ordination process) includes rules against, for example, licking the fingers, scraping the bowl with fingers, or sticking the tongue out. The activities of seeing, pointing, and touching are also strongly rule-governed. The mastery of etiquette is part of a more encompassing effort to mindfully discipline the entire body, as well as speech and mind.

In some of its modern American versions, Buddhism seems opposed to any emphasis on etiquette, standing instead for spontaneity and an egalitarian rejection of all distinctions. Indeed, CHAN SCHOOL discourse has played with violations of etiquette. However, the nondualist rejection of distinctions and the suspension of the assumed norms are only meaningful in terms of shared social norms. Buddhist monasteries are the sites of intensified rather than inverted etiquette, and some highly refined forms of social behavior, such as the tea ceremony, have often spread through the medium of Buddhism.

See also: **Precepts; Robes and Clothing**

Bibliography

Buswell, Robert E., Jr. *The Zen Monastic Experience.* Princeton, NJ: Princeton University Press, 1992.

Dōgen. *Dōgen's Pure Standards for the Zen Community: A Translation of the Eihei Shingi,* tr. Taigen Daniel Leighton and Shohaku Okumura. Albany: State University of New York, 1996.

Hurvitz, Leon. "'Render Unto Caesar' in Early Chinese Buddhism." *Sino-Indian Studies (Liebenthal Festschrift)* 5, no. 3–4 (1957): 81–114.

Prip-Møller, Johannes. *Chinese Buddhist Monasteries: Their Plan and Its Function as a Setting for Buddhist Monastic Life.* London: Oxford University Press, 1937.

ERIC REINDERS

EUROPE

At the beginning of the twenty-first century, the presence of Buddhism in Europe is characterized by a diversity of traditions, schools, orders, and lineages. Since the 1970s interest in Buddhism among Europeans has grown steadily, accompanied by the arrival of Buddhist refugees and immigrants from Asian countries. Of Europe's estimated one million Buddhists, about two-thirds are of Asian ancestry. Nevertheless, Buddhism's public face in Europe and its representation in the media are dominated by convert Buddhists, leaving migrant Buddhists for the most part unseen and unrecognized.

The beginning of Buddhism in Europe can be dated to the mid-nineteenth century, though fragmentary information about Buddhist customs and concepts had trickled into Europe since the seventeenth century. From the 1850s onward, Europe witnessed a boom of translations of Buddhist works, as well as studies and portraits of Buddhism. European philosophers and scholars such as Arthur Schopenhauer (1788–1860), Thomas W. Rhys Davids (1843–1922), and Hermann Oldenberg (1854–1920) helped spread Buddhist concepts through their treatises and translations. These scholars clearly favored the teachings of the Pāli CANON, which they assumed to be pure and original. The first converted European Buddhists appeared during the 1880s in response to these studies; most converts were educated middle-class men. In accordance with the dominance of Pāli Buddhist ideas, a few young men from England and Germany became THERAVĀDA monks in Burma (Myanmar) and Ceylon (Sri Lanka). Most prominent among these were Bennett McGregor (1872–1923), who was ordained as Ananda Metteyya in 1902, and Anton W. F. Gueth (1878–1957), who was ordained as Nyanatiloka in 1904.

Ethical and intellectual interest in the teachings of Theravāda Buddhism gained organizational momentum in Europe with the founding of new Buddhist societies. The first of these was the Society for the Buddhist Mission in Germany, formed by the Indologist Karl Seidenstücker (1876–1936) in Leipzig in 1903. Through lectures, pamphlets, and books, the first professed Buddhists tried to win members from the educated middle and upper strata of society. During the 1920s further Buddhist societies and parishes evolved, many with the support of the Ceylonese reformer ANAGĀRIKA DHARMAPĀLA (1864–1933). Leading Buddhists included Georg Grimm (1868–1945) and Paul Dahlke

The Dharmapāla Center, Kandersteg, Switzerland. Courtesy of Dr. Martin Baumann, University of Lucerne. Reproduced by permission.

(1865–1928) in Germany, and Christmas Humphreys (1901–1983) in England. The schools of Grimm and Dahlke continued their work within small private circles during the Nazi period, when Buddhists were regarded with suspicion as pacifists and eccentrics. With the exception of those who had abandoned Judaism and become Buddhists, however, no official or open persecution of Buddhism took place.

After World War II, small numbers of Buddhists reconstructed former THERAVĀDA-oriented groups or founded new ones. Beginning in the 1950s, Japanese Buddhist traditions, such as Zen, Jōdo Shinshū, and SŌKA GAKKAI, were brought to Europe. Zen became especially popular during the 1960s and 1970s; many local groups were established and Zen teachers began touring Europe. The Zen boom was followed by a sharp rise of interest in Tibetan Buddhism. Beginning in the mid-1970s, high ranking Tibetan teachers conducted preaching tours in Europe. Within two decades, converts to Tibetan Buddhism outnumbered converts to all other Buddhist traditions in many countries.

This rapid increase in the numbers of European Buddhists, accompanied by an expansion of already existing institutions, led to a considerable rise in the number of Buddhist groups and centers. In Britain, for example, the number of Buddhist organizations increased from seventy-four to some four hundred between 1979 and 2000. In Germany, interest in Buddhism resulted in an increase in the number of Buddhist institutions from around forty in 1975 to more than five hundred meditation circles, groups, centers, and societies by 1999. Comparable growth rates occurred in other European countries, such as Italy, Austria, Switzerland, France, the Netherlands, and Denmark. Eastern European countries also witnessed a growing interest in Buddhism following the political changes of 1989. Numerous Buddhist groups, Tibetan and Zen in particular, were founded in Poland, the Czech Republic, Hungary, and western Russia. Visits by European and North American Buddhist teachers, as well as a longing for spiritual alternatives to the established Roman Catholic and Orthodox churches, brought about a steady growth of Buddhism in Eastern Europe.

In addition to Western convert Buddhists, considerable numbers of Asian Buddhists have immigrated to Europe since the 1960s (see Table 1). In France, especially in Paris, large communities of refugees from Vietnam, Laos, and Cambodia have emerged. In Great

TABLE 1

Estimated Buddhists in selected European countries in the late 1990s

Country	Buddhists total	Buddhists from Asia	Percentage of population
France	350,000	300,000	0.6%
Britain	180,000	130,000	0.3%
Germany	170,000	120,000	0.2%
Italy	75,000	25,000	0.1%
Netherlands	33,000	20,000	0.2%
Switzerland	25,000	20,000	0.3%
Austria	17,000	5,000	0.2%
Denmark	10,000	7,000	0.1%
Hungary	7,000	1,000	0.1%
Poland	5,000	500	0.02%
Russia	1,000,000	vast majority	0.7%

SOURCE: Baumann (2002).

Britain, the Netherlands, and other Western European nations, refugees, immigrants, and businesspeople from Asian countries have found work or asylum. In the process of settling down, religious and cultural institutions were established to help immigrants preserve their ethnic identity and build a home away from home.

Still, relative to their absolute numbers, Asian Buddhists in Europe have established few Buddhist institutions. The rapid rise in the number of Buddhist centers and societies is largely due to the work of convert Buddhists, who, in addition to following established forms of Theravāda, MAHĀYĀNA, and Tibetan Buddhism, also founded new Buddhist orders. These include the Arya Maitreya Mandala order, founded by the German lama Govinda (1898–1985) in 1933, and the Friends of the Western Buddhist Order, established by the British Sangharakshita in 1967. In many countries, however, Zen and Tibetan Buddhism remain foremost, superseding the early dominance of Theravāda.

During the 1980s and 1990s, Buddhism in Europe became firmly established in organizational form. In addition to the numerous local Buddhist groups and centers, in many countries national umbrella societies were created to enhance intra-Buddhist dialogue and activity. In Austria, Switzerland, Germany, the Netherlands, and Italy, such national societies have become well respected representatives of Buddhism. The European Buddhist Union was founded in 1975, but this organization has had little impact. Austria officially recognized Buddhism as a religion entitled to special rights, such as school teaching and broadcast time, in 1983. Representatives of the various Buddhist traditions in Germany adopted what they called a "Buddhist Confession" in 1985, although they failed to win state recognition.

The dynamic growth during the 1970s and 1980s included a professionalization of European Buddhism in terms of leadership, book and journal marketing, and the staging of public conventions. In addition, an increasing number of female and male convert Buddhists took on professional roles by becoming priests, nuns, monks, or full-time lay teachers. A second generation of European Buddhist teachers is maturing, an important development that has not yet caught on among immigrant Buddhist communities. Though Buddhism is likely to remain a minority tradition in Europe during the twenty-first century, secure foundations have been laid, ensuring that Buddhism will become an accepted part of Europe's landscape of religions.

See also: **Buddhist Studies; United States; Zen, Popular Conceptions of**

Bibliography

Almond, Philip C. *The British Discovery of Buddhism.* Cambridge, UK: University Press, 1988.

Batchelor, Stephen. *The Awakening of the West: The Encounter of Buddhism and Western Culture.* Berkeley, CA: Parallax, 1994.

Baumann, Martin. "Global Buddhism. Developmental Periods, Regional Histories, and a New Analytical Perspective." *Journal of Global Buddhism* 2 (2001): 1–43.

Baumann, Martin. *Buddhism in Europe: An Annotated Bibliography,* 3rd revision, March 2001. Available from www.globalbuddhism.org/bib-bud.html.

Baumann, Martin. "Buddhism in Europe: Past, Present, Prospects." In *Westward Dharma: Buddhism beyond Asia,* ed. Charles S. Prebish and Martin Baumann. Berkeley: University of California Press, 2002.

Hecker, Hellmuth. *Lebensbilder deutscher Buddhisten. Ein bio-bibliographisches Handbuch,* 2nd edition, 2 vols. Konstanz, Germany: University of Konstanz, 1996, 1997.

Obadia, Lionel. *Bouddhisme et Occident: La diffusion du bouddhisme tibétain en France.* Paris: L'Harmattan, 1999.

Rawlinson, Andrew. *The Book of Enlightened Masters: Western Teachers in Eastern Traditions.* Chicago and La Salle, IL: Open Court, 1997.

Waterhouse, Helen. *Buddhism in Bath: Adaptation and Authority.* Leeds, UK: Community Religions Project, Leeds University, 1997.

MARTIN BAUMANN

EVIL

A word that closely approximates the English word *evil* is the Sanskrit and Pāli term *pāpa,* which can be used to describe anything bad, wicked, troublesome, harmful, inauspicious, vile, or wretched. Although Buddhists have formulated various interpretations of the evils and misfortunes that befall human beings, from an ethical perspective they regard evil as the consequence of previous harmful actions that, by the cause-and-effect laws of KARMA (ACTION), return to beleaguer the perpetrator. In its chapter on *pāpa,* the DHAMMAPADA (*Words of the Doctrine*) articulates the moral dimensions of the notion of evil as wrongdoing that brings about further harm and unfortunate consequences in this life and the next: Evil conduct should be avoided just as poison is avoided, for it results only in sorrow.

The MAINSTREAM BUDDHIST SCHOOLS do not face the problem of theodicy in its classic form, which arises in monotheistic traditions that accept an all powerful, all knowing, and fully benevolent creator deity who still apparently allows suffering and misfortune to strike the innocent. For one thing, Buddhists do not accept the notion of a creator god who could be held accountable for evil. Instead, evil is simply an inevitable feature of SAṂSĀRA, or the cycle of REBIRTH; those who acknowledge the first noble truth recognize that life in saṃsāra entails DUḤKHA (SUFFERING). That which humans may be inclined to call evil (i.e., suffering) has been from eternity a necessary condition of life in impermanence, which ceases completely only upon the attainment of NIRVĀṆA.

Buddhism also offers a thorough explanatory account for what prompts immoral deeds: The condition of SENTIENT BEINGS in saṃsāra is to be beset by ignorance and craving. Sentient beings are deeply mired in greed, hatred, and delusion, which are the roots of harmful acts. Harmful acts bear consequences for oneself and others, implicating the wicked further into a cycle of evil and suffering.

Yet as Buddhist doctrine developed philosophically, a distinctive form of theodicy emerged in some traditions within the MAHĀYĀNA. As Peter Gregory argues, the Chinese AWAKENING OF FAITH (DASHENG QIXIN LUN) poses questions about the presence of ignorance in light of the TATHĀGATAGARBHA doctrine, which holds that all beings contain the germ of enlightenment and are, in their true nature, intrinsically enlightened. If the mind is by nature enlightened, how did it come to be defiled by ignorance and suffering? For Gregory this philosophical problem exposes a fundamental issue that Buddhist karma theory does not satisfactorily resolve. Although karma theory accounts for the apparent injustices in the world, it does not ultimately explain the metaphysical fact of why human beings find themselves in such a world to begin with. Although early Buddhists chose to avoid metaphysical vexations of this sort, later Buddhist philosophers did attempt to tackle such questions.

Moreover, from the soteriological point of view, there is a long tradition in Buddhism of identifying the religious life as poised beyond the dualism of good and evil. The *Dhammapada* asserts: "But one who is above good and evil and follows the religious life, who moves in the world with deliberation, that one is called a mendicant" (267). Indeed the quest for nirvāṇa is the aspiration to transcend the world of karma and morality, and thus good and evil, altogether.

Karma theory notwithstanding, Buddhists have throughout their long history accommodated theistic and animistic accounts of evil in more pedestrian ways, and they have developed technologies (e.g., spells, deity propitiation, astrological advice) to ward off evil. Some scholars, such as Gananath Obeyeskere and Melford Spiro, have suggested that karma theory provides little sense of comfort or control over the day-to-day depredations that are regarded as evil. In this view, while the notion of karma provides an exhaustive and failsafe account of the causes of evil, it is not always psychologically or experientially satisfying. Past immoral deeds that result in present suffering are both remote and unknown since few have memory of previous lives. Moreover, it is the nature of evil to victimize those upon whom it falls, and to exert itself in an immediate way as an imposition from the outside. Such cruelties as accidents, sudden illnesses, and premature death arrive unannounced and unforeseen, often visiting the apparently innocent and striking with powerful and unyielding vengeance. Viewing evil as the result of malevolent influences from meddlesome deities or inauspicious arrangements of celestial bodies, while not entirely consistent with karma theory, provides an immediate recourse for warding off, or at least containing, misfortune by ritual and apotropaic means.

Finally, Buddhists have also found meaning in evil through mythology. The cosmogonic myth recounted in the *Aggañña-sutta* (*Knowing the Beginning*) provides an account of the origins of evil in the gradual descent

Māra, the Evil One, attacks the Buddha. (Tibet, eighteenth century.) The Art Archive/Dagli Orti. Reproduced by permission.

of originally divine beings. These beings are at first celestial, incorporeal, and entirely happy, but they devolve into earth-dwelling, corporeal, and ultimately thieving, deceitful, and violent creatures. As the celestial beings come to crave food and begin to taste the savory crust of the earth, they introduce scarcity to the world, followed by competition, thieving, and the taking up of sticks against one another. In this myth, a world without evil can be imagined, and the "fall" of the world into evil is attributed ultimately to sensual desire. The chain of events that leads to the presence of evil in the world is driven by DESIRE and greed.

Another mythic complex, widely depicted in Buddhist art and legend, centers on MĀRA, a Satan-like deity of lust and death. Māra, accompanied by his legions of demonic forces and his temptress daughters, arrives to menace Gautama as he sits under a pipal tree on the night of his enlightenment. Māra is able to assume shapes and disguises and to harness all manner of demonic forces to oppose the Buddha's enlightenment. Once recognized, however, Māra is powerless, suggesting perhaps that evils are illusory and defeated when exposed. Māra symbolizes all that the Buddha conquers: ignorance, darkness, craving, lust, and destruction. With the conquest of Māra, the round of rebirth ceases, and death is vanquished.

See also: **Death**

Bibliography

Gregory, Peter. "The Problem of Theodicy in the *Awakening of Faith.*" *Religious Studies* 22, no. 1 (1986): 63–78.

Harvey, Peter. *An Introduction to Buddhist Ethics: Foundations, Values, and Issues.* Cambridge, UK: Cambridge University Press, 2000.

Ling, Trevor Oswald. *Buddhism and the Mythology of Evil: A Study in Theravāda Buddhism.* London: Allen and Unwin, 1962.

Norman, K. R., trans. *The Word of the Doctrine (Dhammapada).* Oxford: Pāli Text Society, 1997.

Obeyesekere, Gananath. "Theodicy, Sin, and Salvation in a Sociology of Buddhism." In *Dialectic in Practical Religion,* ed. E. R. Leach. Cambridge, UK: Cambridge University Press, 1968.

Spiro, Melford E. *Buddhism and Society: A Great Tradition and Its Burmese Vicissitudes,* 2nd edition. Berkeley: University of California Press, 1982.

MARIA HEIM

EXISTENCE. *See* Cosmology

EXOTERIC-ESOTERIC (KENMITSU) BUDDHISM IN JAPAN

Kenmitsu, or exoteric-esoteric, Buddhism is a scholarly term for the dominant system of Buddhist thought and practice in medieval Japan. It encompasses a wide variety of beliefs, doctrines, rituals, deities, traditions, and ecclesiastical structures that were characteristic of the mainstream religious institutions of the period. At their core were esoteric (*mitsu*) teachings and practices that gave cohesion to the entire system. In addition, there were exoteric (*ken*) doctrines, which differed from one institution to another, though each considered its own doctrines to be a rational explanation of the hidden truths found in esoteric practices. This system emerged in Japan around the tenth century, and it functioned as Buddhism's medieval orthodoxy. Subsumed under it were many beliefs, practices, and sites that are now identified as Shintō. As the dominant religious worldview, Kenmitsu Buddhism gave structure to medieval society and provided legitimacy to the ruling authorities. Over time, it became diversified and elaborated in a variety of ways. During the twelfth and thirteenth centuries a number of reformers and dissenting figures began to appear and challenge its claims. But these were inconsequential at the time, and the Kenmitsu system endured for the most part until the fifteenth or sixteenth century.

The Kenmitsu theory

Kenmitsu Buddhism as a scholarly designation was proposed by the Japanese historian Kuroda Toshio (1926–1993). In doing so Kuroda sought to dislodge the prevailing view of Buddhism's development that dominated scholarship in the late nineteenth and twentieth centuries. This view was built around a threefold historical classification: (1) Buddhism of the Nara period (710–784), comprising six schools based at the major temples of Nara—Kusha, Hossō, Jōjitsu, Sanron, Kegon, and Ritsu; (2) Buddhism of the Heian period (794–1185), consisting of the Tendai school centered on Mount Hiei near Kyoto and the Shingon school at Tōji in Kyoto and on Mount Kōya near Osaka; and (3) Buddhism of the Kamakura period (1185–1333), encompassing three schools of PURE LAND BUDDHISM (Jōdoshū, Jōdo Shinshū, and Jishū), two schools of Zen (Rinzai and Sōtō), and the NICHIREN SCHOOL. Each new phase of Buddhism's development was portrayed as a reaction to the previous stage and an improvement on it, and the Kamakura schools were perceived as the apex of Japanese Buddhism. Since the Kamakura period was considered the beginning of the medieval era, the Kamakura schools were treated as the prevailing form of Buddhism then, and the Nara and Heian schools as precursors to it. Hence, the primary focus was on Kamakura Buddhism, which indeed evolved into the largest and most pervasive schools of Buddhism at the close of the medieval period.

The Kenmitsu theory offered by Kuroda critiqued this model in several ways. First, it questioned the historical periodization on which it was based. Kuroda claimed that the medieval era began not in the twelfth century with the Kamakura period, but in the tenth century with the emergence of an estate-based economy that supported elite society and religious institutions alike. This social, economic, and political structure persisted until the fifteenth or sixteenth century, and was controlled conjointly by three ruling elites: the imperial court and aristocracy, the warrior government and its functionaries, and the leading religious institutions. In this medieval context the religion that dominated Japan was Kenmitsu Buddhism.

The second critique was that the dominant forms of medieval religion were not the new Pure Land, Zen, and Nichiren movements, but rather Tendai, Shingon, and NARA BUDDHISM. These possessed the largest number of clerics, temples, and resources in medieval times, and were the ones most frequently mentioned in medieval documents and texts. With a few exceptions, the new movements developed into influential religious organizations only in the late 1400s or early 1500s. Hence, Nara and Heian Buddhism should be considered the norm for medieval Japan instead of Kamakura Buddhism. And the new Kamakura movements should be regarded as fringe groups rather than as mainstream religion.

The third critique found in the Kenmitsu theory was of the concept of sects or discrete schools of Buddhism. Beginning in the Tokugawa period (1603–1868) Buddhism was structured into individual sectarian organizations, each with an orthodox body of teachings, a centralized religious authority, a defined set of rituals, a liturgical calendar, an apologetic history, and a hierarchy of member temples. Buddhist schools such as Tendai, Sōtō Zen, or Pure Land's Jōdoshū thus became distinct, independent entities. This sectarian structure, according to Kuroda, has been mistakenly projected onto the medieval setting, thereby producing a distorted view of religion. The Kenmitsu theory presented medieval Buddhism as less rigidly segmented and the boundaries between groups as more permeable. Religious institutions such as monasteries, temples, chapels, wayside shrines, and private meetinghouses all existed, but people could easily cross lines to participate in multiple settings. Priests of the Nara monasteries, for instance, studied the teachings across the various Nara schools as correlative philosophies rather than as rival sectarian dogma. Likewise, Tendai and Shingon clerics frequently looked beyond their own doctrinal circles and sought instruction in other settings or guidance from other masters. The fluidity of religious activity across putative schools contributed to the creation of a systemwide medieval orthodoxy in the form of Kenmitsu Buddhism.

The actual content of Kenmitsu Buddhism varied from one institution to another, but it was predicated on the assumption that esoteric practices (rituals, chants, meditations, prayers, invocations, use of sacred texts, physical austerities, etc.) had the capacity to actualize Buddhahood in this world and to engage the vast and complex spirit world of MAHĀYĀNA Buddhism. Such practices were the stock and trade of most religious institutions and were passed down in master–disciple lineages through secret transmissions and initiation ceremonies. Attached to these practices were a variety of ideas explaining and legitimizing them. This secret lore constituted the esoteric teachings (*mikkyō*) of Kenmitsu Buddhism. Beyond them were the exoteric teachings (*kengyō*), the systems of thought and doctrine, which were likewise a major enterprise of medieval institutions. Those doctrines and philosophies operated alongside esoteric teachings and were considered supportive of them. But exoteric teachings usually differed across institutions, thus distinguishing them from each other. What drew them together, however, was their common recognition of the efficacy of esoteric practices and their perpetuation of them as the core of Buddhism. In every major tradition, esoteric practices were considered primary and exoteric teachings secondary. This shared recognition gave cohesion to Kenmitsu Buddhism as Japan's medieval orthodoxy.

Japan's medieval Buddhist establishment

One major center of Kenmitsu Buddhism was Enryakuji, the Tendai monastic complex on Mount Hiei, founded by SAICHŌ (767–822). Tendai doctrine revolved around the LOTUS SŪTRA (SADDHARMAPUṆḌARĪKA-SŪTRA) and the teachings of ZHIYI (538–597), founder of the parent Tiantai tradition in China. But Saichō also adopted esoteric teachings, which were introduced into Japan by his contemporary KŪKAI (774–835). Later generations of Tendai leaders such as ENNIN (794–864) and Enchin (814–891) traveled to China, trained extensively in esoteric Buddhism, and brought back what they learned to Mount Hiei. The ideas and doctrines proposed by them, and also by Annen (841–889?), a major systematizer of Tendai thought, yoked esoteric teachings inextricably to Tendai doctrine. With these teachings the conceptual framework of Kenmitsu Buddhism was firmly established on Mount Hiei. In the tenth century, as members of Kyoto's aristocracy entered the Tendai clergy in increasing numbers and occupied positions of ecclesiastical authority, Mount Hiei inculcated its Kenmitsu understanding of Buddhism in them. Under their leadership Mount Hiei rose to eminence and began to exercise considerable social, political, and economic influence in Japan. Throughout the medieval period Mount Hiei remained a force to be reckoned with and, wherever it asserted its influence, it extended its Kenmitsu construction of Buddhism. Kuroda claimed that the crowning formulation of Kenmitsu Buddhism on Mount Hiei was ORIGINAL ENLIGHTENMENT (HONGAKU) thought, which became prominent around the twelfth century. This strand of teaching was built on the idea of the inherent and immediate enlightenment of all things, and it was preserved through master–disciple lineages and secret transmissions. But other scholars have questioned Kuroda's claim, pointing out that these teachings were not considered esoteric Buddhism proper, but rather a tradition of exoteric doctrine on Mount Hiei.

The Shingon and Nara temples were also included in the framework of Kenmitsu Buddhism. Kūkai, the founder of Shingon in Japan, was largely responsible for introducing the vocabulary of esoteric and exoteric Buddhism and developing the discourse around which the Kenmitsu order could coalesce. In his hierarchy of teachings he placed esoteric Buddhism at the top, above the exoteric teachings of Tendai and various Nara schools of thought—Hossō, Sanron, and Kegon. These views and this vocabulary became the default religious premises of the institutions that Kūkai organized, Tōji and the Shingon monastery on Mount Kōya. The temples of Nara also opened their doors to the wealth of rituals, initiations, and esoteric practices that Kūkai commanded. His establishment in 822 of the Kanjōdō hall at the powerful Tōdaiji temple, where esoteric initiations were to be performed, marked the beginning of Nara's full-scale appropriation of esoteric Buddhism. Hence, throughout the medieval period the Shingon and Nara institutions constructed their systems of doctrine and exoteric thought on a foundation of esoteric ritual and practice, just as Mount Hiei did. Though Kuroda tended to highlight the role of Mount Hiei more, it is clear that the Nara temples also flourished in this Kenmitsu culture, and built up not only religious authority but also social, political, and economic influence.

Kenmitsu Buddhism, as it pervaded the major religious institutions, emerged as the orthodox worldview of medieval Japan. It also functioned as a legitimizing ideology for the social and political order. The interaction between religious and nonreligious authorities occurred at several levels and in various modes. Society at large recognized Buddhism's capacity to engage the spirit world and to deliver humans from illusion and misfortune. The rituals and practices of esoteric Buddhism were largely aimed at these goals—from actualizing buddhahood in the body itself (*sokushin jōbutsu*) to securing good fortune and averting calamity. Hence, the imperial court, aristocracy, warrior government, and other agents of power relied on the Buddhist clergy to perform these functions in their behalf. They in turn became major adherents, supporters, and patrons of Buddhism—sponsoring rituals, building temples, and sending offspring into the ranks of clergy. But medieval Buddhism did not merely provide religious support to the privileged and powerful; it also served as one of the governing agents of Japan. That is why Kuroda included the large religious institutions among the medieval ruling elites (*kenmon*), alongside the imperial court and the warrior government. Each had its own sphere of influence, claim to authority, network of functionaries, economic base in the estate system, and means of enforcement. The religious sector, unlike the others, also used RITUAL and thaumaturgic powers to assert its influence. But none of the three could gain ascendancy over the other two, and thus had to work in collaboration with them, even while maneuvering for advantage whenever possible. Kenmitsu Buddhism articulated the nature of this relationship as the interdependence and mutual support of Buddhist teachings (*Buppō*) and royal law (*ōbō*). Each flourished only when they worked together, likened by medieval apologists to the two wheels of a cart or the two wings of a bird. This ideology of mutual dependence and benefit was articulated by the Buddhist establishment, but also embraced by the other ruling elites, for it confirmed and bolstered their authority too.

The dominance of Kenmitsu Buddhism

Kenmitsu Buddhism's ritual power was considered efficacious in engaging a vast range of spirits and sacred beings including buddhas, bodhisattvas, deities of heaven and earth, spirits of the dead, demons, ominous spirits, and also local gods (*kami*), the class of deities associated with Shintō. One of the contributions of Kuroda's theory was to refute the idea that Buddhism and Shintō have been separate and distinct religions. This, he argued, is largely a modern conceptualization arising from the forced separation of buddhas and gods and their religious institutions by the government during the Meiji period (1868–1912). This successful partition consolidated the idea of Buddhism and Shintō as independent religions, which was then superimposed on earlier periods of Japanese history. What is now known as Shintō, Kuroda claimed, was actually submerged in Kenmitsu Buddhism during medieval times. Rituals to gods were performed alongside rituals to Buddhist deities, and shrines to gods were integrated with Buddhist temples, as exemplified by the Kasuga Shrine and Kōfukuji temple complex in Nara. Moreover, a variety of explanations and rationalizations of the gods emerged in Kenmitsu doctrine. They ranged from the idea that the gods are protectors of the buddhas and Buddhism to the belief that the gods themselves seek Buddhist liberation and enlightenment, just as humans do. The most important and pervasive interpretation, though, was the *honji suijaku* principle: that the gods are none other than worldly manifestations of the buddhas and bodhisattvas in Japan, and that the buddhas and bodhisattvas are the true essence of gods. Hence, they cannot be separated, and certainly should not be seen as rivals. This view provoked widespread pairings of specific gods with particular buddhas or bodhisattvas in medieval religious institutions, so that the sun goddess Amaterasu was frequently identified with Dainichi (Mahāvairocana) Buddha. Such perceptions held sway as part of Kenmitsu Buddhism throughout the medieval period, and persisted widely until the nineteenth century when Shintō was forcibly extracted from Buddhism.

The dominance of Kenmitsu Buddhism in medieval Japan—in the major religious institutions, in its partnership with other ruling elites, and in the very fabric of popular belief and practice—casts the so-called new schools of Kamakura Buddhism in a very different light. Previously they were seen as the culmination and highest expression of Buddhism in the medieval period. But the degree to which they diverged from the Kenmitsu standard suggests that they were more an anomaly of the period. Mount Hiei was where most of the founding figures of the new Pure Land, Zen, and Nichiren movements received their first inspirations. But in each case they left Mount Hiei because of disenchantment with one aspect or another of the Buddhism there. They criticized the ambitions and self-indulgences of priests in the religious hierarchy, and they championed streamlined religious alternatives—chanting Amida (AMITĀBHA) Buddha's name, practicing Zen meditation, or chanting the title of the *Lotus Sūtra*—which challenged the authority and relevance of esoteric practices and exoteric doctrines. The reaction of Mount Hiei and the Nara centers of Kenmitsu Buddhism was twofold: to suppress these dissenting groups and to initiate reforms of their own. Some mainstream priests actually embraced these alternative practices, but sought to integrate them into the Kenmitsu framework. The dissenting movements in many cases survived suppression, but tended to hover at the margins of medieval Japan's religious world, attracting only meager followings. Those that gained institutional stability and strength in the 1300s and 1400s usually did so by building ties with Kenmitsu institutions or by developing similar religious functions. Zen's Rinzai monasteries, for instance, performed rituals for the benefit of their imperial, aristocratic, and warrior patrons. But the new Buddhist movements were largely peripheral and were frequently regarded as aberrant or even heretical.

Kenmitsu Buddhism finally lost its hold on Japan during the so-called Warring States period (1467–1568). Its decline coincided with the disintegration of medieval Japan's political and economic order. Though Kenmitsu Buddhism dominated religious affairs throughout medieval times, it never completely functioned as a seamless, monolithic system, especially as internal tensions and contradictions arose from it. The dissenting Kamakura movements were one product of these tensions, and they eventually became the successors of Kenmitsu Buddhism itself. With the emergence in the fifteenth and sixteen centuries of powerful new religious organizations such as Pure Land's Jōdo Shinshū, Nichiren's congregational alliances of Kyoto, and Zen's Sōtō school, the ascendancy of Kamakura Buddhism over Kenmitsu was finally realized.

See also: **Huayan School; Japan; Japanese Royal Family and Buddhism; Kamakura Buddhism, Japan; Meiji Buddhist Reform; Shingon Buddhism, Japan; Shintō (Honji Suijaku) and Buddhism; Tiantai School**

Bibliography

Abé, Ryūichi. *The Weaving of Mantra: Kūkai and the Construction of Esoteric Buddhist Discourse.* New York: Columbia University Press, 1999.

Adolphson, Mikael S. *The Gates of Power: Monks, Courtiers, and Warriors in Premodern Japan.* Honolulu: University of Hawaii Press, 2000.

Dobbins, James C., ed. *The Legacy of Kuroda Toshio.* Special issue. *Japanese Journal of Religious Studies* 23, nos. 3–4 (Fall 1996).

Dobbins, James C. "Envisioning Kamakura Buddhism." In *Re-Visioning "Kamakura" Buddhism,* ed. Richard K. Payne. Honolulu: University of Hawaii Press, 1998.

Grapard, Allan G. *The Protocol of the Gods: A Study of the Kasuga Cult in Japanese History.* Berkeley: University of California Press, 1992.

Kuroda Toshio. *Nihon chūsei no kokka to shūkyō* (State and Religion in Medieval Japan). Tokyo: Iwanami Shoten, 1975.

Kuroda Toshio. *Jisha seiryoku—Mō hitotsu no chūsei shakai* (The Power of Temple-Shrine Complexes—Another Medieval Society). Tokyo: Iwanami Shoten, 1980.

Kuroda Toshio. *Nihon chūsei no shakai to shūkyō* (Society and Religion in Medieval Japan). Tokyo: Iwanami Shoten, 1990.

Kuroda Toshio. "Shintō in the History of Japanese Religion." In *Religions of Japan in Practice,* ed. George J. Tanabe, Jr. Princeton, NJ: Princeton University Press, 1999.

Satō Hirō. *Nihon chūsei no kokka to Bukkyō* (State and Buddhism in Medieval Japan). Tokyo: Yoshikawa Kōbunkan, 1987.

Stone, Jacqueline I. *Original Enlightenment and the Transformation of Medieval Japanese Buddhism.* Honolulu: University of Hawaii Press, 1999.

Taira Masayuki. *Nihon chūsei no shakai to Bukkyō* (Society and Buddhism in Medieval Japan). Tokyo: Hanawa Shobō, 1992.

JAMES C. DOBBINS

F

FAITH

Few notions elicit more debate and vague associations than the family of concepts associated with the word *faith* and its various approximate synonyms (e.g., *belief*). Needless to say, the English *faith* has no exact equivalent in the languages of Asia. The word means many things in English and in other Western languages as well, and the proximate Asian equivalents also have many meanings in their Asian contexts. This is not to say that *faith* cannot be used as a descriptive or analytical tool to understand Buddhist ideas and practices, yet one must be aware of the cultural and polemic environments that shaped Buddhist notions of faith.

Semantic range

The most common English theological meanings are the ones that have the most questionable similarity to historical Buddhist belief and practice: acceptance of and secure belief in the existence of a personal creator deity ("belief in"), acceptance of such deity as a unique person with a distinctive name, the unquestioned acceptance of this deity's will, and the adoption of the articles of dogma believed to express the deity's will. Buddhist notions tend to occupy a different center in the semantic field: serene trust, confident belief that the practice of the dharma will bear the promised fruit, and joyful surrender to the presence or vision of one or many "ideal beings" (BUDDHAS, BODHISATTVAS, etc.). The articles of belief and systems of practice that constitute the Buddhist PATH are seldom set up explicitly as direct objects of faith, but confessions of trust and declarations of commitment to various aspects of the path are common ritual practices (taking the REFUGES, taking vows, etc.).

The objects of faith can be all, any, or only one among the multiple buddhas, bodhisattvas, and deities of Buddhism. Nevertheless, Buddhists often confess their total trust in a particular deity or buddha or bodhisattva identified by a unique name and by personal attributes that are considered distinctive and superior to those of any other deity (e.g., the cult of AMITĀBHA or the cult of Shugs ldan).

A sense of the range of Buddhist conceptions of "faith" can be derived from a glance at some of the classical Asian terms that are rendered into English as *faith.* The term *śraddhā* (Pāli, *saddhā*), for instance, may signify belief, but generally refers more to trust and commitment. It is sometimes glossed as "trust or reliance on someone else" (*parapratyaya, Abhidharmakośa* VI. 29), but, etymologically, it derives from an old Indo-European verb meaning "to place one's heart on (a desire, goal, object, or person)," which appears in Latin in the verb *crēdō,* and subsequently in English as *creed, credence,* and so on.

A connection between this mental state and other positive states is suggested in a variety of ways. For instance, in the *abhidharma* literature the word *śraddhā* refers to one of the mental factors that are always present in good thoughts (*kuśalamahābhūmika, Abhidharmakośa* II. 23–25). Already in the sūtra/*sutta* literature, *śraddhā* is one of the five mental faculties necessary for a good practice (the five *indriyas* or five *balas*), which include MINDFULNESS and persevering courage.

These meanings are associated also with the idea of conviction, committed and steadfast practice, or commitment as active engagement, a range of concepts expressed with the term *adhimukti* or *adhimokṣa* (Pāli, *adhimutti* or *adhimokkha*). The attitude or cognitive-affective state expressed by this word is characteristic of the preliminary stage in a bodhisattva's career: the stage of acting (*caryā*) on one's commitment (*adhimukti*), or *adhimukticaryābhūmi.*

Examined from the perspective suggested by the above range of usages, faith would be a sui generis psychological state, an extension of the ability to trust or rely on someone or something. In this aspect of the denotation of *śraddhā,* and *adhimokṣa,* faith is also a virtue necessary for concentrated MEDITATION, and is closely related to, if not synonymous with, the disciple's ardent desire for self-cultivation or the zeal required for such cultivation. In this context, faith is also the opposite of, or an antidote against, the sluggishness, dejection, and discouragement that can arise during long hours of meditation practice.

However, such monastic or contemplative definitions of *faith* do not exhaust the Buddhist repertoire. As noted previously, Buddhist concepts of faith include as well affective states associated with the attachment and trust of devotion. Such states are sometimes subsumed under the category of *prasāda* (the action noun corresponding to *prasannacitta*). This term has a long history in the religious traditions of India; it means etymologically "settling down," and evokes meanings of "serenity, calm, aplomb," as well as conviction and trust. Furthermore, among its many usages, it expresses both the "favor" of the powerful (their serene largess, their grace) and the acceptance or recognition of this favorable disposition on the part of the weaker participant in the relationship (serene trust, confident acceptance). The latter feeling is not only serene trust in the wisdom of a teacher or in the truth of the teachings, but the joyful acceptance of the benevolent power and benediction of sacred objects and holy persons. Thus the proper state of mind when performing a ritual of devotion is a *prasannacitta*: a mind in the state of *prasāda,* that is, calmly secure, trusting, devoted, content, and loyal.

East Asian usages

These Indian concepts were usually rendered in Chinese with a term denoting trust, *xin,* where the accent is on confidence, rather than on a surrender of one's discursive judgment. Nonetheless, *xin* also could denote surrender and unquestioned acceptance, absolute trust, and a believing mind and will. The later meanings played a major role in both nonliterate practice and the theologies of faith of some of the literate schools.

The first element in this polarity (faith that does not exclude knowledge or direct apprehension of religious truths) is seen, for instance, in the classical CHAN SCHOOL notion of *xinxin*: "trusting the mind." This refers to the conviction that the searching mind is the object of its own search—that is, buddha-nature. Such conviction is understood as a nonmediated, nonreasoned confidence born of the immediate apprehension of a presence. Expressed in terms of a process or a practice, this faith is the experience of the mind when one is not manipulating or organizing its contents with discursive thoughts. The trusting mind itself becomes the object of trust.

This is the theme of the *Xinxinming* (*Stanzas on Trusting the Mind*), a poem attributed to the "Third Patriarch" of Chan Buddhism, Sengcan (d. ca. 606 C.E.), in which "mind" or "thought" is the perfect goal of the religious aspiration that is the act of faith. It is "perfect like vast empty space, lacking nothing, having nothing in excess." What keeps us from experiencing the mind in this way is our penchant for "selecting and rejecting." By contrast, "the trusting mind does not split things into twos"; not splitting things into twos is the meaning of "trusting the mind" (or "the trusting mind" *xinxin*).

The idea of faith (*xin*) also appears in a formulation attributed to Gaofeng Yuanmiao (1238–1295), who describes three essential aspects of meditation practice (*chan yao*). These are: the faculty of faith, persevering commitment, and DOUBT. Faith is "the great faculty of trusting" (*daxingen*), which links the idea to the earlier abhidharmic notions of trust and faith as a natural faculty. It is clear that this trust precedes full knowledge or understanding because the other two aspects of practice are great tenacity of purpose or persevering commitment (*dafenzhi*) and a great feeling of doubt or intensely felt doubt (*dayiqing*).

This use of the term *xin* is ostensibly different from the meanings accepted by other important strands of the East Asian tradition in which we find an opposition between examined trust and the surrender of self-knowledge. The PURE LAND SCHOOLS (Chinese, *jingtu*; Japanese, *jōdo*) in particular understood that the *prasannacitta* of the Indian tradition implied a surrender of the will to pursue a life of holiness or the desire to attain awakening by one's own efforts. However, even among the most radical formulations of the Pure Land traditions, where the trusting practitioners are clearly separated from the object of their faith and are incapable of achieving holiness on their own, the desired state of mind has the distinct marks of Buddhist notions of mind and faith. Thus, in some of the more radical Jōdo shinshū formulations the devotee's surrender is not so much an act of belief as an acceptance of grace: One surrenders one's own capacity to discriminate and believe, and one accepts the Buddha's own believing mind (*shinjin*), so that one's faith is in fact adopting, as it were, the Buddha's own trustworthy mind (*shinjin*)—sharing the merits, wisdom, and compassion of the very object of faith. Affectively, this theological view is linked with the ideal of joyful trust (*shingyō*), the joy and bliss of trusting, which ultimately, or eschatologically, may be said to be synonymous with the joy of seeing the Buddha Amitābha face to face (at the time of death or in the pure land).

Summary Interpretation

Ideals of nondiscursive apprehension straddle the dividing line between faith and knowledge, humble surrender and recognition of a state of liberation that cannot be acquired by the individual's will. In some ways the tradition seems to assume that one has faith in that which one respects and trusts, but also in that which one wishes to attain, and that which one imagines oneself to be or able to become.

See also: **Pure Land Buddhism; Pure Lands**

Bibliography

de Certeau, Michel. "What We Do When We Believe." In *On Signs,* ed. Marshall Blonsky. Baltimore, MD: Johns Hopkins University Press, 1985.

Gómez, Luis O., trans. and ed. *The Land of Bliss: The Paradise of the Buddha of Measureless Light: Sanskrit and Chinese Versions of the Sukhāvatīvyūha Sūtras* (1996), 3rd printing, corrected edition. Honolulu: University of Hawaii Press, 2000.

Gómez, Luis O. "Prayer: Buddhist Perspectives." In *Encyclopedia of Monasticism,* Vol. 2, ed. William M. Johnston. Chicago: Fitzroy Dearborn, 2000.

Gómez, Luis O. "Spirituality: Buddhist Perspectives." In *Encyclopedia of Monasticism,* Vol. 2, ed. William M. Johnston. Chicago: Fitzroy Dearborn, 2000.

Hara, Minoru. "Śraddhā in the Sense of Desire." In *Études bouddhiques offertes a Jacques May,* ed. J. Bronkhorst, K. Mimaki, and T. Tillemans. Special issue. *Asiatische Studien/Études Asiatiques* 161, no. 1 (1992): 180–193.

Lopez, Donald S., Jr. "Belief." In *Critical Terms for Religious Studies,* ed. Mark C. Taylor. Chicago: University of Chicago Press, 1998.

Park, Sung-bae. *Buddhist Faith and Sudden Enlightenment.* Albany: State University of New York Press, 1983.

Smith, Wilfred Cantwell. *Faith and Belief.* Princeton, NJ: Princeton University Press, 1979.

LUIS O. GÓMEZ

FAMENSI

Famensi, or Monastery of the Gate of the Dharma, was founded in the Northern Wei dynasty (386–534) at Fufeng in Shaanxi province, about 110 kilometers west of modern Xi'an. One of only four Chinese monasteries believed to possess a true body relic of the Buddha, it was closely associated with no fewer than seven emperors of the Tang dynasty (618–907). Originally called Chongzhensi, it was renamed Famensi in 1003.

In 1981 after heavy rainfall, the thirteen-story octagonal brick pagoda of the Famensi, built in 1609, finally collapsed. Excavations in April 1987 revealed not only the circular foundations of the brick pagoda, but also the square foundations of a Tang dynasty wooden pagoda, with steps, a corridor, and three stone chambers, unusually constructed to allow access from the outside. History records that in 631, 660, 704, 760, 790, 819, and 873, the relics were recovered and conveyed to the capital.

Most of the objects found in the excavation date from 874, after which the entire deposit remained untouched. A pair of large stone tablets, engraved with a text written in 874 by monk Juezhi of the Xingshan Monastery and placed at the inner end of the corridor, give precise details of the 122 gold and silver objects presented in 874 by emperors Yizong and Xizong.

The first chamber of the crypt contained a stone STŪPA, painted both outside and inside, enshrining an elaborate model gilt-bronze stūpa, itself containing a tiny silver-gilt RELIQUARY holding one of the four "finger-bone" relics. In the second chamber, a larger shrine, dedicated in 708, contained a second relic. Beyond it, and close to the doors leading to the innermost chamber of the crypt, was a large cylindrical box containing a number of celadon bowls and dishes, the so-called *mi se* or secret color ware, sent as tribute to the court from the Yue kilns in Zhejiang province. A third relic was found in a tiny solid gold stūpa, the innermost of a series of eight nesting caskets, in the third and innermost chamber, which was filled with the majority of the accompanying gold, silver-gilt, glass, and sandalwood offerings. Finally, sealed in a cavity beneath the rear wall of the innermost chamber, a fourth relic was enshrined in a tiny jade coffin, inside a very small crystal sarcophagus, within a silver-gilt casket bearing forty-five esoteric Buddhist images, protected by a larger iron casket. The other three relics, carved from jade, were all close copies of this fourth relic. About two inches long, it is made of a softer substance resembling bone, hollow and engraved on the inside with the seven stars of the Northern Dipper.

According to the inventory tablet, the iron casket and crystal sarcophagus (with its enclosed jade coffin), were brought from the monastery to the capital in 873. Along with the painted stone stūpa and the gilt-bronze pagoda from the first chamber, they may well be the earliest items in the entire deposit, followed by the larger stone stūpa in the second chamber, and a set of miniature embroidered garments, including a skirt presented by Empress Wu (r. 684–705), which is also mentioned in the inventory tablet.

While a full report of the excavation has yet to be published, this incredible array of sumptuous objects has already provided invaluable evidence for metalworking and textile techniques of the late Tang period, the tributary system, ritual implements (water vessels, staffs, incense burners and stands, containers for incense) and evidence of the practice of esoteric Buddhism at the Tang court.

See also: **Maṇḍala; Relics and Relics Cults; Ritual Objects**

Bibliography

Wang, Eugene Y. "Of the True Body: The Famensi Relics and Corporeal Transformation in Tang Imperial China." In *Body and Face in Chinese Visual Culture,* ed. Wu Hung et al. Cambridge, MA: Harvard Asia Center and Harvard University Press, 2003.

Whitfield, Roderick. "Discoveries from the Famen Monastery at Fufeng and the Qingshan Monastery at Lintong, Shaanxi Province." In *The Golden Age of Chinese Archaeology: Celebrated Discoveries from the People's Republic of China,* ed. Yang Xiaoneng. New Haven, CT, and London: Yale University Press, 1999.

RODERICK WHITFIELD

FAMILY, BUDDHISM AND THE

Given that Buddhism is regularly understood as a monastic movement dedicated to "leaving the family" (*pravrajyā*), the technical term for becoming a monk or nun, it might seem odd to ask about Buddhism's relationship to the family. Why, after all, would Buddhism as a religion of renunciation have anything to do with family life? However, a closer look at the structure of Buddhist rhetoric, as well as Buddhism's various societal roles, reveals that Buddhism's relationship to the family and family values has several unexpected layers.

Arguably there are at least four basic categories of Buddhist discourse that focus on familial issues: (1) a discourse on the negative aspects of family life, the language of renunciation; (2) a symbolic language in which identity within the monastic setting is understood as a kind of replication of the patriarchal family, a kind of corporate familialism; (3) guidelines for correct conduct at home, pastoral advice from the Buddhist establishment; and (4) specific lineage claims that sought to establish an elite family within the monastic family, a more specialized form of corporate familialism.

As for the first, the language of renunciation, statements regarding the unsatisfactory and even dangerous aspects of family life are typical throughout the Buddhist world. According to this logic, life in the family is fraught with burning desires and gnawing concerns. Consequently, life at home is essentially the environment in which patterns of conduct and thinking develop that will continue to bind one in the cycle of birth and death (SAṂSĀRA), and keep one from making progress toward NIRVĀṆA. Among these statements about the generic risks of family life, one can also find more specific statements about the physical dangers that women court as they follow the prescribed life cycle within the family, the risks of childbirth being paramount. In sum, in this sphere of discourse Buddhist authorities encourage reflection on the benefits of leaving the encumbering and dangerous domain of family life in order to pursue higher spiritual goals.

The second sphere of family rhetoric appears when Buddhist renunciants began to settle down into landowning religious groups, roughly two centuries before the beginning of the common era. At this point, even as the evils of family life were still espoused, monastic relations were explained via a kind of corporate familialism. Apparently, the Buddhists began to construct an ulterior family, actually a purer form of patriarchy, that was to solidify and legitimize Buddhist identity within the perimeter of the monastic walls. Thus, in formally gaining the identity of a monk or nun, one joined the Buddha in a kind of fictive kinship that sealed one's Buddhist identity with a kind of "naturalness" and facilitated harmony within the monasteries. In fact, the ritual for becoming a monk or nun seems to have been conceived as a kind of rebirth back into one's "original" family, and one was thereafter called "a son of the Buddha." This motif of rebirth is clear, too, in the way that one's "age" and seniority within the monastery is determined not by real age, but by the number of years that have passed since one's ORDINATION.

The third sphere of family discourse in Buddhism appears in the way that Buddhist authorities, likely from the earliest phases of the religion, prescribed proper conduct for those who remained in the family. These moral guidelines define the life to be maintained at home: One is to be obedient to seniors and considerate of others' needs, while also adhering to the generic set of Buddhist precepts—not killing, stealing, lying, and so on. Given these statements, and particularly those that urge filial submission to one's parents and seniors, one can see that Buddhist discourse was, and still is, intent on stabilizing and even bolstering the family. The reasons for Buddhism's advocacy of traditional family practice are complex, but one important reason is that Buddhist monasteries relied on families to support them financially. In fact, to facilitate exchanges between the family and the monastery, Buddhist discourse often emphasized that one is only a good, filial son at home if one patronizes the Buddhist monasteries. These injunctions could also be focused on ancestor care, where it was argued that living descendents ought to patronize Buddhist monastics in order to enlist their spiritual power, which could be directed toward caring for the deceased family members in the afterworld. In short, Buddhist monastics inserted themselves within the sphere of at-home family values by arguing that the family's life cycle needed to involve patronage of Buddhist monasteries.

As for the last category of familial rhetoric, at different times in Buddhist history there appeared mystical genealogies in which a higher Buddhist family was established within the already domestic space of the Buddhist establishment. Thus, in tantric Buddhism in India and Tibet, as well as in the CHAN SCHOOL of Buddhism in East Asia, it was claimed that certain monks were more directly related to the Buddha than other Buddhist monks or nuns. In both cases, the language of fathers and sons was relied upon to explain why certain monks should be taken to be living representatives of the tradition, with truth, authority, and legitimacy flowing directly down the lineage from the Buddha to the present master. In fact, intricate logics emerged wherein these elite "sons of the Buddha" were put in charge of guiding other less connected Buddhists back to their true familial relationship to the Buddha.

In sum, though Buddhism sought to escape the family, this very effort to leave domesticity was itself domesticized and remade into a Buddhist family. Moreover, this new Buddhist family established a symbiotic relationship with the lay family, encouraging its stability and productivity, along with a pro-Buddhist orientation. Finally, even within the familial space of the monasteries, other hyper-families appeared, suggesting an ongoing need to re-create identity and authority according to patriarchal logics, along with the sense that sameness and difference in social space are best handled via familial rhetorics that are both inclusive and hierarchizing.

See also: **Laity; Monasticism; Monks; Nuns; Women**

Bibliography

Cabezón, José Ignacio, ed. *Buddhism, Sexuality, and Gender.* Albany: State University of New York Press, 1992.

Cole, Alan. "Upside Down/Right Side Up: A Revisionist History of Buddhist Funerals in China." *History of Religions* 35, no. 4 (1996): 307–338.

Cole, Alan. *Mothers and Sons in Chinese Buddhism.* Stanford, CA: Stanford University Press, 1998.

Cole, Alan. "Homestyle Vinaya and Docile Boys in Chinese Buddhism." *Positions: East Asia Cultures Critique* 7, no. 1 (1999): 5–50.

Faure, Bernard. *The Red Thread: Buddhist Approaches to Sexuality.* Princeton, NJ: Princeton University Press, 1998.

Schopen, Gregory. *Bones, Stones, and Buddhist Monks: Collected Papers on the Archaeology, Epigraphy, and Texts of Monastic Buddhism in India.* Honolulu: University of Hawaii Press, 1997.

ALAN COLE

FANWANG JING (BRAHMĀ'S NET SŪTRA)

The *Fanwang jing* (*Brahmā's Net Sūtra*) is a highly regarded apocryphal text in East Asian Buddhism that provided a set of uniquely MAHĀYĀNA precepts. According to tradition, the sūtra was spoken by the Buddha, recorded in Sanskrit in India, and then translated by KUMĀRAJĪVA (350–409/413) into Chinese in 406. In fact, however, it is now known that the *Fanwang jing* was composed in China by unknown author(s), sometime during the middle of the fifth century C.E. The sūtra purports to be the last chapter of a longer Sanskrit text, and its full title is *Chapter on the Mind Ground of the Bodhisattvas of the Fanwang jing.* However, there is no conclusive evidence that this framing text ever existed.

The *Fanwang jing* consists of two fascicles: The first enumerates the stages of practice of the bodhisattva PATH, and the second, which had been circulating as an independent text, contains a list of the ten major and forty-eight minor PRECEPTS. The set of precepts illustrated in the *Fanwang jing* is popularly called the "bodhisattva precepts" or the "*Fanwang* precepts"; thus the second fascicle on its own is often called the *Sūtra of Bodhisattva Precepts* and is used in East Asian countries as a bodhisattva PRĀTIMOKṢA (collection of rules). Traditionally, East Asian Buddhist monks and nuns are ordained using a set of rules drawn from the *Sifen lu* (Four-Part Vinaya) of the Indian DHARMAGUPTAKA school. The *Fanwang* precepts were rarely used by themselves for ordination in China and Korea but instead were treated as a supplementary set of Mahāyāna precepts.

Composed at a time when mainstream Buddhist and Mahāyāna texts on monastic discipline had just been transmitted into China, the contents of the *Fanwang jing* reflect Chinese Buddhist concerns about the impact a foreign morality would have on the indigenous culture. These concerns are reflected in the emphasis placed in the sūtra on filial piety and obedience, two subjects of vital concern to Confucians. In addition, several minor precepts concern the relationship between the Buddhist order and the state, which claim Buddhism's autonomy from secular power. Also of particular interest is that whereas VINAYA rules are intended only for monks and nuns, the *Fanwang* precepts are said to apply universally to both the LAITY and monastics, as illustrated by the sūtra's stated audience of monks, nuns, laypeople, and bodhisattvas. In some instances, the sūtra notes that certain precepts are intended either for laypeople or for members of the Buddhist order. For example, the major precepts against killing, stealing, and illicit sexual activity apply both to members of religious orders and to lay believers, whereas the fifth major precept, a prohibition against selling liquor, was principally directed at the laity.

Numerous commentaries were written on the *Fanwang jing,* representing the significant role its Mahāyāna bodhisattva precepts played in East Asian Buddhism. Many leading scholars in China, including ZHIYI (538–597) and FAZANG (643–712), wrote commentaries on the text, most focusing on the second fascicle. In Korea, more than fifteen commentaries are known to have been written on the sūtra, including works by the eminent monks WŎNHYO (617–686), Sŭngjang (d.u.), Ŭijŏk (d.u.), and Taehyŏn (fl. 753). Six of these commentaries are extant, coming primarily from the Silla period. In Japan, SAICHŌ (767–822) made the *Fanwang jing* one of the most influential texts in Japanese Buddhism by arguing that its set of precepts should serve as the sole basis for ORDINATION in the Tendai school, the Japanese branch of the TIANTAI SCHOOL.

See also: **Apocrypha; Mahāyāna Precepts in Japan**

Bibliography

Groner, Paul. "The *Fan-wang ching* and Monastic Discipline in Japanese Tendai: A Study of Annen's *Futsū jubosatsukai kōshaku.*" In *Chinese Buddhist Apocrypha,* ed. Robert E. Buswell, Jr. Honolulu: University of Hawaii Press, 1990.

EUNSU CHO

FASTING.

See **Ascetic Practices**

FAXIAN

Faxian (ca. 337–ca. 418) is the first Chinese monk whose travel to India is documented. Not only did Faxian bring firsthand knowledge of India to China, he also brought back a series of scriptures.

After being ordained at the age of twenty, Faxian recognized that the VINAYA (canon of monastic rules) available in China was incomplete. He therefore vowed to travel to India to search for Vinaya texts. He left Chang'an in 399 and proceeded via DUNHUANG and across the Pamir mountains into Uddiyana in northwestern India. Between 405 and 407, Faxian studied in Pāṭalīputra, then in Tāmralipti in eastern India, and later in Sri Lanka. He set sail for home in 411, and after an odyssey that lasted until 413 he landed at the Shandong Peninsula. During his fifteen-year pilgrimage, Faxian had traveled to approximately thirty kingdoms.

Faxian went to Jiankang (Nanking) and began translating the texts he had collected in India and Sri Lanka. Two of these were of the Vinaya of the MAHĀSĀṂGHIKA SCHOOL (T1425, T1427), two were MAHĀYĀNA scriptures (T376, T745), and one was a HĪNAYĀNA scripture (T7). Faxian continued to work on translations until his death between 418 and 423.

Faxian, like later Chinese monks, conceived of his travel to India as a "search for the dharma," which involved venerating holy sites, studying with Indian masters, and collecting texts. His trip inspired later generations of pilgrims, including XUANZANG (ca. 600–664) and YIJING (635–713). The major source of information about Faxian's travels is his *Faxian zhuan* (*Record of Faxian,* T2085), written in 416, which is an important document for South Asian and Buddhist history.

See also: China

Bibliography

Giles, Herbert A., trans. *The Travels of Fa-hsien (399–414 A.D.), or, Record of the Buddhistic Kingdoms* (1923). London: Routledge and Kegan Paul, 1956.

Shih, Robert, trans. and ed. *Biographies des moines éminents (Kao seng tchouan) de Houei-kiao.* Louvain, Belgium: Institut Orientaliste, 1968.

ALEXANDER L. MAYER

FAXIANG SCHOOL

Called the *Weishi* (Sanskrit, *Vijñaptimātra*; Consciousness-only) school by its proponents, and the *Faxiang* (dharma characteristics) school by its opponents, this was the third major introduction of the YOGĀCĀRA SCHOOL of Buddhism into China. Competing versions of Yogācāra had dominated Chinese Buddhism since the beginning of the sixth century, first with the Northern and Southern Dilun schools, which followed, respectively, the opposing interpretations by Bodhiruci and Ratnamati of the *Dilun* (Vasubandhu's commentary on the *Shidi jing*; Sanskrit, *Daśabhūmika-sūtra*). Thereafter, a different brand of Yogācāra was introduced by the translator PARAMĀRTHA (499–569) in the mid-sixth century. Disputes between these three schools, as well as various hybrids of Yogācāra and TATHĀGATAGARBHA, had become so pervasive by the time of XUANZANG (ca. 600–664) that he traveled to India in 629 believing that texts as yet unavailable in China would settle the discrepancies. Instead he found that the Indian understanding of Yogācāra differed in many fundamentals—doctrinally and methodologically—from what had developed in China, and on his return to China in 645 he attempted to narrow the differences by translating over seventy texts and introducing Buddhist LOGIC.

Because the novel teachings Xuanzang conveyed represented Indian Buddhist orthodoxy and because the Chinese emperor lavished extravagant patronage on him, Xuanzang quickly became the preeminent East Asian Buddhist of his generation, attracting students from Korea and Japan, as well as China. Two of his disciples, the Korean monk WŎNCH'ŬK (613–696) and the Chinese monk KUIJI (632–682) bitterly competed to succeed Xuanzang upon his death, their rivalry largely centering on divergent interpretations of the *Cheng weishi lun* (*Treatise on Establishing Consciousness-Only*), a commentary on Vasubandhu's *Triṃśikā* (*Thirty Verses*) that, according to tradition, Kuiji helped Xuanzang compile from ten Sanskrit commentaries. Kuiji is considered by tradition to be the first patriarch of the Weishi (or Faxiang) school.

Kuiji wrote many commentaries on such works as the *Vimalakīrtinirdeśa-sūtra,* the HEART SŪTRA, the LOTUS SŪTRA (SADDHARMAPUṆḌARĪKA-SŪTRA), the Madhyāntavibhāga, and Buddhist logic texts, but his commentaries on the *Cheng weishi lun* and an original treatise on Yogācāra, *Fayuan yilin zhang* (*Essays on the Forest of Meanings in the Mahāyāna Dharma Garden*), became the cornerstones of the Weishi school. Hui Zhao (650–714), the second patriarch, and Zhi Zhou (668–723), the third patriarch, wrote commentaries on the *Fayuan yulin chang,* the *Lotus Sūtra,* and the *Madhyāntavibhāga*; they also wrote treatises on Buddhist logic and commentaries on the *Cheng weishi lun.* After Zhi Zhou, Faxiang's influence declined in China, though its texts continued to be studied by other schools. In the late nineteenth and early twentieth centuries Faxiang enjoyed a revival among Chinese philosophers such as Yang Wenhui (1837–1911), Ouyang Jingwu (1871–1943), TAIXU (1890–1947), and Xiong Shili (1883–1968), who sought a bridge between native philosophy and Western philosophy, especially in the field of epistemology.

Faxiang (Korean, Pŏpsang; Japanese, Hossō) was influential in Korea during the unified Silla (668–935) and Koryŏ dynasties (918–1392), but faded with the decline of Buddhism in the Chosŏn dynasty (1392–1910). Similarly, Hossō, initially transmitted to Japan from China and Korea, was prominent during the Nara period (710–784), but withered under attack in the Heian period (794–1185) from rival Tendai and Shingon schools. The Hossō monk Ryōhen (1194–1252) rebutted those attacks in his *Kanjin Kakumushō* (*Précis on Contemplating the Mind and Awakening from the Dream*), but Hossō, though surviving, declined nonetheless.

Most East Asian Buddhist schools, along with Faxiang, accepted many standard Yogācāra doctrines, such as the eight consciousnesses, three natures, and mind-only, though each school quibbled about specifics. The two doctrines that drew the most attacks were the Faxiang rejection of tathāgatagarbha ideology for being too metaphysically substantialistic and the Faxiang doctrine of five seed-families (Sanskrit, *pañcagotras*; Chinese, *wu xing*), which held that one's potential for awakening was determined by the good seeds already in one's consciousness stream. Practitioners of the HĪNAYĀNA, PRATYEKABUDDHA, and MAHĀYĀNA paths, as well as those who were undecided about practice, could fulfill these paths only by bringing the respective seeds of whichever path they contained to fruition. A fifth seed-family, ICCHANTIKA, being devoid of the requisite seeds, can never and would never desire to achieve awakening. Since the other East Asian Buddhist schools held that all beings possess buddha-nature incipiently as tathāgatagarbha, and thus all have the potential for awakening, they found the *icchantika* doctrine unacceptable. However, Faxiang did not treat the *icchantika* as an ontological category or predestination theory; it referred only to someone incorrigible, someone who, in recent lives, remains impervious to the teachings of Buddhism. Anyone desiring enlightenment, by definition, cannot be an *icchantika.*

Bibliography

Lusthaus, Dan. *Buddhist Phenomenology: A Philosophical Investigation of Yogācāra Buddhism and the Ch'eng Wei-shih lun.* London and New York: RoutledgeCurzon, 2002.

Sponberg, Alan. "The Vijñaptimātratā Buddhism of the Chinese Monk K'uei-chi (A.D. 632–682)." Ph.D. diss. University of British Columbia, Vancouver, 1979.

Weinstein, Stanley. "The Kanjin Kakumushō." Ph.D. diss. Harvard University, 1965.

DAN LUSTHAUS

FAZANG

Fazang (also known as Xianshou, 643–712) was born into a family of Sogdian origin in the Chinese capital of Chang'an. He was a consummate Buddhist exegete in the Indian mold and at one point worked with the Khotanese translator ŚIKṢĀNANDA (652–710) on a translation of the HUAYAN JING (*Avataṃsaka-sūtra, Flower Garland Sūtra*). Fazang's works in the standard edition of the Chinese Buddhist canon are: five commentaries on MAHĀYĀNA sūtras, including two on the *Huayan jing*; two commentaries on treatises of NĀGĀRJUNA and Sāramati; two commentaries on the Chinese apocryphon AWAKENING OF FAITH (DASHENG QIXIN LUN); and thirteen treatises on the *Huayan jing* and related matters. Fazang was a disciple of Zhiyan (602–668), and eventually these two were enshrined as the second and third patriarchs of the HUAYAN SCHOOL.

Fazang's *Huayen wujiao zhang* (*Treatise on the Five Teachings of Huayan*) presents a very technical Huayan system, which he refers to as the "perfect teaching of the one vehicle" (*yicheng yuanjiao*) or "*dharmadhātu* dependent origination" (*fajie yuanqi*). The system is based on the six characteristics: the universal, the separate, the same, the different, the coming-into-being, and the disintegrating. These six reveal an inexhaustible and perfect fusion, a fusion without obstruction. By means of this teaching, when one defilement, say greed, is cut off, all are cut off, and when one merit is perfected, all are perfected. When the practitioner first produces the thought of awakening (*bodhicitta*), he has simultaneously completed perfect awakening (*samyaksaṃbodhi*). Cause (practice) and effect (awakening) are at the same time. If, as some have suggested, the *Huayan jing* is associated with the Central Asian Buddhist center of Khotan, then this Huayan system is truly a Central Asian/Chinese development. Later, ZONGMI (780–841) declared Huayan identical to the highest of the three theses (*zong*) of Chan.

Bibliography

Cook, Francis H. *Hua-yen Buddhism: The Jewel Net of Indra.* University Park: Pennsylvania State University Press, 1977.

Fontain, Jan. *The Pilgrimage of Sudhana: A Study of Gaṇḍavyūha Illustrations in China, Japan, and Java.* The Hague, Netherlands: Mouton, 1967.

JEFFREY BROUGHTON

FESTIVALS AND CALENDRICAL RITUALS

Buddhists have divided up time according to various calendrical systems. In Sri Lanka and Southeast Asia, for example, the most lasting and fundamental system has been the ancient Indian lunar calendar, whose twelve months and forty-eight six- to nine-day weeks commence with sabbaths determined by the four phases of the lunar cycle: new moon, waxing moon, waning moon, and, most importantly, the full-moon day (Pāli, *uposatha*; Sanskrit, *upoṣadha* or *poṣadha*). Larger expanses of time have been calculated as numbers of years since the final passing away (Pāli, *parinibbāna*; Sanskrit, *parnirvāṇa*) of the Buddha (*Buddha Varṣa*, abbreviated B.E. or B.V. and commencing in 543 B.C.E.); since the dawn of the imperial Śaka Era (*Śakasaṃvat*, abbreviated S.S. and commencing in 78 C.E.); and since the emergence of various dynasties in different regions. More recently, as a result of colonialism and international practice, time has been calculated as the number of years before and since the start of the common era. These various eras in turn are but fleeting moments in saṃsāra's vast expanse of ages (*yuga*) and eons (*kappa*; kalpa).

Within that expanse, it is considered a rare achievement to be reborn during a *Buddha Varṣa*: a time when a Buddha, his teachings, his corporeal relics, and his community of monks and nuns still exist. According to the late canonical Pāli text the *Buddhavaṃsa* (*Chronicle of Buddhas*, ca. second century B.C.E.), there have been only twenty-four such Buddha eras in "one hundred thousand plus four incalculable numbers of eons." During such rare periods, including the present one, it is possible to advance along the PATH to NIRVĀṆA by learning and practicing the Buddha's teachings. Because such directed progress on the path is not possible in the hiatuses between Buddha eras, every moment in this or any other Buddha era is soteriologically charged. While the ideal is certainly to cultivate Buddhist virtues constantly, from an early date Buddhists throughout the region have considered it especially efficacious to perform such activities on the above-mentioned lunar sabbaths.

Long before the time of the Buddha, South Asians already were focusing their religious activities (such as performing sacrifices and other rituals, and preaching their different messages) on these lunar sabbaths. According to the second book of the *Mahāvagga* (*Great Section*) of the Pāli VINAYA (monastic code), early in his career the Buddha was approached by King Seniya Bimbisāra of Magadha, who requested that the Buddha allow his monks to assemble on these days because non-Buddhists used them for public preaching and thereby gained the hearts and adherence of listeners. The Buddha permitted this, and after people complained that the assembled monks just sat in silence, he further permitted them to preach the dharma to laypeople on lunar sabbaths. Moreover, he established for them the ritual of recitation of the Buddhist monastic disciplinary rules embodied in the Pātimokkha (Sanskrit, PRĀTIMOKṢA). Down to the present day, this recitation of the Pātimokkha on each full-moon day by all ordained (*upasampadā*) Buddhist clergy residing inside a particular monastic boundary (*sīma*), complete with ceremonies and judicial practices and penalties, has constituted the primary monastic ritual by which Buddhist monks and nuns have maintained their collective purity and sense of communitas. Even today it proceeds very much as outlined in the ancient vinaya texts, with a leading monk or nun thrice professing his or her purity as regards each of the major categories of the Pātimokkha rules. Those assembled either profess, through silence, their own purity regarding the rules, or they confess transgressions that have occurred, for which punishments and restorative acts are prescribed in the vinaya texts.

The yearly cycle constituted by these monthly monastic rituals is punctuated by the three-month "rains-retreat" (Pāli, *vassa*; Sanskrit, *varśa*). The retreat is said in the *Mahāvagga* to have been established by the Buddha in response to criticisms that his monks and nuns harmed microscopic creatures by traveling during the rainy season. This period of heightened practice and restrictions on travel away from the monastery begins on the full-moon day that corresponds to July/August (or, in the case of "late *vassa*," August/September) and ends on the full-moon day that corresponds to October/November (or November/December). Though this period does not exactly correspond with the actual monsoons in Sri Lanka and Southeast Asia, the retreat continues to be observed according to the ancient reckoning. Special ceremonies attend the full-moon days that mark the beginning and end of the *vassa* season, whether according to the "early" or the "late" calculation. Gathering for *vassa*, the monks or nuns in a particular monastic boundary recite the Pātimokkha with special intention and additional vows appropriate to the occasion. The full-moon day that marks the end of *vassa* is singled out as especially significant, for here the usual Pātimokkha recitation is replaced with Pavāraṇā (Invitation), in which the assembled monks and nuns are invited to point out the transgressions of others observed during the *vassa* coresidence.

While regular Pātimokkha recitations and the special rituals associated with the rains-retreat are

A woman participating in traditional Cambodian New Year celebrations pours water over a statue of the Buddha at a temple in Phnom Penh, 2001. AP/Wide World Photos. Reproduced by permission.

intended primarily to assist monks and nuns in their discipline, they have important implications for the LAITY as well. In a general sense, these rituals produce certainty about the purity of the monks and nuns to whom one offers alms (*dāna*) and from whom one hears sermons or receives PRECEPTS, thereby guaranteeing the efficacy of such activities in a layperson's presumably longer march toward nirvāṇa. More specifically, over time lay calendrical rituals and festivals have emerged to correspond with the rituals in the monastery.

Thus, from a very early date, it has been considered appropriate for all Buddhists to make the lunar sabbaths, and especially the full-moon days, occasions for enhanced religious activity. At the very least, ordinary lay Buddhists will try to visit the local temple on such days in order to make offerings (*pūjā*) to a buddha image, bodhi tree, or STŪPA after reciting praises of the Buddha (*namaskāra*), the three REFUGES (*tisaraṇa*), and the five precepts (*pañcasīla*). The more pious members of a given lay community adopt an especially rigorous disciplinary regimen for the day, taking on three extra precepts (not to sit on elevated or comfortable seats, not to eat after 12:00 noon, and not to adorn the body with perfumes and jewelry), in addition to the ordinary five; the third precept, chastity (*kamesu micchācāra*), is replaced with celibacy (*brahmacariya*). These "Eight Precept holders" wear special clothes (a white version of the traditional monastic robes) and are honored with special forms of address and provision usually reserved for monks and nuns. They spend the day in the temple listening to sermons, studying and reciting the dharma, performing *pūjā*, and meditating, returning to their homes only in the night or the following morning.

Corresponding to the centrality accorded the *vassa* season in the yearly monastic ritual calendar, lay Buddhists also perform special rites on full-moon days, which mark the beginning and end of the retreat. Employing an ancient Pāli formula, temple patrons inaugurate *vassa* by ceremonially inviting monks within a particular monastic boundary to come to their temple for the retreat, and they mark the end of the season with elaborate festivities, such as processions and almsgivings, that culminate in the presentation of monastic robes (*kaṭhina puññakamma*), either to the monks themselves or to an image of the Buddha or a stūpa.

Certain other full-moon days are also singled out for special festivals. Most important among them is the full-moon day corresponding to April/May (Vesākha), on which day the Buddha is believed to have been born, to have achieved enlightenment, and to have reached *parinirvāṇa*. On this day Buddhists throughout the region erect colorful billboard-like displays containing pictures of the life of the Buddha, of JĀTAKA or historical stories, and of scenes in various HEAVENS and HELLS, in addition to decorating their homes with banners, flags, and lanterns. Festive foods are eaten, and in more recent times Buddhists have begun to send cards and sing carols paralleling the Christian celebration of Christmas and Easter. Vesākha is also a popular occasion for PILGRIMAGE to sites of religious significance. Similarly, though on a smaller scale, various events in the life of the Buddha and in Buddhist history that are believed to have occurred on particular full-moon days are remembered and celebrated on those days across the Buddhist world. In some countries certain of these days are considered especially significant. Thus, for example, modern Sri Lankan Buddhists place special emphasis on the full-moon day corresponding to June/July (Sinhala, Poson), when Mahinda is believed to have brought Buddhism to Sri Lanka for the first time; this season is marked by pilgrimages and processions to the mountain where he first encountered the Sri Lankan king, by the offering of food and drink to pilgrims, and by such modern entertainments as television dramas, concerts of devotional music, and "haunted houses."

Quite apart from these pan-Buddhist and large-scale rituals and festivals, individual Buddhist families often observe rites on a calendrical cycle, punctuated by the day each month or each year when they take alms (*dāna*) to the monks at a chosen temple, or yearly death anniversaries when they make special offerings of food, robes, and other requisites. Individual temples may also sponsor calendrical rites and festivals to celebrate their founding or the birthday or death anniversary of an incumbent monk, or to raise funds for temple improvement projects.

Throughout the region there are also calendrical rites and festivals associated with indigenous as well as originally Hindu deities, which, though only quasi Buddhist, have been absorbed into the Buddhist milieu. In Sri Lanka, the month that culminates in the full-moon day corresponding to July/August (Sinhala, Äśala) is the primary period for annual festivals and processions honoring various such deities. The most famous of these is the Kandy Perahera, in which the guardian deities of the island, together with the tooth relic of the Buddha, are paraded through the streets of the last Sri Lankan Buddhist royal capital amidst rites that derive from both Buddhism (e.g., *paritta*-chanting, sermons, almsgiving) and Hinduism (e.g., *pūjā* to images of the deities, mantra-chanting). The celebration of the Lunar New Year, in mid-April, is another example of a calendrical festival that, though not specifically Buddhist, nevertheless entails various Buddhist rituals, such as the presentation of the first rice of the year to a temple and vows to Buddhist deities.

In modern times, Buddhist countries also use the Roman calendar, within which secularized calendrical festivals are observed. Thus, the Western New Year might be celebrated on the night of December 31, even by those who will celebrate the traditional New Year in April; though full-moon days are holidays, with attendant laws (such as prohibitions on the sale of alcohol) to keep them sacred, Saturdays and Sundays enjoy the same status. National festivals tend to be calculated according to the Roman calendar, such as Sri Lanka's National Day on February 4, the Thai King's Birthday on December 5, or May Day, which is celebrated by workers all over the region. These national festivals are often attended by colorful street displays that parallel the strictly Buddhist festivals described above, Buddhist rites such as almsgivings and processions, and the active participation of Buddhist clergy.

East Asian festivals

In East Asia, Buddhist celebrations have been incorporated into a greater festival year that includes observances that might be defined as primarily Confucian, Daoist, "folk," or Shintō, depending on the country. Of particular note are the Buddha's birth, enlightenment, and *parinirvāṇa,* which are commemorated on separate days (unlike the situation in Theravāda countries, where they are all celebrated on the full-moon day of Vesākha, or April/May). The festival of the Buddha's birthday, in modern times, falls on April 8, and features the bathing of images of the infant Gautama, who is represented at the moment of his birth, standing with one hand pointed to the sky declaring his supremacy in the world. The rite has been traced back as early as the fourth century in China, and may have its roots in India. In Japan this event overlaps with the festival of flowers known as Hana matsuri. The Buddha's enlightenment day (Japanese, *jōdō-e*) is celebrated on December 8, and marks not only his attainment of BODHI (AWAKENING), but the end of his period of severe austerities. In the CHAN SCHOOL, this day is sometimes preceded by a one-week period of intensive meditation, often involving never lying down to sleep. The commemoration of the Buddha's death and *parinirvāṇa* (Japanese, *nehan-e*) falls on February (or March) 15. This celebration has been traced as far back as the sixth century in China, and may also have its origins in India. In Japan, the celebration held in Buddhist temples involves exhibitions of large paintings of the Buddha reclining on his deathbed.

Of greater importance and more generally popular is the celebration of the GHOST FESTIVAL (Japanese, Obon), which falls on July (or August) 15. This is a time when family graves are cleaned and when the spirits of departed ancestors are received on household altars. Its Buddhist roots are found in the story of the Buddha's disciple MAHĀMAUDGALYĀYANA, who, at the Buddha's recommendation, gave offerings to the monks in order to allay the sufferings of his mother who had been reborn in hell, an act that emphasized the ethic of filial piety.

Perhaps of lesser connection to Buddhism in East Asia is the celebration of the New Year, which is also understood to be a time for welcoming the dead, as well as an occasion for renewal and the reassertion of relationships. In Japan, it is especially a time to visit Shintō shrines, although on New Year's Eve people may go to temples to help ring the temple bell 108 times, signifying the elimination of the 108 defilements (Sanskrit, *kleśa*). In Tibet, on the other hand, the celebration of the New Year (Lo gsar) serves to reaffirm Buddhist supremacy over indigenous forces, and, since the time of TSONG KHA PA (1357–1419), it has segued into the celebration of the Great Prayer Festival (Smon lam chen mo).

Bibliography

Ch'en, Kenneth K. S. *Buddhism in China.* Princeton, NJ: Princeton University Press, 1964.

DeVisser, Marinus Willem. *Ancient Buddhism in Japan: Sūtras and Ceremonies in Use in the Seventh and Eighth Centuries A.D. and Their History in Later Times.* Paris: Paul Geuthner, 1928.

Holt, John C. *Discipline: The Canonical Buddhism of the Vinayapiṭaka.* Delhi: Motilal Banarsidass, 1981.

Horner, I. B., trans. *The Book of the Discipline (Vinayapiṭaka),* Vol. 4: *Mahāvagga.* London: Luzac, 1971.

Horner, I. B., trans. *The Minor Anthologies of the Pāli Canon,* Part 3: *Chronicle of Buddhas (Buddhavaṃsa)* and *Basket of Conduct (Cariyāpiṭaka).* London: Pāli Text Society, 1975.

Robertson, Alec. *The Triple Gem and the Uposatha: Buddhist Ethics and Culture.* Colombo, Sri Lanka: Colombo Apothecaries' Company, 1971.

Seneviratne, H. L. *Rituals of the Kandyan State.* Cambridge, UK: Cambridge University Press, 1978.

Wijayaratna, Mohan. *Buddhist Monastic Life: According to the Texts of the Theravāda Tradition,* tr. Claude Grangier and Steven Collins. Cambridge, UK: Cambridge University Press, 1990.

JONATHAN S. WALTERS

FILIALITY.

See **Family, Buddhism and the**

FOLK RELIGION: AN OVERVIEW

Folk religion refers to beliefs and practices that are not specifically marked as Buddhist. The term covers a broad range of phenomena, including worship of local deities, healing practices, the banishment of demons by priests (exorcism), providing offerings to the ANCESTORS to bring them comfort in the afterlife, divination, and other ritual activities seeking good fortune, health, or salvation.

Separating Buddhism from its background (folk religion) is neither easy nor objective. *Folk religion* is usually a second-order description, an attempt by debating parties to insulate an imaginary form of pure Buddhism from less desirable activities occurring in the background. The reality, however, is always more complicated: Elements subsumed under the label of folk religion are mixed together, coherently, with what unreflective authors want to isolate as true, authentic Buddhism. Early biographies of the historical Buddha, for instance, describe how before the Buddha was born his father consulted the state oracle, who prophesied that his son was destined for greatness. The soothsayer, Atiśa, stated that the young prince would become either a great ruler or a majestic world-renouncer. Similarly, most accounts of the Buddha's enlightenment note that after six futile years of practicing austerities, the Buddha-to-be accepted a bowlful of rice and milk from a laywoman named Sujātā. Sujātā presented the gift to the buddha because she mistook him for a tree spirit whose succor she had sought in conceiving a son. Although one might be tempted to discriminate between the folk elements and the more orthodox components in these two episodes, the early texts portray all the elements as integral parts within a healthy, sensible, unitary worldview. In the case of Atiśa, divining the future, especially when it involves the well-being of the state, is deemed perfectly consistent with Śākyamuni's path to buddhahood. Religious awakening, politics, and predicting the future (the latter two often considered to be folk corruptions) are not considered separate realms. Similarly, rather than distinguishing between a pure Buddhist intent and a debased folk practice, the early accounts of Sujāta's offering make no negative judgment about her devotions. Offerings to wandering holy men are believed to bring good fortune, to fulfill a laywoman's ethical obligations, and to further the cause of spiritual progress.

The category of folk religion is also murky because, especially in the premodern period, most Buddhists have not attempted to enforce clear distinctions between what is Buddhist and what is not. Definitions of what counts as Buddhist tend to be inclusive rather than exclusive. The earliest Buddhist communities absorbed much from their background, including belief in the power of holy men; a REBIRTH cosmology that placed human beings on a vertical continuum with gods, demigods (asura), animals, hungry ghosts (preta), and beings in HELLS; a universe animated by spirits of trees, rivers, and mountains; and the ability of talented individuals to perform miracles and see other realms. Even in the Indian context, then, Buddhism possessed what may be considered fuzzy margins. As Buddhism moved out of the Indian sphere and came into contact with other cultures, not only did these original background elements travel as part of Buddhism, but Buddhism also melded easily with the established beliefs and practices in new settings. Ancient deities, famous holy places, and long-standing ritual practices could all be included within the Buddhist sphere.

Modern scholarship focuses on three forms of folk religion: local gods, spirit-mediums, and family religion. Many deities deriving from Brahmanical religion were assimilated into the emerging Buddhist worldview. MĀRA, who appears in the Vedas, came to represent death and evil; he tried to prevent the Buddha from achieving enlightenment and carrying on his ministry. Brahmā and INDRA (Śakra Devānām Indra) were also accepted into the Buddhist pantheon and assigned specific planes in the Buddhist heavens. Other powerful figures in the pre-Buddhist underworld were given roles in later Buddhist mythology, including King Yama (Yama rāja), lord of the underworld, and Hāritī, mother of demons. Native gods in various cultures outside of India were also positioned in relation to Buddhism. As modern ethnographies have shown, monks and laypeople draw on the gods of the region in which they live to achieve a wide range of purposes, ranging from this-worldly to transcendent, all included within Buddhism. Another way to localize Buddhist deities was to place them in recognizable contexts. Thus, Mount Wutai in China was the site where Mañjuśrī Bodhisattva manifested himself as early as the beginning of the Tang dynasty (618–907); in Japan, Buddhist deities in the Kōfuku Temple were correlated with their indigenous counterparts in the Kasuga Shrine in Nara starting in the eighth century; and in Tibet the DALAI LAMA was considered a reincarnation of Avalokiteśvara Bodhisattva beginning in the seventeenth century.

Spirit-mediums (sometimes called shamans) are people who perform various religious rituals (exorcisms, séances, healing rites, divinations) while temporarily incarnating deities. Sometimes the deities are recognizably Buddhist; other times they are considered local ghosts or spirits. Spirit-mediums are drawn from the ranks of the local Buddhist institution, or Buddhist priests attempt to assert their dominance over a class of local spirit-mediums. Some of the best studies of the problem of folk religion deal with spirit-mediums in Thailand (Tambiah), Burma (Spiro), Tibet and the Himalayas (Mumford), China (Strickmann), and Japan (Blacker).

Most traditional Asian cultures treat the ancestors with veneration and emphasize the importance of providing for their salvation. Hence Buddhist rites are often performed in order to bring relief to the ancestors in the afterlife. Providing offerings to monks, patronizing temples, commissioning statues, making prayers at home—almost any Buddhist ritual action has been harnessed to the interests of the ancestral cult. Using early Indian stone inscriptions, Gregory Schopen has recently shown that the concern with filial piety was not unique to Chinese Buddhism, but had developed in India earlier as well.

Folk religion is a contested term. It is sometimes still deployed in an unreflective manner, set up in contrast to a presumably pure or more orthodox form of Buddhism. One should also beware of unacknowledged bias in the use of terms like *popular religion* (rather than monastic doctrine), *little tradition* (as opposed to an intellectual great tradition), or benighted *practice* (versus enlightened beliefs). *Folk religion* in the derogatory sense has been used by both Buddhists and opponents of Buddhism. Yet responsible studies continue to use the term in new ways. Recognizing that it artificially separates Buddhist phenomena from non-Buddhist phenomena, scholars are taking folk religion more seriously and searching for the interrelations between Buddhist and non-Buddhist forms of religion.

See also: **Confucianism and Buddhism; Cosmology; Daoism and Buddhism; Entertainment and Performance; Ghosts and Spirits; Hinduism and Buddhism; Local Divinities and Buddhism; Merit and Merit-Making; Shintō (Honji Suijaku) and Buddhism**

Bibliography

Blacker, Carmen. *The Catalpa Bow: A Study of Shamanistic Practices in Japan.* London: Allen and Unwin, 1975. Revised edition, 1986.

Grapard, Allan G. *The Protocol of the Gods: A Study of the Kasuga Cult in Japanese History.* Berkeley: University of California Press, 1992.

Ling, Trevor O. *Buddhism and the Mythology of Evil: A Study in Theravada Buddhism.* London: Allen and Unwin, 1962.

Mumford, Stan Royal. *Himalayan Dialogue: Tibetan Lamas and Gurnung Shamans in Nepal.* Madison: University of Wisconsin Press, 1989.

Schopen, Gregory. "Filial Piety and the Monk in the Practice of Indian Buddhism: A Question of 'Sinicization' Viewed from the Other Side" (1984). Reprinted in *Bones, Stones, and Buddhist Monks: Collected Papers on the Archaeology, Epigraphy, and Texts of Monastic Buddhism in India,* by Gregory Schopen. Honolulu: University of Hawaii Press, 1997.

Spiro, Melford E. *Buddhism and Society: A Great Tradition and Its Burmese Vicissitudes,* 2nd edition. Berkeley: University of California Press, 1982.

Strickmann, Michel. *Chinese Magical Medicine.* Stanford, CA: Stanford University Press, 2002.

Tambiah, Stanley J. *Buddhism and the Spirit Cults in North-East Thailand.* Cambridge, UK: Cambridge University Press, 1970.

Teiser, Stephen F. *The Ghost Festival in Medieval China.* Princeton, NJ: Princeton University Press, 1988.

Yü, Chün-fang. *Kuan-yin: The Chinese Transformation of Avalokiteśvara.* New York: Columbia University Press, 2001.

STEPHEN F. TEISER

FOLK RELIGION, CHINA

Much has been written about Buddhism's conversation with Confucianism and Daoism since its arrival in China by the first century C.E. While the role of these two systems of ideas and values in Chinese culture cannot be denied, it must be kept in mind that the religious attitudes of the vast majority of the Chinese people never were directly derived from Confucianism or Daoism, but rather from folk religion. Folk (or popular) religion negotiates the relationship of the individual, the family, and the local community with the spirit world by means of beliefs and practices that are transmitted outside the canonical scriptural traditions of China. Often this transmission is oral, but there also exists a long tradition of popular written texts recording myths, rituals, and scriptures. Buddhism's success in China can be measured directly by its impact on this religion of the people.

One major area of Buddhist influence on Chinese folk religion concerns conceptions of the afterlife. Pre-Buddhist ideas distinguished between various paradisiacal realms and a vaguely defined underworld called the Yellow Springs, but there seems to have been no clear link between one's posthumous fate and one's conduct while living. The introduction of such a link by means of the concepts of KARMA (ACTION), REBIRTH, and hell (or purgatory) led to a fundamental restructuring of Chinese conceptions of the afterlife, furnishing it with a complete set of HELLS, reigned over by ten kings, in which the soul of the deceased undergoes a series of punishments in accord with its karmic burden before eventually being reborn. By the seventh century, this new view of the afterlife had already gained some acceptance, and in the following centuries new texts and liturgies for its propagation and ritual negotiation emerged.

Karma linked the afterlife with individual effort, which created the terrifying realm of hell, but also opened up new possibilities for salvation. Here, too, Buddhism made a major contribution by offering the saving compassion of its buddhas and bodhisattvas. From the third century onward, PURE LAND BUDDHISM became the most popular school in China, holding out as it did the hope of rebirth into AMITĀBHA Buddha's Western Paradise. The Bodhisattva Avalokiteśvara, who until the tenth century was mostly portrayed as male, gradually came to be visualized as female. Eventually he became the goddess Guanyin, the quintessential personification of compassion and one of the most widespread deities of folk religion. Other Buddhist figures that played an important role in folk religion include Kṣitigarbha (Dizang Wang Pusa), MAITREYA (Mile Fo), Yama (Yanluo Wang), the Eighteen ARHATS (Lohan), and MAHĀMAUDGALYĀYANA (Mulian).

Buddhist saints—revered masters or miracle workers—sometimes became objects of worship, their mortuary STŪPAS or mummified bodies attracting large numbers of pilgrims praying for blessings and protection. A very popular deity in modern Chinese folk religion, the Living Buddha Jigong (Jigong Huofo), originated in stories surrounding an unconventional Buddhist monk who lived in Hangzhou, Zhejiang province, around the turn of the thirteenth century. While the cult of Jigong spread far beyond its Hangzhou home base, the Patriarch of the Clear Stream (Qingshui Zushi) is an example of a regional deity that developed from the cult of an eleventh-century miracle-working Buddhist monk in Fujian province and remains largely confined to the Anxi area of Fujian and areas settled by Anxi emigrants in Taiwan and Southeast Asia. As bodhisattvas, buddhas, and eminent monks became deities within Chinese folk religion, they were also removed from the doctrinal control of the SAṄGHA and often took on novel features. The cult of Qingshui Zushi, for example, adopted more and more Daoist elements, so that today its Buddhist origins are barely recognizable. The Bodhisattva Avalokiteśvara, in the guise of the female Guanyin, became a multifunctional deity who, among many other concerns, is believed to grant children to her faithful, thus earning her the name Songzi Guanyin (Child-Giving Guanyin).

While Buddhism contributed new deities to folk religion, it in turn adopted popular deities into its own pantheon, albeit usually only in a subservient position. There exist many stories of Buddhist pioneers converting local deities or demons to Buddhism and making them guardian spirits of their newly founded monasteries, thus symbolically subordinating local religion to Buddhism. The most famous case of such subordination is the adoption of the powerful folk deity Guan Gong as a tutelary spirit of Buddhist shrines.

In spite of such attempts at symbolic hegemony, Buddhism never came to dominate Chinese folk religion, either symbolically or institutionally. The saṅgha's deliberate separation from local communities limited its influence on their religious life, but gave it at the same time opportunities for ritual interaction. The strong association of Chinese Buddhism with concepts of the afterlife combined with the saṅgha's separateness to provide Buddhist monks and nuns with unique qualifications as providers of ritual services for the dead. In many areas of China, mortuary rites and rituals performed for the benefit of ghosts are predominantly supplied by Buddhist practitioners. Such practitioners include not only formally ordained monks and nuns, but also the followers of Buddhist-inclined lay sects, which in some areas had a more immediate impact as carriers of Buddhist ideas than the mainstream saṅgha. An example is the role of the Dragon Flower Sect (Longhua Pai) in nineteenth-century Taiwan, where, in the absence of a well-established monastic community, sectarians fulfilled many of the ritual functions that elsewhere were the domain of the ordained Buddhist clergy. Such sects arose in large numbers from the fourteenth century onward. They drew their inspiration ecumenically from all religious traditions of China, but in many of them the soteriological promise of the Pure Land combined with the eschatological expectation of the buddha Maitreya to infuse them with a distinctly Buddhist flavor. For this reason they have at times been characterized as "folk Buddhist."

In these ways Buddhism helped to shape Chinese folk religion and was in turn shaped by it. In the process, it contributed a significant number of the pieces that make up the rich mosaic of religious life in Chinese communities.

See also: **Apocrypha; Confucianism and Buddhism; Daoism and Buddhism; Entertainment and Performance; Ghosts and Spirits; Local Divinities and Buddhism; Merit and Merit-Making; Syncretic Sects: Three Teachings**

Bibliography

Dean, Kenneth. *Taoist Ritual and Popular Cults of Southeast China.* Princeton, NJ: Princeton University Press, 1993.

Overmyer, Daniel L. *Folk Buddhist Religion: Dissenting Sects in Late Traditional China.* Cambridge, MA: Harvard University Press, 1976.

Teiser, Stephen F. *The Ghost Festival in Medieval China.* Princeton, NJ: Princeton University Press, 1988.

Teiser, Stephen F. *The Scripture on the Ten Kings and the Making of Purgatory in Medieval Chinese Buddhism.* Honolulu: University of Hawaii Press, 1994.

Yü, Chün-fang. *Kuan-yin: The Chinese Transformation of Avalokiteśvara.* New York: Columbia University Press, 2001.

PHILIP CLART

FOLK RELIGION, JAPAN

Folk religion (*minkan shinkō* or *minzoku shūkyō*) is the unifying element underlying Japanese religious structure, the "frame of reference," as Miyake Hitoshi has termed it ("Folk Religion," p. 122), through which the religious traditions of Shintō and Buddhism have become rooted in Japan. Folk religion is generally considered to encompass a variety of customs, practices and ideas, including rituals, festivals and events linked to the calendrical cycle and to individual and social life cycles; concepts relating to the spirits of the dead and to other worlds; the use of AMULETS AND TALISMANS and divination; belief in the capacity of various figures of worship to bestow worldly benefits on petitioners; and concepts of spirit possession and shamanism.

The relationship between Buddhism and folk religion in Japan has been, and remains, one of interaction and mutual reinforcement. From its initial entry onward Buddhism has assimilated and adapted to existing folk ideas and practices, simultaneously shaping and influencing their development, while Buddhist ideas and practices have often taken hold through integrating with folk ideas and practices.

This process of mutual influence can be seen from the time Buddhism first entered Japan, bringing with it with Daoist concepts and practices relating to divination, oracles, and the calendar. These became embedded in Japanese folk religious structure: Cycles of lucky and unlucky days and years became part of folk religious consciousness, commemorated through rituals and practices, including the drawing of oracle lots and rituals for preventing misfortunes, that were carried out at Buddhist temples. Buddhist festivals—such as the summer Obon or Festival for the Sprits of the Dead—also became part of the annual round of observances followed by the Japanese.

Buddhism, folk religion, and the dead

Perhaps the main area of interaction between Japanese folk religion and Buddhism has been in relation to the spirits of the dead, ANCESTORS and concepts of other worlds. Before the advent of Buddhism, folk traditions envisaged the spirit as departing from the body at DEATH but remaining essentially tied to this world and reluctant to depart from its kin. Although the spirits of the dead could become benevolent protective deities, they were also inherently dangerous and fearsome, capable of possessing the living or afflicting them in various ways; the realms of death were dark and perilous. Buddhism offered more sophisticated and ultimately more positive visions of what lay beyond death, and offered means of subduing possessing spirits and pacifying the dead through rituals conducted by priests and, especially in earlier times, by ascetics who claimed exorcistic powers. Such notions and practices were readily assimilated into a folk tradition in which shamanic practitioners (including members of mountain cults who were deeply influenced by Buddhism) played a vital role in the religious life of ordinary people. Such practitioners continue to exist, and the new religions that have emerged in more recent times have drawn extensively from this folk/Buddhist shamanic tradition.

Buddhist funerary rituals offered a means of averting the dangers of pollution by purifying the dead of their sins and leading them safely from this realm to the next, thus transforming their spirits into benevolent ancestors existing in a mutually beneficial relationship with their living kin. Buddhism's concepts of other realms, of HELLS for the wicked and REBIRTH in the Pure Land for the virtuous, offered a moral vision of death and the beyond, while its rituals offering merit transference from the living to the dead enabled the living to aid their departed kin in the afterlife.

While these Japanese concepts of death and the ancestors show an obvious Buddhist influence, it is also clear that folk concepts have had an impact on Buddhism in Japan. The notion of the spirit of an ancestor being led elsewhere yet remaining in close contact with the living depends upon an implicit belief in an after-death existence that appears to conflict with standard Buddhist notions of transmigration—a dilemma never resolved in Japan, where Buddhist sects may articulate both concepts simultaneously—and represents a folk transformation of Buddhism. The relationship between the living and the dead remains central to Japanese Buddhism, which since early medieval times has been the primary medium through which death rituals and ancestor veneration have been carried out. Most Japanese households continue to use family Buddhist altars to memorialize their ancestors and most Japanese continue to envisage the dead through ideas framed by Buddhist rites and deeply influenced by folk beliefs.

Folk religion, Buddhism, and worldly benefits

Another major area of folk-Buddhist interaction concerns Buddhism's reinforcement and expansion of existing folk beliefs about the role of figures of worship in providing worldly benefits (*genze riyaku*). In pre-Buddhist Japan spiritual entities such as clan tutelary deities were petitioned for protection and aid; adapting to this tradition, Japanese Buddhism portrayed its figures of worship—BUDDHAS and BODHISATTVAS such as Bhaiṣajyaguru (Japanese, Yakushi; the buddha of healing) and Avalokiteśvara (Kannon; the bodhisattva of compassion)—as powerful agents capable of granting benefits and interceding to heal illness and provide happiness and good fortune to those who worshiped them. Buddhist sūtras, notably the LOTUS SŪTRA (SADDHARMAPUṆḌARĪKA-SŪTRA) provided accounts of miraculous happenings and promises of worldly benefits for those who follow the Buddhist way. Such notions have consistently been emphasized by proselytizing Buddhist itinerants and priests who have composed numerous stories and miracle tales relating to Buddhist figures of worship. Icons and statues of popular figures such as Avalokiteśvara and sacred places such as temples have been portrayed in such stories as sources of spiritual power and benefits that can be accrued by all. Buddhist temples have become primary sites for making petitions for worldly benefits, and primary sources of protective devices such as talismans and amulets, which are widely used in Japan. In the provision of worldly benefits there are few if any distinctions between "elite" monastic centers and "popular" temples; often the two are synonymous, with the monastic practitioners of purportedly elite institutions actively promoting the miraculous powers of the statues, icons, and relics at their institutions. Some scholars argue that there exists a "common religion" (Reader and Tanabe) centered on worldly benefits, in which elite and popular, institutional (Buddhist) and folk religion are effectively parts of one dynamic.

Folk heroes and pilgrimage customs

One of the most striking popular figures of worship who grants worldly benefits is Kōbō Daishi, who can be seen as an exemplar both of the folk transformations of Buddhism and of Buddhist influence on folk religion. Kōbō Daishi is the posthumous name of KŪKAI (774–835), founder of the Shingon Buddhist tradition and of numerous temples in Japan. Shingon Buddhist sources suggest that Kūkai entered into eternal meditation at death, and the sect promoted him, in his posthumous guise as Kōbō Daishi, as a transcendent miracle worker who could bring benefits to the faithful. Cults of worship developed around him, portraying him as an itinerant who dispenses rewards to the worthy and retribution to the venal. PILGRIMAGE routes—most notably an eighty-eight-temple circuit around Shikoku, the island of Kūkai's birth—also developed around this cultic figure; he has transcended sectarian boundaries and become the focus of an extensive folk faith, still vibrant in modern Japan. A study by Kaneko Satoru (*Shinshū shinkō to minzoku shinkō*, 1991) shows that the pilgrimage and veneration of Kōbō Daishi are deeply embedded in the folk customs of Shikoku, and that such folk practices and attitudes permeate the lives of people who officially belong to orthodox sectarian Buddhism but whose daily lives and localized faith are rooted in Kōbō Daishi and pilgrimage-centered folk religion.

The interactions between Buddhism and folk religion in Japan have been extensive. Folk religion is the underlying stratum upon which Buddhism and other traditions have built their foundations and through which they have responded to the needs and views of Japanese people.

See also: **Divinities; Festivals and Calendrical Rituals; Ghost Festival; Ghosts and Spirits; Japan; Local Divinities and Buddhism; Merit and Merit-Making; Shingon Buddhism, Japan; Shintō (Honji Suijaku) and Buddhism**

Bibliography

Blacker, Carmen. *The Catalpa Bow: A Study of Shamanistic Practices in Japan* (1975). Richmond, UK: Curzon, 1999.

Hori, Ichirō. *Folk Religion in Japan: Continuity and Change.* Chicago: University of Chicago Press, 1968.

Kaneko Satoru. *Shinshū shinkō to minzoku shinkō.* Kyoto: Nagata Bunshōdō, 1991.

Miyake Hitoshi. "Folk Religion." In *Japanese Religion,* ed. Hori Ichirō et al. Tokyo: Kōdansha, 1981.

Miyake Hitoshi. *Shugendō: Essays on the Structure of Japanese Folk Religion.* Ann Arbor: Center for Japanese Studies, University of Michigan, 2001.

Reader, Ian. *Religion in Contemporary Japan.* Basingstoke, UK: Macmillan; Honolulu: University of Hawaii Press, 1991.

Reader, Ian, and Tanabe, George J., Jr. *Practically Religious: Worldly Benefits and the Common Religion of Japan.* Honolulu: University of Hawaii Press, 1998.

IAN READER

FOLK RELIGION, SOUTHEAST ASIA

The folk religions of THERAVĀDA Southeast Asia combine elements of local spirit religions, local versions of Brahmanism, and Buddhism. The combination of Buddhism, Brahmanism, and spirits is a total ritual system with as much internal tension as consistency. This is because, while Buddhism is doctrinally opposed to spirit religions, it recognizes and respects Brahmanism. Buddhism's opposition to spirits is not based on the grounds that these religions are false; the problem is that spirits are worldly powers, and people bent on salvation should not concern themselves with them. The Brahmanical DIVINITIES (*devatā*), on the other hand, are seen as supernatural protectors of Buddhism, so interaction with them is considered wholesome. In practice, however, laypersons consider interaction with the spirits to be a practical necessity, and even monks must deal with them on occasion.

Spirit religion

The spirit religions have their roots in the pre-Buddhist past. There is remarkable consistency among the various versions of these religions across Southeast Asia, among both Buddhist and non-Buddhist groups. Spirits are invisible beings with humanlike wills and emotions that are associated with specific places and objects. The spirits have the power to harm humans, and they will do so if they feel that humans have trespassed on their territory, or if they have not been properly propitiated. In Burma, spirits are called *nat.* In Thailand and Laos they are know as *phi,* and in Cambodia as *neak taa* or *kmauit.*

Spirits are seen as, among other things, guardians of morality, particularly as regards proper community, family, and sexual relationships. This is illustrated by the Northern Thai tale of a prince who was visiting a friend, the ruler of a neighboring principality. While there he had an adulterous liaison with his friend's chief wife, the reigning princess. On his return home, he had to ride across the mountains through the forest, where a powerful spirit caused him to drown in a stream as punishment for his wrongdoing.

As guardians of proper human relations, spirits provide benefits to communities more than to individuals. Spirit rites are important markers and maintainers of social solidarity in villages, families, and lineages. Benefits are believed to come to individuals when they turn to individual spirits for help with personal problems. Spirits can heal and find lost objects, among other things. People first seek the help of local spirits. If that fails they turn to professional spirit mediums who are said to serve particularly effective spirits.

Spirits that have been domesticated—that is, turned from things of the wild into elements of the human community—are powerful sources of protection for the people who honor them. The places they protect range in scale from whole kingdoms to individual rooms of the home. Generally speaking, the larger the place a spirit protects, the more powerful the spirit. On the other side of the coin, the smaller the spirit, the more likely it is to be offended by the wrongdoings of particular individuals. The bedroom spirit is the most dangerous of all if one offends it by committing an improper sexual act in its presence. Great spirits will afflict whole communities that offend them (for instance, by withholding rain), but will only punish individuals of equivalent rank. The tutelary spirit of a kingdom may harm a king, but is unlikely to concern itself with the misdeeds of a peasant.

The Buddhist cultures of Southeast Asia make a strong distinction between wild and civilized spaces, that is, between nature and culture. Wild spaces, such as the forests and mountains, are regarded as dangerous and said to be filled with potentially harmful spirits. Humans encroaching on these spaces—for instance, to clear woodlands for agricultural fields—must take care to address the leading spirit of that place and ask permission to undertake human activities. The spirit, and its attendant lesser spirits, are then invited to protect that place on behalf of humans. For their part, humans must make regular offerings to the spirits. These offerings can be as simple as small portions of food, often accompanied by tobacco and liquor, which are offered with humble words by the local farmer or householder, or the offerings may be as elaborate as large-scale animal sacrifices lasting one or two days and requiring the participation of specialized priests.

In addition to the spirits of wild places, spirits of the dead are also important. Like the spirits of the wild, they are bound to and protect designated spaces. One dramatic example is the ancient use of ritual homicide (human sacrifice) to create powerful tutelary spirits. It was sometimes the practice when building entrance gates to walled cities to seize an unsuspecting passerby, kill him or her, and bury the body beneath the foundations of the gate. The resulting spirit was considered to be particularly ferocious, having been ripped so wantonly from this life. The spirit was given offerings and beseeched to turn its rage against strangers seeking to enter the city for wrongful purposes. This spirit would receive generous offerings each year as part of the city's elaborate set of sacrifices to its guardian spirits. On a less gruesome note, the spirits of powerful and revered leaders are often enshrined as the protective divinities of the people and places they once ruled. Since these rulers were Buddhists in their own lives, unlike their wild counterparts, they are likely to be moral beings and inherently benign. They, like some converted spirits of the wild, serve as protectors of the faith as well as protectors of the land and people. Burma (Myanmar), in particular, constructed a highly elaborate state cult of tutelary divinities drawn from the spirits of deceased rulers.

Brahmanism

Brahmanism (in its Southeast Asian form) tends to be directly concerned with male spiritual potency. This potency is applied for the benefit of all people, male or female, but the source of the power is closely connected with maleness. This operates at the individual level. Every man has a certain level of spiritual power or effectiveness that derives from a combination of good KARMA (ACTION) and textual knowledge. This spiritual potency can be built and displayed through conspicuous acts of Buddhist piety—especially temporary ordination as a novice or monk—and knowledge of certain ritual texts. Particularly pious and powerful men may come to be known as learned masters (*ācāriyas*) or

Brāhmaṇas. In their capacity as *ācāriyas* they are considered to be half layman and half monk, and they serve as congregation leaders of Buddhist temples (vihāras or *āvāsas*), where they mediate between the world of the LAITY (*gharāvāsa*) and the sacred world of the monkhood (SAṄGHA). Although this office is not specified in the Buddhist CANON, it is extremely important to the everyday practice of Buddhism in Southeast Asia. In their capacity as Brāhmaṇas, spiritually powerful men can also serve as healers and as priests to the Vedic gods, particularly INDRA, Brahmā, and the Lords of the Four Quarters. In urban areas this service can be a profession.

Even men who do not take this profession or wear such exalted titles seek to acquire some degree of personal spiritual potency. The male literacy rate was traditionally quite high in Southeast Asia, in part because a knowledge of the Brahmanical religious texts was the best means to such potency. Even illiterate men are likely to have some practical ritual or magical knowledge, for such things are a necessity in daily life. The Brahmanical texts contain varieties of ritual knowledge. They include, for example, knowledge of the direction in which the earth-dragon lies in each season, which is important to consider when building a house or plowing a field. Various kinds of numerical magic squares figure as means of calculating auspicious days and directions for undertaking certain activities, such as setting out on a journey. There are also texts to be recited as spells for healing, love, and protection. In addition, certain texts contain the words required for sacrifices to the Vedic gods. In each case, however, the texts contain only the words for the rite. Knowledge of the proper materials to use and the proper performance of the rites must be learned from a teacher.

See also: **Ancestors; Death; Festivals and Calendrical Rituals; Ghosts and Spirits; Hinduism and Buddhism; Local Divinities and Buddhism; Merit and Merit-Making**

Bibliography

Archaimbault, Charles. "Religious Structures in Laos." *Journal of the Siam Society* 52 (1964): 57–74.

Chouléan, Ang. *Les êtres surnaturels dans la religion populaire Khmère.* Paris: Cedorek, 1986.

Lemoine, Jacques, and Eisenbruch, M. "The Practice and the Power of Healing by the Hmong Shamans and the Cambodian Traditional Healers of Indochina." *Homme* 37, no. 144 (1997): 69–103.

Spiro, Melford E. *Buddhism and Society: A Great Tradition and Its Burmese Vicissitudes*, 2nd edition. Berkeley: University of California Press, 1982.

Tambiah, Stanley J. *Buddhism and the Spirit Cults in North-East Thailand.* Cambridge, UK: Cambridge University Press, 1970.

MICHAEL R. RHUM

FOREST MONKS. *See* **Wilderness Monks**

FOUR NOBLE TRUTHS

The four noble truths are known best for their appearance in the classic *Turning of the Wheel of Dharma* (*Dharmacakrapravartana-sūtra*). This address appears in the Pāli, Sanskrit, Tibetan, and Chinese canons of various Buddhist schools, with relatively little variation in the actual content and terminology of the speech itself. The larger setting for this speech begins with the enlightenment of Gautama Buddha (566–486 B.C.E. or 470–350 B.C.E.). In the *Basket of Discipline* (*Vinaya-piṭaka*), a lengthy sequence describes how the Buddha left his five companions to pursue his own path toward enlightenment. He ate a bowl of rice porridge, and sat down under a pipal tree, vowing not to move until he was enlightened. Successively, during that night, in a series of three watches (each watch was about three hours long), the Buddha realized the four noble truths. During the first watch, he became aware of each of the four truths; during the second watch, he realized that he had to fully *know* the truth of each of the four truths; and during the third watch, he knew that he had, in fact, realized just how each truth was true. With that, he knew that he had reached BODHI (AWAKENING), that he had escaped the endless cycle of birth and death and had experienced NIRVĀṆA.

The Buddha spent the next seven weeks in a state of bliss, enjoying his newfound experience of enlightenment. A divinity from the heavens came down and asked the Buddha when he would begin to teach what he had just realized. The Buddha refused to teach, saying that what he had realized was far too difficult for other beings to know for themselves. After the divinity convinced him that there were others who could learn what he had to teach, the Buddha agreed to teach. He took time deciding to whom his first teaching should be delivered, and settled on his five companions from whose company he had parted in order to seek his own enlightenment. After he approached them and convinced them that he had attained the state in which there is no death or suffering (that is, the state of nirvāṇa), they settled down to listen to this first talk. The Buddha's first talk on dharma is titled "Turning of the Wheel of the Law" because after he spoke to his five former companions, explaining the four noble truths and the middle way of the eightfold PATH, one of them, Kauṇḍinya, cultivated the eye of dharma—that is, he became fully enlightened. When he was enlightened, Gautama Buddha had turned the wheel of dharma in this world for the first time, and nothing could stop the teaching of dharma and the enlightenment of other beings.

The four noble truths

The story of the Buddha's enlightenment and the turning of the wheel of dharma is the setting for the Buddha's first talk on dharma to an audience. He explains that his companions should pursue the middle way, avoiding the extremes of self-indulgence and self-mortification, and then lays out the four noble truths and the eightfold path. The four noble truths present the fact of suffering in this world and the means to end suffering in the following verses:

> This, bhikkhus, is the noble truth that is suffering. Birth is suffering; old age is suffering; illness is suffering; death is suffering; sorrow and grief, physical and mental suffering, and disturbance are suffering. Association with things not liked is suffering, separation from desired things is suffering; not getting what one wants is suffering; in short, the five aggregates of grasping are suffering.
>
> This, bhikkhus, is the noble truth that is the arising of suffering. This is craving that leads to rebirth, is connected with pleasure and passion and finds pleasure in this or that; that is, craving for desire, existence, and the fading away of existence.
>
> This, bhikkhus, is the noble truth that is the ending of suffering. This is the complete fading away and ending of that very craving, giving it up, renouncing it, releasing it, and letting go.
>
> This, bhikkhus, is the noble truth that is the way leading to the ending of suffering. This is the eightfold path of the noble ones: right view, right intention, right speech, right action, right livelihood, right effort, right mindfulness, and right concentration. (*Book of Kindred Sayings* [*Saṃyutta-nikāya*], vol. 5, line 410ff)

DUḤKHA (SUFFERING; Pāli, *dukkha*), the first of the four noble truths, is defined in the first verse above. Suffering in the Buddhist sense means far more than suffering is usually understood in a Judeo-Christian context. For Buddhists, anything that one wants and does not have is suffering. Having something that one does not want is also suffering. Clinging to the five SKANDHA (AGGREGATE) that make up a person is suffering. In other words, if a person holds onto any aspect of his or her being, whether the physical body, feelings, perceptions, formations, or consciousness, in the hope that any of those things exists permanently, that person will experience suffering. BUDDHAGHOSA, a Buddhist commentator who lived during the late fourth and early fifth centuries C.E. in what is now Sri Lanka, explained that there were three kinds of suffering: suffering that is inherent in a thing, suffering that emerges because things change, and suffering that develops because something else influences an experience. An example of the last type of suffering would be the pain from an earache or a toothache that arises because of an infection. In short, all life is suffering, according to the Buddha's first sermon.

The second truth is *samudaya* (arising or origin). To end suffering, the four noble truths tell us, one needs to know how and why suffering arises. The second noble truth explains that suffering arises because of craving, desire, and attachment. Because one wants to avoid things that cause discomfort, and because one wants to have things that bring pleasure, these "desires" are the origin of suffering. If one does not desire things, then one will not experience suffering. If one wants to avoid the suffering that comes from thinking that the self (who "I" am) is permanent and unchanging, then one should not be attached to the idea of a self.

The third truth follows from the second: If the cause of suffering is desire and attachment to various things, then the way to end suffering is to eliminate craving, desire, and attachment. The third truth is called *nirodha,* which means "ending" or "cessation." To stop suffering, one must stop desiring.

The Buddha taught the fourth truth, *mārga* (Pāli, *magga*), the path that has eight parts, as the means to end suffering. Taken together, the four truths present a concise and logical analysis of the cause of human suffering and an equally straightforward solution to the problem of human suffering: the eightfold path.

The eightfold path

The eightfold path is the middle way that the Buddha described during his first sermon, the way between the two extremes of self-indulgence and self-mortification. The eight limbs of the path consist of: right view, right intention, right speech, right action, right livelihood, right effort, right mindfulness, and right concentration. These are not sequential, because each one depends upon the other: They are meant to be followed and practiced in cooperation with one another. One cannot fully perfect the first step (for example, right view) until the last one, right concentration, is perfected. When all are practiced and perfected, then one attains enlightenment. Each of these components of the path is "right" in the sense that it is an ideal that should be undertaken and practiced seriously. One should follow the path not just because the Buddha taught it but because this is the way to attain the same perfection and enlightenment that Gautama Buddha reached while sitting under the bodhi tree. The word for *right* (Pāli, *sammā*; Sanskrit, *samyañc*) in each of the compounds that are found in the fourth truth can be translated as right, proper, or good; the meaning becomes clearer when contrasted with its opposite (Pāli and Sanskrit, *pāpa*), which means wrong, bad, or even EVIL.

Buddhaghosa grouped the eightfold path into three different stages, as shown in Table 1. According to Buddhaghosa, *right view* means having nirvāṇa as one's goal through eliminating ignorance. One should strive to see clearly, always envisioning reaching nirvāṇa in one's mind. Other commentaries have explained that right view means understanding the four noble truths. *Right intention* (sometimes translated as *right thought*) involves thinking according to the Buddha's teachings, and always directing one's intentions and thoughts toward nirvāṇa, with keen attention to the proper ways of understanding the world. If one has abandoned wrong intentions or thoughts, then one knows that one is on the way to developing right intention. Some commentaries also explain that right intention involves the cultivation of *maitrī* (loving-kindness; Pāli, *mettā*) toward all other beings. Taken together, Buddhaghosa wrote that both right view and right intention make up *right wisdom*, for one is then focused on the ultimate goal of the Buddha's teachings, which is nirvāṇa.

The second group, *right ethical conduct* (sometimes translated as *right morality*), is more readily understood than the first. *Right speech* means not lying, not engaging in gossip, not slandering others, and not speaking harshly. *Right action* involves not killing living things, not stealing, and not engaging in sexual misconduct. When one practices *right livelihood*, one avoids careers or jobs that harm others. Specifically, one should not earn a living by engaging in trading weapons, slaughtering animals, dealing in slavery, selling alcohol or other intoxicants, or selling poisons. When one practices right speech, right action, and right livelihood, one lays the proper ethical foundation for the other remaining stages of the path.

TABLE 1

Buddhaghosa's three stages of the eightfold path

Right wisdom	right view right intention
Right ethical conduct	right speech right action right livelihood
Right concentration	right effort right mindfulness right concentration

The third and last group of the eightfold path, *right concentration*, includes right effort, right MINDFULNESS, and right concentration. Each of these limbs of the path requires focus and deliberate cultivation of certain meditative practices. *Right effort* means deliberately preventing undesirable mental attitudes, such as sensual desire, hatred, sluggishness, worry and anxiety, and doubt, as well as deliberately letting go of such attitudes if they have already arisen. Right effort means bringing about and maintaining positive mental attitudes, such as the seven factors of enlightenment: mindfulness, investigation of phenomena, energy, rapture, tranquility, concentration, and equanimity. *Right mindfulness* means cultivating an awareness of one's body, one's feelings, one's mind, and of mental objects. The development of mindfulness is explained in detail in *The Foundations of Mindfulness* (Pāli, *Satipaṭṭhāna-sutta*); it involves simply watching and observing, for example, one's body or mind. Right mindfulness is then accompanied by meditative practices of *right concentration*, which enable one to develop "one pointedness of mind." By closing the doors of the senses to the outside world, one focuses on one of a variety of objects that are designed to enable the practitioner to attain specific mental states that lie beyond one's usual daily consciousness.

Taken as a whole, the four noble truths and the eightfold path are emblematic of all of the Buddha's teachings. Because the Buddha is said to have taught these in his first sermon, they represent the most fundamental teachings of Buddhism. The four noble truths are woven throughout all of the Buddhist worlds; they appear in countless texts, and the story of the Buddha's enlightenment has been told even in fourteenth-century Japanese Nō plays. The eightfold path, too, is representative of the path to enlightenment. The eight stages of the path are broadly designed to take a practitioner from the initial steps of right intention and right view—being properly focused on the attainment of nirvāṇa—to the more strenuous meditation practices that enable one to cultivate awareness and insight and one pointedness of mind.

However, because the four noble truths and the eightfold path are construed so broadly, it is difficult to talk about them as specific and explicit guides to the practices that lead to nirvāṇa. While there are certain practices enumerated in the commentaries on the four noble truths and the eightfold path, the first talk on dharma in which the Buddha lays out the teachings contains no specific instructions on how one should recognize the truth of the four noble truths and the eightfold path. The Buddha himself simply states that he *knew* that he had to know the truth of the four noble truths for himself, and that he came to realize the truth of the four noble truths. The Buddha then instructs his audience to do the same. In short, the four noble truths and the eightfold path are illustrative of the progressive path toward enlightenment, rather than being specific teachings on how one should meditate in order to reach enlightenment.

There are other meditation practices that employ the four noble truths and the eightfold path, such as the practice of the foundations of mindfulness. In that practice, one meditates upon the ways in which mental objects such as the four noble truths or the eightfold path are constructed in the world, how they come to be, and how they pass away. Buddhist texts also offer an extensive set of teachings on how to meditate in order to reach enlightenment that incorporate the four noble truths and the eightfold path as objects of contemplation. At the same time, however, there are countless references to the significance of the four noble truths as a means to fully understand the dharma and to fully comprehend the right view that will lead one to nirvāṇa.

The four noble truths are often employed as an organizing principle to describe the more detailed and complex set of teachings that are the framework for more specific meditation practices. As a representation of the enlightenment that the Buddha reached, and as an illustration of the path that others might follow to gain enlightenment, the four noble truths are the most significant teaching in all of Buddhism's varied schools and traditions.

See also: **Meditation; Prajñā (Wisdom); Pratītyasamutpāda (Dependent Origination)**

Bibliography

Anderson, Carol S. *Pain and Its Ending: The Four Noble Truths in the Theravāda Buddhist Canon.* Richmond, UK: Curzon, 1999.

Bodhi, Bhikkhu. *The Noble Eightfold Path: The Way to the End of Suffering,* 2nd edition. Kandy, Sri Lanka: Buddhist Publication Society, 1994.

Bond, George D. *The Word of the Buddha: The Tipiṭaka and Its Interpretation in Theravāda Buddhism.* Colombo, Sri Lanka: M. D. Gunasena, 1982.

Dalai Lama XIV. *The Four Noble Truths: Fundamentals of the Buddhist Teachings, His Holiness the XIV Dalai Lama,* tr. Thupten Jinpa, ed. Dominique Side. London: Thoresons, 1998.

Griffith, Paul. "Concentration or Insight: The Problematic of Thervāda Buddhist Meditation-Theory." *Journal of the American Academy of Religion* 44 (1981): 605–624.

Matthews, Bruce. *Craving and Salvation: A Study in Buddhist Soteriology.* Waterloo, ON: Wilfred Laurier University Press, 1983.

Norman, K. R. "The Four Noble Truths." In *Collected Papers,* Vol. 2. Oxford: Pāli Text Society, 1990–2001.

Norman, K. R. "Why Are the Four Noble Truths Called Noble?" In *Collected Papers,* Vol. 4. Oxford: Pāli Text Society, 1990–2001.

Rahula, Walpola. *What the Buddha Taught,* 2nd edition. New York: Grove Press, 1974.

Sumedho, Bhikkhu. *The Four Noble Truths.* Hertfordshire, UK: Amaravati, 1992.

CAROL S. ANDERSON

G

GANDHĀRA. *See* **India; India, Northwest**

GĀNDHĀRĪ, BUDDHIST LITERATURE IN

Gāndhārī, formerly known as Northwestern Prakrit, is a Middle Indo-Aryan vernacular of the ancient region of Gandhāra in the northwest of the Indian subcontinent around modern Peshawar in northern Pakistan. Gāndhārī is closely related to its parent language, Sanskrit, and to its sister language, Pāli. Gāndhārī was written in the Kharoṣṭhī script, running from right to left, unlike all other Indo-Aryan languages that were written in Brāhmī script and its derivatives, which ran from left to right. In the early centuries of the common era, Gāndhārī was used as a religious and administrative language over a wide area of South and Central Asia.

For many years, Gāndhārī was attested primarily in Buddhist inscriptions, coin legends, and secular documents. Only one manuscript of a Buddhist text, the *Gāndhārī Dharmapada,* discovered near Khotan in Chinese Central Asia in 1892, was known. But in the 1990s, many fragmentary Gāndhārī manuscripts on birch bark and palm leaf came to light. Most of these now belong to three major collections: the British Library scrolls, the Senior scrolls, and the Schøyen fragments. These texts are still being studied and published, so that knowledge of Buddhist literature in Gāndhārī is at a preliminary stage. But the texts clearly show that, as previously suspected, Gāndhārī was one of the major Buddhist languages, with an extensive literature that probably constituted one or more independent canons or proto-canons.

The Gāndhārī manuscripts date from about the first to third centuries C.E. They include the oldest surviving manuscript remains of any Buddhist tradition and present a unique source for the study of the formation of Buddhist literature. Although the circumstances of their discoveries are not well documented, most of the manuscripts apparently came from Buddhist monastic sites in eastern Afghanistan, such as Hadda and BĀMIYĀN, where they were buried in clay pots or other containers.

The twenty-nine British Library scrolls constitute a diverse collection of texts and genres written in various hands and formats. The most prominent genres are legends (AVADĀNA or *pūrvayoga*), sūtras, scholastic and ABHIDHARMA texts, and commentaries on groups of verses. The Senior collection, consisting of twenty-four scrolls, is more unitary in that all of the manuscripts were written by the same scribe and most of them are sūtras. The Schøyen fragments comprise over one hundred small remnants from miscellaneous texts, very few of which had been identified as of 2002.

Gāndhārī sūtras include versions of well-known texts such as the *Rhinoceros Sūtra* (Pāli, *Khaggavisāṇa-sutta*) and the *Saṅgīti-sūtra,* both in the British Library collection. The same collection also includes a fragment of a group of short sūtras arranged on a numerical basis, like the *Aṅguttaranikāya* of the Pāli canon and *Ekottarikāgama* of the Sanskrit canon. Among the many sūtras in the Senior collection are Gāndhārī versions of the *Sāmaññaphala-sutta,* which is part of the *Dīghanikāya* in the Pāli canon, and of the *Cūḷagosiṅga-sutta* of the Pāli *Majjhimanikāya,* as well as several others that correspond to *Saṃyuttanikāya* suttas, such as the *Veḷudvāreyya-sutta* and *Pariḷāha-sutta.* The Schøyen collection includes fragments of a Gāndhārī version of the MAHĀPARINIRVĀṆA-SŪTRA.

The Gāndhārī sūtras are broadly similar to the parallel texts in Pāli, Sanskrit, Chinese, and Tibetan, but they differ significantly in structure, contents, and wording. The same is true of Gāndhārī versions of other canonical or paracanonical texts, such as the *Dharmapada* (Pāli, DHAMMAPADA), which is attested both in the Khotan *Dharmapada* scroll and in a small fragment in the British Library collection. The paracanonical *Songs of Lake Anavatapta* (*Anavatapta-gāthā*) is similarly preserved in two fragmentary scrolls in the British Library and Senior collections.

But the majority of the Gāndhārī texts have no known parallels in other Buddhist traditions, and many of them are evidently peculiar to the Gandhāran regional tradition. For example, several of the British Library *avadānas* are marked as local literature by references to historical figures of Gandhāra, such as the Great Satrap Jihonika. Such references provide important clues for the dating of these texts in or around the first century C.E. In general, the Gāndhārī *avadānas* and *pūrvayogas* are characterized by an extremely terse style, indicating that they are summaries of longer stories, designed to serve as mnemonic aids for expanded oral presentations. This makes them difficult to interpret when no parallels are available.

The *abhidharma* and other scholastic texts in the British Library and Schøyen collections also have few, if any, direct parallels, and thus appear to be products of local monastic scholarship that were not preserved in the Buddhist literatures of other regions. Prominent in the British Library collection are commentaries on series of verses of the type that in other Buddhist literatures are found in texts such as the *Sutta-nipāta*, *Dhammapada*, and *Theragāthā*. But the selection and ordering of these verses is peculiar to these texts, and as yet is not clearly understood.

The doctrinal content of the Gāndhārī Buddhist literature is consistently representative of mainstream or HĪNAYĀNA Buddhism. With a few possible exceptions among the Schøyen fragments, which represent a slightly later phase of Gāndhārī literature, they contain no reference to MAHĀYĀNA texts or ideas. Although it is difficult to identify specific sectarian affiliations for many of the Gāndhārī texts, at least some of the British Library scrolls probably represent the literature of the DHARMAGUPTAKA school, since they were found inside a pot that bore a dedicatory inscription to that school. A Dharmaguptaka affiliation is also supported by the British Library *Saṅgīti-sūtra*, which is similar to the version of the same sūtra preserved in the Chinese *Dīrghāgama* (*Chang ahan jing*), which is probably a Dharmaguptaka collection.

The discovery of extensive remains of a Buddhist literature in Gāndhārī, hitherto almost entirely unknown, provides support for the long-standing "Gāndhārī hypothesis," according to which many of the earliest Chinese Buddhist translations were derived from Gandhāran archetypes. This confirms that Gandhāra was the principal jumping-off point for the spread of Buddhism from its Indian homeland into Central Asia and China.

See also: **India, Northwest; Mainstream Buddhist Schools; Pāli, Buddhist Literature in; Sanskrit, Buddhist Literature in**

Bibliography

Allon, Mark. *Three Gāndhārī Ekottarikāgama-Type Sūtras: British Library Fragments 12 and 14.* Seattle: University of Washington Press, 2001.

Allon, Mark, and Salomon, Richard. "Kharoṣṭhī Fragments of a Gāndhārī Version of the Mahāparinirvāṇasūtra." In *Buddhist Manuscripts,* vol. 1, ed. Jens Braarvig. Oslo, Norway: Hermes, 2000.

Boucher, Daniel. "Gāndhārī and the Early Chinese Buddhist Translations Reconsidered: The Case of the *Saddharma-puṇḍarīkasūtra.*" *Journal of the American Oriental Society* 118, no. 4 (1998): 471–506.

Brough, John, ed. *The Gāndhārī Dharmapada.* London: Oxford University Press, 1962.

Fussman, Gérard. "Gāndhārī écrite, Gāndhārī parlée." In *Dialectes dans les littératures indo-aryennes,* ed. Colette Caillat. Paris: Collège de France, l'Institut de Civilisation Indienne, 1989.

Konow, Sten, ed. *Kharoshṭhī Inscriptions, with the Exception of Those of Aśoka,* Vol. 2, part 1: *Corpus Inscriptionum Indicarum.* Calcutta: Government of India, 1929.

Lenz, Timothy. *A New Version of the Gāndhārī Dharmapada and a Collection of Previous-Birth Stories: British Library Kharoṣṭhī Fragments 16 and 25.* Seattle: University of Washington Press, 2002.

Salomon, Richard. "Kharoṣṭhī Manuscript Fragments in the Pelliot Collection, Bibliothèque Nationale de France." *Bulletin d'Études Indiennes* 16 (1998): 123–160.

Salomon, Richard. *Ancient Buddhist Scrolls from Gandhāra: The British Library Kharoṣṭhī Fragments.* London: British Library; Seattle: University of Washington Press, 1999.

Salomon, Richard. *A Gāndhārī Version of the Rhinoceros Sūtra: British Library Kharoṣṭhī Fragment 5B.* Seattle: University of Washington Press, 2000.

RICHARD SALOMON

GANJIN

Ganjin (Chinese, Jianzhen; 688–763) was a Chinese monk who played a major role in the establishment of Buddhism in Japan. In 742 Ganjin accepted an invitation from two Japanese emissaries to introduce orthodox ORDINATION rituals to Japan. At that time a legitimate order of monks (SAṄGHA) did not yet exist in Japan and proper ceremonies to establish an order could not be conducted since Japan lacked the quorum of ten senior bhikṣu (fully ordained monks) to preside over the ordination ceremony as required by VINAYA regulations.

During a twelve-year ordeal, Ganjin and his followers endured five shipwrecks, which cost Ganjin his eyesight and took the lives of thirty-six of his disciples, before they finally arrived in Japan in 754 on their sixth attempt to cross the sea. Once in Japan, Ganjin constructed an ordination platform at Tōdaiji temple in the capital city of Nara and founded a new monastery, the Tōshōdaiji, to serve as a center for the study of VINAYA doctrines. In 754 alone Ganjin and his Chinese compatriots ordained more than four hundred new Japanese bhikṣu. Today, Ganjin is still revered as the founding patriarch of Japan's Vinaya school (Risshū), which adheres to the commentaries on vinaya by DAOXUAN (596–667). In addition to establishing Japan's first properly constituted saṅgha, Ganjin also introduced Chinese medical knowledge, Chinese calligraphy, and the texts and doctrines of the TIANTAI SCHOOL (Japanese, Tendai) of Buddhism. His biography, the *Tō daiwajō tōsei den* (*Biography of the Great Master of Tang China Who Journeyed to the East*; 779) by Genkai (Ōmi no Mifune, 722–785), is one of the early classics of Japanese Buddhist literature.

Bibliography

Tamura, Kwansei. "Ganjin (Chien-Chen): Transmitter of Buddhist Precepts to Japan." *Young East* (Tokyo) 6, no. 4 (1980): 4–6.

WILLIAM M. BODIFORD

GAVĀṂPATI

Gavāṃpati (Pāli, Gavampati) is a disciple of the Buddha, one of the first ten to be ordained and to have known the state of ARHAT. His name means "guardian of the cows" or "bull." Gavāṃpati is mentioned first of all in the VINAYA or monastic codes of the various schools. These sources report on Gavāṃpati's appearance after the ordination of Yaśa, an early convert, whose example Gavāṃpati seeks to emulate. Gavāṃpati is introduced as a friend of Yaśa's; like Yaśa, Gavāṃpati comes from a rich Vārāṇasī family. The episode, described precisely in the Pāli Vinaya, is also evoked, with few differences, in Sanskrit texts (*Saṅghabhedavastu* [*Section on the Schism in the Community*], *Catuṣpariṣat-sūtra* [*Sūtra on the* (*Establishment of the*) *Fourfold Assembly*]) and in their Chinese translations.

The *Theragāthā* (v. 38) mentions Gavāṃpati's supranormal powers and calls him a man of great wisdom "who has surpassed all attachments and reached the far shore of existence" (Norman, p. 5). His mythical nature is explained in the text's commentary (*Theragāthā-aṭṭhakathā*): During three prior lives, Gavāṃpati accumulated merits that allowed him, in a fourth life, to live in a heavenly realm, where he resides in a sumptuous house, the Serīssakavimāna (Palace of Acacias). In his fifth life, in Gautama's time, Gavāṃpati saved a group of monks by stopping a river's flood waters so that the waters remained standing in the air, like a mountain. Echoing this theme, the Vinaya of both the Mahīśāsakas and the Dharmaguptakas shows how Gavāṃpati helped the Buddha and his retinue cross the Ganges on their way to Kuśinagara. Finally, both the *Pāyāsi-sūtra* and the *Dhammapada-aṭṭhakathā* (*Commentary on the Word of the Doctrine*) emphasize that Gavāmpati resides, in a timeless fashion, in the Palace of Acacias.

Gavāṃpati's unusual personality is even more obvious in the texts of north Asian schools. Jean Przyluski showed how Tibetan and Chinese texts glorify Gavāṃpati at the moment of his *parinirvāṇa.* Gavāṃpati was summoned to the Rājagṛha Council after the Buddha's death. A young monk came to his celestial palace to invite him, but Gavāṃpati immediately understood that the Buddha had passed away, and decided that he, too, would accomplish his *parinirvāṇa.* Then, he performed a series of wonders: He sprang into space; his body started to radiate water and fire;

his hands touched the sun and the moon; and, finally, his body wasted away while the river of his waters reached the land of men, and Rājagṛha, putting an end to the dry season.

Przyluski considered this story to be the expression of a pre-Buddhist myth that belongs more to the Asia of monsoons than to Indo-European stock. He proposed the hypothesis that Gavāṃpati was the incarnation of dry winds chasing the waters away, and that his *parinirvāṇa* could be interpreted as a bull-sacrifice that brought the drought to an end. Some scholars have criticized this thesis. Nevertheless, there remain textual facts that are disconnected from any known cult in Indian Buddhism or in the MAHĀYĀNA tradition and that feature Gavāṃpati's strange powers over water.

Within the context of Southeastern Asian Buddhism, Gavāṃpati has become a preeminent character because his textual dimension is enhanced by his ritual dimension. The Sanskrit text of the *Mahākarmavibhaṅga* states that "The saint, Gavāṃpati, converted people in . . . the Golden Land [Suvarṇabhūmi]," a region identified with Lower Burma (Myanmar) or with the central plain of Thailand. The *Sāsanavaṃsa,* a late historical chronicle, tells more specifically that Gavāṃpati was the first to preach the Buddha's doctrine in the Mon kingdom of Thaton. Ancient Mon inscriptions confirm this legend, and one of them points out that Gavāṃpati founded Śrī Kṣetra, the ancient capital city of the Pyus. Some Pagan inscriptions add that a cult, which probably disappeared around the fourteenth century, developed around his images. According to Gordon H. Luce, the limited number of statuettes of the "Fat Monk" found at Pagan are indeed those of Gavāṃpati. Such images are today innumerable in Thailand, where they are called Kachai, Mahakachai, or Sangkachai when they represent the fat monk seated in meditative fashion, and Phagawam when they show him covering his eyes or other bodily orifices. These images are venerated for their protective virtues and for the symbol of renunciation of the senses they express.

Therefore, it is mostly in Thailand, but also in Laos, Cambodia, and in the Shan states, that the Mon cult of Gavāṃpati has survived. Several local texts in Pāli, Thai, and Lao (such as *Gavampati-sutta, Gavampatinibbāna,* or *Kaccāyananibbāna*) tell the story of a monk who resembled too closely the Buddha and so was often confused with him. He therefore decided to transform himself into a shapeless being and to take on another name, Gavāṃpati. This tradition was then extended to another disciple, Mahākaccāyana.

See also: **Disciples of the Buddha; Folk Religion, Southeast Asia**

Bibliography

Lagirarde, François. "Gavampati et la tradition des quatre-vingts disciples du Bouddha: textes et iconographie du Laos et de Thaïlande." *Bulletin de l'Ecole Française d'Extrême-Orient* 87, no. 1 (2000): 57–78.

Luce, Gordon H. *Old Burma-Early Pagan.* Locust Valley, NY: J. J. Augustin, 1969.

Norman, K. R., ed. and trans. *The Elders' Verses,* Vol. 1. London: Pāli Text Society, 1969.

Przyluski, Jean. *Le concile de Rājagṛha: Introduction à l'histoire des canons et des sectes bouddhiques.* Paris: Paul Geuthner, 1928.

Shorto, H. L. "The Gavampati Tradition in Burma." In *R.C. Majumdar Felicitation Volume,* ed. Himansu Bhusan Sarkar. Calcutta: K. L. Mukhopadhyay, 1970.

FRANÇOIS LAGIRARDE

GELUK. *See* **Dge lugs (Geluk)**

GENDER

Buddhist perspectives on gender are multiple, diverse, and often contradictory, varying widely over time and space. This entry will first focus on early or mainstream Buddhism in India (especially as represented by the Pāli canon), and then discuss views of gender particular to MAHĀYĀNA and TANTRA. Emphasis throughout will be on the ideology of gender expressed through Buddhist textual discourse rather than the actual status of Buddhist men and women historically.

Gender in early Buddhism

According to an important Buddhist cosmogonical myth found in the Pāli *Agañña-sutta* (*Knowing the Beginning*), the ideal "Golden Age" that initiates each cycle of world creation is characterized by ethereal human beings who are identical, sexless, and androgynous. It is only when they become greedy for food that sexual differentiation into male and female genders occurs, quickly leading to further moral decline in the form of passion, lust, and jealousy. Gender distinctions thus constitute a fallen and imperfect condition and are a sign of humanity's moral decline. A necessary corollary of this is that as individual beings perfect themselves by following the Buddhist PATH, they return, to some extent, to this genderless ideal. Since sexual differentiation brought about passion and lust, it follows that those who eradicate passion and lust would reverse the process of differentiation. Symbolically, this is suggested by the androgynous behavior and appearance of Buddhist MONKS and NUNS, with their shaved heads, baggy robes, and identical forms of practice. Doctrinally, it is reinforced by early Buddhism's frequent insistence on the irrelevance of gender in spiritual matters and the equal ability of men and women to attain liberation. Women are repeatedly described as being fully capable of attaining NIRVĀṆA (as well as other spiritual goals), and there are many examples of highly accomplished women throughout the early literature. The Buddha's direct disciples included many *arhatīs* (female ARHATS) who were highly esteemed for their moral discipline, meditation, and learning. The liberation of a woman is identical to the liberation of a man, as are the qualities that lead to it.

This tendency toward androgyny and gender equality in matters of the dharma must be balanced, however, against a range of conflicting views equally well represented in early Buddhist literature. Despite the idealization and symbolic appropriation of the androgyny of the Golden Age, for example, it appears that once gender distinctions have developed, they must be observed and maintained. This is apparent in the way early Buddhist texts describe the Buddhist community as a "fourfold community" consisting of "monks, nuns, laymen, and laywomen," with the distinction by gender being considered just as fundamental as the distinction between monastics and LAITY. This sense of the separation and complementarity of the two genders is pervasive throughout early Buddhist literature: There is an order of monks and an order of nuns, the Buddha has two chief male disciples and two chief female disciples, and the lives of men and women are treated separately in complementary texts such as the *Theragāthā* (*Verses of the Elder Monks*) and *Therīgāthā* (*Verses of the Elder Nuns*). Real, rather than symbolic, gender ambiguity is problematic and cannot be tolerated. In fact, proper male or female gender had to be officially confirmed at the time of ORDINATION, and people of ambiguous gender of various types were barred from entering the SAṄGHA.

Distinction between the genders is further reinforced by a consistent hierarchy in which male gender is made superior to female gender. The higher status of men over women is again pervasive throughout early Buddhist literature. Thus, the order of nuns is subordinate to the order of monks, seniority for nuns is calculated separately from and is lower than seniority for monks, and giving alms to a nun results in less merit for the donor than giving alms to a monk (a belief that has adversely affected the order of nuns throughout history). Moreover, this inferiority of women is not merely a matter of social convention, but is, in fact, karmically significant. Male or female gender is determined at the time of conception by one's KARMA (ACTION), with male gender being an indication of better karma than female gender. In cases of spontaneous sex change (several of which are attested in the Pāli Vinaya), the change from male into female is the result of a powerful evil deed, while the change from female into male is the result of a powerful good deed. The same is true of sexual transformations that occur through REBIRTH: In Buddhist stories, women sometimes aspire to be reborn as men (and succeed in doing so by performing good deeds), whereas men never aspire to be reborn as women (but occasionally are as a result of bad deeds).

Early Buddhist views of female gender are further affected by the demands of male celibacy. Because of the threat women pose to this celibacy, there is often a tendency in these male-authored texts to associate female gender with sexuality and lust, and to demonize women as immoral and dangerous temptresses out to divert male renunciants from the path. Women are described as being "wholly the snares of MĀRA," and are said to be driven by uncontrollable lust and "never sated with sexual intercourse and childbirth." The impurity of the female body is also emphasized, and female biological processes such as menstruation are depicted as being filthy and polluting. Alternatively, women (especially virtuous Buddhist laywomen) are sometimes highly idealized as nurturing wives and mothers or celebrated for their feminine beauty and fertility. But whether idealized as madonnas or demonized as whores, such persistent gender stereotypes tend to weaken the tradition's clear statements of gender equality in matters of the dharma.

It is also true that beyond the status of arhatship, early Buddhist texts are more ambivalent about women's spiritual capabilities. In many texts, we find a list of the woman's "five hindrances" or those positions in the cosmos that are unavailable to her as a woman—including the position of buddhahood. Thus, BUDDHAS in the early tradition are never female, a view most likely due to the well-established notion that a buddha's body is characterized by the thirty-two marks of the "Great Man," including the mark of having the penis encased in a sheath. Even becoming a BODHISATTVA was an impossibility for a woman (at least according to the Pāli sources) because one of the five requirements for making the bodhisattva vow was male gender. Nevertheless, since these sources envision both bodhisattvahood and buddhahood as exceedingly rare anyway and perceive arhatship as the only viable goal, this limitation has perhaps been less significant in practice than the unequivocal endorsement of women's ability to attain nirvāṇa.

Overall, then, early Buddhist attitudes toward women and gender take a variety of different forms, some of which Alan Sponberg (1992) has usefully characterized as "soteriological inclusiveness," "institutional androcentrism," and "ascetic misogyny." In the present-day THERAVĀDA cultures of Southeast Asia, many of these views persist, but are also affected by modern developments, such as the greatly increased role of the laity and the global movement for women's rights.

Gender in Mahāyāna Buddhism

All of the views on gender described above for early Buddhism, including the most misogynistic, continue to be found in the Mahāyāna traditions. Nevertheless, the advent of Mahāyāna also heralds some new notions of gender and significant adaptations of earlier ideas. In general, it is often said that female gender is revalorized to some degree in Mahāyāna thought. This may (or may not) be true, but one should be careful to draw a distinction between symbolic representation and historical reality. The revalorization of female gender symbolically does not necessarily imply a better status for women in Buddhism historically. There is no evidence, for example, that the position of women within Indian Mahāyāna was any better than in the mainstream tradition.

In the Mahāyāna tradition, the earlier religious goal of becoming an arhat was replaced by the new religious goal of becoming a bodhisattva (and eventually a buddha)—something every Mahāyānist should do. Thus, the bodhisattva path was open to both men and women equally, and Mahāyāna texts are often noted for their use of gender-inclusive language, frequently addressing themselves to those "good sons" and "good daughters" who adhere to the Mahāyāna teaching. Mahāyāna literature is also full of positive portrayals of women, who function not merely as "good daughters," but even as advanced spiritual teachers to men and full-fledged female bodhisattvas. Mahāyāna texts are not consistent, however, about what level of bodhisattvahood a woman can attain without first becoming a man. Some of the most restrictive texts claim that as soon as a woman becomes a bodhisattva, she will never be reborn as a female again. Other texts, however, claim that bodhisattvas of quite an advanced degree can be female, though they ultimately must become male. Nevertheless, we also find in the Mahāyāna tradition the depiction of female bodhisattvas of the very highest order, such as Tārā in India and Tibet and Guanyin in China, both of whom developed into major objects of worship and cult.

Further complicating this matter is the narrative theme of sexual transformation found in many Mahāyāna texts, such as the LOTUS SŪTRA (SADDHARMAPUṆḌARĪKA-SŪTRA) and *Vimalakīrtinirdeśa-sūtra* (*Discourse on the Teaching of Vimalakīrti*). In episodes that make use of this theme, a woman is depicted as being an advanced bodhisattva who has attained the highest wisdom and understands the true nature of reality. Despite these obvious capabilities, she is challenged in some way by a man, who expresses doubts about the spiritual abilities of women, often asserting the idea that a woman cannot attain buddhahood. The woman then refutes this idea by instantaneously changing her sex and becoming a man (sometimes a fully enlightened buddha). These episodes of sexual transformation have been interpreted in a number of different ways. Most simply, they can be seen as Mahāyāna attempts to refute the traditional idea that a woman could not attain buddhahood or advanced bodhisattvahood within the present life. Such episodes suggest that women can, in fact, attain these states, yet they also depict these women transforming themselves into men, thus ultimately holding to the technical requirement of a male body. Alternatively, however, these episodes can also be interpreted in light of the Mahāyāna philosophical notion of ŚŪNYATĀ (EMPTINESS). Mahāyāna philosophy maintains that all phenomena are "empty" of any inherent self-existence, and all conceptual distinctions are thus relative in nature and not ultimately real—including distinctions of gender. "Male" and "female" are nothing more than conventional categories, and for one who does not cling to such categories, they are as fluid and malleable as a magical creation. In this interpretation, then, the sexual transformation is not to be perceived as a necessary step or prerequisite for buddhahood, but rather, as a teaching device—a playful performance by means of which the female bodhisattva demonstrates to her male challenger the essencelessness of all dharmas. This interpretation is supported by the fact that the sexual transformation is often accompanied by statements asserting the truth of emptiness and the ultimate irrelevance of all gender distinctions. It is also compromised, however, by the fact that it is always women who transform themselves into men (not vice versa), and that most of these transformations appear to be real and permanent. Episodes involving the theme of sexual transformation thus ultimately remain ambiguous. Nevertheless, they do at least demonstrate that the Mahāyāna's insistence on emptiness and the relative nature of all distinctions was explicitly and frequently applied to gender. Similar ideas are also found in schools that derive from the Mahāyāna; in the CHAN SCHOOL, for example, the irrelevance of gender in light of all beings' possession of buddha-nature is a common theme.

In addition to the positive portrayal of female characters, Mahāyāna thought also revalorizes feminine gender on the symbolic level by identifying *prajñāpāramitā* or the "perfection of wisdom" as a female goddess. The goddess Prajñāpāramitā is worshiped and praised as the "mother of all buddhas" (since it is she who "gives birth" to buddhahood) and she is frequently represented in Pāla-period Buddhist art. Since *prajñā* is a feminine noun, wisdom itself is also seen as a feminine quality and is often paired with a masculine quality equally necessary for the attainment of buddhahood—compassionate skillful means or UPĀYA (a masculine noun). The attainment of buddhahood is then envisioned symbolically as the union of male and female forces, whose complementarity and interdependence are emphasized. This type of gender symbolism becomes significantly more pronounced, however, with the advent of tantra.

Gender in tantric Buddhism

Tantric or VAJRAYĀNA Buddhism represents a stark departure from both the mainstream and Mahāyāna traditions in its emphasis on the category of gender. Gender, in fact, becomes absolutely central: Whereas other forms of Buddhism may have certain attitudes about gender, tantric thought is inseparable from its gender ideology. This makes it difficult to isolate the discussion of gender from a more thorough consideration of tantric philosophy and practice. Nevertheless, this discussion will limit itself to a consideration of gender symbolism, female roles, and male attitudes toward women characteristic of the tantric tradition.

The gender symbolism involving the union of male and female qualities to produce the ultimate goal of enlightenment (noted above for Mahāyāna thought) comes to full force and becomes explicitly sexual in tantric Buddhism, especially in the highest and most esoteric class of tantras, the *Anuttarayoga Tantras* (*Highest Yoga Tantras*). These texts are pervaded by a sexual symbolism in which the female (often symbolized as a lotus) stands for prajñā or wisdom, the male (often symbolized as a *vajra* or thunderbolt) stands for *upāya* or skillful means, and male-female sexual union stands for the joining of wisdom and means in the great bliss of perfect enlightenment. In tantric art, this is often symbolized by depicting buddhas and bodhisattvas in sexual union with female consorts. In Tibet, where they were to become very popular, these depictions are known as *yab-yum* or "father-mother" images. The same symbolism is also physically enacted through a highly esoteric form of yoga involving ritualized sexual intercourse between male and female lay tantric practitioners, who together strive to produce the great bliss of perfect enlightenment within their own bodies. Even monastic tantric practitioners bound by the vow of celibacy engage in this sexual yoga—although in their case, the union takes place within the meditator's own mind. The symbolism of sexual union is thus basic to tantric ideology and practice.

Within this sexual symbolism, it is the polarity, complementarity, and interdependence of the two genders that is emphasized. Buddhahood is envisioned as a perfect integration of male and female qualities, which join together seamlessly yet retain their distinctive natures. Philosophically, the union of male and female also stands for the overcoming of all dualistic thinking (including distinctions of gender) and the attainment of an enlightened perspective of emptiness. At the same time, however, female gender alone is sometimes explicitly privileged. Thus, for the first time in the Buddhist tradition, we see the depiction of true female buddhas such as Vajrayoginī, sometimes in consort with male partners but often alone, as well as other divine and powerful female figures such as goddesses, *yoginīs*, and ḌĀKINĪS. Such images were made the object of complex visualization and meditation practices, as well as worship and cult.

The dramatic revalorization of female gender that is characteristic of tantric symbolism also applies to men's and women's roles as depicted in tantric texts.

Perhaps the most striking aspect of higher tantric practice is the prevalence of women's participation, particularly in connection with the sexual yoga mentioned earlier. In tantric literature, women are often depicted as accomplished tantric practitioners and the teachers and founders of specific tantric techniques. Exemplary women such as Princess Lakṣmīṅkarā in India or Ye shes mtsho rgyal in Tibet are remembered and eulogized as respected tantric gurus, while the life stories of many of the most important male "founders" of tantric Buddhism mention female teachers and consorts. Male practitioners are repeatedly instructed to serve and worship their female consorts as goddesses and to see all human women as divine. Moreover, women are often depicted as reservoirs of spontaneous and enlightened wisdom, which is contrasted with the stale intellectualism of men. A constant theme in tantric biographies, in fact, is that of the male practitioner who is stuck in habitual patterns of thought and behavior until spurred on to a new realization through his encounter with a wise and enlightened woman (often described as a ḍākinī or "sky-going" goddess).

Exactly how this dramatic revalorization of female gender on both the symbolic and literary levels relates to the actual status of women in tantric communities historically is open to considerable debate. While it is clear in the case of India that some historical women, such as Princess Lakṣmīṅkarā, must have attained positions of great prominence, the status of ordinary female practitioners is far less certain. Female gender is indeed valorized in tantric literature, but perhaps this valorization is largely for the benefit of men. One could argue, in fact, that the constant attention paid to women merely demonstrates that the vast majority of tantric texts assume the perspective of a male subject. Likewise, though wise and enlightened women often appear in tantric biographies, the biographies themselves are overwhelmingly about men, while many of the women are ethereal *ḍākinīs* encountered in dreams and visions who seem to lack the historical specificity of the men. Finally, it is also important to place the revalorization of female gender within the larger context of tantric Buddhism's use of transgressive sacrality. One of the basic principles of higher tantric practice is to overcome all dualistic thinking through the intentional violation of societal taboos and the breaking of social conventions (such as we see in the practices of sexual intercourse, meat eating, and liquor drinking). From this perspective, the valorization of women (often low-caste women) as pure and goddess-like is effective precisely because it overturns the conventional assumption that women are inferior and impure. Thus, it may be the case that women, no matter how glorified, function more as a symbolic resource for men than as independent agents and subjects.

In any case, it is not at all clear that the tantric valorization of female gender has had any discernible effect on the general status of women in tantric-influenced cultures, such as that of Tibet. Nevertheless, this does not mean that women themselves cannot make use of tantric gender symbolism in new ways, and this is indeed a recent trend among modern female practitioners, particularly in Euro-American Buddhism in the West.

See also: **Body, Perspectives on the; Mainstream Buddhist Schools; Sexuality; Women**

Bibliography

Blackstone, Kathryn R. *Women in the Footsteps of the Buddha: Struggle for Liberation in the Therīgāthā.* Richmond, UK: Curzon, 1998.

Cabezón, José Ignacio, ed. *Buddhism, Sexuality, and Gender.* Albany: State University of New York Press, 1992.

Harvey, Peter. "Sexual Equality." In *An Introduction to Buddhist Ethics: Foundations, Values, and Issues.* Cambridge, UK: Cambridge University Press, 2000.

Klein, Anne Carolyn. *Meeting the Great Bliss Queen: Buddhists, Feminists, and the Art of the Self.* Boston: Beacon, 1995.

Lang, Karen Christina. "Lord Death's Snare: Gender-Related Imagery in the *Theragāthā* and the *Therīgāthā.*" *Journal of Feminist Studies in Religion* 11, no. 2 (1986): 63–79.

Paul, Diana. *Women in Buddhism: Images of the Feminine in the Mahāyāna Tradition,* 2nd edition. Berkeley: University of California Press, 1985.

Schuster, Nancy. "Changing the Female Body: Wise Women and the Bodhisattva Career in Some Mahāratnakūṭasūtras." *Journal of the International Association of Buddhist Studies* 4, no. 1 (1981): 24–69.

Sponberg, Alan. "Attitudes toward Women and the Feminine in Early Buddhism." In *Buddhism, Sexuality, and Gender,* ed. José Ignacio Cabezón. Albany: State University of New York Press, 1992.

Tsomo, Karma Lekshe, ed. *Buddhist Women across Cultures: Realizations.* Albany: State University of New York Press, 1999.

Wilson, Liz. *Charming Cadavers: Horrific Figurations of the Feminine in Indian Buddhist Hagiographic Literature.* Chicago: University of Chicago Press, 1996.

Yuichi, Kajiyama. "Women in Buddhism." *Eastern Buddhist* 15, no. 2 (1982): 53–70.

REIKO OHNUMA

GENSHIN

Genshin (Eshin *Sōzu*, 942–1017) was a Japanese Tendai Buddhist master who is best known for his teachings on PURE LAND BUDDHISM. Genshin helped popularize the deathbed *nenbutsu* ritual, in which the dying believer has a vision of Amida (AMITĀBHA) Buddha and his retinue coming to usher the person into the Pure Land paradise. Genshin's most famous work, *Ōjōyōshū* (*Collection of Essentials on Birth in the Pure Land*), left an indelible mark on the thought and practice of Pure Land Buddhism in Japan, influencing later masters such as HŌNEN (1133–1212) and SHINRAN (1173–1262).

Though Genshin is remembered principally for the *Ōjōyōshū,* he was also a proponent of mainstream Tendai beliefs, particularly in his later years. He compiled an important work on the Tendai doctrine of universal enlightenment found in the LOTUS SŪTRA (SADDHARMAPUṆḌARĪKA-SŪTRA), and he organized the Shakakō, a religious association that constantly tended the icon of Śākyamuni Buddha in Ryōzen'in hall at Yokawa on Mount Hiei. Thus, Genshin's Pure Land teachings, though largely separated nowadays from their original context, were simply part of Mount Hiei's Tendai culture during his period.

The *Ōjōyōshū* is a compendium of quotations from scriptures, commentaries, and treatises on all aspects of Pure Land belief and practice. It may not have had an extensive readership in Genshin's lifetime, but became widely known in subsequent centuries. Thematically, it focuses on the *nenbutsu,* the practice of contemplating Amida Buddha, particularly in meditative visualization, and of invoking his name as a verbal chant. Overall, the *Ōjōyōshū* presents visualization of the Buddha and his resplendent world as the superior practice for birth in the Pure Land. But it also recommends vocal invocation of his name as an important practice for those incapable of meditation.

Among the practices outlined in the *Ōjōyōshū,* and also developed by the Nijūgo zammaie (Twenty-five Member Meditation Society) on Mount Hiei, was the deathbed *nenbutsu* ritual. It was based on passages in the Pure Land scriptures indicating that Amida Buddha and his retinue would come to meet believers (*raigō*) on their deathbed to usher them into the Pure Land. There thus developed the practice of sequestering the dying, surrounding them with spiritual friends, erecting an image of Amida before them, urging them to chant the *nenbutsu,* keeping their mind undistracted and focused on the next life, and thereby assisting them in a final vision of the Buddha coming to greet them at death. This ritual gradually spread and became especially popular among Kyoto aristocrats, though later PURE LAND SCHOOLS did not all adopt it.

Genshin's lasting influence is reflected in the fact that one of Mount Hiei's two dominant doctrinal lineages, the Eshinryū, traced its beginnings to him.

See also: **Japan; Nenbutsu (Chinese, Nianfo; Korean, Yŏmbul)**

Bibliography

Andrews, Allan A. *The Teachings Essential for Rebirth: A Study of Genshin's Ōjōyōshū.* Tokyo: Sophia University, 1973.

Dobbins, James C. "Genshin's Deathbed Nembutsu Ritual in Pure Land Buddhism." In *Religions of Japan in Practice,* ed. George J. Tanabe, Jr. Princeton, NJ: Princeton University Press, 1999.

Horton, Sarah Johanna. "The Role of Genshin and Religious Associations in the Mid-Heian Spread of Pure Land Buddhism." Ph.D. diss. Yale University, 2001.

Reischauer, August Karl. "Genshin's Ōjōyōshū: Collected Essays on Birth into Paradise." *Transactions of the Asiatic Society of Japan,* second series 7 (1930): 16–97.

JAMES C. DOBBINS

GHOST FESTIVAL

The Ghost Festival is the Buddhist-inspired festival held throughout China and East Asia on the full moon (fifteenth day) of the seventh lunar month. In modern China it is known as the Ghost Festival (*guijie*) or Rite of Universal Salvation (*pudu*). Older sources describe it as the Yulanpen Festival; various Sanskrit etymologies have been provided for the term *yulanpen,* which refers to "the bowl" (*pen*) in which food offerings are placed for bringing aid to the ancestors suffering the fate of "hanging upside-down" (*yulan*) in purgatory. In Japan the festival is known as *urabon* (the Japanese pronunciation of *yulanpen*) or more colloquially as *Obon,* the Bon festival, while in Korea it is called *manghon il,* "Lost Souls' Day."

Most of the components of the festival were known in early Indian Buddhism, but it was only in China that they coalesced into a single mythological and ritual unit. Indian saṅghas observed a rain retreat that ended with a monastic ritual in the middle of the seventh

Japanese Americans light candles during Obon, the Ghost Festival commemorating the ancestors, at Senshin Buddhist Temple, Los Angeles, 1991. © Don Farber 2003. All rights reserved. Reproduced by permission.

month. In India monks and laypeople engaged in a cycle of exchange, laypeople providing food, clothing, and other necessities to the professionally religious, who in turn supplied instruction and the chance of improving one's REBIRTH. ANCESTORS and filial piety were always important parts of Indian religion, and one of the DISCIPLES OF THE BUDDHA, MAHĀMAUDGALYĀYANA, was well known throughout Buddhism for his abilities to travel to heaven and hell.

Uniting all these elements, the Ghost Festival was celebrated in China as early as the fifth or sixth century. By that time canonical scriptures, probably composed in China, provided a Buddhist rationale for the practice. According to the *Yulanpen jing* (*Yulanpen-sūtra*), Mahāmaudgalyāyana searches the cosmos for his mother. He finds her reborn in hell for her evil deeds, but is unable to release her from torment. He appeals to the Buddha, who founds the Yulanpen Festival and decrees that all children can bring salvation to their parents by making offerings to monks on the full moon of the seventh lunar month. In practice the festival was part of the cycle of holy days, Buddhist and non-Buddhist, linked to the lunar calendar. With laypeople flocking to monasteries on behalf of their ancestors, the ritual was one of the highlights of the religious year, a kind of Buddhist mirror to the New Year, held six months earlier. The story of Mahāmaudgalyāyana proved that one could be both a monk—one who renounces family and leaves home—and a son who fulfills his obligations to his ancestors. Tang-dynasty (618–907) commentaries on the *Yulanpen-sūtra* emphasize the importance of filial piety (*xiao*), the central ideal of the Chinese kinship system. Thus, the festival symbolized the accommodation between monasticism and lay life.

In later centuries the Ghost Festival moved increasingly out of the Buddhist sphere and into other domains of Chinese social life. The legend of

Mahāmaudgalyāyana (Mulian in Chinese) was retold in popular entertainments and enacted in a wide range of operas sung in local dialects. Storytellers and artists were especially interested in his tours of the various compartments of hell and in his mother's misdeeds. Focusing on a boy's devotion to his mother, the myth was part of the emerging Buddhist discourse about GENDER, female pollution, and the special forms of salvation required for women. The Daoist religion developed its own analogue to the festival, celebrated on the same day, in which offerings to the Daoist deity known as "Middle Primordial" (Zhongyuan) brought salvation to the ancestors. The mythology of Mulian became part of the Daoist celebration and worked its way, in both Buddhist and Daoist guises, into funerary rituals performed by local priests all over China.

The *Yulanpen jing* and its associated rituals were carried to Japan by the seventh century, when the state sponsored the chanting of the text by Buddhist monks. Beyond the reaches of government and monastic control, the festival of Obon later became an expression of Japanese local culture. In modern times many communities sponsor local troupes who perform dances. In both urban and rural Japan most people still return to their family home to observe the holiday, visiting gravesites, honoring spirit tablets, and taking part in festivities.

See also: **Ancestors; Daoism and Buddhism; Death; Ghosts and Spirits; Hells; Intermediate States**

Bibliography

Cole, Alan. *Mothers and Sons in Chinese Buddhism.* Stanford, CA: Stanford University Press, 1998.

Glassman, Hank. "The Tale of Mokuren: A Translation of *Mokuren-no-sōshi.*" *Buddhist Literature* 1 (1999): 120.

Johnson, David, ed. *Ritual Opera, Operatic Ritual: "Mu-lien Rescues His Mother" in Chinese Popular Literature, Papers from the International Workshop on the Mu-lien Operas.* Berkeley, CA: Institute for East Asian Studies, 1989.

Mair, Victor H., trans. "Maudgalyāyana." In *Tun-huang Popular Narratives.* Cambridge, UK: Cambridge University Press, 1983.

Teiser, Stephen F. *The Ghost Festival in Medieval China.* Princeton, NJ: Princeton University Press, 1988.

Weller, Robert P. *Unities and Diversities in Chinese Religion.* Seattle: University of Washington Press, 1987.

STEPHEN F. TEISER

GHOSTS AND SPIRITS

By the time of the Buddha, around the fifth or sixth centuries B.C.E., there already existed the Brahmanic notion of a deceased person spending one year as a troublesome, disembodied spirit, or preta, wreaking domestic havoc to coerce still living relatives into performing the śrāddha rites that would provide the deceased with a new body suitable for joining ANCESTORS, as a *pitṛ*, in heaven.

In early Buddhist scriptures, the figure of the *peta* (a Pāli equivalent of both Sanskrit *preta* and *pitṛ*) is retained, but is transformed from an intermediary, disembodied stage into a fresh rebirth in its own right, though one in which the *peta* is still dependent upon sacrificial assistance from living relatives.

In the *Petavatthu* (*Peta Stories*), the canonical text dealing exclusively with the *peta,* some *petas* are said to endure an existence of total and continual suffering, in which they sustain themselves, if at all, on impurities. They exhibit a wretched appearance, and they are frequently found dwelling in such places as the latrine of a former monastery, at doorposts and crossroads, in moats, in forests, or in cemeteries where they feed off the flesh of corpses.

In the MAHĀYĀNA tradition, the preta is frequently depicted as a "hungry ghost," a creature with a huge belly, but with a needle-shaped mouth through which it is impossible to pass sufficient nutriment to assuage the enormous pangs of hunger.

No such description is found in the *Petavatthu,* according to which there are, in addition to those *petas* already mentioned, other *petas* who are said to resemble *devatās* (inhabitants of the various heavenworlds) of great psychic power, save for some deficiency that prevents them from fully enjoying the benefits normally associated with their world. Most notable of these are the *vimānapetas* (*petas* owning celestial mansions), who seem to be little different from other *vimāna*-owning *devatās,* except that their heavenly bliss is interrupted at regular intervals by their being devoured by a huge dog, or by their having to consume the flesh they have already, as "back-biters," gouged from their own backs.

Though they often seem to dwell cospatially with humans, *petas* belong to a different plane, or dimension. This dimension clearly emerges to be the heavenworld associated with the Four Great Kings, who police that world, which extends from the earth's surface to the summit of Mount Meru, with their troops of YAKṢAS, nāgas, *gandharvas,* and *kumbhaṇḍas.* All manner of other nonhuman creatures, such as *piśācas, bhūtas,* and eclipse-causing asuras, are assigned to that world, as are lesser deities, such as household *devatās,* tree *devatās,* guardian spirits of lakes, and so on. As Buddhism spread further into Asia, the various local deities and the like that Buddhism encountered were also assigned to this world.

Despite the fact that rebirth as a deva and rebirth as a *peta* are deemed discrete types of REBIRTH, the *devatā* and the *peta* seem to represent twin extremes of a whole spectrum of nonhuman beings dwelling in the heavenworld associated with the Four Great Kings. They are differentiated solely by the degree to which each is able to enjoy the pleasures of that world.

Individuals become *petas* due largely to their failure in a former life to show charity to enlightened members of the SAṄGHA, or to demerit stemming from some previously committed evil deed. In order to understand the former, it is necessary to recall the earlier Vedic practice of pouring an oblation into the sacrificial fire to create a sphere of personal well-being embracing not only this life but also the life to come. In the Buddhist period, the saṅgha performs a function similar to the sacrificial fire, in that, through donating alms to the saṅgha, one brings into being a counterpart of those alms on the divine plane for one's use after death. If one neglects to give alms, one naturally finds, in the life to come, no source of sustenance.

Such postmortem deprivation of the Buddhist *peta* echoes the inability of the Brahmanic preta to join the *pitṛs* due to lack of a suitable body. And just as the latter's predicament could be rectified by relatives performing the śrāddha rites, so could the *peta* have its deprivation ameliorated through still living friends and relatives offering a gift to the saṅgha on the *peta*'s behalf and then assigning the fruit of that donation to the benefit of the *peta* concerned. Whatever deprivation the *peta* had been experiencing is immediately rectified and the *peta* is, henceforth, able to enjoy the pleasures and comforts associated with the heavenworld. This practice, wrongly referred to as a "transfer of merit," involves no transfer of merit whatsoever; rather, the *peta* is simply assigned the divine counterpart of the alms offered to the saṅgha on the *peta*'s behalf.

There is, however, one proviso: If the reason for existence as a *peta* is due to, or complicated by, previous demerit, assistance cannot take place until that demerit has been exhausted. Moreover, it is said that part of such a *peta*'s plight is that living relatives forget that he or she ever existed, and thus fail to offer alms on the *peta*'s behalf. For this reason, modern Sinhalese Buddhists, when bestowing alms, do so in the name of any former relatives they may have overlooked.

Although black magicians sometimes commandeer *petas* against their will to do the magician's bidding, they more often enlist the more willing assistance of other nonhuman beings, such as malevolent yakṣas and *bhūtas,* to achieve their ends, just as some of the latter have, on occasion, been transformed by powerful monks into Dharma-protectors.

Although the ORDINATION of nonhumans is not permitted by the Vinaya, it is nonetheless practiced (e.g. in modern Thailand), and it is encouraged by certain Mahayana scriptures, such as the FANWANG JING (BRAHMĀ'S NET SŪTRA). In East Asia (especially in Japan), ordination frees nonhuman beings from *preta* status.

A Buddhist festival known as the Ullambana is still held annually in East and Southeast Asia. The festival is aimed at assuaging the suffering of "hungry ghosts."

See also: **Cosmology; Death; Ghost Festival; Hells; Merit and Merit-Making**

Bibliography

Kyaw, U Ba, trans. *Peta Stories,* edited and annotated by Peter Masefield. London: Pāli Text Society, 1980.

Masefield, Peter, trans. *Vimāna Stories.* Oxford: Pāli Text Society, 1989.

PETER MASEFIELD

GUANYIN. *See* **Bodhisattva(s)**

GYŌNEN

Gyōnen (1240–1321) was a brilliant Japanese scholar-monk of the Kegon school (Chinese, Huayan) who lived in the great monastic center of Tōdaiji in Nara. Born into the aristocratic Fujiwara clan, Gyōnen entered the priesthood at the age of sixteen and at eighteen moved to the Kaidan'in (Hall of Ordination) at

Tōdaiji, where he later became abbot and remained for the rest of his life.

With an eclectic approach to scholarship and practice, Gyōnen dedicated himself to exhaustive studies of nearly every school of Buddhism, writing monographs on Buddhist thought and history from the age of twenty-eight, beginning with his *Hasshū kōyō* (*Essentials of the Eight Doctrines*), a survey of the core doctrines of the eight established schools of Buddhism in Japan in his time. Lucid and extremely informative, this work has served as a textbook for students of Buddhist thought from the thirteenth century into the modern period. Writing in Chinese, Gyōnen went on to compose more than 125 learned works, exploring sūtra exegesis, biography, ritual music, and so on. He also wrote the first detailed histories of individual schools in Japan and survey histories of Buddhism as a whole, carefully tracing the lineage, authoritative scriptures, and doctrinal evolution of all major traditions from their origins in India or China to Japan. Gyōnen has had a profound impact upon Japanese BUDDHIST STUDIES, not only through the wealth of information his writings contain (modern Buddhist dictionaries in East Asia frequently use Gyōnen's works as source material), but also because his historical view defining Buddhism as a collection of schools identified by a doctrinal and transmission lineage became the normative Japanese approach to the study of religion, an approach that began to be challenged only at the end of the twentieth century.

See also: **Huayan School; Japan**

Bibliography

Blum, Mark. *The Origins and Development of Pure Land Buddhism: A Study and Translation of Gyōnen's* Jōdo Hōmon Genrushō. Oxford and New York: Oxford University Press, 2002.

Ketelaar, James. *Of Heretics and Martyrs in Meiji Japan: Buddhism and Its Persecution.* Princeton, NJ: Princeton University Press, 1990.

MARK L. BLUM

H

HACHIMAN

Hachiman is one of the most popular Shintō deities. Originally a tutelary deity of a clan in Kyushu (southern Japan), Hachiman gained official recognition in the eighth century within the framework of state Buddhism. Until the anti-Buddhist persecution of 1868, Hachiman was worshiped as a "great bodhisattva" (*daibosatsu*) and functioned as a protector of Buddhism and of Japan.

See also: **Japan; Shintō (Honji Suijaku) and Buddhism**

FABIO RAMBELLI

HAIR

Manipulation of hair carries cultural meanings in most societies. In traditional India, individuals within society kept their hair controlled by some form of grooming. Controlled social hair stands in sharp contrast to ascetic hair, which is either left ungroomed to form a matted mass or completely shaved. The Buddha and Buddhist MONKS share this feature with other world-renouncing ascetics, including Hindu *sannyāsis* and Jain monks: They are all shaven-headed.

Early texts state that the Buddha cut his hair to two-fingers' breadth in length when he renounced the world. His hair (and beard) remained at that length for the rest of his life, curling to the right. This is the way the Buddha is depicted in art. A stock phrase in Buddhist scriptures states that a monk "cuts his hair and beard and goes from home to the homeless state." Shaving the head has remained a distinctive feature of Buddhist monks and NUNS. Hairs of the Buddha, along with his nail parings, also came to be enshrined and venerated as relics.

Shaving symbolized an individual's separation from society, marked both by the monk's withdrawal from home and social institutions and by his exclusion from socially sanctioned structures for sexual expression. All ritually shaven individuals, both ascetics and nonascetics, such as criminals and widows, live celibate lives. Scholarship in a variety of disciplines has recognized the sexual symbolism of hair. Removing hair at ascetic initiation symbolically returns the ascetic to a prepubertal state of a sexually undifferentiated infant. Removing hair implies the uprooting of sexual desires.

Hair has remained a focus of attention and anxiety among Buddhist monks. Anthropologists have noted that young monks often express rebellion against authority and left-wing political allegiances by allowing their hair to grow a little longer.

See also: **Ordination; Relics and Relics Cults; Sexuality**

Bibliography

Hiltebeitel, Alf, and Miller, Barbara D., eds. *Hair: Its Power and Meaning in Asian Cultures.* Albany: State University of New York Press, 1998.

PATRICK OLIVELLE

HAKUIN EKAKU

Hakuin Ekaku (1686–1768) was a Japanese Zen monk who worked to reform Rinzai Zen, and from whom modern Rinzai lineages in Japan are descended. For Zen monks, he is known as an artist, scholar, and systematizer of DOUBT in KŌAN study. He stressed that kōan introspection, especially the cultivation of doubt, was the only means to SATORI (AWAKENING) and that initial sudden awakening had to be followed with more kōan study (*gogo*) to deepen the experience.

See also: **Chan School**

Bibliography

Yampolsky, Philip B., trans. *The Zen Master Hakuin: Selected Writings.* New York and London: Columbia University Press, 1971.

JOHN JORGENSEN

HAN YONGUN

Han Yongun (Manhae, 1879–1944) was a monk, poet, and critic of the Japanese colonial rule of Korea. He was born in present-day Hongsŏng in South Ch'ungch'ŏng province in Korea. He took full ordination in 1905 and devoted his life to Buddhist reformation, exploring ways of Buddhist engagement in society. By aiming to make Buddhism socially engaged, and thus accessible to the public, his *Chosŏn Pulgyo yusin non* (*Treatise on the Reformation of Korean Buddhism*) provided a rationale and blueprint for the modern reform of the Korean order. Areas of reform included: modernization of the monastery education, development of propagation methods, simplicity of rituals, and centralization of the SAṄGHA. Han offered leadership to the Buddhist youth movement that sought further Buddhist reforms and the saṅgha's independence from the Japanese regime.

In 1914 Han published the *Pulgyo taejŏn* (*Great Canon of Buddhism*), a digest of Buddhist scriptures in Korean vernacular intended to provide the gist of Buddhist teachings to laypeople and to help guide their religious lives. As a certified Sŏn master, Han emphasized mind cultivation through Sŏn (Chinese, Chan) meditation, considered the fountainhead of all other activities in life.

In addition, Han's social and literary activities occupied a great part of his life. He was one of the thirty-three leaders of the March First Movement, which proclaimed Korean independence from imperial Japan in 1919, and he assisted in drafting the Korean "Declaration of Independence" for the movement. In 1926 he published a collection of his poems, *Nim ŭi chimmuk* (*The Silence of the Beloved*). This collection earned him a name as the first modern nationalist poet. He also left 163 Chinese poems, thirty-two *sijo* poetic compositions, and five novels. In 1944 Manhae died of palsy at the age of sixty-five.

See also: **Chan School; Engaged Buddhism; Korea; Nationalism and Buddhism**

Bibliography

An Pyong-jik. "Han Yongun's Liberalism: An Analysis of the Reformation of Korean Buddhism." *Korea Journal* 19, no. 12 (1979): 13–18.

Han Yongun chŏnjip (*The Collected Works of Han Yongun*). Seoul: Sin'gu Munhwasa, 1973.

Lee, Peter, trans. *The Silence of Love: Twentieth-Century Korean Poetry.* Honolulu: University Press of Hawaii, 1980.

PORI PARK

HEART SŪTRA

A text of fewer than three hundred Chinese characters in its earlier short version, the *Heart Sūtra* (Sanskrit, *Prajñāpāramitāhṛdaya*; Chinese, *Boruo boluomiduo xin jing*) was given to the great translator XUANZANG (ca. 600–664) to recite for protection on his pilgrimage to and from the holy land in India. Through his successful use of the sūtra and its concise eloquence, the text became the single most commonly recited and studied scripture in East Asian Buddhism. The *Heart Sūtra* is thought to embody the most profound teaching of *prajñāpāramitā*, the perfection of PRAJÑĀ (WISDOM), and it is recited in rituals by participants in the CHAN SCHOOL, the TIANTAI SCHOOL, and other traditions.

The longer version of the *Heart Sūtra* has a conventional sūtra opening in which ĀNANDA recites the teaching as given by Śākyamuni Buddha on Vulture Peak, followed by a formal conclusion. The short version lacks these framing elements, consisting solely of Avalokiteśvara's explanation of the identity of form and ŚŪNYATĀ (EMPTINESS), as well as a MANTRA. Based on literary evidence, Jan Nattier has argued that the short version was constructed initially in Chinese and then translated into Sanskrit. If correct, this would be an otherwise unknown sequence in Buddhist literary history.

The *Heart Sūtra* opens with the statement that Avalokiteśvara understood the emptiness of all things and was thus liberated from all suffering. Addressing ŚĀRIPUTRA, the stand-in for the ABHIDHARMA understanding of Buddhism in this scriptural genre, Avalokiteśvara then describes the perfect equivalence of emptiness and form; that is, emptiness is not a separate realm underlying or transcending the mundane world, but a different aspect of that same world, or a transcendent realm entirely identical with mundane reality. With concise but systematic thoroughness, the text denies the ultimate reality of virtually all aspects of that mundane world, including such quintessential Buddhist teachings as the FOUR NOBLE TRUTHS of DUḤKHA (SUFFERING), its cause, its elimination, and the PATH to that end. With a wordplay on attainment, taken first as sensory apprehension and then as the achievement of spiritual goals, the *Heart Sūtra* describes the perfection of wisdom as the source of the enlightenment of all the buddhas. Finally, it identifies the perfection of wisdom with a mantra: *gate gate pāragate pārasaṃgate bodhi svāhā.* The grammar of this phrase is obscure (as is the case for mantras in general), even more so for East Asian users of the text, but it is usually understood to mean roughly "gone, gone, gone beyond, gone completely beyond; enlightenment; hail!"

See also: **Prajñāpāramitā Literature**

Bibliography

Lopez, Donald S., Jr. *The Heart Sūtra Explained: Indian and Tibetan Commentaries.* Albany: State University of New York Press, 1988.

Lopez, Donald S., Jr. *Elaborations on Emptiness: Uses of the Heart Sūtra.* Princeton, NJ: Princeton University Press, 1996.

McRae, John R. "Ch'an Commentaries on the Heart Sūtra." *Journal of the International Association of Buddhist Studies* 11, no. 2 (1988): 87–115.

Nattier, Jan. "The Heart Sūtra: A Chinese Apocryphal Text?" *Journal of the International Association of Buddhist Studies* 15, no. 2 (1992): 153–223.

JOHN R. MCRAE

HEAVENS

Buddhist COSMOLOGY recognizes a hierarchy of heavens (*svarga*) comprising the six heaven realms of the "world of the senses" (*kāmaloka*) inhabited by their respective gods, and the various heavens of the pure form and formless worlds inhabited by the various classes of higher gods known as *brahmās.* These heavens are places where any being can potentially be reborn. Existence in these heavens is essentially the fruit of wholesome (*kuśala*) or meritorious (*puṇya*) KARMA (ACTION), and is exceedingly pleasant. Indeed, in the higher heavens there is a complete absence of physical and mental pain.

REBIRTH in the heaven realms of the world of the senses is a result of the practice of generosity (*dāna*) and good conduct (*śīla*), while rebirth in the higher *brahmā* heavens is a result of the development of sublime peace and wisdom through the practice of calm and insight MEDITATION. While life in these heaven realms is long and happy, it must eventually come to an end with the exhaustion of the good karma of which it is the fruit. Rebirth in a lower and less pleasant realm is then a distinct possibility. To this extent, heavenly existence is not entirely free of DUḤKHA (SUFFERING) and falls short of the ultimate Buddhist goal of NIRVĀṆA, which constitutes a complete and final freedom from the sufferings of the round of rebirth. Nonetheless, to be reborn in one of these heaven realms has often been presented and viewed, even in some of the earliest Buddhist texts (such as the *Sigālovāda-sutta*), as forming a step in the right direction and an intermediate goal on the way to nirvāṇa. The goal of rebirth in heaven has thus been considered an appropriate aspiration of especially the Buddhist LAITY, but also anyone else who finds the demands of the practice that leads to nirvāṇa daunting. The underlying outlook here is connected with the notion of the gradual and inevitable decline of the Buddha's teaching, which means that the further removed we are in time from the Buddha himself, the harder it becomes to reach the ultimate goal. Thus, even the great fifth-century monastic commentator of the THERAVĀDA tradition, BUDDHAGHOSA, writes at the conclusion of his manual of Buddhist theory and practice, *Visuddhimagga* (*The Path of Purification*), that he hopes not for nirvāṇa in his lifetime but to experience the joys of rebirth in the Heaven of the Thirty Three and subsequently to attain nirvāṇa having seen and been taught by the next buddha, MAITREYA (Pāli, Metteyya).

In certain MAHĀYĀNA sources the PURE LANDS of buddhas, while technically distinct from the heavens described above, perform a religiously analogous function. Rather than struggle for enlightenment here and now, far removed from the Buddha in time and space, and in circumstances that are somewhat unpropitious, it is better to aspire to be reborn in a pure land such as Sukhāvatī, the Realm of Bliss of the Buddha AMITĀBHA/Amitāyus, where in the presence of a living buddha conditions are more conducive and enlightenment almost a certainty.

See also: **Dāna (Giving); Divinities; Indra**

Bibliography

Reynolds, Frank E., and Reynolds, Mani B., trans. *Three Worlds According to King Ruang: A Thai Buddhist Cosmology.* Berkeley: University of California Press, 1982.

Sadakata, Akira. *Buddhist Cosmology: Philosophy and Origin.* Tokyo: Kosei, 1997.

RUPERT GETHIN

HELLS

Hells play an important part in virtually all Buddhist traditions, past and present. As the lowest of the six (or sometimes five) paths of REBIRTH, hell is one of the most colorful parts of Buddhist COSMOLOGY, mythological reflection, and practice. The hells are the worst (and therefore the best) example of the fate that greets the unenlightened after DEATH, just as a pleasurable rebirth in heaven serves as a positive incentive. Although one might be tortured for a lifetime in hell, rebirth there is, like all phenomena in Buddhism, temporary, leading either to further misery or escape from rebirth altogether. Various etymologies have been offered for the Sanskrit *naraka* and Pāli *niraya.* The normal Tibetan translation is *dmyal ba,* while Chinese usage is usually *diyu* (Japanese, *jigoku*), literally "subterranean prisons."

Number and arrangement of hells

Buddhist ideas of hell grew out of Vedic conceptions and share much with Brahmanical (and later Hindu) views of the underworld. Early Buddhist sources voice different opinions about the names, number, and location of the hells. Some texts discuss one great hell with four doors, each leading to four smaller hells; some claim there are five hells; some refer to seven unnamed hells; some mention ten specific cold hells; some refer to eighteen, thirty, or sixty-four hells. In the most common system, eight hells are located, one on top of another, underneath the continent of Jambudvīpa. Closest to the surface is (1) Saṃjīva, the hell of "reviving," where winds resuscitate victims after torture. Beneath it lie: (2) Kālasūtra, named after the "black string" that cuts inhabitants into pieces; (3) Saṃghāta, where inmates are "dashed together" between large objects; (4) Raurava, "weeping," and (5) Mahāraurava, "great weeping," which describe how denizens behave; (6) Tapana, "heating," and (7) Pratāpana, "greatly heating," which describe the tortures applied to residents; and (8) Avīci, "no release" or "no interval," where there is no rest between periods of torture. Each hell has sixteen smaller compartments, named after the method of punishment: (1) black sand, (2) boiling excrement, (3) five hundred nails, (4) hunger, (5) thirst, (6) copper pot, (7) many copper pots, (8) stone mill, (9) pus and blood, (10) trial by fire, (11) river of ashes, (12) ball of fire, (13) axe, (14) foxes, (15) forest of swords, and (16) cold.

Representations of hells in art and literature

Most accounts of the hells include elements of morality, deliverance, and entertainment. When understood properly, the underworld demonstrates the ineluctability of KARMA (ACTION). Every deed has a result, and if on balance one's life is particularly evil, then one is likely to be reborn in hell. The entire cosmos is ranked; the various scales of measurement reflect an underlying moral hierarchy. The hells are situated below the other five paths, and hell beings lead a longer life than humans or animals. The natural order thus seems to maximize punishment. Some texts name the specific bad deeds that merit rebirth in specific hells: The more evil the deed, the more painful the form of punishment.

Pointing beyond the realm of karma, most accounts of hell contain a soteriology, or theory of salvation. Literary descriptions of the tortures in hell encourage the reader to cultivate roots of goodness (*kuśalamūla*), leading to a better rebirth and eventually release from the pain of sentient existence. Paintings of the wheel of rebirth usually portray a BODHISATTVA or other saint bringing aid to hell beings, emphasizing that suffering can be conquered. And most images of the hell regions are juxtaposed to pictures of life in paradise or to portraits of buddhas who have transcended birth and death.

In whatever genre they occur—folktales, drama, paintings, fictional accounts, or scholastic compendia—representations of the Buddhist hells are usually entertaining. Repetition is a common device in hell narratives: The inmates of the various compartments are tortured not once or twice, but three times. Their pains are described in grisly detail: People are not simply ground to bits, but every component of the body (skin, bone, marrow, muscle, sinew, pus, blood, etc.) is discussed. Although Buddhist ethics are founded on nonkilling, Buddhist accounts of the underworld dwell on the violence meted out to average sentient beings. Alongside this graphic interest in the use of force, there is an equally strong comic strain. Many stories of Buddhist near-death experience involve mistaken identity, in which the protagonist is erroneously sentenced to someone else's punishment. Even austere philosophical sources list the cold hells, three of which are named onomatopoetically after the sounds of chattering teeth: Atata, Hahava, Huhuva.

Attitudes toward hells

Buddhists take a wide range of attitudes toward the hells. Like most teachings, the hells can be regarded as an expedient device, an effective way of motivating people to follow the Buddhist PATH. The hells have also been interpreted as psychological metaphors, as summations of the state of mind one engenders by doing EVIL. While certainly authentic, these two interpretations do not exhaust Buddhist views of hell.

Tours of hell are found throughout Buddhist cultures. MAHĀMAUDGALYĀYANA, one of the DISCIPLES OF THE BUDDHA who was most skilled in supernatural powers, was especially famous for his travels up and down the cosmic ladder. His tours of the underworld are recounted in sources ranging from Mūlasarvāstivāda mythology of the first few centuries C.E., to the MAHĀVASTU (Great Story) in the fifth century, to popular literature in China, Tibet, Japan, Korea, and Thailand. Judging from the narratives of *delok* storytellers in Tibet, the hells are one of the most frequent destinations of modern spirit-mediums as well.

The hells supply a rich fund of mythology for Buddhist preachers. Dharma talks use the tortures of hell to spark reflection on the law of karma and to encourage ethical action. Stories of what happens after death replay the process of warning, reflection, and conversion. Some tales portray the lord of the underworld, King Yama, questioning the dead about the "three messengers" (old age, sickness, and death) they have seen while alive. Most people ignore these signs of impermanence, perpetuating egocentrism and evil deeds. Under Yama's questioning after death, people who awaken to the perils of attachment can be released from suffering.

Many saviors are paired with King Yama's unbending administration of impersonal law. Bodhisattvas like

The Hell of Shrieking Sounds. (Japanese painting, Kamakura period, ca. 1200.) © Seattle Art Museum/Corbis. Reproduced by permission.

Kṣitigarbha (Chinese, Dizang; Japanese, Jizō) and Avalokiteśvara (Chinese, Guanyin; Japanese, Kannon) specialize in rescuing sentient beings from the torments of hell. Visions of the hell regions are also supposed to motivate believers. NĀGĀRJUNA's *Dazhidu lun* (*Commentary on the Great Perfection of Wisdom*) discusses the hells under the category of "vigor" (*vīrya*), one of the virtues of the bodhisattva. Reflecting on the pain people experience in the hells, the bodhisattva is supposed to develop greater energy. Surveying the underworld makes the bodhisattva think, "The causes of this painful karma are created through ignorance and the passions. I must be vigorous in cultivating the six perfections and amassing virtue. I will eliminate the sufferings of sentient beings in the five paths, give rise to great compassion, and augment my vigor" (*Dazhidu lun, Mahāprajñāpāramitā śāstra,* trans. Kumārajīva (350–413), T1509:25.177c).

See also: Icchantika

Bibliography

Feer, Leon. "L'enfer indien." *Journal Asiatique,* ser. 8, 20 (September–October 1892): 185–232; ser. 9, 1 (January–February 1893): 112–151.

Kloetzli, Randy. *Buddhist Cosmology, from Single World System to Pure Land: Science and Theology in the Images of Motion and Light.* Delhi: Motilal Banarsidas, 1983.

La Vallée Poussin, Louis de. *Abidharmakośabhāṣyam,* Vol. 2., tr. Leo Pruden. Berkeley, CA: Asian Humanities Press, 1988.

Matsunaga, Daigan, and Matsunaga, Alicia. *The Buddhist Concept of Hell.* New York: Philosophical Library, 1972.

Pommaret, Françoise. *Les revenants d'au-delà dans le monde tibétain: sources littéraires et tradition vivante.* Paris: Éditions du Centre National de la Recherche Scientifique, 1989.

Reischauer, A. K. "Genshin's Ojo Yoshu: Collected Essays on Rebirth into Paradise." *Transactions of the Asiatic Society of Japan,* second ser., 7 (1930): 16–97.

Reynolds, Frank E., and Reynolds, Mani B., trans. *Three Worlds According to King Ruang: A Thai Buddhist Cosmology.* Berkeley: University of California, Center for South and Southeast Asian Studies, 1982.

Sawada, Mizuhō. *(Shūtei) Jigoku hen: chūgoku no meikaisetsu.* Tokyo: Hirakawa shuppansha, 1991.

Teiser, Stephen F. *"The Scripture on the Ten Kings" and the Making of Purgatory in Medieval Chinese Buddhism.* Honolulu: University of Hawaii Press, 1994.

STEPHEN F. TEISER

HELLS, IMAGES OF

Images of Buddhist HELLS are found largely in Central and East Asia. Although descriptions of hell exist within early Buddhist literature, hell was not a popular subject for depiction in India. The earliest extant Chinese images date to the fifth century and appear within representations of Buddhist COSMOLOGY. These hell images are components of singular carved statues (often referred to as *cosmological buddhas*), as well as larger painted cave programs. The hells are hierarchically placed at the bottom, with the earthly and heavenly realms above. Although the *Shiji jing* (*Scripture of Cosmology*) is fairly lengthy in the number and description of the various hells, the representations themselves are abbreviated. Numerous hell scenes in various media were produced between the seventh and eleventh centuries and were preserved in the DUNHUANG caves of northwestern China. This hell imagery consists mainly of three distinct iconographic programs: imagery related to Dizang Bodhisattva (Sanskrit, Kṣitigarbha; Japanese, Jizō Bosatsu), to the Ten Kings of Hell, and to Mulian (Sanskrit, MAHĀMAUDGALYĀYANA).

Dizang and the Ten Kings of Hell

Images of Dizang Bodhisattva were often used in funerary rituals by relatives who viewed him as a savior of souls trapped in the various hells. Dizang is shown dressed either as a monk carrying a staff or as a princely bodhisattva. A number of hanging silk paintings show Dizang in the company of the Ten Kings of Hell, over whom he presides. Yet it is also common for the Ten Kings to be depicted independent of Dizang, ruling over their respective courts. The Chinese term for hell, *diyu,* translates as "subterranean prison," and the Ten Kings are thus depicted as judges. The exception is King Yama, who is always in regal attire. Yama was the original king of the Indian Buddhist underworld, and it is in his court that the karmic mirror, showing an individual's deeds, is often found. Variations often show all Ten Kings in royal trappings, leading to the common usage of the term *Ten Yamas.* Monkey-faced or military-attired attendants keep track of a soul's crimes and aid in meting out the appropriate punishment. One common representational element found in virtually all hell imagery is that of the naked sinner in a *cangue,* a form of earthly punishment commonly seen in medieval China and Japan. Also critical to hell imagery is a preponderance of flames and blood. Yet unlike hell in a Judeo-Christian sense, Buddhist hells are not permanent, but a means to expiate bad KARMA (ACTION) before moving on to the next REBIRTH.

Several hand scrolls depicting the Ten Kings were found at Dunhuang. These scrolls hint at the usage of hell imagery within a public sphere. Monks would edify the laity with visions of the torments of hell that awaited them, or more importantly, their deceased relatives. The belief in the apocryphal *Shi wang jing* (*Scripture of the Ten Kings*) led to their worship as intercessors who could move the deceased more quickly through the realms of hell to the promised Pure Land. Worship of the Ten Kings centers on the idea that each soul passes in front of each of the kings at predetermined points over a three-year duration. On these days, offerings need to be made to each of the Ten Kings. Besides hand scrolls, Ten Kings imagery also exists in smaller booklet format, indicating mass production as well as a more personal use.

Depictions of hell far exceeded literary descriptions in both variety and detail, a fact most likely due to anxiety for the welfare of the dead. In the *Scripture on the Ten Kings,* no hells are actually described. Works can be found that are consistent in their depiction of the Ten Kings and their courts while greatly varying in the tortures shown. The largest sculpted depiction of hell scenes can be found at Baodingshan in Sichuan province in China. The worshipper at Baodingshan is confronted with an immediate reminder of how his present actions will affect his future fate—a twenty-five-foot-high sculpted depiction of the wheel of life, of which the six destinies of rebirth are one portion.

Kṣitigarbha (Dizang) Bodhisattva rescuing vicitms from the torments of hell, from a painting at Dunhuang. (Chinese, eighth century.)

Hell is one of the six possibilities, the others being hungry ghost, animal, asura, human, or deva. The worshipper then moves around to the other side of the grotto where he first encounters the promise of the Pure Land, then the grim realities of hell. This hell tableau includes Dizang and the Ten Kings set above a chaotic grouping of eighteen hells. Engraved texts aid the worshipper by both identifying the sins committed and providing the necessary ritual hymn to recite in order to gain release. Unique to this hell grouping is a sculpted section devoted specifically to admonitions against alcohol consumption by, or sale to, the clergy. Also unusual is a depiction of a Freezing Hell, which is more common in Tibetan and Mongolian descriptions of hell.

In Japan, the pains of hell, along with the Pure Land's rewards, may have been imported in the seventh century from China, although extant hell imagery dates mainly to after the eleventh century. King Yama takes the form of Emma-Ō, being portrayed as a judge in both painted and sculpted form. There are also several twelfth-century versions of hell, collectively referred to as the *Jigoku zoshi* (*Hand Scrolls of Buddhist Hells*). These painted works are distinctive in the imagery shown. Although they share characteristics with Chinese hell imagery, such as the Hell of Feces and Filth and the Hell of Grinding, the Japanese works also include unique representations, such as the Hell of Cocks, for those cruel to living things; the Hell of Worms, for those who commit adultery or theft; and the Hell of Pus and Blood, in which the damned are tortured by being repeatedly stung by large wasps. Hungry ghosts are often linked to hell imagery, although technically they are not hell dwellers, but another option on the six destinies of rebirth. The best-known imagery depicting hungry ghosts is the twelfth-century Japanese work entitled *Gaki zoshi* (*Hungry Ghosts Hand Scroll*).

Mulian

The last iconographic program is that of Mulian, one of the ten chief DISCIPLES OF THE BUDDHA. Mulian goes in search of his deceased mother only to discover that she is not in a heavenly realm. The *Yulanpen jing*, colloquially referred to as "Scripture of Mulian Rescuing His Mother from the Underworld" was represented in a variety of media, including BIANWEN (transformation texts), which were used to propagate the Buddhist faith among the uneducated, and their accompanying BIANXIANG (TRANSFORMATION TABLEAUX), both of which first appeared in late Tang dynasty China (618–907). Celebrations of the annual GHOST FESTIVAL often included theatrical productions of the Mulian story as well. Murals of the Mulian story in Cave 19 at Yulin, near Dunhuang, depict his travels through the hell regions. These works afforded worshippers explicit glimpses into the horrors of hell as Mulian worked his way down to the Hell of the Iron Bed, where his mother was being tortured for keeping alms meant for the clergy. Hells seen along the way included Knife Mountain Hell, where one was repeatedly sliced open by knives while attempting to scramble out, or

Boiling Cauldron Hell, where Horsehead or Oxhead, minions of the Ten Kings, ensured that the sinner stayed within a vat of boiling oil. Mulian eventually would find and free his mother, but not before reinforcing the Buddhist belief in karmic retribution.

Bibliography

Fan Jinshi, and Mei Lin. "An Interpretation of the Maudgalyāyana Murals in Cave 19 at Yulin." *Orientations* no. 27 (November 1996): 70–75.

Howard, Angela Falco. *The Imagery of the Cosmological Buddha.* Leiden, Netherlands: Brill, 1986.

Kucera, Karil. "Lessons in Stone: Baodingshan and Its Hell Imagery." *Bulletin of the Museum of Far Eastern Antiquities* no. 67 (1995): 79–157.

Mair, Victor. *T'ang Transformation Texts: A Study of the Buddhist Contribution to the Rise of Vernacular Fiction and Drama in China.* Cambridge, MA, and London: Council on East Asian Studies, Harvard University Press, 1989.

Matsunaga, Daigan, and Matsunaga, Alicia. *The Buddhist Concept of Hell.* New York: Philosophical Library, 1972.

Teiser, Stephen F. *The Ghost Festival in Medieval China.* Princeton, NJ: Princeton University Press, 1988.

Teiser, Stephen F. *The Scripture on the Ten Kings and the Making of Purgatory in Medieval Chinese Buddhism.* Honolulu: University of Hawaii Press, 1994.

Visser, Marinus Willem de. *The Bodhisattva Ti-tsang (Jizo) in China and Japan.* Berlin: Oesterheld, 1914.

KARIL J. KUCERA

HERMENEUTICS

The term *hermeneutics* derives from the Greek god Hermes, the messenger of the gods, whose task was to communicate between gods and humans. Since both sides had different languages and worldviews, it was necessary to interpret a god's wishes in ways that humans could comprehend. In addition, Hermes had to understand the god's intentions and how to translate them.

In its earliest uses in Western thought, hermeneutics was mainly associated with biblical exegesis, and specifically with the rules and standards that should guide interpretation of scripture. During the twentieth century, its scope was considerably widened, and it is now generally seen as a fundamental aspect of all the humanities and social sciences. It should be noted, however, that the term *hermeneutics* is not generally conceived as applying to all interpretation, but rather to the rules and methods that guide it.

In the Indian Buddhist context, hermeneutical literature is mainly concerned with identifying the intention (*abhiprāya*) behind scriptural statements, particularly those that are viewed as being in conflict with other statements. The Buddhist case presents special difficulties for interpretation because of the vastness of Buddhist scriptural literatures and the plethora of conflicting doctrines and practices. According to Buddhist tradition, the Buddha traveled from place to place teaching those who came to him with questions. He is compared to a skilled physician who provides different medicines specific to particular illnesses. The Buddha taught each person or group what would be most helpful soteriologically; he was not principally concerned with creating an internally consistent doctrinal system. Thus, after his death, his followers were left with a corpus of texts that all claimed canonical status, but that contained often contradictory teachings.

From an early period, Indian Buddhist exegetes strove to differentiate those statements that were of "provisional meaning" (*neyārtha*) from those of "definitive meaning" (*nītārtha*). The former were expedient teachings given to a particular person or group, but they do not represent the Buddha's final thought, while the latter reflect the (often hidden) intention behind his teaching.

Buddhist hermeneutics became even more difficult around the first century C.E. when large numbers of new texts began to appear that purported to have been spoken by the Buddha when he was alive, but that often differed in style, content, and doctrine from the texts contained in earlier canons. These were the sūtras of the MAHĀYĀNA school, which claimed to supersede earlier teachings, most of which were said to be of merely provisional meaning. Within this new literature, however, there were even more conflicting doctrines. Many texts contained statements attributed to the Buddha that claimed that a particular teaching should be viewed as his final thought, but these statements were sometimes contradicted by other sūtras.

Buddhist exegetes generally responded to this situation by privileging certain texts and basing their interpretive schemas on them. Some of the new Mahāyāna texts provided specific guidelines for interpretation. The SAṂDHINIRMOCANA-SŪTRA (Tibetan, *Dgongs pa nges par 'grel pa'i mdo*; *Sūtra on Unfurling the Real Meaning*), for example, states that Buddha's teachings may be divided into three "wheels of doctrine" (*dharmacakra*). The first two wheels—comprising certain HĪNAYĀNA doctrines and teachings relating to ŚŪNYATĀ (EMPTINESS) in Perfection of Wisdom sūtras—are said to be of provisional meaning, while the third (the teachings of the *Saṃdhinirmocana*) is said to be definitive.

In some Mahāyāna sūtras, an alternative strategy is proposed: The level of a particular text is determined by subject matter. The most advanced sūtras are those that directly discuss emptiness, a doctrine only taught to the most advanced disciples. Thus, if a sūtra examines emptiness as its main object of discourse, it should be viewed as representing Buddha's definitive intention.

Tibetan exegetes generally based their interpretive schemas on Indian precedents. Several, for example, used the "three wheels of doctrine" model as a basis for differentiating interpretable from definitive scriptures. In his *Legs bshad snying po* (*Essence of Good Explanations*), TSONG KHA PA (1357–1419) divided his presentation into two sections, one based on the *Saṃdhinirmocana-sūtra,* the main scriptural source for the YOGĀCĀRA SCHOOL, and the other on the *Akṣayamatinirdeśa-sūtra* (Tibetan, *Blo gros mi zadpas bstan pa'i mdo*; Chinese, *Achamo pusa jing; Discourse Taught by Akṣayamati*), which he considered to be definitive for MADHYAMAKA SCHOOL hermeneutics. Other Tibetan exegetes altered the three wheels schema, and claimed that the first wheel was comprised of Hīnayāna teachings, the second of Mahāyāna teachings, and the third and definitive wheel was declared to be the tantric teachings of VAJRAYĀNA.

East Asian exegetes faced all the same problems as their counterparts in India and Tibet, but they also encountered difficulties related to the haphazard nature of textual transmission to the region. Unlike the relatively ordered transmission of texts to Tibet, Buddhist literature came to China via numerous different routes, and there was little coordination in these efforts. Sometimes a commentary would arrive in China before the root text, and the Chinese were faced with an enormous imported literature containing various competing and incompatible claims to authority. Several Chinese Buddhist exegetes developed classification schemes (*panjiao*), which were generally based on a particular text (or a related group of texts) and which ranked scriptures hierarchically. One of the most important of these was the Tiantai schema, which was based on the LOTUS SŪTRA (SADDHARMAPUṆḌARĪKA-SŪTRA; Chinese, *Miaofa lianhua jing*) and divided the Buddha's teaching career into five periods and eight teachings (*wushi bajiao*). FAZANG (643–712) and the HUAYAN SCHOOL had an alternative five-teaching schema, which culminated in the Perfect Teaching (*yuanjiao*) of the HUAYAN JING (Sanskrit, *Avataṃsaka-sūtra*; *Flower Garland Sūtra*).

In Japan, the Kamakura period (1185–1333) saw the development of indigenous Buddhist schools, and most of these also developed their own classification systems. NICHIREN (1222–1282), for example, used the *Lotus Sūtra* as the basis for his teachings, and the Zen, Esoteric, and Pure Land schools also developed ranking systems in which their own doctrines and scriptures were placed at the top of the doctrinal hierarchy, while others were relegated to inferior positions.

Most traditional Buddhist exegetes have been involved in what the German philosopher Hans-Georg Gadamer (1900–2002) dismissed as the "Romantic endeavor," that is, attempting to discern the intention of the purported author of their scriptures (i.e., the Buddha). Underlying their efforts was a shared conviction that the experience of buddhahood is available to all and that as one approaches it, one's mind more and more closely approximates that of the Buddha. Thus it is assumed that competent exegetes are able to re-create the true intentions underlying apparently contradictory scriptural statements and arrive at interpretations that accurately reflect the Buddha's ultimate intent, which is assumed by traditional Buddhists to be free from contradiction.

See also: **Commentarial Literature; Scripture**

Bibliography

Broido, Michael M. "Some Tibetan Methods of Explaining the Tantras." In *Contributions on Tibetan Language, History and Culture: Proceedings of the 1981 Csoma de Körös Symposium,* ed. Ernst Steinkellner and H. Tauscher. Vienna: Wiener Studien zur Tibetologie zur Buddhismuskunde, 1983.

Chegwan. *T'ien-t'ai Buddhism: An Outline of the Fourfold Teachings,* tr. Buddhist Translation Seminar of Hawaii, ed. David W. Chappell. Honolulu: University of Hawaii Press, 1983.

Gregory, Peter N. *Tsung-mi and the Sinification of Buddhism.* Princeton, NJ: Princeton University Press, 1991.

Lopez, Donald S., Jr., ed. *Buddhist Hermeneutics.* Honolulu: University of Hawaii Press, 1988.

Powers, John. *Hermeneutics and Tradition in the Saṃdhinirmocana-sūtra.* Leiden, Netherlands: Brill, 1993.

Ruegg, David S. "Purport, Implicature, and Presupposition: Sanskrit *Abhiprāya and Tibetan dGoṅs pa/dGoṅs gźi* as Hermeneutical Concepts." *Journal of Indian Philosophy* 13 (1985): 309–325.

JOHN POWERS

HIMALAYAS, BUDDHIST ART IN

The wide geographic area covered by the Himalayan range and reaching from Kashmir in the west to Mongolia in the east includes several civilizations dedicated to Buddhism, often in close symbiosis with other religions. The strength of autochthonous traditions and the different ways in which Buddhism was imported from foreign cultures resulted in different types of Buddhist art in this region.

Kashmir

Sarvāstivāda Buddhism was the dominant religion in Kashmir until the sixth century; from the eighth to the twelfth centuries MAHĀYĀNA Buddhism was also a strong force. During this period Buddhist art in Kashmir developed a characteristic national style embodying elements from Gupta India and Gandhāra, and even from Syrian-Byzantine styles.

No early Kashmiri Buddhist monastery remains intact, but in structure and style they were probably similar to the still existing brahmanical structures. In Parihāsapura (Paraspor), there are remains of temples and of a STŪPA that date to the first half of the eighth century. The square halls and chapels of these structures were characterized by lantern-ceilings consisting of superimposed intersecting squares and tympana of triangular gables over openings in the facade that enclosed a trefoil arch. The chapels had fluted pillars and stepped pyramidal roofs. A special type of building design was the *pañcāyatana* form, which consisted of a cubic structure with entrances in all four walls and a large central tower and smaller caitya-like elements at all four corners.

The remains of stūpas allow scholars to reconstruct their original appearance. The stūpa in Huviṣkapura (Uṣkur), located inside a large courtyard, includes terra-cotta and stucco fragments that show Gandhāra influences. Other remains at Sadarhadvāna (Hārvan), datable to between 400 and 500 C.E., can be reconstructed by terra-cotta plaques showing miniature stūpas. The enormous Caṅkuna-stūpa at Parihāsapura, datable to the first half of the eighth century, had a large square double platform with projecting staircases on each side and indented corners, making it somewhat similar to the BOROBUDUR in Java.

Only a few early Kashmiri Buddhist sculptures in stone have survived, including a life-size standing bodhisattva unearthed at Pāṇḍrēṇthan (Purāṇādhisthāna), datable to the seventh or eighth century. Stucco and terra-cotta fragments, stylistically comparable to Haḍḍa and Taxila, were found in the ruined stūpa at Uṣkur. Sculptures in bronze are also well documented; their yellowish brass material, often with inlays of copper and silver, is typical. Beginning in the eighth century, standing figures of Buddha Śākyamuni wore garments with stylized folds, sometimes including a capelike "cloud-collar" around the neck. The Buddha was also often represented seated and wearing a crown. The stylistic roots for such representations may be found in Bengal. Kashmiri bodhisattvas were generally ornamental, with a luxuriant surface. Avalokiteśvara is often shown seated in a pensive mood, a form probably derived from Gandhāra models. There are also examples of other bodhisattvas, such as MAITREYA or Vajrapāṇi, as well as goddesses like Tārā clad in tight bodices accentuating their feminine appearance. After the eighth century, fierce deities of the tantric pantheon were also represented.

An impression of what the lost Buddhist murals in Kashmir must have looked liked may be gained from the enormously rich twelfth-century wall paintings in Ladakh, especially those at ALCHI, which were probably executed by Kashmiri artists.

Nepal

Nepal's proximity to Northern India influenced the Buddhist art in Nepal on many levels; these Indian influences were later integrated into existing local traditions. The earliest still existing monuments were stūpas. The four AŚOKA stūpas erected at the cardinal points near the entrances to the city of Pāṭan are related to basic Indian forms of the third century, as exemplified by the Great Stūpa of SĀÑCĪ. The stūpas at Pāṭan have flat tumulus-like cupolas on low walls, small shrines for reliefs of buddhas, and square *harmikās* (pavilion-like blocks of stone atop the domelike stūpas) that show Pāla influence. The large Svayambhūnāth stūpa to the west of Kathmandu, first erected around 400 C.E., is dedicated to the five tathāgatas. It shows a relationship to a Mauryan tumulus, but pairs of eyes painted onto the four sides of the *harmikā* are a Nepalese characteristic. They symbolize the all-seeing eyes of the supreme *ādi-buddha.* The stūpa is designed as a representation of the axis of the world, and it is thus surrounded by four shrines marking each of the heavenly directions. The plan of the second monumental stūpa of Bodhnāth in Bhatgāon (Bhaktapur) is related to the concepts of a MAṆḌALA. It is also orientated to the four heavenly directions; it has a flat large tumulus on a three-step foundation, as well as eyes on the *harmikā.*

A mural depicting a many-headed, many-armed bodhisattva Avalokiteśvara at the ancient Buddhist center of Alchi, in Ladakh, India. © Hulton/Archive by Getty Images. Reproduced by permission.

One hundred and eight niches in the low base of the *aṇḍa* contain statues of AMITĀBHA.

The earliest representations of monastic architecture in Newari style are found in illustrations of *prajñāpāramitā* sūtras that date to 1015. These buildings were characterized by a combination of plain brick walls, with roofs, doors, and windows made of elaborately decorated wood, a style possibly derived from Gupta architecture. Such structures are also characterized by slanting struts supporting the weight of the projecting roofs, which sometimes have Chinese-looking upturned corners.

In Nepal, there is a close technical and structural parallelism between nonreligious and monastic buildings, whether Buddhist or brahmanic. Three or four upper stories were often added to such buildings beginning in about the fourteenth century. Nepalese monasteries and temple complexes consisted of a square courtyard surrounded by buildings, with a main chapel at the end of the central axis. The center of the courtyard was sometimes occupied by a caitya or a maṇḍala structure.

The coexistence of Buddhism and Brahmanism in Nepal resulted in a similarity in iconographical types and forms. The earliest stone and wood sculptures of bodhisattvas in the Licchavi period (300–850) show a relationship to Kushan or Gupta art, but certain influences from Sārnāth may also be observed. During the Thakuri phase (beginning about 1480) some Pāla influences became apparent, and between the fourteenth and seventeenth centuries, there develops a distinctive Newari style that can no longer be labeled as a regional variety of Indian art. In this style, the sculptural surfaces, especially of bronze figures, is smooth and usually gilded. There are no obvious stylistic changes over longer periods, although a predilection for sensual representations of Avalokiteśvara and the female deity Vasudhārā began in the eleventh century. After 1278 Newari artists were frequently employed by Tibetan monasteries, including the famous Aniko.

In part because of differences in architectural structures, murals played a much smaller role in Buddhist painting in Nepal than in Ladakh or Tibet. Instead, narrative scenes and holy figures of the pantheon were painted on cotton and mounted as movable hanging scrolls (*paṭa* or *paubhā*) to be shown during appropriate ceremonies, a tradition that continued well into the eighteenth century. The earliest dated piece is a maṇḍala of the deity Vasudhārā from the year 1367. These scrolls are characterized by detailed and elegant execution, the use of primary colors (especially red), the hieratic frontality of central figures, and visual order and spatial symmetry.

Another characteristic field of Buddhist painting in Nepal are illustrations in manuscripts on palm leaf or paper, an art practiced since the first half of the eleventh century. The roots for this form may be found in Eastern India, but the Nepalese paintings are more expressive and painterly than Indian Pāla versions. During the first half of the seventeenth century, a new stylistic tradition developed as Nepalese artists came under the influence of Rajput paintings.

Ladakh and western Tibet

Buddhist art in the regions of Ladakh, Spiti, and Guge in western Himalaya mainly came to life under the influence of the "second spread" (*bstan pa phyi dar*) of Buddhism, which was started by Rin chen bzang po (958–1055) and sponsored by the local royal families. Rin chen bzang po is said to have founded many temples, although only few such reports can be substantiated historically. The new religious trends, with roots in Northern India and Kashmir, were characterized by a cosmic conception centered on the transcendental Buddha Vairocana and the four tathāgatas. This focus is reflected clearly in iconography. Influences from Nepal can also be traced. Later, artists in central Tibet, under the influence of the Bka' gdams pa (Kadampa order), introduced sexually tinted *yab-yum* figures in sculpture and painting ("yab-yum," literally "father-mother," is a couple in an erotic embrace—he a tantric deity, she the embodiment of transcendental wisdom, or prajñā). After the sixteenth century, when the DGE LUGS (GELUK) order became the leading power, Tibetan art shows Chinese influence, especially in monastic architecture, and monasteries of this period often look like fortresses.

Nyar ma, near the capital Leh, is the only monastery in Ladakh that can be confirmed as having been founded by Rin chen bzang po, in about 1000 C.E. This monastery was an influential religious center during the eleventh and twelfth centuries, but only ruined foundations of the buildings remain. Another early building is a small temple at Lamayuru Monastery (Gyung drung dgon pa) in the Indus valley. This building contains murals and a sculpture of Vairocana flanked by the four tathāgatas. The other buildings at Lamayuru were redecorated later.

The temples in the village of Alchi (A lci) on the left bank of the Indus, to the east of Leh, occupy an exceptional position in the Himalayan history of Buddhist architecture and wall painting. While the structures of the walls follow the local Ladakhi-Tibetan tradition, the wooden facade and pillars, elements of the ceilings, and especially the wall paintings, clearly represent Kashmiri traditions, and were probably executed by Kashmiri artists invited to western Tibet by Rin chen bzang po. Whereas the congregation hall (*Du khang*) was erected and decorated early in the twelfth century, the three-storied temple (Gsum brtsegs) dates slightly later to around 1200 C.E. The murals at Alchi are extremely elegant and stylistically quite different from paintings in Tibetan style. The secular scenes depicting male and female donors in royal attire show Indian and Central Asian influence, whereas the Great Stūpa, which is actually a *pañcāyatana* chapel, and its murals belong to the same period as the early Alchi temples. Rich wall paintings of male and female deities united in the *yab-yum* position correspond to a typical Tibetan style. The only known temple complex in a style closely related to that of Alchi are the four chapels and a *pañcāyatana* building in the small village of Mang rgyu, which is located in a valley near Alchi.

Whereas many of the earlier temples in Ladakh were built on flat ground near villages, beginning in the fifteenth century most monastic complexes were constructed on hills. These fortresslike complexes consisted of several courtyards with temples. Painted and sculpted icons used the tantric iconography of Tibetan Buddhism. A typical example is Spituk (Dpe thub) near Leh. The temples at Tiktse (Khrig rtse) and Likir (Klu dkyil) show later repainting and restoration. The wealthy 'Brug pa monastery at Hemis consists of several large buildings, some with murals from the eighteenth century.

Five cave temples above the village of Saspol (Sa spo la) opposite Alchi house rich murals with a wide spectrum of iconography. These show Śākyamuni, the Sukhāvatī Paradise, many bodhisattvas, protective deities, and monks.

The important temple complex at Tabo (Rta bo) in Spiti was founded in 996 by Rin chen bzang po and the religious king Ye shes 'od. The walls (*lcags ri*) surround eight asymmetrically arranged temple buildings.

The temple and other buildings of the religious compound at Alchi in Ladakh, India. © Craig Lovell/Corbis. Reproduced by permission.

The entrance hall (*sgo khang*) includes murals from 996 that show influences from Central Asia, especially in the representation of human figures. The main hall (*Gtsug lag khang*), which was renovated in 1042, is divided by rows of pillars into three naves with a circumambulation route at its end. The walls show a Sarvavid-Vairocana maṇḍala; the main figures are affixed as sculptures to the walls and are surrounded by paintings. The wooden portals are framed by panels of sculptures with scenes from Śākyamuni's life, probably executed by Kashmiri artists. There are also remarkable painted portraits of royal patrons, nobles, and monks with their names added. Several other chapels are dedicated to different deities.

The group of temples at Tholing (Mtho lding), the religious center of the kingdom of Gu ge, was founded at the end of the tenth century by Ye shes 'od and Rin chen bzang po, who served as the first abbot. The layout was modeled after the Tibetan monastery BSAM YAS (SAMYE). The rectangular outer walls surround a row of small chapels. The greatest building in the center, dedicated by Ye shes 'od, is accentuated with stūpas over its four corners, resulting in a pyramidal effect, the arrangement of which, together with the interior decoration, represents a Vajradhātu maṇḍala. The masonry structure is Tibetan; the Chinese-style copper roofs were added during the fifteenth century. There are several other buildings, including a congregation hall (*'Du khang*). The hall for initiations (*Gser khang*) has three stories representing the three bodies of a buddha and a maṇḍala-like plan with chapels; the wooden columns are in Central Asian style and are similar to the wooden portal of the White Temple (Lha khang dkar po).

The surviving murals in the temples at Tsaparang (Rtsa pa brang), only ten kilometers from Tholing, and the later capital of Gu ge, were painted during the fifteenth and sixteenth centuries and are related to those of Gyantse (Rgyal rtse). The White Temple had twenty-two stucco statues affixed to its walls; these were destroyed during the Cultural Revolution. Remaining murals show scenes from Śākyamuni's life. The Red Temple (Lha khang dmar po), built during the fifteenth century, has murals with tathāgatas executed about two centuries later.

Central and eastern Tibet

Whereas Ladakh and western Tibet were strongly influenced by the art of Kashmir, the Buddhist art of central and eastern Tibet was in its formative period stimulated by the introduction of Buddhism from India, via Nepal, and from Central Asia, and in its later phase from China. Characteristic local styles were the result of mingling adaptations with autochthonous traditions, especially in architecture.

The JO KHANG in Lhasa, its founding in the eighth century attributed to King Srong btsan sgam po, is close to Indian Gupta models. There are three stories over a square plan, the third story probably constructed later. The five inner chapels are surrounded by corridors for circumambulation. The wooden chapel doors and heavy columns are decorated with carvings resembling a mid-seventh century Newari style. The projecting Chinese-style roofs were built later. The principal chapel contains a sculpture of the eastern tathāgata, AKṢOBHYA, as its main image, with sculptures of Amitābha and Maitreya in side chapels. The original monumental murals are lost; the existing paintings were executed in the twelfth century and show Tibetan style with some Nepalese and Pāla influences.

The temple complex of Bsam yas (Samye) in the Tsangpo valley was founded in 779 by King Khri srong lde btsan. The layout comprises several buildings and four outer *chörten* (*mchod rtens*), or stūpas, which were based on maṇḍala concepts. The three-storied central temple (*dbu rtse*) symbolizes Mount Sumeru as axis mundi. The circular perimeter wall stood for the chain of mountains surrounding the world (*lchags ri*). The differing architectural structures of the three stories reflect the pluralism of religious and stylistic sources from India, Khotan, and China. Turrets at the four corners of the upper story transform it into a *pañcāyatana* structure. The wall paintings in the chapels symbolize the ascent of the adept through the spiritual layers of the Buddhist religion.

The extremely dilapidated temple of Yemar (Gye dmar) in the Khangmar county, erected early in the eleventh century, holds an important position in art history. Three chapels inside a processional path (*skor lam*) house larger than life-size clay figures of buddhas, bodhisattvas, and guardian deities, which were originally colored and gilded. The figures are characterized by fine molding of the faces and the folds of garments, the latter featuring rich ornamental medallions showing Central Asian influence. The figures represent a Tibetan substyle with Pāla and Central Asian elements. All the murals have disappeared.

A highlight of the later phase of Tibetan art is the temple complex Dpal khor chos sde at Gyantse (Rgyal rtse), formerly the third-largest city in Tibet. Gyantse is crowned by a fortress (*rdzong*), destroyed in 1904 by the Younghusband expedition, but partly reconstructed. The temple complex was founded in 1418 by a Gyantse prince and comprised many buildings and eighteen colleges run by different Buddhist schools, including SA SKYA (SAKYA), KARMA PA, Dge lugs (Geluk), and others. Most of the buildings were destroyed during the Cultural Revolution. Most important is the building of the Sku 'bum, erected and decorated between 1427 and 1442. Its ground plan has the character of a maṇḍala and its four-storied elevation resembles an "auspicious stūpa with many doors," the so-called *Bkra shis sgo mang mchod rten*. The building contains seventy-two temples and chapels that are decorated with sculptures and paintings of more than twenty-seven thousand deities. These images illustrate the esoteric and cosmological speculations of the Sa skya school, which are experienced by adepts during circumambulation. A central figure is that of the transcendental Vajradhara, located in the fourth story. The stucco statues and the paintings represent a typical Tibetan style called "school of Gyantse," into which foreign influences have been fully integrated.

Beginning in the fifteenth century, temple plans in Tibet develop according to different systems, culminating in complex monastic cities like Dga ldan, especially under the influence of the Dge lugs order. An increasing Chinese influence is noticeable, mainly in roof structures. Examples are the Kumbum (Sku 'bum; Chinese, Ta'ersi) at the birthplace of TSONG KHA PA (1357–1419) in Amdo, and Labrang Tashi Khyil (Bla brang bKra shis dkyil), founded in 1710 by the Dge lugs order.

A special position in Tibetan architecture is occupied by the political and religious center of the POTALA on the Red Mountain at Lhasa. Since the fifth DALAI LAMA started construction on the White Palace in 1645, the fortresslike palace and temple complex, rising thirteen stories and covering more than 100,000 square meters, served as a residence for the dalai lamas. The palace comprises halls, chapels, shrines, *chörtens*, and libraries, as well as quarters for administration and living. Its architectural style is a combination of Tibetan and Chinese features, but it has a uniquely Tibetan appearance. It has slightly slanting stone walls and golden roofs for the main buildings, and it is filled with murals, paintings, and sculptures of historical figures from the seventh to the seventeenth century and of deities of the pantheon, along with many other treasures. The rich interior wooden structures are heavily painted.

In Tibet, sculptures that were not permanently fixed into an architectural context were rarely executed in stone, but rather in stucco, clay, and metal. The center of bronze casting was Kham in western Tibet, especially Sde dge (Derge); the technique was *cire perdue*, often gilded. Foreign influences, especially from Pāla and Sena in eastern India, are obvious during early periods in western Tibet and Ladakh. During the Yuan period (1279–1368) in China, artists from Nepal were also active. Different local stylistic varieties exist over longer periods. Whereas icons used in rituals were subject to formal rules and measurements of iconography, the portraits of historical saints and monks show tendencies toward realism.

Paintings not executed on walls of temples may be grouped into two categories: mobile hanging scrolls (*thang ka*) and book illustrations. *Thang kas,* which show Chinese influences, were painted mainly in gouache on cotton or paper and framed in elaborate mountings, often of brocade. Icons were governed by strict rules of iconometry; illustrations of texts or biographies and views of temples were more freely represented. The different styles were connected to the spread of religious schools, but beginning in the fourteenth century there was a stylistic unification connected with the spread of the Sa skya order over Tibet. Chinese influences are obvious after the fifteenth century in landscape images, even when these images serve only as settings for compositions centered on figures.

Mongolia

Knowledge about Buddhist art of the Mongolian region is limited, partly because many monuments have been destroyed through the centuries. Only a few lamaistic monasteries remain, their architectural structure and style exhibiting a mingling of autochthonous and Tibetan traditions, with increasing Chinese influence beginning in the eighteenth century. Beginning in the sixteenth century, Buddhist monasteries in Mongolia were established as centers of cities. Buildings in Tibetan style, like the temple in the monastery Erdeni Zuu, erected in 1586, had a square plan with enclosing walls that were crowned by stūpas. Erdeni Zuu has 108 small stūpas on its walls, as well as three temples and a stūpa inside. The temple Wudang-zhao, erected in 1749 in Inner Mongolia, looks purely Tibetan and contains wall paintings of Śākyamuni, Yamāntaka, and Tsong kha pa in its three stories. The most important temple in Mongolian style was located at Maidari, but it was destroyed in 1938. The Da Kürij-e of 1651 is crowned by an upper story with a roof in the form of a Mongolian tent. Monastic buildings in Sino-Tibetan style, like the Dalailama Temple of 1675 at Erdeni Zuu, are characterized by Chinese roofs. Stūpas, called *suburgan* in Mongolian, resemble Tibetan *chörten* in form and style.

The sculptor Bogdo Gegen Zanabazar (1635–1723), trained at Lhasa as both a religious patriarch and an artist, created in Outer Mongolia a tradition of bronze sculpture with characteristic drum-shaped pedestals that exhibits simplicity and excellent workmanship. Slight influences from Nepal and China are observable. Another school of Dolonnor at Urga in Inner Mongolia is stylistically closer to China.

Buddhist painting in Mongolia is directly related to that of Central Tibet, the paintings mostly being framed with silk brocades from China. Typical are hanging scrolls formed by application of textiles in different colors and showing maṇḍalas or icons.

Bhutan

Most early monuments and buildings in Bhutan were destroyed during an earthquake in 1896. Monastic complexes have three-story temples at the end of a square court with habitations at the sides. The upper stories contain chapels, with the most important chapel at the top center. The slightly projecting roofs are designed like those in secular mansions. Typical for Bhutan are monastic fortresses (*rdzong*) with inner courts containing religious and secular wings and surrounded by galleries. The main building has five floors with chapels. The court of Tashi chödzong (Bkra shis chos rdzong) at Thimbu is used for religious dance festivals. The compact structure at Paro (Spa gro) was burnt, but reconstructed in 1864; today it is a museum.

See also: **Central Asia, Buddhist Art in; Huayan Art; India, Buddhist Art in; Monastic Architecture; Mongolia; Nepal; Silk Road; Tibet**

Bibliography

Aris, Michael. *Bhutan: The Early History of a Himalayan Kingdom.* Warminster, UK: Aris and Phillips, 1979.

Berger, Patricia, and Bartholomew, Terese Tse. *Mongolia: The Legacy of Chinggis Khan.* London: Thames and Hudson, 1995.

Bernier, Ronald M. *The Temples of Nepal: An Introductory Survey.* Kathmandu, Nepal: Voice of Nepal, 1970.

Chayet, Anne. *Art et archéologie du Tibet.* Paris: Picard Editeur, 1994.

Fontein, Jan. *The Dancing Demons of Mongolia.* London: Lund Humphries, 1999.

Francke, A. H. *Antiquities of Indian Tibet,* 2 vols. Reprint, New Delhi: S. Chand, 1972.

Gega Lama. *Principles of Tibetan Art: Illustrations and Explanations of Buddhist Iconography and Iconometry According to the Karma Gadri School.* Antwerp, Belgium: Karma Sonam Gyamtso Ling, 1981.

Genou, Charles (text), and Inoue, Takao (photographs). *Peinture Bouddhique du Ladakh.* Geneva, Switzerland: Edition Olizane, 1978.

Goepper, Roger (text), and Poncar, Jaroslav (photographs). *Alchi: Ladakh's Hidden Buddhist Sanctuary: The Sumtsek.* London: Serindia, 1996.

Goetz, Hermann. *Studies in the History and Art of Kashmir and the Indian Himalaya.* Wiesbaden, Germany: Harrassowitz, 1969.

Hein, Ewald, and Boelmann, Günther. *Tibet: Der Weisse Tempel von Tholing.* Ratingen, Germany: Melina-Verlag, 1994.

Heissig, Walter, and Müller, Claudius. *Die Mongolen,* 2 vols. Innsbruckm Austria: Pinguin-Verlag, and Frankfurt/Main, Germany: Umschau-Verlag, 1989.

Kak, Ram Chandra. *Ancient Monuments of Kashmir.* Reprint, New Delhi: Sagar, 1971.

Khosla, Romi. *Buddhist Monasteries in the Western Himalaya.* Kathmandu, Nepal: Ratna Pustak Bhandar, 1979.

Klimburg-Salter, Deborah E., ed. *Tabo: A Lamp for the Kingdom, Early Indo-Tibetan Buddhist Art in the Western Himalaya.* Milan, Italy: Skira Editore, 1997.

Orientations Magazine Ltd., ed. *Art of Tibet: Selected Articles from* Orientations, *1981–1997.* Hong Kong: Orientations, 1998.

Pal, Pratapaḍitya. *The Art of Tibet.* New York: Asia Society, 1969.

Pal, Pratapaditya. *Bronzes of Kashmir.* New York: Hacker Art Books, 1975.

Pal, Pratapaditya. *The Arts of Nepal,* Part 2: *Painting.* Leiden, Netherlands: Brill, 1978.

Regmi, D. R. *Ancient and Medieval Nepal.* Kathmandu, Nepal: 1952.

Ricca, Franco, and Lo Bue, Erberto. *The Great Stūpa of Gyantse: A Complete Tibetan Pantheon of the Fifteenth Century.* London: Serindia, 1993.

Schroeder, Ulrich von. *Indo-Tibetan Bronzes.* Hong Kong: Visual Dharma, 1981.

Singer, Jane Casey, and Denwood, Philip, eds. *Tibetan Art: Towards a Definition of Style.* London: Laurence King, 1997.

Snellgrove, David, and Skorupski, Tadeusz. *The Cultural Heritage of Ladakh,* 2 vols. Warminster, UK: Aris and Phillips, 1977.

Tucci, Giuseppe. *Indo-Tibetica* (English edition), Vols. 1–4. New Delhi: Aditya Prakashan, 1988–1989.

Vitali, Roberto. *Early Temples of Central Tibet.* London: Serindia, 1990.

Wiesner, Ulrich. *Nepalese Temple Architecture: Its Characteristics and Its Relations to Indian Development.* Leiden, Netherlands: Brill, 1978.

ROGER GOEPPER

HĪNAYĀNA

Hīnayāna is a pejorative term meaning "Lesser Vehicle." Some adherents of the "Greater Vehicle" (MAHĀYĀNA) applied it to non-Mahāyānist schools such as the THERAVĀDA, the Sarvāstivāda, the MAHĀSĀṂGHIKA, and some fifteen other schools. This encyclopedia uses the term MAINSTREAM BUDDHIST SCHOOLS instead of *Hīnayāna.*

JOHN S. STRONG

HINDUISM AND BUDDHISM

The term *Hinduism* as used in this entry (but not usually elsewhere) covers the whole Brahmanical tradition, which initially expresses itself in Vedic and its ancillary literature and is in its later phases characterized by its acceptance of the authority of the Veda. Hinduism understood in this manner is no monolithic whole, and a discussion of the importance of Hinduism in the development of Buddhism is not possible without some understanding of the development of Hinduism itself.

Vedic religion and Buddhism

Little is known about religion in early India beyond what can be learned from the corpus of texts collectively known by the name *Veda.* Vedic literature is extensive and was produced over a very long period: The earliest parts of the *Ṛgveda* were composed many centuries before the Vedic Upaniṣads, which constitute the most recent part of this corpus. Vedic literature is expressive of what is commonly called Vedic religion. Vedic religion did not remain static, yet manifests as a whole a clear continuity. It is on the other hand becoming increasingly clear that early Indian religions cannot be reduced to Vedic religion alone. There were other, non-Vedic, religions that, unlike Vedic religion, have left no early texts.

Some of those non-Vedic religions will be referred to here collectively as the *Śramaṇa* (mendicant) movement. Buddhism originally belonged to the Śramaṇa movement, as did Jainism and other religious currents. The Śramaṇa movement also came to exert an important influence on later forms of Vedic religion, more commonly known by the name of Brahmanism. This means that at least some of the ideas and ideals that characterized the Śramaṇa movement came to be absorbed into Brahmanism and are not necessarily borrowings from Buddhism and Jainism. At least in part on account of these influences, the Brahmanical tradition underwent profound changes. Many later forms of Hinduism therefore share certain notions with Buddhism that early Hinduism (i.e., Vedic religion) does not contain.

Which were the ideas and ideals that characterized the Śramaṇa movement? The single most important idea is the doctrine of KARMA (ACTION): the belief that acts bring about their retribution, usually in a following existence. Connected with this belief is the religious aim of finding liberation from the eternal cycle of rebirths (SAṂSĀRA). Various methods to reach this aim existed. Buddhism primarily distinguished itself from other currents within the Śramaṇa movement by its specific method, which consisted of a psychological strategy for destroying desire.

Several features of early Buddhism can be understood in the light of the fact that it arose out of the Śramaṇa movement. It shared with this movement the general ideas of karma and REBIRTH, and the ideal of liberation from the eternal cycle of rebirths. It distinguished itself through its specific understanding of karma, and through the method it preached.

Early Buddhism, then, was a special development of, and within, the Śramaṇa movement. As such it had little to do with early Hinduism, that is, Vedic religion. It was not a development of, or a reaction against, Hinduism, nor was it conceived of as one. It is not, therefore, necessary to study the Veda in order to understand most aspects of early Buddhism. Nor does it make sense to claim that Buddhism is a branch of Hinduism, unless, of course, one chooses to redefine the term *Hinduism* in a way that suits this purpose, as some thinkers have done.

The fact that the youngest parts of Vedic literature have themselves undergone the influence of ideas belonging to the Śramaṇa movement complicates the picture to some extent. One of the ideas current in at least some circles belonging to the Śramaṇa movement concerned the true nature of the "self." It was believed that the self, by its very nature, never acts. Insight into the true nature of the self entailed the realization that one never acts and has never acted. Retribution of acts no longer concerns those who have realized that they have never acted to begin with. This belief about the true nature of the self found its way into certain passages of the Vedic Upaniṣads, in a suitably adjusted form: The self, it is here stated, is really identical with Brahman, the highest principle of the universe. Some Upaniṣadic passages freely admit that this knowledge had not been known to the Vedic Brahmins until it was revealed to them by others. The most orthodox continuation of Vedic religion went on ignoring this "knowledge" for another millennium, most notably in the Mīmāṃsā system of Vedic hermeneutics.

The Buddhist doctrine of no-self (anātman) is to be understood against the background of the Śramaṇa belief in the inactive nature of the self. Early Buddhism rejects the idea that knowledge of the true nature of the self leads to liberation (it does not say, but it does suggest, that such an inactive self does not exist at all). In rejecting this idea, the early Buddhist texts do not so much express disagreement with Vedic religion, which had only recently accepted the idea in some of its texts, but with the milieu from which the Vedic text had borrowed this idea, that is, certain circles within the Śramaṇa movement. This is not to deny on principle that the Buddha, or the early redactors of the Buddhist CANON, may have been acquainted with the contents of some of the Upaniṣads, as is claimed by some scholars (unfortunately scholarly research has produced few, if any, convincing reasons to believe that this must have been the case). But in this context it is no doubt important that the canonical passages that present the doctrine of no-self do not link the view criticized with Vedic religion or with the Upaniṣads.

There are, to be sure, passages in the early Buddhist canon that do depict encounters between the Buddha and representatives of Vedic religion. The subject matter of these discussions frequently focuses on the position of Brahmins in society, and on the question of who is a true Brahmin (answer: a Buddhist practitioner), what is the right sort of sacrifice (answer: faith, training in the precepts, and other Buddhist virtues), and so on. There may be no canonical passages in

The Hindu deities Brahmā and Indra invite the Buddha to preach. (Gandhāra, first–second century.) © Scala/Art Resource, NY. Reproduced by permission.

which a Brahmin is presented as defending points of view that are associated with the Vedic Upaniṣads. This confirms the conclusion that Buddhism did not arise as a reaction against Vedic religion in any of its forms. However, the preaching Buddha and his early followers did come across Vedic Brahmins and had to take position with regard to their views; traces of these confrontations have been preserved in the Buddhist canon.

Philosophy

It was pointed out above that Hinduism underwent major developments during which it absorbed several features from the Śramaṇa movement. Once Buddhism had been established as an independent tradition, Hinduism started to absorb certain features directly from Buddhism. An important form of interaction between the two was, for a long time, that of intellectual debate. This explains that mutual influence is clearly discernible in the systems of thought (philosophy) that developed within the two religions.

Surviving texts—both Chinese translations and original manuscripts dating from the first centuries of the common era, along with indirect evidence—support the view that systematic philosophy arose in Buddhism before it made its appearance in Hinduism. Perhaps the first to systematize Buddhist teachings into a coherent whole were the Sarvāstivādins, who elaborated a vision of the world in which no composite wholes were believed to exist: Only the ultimate constituents of all there is (called *dharmas*) really exist. In a similar manner no entities extended in time were considered to exist. As a result only momentary dharmas have real existence. The false impression that there are composite things is due to the words of language: A chariot is in the end just a word, or exists merely by virtue of the word.

One of the two major Hindu ontologies that arose in the early centuries of the common era, Vaiśeṣika, can be understood as a reaction against Sarvāstivāda ontology. Vaiśeṣika agreed with Sarvāstivāda that there is a close parallelism between the objects of phenomenal reality and the words of language. Where, however, the latter combined this point of view with the conviction that the objects of phenomenal reality do not really exist, because they are composite, the former did not share this conviction. For Vaiśeṣika, composite objects exist just as much as their constituent parts: They exist beside each other. This implies that a jar and the two halves that constitute it are together three different things. There are other features that Vaiśeṣika shares with Sarvāstivāda, which confirm that the former, while opposing the latter, was created under its influence.

The other major Hindu ontology of that period is Sāṃkhya, which does not appear to have been deeply influenced by Buddhist thought. Sāṃkhya is linked to Yoga, a form of spiritual practice. Yoga, which was originally quite distinct from Buddhism, soon came to undergo its influence. Some early evidence for this influence is already discernible in the *Mahābhārata,* and Buddhist influence has become strong and unmistakable in the classical texts of Yoga, the *Yoga Sūtra* and the *Yoga Bhāṣya,* both attributed to a Patañjali by the early tradition.

Hindu linguistic philosophy, whose classical representative is Bhartṛhari (fifth century C.E.), has been influenced by Buddhist thought in various ways. Let it suffice here to point out that the notion of words and sentences as entities that are different from the physical sound that produces them—often referred to by the term *sphoṭa*—corresponds to several linguistic dharmas that had been postulated in Sarvāstivāda.

Systematic Vedānta philosophy, whose earliest surviving texts date from the middle of the first millennium C.E., owes so much to Buddhist influence that one chapter of the *Āgamaśāstra* of Gauḍapāda—supposedly the teacher of the teacher of the famous Vedāntin Śaṅkara (ca. 700 C.E.)—is to all intents and purposes a Buddhist text. Śaṅkara himself has been accused of being a pseudo-Buddhist, which shows that some of his early Hindu opponents did not fail to see the extent to which Buddhist influence is recognizable in his work.

Other forms of interaction

There can be no doubt that Hinduism and Buddhism have interacted in many other ways during their long coexistence in South Asia. Unfortunately the surviving literature does not shed light on all of them. The idea, for example, that the great Hindu epic called *Mahābhārata* was composed as a Hindu "riposte" to Buddhism (Biardeau), though interesting, remains for the time being speculative. There is, however, one area in which interaction between Hinduism and Buddhism has left clear traces: the complex of religious practices and beliefs commonly known by the name TANTRA. Both texts belonging to Hinduism and others belonging to Buddhism testify to the strong interest in the forms of ritual, the use of MANTRAS and MAṆḌALAS, the sexual symbolism, and other features that come together under this label. Buddhist and Hindu tantric deities often share the same characteristics: Both are smeared with ashes, drink blood from skulls, have the third eye that is typical of the Hindu god Śiva, wear Śiva's sickle moon in their matted hair, and so on. Sometimes Buddhist tantric texts refer to major Hindu deities by their Hindu names. Similar ideas about the nature of the mystical body, with its various nerve centers and channels, are found in texts belonging to both religions. The interaction between Buddhist and Hindu tantrism was undeniably intense, and here it seems that it was most often the Buddhists who borrowed from the Hindus. Indeed, it has been observed that it is particularly unlikely that the Buddhist doctrinal tradition could have developed an offshoot so completely foreign to itself as tantra on its own accord (Goudriaan). At the same time the idea of a common "religious substratum" cannot be rejected outright (Ruegg).

It should be clear from this short survey that at no moment of its existence in India was Buddhism completely isolated from its non-Buddhist surroundings. There are no doubt aspects of Buddhism on which those surroundings exerted a less identifiable influence than on others. It is also likely that the interaction with the non-Buddhist world was more intense during some periods than others. It is not at all implausible that Buddhist MONKS and NUNS, who spent most of their time in major monastic centers that were supported by the local ruler, would care little about the thoughts or practices of outsiders. However, not all Buddhists lived in such circumstances. There were monks and nuns who, through choice or necessity, spent much of their time outside monastic communities. And there were, of course, many Buddhists who were neither monk nor nun. Early and late Buddhism in India would seem to have interacted most intensely with non-Buddhists. But even the most isolated and protected monastic scholars of the middle period had to take heed of the thoughts of others, because they might be obliged to enter into debate with them.

See also: **Anātman/Ātman (No-Self/Self); Dharma and Dharmas; India; Jainism and Buddhism; Sarvāstivāda and Mūlasarvāstivāda**

Bibliography

Biardeau, Madeleine. *Le Mahābhārata: Un récit fondateur du brahmanisme et son interprétation,* 2 vols. Paris: Editions du Seuil, 2002.

Bronkhorst, Johannes. *The Two Traditions of Meditation in Ancient India,* 2nd edition. Delhi: Motilal Banarsidass, 1993. Reprint, 2000.

Bronkhorst, Johannes. *The Two Sources of Indian Asceticism,* 2nd edition. Delhi: Motilal Banarsidass, 1998.

Bronkhorst, Johannes. "Die buddhistische Lehre." In Heinz Bechert et al., *Der Buddhismus I: Der indische Buddhismus und seine Verzweigungen.* Stuttgart, Germany: W. Kohlhammer, 2000.

Gombrich, Richard F. *How Buddhism Began: The Conditioned Genesis of the Early Teachings.* London and Atlantic Highlands, NJ: Athlone, 1994.

Goudriaan, Teun; Gupta, Sanjukta; and Hoens, Dirk Jan. *Hindu Tantrism.* Leiden, Netherlands: Brill, 1979.

Oetke, Claus. *"Ich" und das Ich: Analytische Untersuchungen zur buddhistisch-brahmanischen Ātmankontroverse.* Stuttgart, Germany: Franz Steiner, 1988.

Ruegg, David Seyfort. "A Note on the Relationship between Buddhist and 'Hindu' Divinities in Buddhist Literature and Iconology: The Laukika/Lokottara Contrast and the Notion of an Indian 'Religious Substratum.'" In *Le Parole e i Marmi: Studi in onore di Raniero Gnoli nel suo 70° compleanno,* a cura di Raffaele Torella. Rome: Istituto Italiano per l'Africa e l'Oriente, 2001.

Sanderson, Alexis. "Vajrayāna: Origin and Function." *Buddhism into the Year 2000: International Conference Proceedings.* Bangkok and Los Angeles: Dhammakaya Foundation, 1994.

Snellgrove, David L. *Indo-Tibetan Buddhism: Indian Buddhists and Their Tibetan Successors.* London: Serindia, 1987.

JOHANNES BRONKHORST

HISTORY

The difference between notions of history in Buddhist literature and those typical in contemporary secular culture is evident when one contrasts certain popular Buddhist narratives with the accounts of modern scholars. One such contrast concerns the very beginning of Buddhism. Historically, scholars say, Buddhism began with the teaching activity of Śākyamuni, the historical Buddha, roughly twenty-five hundred years ago in northern India. Early Buddhist narratives, on the other hand, envision a teaching and indeed a universe with no beginning, say that there were twenty-four BUDDHAS who appeared before Śākyamuni, and recount that Śākyamuni himself remembered his numerous previous lives during the night of his awakening. In the LOTUS SŪTRA (SADDHARMAPUṆḌARĪKA-SŪTRA), Śākyamuni reveals that he is eternal and universal, appearing over and over again in innumerable worlds and communicating the all-inclusive and superlative teaching that is the subject of this sūtra. Scholars tell us that the *Lotus Sūtra* was composed around 200 C.E. as an expression of a sectarian movement that eventually gave rise to distinct schools of Buddhism, such as the TIANTAI SCHOOL in China in the 500s and Tendai in Japan in the 800s, as well as the Japanese NICHIREN SCHOOL in the 1200s. In fact, scholarship shows, there is no evidence that any of the discourses were recorded during the lifetime of the historical Buddha; whatever Śākyamuni may have taught, recorded Buddhist teachings were embellishments and often fabrications of his words. What the scholarly work and traditional narratives have in common seems only to be a desire to connect their accounts with Śākyamuni Buddha.

History in its barest sense is a narrative account that connects the present to the past in anticipation of an open future. The recognition of the world as a meaningful sequence of events, one leading to another, lends the word its common double usage: *History* means both the events themselves and the account of events. Modern scholars also use the word *historiography* for any written accounts of the past, although they sometimes restrict this term to critical accounts that evaluate multiple sources and try to establish "what actually happened." Thus *historicity* refers to historical factuality or reality, of a person like Śākyamuni for example. The naturalistic attitude in modern scholarship differentiates fact from fiction and history from myth or legend. This distinction is not at all obvious in traditional histories and stories, which often bear witness to transcendent spiritual realities at work in the course of time.

A few scholars contend that Buddhism has no use for history at all since its doctrines imply that change over time is inherently meaningless. They see Buddhism as sharing an Indian worldview where time is cyclical and events (like the Buddha's awakening) are repeatable, where true reality transcends time. They find no writing in pre-Muslim India at all that deserves the name of history. Scholars like Robert Frykenberg argue that this view is a simplistic stereotype. A. K. Warder proposes that the story of the Buddha's life, the record of episodes after his death in early VINAYA literature, and the separate accounts of various schools after their schism, all clearly indicate a sense of history in Indian Buddhism. Buddhist literature in all of Asia contains a rich array of historical schemes used to make sense of a changing world.

The seeming lack of historical consciousness in Buddhism has also become a point of intense discussion in interreligious dialogue linking history and ethics. Jewish and Christian theologians often say that Buddhist PHILOSOPHY overlooks the possibility that ultimate reality (be it God or ŚŪNYATĀ [EMPTINESS]) is of consequence to humans only in the vicissitudes of history—that to overcome historical EVIL we need ethical action, not liberation from KARMA (ACTION), or that any ultimate liberation will come only eschatologically, through history. Buddhists, for their part, do not recognize a historical battle between good and evil with only humans on earth at stake. They stress insight into the nature of the cosmos and the self more than ethical imperatives or an understanding of anthropocentric history. MAHĀYĀNA Buddhist answers have emphasized the timeless inseparability of NIRVĀṆA and SAṂSĀRA, the endless activity of the BODHISATTVA, and the perpetual danger of absolutizing the distinction between good and evil. (Another philosophical response is discussed at the end of this entry.) In any case, historical scholarship has found ample evidence that Buddhism has been anything but ahistorical.

Patterns of didactic history: National order and eschatological decline

All scholars recognize the Buddhist chronicles or VAṂSA literature of Sri Lanka as historical in some sense. These works, composed by Buddhist monks, began in the sixth century C.E. and were continually supplemented until the British occupation in the early 1800s. In the *Mahāvaṃsa* (*The Great Chronicle*), Śākyamuni Buddha visits the island and proclaims that it will become the repository of his teachings. A sequence of kings promotes the DHARMA and protects the SAṄGHA, at times against foreign invaders, and Sri Lanka appears as a model for an ideal Buddhist nation. This work organizes past events to demonstrate not only the effects of karma and the reality of ANITYA (IMPERMANENCE) but also the necessity of meritorious works and deeds for a better future. Its concern is to understand the progression of human society within a Buddhist worldview; a sense of right intention (a soteriological practice enjoined by the noble eightfold PATH) rather than factual accuracy guides its author. To modern critical sensibilities, the *Mahāvaṃsa* mixes myth and history, religious doctrine and political motive. Its genealogies and arrangement of recognizable events make it historical, but it is didactic history with an agenda: to promote the welfare of the saṅgha through the centuries by legitimizing the Buddhist state.

The motif of a perfect order in the Sri Lankan chronicles contrasts with the motif of decline in Indian and East Asian Buddhist literature. According to some early Indian literature, the dharma will vanish after five hundred years, a doctrine that has been called DECLINE OF THE DHARMA. Later texts say that it was the *true dharma* that disappeared. East Asian texts tell of three ages. In the first, the true dharma flourished and awakening was attainable. The following age of the *semblance dharma* meant that practice, but no attainment, was possible. In the third or current era of the *final dharma*, lasting some ten thousand years or virtually all countable time, not even practice is efficacious. Deleterious events, harmful deeds, and political circumstances are the cause of this deterioration; even the Buddhadharma is impermanent. Some texts place this scheme in a larger cycle where a period of ascent begins after the three ages of decline and culminates in the coming of MAITREYA, the future Buddha. Karmic conditions governing an entire people, indeed all humankind, must be right for Buddhism to thrive.

Modern scholarship finds that a substantial body of Buddhist literature demonstrates a sense of progression (or decline) through time, and of distinct historical period and the causes for their difference. Jan Nattier argues that the variety of schemes and timetables were in part an attempt to resolve discrepancies, evident to the writers, between previous predictions and current historical conditions, and between the differing teachings of Buddhist schools. In this literature, human actions are significant for changing the world; the future is not the repetition of the past, and the era in which one lives matters greatly, especially when the march of time is toward decline. Instead of encouraging an attitude of hopelessness and inevitability, in medieval East Asia the doctrines of decline generated new teachings, interpretations, and even schools that proclaimed themselves necessary to address an age of crisis where traditional approaches no longer worked. Such doctrines often served to renew rather than weaken Buddhism.

History as seamless transmission and as comprehensive vision

In China, Buddhist texts of various schools often emphasize LINEAGE, the linear succession of patriarch teachers from Śākyamuni to the present. The case of the CHAN SCHOOL is particularly instructive. Although its texts contain divergent lineage charts and a wide variety of stories connecting teachers and disciples, one story line in particular has been popularized: In the sixth century the Indian patriarch BODHIDHARMA brings the correct understanding of the dharma to China—a nonverbal understanding achieved through sitting MEDITATION and enlightenment, with no place for scriptural study. Bodhidharma's robe, symbolizing the direct transmission of mind from Śākyamuni Buddha through the generations, is passed to his successors one at a time when they too realize this ineffable truth. The sixth patriarch HUINENG (ca. 638–713) recognizes several successors, and their lineages eventually form the five houses of Chan and later the seven schools. Teachers in the two extant schools, Linji (Japanese, Rinzai) and Caodong (Sōtō), can therefore trace their lineage to Tang China and back to Śākyamuni himself; what the "true dharma eye" sees is retained in an unbroken history.

The research of modern scholars demonstrates that this story line is largely a fabrication that served to legitimize the teachings and practices of a particular group, or to secure its place in a society of competing interests. Taken together, early DUNHUANG chronicles, Song-period *lamp histories,* and other texts present a far more complicated picture of lineages, schools, rivalries, and projections into the past. One might see the lineage charts as evidence of the lack of historical consciousness, insofar as they flatten time into a "continuous expression of a golden moment of the past" (McRae, p. 353) where the primordial event of enlightenment can be ever repeated. Another interpretation understands the lineage charts as proof-texts that the school has transmitted a thread of truth through history and in the midst of a chaotic world.

Be that as it may, there is ample evidence of Chinese Buddhist historical writing in other records that extend beyond biographies of the Buddha and the patriarchs. Beginning in the fifth century, accounts modeled after dynastic and secular histories tried to demonstrate that Buddhism was truly Chinese and did in effect help to make it so. In the Song and Yuan eras, *universal histories* recounted developments of Buddhism over long periods, usually culminating in a particular school such as Tiantai that deemed itself superior because it included but surpassed all previous teachings. Occasionally these histories tested the reliability of their sources and their chronologies. Though these texts often mix realistic geography with mythical COSMOLOGY, they show that Buddhists in China also incorporated critical methods in composing history as a comprehensive vision.

History as regeneration of a cosmological order

Buddhist Tibet is distinguished by its layers of historical writing. According to one group of popular stories, Tibet is converted to Buddhism in the eighth century when the great Indian master, PADMASAMBHAVA, wields his magical powers to subdue local spirits and demons and persuades them to take an oath to protect the dharma from then on. He establishes Tibet's first monastery at BSAM YAS (SAMYE). His ability to see the future as well as the past inspires him to hide certain "treasures," including texts imparting ancient or even timeless wisdom that will be discovered in future times when they are needed and can be understood. Many stories celebrate great lamas through the centuries as treasure discoverers. Chronicles about the Tibetan empire, from 650 to the early 800s C.E., also tell of the introduction of Buddhism from China. The very first emperors marry Chinese princesses who bring the new religion to the land. Then about 760 Khri srong lde btsam (Tri Songdetsen) expands the empire into rival China and patronizes Indian Buddhism; it is he who invites Padmasambhava and establishes the first monastery. About 850 the last emperor persecutes Buddhism and initiates the dark ages lasting a century, until Buddhism is revived. Tibet appears as a field of saṃsāra ripe for the salvific work of numerous bodhisattvas, many appearing as rulers. Their dominion, in some accounts, is like that of the Buddha Vairocana in his own realm.

Modern scholarship reads these accounts as embellished legends recorded centuries later and meant to associate the unification of Tibet with the arrival and flourishing of Buddhism. The later chronicles, along with numerous genealogies and sectarian histories, were composed to ensure political continuity and preservation of a tradition. The "treasure" texts are apocryphal revelations that link a later time to the imperial period. Like the rich tradition of various lamas' autobiographies, they show an awareness of the development and differentiation of time periods. Yet the idea of reincarnation and the reappearance of bodhisattvas, such as Avalokiteśvara in the person of the DALAI LAMA, extend the sense of historical time far beyond the scope of merely human activity.

Visionary history, critical history, and history as the field of emptiness

Japanese historical writing includes both works that mix eschatological history with indigenous motifs, and others that criticize the scheme of decline and the sectarian biases of Buddhist comprehensive histories. The monk Jien's *Gukanshō* (*Miscellany of Ignorant Views*) of 1219 attempts to explain the tumultuous present by the karmic influences of previous times, leading to this age of the final dharma. The emperors, who are of divine origin and occasionally are incarnations of the Buddha, can still wield the dharma and gain the gods' blessings to arrest the decline and establish peace and order. This work envisions a single course of events that shape the nation, have human as well as divine causes, and lead to a variable future depending upon the actions of the rulers. It exemplifies visionary history, a supernatural interpretation of why the present is as it is and how the future can be better. A hundred years later the Pure Land monk GYŌNEN (1240–1321) wrote an account titled the *Sangoku buppō denzū engi* (*Circumstances of the Transmission of the Buddhadharma in the Three Countries of India, China, and Japan*) that disputes the prevailing philosophy of final dharma and explains Japanese Buddhism in terms of Indian and Chinese Buddhism. The transhistorical, unconditioned dharma is mediated by geographical and cultural factors. Gyōnen's work counts as international, if idealized, religious history.

TOMINAGA NAKAMOTO's more realistic work of 1745, *Shutsujō kōgo* (*Emerging from Meditation*) argues that Buddhism develops by reforming what came before and then appealing to the authority of the founder in order to justify the reforms as a return to original teachings—as if no essential change had taken place. His work articulates several criteria of textual criticism to uncover this process, and concludes that Śākyamuni Buddha could not have taught Mahāyāna Buddhism. His writing represents a rare instance of critical history in the service of Buddhism. Yet as late as 1935 the Pure Land thinker Soga Ryōjin, rejecting naturalist as well as nationalist and Marxist explanations, proposed that Buddhist history is the time-transcendent dharma being realized in time by those who experience and practice it.

Twentieth-century Japanese Buddhist philosophers offer some of the very few attempts to formulate a specifically Buddhist interpretation of what makes history possible. Nishitani Keiji argues that śūnyatā is what enables history to be free of predetermination and thus to be real. For the future to remain open and historical existence to be meaningful, emptiness must underlie each and every moment thus ensuring its absolute newness. Nishitani's history as the field of emptiness does not consider the discrimination required by historians to select events of primary significance. But it does envision the task, common to the Buddhist senses of history sketched here, that the present must be accounted for not only in terms of the past with an eye to the future, but also as a moment in a cosmos that is beginningless, endless, and conditioned by timeless truth.

Bibliography

Beasley, W. G., and Pulleyblank, E. G., eds. *Historians of China and Japan.* London: Oxford University Press, 1961.

Bechert, Heinz. "The Beginnings of Buddhist Historiography: *Mahāvaṃsa* and Political Thinking." In *Religion and the Legitimation of Power in Sri Lanka,* ed. Bardwell L. Smith. Chambersburg, PA: Anima Books, 1978.

Blum, Mark L. *The Origin and Development of Pure Land Buddhism: A Study and Translation of Gyōnen's* Jōdo Hōmon Genrushō. Oxford and New York: Oxford University Press, 2002.

Brown, Delmer, and Ishida, Ichiro. *The Future and the Past: A Translation and Study of the* Gukanshō. Berkeley and Los Angeles: University of California Press, 1979.

Frank, Herbert. "Some Aspects of Chinese Private Historiography in the Thirteenth and Fourteenth Centuries." In *Historians of China and Japan,* ed. W. G. Beasley and E. G. Pulleyblank. London: Oxford University Press, 1961.

Frykenberg, Robert Eric. *History and Belief: The Foundations of Historical Understanding.* Grand Rapids, MI: Eerdmans, 1996.

Gyatso, Janet. *Apparitions of the Self: The Secret Autobiographies of a Tibetan Visionary.* Princeton, NJ: Princeton University Press, 1998.

Kapstein, Matthew T. *The Tibetan Assimilation of Buddhism: Conversion, Contestation, and Memory.* Oxford and New York: Oxford University Press, 2000.

Maraldo, John. "Is There Historical Consciousness within Ch'an?" *Japanese Journal of Religious Studies* 12, nos. 2–3 (1985): 141–172.

Maraldo, John C. "Hermeneutics and Historicity in the Study of Buddhism." *Eastern Buddhist* 19, no. 1 (Spring 1986): 17–43.

McRae, John. "Encounter Dialogue and the Transformation of the Spiritual Path in Chinese Ch'an." In *Paths to Liberation: The Mārga and Its Transformations in Buddhist Thought,* ed. Robert E. Buswell, Jr., and Robert M. Gimello. Honolulu: University of Hawaii Press, 1992.

Nattier, Jan. *Once upon A Future Time: Studies in a Buddhist Prophecy of Decline.* Berkeley, CA: Asian Humanities Press, 1991.

Nishitani Keiji. *Religion and Nothingness.* Berkeley: University of California Press, 1982.

Perera, L. S. "The Pali Chronicle of Ceylon." In *Historians of India, Pakistan, and Ceylon,* ed. C. H. Philips. London: Oxford University Press, 1961.

Schmidt-Glintzer, Helwig. *Die Identität der buddhistischen Schulen und die Kompilation buddhistischer Universalgeschichten in China.* Wiesbaden, Germany: Franz Steiner, 1982.

Soga Ryōjin. "Shinran's View of Buddhist History," tr. Jan Van Bragt, with an introduction by Yasutomi Shin'ya. *Eastern Buddhist* 32, no. 1 (2000): 106–129.

Sørensen, Per K. *Tibetan Buddhist Historiography: The Mirror Illuminating the Royal Genealogies.* Wiesbaden, Germany: Harrassowitz, 1994.

Tominaga Nakamoto. *Emerging from Meditation,* tr. Michael Pye. Honolulu: University of Hawaii Press, 1990.

Warder, A. K. *An Introduction to Indian Historiography.* Bombay: Popular Prakashan, 1972.

JOHN C. MARALDO

HŌNEN

Hōnen (Genku, 1133–1212) was a renowned master of PURE LAND BUDDHISM in medieval Japan. He is best known for his advocacy of the verbal *nenbutsu* as the exclusive practice for birth in the Pure Land paradise of the Buddha Amida. Hōnen is recognized as the founder of an independent Pure Land movement in Japan and of the Jōdoshū, or Pure Land school.

Hōnen was born in Mimasaka province (present-day Okayama prefecture) and entered the priesthood as a boy in 1141. In 1145 or 1147 he was sent to train at the Enryakuji, the preeminent Tendai monastic complex on Mount Hiei near Kyoto. There he studied a variety of Tendai traditions, but gravitated to its Pure Land teachings and practices. In 1150 he took up residence at the Kurodani hermitage on Mount Hiei, which was headed by the Tendai master Eikū (d. 1179) and devoted primarily to Pure Land practices. Hōnen explored widely other forms of Buddhism, and visited major temples in Nara and Kyoto. But the main influence on him came from the writings of the Chinese Pure Land master Shandao (613–681).

In 1175 Hōnen left Mount Hiei in order to spread the Pure Land teachings in Kyoto; he resided for many of his remaining years at Ōtani on the east side of the city. Over time he became a Pure Land teacher of great renown, attracting aristocrats, samurai, and clerics, as well as lowly members of society. His primary message, based largely on his interpretation of Shandao's teachings, was that invoking or chanting AMITĀBHA (Amida) Buddha's name is the one and only practice assuring birth in the Pure Land, where Buddhist enlightenment would be certain. This teaching came to be known as the "exclusive *nenbutsu*" (*senju nenbutsu*). It is the message Hōnen articulated in his foremost doctrinal treatise, *Senchaku hongan nenbutsu shū* (*Passages on the Selection of the Nenbutsu in the Original Vow*), composed in 1198.

The established monasteries, Enryakuji on Mount Hiei and Kōfukuji in Nara, raised objections to Hōnen's movement in 1204 and 1205, and called for its ban. In 1207 the court executed four of his followers, and banished Hōnen and several disciples from the capital. Though Hōnen was revolutionary in his exclusive *nenbutsu* teaching, he was always an upstanding priest, observant of the Buddhist precepts, and he even administered the precepts to others. He also continued to practice Pure Land meditative visualizations throughout his life. Hōnen was allowed to return to Kyoto in 1211, and died at Ōtani in 1212. Many followers considered him a wordly incarnation of Amida's companion bodhisattva Seishi, or even of Amida Buddha himself.

See also: **Nenbutsu (Chinese, Nianfo; Korean, Yŏmbul); Pure Land Schools**

Bibliography

Andrews, Allan A. "The *Senchakushū* in Japanese Religious History: The Founding of a Pure Land School." *Journal of the American Academy of Religion* 55, no. 3 (1987): 473–499.

Coates, Harper Havelock, and Ishizuka, Ryugaku, trans. *Hōnen, the Buddhist Saint: His Life and Teaching* (1925), 5 vols. Reprint, Kyoto: Society for the Publication of Sacred Books of the World, 1949.

Kleine, Christoph. *Hōnens Buddhismus des Reinen Lande: Reform, Reformation oder Häresie.* Frankfurt, Germany: Peter Lang, 1996.

Senchakushū English Translation Project, trans. and ed. *Hōnen's Senchakushū: Passages on the Selection of the Nembutsu in the Original Vow (Senchaku hongan nembutsu shū).* Honolulu: University of Hawaii Press, 1998.

JAMES C. DOBBINS

HONJI SUIJAKU

The term *honji suijaku* (literally, "the original ground and its traces") refers to a particular interpretation of the interaction between Buddhism and Japanese local cults. The term was used in medieval Japan to mean that Indian and Buddhist divinities constituted the "original ground" (*honji*) of their Japanese manifestations as local *kami,* defined as "traces" (*suijaku*).

See also: **Shintō (Honji Suijaku) and Buddhism**

Bibliography

Teeuwen, Mark, and Rambelli, Fabio, eds. *Buddhas and Kami in Japan: Honji Suijaku as a Combinatory Paradigm.* London and New York: Routledge Curzon, 2003.

FABIO RAMBELLI

HŌRYŪJI AND TŌDAIJI

Hōryūji (Temple of the Exalted Law), located in Ikaruga Village (Nara) and first founded by Prince Shōtoku (574–622), was rebuilt after a 670 fire under royal patronage. Long associated with Hossō (FAXIANG SCHOOL) teachings, the temple owes its survival to its celebration of Shōtoku's memory. Hōryūji's west and east precincts contain an extraordinary number of ancient buildings, images, and treasures dating from the seventh, eighth, and later centuries. Several seventh-century images at Hōryūji are associated by inscription or legend with the prince: gilt-bronze representations of Yakushi (Bhaiṣajyaguru) and Shaka (Śākyamuni) on the primary altar, a gilded wood image of Kannon (Avalokiteśvara) in the Dream Hall, and a seated Miroku (MAITREYA) at neighboring Chūgūji. A large eleventh-century hagiographical painting of Prince Shōtoku drew visitors to the Painting Hall (Edono), while memorial rites before his portrait were conducted at the Shōryōin.

Tōdaiji (Great Eastern Temple), located in the former capital Heijō-kyō (Nara), was begun in the mid-eighth century by the sovereign Shōmu (r. 723–749) as a state-supported centerpiece to a Chinese-style provincial temple system. Tōdaiji served as headquarters of the Kegon school (HUAYAN SCHOOL), but in fact functioned as the central venue for ordination and study of Buddhism more broadly. Shōmu commissioned for its central icon a colossal gilt-bronze Rushana (Vairocana) dedicated in 752. After Shōmu's death, his consort Kōmyō offered their massive collection of precious and imported objects to the temple, much of which survives. Burned twice in civil wars (1180 and 1567), Tōdaiji has been repeatedly revived. Several precincts and storehouses preserve sculptures from the eighth and thirteenth centuries, as well as temple treasures, documents, and books.

See also: **Japan, Buddhist Art in; Monastic Architecture; Shōtoku, Prince (Taishi)**

Bibliography

Cunningham, Michael R., ed. *Buddhist Treasures from Nara.* Cleveland, OH: Cleveland Museum of Art, 1998.

Guth, Christine M. E. "The Pensive Prince of Chūgūji: Maitreya Cult and Image in Seventh-Century Japan." In *Maitreya the Future Buddha,* ed. Helen Hardacre and Alan Sponberg. Cambridge, UK: Cambridge University Press, 1988.

Kurata Bunsaku, ed. *Hōryūji, Temple of the Exalted Law: Early Buddhist Art from Japan.* New York: Japan Society, 1981.

Mino, Yutaka, ed. *The Great Eastern Temple: Treasures of Japanese Buddhist Art from Tōdaiji.* Chicago: Art Institute of Chicago, 1986.

Sugiyama, Jirō. *Classic Buddhist Sculpture: The Tempyō Period,* tr. Samuel Crowell Morse. New York: Kodansha International and Shibundo, 1982.

KAREN L. BROCK

HUAYAN ART

The comprehensive and multidimensional vision of reality as expounded in the HUAYAN JING (Sanskrit, *Avataṃsaka-sūtra; Flower Garland Sūtra*) has provided a wealth of inspiration to Buddhist artists in all the Asian cultures in which the scripture was received. Not only is the text filled with exalted visions and holy themes, but its elaborate descriptions of "ocean-like assemblies" and the "jewels of Indra's Net" fired the imagination of the faithful. Hence it is no coincidence that in time an established set of themes associated with the various chapters of the *Avataṃsaka-sūtra* was developed. Most popular of these is the opening scene in which Śākyamuni Buddha, after his enlightenment, attains the transcendental body (dharmakāya) of Vairocana, the Cosmic Buddha. Later a pictorial scheme became popular in which the central scenes were represented together as the "nine assemblies in seven locations."

Each of these scenes is depicted as a standard buddha assembly with a seated Vairocana surrounded by all the BODHISATTVAS, ARHATS, DIVINITIES, and protectors. Another important *Avataṃsaka*-related theme is provided by the *Gaṇḍavyūha,* a text that is an integral part of the long version of the *Avataṃsaka-sūtra.* This embedded scripture describes the youth Sudhana's spiritual journey in search of enlightenment. Some secular powers used its cosmological and encompassing vision of totality in order to adopt the authority and perceived enlightenment of a Buddhist theocracy. Hence the *Avataṃsaka-sūtra* inevitably came to be associated with the divine mandate of various ruling houses in East Asia.

China

Among the earliest expressions of Huayan-related art in China are the so-called cosmic buddhas, images in stone and bronze that depict the standing Vairocana. What distinguishes these images from other standing buddhas is the fact that their robes are adorned with numerous small images of buddhas and other beings meant to represent the totality of the DHARMADHĀTU (dharma realm). The monumental BUDDHA IMAGES in the YUN'GANG caves outside of Datong in northern Shanxi are the earliest examples of Buddhist art in China relating to Vairocana. Stone sculptures dating from the late Northern Wei (386–534) and Northern Qi (550–577) found at the site of the Longxing Monastery in Shandong feature Vairocana images whose robes are painted with scenes of the *dharmadhātu.*

The HUAYAN SCHOOL of Buddhism reached unprecedented popularity during the late seventh century through the efforts of the third Huayan patriarch FAZANG (643–712). With solid backing from Empress Wu Zedian (r. 684–704) and the imperial court, the creations of various monuments associated with the Huayan school and its cosmology were initiated as part of a new cult of KINGSHIP in which the empress played the role of a cakravartin (wheel-turning ruler). One of the most famous Huayan-related images made around this period is the large Vairocana image carved in the grotto of the Fengxian Monastery in the LONGMEN complex of grottoes. The 13.5-meter-high image is carved in the style characteristic of Buddhist sculptural art as it flourished in the central provinces during the second half of the seventh century. Iconographically it does not bear any distinctive marks or characteristics that clearly identify it with Vairocana. This indicates that at the time of its making a distinct Huayan iconography had not yet developed. However, this appears to have changed in the following decades. Images of the adorned Vairocana wearing crowns and jewelry, symbols representing the transcendent and cosmic nature of this buddha, are found among the Buddhist carvings of Sichuan in sites such as Wanfo cliff in Guangyuan and at Feixian Pavilion in Pujiang.

The Huayan school remained influential throughout the Tang and left a strong imprint on the future development of Chinese Buddhism. Wall paintings and votive banners thought to date from the eighth century and featuring *dharmadhātu* tableaux—in essence an illustrated guide to the *Avataṃsaka-sūtra*'s "nine assemblies in seven locations"—have been found in the Mogao caves in DUNHUANG.

During the late Tang dynasty (618–907), Sichuan province developed a strong Huayan cult that is especially reflected in the expressive narrative stone carvings of Dazu. Some of the sculptural groups here give evidence of a merger between the imagery of Huayan and that of the MIJIAO (ESOTERIC) SCHOOL, a development that culminated in the creation of the pilgrimage center on Mount Baoding to the north of Dazu during the middle of the Southern Song dynasty (1127–1279). This important pilgrimage site features monumental sculptural groups in stone depicting central scenes and tableaux of the *Avataṃsaka-sūtra* and related scriptures.

During the Northern Song (960–1127), the *Gaṇḍavyūha* reached new heights of popularity through the printing of the illustrated text of Sudhana's journey by master Foguo (eleventh–twelfth centuries), a monk of the Yunmen branch of the CHAN SCHOOL. The presence of Huayan imagery within the context of Chan Buddhism shows the extent to which the former tradition influenced other schools of Chinese Buddhism during the Song dynasty.

The Khitan rulers of the Liao empire (907–1125) were devout Buddhists and the Huayan school enjoyed special patronage. Numerous monasteries were built, including many belonging to the Huayan school. Among these were the Higher and Lower Huayan monasteries in Datong, where an impressive group of wooden sculptures stand on an altar in the center of the temple building, creating a MAṆḌALA-like arrangement with a figure of Vairocana in the center surrounded by attending bodhisattvas.

Holy Buddhist mountains such as Mount Emei in Sichuan and Mount Wutai in northern Shanxi province, being the abodes of the bodhisattvas Samantabhadra and Mañjuśrī, respectively, the primary attendants of Vairocana Buddha, have long been associated with the Huayan Buddhist tradition.

Korea

Huayan (Korean, Hwaŏm) Buddhism reached the Korean peninsula during the late seventh century, where it soon achieved the same importance and popularity as in China. A number of prominent monks, including ŬISANG (625–702) and his contemporary WŎNHYO (617–686), actively propagated the teachings prior to the actual founding of the Hwaŏm school in the early eighth century. During the eighth century a number of monasteries belonging to the Hwaŏm school were built in different parts of the country. Outside the Silla capital of Kyŏngju, King Kyŏngdŏk (r. 742–765) constructed SŎKKURAM, a manmade grottolike sanctuary, as a symbol of the close link between royal power and Buddhism. It would appear that the central buddha image at Sŏkkuram, an impressive sculpture in polished granite, was meant to depict Śākyamuni Buddha at the moment he manifests as Vairocana in accordance with the opening chapter of the *Avataṃsaka-sūtra.* The image is iconographically identical to ordinary images of Śākyamuni, but the context of the shrine itself, with its central altar and special rounded ground plan (perhaps a symbolic representation of the *dharmadhātu*), as well as the secondary images carved in relief along the sides, suggest that the Sŏkkuram Buddha is actually a representation of Vairocana.

Vairocana, the Cosmic Buddha. (Chinese bronze sculpture, Sui dynasty, 581–618.) The Art Archive/Dagli Orti. Reproduced by permission.

During the ninth century, Esoteric Buddhism became increasingly popular in Korea, and many of its elements, such as its ritual practices and its art, were adopted by other schools of Korean Buddhism. Among other things this process resulted in the creation of Vairocana images that reflect the dual influence of both Hwaŏm and Esoteric Buddhism (Korean, *milgyo*). Vairocana images in early Korean Buddhism are always unadorned, that is, they are without crowns and bodily ornaments. It is only during the Koryŏ dynasty (918–1392) that adorned images chiefly associated with Esoteric Buddhism become prominent.

With the first printing of the Buddhist CANON during the eleventh century, which established the Buddhist scriptures in their definitive form, the Koreans also fixed the associated iconography. It became common to carve frontispieces on the blocks with an opening chapter of a given scripture, whereby iconographical forms and typologies became standardized. This was also the case with the *Avataṃsaka-sūtra,* which enjoyed a special popularity during the Koryŏ. Hence, all the major themes and scenarios of the sūtra were illustrated with explanatory cartouches inserted throughout.

During the Chosŏn dynasty (1392–1910) the importance of Hwaŏm Buddhism as an intellectual tradition declined. However, its imagery and cosmology still captivated the minds of the Korean Buddhists. This is especially evident in the tradition associated with the distinctly Korean votive paintings (Korean, *t'aenghwa*) hung above the main altars of temple buildings. Among the many themes depicted is that of the *dharmadhātu* with the "nine assemblies in seven locations." Interestingly, this follows more or less the same iconographical arrangement as the similar, but much earlier, Chinese Buddhist paintings from Dunhuang.

Japan

The teachings associated with Huayan (Japanese, Kegon) Buddhism were transmitted to Japan from China and Korea during the late seventh century, and the Kegon school became one of the leading denominations of Japanese Buddhism during the Nara period (710–794). During the eighth century a number of temples were established under imperial patronage for the Kegon school in the capital. Among these, Tōdaiji, located in the center of Nara, is the most important and imposing. In this temple Emperor Shōmu (r. 724–749), imitating Empress Wu Zedian, established the Kegon school as an imperial cult. To this end he had cast in bronze a sixteen-meter-high image of Vairocana Buddha, the largest such image in the world at that time. The lotus petals of its enormous seat are adorned with engraved scenes of the *dharmadhātu* and imagery from the *Avataṃsaka-sūtra*. The image was dedicated in a large ceremony in 752.

During the ninth century the Kegon school declined with the transfer of the capital to Heian (Kyoto) in 794 and the rise of Tendai and SHINGON BUDDHISM. However, even after its decline the Kegon school continued to exert considerable influence on Japanese Buddhism. During the late Heian period the charismatic monk Myōe KŌBEN (ca. 1173–1232) continued to transmit Kegon doctrines and practices at Kōzanji outside Kyoto. Due to his influence many pieces of religious art associated with the *Avataṃsaka-sūtra* were created, including paintings of the *dharmadhātu* and Sudhana's journey.

Southeast Asia

The *Avataṃsaka-sūtra* also became popular in Southeast Asia, where we find Sudhana's journey prominently displayed among the reliefs decorating the three-dimensional maṇḍala edifice of BOROBUDUR in Java, which was part of the Śailendra kingdom (ca. 750–860). Images in bronze and stone of Vairocana and other buddhas and bodhisattvas associated with the imagery of the *Avataṃsaka-sūtra* have also been found elsewhere in Java, most notably in the vicinity of Prambanam in the central part of the island.

See also: **Central Asia, Buddhist Art in; China, Buddhist Art in; Hōryūji and Tōdaij; Japan, Buddhist Art in; Korea, Buddhist Art in; Southeast Asia, Buddhist Art in**

Bibliography

Foguo chanshi Wenshu zhinan tu zan (Hymns on Chan Master Foguo's Pictures on Mañjuśrī Pointing the Way to the South). In *Dai-Nihon zōkuzōkyō* 1021.58: 592a–619b.

Fontein, Jan. *The Pilgrimage of Sudhana: A Study of Gaṇḍavyūha Illustrations in China, Japan, and Java.* Paris and the Hague, Netherlands: Mouton, 1967.

Fontein, Jan. *The Sculpture of Indonesia.* Washington, DC: National Gallery of Art; New York: Harry N. Abrams, 1990.

Howard, Angela Falco. *The Imagery of the Cosmological Buddha.* Leiden, Netherlands: Brill, 1986.

Ishida Hichitoyo. "Kegon kyō kai" (Paintings [relating to the] *Avataṃsaka Sūtra*). *Nihon no bijutsu* 11, no. 270 (1988).

Kobayashi, Takeshi. *Nara Buddhist Art: Todai-ji.* New York: Weatherhill; Tokyo: Heibonsha, 1975.

Kōsan-ji ten: Treasures of Kōsan-ji Temple. Kyoto: Kyoto National Museum, Asahi Shimbun, Kyoro, 1981.

Mun Myŏngdae. "Silla hadae Pirosana pulsang chogak ŭi yŏn'gu" (A Study of Vairocana Buddha Sculptures from the later Silla). *Misul ch'waryo* 21 (1977): 16–40; 22 (1978): 28–37.

Mun Myŏngdae. *Han'guk chogak sa* (The History of Korean Sculpture). Seoul: Yŏrhwa Tang, 1984.

Mun Myŏngdae. *Sŏkkuram pulsang chogak ŭi yŏn'gu* (A Study of the Buddhist Sculptures in Sŏkkuram). Seoul: Tongguk University, 1987.

Sørensen, Henrik H. "The Hwaŏm Kyŏng Pyŏnsang to: A Yi Dynasty Buddhist Painting of the Dharma Realm." *Oriental Art* 34, no. 2 (1988): 91–105.

Sørensen, Henrik H. "The Tang Buddhist Sculptures at Feixian Pavilion in Pujiang, Sichuan." *Artibus Asiae* 63, nos. 1–2 (1998): 33–67.

Su Bai et al., eds. *Masterpieces of Buddhist Statuary from Qingzhou City.* Beijing: Beijing Chinasights Fine Arts, 1999.

Yukata Mino, ed. *The Great Eastern Temple: Treasures of Japanese Buddhist Art from Tōdai-ji.* Chicago: Art Institute of Chicago, Indiana University Press, 1986.

HENRIK H. SØRENSEN

HUAYAN JING

The *Huayan jing,* a key MAHĀYĀNA scripture, is among the most influential texts in the history of East Asian

Buddhism. The scripture's cosmic vision of infinite and perfectly interfused worlds and its exalted depictions of an all-encompassing realm of reality inspired the formation of the HUAYAN SCHOOL, which adopted its name. In Chinese its full title is *Dafangguang fo huayan jing.* It is often referred to as the *Avataṃsaka-sūtra* (an abbreviation of *Buddhāvataṃsaka-nāma-mahāvaipulya-sūtra,* a reconstruction of the Sanskrit title), and is also known by the English titles *Flower Garland Scripture* or *Flower Ornament Scripture.* The exact provenance of the text is uncertain. It was probably compiled around the third or fourth century C.E., perhaps in Central Asia. The scripture is of encyclopedic proportions and was composed by bringing together a number of shorter scriptures, some of which are preserved in extant Sanskrit versions or Chinese translations. The two best known of these constituent texts are the *Daśabhūmika-sūtra* (*Ten Stages Scripture*) and the *Gaṇḍavyūha-sūtra,* both of which circulated widely as independent texts.

The first Chinese translation, in sixty fascicles and thirty-four chapters, was completed by Buddhabhadra (359–429) from 418 to 421. Another translation, in eighty fascicles and thirty-nine chapters, was finished during the 695 to 704 period by the Khotanese monk ŚIKṢĀNANDA (652–710). A third forty-fascicle translation, consisting of only the final chapter of the other two versions, was done from 795 to 798 by Prajña. There is also a Tibetan translation, which has forty-five chapters and is similar in scope to Śikṣānanda's version. Chinese scholars wrote a number of commentaries on the scripture, the most important of which are those by FAZANG (643–712) and CHENGGUAN (738–840), two patriarchs of the Huayan school.

Traditionally the *Huayan jing* is considered to be the first scripture preached by the Buddha, directed toward an audience of advanced BODHISATTVAS. Its contents were supposedly revealed just after the Buddha's realization of awakening, as he was deeply immersed in a profound samādhi that illuminates the true nature of reality. In accord with the text's arcane purport, its main buddha is Vairocana, the cosmic embodiment of the Buddha's body of truth (dharmakāya). The contents of the scripture take on monumental proportions, covering a wide range of Mahāyāna beliefs, doctrines, and practices. Drawing heavily on rich traditions of Buddhist COSMOLOGY, the text is replete with mythical elements, including elaborate descriptions of otherworldly realms where limitless buddhas and bodhisattvas manifest sublime spiritual powers and perform the work of universal salvation. The scripture makes extensive use of visual metaphors, especially images of light and space, in its depictions of an infinite universe in which all things interpenetrate without obstruction.

A central theme that runs throughout the whole text is the cultivation of the bodhisattva PATH, with its distinct stages, practices, and realizations. Chinese exegetical works analyze the scripture's depiction of the bodhisattva path in terms of fifty-two stages, which include ten faiths, ten abodes, ten practices, ten dedications, and ten stages. The path culminates with the attainment of the two levels of equal and sublime enlightenment. The bodhisattva path is retold in a dramatic fashion in the last (and by far longest) chapter, which relates the pilgrimage of the youth Sudhana who, during his search for enlightenment, meets various teachers, each of whom represents one of these specific stages. With respect to its doctrinal orientations, the scripture makes extensive use of the TATHĀGATAGARBHA doctrine and the attendant concept of Buddha nature, which are integrated into a larger theoretical framework that also incorporates the MADHYAMAKA SCHOOL's teachings on ŚŪNYATĀ (EMPTINESS) and the YOGĀCĀRA SCHOOL's theories of consciousness and reality.

Bibliography

Cheng-chien Bhikshu, trans. *Manifestation of the Tathāgata: Buddhahood According to the Avataṃsaka Sūtra.* Boston: Wisdom, 1993.

Cleary, Thomas, trans. *The Flower Ornament Scripture,* 3 vols. Boston and London: Shambala, 1984–1987. Also published as a one-volume edition.

MARIO POCESKI

HUAYAN SCHOOL

The Huayan school is one of the uniquely Chinese traditions of Buddhism that emerged during the Sui (581–618) and Tang (618–907) dynasties. It is especially known for its comprehensive and rarefied system of religious philosophy, which is widely regarded as a pinnacle of doctrinal development in medieval Chinese Buddhism. Huayan teachings also exerted a significant influence on the doctrinal evolution of other Buddhist traditions throughout East Asia. Huayan's formation was related to and inspired by the HUAYAN JING (Sanskrit, *Avataṃsaka-sūtra; Flower Garland Sūtra*), and the school adopted its name from the scripture's title. Key Huayan concepts and doctrines, such as mutual interpenetration and identity, are based on religious motifs and discussions presented in the *Huayan jing.* Nonetheless, the Huayan school also drew on other texts and traditions, and was predisposed toward imaginative theoretical innovation. Accordingly, the full range of its teachings goes beyond parameters set by the *Huayan jing* and other canonical sources, and involves novel philosophical reflections on the nature of reality.

The mature Huayan system represents an ingenious amalgamation of mythopoetic motifs and doctrinal tenets of Indian provenance, on one hand, with philosophical outlooks and spiritual sentiments representative of indigenous Chinese religious and intellectual traditions, on the other. While they incorporate the main streams of MAHĀYĀNA scholasticism and substantiate their arguments by referring to an array of canonical sources, the writings of the Huayan patriarchs also reveal an unmistakably Chinese concern for harmony and balance, and a tendency to valorize the phenomenal realm. For that reason, the formation of the Huayan school is regarded as one of the culminating chapters in the sinification of Buddhism, especially in the transformation of doctrine.

The establishment of Huayan as a distinctive system of religious philosophy and practice was largely the work of a few brilliant monks active during the Tang dynasty, who were retroactively recognized as the tradition's patriarchs. Although there was relatively little original doctrinal development that occurred after them, Huayan teachings continued to be admired as a theoretical hallmark of Chinese Buddhism. They also left imprints on the evolution of Buddhist SOTERIOLOGY, especially as some of their key elements were absorbed into other traditions, such as the CHAN SCHOOL. Early on, Huayan was also transmitted to Korea and Japan, where it had a significant impact on the evolution of native Buddhist traditions. The Huayan worldview also exerted influence on other religious and philosophical traditions, such as neo-Confucianism, and it continues to provide a compelling vision with contemporary relevance.

Early history

The gradual formation of a loosely defined and broadly constituted Huayan tradition started soon after the first Chinese translation of the *Huayan jing* was made by Buddhabhadra (359–429) between 418 and 421. Before long, the scripture's influence was felt in different spheres of medieval Chinese Buddhism. In the scholastic arena, the text inspired doctrinal speculations, gave rise to exegetical traditions, and appeared in taxonomies of teachings (*panjiao*), where it was typically treated as a repository of the Buddha's most profound teachings. The *Huayan jing* also had broad popular appeal. It became a focal point of various cultic activities, including religious rites and vegetarian feasts, and it motivated pious acts such as chanting and copying. The text also inspired artistic responses, evident in the production of numerous images and painting of Vairocana, the cosmic buddha who is its central deity.

The history of Huayan as a distinct school of Chinese Buddhism is usually discussed in reference to its famous five patriarchs, all of whom were creative thinkers who left their indelible marks on the history of East Asian Buddhism. Such a view of Huayan history is somewhat problematic, inasmuch as at the time of the early patriarchs there was no awareness of Huayan as an independent tradition and no notion of a patriarchal succession. The first four patriarchs were retroactively recognized as such only after their deaths, as the notion of spiritual LINEAGE became an important organizing principle, marker of religious orthodoxy, and source of legitimacy, largely due to the influence of the Chan school. Even so, there is no gainsaying the fact that the writings of the Huayan patriarchs are the core of Huayan's unique worldview, and that they encompass the main doctrinal and soteriological perspectives identified with the tradition.

Dushun. The putative first patriarch, Dushun (557–640), is an enigmatic figure who embodies both the popular and intellectual streams of the nascent Huayan movement. Also known as Fashun, he was revered by his contemporaries as a thaumaturge and meditation master, who was also recognized as a leading figure in local cultic traditions centered on the *Huayan jing.* His historical position in the doctrinal evolution of Huayan is based on his reputed authorship of *Fajie guanmen* (*Discernments of the Realm of Reality*), a seminal text that formulates some of the basic principles and themes of the mature Huayan system, most notably the causal relationship between principle (*li*) and phenomena (*shi*). Although recent scholarship has raised doubts about Dushun's authorship of this text, the evidence is not conclusive.

Zhiyan. Dushun was one of the teachers of Zhiyan (602–668), the second patriarch and the architect of the basic structure of Huayan's doctrinal system.

Zhiyan came from a gentry family and was born in the vicinity of the capital. A quiet monk of scholastic bent and keen intelligence, he was steeped in the scholastic traditions of his time. Following his entry into monastic life in his youth, he mastered the doctrines of the Dilun and Shelun schools, which emerged during the sixth century in response to the transmission of TATHĀGATAGARBHA doctrine and the YOGĀCĀRA SCHOOL into China. Dilun was an exegetical tradition based on VASUBANDHU's commentary to the *Daśabhūmika-sūtra* (*Ten Stages Scripture*), while Shelun was a Chinese version of the Yogācāra tradition that was based on PARAMĀRTHA's (499–569) translation of ASAṄGA's *Mahāyānasaṃgraha.* Zhiyan was also well versed in the VINAYA and had studied key Mahāyāna scriptures, such as the NIRVĀṆA SŪTRA, as well as earlier commentaries on the *Huayan jing,* especially the one written by Huiguang (468–537). Zhiyan used his extensive learning and doctrinal mastery in his study and thorough analysis of the *Huayan jing.* He wrote a ten-fascicle commentary on the scripture and a few shorter works. In them, he formulated some of the key doctrines that became hallmarks of Huayan thought, such as nature origination (*xingqi*) and conditioned origination of the realm of reality (*fajie yuanqi*).

Fazang. During his most productive years Zhiyan lived a quiet life at Mount Zhongnan, south of Chang'an, and he shunned the public limelight. In contrast, his brilliant disciple FAZANG (643–712) was at the center of the empire's cultural, religious, and political life, and was a recipient of great public recognition and imperial support. An exceptional scholar, creative thinker, and prolific writer, Fazang is regarded as the great systematizer of Huayan philosophy and effectively the founder of the tradition. Born in Chang'an of Sogdian ancestry, Fazang entered the monastic order only after Zhiyan's death. As a young man he participated in XUANZANG's (ca. 600–664) translation project, but left because of doctrinal disagreements. Later he was involved in ŚIKṢĀNANDA's (652–710) new translation of the *Huayan jing,* undertaken under imperial auspices. Fazang had an illustrious career, which was greatly helped by the unflagging patronage of Empress Wu Zetian, or Wu Zhao (r. 684–705). A record of Fazang's teaching presented to the empress is preserved as *Jin shizi zhang* (*Treatise on the Golden Lion*), a popular summary of Huayan doctrine whose title is derived from a statue in the imperial palace that was used by Fazang to illustrate his ideas.

Fazang was greatly successful in popularizing Huayan. His influence was such that the Huayan school is also often called the Xianshou school, after the honorific name Empress Wu bestowed on Fazang. His major works include a large (twenty-fascicle) commentary on Buddhabhadra's translation of the *Huayan jing,* entitled *Huayan jing tanxuan ji* (*Record of Exploration of the Huayan jing's Mysteries*); *Huayan wujiao chang* (*Treatise on the Five Teachings of Huayan*), which elaborates on his fivefold doctrinal taxonomy; and *Wangjin huanyuan guan* (*Contemplation of Ending Falsehood and Returning to the Source*), which deals with the philosophical and applied aspects of Huayan meditation. Fazang also wrote a history of the transmission of Huayan in China, *Huayan jing zhuan ji,* and an authoritative commentary titled *Qixin lun yi ji* on the AWAKENING OF FAITH (DASHENG QIXIN LUN), an important text that had profound influence on the development of Fazang's thought.

Huiyuan. After Fazang's death, his student Huiyuan (ca. 673–743) completed *Kanding ji,* an abbreviated commentary on Śikṣānanda's new translation of the *Huayan jing,* which was started by Fazang but left unfinished. Huiyuan also wrote a few additional works, but despite the prominent status he enjoyed during his lifetime he was subsequently ostracized and his teachings were labeled as heterodox. This censure was largely due to Huiyuan's divergence from aspects of Fazang's thought, especially his critique of Fazang's inclusion of the sudden teachings (*dunjiao*) in his fivefold taxonomy of teachings.

Chengguan. Huiyuan's strongest critic was CHENGGUAN (738–839), who came to be recognized as the fourth patriarch. Since he studied under a disciple of Huiyuan decades after Fazang's death, Chengguan's recognition as a Huayan patriarch was based on his high stature and his contributions to the evolution of Huayan doctrine, rather than on his direct connection with Fazang.

An exceptional scholar of prodigious learning and deep religious commitment, Chengguan mastered a broad range of canonical literature. In addition, he studied the teachings of other Buddhist traditions, especially Chan, Tiantai, and Sanlun, and he was learned in non-Buddhist literature, including the Confucian and Daoist classics. Chengguan had a highly successful monastic career during which he served under seven Tang emperors and he was a recipient of numerous imperial honors, including the titles of national teacher, grand recorder of monks, and controller of the clergy. Chengguan's magnum opus is his monumental commentary on Śikṣānanda's translation of the *Huayan jing,* which he supplemented with a subcommentary. A masterpiece of medieval exegetical literature, Chengguan's work superseded all earlier commentaries and was recognized as an authoritative study of the scripture. The commentary exceeds the scope and length of the scripture and is unrivaled in its comprehensive coverage and subtle analysis. Chengguan's major contribution to Huayan's doctrinal evolution was his theory of the four realms of reality (DHARMADHĀTU). He was also the first Huayan scholar to take into account the teachings of the Chan school, which he studied during his early years.

Zongmi. The connection with Chan was further extended by Chengguan's student ZONGMI (780–841), the fifth and last of the Huayan patriarchs. Born into a gentry family in Sichuan, Zongmi received a classical education in his youth. He became interested in Chan during his twenties, and before long decided to enter the monastic order. Zongmi became a student of Chengguan in 812 after his move to Chang'an. Subsequently he had a successful clerical career and authored a number of works that cover a broad range of topics. Zongmi's position within Huayan is somewhat ambiguous because his writings do not focus directly on the *Huayan jing,* and because he was also recognized as a member of the Chan lineage. He made lasting contribution to the rapprochement between Chan and the doctrinal traditions of Buddhism (*jiao*), represented mainly (but not exclusively) by Huayan. He also introduced changes in his doctrinal taxonomy by including the teachings of Confucianism and Daoism, and by elevating the TATHĀGATAGARBHA theory to a place of preeminence at the expense of the perfect teaching represented by the *Huayan jing.*

Li Tongxuan. Another notable figure during the Tang period was Fazang's contemporary Li Tongxuan (635–730), a lay recluse whose whole life is shrouded in mystery. Li's major work was his commentary on the *Huayan jing* (in forty fascicles), and he also wrote a few shorter works. Li studied Fazang's writings, but his exegesis of the scripture often adopts a different approach and puts forward novel ideas and interpretations. Although he was not widely recognized during his lifetime, Li's writings became popular after the Tang period among Chan monks, and they were transmitted to Japan and Korea, where they achieved high acclaim.

Further spread and influence

With Zongmi, the patriarchal tradition came to an end. Yet, that was not the end of Huayan history in China. Huayan continued to be studied as a major system of Buddhist philosophy. Its key tenets also became diffused as part of a general Chinese Buddhist worldview and they were gradually absorbed into other Buddhist schools. Huayan influences can be found in the records of many Chan teachers, including Dongshan (807–869), Caoshan (840–901), Fayan (885–958), and Dahui ZONGGAO (1089–1163). Huayan concepts and teachings, such as nature origination, were also absorbed into the TIANTAI SCHOOL. Huayan influences are evident in the writings of ZHANRAN (711–782), who revived Tiantai's sagging fortunes during the Tang, even as he tried to demonstrate the superiority of Tiantai over Huayan. The increasing scope of Huayan influences became a point of contention during the Tiantai debates of the Northern Song period (960–1126), as proponents of the Shanwai (Off Mountain) faction of Tiantai were criticized by ZHILI (960–1028) and his Shanjia (Home Mountain) faction for their unwarranted adoption of Huayan metaphysics, mainly derived from the writings of Chengguan and Zongmi. There was also a modest Huayan revival during the Song, spearheaded by the reputed "four masters"—Daoting, Shihui, Xidi, and Guanfu—but their main focus was on commenting on the works of the Tang patriarchs rather than on charting new paths of doctrinal development for the school.

Korea. Beyond China, Huayan entered Korea (where it is known as Hwaŏm) at an early stage of the tradition's history. The first transmitter and leading Hwaŏm figure during the Silla period (668–935) was ŬISANG (625–702). Ŭisang traveled to China and became a student of Zhiyan at Mount Zhongnan. He was a senior colleague of Fazang and the two formed a lasting friendship. After returning to his native land in 671, Ŭisang was successful in establishing Hwaŏm as a major Buddhist tradition on the Korean peninsula. He built a number of monasteries and secured the official patronage of the royal court, which bestowed on him the title of national teacher. Ŭisang's major work, the brief *Hwaŏm ilsŭng pŏpkye to* (*Chart of the Huayan One-Vehicle Realm of Reality*), was presented to Zhiyan during his stay in China and it remains a classic exposition of Huayan thought.

Because of the great influence of Ŭisang and his disciples, Hwaŏm became the primary theoretical system of Korean Buddhism and served as the foundation for the subsequent doctrinal evolution of the native tradition, even after Chan (or Sŏn in Korean) became established as the predominant Buddhist school. Another major figure during the Silla period was Ŭisang's friend WŎNHYO (617–686), arguably the foremost scholar in the history of Korean Buddhism. Although not formally affiliated with the Hwaŏm tradition, Wŏnhyo was deeply influenced by Hwaŏm ideas and teachings, which shaped his creation of an integrated system of Buddhist philosophy that attempted to harmonize the differences of the various schools. Some of Wŏnhyo's writings were transmitted to China and his commentary on the *Awakening of Faith* exerted considerable influence on Fazang's thought.

Hwaŏm continued to be a major tradition of Korean Buddhism into the early part of the Koryŏ dynasty (918–1392). Its predominant position was supplanted by the resurgent Sŏn school, but Korean thinkers were able to create an integrated Buddhist tradition that incorporated teachings and practices from both of these schools. Major contributions in that direction were made by CHINUL (1158–1210), the most prominent monk of the period, who created a successful synthesis that incorporated both Hwaŏm scholasticism and Sŏn meditation practice. Chinul was also fond of Li Tongxuan's commentary on the *Huayan jing,* which became an important text in Korean Buddhism thanks to his advocacy. Chinul's vision of an integrated and ecumenical Buddhist church became normative within Korea and, notwithstanding its past and present detractors, remains a principal model for a distinctive native tradition, in which Hwaŏm thought plays a more central role than it does in any other contemporary Buddhist tradition.

Japan. Huayan also entered Japan (where it is known as Kegon) at an early date. In 740 the Korean monk Simsang (or Shinjō in Japanese, d. 742), a disciple of Fazang, was invited by Emperor Shōmu (r. 724–749) to lecture on the *Huayan jing* at Konshōji (later renamed Tōdaiji) in Nara, the Japanese capital. The invitation was extended at the urging of Rōben (689–773), a descendant of Korean immigrants and a specialist in the doctrine of the Hossō school (Chinese, FAXIANG SCHOOL). As a leading Buddhist figure with good political connections, Rōben was instrumental in the establishment of Kegon as one of the eight schools of NARA BUDDHISM, which functioned as traditions of Buddhist learning rather than as independent sects. Rōben was also involved in the construction of the great Buddha at Tōdaiji, and subsequently he became the monastery's chief priest. The great Buddha, representing Vairocana as the principal Buddha of the Huayan universe, was consecrated in 752 under the auspices of Emperor Shōmu. Tōdaiji emerged as a focal institution for Kegon studies (and the study of other scholastic traditions) and a prominent center of Buddhist culture. Despite its turbulent history, including its destruction in 1180, the rebuilt monastery and its great Buddha statue remain potent symbols of Kegon's prominent place in Japanese Buddhism.

While interest in the study of the Nara schools declined during the Heian period (794–1185), there were prominent scholar-monks during the following Kamakura era (1185–1333) who continued the tradition of Kegon learning. Well-known examples include Myōe KŌBEN (1173–1232) and GYŌNEN (1240–1321). Known as a restorer of the Kegon tradition, Myōe was also well versed in the teachings of esoteric Buddhism and Chan, and he was known for his strict observance of the precepts. His supporters included a number of prominent aristocrats, and he was successful in turning Kōzanji, a monastery located in the vicinity of Kyoto, into a center of Kegon studies. Gyōnen, a Kegon monk of extensive learning, was known for his expertise in the vinaya. He moved to Tōdaiji in 1277 and afterwards he lectured on the *Huayan jing.* He also presented lectures on Fazang's *Wujiao zhang* at the imperial court, which later awarded him the title of national teacher. Although Gyōnen is chiefly associated with the Kegon school, he was well versed in the teachings of other schools of Buddhism, as can be seen from one of his principal works, *Hasshū kōyō* (*Outline of the Eight Schools*), which is still read as a popular summary of the history and doctrines of the major schools of Japanese Buddhism.

Beyond the narrowly defined Kegon tradition, evidence of Huayan influences can be found in the writings of other major figures in the history of Japanese Buddhism. One such example is KŪKAI (774–835), the founder of SHINGON BUDDHISM, who drew on Huayan doctrine in his systematization of esoteric Buddhism, and who ranked Huayan just below Shingon in his tenfold taxonomy of the Buddhist teachings. Another example is SAICHŌ (767–822), the founder of Tendai, who studied Huayan texts during his formative years and whose writings reflect the influence of Huayan ideas.

Taxonomies of teachings

Like other taxonomies of teachings (or "classified teachings"; *panjiao*) created by medieval Chinese scholiasts, Huayan taxonomies involve the ordering of the major doctrines of Buddhism and exemplify the Chinese penchant for order and hierarchy. Within a given taxonomy each doctrine is recognized as a meaningful part of the totality of Buddhist teachings, while the whole structure performs the hermeneutical function of relating diverse Buddhist traditions to each other and integrating them into a comprehensive conceptual framework. At the same time, within such a rigid hierarchical ordering, all teachings, with the exception of the highest teaching, are judged to convey only partial understanding of the ultimate truth. The best-known Huayan taxonomy is the fivefold classificatory scheme created by Fazang. Within it, the lowest level is represented by the HĪNAYĀNA teaching, which reveals the emptiness of self but not the emptiness of phenomena (dharma). Next comes the elementary teaching of Mahāyāna, which consists of two parts: the Faxiang version of Yogācāra and the Madhyamaka/Sanlun teaching of ŚŪNYATĀ (EMPTINESS). At the third level there is the advanced teaching of Mahāyāna, which is identified with the tathāgatagarbha doctrine (combined with the earlier type of Yogācāra that was transmitted to China by Paramārtha). That is followed by the sudden teaching, which involves the abandonment of words and concepts and the immediate realization of reality. Finally, at the pinnacle there is the perfect teaching that consummately reveals the whole truth without the slightest deficiency or partiality; Fazang identifies this teaching exclusively with the *Huayan jing.* While Fazang's fivefold nomenclature was based on earlier classificatory schemes developed by Zhiyan, who himself drew on taxonomies formulated by pre-Tang scholars such as Huiguang, his taxonomy represents an important point of departure inasmuch as it is the first one to present Huayan as being absolutely superior to all other traditions.

Fazang was criticized by his disciple Huiyuan for including the sudden teaching in his doctrinal taxonomy. Huiyuan argued that the sudden teaching does not qualify as a separate category because it has no doctrinal content specific to it. Following criteria employed in Tiantai taxonomies, he also noted that the sudden teaching refers to the manner of instruction and thus does not belong to Fazang's classification, given that its basic organizing principle is the content of the teaching rather than the manner in which it is communicated. Fazang's doctrinal taxonomy was defended by Chengguan, who argued (perhaps not entirely convincingly) that Huiyuan's critique was unwarranted, since he failed to realize that the sudden teaching corresponded to the newly formed Chan tradition. By identifying Chan with the sudden teaching, Chengguan was able to assign Chan a high position within his taxonomy and integrate it into the Buddhist mainstream, while still subordinating it to Huayan.

Doctrines

Huayan's system of religious philosophy and practice is a vast conglomeration of abstruse doctrines, expounded by recourse to a highly technical vocabulary. At its core is a holistic vision of the universe as a dynamic web of causal interrelationships, in which each and every thing and event is related to everything else as they interpenetrate without any obstruction. The Huayan depiction of reality is an ingenious reworking of the central Buddhist doctrine of PRATĪTYASAMUTPĀDA (DEPENDENT ORIGINATION), which postulates that things are empty of self-nature and thus lack independent existence, and yet they exist provisionally as they are created through the interaction of various causal factors. In Huayan's discussion of causality, the focus shifts away from the correlation between emptiness and form representative of PRAJÑĀPĀRAMITĀ LITERATURE and toward the relationship between individual phenomena or events (*shi*) and the basic principle(s) of reality (*li*). The causal relationship between phenomena and principle is that of mutual inclusion, interpenetration, and identity. That relationship is elaborated in Chengguan's doctrine of the four realms of reality (*dharmadhātu*): (1) the realm of individual phenomena (*shi fajie*); (2) the realm of principle (*li fajie*); (3) the realm of nonobstruction between principle and phenomena (*lishi wuai fajie*); and (4) the realm of nonobstruction between all phenomena (*shishi wuai fajie*).

The last two realms are also explained by the doctrines of nature origination and dependent origination of the realm of reality, respectively. According to Fazang's explanation of nature origination, all phenomena are ultimately created based on the "nature," which stands for the emptiness or suchness of things. Therefore, the nature is the source of all phenomena, and yet it does not exist outside of them. In that sense, the theory does not postulate a dichotomy between the absolute and phenomenal orders, but rather elucidates the interdependent relationship between ultimate reality and phenomenal appearances. The doctrine of dependent origination of the realm of reality goes a step further and shifts the focus to the causal relationship that obtains between individual phenomena. Based on the notions of lack of self-nature and the dependent origin of all things, it postulates that each phenomenon is determined by the totality of all phenomena of which it is a part, while the totality is determined by each of the phenomena that comprise it. Therefore, each phenomenon is determining every other phenomenon, while it is also in turn being determined by each and every other phenomenon. All phenomena are thus interdependent and interpenetrate without hindrance, and yet each one of them retains its distinct identity.

According to Huayan's viewpoint, any individual thing or phenomenon, being empty of self-nature and thus identical to the principle, can be seen both as a conditioning cause of the whole and as being caused by the whole. In addition, every phenomenon conditions the existence of every other phenomenon and vice versa. Accordingly, nothing exists by itself, but requires everything else to be what it truly is. The Huayan analysis of causality is not concerned with temporal sequencing and does not postulate causal processes that involve a progressive unfolding of events. Instead, its philosophy represents an attempt to elucidate the causal relationships that obtain among all phenomena in the universe at any given time.

A popular metaphor that exemplifies Huayan's notion of mutual interpenetration of all phenomena is that of Indra's net. The image of Indra's net of jewels originally comes from the *Huayan jing,* which describes how in the heaven of the god Indra there is a vast net that extends infinitely in all directions. Each knot of the net holds a gleaming jewel, and because the net is limitless in size it contains an infinite number of jewels. As the multifaceted surface of each jewel reflects all other jewels in the net, each of the reflected jewels also contains the reflections of all other jewels; thus there is an unending process of infinite reflections.

Notwithstanding the complex and recondite character of much of Huayan doctrine, its principles found resonance within large segments of the Buddhist world in East Asia. As they became key influences on religious and intellectual life, they were absorbed as elements of the native cultures. Huayan thinkers constructed a compelling and deeply satisfying worldview that was distinctly Chinese, yet based on essential concepts and teachings presented in the Buddhist canon. Huayan religious philosophy still retains its relevance to vital human concerns and has stimulated a significant cross-fertilization of ideas and viewpoints with modern philosophical and humanistic movements, including ENGAGED BUDDHISM and environmentalism.

Bibliography

Chang, Garma C. C. *The Buddhist Teaching of Totality: The Philosophy of Hwa Yen Buddhism.* University Park and London: Pennsylvania State University Press, 1971.

Cleary, Thomas. *Entry into the Inconceivable: An Introduction to Hua-yen Buddhism.* Honolulu: University of Hawaii Press, 1983.

Cook, Francis H. *Hua-yen Buddhism: The Jewel Net of Indra.* University Park and London: Pennsylvania State University Press, 1977.

Gimello, Robert. "Apophatic and Kataphatic Discourse in Mahāyāna: A Chinese View." *Philosophy East and West* 26, no. 2 (1976): 117–136.

Gimello, Robert. "Li T'ung-hsüan and the Practical Dimensions of Hua-yen." In *Studies in Ch'an and Hua-yen,* ed. Robert M. Gimello and Peter N. Gregory. Honolulu: University of Hawaii Press, 1983.

Gregory, Peter N. *Tsung-mi and the Sinification of Buddhism.* Princeton, NJ: Princeton University Press, 1991.

Gregory, Peter N., trans. *Inquiry into the Origin of Humanity: An Annotated Translation of Tsung-mi's Yüan jen lun with a Modern Commentary.* Honolulu: University of Hawaii Press, 1995.

MARIO POCESKI

HUINENG

Huineng (ca. 638–713) is the putative sixth patriarch of the Chinese CHAN SCHOOL. It is best to recognize two Huinengs, historical and legendary. Very little is known of the rather insignificant historical figure, who was an early Chan teacher of regional prominence in the far south, perhaps a member of a local gentry family. Even his most famous student and promoter, Heze Shenhui (684–758), remembered virtually nothing about his master's biography. The dates given for Huineng's life are at least approximately correct, but they derive from a later legendary source.

The far more important legendary image of Huineng is based primarily on the PLATFORM SŪTRA OF THE SIXTH PATRIARCH (LIUZU TAN JING), which appeared around 780. Here Huineng is depicted as an illiterate and impoverished layman whose grandfather had been banished to the far south and who supported his mother by the very humble endeavor of collecting firewood. Hardworking and filial, in spite of his total lack of social advantages this Huineng possessed innate spiritual insight. This gift led him to the monastic training center of Hongren (601–674), described in the *Platform Sūtra* as the "fifth patriarch" of Chan. After eight months as a menial worker at Hongren's monastery in central China (Hubei province), Huineng composed a verse in response to one by Shenxiu (ca. 606–706), known historically as the central figure of the so-called Northern school of Chan. Because of the insight supposedly shown in his verse, that very night Hongren taught Huineng the ultimate teachings of Chan (based on the DIAMOND SŪTRA), appointed him the sixth patriarch, gave him the robe and bowl of the founding patriarch BODHIDHARMA (ca. early fifth century), and sent him away to protect him from jealous rivals. After spending sixteen years in hiding, Huineng announced his identity and became ordained as a Buddhist monk, after which he taught at Caoqi (Guangdong province) until his death.

Precisely because of his historical obscurity, Chan lineages from the late eighth century onward were easily able to identify themselves with him. Accounts connecting him with Nanyue Huairang, and through him Mazu DAOYI (709–788) and the later Linji (Japanese, Rinzai) lineage, as well as with Qingyuan Xingsi, and through him Shitou Xiqian (700–790) and the later Caodong (Japanese, Sōtō) lineage, are palpably fictional. However, those accounts are of foundational importance to the Chan tradition, and they draw on the legendary image of Huineng to create a totalistic explanation of Buddhist spiritual training that fits the contemporary Chinese social world.

The thorough fictionality of the legendary image of Huineng only indicates its great literary and mythopoeic power. This image resonates deeply with Buddhist and native Chinese mythic themes: Social standing and family identity were theoretically unimportant in the face of true virtue and insight, which is personified in the most humble of figures. The interaction between Hongren, Shenxiu, and Huineng dramatized and helped define for later readers the generational dynamics of Chan religious training, in which the achievement of enlightenment gives one access to authority within the lineage.

In the Chan tradition, Huineng is associated with the "sudden" teaching, whereby enlightenment occurs in a single instantaneous transformation. This is often contrasted with the "gradual" teaching, whereby one moves toward enlightenment through progressive stages. Members of both the Linji and Caodong lineages generally claim the subitist teaching for themselves and criticize the other as gradualist.

Bibliography

McRae, John R. *Seeing through Zen: Encounter, Transformation, and Genealogy in Chinese Chan Buddhism.* Berkeley: University of California Press, 2003.

JOHN R. MCRAE

HUIYUAN

Huiyuan (334–416) is an important vaunt-courier of the PURE LAND SCHOOLS of Buddhism. As a young man Huiyuan applied himself to Confucian and Daoist studies until he met DAO'AN (312–385), whereupon he took the tonsure to become Dao'an's disciple. After their monastery suffered military attack in 378, Huiyuan moved to South China, settling on Lushan (Mount Lu), where he remained until his death. Huiyuan thereafter established an extremely vibrant monastic and lay community that, in its devotion to doctrinal study, practice, and rigorous maintenance of the precepts, became a model for later Buddhist monasteries. His correspondence with KUMĀRAJĪVA (350–409/413), later compiled as the document *Dasheng dayizhang* (*The Chief Ideas of the Māhāyana*), is an important resource for understanding the difficulties faced by the Chinese Buddhist community in understanding such concepts as ŚŪNYATĀ (EMPTINESS), *dharmakāya,* and momentariness.

Huiyuan is also known as the first leader in China of organized ritual practice aimed at rebirth in the Pure Land of AMITĀBHA Buddha. Huiyuan's group of monastic and lay Buddhists, in its devotion to samādhi via *nianfo* (Japanese, *nenbutsu*) practice, may have been the first of its kind. Aside from a preface to a collection of *nianfo* samādhi poems, everything known about Huiyuan's Pure Land activities comes from sources written in the eighth century or later, when there was great interest in Pure Land thought and history. But Tang and Song period Pure Land scholars regarded Huiyuan and what some called his White Lotus Society as having played a foundational role in establishing Pure Land thought and practice in China, and some recognized Huiyuan as the first Chinese patriarch of this school.

See also: **Nenbutsu (Chinese, Nianfo; Korean, Yŏmbul)**

Bibliography

Liebenthal, Walter. "Shih Hui-yuan's Buddhism." *Journal of the American Oriental Society* 70 (1950): 243–259.

Zürcher, E. *The Buddhist Conquest of China: The Spread and Adaptation of Buddhism in Early Medieval China.* Leiden, Netherlands: Brill, 1959.

MARK L. BLUM

HWAŎM SCHOOL. *See* **Huayan School**

HYESIM

Hyesim (Chin'gak *kuksa,* 1178–1234) was an eminent Sŏn (Chinese, Chan) school master from the mid-Koryŏ dynasty. Like many other Koryŏ- and Chosŏn-era figures, he entered the Buddhist order with a strong Confucian background. Hyesim passed the highest-ranking civil service exam and taught at a Confucian institute. But in 1202, after the death of his mother (who had adamantly opposed his wishes to be ordained), he joined CHINUL's Susŏnsa (Cultivation of Chan) Society and became his disciple. After studying with Chinul for a period of time, Hyesim went off on his own to practice in places such as Osan and Chirisan, learning from a number of different masters. He eventually returned to Chinul, who acknowledged his disciple's attainment of enlightenment. When Chinul passed away in 1210, Hyesim was pressed into taking the mantle of leadership of the society, thus becoming its second patriarch. He spent the rest of his life expanding the society, studying the *kanhwa* meditation technique developed by Chinul, and writing and compiling voluminously.

Most renowned of Hyesim's extensive works are the *Sŏnmun gangyo* (*Essentials of the Sŏn School*) and the *Sŏnmun yŏmsong chip* (*Enlightenment Verses of the Sŏn School*). The latter is a massive collection of edifying ancient precedents from Chan and pre-Chan Buddhist literature, which has been viewed as an important source for adherents of KŌAN (Korean, *kongan*) meditation throughout East Asia down to the present day. Hyesim passed away at the age of fifty-seven and received the posthumous title National Master Chin'gak (True Enlightenment).

See also: **Chan School**

Bibliography

Buswell, Robert E., Jr. *The Collected Works of Chinul.* Honolulu: University of Hawaii Press, 1983.

A. CHARLES MULLER

HYUJŎNG

The Buddhist monk Hyujŏng (1520–1604) lived during the Chosŏn dynasty (1392–1910) in Korea, when Buddhism, marginalized by an aggressively neo-Confucian state, eked out survival in the form of so-called Mountain Buddhism. Buddhist monasteries were under the control of the government and Buddhist monks, placed at the bottom of the Chosŏn social spectrum, were prohibited from entering the capital.

Hyujŏng is also known as Ch'ŏnghŏ taesa (Master Ch'ŏnghŏ) or Sŏsan taesa (Master of Western Mountain) because he resided primarily on Mount Myohyang, also known as Sŏsan (Western) Mountain. His secular name was Ch'oe Hyŏnŭng; Hyujŏng is his dharma name. He was orphaned at the age of ten, and raised by Yi Sajŭng, a Confucian scholar who was a local government official. After being educated in the Confucian classics at home, Hyujŏng entered the Sŏnggyun'gwan, an academy for the Confucian elite. He failed the rigorous civil service examination necessary for government office, however, and then embarked on a period of travel, during which time he was introduced to MAHĀYĀNA Buddhist texts at Mount Chiri. This experience set the stage for his decision to become a monk. He later studied Sŏn (Chinese, Chan) under the guidance of Master Puyong Yŏnggwan (1485–1571), who eventually recognized his enlightenment.

During his career as a Sŏn monk, Hyujŏng did not ignore the importance of *kyo* (doctrinal teaching); he acknowledged that doctrine is a companion to practice. In his work *Sŏn'ga kwigam* (*Speculum on the Sŏn School*), he states "Sŏn is the mind of the Buddha and doctrine is his word." However, he never thought doctrine to be the equal of meditation. This is clear in his theory of *sagyo ipsŏn,* which means "abandon doctrine and enter Sŏn." Hyujŏng authored a number of texts on the relation between Sŏn and doctrine, and the importance of Sŏn practice for attaining enlightenment. The most important are *Sŏn'gyo sŏk* (*The Exposition of Sŏn and Doctrine*), *Sŏn' gyo kyŏl* (*The Secret of Sŏn and*

Doctrine), and *Simbŏp yoch'o* (*The Essential Excerpts of the Teachings of Mind*). He also wrote books attempting to incorporate the three main traditions in East Asian thought—Confucianism, Daoism, and Buddhism—into a Sŏn framework, such as *Samga kwigam* (*Speculum on the Three Teachings*).

Hyujŏng also played a role in Korean political history as the organizer of the so-called Monk's Militia that helped repel the Japanese invasion of 1592. Depending on one's point of view, this can be seen as a highly successful manifestation of the Korean tradition of *hoguk pulgyo* (state-protection Buddhism) or as a striking example of the distorting influence of political involvement on Korean Buddhism. Considering the strongly Confucian tenor of the culture at that time, however, and the fact that Hyujŏng was raised in the home of a Confucian scholar, it might not be surprising that he chose a more actively patriotic course.

See also: **Chan School; Confucianism and Buddhism; Korea; Yujŏng**

Bibliography

Buswell, Robert E., Jr. "Buddhism under Confucian Domination: The Synthetic Vision of Sŏsan Hyŭjŏng." In *Culture and the State in the Late Chosŏn Korea*, ed. JaHyun Kim Haboush and Martina Deuchler. Cambridge, MA: Harvard University Asia Center, 1999.

Kim, Yŏng-t'ae. "Master Hyujŏng: His Thought and Dharma Lineage." In *Buddhism in the Early Chosŏn: Suppression and Transformation*, ed. Lewis R. Lancaster and Chai-shin Yu. Berkeley: Institute of East Asian Studies, 1996.

SUNGTAEK CHO

I

ICCHANTIKA

The notion of the *icchantika* (loosely rendered into English as "hedonist" or "dissipated") is the closest Buddhism comes to a notion of damnation or perdition. *Icchantika* refers to a class, or "lineage" (Sanskrit, *gotra*), of beings who are beyond all redemption and lose forever the capacity to achieve NIRVĀṆA (Sanskrit, *aparinirvāṇagotraka*). The NIRVĀṆA SŪTRA defines the *icchantika* as one who "does not believe in the law of causality, has no feeling of shame, has no faith in the workings of KARMA, is unconcerned with the present or the future, never befriends good people, and does not follow the teachings of the Buddha." The term is often employed polemically in MAHĀYĀNA texts, as for example the LAṄKĀVATĀRA-SŪTRA (*Discourse of the Descent into Laṅka*), to refer to beings who are antagonistic toward the Mahāyāna canon. Their destiny is typically an eternity in the HELLS. Some BODHISATTVA *icchantikas* intentionally choose this spiritual lineage because they "cherish certain vows for all beings since beginningless time" (*sattvānādikālapraṇidhānata*), and they wish to help all beings gain nirvāṇa.

The *icchantika* doctrine has long been controversial in Mahāyāna because it seems to contradict an axiom of many strands of Buddhism: the innate presence of the buddha-nature, or TATHĀGATAGARBHA, in all sentient beings. The Chinese commentator DAOSHENG (ca. 360–434), for example, debunked the theory and even had the audacity to question the accuracy of passages in sūtra translations that mentioned the lamentable destiny of *icchantikas.* With the prominent exception of the FAXIANG SCHOOL, the Chinese branch of Yogācāra, East Asian Buddhists resoundingly rejected the *icchantika* doctrine in favor of the notion that all beings, even the denizens of hell, retained the capacity to attain enlightenment.

See also: **Cosmology; Path**

Bibliography

Buswell, Robert E., Jr. "The Path to Perdition: The Wholesome Roots and Their Eradication." In *Paths to Liberation: The Mārga and Its Transformations in Buddhist Thought,* ed. Robert E. Buswell, Jr. and Robert M. Gimello. Honolulu: University of Hawaii Press, 1992.

Suzuki Daisetz Teitaro. *Studies in the Laṅkāvatāra Sūtra* (1930). London and Boston: Routledge and Kegan Paul, 1972.

ROBERT E. BUSWELL, JR.

IGNORANCE. *See* **Pratītyasamutpāda (Dependent Origination)**

IKKYŪ

Born in Kyoto to a court lady-in-waiting and, according to some sources, the young sovereign Gokomatsu (1377–1433), Ikkyū Sōjun (1394–1481) became an acolyte at age five at the Zen temple Ankokuji. He later trained under two harsh, iconoclastic Zen masters, first Ken'ō Sōi (d. 1414) and then Kasō Sōdon (1352–1428). Kasō granted his student the name Ikkyū (One Pause) after he had an awakening experience in 1418. Around 1425 Ikkyū moved to Sakai, where he reveled in an independent, pleasure-loving way of life. At age seventy-seven, he fell in love with the blind minstrel Lady Mori, and may have fathered a daughter with her. At eighty, he was appointed abbot of the great Zen monastery Daitokuji, which had been mostly destroyed in the Ōnin war (1467); Ikkyū completely rebuilt it in the last years of his life.

Ikkyū is a Zen master beloved as much for his outlandish jokes and erotic affairs as for his ascetic meditation practice. One New Year's Day he appeared in the streets of Kyoto brandishing a human skull on a pole, claiming that this reminder of death should not dampen the day's spirit of celebration. Ikkyū refused to receive or grant official dharma transmission, compared the Zen of his day to a wooden sword—all show and no substance—and flouted convention by frequenting bars and brothels. He is well known for his literary works, including *Skeletons* (*Gaikotsu*), *Crazy Cloud Collection* (*Kyōunshū*), and many other poems and prose works, as well as calligraphy and paintings.

See also: **Chan Art; Chan School; Japanese, Buddhist Influences on Vernacular Literature in**

Bibliography

Arntzen, Sonya. *Ikkyū and the Crazy Cloud Anthology: A Zen Poet of Medieval Japan.* Tokyo: University of Tokyo Press, 1987.

Berg, Stephen, trans. *Crow with No Mouth: Ikkyū, Fifteenth Century Zen Master.* Reprint. Port Towsend, WA: Copper Canyon Press, 2000.

Sanford, James. *Zen-Man Ikkyū.* Chico, CA: Scholar's Press, 1981.

SARAH FREMERMAN

IMPERMANENCE. *See* **Anitya (Impermanence)**

INDIA

For Buddhists, India is a land of many buddhas. From time immemorial, bodhisattvas have been born within India's borders, have awakened there, and have attained final NIRVĀṆA. As the buddha of our present era, Śākyamuni is crucial but not unique: The dharma he taught has been found and lost countless times over the ages. This myth of buddhahood has profoundly affected traditional biographies of Śākyamuni, a fact that limits their utility as evidence for "what really happened."

Historians accept that Śākyamuni lived, taught, and founded a monastic order. But they cannot easily accept most details included in his biographies. Available sources are twofold—textual and archaeological—and neither is satisfactory. Textual sources cannot be fully trusted, since even the earliest extant texts date to five centuries after Śākyamuni's death; archaeological sources are older, but sparser in their details. For this reason, scholars cannot agree upon the century in which Śākyamuni lived. One chronology places his life circa 566 to 486 B.C.E.; a second, circa 488 to 368 B.C.E., and other dates are proposed as well. Scholars do not know all the doctrines Śākyamuni taught, nor how people regarded him in his own day. Lacking even such basic knowledge, one can consider the social milieu of Buddhism's origins in only the most general terms.

The social milieu of early Buddhism (fifth or fourth century B.C.E)

To understand the rise of Buddhism, one must look to a world in transition. Approximately one millennium before Siddhārtha Gautama—the man who was to become the Buddha Śākyamuni—was born, waves of nomads, the Indo-Āryans, crossed the mountain passes of Afghanistan in approach to South Asia. Little is known about these people. What is known comes from their sacred Vedas, collections of hymns and lore to be used in the performance of ritual. These texts represent the Indo-Āryans as proud warriors, noble masters of the world who by 1000 B.C.E. began replacing their caravans with agrarian settlements. As agricultural production increased, villages developed into towns, and towns into cities.

As the Indo-Āryans settled, Vedic lore increasingly became the dominant ideology of the Gangetic plain in North India. Vedic Brahmin priests performed rituals, told stories of the gods, and explained the working of the universe; they even guaranteed supporters a favorable place in the afterlife. But the Vedas had been composed when the Indo-Āryans were nomad-warriors. Although the Brahmins held that their sacred knowledge was valid in this new urban context, some found that a hollow claim. Men like Siddhārtha Gautama were not satisfied by the ordinary patterns of daily life, or the Vedic legitimations thereof. Such men left their families and wandered out of the cities to become śramaṇas (seekers). Siddhārtha was to become the most successful critic of the Vedic Brahmins, and the most famous representative of India's seeker movement.

The problem, as Siddhārtha saw it, was that the Vedic priests of his day did not merit their high social status. Those Brahmins claimed to be the offspring of Brahmā (the creator god), and thus to be conduits of supermundane power (Brahman) in the human world. When the seeker Siddhārtha encountered these priests, however, he did not find them upright or learned gods-on-earth. To the contrary, Buddhist texts present them as beguiled by the wealth and tumult of urban India. They come across as greedy, foolish, proud men who hide their fraud behind high-flown claims to supremacy based upon the ancient names of their clans and caste.

By considering the institutional foundation of Buddhism in its sociohistorical context, one finds Śākyamuni to have been a critic and innovator whose institutional genius lay in his ability to legitimate new rituals of social engagement appropriate to the economic situation of his day through claims that he was merely reforming a broken social-spiritual order. For instance, verse 393 in DHAMMAPADA (*Words of the Doctrine*) reads: "One is not a Brahmin because [one wears] dreadlocks, or due to one's clan or caste. It is due to truth and dharma that one is pure, and is a Brahmin." This verse promises that Buddhist "Brahmins," unlike the Vedic, are not frauds, for their brahminhood is guaranteed by the imprimatur of Śākyamuni himself, the teacher of true dharma. Vedic priests, by contrast, were not only frauds, but dangerous frauds. For by denouncing these priests' brahminhood, Śākyamuni also denied the efficacy of their rituals. In their place he offered his own disciples, who had realized FOUR NOBLE TRUTHS and become worthy "Brahmins." The multiple connotations of the word *ārya*—the ethnonym for India's conquerors, the adjective *noble*, a description of Buddhist truths—connect Śākyamuni's religious innovations with hallowed memories of the past. In sum, rather than sponsor elaborate Vedic rites or pay the fees of Vedic priests, the laity were directed to make offerings of food, clothing, and medicine to Śākyamuni and his SAṄGHA (community of monks). This was presented as a truly efficacious way to earn spiritual merit, ensuring a family member's favorable afterlife. As receivers of gifts, Buddhist monks were ideally suited to the new urban landscape of northern India.

The saṅgha and social norms (fifth or fourth century B.C.E.)

According to Buddhist lore, the saṅgha was founded when Śākyamuni taught the *Dharmacakrapravartana-sūtra* (*Turning the Wheel of the Law*) to five men who had been his companions when he undertook intense ascetic rigors before he attained buddhahood. Swiftly, Śākyamuni attracted many more followers, ascetics, and seekers to his community. As the saṅgha's reputation spread, it earned support from wealthy merchants and kings. Such patronage was necessary, for this community was comprised of bhikṣus (beggars living on alms). Thus, monastic rule books represent Śākyamuni as fervent in his pursuit of a monastic "good neighbor" policy. For as a social institution, Buddhism was woven into a web of parallel institutions—economic, political, familial, medical, cultural—that had no necessary stake in the saṅgha's perpetuation. Potential donors had definite expectations about how bhikṣus should comport themselves. If monks transgressed those expectations, they stood to lose support. It is thus crucial to recognize that although Buddhist monks took the radical step of leaving their families, the Buddhist saṅgha was neither a radical nor an antisocial institution. It did not strive to undermine fundamental social canons. Indeed its rules often legitimated and conserved those canons.

Tensions between the saṅgha's identity as a community of beggars, and its need to conform to public norms of behavior, are exemplified by stories about founding the order of NUNS. When asked to admit his foster-mother, MAHĀPRAJĀPATĪ GAUTAMĪ, as the first female *bhikṣuṇī*, Śākyamuni refused, even though he admitted that women are as capable as men of becoming arhats. The rationale given for his reluctance was that *bhikṣuṇīs* would be like blight in a field of sugarcane, weakening the saṅgha's vitality. Śākyamuni prophesied that if he founded an order of nuns the saṅgha would remain true to his teachings for five hundred years only, whereas if he did not admit women, his male brotherhood would survive one thousand years without decay. Ultimately Śākyamuni relented, after pledging Mahāprajāpatī and all future nuns to accept eight extraordinary rules, which thoroughly subordinated the female *bhikṣuṇīs* to the male bhikṣus. In sum, the male institution's reluctance to grant unreserved legitimacy to its female counterpart reflected a broader cultural ambivalence in India concerning women, one that was misogynist in its value judgments, even while it recognized the inevitability of women's social presence.

The Buddha's death and the First Council (fifth or fourth century B.C.E.)

If the saṅgha was founded with Śākyamuni's first sermon, his death forced it to be reborn. Without a single, universally accepted voice of authority, Buddhist monks became increasingly divided over wisdom, practice, conduct, and religious goals. The ongoing history of the saṅgha presents a tug-of-war between, on the one hand, individuals or groups seeking to conserve what they considered the core of Śākyamuni's religion, and on the other hand, the continuing need to conform to changing social, cultural, political, and economic structures.

The first example of such a battle comes from the stories of Śākyamuni's own life, when his cousin, DEVADATTA, attempted to supplant him as the saṅgha's leader. The sources suggest that this rebellion was swiftly quashed by ŚĀRIPUTRA and MAHĀMAUDGALYĀYANA, Śākyamuni's chief disciples. After Śākyamuni's death, however, a more comprehensive strategy was needed to keep the saṅgha whole. That strategy is contained in the legend of a First Council: a convocation held in the city of Rājagṛha during the first summer after Śākyamuni's death. Buddhist traditions claim that this council was comprised of five hundred monks, all arhats. It was presided over by Mahākāśyapa, an early convert and the most accomplished monk still alive. The purpose of this council was to recollect all Śākyamuni's teachings, and thus to establish the discourses (sūtra), monastic rules (VINAYA), and formal doctrines (ABHIDHARMA) that would sustain the unified saṅgha in Śākyamuni's absence. Scholars do not regard narratives about this council as historically credible. Nevertheless, one can certainly see its rhetorical value. Buddhists could affirm that within one year of Śākyamuni's final nirvāṇa, all of his pronouncements were recited, confirmed as the legitimate BUDDHAVACANA (WORD OF THE BUDDHA) by a congregation of perfect men, and set in their appropriate canonical baskets.

Schism after schism (fourth through second century B.C.E.)

The same institutional memory that lauds this "orthodox" meeting also tells of other, "dissident" monks, who rejected the council's authority. Accordingly, even if scholars knew that a council of elite disciples really did convene in the year after Śākyamuni's death, they still could not reckon how many subgroups existed within the saṅgha that followed a dharma and vinaya owing nothing to Rājagṛha's convocation. The meeting held in Rājagṛha is remembered as only the first of several. As time progressed, the ideally unified saṅgha splintered into numerous disparate sects (*nikāya*), each claiming to faithfully preserve Śākyamuni's dharma and vinaya. It is difficult to give a precise account of these later councils, for each sect relates this history from its own biased point of view. Nevertheless, the most important of these later councils can be dated to approximately one hundred years after Śākyamuni's death, and placed in the north Indian city of Vaiśālī. At issue were several practices of Vaiśālī's saṅgha, which some from outside the city considered violations of the vinaya. With the exception of Theravāda materials, all other sources agree that the dispute was resolved and that the "lax practices" of the Vaiśālī monks were declared unacceptable, a verdict apparently accepted by the Vaiśālī monks themselves. Thus, for the time being, the unity of the saṅgha was restored.

Some time after the council at Vaiśālī, however, a more far-reaching dispute erupted, which resulted in the first schism in the Buddhist community: a division between one group that styled itself the Sthaviravāda (Pāli, THERAVĀDA; The Teaching of the Elders) and a second group that called itself the MAHĀSĀṂGHIKA SCHOOL (The Great Assembly, or "Majorityists"). Accounts vary as to the cause of the dispute; according to some, the disagreement was occasioned by the so-called five points of a certain Mahādeva, which concerned the fallibility of the ARHAT. It now seems more plausible, however, that these points arose later and occasioned a schism within the Mahāsāṃghika subgroup itself. More likely is that the original dispute was provoked by the addition of some new vinaya rules by the group that styled themselves the "Elders," which were rejected by the more conservative Mahāsāṃghikas. In any event, the division between the Mahāsāṃghika and the Sthaviravāda is universally accepted within the tradition as the first real schism to split the Buddhist community. All the schools that subsequently emerged within Indian Buddhism are offspring of one of these two main groups.

The schism between the Mahāsāṃghika and the Sthaviravāda was but one example of centrifugal forces that had long been present in the saṅgha. Multiple claims to authority, differences of language, of location, and of monastic rules, as well as burgeoning differences over doctrine and religious practice all contributed to the further division of the saṅgha into numerous *nikāyas*, as the Sthaviravāda and Mahāsāṃghika sects both ruptured internally. Though the absolute number of *nikāyas* is not known, it is popularly held that several centuries after Śākyamuni's nirvāṇa, the saṅgha had split into eighteen separate *nikāyas*. Some of these *nikāyas* were distinguished by little more than geography, others by unique doctrines, and still others in terms of their ritual practice. Each *nikāya* possessed its own canon, grounding its own profession of orthodoxy. Unfortunately, with the exception of the Theravāda's canon in Pāli, and scattered fragments from other *nikāyas,* little of this once vast literary corpus survives.

Institutionalization and the worship of stūpas (fifth through third century B.C.E.)

Monastic competition after Śākyamuni's death was not the only agent of institutional change. Traditional tellings of Śākyamuni's biography do not end with his final nirvāṇa in Kuśinagara. These narratives describe the people gathered at Śākyamuni's death as observing a body progressively emptied of personal vitality. The body was cremated. But a dispute soon arose over who owned the funerary remains. The people of Kuśinagara claimed these relics (*śarīra*) for themselves, since Śākyamuni had chosen their territory for his final nirvāṇa. But the people of other territories swiftly demanded relics as well. To stave off war, equal shares of Śākyamuni's remains were given to all. Each of these measures was then housed in a memorial STŪPA.

Why would people have been willing to go to war over the funerary fragments of a dead holy man? Here one finds a window onto early Indian Buddhism. Stūpas associated with Śākyamuni provided sacred sites at which lay and monastic Buddhists alike were able to enter his otherwise inaccessible presence. Once in that presence, they could make offerings and reap merit. Thus, stūpas promised spiritual power to the kings who controlled them, and particularly prestigious sites would also have generated great revenues from pilgrims who traveled from far and near for worship. Similarly, caityas (shrines commemorating places visited, and objects used, by Śākyamuni) also became pilgrimage centers.

PILGRIMAGE was enormously important in Buddhism's development. Laymen, laywomen, monks, and nuns all encountered one another traversing the Ganges basin, from sacred site to sacred site. Such shared ritual, in turn, became the foundation of a shared religious identity, an all-inclusive community called "the fourfold assembly" in Buddhist texts. But even though patterns of worship gave the laity a bona fide position within this assembly, the institutionalization of pilgrimage also granted additional duties and opportunities to the monks. Large monastic communities grew up around major stūpas; these monasteries' inhabitants served as caretakers, priests, and teachers. Acting for the good of the buddha, of their brotherhood, and of their kingdom, monks made Buddhism a fixture of the Indian religious landscape for nearly two millennia.

Aśoka Maurya (third century B.C.E.)

Artifacts dating to the reign of AŚOKA, ruler of the Mauryan dynasty (third century B.C.E.), provide the oldest extant evidence for Buddhism in India. Aśoka was an important early patron of the saṅgha, and his exertions on its behalf are celebrated in traditional Buddhist writings from Sri Lanka to China. Legend holds that Aśoka raided the original group of stūpas in order to redistribute Śākyamuni's relics into eighty-four thousand stūpas, making that presence available throughout his kingdom. Aśoka is said to have held a grand council in order to reestablish a single orthodoxy within the saṅgha; he also supposedly made pilgrimage to all the places important to Śākyamuni's life.

Though hyperbolic, these literary paeans point to Aśoka's prominent role in Buddhism's institutionalization. Archaeological remains provide more precise, through less glorified, evidence of Aśoka's activities. Among the many edicts Aśoka incised on pillars and boulders, several speak to his interest in Buddhism. The Bhābrā edict, for instance, recommends a set of seven texts for Buddhist monks and laity to read and study (all the texts focus on ethics, suggesting that, for Aśoka, good Buddhists were also good citizens). The Kauśāmbī edict denounces disunity within the saṅgha, ordering schismatic monks to return to lay status. The Nigliva inscription tells that Aśoka doubled the size of a stūpa dedicated to a past buddha named Konākamana. In short, although sectarian Buddhist writings on the religion's early historical development cannot be trusted in their details, archaeological evidence from Aśoka's reign allows us to accept these texts' broad characterization of this era, when worship focused on stūpas, devoted Buddhists made pilgrimages, and nostalgic tales of Śākyamuni's harmonious saṅgha contrasted with the sharp-edged glare of contemporary circumstances.

A time of change and development (second century B.C.E. to fourth century C.E.)

The Mauryan empire did not long survive Aśoka. It was followed by five centuries of political turmoil, during which indigenous dynasties and foreign invaders vied for supremacy. Although Buddhism established a base identity during Mauryan times, the succeeding era of political competition and social diversification fostered new doctrinal and institutional expressions. During these centuries, monastic spats increased the number of *nikāyas* to eighteen, or more. Additionally, monasteries and pilgrimage centers were increasingly founded outside the Gangetic basin: in the South (Amarāvatī, Nāgārjunīkoṇḍa), central India (Bārhut, SĀÑCĪ), and the Northwest (Takṣaśīla, Haḍḍa, BĀMIYĀN). A tradition of representing the buddha in iconic form developed during this period as well, alongside numerous regional styles.

Religious creativity was not the sole property of Buddhists, however. This era also saw innovations in Hinduism, leading to its increased popularity. The Mauryan dynasty was succeeded in north India by the Śuṅga, whose first ruler, Puṣyamitra (187–151 B.C.E.), showed a strong interest in Vedic ritual, and governed with the support of Vedic Brahmins. Buddhists number Puṣyamitra among the saṅgha's greatest enemies. In central India during this same century, a Greek legate erected a pillar in Kṛṣṇa's honor. Still, such developments do not signal Buddhism's eclipse. One of the Indo-Greek kings, Menander (ca. 150 B.C.E.), is claimed as a Buddhist convert, while the Kushan royal Kaṇiṣka (first or second century C.E.) sought to emulate Aśoka through his largesse and close stewardship of the saṅgha.

The *bodhisattvayāna* (second to first century B.C.E.)

The Buddhist saṅgha was a ritual community pledged simultaneously to the preservation of an ultimate truth and the legitimation of social norms. As social forms, economic systems, and rulers changed, Buddhist monks devised new, locally appropriate expressions of their core principles. The fact that so many *nikāyas* came into being so quickly testifies to the ideological ferment of this time.

A backlash against this turmoil produced the most comprehensive breach in Buddhism's early history. Each *nikāya* claimed orthodoxy, inspiring some partisans to adopt stalwart sectarian identities. But other Buddhists found this strident sectarianism a violation of Śākyamuni's ideals. These latter viewed their brethren as backsliding from the original intent of the renunciant's life. Zealous to recover that origin, they accused those monks of being hypocritical, hedonistic, lazy, and unstudied in the rules of conduct. These reformers singled themselves out by advocating living in forests, an optional practice for all monks. But even more importantly, these monks sought to reform Buddhism by declaring themselves to be bodhisattvas, riding the bodhisattva-vehicle (*bodhisattvayāna*) to perfect buddhahood.

Institutionally, this *bodhisattvayāna* had a diffuse origin. It cannot be traced to a single social group, *nikāya*, locale, or founder. Its members did not claim to be the First Council's heir, and thus to form a new *nikāya*. Rather, these bodhisattvas were united by a common vision, for which *nikāya* membership was beside the point. They held that bodhisattvahood, and ultimately buddhahood, was the only legitimate aspiration for Śākyamuni's followers.

This *bodhisattvayāna* was adopted by monks and laity alike. For the renunciants, monastic vows and bodhisattva's vows were not in conflict. To the contrary, by aspiring to become Śākyamuni's equal, a monk demonstrated just how seriously he took his renouncer's role. For the laity, too, to articulate a bodhisattva's vows was to signal one's serious religious intent. Most *nikāyas* held that only monks can become arhats; individuals who aspired thus were expected to abandon lay life. But the nature of the bodhisattva path made it such that a bodhisattva could marry, work, raise a family, and still be spiritually adept. Thus the same vow that enabled bodhisattva monks to aggrandize themselves as Śākyamuni's legitimate heirs, allowed bodhisattva laity to aggrandize almsgiving and worship as significant accomplishments on the path to buddhahood.

From *bodhisattvayāna* to Mahāyāna (first century B.C.E. to second century C.E.)

The fact that the *bodhisattvayāna* developed simultaneously in many centers makes it difficult to speak of an origin per se, or even a single *bodhisattvayāna*. However, there is one aspect of religious life that these scattered bodhisattvas did share in common: a desire to learn more about how they should live, practice, and think as bodhisattvas. The *nikāyas* had little to say about the bodhisattva figure, and what information their canons did provide was general and retrospective.

In the centuries after Śākyamuni's nirvāṇa, members of the *nikāyas* composed (or edited) sūtras, but they presented their work as the Buddha Śākyamuni's. Bodhisattvas were no exception to this practice. By the first century B.C.E., a new genre of Buddhist literature was being written, focusing upon the path and practices of bodhisattvas. The first works of this literature are lost. The earliest texts that do still exist, from circa first century C.E., reveal this bodhisattva movement to have been diffuse and numerically insignificant. But they also begin to use a distinctive name, MAHĀYĀNA (Great Vehicle). The Mahāyāna began as a minor reform movement within the constraints of *nikāya*-

Buddhism. It soon developed new and distinct forms of the religion.

The wide range of subjects one finds in early Mahāyāna sūtras is suggestive of the diverse origins from which it arose. These sūtras show that Mahāyānists were concerned with reforming Buddhism on a number of fronts: doctrinal, sociological, soteriological, cultic, and mythological. Some severely criticize Buddhists who do not take the bodhisattva vow, while others contain no such polemic; some speak to a monastic milieu, while others champion lay bodhisattvas. This early Mahāyāna was heterogeneous, with bodhisattvas even disputing other bodhisattvas in an open-ended process of decentralized change.

Institutionalization of the Mahāyāna (second to twelfth century C.E.)

Although sūtras provide the first evidence for the Mahāyāna's existence, few contemporaneous material artifacts show their influence. That is to say, archaeological data do not suggest that the Mahāyāna directly affected monastic life, patronage, ritual, or even education during the first, second, or third centuries C.E. Only in the fifth century is there significant public evidence of Mahāyāna Buddhism in India.

The "underground" nature of Mahāyāna at its inception is one factor in this slow transition from spiritual movement to public institution. But an important catalyst toward change came in 320 C.E., when Candragupta I founded a dynasty that united north India as a single state for the first time since Aśoka. The changes initiated by Candragupta's ascension are so numerous that 320 C.E. is often cited as the first in a new era of Indian history. For explaining the Mahāyāna's institutionalization, however, the most profound development was economic.

Before the Guptas, monetary exchange formed the basis of the north Indian economy. A money-economy circulates wealth through direct transactions between people. *Nikāya*-Buddhism was well suited to such a system because the *nikāyas* emphasized the worth of the monks (or the stūpas they controlled) as recipients of donation. Indeed, Buddhism gained such prominence in the centuries after Śākyamuni's death in large part because its ideology justified the accumulation of money, and provided a way to benefit from that accumulation even after death. Beginning with the Gupta dynasty, however, this money-economy began to give way to one based upon ownership of land. The Guptas did not attempt to govern their entire territory directly from their capital city. Rather, as "Lords of the Earth," the Guptas permitted petty kings to retain residual control over their regions, and gave fields and villages to Brahmins, who then administered those lands. Thus, beginning with the Guptas, wealth became less associated with amassing money than with holding jurisdiction over a quasi-independent territory; one did not have prestige because one could enter into many exchange relationships, but due to one's close alliance with the imperial suzerain.

For Buddhism this meant that the wealth, position, and surplus resources of the merchants who had made up the bulk of the religion's early lay followers were diminished, leaving only members of the royalty and Buddhists themselves as donors. As possession of land became essential for Buddhism's survival, Buddhist institutions were ever more dependent upon direct royal patronage. This required Buddhists to adjust the tenor and focus of their religious productions, and directly address royal concerns in Buddhist media.

The Mahāyāna was particularly well suited to this new economy. Its sūtras had long used royal imagery when speaking of buddhas and bodhisattvas. Thus, the PRAJÑĀPĀRAMITĀ LITERATURE (Perfection of Wisdom texts) describes bodhisattvas as fearless heroes, wearing armor while mounted on the great vehicle. Buddhas, similarly, are presented by the Mahāyāna as lords, each of his own personal buddha-land, surrounded by divine retinues; they engage in demonstrations of mutual admiration and support; they send bodhisattva emissaries to one another. In the fifth century, these literary tropes begin to make their mark on public art and inscriptions, revealing the symbolic maneuvers by means of which Mahāyāna Buddhism became prominent in India.

The institutionalization of Indian Mahāyāna Buddhism reached its apogee in the great monastery at Nālandā, which, as a center for higher education, attracted students to Northern India from throughout Asia. As delineated by the seventh-century pilgrim XUANZANG (ca. 600–664), Nālandā's foundation dated to the imperial Guptas. In the early fifth century, one king built a monastery at a lucky spot in this town. Over the next century, subsequent Gupta rulers added to that establishment. Eventually, devout rulers from other parts of India, and even other countries, made their own donations of buildings and resources. By Xuanzang's day, Nālandā had become the preeminent Buddhist university. Its endowment included several hundred villages; its dormitories housed

Tibetans light butter lamps for world peace at Bodh Gayā, India, 1997. Bodh Gayā is where the Buddha achieved enlightenment and is Buddhism's most sacred pilgrimage site.

several thousand students. And although a liberal education was possible—including the Vedas, medicine, and art—every student was required to study Mahāyāna literature as well. In later centuries, Nālandā was supplemented, and then surpassed, by two other Mahāyāna universities, Otantapūri and Vikramaśīla; both were established by the Pāla dynasty that ruled in India's Northeast from about 750 to 1150 C.E. Furnished with ample lands by their Pāla patrons, these great monasteries were eventually depopulated, their books destroyed, during the thirteenth-century Muslim conquest of north India.

The end of Buddhism in India (seventh to thirteenth century C.E.)

The fact that Mahāyānists came to have a significant public presence does not mean that *nikāya*-Buddhism was eclipsed. A census of monks, made by Xuanzang in the seventh century, reveals that monks who were primarily identified with the *nikāyas* still outnumbered Mahāyānists. Yet, of the original eighteen-plus *nikāyas*, only four remained vital, and almost half of all *nikāya*-Buddhists belonged to the Saṃmitīya sect, whose tenets were the object of considerable intra-Buddhist polemic.

When Xuanzang's census is compared with an account given by FAXIAN (ca. 337–418) in the fifth century, however, one notices that the Mahāyāna's institutional gains took place in a landscape within which Buddhism as a whole had become less prominent. The same economic developments that supported the Mahāyāna also instigated an effloresence of sectarian Hinduism devoted to VIṢṆU and Śiva. Like the Buddhists, these Hindus sought royal patronage. But unlike the Buddhists, the Hindus were effective allies for kings who needed to socialize indigenous and tribal peoples. Brahmin legal codes, rooted in the Vedas, legitimated a strictly stratified society, and gave every person a fixed place within that society. Such codes eventually gave rise to a "caste system." Though Buddhist texts take the existence of "caste" for granted, they attempt neither to justify this social system, nor to disseminate it. From the point of view of India's rulers, Buddhist monks were less effective ideologues than Brahmins. In turn, as Brahmins held primary responsibility for transforming villagers and tribals into royal subjects, those peoples came to identify themselves with the Brahmins' own gods. Thus, although Buddhism flourished in the post-Gupta period, the religion became increasingly rarified and disengaged from the immediate interests of the common masses.

This transformation of Buddhism's social base was, ultimately, the cause of its downfall in India. Buddhist monks became increasingly professionalized: intellectuals in "ivory towers," uninvolved in the day-to-day lives of common folk. The destruction of the great monasteries (Nālandā in 1197; Vikramaśīla in 1203) by invading Turks provided the coup de grace. Lacking strong royal support, and long since having lost that of the populace, India's Buddhist monks had nowhere to turn. A travelogue written by Dharmasvāmin, a monk from Tibet, reveals that by the mid-thirteenth century there were almost no self-professed Buddhists remaining in India.

Over the preceding two millennia, Buddhist institutions, ritual practices, ideas, ideals, and ways of life had become a part of the social landscape in almost every Asian land. These regional and national Buddhisms all looked back to Śākyamuni for authority, though the incredible diversity of their forms and expressions might have astounded him. Despite Buddhism's demise in its first home, its traditions continued to thrive.

The revival of Buddhism in India (nineteenth to twenty-first century C.E.)

The nineteenth and twentieth centuries saw a resurgence of Buddhism in India. The first concerted attempt toward reintroducing Buddhism to the land of its origin was made in 1891, when ANAGĀRIKA DHARMAPĀLA (1864–1933), the son of a wealthy furniture dealer in Sri Lanka, visited BODH GAYĀ, the site of Śākyamuni's awakening. Distressed by the sorry neglect of this site, he founded the Mahā Bodhi Society with the aim of fostering its restoration. Dharmapāla's motives were missionary as well as devotional. Educated in the Christian missionary schools of colonial Sri Lanka, Dharmapāla imagined that a renewed Bodh Gayā would serve as a center for the propagation of Śākyamuni's teachings. The fact that this small town is now filled with monasteries and hostels serving pilgrims from all over the world is the realization of Dharmapāla's dream.

However, in terms of the re-creation of a native Indian Buddhism, no figure has been more important than Dr. Bhimrao Ramji AMBEDKAR (1891–1956). As a leader of India's Untouchables, Ambedkar renounced Hinduism in favor of Buddhism, believing that this conversion would lead to greater respect for his downtrodden people. Ambedkar himself has now become a central figure of reverence for India's neo-Buddhist movement.

In 1959 Tenzin Gyatso, the fourteenth Dalai Lama, escaped to India, soon followed by many thousands of his countrymen. In exile, the Tibetans have remained vigorous patrons of Buddhism: establishing monastic centers that serve their own people as well as the curious who visit India to learn about Buddhism. Indeed, as Buddhism became a religion with a global reach during the latter half of the twentieth century, all evidence has shown a burgeoning appreciation within India itself for its Buddhist heritage.

See also: **Ajaṇṭā; Councils, Buddhist; Hinduism and Buddhism; India, Buddhist Art in; India, Northwest; India, South; Mainstream Buddhist Schools**

Bibliography

Ahir, D. C. *The Pioneers of Buddhist Revival in India.* Delhi: Sri Satguru, 1989.

Allchin, F. R. *The Archaeology of Early Historic South Asia: The Emergence of Cities and States.* Cambridge, UK: Cambridge University Press, 1995.

Almond, Philip C. *The British Discovery of Buddhism.* Cambridge, UK: Cambridge University Press, 1988.

Bareau, André. *Les sectes bouddhiques du petit véhicule.* Saigon, South Vietnam: École Française d'Extrême-Orient, 1955.

Bechert, Heinz, and Gombrich, Richard, eds. *The World of Buddhism: Buddhist Monks and Nuns in Society and Culture.* London: Thames and Hudson, 1984.

Chakravarti, Uma. *The Social Dimensions of Early Buddhism.* Delhi: Oxford University Press, 1987.

Dutt, Sukumar. *Buddhist Monks and Monasteries of India: Their History and Their Contribution to Indian Culture.* London: Allen and Unwin, 1962.

Hirakawa, Akira. *A History of Indian Buddhism: From Śākyamuni to Early Mahāyāna,* tr. Paul Groner. Honolulu: University of Hawaii Press, 1990.

Joshi, Lal Mani. *Studies in the Buddhistic Culture of India, during the Seventh and Eighth Centuries A.D.* Delhi: Motilal Banarsidass, 1967.

Lamotte, Étienne. *History of Indian Buddhism: From the Origins to the Śaka Era,* tr. Sara Webb-Boin. Louvain, Belgium: Peeters Press, 1988.

Legge, James, trans. *A Record of Buddhistic Kingdoms: Being an Account by the Chinese Monk Fa-Hien of His Travels in India and Ceylon (A.D. 399–414) in Search of the Buddhist Books of Discipline.* New York: Dover, 1965.

Masefield, Peter. *Divine Revelation in Pali Buddhism.* Colombo, Sri Lanka: Sri Lanka Institute of Traditional Studies, 1986.

Mitra, Debala. *Buddhist Monuments.* Calcutta: Sahitya Samsad, 1971.

Mus, Paul. *Barabuḍur: Sketch of a History of Buddhism Based on Archaeological Criticism of the Texts,* tr. Alexander W. MacDonald. New Delhi: Sterling, 1998.

Nattier, Janice J., and Prebish, Charles S. "Mahāsāṅghika Origins: The Beginnings of Buddhist Sectarianism." *History of Religions* 16 (1977): 237–272.

Ray, Himanshu P. *The Winds of Change: Buddhism and the Maritime Links of Early South Asia.* Delhi: Oxford University Press, 1994.

Ray, Reginald A. *Buddhist Saints in India: A Study in Buddhist Values and Orientations.* Oxford and New York: Oxford University Press, 1994.

Roerich, George, trans. *Biography of Dharmasvamin (Chag lo tsa-ba Chos-rje-dpal), a Tibetan Monk Pilgrim.* Patna, India: K. P. Jayaswal Research Institute, 1959.

Sarkar, H. *Studies in Early Buddhist Architecture of India.* Delhi: Munshiram Manoharlal, 1993.

Schopen, Gregory. *Bones, Stones, and Buddhist Monks: Collected Papers on the Archaeology, Epigraphy, and Texts of Monastic Buddhism in India.* Honolulu: University of Hawaii Press, 1997.

Snellgrove, David L. *Indo-Tibetan Buddhism: Indian Buddhists and Their Tibetan Successors.* Boston: Shambala, 1987.

Stein, Burton. *A History of India.* Oxford: Blackwell Publishers, 1998.

Strong, John S. *The Legend of King Aśoka: A Study and Translation of the Aśokāvadāna.* Princeton, NJ: Princeton University Press, 1983.

Thapar, Romila. *Aśoka and the Decline of the Mauryas.* Delhi: Oxford University Press, 1983.

Walters, Jonathan S. *Finding Buddhists in Global History.* Washington, DC: American Historical Association, 1998.

Warder, Anthony Kennedy. *Indian Buddhism.* Delhi: Motilal Banarsidass, 1970.

Xuanzang. *The Great Tang Dynasty Record of the Western Regions,* tr. Li Rongxi. Berkeley, CA: Numata Center for Buddhist Translation and Research, 1996.

Yijing. *Buddhist Monastic Traditions of Southern Asia: A Record of the Inner Law Sent Home from the South Seas,* tr. Li Rongxi. Berkeley, CA: Numata Center for Buddhist Translation and Research, 2000.

Zelliot, Eleanor. *From Untouchable to Dalit: Essays on the Ambedkar Movement.* New Delhi: Manohar, 1992.

RICHARD S. COHEN

INDIA, BUDDHIST ART IN

Sometime around the fifth century B.C.E., the historical Buddha Śākyamuni encouraged his disciples to spread his teachings in all directions. Although Buddhism was thus established as a missionary religion, the earliest remaining artworks devoted to the Buddhist tradition date from the mid-third century B.C.E. After that time, however, Buddhist arts and teachings flourished together, propagating outward from their Indian home to the farthest points of Asia, until the advent of Muslim hegemony, when Buddhism virtually ceased on the Indian subcontinent. Today India is mainly of historical interest to scholars and art historians of Buddhism; to Buddhists, however, India is home to the most important PILGRIMAGE sites. India is the land where Buddha Śākyamuni lived, taught, and died, as well as where the familiar and beloved arts and literature of Buddhism first developed. Indeed, much of the history of India's culture is only known through the accounts of travelers and pilgrims and through the arts and literature they brought home with them. Particularly important are the many Buddhist pilgrims from China—especially FAXIAN (ca. 337–418) in the late fourth century C.E. and XUANZANG (ca. 600–664) in the seventh century—and the countless merchants and monks who traveled along the SILK ROAD and to Southeast Asia.

The materials used for Buddhist arts in India range from precious metals to the cliffs that edge the Deccan plateau. Artworks made of more ephemeral materials, such as clay or wood, have not survived but were probably made in abundance starting in the second century B.C.E. The most prominent medium is stone relief sculpture, sometimes carved nearly in the round, along with the context of the sculptures—monumental reliquary mounds (STŪPAS) and architecture in brick or stone. Although today most Indian Buddhist sculptures are found in museums, they once were part of stūpa railings, were arrayed in niches on the exterior walls of temples, or were placed on altars with other images. Free-standing sculptures were also important; bronze-casting achieved a high degree of perfection in south India and in Kashmir, where they inlaid the bronze with silver. Mural painting in dry-fresco was established early in India, culminating in the preserved works at AJAṆṬĀ in the fifth century C.E., but influencing later mural painting throughout Buddhist Asia. Manuscript illuminations and sacred writings on palm leaves were specialties in Pāla northeast India, providing models for the vast corpus of Hi-

The exterior of cave 19 at Ajaṇṭā, Maharashtra, India. © Archivo Iconografico, S.A./Corbis. Reproduced by permission.

malayan books. RITUAL OBJECTS, usually made of metal alloys, were always in demand for Buddhist ceremonies and initiations.

The themes of the earliest Buddhist arts in India celebrate nature's abundance, ironically in Western eyes, around the stūpas that commemorate the Buddha's death. The flourishing forces of water, plant life, and animals and spirits are all evoked in the reliefs at Bhārhut and SĀÑCĪ. The motivation for this "iconography of abundance" has piqued the curiosity of many generations of art historians. When MAHĀYĀNA Buddhism arose in India, with its emphasis not on the humanity of the Buddha Śākyamuni but on his spiritual attainment, another irony was embodied by representing this ethereal spirit in physical form. Images of the Buddha and BODHISATTVAS became the focus of devotion and complicated meditations. The primacy and the very existence of bodhisattvas, beings whose only purpose is to devote their enlightened energies to the benefit of others, may have been the impetus for formulating images of the Great Persons (*Mahapuruṣas*) in the first century C.E.

Pillars and edicts of the Mauryan emperor Aśoka (mid-third century B.C.E.)

An apparent convert to Buddhism, Emperor Aśoka (r. ca. 268–232 B.C.E.) of the Mauryan period sponsored the first large-scale and most well-known Indian imagery. After witnessing the carnage at an excessively bloody battle in Orissa, it is said that Aśoka took up the Buddhist cause of nonviolence. Throughout his empire, at crossroads and places sacred to Buddhists, Aśoka had monolithic pillars engraved with political edicts and Buddhist precepts. Most of the messages are in the Brāhmī script, the earliest writing used in India. Only about thirty of the Mauryan-period columns remain. The capitals of the pillars are composite, with inverted lotus-petal bells, an abacus, and crowning animals. The pillars are made from one shaft of sandstone (monolithic) from thirty- to forty-feet high, sunk deep into the ground, and polished by the application of heat, which gives them a glassy and durable finish.

The modern flag of India includes the Aśokan lion capital as an emblem of the unification of India under one government during the Mauryan period. Its powerful silhouette of four addorsed lions once supported an enormous wheel that symbolized the Buddha's first sermon, the "turning of the Wheel of the Dharma" (*dharmacakrapravartana*), which took place near Sārnāth. The lions are carved in a highly abstract way reminiscent of the composite lion capitals of Achaemenid Persia, but all other features of these free-standing pillars are purely Indian. The four lions facing in four directions probably signify the sovereignty of both Aśoka, since the pillar was erected near the capital of his kingdom, and of the truths taught by the Buddha, whose clan, the Śākyas, used the lion as their emblem. Around the abacus are four small wheels alternating with naturalistically carved animals (lion, elephant, bull, horse), which have great significance to indigenous clan traditions. The lion is especially associated with royalty and power in India. The pillars themselves also signify the pan-Indian idea of the axis of the world (*axis mundi*) that links the cosmic waters below with the sun above. Floral motifs, such as the palmettes and rosettes sometimes found on the Aśokan capitals, are more familiar in distant Mediterranean regions, but their appearance in India can be explained by the trade relations of India with the West and by the incursion of Alexander the Great into the northwest provinces of India.

Stūpas and stone reliefs (second century B.C.E. to first century C.E.)

In addition to free-standing pillars, Aśoka had stūpas, or reliquary mounds, erected in India, Sri Lanka, and Nepal to commemorate the Buddha and to designate worship and teaching centers. According to legend, Aśoka opened up the original eight stūpas containing the Buddha's relics and redistributed them in eighty-four thousand simple burial mounds.

The earliest known monumental stūpa was erected at Bhārhut in Madhya Pradesh in about 100 to 80 B.C.E. Constructed in red sandstone, it consisted of a central burial mound, now lost, surrounded by elaborate railings (*vedikā*) with four gates (*toraṇa*) carved with reliefs. Most of the fragments from Bhārhut are on display at the Indian Museum in Calcutta. The reliefs emphasize the abundance of nature in their depictions of YAKṢAS and *yakṣīs* (male and female fertility spirits), lotuses, elephants, and composite water creatures. Medallions with vignettes of the Buddha's life, as well as stories of his previous births (JĀTAKA), are carved in a low-relief style, often using continuous narration, with the same characters appearing more than once, in a shallow, almost two-dimensional space. The carvings accentuate geometric patterns, including elaborate tattoos on some of the figures.

The Buddha himself does not appear in any of these narratives. His presence is indicated by aniconic symbols, such as his footprints, an empty seat beneath the bodhi tree under which he became enlightened, the *dharmacakra* or Wheel of the Dharma that he set in motion, or a parasol over a horse with no rider to indicate that he left his princely home. Some consider these aniconic images to be representations of shrines or pilgrimage sites, and therefore not merely symbols of the Buddha's person. Images of the Buddha are not used until the Kushan period in the north and the late second century C.E. in south India.

The Great Stūpa at SĀÑCĪ, first erected during Aśoka's reign, was completed and elaborated around the beginning of the first century C.E. with railings, balustrades, and gates covered with narrative relief carvings. Reliefs of city scenes describe the sophisticated urban culture of ancient India. Probably because many of the relief panels were sponsored by a guild of ivory carvers, the scenes emulate the precise density of small-scale reliefs. The natural liveliness of these carvings shows a significant change from the geometric style used at Bhārhut. Impressive scenes abound on the elaborate gateways that narrate the life of the Buddha and some of the *jātaka* stories. Nature, demons, and mythical creatures are all portrayed with great imagination, utilizing a vast visual vocabulary culled from indigenous sources, as well as adaptations of Western composite creatures and plant life.

On the eastern Deccan, the broad central plateau of India, the Buddhist center at Amarāvatī (Andhra Pradesh, Śātavāhana period, second century C.E.) was the site of a large stūpa that was faced and surrounded by elegantly carved white-green limestone slabs. The stūpas themselves are gone, but many of the railings and facing slabs can be seen in Indian and Western museums. Many of the slabs reproduce in section the whole stūpa with its intricate railings and gateways. The narrative scenes are taken mainly from the life of the Buddha, although the Buddha image is still not shown. The style is naturalistic, as at Sāñcī, but uses more layering of figures to give a greater sense of depth. Figures are rounded, like those at Sāñcī, but the outlines are slightly elongated and nervous in their movements. Remains of temples and monastic dwellings have also been found at Amarāvatī and at the related sites of Ghaṇṭaśālā, Jaggayyapeṭa, and later at Nāgārjunakoṇḍa (third century C.E.).

Stūpas and monastic centers were usually patronized by guilds and by individuals, both lay devotees and monks or nuns, not by royalty or wealthy merchants. This public interest aspect of stūpas is reflected in everyday scenes from the Buddha's life, usually depicted in the reliefs, rather than scenes of royal and godly figures in palace halls. This patronage may also have contributed to the prohibition against using BUDDHA IMAGES: Lay Buddhists may have felt that you should not represent in art a person who had entered NIRVĀṆA, a TATHĀGATA (one who has gone), the name most often used to refer to the Buddha in the texts.

Rock-cut architecture (first century B.C.E. to second century C.E.)

Beginning in the first century B.C.E., rock-cut or CAVE SANCTUARIES and monasteries carefully imitated wooden structures of the day. In the centuries around the beginning of the common era the rock-cut worship hall (caitya) and monastery (vihāra) became established forms in northern and central India. The earliest site known is Bhājā (100 to 70 B.C.E., contemporary with Bhārhut) in Maharashtra, where a large caitya hall and many small monastic dwellings were excavated. Its imitation of wooden constructions includes the use of actual wood beams in the hall's barrel ceiling; wooden architectural sculpture and balconies once adorned the front. Other rock-cut sites, all found along the high escarpment in Maharashtra, are Pitalkhorā (also 100–70 B.C.E.), Bedsā (early first century C.E.), and Nāsik and Kānheri (both about 125–130 C.E.).

The largest caitya hall is at Kārlī, Maharashtra, carved out of a stone cliff in about 50 to 75 C.E. near Bombay. It has a navelike form, 125-feet in length including apse and colonnade, and has stone reliefs of a palatial facade; a free-standing lion-topped pillar marks the entrance. An enormous horseshoe-shaped window with a wooden lattice filters light into the hall, illuminating the monolithic stūpa at the apse-end of the hall. This window shape and lattice decoration characterizes Indian facades to this day. An elaborately sculpted veranda has high-relief elephants "supporting" the side walls and voluptuous couples on either side of the main door. Figures ride animals on the interior column capitals and the facade has multiple balconies decorated with reliefs of smiling people. Overall, Kārlī shows a sensuous environment equal to that created on Sāñcī's carved gateways in miniature, here on a large scale carved right out of the living rock.

The Buddha image: Mathurā and Gandhāra (Kushan period, first to third centuries C.E.)

The beginnings of figural sculpture of the Buddha in India is a controversial and intriguing study in the motives for image-making, as well as the development of both indigenous and adapted styles. Two sites—Mathurā, Uttar Pradesh, in northern India, and the Gandhāra region in present-day Pakistan—sponsored parallel versions of Buddha images and narrative reliefs at least as early as the first century C.E. (some fragments may be from the first century B.C.E.). The Kushan rulers, under whom this new trend in Buddhist imagery arose, came from Central Asia and dominated the area from Bactria to the Gangetic plain. Buddhism was spreading actively along the Silk Road through Central Asia at this time, making Gandhāra a fertile site for trade in artworks in service of the faith. Mathurā, the Kushan southern capital, had long been an artistic center, and artists there also made images for the monastic centers that had spread throughout northern India.

The Mathurā images follow indigenous forms with geometric, full volumes and attributes signifying a spiritual being (called *lakṣaṇa*). The solid power of the Mathurā buddhas follow the prototype of the village yakṣas found so frequently around stūpas—nature

Buddha Preaching the First Sermon, Sārnāth, India, about 465–485, buff sandstone. Archaeological Museum, Sārnāth. Reproduced by permission. This Buddha image embodies the Gupta style that became an international model for Buddhas throughout Asia.

spirits standing apart from the everyday world. The Gandhāra images resemble Hellenistic figural and relief traditions first imported with Alexander the Great when he conquered the area in 327 B.C.E. The Gandhāra buddha looks like a perfect, sensuous human being—a nobleman wearing heavy monk's robes.

Narrative reliefs of the Buddha's life also flourished at this time, especially in the Gandhāra region, now freely using the figure of the Buddha in the scenes. The Gandhāra scenes are very like those found on Roman sarcophagi—set pieces in niches separated by Western-style columns and pediments. Reliefs from the third and fourth centuries at Amarāvatī in south India also began to include images of the Buddha.

Gupta period "classical" style (fourth to sixth centuries C.E.)

The disparate styles of Kushan Mathurā and Gandhāra blended into an eloquent compromise during the fifth-century C.E. hegemony of the famous Gupta clan. The Gupta "classical" style became the prototype for Buddha images throughout Asia. A sandstone image found at Sārnāth, the site of the Buddha's first sermon, exemplifies this style—sensuous human volumes combined with abstract religious symbolism. The ornamental finesse of this style was to be admired and imitated throughout South and Southeast Asia for centuries. It also provided the visual vocabulary for much of the religious art in Central Asia, China, Korea, and Japan. Although in India the remaining Gupta period images are usually stone, metal-cast images were also commissioned and exported. A larger than life-size copper alloy sculpture weighing about one metric ton was found at Sultāngañj in Bihar.

The Guptas arose as the first major Indian dynasty since the Mauryas, but they maintained missionary and trade relationships with Central, Southeast, and East Asia. Although the rulers were themselves mostly Hindu, they sponsored a rich environment for the flourishing of a variety of art forms and dedications, from Hindu plays to Buddhist monuments. Mathurā continued to be a major artistic center, but Sārnāth arose as the leading innovator of the style. As the Buddha image became firmly established as the primary focus of Buddhist devotions, aniconic expressions of the religion, such as the stūpa, became less important in India in favor of temples to enshrine statues of Buddhist figures. During the fifth century, Gupta-style buddhas were placed at each of the gateways of the Great Stūpa at Sāñcī.

The multi-tiered MAHĀBODHI TEMPLE tower at BODH GAYĀ in Bihar, the site where the Buddha reached enlightenment, was first built during the Gupta hegemony. A descendant of the bodhi tree under which the Buddha sat is enshrined there and the site remains a major pilgrimage destination for Buddhists. The outer facets of the temple have enumerable niches for Gupta-style images of the Buddha and bodhisattvas. Miniature votive temples are placed around the main structure, intermingled with remains of earlier stūpa railings, shrines, and altars, providing important archaeological evidence of the development of pilgrimage site arts. At Bhārhut and Sāñcī there are clear reliefs showing what the earlier Bodh Gayā shrines looked like.

The classic Gupta proportions and spiritually charged detail appealed to patrons of Buddhist arts throughout India. Art and artists from Sārnāth were exported especially to the Deccan and southern India, as well as to Orissa and northeastern India. From there the style spread to Sri Lanka and Southeast Asia. Art and artists from Mathurā, the northernmost center of the Gupta style, were exported north toward Kashmir and the Gandhāra region. From there the style spread through Central Asia along the silk routes into western China, where it ultimately influenced Buddhist arts of the Tang dynasty (618–907).

Painting and sculpture at Ajaṇṭā (fifth century C.E.) and related sites

New rock-cut architecture was excavated beginning in the fifth century, serving both Buddhist and Hindu worship needs. The best-known group of Buddhist caitya halls and vihāras is at Ajaṇṭā on the eastern Deccan (Maharashtra, latter half of the fifth century). Dry-fresco murals on many of the walls portray the previous lives (*jātakas*) of the Buddha, as well as Buddhist saints and divine beings. Figures seem to glow in the dark interior because of the use of brilliant color and white highlights. Although the images use courtly, sophisticated compositions, they evoke a strong spiritual presence. Remarkable for their rich modeling and palatial imagery, these paintings also provided models for designs in Sri Lanka and especially for the murals of rock-cut halls in Central Asia and China for the next three centuries.

Imitations of wooden facades and high-relief sculptures at Ajaṇṭā cut into the caitya halls and vihāra walls also carried forward the Gupta opulence into ever more elaborate displays. The style and skill of the painting and sculpture at Ajaṇṭā continued to flourish in India in works dedicated to Hinduism, Jainism, and Buddhism. Auraṅgābād, also in Maharashtra, was an important site for both rock-cut and structural Buddhist architecture, as well as relief sculpture. Buddhist and Hindu rulers excavated the long cliff at Ellorā on the Deccan from the seventh to the ninth centuries.

Final phase of Buddhist art in India (sixth to twelfth centuries C.E.)

Buddhist structural architecture, sculpture, and manuscript illumination continued in India until the twelfth century. Two major sites were Nāgārjunakoṇḍa on the Deccan plateau and Nālandā in the northeast. Both rock-cut and structural com-

Buddha Śākyamuni Becoming Enlightened, Bodh Gayā, India, about 850, black schist. Los Angeles County Museum of Art. Reproduced by permission. This Pāla style sculpture illustrates the moment when the Buddha became enlightened as he sat beneath the Bodhi tree—notice the leaves arranged at the top of the throne—and touched the earth (*bhūmisparśa-mudrā*) to affirm that through his many lives he had achieved moral perfection. This style influenced the Mahāyāna and Vajrayāna arts throughout South, Southeast, and East Asia.

plexes served as universities for Buddhist scholars from all over Asia and as monasteries for monks and nuns. The Gandhāra region and Kashmir in northwestern India remained strong producers of distinctive arts that combined the humanistic Gandhāra ideal with Gupta spiritual sensibilities.

Buddhist stone and metal-cast sculptures, as well as manuscript illustrations, of the Pāla and Sena dynasties in northeastern India (eighth to twelfth centuries) are well known for their supreme elegance and fine detail. Usually called the Pāla style, this lithe and refined tradition was exported to Burma, Java, Nepal, Tibet, and China, especially in service of the Mahāyāna and VAJRAYĀNA Buddhist traditions. By the beginning of the thirteenth century the Pāla style was declining in Bihar and Bengal, until this last stronghold of Buddhist art in India finally collapsed under the advent of the Muslims in the northern regions of India.

See also: **Buddha, Life of the, in Art; India; India, Northwest; India, South; Jātaka, Illustrations of; Monastic Architecture**

Bibliography

Craven, Roy C. *Indian Art: A Concise History,* revised edition. London and New York: Thames and Hudson, 1997.

Dallapiccola, Anna L., and Lallemant, Stephanie Zingel-Avé, eds. *The Stūpa: Its Religious, Historical, and Architectural Significance.* Wiesbaden, Germany: Steiner, 1980.

Dehejia, Vidya. *Indian Art.* London: Phaidon, 1997.

Dumoulin, Heinrich. "The Mystery of Personhood in Buddhist Art." In *Understanding Buddhism: Key Themes,* tr. Joseph O'Leary. New York and Tokyo: Weatherhill, 1993.

Fisher, Robert E. *Buddhist Art and Architecture.* London and New York: Thames and Hudson, 1993.

Harle, James C. *The Art and Architecture of the Indian Subcontinent.* Middlesex, UK: Penguin, 1986.

Huntington, Susan L. *The Art of Ancient India: Buddhist, Hindu, Jain.* New York and Tokyo: Weatherhill, 1985.

Huntington, Susan L., and Huntington, John C. *Leaves from the Bodhi Tree: The Art of Pala India (8th–12th centuries) and Its International Legacy* (exhibition catalogue, Dayton Art Institute). Seattle and New York: University of Washington Press, 1990.

Irwin, John. "Aśokan Pillars: A Reassessment of the Evidence, Parts I–IV." *Burlington Magazine* 115 (1973): 706–720; 116 (1974): 712–727; 117 (1975): 631–643; 118 (1976): 734–753.

Maxwell, Thomas S. "Cult Art in the Buddhist Systems." In *The Gods of Asia: Image, Text, and Meaning.* Delhi: Oxford University Press, 1997.

McArthur, Meher. *Reading Buddhist Art: An Illustrated Guide to Buddhist Signs and Symbols.* London: Thames and Hudson, 2002.

Michell, George. *The Penguin Guide to the Monuments of India, Vol. 1: Buddhist, Jain, Hindu.* London: Viking, 1989.

Rosenfield, John M. *The Dynastic Arts of the Kushans.* Berkeley and Los Angeles: University of California Press, 1967.

Schopen, Gregory. "On Monks, Nuns, and Vulgar Practices: The Introduction of the Image Cult into Indian Buddhism." *Artibus Asiae* 49 (1988–1989): 153–168.

GAIL MAXWELL

INDIA, NORTHWEST

By the first century C.E., distinct regional styles of Buddhist art, architecture, and literature had emerged on the northwestern Indian subcontinent. Buddhist materials from the borderlands of modern India, Pakistan, and Afghanistan reflect prolonged contact between Indian, Iranian, Central Asian, and Hellenistic cultural traditions. As a pivotal transit zone for the movement of people, practices, and ideas both into and out of South Asia, the northwestern frontier was a dynamic launching pad for the early transmission of Buddhism to Central Asia and China.

Numerous Buddhist centers in the Northwest were located on the "northern route" (*uttarāpatha*), a major artery for trade and travel that connected the northwestern frontiers with the Buddhist homeland in northeastern India. Mathurā, a city located on the northern route south of modern New Delhi, was a significant node for trade and administration and an important center for Buddhist, Hindu, and Jain art and literature. Mathurā had close ties with Kashmir in the western Himalayas, where the Sarvāstivādin tradition of ABHIDHARMA scholasticism developed. The northern route linked Mathurā with Taxila (Takṣaśīla), an ancient metropolis on the northern route near modern Islamabad in Pakistan, where extensive archeological remains of stūpas and monasteries have been excavated. Gandhāran art and the Gāndhārī language (written in the Kharoṣṭhī script) were transmitted together with Buddhism beyond the Gandhāran heartland in northwestern Pakistan to Central Asia. Buddhist art and architecture in Afghanistan at sites such as Haḍḍa (south of Jalalabad), Bagrām (north of Kabul), and BĀMIYĀN led French art historian Alfred Foucher to label paths across the Hindu Kush to Bactria and western Central Asia the *Vieille Route* (Ancient Route). Buddhist petroglyphs and inscriptions in the upper Indus River valley indicate that Buddhist travelers also followed capillary routes across the Karakoram Mountains of northern Pakistan to eastern Central Asia.

Buddhism was established in Northwest India during the late centuries B.C.E. and the early to mid first millennium C.E. Afghanistan, Gandhāra, and the lower Indus River valley were Achaemenid provinces until 327 to 326 B.C.E., when Alexander of Macedon attempted to conquer these areas. The Mauryan emperor AŚOKA (r. ca. 268–232 B.C.E.) provided the impetus for the introduction of Buddhism in the Northwest. A devout lay Buddhist, Aśoka had two sets of major rock edicts in Kharoṣṭhī inscribed in northwestern Pakistan,

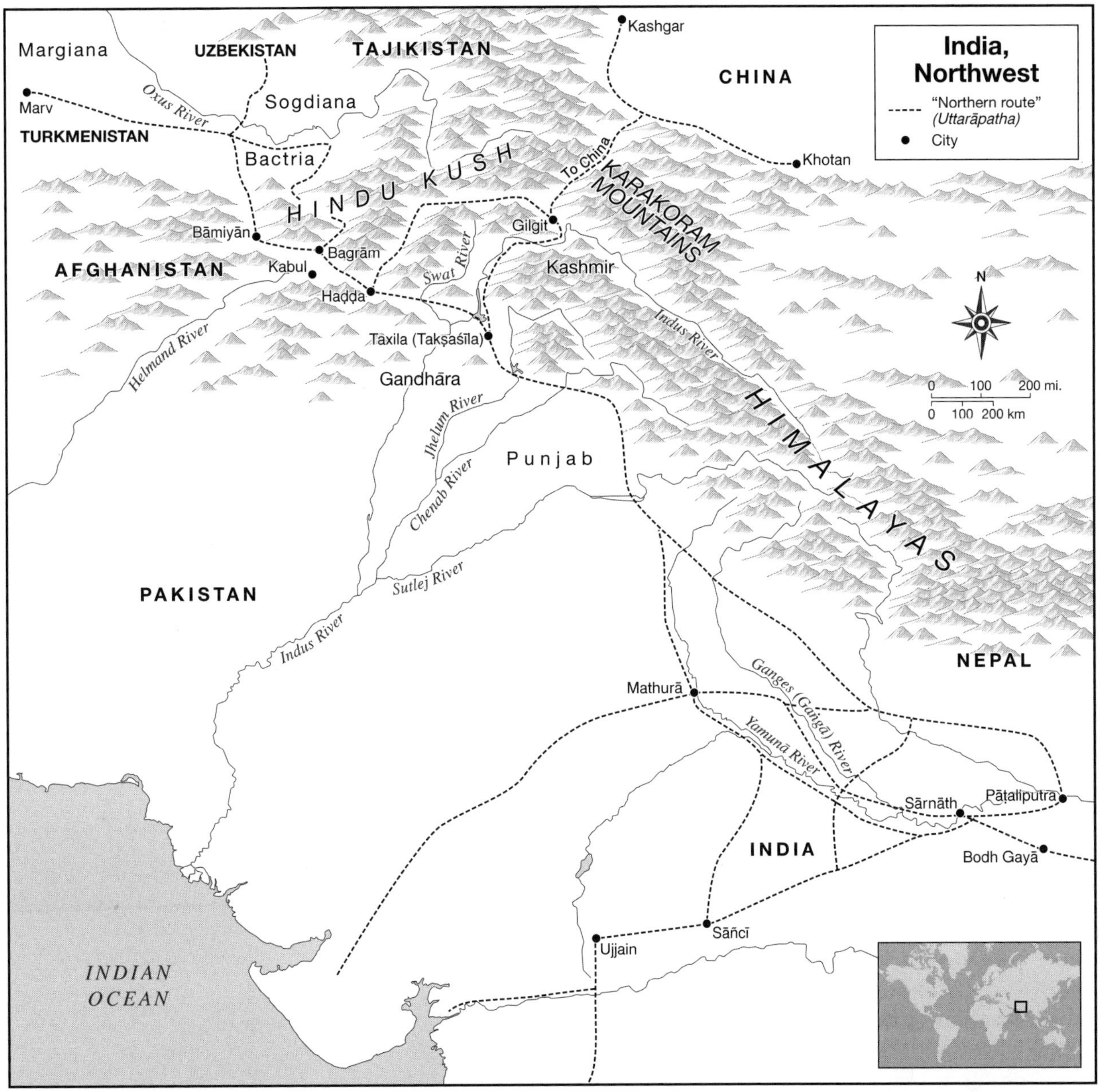

Buddhist centers on the "northern route" (*uttarāpatha*). XNR Productions, Inc. Reproduced by permission of the Gale Group.

with shorter versions in Greek and Aramaic in eastern Afghanistan and Taxila. Foundations of large early stūpas at Taxila and at Butkara in the Swat valley probably belong to the Mauryan period, and may be connected with Aśoka's patronage. Menander, one of Alexander's Indo-Greek successors who ruled the Punjab around 150 B.C.E., was a patron of Buddhism, according to Pāli and Chinese literary traditions. Saka (or Indo-Scythian) and Parthian rulers of the Northwest continued to support Buddhist institutions, since the names and titles of these Iranian rulers appear on coins and in Buddhist inscriptions and texts of the first century B.C.E. and first century C.E.

During the Kushan period in the early centuries C.E., Buddhism began to expand beyond the northwestern frontiers of South Asia. The Kushan empire extended from Bactria to Bengal at the beginning of the second century C.E. during the reign of Kanishka, who is portrayed in Chinese and Central Asian Buddhist literature as the greatest Buddhist royal patron after Aśoka. In the post-Kushan period, local rulers and other patrons maintained Buddhist monastic communities where surplus resources for donations were available. Buddhist monastic communities in Bāmiyān in central Afghanistan and Gilgit in northern Pakistan evidently remained connected with Buddhist centers in

Central Asia in the late first millennium C.E. Buddhism in the Northwest gradually declined as lay support diminished and Hinduism and Islam eventually became more prevalent.

Discoveries of inscribed reliquaries and archeological excavations of stūpas and monasteries provide material evidence for a wide spectrum of Buddhist practices in Northwest India. A growing number of Kharoṣṭhī inscriptions record the donation of reliquaries containing physical relics (*śarīra*). Stūpas built to enclose these relics replicated the presence of the Buddha. The primary STŪPA was typically surrounded by smaller stūpas and columns, which often contained secondary relic deposits. Permanent Buddhist monastic structures consisting of cells for monks and nuns around open rectangular courtyards were usually built near stūpas. Such Buddhist sacred complexes were often decorated with stone and stucco sculptures. Art produced by Gandhāran workshops incorporated Indian, Iranian, and Hellenistic elements in distinctive iconographic patterns. Gandhāran Buddhist art of the Northwest continued to have an impact on Buddhist artistic traditions of Central Asia and China, where worship of images played a prominent role in popular practice.

Several narratives associated with the Buddha's previous lives have Northwest India as their setting, although the historical Buddha did not visit this region during his lifetime. The earliest conversion of Kashmir, the Indus valley, and Gandhāra to Buddhism is attributed to a disciple of ĀNANDA named Madhyāntika (Pāli, Majjhantika). MAINSTREAM BUDDHIST SCHOOLS in Northwest India included Śrāvakayāna (or HĪNAYĀNA) sects that were active in the transmission of Buddhism to Central Asia and China. Kharoṣṭhī inscriptions record donations of relics, images, water pots, utensils, and other gifts to teachers of the DHARMAGUPTAKA, Sarvāstivādin, MAHĀSĀṂGHIKA, Mahīśāsaka, and Kāśyapīya schools. For example, a clay pot dedicated to the Dharmaguptakas contained early Buddhist manuscripts from the first century C.E. Another collection of Buddhist manuscripts from the second or third to seventh centuries C.E. may have come from the library of a Mahāsāṃghika monastery in Bāmiyān. Parts of the MŪLASARVĀSTIVĀDA-VINAYA are preserved among Buddhist Sanskrit manuscripts from the sixth to seventh centuries C.E. found near Gilgit in the 1930s. Manuscripts from Bāmiyān and Gilgit include several MAHĀYĀNA texts, which are apparently absent in earlier Kharoṣṭhī manuscript collections. Further research in the relationships between Buddhist manuscripts from the Northwest and Buddhist texts translated into Chinese and Central Asian languages should clarify patterns of textual transmission.

With new discoveries of Buddhist inscriptions and manuscripts and additional excavations of Buddhist sites in northwestern India, Pakistan, and Afghanistan, it is becoming increasingly clear that the northwestern borderlands of Kashmir, Gandhāra, and Bactria linked older Buddhist communities in the Indian homeland with those developing in Central Asia during the first millennium C.E. Therefore, the Northwest played a critical role in the movement of Buddhist institutions, ideas, and practices beyond the Indian subcontinent to Central Asia and China.

See also: **Gāndhārī, Buddhist Literature in; Hinduism and Buddhism; India; India, Buddhist Art in; India, South; Islam and Buddhism; Sarvāstivāda and Mūlasarvāstivāda**

Bibliography

Errington, Elizabeth, and Cribb, Joe, eds. *The Crossroads of Asia: Transformation in Image and Symbol in the Art of Ancient Afghanistan and Pakistan.* Cambridge, UK: Ancient India and Iran Trust, 1992.

Foucher, Alfred. *La vieille Route de l'Inde de Bactres à Taxila,* 2 vols. Paris: Les éditions d'art et d'histoire, 1942–1947.

Fussman, Gérard. "Upāya-kauśalya: L'implantation du bouddhisme au Gandhāra." In *Bouddhisme et cultures locales: Quelques cas de réciproques adaptations,* ed. Fukui Fumimasa and Gérard Fussman. Paris: École Française d'Extrême-Orient, 1994.

Hinüber, Oskar von. "Expansion to the North: Afghanistan and Central Asia." In *The World of Buddhism: Buddhist Monks and Nuns in Society and Culture,* ed. Heinz Bechert and Richard Gombrich. London: Thames and Hudson, 1984. Reprint, 1998.

Lamotte, Étienne. *History of Indian Buddhism from the Origins to the Śaka Era,* tr. Sara Webb-Boin. Louvain-la-Neuve, Belgium: Université catholique de Louvain, Institut Orientaliste, 1988.

Marshall, John. *Taxila: An Illustrated Account of Archaeological Excavations Carried Out at Taxila under the Orders of the Government of India between the Years 1913 and 1934,* 3 vols. Cambridge, UK: Cambridge University Press, 1951.

Salomon, Richard. *Ancient Buddhist Scrolls from Gandhāra: The British Library Kharoṣṭhī Fragments.* London: British Library; Seattle: University of Washington Press, 1999.

Zwalf, Wladimir. *A Catalogue of the Gandhāra Sculpture in the British Museum,* 2 vols. London: British Museum, 1996.

JASON NEELIS

INDIA, SOUTH

Evidence for the history of Buddhism at the southernmost end of the Indian subcontinent (defined here as the modern states of Karnataka, Andhra Pradesh, Kerala, and Tamilnadu) is highly fragmented, a scattered collection of inscriptions, archaeological ruins, art-historical remains, and a few texts. Yet Buddhist institutions clearly once flourished in South India. From the edicts of AŚOKA (third century B.C.E.) and the written testimony of Chinese pilgrims to the presence of Buddhist interlocutors in Hindu and Jain texts for more than a millennium, Buddhists obviously played significant roles in the South Indian religious landscape until at least the fourteenth century. Yet what sort of Buddhism flourished there? What did it mean to be a "Buddhist" in early medieval South India? What kinds of interactions took place among Buddhists, Hindus, and Jains? Answers to such questions remain elusive.

With no direct references to Buddhism found in any extant Malayalam or Kannada text, both Kerala and Karnataka harbor Buddhist archaeological records that are difficult to interpret. Only a meager collection of Buddhist images has been unearthed in Kerala, all roughly datable to the sixth through tenth centuries C.E. In Karnataka, the record expands ever so slightly, from the STŪPA at Vanavāsī (third century C.E.) to the fifth-century caitya at Aihole and evidence of tantric worship at Balligāve (eleventh century). STŪPAS and caityas attest to some sort of institutional organization, royal or lay patronage, and active practices of worship, but the inscriptional record provides no further evidence concerning the status or use of such structures.

Two more substantial bodies of evidence can be found in the archaeological ruins of Andhra Pradesh and in the Tamil literary record. While neither presents a complete picture of Buddhist life and practice in the South, each does provide a richer range of material for interpretation.

The impressive ruins of Amarāvatī, Nāgārjunakoṇḍa, and other sites in Andhra Pradesh constitute the earliest evidence for Buddhism in the South (second century B.C.E.). Although no textual production can be located here with any certainty, these grand stūpas or *mahācaityas*, with their rich inscriptional records, narrative friezes, and hundreds of Buddhist sculptures, bespeak flourishing centers of Buddhist practice through at least the twelfth century. Due both to the traditional association of Amarāvatī and Nāgārjunakoṇḍa with NĀGĀRJUNA (the great Madhyamaka philosopher of the second century C.E.) and to the nature of the images found there, Andhra Buddhism has long been labeled "MAHĀYĀNA" by scholars. The narratives of the Buddha's lives carved in stone, the belief that each stūpa contained relics of the Buddha's earthly body, and the inscriptional references to lay donors (many of them women of the Īkṣvāku royal dynasty that ruled from Nāgārjunakoṇḍa) all point to flourishing centers of Buddhist worship, where monastic and lay devotees honored the remains of the Buddha, contemplated the lessons of his many lives, and worshiped in myriad ways the figures of buddhas past and future.

Turning southward to the Tamil-speaking region, the true treasure trove of Buddhist artifacts is Nākapaṭṭiṉam, a coastal site mentioned in Sri Lankan, Burmese, and Chinese sources from which over three hundred images have been recovered. Buddhist sculptures found in the midst of Hindu places of worship, such as the six-foot standing Buddha from the Kāmākṣīyammaṉ Temple in Kāñcīpuram (fourth century C.E.), attest to a long Buddhist influence in the Tamil region. Yet does the presence of a Buddha image mean that a Hindu temple was once truly "Buddhist"? A seventh-century inscription from Māmallapuram, listing the Buddha as an incarnation of the Hindu deity Viṣṇu, suggests a more complex scenario. Does a Buddha image imply a strong sense of Buddhist sectarian affiliation, or had the Buddha simply been absorbed into the wider South Indian pantheon by the seventh century?

What emerges uniquely in South India from the Tamil-speaking region is a Buddhist literary record in languages other than Sanskrit. The three famed Pāli commentators of the fourth and fifth centuries, for example—BUDDHAGHOSA, Buddhadatta, and Dhammapāla—claim some connection to beautiful monasteries patronized by beneficent Tamil kings. Through the twelfth-century works of Buddhappiya and Kassapa, eminent THERAVĀDA monks associate themselves with southern India, with monasteries from Nākapaṭṭiṉam to Kāñcīpuram.

Tamil is unique among the regional literary languages of India for its two premodern Buddhist works. The older of the two remaining pieces of Buddhist literature composed in Tamil, the *Maṇimēkalai*, attributed to Cāttaṉār and dated to roughly the sixth century, narrates the story of a young courtesan who gradually turns away from that life to embrace Buddhism. The *Maṇimēkalai* presents its audience with a long and stylistically beautiful narrative meditation on the arising of the conditions that propel its heroine to eventual enlightenment, culminating in two densely terse chapters on Buddhist LOGIC and PRATĪTYASAMUTPĀDA (DEPENDENT ORIGINATION). With the settings of its stories ranging from luxurious Tamil cities to Kapilavastu and the shores of a Southeast Asian island kingdom known as Cāvakam, the *Maṇimēkalai* clearly attests to a vibrant literary culture in Tamil that counted Buddhists, sophisticated in their knowledge of Buddhist tradition and highly technical philosophical language, among its participants.

Further evidence of Buddhist literary culture in the South can be found in the *Vīracōḻiyam,* an eleventh-century treatise on Tamil grammar and poetics attributed to Puttamittiraṉ and accompanied by a commentary thought to have been composed by the author's student, Peruntēvaṉār. As the first Tamil grammar to claim direct appropriation of Sanskrit poetic theory (in its treatment of *alaṅkāra* or "poetic ornamentation"), the *Vīracōḻiyam* explicitly forges a new Tamil-Sanskrit hybrid language in the name of Buddhism. Claiming that the literary language he describes first issued forth from the mouth of Avalōkitaṉ (Avalokiteśvara), Puttamittiraṉ pioneers a new poetic style for his own sectarian community. The commentary then substantiates that project by gathering together examples of Tamil Buddhist poetry in illustration of this new Sanskrit-Tamil hybrid. Such scattered poetic phrases—many alluding to Tamil versions of JĀTAKA stories and to songs in praise of the Buddha and his many wonderful qualities—are, unfortunately, all that remain (apart from the *Maṇimēkalai,* which the commentator never cites) of what must have once been a considerable corpus of Buddhist devotional, philosophical, and narrative poetry in Tamil.

Evidence for the presence of Buddhists in southernmost India thus presents us with a series of disparate snapshots, some more in focus than others. Whether the substantial archaeological finds in southern Andhra Pradesh bear any relevance for understanding the Buddhist literary record in Tamil, or whether the scattered Buddhist images recovered from paddy fields across the region reveal anything of "Buddhism" per se in the South, are questions that await further research.

See also: **India; India, Buddhist Art in; India, Northwest**

Bibliography

Alexander, P. C. *Buddhism in Kerala.* Annamalainagar, India: Annamalai University, 1949.

Hikosaka, Shu. *Buddhism in Tamilnadu: A New Perspective.* Madras, India: Institute of Asian Studies, 1989.

Hiremath, Rudrayya Chandrayya. *Buddhism in Karnataka.* New Delhi: D. K. Printworld, 1994.

Monius, Anne. *Imagining a Place for Buddhism: Literary Culture and Religious Community in Tamil-Speaking South India.* New York: Oxford University Press, 2001.

Richman, Paula. *Women, Branch Stories, and Religious Rhetoric in a Tamil Buddhist Text.* Syracuse, NY: Maxwell School of Citizenship and Public Affairs, Syracuse University, 1988.

Schalk, Peter. *Pauttamum Tamiḻum: Inventory, Investigation and Interpretation of Sources Pertaining to Buddhism among Tamilar in Pre-Colonial Tamiḻakam and Īḻam (Ilaṅkai).* Uppsala, Sweden: Uppsala University, 2002.

Sivaramalingam, K. *Archaeological Atlas of the Antique Remains of Buddhism in Tamilnadu.* Madras, India: Institute of Asian Studies, 1997.

Subramanian, K. R. *Buddhist Remains in Andhra and the History of Andhra between 224 and 610 A.D.* Madras, India: Diocesan Press, 1932.

ANNE E. MONIUS

INDONESIA AND THE MALAY PENINSULA

The geography of the Malay Peninsula and of Indonesia helps to explain the role the region played in the early spread of Buddhism to Southeast Asia and China. The peninsula includes the modern nation-states of Malaysia and Singapore and the southern portion of Thailand. Malaysia occupies the end of the peninsula, with the small city-state of Singapore at its southern tip on the Sunda Strait. Malaysia shares its northern border, halfway up the peninsula, with Thailand. For purposes of examining the role of ancient Buddhism, the entire peninsula can be seen as a single geographical area. Some twenty-five miles from Singapore, across the Sunda Strait, is the island of Sumatra, one of about three thousand islands that make up the archipelago of modern Indonesia. The peninsula and the islands, surrounded by water, are an environment that produces cultures that rely on boats. Likewise, the peninsula is located about halfway between India and China along the route taken by trading vessels. The area was a crossroads for both local and international trade and communication. It is thus not surprising that most of the earliest evidence for Buddhism in Southeast Asia comes from the peninsula, and that both the peninsula and the islands reveal in their art, culture, and religion very direct and frequent interchanges with South Asia.

These interchanges, based on trading activities, brought Buddhism and Hinduism to Southeast Asia. There is archeological evidence on the Malay Peninsula for the presence of both Hinduism and Buddhism from about the fifth century C.E. Both these Indic religions are present together for centuries to follow at sites on the Malay Peninsula and in Indonesia, specifically on the islands of Sumatra, Java, and Bali. While one religion may have been favored over the other at certain times and places, they rarely were set in opposition to one another. Indeed, as on Bali today, they tended to blend together.

The evidence for Buddhism comes from three sources: Chinese histories, local inscriptions, and art. The Chinese histories that mention early Southeast Asian polities have been very thoroughly explored by scholars. The Chinese sources present the Indian impact starting in the first century C.E., and at times references to Buddhism can be discerned for this early period. By around the fifth century, there are reports from Chinese monks who traveled by ship to and from India, and who thus passed through Southeast Asia. One monk, YIJING (635–713), stopped in the capital of Śrīvijaya in 671 on his way to India in order to study Sanskrit. The capital is believed to have been Palembang on Sumatra. Yijing returned to Palembang after ten years in India to live again in Śrīvijaya from 685 to 695 (with one visit to China in 689), and it is there that he translated Indian texts into Chinese and wrote his memoirs.

Srivijaya remained a center for Buddhist studies for hundreds of years. The famous Indian monk ATISHA (982–1054) went to Sumatra to study with the Buddhist teacher Dharmakīrti. Atisha later traveled to Tibet in 1042 and founded the Kadam lineage, which became the DGE LUGS (GELUK) school of Tibetan Buddhism.

The second category of evidence for Buddhism on the Malay Peninsula and in Indonesia is inscriptions. The earliest inscriptions, mostly written on stone, date from around the fifth to the eighth centuries C.E. They are written in Indian-related scripts in Sanskrit, and often include phrases from, or similar to those in, Buddhist texts. The dating of these inscriptions, scattered at various sites, is generally based on paleography (that is, the style of the letters), which gives rise to varying opinions by scholars. Most of these inscriptions hold little historical information, but they tell us that Buddhism was practiced by some of the population and sometimes the school of Buddhism can be broadly identified. When the early Buddhist inscriptions are compared to those of similar date that relate to Hinduism, it appears that Hinduism was associated with those in power, the local chiefs or kings. Hinduism in Southeast Asia served the role of building royal power more frequently than did Buddhism during this early period.

A Buddhist ceremony at Jakarta, Indonesia, 1994. © Don Farber 2003. All rights reserved. Reproduced by permission.

When one thinks of Buddhism in Java, it is the Central Javanese period (seventh to tenth centuries) and the truly spectacular monument of BOROBUDUR that come to mind. Borobudur is but one of the many Buddhist monuments built during this time, when hundreds of Buddhist images in stone and bronze were also made. Hinduism was practiced here as well, and the old theory that the two religions represented contending dynasties is today discounted. The coexistence of Buddhism and Hinduism continued when the cultural center of Java moved to the east. During the Majapahit period (fourteenth and fifteenth centuries), Śiva and the Buddha were worshiped, both with tantric texts and rituals.

Today, most of the population of Indonesia and the Malay Peninsula is Muslim. Islam appeared in Sumatra by the ninth century C.E. and by the sixteenth century had come to dominate most of the Indonesian islands and the Malay Peninsula up to about the border with modern Thailand. Although Thailand is today overwhelmingly Buddhist, its southern peninsular region has a large Muslim minority. Modern Thai Buddhism is not related to the earlier Buddhism of the peninsula, but is connected to that of Burma and Sri Lanka. Buddhism is also practiced in Singapore, but this is Buddhism of the large expatriate Chinese community. It is only on the tiny island of Bali that echoes of the region's early Buddhism remain today, blended with Hinduism in a unique local religion and culture.

See also: **Hinduism and Buddhism; Indonesia, Buddhist Art in; Islam and Buddhism; Southeast Asia, Buddhist Art in**

Bibliography

Coèdes, George. *The Indianized States of Southeast Asia,* tr. Susan Brown Cowing. Honolulu: East-West Center Press, 1968.

Jacq-Hergoualc'h, Michel. *The Malay Peninsula: Crossroads of the Maritime Silk Road (100 B.C.–1300 A.D.),* tr. Victoria Hobson. Leiden, Netherlands: Brill, 2002.

Miksic, John N., ed. *The Legacy of Majaphit.* Singapore: National Heritage Board, 1995.

Soekmono, R. *The Javanese Candi: Function and Meaning.* Leiden, Netherlands: Brill, 1995.

ROBERT L. BROWN

INDONESIA, BUDDHIST ART IN

The oldest Buddhist objects in Indonesia date from around the seventh century C.E. The major early focus of Buddhist activity in the archipelago lay in southeast Sumatra, where the kingdom of Śrīvijaya was centered. By the late seventh century this kingdom had attained an important position in conducting trade between the Indian Ocean and the South China Sea. The Chinese Buddhist pilgrim YIJING (635–713), who traveled to India in ships belonging to the ruler of this kingdom in 672 C.E., described Buddhism as flourishing in Śrīvijaya's capital, with a large monastery where he learned Sanskrit.

A large granite standing Buddha image has been found at Seguntang Hill, on the fringe of the city. Such stylistic elements as emphasis on the folds of his robe are reminiscent of art from the Amarāvatī area in India, but it is more likely that the earliest Indonesian Buddhist art was influenced by Sri Lanka, where this style lasted longer than in southern India. Two other important bronze Buddha images found much farther east, at Sikendeng on Sulawesi and Kota Bangun on east Borneo, share these same features. They date from approximately the same period and demonstrate the extent to which Buddhism had already spread. Bronze images from the eighth century indicate that Buddhism made its presence felt as far east as Lombok during this period.

The corpus of art directly associated with Sumatra during this period is scanty, but combined with statuary found in politically and culturally allied areas of the Malay Peninsula around the Isthmus of Kra and Kedah, images of Avalokiteśvara enable us to draw the inference that a generalized cult of this bodhisattva was common in this region. A bronze of the bodhisattva Tārā and an Avalokiteśvara presumably from this period have also been found in Lombok.

By the late eighth century, MAHĀYĀNA Buddhist imagery also began to appear in central Java. Between about 780 and 850 C.E., this region produced unsurpassed works of sculpture and architecture. Some images bear indications of continued connections with centers of Buddhism in Sri Lanka and south India, such as Negapatam, while by the late ninth century connections with the monastery at Nālandā in what is now Bangladesh are also visible.

Among the important complexes of Buddhist architecture constructed in central Java, the best known is the great site of BOROBUDUR. Few free-standing STŪPA were built; instead most Javanese structures consisted of temples with chambers for statuary. The main image at Kalasan, erected around 780 C.E., was a large Tārā (now lost). Around 800 C.E. a major revolution in Javanese Buddhism marked by intense interest in MAṆḌALAS resulted in the reconstruction of all major sites. At Sewu, an earlier complex was altered to create a cruciform building with enclosed circumambulation pathway. A group of over two hundred stone structures formed a huge three-dimensional maṇḍala. Major deities worshipped there may have included the bodhisattva Mañjuśrī and the buddha Vairocana.

Relief sculpture depicting the entourage of Māra surrounding the Buddha at the great eighth- and ninth-century Buddhist site of Borobudur in Java, Indonesia. © Charles and Josette Lenars/Corbis. Reproduced by permission.

At Plaosan Lor, several types of structures were built in the early ninth century C.E. The two principal remaining buildings consist of approximately identical two-storied edifices with rectangular floor plans, each divided into three rooms. Against the east wall of each edifice, facing west, was a low stone bench upon which nine images were placed, three in each cella. The central images, probably of bronze, have all disappeared. They were flanked by other figures of stone that still remain. Among the bodhisattvas tentatively identified are Mañjuśrī, Avalokiteśvara, MAITREYA, and Kṣitigarbha.

Mañjuśrī was an important figure in the Javanese Buddhist pantheon. Among the most beautiful surviving images is a silver Mañjuśrī from the village of Ngemplak. Another popular subject was Jambhala, god of wealth. Other important artistic expressions from this culture include *vajra* (thunderbolts) and *ghaṇṭā* (bells), sometimes combined into a single object. These may have been associated with the cult of Mahāvairocana Sarvavid, who became important around the second half of the ninth century.

Central Javanese civilization suffered a catastrophic decline in the early tenth century. What caused the decline is not clear, but complex art was no longer produced there. It took more than three hundred years before a new wave of Buddhist art arose in Java, by which time the center of activity had shifted toward the east.

During this gap in the Javanese record, the Sumatran kingdom of Śrīvijaya also came to an end. During the eleventh and twelfth centuries, two other important complexes of Buddhist art arose on that island. One complex, at an isolated hinterland site known as Muara Takus, consists mainly of a stūpa of unusual elongated shape, made of brick, together with several other foundations of now-ruined structures. No statuary has been reported from Muara Takus, but pieces of inscribed gold foil attest to the site's esoteric affiliation.

The other important site, Padang Lawas, in the hinterland of North Sumatra, consists of numerous brick complexes scattered over a wide area. Statuary and inscriptions from Padang Lawas indicate affinities with KĀLACAKRA Buddhism: a shattered Heruka image and inscriptions describing the ecstasy of the initiates occasioned by the aroma of burning corpses, and the demonic laughter that they are inspired to emit.

Buddhism continued to be practiced in Sumatra into the fourteenth century. A huge Bhairava image over four meters tall, found at Padang Reco in West Sumatra, depicts an initiate with sacrificial skull bowl and knife, standing on a corpse resting on a pile of skulls.

A major Buddhist center named Jago was erected around 1280 C.E. in an east Javanese kingdom named Singasari. The walls of the sanctuary base were embellished with reliefs of mixed Hindu and Buddhist character. Its interior was equipped with an elaborate system for lustrating statues. These include some of the most beautiful images ever created in Java, including a beautiful Sudanakumāra and an impressively ugly Hayagrīva. The main statue was probably an Amoghapāśa, of which several copies were made. One of these copies was found in Sumatra, probably sent there as a token of Singasari's conquest of Malayu, the Sumatran successor to Śrīvijaya.

Another triumph of Javanese Buddhist art was created either in the last years of Singasari, or in the early phase of its successor kingdom, Majapahit. This image, of Prajñāpāramitā, was found at the site of Singasari's capital. Similar statues were also carved around the same time, one of which was also found at Malayu's capital, Muara Jambi. Inscriptions show that a Majapahit queen personally identified with this deity.

See also: **Cave Sanctuaries; Folk Religion, Southeast Asia; Indonesia and the Malay Peninsula; Monastic Architecture; Southeast Asia, Buddhist Art in**

Bibliography

Bernet Kempers, August Johan. *Ancient Indonesian Art.* Amsterdam: C. P. J. van der Peet; Cambridge, MA: Harvard University Press, 1959.

Dumarçay, Jacques. *The Temples of Java,* tr. Michael Smithies. Kuala Lumpur, Malaysia: Oxford University Press, 1986.

Fontein, Jan, ed. *The Sculpture of Indonesia.* New York: Abrams, 1990.

Lunsingh Scheurleer, Pauline, and Klokke, Marijke J. *Ancient Indonesian Bronzes: A Catalogue of the Exhibition in the Rijksmuseum Amsterdam.* Leiden, Netherlands: Brill, 1988.

Miksic, John N., ed. *Indonesian Heritage,* Vol. 1: *Ancient History.* Singapore: Archipelago Press, 1996.

Satyawati Suleiman. *The Archaeology and History of West Sumatra.* Jakarta, Indonesia: Berita Pusat Penelitian Arkeologi Nasional Number 12, 1977.

Schnitger, F. M. *Forgotten Kingdoms in Sumatra.* Leiden, Netherlands: Brill, 1964.

Subhadradis Diskul, M. C., ed. *The Art of Śrīvijaya.* Kuala Lumpur, Malaysia, and New York: Oxford University Press, 1980.

JOHN N. MIKSIC

INDRA

Indra, also known as Sakka (Pāli) and Śakra (Sanskrit), is initially the Vedic lord of the heavens. Indra is incorporated into Buddhism in several ways. He is said to have been converted and to have attained the first stage of realization on the path (stream winner) in the *Group of Long Discourses* (Pāli, *Dīghanikāya*) (II. 288). He is typically portrayed as a guardian of the religion and the chief deity in the heaven of the thirty-three gods. In some versions of the Buddha's life story, Indra receives the infant Buddha as he emerges from his mother's side and then bathes him. Likewise, when the recently enlightened Buddha is reluctant to share his insight with the world, it is Indra (along with Brahmā) who convinces him to teach. Indra also accompanies the Buddha to the heaven of the thirty-three gods to preach to his mother, and it is Indra who provides the ladder on which the Buddha descends. Iconographically, Indra is often depicted as subservient to the Buddha. In Gandhāran sculpture, for instance, he is sometimes depicted, along with Brahmā, worshipping the Buddha, sometimes holding an umbrella to shade him from the sun, or sometimes holding the Buddha's alms bowl.

The image of Indra's net, which stretches infinitely across the heavens, becomes important in the MAHĀYĀNA tradition—particularly in the HUAYAN SCHOOL and its text, the HUAYAN JING (Sanskrit, *Avataṃsaka Sūtra*; *Flower Garland Sūtra*)—as a metaphor for the interconnectedness of all beings. This image has been frequently adopted by modern Buddhist activists. Indra continues to be an important deity in a number of Southeast Asian countries, both as the model ruler and active force. In legend, he frequently appears as a deus ex machina, sometimes in disguise to test the BODHISATTVA, more frequently to assist devotees in their merit-making. He is venerated at the end of the year as Thagya Min in Myanmar (Burma). Elsewhere, Indra is invoked to protect those gathered at festivals and important ceremonies.

See also: **Divinities; Hinduism and Buddhism**

Jacob N. Kinnard

INGEN RYŪKI

Ingen Ryūki (Chinese, Yinyuan Longqi; 1592–1673), although unknown from Chinese sources, was the founder of the Ōbaku sect of Japanese Zen and was the most prominent figure in introducing Ming dynasty-style Buddhism to Japan. After completing the restoration of Wanfu Monastery on Mount Huangbo in China, Ingen arrived in Japan in 1654 at the invitation of the Nagasaki Chinese community. He reinvigorated Zen training in the Nagasaki area and was invited to Kyoto in 1655. In 1658 Ingen traveled to Edo and impressed many important officials, including the shogun, who granted him land in 1665 for the founding of Ōbaku-san Mampukuji in the Uji area. The name and style of the monastery was copied from Ingen's home monastery. By 1745 the Ōbaku sect had 1,043 monasteries in its network; 431 of them are still in operation today.

Wanfu Monastery belonged to one of the many branches of the Linji lineage of the Chinese Chan school and did not form an independent sect in China. Thus, Ingen's teachings were not substantially different from other Japanese Rinzai Zen branches. Major differences can be found, however, in his emphasis on vinaya and on following the *Ōbaku shingi* (*Pure Rules for the Ōbaku Sect*) and maintaining Ming dynasty-style music, rituals, and robes. The Ōbaku sect's social engagement, differing use of text, and its acceptance of Pure Land practices are also significant. Chinese-style arts also played a role at Mampukuji, where Chinese artists were employed, and Ingen is famous for his calligraphy.

Bibliography

Baroni, Helen J. *Ōbaku Zen: The Emergence of the Third Sect of Zen in Tokugawa Japan.* Honolulu: University of Hawaii Press, 2000.

A. W. Barber

INITIATION

Initiation (or "consecration" in tantric Buddhism) brought a candidate into the maṇḍala of buddha families and, most frequently, authorized the individual to visualize himself or herself as some form of a buddha or bodhisattva. Only partly similar to initiation rituals in the Mediterranean mystery religions, Buddhist initiation was initially patterned on political rites of coronation that had been developed in the early medieval period of India (ca. 500–1200 C.E.). As such, the individual was consecrated or anointed with water at a specific moment in the ceremony; the ritual derived its name, *abhiṣeka,* from this process of anointing (*Öabhiṣic* means "to asperse"). The term *abhiṣeka* also denotes rituals employed in the bathing of images, such as pouring fragrant water on a Buddha statue during the Buddha's birthday celebrations, and the cleansing aspect of the consecration ritual was never entirely lost.

Buddhists had consistently relied on formal rites of passage, whether those of taking refuge (*śaraṇagamana*) for the laity, or lower and higher ordination (*pravrajyā* and *upasampadā*) for monks and nuns. Mahāyānist authors had developed a new ceremony for the assumption of the bodhisattva vow and had eventually termed it "bodhisattva ordination" (*bodhisattva-upasampadā*). The idea of royal consecration, however, was first applied to the bodhisattva Maitreya, who was said to be the crown prince (*yuvarāja*) of the dharma, as the successor to Śākyamuni Buddha, who was denoted the king of the dharma. Thus, consecration indicated a political metaphor, which assumed a position of increasing importance during the fifth- and sixth-century transition between the classical Gupta and the early medieval period of India. As Mahāyāna developed this metaphor, a mythic rite of consecration became applied to all bodhisattvas who reached the tenth stage of the Mahāyāna path, so that the bodhisattva at the tenth stage became consecrated (*abhiṣikta*) in the heavenly realm of *Akaniṣṭḥa* by all the buddhas.

With tantric Buddhism, the initiation rite went from a narrative applied to exalted bodhisattvas to a new rite of passage indicating the entrance into a new vehicle, the vehicle of mantras, or the adamantine vehicle (Vajrayāna). Initiation into this vehicle, employing the imperial metaphor, meant that the candidate was consecrated as the head of a ritual family (*kula*) through a Buddhist form of the medieval Indian coronation ritual. While details vary between texts and lineages, by the eighth century the normative initiation ritual involved a day of preparation and a day of consecration. The preparatory day was devoted to the consecration of the site, which included a request for permission from the snake spirits and autochthonous gods to hold the ceremony. The preparatory day also included the performance of a fire ritual (*homa*) for the sake of purity and auspiciousness. After the maṇḍala was constructed and consecrated by the master, the candidate would be prepared by some teaching. After being presented with a piece of *kusha* or other variety of grass, the candidate would be told to place the consecrated grass under the pillow and to remember whatever dreams might occur in the night. Auspicious dreams (e.g., a sunrise or a view from the pinnacle of a high mountain) would mean that the candidate was appropriate; conversely, inauspicious dreams (e.g., imprisonment or losing one's way in a unknown place) might convince the master than the candidate was inadequate to the task, and cause the consecration to be canceled or postponed.

On the day of the consecration, the candidate would be brought in, sometimes blindfolded, to relate the dreams. The blindfold or screen would then be removed and the maṇḍala revealed. The master would then have the candidate throw a flower into the maṇḍala to determine which of the five families (buddha, *vajra, ratna, padma,* or karma) the person belonged to, so that the appropriate MANTRA and form of the buddha could be conferred. The candidate was then consecrated by anointing from a pot of water, by conferring a vajra-scepter, by bestowing a ritual bell, by placing a crown on the candidate's head, by entrusting a buddha's mantra to the candidate, and by granting the candidate a new name. Other subsidiary consecrations could be added as well, but the above were standard, although the order in which they were granted would vary with the event or lineage. The candidate was instructed especially in the proper use of the mantra and in the ritual of contemplation on the buddha, and was further granted the authority (in some traditions) to become a teacher. Vows of secrecy were essential to this process, even though the content of the secrets continued to change as the understanding of the ritual and its literature progressed. Other vows would include nonrepudiation of mantras, acquiescence to the authority of the buddhas, and acquiescence to the authority of the candidate's master (who was the buddhas' representative), all allied with the general commitment to cultivate the attitudes associated with the Mahāyāna. Increasingly, the candidate was instructed to visualize himself as the buddha or bodhisattva on whom the flower fell during the maṇḍala rite. Finally, the candidate was granted the authority to perform rituals (especially fire rites) associated with pacification, accumulation, subjugation, and destruction; these were traditionally exercised on behalf of patrons and so represented the newly consecrated master's potential source of income.

By the late eighth century, the development and institutionalization of the new "perfected" (*siddha*) figures in Indian Buddhism led to a change in some of the initiatory rituals. In *siddha*-inspired literature, the above rites all came to be subsumed into the category of the "jug" or "ewer" consecration, since the candidate's aspersion from a pot was its hallmark. Added to this were three new forms of consecration, derived from *siddha* rituals, for ascension to kingship over celestial sorcerers (VIDYĀDHARA): the secret consecration, the insight/gnosis consecration, and the fourth consecration. The first was secret, for the master was to copulate with a woman (often a prostitute), and the candidate was instructed to consume the ejaculate. In the insight/gnosis consecration, the candidate himself copulated with the consort, experiencing great bliss as a symbol of liberation. The fourth consecration was the revelation of a symbol to the candidate, who was expected to understand its significance.

These new rituals were not introduced without comment, for they represented a dramatic reorientation toward the fundamental values of Buddhist clerical celibacy. Although multiple opinions on their desirability or necessity were voiced throughout the ninth to twelfth centuries, they were eventually enacted almost exclusively in a visualized form, rather than the literal enactment seen earlier. Over time, the new consecrations were combined with new forms of yoga developed from non-Buddhist analogs and a new set of vows and sacraments (*samaya*) were added to provide a framework for the yogin's subsequent behavior.

See also: **Mahāsiddha; Tantra**

Bibliography

Davidson, Ronald M. *Indian Esoteric Buddhism: A Social History of the Tantric Movement.* New York: Columbia University Press, 2002.

Lessing, Ferdinand D., and Wayman, Alex, trans. *Mkhas Grub Rje's Fundamentals of the Buddhist Trantras.* The Hague, Netherlands, and Paris: Mouton, 1968.

Snellgrove, David L. "The Notion of Divine Kingship in Tantric Buddhism." In *La Regalità Sacra: Contributi al Tema dell' VIII Congresso Internazionale di Storia delle Religioni.* Leiden, Netherlands: Brill, 1959.

Snellgrove, David L. *Indo-Tibetan Buddhism: Indian Buddhists and Their Tibetan Successors,* 2 vols. Boston: Shambhala, 1987.

Strickmann, Michel. "The Consecration Sūtra: A Buddhist Book of Spells." In *Chinese Buddhist Apocrypha,* ed. Robert E. Buswell. Honolulu: University of Hawaii Press, 1990.

Strickmann, Michel. *Mantras et mandarins: Le bouddhisme tantrique en Chine.* Paris: Gallimard, 1996.

RONALD M. DAVIDSON

INOUE ENRYŌ

Inoue Enryō (1858–1919) was an Ōtani-branch Jōdo Shin philosopher and educator. Born into a Jōdo Shin family in Japan's Niigata region, Inoue eventually studied philosophy with Ernest Fenollosa, graduating with a degree in that subject from Tokyo Imperial University in 1885. Inoue was highly critical of the Buddhist clergy of his day and decided that the best way to work for the revitalization of Buddhism in Japan was as a layman. He renounced his status as a Shin cleric in the late 1880s.

Inoue was convinced that philosophy was the key to understanding absolute truth and that Buddhism, properly understood, was consonant with both Western philosophical and modern scientific understandings of the world. To promote the study of philosophy, particularly his Hegelian-tinged, Buddhist philosophical rationalism, Inoue founded the Tetsugakukan (Academy of Philosophy; later Tōyō University) in 1887. An ardent nationalist and opponent to Christianity in Japan, Inoue was a vigorous apologist for Buddhism. Inoue argued that Buddhism provided the best ideological support for modernizing the Japanese nation-state and served as a bulwark against Western missionaries, offering its emotional dimension (the Pure Land traditions) to the masses and its profound intellectual facets (Tendai and Kegon thought) to the elite.

In an effort to uplift those he viewed as the ignorant masses (*gumin*) and combat Christian missionary influence, Inoue promoted various Buddhist social reform activities, including the founding of orphanages, reform schools, and hospitals, as well as more active proselytization efforts by Buddhist organizations. Ever the rationalist, Inoue also embarked on an ambitious project to catalogue and analyze numerous accounts of supernatural phenomena throughout Japan with an eye to debunking empirically the supernatural tales that loomed large in Japanese popular culture.

See also: **Meiji Buddhist Reform; Philosophy**

Bibliography

Figal, Gerald. *Civilization and Monsters: Spirits of Modernity in Meiji Japan.* Durham, NC, and London: Duke University Press, 1999.

Snodgrass, Judith. "The Deployment of Western Philosophy in the Meiji Buddhist Revival." *Eastern Buddhist* 30/2 (1997): 173–198.

RICHARD M. JAFFE

INTERMEDIATE STATES

Intermediate state (Sanskrit, *antarābhava*; Chinese, *zhongyou*; Tibetan, *bardo*) is the interim between death and the next birth. The term refers both to the postmortem state of transition and to the subtle entity that abides in that state. During the early period of Buddhism in India, the status of the intermediate state between lives was a subject of some controversy. The doctrine was not accepted by some early Buddhist schools, including the THERAVĀDA, Vibhajyavāda, MAHĀSĀṂGHIKA, and MAHĪŚĀSAKA. The schools that accepted some version of the theory were the Sarvāstivāda, SAUTRĀNTIKA, Saṃmitiya, Pūrvaśaila, and Dārṣṭāntika.

The doctrinal controversy is described briefly in the *Kathāvatthu* (*Points of Controversy*) of Moggaliputta Tissa (second century B.C.E.). There the problem focuses on how to properly interpret the expression "completed existence within the interval" (*antarābhavūpagaṃ*). Some argued that this phrase referred to the existence of an actual intermediate period between death and rebirth. Others held that such an intermediate period was never taught explicitly by the Buddha and thus does not exist. According to opponents of the intermediate state doctrine, since the Buddha taught that there are only three realms of existence—desire (*kāmadhātu*), form (*rūpadhātu*), and formlessness (*arūpadhātu*)—an intermediary realm cannot be accepted as valid. Even proponents of the doctrine were not always in agreement as to how this intervening realm should best be understood. There were a number of detailed early doctrinal expositions of the intermediate state written in India, such as the second-century compilation *Mahāvibhāṣā* (*Great Exegisis*), a Sarvāstivāda ABHIDHARMA commentary. VASUBANDHU codified the doctrine in his fifth-century ABHIDHARMAKOŚABHĀṢYA, and this became the standard presentation and subsequently the basic model adopted in East Asia and Tibet.

In this monumental work, which represents essentially the position of the Mūlasarvāstivāda school, Vasubandhu compiled all previous arguments in favor of interim existence and offered descriptions of the intermediate state and the liminal entity who abides there. His presentation can be encapsulated in six basic points:

1. The duration of the intermediate state is divided into seven short phases, each lasting no more than a week, for a total of up to seven weeks or forty-nine days;
2. The entity that abides in this interim state is defined as a being that arises between the moment of death and the next state of birth on its way to a new existence;
3. Because this being subsists on fragrance it is called a *gandharva,* meaning literally "that which eats (*arvati*) odors (*gandham*)";
4. The shape and form of this liminal entity resembles that of the beings in the realm where it is to be reborn;
5. Its senses are intact, though in subtle forms; no one can resist it, it cannot be turned away, and it can only be seen by those of its own class and by those with pure divine eyes;
6. Rebirth occurs when the mind (*mati*) of the *gandharva* is troubled by the sight of its future parents having sexual intercourse and when the emotional quality of that mind propels it into a new existence. Accordingly, when the *gandharva* enters the womb it becomes male if it is attracted to its future mother and repulsed by its father, or female if attracted to its future father and repulsed by its mother. These agitated thoughts of desire and repulsion cause the mind to cohere to the semen and blood mixed in the womb just prior to conception. At the point of conception, the psychophysical SKANDHA (AGGREGATES) gradually become coarse and coagulate, the intermediate-state being dies, and a new life is conceived.

There are three conditions, therefore, necessary for conception: The mother must be healthy, the parents must be engaged in sexual intercourse, and a *gandharva,* an intermediate-state being, must be present. These six basic components of the Buddhist intermediate-state doctrine had been formalized by at least the fifth century C.E.

The doctrine is expounded also in a number of Buddhist MAHĀYĀNA sūtras influenced by Abhidharma interpretations, most notably the *Garbhāvakrāntinirdeśa-sūtra* (*Sūtra on Entering the Womb*) and the *Saddharmasmṛtyupasthāna-sūtra* (*Sūtra on Stability in Mindfulness of the True Dharma*). The *Garbhāvakrāntinirdeśa-sūtra* is extant in four recensions, the earliest being a Chinese translation. The later versions from the MŪLASARVĀSTIVĀDA-VINAYA detail the progression of the intermediate-state being from the final moment of death, to conception in the future mother's womb, and subsequently through each week of fetal development. This particular version of the *Garbhāvakrāntinirdeśa* appears to have been the primary source for the descriptions of the intermediate state found in the *Yogācārabhūmi* (*States of Yoga Practice*). The *Saddharmasmṛtyupasthāna-sūtra* is noteworthy in that it includes elaborate discussion of as many as seventeen individual intermediate states. Some features of this exposition accord with earlier Abhidharma formulations, while others resemble later tantric descriptions similar to those found in Tibetan literature.

Over time the doctrine of the intermediate state was reformulated and embellished within the soteriological framework of Tantric Buddhism. A distinctive feature of the tantric reinterpretation of the doctrine was the proliferation of the intermediate state, originally a single period, into a series of distinct and separate phases. Some Buddhist tantric systems enumerated as many as three, four, five, and even six individual intermediate states. This expansion of the concept of interim existence was derived in part by a conflation of the earlier Abhidharma doctrine of the intermediate state with the Mahāyāna idea of a buddha's three bodies (*trikāya*): truth body (*dharmakāya*), enjoyment body (*saṃbhogakāya*), and emanation body (*nirmāṇakāya*). The combination of these conceptual elements was grafted onto an advanced twofold yogic system, which the Tibetans were later to classify as Supreme Yoga Tantra (Sanskrit, *anuttarayoga-tantra*; Tibetan, *rnal 'byor bla na med pa'i rgyud*), involving the successive stages of generation (Sanskrit, *utpannakrama*; Tibetan, *bskyed rim*) and completion (Sanskrit, *sampannakrama*; Tibetan, *rdzogs rim*). This particular tantric program does not appear to have been introduced into China or Japan, but it did enter Tibet as early as the eleventh century through the efforts of Tibetan disciples of Indian tantric adepts (siddha).

One of the most famous and influential of these Indian siddhas was NĀROPA (1016–1100), who codified a diverse system of tantric instruction that would come to be widely known in Tibet as the "Six Doctrines of Nāropa" (Tibetan, *Nā ro chos drug*). In Nāropa's system the intermediate state was expanded to include three separate states:

1. The long period between birth and death, which was identified as the "intermediate state of birth-to-death";
2. The interval between sleep and waking consciousness called the "intermediate state of dreams";
3. The intervening period between death and rebirth identified as the "intermediate state of becoming."

The tradition argued that all three intermediate states provide particularly fruitful opportunities for tantric practice leading eventually to buddhahood itself. The aim of such practice was to actually become embodied as a buddha using special tantric techniques of yoga and contemplation to mix or blend (Tibetan, *bsres ba*) one's experience with the three bodies of a buddha during each of the three transitional periods—in meditation during life, in dreams during sleep, and in the interim state after death. In Tibet this practice of blending the intermediate states with the three embodiments of buddhahood is commonly referred to as "bringing the three bodies to the path" (*sku gsum lam 'khyer*).

In Tibet the tantric reinterpretation of the intermediate state inspired even further innovations. In time there emerged several Tibetan religious systems that posited multiple intermediate states beyond the three separate interim periods developed previously by Indian siddhas like Nāropa. The ritual and literary tradition of the famous TIBETAN BOOK OF THE DEAD (*Bar do thos grol chen mo,* pronounced Bardo thödol), for example, enumerates six individual states, including the three described in Nāropa's scheme and adding:

4. The intermediate state of meditative stabilization;
5. The intermediate state of dying; and
6. The intermediate state of reality-itself, wherein the deceased encounters the true nature of reality manifest as a radiant display of one hundred peaceful and wrathful deities.

In particular, the concept of the intermediate state of reality-itself is derived from the unique doctrines of the Great Perfection tradition that began to emerge in Tibet in the eleventh century and became fully systematized by the late fourteenth century. The Tibetan Great Perfection tradition was promoted largely by the RNYING MA (NYINGMA) and non-Buddhist BON orders.

As for the formal doctrine of the intermediate state in its ritual dimension, Buddhist funeral rites in Tibet and East Asia are timed ideally to coincide with the forty-nine days of postmortem intermediate existence, although it is not uncommon for this prolonged period to be abbreviated depending on the resources and influence of the deceased's family. In Tibet the fully developed liturgical sequence, inscribed in specialized texts such as those belonging to the *Tibetan Book of the Dead,* consists of a variety of offerings for generating merit, tantric initiation rites for the ripening of virtues, prayers of confession and reconciliation in the purification of nonvirtuous karma, and guidance rites for leading the deceased through the perilous intermediate state into the next life.

In East Asia the doctrine of the intermediate state is linked to bureaucratic notions of the judgment of ten postmortem kings and to rituals performed for the benefit of the deceased presumed to be undergoing a kind of purgatory, a period in which the good and bad deeds of the departed are put under judicial review. The ritual actions performed by the living for the penitent dead include the dedication of merit, almsgiving, and the recitation of Buddhist scripture. The general assumption underlying the intermediate-state funeral rites in Tibet and East Asia is that actions performed by the living affect directly the condition of the dead. Buddhist funerals are thus designed to provide for the dead a means of expediting safe passage over death's threshold and of ensuring an auspicious future destiny.

See also: **Cosmology; Death; Mainstream Buddhist Schools; Rebirth; Sarvāstivāda and Mūlasarvāstivāda**

Bibliography

Bareau, André. "Chuu." In *Hōbōgirin,* ed. Jacques May. Paris and Tokyo: L'Academie des Inscriptions et Belles-Lettres, Institut de France, 1979.

Cuevas, Bryan J. "Predecessors and Prototypes: Towards a Conceptual History of the Buddhist Antarābhava." *Numen* 43, no. 3 (1996): 263–302.

Evans-Wentz, W. Y., and Kazi Dawa Samdup, eds. and trans. *The Tibetan Book of the Dead* (1927). New York: Oxford University Press, 2000.

Kritzer, Robert. "Antarābhava in the Vibhāṣā." *Nōtom Damu Joshi Daigaku Kirisutokyō Bunka Kenkyojo Kiyō* (*Maranata*) 3, no. 5 (1997): 69–91.

Kritzer, Robert. "Rūpa and the Antarābhava." *Journal of Indian Philosophy* 28 (2000): 235–272.

Lati Rinbochay, and Hopkins, Jeffrey, trans. *Death, Intermediate State, and Rebirth in Tibetan Buddhism.* Ithaca, NY: Snow Lion, 1979.

Teiser, Stephen F. *The Scripture on the Ten Kings and the Making of Purgatory in Medieval Chinese Buddhism.* Honolulu: University of Hawaii Press, 1994.

Wayman, Alex. "The Intermediate-State Dispute in Buddhism." In *Buddhist Studies in Honor of I. B. Horner,* ed. L. Cousins, Arnold Kunst, and K. R. Norman. Dordrecht, Netherlands, and Boston: Reidel, 1974.

BRYAN J. CUEVAS

IPPEN CHISHIN

Ippen Chishin (1239–1289) was an itinerant monk who popularized Pure Land Buddhist faith in rural areas of Japan during the Kamakura period (1185–1333). His teachings emphasized the doctrine of Other Power (*tariki,* reliance on the saving power of AMITĀBHA Buddha alone), the practice of dancing while chanting Amitābha Buddha's name (*nenbutsu odori*), and the distribution of paper tallies to confirm one's connection to Amitābha Buddha. Today Ippen Chishin is revered as the founder of the Jishū (Time) denomination in Japan.

See also: **Japan; Kamakura Buddhism, Japan; Pure Land Buddhism; Pure Land Schools**

WILLIAM M. BODIFORD

ISLAM AND BUDDHISM

The historical meeting between the various powerful states that drew political legitimacy from either Islam or Buddhism was a violent one. The Arab conquest of Bukhara (in present-day Uzbekistan) in 696 C.E., in which a mosque replaced a monastery, and the Turkic destruction of the important Buddhist monasteries of Nālandā and Vikramaśīla in India in 1202, are widely recognized as the end of Indian Buddhism. Similar devastation was glorified in a Turkic folksong recorded in Al-Kashgari's twelfth-century dictionary, which revels in the desecration of Buddhism during the tenth-century Karakhanid attack on the Uygur Buddhist kingdom of Turfan along the SILK ROAD. With the Inner Asian imperial revival of Buddhism in the twelfth century, however, the direction of religious violence was reversed. The Kara Khitais launched pogroms against Muslims, and Hülegü, a supporter of the Tibetan Phag mo gru pa, killed the 'Abbasid Caliph in 1256.

Of course there were exceptions to these norms of imperial violence. Kabūl Shāh converted to Islam only in 814. When BĀMIYĀN and Gandhāra were seized in 711, Buddhism and Islam coexisted. When Sind was conquered it was decreed that Buddhists, like Christians and Zoroastrians, should be taxed though not killed, as was the case during the reign of Zayn al-'abidīn in Kashmir (1420–1470). Early Arabic sources also note that sometimes Buddhists and Muslims were military allies. Tāranātha's *Rgya gar chos 'byung* (*History of Buddhism in India,* 1608), in accord with other Indian sources, notes that Buddhists rejoiced in the Muslim destruction of Hinduism and records that Buddhists even acted as agents and intermediaries for the Turkic assault on Magadha in central India. The Buddhist–Muslim encounter has manifested a full range of experiences and dialogues.

Arabic translations of Indian Buddhist works reflect the earliest engagement between Buddhism and Islam. These include the animal tales of the *Kalīla wa-Dimna* (*Kalila and Dimna,* ca. eighth century), based on the *Pañcatantra* (*Five Treatises,* ca. 300 C.E.), and the *Kitāb Bilawhar wa-Yūdāsaf* (*The Book of Bilawhar and Yudasaf,* ca. seventh–eighth century), a compilation from various sources of the Buddha biography that became the prototype for the Christian legend of Barlaam and Josaphat. Although these translation projects ceased by the mid-ninth century, Muslim scholars continued to describe and interpret the Buddhist tradition. In the tenth century, Ibn al-Faqīh and Yāqūt described in detail the Buddhist architecture, ritual, and doctrine as witnessed at Nowbahar in Afghanistan. Similarly, Jayhānī's description of Buddhism in his now lost gazetteer *Kitāb al-masālik* (*The Book of Roads*) provided material on Buddhist thought for both Maqdisī and Gardīzī in their brief descriptions of religion in

India. More detailed descriptions of the dharma, as well as the standard categorization of Indian religions, are found in Ibn al-Nadīm's *Fihrist* (*Catalogue,* 987) and Shahrastānī's *Kitāb al-milal wa-n niḥal* (*The Book of Religions and Faiths,* 1125), works superseded only by Rashīd al-Dīn's *Ta'rīkh al-Hind* (*History of India,* ca. 1305/6), which explores at length the Buddha and Buddhist concepts of time as presented by the Kashmiri monk Kamalaśri (dates unknown).

Muslim engagement with Buddhism, however, was not limited to theological and historical works. Islamic architecture derived inspiration from and appropriated localized Buddhist forms across Asia. And in opposition to Islam's well-known iconoclasm, an extensive Muslim trade in Buddhist icons flourished through the tenth century. Indeed, over time the term *bot* (idol, presumably deriving from Buddha) lost its religious significance and became a clichéd metaphor of idealized beauty in Persian poetry.

Extant sources for the Buddhist interpretation of Islam are more limited. The main source is the KĀLACAKRA (*Wheel of Time*), a work composed in India during the early eleventh century at a time of increased Muslim migration, primarily Shi'ite groups fleeing persecution from the Sunni caliphate. The work outlines Muslim dietary laws, circumcision, marriage, the nature of god, and god's relationship to humanity. Why there are not more Buddhist interpretations of Islam is uncertain, though the retreat of Buddhism as a culturally dynamic force certainly played a role.

This retreat was premised on many factors—economics, politics, and most importantly, the growing fusion between Hindu and Buddhist thought, particularly among the laity. A syncretism fueled by Advaita Vedānta and tantric thought also played a role in South Asia's Islamization, as Sufi saints appropriated indigenous Indian religious discourses in transmitting and developing Islam in South Asia. Thus, for a time these traditions engaged one another, and holy sites came to share narratives of sacrality. The most famous of these narratives concerns the footprint on a mountain in Sri Lanka traditionally attributed to the Buddha. In the *Akhbār al-Sīn wa-l-Hind* (*Stories about China and India,* 851), this site was identified as the place where Adam descended after his expulsion from paradise. In the fourteenth century, Ibn Baṭūṭa noted that Muslims, Hindus, and Buddhists all regarded "Adam's Peak" as holy.

Yet amid this South Asian religious multiplicity, Buddhism became intellectually isolated, losing both royal and lay support. Chinese pilgrims to India witnessed this diminishing interest and recorded the concurrent disappearance of Buddhist temples and monasteries. Similarly, artistic remains from the period reflect a systematic shift of royal patronage from Buddhism to Hinduism. Although the Turkic destruction of two monasteries in 1202 is held up as the ultimate demise of Buddhism in India, seventy-eight Hindu temples were also destroyed in the creation of an Indo-Muslim state. Islam was a threat, but Buddhism's inevitable absorption into the amorphous doctrinal and ritual category of Hinduism was a greater one.

This transition occurred so seamlessly in Southeast Asia that when Islam finally arrived, the pre-Hindu layer of Buddhist religious history and culture was largely forgotten except in its famous monuments. In Java, Buddhism eventually merged into tantric Śaivism, only to be displaced by Islam after royal conversion in the fourteenth century, a trajectory also found in Kashmir. More often, Buddhist sources wrote of fearing Hinduization rather than defeat by Muslim forces. The nexus of Buddhism's imminent internal absorption into Hinduism and the external threat posed by Islam is most eloquently captured in the central eschatological myth of the *Kālacakra.* This narrative refashioned the Hindu myth of Viṣṇu's final avatar Kalkin Cakrin into a Buddhist apocalypse where Kalkin rides out of Shambhala, the mythical kingdom where the Buddha's final teachings are preserved, and kills the Muslims who have taken over the world, ushering in an age of pure dharma. This vision of Islamic perfidy has influenced Buddhist representations of Islam up to the present time.

In modern Buddhist states, these negative images are often framed in terms of such categories as ethnonational identity, politics, and demographics, with at times devastating consequences, as witnessed in Burma (Myanmar), where, in Arakan State, a predominantly Muslim area, the Burmese government has carried out policies of institutionalized discrimination including forced labor, restrictions on freedom of movement, and destruction of mosques. Elsewhere, however, dialogue between the traditions is again progressing as Muslim and Buddhist states and citizens grapple with the religious consequences of migration and conversion.

See also: **Indonesia and the Malay Peninsula; Nationalism and Buddhism; Persecutions; Politics and Buddhism; Thailand**

Bibliography

Barthold, V. V. *Turkestan Down to the Mongol Invasion.* Philadelphia: Porcupine Press, 1977.

Beal, Samuel. *Chinese Accounts of India: Translated from the Chinese of Hiuen Tsiang.* Calcutta: Susil Gupta, 1958.

Bechert, Heinz. "The Buddhayana of Indonesia." *Journal of the Pāli Text Society* 9 (1981): 10–21.

de Silva, K. M., et al., eds. *Ethnic Conflict in Buddhist Societies: Sri Lanka, Thailand, and Burma.* Boulder, CO: Westview Press, 1988.

Eaton, Richard M. "Temple Desecration and Indo-Muslim States." In *Essays on Islam and Indian History,* ed. Richard Eaton. New York: Oxford University Press, 2000.

Hasan, Perween. "Sultanate Mosques and Continuity in Bengal Architecture." *Muqarnas* 6 (1989): 58–74.

Huntington, Susan L. *The "Pala-Sena" Schools of Sculpture.* Leiden, Netherlands: Brill, 1984.

I-ching. *A Record of the Buddhist Religion as Practiced in India and the Malay Archipelago (A.D. 671–695),* tr. J. Takakasu. Delhi: Munshiram Manoharlal, 1966.

Ishii, Yoneo. "Thai Muslims and the Royal Patonage of Religion." *Law and Society Review* 28 (1994): 453–460.

Jahn, Karl. *Rashīd al-Dīn's History of India.* The Hague, Netherlands: Mouton, 1965.

Knodel, John, et al. "Religion and Reproduction: Muslims in Buddhist Thailand." *Population Studies* 53 (1999): 149–164.

Lawrence, Bruce B. *Shahrastānī on the Indian Religions.* The Hague, Netherlands: Mouton, 1976.

Newman, John. "Islam in the Kālacakra Tantra." *Journal of the International Association of Buddhist Studies* 21 (1998): 311–371.

Roy, Asim. *The Islamic Syncretistic Tradition in Bengal.* Princeton, NJ: Princeton University Press, 1983.

Smith, Jane I. "Early Muslim Accounts of Buddhism in India." *Studies in Islam* 10 (1973): 87–100.

Tāranātha. *History of Buddhism in India,* tr. Lama Chimpa and Alaka Chattopadhyaya. Delhi: Motilal Banarsidas, 1990.

JOHAN ELVERSKOG

J

JAINISM AND BUDDHISM

Jainism and Buddhism have a common origin in the culture of world-renunciation that developed in India from around the seventh century B.C.E. This common origin can be confirmed by the many similarities between their respective ancient codes of practice, and the two traditions have always shared an acceptance of the transformative powers of human effort in effecting freedom from REBIRTH.

Although evidence beyond that afforded by partisan texts is not available, Jainism can be judged to be the older religion because from a relatively early period it claimed as authoritative a teacher called Pārśva, who can reasonably be dated to around two centuries before the Buddha. Mahāvīra, who is generally credited with being the "founder" of Jainism, appears to have built upon Pārśva's teachings. Jainism eventually located Pārśva and Mahāvīra as the twenty-third and twenty-fourth of a succession of teachers called fordmaker (*tīrthaṅkara*) or conqueror (*jina*). The word *jina* is the source of the Sanskrit name *Jaina,* used to refer to a follower of these teachers, although the earliest term to designate them was *nigaṇṭha* (bondless). While early Buddhism developed a succession of twenty-five buddhas, most likely under the influence of Jainism, both traditions assert that their teachings are uncreated, without beginning or end, and outside the parameters of historical time.

The date of Mahāvīra relies on synchronicity with that of the Buddha, who is now regarded by scholars as having lived in the fifth century B.C.E. Although the two teachers were contemporaries who lived in the same area of the Ganges basin, there is no record of them having met. The *Saṅgīti-sutta* of the *Dīghanikāya* describes the strife that broke out in the Jain community after Mahāvīra's death and the Buddha's contrast of this with the stability of his own teaching and followers. Mahāvīra, under the name of Nigaṇṭha Nātaputta, is conventionally located by early Buddhist scripture within a group of six rival ascetics (*śramaṇa*) who taught a variety of false doctrines. Nigaṇṭha Nātaputta is associated with a "fourfold restraint" with regard to evil, which, in the light of the fact that Mahāvīra taught five "great vows," suggests that the early Buddhists were familiar with members of the community of the earlier Jain teacher, Pārśva.

The Pāli CANON views the Jains in inimical terms and frequently describes ascetic and lay followers of Mahāvīra joining the Buddhist community. Jain doctrine advocated the existence of a permanent soul or life monad (*jīva*) that changed only in respect to its modifications, a standpoint also applied to reality as a whole. Such a view was very much at variance with Buddhist teaching, which denied the possibility of the existence of entities that were not impermanent or conditioned. Buddhism also rejected as fruitless Jainism's strong ascetic ethos, which held that only fasting and intense forms of religious exercise would lead to liberation. A further area of Jain teaching that the Buddhists found inadequate was that of intentionality. Although the Jains were aware of the role of mental attitude in determining the moral tone of an action, the Buddhists accused them of advocating a crude mechanistic approach to agency and retribution.

The Jains, for their part, regarded the Buddhists as incorrigibly lax in their behavior and as promoting a view of the momentary nature of the world that verged on nihilism in that moral retribution could not operate without some kind of permanent self. According to one medieval writer of the Digambara sect, the Buddha himself had originally been a Jain monk who abandoned the true path because of his inability cope with its rigorous demands. Buddhism's claims to be nonviolent were rejected on the grounds that Buddhism lacked Jainism's radical analysis of reality as composed of embodied, eternally existing souls, and the Buddhists, whether renouncers or laity, were portrayed by their vegetarian opponents as habitual meat eaters. MAHĀYĀNA Buddhism's teaching of ŚŪNYATĀ (EMPTINESS) was stigmatized by the Jains as promoting a brand of illusionism where no ethical values could hold sway, while the bodhisattva's supposed postponement of enlightenment to aid others' attainment of the goal was deemed to be illogical because it entailed a possible situation in which all beings could be in a state of liberation at one and the same time, thus voiding the realms of rebirth and liberation of any distinct meaning.

In the light of these differences, it might appear difficult to locate areas of interaction or mutual influence between the two traditions. However, a consistent Jain interest in Buddhist learning can be seen in the use of the term *basket* (*piḍaga*) to refer to their scriptures (like the Buddhist expression *tripiṭaka*) and the fact that the titles of several Jain works are modeled on Buddhist originals. Particularly noteworthy is the eighth-century teacher Haribhadra, who wrote several works in which he pointed to soteriological similarities between Jainism and Buddhism. From the doctrinal perspective, it is likely that the Jains borrowed the term *pudgala* (atom) from Buddhism, where, at least among the Sarvāstivādins and the Vātsīputrīyas, the term carried the sense of the individual perceived as an aggregate. As for ritual, a Buddhist text on mantras, the *Vasudha ¯rādhāraṇī* (*The Magic Formula of the Goddess Vasudhārā*), has been used by the Jains of Gujarat for the last three centuries.

Certain aspects of early Buddhist meditation practice that relate to the suppression of bodily and mental activity and the senses suggest some sort of external influence, most likely Jain, since such techniques are otherwise said to have been rejected by the Buddha. The Buddhists also appear to have been obliged to consider the nature of the Buddha's omniscience in light of the Jain claim that Mahāvīra and other enlightened people were, as a result of the purification of their souls from karmic accretion, literally "all-knowing" with regard to all constituent elements of the universe in every temporal and spatial location simultaneously. Omniscience was ascribed to the Buddha in the early texts only in respect to aspects of the religious path. Later Buddhism attributed to him the capacity to know all objects, but only individually, each at one time.

See also: **Hinduism and Buddhism; Karma (Action)**

Bibliography

Balbir, Nalini. "Jain-Buddhist Dialogue: Material from the Pāli Scriptures." *Journal of the Pali Text Society* 26 (2000): 1–42.

Bollee, W. B. "Buddhists and Buddhism in the Earlier Literature of the Śvetāmbara Jains." In *Buddhist Studies in Honour of I. B. Horner,* ed. L. Cousins, A. Kunst, and K. R. Norman. Boston and Dordrecht, Netherlands: Reidel, 1974.

Bronkhorst, Johannes. "The Buddha and the Jainas Reconsidered." *Asiatische Studien/Etudes Asiatiques* 49 (1995): 333–50.

Dundas, Paul. *The Jains,* 2nd revised edition. London and New York: Routledge, 2002.

Jaini, Padmanabh S. *Collected Papers on Buddhist Studies.* Delhi: Motilal Banarsidass, 2001.

Tatia, N. "The Interaction of Jainism and Buddhism and Its Impact on the History of Buddhist Monasticism." In *Studies in History of Buddhism: Papers Presented at the International Conference on the History of Buddhism at the University of Wisconsin, Madison, August 19–21, 1976,* ed. A. K. Narain. Delhi: B. R. Publishing, 1980.

PAUL DUNDAS

JAPAN

Buddhism in contemporary Japan exhibits several distinctive characteristics. In a country that sometimes prides itself on having achieved a secular society of the sort predicted for modernity by Max Weber, the Buddhist religion often seems marginal to contemporary Japanese culture. Yet surveys of the populace reveal that a large majority (roughly 75%) identifies itself as Buddhist. These same surveys indicate that an even larger majority sees itself as Shintō, suggesting that, at least for many Japanese, being Buddhist does not necessarily entail exclusive allegiance to the religion. Indeed, it is sometimes said that Japanese are born Shintō (i.e., receive blessings from a Shintō shrine at birth) and die Buddhist (receive Buddhist funeral and memorial services). The division of spiritual labor here tells us something not only about the fluid character of religious identities but about one of the primary functions of Buddhism in contemporary society. If Buddhism often seems marginal to public life, it remains central to private life through its role in the care and commemoration of the family dead.

Contemporary organization

The representative institution of contemporary Buddhism is the local temple, which serves as the residence of a married cleric and his family. The temple is supported by a lay membership, for which it provides a calendar of rituals and festivals, occasional pastoral care, and especially funerals and memorial services. Such local institutions usually represent branch temples (*matsuji*) of the many denominations, or schools (*shū*), into which Buddhism is divided. These organizations, registered with the government as religious corporations (*shūkyō hōjin*), are typically centered in a main temple (*honzan*), which serves as symbolic and administrative headquarters. The larger denominations, which can claim thousands of local temples, may include several monastic centers, as well as parochial schools and universities. Whether large or small, the denominations operate as independent religious entities, with their own clergy and real property, their own distinctive scriptures and rituals, and their own lay membership. There is no significant ecumenical body that governs the Buddhist community as a whole. Hence, in institutional terms, Japanese Buddhism is simply the sum of its denominations, and being a Buddhist means being a member of one of the denominations.

The various Buddhist organizations are typically divided into two categories: denominations that trace their origins to ancient and medieval times, and the so-called new religions (*shin shūkyō*), founded in modern times. The former category is often understood as consisting of six sets of denominations, grouped on the basis of their historical association with particular traditional forms of Japanese Buddhism: (1) denominations based at temples in the ancient capital of Nara (e.g., the relatively small Hossō shū, Kegon shū, Risshū, and Shingon risshū); (2) denominations associated with the Tendai tradition; (3) denominations associated with the Shingon tradition; (4) denominations associated with the Pure Land form (e.g., the large Jōdo shū, and still larger Honganji and Ōtani branches of the Jōdo shinshū); (5) denominations associated with Zen (e.g., the large Sōtō shū, the small Ōbaku shū, and the various branches of the Rinzai shū); and (6) denominations associated with the tradition of NICHIREN (e.g., the Nichiren shū and Nichiren shōshū). These groupings do not typically reflect institutional affiliations; contrary to common usage, there is no organization that could be called, for example, the Zen school or the Pure Land school.

In the category of new religions, there is a wide variety of organizations, from small local groups, to large national, and even international, bodies such as the SŌKA GAKKAI. A few date back to the mid-nineteenth century; most of the largest, such as Sōka Gakkai, Reiyūkai, and Risshō kyōseikai, were founded during the first half of the twentieth century and flourished following World War II; still others arose in the last decades of the twentieth century, the most recent sometimes being referred to as the "new new religions" (*shin shin shūkyō*). Occasionally these organizations represent lay movements within a traditional denomination (such as Shinnyoen within a branch of Shingon or, until 1991, Sōka Gakkai within Nichiren shōshū), but for the most part they are wholly independent bodies, typically founded and run by a lay leadership. The older, more established organizations function much like the traditional denominations in providing services to a stable membership of lay households; the newer groups tend to be tailored somewhat more to the spiritual aspirations of individual converts. Some organizations base their teachings primarily on texts of the Buddhist canon, perhaps most often on the LOTUS SŪTRA (SADDHARMAPUṆḌARĪKA-SŪTRA); others have developed a distinctive scriptural corpus, which may combine traditional Buddhist material with elements drawn from other sources. Indeed, within the broad category of new religions are organizations, such as the notorious Aum shinrikyō, so eclectic in their beliefs and practices that it is difficult to identify them as Buddhist.

If the identification of some of the new religions as Buddhist may mask their more complex religious characters, the standard division of contemporary Buddhism into traditional denominations and new religions may also obscure as much as it reveals. The category of traditional denominations, for example, may suggest an orthodox, historically sanctioned heritage reaching back into premodern times, yet many of the contemporary forms of these denominations owe much to the same modern developments that produced the new religions. By the same token, the tendency, ascribed to the new religions, to incorporate into their Buddhism elements drawn from other sources, such as Shintō and popular religion, has an ancient history common to all the traditional denominations.

Still, whether or not they can easily be applied to the contemporary scene, the two categories can be useful in revealing tensions, present throughout the history of Japanese Buddhism, between tradition and innovation, orthodoxy and heterodoxy, elite establishment and popular practice.

Early modern developments

Many of the distinctive characteristics of the contemporary Japanese Buddhist institution have their origins in government policies of the Meiji period (1868–1912) and the long Edo (or Tokugawa) period (1600–1868) that preceded it. In the years immediately following the revolution that overthrew the Tokugawa administration, the new Meiji government sought to establish an officially sanctioned Shintō in support of imperial rule. It thus drew a sharp, and historically dubious, distinction between a native Shintō and the imported Buddhism, and sought institutionally to separate the two—a policy that had the practical effect of a brief but severe persecution of many Buddhist establishments. In the end, the government adopted a policy that at once separated church and state and reasserted state authority over the church: On the one hand, it revoked the old Tokugawa laws governing the clergy, decriminalizing violations of the Buddhist precepts and allowing the clerical marriage that has now become common; on the other hand, it carried forward the Tokugawa practice of legal recognition and regulation of Buddhist organizations, setting the precedent for the pattern of religious corporations that we see today.

The contemporary pattern of separate denominations with branch temples serving a local congregation of member households can be understood as a remnant of the Tokugawa government's administration of Buddhism through what are known as the *honmatsu* and *terauke* systems. The former term refers to the organization of the Buddhist institutions into a fixed set of sanctioned denominations, each governed from a headquarters responsible to the secular authorities. The latter term refers to the practice of requiring lay households to register their members at a recognized local temple. These two systems, developed during the seventeenth century in order to regulate both the Buddhist institutions and the religious options of the populace, had the effect of establishing Buddhism as a branch of government administration and the local temples as the registrars of the citizenry.

Such an arrangement assured Buddhism throughout the Edo period of both government support and popular patronage; and indeed, though the period is sometimes regarded as one of Buddhist decline, in many ways the religion flourished. Not only did many of the sanctioned denominations thrive as institutions, but the period also witnessed a marked growth in the popularity of Buddhist funeral rites and pilgrimage to Buddhist sacred sites that cut across sectarian divides. It also saw the persistence of unauthorized Buddhist communities and the rise of new religious fraternities outside the sanctioned ecclesiastical establishment. And it fostered within that establishment the development of Buddhist centers of sectarian learning (*shūgaku*) that generated scholarship on the history, texts, and doctrines of the various denominations.

The Buddhist sectarian scholarship that developed during the Edo period and continued into the twentieth century did much to frame the modern understanding of the religion. In general, it may be said that such scholarship sought to create a systematic account of the history and teachings of each school: to establish the orthodox tenets (*kyōgi*) of the school, to define the corpus of its scriptural canon, and to provide a history of its origins and transmission. In more modern times, when attempts were made to tell the story of Japanese Buddhism as a whole, these separate sectarian accounts were often simply brought together in a collection of loosely related narratives. Indeed, to this day, the story of Buddhism in Japan is often told primarily through an accounting of the basic doctrines and founding figures recognized by the major denominations (or their groupings into related traditions). Because of the emphasis on the founders, the history of the religion is typically punctuated by the dates of the origins of the schools, which fall into three distinct phases, located in the periods of Nara (710–784), Heian (794–1185), and Kamakura (1185–1333).

The first of these phases covers those schools (traditionally numbered as six) founded in the years between the introduction of Buddhism from the mainland (usually dated 552) and the end of the Nara. The second is associated with the two schools of Tendai and Shingon, introduced near the start of the Heian period. To the last are assigned the traditions of Zen, Pure Land, and Nichiren, all of which look back to founding figures in the Kamakura period. To the extent that these three periods are plotted in a larger historical narrative, it is often one of recurrent spiritual renewal and decline. Thus, the founding of the Heian schools of Tendai and Shingon are seen as a reaction by the founders (SAICHŌ and KŪKAI, respectively) against the stale scholarship and corrupt politics of the Nara Bud-

The Kinkakuji (Golden Pavilion Temple) in Kyoto, Japan, so called because it is covered in gold leaf. © Chris Lisle/Corbis. Reproduced by permission.

dhist establishment, and the rise of the "new Buddhism of the Kamakura" (*kamakura shin bukkyō*) is understood as a reformation, led by famous founders such as HŌNEN, SHINRAN, DŌGEN, and Nichiren, in response to a Heian Buddhism increasingly dominated by the secular concerns of its aristocratic patrons. The period following the Kamakura is often seen as another time of decline, during which the reforming spirit of the Kamakura founders was lost once again.

Needless to say, this neatly articulated account of the history of the various schools, however well it may reflect the self-understanding of the modern denominations, is hardly the whole, or necessarily the most instructive, story of Buddhism in Japan. Not surprisingly, it has been challenged by historians who seek a broader understanding of the character of the religion and its role in society. For such historians, an account that focuses on the sectarian traditions of the schools and the lives and teachings of their founding figures exaggerates not only the historical significance of a few great men but the historical status of the schools themselves. Even in the early modern and modern periods, when the institutional and intellectual definitions of the schools are fairly well established, popular Buddhist belief and practice has often, perhaps typically, been oblivious of sectarian distinctions, and the meaning of such distinctions during the premodern period developed only gradually over a millennium of Japanese history.

Premodern background

The founding of the Nara schools is but a minor note in the early history of Japanese Buddhism, which is itself but part of a larger story of the formation of a central Japanese court and its wholesale importation of continental culture during the seventh and eighth centuries. While the transmission of Chinese Buddhist books and ideas was certainly one feature of this process, far more conspicuous was the creation of a court-supported clerical establishment, housed at great monasteries in and around the capital cities. Much of the subsequent institutional history of Japanese Buddhism revolves around the shifting relations between the central government and the increasingly powerful and independent monastic centers.

Throughout the eighth century, the court sought to bring Buddhism under civil control through the promulgation of regulations (*sōniryō*) governing the ordination, offices, and activities of monks and nuns. Court ambitions for a national Buddhism administered from the capital reached its apogee during the middle of the century, with the government's dedication of the great bronze buddha image of Tōdaiji in Nara and the founding of national monasteries (*kokubunji*) in the provinces. What came to be known as the Nara schools of Buddhism represent simply the curriculum of the scholar monks of Tōdaiji and other officially recognized institutions in the capital, a curriculum of particular Buddhist texts for the study of which the government came to sponsor an annual allotment of ordination rights (*nenbun dosha*).

Though the court would continue to claim authority to regulate the religion, the vision of a national Buddhism did not survive the Nara period. Already in this period, it is clear from government efforts to restrict it that Buddhism was taking on an independent life of its own, in the proliferation of unofficial monasteries sponsored by the laity (*chikishiji*), the development of independent centers of Buddhist practice, often associated with sacred mountains, and the unauthorized activities of popular preachers, healers, wonder-workers, and the like. These trends toward an independent Buddhism would only increase as the religion spread throughout the country and into all levels of society during the succeeding Heian period.

The growing autonomy of Buddhism in the Heian period was occasioned not only by the diffusion of the religion to the populace but by the consolidation of power in the monastic centers. Just as the major aristocratic families came increasingly to dominate the court through the independent means provided by their private land holdings, so too certain monasteries acquired extensive property rights that made them significant socioeconomic institutions. As such, they were players in Heian politics, supported by, and in turn supporting, one or another faction at court; as a result, their elite clergy interacted with, and was itself often drawn from the scions of, the aristocracy. This development produced what is often referred to as Heian "aristocratic Buddhism," with its ornate art and architecture, its elegant literary expression, and its elaborate ritual performance.

The new style of autonomous Buddhist institution is well represented by Tōdaiji, with its historic status as a national shrine, and the great Kōfukuji and Kasuga Shrine complex, with its links to the powerful Fujiwara clan. But the Nara monasteries were challenged and often superseded by institutions in and around the new capital of Heian (modern Kyoto), of which the most historically influential became Enryakuji, on Mount Hiei, and (to a somewhat lesser extent) Tōji. The former was the seat of the Tendai school; the latter was the metropolitan base of the Shingon (which had established itself on isolated Mount Kōya). Like Tōdaiji, Kōfukuji, and other major monasteries, these institutions not only held significant land rights but developed networks of subsidiary temples that made them, in effect, the headquarters of extended organizations. The identity of the Tendai and Shingon organizations was ritually reinforced by the adoption of new, private rites of ordination (*tokudo*) and initiation (*kanjō*) that supplemented and in some cases even replaced the standard rituals of Buddhist clerical practice. Thus, the first steps were taken toward a division of the Buddhist community into ritually distinct and institutionally separate ecclesiastic bodies.

It is sometimes suggested that these great Buddhist institutions went into decline at the end of the Heian, to be replaced by the new Buddhism of the Kamakura period. In fact, such was their power and prestige that they continued to exercise great influence well into medieval times, as what is sometimes called by historians the exoteric-esoteric establishment (*Kenmitsu taisei*). Just as the rise of the provincial warriors in the Kamakura did not displace the old court aristocracy but rather added new layers of power, so too the development of new Buddhist movements did not replace the establishment but introduced additional options of religious belief, practice, and organization. While some of these options were resisted by members of the establishment, others were welcomed and, indeed, incorporated into the catholic Buddhism of the great monasteries.

The decision to resist or accept rested heavily on the degree to which spokesmen for the new movements aggressively sought patronage in order to establish separate institutions. Thus, to cite the two most conspicuous examples of the time, while many within the Nara-Heian establishment saw both the Pure Land preachers' call to faith in AMITĀBHA (Amida) and the Zen masters' emphasis on meditation as legitimate forms of Buddhist teaching, they opposed those versions of the teachings that sought to convert the laity to the new movements as alternatives to other forms of Buddhism. In this issue, we see not simply a familiar institutional struggle for patronage but the rise of a novel model of religious organization, in which the laity identifies with, and becomes, in effect, a member of a particular Buddhist faction. The new model would become increasingly popular during the medieval period (especially in the traditions of Pure Land, Nichiren, and Sōtō Zen) and led to the development of powerful national organizations that could claim millions of adherents. This is the prime institutional development that made possible the formal division of Japanese Buddhism into the denominations of early modern and modern times.

Belief and practice

The outreach to lay believers characteristic of some of the new movements of the twelfth and thirteenth centuries involved not only novel institutional models but new styles of Buddhist belief and practice. Conspicuous among these is a style, sometimes termed "selective Buddhism" (*senchaku bukkyō*), in which the believer is urged to exclusive faith in a particular version of Buddhist teaching and exclusive commitment to a particular form of spiritual practice. So, for example, preachers of the Pure Land movement called for abandonment of the spiritual exercises of the bodhisattva path in favor of faith in the vow of the Buddha Amida to take his devotees into his Western Pure Land. Similarly, followers of the Tendai reformer Nichiren sharply criticized other forms of Buddhism and taught exclusive resort to the *Lotus Sūtra* and its revelation of the ongoing ministry of the Buddha Śākyamuni. In both these movements, the new selective style was justified in part by the doctrine that Buddhist history had entered its "final age" (*mappō*), a period of spiritual decline during which it was no longer possible to achieve buddhahood through the traditional practices of the monastic community.

This new religious style of popular outreach, lay organization, and sectarian faith is often said to constitute a "reformation" of Japanese Buddhism, through which the religion emerged from the confines of the cloister into the lives of ordinary people. Yet this account, based heavily on a model provided by the Pure Land tradition (and influenced in modern times by Western religious historiography), hardly does justice to the full range of Buddhism in the late Heian and Kamakura periods. It does not, for example, adequately account for one of the most conspicuous developments of the age: the renewed emphasis within the Buddhist establishment on monastic discipline and the founding of major centers of Chinese-style monas-

Monks of Tōfukuji, Kyoto, going out to beg for alms, 1992.

tic practice within the new Zen movement. And it tells us little about the religious lives of the bulk of Buddhists, who neither entered the monasteries nor joined the new movements. Hence, historians of the period warn against a narrow focus on the novel teachings of the new Kamakura movements, often preferring to see them against the background of an older, broader religious style of thought and practice that permeated the medieval Buddhist world—a style we may loosely call *mikkyō*, or "esoteric teachings."

The esoteric style developed initially within the schools of Tendai and Shingon but spread widely during the Heian period to influence all forms of Japanese Buddhism. This style was built on a common MAHĀYĀNA vision of universal buddhahood—universal both in the metaphysical sense that the "dharma body" of the buddha was present in all things and all people, and in the soteriological sense that all people could themselves become buddhas through the realization of this presence. Given such a vision—what scholars sometimes call ORIGINAL ENLIGHTENMENT

The famous Zen garden at the Ryōanji, Kyoto, Japan, which probably dates from the late fifteenth century. © Abe Ahn and Tim Ciccone, www.orientalarchitecture.com. Reproduced by permission.

(HONGAKU) thought—the chief religious issue was often cast in terms less of how one might purify and perfect the self than of how one might best contact the realm of universal buddhahood and tap into its power. The new Buddhist movements of the Kamakura period can themselves be seen as variant strategies for answering this question.

Thus, for example, the Pure Land teachings tended to treat the symbol of buddhahood in anthropomorphic terms, as the figure of the Buddha AMITĀBHA, and to understand the universality of enlightenment as the unlimited power of Amitābha's compassionate concern for all beings. The religious strategy, then, was to access this power by surrendering the pride that separated us from Amitābha, humbly accepting his help, and calling his name (*nenbutsu*) in faith and thanksgiving. In contrast, the new Zen movement preferred to think of universal buddhahood less in anthropomorphic than in epistemological terms, as a subliminal mode of consciousness shared by all beings. Here, the prime religious problem lay not in pride but in the habits of thought that obscured the enlightened consciousness, and the chief religious strategy was to suspend such habits, through Zen meditation (*zazen*), in order to "uncover" the buddha mind within.

For its own part, the esoteric tradition itself tended to conceive of buddhahood in cosmological terms, as the hidden macrocosm of which the human world was the manifest embodiment. An elaborate system of homologies was developed between the properties of the buddha realm and the physical features of Japan, between the deities of the Buddhist pantheon and the local gods of Japan, between the virtues of the cosmic buddha and the psychophysical characteristics of the individual, and so on. The chief means of communication between the two realms was ritual practice—recitation of spells and prayers, performance of mystic gestures, repentance, sacrifice, PILGRIMAGE, and the like—through which the forces of the other realm were contacted and channeled into this world, and the people and places of this world were mystically empowered by (or revealed as) the sacred realities of the buddha realm.

This cosmological style of religion is often now held up as one of the key unifying forces of Japanese Buddhism, a force that flows across history, from the

Heian, through the medieval period, and even into modern times; a force that spreads across the boundaries of clerical and lay communities or elite and popular Buddhism—a force, in fact, that reaches beyond Buddhism proper into Shintō and FOLK RELIGION, allowing a remarkable freedom of accommodation between the more universal Buddhist vision and the various local Japanese beliefs and practices. The prevalence of this style may help to explain why Japanese Buddhists tend to think of their dead as ancestral "buddha" (*hotoke*) spirits dwelling in the other world, and why, though the Buddhist denominations today are so sharply divided in formal doctrine and institutional organization, they are so similar in their social function as the intermediaries between the realms of the living and the dead.

See also: **Chan School; Clerical Marriage in Japan; Exoteric-Esoteric (Kenmitsu) Buddhism in Japan; Hōryūji and Tōdaiji; Japan, Buddhist Art in; Japanese Royal Family and Buddhism; Kamakura Buddhism, Japan; Mahāyāna Precepts in Japan; Meiji Buddhist Reform; Nara Buddhism; Parish (Danka, Terauke) System in Japan; Pure Land Schools; Shingon Buddhism, Japan; Shintō (Honji Suijaku) and Buddhism; Tiantai School; Temple System in Japan**

Bibliography

Abé, Ryūichi. *The Weaving of Mantra: Kūkai and the Construction of Esoteric Buddhist Discourse.* New York: Columbia University Press, 1999.

Bielefeldt, Carl. *Dōgen's Manuals of Zen Meditation.* Berkeley: University of California Press, 1988.

Blum, Mark L. *The Origins and Development of Pure Land Buddhism: A Study and Translation of Gyōnen's Jōdo Hōmon Genrushō.* New York: Oxford University Press, 2002.

Bodiford, William. *Sōtō Zen in Medieval Japan.* Honolulu: University of Hawaii Press, 1993.

Collcutt, Martin. *Five Mountains: The Rinzai Zen Monastic Institution in Medieval Japan.* Cambridge, MA: Harvard University Press, 1981.

Dobbins, James C. *Jōdo Shinshū: Shin Buddhism in Medieval Japan.* Honolulu: University of Hawaii Press, 2002.

Fauré, Bernard. *Visions of Power: Imagining Medieval Japanese Buddhism.* Princeton, NJ: Princeton University Press, 1996.

Grapard, Allan G. *The Protocol of the Gods: A Study of the Kasuga Cult in Japanese History.* Berkeley: University of California Press, 1992.

Groner, Paul. *Ryōgen: The Restoration and Transformation of the Tendai School.* Honolulu: University of Hawaii Press, 2000.

Groner, Paul. *Saichō: The Establishment of the Japanese Tendai School.* Honolulu: University of Hawaii Press, 2002.

Jaffe, Richard M. *Neither Monk nor Layman: Clerical Marriage in Modern Japanese Buddhism.* Princeton, NJ: Princeton University Press, 2001.

Kasahara, Kazuo, ed. *A History of Japanese Religion.* Tokyo: Kosei Publishing, 2001.

Ketelaar, James. *Of Heretics and Martyrs in Meiji Japan: Buddhism and Its Persecution.* Princeton, NJ: Princeton University Press, 1990.

Lafleur, William R. *The Karma of Words: Buddhism and the Literary Arts in Medieval Japan.* Berkeley: University of California Press, 1983.

McMullin, Neil. *Buddhism and the State in Sixteenth Century Japan.* Princeton, NJ: Princeton University Press, 1984.

Payne, Richard K., ed. *Re-Visioning Kamakura Buddhism.* Honolulu: University of Hawaii Press, 1999.

Reader, Ian. *Religion in Contemporary Japan.* Honolulu: University of Hawaii Press, 1991.

Ruppert, Brian D. *Jewel in the Ashes: Buddha Relics and Power in Early Medieval Japan.* Cambridge, MA: Harvard University Press, 2000.

Stone, Jacqueline. *Original Enlightenment and the Transformation of Medieval Japanese Buddhism.* Honolulu: University of Hawaii Press, 1999.

Tamamura Yoshio. *Japanese Buddhism: A Cultural History.* Tokyo: Charles Tuttle, 2001.

Tanabe, George J., Jr. *Myōe the Dreamkeeper: Fantasy and Knowledge in Early Kamakura Buddhism.* Cambridge, MA: Harvard University Press, 1992.

Tanabe, George J., Jr., ed. *Religions of Japan in Practice.* Princeton, NJ: Princeton University Press, 1999.

Yamasaki, Taiko. *Shingon: Japanese Esoteric Buddhism.* Boston: Shambala Publications, 1988.

CARL BIELEFELDT

JAPAN, BUDDHIST ART IN

The juxtaposition of the words *Buddhist* and *art* may seem natural, requiring no comment. But this concept is of recent vintage and stems from encounters between traditional societies and modern interpreters. In the case of Japan, the creation of an elite canon of "Buddhist art" took place in the late nineteenth century, building upon earlier precedents. Over the twentieth century, numerous temple buildings, icons, and other objects received state-approved designations as National Treasure, Important Cultural Property, and

Important Art Object. Artifacts not deemed artistically or historically important have receded from view. Many "art objects" left temple precincts for the art market and now reside in museums and private collections both in Japan and abroad. Icons in temple settings, whether on permanent view or revealed periodically, as often submit to the gaze of tourists and photographers as to visiting worshippers or temple congregations.

Japanese Buddhist art refers primarily to sculpture and painting of the seventh through thirteenth centuries, which is perceived to be the most creative period. Canonical objects were commissioned by elite patrons who founded temples and engaged the services of metalworkers, woodcarvers, painters, weavers, and lacquerers—artisans in every media. Initially, people without wealth and property who contributed their labor and skill in the service of the elite would not have participated in the religious practices their productions served. Over time some artisans rose in status as they held lower aristocratic rank or obtained honorary Buddhist titles for their service at court. By the thirteenth century some painters and carvers joined their patrons as donors, even signing their names inside images or on paintings. As Buddhism spread both geographically and socially, groups of devotees visited temples and made monetary donations for the construction and upkeep of images, halls, and festivals. Indeed, by the sixteenth century temples depended on patronage from all levels of society as merchants and artisans grew wealthy at the expense of the aristocratic and military elites.

Many scholars now challenge long-held assumptions about what constitutes "Buddhist art" and whether such a concept remains valid. Art historians and Buddhologists have renewed their scrutiny of objects, sites, practices, and beliefs long forgotten, giving more attention to functions and audiences than to aesthetic properties, and hence opening up later periods and commoner arts to scholarly inquiry. With this process in mind, this entry focuses specifically upon the dynamic of making and using "Buddhist art" in Japan: It only hints at specific objects, their style, iconography, and relationships to other objects. MONASTIC ARCHITECTURE, PORTRAITURE, and arts associated with individual schools of Buddhism are treated in separate entries. Unlike some Asian countries, Japan has preserved material and documentary traces of Buddhist patronage to a remarkable degree. Much that is discussed in this entry would have been equally true for other Buddhist countries.

Consecrated images

The most prominent Buddhist objects are cast, carved, modeled, or painted images of buddhas and bodhisattvas (collectively, *butsuzō*). In the eyes of makers and worshippers, these things were not sculpture, statuary, or painting, but were rather animate, living images that manifested the aura of the deities they represented. Materials—most commonly wood, silk, mineral pigments, and gold—were themselves sacred, prepared and worked by artisans who were part of the Buddhist establishment. When an image was finished, an eye-opening (*kaigen*) ceremony was held in which the officiant dotted in the pupils of the eyes to signify its birth as a sacred image. Once animated, an image would be placed on a temple altar or in a temporary space, to be provided with offerings of light, incense, water, and food.

Large altar platforms in the main halls of Buddhist temples from all periods generally held ensembles of images including BUDDHAS, BODHISATTVAS, and guardian figures. In many cases these images date from different periods and have separate histories, and may have come from other temples or private residences. Whether an altar maintains its originally planned complement of images, or has been changed, a central buddha or bodhisattva image serves as the main icon of the hall. That image is generally larger in scale than attendant deities. In addition to buddha icons and ensembles in the main halls, most temples also established separate halls devoted to a single deity worshipped alone or as part of an ensemble.

Much smaller images, both carved and painted, were often made for particular occasions and may have been used only once or periodically. During ceremonies and lectures, images served as the fundamental deity (*honzon*), were offered greetings, offerings, prayers, music, and the like, and were then de-animated as the ceremony closed. Smaller images could be returned to shrine boxes or temple storehouses. Some images became the focus of monthly or yearly ceremonies or sūtra readings, but many were kept secret, locked away in cabinets that ultimately enhanced their efficacy and aided in their preservation.

Because buddha images must be made to exacting iconographical standards, most in fact copy other images, leaving little room for innovation on the part of their makers, except perhaps in stylistic detail or technique. The act of making and worshipping an image was a good deed, and inscribed or documented examples reveal that buddha images were dedicated to transfer merit to someone else, to cure illness, to improve the KARMA (ACTION) of someone already deceased, to pray for future generations, and to beseech protection of family and state. Such motivations have remained constant for centuries.

Cast, carved, and modeled images

Small images initially came to Japan as the baggage of immigrants from the Korean peninsula during the mid-sixth century. Official accounts of the introduction of the dharma from the Korean peninsula devote considerable attention to gifts of BUDDHA IMAGES, to their circulation among the elite, and to building temples to house them. The first images do not survive, but numerous sixth- and seventh-century examples of both imported and local manufacture remain. Most are of gilt-bronze, less than fifty centimeters in height; their iconographic and stylistic diversity reflects both earlier and contemporary developments on the mainland. Thus Shaka (Śākyamuni), Yakushi (Bhaiṣajyaguru), Miroku (MAITREYA), and Kannon (Avalokiteśvara) predominate. These earliest images are generally not inscribed or recorded in documents, nor do they remain in their original settings.

During the seventh and eighth centuries, members of the court took up image-making on a grand scale, sponsoring a succession of massive projects designed to unite the populace, assert state authority, and create a material presence for the Buddhist establishment to rival those abroad. A succession of increasingly ambitious state temples built in Fujiwara-kyō and Heijō-kyō (among them Hōkōji, Daikandaiji, and Yakushiji) culminated in the building of Tōdaiji, with its colossal cast bronze and gilded image of Rushana (Vairocana), a project modeled directly on Tang-dynasty precedents. Because bronze was too costly for most image production, during the eighth century state and temple workshops employed a variety of carving and modeling techniques to achieve an increasingly lifelike appearance. Hōryūji, Tōdaiji, and Kōfukuji all contain numerous life-size or larger images of clay modeled on a wooden armature, as well as those modeled in lacquer-soaked cloth over a wooden frame. Mineral pigments and gold enhanced the surface of the images.

These costly and time-consuming techniques died out in the late eighth century as a result of patronage shifts and the closing of temple and state workshops. During the late eighth, ninth, and tenth centuries, Buddhism spread throughout the provinces, where local leaders built temples in the mountains and on provincial estates. Image-making in wood proliferated, resulting in a variety of regional styles, iconographies, and carving techniques.

The statue of Vairocana Buddha at Tōdaiji, Nara, Japan. This statue is a seventeenth-century replacement for a destroyed eighth-century original. © Robert D. Fiala, Concordia University, Seward, Nebraska. Reproduced by permission.

Buddha and bodhisattva images were not the only deities within temple precincts in the eighth and later centuries. Powerful local deities (*kami*) played critical roles in the lives of temples and monks, as for instance when in 749 a HACHIMAN shrine was built at Tōdaiji. The making of carved images of *kami* began in the ninth century, and representations of Hachiman at Tōji, Yakushiji, and elsewhere attest their growing importance as protectors of the dharma. Due to the "Separation of Gods and Buddhas" edicts of the 1870s, however, the prominence of *kami* images and the shrines that housed them at Buddhist temples has largely been obscured or forgotten.

During the eleventh century in the capital Kyoto, members of the Fujiwara and ruling families dedicated themselves to temple-building and image-making on a grand scale. To meet their demands, wood-carvers devised an effective method for carving multiple blocks of wood, which were hollowed and reassembled to

This statue depicts the Shintō deity Hachiman as a Buddhist priest. (Japanese sculpture by Kaikei, ca. 1201.) © Sakamoto Photo Research Laboratory/Corbis. Reproduced by permission.

create large numbers of relatively lightweight images in a variety of challenging poses. This "joined woodblock" technique, augmented in the late twelfth century by painted glass eyes and painted or gilded surfaces, became the norm in later centuries. From the eleventh century, carvers and their assistants organized themselves into family-based workshops where such techniques and styles were passed on from one generation to the next.

Hollowing out images created spaces where objects were deposited and inscriptions written. These inscriptions often give the date and circumstances of production, and include the names of donors and carvers. Objects deposited include dedicatory vows, sūtras, smaller images, and personal possessions. Where intact, these collections of objects provide revealing information about the beliefs and practices of image-making.

Painted images

In addition to three-dimensional images installed on temple altars or kept in small shrine boxes, the walls of some temple buildings were themselves painted with ensembles of buddhas (Hōryūji Golden Hall, early eighth century), deities of esoteric maṇḍalas and Shingon patriarchs (Daigoji pagoda, 851), representations of the nine stages of Amida's descent (Phoenix Hall, Byōdōin, 1053), and other subjects. But most walls were never painted or have lost their paintings due to repeated restorations. Instead, buddhas and bodhisattvas were painted on silk, mounted in scroll format, and hung only for special occasions ranging from state-sponsored rites to childbirth or death rituals. The largest of these were the size of temple walls, and represented AMITĀBHA's pure land, the two-world MAṆḌALA of esoteric deities, and depictions of Śākyamuni's *parinirvāṇa.*

Painted images often incorporated a profusion of deities and landscape or architectural settings and local Japanese details. Representations of Amida's descent (*raigō*) for instance, often show Amida (Amitābha) and his entourage descending in a seasonal landscape to a dying believer recognizably in aristocratic dress and surroundings. In some cases, dreams or visions led to the creation of hitherto unseen iconography, as in the case of standing deities, different colorations or attributes, or unusual juxtapositions. Paintings depicting buddhas (*honji*) and their *kami* manifestations (*suijaku*), or shrine and temple precincts, produced from the thirteenth and later centuries, reveal the localization of Buddhist beliefs and practices.

Texts and tales

The arrival of Buddhism in Japan brought with it the written word and an enormous body of sacred literature, including sūtras, commentaries, practice manuals, and miraculous tales. Thousands of manuscripts survive from the eighth century on, some beautifully handwritten or printed, crafted of fine materials, or incorporating painting. Unlike living images installed on altars and wreathed in incense, flowers, and candle light during ceremonies, manuscripts brought individual devotees closer to the dharma, whether they themselves read or wrote the texts, or experienced them through lecture or oral storytelling.

Sūtra-copying was central to Buddhist practice in Japan from the earliest period, as every temple needed copies of basic texts. During the eighth century, most were produced at the state-sponsored workshop at Tōdaiji, but individual monks and lay patrons made their own copies for private use or donation. Like image-making and temple-building, sūtra-copying was an act of devotion and merit, requiring a reverent attitude. Sūtras were copied for a variety of occasions and reasons, and their completion was often accompanied by ceremonies or lectures. In the eleventh-century court, lavish projects to copy the LOTUS SŪTRA (SADDHARMAPUṆḌARĪKA-SŪTRA) mobilized teams of aristocrats who chose the finest materials—colored and decorated paper, gold and silver ink—to create manuscripts of extraordinary beauty and richness. The boom in sūtra-copying in the mid-eleventh century was related to belief that the world had entered the final era of the dharma (*mappō*). Many monks and lay patrons buried hand-copied sūtras in specially designed sūtra mounds (*kyōzuka*), in remote mountain settings where they were protected by local *kami* while awaiting the advent of Miroku (Maitreya). In some cases, letters or picture books of the deceased would be used as the paper for sūtras written out by their descendants on behalf of the departed. But most sūtra-copying projects were a simple matter of ink and paper, and a private vow from the writer; most ended up in temple or family storehouses. This practice of copying sūtras still flourishes at temples and in private homes.

In addition to sūtras, Buddhist literature abounds in biographies and miracle tales, many illustrated. The life of Śākyamuni was among the first narrative sequences to be represented in Japan in both sculpture (Hōryūji pagoda) and painting. But the initial focus on Śākyamuni quickly expanded to include miracle tales, both imported and localized. In the tenth century, the *Sanbōe* (*Illustrations of the Three Jewels*), written on behalf of a princess, included painted depictions of episodes from the history of Buddhism as well as of contemporary Japanese religious festivals and ceremonies.

Many temple icons were believed to have miraculous origins, and these origin tales (*engi*) were frequently illustrated in painted narratives. More extensive painted scrolls treat entire temple histories, from the making of icons, building of halls, to miracles wrought by their deities. A major genre of illustrated narrative was the sacred biography. In addition to Śākyamuni, the life of Prince SHŌTOKU was illustrated repeatedly, first at temples he founded such as Shitennōji and Hōryūji, and at numerous temples that claimed him as founder. At least as early as the eleventh century, painted narrative cycles of famous patriarchs stressed aspects of their lineage and teaching. Interest in the lives of teachers peaked in the thirteenth and fourteenth centuries with the lavish productions of pictorial biographies of Pure Land patriarchs IPPEN CHISHIN, HŌNEN, and Ryōnen produced in numerous copies for distribution to branch temples. Some of these survive in such pristine condition that one wonders if they were ever viewed. The small scale of hand-held narrative scrolls proved unsuitable for more than intimate viewing, but at Dōjōji (Wakayama prefecture) picture-explaining monks (*etoki hōshi*) unroll a large-format scroll to tell the infamous story of Kiyohime's unrequited love for a monk and her transformation into a dragon, which follows the monk to Dōjōji and incinerates him with her fiery breath.

However, large hanging scrolls more commonly served for picture-explaining lectures directed at visitors and pilgrims. Prince Shōtoku's life may have been the first instance of this, but many such wall-sized biographies and origin tales exist from the thirteenth and later centuries, often now worn and tattered from repeated use. In the sixteenth and later centuries many temples and shrines utilized pilgrimage maṇḍala to instruct visitors about the history of their institution, its halls and deities, and miracles that had occurred within their precincts. These paintings served as effective fund-raising devices, as did representations of the six realms of existence (*rokudō*) with their emphasis upon punishment and hell. Such paintings, crude in execution but powerful in message, were carried about by itinerant storytellers who worked the roadsides, festivals, cities, and even private gatherings.

Practical needs

Buddhist temples and their affiliated shrines are repositories of the myriad finely crafted objects used to adorn temple halls, ritual implements employed in ceremonies, articles used by temple inhabitants, and precious gifts donated by lay patrons. These constituted part of a temple's material wealth, and thus could be sold if need dictated. Among the temples noted for their extensive storehouses are Hōryūji (seventh- and eighth-century textiles and metalwork, etc.), Tōdaiji (eighth-century objects in all media of foreign and native manufacture), Tōji and Daigoji (esoteric arts and manuscripts of all periods), Kōzanji (manuscripts and printed books, including those from China and Korea), DAITOKUJI (imported Chinese paintings, calligraphies, and tea utensils), and Kōdaiji (lacquerware and textiles), to name a few.

The many public and private ceremonies conducted at Buddhist temples or even in private residences utilized a variety of finely crafted objects for sacred adornment (*sōgon*) and in actual practice. Painted and woven banners were hung or were carried by participants in processions. Altar tables held ritual implements, incense burners, water dishes, and other items of bronze, gold, and silver. Monastic surplices, altar cloths, seat cushions, and other sacred textiles were made from donated women's garments. Black lacquer with sprinkled gold patterns or precious inlays of silver or mother-of-pearl, adorned tables, cabinets, and boxes for storing objects, clothing, and sacred texts. Large ceremonies and theatrical performances required musical instruments, masks, and costumes.

Because many temples also served as the private retreats for elite patrons, especially noblemen and women who themselves became monks and nuns, many paintings, manuscripts, textiles, lacquerware and other objects housed in temple storehouses cannot properly be characterized as "Buddhist art" even though they were perceived as "temple treasures."

The lower levels of society also participated in the material cultures of Buddhism, especially during the sixteenth and later centuries when a rise in quasi-religious travel by commoners created precursors of contemporary tourism. Temple icons, both carved and painted, were put on periodic display during temple airings and were sometimes sent outside temple precincts for fund-raising purposes. Devotional objects made expressly for purchase by visitors include printed Buddha images and sūtras, AMULETS AND TALISMANS, and painted wooden plaques (*ema*) upon which prayers to specific deities are written. Pilgrims often left paper "calling cards" on temple gates, they piled up stones in the form of a STŪPA, and deposited small carved Buddha images in the rafters of temple halls. In addition to PILGRIMAGE, temples also established vast funerary precincts that have become extraordinary stone graveyards, most notably near the tombs of Prince Shōtoku, KŪKAI, Hōnen, and other holy figures. While such material manifestations of Buddhist practice are not usually termed *art*, they are nonetheless a continuing feature of the visual culture of Buddhist practice in Japan today.

See also: **Chan Art; China, Buddhist Art in; Hells, Images of; Honji Suijaku; Hōryūji and Tōdaiji; Huayan Art; Phoenix Hall (at the Byōdōin); Pure Land Art**

Bibliography

Cunningham, Michael R., ed. *Buddhist Treasures from Nara.* Cleveland, OH: Cleveland Museum of Art, 1998.

Kanda, Christine Guth. *Shinzō: Hachiman Imagery and Its Development.* Cambridge, MA: Harvard University Press, 1985.

McCallum, Donald F. *Zenkōji and Its Icon: A Study in Medieval Japanese Religious Art.* Princeton, NJ: Princeton University Press, 1994.

Morse, Anne Nishimura, and Morse, Samuel Crowell. *Object as Insight: Japanese Buddhist Art and Ritual.* Katonah, NY: Katonah Museum of Art, 1995.

Rosenfield, John M., and ten Grotenhuis, Elizabeth. *Journey of the Three Jewels: Japanese Buddhist Paintings from Western Collections.* New York: Asia Society, 1979.

Sanford, James H.; LaFleur, William R.; and Nagatomi Masayoshi. *Flowing Traces: Buddhism in the Literary and Visual Arts of Japan.* Princeton, NJ: Princeton University Press, 1992.

Sharf, Robert H., and Sharf, Elizabeth Horton, eds. *Living Images: Japanese Buddhist Icons in Context.* Stanford, CA: Stanford University Press, 2001.

Sugiyama, Jirō. *Classic Buddhist Sculpture: The Tempyō Period,* tr. Samuel Crowell Morse. New York: Kodansha International and Shibundo, 1982.

Tanabe, Willa J. *Paintings of the Lotus Sūtra.* New York and Tokyo: Weatherhill, 1988.

ten Grotenhuis, Elizabeth. *Japanese Maṇḍalas: Representations of Sacred Geography.* Honolulu: University of Hawaii Press, 1999.

Yiengpruksawan, Mimi Hall. *Hiraizumi: Buddhist Art and Regional Politics in Twelfth-Century Japan.* Cambridge, MA: Harvard University Press, 1998.

KAREN L. BROCK

JAPANESE, BUDDHIST INFLUENCES ON VERNACULAR LITERATURE IN

Japanese secular literature is grounded in ways of feeling, thinking, and behaving that developed centuries before they were defined by the classifications used today: Shintō (Way of the Gods), the national memory of ancient myths and rituals; Buddhism, a religion teaching spiritual enlightenment, which originated in India circa 500 B.C.E. and spread to Japan through China by the middle of the sixth century C.E.; and Confucian social philosophy, which trickled into Japan from China and was selectively adapted to the country's needs.

It is equally important to stress that Western attitudes concerning proper feeling, thinking, and behavior—through the Christian missions circa 1549–1630, eighteenth-century Enlightenment notions of democracy, Marxism, and such—have left their mark mainly since the Meiji Restoration of 1868. To appreciate Japan's literature is first to come to terms with Japan's own deeply seated ideological roots before attempting to impose values and critical analyses developed in other societies.

Evidence of Buddhist influence on Japanese vernacular literature—both doctrinal and secular writings—can be seen, of course, in obvious references to pagodas, sūtras, and monks. But a more difficult, and far more rewarding, understanding can be found by exploring the aesthetic milieu that informs this literature rooted in a native tradition assimilated with Buddhism and Confucianism. The two oldest surviving Japanese literary works—composed in Chinese—the *Kojiki* (*Record of Ancient Matters,* 712 C.E.) and the *Nihon shoki* (*Chronicles of Japan,* 720 C.E.), have much to offer historically, but say little about Buddhist literature. They offer slight opportunity to share an author's feelings, ideals, and sentiments with the immediacy that distinguishes literature from reporting.

The following short thirty-one-syllable Japanese poem (*waka*) by Buddhist novice Manzei (fl. 704–731) is a rare example of a verse arguably revealing Buddhist influence. This poem first appears in the monumental *Man'yōshū* (*Collection of Ten Thousand Leaves,* ca. 759):

To what	*yo no naka wo*
shall I compare this life?	*nani ni tatoen*
to the white wake	*asaborake*
of a boat rowing away	*kogiyuku fune no*
at the break of dawn.	*ato no shiranami*

The reasons for the late appearance of Buddhist imagery and ideals in Japanese literary works were simply the late development of a comfortable vocabulary to supersede the often abrasive transliterations of Chinese (and even Indian) religious technical terms into the more fluid native language (*yamato kotoba*) and the refinement of a phonetic (*kana*) syllabary to supplant the often stodgy Chinese compounds. The syllabary, traditionally attributed to KŪKAI (774–835), is now believed to have developed gradually, becoming standardized by the late eleventh century. The anonymous *I-ro-ha uta (Syllabary Song),* an *imayō* ("modern-style") verse organizing all but one of the syllabary's sounds ("-*n*-"), first appeared in a work written in 1079, and is still a familiar furnishing of the Japanese literary consciousness. Its message is the ancient Buddhist theme of ANITYA (IMPERMANENCE; *mujō*):

Blossoms glow	*iro ha ni(h)o(h)e to*
but then they scatter,	*chirinuru wo*
and in this life of ours	*wak[g]a yo tare so*
who endures?	*tsune naramu*
Today we cross the dense mound	*u[wi] no okuyama*
of worldly illusion,	*kefu koete*
dissolving our shallow dreams,	*asaki yume mish[j]i*
beyond inebriation.	*[w]ehi mo ses[z]u*

It should be noted, however, that this sense of impermanence, in spite of its terminology and somber shadings, is a powerful affirmation of the value and wonder of every moment of our brief lives. The courtly priest Yoshida Kenkō declares in his *Tsurezuregusa* (*Essays in Idleness,* ca. 1330–1333): "If man were never to fade away like the dews of Adashino, never to vanish like the smoke over Toribeyama, but lingered on forever in this world, how things would lose their power to move us [*mono no aware*]! The most precious thing in life is its uncertainty" (*Seeds in the Heart,* p. 859). Some time later the great Nativist scholar Motoori Norinaga (1730–1801)—no friend of Buddhism—characterized *Genji monogatari* (*The Tale of Genji,* ca. 1007) as a novel of *mono no aware,* though he defined it somewhat differently, possibly as "sensitivity to the wonder of things."

It is also well known that in her defense of fiction ("lies" in the opinion of traditional moralists), Lady Murasaki, the author of *Genji monogatari,* appealed to the Buddhist doctrine of skillful means (*hōben;* Sanskrit, *upāya*), which is so tenaciously argued in the LOTUS SŪTRA (*Saddharmapuṇḍarīka-sūtra;* Japanese, *Myōhō rengekyō*), the source of seven parables whose imagery permeates traditional secular literature. There are many routes to religious enlightenment expressed through a variety of mythologies, modes of practice, and necessary "fictional" devices possible in literature. The blandness of many modern translations of traditional Japanese poetry and literature is often the result of its being sanitized to conform to Western expectations rather than asking the Western reader to suspend disbelief in a fascinating world of alien values and ideas.

The aesthetics of *mono no aware* lead us to the related ideal of "mystery and depth" (*yūgen*), of major importance to the poetry of the *Shinkokinshū* (*New Collection of Ancient and Modern Times,* ca. 1206) and the Muromachi Noh theater. The phrase first appears in a Chinese Buddhist commentary, and the comments of Kamo no Chōmei (1153–1216), the author of *Hōjōki* (*Essays in Idleness*), point to the emotional ideal while reminding us of Buddhism's understanding of the limitations of reason:

> On an autumn evening, for example, there is no color in the sky nor any sound, yet although we cannot give any definite reason for it, we are somehow moved to tears. . . . It should be evident that this is a matter impossible for people of little sensibility to understand. . . . How can such things be easily learned or expressed precisely in words?

How, for example, can we explain why the following poem by Shunzei (1114–1204) moves us? And why should we try?

As evening falls,	*yū sareba*
autumn wind across the moors	*nobe no akikaze*
blows chill into the heart,	*mi ni shimite*
and a quail seems to be crying	*uzura naku nari*
in the deep grass of Fukakusa.	*Fukakusa no sato*

Without minimizing the profound influences of Shintō and Confucianism on traditional Japanese thought and feeling, we must recognize the preeminence of Buddhism in shaping the nation's artistic production, providing much of its imagery and aesthetic direction. The impermanence (*mujō*) behind the ideal of "sensitivity to things" and "mystery and depth," the consciousness of moral retribution between existences (*sukuse,* karma), and myriad half-sensed feelings and images from an antique past inform a rich literature of some five centuries of histories, poetry (*waka, renga,* haiku, . . .), novels (*monogatari*), "essays" (*zuihitsu*), anecdotal "tale literature" (*setsuwa*), theater (Noh, *jōruri,* kabuki, and their modern successors), memoirs (*nikki*), and travel diaries (*kikō*).

But Japanese and English literature, however their fruits may compare or contrast, nevertheless shared a common chronological timeline. The bards of the Old English epic poem *Beowulf* were contemporaries of the guild of reciters (*kataribe*) that produced the *Record of Ancient Matters.*

See also: **Chinese, Buddhist Influences on Vernacular Literature in; Cosmology; Entertainment and Performance; Ikkyū; Poetry and Buddhism; Ryōkan; Shintō (Honji Suijaku) and Buddhism**

Bibliography

deBary, William Theodore; Keene, Donald; Tanabe, George; and Varley, Paul, eds. *Sources of Japanese Tradition,* 2nd edition. Vol. 1: *From Earliest Times to 1600.* New York: Columbia University Press, 2001.

Keene, Donald. *Essays in Idleness: The* Tsurezuregusa *of Kenkō.* New York and London: Columbia University Press, 1967.

Keene, Donald. *Seeds in the Heart: Japanese Literature from Earliest Times to the Late Sixteenth Century.* New York: Henry Holt, 1993.

LaFleur, William R. *The Karma of Words: Buddhism and the Literary Arts in Medieval Japan.* Berkeley and Los Angeles: University of California Press, 1983.

Miner, Earl; Hiroko Odagiri; and Morrell, Robert E., eds. *The Princeton Companion to Classical Japanese Literature.* Princeton, NJ: Princeton University Press, 1985.

Tanabe, George J., Jr., ed. *Religions of Japan in Practice.* Princeton, NJ: Princeton University Press, 1999.

ROBERT E. MORRELL

JAPANESE ROYAL FAMILY AND BUDDHISM

Although the royal family of Japan, headed by the *tennō* (heavenly monarch), has since 1868 been identified by the Japanese media and government with Shintō, it long led a religious life dominated by Buddhism. It was, indeed, the prince-regent SHŌTOKU (574–622) who was identified as having the greatest impact on the early history of Buddhism in Japan, in emphatically supporting Buddhism in early proclamations, in supporting the construction of major temples such as Shitennōji in Ōsaka, and in writing—or, more likely, sponsoring—one or more of the commentaries on Buddhist scriptures that have been attributed to him.

The eighth-century sovereign Shōmu combined a deep faith in Buddhism with an effort to incorporate the faith into his effort to undergird his authority. Following several years of natural disasters and pestilence, while queen Kōgō administered a new and extremely active sūtra-copying bureau, Shōmu hatched a plan to establish a national system of provincial temples and nunneries (*kokubunji*). He surprisingly described himself at the dedication of the Great Buddha at Tōdaiji in Nara as a "slave" of the Three Jewels (a reference to Buddha, his teachings, and his community).

Although the period after Shōmu was infamous for the undue influence of clerics over the ruler, whatever qualms the family and court had vis-à-vis the Buddhists were no longer evident by the early ninth century, when sovereigns balanced support of the Nara schools with that of the new Tendai and Shingon schools. From the 830s on, Buddhist rites formed an increasingly large role in the ritual life of the royal family and court: The Shingon monk KŪKAI successfully petitioned for the inauguration of the annual esoteric Latter Seven-Day Rite (*go-shichinichi mishiho*), to be conducted from January 8 through January 14, simultaneously with the long-established exoteric Misai'e (Gosai'e) rite for the welfare of ruler and realm, and for the construction of the palace chapel, Shingon'in in Kyoto.

Increasing domination of the royal family by the northern Fujiwaras from the late ninth century on was also marked by an effort to promote the ruler's authority in religious terms. For example, the increase in the number and volume of accession rites performatively represented the ruler's sanctity and grace on a grand scale. As part of this effort, the court, in the name of the acceding ruler, sponsored the Great Treasures Offering (*ichidai ichido daijinpō hōbei*) and the Buddha Relics Offering (*ichidai ichido busshari hōken*), both of which were made to native shrines throughout the realm. The offering of remains of the Buddha (housed in small STŪPAS) to non-Buddhist religious institutions and local deities (*kami*), while seemingly odd, was focused especially on Usa Hachimangū shrine in Kyūshū, where the local gods had been venerated since at least the early ninth century as both the spirit of the legendary ancient ruler Ōjin (ca. early fifth century) and the bodhisattva HACHIMAN. Meanwhile, *tennō* were sometimes cremated in Buddhist ceremonies, and the royal family increasingly sponsored Buddhist masses to memorialize their dead.

Prince Shōtoku (574–622), great Japanese patron of Buddhism, between two women of the court.

Royal culture and Buddhism

The retired ruler Uda (867–931) became the first retired *tennō* to become a monk (*in*), entering the Shingon order at Ninnaji Monastery in Kyoto and receiving the *denbō kanjō* initiation as ācārya (*ajari*) there. Thus Uda set the precedent not only for royal relatives to often head Ninnaji but for princes to serve regularly as abbots of the so-called O'muro royal-temple compound (*monzeki*) in Ninnaji beginning in the late eleventh century, and, from the twelfth century on, effectively ruling over the entire Buddhist community. (Cloistered rulers also tended to have close ties with the Tendai temples Onjōji and the *monzeki* Shōren'in, both near Kyoto.)

At the same time, Uda also established the pattern for a former *tennō* to engage in politics while donning clerical robes. From the late eleventh century on, retired sovereigns (*insei*) increasingly replaced the Fujiwaras as rulers, while symbolically demonstrating their religiosity by elaborating on precedents set by figures such as Fujiwara no Michinaga (966–1027) and those around him. Thus, retired *tennō* Shirakawa

(1053–1129) established magnificent temples and multiple stūpas as expressions of his grace, and his son Toba (1103–1156)—on better terms with the Fujiwaras—established the Shōkōmyō'in chapel and treasury (*hōzō*) near Kyoto, housing a Buddhist scriptural collection and other treasures in apparent imitation of the Fujiwara chapel Byōdō'in, also near Kyoto, which similarly featured an Amidist sanctuary and a scriptural treasury (*kyōzō*). This "royal culture" of powerful aristocrats and cloistered sovereigns, particularly with its emphasis on demonstrating largess and religious devotion as well as an increasing interest in acquiring knowledge of esoteric Buddhism—and influence over the clerical appointment system—was one of the primary factors that influenced Tendai and Shingon monks and temples of the medieval era. Under this influence, Buddhists increasingly sought to produce large iconographic collections (the first, Zuzō shō [ca. 1135–1141], was reputedly produced by order of Toba), to establish large treasuries of scriptures and other objects, and to specialize in particular tantric rites (*shuhō*) of concern to the royal family.

Buddhist accession rites and Shintō

Moreover, during the same period, particularly in the O'muro at Ninnaji, the enriching of esoteric Buddhist teachings with worship of native deities produced novel teachings and ritual practices that attempted to confer legitimacy on the ruler, and were later referred to as Goryū Shintō. At the latest, by Go-Uda's accession (late thirteenth century), the ruler often underwent an esoteric Buddhist consecration rite (*sokui kanjō*) as part of the accession process. The initiation of retired *tennō* Go-Daigo in the fourteenth century into what would later be deemed the "controversial" Tachikawa line of Shingon was, indeed, an elaboration of this trend. Moreover, the first use of the term *Shintō* was established in and through the so-called *kenmitsu* institutions of Shingon and Tendai. Even the emphasis on the three royal regalia was forged in the milieu of those institutions to legitimize royal rule amidst the impending split into rival lines: The jewel (*magatama*) was newly emphasized and was commonly compared to the wish-fulfilling jewel and Buddha relics of the treasuries of esoteric temples such as the Shingon temple Tōji.

In spite of the rising prominence of nativist scholars such as Motoori Norinaga (1730–1801), the royal family remained devoted Buddhists until the Meiji restoration in 1868, when mid-level samurai returned the Japanese government from Tokugawa warrior rule to royal rule in the name of the *tennō*. Rituals such as the Latter Seven-Day Rite were no longer held in the palace, and any public relationship between the royal family and the Buddhist community was dissolved—a government policy that has continued to the present.

See also: **Aśoka; Meiji Buddhist Reform; Nationalism and Buddhism; Politics and Buddhism; Tachikawaryū**

Bibliography

Abe Yasurō. "Hōju to Ōken: chūsei to mikkyō girei" (Jewels and royal authority: esoteric Buddhist rites and the medieval era). In *Iwanami kōza tōyō shisō 16: Nihon shisō 2.* Tokyo: Iwanami Shoten, 1989.

Abe Yasurō. "Shukaku hosshinnō to inseiki no bukkyō bunka" (The prince-monk Shukaku and the Buddhist culture of the cloistered-rule era). In *Inseiki no bukkyō,* ed. Hayami Tasuku. Tokyo: Yoshikawa Kōbunkan, 1998.

Amino Yoshihiko. "Igyō no Ōken: Go-Daigo/Monkan/Kenkō" (Awful royal authority: Go-Daigo/Monkan/Kenkō). In *Igyō no Ōken.* Tokyo: Heibonsha, 1987.

Kamikawa Michio. "Accession Rituals and Buddhism in Medieval Japan." *Japanese Journal of Religious Studies* 17, no. 2/3 (1990): 243–280.

Maki Toshiyuki. "Go-Uda tennō no mikkyō juhō" (The ruler Go-Uda's initiation into esoteric Buddhism). In *Kodai/chūsei no shakai to kokka,* ed. Osaka Daigaku Bungakubu Nihonshi Kenkyūshitsu. Osaka, Japan: Seibundō, 1998.

Okano Kōji. "Mudoen senji/isshin ajari/sōzu chokunin" (Royal orders without official monastic identification/aristocratic-appointed ācāryas/directly-appointed bishops). In *Inseiki no bukkyō,* ed. Hayami Tasuku. Tokyo: Yoshikawa Kōbunkan, 1998.

Ruppert, Brian D. *Jewel in the Ashes: Buddha Relics and Power in Early Medieval Japan.* Cambridge, MA: Harvard University Asia Center and Harvard University Press, 2000.

Uejima Susumu. "Fujiwara no Michinaga to insei: Shūkyō to seiji" (Religion and politics: cloistered rule and Fujiwara no Michinaga). In *Chūsei kōbu kenryoku no kōzō to tenkai,* ed. Uwayokote Masataka. Tokyo: Yoshikawa Kōbunkan, 2001.

BRIAN O. RUPPERT

JĀTAKA

Jātaka is the Sanskrit and Pāli term for a particular genre of Buddhist literature. A jātaka is a story in which one of the characters—usually the hero—is identified as a previous birth of the historical Buddha, generally appearing as a man, a deity, or one of the higher animals (but only rarely as a female of any kind). The existence of the jātaka genre is based on the notion that the Buddha, on the night of his enlightenment, attained the recollection of his previous lives, which then, throughout his life, he often had occasion to relate in order to illustrate a point, drive home a moral lesson, or shed light on some situation. It is these stories that constitute the jātakas.

The jātaka genre appears to be very old, for the term *jātaka* is included in an ancient categorization of Buddhist literary styles, and depictions of jātaka stories appear in Indian Buddhist art as early as the second century B.C.E.

All of the lives related in the jātakas are understood to have taken place during the Buddha's BODHISATTVA career, only after he had made a firm vow to become a buddha in the distant future. The general function of the jātakas, then, is to illustrate how the bodhisattva, in life after life, cultivated various virtues and qualities that ultimately contributed to his attainment of buddhahood. Accordingly, most jātakas portray the bodhisattva as an exemplary figure, highlighting such features as his wisdom, compassion, or ascetic detachment. Many jātakas, in fact, are explicitly intended to illustrate the bodhisattva's cultivation of one of the PĀRAMITĀ (PERFECTION) needed for buddhahood. In the *Śāśajātaka,* for example, the bodhisattva is a hare who offers his own body as food to a wandering traveler, thus cultivating the "perfection of generosity." In the *Brāhmaṇajātaka,* he is a boy who refuses to steal even when his brahmin teacher urges him to do so, thus cultivating the "perfection of morality." And in the *Kṣāntijātaka,* he is an ascetic who calmly tolerates the mutilation inflicted on him by an angry king, thus cultivating the "perfection of forbearance." Some jātaka collections are even arranged on this basis: The JĀTAKAMĀLĀ (*Garland of Jātakas*) of Āryaśūra, a famous Sanskrit collection from approximately the fourth century C.E., arranges the bulk of its thirty-four stories (including the three mentioned above) in accordance with the first three of the six perfections; the *Cariyāpiṭaka* (*Collection on [the Bodhisatta's] Conduct*) of the Pāli canon arranges its thirty-five versified jātakas in accordance with the THERAVĀDA list of ten perfections.

The jātaka genre was used to assimilate an enormous amount of traditional Indian folklore into the Buddhist fold, including many tales whose moral lessons were not specifically Buddhist (or that had no moral lesson at all). Any traditional tale could be transformed into a jātaka simply by turning one of its characters into a previous birth of the Buddha. This is especially true of the *Jātakaṭṭhakathā* (*Explanation of the Birth Stories*), a massive Pāli collection of 547 prose and verse jātakas, of which only the verses are considered canonical. Much of the contents of the *Jātakaṭṭhakathā* are likely non-Buddhist in origin, including, for example, many animal fables, folk tales, and fairy tales. Similarly, as the jātaka genre spread to Buddhist cultures outside of India, it often drew on local folklore to domesticate existing jātakas or compose wholly new ones more relevant to new environments.

Jātaka stories exist not only in Sanskrit and Pāli literature, but also in the Chinese and Tibetan canons, as well as in many vernacular languages and texts. Throughout history and throughout the Buddhist world, jātakas have played a major role in the dissemination of Buddhist teachings, being the constant focus of sermons, rituals, festivals, and many varieties of art and performance. The relevance of the jātakas to everyday Buddhist life is perhaps most apparent in the Theravāda cultures of Southeast Asia, where many jātakas of the Pāli tradition are widely known and frequently alluded to in everyday conversation and moral argument.

See also: **Avadāna; Buddha, Life of the; Viśvantara**

Bibliography

Cowell, E. B., ed. *The Jātaka or Stories of the Buddha's Former Births,* 3 vols. Delhi: Motilal Banarsidass, 1990.

Jones, John Garrett. *Tales and Teachings of the Buddha: The Jātaka Stories in Relation to the Pāli Canon.* London: Allen and Unwin, 1979.

Khoroche, Peter, trans. *Once the Buddha Was a Monkey: Ārya Śūra's Jātakamālā.* Chicago: University of Chicago Press, 1989.

Schober, Juliane, ed. *Sacred Biography in the Buddhist Traditions of South and Southeast Asia.* Honolulu: University of Hawaii Press, 1997.

REIKO OHNUMA

JĀTAKA, ILLUSTRATIONS OF

Visual *jātakas* do not simply illustrate verbal *jātakas* (birth stories) but share equal status with them. Each is a unique narrative belonging to a genre of stories existing in a community of memory rather than in a specific verbal version. Except for the *Viśvantara Jātaka,* individual *jātakas* are rarely narrated in isolation. They usually participate in larger texts, which occasionally have counterparts in literary genres. Since these larger texts are expressions of different Buddhisms in various times and places, Jātaka narratives should be viewed in their embedded textual and sociocultural contexts.

Despite the acknowledged antiquity of the 547 Pāli verse *jātakas,* the earliest datable physical *jātaka* narratives are the visual ones on the Bhārhut stūpa railing (ca. first century B.C.E.). With the exception of the coping reliefs, the Bhārhut *jātakas* belong to a larger text that includes other kinds of narratives, such as incidents from the Buddha's life, Avadānas, and "legends" concerning historical figures. The Bhārhut coping takes the form of an *s*-shaped lotus vine-cum-garland, within each of whose lower curves a *jātaka* is narrated. Hence, the coping functions as a unified text of the Jātakamālā (garland of *jātakas*) genre.

The Borobudur stūpa contains another sculpted example of a unified *jātaka* cycle within a larger monumental text, which is possibly an extended biography of the Buddha. Similar cycles proliferate in the murals of the pre-Tang (ca. 421–640 C.E.) Silk Road cave monasteries of Kucha and in various media in Burmese stūpas and temples from the eleventh century onward, especially at Pagan. Burma has the longest and most prolific tradition of visual *jātakas,* which ceramists, painters, and woodcarvers narrate individually, in small groups, or in cycles. For example, glazed tiles line the upper circumambulatory terraces of the Ananda Temple, composing a cycle of 554 *jātakas,* prefaced by events from the Buddha's last birth on the lower terraces. The main hall narratives of Ajaṇṭā's fifth-century caves 1 and 17 compose monumental *jātakāmalās,* which are framed and bracketed by the cave's porch, shrine antechamber, and shrine. The latter narrate important events from the Buddha's ministry and represent cosmic landscapes and beings often shown worshiping the Buddha.

How do visual *jātakas* function? Buddhist texts do not narrate *jātakas* concerning other buddhas and all buddhas perform the same deeds in their last births. Thus, the significant presence of *jātakas* in a Buddhist monastery indicates that Śākyamuni Buddha and his worship are the focus of Buddhist practice and belief there. Further, visual *jātakas* re-create the Bodhisattva's marvelous deeds as models to be imitated and as transcendental actions to be worshiped, characterizing his nature as human and supramundane. Architecture and style express this visually, as in the *jātaka* cycles painted on the sloping ceilings of the Kizil caves and in the idealized naturalism of paintings at Ajaṇṭā. Finally, *jātaka* cycles allow Buddhist pilgrims to follow the Buddha's steps by walking through his previous lives.

See also: **Buddha, Life of the, in Art; Dunhuang; Sūtra Illustrations**

Bibliography

Barua, Beni Madhab. *Bharhut.* Patna, India: Indological Book Corp., 1979.

Cummings, Mary. *The Lives of the Buddha in the Art and Literature of Asia.* Ann Arbor: University of Michigan, Center for South and Southeast Asian Studies, 1982.

Dehejia, Vidya. *Discourse in Early Buddhist Art: Visual Narratives of India.* New Delhi: Munshiram Manoharlal, 1997.

Girard-Geslan, Maud, et al. *Art of Southeast Asia,* tr. J. A. Underwood. New York: Harry N. Abrams, 1998.

Schlingloff, Dieter. *Studies in the Ajaṇṭā Paintings: Identifications and Interpretations.* Delhi: Ajaṇṭā Publications, 1987.

Schlingloff, Dieter. *Guide to the Ajaṇṭā Paintings: Narrative Wall Paintings.* New Delhi: Munshiram Manoharlal, 1999.

Whitfield, Roderick. *Cave Temples of Mogao: Art and History on the Silk Road.* Los Angeles: Getty Conservation Institute and the J. Paul Getty Museum, 2000.

Leela Aditi Wood

JĀTAKAMĀLĀ

Jātakamālā (*Garland of Jātakas*) is the title of a work by the poet Āryaśūra (fourth century C.E.). The title was later adopted by other authors, such as Haribhaṭṭa (early fifth century) and Gopadatta (seventh or eighth century), each of whom gives a personal slant to his own selection of thirty-four legends about the Buddha's previous lives, refashioning them in a mixture of verse and prose. Fourteen of Haribhaṭṭa's retellings survive in the original Sanskrit (the entire work is available in Tibetan), and about half of Gopadatta's *Garland* has so far been retrieved from miscellaneous story collections in Sanskrit.

See also: **Jātaka**

Bibliography

Hahn, Michael. *Haribhaṭṭa and Gopadatta: Two Authors in the Succession of Āryaśūra, on the Rediscovery of Parts of Their

Jātakamālās, 2nd revised edition. Tokyo: International Institute for Buddhist Studies, 1992.

Hahn, Michael, ed. *Haribhaṭṭa's Jātakamālā.* Wiesbaden, Germany: Franz Steiner Verlag, 2002.

Khoroche, Peter, trans. *Once the Buddha Was a Monkey: Ārya Śūra's Jātakamālā.* Chicago: University of Chicago Press, 1989.

PETER KHOROCHE

JEWELS

Jewels occupy important narrative and ritual spaces throughout the history of Buddhism. Buddhism, insofar as it constitutes the faith dedicated to elimination of desire, would seem at first consideration to be a religion at variance with objects that are culturally most directly associated with wealth. However, from an early stage Buddhists incorporated jewels into their teaching as part of a discourse on value.

The Buddha routinely employed the metaphor of the jewel (*ratna*) in a variety of sūtras to refer to the unlimited value of enlightened wisdom, a value that can be seen as represented in the form of an infinitely beautiful and valuable jewel that at the same time stands in contrast to the limitations of material jewels. Likewise, the jewel was often used as a metaphor to depict the conquest of death that is accomplished in Buddhist liberation—an item that, as with the metaphor of the diamond (*vajra*), represents absolute solidity, beauty, and permanence. Both of these metaphors are represented in their quintessential form in the *Gaṇḍhavyūha-sūtra* (*Flower Garland Scripture*), which elaborately deploys jewels and other glittering metaphors to illustrate enlightened vision of the absolute character of the interpenetration of all phenomena (dharma). While such discourse was often abstract, the jewel was also used in the phrase "Three Jewels" (*triratna*) to refer to the Buddhist tradition in its three basic, most treasured, aspects: Buddha, his teaching (dharma), and his community (SAṄGHA).

Jewels have also been an essential feature in iconographic representations of celestial buddhas and BODHISATTVAS of the Mahāyānist and tantric traditions. While the glittering character of the jewels and gold of the Buddha AMITĀBHA's Pure Land Sukhāvatī are well known, a series of buddhas, bodhisattvas, and other beings protective of Buddhism are routinely represented as carrying one or more jewels, which constitutes their so-called *samaya* (attribute). Among such figures are the bodhisattvas Kṣitigarbha (Chinese, Dizang; Japanese, Jizō) and Avalokiteśvara (Chinese, Guanyin; Japanese, Kannon), the female protective deity Śrī-mahādevī (Japanese, Kichijōten), and figures of esoteric Buddhism, such as the Jewel Buddha Ratnasambhava. The so-called seven jewels (*saptaratna*), likewise, represent the splendid treasures of the ideal wheel-turning Buddhist king: the wheel, the white elephant, the deep blue horse, the sacred jewel, the jewel woman, the merchant-artisan, and the military commander. The same term was also used to refer to seven precious substances used in the construction of elaborate Buddhist edifices, such as brilliant STŪPAS.

The jewel was also the subject of the more elaborate discourse of the "wish-fulfilling jewel" (*cintāmaṇi*), which represents the absolute merit (*puṇya*) offered by the Buddhist dharma and scriptures. While originally an image, the term in some East Asian tantric traditions came to be venerated as an object of esoteric ritual, and was even regarded by some in medieval Japanese Shingon as equivalent with Buddha relics—and the greatest treasure of Shingon—or the product of alchemical production that used relics and other precious substances, and was coveted by the sovereign.

See also: **Huayan Jing; Kingship; Refuges; Relics and Relics Cults**

Bibliography

Abe Yasurō. "Hōju to ōken: chūsei to mikkyō girei" (Jewels and royal authority: esoteric Buddhist rites and the medieval era). In *Iwanami kōza tōyō shisō 16: Nihon shisō 2.* Tokyo: Iwanami Shoten, 1989.

Cleary, Thomas, trans. *The Flower Ornament Scripture.* Boulder, CO: Shambhala, 1984.

Cook, Francis D. *Hua-yen Buddhism: The Jewel Net of Indra.* University Park: Pennsylvania State University Press, 1977.

Go yuigō (attributed to Kūkai). *Taishō shinshū daizōkyō* 77, no. 2431.

Ruppert, Brian D. *Jewel in the Ashes: Buddha Relics and Power in Early Medieval Japan.* Cambridge, MA: Harvard University Asia Center and Harvard University Press, 2000.

Uehara Kazu. "Higashi ajia no bukkyō bijutsu ni mirareru mani hyōgen no shosō" (Forms of expression of *cintā*[-*maṇī*] as seen in East Asian Buddhist art). In *Kodai no saishiki to shisō: higashi ajia no naka no nihon,* ed. Nakanishi Susumu. Tokyo: Kadokawa shoten, 1991.

BRIAN O. RUPPERT

JIUN ONKŌ

Jiun Onkō (Jiun Sonja, 1718–1804) was born and raised in Osaka, the son of a masterless samurai and a devoutly Buddhist mother. Forced into the Buddhist clergy at thirteen at the time of his father's death, Jiun became a novice under Ninko Teiki (1671–1750), a master in the Shingon Vinaya sect. This sect stressed both Shingon or Japanese tantric Buddhism and traditional monastic discipline. Under Teiki's influence, and after a period of training in his late teens and early twenties that included Zen and further Confucian studies, Jiun went on to become one of the leading Buddhist scholars and reformers of the Tokugawa period (1603–1868).

Early in his career, Jiun devoted much attention to the study of monastic discipline and the creation of supra-sectarian Buddhist communities that became part of his "Vinaya of the True Dharma" movement. To counteract a moral laxity that he saw in the Buddhist clergy, he advocated a return to what he judged to be a common core of Buddhist thought and practice that he called "Buddhism as it was when the Buddha was alive." Buddhist ethics, the practice of meditation, and, for monks and nuns, the observance of the VINAYA or monastic discipline stood at the center of his movement. Jiun's most famous work, *Jūzen hōgo* (*Sermons on the Ten Good Precepts*), completed in 1774, was an argument for Buddhist ethics as the foundation of the Buddhist way of life. Jiun is also remembered as one of Japan's greatest Sanskrit scholars. Working without the aid of a Sanskrit teacher and without a living tradition of Sanskrit studies, Jiun compiled the one thousand-chapter *Bongaku shinryō* (*Guide to Sanskrit Studies,* 1766) that included information on the geography, history, and customs of India, as well as dictionaries, grammars, and textual studies.

In his later years, Jiun turned his attention to the study of nativism and articulated his own understanding of the positive relationship that existed between Buddhism and Japan's local gods. His interpretation of nativism came to be known as Unden Shintō, or the "Shintō Transmitted by Jiun." When Japan began a period of rapid modernization in the Meiji period (1868–1912), Buddhist leaders who shared Jiun's concerns about the moral laxity of the clergy and the overly sectarian character of Japanese Buddhism drew inspiration from his *Sermons on the Ten Good Precepts,* and Japanese scholars who were learning of new research on Indian Buddhist languages in Europe looked with pride to Jiun's pioneering Sanskrit studies.

See also: **Shingon Buddhism, Japan; Shintō (Honji Suijaku) and Buddhism**

Bibliography

Watt, Paul B. "Sermons on the Precepts and Monastic Life by the Shingon Vinaya Master Jiun (1718–1804)." *Eastern Buddhist* 25, no. 2 (1992): 119–128.

Watt, Paul B. "Jiun Sonja (1718–1804): A Response to Confucianism within the Context of Buddhist Reform." In *Confucianism and Tokugawa Culture,* ed. Peter Nosco. Honolulu: University of Hawaii Press, 1997.

Watt, Paul B. "Shingon's Jiun Sonja and His 'Vinaya of the True Dharma' Movement." In *Religions of Japan in Practice,* ed. George J. Tanabe, Jr. Princeton, NJ: Princeton University Press, 1999.

PAUL B. WATT

JO KHANG

Jo khang is Tibet's earliest and foremost Buddhist temple. It is located in the center of Tibet's capital city, Lhasa. The Jo khang enshrines one of Tibet's most sacred Buddhist images—a statue of the buddha Śākyamuni as a young man, said to have been crafted in India during his lifetime. The monastery takes its name from this icon: Jo bo (pronounced Jowo) means "lord"; *khang* means "house."

The Jo khang has been a major center for Tibetan Buddhist worship and religious practice, drawing pilgrims and devotees from all parts of the Tibetan cultural world for well over a millennium. In common parlance the temple, with its numerous side chapels, adjoining courtyards, walkways, and residential quarters, is referred to simply as the Gtsug lag khang (pronounced Tsuglag khang), perhaps translated as "grand temple" or "cathedral." Western sources often describe it, somewhat misleadingly, as "the Cathedral of Lhasa."

Traditional sources such as the *Maṇi bka' 'bum* (*Hundred Thousand Pronouncements [Regarding] Maṇi*) credit the Tibetan king Srong btsan sgam po (r. ca. 614–650) and his two queens with founding the Jo khang's original temple in approximately 640. According to these accounts, the king's Chinese bride Wencheng carried the Jo bo statue to Tibet as part of her dowry. Arriving in the capital city to inauspicious signs, however, she divined that the landscape of Tibet was like a great supine demoness, obstructing the introduction and spread of the dharma. She advised the king, a new Buddhist convert, and his Nepalese wife Bhṛkuti to erect the Jo khang directly over the demoness's heart. This project was later augmented with twelve temples constructed at other physiognomic locations, where they served as great geomantic nails to pin down and subdue the forces inimical to Buddhism. The Jo khang originally housed a statue of the buddha AKṢOBHYA belonging to Bhṛkuti. After the king's death, the Jo bo was removed from its previous location in the nearby Ra mo che Temple, founded by Wencheng herself, and installed in the Jo khang's inner sanctum.

Modern scholarship now questions the historicity of many details of this episode, including Srong btsan sgam po's exclusive dedication to Buddhism and the existence of his Nepalese queen. However, the narratives of Tibet's Buddhist conversion through the subjugation of local deities continue to play a significant role in the religious life of many Tibetans, affirming the Jo khang's key position in the sacred geography of the Tibetan Buddhist world.

Since its founding, the Jo khang has been enlarged and renovated on numerous occasions, although architectural details from its original foundation are still evident, especially in the carved wooden door frames attributed to Newari craftsmen from Nepal. The temple suffered in the 1960s during the Chinese Cultural Revolution, when part of the complex and much of its original statuary were damaged or destroyed; restoration took place in the early 1970s and again during the early 1990s.

The temple lies at the heart of Lhasa's principal ritual ambulatory, called the *bar skor* (pronounced barkhor) or middle circuit, which skirts its outer walls and surrounding structures. The Jo khang and *bar skor* together continue to form Lhasa's primary public religious space, where pilgrims and devotees daily walk, prostrate, pray, and perform offerings in the temple's many chapels and around the circumambulation path. The site is also a lively marketplace and social scene, where individuals meander through street vendor's stalls and modern Chinese department stores. Since the late 1980s the *bar skor* has also become the principal Tibetan stage for political protest and civil demonstration.

Bibliography

Aris, Michael. *Bhutan: The Early History of a Himalayan Kingdom.* Warminster, UK: Aris and Phillips, 1979.

Gyatso, Janet. "Down with the Demoness." *Tibet Journal* 12, no. 4 (1987): 34–46. Reprinted in *Feminine Ground: Essays on Women and Tibet,* ed. Janice Dean Willis. Ithaca, NY: Snow Lion, 1989.

Larsen, Knud, and Sinding-Larsen, Amund. *The Lhasa Atlas: Traditional Tibetan Architecture and Townscape.* Boston: Shambhala, 2001.

Richardson, Hugh. "The Jo-Khang 'Cathedral' of Lhasa." In *Essais sur l'art du Tibet,* ed. Ariane Macdonald and Yoshiro Imaeda. Paris: Librairie d'Amérique et d'Orient, 1977. Reprinted in *High Peaks, Pure Earth: Collected Writings on Tibetan History and Culture,* ed. Michael Aris. London: Serindia, 1998.

Vitali, Roberto. "Lhasa Jokhang and Its Secret Chapel." In *Early Temples of Central Tibet.* London: Serindia, 1990.

ANDREW QUINTMAN

JUEFAN (HUIHONG)

Juefan Huihong (1071–1128) was a Buddhist monk and poet active primarily during the tumultuous reign of the Chinese emperor Song Huizong (r. 1101–1125). Huihong promoted an approach to Buddhism he called literary Chan (*wenzi* Chan) that incorporated poetry, painting, and scholarship on religious and secular books, with contemporary CHAN SCHOOL practices. Several prominent literati including Zhang Shangying (1043–1122) and Huang Tingjian (1045–1105) befriended Huihong and advocated his literary Chan, helping to ensure his lasting fame.

Huihong became a monk after he lost his parents at the age of fourteen and was ordained at nineteen. During his early years he primarily studied YOGĀCĀRA SCHOOL texts. In 1092 Huihong became a pupil of Zhenjing Kewen (1025–1102), a legendary Chan teacher from the Huanglong collateral branch of the Linji lineage. Between 1092 and 1105, Huihong investigated the sūtras and Chan literature, and visited sacred sites throughout southern China. In 1105 Huihong was jailed for the first of four incarcerations because of his connections to a faction opposed to Huizong's anti-Buddhist policies. Huihong's disfavor at court earned him an exile to Hainan island in 1112–1113. During this time Huihong turned to writing and reading poetry for solace and compiled a treatise on poetic criticism called the *Lengzhai yehua* (*Evening Discourses from a Cold Studio*). In addition, Huihong finished work on his somewhat unorthodox discourse record, the *Linjian lu* (*Anecdotes from the*

Groves [of Chan]), and one of the earliest commentaries to the *Śūraṅgama-sūtra* (Chinese, *Shoulengyan jing; Heroic March Sūtra*). During the last decade of his life, Huihong finished compiling the *Chanlin sengbao zhuan* (*Chronicles of the Saṅgha Jewel within the Groves of Chan*) with eighty-four biographies.

See also: **Chan Art; China; Poetry and Buddhism**

Bibliography

Gimello, Robert M. "Mārga and Culture: Learning, Letters, and Liberation in Northern Sung Ch'an." In *Paths to Liberation: The Mārga and Its Transformations in Buddhist Thought,* ed. Robert E. Buswell, Jr. and Robert M. Gimello. Honolulu: University of Hawaii Press, 1992.

Keyworth, George. "Transmitting the Lamp of Learning in Classical Chan Buddhism: Juefan Huihong (1071–1128) and Literary Chan." Ph.D. diss. University of California, Los Angeles, 2001.

GEORGE A. KEYWORTH

K

KAGYU. *See* Bka' brgyud

KAILĀŚA (KAILASH)

Kailāśa (Kailash) is one of Asia's preeminent sacred mountains. It is located in southwestern Tibet near the borders of India and Nepal. By Himalayan standards Mount Kailāśa is a modest peak, standing at 22,028 feet; yet the stature of its isolated snow-capped dome forms a striking image against the arid plateau. Together with Lake Manasarovar, eighteen miles to the southeast, Kailāśa forms one of the region's richest and most active PILGRIMAGE sanctuaries, revered for nearly two millennia by followers of diverse religious traditions including Jains, Hindus, and members of the indigenous Tibetan BON religion. Beginning in the eleventh century, Mount Kailāśa occupied a central position in the sacred landscape of Tibetan Buddhists, who associate the sanctuary complex with an array of BUDDHAS, tantric deities, and past Buddhist masters. Situated at Asia's watershed, four of the continent's largest rivers originate within fifty miles of the mountain: the Brahmaputra, the Karnali, the Sutlej, and the Indus. Tibetan literature refers to the mountain as Gangs dkar Ti se (White Snow Mountain Ti se); in common parlance, however, it is simply called Gangs rin po che (Precious Snow Mountain).

Mount Kailāśa is popularly associated with Mount Meru, the central pillar of the world system as depicted in Buddhist and Hindu COSMOLOGY. Tibetan descriptive guides to Kailāśa, however, equate the mountain with a site known as Himavat or Himalaya (the Snowy, or the Snow Mountain), one of twenty-four sacred lands (*piṭha*) named in the *Cakrasaṃvara-tantra* as geographic locations efficacious for Buddhist practice (as well as sites "mapped" within the visualized *vajra*-body of the yogin meditator). The mythic narratives of the Cakrasaṃvara literature recount how, in primordial times, these twenty-four lands fell under the dominion of Maheśvara (Śiva), manifesting in the guise of the fierce, blood-thirsty god Bhairava (or Rudra). The buddha Vajradhara, in wrathful form as a Heruka deity, then subdued Bhairava, blessing each location as a MAṆḌALA of the deity Cakrasaṃvara and his retinue. The tradition of identifying Kailāśa within this sacred landscape was especially promoted by members of the BKA' BRGYUD (KAGYU) sect of Tibetan Buddhism, who grouped the peak together with two other important mountain pilgrimage sites in southern Tibet, La phyi and Tsa ri, identified respectively as Cakrasaṃvara's body, speech, and mind. These claims drew criticism from some Tibetan quarters; the renowned scholar SA SKYA PAṆḌITA (SAKYA PAṆḌITA; 1182–1251), for example, argued that the sites associated with Cakrasaṃvara were located not in Tibet but India, and were part of a visionary geography accessible only to highly skilled meditators. Modern scholars such as Toni Huber have begun to track the manner in which important sacred locations of India were "remapped" onto Tibetan soil.

Tibetan tradition credits both the historical Buddha and the Indian adept PADMASAMBHAVA (ca. eighth century) with visits to the mountain. Another important narrative recounts how the poet-yogin MI LA RAS PA (MILAREPA; 1028/40–1111/23) inaugurated Buddhism's ascendancy at Mount Kailāśa by defeating a rival Bon priest, Na ro bon chung, in a contest of miracles. The mountain later became associated with the

Kailāśa (Mount Kailash) in southwestern Tibet, the goal of many pilgrimages, is sacred to both Buddhists and Hindus. © Galen Rowell/Corbis. Reproduced by permission.

followers of Mi la ras pa, principally members of the 'Brug pa and 'Bri gung Bka' brgyud sects, who traveled in great numbers to meditate there.

Pilgrims from all quarters of the Tibetan Buddhist world continue to visit Mount Kailāśa, many remaining in residence for an entire season. Their primary practice is completing the arduous thirty-two mile clockwise circumambulation route around the mountain, often undertaken in a single eighteen-hour day of walking. (Bon pilgrims make the identical circuit in a counterclockwise direction.) Traditional pilgrimage guide books describe a complex array of sacred elements inscribed within the landscape around the mountain, as well as specific religious practices to be undertaken at various points along the trail.

See also: **Space, Sacred**

Bibliography

Allen, Charles. *A Mountain in Tibet: The Search for Mount Kailas and the Sources of the Great Rivers of India.* London: André Deutsch, 1982.

Chang, Garma C. C., ed. and trans. *The Hundred Thousand Songs of Milarepa.* New Hyde Park, NY: University Books, 1962. Reprint, Boston: Shambhala, 1999.

Huber, Toni. "Where Exactly Are Carita, Devikota, and Himavat? A Sacred Geography Controversy and the Development of Tantric Buddhist Pilgrimage Sites in Tibet." *Kailash* 16, nos. 3–4 (1990): 121–164.

Huber, Toni, and Rigzin, Tsepak. "A Tibetan Guide for Pilgrimage to Ti-se (Mount Kailas) and mTsho Ma-pham (Lake Manasarovar)." In *Sacred Spaces and Powerful Places in Tibetan Culture: A Collection of Essays,* ed. Toni Huber. Dharamsala, India: Library of Tibetan Works and Archives, 1999.

Ricard, Mathhieu, ed. and trans. "At Mt. Kailash." In *The Life of Shabkar: The Autobiography of a Tibetan Yogin.* Albany: State University of New York Press, 1994.

ANDREW QUINTMAN

KĀLACAKRA

The Kālacakra Tantra (Tibetan, *Dus kyi 'khor lo'i rgyud*; *Wheel of Time, System of Mysticism*) is the most complex of the numerous VAJRAYĀNA Buddhist systems of mysticism. Although it presupposes and draws on all of the preceeding developments of Indian Buddhism, it is innovative in both its soteriological doctrines and in its mythic prophetic vision. Based on the ancient idea of the homology of the macrocosm and the microcosm, the Kālacakra presents a tantric yogic method for transforming an individual from a suffering, saṃsāric state into the transcendent state of perfect awakening. Drawing on Hindu mythology and historical events, it predicts a conflict between the forces of good and evil out of which a new golden age will be born.

Doctrine

The subject matter of the Kālacakra system has a tripartite structure: the external world (*bāhya*), the self (*adhyātman*), and the transcendent (*para*). The last topic can be subdivided into three: INITIATION (abhiṣeka), practice (sādhana), and gnosis (jñāna). The yoga of the Kālacakra is founded on the idea that the world (the macrocosm) and the self (the microcosm) share essential properties and that a person contains all of the elements of the cosmos. Correspondences between world and self allow the universe to be treated as a unified field for the development of salvific knowledge—gnosis.

In the Kālacakra initiation rites—the entryway to the tantric path—the guru introduces the disciple to the MAṆḌALA, a palace inhabited by deities that represents the disciple's world/self in a purified, awakened state. The maṇḍala provides a new self-image for the disciple: Whereas previously the disciple was enmeshed in the impure, limited, and confused projections of ordinary saṃsāric mind, the mysteries of the maṇḍala revealed in the initiation rites furnish a glimpse of the disciple's potential for the realization of awakening.

During the initial phase of tantric practice—the generation stage (*utpattikrama*)—the practitioner first dissolves ordinary perceptions of self and environment into a perception of emptiness, and then imaginatively generates a vision of self in the form of the buddha deities Śrī Kālacakra (Splendid Wheel of Time) and Viśvamātā (Mother of the Universe), together with their progeny, the rest of the maṇḍala. This stage—explicitly correlated with the process of human conception, birth, and maturation—transforms and divinizes the power of imagination, loosens attachment to mundane concerns, and produces a great store of merit.

The deity Śrī Kālacakra, a vision of self generated by the practitioner of tantra. © Lokesh Chandra. Reproduced by permission.

The second phase of practice—the completion stage (*utpannakrama*)—uses controlled sensory deprivation, mental fixation, and manipulation of respiration and other energies in the body to induce a physiological and psychic condition similar to death. In this state all forms of ideation cease, and the practitioner obtains a vision of the emptiness image (*śūnyatābimbam*). The emptiness image is a gnosis that nonconceptually cognizes the totality of the universe in terms of both conventional truth (the appearances of ordinary phenomena) and ultimate truth (the universal emptiness that is everything's lack of absolute, autonomous existence). Vision of the emptiness image gives rise to imperishable bliss (*akṣarasukha*), so that gnosis and bliss are inseparably fused. Repeated cultivation of this experience purifies the mind of obscurations, finally culminating in the practitioner's achievement of the transcendent, perfect awakening of a buddha.

Myth

According to the Kālacakra tradition, the Buddha taught this tantra at the Dhānyakaṭaka stūpa in South India to King Sucandra, ruler of Shambhala, a vast empire located in Central Asia. The Kālacakra was

Cakrin, twenty-fifth Kalkin of Shambhala. A prophecy of the Kālacakra says that at the end of the current age of degeneration, Cakrin will conquer the followers of the "barbarian religion," inaugurating a new golden age. © Lokesh Chandra. Reproduced by permission.

preserved in Shambhala by Sucandra's successors, the sixth of whom—Yaśas—was given the title Kalkin for unifying all of the castes of Shambhala within a single Vajrayāna family. Also, the Kālacakra prophesies that at the end of the current age of degeneration, the twenty-fifth Kalkin of Shambhala—Cakrin—will lead the Hindu gods and the army of Shambhala in battle at Baghdad against the followers of the "barbarian religion" Islam. Kalkin Cakrin's defeat of the forces of Islam will mark the end of the age of degeneration and the beginning of a new golden age.

The preceding is a Buddhist rewriting of the earlier Hindu myth of Kalki updated to suit historical conditions contemporaneous with the origin of the Kālacakra. In the Hindu myth it is prophesied that the great god VIṢṆU will incarnate as a brahman warrior named Kalki in the village of Shambhala. At the end of the age of degeneration, Kalki will eradicate barbarians and unruly outcastes, thus reestablishing brahman supremacy and initiating a new golden age.

The Kālacakra first appeared in India during the early decades of the eleventh century C.E., when, in the name of Islam, Sultan Mahmud of Ghazni conducted expeditions of plunder and iconoclastic destruction in northwestern India. Thus the Kālacakra's retelling of the prophetic myth of Kalki replaces a brahman Hindu hero with a Buddhist messiah in response to the traumatizing depredations of the Muslim invaders of India.

History

The most important texts of the Kālacakra system contain a date that enables scholars to determine that they were completed between 1025 and approximately 1040. The authors of these works disguised their identities with mythic pseudonyms, but among the known early masters of the tradition is Piṇḍo (tenth–eleventh century), a brahman Buddhist monk born in Java who taught the famous Dīpaṃkaraśrījñāna (ATISHA; 982–1054), and Nāropāda (d.u.–ca. 1040), the renowned Vajrayāna teacher of Nālandā monastic university. The Kālacakra flourished among the Buddhist intelligentsia of northern India from the eleventh through the thirteenth centuries, and it continued to be studied and practiced in India until at least the end of the sixteenth century.

From northern India the Kālacakra spread to Nepal and Tibet, and from Tibet it was transmitted to Mongolia and China. The Tibetans produced a vast literature on the system, and continue to study and practice the Kālacakra. During the last decades of the twentieth century, the fourteenth DALAI LAMA of Tibet performed the Kālacakra initiation rites on numerous occasions in Asia and in the United States, fostering the continued cross-cultural diffusion of this important Vajrayāna tradition.

See also: **Hinduism and Buddhism; Islam and Buddhism; Tantra**

Bibliography

Lamrimpa, Gen. *Transcending Time: An Explanation of the Kālachakra Six-Session Guru Yoga,* tr. B. Alan Wallace. Boston: Wisdom, 1999.

Newman, John. "Eschatology in the Wheel of Time Tantra." In *Buddhism in Practice,* ed. Donald S. Lopez, Jr. Princeton, NJ: Princeton University Press, 1995.

Newman, John. "Itineraries to Sambhala." In *Tibetan Literature: Studies in Genre,* ed. José Ignacio Cabezón and Roger R. Jackson. Ithaca, NY: Snow Lion, 1996.

Newman, John. "Islam in the Kālacakra Tantra." *Journal of the International Association of Buddhist Studies* 21, no. 2 (1998): 311–371.

Newman, John. "Vajrayoga in the Kālacakra Tantra." In *Tantra in Practice,* ed. David Gordon White. Princeton, NJ: Princeton University Press, 2000.

Sopa, Geshe Lhundub; Jackson, Roger; and Newman, John. *The Wheel of Time: The Kālachakra in Context.* Ithaca, NY: Snow Lion, 1991.

JOHN NEWMAN

KAMAKURA BUDDHISM, JAPAN

Kamakura Buddhism is a modern scholarly term referring to a phase in the development of Japanese Buddhism coinciding with the Kamakura period (1185–1333). The term also refers to several new Buddhist movements that appeared during that time, specifically, Pure Land, Zen, and Nichiren. These movements eventually became the dominant schools of Buddhism in Japan. Kamakura Buddhism is typically contrasted to NARA BUDDHISM and Heian Buddhism, which denote other forms of Buddhism and the periods in which they emerged. These three categories—Nara, Heian, and Kamakura Buddhism—provide a historical periodization as well as a conceptual framework for the classification of Buddhist schools. Of the three, Kamakura Buddhism is frequently portrayed as the most significant, especially in light of the large memberships of its modern denominations. This threefold classification appears in most surveys of Japanese Buddhism, although some scholars question whether it accurately reflects the character of Buddhism in each historical period and the actual course of its development.

The foundations on which Kamakura Buddhism arose were the religious traditions of the Nara (710–784) and Heian (794–1185) periods. These periods correspond to the time when Japan's capital was located first in the city of Nara and then in Heian (Kyoto). The Kamakura period is likewise named after a city, Kamakura, where the first warrior government was established in 1185. Hence, the periodization of Japanese history, as well as the classification of its Buddhist schools, has arisen as an extension of Japan's geography and political history. There are questions whether this political framework offers the best structure for categorizing and analyzing Japanese Buddhism, but it has become the most common template used in presentations of Japanese Buddhism.

Nara and Heian Buddhism

Nara Buddhism is typically equated with six schools, or more properly six traditions, of Buddhist scholarship. These developed during the eighth century at major monasteries in and around Nara, such as Tōdaiji, Kōfukuji, Gangōji, Daianji, and Tōshōdaiji. The six consist specifically of: (1) Kusha, the study of the ABHIDHARMAKOŚABHĀṢYA, a treatise that analyzes all things into atomistic units; (2) Hossō, the study of YOGĀCĀRA, a philosophy attributing this atomistic reality to mind only; (3) Jōjitsu (Chinese, Chengshi), the study of a treatise that recognizes discrete elements at a conventional level, but not at an absolute level; (4) Sanron, the study of MADHYAMAKA, a philosophy using emptiness as a concept to refute the standard ideas of existence and nonexistence; (5) Kegon (Chinese, HUAYAN), a philosophy of interdependence and mutual identification among all things; and (6) Ritsu (Sanskrit, VINAYA), a systematic exposition of the rules, procedures, and lifestyle applying to the Buddhist clergy.

These six schools represent a complex body of knowledge transplanted from the Asian mainland and studied by clerics as correlative systems rather than as competing philosophies. The state sanctioned and supported the monasteries in which they flourished, and sought to make Buddhist learning and the entire Buddhist order its own preserve. It oversaw who could become priests and nuns, and issued regulations governing them. Such control, aimed at protection of the state and concrete benefits, is considered a defining characteristic of Nara Buddhism. Despite the state's efforts, Buddhist beliefs and practices began to spread more widely in the population, primarily through itinerant Buddhist preachers such as Gyōki (or Gyōgi, 668–749).

Heian Buddhism refers specifically to the Tendai and Shingon schools, which emerged at the beginning of the Heian period (794–1185) and quickly dominated religious affairs in Japan. This new phase commenced soon after the imperial capital was moved from Nara to Kyoto in an attempt to distance the government from the encroaching influence of the Nara temples. Heian Buddhism arose in a sense as a reaction to Nara Buddhism, and also as a continuing expansion of Buddhism from the Asian continent. The Heian founders, SAICHŌ (767–822) of Tendai and KŪKAI (774–835) of Shingon, studied Buddhism in China and introduced into Japan trends they encountered there, along with adaptations of their own. Each considered his own form of Buddhism superior to

The Great Buddha of Kamakura, Japan. (Japanese, bronze, 1252.) © Edifice/Corbis. Reproduced by permission.

those preserved in the Nara temples. The Tendai tradition that Saichō established claimed the LOTUS SŪTRA (SADDHARMAPUṆḌARĪKA-SŪTRA) as its core text; propounded the doctrines of emptiness, provisional reality, and the middle way; and developed a complex monastic program of meditative training and rituals, influenced in part by Kūkai's esoteric teachings. Saichō also sought to make his monastic community, located on Mount Hiei northeast of Kyoto, independent of the Nara Buddhist organization by developing his own procedures for ordaining clerics based on MAHĀYĀNA precepts.

Kūkai, for his part, advanced the Shingon idea of the all-pervasive presence of Dainichi (Mahāvairocana) Buddha and the actualization of buddhahood through physical, verbal, and mental acts of ritual. Instead of distancing himself from Nara Buddhism, Kūkai introduced Shingon esoteric ritual into Tōdaiji and other temples, and at the same time developed his own Shingon institutions at Tōji in Kyoto and on Mount Kōya near Osaka. Tendai and Shingon Buddhism thus took their place alongside Nara Buddhism as the religious establishment of Japan, and in many ways superseded it. Both operated in partnership with the ruling powers, creating a religious and ideological foundation for governance. Materially, they benefited from the burgeoning estate system in the Japanese medieval economy, which richly endowed their temples and monasteries and allowed them to develop elaborate traditions of religious training, ritual, doctrine, and iconography. Their beliefs, practices, and institutions, especially those found on Mount Hiei, were the matrix from which Kamakura Buddhism arose.

The emergence of Kamakura Buddhism

Kamakura Buddhism is commonly presented as a reaction to Heian Buddhism, just as Heian is considered a reaction to Nara Buddhism. By the twelfth century the burgeoning Tendai and Shingon institutions, combined with the Nara temples, formed the prevailing religious order of Japan, frequently referred to as the eight schools (*hasshū*). The fledgling movements that eventually grew into the Kamakura schools emerged out of this milieu and to a certain extent reacted against it. Their teachings and practices were inspired by the existing traditions, and their founders received training at established monasteries and temples, particularly on Mount Hiei. But they approached mainstream Buddhism selectively, embracing some teachings and rejecting others. All three forms of Kamakura Buddhism—Pure Land, Zen, and Nichiren—thus developed different orientations from Tendai, Shingon, and Nara Buddhism, and quickly diverged from their norm.

PURE LAND BUDDHISM was perhaps the largest and most pervasive segment of Kamakura Buddhism. The specific Japanese schools commonly classified in the Pure Land category are the Jōdoshū school founded by HŌNEN (1133–1212), the Jōdo Shinshū school founded by SHINRAN (1173–1263), and the Jishū school founded by IPPEN CHISHIN (1239–1289). All three lived during the Kamakura period, and emphasized devotion to AMITĀBHA Buddha and rebirth in his Pure Land paradise. Pure Land beliefs and practices had already emerged as prominent elements in Japanese Buddhism, particularly on Mount Hiei and in aristocratic society. But the Kamakura founders stressed them even more, often to the exclusion of other forms of Buddhism. Hōnen, who was the most prominent Pure Land master of his time, advocated exclusive practice of the *nenbutsu*, invoking or chanting the name of the Buddha Amitābha in the form *Namu Amida Butsu*. Shinran, who was his disciple, believed that it is Amitābha's power that leads people to enlightenment in the Pure Land and that infuses them with *nenbutsu* practice and FAITH (*shinjin*). Ippen, an itinerant Pure Land holy man, considered the *nenbutsu* an act wherein the Buddha and the believer merge, and he spread the *nenbutsu* widely through distribution of amulets inscribed with it. Hōnen's initiatives inspired an independent Pure Land movement, but also provoked a harsh reaction from established temples and monasteries, resulting in his banishment from Kyoto for four years. Shinran's following, which grew to be a mass movement two centuries later, was distinctive in that its clergy, in accord with his example, forsook Buddhism's clerical celibacy, and married and begot families. And Ippen's activities led to an extensive network of *dōjō* (congregational meeting places) of *nenbutsu* practitioners.

Zen, the second form of Kamakura Buddhism, consists of the Rinzai school, founded by Eisai (or Yōsai, 1141–1215) and others, and the Sōtō school, begun by DŌGEN (1200–1253). Both were monks on Mount Hiei, and both traveled to China for further training in monasteries. Each emphasized Zen meditation as a crucial religious practice, though for somewhat different reasons. Eisai considered Tendai Buddhism on Mount Hiei to be in decline, and he sought to revitalize it by introducing China's method of Zen training (and also by emphasizing clerical precepts anew). But Mount Hiei rejected his initiatives. Eisai, nonetheless, found an ally in the recently established warrior government, which first supported him as a Zen master in the city of Kamakura and later sponsored his new Zen monastery, Kenninji, in Kyoto. These institutions, along with others established by subsequent Chinese and Japanese masters, became the basis for the Rinzai branch of Zen. Dōgen, for his part, also trained on Mount Hiei and then at Kenninji before traveling to China. He regarded the Zen method he learned there as Buddhism's most authentic form, and upon returning to Japan he quickly built a following around it, separate from his previous affiliations. Eventually he received patronage from a regional lord who enabled him to establish a monastery, Eiheiji, in the remote province of Echizen. The monastic rules and routines that Dōgen formulated there became the starting point of Sōtō Zen in Japan. At the heart of his teaching and monastic community was Zen MEDITATION, which he considered the very practice of enlightenment.

Nichiren Buddhism, known widely in medieval times as the Hokkeshū, or Lotus school, comprises the third tradition of Kamakura Buddhism, which is named after its founder NICHIREN (1222–1282). Nichiren was active somewhat later than the other Kamakura founders, but like most of them he was trained for a period in Tendai Buddhism on Mount Hiei. Early in his career he was exposed to various forms of Buddhism including Pure Land, Zen, and Shingon, but on Mount Hiei he fixed upon the *Lotus Sūtra,* Tendai's central scripture, as the highest teaching. While utilizing Tendai terminology and doctrine to articulate his ideas, over time Nichiren came to emphasize single-minded and exclusive devotion to the *Lotus,* and he promoted the practice of the DAIMOKU, chanting the title of the sūtra in the form *Namu Myōhō-renge-kyō* as the quintessential expression of the *Lotus Sūtra*'s truth and power. This practice existed in certain Tendai circles prior to Nichiren's time, but he championed it with a fervor surpassing all previous proponents. At the same time, Nichiren began to criticize other forms of Buddhism—specifically, Pure Land, Zen, Shingon, and Ritsu. This action earned him the enmity of the warrior government in Kamakura, which patronized them. On two occasions the government banished Nichiren to remote parts of Japan as punishment. These events marginalized Nichiren and his following, even as he continued to attract believers, including a significant number of women, to his Lotus teachings.

Kamakura Buddhism as a scholarly category

The classification of the Pure Land, Zen, and Nichiren movements as Kamakura Buddhism occurred largely in the late nineteenth and early twentieth century. Scholars then began to identify Kamakura times as a period of significant and lasting change in Japanese religion. To highlight this change they coined the terms *New Buddhism,* to refer to the six schools traceable to the Kamakura period, and *Old Buddhism,* to indicate the eight schools originating in Nara and Heian times. Scholars further attributed distinct characteristics and orientations to New Buddhism that set it apart from the earlier forms. Specifically, New Buddhism tended to reduce religious practice to a single simple activity that could be performed by most people, such as the *nenbutsu,* Zen meditation, or the daimoku. New Buddhism was oriented more to the salvation of regular people than to the lofty goals and arduous lifestyle of monastic elites. Such practices were not predicated on a mastery of complex doctrine, but usually involved a simple religious stance of faith, sincerity, and devotion. Also, such practices did not require the intercession of priests, but could be performed on an individual basis. This focus on specific uncomplicated religious practices made New Buddhism more exclusivistic, distilling religion to the bare essentials, in contrast to Old Buddhism, which was more inclusivitic, integrating a vast array of practices, beliefs, texts, deities, rituals, and ecclesiastical ranks into a multifaceted religious culture. In the process, New Buddhism set aside many of the magical and apotropaic concerns of Old Buddhism in order to concentrate on personal salvation. Overall, the new Kamakura movements are portrayed as the democratization of Japanese Buddhism—that is, the extension of Buddhism beyond a predominantly upper-class, male, clerical elite to include lowly, female, and lay adherents. This view of Japan's religious development has dominated scholarship for the last century, though it has been subject to a variety of refinements and critiques.

A by-product of this characterization of Kamakura Buddhism has been the tendency to compare it to the Protestant Reformation in Europe. In fact, the example of the Reformation may have influenced the way scholars conceived of Kamakura Buddhism and the features they highlighted. The parallels most often cited between the two are an emphasis on faith, the emergence of a married clergy, the decentralization of religious authority, and the diminished role of clerical intercessors. Among the various forms of Kamakura Buddhism, Shinran's school, the Jōdo Shinshū, has attracted the greatest attention. Shinran himself is frequently compared to Martin Luther. Were it not for Shinran and his school, however, it is questionable how germane the Reformation model would be for analyzing Japanese Buddhism. The tendency to equate Kamakura Buddhism to the Protestant Reformation has declined in recent decades, especially as scholars examine Japanese Buddhism in greater depth and identify dissimilarities. Nonetheless, the terminology of reform has persisted, even though Kamakura is now treated as its own distinct example of reform.

One difficulty in attributing special characteristics to this New Buddhism is that many of the reforms identified in it also occurred in Old Buddhism. Hence, one of the refinements to the category of Kamakura Buddhism has been to extend its boundaries to include various movements and new developments in the Heian and Nara schools too. It is well known, for instance, that various eminent priests of Tendai, Shingon, and the Nara temples were drawn to the *nenbutsu* as a religious practice, and some to Zen meditation also. In addition, various clerics from Nara, such as Jōkei (1155–1213) and Myōe KŌBEN (1173–1232), promoted popular and easily practiced devotions to Buddhist deities, including Śākyamuni Buddha, the future Buddha MAITREYA, and the Bodhisattva Mañjuśrī. Though not as widespread as Pure Land devotions to Amitābha, these practices were often conducted in a similar manner—for instance, chanting the name of the buddha or bodhisattva before an enshrined image or sacred object. Another initiative in Old Buddhism was to revive the Buddhist PRECEPTS, just as Eisai sought to do alongside Zen meditation in his monastery. Ostensibly, this was done to revitalize the Buddhist order, which was considered lax and in decline. But administering the Buddhist precepts was not limited to clerics. Nara proponents such as Eison (1209–1290) developed mass ceremonies for administering lay precepts to ordinary people as well. Thus, Old Buddhism responded to their needs and religious proclivities as much as New Buddhism did. This wave of popular practice, however, did not displace traditional rituals and doctrine in the established temples, but emerged alongside them. In fact, some learned priests such as GYŌNEN (1240–1321) and Kakuzen (b. 1143) compiled systematic accounts of doctrine, compendiums of beliefs and practices, and historiographies of Buddhism as another way of revitalizing their schools. Hence, Old Buddhism was equally caught up in the religious ferment of the Kamakura period, even while maintaining its traditions of the past.

The most important critique of Kamakura Buddhism as a scholarly concept is found in the alternative theory of medieval Japanese religion proposed by the historian Kuroda Toshio (1926–1993). This theory centers on the idea that the dominant form of religion in medieval times was Kenmitsu, or exoteric-esoteric, Buddhism. Specifically, this refers to an array of practices and assumptions found widely in the temples, monasteries, and organizations of Tendai, Shingon, and Nara Buddhism, rather than in the new Pure Land, Zen, and Nichiren movements. Kenmitsu Buddhism was, in short, Japan's medieval orthodoxy, binding together the mainstream institutions through commonly recognized esoteric rituals, even while they diverged on exoteric doctrine. Esoteric ritual was considered efficacious in achieving both spiritual and worldly goals, so the ruling powers of Japan looked to Kenmitsu Buddhism for support and, in turn, patronized and promoted it. Inherent in this depiction of religion is the supposition that the new Kamakura movements were, at best, minor participants in medieval culture and, at worst, heretical fringe groups. The upshot of this view is that Nara and Heian Buddhism are recognized as greater and longer influences on Japan's history than is commonly acknowledged. The Kamakura Buddhism model thus reflects a projection back onto medieval times of the early modern and modern religious order, since most of its institutions gained prominence only around the fifteenth and sixteenth centuries, toward the end of the medieval period.

The Kenmitsu theory offers a critique of the presumption that Kamakura Buddhism was the focal point and the most representative expression of medieval Japanese religion. This critique is built on an astute analysis of medieval religious institutional culture, and it provides an important correction to the tendency to inflate the significance of the new Pure Land, Zen, and Nichiren movements in medieval Japan. But whether the Kenmitsu theory can actually lay to rest the Kamakura Buddhism model is another question. For all its shortcomings, the model underscores the point that over time Japan underwent notable changes in its religious outlook and practice, which are embedded in the dominant forms of Japanese Buddhism today, and that those changes had their inception, if not their heyday, in the Kamakura period. This assumption is so pervasive in the study of Japanese Buddhism that the Kamakura model is likely to continue as an important category in explaining the development of Buddhism in Japan.

See also: **Chan School; Exoteric-Esoteric (Kenmitsu) Buddhism in Japan; Japan; Nenbutsu (Chinese, Nianfo; Korean, Yŏmbul); Nichiren School; Shingon Buddhism, Japan; Tiantai School**

Bibliography

Bellah, Robert N. "The Contemporary Meaning of Kamakura Buddhism." *Journal of the American Academy of Religion* 42, no. 1 (1974): 3–17.

Dobbins, James C., ed. *The Legacy of Kuroda Toshio.* Special issue. *Japanese Journal of Religious Studies* 23, nos. 3–4 (Fall 1996).

Dobbins, James C. "Envisioning Kamakura Buddhism." In *Re-Visioning "Kamakura" Buddhism,* ed. Richard K. Payne. Honolulu: University of Hawaii Press, 1998.

Foard, James H. "In Search of a Lost Reformation: A Reconsideration of Kamakura Buddhism." *Japanese Journal of Religious Studies* 7, no. 4 (1980): 261–291.

Ienaga Saburō. *Chūsei Bukkyō shisōshi kenkyū* (A Study of the Intellectual History of Medieval Buddhism), revised edition. Kyoto: Hōzōkan, 1955.

Kuroda Toshio. "Bukkyō kakushin undo no rekishi teki seikaku" (The Historical Character of Buddhism's Reform Movement). In *Nihon chūsei no shakai to shūkyō* (Society and Religion in Medieval Japan). Tokyo: Iwanami Shoten, 1990.

Matsunaga, Daigan, and Matsunaga, Alicia. *Foundation of Japanese Buddhism,* Vol. 2: *The Mass Movement: Kamakura and Muromachi Periods.* Los Angeles and Tokyo: Buddhist Books International, 1976.

Morrell, Robert E. *Early Kamakura Buddhism: A Minority Report.* Berkeley, CA: Asian Humanities Press, 1987.

Payne, Richard K., ed. *Re-Visioning "Kamakura" Buddhism.* Honolulu: University of Hawaii Press, 1998.

Ōsumi Kazuo. "Buddhism in the Kamakura Period." In *The Cambridge History of Japan,* Vol. 3: *Medieval Japan,* ed. Kozo Yamamura. Cambridge, UK: Cambridge University Press, 1990.

Stone, Jacqueline I. *Original Enlightenment and the Transformation of Medieval Japanese Buddhism.* Honolulu: University of Hawaii Press, 1999.

Weinstein, Stanley. "The Concept of Reformation in Japanese Buddhism." In *Studies in Japanese Culture,* Vol. 2, ed. Saburō Ōta. Tokyo: Japan Pen Club, 1973.

JAMES C. DOBBINS

KARMA (ACTION)

The term *karma,* which literally means "action," is frequently used in the context of what can be called the doctrine of karma: the belief that acts bring about their retribution, usually in a subsequent existence. This belief is nowadays shared by many Hindus, Buddhists, Jainas, and others, but the details can vary considerably between different believers. In order to understand the doctrine of karma in Indian Buddhism it will be necessary briefly to explore its historical background.

Buddhism was originally one of the religious currents that made up the so-called Śramaṇa (mendicant) movement. Other religious currents belonging to the same movement were Jainism and Ājīvikism; there were no doubt more such currents, but no details about them have survived. All these currents shared the conviction that acts will bring about their retribution. Moreover, they all seem to have shared the aspiration to end the endless cycle of rebirths that results from acts and their consequences. Buddhism, too, was based on these convictions, and it, too, was driven by the aspiration to free its practitioners from the results of their acts, that is, from REBIRTH.

The surviving sources indicate that, outside Buddhism, especially two methods believed to lead to the desired goal had found acceptance among practitioners. On the one hand there were those who drew the conclusion that, if acts are responsible for the consequences that one tries to avoid, the solution can only lie in the practice of complete motionlessness of body and mind. This form of asceticism, preferably performed until death, found followers among the Jainas, the Ājivikas, and elsewhere. There were, however, others who preferred a second method. This method is, in its conception, as simple as it is elegant. If acts lead to undesired consequences, it is sufficient to realize that one has never committed those acts to begin with. And indeed, one has never committed those acts, because that which one really is, one's true self (ātman), does not act by its very nature. This second method, in which transcendental insight plays a central role, found entrance into the Vedic Upaniṣads and is almost omnipresent in later Hindu religious literature.

Both of these methods are based on a simple and straightforward notion as to what are acts; clearly all forms of bodily and mental motion, and only bodily and mental motion, are involved here. Complete physical and mental immobility would obviously be a poor, or exaggerated, response if only certain acts (such as, for example, only morally relevant acts) have karmic consequences.

Early Buddhism did not accept these two methods because it did not share with the other religious currents of that period this specific notion of karma. Early Buddhism does not identify bodily and mental motion, but DESIRE (or thirst, *tṛṣṇā*), as the cause of karmic consequences. Neither physical and mental immobility nor insight into the true nature of a presumed self will have any effect on the presence of desire, which means that Buddhism had to find a different method. This is what the Buddha is reported to have done; his method is psychological, and it is said to destroy desire.

It should be clear from the above that the Buddhist understanding of the doctrine of karma and the Buddhist PATH to liberation are intricately linked. Both the rejection of extreme ASCETIC PRACTICES and the doctrine of no-self (though variously interpreted, even by the later Buddhists themselves) owe their origin to the specifically Buddhist understanding of the doctrine of karma.

The authentic Buddhist path to liberation, however, is difficult to understand and difficult to practice. Moreover, it appears that the canonical passages that describe it were not sufficiently clear even to many early Buddhist converts. This would explain why Buddhism in India, from its early days onward, time and again reintroduced, in various shapes, the methods that had been rejected by its founder. In particular, already in canonical times, ascetic practices that were centered on the suppression of mental activity made their way into Buddhism. More recent texts speak of the suppression of all activity, both mental and physical, as a desirable aim. An idea that is structurally similar to the non-Buddhist ātman doctrine found its way into the Buddhist canon in the form of the Buddhist anātman (no-self) doctrine; in both cases the doctrine implies the realization that one does not really act. More recent developments in Indian Buddhism introduce notions, such as that of the TATHĀGATAGARBHA, that are even more similar to the initially rejected ātman doctrine.

The causal process leading to karmic retribution is described, from canonical times onward, in terms of the causal chain of items called PRATĪTYASAMUTPĀDA (DEPENDENT ORIGINATION). This causal chain has been variously interpreted and elaborated in the Buddhist scholastic tradition.

However, problems linked to karmic retribution remained. How, indeed, should one imagine that a bad deed committed in one life will give rise to punishment in another one without the intervention of a conscious and all-powerful agent who keeps account of all the acts carried out by all living beings? The problem of karmic retribution presented itself to various non-Buddhists in India as well, who often solved it precisely by postulating the existence of a creator God who was in charge of it. Buddhism, on the other hand, had no place for a creator God. The workings of karmic retribution, though essential to Indian Buddhists, remained therefore a mystery to many of them.

A daring attempt to solve this mystery finds expression in the YOGĀCĀRA SCHOOL of Buddhist thought, and most clearly in the writings of VASUBANDHU (ca. fourth century C.E.), who presumably converted to Yogācāra later in life. It starts from the question of what exactly links an act with its (often much later) retribution. In his early work, the ABHIDHARMAKOŚABHĀṢYA, Vasubandhu stated already that this link is constituted by a series of mental events. Furthermore, he conceived of the initial intentional act, too, as a mind-event. Its fruition, however, is not normally a mind-event, but an event in the world. How is this to be explained? Vasubandhu does not attempt to answer this question in his *Abhidharmakośabhāṣya.* In his later *Viṃśikā* (*Twenty Verses*) he does. In this work, he offers the solution that the fruition of an act, like the act itself and the intermediate sequence, must be a mind-event. That is to say, acts and their consequences, and therefore the whole world, are nothing but mind-events. Vasubandhu opts here for idealism in order to solve a problem that resulted from the doctrine of karma.

The Buddhist doctrine of karma, then, is intimately linked to the specific ways to liberation accepted by Indian Buddhists in the course of time, but also to certain doctrinal developments.

See also: **Anātman/Ātman (No-Self/Self); Critical Buddhism (Hihan Bukkyō); Hinduism and Buddhism; India; Jainism and Buddhism**

Bibliography

Bronkhorst, Johannes. "The Buddha and the Jainas Reconsidered." *Asiatische Studien/Études Asiatiques* 49, no. 2 (1995): 333–350.

Bronkhorst, Johannes. *Karma and Teleology: A Problem and Its Solutions in Indian Philosophy.* Tokyo: International Institute for Buddhist Studies, 2000.

Cox, Collett. "Dependent Origination: Its Elaboration in Early Sarvāstivādin Abhidharma Texts." In *Researches in Indian and Buddhist Philosophy: Essays in Honour of Professor Alex Wayman,* ed. Ram Karan Sharma. Delhi: Motilal Banarsidass, 1993.

La Vallée Poussin, Louis de. *L'Abhidharmakośa de Vasubandhu: Traduction et Annotations* (1923). Brussels: Institut Belge des Hautes Etudes Chinoises, 1980.

Potter, Karl H., ed. *Encyclopedia of Indian Philosophies,* Vol. 8: *Buddhist Philosophy from 100 to 350 A.D.* Delhi: Motilal Banarsidass, 1999.

Schmithausen, Lambert. "Zur zwölfgliedrigen Formel des Entstehens in Abhängigkeit." *Hōrin: Vergleichende Studien zur japanischen Kultur* 7 (2000): 41–76.

Willemen, Charles; Dessein, Bart; and Cox, Collett. *Sarvāstivāda Buddhist Scholasticism.* Leiden, Netherlands: Brill, 1998.

JOHANNES BRONKHORST

KARMA PA

Karma pa is an appellation given to the spiritual head of the Karma BKA' BRGYUD (KAGYU), a major branch of the larger Bka' brgyud sect of Tibetan Buddhism. The term *Karma pa* is commonly etymologized as "Man of (Enlightened) Action (karma)." The Karma pas are considered to form the first institutionalized succession of reincarnated masters (*sprul sku,* pronounced *tulku*) in Tibet, a process whereby a young child is recognized as the reembodiment of a recently deceased master and raised to continue the latter's religious and political activities. In a tradition perhaps unique to the Karma pas, prior to his death each hierarch is said to compose a letter predicting the date and location of his future rebirth. Entrusted to a close disciple, this prediction letter then forms the basis for seeking out the prelate's next incarnation.

The Karma pas are traditionally believed to be the custodians of a black crown fashioned from the hair of 100,000 ḌĀKINĪ goddesses, invisible to all save those of great spiritual merit. In the early fifteenth century, the Ming emperor Yongle offered the fifth Karma pa a physical replica, which has since become one of the lineage's most sacred relics, believed to confer liberation upon those who merely see it. For this reason, the Karma pas are sometimes called the Black Crowned (*zhwa nag*) and have somewhat unwittingly received the title Black Hat Lama in the West. While they have occasionally been the target—and the source—of polemical sectarian attack, the Karma pas (like the Dalai Lamas) are traditionally understood by Tibetans to be emanations of the Bodhisattva of Compassion, Avalokiteśvara. They rank among Tibet's greatest religious figures, revered for their learning and exposition as well as their mastery of yogic and meditative disciplines, and at times they have wielded tremendous secular influence and political power.

The line of Karma pas originated during the twelfth century with the first Karma pa, Dus gsum mkhyen pa (Dusum Khyenpa, 1110–1193), a close disciple of Sgam po pa Bsod nams rin chen (Gampopa Sönam Rinchen, 1079–1153), who had studied under the famous yogin MI LA RAS PA (MILAREPA, 1028/40–1111/23). Dus gsum mkhyen pa established several important monasteries, including Karma Dgon (Karma Gön) in eastern Tibet and, in 1187, Stod lung Mtshur phu (Tölung Tshurphu), northwest of Lhasa. The latter was expanded during subsequent generations, becoming one of the region's leading institutions and serving as the main seat of the Karma pas and the Karma Bka' brgyud. Dus gsum mkhyen pa's successor, the second Karma pa, Karma Pakshi (1204–1283), is remembered especially for his prowess in meditation and the performance of magical feats. Patronized for a time by the Mongol emperor Kublai Khan (r. 1260–1294), he

The seventeenth Karma pa, O rgyan 'phrin las rdo rje (Orgyan Trinle Dorje), in Dharamsala, India, in 2000. AP/Wide World Photos. Reproduced by permission.

established ties with the Yuan court in China. The third Karma pa, Rang 'byung rdo rje (Rangjung Dorje, 1284–1339), advanced his predecessor's affiliation with the Mongol court by supervising Emperor Toghun Temur's (r. 1333–1368) ascension to the throne. He was also influenced, like his predecessor, by the RNYING MA (NYINGMA) sect's teachings on the Great Perfection (*rdzogs chen*), and he authored several important treatises on tantric theory and practice.

The fourth Karma pa, Rol pa'i rdo rje (Rolpe Dorje, 1340–1383), and the fifth Karma pa, De bzhin gshegs pa (Dezhin Shekpa, 1384–1415), continued to develop ties with the Chinese court—the former with Toghun Temur and the latter serving as guru to the Ming dynasty emperor Yongle (r. 1402–1424), a position of great influence. While the sixth Karma pa, Mthong ba don ldan (Thongwa Dondan, 1416–1453), did not actively pursue the political connections established by his predecessors, he is known for reinvigorating the ritual practice of the Karma Bka' brgyud, authoring numerous meditation and liturgical manuals. The seventh Karma pa, Chos grags rgya mtsho (Chödrak Gyatso, 1454–1506), is remembered primarily for his philosophical writings on logic and epistemology. His voluminous work on the topic of *pramāṇa* is still used as a principal textbook in many Bka' brgyud monasteries. The eighth Karma pa, Mi bskyod rdo rje (Mikyö Dorje, 1507–1554), was likewise a prolific scholar whose writings encompassed Sanskrit linguistics, poetry, and art, as well as MADHYAMAKA SCHOOL philosophy and TANTRA. Several of his works sparked a heated debate with DGE LUGS (GELUK) scholars by criticizing the views of their founder, TSONG KHA PA (1357–1419), and his *Thun bzhi bla ma'i rnal 'byor* (*Four Session Guru Yoga*) remains an important, widely practiced meditation text. The ninth Karma pa, Dbang phyug rdo rje (Wangchuk Dorje, 1604–1674), is revered for his seminal writings on the theory and practice of MAHĀMUDRĀ. However, with the ascendance of the Mongol backed Dge lugs hierarchs, he also witnessed the decline of his sect's political influence in central Tibetan politics. His successor, the tenth Karma pa, Chos kyi dbang phyug (Chökyi Wangchuk, 1604–1674), was thus forced into virtual exile near the Sino-Tibetan border in the east. As the civil war in Tibet waned, Chos kyi dbang phyug returned to Lhasa where he forged ties with Tibet's new religious and political leader, the fifth DALAI LAMA Ngag dbang blo bzang rgya mtsho (Ngawang Lozang Gyatso, 1617–1682).

The eleventh Karma pa, Ye shes rdo rje (Yeshe Dorje, 1676–1702), and twelfth Karma pa, Byang chub rdo rje (Changchub Dorje, 1703–1732), both lived relatively short lives, although the latter made an important journey through Nepal together with his disciple, the brilliant scholar and Sanskritist Situ Chos kyi 'byung gnas (Chökyi Jungne, 1700–1774). The life of thirteenth Karma pa, Bdud 'dul rdo rje (Dudul Dorje, 1733–1797), was, for the most part, lived outside the sphere of politics. He is especially remembered for his love of birds and animals, to whom he is said to have taught the dharma. Together with his predecessor, the fourteenth Karma pa, Theg mchog rdo rje (Thekchok Dorje, 1798–1868), witnessed a revival of Bka' brgyud doctrine in the eastern Tibetan province of Khams, as part of the so-called Eclectic (*ris med*) Movement of which his disciple Kongs sprul Blo gros mtha' yas (Kongtrul Lodrö Thaye, 1813–1899) was a leading voice. The fifteenth Karma pa, Mkha' khyab rdo rje (Khakhyab Dorje, 1871–1922), the latter's principal disciple, continued to support this movement and left an ample body of collected writings. The sixteenth Karma pa, Rang 'byung rig pa'i rdo rje (Rangjung Rigpe Dorje, 1924–1981), faced the Communist Chinese occupation of Tibet; he fled to India in 1959 and established an exile seat at Rumtek Monastery in

Sikkim. He traveled widely throughout Europe and North America prior to his death in a Chicago hospital, establishing numerous Tibetan Buddhist centers and attracting a large following of Western devotees. The seventeenth Karma pa, O rgyan 'phrin las rdo rje (Orgyan Trinle Dorje, b. 1985), was enthroned at Mtshur phu Monastery in Tibet on September 27, 1992. In late December 2000 he escaped into exile, establishing a temporary residence in Dharamsala, India, where he continued to reside as of 2003. Although his identification as the Karma pa has been disputed by a small number of followers, O rgyan 'phrin las rdo rje maintains the support of the majority of the Tibetan and Western Buddhist community, including the Dalai Lama.

Bibliography

Douglas, Nik, and White, Meryl. *Karmapa: The Black Hat Lama of Tibet.* London: Luzac, 1978.

Hilton, Isabel. "Flight of the Lama." *New York Times Magazine* (March 12, 2000): 50–55.

Karma Thinley. *The History of the Sixteen Karmapas.* Boulder, CO: Prajña Press, 1978.

Martin, Michele. *Music in the Sky: The Life, Art, and Teaching of the 17th Karmapa Ogyen Trinle Dorje.* Ithaca, NY: Snow Lion, 2003.

Richardson, Hugh. "The Karma-pa Sect: A Historical Note." *Journal of the Royal Asiatic Society* (1958): 139–164, and (1959): 1–18. Reprinted in *High Peaks, Pure Earth: Collected Writings on Tibetan History and Culture,* ed. Michael Aris. London: Serindia, 1998.

Richardson, Hugh. "Chos-dbyings rdo-rje, the Tenth Black Hat Karma-pa." *Bulletin of Tibetology,* new series 1 (1987): 25–42. Reprinted in *High Peaks, Pure Earth: Collected Writings on Tibetan History and Culture,* ed. Michael Aris. London: Serindia, 1998.

Sperling, Elliot. "The 5th Karma-pa and Some Aspects of the Relationship between Tibet and the Early Ming." In *Tibetan Studies in Honor of Hugh Richardson,* ed. Michael Aris and Aung San Suu Kyi. New Delhi: Vikas, 1980.

Williams, Paul M. "A Note on Some Aspects of Mi Bskyod Rdo Rje's Critique of Dge Lugs Pa Madhyamaka." *Journal of Indian Philosophy* 11 (1983): 125–145.

ANDREW QUINTMAN

KARUṆĀ (COMPASSION)

Karuṇā (compassion), along with PRAJÑĀ (WISDOM), is one of the two virtues universally affirmed by Buddhists. Basically, karuṇā is defined as the wish that others be free of suffering, in contradistinction to *maitrī* (love; Pāli, mettā), which is the wish that others be happy. Compassion is a quality that a buddha is believed to possess to the greatest possible degree, and that Buddhists still on the path strive to cultivate.

The texts of the THERAVĀDA and other MAINSTREAM BUDDHIST SCHOOLS make it clear that the Buddha Śākyamuni was deeply motivated by compassion. The JĀTAKA stories describe how, in his previous lives as a BODHISATTVA, the Buddha sometimes sacrificed his life to relieve the suffering of another, as when he fed his body to a hungry tigress unable to feed her cubs. In his final life, after his awakening under the bodhi tree, he decided to teach, rather than enter final NIRVĀṆA, out of compassion for those few who might understand his message. He also sent forth his monks to preach the dharma "for the benefit of the many, for the welfare of the many." Among the rules established by the Buddha for lay and monastic followers are numerous prohibitions against harming others, motivated at least in part by a desire to avoid causing unnecessary suffering; indeed, nonharming (*ahiṃsā*) often has been defined as essential to practicing the dharma. The Buddha also encouraged his followers, in their meditative life, to immerse themselves in the four immeasurable states (*brahmāvihāra*): love, compassion, sympathetic joy, and equanimity, which are extended to all beings throughout the cosmos.

With the emergence of the MAHĀYĀNA some four centuries after the Buddha's death, compassion took on added significance. Such texts as the *Prajñāpāramitā* (*Perfection of Wisdom*) sūtras, the LOTUS-SŪTRA (SADDHARMAPUṆḌARĪKA-SŪTRA), and the *Gaṇḍavyūha-sūtra,* as well as countless treatises and commentaries, articulated a new vision of the Buddha, bodhisattva, and ordinary practitioner. The Buddha now was seen as eternal, omniscient, and infinitely compassionate. To act compassionately, the Buddha was capable of myriad metamorphoses and manifestations, including the creation of PURE LANDS (or buddha-fields) in which suffering beings might have their troubles eased and their progress toward awakening hastened.

The bodhisattva became a normative ideal for Mahāyāna practitioners, penetrating to the emptiness at the core of all persons and phenomena, yet driven by compassion so great that he or she not only wished all beings freed from suffering, but resolved to effect that freedom personally, regardless of the hardships involved. In some Mahāyāna texts, the bodhisattva's compassion is such that he or she vows to postpone awakening until others are freed. In other texts, compassion drives the bodhisattva to try to become a buddha as swiftly as possible so he or she can maximally benefit others. In either case, the bodhisattva sought to develop *bodhicitta,* the dedication to enlightenment for the sake of others, and UPĀYA, the skill-in-means, guided by wisdom, that enables one to act in the world effectively—and sometimes unconventionally—for the benefit of suffering beings. In general, compassion was seen as indispensable to the attainment of buddhahood, as one of the two "wings" (the other being wisdom) without which one could not ascend to awakening. Perfected, it would issue in the "Form Body," through which a buddha assists others, as perfected wisdom would become the transcendent, gnostic "Dharma Body."

Mahāyāna philosophers celebrated and analyzed compassion. CANDRAKĪRTI (ca. 600–650 C.E.) praised compassion as the original seed of the buddhas. Dharmakīrti (ca. 600–660 C.E.) framed logical arguments to prove that compassion could be developed infinitely. ŚĀNTIDEVA (ca. 685–763 C.E.), in his *Bodhicaryāvatāra* (*Entry to Enlightened Conduct*), attempted to demonstrate on rational grounds why one should be compassionate, to articulate why compassion should extend even to one's enemies, and to provide meditative methods through which one might develop compassion, including the "great mystery" of imaginatively exchanging oneself with others. Other Mahāyāna methods for developing compassion included thinking of all sentient beings as one's mother (which, according to Buddhist metaphysics, they have been), and then directing the same compassionate thoughts toward them as one would to one's own mother. Another method was the visualization practice of "giving and taking," in which one inhales the sufferings of others as smoke, then exhales to them one's own virtues in the form of light. The tantric traditions that grew out of the Mahāyāna milieu also emphasized compassion as a crucial prerequisite for their complex and sometimes dangerous meditations. Indeed, because of the power evoked by tantric practitioners, compassion was, if anything, even more important for them, though its expression, in images sometimes filled with sexuality and wrath, could seem shocking.

Mahāyāna compassion also was personified, most notably in the bodhisattva Avalokiteśvara, who looks down compassionately on the world and responds to its cries of anguish. An important focus of worship for Indian Mahāyāna Buddhists, Avalokiteśvara assumed over a hundred forms, including the four-armed holder of the mantra OṂ MAṆI PADME HŪṂ, a thousand-armed and eleven-headed version, and wrathful tantric manifestations. If anything, Avalokiteśvara grew in stature as Buddhism spread beyond India. Among many transformations, he became the female bodhisattva Guanyin in China, the Dalai Lamas in Tibet, and the *dhamma*-protecting bodhisattva Nātha in Sri Lanka. Similarly, various meditative and ritual expressions of compassion evolved in various Asian cultures. These include Sri Lankan attempts to transfer merit to deities who have gathered in a sacred bodhi tree; the Chan Buddhist promise to save all beings, numberless though they be; the widespread practice of purchasing animals, then setting them free; and funeral and memorial rites throughout Buddhist Asia.

Over the centuries, Buddhists reflecting on compassion have faced numerous dilemmas. They have had to balance analytical deconstruction of the "person" with the person-oriented sentiment involved in concern for others. Buddhists have tried to understand the degree to which compassion that is developed in meditation can or should be translated into concrete action in the world. They have also wrestled with establishing criteria for determining which sort of action is truly compassionate, and which is selfish and destructive. These issues have become especially pressing in the modern era as Buddhist traditions have interacted with those of the West, and with those of emerging nations in Asia. Buddhists have pondered seriously whether the imperative to compassion countenances unconventional behavior by spiritual teachers, active resistance to social and political oppression, or acquiescence to war and other forms of violence, including simple anger. Many modern Buddhist thinkers, including the fourteenth DALAI LAMA (1935–) and THICH NHAT HANH (1926–), have wrestled with these issues and have found no easy answers. Nevertheless, Buddhist leaders have insisted that compassion remains absolutely integral to the practice of Buddhism, and must be developed to the greatest possible degree, now as in the time of the Buddha.

See also: **Bodhicitta (Thought of Awakening); Engaged Buddhism**

Bibliography

Aronson, Harvey B. *Love and Sympathy in Theravāda Buddhism.* Delhi: Motilal Banarsidass, 1980.

Dalai Lama XIV. *Ethics for the New Millennium.* New York: Riverhead Books, 1999.

Dayal, Har. *The Bodhisattva Doctrine in Buddhist Sanskrit Literature.* Delhi: Motilal Banarsidass 1975.

Newland, Guy. *Compassion, a Tibetan Analysis: A Buddhist Monastic Textbook.* Boston: Wisdom, 1985.

Queen, Christopher S., and King, Sallie B., eds. *Engaged Buddhism: Buddhist Liberation Movements in Asia.* Albany: State University of New York Press, 1996.

Śāntideva. *The Bodhicaryāvatāra,* tr. Kate Crosby and Andrew Skilton. Oxford and New York: Oxford University Press, 1996.

Watson, Burton, trans. *The Lotus Sutra.* New York: Columbia University Press, 1993.

Williams, Paul. *Altruism and Reality: Studies in the Philosophy of the Bodhicaryāvatāra.* Richmond, UK: Curzon, 1998.

ROGER R. JACKSON

KEGON SCHOOL. *See* **Huayan School**

KHMER, BUDDHIST LITERATURE IN

Until the twentieth century, most vernacular literature composed or known in Cambodia, including literature intended primarily for entertainment, articulated Buddhist themes concerning COSMOLOGY and HISTORY, moral and ethical values, RITUAL, and the biography of the Buddha. Thus, to a large extent, it is possible to argue that the history and development of Khmer literature in Cambodia is at once the history and development of its vernacular religious literature. Khmer literature is generally divided into the following periods: pre-Angkorian (seventh to ninth centuries); Angkorian (ninth to fifteenth centuries); middle or post-Angkorian (sixteenth to nineteenth centuries); French protectorate or early modern (mid-nineteenth to early twentieth centuries); and contemporary or modern (mid-twentieth century to the present).

The Khmer language belongs to the subgroup of the Austro-Asiatic language family that includes Mon and Khmer. Khmer writing, derived from Sanskrit, developed after the second century C.E. when Indian traders and migrants to the region began to introduce Sanskrit writing and literature, and Indian art forms, religious ideas, and ideologies of KINGSHIP and government. The first dated inscription in Khmer appeared in 612 C.E., roughly concurrent with several dated Cambodian inscriptions in Sanskrit. The dual use of both vernacular and Sanskrit inscriptions continued throughout the following centuries with the emergence of the Khmer kingdom of Angkor, which dominated the region between the ninth through thirteenth centuries. Pāli became important as a scriptural and literary language after THERAVĀDA Buddhism rose to prominence in the thirteenth century.

The processes of both *Indianization* and *vernacularization* in Southeast Asia, including the Khmer regions, have received a great deal of scholarly attention. Colonial era scholarship tended to view Southeast Asia as an empty but fertile ground in which a "superior" Indian culture was implanted and took root, giving rise to a whole new Indianized civilization. More recently, scholars have suggested that the absorption of Indian cultural motifs and ideas was possible because they were similar or complementary to existing indigenous cultural forms. Thus the process was perhaps not a wholesale Indianization, but rather a selective process of cultural borrowing and adaptation, with influences moving in both directions. Among the most important borrowings from India for the Khmer was the introduction of Sanskrit writing and literature. Archaeological evidence from pre-Angkorian and Angkorian periods shows that the Khmer utilized both Sanskrit and Khmer for inscribing their religious, literary, and political lives. The clear division of labor between the two languages has been much commented on by scholars: Sanskrit was nearly always the medium for expressive literary purposes such as extolling the virtues of the gods, while Khmer was employed for more documentary purposes such as listing donations of slaves to temples. Sheldon Pollock has theorized that the attraction of Sanskrit as a cosmopolitan language was aesthetic; it provided a powerful medium for imagining the world in a larger, more complex way. *Vernacularization,* the turn away from Sanskrit to the use of localized languages such as Khmer for literary production, began to occur in Cambodia after the fifteenth century. By this time, Sanskrit and Pāli loan words had been absorbed into Khmer and the Khmer had developed a literary idiom of their own for expressing cosmopolitan ideas, evident in the Khmer classical literature composed during the middle or post-Angkorian period.

The most profound example of the ways in which aspects of the Indian literary imagination were absorbed and adapted by the Khmer is that of the *Rāmāyaṇa,* known in Khmer as the *Rāmakerti* (pronounced

"Ream-ker"), the *Glory of Rām.* The outlines of the story, widely known among the Khmer population since at least the time of Angkor, maintain some of the main elements of the Indian *Rāmāyaṇa* while at the same time adapting them in critical ways. Known in Khmer as Rām, the hero of the epic is rendered as a BODHISATTVA, thus transforming the story into the favorite theme of Khmer literature: the biography of the Buddha. The *Rāmakerti* appears as one of the most ubiquitous subjects of Khmer art; it is painted as temple murals, carved into bas-reliefs on the galleries of Angkorian buildings, reenacted in elaborate traditional dance forms, composed in literary versions, and retold in many oral versions, including shadow puppet plays known as *spaek dhaṃ.* At least one version of the text has also been used as a manual for the practice of tantric forms of Buddhist meditation in which the Buddhist adept follows the journey of *Rām* in his quest to retrieve his wife Sītā as a form of esoteric spiritual instruction.

While the Khmer *Rāmakerti* is generally considered to be the greatest work of Khmer literature, it is not the only one that is celebrated and influential. Equally beloved by Khmer have been versions of the Buddhist JĀTAKA depicting the moral development of the Bodhisattva in his many lives as he moves toward buddhahood. The best known and revered of the Buddha's life stories, at least since the eighteenth century, are his last ten lives, appearing in Cambodia in a single compilation known as the *Dasajātaka.* The narrative of the Bodhisattva's penultimate life, the *Mahāvessantara-jātaka* (also called the *Mahājāt*), is the most popular of these *jātaka,* redacted in many different manuscript and later print versions. *Jātaka* stories were also rendered into *sātra lpaeṅ,* a genre of narrative poetry intended for entertainment which often contained long descriptions of magical battles and other feats performed by the Bodhisattva. This genre appears to have developed beginning in the sixteenth century as part of the process of vernacularization. *Cpāp* or "codes of conduct" constituted another prominent genre of vernacular literature in Cambodia known since at least the seventeenth century. Didactic poetry intended to transmit religious values and practical advice for living, the *cpāp* were composed in stylized meters (to aid memorization) and sung by parents or teachers to children.

By the latter half of the nineteenth century, prominent vernacular texts used in Buddhist education (but also known more widely through artistic representations, sermons, and stories) included not only the texts already mentioned, but also several works of Siamese composition that had been translated into Khmer versions: the *Trai Bhūm* (a cosmological text), the *Maṅgalatthadīpanī* (a narrative commentary on the *Maṅgala-sutta*), and the *Paṭhamsombodhi* (a biography of the Buddha). Also in evidence in monastic collections during the period were manuals (*kpuon* or *tamrā*) on ritual, medicine, and astrology. *Buddh Daṃnāy* texts, prophesies of the Buddha concerning the arrival of the Buddhist *dhammik,* or righteous king, circulated in written and oral forms. Folk stories loosely based on Buddhist themes were transmitted orally until the early part of the twentieth century when Buddhist writers such as Ukñā Suttantaprījā Ind, author of the ethics manual *Gatilok* (1921), began to collect and record Khmer oral stories. While French colonial scholars during the protectorate period were often critical of the "fanciful" nature of Khmer vernacular works, their objections have been countered by Khmer scholars. Keng Vansak, a Khmer literary scholar, has argued that Khmer writers have been concerned not with literal representations of reality, but rather with representing the moral experience of social life, which often presents human beings with "insolvable contradictions" between their aspirations for moral perfection and their situatedness in a world of social and political bonds.

Along with the works already described, Khmer Buddhists used vernacular versions of canonical texts. By the eighteenth and nineteenth centuries (and likely earlier), many texts based on Pāli canonical sources such as the *jātaka* and the DHAMMAPADA were translated into a genre of texts known as *samrāy,* consisting of interwoven Pāli verses and their Khmer translations, followed by commentary in Khmer. Most of the *samrāy* that survive in existing collections of Khmer manuscripts date from no earlier than the nineteenth century, when monastic libraries were reconstituted following a long period of warfare in Cambodia. During the twentieth century, many Khmer *samrāy* originally composed on palm leaf were republished as print texts with little or no change from the originals. Although traditionalist members of the Khmer saṅgha initially resisted the use of print for religious texts, by the 1920s monks and scholars turned to the use of print rather than palm leaf (*sḷik ṛit*) or accordion-folded mulberry bark paper (*krāṃṅ*) for disseminating their works. Among the earliest vernacular texts published in print in the 1920s were segments of the VINAYA and the *Siṅgālovāda-sutta.* A full edition of the Pāli *Tipiṭaka,* with Khmer translation, was finally issued in 1969 by the Buddhist Institute, although many Pāli texts had already been translated and published in single editions from the 1920s on. Although print is the principal medium for religious texts in Cambodia today, both palm leaf and *krāṃṅ* manuscripts continue to be used and venerated, though rarely produced. Scholars estimate that 98 percent of Cambodia's rich collection of manuscripts was lost or destroyed during the Khmer Rouge period (1975–1979).

See also: **Cambodia; Southeast Asia, Buddhist Art in**

Bibliography

Bizot, François. *Ramaker ou l'amour symbolique de Ram et Sita.* Paris: École Française d'Extrême-Orient, 1989.

Bizot, François. *Le Chemin de Lanka.* Paris: École Française d'Extrême-Orient, 1992.

Guesdon, Joseph. "La Littérature khmère et le Buddhisme." *Anthropos* 1 (1906): 91–109.

Iyengar, K. R. Srinivasa, ed. *Asian Variations in Rāmāyaṇa.* New Delhi: Sahitya Akademi, 1983.

Jacob, Judith. *Cambodian Linguistics, Literature, and History: Collected Articles,* ed. David A. Smyth. London: School of Oriental and African Studies, University of London, 1993.

Jacob, Judith. *The Traditional Literature of Cambodia: A Preliminary Guide.* London: Oxford University Press, 1996.

Keng Vansak. "Réflexions sur la littérature khmère." *Revue française* 206 (1968): 31–34.

Khing Hoc Dy. *Contribution à l'histoire de la littérature khmère: littérature de l'époque "classique" (XVème–XIXème siècles).* Paris: Editions L'Harmattan, 1991.

Khing Hoc Dy. *Ecrivains et expressions littéraires du Cambodge au XXème siècle,* Vol. 2. Paris: Editions L'Harmattan, 1993.

Khing Hoc Dy, and Mak Phoeun. "Cambodia." In *South-east Asia: Languages and Literatures,* ed. Patricia Herbert and Anthony Milner. Honolulu: University of Hawaii Press, 1989.

Lī Dhām Teṅ. *Aksarsāstr Khmaer* (Khmer Literature). Phnom Penh, Cambodia: Seô óuon Huot, 1961.

Nepote, Jacques, and Khing Hoc Dy. "Literature and Society in Modern Cambodia." In *Essays on Literature and Society in Southeast Asia,* ed. Tham Seong Chee. Singapore: Singapore University Press, 1981.

Pollock, Sheldon. "The Cosmopolitan Vernacular." *Journal of Asian Studies* 57, no. 1 (1998): 6–37.

Pou, Saveros. *Etudes sur le Rāmakerti: XVI–XVII siècles.* Paris: École Française d'Extrême-Orient, 1977.

Pou, Saveros. *Rāmakerti: XVI–XVII siècles.* Paris: École Française d'Extrême-Orient, 1977.

Pou, Saveros. "Khmer Epigraphy." In *Sculpture of Angkor and Ancient Cambodia: Millennium of Glory,* ed. Helen Ibbitson Jessup and Thierry Zephir. Washington, DC: National Gallery of Art, 1997.

Thierry, Solange. *Le Cambodge des contes.* Paris: Editions L'Harmattan, 1985.

ANNE HANSEN

KIHWA

Kihwa (1376–1433) was a Korean monk of the late Koryŏ/early Chosŏn periods. He was also known by the monastic name Hamhŏ Tukt'ong. Kihwa was typical of the Sŏn (Chan) school masters of his time; he taught his followers the Imje (Linji) oriented *kong'an* (KŌAN) method, along with other standard aspects of Sŏn practice. At the same time, he was one of the most focused and energetic advocates of the intrinsic resonance between meditation practice and scriptural study.

Kihwa is considered by many scholars of Korean Buddhism to be one of the best writers of the Korean tradition. He wrote important commentaries on the *Yuanjue jing* (*Perfect Enlightenment Sūtra*), the *Jin'gang jing* (DIAMOND SŪTRA), and the *Chan Yongjia ji* (*Collection of Yongjia of the Chan School*). Kihwa was distinguished by his mastery of Chinese philosophy, but he eventually set aside his Confucian studies in favor of Buddhism. This philosophical background, coupled with his literary talents, served him well when he defended the Buddhist establishment against a rising neo-Confucian ideological movement. The treatise that Kihwa wrote in defense of Buddhism on this occasion, the *Hyŏnjŏng non* (*Articulating the Correct*), is considered one of the great works in Korean intellectual history. In this work, Kihwa argued that the three traditions of Confucianism, Daoism, and Buddhism are in basic agreement at a fundamental philosophical level. Kihwa passed away while residing at Chŏngsusa, located at the southern tip of Kanghwa Island, where his tomb can still be visited.

See also: **Confucianism and Buddhism; Korea**

Bibliography

Buswell, Robert E., Jr. "Buddhism under Confucian Domination: The Synthetic Vision of Sŏsan Hyŭjŏng." In *Culture and the State in the Late Chosŏn Korea,* ed. JaHyun Kim Haboush and Martina Deuchler. Cambridge, MA: Harvard University Asia Center, 1999.

Muller, A. Charles. *The Sūtra of Perfect Enlightenment: Korean Buddhism's Guide to Meditation, with Commentary by the Sŏn Monk Kihwa.* Albany: State University of New York Press, 1999.

A. CHARLES MULLER

KINGSHIP

Throughout Asia, rulers channeled the rich resources of Buddhist symbolism to reinforce their authority and to authenticate their political imagination. Close linkages between Buddhism and kingship are evident even during the time of the Śākyamuni Buddha. When the Buddha reached Rājagṛha, capital of the kingdom of Magadha, King Ajātaśatru came out with his retinue to welcome him. Later Ajātaśatru was involved in the first of the Buddhist councils, held at Rājagṛha. King Prasenjit of Kośala also sought to identify himself with the Buddha. He is quoted in the *Majjhimanikāya* as saying, "The Lord is a Kośalan and so am I."

It is apparent from the Pāli texts that Buddhism formulated its theoretical position on the subject early in its history in recognition of the significance of kingship to the religion. B. G. Gokhale discerned three such ideological strands. First was the theory of *mahāsammatta* (the great elect), anchored in the Buddha's nostalgia for tribal republicanism; second was the theory of mutually exclusive spheres of *dhamma* (Sanskrit, dharma) and *ana* (politics), an expression of monastic skepticism about the increasingly militant Indian monarchies; and third was the theory of an invincible *dhamma,* that is, *dhamma* as a cosmocratic principle underpinning the political philosophy of a cakravartin (wheel-turning king). The second theory, however, seems to be either a variation or extension of the doctrine of *mahāsammata,* premised as it is on the superiority of the tribal republican model, under increasing pressure from the emergent centralized states. Indeed, only the doctrines of *mahāsammata* and cakravartin formed the kernel of the Buddhist concept of kingship and were invoked by rulers as sacred symbols of power.

The theory of *mahāsammata* depicts the gradual degeneration of humankind from the primeval stage of perfect purity and the consequent need for the reorganization of society. According to this theory, the people assembled and chose by common consent the strongest and the finest person among them as their leader. They asked him to perform judicial tasks on their behalf and agreed to pay part of their produce in return for his services. He was called rāja (king) because he brought happiness to the people, and kṣatriya (warrior) because he protected their fields. The Buddha's sympathy for this tribal-republican model of the political process is evident in the constitution of the SAṄGHA and the Buddha's denunciation of kings as poisonous snakes or robbers violating people's property.

However, with the increasing growth of centralized monarchical power, Buddhism had to grudgingly accept the "necessary evil" of monarchy. It revised its initial principle of "tribal-republicanism" and adopted the ideal of cakravartin, encapsulating a normative kingship known as *dhammiko dhammarāja,* the king as an upholder of the *dhamma.* Evidently Buddhism sought to inject into the institution of kingship its own conceptions and worldview. A cakravartin king was said to possess seven JEWELS, including a wheel of divine attributes that rolls unhindered and unchallenged over the earth. The wheel's ever-onward movement symbolizes the ceremonial conquests of its possessor (the cakravartin) over all the lands where it goes. The cakravartin king of the Pāli canons is paired with the Buddha as his secular counterpart and conqueror of the universe not by arms, but by force of righteousness. He is described as generously endowed with the ten *rājadharmas* of liberality, good conduct, nonattachment, straightforwardness, mildness, austerity, nonanger, noninjury, patience, and forbearance. The cakravartin of the Pāli texts is clearly shown to possess divine attributes, but in China, where translators rendered the term as a divine emperor with flying wheels or a flying emperor (*feixing huangdi*), the supranormal aspect of the concept became additionally clear. In subsequent centuries Buddhism further revised its ideas of cakravartin in ways that suggest its acknowledgment of the centrality of force to the institution of kingship. According to the new definition found in the ABHIDHARMAKOŚABHĀṢYA of VASUBANDHU (ca. fourth century C.E.), there are four kinds of cakravartin: gold-wheel, silver-wheel, bronze-wheel and iron-wheel, the last one taking recourse to violence and yet entitled to the glory of ideal Buddhist kingship.

King AŚOKA (ca. 300–232 B.C.E.) was elevated in Buddhist historiography as an archetypal exemplar of Buddhist kingship because his conquests, stretching from the Himalayas to the ocean, realized the imperial ideals of ancient India, and his espousal of the dharma and support of the saṅgha were singular achievements in the history of Buddhism. Several eminent historians of early India, notably A. L. Basham and Romila Thapar, have persuasively argued that Buddhism developed its concept of cakravartin in the post-Aśokan era on the basic model provided by Aśoka's political career and philosophy. They have pointed out that at the time of Aśoka the Buddhist ideal of cakravartin was not yet systematized, otherwise Aśoka would have demonstrated his affiliation with it in his inscriptions. V. S. Agrawala also subscribes to this view, noting in his work *The Wheel Flag of India* (1964), that Aśoka's appellation *Priyadarśi* and the name *Sudassana,* a cakravartin king figuring in the *Mahāsudassana-sūtta,* have the identical meaning of "good in appearance." It is also noteworthy that the career of a cakravartin king in the Buddhist texts closely parallels the career of Aśoka. Like Aśoka, the mythical cakravartin kings heed counsel from both Brahmins and mendicants, work for the happiness of their subjects, propagate and patronize Buddhism, and protect the dharma.

Several centuries later, with the rise of powerful Kushan states whose rulers styled themselves as *devaputra* (son of heaven), and the attendant influence of foreign ideas and institutions, the Buddhist recognition of the king's status as god-incarnate became less ambiguous, as is testified by the SUVARṆAPRABHĀSOTTAMA-SŪTRA, which describes kings as "son of gods" and "born in the mortal world by the authority of the great gods."

Several rulers of Southeast Asia invoked and sought to trace their ancestry to *mahāsammata,* which represented to them the first Buddhist ruler in history. Devānampiyatissa (247–207 B.C.E.) of Sri Lanka was the first known foreign ruler in history to connect himself to Aśoka and to extend patronage to Buddhism. Soon thereafter, Duṭṭhagāmaṇī (107–77 B.C.E.) placed a relic of the Buddha on his spear to sacralize his war against the Tamil invaders. In subsequent centuries rulers both in the THERAVĀDA and MAHĀYĀNA traditions employed the versatile symbolism held out by Buddhism—rulers as cakravartin and as BODHISATTVAS. The influential Chinese monk Faguo declared, "Emperor Taizu is an enlightened ruler and fond of Buddha. He is the Tathāgata of today." Liang Wudi and Sui Wendi of sixth-century China, King Chinhŭng (r. 540–576) of Silla, Prince SHŌTOKU (574–622) of Japan, Jayavarman II (r. 802–c. 834) of Angkor, and King Chakkraphat (r. 1548–1569) of Thailand are some other famous examples of the close interface between Buddhism and kingship.

See also: **Politics and Buddhism**

Bibliography

Agrawala, Vasudeva Sharana. *The Wheel Flag of India: Chakra-Dhvaja, Being a History and Exposition of the Meaning of the Dharma-Chakra and the Sarnath Lion Capital.* Varanasi, India: Prithivi Prakashan, 1964.

Basham, A. L. *The Wonder That Was India: A Study of the Culture of the Indian Subcontinent before the Coming of the Muslims.* London: Sidgwick and Jackson, 1954.

Chakravarti, Uma. *The Social Dimensions of Early Buddhism.* Delhi and Oxford: Oxford University Press, 1987.

Gokhale, B. G. "Early Buddhist Kingship." *Journal of Asian Studies* 26, no. 11 (1966–1967): 15–22.

Gokhale, B. G. "The Early Buddhist View of the State." *Journal of the America Oriental Society* 89, no. 4 (1969): 731–738.

Strong, John S. *The Legend of King Aśoka: A Study and Translation of the Aśokāvadana.* Princeton, NJ: Princeton University Press, 1983.

Tambiah, Stanley J. *World Conqueror and World Renouncer: A Study of Buddhism and Polity in Thailand against a Historical Background.* Cambridge, UK: Cambridge University Press, 1976.

Tambiah, Stanley J. *The Buddhist Conception of Universal King and Its Manifestations in South and Southeast Asia.* Kuala Lumpur, Malaysia: University of Malaya, 1987.

Thapar, Romila. *Aśoka and the Decline of the Mauryas,* 2nd edition. Bombay: Oxford University Press, 1973.

PANKAJ N. MOHAN

KIZIL. *See* Cave Sanctuaries; Central Asia, Buddhist Art in

KLONG CHEN PA (LONGCHENPA)

Klong chen pa (Longchenpa, 1308–1363) is widely acknowledged as the greatest writer on the *Rdzogs chen* (*Great Perfection*) teachings of the RNYING MA (NYINGMA) school of Tibetan Buddhism. He was born in the Grwa valley in the G.yu ru region of central Tibet. At the age of twelve he took ordination and was given the name Tshul khrims blos gros. In this monastic setting, he received a thorough Buddhist training, exhibiting a particular talent for composing poetry, a skill that would continue to shape his later writings.

Klong chen pa had an immeasurable impact on the development of *Rdzogs chen.* From the eleventh through the fourteenth centuries, the *snying thig* (seminal heart) traditions had produced some of the most creative innovations ever seen in Tibetan Buddhism. But only with Klong chen pa were these scattered and often contradictory developments systematized. Drawing upon his extensive studies of these earlier writings, Klong chen pa detailed a cohesive set of contemplative practices that culminate in patterns of light and emptiness flowing effortlessly from within the body. He presented these visions within the context of wider *snying thig* theories on topics including how the buddhas emanate into the world, how the universe came into existence, and how mind emerges from sleep into dreaming or from the moment of DEATH into the INTERMEDIATE STATE (*bar do*).

In his mid-twenties, Klong chen pa gave up the monastery to live as an itinerant ascetic in the Tibetan wilderness. It was during these years, probably around 1336, that he first met his main teacher, Kumārarāja (1266–1343). From this master, he received the Great Perfection teachings according to the *Vima snying thig* (*Seminal Heart of Vimalamitra*) tradition. This meeting engendered a major shift in Klong chen pa's thought; for the rest of his life, his attentions would focus on the *snying thig*. On the basis of Kumārarāja's teachings, Klong chen pa composed his *Bla ma yang thig* (*Seminal Quintessence of the Lama*), a commentary to the *Vima snying thig*.

To further consolidate his command of the *snying thig*, Klong chen pa next turned to the more recently revealed *gter ma* (treasure) teachings of the *Mkha' 'gro snying thig* (*Seminal Heart of the Ḍākinīs*). His authority over this system was secured when a disciple, while channeling a series of female ḌĀKINĪ, recognized Klong chen pa as the reincarnation of the *Mkha' 'gro snying thig*'s discoverer, Tshul khrims rdo rje (1291–1315/17). Thus inspired, Klong chen pa composed his commentary on the system, his *Mkha' 'gro yang thig* (*Seminal Quintessence of the Ḍākinīs*). Later still, he synthesized the two systems of the *Vima snying thig* and the *Mkha' 'gro snying thig* in his masterful *Zab mo yang thig* (*Seminal Quintessence of the Profound*).

The fourteenth century was a critical time in Tibetan history, when the SA SKYA (SAKYA) sect's hegemony (1260–1358) was toppled in a civil war. As these events took shape, Klong chen pa came to be regarded as an ally of the 'Bri gung sgom chen, Kun dga' rin chen, a major rival to the ultimately victorious new Tibetan leader, Tai Situ Byang chub rgyal mtshan (1302–1364). Klong chen pa was exiled to Bhutan, where he lived for a number of years at a monastery he founded called Thar pa gling, near Bum thang. While there, he fathered a daughter and a son. The latter, Sprul sku grags pa 'od zer, would become a significant *snying thig* teacher in his own right. Eventually, with the help of his lay patrons, Klong chen pa reconciled with the new Tibetan king and was allowed to return to Tibet around 1360.

Klong chen pa composed many of his most famous works while living at his hermitage atop Gang ri thod dkar, in central Tibet. He was a prolific writer, known for his ability to synthesize a rich array of materials and literary styles. His foremost writings were gathered into several collections: The *Mdzod bdun* (*Seven Treasuries*) are his most famous works, presenting the whole of Buddhist thought from a *snying thig* viewpoint; the *Ngal gso skor gsum* (*Resting at Ease Trilogy*) and the *Rang grol skor gsum* (*Natural Freedom Trilogy*) provide in-depth introductions to *Rdzogs chen*; the *Mun sel skor gsum* (*Dispelling the Darkness Trilogy*) are three commentaries on the *Guhyagarbha Tantra*; and the *Snying thig ya bzhi* (*Seminal Quintessence in Four Parts*) is a redaction of his three *snying thig* commentaries together with their predecessors, the *Vima snying thig* and the *Mkha' 'gro snying thig*.

See also: **Tibet**

Bibliography

Germano, David, and Gyatso, Janet. "Lonchenpa and the Possession of the Ḍākinīs." In *Tantra in Practice*, ed. David Gordon White. Princeton, NJ: Princeton University Press, 2000.

Guenther, Herbert V., trans. and ed. *Kindly Bent to Ease Us: From the Trilogy of Finding Comfort and Ease, Ngal-gso skor-gsum*, 3 vols. Berkeley, CA: Dharma, 1975.

Rinpoche, Dudjom. *The Nyingma School of Tibetan Buddhism: Its Fundamentals and History*, 2 vols., tr. Gyurme Dorje and Matthew Kapstein. Boston: Wisdom, 1991.

Thondup, Tulku. *Buddha Mind: An Anthology of Longchen Rabjam's Writings on Dzogpa Chenpo*. Ithaca, NY: Snow Lion, 1989.

JACOB P. DALTON

KŌAN

Kōan (Chinese, *gong'an*; Korean, *kongan*; "case for judgment" or "public case") is an administrative and legal term that was first adopted by the Chan (Korean, Sŏn; Japanese, Zen) school in Song-dynasty China

(960–1279). The Japanese pronunciation of the term, *kōan,* has become standard in English usage. The term mainly refers to the usually enigmatic, frequently startling, and sometimes shocking stories about legendary Chan masters' encounters with disciples and other interlocutors. The kōan may be the most distinctive feature of Chan Buddhism, where it is understood as an unmediated articulation of enlightenment (Chinese, *wu*; Japanese, *satori*; awakening). Since the tenth century, Chan students throughout East Asia have studied and pondered kōans in order to gain a sudden breakthrough of insight into the minds of the ancient Chan masters and into their own primordial buddha-minds.

The best-known kōan is probably the one about the Tang-dynasty (618–907) Chan master Zhaozhou Congshen (778–897), who reportedly was asked: "Does a dog have the buddha-nature or not?," to which he replied "It doesn't" (Chinese, *wu*; Japanese, *mu*; Korean, *mu*), or simply "no." Zhaozhou's answer poses an impossible and confusing contradiction of the MAHĀYĀNA Buddhist notion, central to all of Chan, that every sentient being is endowed with the buddha-nature or TATHĀGATAGARBHA. Another famous kōan is the one about the master Nanquan Puyuan (748–835), who is said to have challenged two monks who were fighting over the ownership of a cat to demonstrate their enlightened minds to him on the spot. When neither could do so, Nanquan Puyuan hacked the cat in two, in gross violation of the Buddhist precept against killing. Other kōan stories about Tang Chan masters describe shouting, hitting, and other erratic behavior, although some kōan stories seem utterly mundane, such as when Zhaozhou is said to have told a student who asked for instruction to go wash his breakfast bowls.

Kōans are understood to embody the enlightened minds of the ancient Chan masters and to communicate a truth that cannot be expressed in ordinary discourse. Many kōans, like "Zhouzhou's dog" and "Nanquan's cat," can be interpreted as being about transcending habitual dichotomies like subject and object, and recognizing the oneness of everything in the universe, but such rational analysis is considered foolish and futile. Truly comprehending a kōan is thought to entail a sudden and direct nondualistic experience of an ultimate reality, which fundamentally differs from any intellectual understanding.

Since the tenth century, kōan commentary has been a favorite means of instruction in all the East Asian Chan schools, and later kōans also came to be used as objects for meditation. Although initially only stories that were held up for special comment by a later Chan master were considered kōans, eventually virtually any story about a Chan master could be called a kōan. The term also came to refer to any phrase or saying that was used to challenge students of Chan, such as "Why did Bodhidharma come to the West?" or "What is the sound of one hand clapping?"

Kōan literature

It is uncertain when exactly kōans first began to be produced. Early Chan materials from the sixth and seventh centuries show that kōans were not a feature of early Chan, although the later tradition created many kōan stories about the early masters.

It is the Chinese Chan masters of the eighth to mid-tenth centuries who most often are the protagonists of kōan stories, but few facts about this so-called golden age of Chan exist and no sources that contain kōans can be reliably dated to that period. The earliest datable source for kōans is the groundbreaking genealogical Chan history, the *Zutang ji* (Korean, *Chodang chip*; *Collection from the Hall of the Patriarchs*) from 952. Later genealogical Chan histories are also important sources for kōans, but the most influential was the *Jingde chuandeng lu* (*Records of the Transmission of the Lamplight* [*of enlightenment compiled during the*] *Jingde Era*) from 1004, and many of the most commonly used kōans come from this work. Kōans can also be found in collections focusing on individual Chan masters. Such collections, which are known as "recorded sayings" or "discourse records" (Chinese, *yulu*), were first published during the Song dynasty.

Early in the Song it became common for Chan masters to sermonize on select kōans and offer their own comments (usually just as enigmatic as the original stories), often with verses expressing their understanding. This gave rise to a number of published collections of kōans with appended commentary by a specific master. These collections themselves sometimes became the object of several levels of commentary by still other Chan masters, creating complex and multilayered works of literature. The most famous of these compilations is Yuanwu Keqin's (1063–1135) *Biyan lu* (Japanese, *Hekigan roku*; *Blue Cliff Record*), which itself has become a common subject of commentary by modern Japanese and Western Zen masters.

Kōan commentary and other types of kōan literature are best understood as literary genres created by a Song-dynasty Chan school that was looking back to an age of semimythical ancestors. Song Chan masters themselves are almost never the subject of kōan stories. An important audience for this literature has always been the secular educated elite, whose support has been crucial to the fortunes of all the East Asian Chan schools.

Kanhua Chan

In the eleventh century, some Chinese Chan masters began to assign particular kōans to individual students to ponder; in several accounts such mulling over a kōan is reported to have led to an enlightenment experience for the student. Initially, this seems to have been a general contemplation of the kōan that was not specifically associated with formal meditation.

However, in the twelfth century a new meditative technique developed in which the kōan became the subject of intense reflection. This form of meditation, which had no counterpart in traditional Indian meditation practice, became known as *kanhua* Chan (Korean, *kanhwa* Sŏn; Japanese, *kanna* Zen; "Chan of observing the key phrase" or "kōan introspection Chan") and was first formulated by Dahui ZONGGAO (1089–1163) of the Linji Chan tradition. Dahui directed his students to meditate on the crucial part of a kōan, the *huatou* (Korean, *hwadu*; Japanese, *watō*; critical phrase, keyword, or punchline). In Dahui's favorite kōan, "Zhaozhou's dog," the word *wu* (no) is the *huatou.* According to Dahui, prolonged and intense attention to the *huatou,* maintained not only in sitting meditation but in all activities, will cause a huge "ball of DOUBT" to form, which will eventually burst into an enlightenment experience.

Scholars have commonly accepted the Chan school's own view of the development of *kanhua* Chan as a response to a "spiritual decline" in the Song and an effort to preserve the wisdom and insights of the great Tang Chan masters. However, in "The 'Shortcut' Approach of *K'an-Hua* Meditation" (1987) Robert Buswell argues that *kanhua* Chan can be better understood as a culmination of internal developments in Chan "whereby its subitist rhetoric came to be extended to pedagogy and finally to practice." In "Silent Illumination, *Kung-an* Introspection, and the Competition for Lay Patronage in Sung-Dynasty Ch'an" (1999) Morten Schlütter suggests that Dahui championed *kanhua* Chan, in large part, as a corrective to the MOZHAO CHAN (Japanese, *mokushō*; silent illumination) meditation that was taught in the rival Caodong tradition of Chan, which Dahui condemned as quietistic and not leading to enlightenment. Dahui seems especially concerned that Caodong masters were teaching silent illumination to members of the secular educated elite, and competition for patronage was clearly an element in the dispute.

Kōan use after Dahui

Dahui's development of *kanhua* Chan exerted an enormous influence on kōan use and Chan meditation in all of East Asia. However, it is important to be aware that the older practices of kōan study and kōan commentary were never abandoned and continued to exist alongside the practice of *kanhua* Chan.

In Japan, *kanhua* Chan was taken up in the Rinzai (Chinese, Linji) sect of Zen, where kōans were eventually systematized by the reformer HAKUIN EKAKU (1686–1768) and his disciples into a curriculum of five main levels. Students meditate on the *huatou* (Japanese, *watō*) of a series of kōans and have to pass each kōan in meetings with the Zen master (known as *sanzen* or *dokusan*) by giving the answers considered correct in their Zen master's particular lineage. The answers, and answers to related follow-up questions, are supposed to be kept secret, but, in fact, crib-sheets exist. However, Zen masters are thought to be able to distinguish an answer that demonstrates true insight (Japanese, *kenshō*) from one that has simply been memorized. Finishing the entire kōan curriculum to the satisfaction of the Zen master ends the training of a student, who is now ready to function as a Zen master. However, completing the curriculum takes many years, and most students leave long before completion to take over their family temples.

The founder of the Japanese Sōtō (Chinese, Caodong) sect of Zen, DŌGEN (1200–1253), who became heir to the Caodong tradition of Chan, did not advocate *kanhua* Chan meditation, and it has never been employed in the Sōtō sect. However, Dōgen often commented on kōans as a means of instruction, and medieval Sōtō students were formally trained in kōan commentary. After reforms in the eighteenth century the Sōtō sect sought to differentiate itself from the Rinzai sect and kōan use became rare in Sōtō.

In Korea, Dahui's *kanhua* Chan quickly took root, mainly through the efforts of the great Sŏn master CHINUL (1158–1210) and his disciple HYESIM (1178–1234), and *kanhua* Chan eventually came to dominate Korean Buddhist meditation practice. In Korean Sŏn, a student will usually only contemplate a few kōans over a lifetime, based on the notion that resolving one kōan is resolving them all.

In China, *kanhua* Chan became a standard for Chan meditation soon after Dahui, even in the Caodong tradition that Dahui had criticized. *Kanhua* Chan continues to be important in Chinese Chan through the twentieth century, although earlier types of meditation, similar to silent illumination, are also considered legitimate.

See also: **Chan School; China; Japan; Korea; Meditation**

Bibliography

Bodiford, William M. *Sōtō Zen in Medieval Japan.* Honolulu: University of Hawaii Press, 1993.

Buswell, Robert E., Jr. "The 'Short-Cut' Approach of *K'an-Hua* Meditation: The Evolution of a Practical Subitism in Chinese Ch'an Buddhism." In *Sudden and Gradual: Approaches to Enlightenment in Chinese Thought,* ed. Peter N. Gregory. Honolulu: University of Hawaii Press, 1987.

Cleary, J. C., and Cleary, Thomas, trans. and eds. *The Blue Cliff Record.* Boston: Shambhala, 1977.

Foulk, T. Griffith. "The Form and Function of Kōan Literature: A Historical Overview." In *The Kōan: Texts and Contexts in Zen Buddhism,* ed. Steven Heine and Dale S. Wright. New York: Oxford University Press, 2000.

Hoffmann, Yoel, trans. and ed. *The Sound of the One Hand: 281 Zen Kōans with Answers.* New York: Basic Books, 1975.

Hori, G. Victor Sogen. "Teaching and Learning in the Rinzai Zen Monastery." *Journal of Japanese Studies* 20, no. 1 (1994): 5–35.

Hsieh, Ding-hwa Evelyn. "Yüan-Wu K'o-Ch'in's (1063–1135) Teaching of Ch'an *Kung-an* Practice: A Transition from Literary Study of Ch'an *Kung-an* to the Practical *K'an-Hua* Ch'an." *Journal of the International Association of Buddhist Studies* 17, no. 1 (1994): 66–95.

Schlütter, Morten. "Silent Illumination, Kung-an Introspection, and the Competition for Lay Patronage in Sung-Dynasty Ch'an." In *Buddhism in the Sung,* ed. Peter N. Gregory and Daniel Getz. Honolulu: University of Hawaii Press, 1999.

MORTEN SCHLÜTTER

KŌBEN

Kōben (Myōe; 1173–1232), a Japanese Shingon-Kegon monk, embraced traditional Buddhist practices in reaction to reformers like HŌNEN (1133–1212), who founded the Pure Land school based on the rejection of all practices except for the recitation of the name of AMITĀBHA Buddha. Orphaned at the age of eight, Kōben was raised by his uncle, a Buddhist priest, and lived a life of study and practice in monasteries. In 1204 he was granted his own monastery, Kōzanji, in the outskirts of Kyoto, and he spent the rest of his life there and at his hometown in Wakayama prefecture, studying, meditating, and writing.

Trained primarily as a Shingon monk, Kōben revived ritual practices and devised new ones for the purpose of transforming doctrinal teachings into actual experience and vision. He popularized Esoteric Buddhist practices, such as the MANTRA of Radiance (*komyo shingon*), which is still chanted widely today. He was also a prolific poet and kept a diary of his meditative dreams over a period of forty years. Using poetry and meditation, Kōben transfigured the world around him into the idealized realm of his dreams, and he even cut off his right ear to prove to himself that he was not attached to this world.

His active imagination, however, did not prevent him from exercising his critical faculties. Kōben wrote a lengthy, scathing attack to show that Hōnen's exclusive practice of recitation not only rejected traditional Buddhism but also misrepresented the Pure Land tradition. Kōben is therefore remembered primarily as a defender and reviver of traditional Buddhism and the practice of RITUAL and MEDITATION.

See also: **Japan; Pure Land Buddhism**

Bibliography

Brock, Karen L. "My Reflection Should Be Your Keepsake: Myōe's Vision of the Kasuga Deity." In *Living Images: Japanese Buddhist Icons in Context,* ed. Robert E. Sharf and Elizabeth Horton Sharf. Stanford, CA: Stanford University Press, 2001.

Morrell, Robert E. *Early Kamakura Buddhism: A Minority Report.* Berkeley, CA: Asian Humanities Press, 1987.

Tanabe, George J., Jr. *Myōe the Dreamkeeper: Fantasy and Knowledge in Early Kamakura Buddhism.* Cambridge, MA: Harvard University Press, 1992.

GEORGE J. TANABE, JR.

KONJAKU MONOGATARI

Konjaku monogatari (or *Konjaku monogatarishū, Collection of Tales Now Past*) is a monumental collection of popular stories (*setsuwa*), mostly emphasizing

Buddhist themes, compiled during the twelfth century. The portion still extant today consists of twenty-nine books containing more than one thousand stories grouped into three geographic categories: tales of India, tales of China, and tales of Japan. The tales of India consist of the biography of Śākyamuni Buddha, as well as stories of his disciples and his previous lives (JĀTAKA). The tales of China concern the introduction and propagation of Buddhism, as well as miracles, both Buddhist and non-Buddhist. The tales of Japan are divided into Buddhist themes and secular themes, which tell of famous warriors, ghosts, strange animals, and humorous events. *Konjaku monogatari* is an indispensable work for understanding the role of Buddhism in Japanese culture. Its stories have served as the basis for countless subsequent retellings in the form of dramas, short stories, novels, and screenplays.

See also: **Japanese, Buddhist Influences on Vernacular Literature in**

WILLIAM M. BODIFORD

KOREA

Korean Buddhism must be considered within the larger context of the East Asian MAHĀYĀNA tradition. Broadly speaking, the creative period of Chinese Buddhism was over by the end of the twelfth century, after which Chinese Buddhism ceased to have a significant impact on Korean Buddhism. Furthermore, no indigenous developments within Korean Buddhism radically altered its character after the twelfth century; by and large, the basic identity of Korean Buddhism was formed by this time, in clear contrast with Japanese Buddhism, which began to develop its highly idiosyncratic forms after the thirteenth century. This does not mean that Korean Buddhism ceased to develop, but that its fundamental character was established long ago.

After the thirteenth century, denominational differences within Korean Buddhism became less significant until the entire Korean SAṄGHA eventually became a single order. This process, which took more than six hundred years, culminated in the establishment of the Chogyejong (CHOGYE SCHOOL or order) in 1941. The Chogye order, which practically represents the entirety of modern Korean Buddhism, considers itself a scion of the CHAN SCHOOL (Korean, Sŏn; Japanese, Zen), but it actually embraces many of the diverse forms of East Asian Buddhist thought and practice that had flowed into Korea beginning in the fourth century C.E. This feature of Korean Buddhism has led scholars to characterize it as *t'ongbulgyo,* a "holistic Buddhism" that is free from sectarian differences and doctrinal conflicts.

Introduction of Buddhism into the Three Kingdoms

When Buddhism came to Korea in the latter half of the fourth century, the peninsula was divided into three kingdoms, each ruled by an ancient tribal confederation trying to expand its territory at the expense of the others. The religious beliefs and practices of the people were predominantly animistic; they believed in deities that resided in nature, and they worshipped the ancestral spirits of tribal leaders. With the establishment of monarchies, however, Korean society moved beyond its tribal stage and was ready to entertain a new religion with a universalistic ethos.

Among the three kingdoms, Koguryŏ (37 B.C.E.–618 C.E.) in the north was the earliest to form a centralized state and was by far the most powerful. Although some evidence suggests that Buddhism had been known earlier, it was in 372 C.E., during the reign of King Sosurim (r. 371–384), that Buddhism was officially introduced into Koguryŏ. Sosurim maintained a tributary relationship with the Former Qin (351–394) in northern China, and its king, Fujian (r. 357–385), an ardent supporter of Buddhism, sent a monk-envoy named Sundo (d.u.), with Buddhist images and scriptures, to Koguryŏ. Significantly, in that same year Sosurim also established the T'aehak, an academy for Confucian learning. The following year he promulgated legal codes, laying the foundation for a centralized bureaucratic state.

Around the time Buddhism came to Koguryŏ, the Paekche kingdom (18 B.C.E.–660 C.E.), which occupied the southwestern part of the peninsula, was introduced to Buddhism by the Eastern Jin in southern China, with which Paekche had a close diplomatic relationship. As with Koguryŏ, the new religion came to Paekche at the time the kingdom, in particular King Kŭn Ch'ogo (346–375), was consolidating royal control over tribal powers.

The kingdom of Silla (57 B.C.E.–935 C.E.), which held the southeastern corner of the peninsula, was the last of three kingdoms to be introduced to Buddhism. When Buddhism first came to Silla during the reign of King Nulchi (417–447), it met strong resistance from ruling aristocratic families that were deeply rooted in tribal religious practices. The martyrdom of Ich'adon, a loyal minister, provoked King Pŏphŭng (r. 514–540) to finally recognize the new religion in 527 C.E. Pŏphŭng had promulgated legal codes for the kingdom in 520, and he prohibited killing throughout the land two years after recognizing Buddhism.

Buddhism introduced a number of new religious practices and ideas to Korea: Buddhist MONKS were clearly set apart from the rest of the society; images of BUDDHAS and BODHISATTVAS offered a clear focus for devotion; and Buddhist scriptures contained soaring philosophical ideas with an expansive COSMOLOGY and advanced moral teaching. In addition, a host of new cultural phenomena accompanied Buddhism, including architecture, craftsmanship, a writing system, calendrics, and medicine. Buddhist monks were not simply religious figures, they were magicians, doctors, writers, calligraphers, architects, painters, and even diplomats and political advisers. Although many years passed before Korean Buddhists had a solid understanding of the philosophical subtleties of Buddhist teachings, its material culture alone was sufficient to win the hearts of the kings and nobles, as well as the common people.

Expansion of Buddhist influence

It was Silla, the least developed of the three kingdoms, that benefited most from Buddhism after Silla leaders turned Buddhism into a powerful ideology of the state. As a source of religious patriotism, Buddhism played an important role in Silla's unification of the divided peninsula. King Chinhŭng (r. 540–576), the successor of Pŏphŭng, was the first Silla monarch who allowed his subjects to become monks. Pŏphŭng himself became a monk at the end of his life, taking the Buddhist name Pŏbun (Dharma Cloud), an act that demonstrated the unity of the state and the saṅgha. Beginning with Pŏphŭng, many Silla rulers adopted Buddhist names, including Śuddhodana, Māyā, and Śrīmālā, for themselves and their families. Buddhism had clearly become a force for legitimizing royal authority.

Eminent monks, such as Wŏn'gwang (d. 630) and Chajang (ca. seventh century), became spiritual leaders of both the saṅgha and the state. Wŏn'gwang is best known for his *sesok ogye* (five precepts for laypeople), which he presented at the request of two patriotic youths. The precepts stipulated that one must serve the sovereign with loyalty, serve parents with filial piety, treat friends with sincerity, never retreat from the battlefield, and not kill living beings indiscriminately. Instead of offering the traditional five precepts, Wŏn'gwang adapted Buddhist ethics to the pressing needs of the Silla kingdom during a crucial period of its history.

Chajang, a Silla nobleman, traveled to Tang China in 636 and spent seven years studying Buddhism. Upon his return, he was given the title of *taegukt'ong* (Grand National Overseer), one who supervises the entire saṅgha. Chajang established the ordination platform for monks at T'ongdo Monastery and strictly enforced the Buddhist VINAYA throughout the saṅgha. He is also credited with building a magnificent nine-story pagoda in the compound of Hwangnyong Monastery, the national shrine of Silla.

Although the rulers and aristocratic families were attracted to Buddhism mainly for its material benefits, such as the protection of the state and the welfare of the family, many monks avidly studied and lectured on important Chinese Buddhist texts. Almost all the major Mahāyāna texts, which had played an important role in the formative period of Chinese Buddhism, were introduced into Korea. Buddhist monks from Koguryŏ and especially Paekche subsequently played seminal roles in the transmission of Buddhism and Sinitic culture to Japan.

Buddhist thought flourished in Korea once the Silla rulers unified the three kingdoms in 680. The contributions of the eminent monks ŬISANG (625–702) and WŎNHYO (617–686) were particularly important. Ŭisang had traveled to China and studied under Zhiyan (602–668), the second patriarch of the HUAYAN SCHOOL. Upon his return to Silla, he became the founder of the Korean Hwaŏm (Huayan) school, the most influential doctrinal school in Korean Buddhism. The founding of many famous monasteries in Korea, such as Hwaŏmsa, Pusŏksa, and Pŏmŏsa, are attributed to Ŭisang, and his *Hwaŏm ilsŭng pŏpgye to* (*Chart of the One-Vehicle Dharma-Realm of Huayan*) sets forth the gist of Hwaŏm philosophy in the form of 210 Chinese characters arranged in a square diagram.

Wŏnhyo, commonly regarded as the greatest thinker in Korean Buddhism, was a prolific writer who produced no less than eighty-six works, of which twenty-three are extant either completely or partially. By his time, most of the important sūtras and treatises had flowed into Korea from China, and they were causing a great deal of confusion for Silla Buddhists, as they had for the Chinese. It was Wŏnhyo's genius to interpret all of the texts known to him in a way that would reveal their underlying unity of truth without sacrificing the distinctive message of each text. He found his hermeneutical key in the famous Mahāyāna text, the AWAKENING OF FAITH (DASHENG QIXIN LUN). Wŏnhyo's commentaries on this text influenced FAZANG (643–712), the great systematizer of Huayan thought.

But Wŏnhyo was more than a scholar-monk. He tried to embody in his own life the ideal of a bodhisattva who works for the well-being of all SENTIENT BEINGS. Transcending the distinction of the sacred and the secular, he married a widowed princess, visited villages and towns, and taught people with songs and dances. Silla Buddhism fully matured during Wŏnhyo's time, not only in terms of its doctrinal depth but also its ability to engage the common people.

Beginning in the late eighth century, the unified Silla dynasty began to show signs of disintegration due to conflicts within the ruling class and the rise of local warlords. During this period of political turmoil the Sŏn or Chan school of Buddhism was introduced into Korea from Tang China. Numerous Sŏn centers were soon established, mostly in provinces far away from the Silla capital of Kyŏngju and under the patronage of local warlords and magnates. Most of the founders of the NINE MOUNTAINS SCHOOL OF SŎN (Kusan Sŏnmun) received transmission in China from members of the dharma-lineage of the famous Mazu DAOYI (709–788). Their new approach to Buddhism soon created conflict with the older schools of doctrinal Buddhism (Kyo), bifurcating the Korean saṅgha.

Buddhism in the Koryŏ dynasty

The long political turmoil of the late Silla period ended with the redivision of the Korean peninsula into three kingdoms and the rise of Wang Kŏn (r. 918–943), a local warlord who founded a new dynasty, the Koryŏ (918–1392). Although the political climate had changed, the intimate relationship between Buddhism and the state did not. Buddhism became even more firmly established as the state religion. Wang Kŏn was a pious Buddhist and attributed his political success to the protective power of the buddhas. He was also a firm believer in geomancy, and he constructed numerous Buddhist monasteries according to geomantic principles with a view to curbing evil forces emanating from unfavorable places. Following his example, the succeeding Koryŏ monarchs became ardent supporters of Buddhism. During the reign of King Kwangjong (949–975), the state established a monks' examination system that was modeled on the civil service examination. Titles were conferred upon the monks who passed the examination, according to their ranks. The highest honor belonged to the royal preceptor (*wangsa*) and the posthumous national preceptor (*kuksa*). In short, the Buddhist saṅgha became part and parcel of the state bureaucracy, and the idea of *hoguk pulgyo* (state-protection Buddhism) became firmly entrenched during the Koryŏ dynasty.

In the latter half of the eleventh century, a new school arose and changed the denominational dynamics of the Koryŏ saṅgha. ŬICH'ŎN (1055–1101), the fourth son of King Munjong, became a Hwaŏm monk at the age of eleven. At thirty-one he traveled to Song China, where he met many illustrious Chinese masters, who inspired him to establish a new order, the Ch'ŏnt'aejong (TIANTAI SCHOOL) in Koryŏ, a decision rooted in his determination to resolve the severe conflict between Sŏn and Kyo (doctrinal Buddhism) in the Koryŏ saṅgha. Ŭich'ŏn was critical of Sŏn's iconoclastic rhetoric, which he believed ignored scriptural learning. He wanted his new school to balance doctrinal study (*kyo*) and MEDITATION (*kwan*). Ŭich'ŏn's leadership and royal background soon made Ch'ŏnt'ae a flourishing order, but the conflict continued to intensify. Not long after Ŭich'ŏn, the Nine Mountains school of Sŏn began to consolidate under a new name, the Chogyejong.

A century later, a Sŏn monk named CHINUL (1158–1210) led a quiet monastic reform movement in order to purify the Koryŏ saṅgha, which he believed was in a state of serious moral and spiritual decay. Convinced through his encounter with the writings of the Hwaŏm exegete Li Tongxuan (635–730) that Sŏn's "sudden enlightenment" (*tono*) approach could also be found in Hwaŏm teaching, Chinul concluded that there was no discrepancy between Sŏn and Kyo. Chinul established a comprehensive approach to Sŏn that balanced "sudden enlightenment" with "gradual cultivation," and he permitted both a Hwaŏm method of "sudden enlightenment" and the "extraordinary" (*kyŏgoe*) method of *hwadu* (KŌAN) meditation. Chinul's Sŏn teaching, set forth in many of his writings, became the foundation for the thought and practice of Korean Sŏn Buddhism to the present day.

Koryŏ Buddhism is also noted for its monumental woodblock editions of the Chinese Buddhist canon, the first of which is said to have been commissioned by King Hyŏnjong (1009–1031) in the hope of protecting the country from invading Liao forces. This edition was burned by Mongols in 1232. King Kojong (1213–1259) commissioned another edition of the canon on Kanghwa Island, where he had fled after the Mongol invasion. This edition, which consisted of more than eighty thousand woodblocks, took sixteen years to complete (1236–1251); it is still preserved in the Tripiṭaka Hall of Haein Monastery near Taegu.

Buddhism during the Chosŏn dynasty

Supported by the court and the nobles, the Koryŏ saṅgha enjoyed considerable economic prosperity. Large monasteries became major landowners after the donation of land and serfs by the kings and influential families, and many monasteries developed into financial powers by pursuing various commercial enterprises. The saṅgha's economic power became so immense that it generated much complaint and criticism toward the end of the dynasty. Lesser bureaucrats were especially strong critics, influenced by neo-Confucianism, a new ideology introduced from Song China in the late thirteenth century.

With the collapse of the Koryŏ regime, Buddhism came under further attack. The new Chosŏn dynasty (1392–1910), which was built upon neo-Confucian ideology, severed its official relationship with Buddhism. Land holdings were confiscated and hundreds of monasteries were disbanded. As anti-Buddhist measures grew more severe, people were prohibited from ordaining, monks were not allowed to enter the capital city, the monks' examination system was abolished, and the various Buddhist denominations were forced to consolidate. Only two denominations, Sŏnjong and Kyojong, were left, all others being absorbed into them. In short, Buddhism was forced out of mainstream society, and monks were downgraded to the lowest social stratum.

It was during this period of PERSECUTION that the denominational identities of the traditional Buddhist schools disappeared and the ascendancy of Sŏn began. Less dependent, perhaps, upon institutional and doctrinal structures, Sŏn withstood the persecution better than Kyo and managed to maintain its tradition deep in the mountain areas.

Buddhism experienced a short revival during the sixteenth century when HYUJŎNG (1520–1604) became the most important leader of the Chosŏn saṅgha, both Sŏn and Kyo. Although a Sŏn master, Hyujŏng demonstrated an accommodating attitude toward doctrinal studies. He argued that Kyo is the word of the Buddha, whereas Sŏn is his mind. Although he believed in their essential unity, Hyujŏng taught that a monk's training should begin with Kyo, but eventually the trainee must move on to Sŏn in order to attain perfection. Hyujŏng thus established the principle of "relinquishing Kyo and entering into Sŏn" (*sagyo ipsŏn*), which is still followed among Korean monks today.

Hyujŏng and his followers, especially YUJŎNG (1544–1610) and Yŏnggwan (1485–1571), also played an important role in mobilizing the monks' militia against Japanese forces during the Hideyoshi invasion (1592–1599). Although Buddhist monks were held in contempt in the strongly anti-Buddhist Confucian society, they were ironically the salvation of the state during this national crisis. Many monks were subsequently given high honorific military titles, and their improved status continued for a while after the war.

On the whole, during the Chosŏn period, Buddhism fell from the place of high respect and honor that it had enjoyed during the Silla and Koryŏ periods, and it remained largely confined to the countryside, isolated from mainstream intellectual and cultural life. Nevertheless, monks of high learning and character continued to flow into the saṅgha, providing leadership during a difficult period.

Modern period

During the Japanese colonization of Korea (1910–1945), Korean Buddhism faced new challenges. The Japanese policy toward Buddhism was inconsistent. Although the Japanese government lifted the ban on monks' entry into metropolitan areas and allowed most religious activities, the government-general also tried to control the Korean saṅgha and to force its merger with one or another Japanese sect of Buddhism. The *sach'allyŏng* (Monastery Act) placed the Korean saṅgha under political surveillance by imposing a hierarchical organization on the monasteries and by requiring state approval for the appointment of the abbots. An important development in Korean Buddhism under colonial rule was the emergence of married priests (*taech'ŏsŭng*), an influence of Japanese Buddhism, which eventually became a major source of conflict in the saṅgha after Korean independence.

Government persecution during the Chosŏn period had forced the amalgamation of schools and sects, and the denominational identities of Korean Buddhism were essentially obliterated, with the exception of the distinction between Sŏn and Kyo, although even this distinction became practically meaningless after the ascendance of Sŏn. Efforts were made during the Japanese colonial period to define the character of Korean Buddhism by giving it a denominational name. In view of its predominantly Sŏn character, it adopted in 1941 the name Chogyejong, after the old Koryŏ Sŏn order.

Lanterns on the river during the Buddha's birthday celebrations, Seoul, South Korea, 1990.

After independence, a struggle broke out between celibate monks (*pigusŭng*) and married clergy over control of the monasteries, resulting in the schism of the saṅgha in 1962 into two denominations: the celibate Chogye order and the much smaller T'aego order for married priests. Although new sects such as Ch'ŏnt'aejong and Chin'gakchong arose during the 1960s, the Chogye order represents virtually all of Korean Buddhism today. It is administered by its national office (*ch'ongmuwŏn*) based at the Chogye monastery in Seoul. A comprehensive program of ordination and training of monks is provided by four main Chogye monasteries: Haeinsa, Songgwangsa, T'ongdosa, and Sudŏksa. Having separate quarters and facilities for Sŏn meditation, doctrinal studies, vinaya studies, and Pure Land recitation, these comprehensive monasteries are called *ch'ongnim* ("grove of trees," referring to the large body of monks residing there), and they are distinguished from other large and small monasteries.

In modern times, the Chogye order is organized on the basis of three important levels of distinction. These distinctions are by no means rigid, but they reveal the nature and spirit of contemporary Korean Buddhism.

First, monastic communities of celibate monks and nuns are distinguished from lay Buddhists, a distinction familiar throughout the Buddhist world. In Korea, a further distinction exists between the monks who are engaged in *chŏngjin* (meditation practice) or *kongbu* (doctrinal study) and those who provide *woeho* (external support) for them. The first group is devoted to some form of spiritual cultivation, while the other is responsible for the maintenance of the monastery, food preparation, financial management, construction and repair of buildings, ritual services for lay Buddhists, and other works. This distinction, which dates back to the Chosŏn period when Buddhism was persecuted by the state, is more than a division of labor; it constitutes a nearly polar division within the Korean saṅgha, especially in large well-established monasteries.

Monks devoted to study are further distinguished in that some practice Sŏn in the meditation hall under the guidance of Sŏn masters, while others study scriptures and doctrines in the lecture hall. These two groups do not have equal status because scriptural study, which is expected of every monk, is regarded as a preparatory step toward meditation, and the authority of the Sŏn master is incomparably higher than that of the lecturer. This distinction reflects the primarily Sŏn orientation of Korean Buddhism, with doctrinal or scriptural study occupying a subordinate or subsidiary position.

At the beginning of the twenty-first century, it is estimated that more than ten million Buddhists live in Korea, mainly in the South. (Although some Buddhist monasteries exist in North Korea, the number of practicing Buddhists is negligible, if they do indeed exist.) Buddhism strengthened its urban presence considerably during the 1980s and 1990s in response to increased activity by Christian churches in South Korea. Many urban centers of Buddhism were established by the traditional influential monasteries, and some independent Buddhist centers have arisen, drawing large numbers of middle- and upper-class Koreans. Meanwhile, many monks with keen social consciences are leading movements dedicated to various social, political, and environmental causes, including the reconciliation of North and South Korea.

Buddhism has left an indelible mark upon the Korean people and their culture. The vast majority of Korean cultural monuments and treasures derive from Buddhism, and many names of towns and mountains are of Buddhist origin. Stories and legends with Buddhist motifs abound, as do novels and films based on Buddhist themes. For centuries Buddhism has provided Koreans with a way to cope with major misfortunes or crises in life. The belief in the law of karma and the cycle of birth-and-death has become a part of the Korean psyche, and the Buddhist teaching that life is impermanent and full of suffering has been fundamental to the Korean worldview ever since the arrival of Buddhism in the fourth century.

See also: **Korea, Buddhist Art in; Korean, Buddhist Influences on Vernacular Literature in; Printing Technologies**

Bibliography

Buswell, Robert E., Jr., trans. *The Korean Approach to Zen: The Collected Works of Chinul.* Honolulu: University of Hawaii Press, 1983.

Buswell, Robert E., Jr. *The Formation of Ch'an Ideology in China and Korea: The Vajrasamādhi-Sūtra, A Buddhist Apocryphon.* Princeton, NJ: Princeton University Press, 1989.

Buswell, Robert E., Jr. *Tracing Back the Radiance: Chinul's Korean Way of Zen.* Honolulu: University of Hawaii Press, 1991.

Buswell, Robert E., Jr. *The Zen Monastic Experience: Buddhist Practice in Contemporary Korea.* Princeton, NJ: Princeton University Press, 1992.

Buswell, Robert E., Jr., ed. *Currents and Countercurrents: Korean Influences on the Buddhist Traditions of East Asia.* Honolulu: University of Hawaii Press, 2004.

Keel, Hee-Sung. *Chinul: The Founder of the Korean Sŏn Tradition.* Berkeley, CA: Institute of South and Southeast Asian Studies, 1984.

Keel, Hee-Sung. "Word and Wordlessness: The Spirit of Korean Buddhism." In *The Buddhist Heritage,* ed. Tadeusz Skorupski. Tring, UK: Institute of Buddhist Studies, 1989.

Lancaster, Lewis R., ed. *Religion and Society in Contemporary Korea.* Berkeley, CA: Institute for East Asian Studies, 1992.

Lancaster, Lewis R., and Yu, Chai-shin, eds. *Introduction of Buddhism to Korea: New Cultural Patterns.* Berkeley, CA: Asian Humanities Press, 1989.

Lee, Peter H., trans. *Lives of Eminent Korean Monks: The Haedong Kosŭng Chŏn.* Cambridge, MA: Harvard University Press, 1969.

Lee, Peter H., ed. *Sourcebook of Korean Civilization,* 2 vols. New York: Columbia University Press, 1993/1996.

Lee, Young Ho, trans. "The Ideal Mirror of the Three Religions (Samga Kwigam) of Ch'ŏnghŏ Hyujŏng." *Buddhist-Christian Studies* 15 (1995): 139–187.

Muller, A. Charles, trans. *The Sūtra of Perfect Enlightenment: Korean Buddhism's Guide to Meditation.* Albany: State University of New York Press, 1999.

Park, Sung Bae. *Buddhist Faith and Sudden Enlightenment.* Albany: State University of New York Press, 1983.

HEE-SUNG KEEL

KOREA, BUDDHIST ART IN

Buddhism, over the one and a half millennia since its introduction to Korea in the fourth century, has inspired the creation of uniquely Korean traditions in Buddhist art. Korean monarchs and members of the ruling class from the sixth to the fourteenth centuries were patrons of the Buddhist religion and supported the creation of artistic and ceremonial objects and the construction of the most famous Buddhist monasteries and pagodas in Korea. Buddhism lost these influential patrons during the Chosŏn dynasty (1392–1910), but thereafter gradually permeated among ordinary folk, a change that is reflected in the country's Buddhist art.

Buddhist monastery architecture

Korea's Three Kingdoms—Koguryŏ (37 B.C.E.–668 C.E.), Paekche (18 B.C.E.–660 C.E.), and Silla (57 B.C.E.–935 C.E.)—built great monasteries in their capitals or nearby, judging by the historical records and the architectural remnants. The latter include Kŭmgangsa near P'yŏngyang (probably from the early sixth century); Hwangnyongsa (founded in 553) with its legendary nine-story wooden pagoda (destroyed in 1234 by the Mongols, except for the foundation stones, now visible after excavation) and Punhwangsa (built in 634, only three stories survive of the original nine-story pagoda built of brick imitating stone), both in the Silla capital of Kyŏngju; and Mirŭksa (built by King Mu of Paekche in the early seventh century) in Iksan.

Korean Buddhist monasteries feature architectural elements similar or identical to those of secular buildings introduced from China. In general, there is little difference in architectural style between sacred and secular buildings in East Asia. The monasteries of the Three Kingdoms consisted of a lecture hall, a main hall with Buddhist images (also known as *kŭmdang,* or Golden Hall, the focus of worship), a pagoda, and a temple gate arranged along a north-south axis. Later, many more image halls (*pŏptang*) were added to the complex according to the scale of the monastery. These ceremonial halls are dedicated to a specific buddha or bodhisattva and other Buddhist deities—thus Piro chŏn for Vairocana; Taeung chŏn (Hall of the Great Hero) and Yŏngsan chŏn (Hall of Vulture Peak), both for Śākyamuni Buddha; Muryangsu chŏn (Hall of Infinite Life) and Kŭngnak chŏn (Hall of Utmost Bliss), both for AMITĀBHA Buddha; Yaksa chŏn for the Medicine Buddha, Bhaiṣajyaguru (Yaksa Yŏrae); Mirŭk chŏn for MAITREYA; Kwanŭm chŏn for Avalokiteśvara; Chijang chŏn for Kṣitigarbha; Sipwang chŏn for the Ten Kings; Nahan chŏn for ARHATS; and Chosa dang for a monastery's founding teachers. Sometimes three buddhas, who embody past, present, and future, are enshrined in one hall. Besides the bell and drum pavilions, there were additional buildings for the storage of Buddhist scriptures, lecture and meditation halls, monks' living quarters, and kitchens.

Pagodas and reliquaries

Multistoried pagodas (*t'ap*), built in the center of the monastery's courtyard for daily circumambulation, were originally reliquaries of the historical Buddha Śākyamuni, but increasingly came to serve as commemorative monuments. Simple, monumental granite stone pagodas were built with minimal adornment. The finial was designed in the form of an ancient Indian stūpa. The relic chamber in wooden pagodas was located in the foundations beneath the central pole, while in stone pagodas it was located above ground just below the central mast. From the late seventh century "twin pagodas," a Chinese innovation introduced for the sake of symmetry, began to appear. King Sinmun built Kamŭnsa (twin pagodas) in 682 in memory of his father King Munmu, who unified the Three Kingdoms under the rule of Silla. STŪPAS (*pudo*), mostly octagonal single-story stone monuments, served to enshrine the relics of eminent monks.

RELIQUARY containers were exquisitely crafted in ceramic, gilt bronze, silver, gold, and glass. The outer container is usually a square or rectangular box. The innermost reliquary, which contains the relic of the true body of the Buddha (the remains after cremation), is a tiny crystal or glass bottle with an exquisite gold or openwork stopper. Gilt-bronze images and written Buddhist sūtras, both representing the dharma body, were also deposited in reliquaries. In the five-story granite stone pagoda in Iksan Wanggung-ni was found a copy of the DIAMOND SŪTRA in seventeen gold sheets, on which is embossed the entire text in majestic regular script style, the only known example in East Asia. Reliquaries from the unified Silla period (668–935) were often in the shape of a miniature pagoda or palanquin with a bejeweled canopy and musicians or guardian kings at the corners. Stūpas of eminent monks from the Chosŏn period (fourteenth to seventeenth centuries) yielded white ceramic and brass reliquaries in the form of simple covered bowls.

Buddhist paraphernalia

Bronze bells, censers, incense boxes, *kuṇḍikā* (water bottles), and flower vases can all be categorized as Buddhist RITUAL OBJECTS and ceremonial paraphernalia; such objects were executed with considerable craftsmanship since the Three Kingdom period. A Paekche gilt-bronze censer from the late sixth century, excavated in Nŭngsan-ri site in Puyŏ, shows a superb combination of traditional ideas in its dragon support and its lotus bowl and cover in the shape of the legendary Penglai paradise mountain surmounted by a phoenix. During the Unified Silla period, magnificent bells were cast in bronze as seen in the huge Pongdŏksa bell. The refinement of design with floral bands and elegant airy *apsaras* kneeling on clouds, as well as the profound sound and superb casting technique, is unmatched in East Asia. In the Koryŏ period (918–1392) incense containers and bottles for private use and for altars were made of lacquer or bronze. They were often decorated with tiny and elegant inlaid designs executed with mother-of-pearl on lacquer vessels or with silver on bronze vessels.

Buddhist sculpture and painting

Buddhist images of Śākyamuni, Amitābha, the Medicine Buddha Bhaiṣajyaguru, and the Universal Buddha Vairocana, who were enshrined in the *kŭmdang*, are the focus of worship. No large bronze images, prior to the ninth century, have survived, but small votive gilt-bronze images (ten to thirty centimeters in height and dated between the seventh and ninth centuries) have been excavated from temples, residential sites, and pagodas. These images were for personal altars or for ritual offering. From the earliest period (sixth century) Buddha images portrayed characteristically Korean broad faces with high cheekbones, while the drapery styles, which show influence from the Six Dynasties in China, are characterized by the symmetrical arrangement of garments and an emphasis on frontality. Maitreya Bodhisattva (Mirŭk posal), the Future Buddha, was worshiped in royal and aristocratic circles in the early seventh century in all of the Three Kingdoms. Some of the finest images demonstrate Korean mastery of the lost-wax bronze-casting technique and refinement in every detail. Avalokiteśvara Bodhisattva (Kwanseŭm posal) was one of the most popular images throughout history in Korea. The Avalokiteśvara image excavated from Sŏnsan, a small bronze masterpiece, effortlessly conveys a gentleness in facial expression, a gracefully raised right hand with lotus bud, and the fluent style of sashes and skirt.

Maitreya Bodhisattva. (Korean, gilt bronze, Paekche, seventh century.) National Museum of Korea. Reproduced by permission.

A new style of thin monastic garment worn with the left shoulder bare appears in most eighth- and ninth-century Buddha images in Korea, after Korean monks began traveling to Tang China, Central Asia, and as far as India. Monumental granite stone images (all their original coloring is now lost) were carved from the seventh century and enshrined in cave temples (e.g., the Amitābha Buddha triad in Kunwi in North Kyŏngsang province); during the seventh to ninth centuries they were also placed in natural environments, such as Namsan, the sacred Buddhist mountain in Kyŏngju. The SŎKKURAM Buddha image from the mid-eighth century is unquestionably one of the great masterpieces of the world in its outstanding concept and execution in rough textured granite. In the Koryŏ and Chosŏn dynasties, Buddhist images wearing heavy garments covering both shoulders were made in all kinds of materials, in particular bronze, clay, and wood. Especially in the Chosŏn period, large carved wooden altarpieces depicting the pantheon of buddhas, bodhisattvas, arhats, and guardian kings in high relief were frequently placed behind three-dimensional main buddhas in the worshiping halls.

The paintings of sacred images on the walls of monastery must have been practiced in Korea at the same time the sculptured images were executed, but despite written records in the SAMGUK YUSA (MEMORABILIA OF THE THREE KINGDOMS), no visual material has survived.

Sagyŏng (handwritten and hand-painted Buddhist scriptures) flourished during the Koryŏ dynasty. The most frequently copied sūtras of the Koryŏ dynasty were the HUAYAN JING (Korean, *Hwaŏmgyŏng*), *Amitābha Sūtra* (Korean, *Amit'agyŏng*), and LOTUS SŪTRA (SADDHARMAPUṆḌARĪKA-SŪTRA; Korean, *Pŏphwagyŏng*). *Sagyŏng* took the form of precious

Amitābha Buddha. (Korean, Koryŏ, gold, colors on silk, 1306.) Nezu Institute of Fine Arts. Reproduced by permission.

illuminated manuscripts in which the title, the exquisite miniature paintings of the dazzling frontispiece, and the text were decorated and written in gold or silver on dark indigo-dyed paper made from the inner bark of the mulberry. During the thirteenth and fourteenth centuries, Koryŏ became the center of illuminated manuscript production in East Asia.

In the Koryŏ period, when Buddhism prospered under royal and aristocratic patronage, Pure Land Buddhist paintings of Amitābha, Water Moon Avalokiteśvara, and Kṣitigarbha flourished. These paintings were rendered on hanging silk scrolls in various sizes, depending on their use; smaller scrolls were for private altars, and larger ones for temples. The images are outlined in red or black ink and painted with mineral colors, including cinnabar red, malachite green, and lead white. These principal colors, finely ground and prepared with a binder, were first applied on the back of the silk, then on the front, in order to ensure the durability of the colors and to intensify the hue. Gold for exposed parts of the Buddha's body and decorative motifs were applied on top of this. Facial details were drawn and the image would be completed during an eye-dotting ceremony. In the Chosŏn dynasty Buddhist paintings of large figural groups were often executed on hemp. Mineral pigments on such paintings were applied only to the front surface. As a consequence, some colors, especially red and green, have been lost from paintings dating from the sixteenth and seventeenth centuries. A new type of painting, in which Buddhist images were mixed with native Korean spirits and deities, began to emerge in the second half of the Chosŏn dynasty.

See also: **Chan Art; China, Buddhist Art in; Huayan Art; Monastic Architecture; Portraiture; Pure Land Art**

Bibliography

The Art of Śarīra Reliquary. Seoul: National Museum of Korea, 1991.

Best, Jonathan W. "Early Korean Buddhist Bronzes and Sui Regional Substyles: A Contextual Study of Stylistic Influence in the Early Seventh Century." In *Sambul Kim Won-yong kyosu chŏngnyŏn t'oeim kinyŏm nonch'ong.* Seoul: Ilchisa, 1987.

Fontein, Jan. "Masterpieces of Lacquer and Metalwork." *Apollo* (August 1968): 114–119.

Hwang, Su-young. *Han'guk ŭi pulsang* (Korean Buddhist Sculpture). Seoul, 1990.

Kang, Woo-bang. *Pulsari Changŏm* (The Art of Śarīra Reliquary). Seoul: National Museum of Korea, 1991.

Kim, Hongnam. *The Story of a Painting: A Korean Buddhist Treasure from the Mary Jackson Burke Foundation.* New York: Asia Society Galleries, 1991.

Kim, Lena. "Buddhist Sculpture." In *Korean Art Treasures,* ed. Youngsook Pak and Roderick Whitfield. Seoul: Ye-gyŏng, 1986.

Kim, Lena. "Tradition and Transformation in Korean Buddhist Sculpture." In *Arts of Korea,* ed. Judith Smith. New York: Metropolitan Museum of Art, 1998.

Lee, Junghee. "Sixth Century Buddhist Sculpture." *Korean Culture* 2, no. 2 (1981): 28–35.

McCallum, Donald F. "Korean Influence on Early Japanese Buddhist Sculpture." *Korean Culture* 3, no. 1 (1982): 22–29.

Mun, Myong-dae. *Han'guk chogaksa* (History of Korean Buddhist Sculpture). Seoul: Yorhwadang, 1984.

Pak, Youngsook. "The Korean Art Collection in the Metropolitan Museum of Art." In *Arts of Korea,* ed. Judith Smith. New York: Metropolitan Museum of Art, 1998.

Pak, Youngsook. "Grundzüge der koreanischen Architektur." In *Korea: Die Alten Königreiche.* Munich, Germany: Hirmer Verlag, 1999.

Pak, Youngsook, and Whitfield, Roderick. *Handbook of Korean Art: Buddhist Sculpture.* Seoul: Yekyong, 2002.

Sørensen, Hendrik Hjort. *The Iconography of Korean Buddhist Painting.* Leiden, Netherlands: Brill, 1989.

YOUNGSOOK PAK

KOREAN, BUDDHIST INFLUENCES ON VERNACULAR LITERATURE IN

Buddhism had an enormous impact on the development of Korean vernacular literature, primarily in premodern Korea. Buddhism's influences on the Korean language and vocabulary are also noteworthy, a legacy still apparent in contemporary Korea. Buddhist literature constituted the mainstream of Korean literature before the Chosŏn dynasty (1392–1910) and a substantial part of Korean literature during and after that period. The development of the Korean script, Korean verse and prose forms, and the Korean language were all closely associated with Buddhism.

Yongbi ŏch'ŏn'ga (*The Songs of the Flying Dragons According to Heaven,* 1445), a eulogy of the founding of the Chosŏn dynasty, was the first literary work composed in the indigenous Korean script. This phonetic script was originally promulgated in the edict *Hunmin chŏngŭm* (*Correct Sounds to Instruct the People*) and it came to be known as *Han'gŭl* (one and great letters) during the twentieth century. Heavily influenced by Buddhism, the *Songs of Flying Dragons* became a model for epic poems in vernacular Korean. Buddhism also had an impact on writing style. The interpretive text outlining the Han'gŭl writing system, *Hunmin chŏngŭm,* was published around 1446 and was modeled after Buddhist canonical scriptures in its use of prose narration followed by reiteration in verse. Numerous Buddhist texts were translated into Han'gŭl, including Buddhist miracle tales and classical Chinese and Sanskrit MANTRAS. In addition, a number of narrative songs (*kasa*) and short lyric poems (*sijo*), novels, Confucian edification works, and textbooks were composed in vernacular Korean under Buddhist influence.

Examples of Buddhist vernacular literature in Han'gŭl

The promulgation of Han'gŭl in 1446 signaled the blossoming of Korean vernacular literature. Prior to devising its own writing system, Korea had used Chinese characters for transcription, even though they were not always appropriate to a Korean setting. A Korean alphabet was thus devised under the leadership of King Sejong (1418–1450). However, Confucian scholar-officials of the Chosŏn government, led by Ch'oe Malli (ca. mid-fifteenth century), strongly opposed the use of Korea's own script on the grounds that it would violate the policy of respecting the senior state, China. They even labeled the Korean alphabet a "debased" writing system that was inferior to that of China, calling it *ŏnmun* (vulgar language) or *amk'ŭl* (language for women), a tradition that continued into the twentieth century. As a result, the Korean alphabet became marginalized and for many years it was primarily used by women and commoners who could not read classical Chinese.

The translation of important Mahāyāna Buddhist texts, such as the LOTUS SŪTRA (SADDHARMAPUṆḌARĪKA-SŪTRA), marked the first major use of Han'gŭl. A wide range of Buddhist texts were rendered into vernacular Korean in order to propagate Buddhist teachings while, at the same time, diffusing the newly invented Han'gŭl. Translated works included *Sŏkpo sangjŏl* (*A Detailed Biography of the Buddha Śākyamuni,* 1447); *Wŏrin ch'ŏn'gangjigok* (*The Songs of the Moon's Reflection on a Thousand Rivers,* 1449); *Wŏrin sŏkpo* (*The Moon's Reflection on the Buddha's Lineage,* 1459); and *Pumo ŭnjung kyŏng* (*The Sūtra of Parental Gratitude,* 1563). *A Detailed Biography of the Buddha Śākyamuni* depicted the eight principal stages in the Buddha's life, and it catalyzed the development of vernacular Korean literature from the fifteenth to the sixteenth centuries. The earliest Buddhist poem written in vernacular Korean, *The Songs of the Moon's Reflection on a Thousand Rivers,* is comparable to one of the masterpieces of Indian literature, BUDDHACARITA (*Acts of the Buddha*), a narrative of the life of Śākyamuni. *The Moon's Reflection on the Buddha's Lineage* is a combined publication of the aforementioned two works. A Chinese Buddhist apocryphal work, *The Sūtra of Parental Gratitude* was translated to promote the pan-Asian ideal of filial piety. Han'gŭl was also used to transliterate anthologies of Sanskrit mantras, including *Odae chinŏn* (*The Five Great Mantras,* 1485).

Another important area of Korean Buddhist literature in Han'gŭl is vernacular novels. *Ku unmong* (*The*

Cloud Dream of the Nine, 1687–1688) by Kim Manjung (1637–1692) is a typical Buddhist novel that portrays all the fame and glory of the human world as a dream, making the Buddhist notion of ŚŪNYATA (EMPTINESS) its primary theme. *Sassi namjŏng ki* (*The Story of Lady Sa,* ca. 1689–1692) serves as a prototype for later novels, taking the promotion of virtue and reproval of vice as its main theme. *Onggojip chŏn* (*The Tale of a Stubborn Person Ong*), *Sim Ch'ŏng chŏn* (*The Tale of Sim Ch'ong*), and *Hŭngbu chŏn* (*The Tale of Hŭngbu*), all composed in the late Chosŏn period, adopted the Buddhist motifs of karmic fruition and promotion of virtue. Korean vernacular literature gained wider readership in the mid-nineteenth century, about the time that the classical Confucian novel in Chinese entered its period of decline.

Koreans composed literature in classical Chinese before the invention of the Korean alphabet. Unlike China and Japan, however, Korea did not have a strong tradition of fictional prose narratives before the seventeenth century. The promulgation of the Korean script brought popular literary forms, including fiction, to prominence. In particular, political, social, and economic diversification resulting from the invasions of Japan and Qing China from the end of the sixteenth century to the mid-seventeenth century was matched by cultural diversification, and the vernacular novel was a product of this milieu. Han'gŭl versions of the novel came to be particularly popular among women and lay readers, who were unfamiliar with Chinese writing, and vernacular novels gained a wide readership. Buddhist vernacular literature did not appeal to the literati, however, due in part to the dominance of Confucianism during the Chosŏn period.

Buddhist influences on Korean language and vocabulary

Buddhism also exerted considerable influence on the Korean language and vocabulary. Contemporary scholars have argued that Han'gŭl originated from symbol letters (*puhoja*), a kind of signifier used in Buddhist literature in classical Chinese during the Koryŏ dynasty (918–1392). Some Korean and Japanese scholars have begun studying *puhoja* as the possible origin of the Korean alphabet and they have noted its use in Buddhist canonical texts during the Koryŏ period. An ardent debate in Korean academe rages over this issue.

Many Korean geographical names are associated with Buddhism. For instance, Mount Sŏrak (Snowy Peak), one of the most beautiful mountains in Korea, is considered the Korean counterpart of the Himalayas, the birthplace of the Buddha. Much of Korean cultural language involves Buddhist words or is associated with Buddhism. A representative example is the word *ip'an sap'an,* which originally referred to practicing monks who studied both doctrine and meditation (*ip'an*) and to administrative monks (*sap'an*). In addition, there are some difference in the way similar terms are used in China and Korea. For example, the terms *pigu* (Chinese, *biqiu*; monk) and *piguni* (Chinese, *biqiuni*; nun) are still used in Korea, but they are no longer recognized in China. Moreover, the meaning of some Buddhist terminology has changed. For instance, the meditative term *musim* (no mind, or no false mind) today means "heartlessness." The original meaning of *ŏp* (karma) referred to both good and bad actions; now it signifies only evil actions. Furthermore, the Buddhist terms that entered everyday parlance often had derogatory meanings, a product of the Confucian dominance of premodern Korea. Since the Chosŏn period, in particular, the meaning of certain Buddhist terms has become derogatory; thus, *ip'an sap'an* came to signify "a brawling situation." Originally the term *yadan pŏpsŏk* referred to "an outdoor sermon"; it is now used in a negative sense to mean "an extremely noisy situation."

Historically, Buddhist literature played a leading role in the formation of vernacular Korean literature. By the late nineteenth century, the importation of Western civilization and culture caused traditional verse and prose forms to give way to new forms. Although the *Nim ŭi ch'immuk* (*Silence of Love,* 1926) by monk HAN YONGUN (1879–1944) is considered one of the masterpieces of modern Korean poetry, vernacular Buddhist literature in Han'gŭl was not generally perceived as literary. It is only in recent years that Buddhist literature has regained a growing readership in Korea.

See also: **Chinese, Buddhist Influences on Vernacular Literature in; Korea; Languages; Poetry and Buddhism**

Bibliography

Bantly, Francisca Cho. *Embracing Illusion: Truth and Fiction in The Dream of the Nine Clouds.* Albany: State University of New York Press, 1996.

Lee, Peter H. *Korean Literature: Topics and Themes.* Tucson: University of Arizona Press, 1966.

Rutt, Richard, trans. *A Nine Cloud Dream.* In *Virtuous Women: Three Classic Korean Novels,* ed. Richard Rutt and Kim chong-un. Seoul: Royal Asiatic Society, 1974.

Sa, Chaedong. *A Study of the History of Korean Narrative Literature (Han'guk sŏsa munhak ŭi yŏn'gu)*, 5 vols. Taejon, Korea: Chungang munhwasa, 1995.

Shim, Jae-ryong. *Korean Buddhism: Tradition and Transformation.* Seoul: Jimmundang, 1999.

A Study of Korean Buddhist Literature (Han'guk Pulgyo munhak yŏn'gu), 2 vols. Seoul: Han'guk Munhak Yŏn'guso, Dongguk University Press, 1988.

Yi, Sŭngjae. "The Philological Meaning of Symbol Letters" (Puhoja ŭi munjaron chŏk ŭiŭi). In *Studies of the Korean Language (Kugŏhak)* 38 (2001): 89–116.

JONGMYUNG KIM

KUIJI

Kuiji (Dasheng Ji, Ci'en *Dashi*; 632–682) was the dharma-name of a prominent Tang dynasty (618–907) scholar and monk. Scion of a family of politically powerful generals, Kuiji was orphaned as a young child and ordained in his teens. Assigned to the imperially sponsored translation team of the renown pilgrim-monk XUANZANG (ca. 600–664), Kuiji soon established himself as one of Xuanzang's most capable protégés. After Xuanzang's death, Kuiji went on to write a series of voluminous commentaries and doctrinal essays based on his understanding of the Dharmapāla lineage of Indian *vijñaptimātra-yogācāra* philosophy. He was posthumously designated the first patriarch of what was eventually styled the FAXIANG SCHOOL of Chinese Buddhism, which represented the second main transmission of the YOGĀCĀRA SCHOOL into East Asia.

Kuiji's presentation of *vijñaptimātra-yogācāra* thought was based principally on the *Cheng weishi lun,* a translation of VASUBANDHU's fourth-century *Triṃśikā (Thirty Verses)*, substantially supplemented with a selective synopsis of ten Indian commentaries. This work was officially a product of Xuanzang's translation project, although its preface indicates the key role Kuiji played in selecting and adjudicating the various doctrinal controversies excerpted from the divergent Indian commentarial traditions. The result was a highly technical and doctrinally conservative presentation of Yogācāra thought, one very different from, and in conflict with, the PARAMĀRTHA school of Yogācāra thought already popular in China. This, coupled with the fickleness of imperial patronage after Xuanzang's death, led to the eventual decline of Kuiji's influence, a fate already evident during the latter part of his life as his main rival FAZANG (643–712) rose in prominence under the sponsorship of the royal consort, who was eventually to declare herself the Empress Wu.

Bibliography

Sponberg, Alan. "Meditation in Fa-hsiang Buddhism." In *Traditions of Meditation in Chinese Buddhism,* ed. Peter N. Gregory. Honolulu: University of Hawaii Press, 1987.

ALAN SPONBERG

KŪKAI

Kūkai (774–835) was a ninth-century Japanese figure renowned for his introduction of esoteric Buddhism into early Heian society. In his youth Kūkai studied Confucianism and Chinese literature at Daigaku, the state college. But he soon dropped out of Daigaku and joined a throng of privately ordained priests and nuns (*shido sō*), and he avidly trained in Buddhism. In 804, at age thirty-one, Kūkai hastily received official ORDINATION and was chosen to be part of the Japanese diplomatic mission to Tang China. Under the guidance of Master Huikou (746–805) of Qinglongsi in the capital city of Chang'an, Kūkai studied a system of esoteric Buddhism grounded in the *Mahāvairocana-sūtra* (Japanese, *Dainichikyō*) and the *Tattvasaṃgraha* or *Vajraśekhara-sūtra* (or *Tantra*; Japanese, *Kongōchōkyō*). Shortly after Huikou's death, Kūkai returned to Japan, carrying with him over 210 new Buddhist scriptures.

Kūkai was the first to invent a paradigm for separating esoteric and exoteric Buddhism (*Ben kenmitsu nikyōron*) and then to understand their complementary relationship (*Hannya shingyō hiken, Himitsu mandara jūjūshinron*). Kūkai's creation of a theory of ritual language (*Shōji jissōgi, Unjigi*) enabled the early Heian clergy to achieve integration between their textual studies and ritual practices, and accelerated their adoption of esoteric Buddhism. Kūkai also founded the Latter Seven-Day rite (*Goshichinichi mishihō*), the New Year esoteric Buddhist ceremony at the palace, and the ritual service aimed at legitimating the Japanese ruler as a cakravartin (wheel-turning monarch). Kūkai's ritual initiated the rapid integration of esoteric Buddhist rites into the ceremonies of the royal court, a process that led to the rise of Buddhism as the dominant ideology of the state. In medieval Japan, Kūkai became one of the most popular Buddhist saints; he was worshiped as a savior who lived on in his seat of endless meditation on Mount Kōya.

See also: **Exoteric-Esoteric (Kenmitsu) Buddhism in Japan; Shingon Buddhism, Japan**

Bibliography

Abé, Ryūichi. "Saichō and Kūkai: Conflict of Interpretations." *Japanese Journal of Religious Studies* 22 (1995): 1–2.

Abé, Ryūichi. *The Weaving of Mantra.* New York: Columbia University Press, 1999.

Groner, Paul. *Saichō: The Establishment of Japanese Tendai School.* Berkeley: Center for South and Southeast Asian Studies, University of California at Berkeley, 1984.

Hakeda, Yoshito. *Kūkai: Major Works.* New York: Columbia University Press, 1976.

RYŪICHI ABÉ

KUMĀRAJĪVA

Kumārajīva (350–409 or 413), the most important translator in East Asian Buddhist history, was born to a noble family in Kucha, a center of largely MAINSTREAM BUDDHIST SCHOOLS on the northern branch of the SILK ROAD. His native language, now known as Tokharian B, belonged to the Indo-European family. Under the guidance of his mother, Kumārajīva became a monk while still a boy, then traveled with her to Kashmir to study Buddhist philosophy of the Sarvāstivāda school. While continuing his studies in Kashgar (roughly between Kucha and Kashmir), Kumārajīva was converted to the MAHĀYĀNA by a monk who was a former prince of Yarkand, in the Khotan area, along the southern SILK ROAD. Eventually, Kumārajīva converted his earlier Indian teacher to the Mahāyāna.

In 383 a Chinese army occupied Kucha and took Kumārajīva away as a captive. He was held for some two decades in Liangzhou near DUNHUANG in the Gansu corridor, where he presumably learned to speak and read Chinese. When the Later Qin regime conquered Liangzhou in 401, Kumārajīva was taken to the Chinese capital of Chang'an, where he was immediately put at the head of a large translation staff.

Although a brilliant scholar, Kumārajīva was painfully aware of his own failings as a monk. While in Chang'an he was forced by the ruler to sire numerous children, in the hopes of producing offspring as gifted as their father. Nothing is known of them.

There are four aspects to Kumārajīva's greatness. First and most important is the volume, variety, and richness of his translations. Kumārajīva and his staff translated seventy-four works in 384 fascicles, including the *Amitābha-sūtra* (402), about the Pure Land paradise in the west; a new and more readable *Pañcaviṃśatisāhasrikāprajñāpāramitā-sūtra* (*Perfection of Wisdom in 25,000 Lines,* 404), a basic *prajñāpāramitā* text; the *Dazhidu lun* (*Great Perfection of Wisdom Treatise,* 405), a massive commentary attributed to Madhyamaka philosopher NĀGĀRJUNA (ca. second century C.E.), but edited and probably compiled by Kumārajīva; the LOTUS SŪTRA (SADDHARMAPUṆḌARĪKA-SŪTRA, 406), the single most important Mahāyāna scripture in all of East Asian Buddhism; the *Vimalakīrtinirdeśa-sūtra* (406), a very readable scripture about a wise lay bodhisattva; and the *Zhonglun* (*Treatise on the Middle,* 409?), Nāgārjuna's *Mādhyamakakārikā* (*Verses on Madhyamaka*) and commentary. The translations produced by Kumārajīva's team borrowed significantly from predecessors such as Zhi Qian (fl. mid-third century) and are known for their fluent and readable style. In cases where multiple Chinese translations exist, it is always Kumārajīva's version that is used.

The second aspect of Kumārajīva's greatness is that individual translations or groups of texts became the bases for distinctive exegetical traditions, especially the *Tattvasiddhi-śāstra* (Chinese, *Chengshi lun*; *Completion of Truth*) and the "Three Treatises" or *Sanlun* of the MADHYAMAKA SCHOOL. Third, Kumārajīva's texts contained much more than doctrine; they also included various types of songs and poetry, legends and stories, literary styles and motifs, and a vast repertoire of religious images. Fourth, and certainly not least, is that Kumārajīva taught a group of gifted students who wrote texts that formed the foundation of East Asian Buddhism, including SENGZHAO (374–414), DAOSHENG (ca. 355–434), Sengrui (also Huirui; 352–436), and others.

See also: **Paramārtha; Śikṣānanda**

Bibliography

Ch'en, Kenneth Kuan Sheng. *Buddhism in China: A Historical Survey.* Princeton, NJ: Princeton University Press, 1964.

Liu Mau-Tsai. *Kutscha und seine Beziehungen zu China vom 2. Jh. v. bis zum 6. Jh. n. Chr.,* 2 vols. Wiesbaden, Germany: Harrassowitz, 1969.

Robinson, Richard H. *Early Mādhyamika in India and China.* Madison: University of Wisconsin Press, 1967.

Tsukamoto Zenryū. *A History of Early Chinese Buddhism: From Its Introduction to the Death of Hui-yüan*, tr. Leon Hurvitz. Tokyo and New York: Kodansha, 1985.

Zürcher, E. *The Buddhist Conquest of China: The Spread and Adaptation of Buddhism in Early Medieval China.* Leiden, Netherlands: Brill, 1959 (1972).

JOHN R. MCRAE

KYŎNGHŎ

Kyŏnghŏ Sŏngu (1849–1912) was among the few important Sŏn (CHAN SCHOOL) Buddhist leaders in nineteenth-century Korea. His rise to eminence took place at a time when Buddhist institutions were in cultural and political decline after almost six hundred years of Confucian domination.

In 1879, after secluding himself in a hut for several months in order to practice intense *kongan* (KŌAN) meditation, Kyŏnghŏ became enlightened. Subsequently his fame spread far and wide and hundreds of followers gathered to receive his instructions. In the following decades he revived Sŏn practice greatly and set up different monasteries as training centers. Kyŏnghŏ also contributed to the renaissance of Korean Buddhism by organizing Buddhist societies on behalf of the laity.

Kyŏnghŏ passed away in his hermitage on Kapsan in 1912. His lineage of Sŏn was continued by several important disciples, all of whom have left their imprint on contemporary Buddhism in Korea.

Kyŏnghŏ did not write any major works, but he left behind a large number of instructions for meditation, exhortations to practice, and occasional pieces, as well as many songs and poems in praise of Sŏn in particular and Buddhism in general. Among these his *Odo ka* (*Song of Enlightenment*) is the most important. Much of this material was compiled posthumously by his disciples and subsequently published. Kyŏnghŏ also compiled a manual for Sŏn practitioners entitled *Sŏnmun ch'waryo* (*Important Points of Sŏn Buddhism*), which is still in use today.

See also: **Chan School; Korea**

Bibliography

Kyŏnghŏ chip (*Collected Works of Kyŏnghŏ*), ed. Han Yongun. Seoul: Poryon'gak, 1979. Reprint of Chungang Sŏnwŏn Chang edition, 1942.

Kyŏnghŏ pŏbŏ (*The Dharma Talks of Kyŏnghŏ*), ed. Kyŏnghŏ Songu Sŏnsa Pŏbŏ Chip Kanhaeng Hoe. Seoul: Inmul Yŏn'gu, 1981.

Sŏnmun ch'waryo (*Important Points of Sŏn Buddhism*), ed. Kyŏnghŏ Sŏngu. Seoul: Poryŏn'gak, 1982.

Sørensen, Henrik H. "The Life and Times of the Korean Sŏn Master Kyŏnghŏ." *Korean Studies* 7 (1983): 7–33.

HENRIK H. SØRENSEN

L

LAITY

The laity in Buddhism makes up two of the four constituent parts of the SAṄGHA (monks, nuns, laymen, and laywomen) and the great majority of Buddhists. The ordained differ from the laity by virtue of their renunciation of the householder's life and observance of a strict code of behavior, which make them worthy and deserving, a pure and holy "field of merit." Laypeople acquire merit through giving food, clothing, shelter, and other material support to the ordained, and merit-making by laity to the ordained has been a central aspect of lay life in all Buddhist societies. Prohibitions on the ordained acquiring individual wealth, as well as prohibitions on sexual activity, make the ordained dependent upon laity for their living and the perpetuation of a religious order.

The textual legacy

Laity in early Buddhist texts are referred to as *upāsaka* (laymen) and *upāsikā* (laywomen), devoted followers of Buddhist teaching, and they are distinguished from ordinary householders. Lay followers should take proper care of the monks during the retreats, hear the dharma expounded at that time and on the monthly Poṣadha (Pāli, *Uposatha*) days, take the three refuges, follow the first five *śīlas* or moral rules (refraining from taking life, stealing, unchastity, lying, and taking intoxicants), offer robes to the monks at the end of the rainy season, undertake PILGRIMAGE, and venerate STŪPAS containing relics of the Buddha. The *Sigalovāda-sutta* (*Discourse to Sigala*) urges laity to revere their parents, spouses and children, friends and companions, and religious teachers. Instructions specifically for women direct them in various texts to be capable in work, to manage servants well, to be physically attractive to their husbands, and to manage his fortune well.

THERAVĀDA Buddhism has traditionally emphasized a strong distinction between the ordained and the laity. The *nikāyas* show that laity can reach the first three stages of sanctity (*sotāpanna, sakadāgāmi,* and *anāgāmi*), but they cannot become arhats. Instead, they aim for a better rebirth. Recent studies suggest, nevertheless, that the *Sutta Piṭaka* also contains a second, contrasting view on the laity, holding that laity can attain enlightenment. The *Mahāvagge Maṇḍapeyyakathā* depicts the Buddha teaching the FOUR NOBLE TRUTHS and the eightfold path to the laity, and the *Nakulapitā-sutta* (*Discourse to Nakulapitā*) has the Buddha teaching a layman about the five aggregates and the error of confusing these with the self.

With the appearance of early MAHĀYĀNA in the first century, new concepts and practices developed, widening the laity's scope. The cardinal idea of emptiness undermined all conceptual oppositions, including that between monastics and laity. The idea of the BODHISATTVA who purposefully remains in the world to save others further undermined the dichotomy separating the ordained and laity, and the idea of the lay bodhisattva emerged.

The quintessential example of the lay bodhisattva is the layman VIMALAKĪRTI, in the *Vimalakīrtinirdeśa* (*The Teaching of Viamalakīrti*), composed between the first century B.C.E. and first century C.E. Vimalakīrti expounds on the nature of emptiness, exhibiting his wisdom to an immense assembly of holy men and bodhisattvas. He ridicules their doctrinal abstractions and pretensions to a higher status than the

Laypersons dip lotus flowers in holy water and sprinkle it on themselves at Phra Kaew Monastery, Bangkok, Thailand, 1991.

laity. Other sūtras continue the themes of this work, sometimes introducing laywomen as the protagonists. Two such examples are Vimalakīrti's daughter in the *Candrottarādārikāvyākaraṇa-sūtra* (*Discourse on the Prediction Made about the Girl Candrottarā*) and Queen Śrīmālā in the *Śrīmālādevīsiṃhanāda-sūtra* (*Lion's Roar of Queen Śrīmālā*).

Other Mahāyāna texts present filial piety as a kind of Buddhist morality, in a concession to the prominence of this principle especially among the laity in East Asia. The central role of the priesthood in funerary and ancestral rites in East Asian Buddhism stems from the elevation of filial piety as an ethical ideal in such works as the *Ullambana-sūtra.*

Laity in Theravāda countries

Lay life in Theravāda countries is greatly influenced by the custom of men entering a Buddhist monastery for a period of time, later returning to lay life. Nearly all Burmese men and about half the men in Thailand, Laos, and Cambodia have spent at least one rains-retreat, and often much longer, as an ordained monk. This means that the laity of several Theravāda countries has significant personal experience of monastic life, unparalleled by any comparable custom in countries where Mahāyāna predominates. This custom creates close ties between laity and the ordained and expands the range of religious experience for lay men. Women are excluded because the tradition of valid ORDINATION for NUNS is believed to have died out.

Lay practice revolves around the precepts and merit-making activities. Laypeople observe the five basic precepts already discussed, and on holy days they may take a further five: refraining from sex, eating after noon, perfumes and adornments, seeing public entertainments, and the use of grand beds. Giving food to monks on a daily basis is a widespread practice, as is contributing to such ceremonies as a man's ordination, New Year's, an abbot's promotion, meals for monks, presentation of robes, cremations, and to general monastery fund-raising or repairs. Donations may take the form of money, items involved in a particular ceremony, or they may be things monks are allowed to own, such as bedding, a razor, an umbrella, or a needle and thread. Founding and supporting schools and hospitals is also religiously meritorious. The performance of meritorious giving thus creates and strengthens the connections between monastic and lay society.

Laity in Mahāyāna countries

In East Asia ritual merit transfer is the basic motif structuring the relation between laity and the ordained. In essence, descendants make gifts to monastics, who transfer the merit to descendants' ancestors in order to ensure them a better REBIRTH or a more comfortable existence in the other world. Merit transfer has also become institutionalized in the mid-summer GHOST FESTIVAL, based on the *Ullambana-sūtra.*

A wide variety of devotional practices are performed by lay Buddhists in China, Korea, and Japan, including veneration of such sacred objects as Buddhist images, relics, and stūpas; copying and reciting sūtras, prayers, and formulas; use of Buddhist rosaries, AMULETS AND TALISMANS; pilgrimage; and participation in cults and rites for particular buddhas and bodhisattvas, including Śākyamuni, MAITREYA, AMITĀBHA, Avalokiteśvara, Kṣitigharba, Bhaiṣajyaguru, Samantabhadra, Acalā, and others.

Chinese laity formed societies for reciting the Buddha's name, for study, and for publication as early as the Six Dynasties (222–589). The tradition of the learned layman in China had a prototype in Pang Yun (born ca. 740), "Layman P'ang," whose Chan sayings were later collected as *Pang jushi yulu* (*The Recorded Sayings of Layman Pang*). He gave away his house and sank his possessions in a boat, taking up a wandering life and studying under several Chan masters, though not becoming a monk.

A Buddhist revival in the late Ming dynasty (1368–1644) grew out of a lay movement of provincial gentry, who underwrote the founding of monasteries, sponsored the clergy, and enthusiastically practiced Buddhist devotions. Gentry went on pilgrimage to Buddhist monasteries, composed poems about them, and restored them. They corresponded with monks, attended lectures, chanted Buddhist texts and the Buddha's name, and burned incense. They organized lay associations with names like Lotus Society for pure land devotions, or associations for liberating captive animals. They participated in public rites called "Bathing the Buddha" for the Buddha's birthday and the Ghost Festival.

During the late Qing dynasty (1644–1911) and the Republican period (1911–1920), the number of Buddhist lay societies grew rapidly, attracting literati and bourgeoisie adherents. Merit clubs operated vegetarian restaurants in the cities, and study groups met to discuss sacred texts or to hear lectures by visiting monks. Recitation clubs gathered to recite the Buddha's name in the hope of being reborn in the Western Pure Land. Founded by a Hangzhou businessman in 1920, the Right Faith Society operated a clinic and a boys' primary school, also providing soup kitchens, free coffins for the poor, and a widows' home. The Buddhist Pure Karma Society, founded in Shanghai in 1925, ran an orphanage and a clinic dispensing free medicine; it also broadcast a nightly radio program.

In ancient Korea, lay practice centered on worship of both Maitreya and Amitābha. Chanting Amitābha's name was a central lay practice. Pure land faith was propagated through Buddhist folk tales from the unified Silla dynasty (668–935) that were later incorporated into a history, SAMGUK YUSA (MEMORABILIA OF THE THREE KINGDOMS, 1285). This work reflects strong lay participation in Buddhism and also shows that lay associations were formed around pure land practice.

Ancient and medieval Japan exhibited a rich variety of lay Buddhist practices, including pilgrimage to famous monasteries and sacred mountains or around circuit routes devoted to Avalokiteśvara or the historical Buddhist figure KŪKAI (774–835); sponsoring Buddhist art works and ceremonies; and building or repairing temples. The Great Buddha statue of Tōdaiji in Nara was completed in 752, in part by lay contributions organized by the lay Buddhist En no Ubasoku (from Sanskrit *upāsaka*).

Classical literature is replete with images of laity. In 984 a lay noble, Minamoto Tamenori, completed the *Sanbōe* (*Illustrations of the Three Jewels*), an illustrated collection of Buddhist tales in three volumes, as a guide to Buddhism for an imperial princess. It included tales of Japanese Buddhists, the miracles achieved through their devotions, and stories of meritorious people whose good deeds produced rewards in this life and the next.

Especially after periods of warfare, many widows adopted a semimonastic style of life, taking the tonsure though not necessarily living in a monastery, forming societies to commission or repair statues, and devoting themselves to prayers for the souls of the dead. Sometimes such women congregated near a monastery and performed tasks like laundry and food provisioning for the monks.

Monks receive alms from lay Buddhists at Phra Dhammakāya Monastery near Bangkok, Thailand, 1991. © Don Farber 2003. All rights reserved. Reproduced by permission.

During the Edo period (1600–1868), the entire population was legally required to affiliate with a Buddhist monastery. These inalterable, exclusive affiliations were established by family units and passed down through generations. In return for supporting the monasteries and their priests, the priests performed the family's funerals and periodic ancestral rites. Although the legal obligation of monastery affiliation dissolved in the 1870s, the fact of family graves and records being kept by the monasteries means that these affiliations have largely been preserved.

Laity established associations for pilgrimage and for the recitation of Amitābha's name or the title of the LOTUS SŪTRA (SADDHARMAPUṆḌARĪKA-SŪTRA). Stories of the ideal layperson, based on historical individuals, were published by the True Pure Land sect during the Edo period in collections called *ōjōden* (tales of rebirth [in the pure land]). These tales vividly illustrated valued traits: filial piety, honesty, compassion, devotion to reciting Amitābha's name, and strong conviction of the certain rebirth in the Western Pure Land.

Laity and modernization

The modernization of Buddhist societies has brought sweeping changes. The extension of the franchise and expanded political participation in secular life colored religious life, creating the expectation that laity should be able to influence the character of Buddhist institutions. The spread of literacy has enabled laity to read and interpret sacred scripture with increasing independence from the ordained. Higher education hones a critical spirit and encourages skepticism regarding clergy's preeminence over the laity and their monopoly over funerals and other rituals. The prestige of science and rationality in modernizing societies further nurtures a critical view of traditional religious beliefs, practices, and institutions.

The encounter with Christian missionaries and Western imperialism was an important catalyst to Buddhist revival movements, and laymen have frequently played significant roles. The lay branch of the Buddhist Theosophical Society, founded in Sri Lanka in 1880, created a press, the Buddhist English School (later Ananda College), and a newspaper, *The Buddhist.* Prominent laity like ANAGĀRIKA DHARMAPĀLA (born David Hewavitarne, 1864–1933) acquired their first experience of activism in the Buddhist Theosophical Society and in the Young Men's Buddhist Association (later renamed the All-Ceylon Buddhist Congress), founded in Colombo in 1898 by C. S. Dissanayake.

Dharmapāla founded the first international Buddhist organization, Mahābodhi Society, in Colombo in 1891, later starting a revival of Buddhism in India, beginning with a project to restore BODH GAYĀ. Dharmapāla linked his support for Buddhism to the struggle for Indian independence, so that Buddhist advocacy was inseparable from the call for political independence. The Indian Buddhist revival did not become a mass movement, however, until the leadership of Bhimrao Ramji AMBEDKAR (1891–1956), an attorney trained in the United States and Britain who worked for the legal emancipation of the Untouchables. Despairing of integrating the Untouchables into Hindu caste society, he converted to Buddhism in 1950. When he called on all Untouchables to convert, mass conversions followed in several Indian states.

In late nineteenth- and early twentieth-century Japan, Buddhist reform movements arose, frequently led by groups of priests and laymen, calling for free inquiry into traditional beliefs and practices, rejecting superstition, and striving to articulate a modern Buddhist ethic. One such association, Bukkyō Seitō Dōshikai, published a widely circulated journal called *Buddhism* (*Bukkyō*), sought inspiration from Unitarianism, embraced skepticism, and even questioned whether Mahāyāna is true Buddhism. Other reformers admired socialism, affirmed equality, and called for reform of authoritarian sectarian organizations. Still others aligned Buddhism with nationalism, such as Nation's Pillar Society (Kokuchūkai), founded in 1914 by a Nichiren priest who later disrobed and wrote in defense of marriage, Tanaka Chigaku (1861–1939).

Buddhist new religious movements in Japan

The formalism inherent in the historical origins of Japanese temple affiliations has made the country a fertile area for the founding of new religious movements expanding the scope of lay Buddhism. In the early twentieth century Buddhist new religions emerged, based on the belief that the laity possess all necessary qualifications to perform funerals and ancestral rites without clerical mediation. Reiyūkai Kyōdan, founded in 1930, and its offshoot Risshō Kōseikai, founded in 1938, are two such examples. Both derive from Nichiren Buddhism and emphasize ancestor worship through the *Lotus Sūtra*.

After World War II, many more Buddhist new religions emerged. The largest is SŌKA GAKKAI, which was founded in 1930 but which did not become a mass movement until after 1945. Its main religious practices are chanting the title of the *Lotus Sūtra* and studying its doctrines. It founded a political party in 1964. Sōka Gakkai was originally affiliated with a branch of the NICHIREN SCHOOL, Nichiren Shōshū, but this connection was abolished in 1991. Sōka Gakkai maintains an extensive program of peace work and branches throughout the world. With membership estimated at seventeen million, it is one of the largest—if not the largest—Buddhist lay associations in history.

In recent years Buddhist new religions deriving from Shingon Buddhism, such as Agon-shū, Shinnyoen, and Gedatsukai, have been founded. In 1995 the Buddhist new religion Aum Shinrikyō, founded in 1986, carried out an attack on the Tokyo subway system that killed twelve people and required some five thousand to be hospitalized. The founder, Asahara Shōkō, hoped to cause Armageddon to fulfill his prophecy of the millennium. This group had no affiliation with any branch of Japanese Buddhism; it drew its main doctrines from Tibetan Buddhism mixed with the founder's eclectic readings in Christianity and Western millenarianism.

See also: **Merit and Merit-making; Monasticism**

Bibliography

Barua, Dipak Kumar. *An Analytical Study of Four Nikāyas.* Calcutta: Ribindra Bharati University, 1971.

Beyer, Stephan. *The Cult of Tara: Magic and Ritual in Tibet.* Berkeley: University of California Press, 1973.

Brook, Timothy. *Praying for Power: Buddhism and the Formation of Gentry Society in Late-Ming China.* Cambridge, MA: Harvard University Press, 1993.

Bunnag, Jane. *Buddhist Monk, Buddhist Layman: A Study of Urban Monastic Organization in Central Thailand.* Cambridge, UK: Cambridge University Press, 1973.

Dutt, Nalinaksha. "Place of Laity in Early Buddhism." *Indian Historical Quarterly* 21 (1945): 163–183.

Fuller, Ruth Sasaki; Iriya Yoshitake; and Fraser, Dana R.; trans. *The Recorded Sayings of Layman P'ang: A Ninth-Century Zen Classic.* New York: Weatherhill, 1971.

Gombrich, Richard, and Bechert, Heinz, eds. *The World of Buddhism: Buddhist Monks and Nuns in Society and Culture.* London: Thames and Hudson, 1991.

Hirakawa, Akira. *A History of Indian Buddhism: From Sakyamuni to Early Mahayana,* tr. Paul Groner. Honolulu: University of Hawaii Press, 1990.

Lancaster, Lewis, and Yu, C. S., eds. *Assimilation of Buddhism in Korea: Religious Maturity and Innovation in the Silla Dynasty.* Berkeley, CA: Asian Humanities Press, 1991.

Malalgoda, Kitsiri. *Buddhism in Sinhalese Society 1750–1900: A Study of Religious Revival and Change.* Berkeley and Los Angeles: University of California Press, 1976.

Samuels, Jeffrey. "Views of Householders and Lay Disciples in the *Sutta Piṭaka*: A Reconsideration of the Lay/Monastic Opposition." *Religion* 29 (1999): 235–238.

Tambiah, Stanley J. *Buddhism and the Spirit Cults of North-East Thailand.* Cambridge, UK: Cambridge University Press, 1970.

Teiser, Stephen F. *The Ghost Festival in Medieval China.* Princeton, NJ: Princeton University Press, 1988.

Welch, Holmes. *The Buddhist Revival in China.* Cambridge, MA: Harvard University Press, 1968.

HELEN HARDACRE

LALITAVISTARA

The *Lalitavistara,* of late but uncertain date (ca. fourth century C.E.), is an important Sanskrit biography that recounts in both prose and verse the life of the Buddha from his preexistence in Tuṣita heaven to his first sermon at Sārnāth. Originally written in Sanskrit, it is Mahāyānist in its view of Śākyamuni, embellishing his life story with accounts of miracles and evidence of his supernatural nature.

See also: **Buddha, Life of the; Sanskrit, Buddhist Literature in**

Bibliography

Bays, Gwendolyn, trans. *The Voice of the Buddha: The Beauty of Compassion,* 2 vols. Berkeley, CA: Dharma, 1983.

JOHN S. STRONG

LAMA

A lama is a Tibetan Buddhist teacher. In the most narrow sense, the term *bla ma* (pronounced "lama") refers to a lay or ordained religious instructor. It is also commonly used by Tibetans as a title for *tulku* (*sprul sku*), a reincarnated teacher. The prominent position of the lama in Tibetan Buddhism gave rise, first in China and then in the West, to the misnomer *Lamaism* to refer to Tibetan religion.

The term *bla ma* was one of countless neologisms invented by early Buddhist translators active in seventh- and eighth-century Tibet. It was coined to render the Sanskrit term *guru,* commonly glossed in India as "heavy," in apparent reference to the great burden of good qualities and responsibilities the religious guide carries. The Tibetan word *bla* was already endowed with considerable religious weight, referring to the life-force or spirit of an individual or corporate entity, such as a family or a community. The *bla* is mobile, able to establish residence in numerous external places or objects called *bla gnas,* or "*bla* support." Damage to the *bla gnas* is harmful, even fatal, to the person to whom it belongs. More perilous still is the ever-present danger that the *bla* might wander away or be stolen by demons, to the detriment of the person or group. Rituals are commonly performed to prevent the loss of the *bla* and call it back when it has departed.

Bla also caries the senses of "high," "appropriate," and "lord," and was used to translate the Sanskrit terms *pati* (lord) and *ūrdhvam* (elevated). The second part of the word, *ma,* can be read as either a substantive marker, a negative particle, or "mother." The multivalence of both syllables has led to near-countless etymologies of the term by Tibetan and Western exegetes alike, among them "highest" (literally, "none above") and "exalted mother."

The lama, incarnate or otherwise, occupies a central role in Tibetan Buddhism. This status can in part be attributed to the influence of tantric Buddhism. The tantric guru serves as the conduit for the teachings, transmitting secret instruction and rites though a series of initiations. The tantric practitioner is enjoined to view his or her guru as a buddha, more precious than any other BUDDHAS or BODHISATTVAS. Because of this the lama is considered in Tibet to be the fourth jewel, equal if not superior to the buddha, dharma, and SAṄGHA.

This exalted status is perhaps a reason for the invention of *Lamaism,* a term that has its roots in eighteenth-century China. Since the thirteenth century, powerful Tibetan lamas interacted with Mongol and Chinese imperial rulers, who referred to the lamas as *seng,* the term for Chinese monks. In the eighteenth century, however, the category of the Tibetan Buddhist master was differentiated from *seng* and transliterated as *lama.* This gave rise to the term *lama jiao,* the religion of *bla ma,* whence came the English *Lamaism.* The term was adopted by Western travelers and scholars of Tibet who routinely viewed Tibetan religion as a debased mingling of indigenous Tibetan animism with "pure" Indian Buddhism, and hence literally unworthy of being called Buddhism. Though usage persists, the term *Lamaism* is considered offensive by Tibetans and is by and large dropping out of circulation.

Bibliography

Lessing, Ferdinand. "Calling the Soul: A Lamaist Ritual." *Semitic Philology* 11 (1951): 263–284.

Lopez, Donald S., Jr. *Prisoners of Shangri-La: Tibetan Buddhism and the West.* Chicago: University of Chicago Press, 1998.

Nebesky-Wojkowitz, Réne de. *Oracles and Demons: The Cult and Iconography of the Tibetan Protective Deities.* Kathmandu, Nepal: Book Faith India, 1993.

Sperling, Elliot. "The Fifth Karma-pa and Some Aspects of the Relationship between Tibet and the Early Ming." In *Tibetan Studies in Honour of Hugh Richardson: Proceedings of the In-*

ternational Seminar on Tibetan Studies, ed. Michael Aris and Aung San Suu Kyi. Warminster, UK: Aris and Phillips, 1980.

Tseten Zhabdrung. "Research on the Nomenclature of the Buddhist Schools in Tibet," tr. Tenzin Dorjee. *Tibet Journal* 11, no. 3 (1986): 40–50.

ALEXANDER GARDNER

LANGUAGE, BUDDHIST PHILOSOPHY OF

The earliest Buddhist discussions of language are found in the canonical literature, where the principal focus is on the correct use of speech. In *Majjhimanikāya* (*Middle Length Discourses*) 58, for example, the Buddha advises his followers to consider before they speak whether what they are about to say is factual, true, beneficial, endearing, and agreeable to others. If what one was thinking of saying is false or harmful, then one should not say it at all. If it is true and beneficial but is likely to be unpleasant to the hearer, then one should wait for a suitable occasion to say it. Even if what one has an urge to say meets all those criteria, one should still wait for the correct time to say it. Being mindful of one's speech is said in that canonical text to be a natural manifestation of kindness and sympathy for others.

As Buddhist scholasticism developed in India, scholastics became increasingly occupied with criticizing non-Buddhist schools and defending Buddhism against criticisms made by non-Buddhists. Among the many topics that were debated by scholastics, one of the most important was the issue of the authority of scriptures. It was in the context of discussing this issue that most of the Buddhist reflections on the nature of language occurred.

In such Pāli canonical sources as the *Suttanipāta*, the Buddha is portrayed as telling his followers that the Vedas had been composed by unscrupulous Brahman priests who were intent on duping people into hiring them to perform expensive religious rituals. In defending the authority of the Vedas against Buddhists and other critics, scholastics within the Brahmanical tradition devised two different and mutually incompatible strategies. The first strategy consisted in attributing the Vedic texts to God. The argument was that God, being omniscient and benevolent, could neither deceive nor be deceived, and therefore every text composed by him is necessarily reliable. The second strategy consisted in claiming that the Vedic texts had never been composed by anyone and were therefore eternal. The argument here was that errors occur in texts only because of the limited knowledge and integrity of imperfect authors. But if a text has no author at all, then it has no author whose limitations are liable to introduce errors into the text. An authorless text is therefore error-free and hence perfectly reliable. Both of these Brahmanical strategies involved claiming that the language of the Vedic texts was different from any ordinary human language. Various features of the Vedic form of Sanskrit were adduced as evidence that Vedic Sanskrit was eternal and unevolving and that it was the ultimate source of all human languages, which could therefore all be seen as corrupted versions of the pristine Sanskrit language. Moreover, it was claimed that the relationship between a Sanskrit word and the object that it denotes is eternally fixed. The Sanskrit name for any object is the object's true name; its name in any other language was merely a matter of human convention and convenience. The Brahmanical writer Bhartṛhari (fifth century), against whose views several Buddhist scholastics articulated their views on language, argued that knowledge from the Veda surpassed both personal experience and reasoning, since both empirical investigation and logic are limited to the particular limitations of the individual, while the Veda has none of these human limitations.

Disagreeing with the Brahmanical view that Sanskrit has a privileged place among all languages and is the only legitimate language for rituals, the Buddha strongly advised that dharma teachers should communicate in the vernacular language of their audience. No language is intrinsically more pure or expressive than any other; a language is expressive only if it is understood by both the speaker and the hearer.

Among the first of the Buddhist scholastics to argue extensively against the Brahmanical tradition on issues of language was DIGNĀGA (fl. ca. 500 C.E.). Dignāga's principal claim was that all language is nothing more than a system of signs governed by conventional rules that are established by the consensus of the language-using community. Since language consists of signs, the interpretation of language is nothing but a special application of inference. In much the same way that the observation of a column of smoke could be taken as a sign that fire is burning somewhere, the spoken or written word *fire* can be seen as a sign that the person who uses it is thinking something about fire.

Two important claims about language follow from the claim that linguistic interpretation is a species of inference. First, it follows that since all inference is fallible, any knowledge communicated through any language is also fallible. Second, it follows that since the knowledge gained through inference is much more vague and imprecise than knowledge gained through direct experience, linguistically communicated knowledge is much less precise and of lower practical value than knowledge gained through direct experience. This means that any body of scripture, whether the Veda or the canonical literature of Buddhism, is of limited value. Only personal experience can be fully trusted. DHARMAKĪRTI (ca. 600–ca. 660) and other Buddhists who followed Dignāga argued that what made Buddhist canonical literature valuable was that it contained advice that, when followed properly, would help people reduce the amount of suffering that they experience in the world. Buddhist canonical sources, in other words, were seen as valuable not because they tell the truth, as the Brahmans claimed the Vedas do, but because they suggest methods by which people may discover the truth for themselves.

Although Indian Buddhist apologists were critical of many Brahmanical views concerning language, one belief that was never questioned was that MANTRAS had the power to heal and achieve various other results in the physical world. The Buddha forbade monks uttering mantras for material gain, but he also forbade monks the practice of MEDICINE for profit. The warning against mantras was therefore only against the Brahmanical practice of reciting them for material reward. Philosophers such as Dharmakīrti and his followers, while being opposed to the recitation of mantras for personal rewards, expressed their conviction that mantras have the power to alter conditions in the material world and thus must be used with discretion and compassion.

See also: **Buddhavacana (Word of the Buddha); Dhāraṇī; Languages; Logic**

Bibliography

Ganeri, Jonardon. *Philosophy in Classical India.* London: Routledge, 2001.

Hayes, Richard P. *Dignāga on the Interpretation of Signs.* Boston and Dordrecht, Netherlands: Kluwer, 1988.

Tillemans, Tom J. F. *Scripture, Logic, and Language: Essays on Dharmakīrti and His Tibetan Successors.* Boston: Wisdom, 1999.

RICHARD P. HAYES

LANGUAGES

As it spread throughout Asia, Buddhism succeeded in crossing a remarkable number of linguistic boundaries, in some cases being transposed into languages very different from those spoken in India. Its doctrines came to be presented orally in numerous languages and dialects, and its canonical literature, once written down, was translated into over a dozen languages even in premodern times. Since the historical sources do not permit scholars to identify all the languages used for oral presentations of the teaching, the following entry will focus on written expressions, considering oral transmission during only the early period of Indian Buddhism.

Whether any words of the Buddha are preserved in his own tongue is a matter of dispute. The THERAVĀDA claims that Pāli, the Middle Indian language used by that school for its scriptures, was the language of the Buddha. Modern research, however, has convincingly shown Pāli to be a western, or rather a west-central, dialect of Middle Indian, while the Buddha himself must have spoken an eastern dialect, most probably Old Māgadhī, the local language of the area in which he wandered, or perhaps some form of "Gangetic koine." Not a single utterance of the Buddha is preserved in that language, but certain words and forms in the Pāli canon reveal traces of a transposition from the eastern into the western dialect. Therefore it is safe to assume that during the early phases of its transmission, the word of the Buddha was transposed into local dialects wherever Buddhist monks traveled and taught.

The Buddha himself is said to have regulated the use of languages or dialects for the spread of his teaching. According to a difficult passage preserved in various vinayas, two monks, both former brahmins, asked the Buddha for permission to redact the teaching in a form corresponding to (Vedic) Sanskrit in order to avoid corruptions. The Buddha, however, declined the request and apparently ordered that everybody should transmit his teaching in their own (spoken) language. This passage is generally understood as permitting the use of the various vernaculars for the spread of the doctrine; it is consistent with the exoteric nature of Buddhism and its basic intention of making its doctrines accessible to everybody, in deliberate contrast to brahminical restrictions.

It is questionable whether any kind of Urkanon took shape during the lifetime of the Buddha or soon after.

Initially, preservation of the teachings with their wording unaltered was not considered a necessary criterion of authenticity, and this contributed greatly to fostering linguistic diversity and spreading the teaching as Buddhism left its homeland in the Ganges plain. The texts that had hitherto been transmitted orally were then transposed into other more or less supraregional Middle Indian dialects to facilitate understanding and wider dissemination. At present we know of only two, Pāli and Gāndhārī, Pāli being a western dialect, whereas Gāndhārī was widely used in the northwestern part of the subcontinent and, with the growth of the Kushan empire, in Bactria and Central Asia. Pāli became the canonical language of the Theravāda school, and Gāndhārī that of the DHARMAGUPTAKA. Considerably later sources mention other Prakrits used by various schools, namely Paiśācī, Apabhraṃśa, and Maddhyoddeśika. Apabhraṃśa is assigned to the Saṃmatīyas or to the Sthaviras, and Maddhyoddeśika to either the Sthaviras or the MAHĀSĀṂGHIKA SCHOOL.

All schools must at first have transmitted their canonical texts in Prakrit. Some of them, like the Theravāda, retained their Middle Indian language, while others participated in the so-called Sanskrit renaissance and started to Sanskritize their received literature. Sanskritization was apparently a gradual process permitting schools that were spread over a vast area to undergo different regional developments. The literature of the (Mūla-)Sarvāstivāda is preserved only in Buddhist Sanskrit, but its older layers reveal many traces of the underlying Prakrit. Surviving fragments suggest that the Dharmaguptakas also took part in the process of Sanskritization, at least in Central Asia. The growing number of fragments found in Afghanistan since 1994 supports the view that the Mahāsāṃghikas, and especially the Lokottaravāda, used a specific mixture of Prakrit and Sanskrit that may be termed Buddhist Hybrid Sanskrit in the true sense, and which was probably referred to as Maddhyoddeśika (intermediate recitation), a term not yet fully understood.

Retention or translation

When Buddhism began to spread beyond the Indian subcontinent, missionaries and local followers were confronted with the problem of how to communicate the teaching, the rituals, and the literature in a totally different linguistic environment. Basically, two possibilities offered themselves: to preserve the Indian language used so far, or to translate into the local language. Preserving the Indian original offered practitioners several advantages, among them a sense of the sacredness of oral and written texts derived from their use of the holy language supposedly spoken in the homeland of the Buddha or even by the Buddha himself; continuing access to other Indian sources; and, very importantly, unambiguousness in terminological matters. It also provided a useful common currency in a multiethnic and multilingual environment, no small issue when a Buddhist missionary movement came to be supported by the ruling powers for its unifying potential. On the other hand, Indian languages would have been incomprehensible to most followers outside India and a deterrent to prospective converts, especially in areas where non-Indo-European languages were spoken. This unintelligibility would have facilitated their readiness to exchange the Indian original for a more suitable vernacular, even if it necessitated the gargantuan task of finding at least approximate equivalents in the target language for difficult Indian Buddhist terminology. Discussions preserved in several Chinese and Tibetan treatises clearly show that some translators were well aware of the methodological, philological, and cultural problems involved in the translation process; their reflections on these problems resulted in attempts to establish guidelines for bridging the linguistic and cultural divide.

In the course of history both these possibilities—retention of the Indian original and translation into the vernacular—were employed, sometimes side by side. Several times the vernacular chosen for translation became itself a transregional "church" language (i.e., the idiom used for canonical scriptures and liturgical purposes) when its specific form of Buddhism crossed further linguistic borders, as in the case of Chinese and Tibetan. Although no Buddhist tradition developed prescriptions for or against the use of a specific language, in most cases one observes a slowly but steadily increasing tendency to regard the language of the written canonical texts as sacred, and this greatly reduced the original openness to linguistic changes characteristic of the early period of oral transmission in India. Wherever the language of the canonical literature was not identical with the vernacular, sooner or later the vernacular came to be used for the production of a sometimes very rich noncanonical Buddhist literature consisting of commentaries, story collections, manuals, poetry, devotional texts, and the like, and sometimes this led to the development of a new literary language in its own right. Examples are the use of Newari, Tamil, and Old Javanese alongside Sanskrit, and Thai, Japanese, and Mongolian alongside Pāli, Chinese, and Tibetan, respectively.

Central Asia. A most interesting case exemplifying the various possibilities is Central Asia, where various forms of Buddhism coexisted during the second half of the first millennium. First, there were some ethnic groups, notably speakers of the two dialects of Tocharian (the easternmost form of western Indo-European), of the two Saka dialects, Tumshuq and Khotanese (Middle Iranian), and of Uigur (a Turkish language), who continued to use Sanskrit as their "church" language, but also translated scriptures into their vernacular and composed their own Buddhists texts. That these ethnic groups transmitted scriptures in Sanskrit is proven by the existence of a considerable number of bilingual manuscripts and texts, manuscripts where glosses in one of the local languages are added to a Sanskrit text between the lines, as well as texts, at least in the case of the Tocharians and Uigurs, where the Sanskrit original and the vernacular translation alternate word by word or sentence by sentence in the same line. Second, there were the Chinese and the Tibetans, both of whom translated Buddhist literature into their own languages from the very beginning of missionary activity in their countries. Finally, there is the specific case of the Sogdians, speakers of another Middle Iranian language, whose merchants must have been instrumental in spreading Indian Buddhism and its literature from the Kushan empire to China. When they started in the second half of the first millennium to translate Buddhist texts into Sogdian, they did so from Chinese translations of Indian originals. All this can be gleaned from Central Asian manuscript finds, and specifically from the walled-up library in DUNHUANG, where texts in all these different languages were found side by side.

According to Jan Nattier no translation of an Indian Buddhist text into a vernacular is found west of Kashgar, the westernmost town in the Tarim basin. So far, recent manuscript finds in Afghanistan confirm her view, since nearly all the texts are written in Indian languages. There is only one exception—a Buddhist text in Bactrian, yet another Middle Iranian language, but at present it is not clear whether it is a translation or a ritual text written in the vernacular for a specific purpose.

China and East Asia. As soon as Buddhism reached China it proved necessary to translate its texts into Chinese. One reason for this must have been the extreme grammatical and phonetic differences between Indian languages and Chinese; another reason was the sheer foreignness of Buddhism to the Chinese, whose highly sophisticated and literary culture was distinguished by rather different value systems and aesthetic perceptions. Translation techniques went through various models and periods, starting with the second-century translator AN SHIGAO, who made extensive use of the vocabulary and other features of the spoken language. This tendency to incorporate vernacular elements was followed by a period that was characterized by an attempt to employ Daoist vocabulary to express Buddhist terms and ideas, and to write in a more literary mode. A new standard was set during the fifth century when the famous translator KUMĀRAJĪVA (350–409/413) introduced the translation bureau, a team of Chinese and foreign specialists who, usually under state patronage, jointly took care of the various steps involved in the translation process. Similar institutions were set up several times in the history of Central and East Asian Buddhism—for example, in Tibet during its imperial age, and later in Central Asia and China for the translations of the Tangut, Mongol, and Manchu versions of the *tripiṭaka.*

As Chinese culture became paradigmatic throughout East Asia, Buddhism went along with it. In its Sinitic form, Buddhism spread to Korea, Japan, and Vietnam, and literary Chinese became the "church" language of Buddhist literature throughout East Asia. In Central Asia, as mentioned above, Chinese translations served as the basis for all the translations into Sogdian, but also for many into Uigur and some into Tibetan. Between the eleventh and thirteenth centuries, a considerable number of translations—first of Chinese, then also of Tibetan translations of Buddhist texts—were further translated into Tangut or Xixia, another Sino-Tibetan language used in the Tangut empire northwest of China, before its destruction by Genghis Khan.

Tibet and Mongolia. Buddhism reached Tibet around the seventh century. From the very beginning, apparently, texts were translated into the vernacular, but they did not encounter an existing literary heritage as they had in China; indeed the traditional sources inform us that the Tibetan script was created specifically to translate Buddhist materials. A few of the early translations are preserved. Their grammar is often awkward, if not contrary to Tibetan usage, because of their attempt to reproduce the word order of the Indian original, and different Tibetan words are employed to express the same Buddhist term. Another difference from the situation in China concerned the role of Buddhism in Tibet: It appears that from the beginning Buddhism served domestic political purposes and received considerable support from the royal court. This close relationship with royal power led at the beginning of the ninth century to a singular event in the translation history of Buddhist literature. With a view to setting general standards for translation methods and producing renditions intelligible to everybody, the king issued a decree laying down compulsory rules for translators. To implement the decree, a royal translation bureau published a list of about ninety-five hundred Sanskrit technical terms and their standard Tibetan equivalents, together with a treatise explaining the translation of some four hundred Buddhist terms. After that, fresh translations were made and the older ones revised according to these new rules, which continued to be observed after the fall of the royal dynasty in the mid-ninth century until the end of the translation period in the fifteenth century. This led to a unique phenomenon in the Buddhist world: The language of nearly all Tibetan translations is extremely standardized and, usually without violating the rules of Tibetan grammar, faithful to the Sanskrit originals to a degree never again reached in any other language used for translating Buddhist texts.

Like Buddhist Chinese for East Asia, Classical Tibetan became the "church" language for much of Central Asia. In the final period of their Buddhist tradition, the Uigurs translated several works from Tibetan. After the Mongols arrived in the domain of Tibetan Buddhism in the sixteenth century, Tibetan texts were continuously translated into Mongolian. During the eighteenth century Chinese emperors even supported complete Mongolian translations of the Bka' 'gyur (Kanjur) and Bstan 'gyur (Tanjur), the two collections of canonical translations in Tibetan. Mongolian lamas wrote works in Mongolian, but Mongolian never succeeded in replacing Tibetan as the prime language for ritual and literature. From Inner Mongolia in the east to Buryatia and the Kalmyk steppe in the west, Mongols continued to study Buddhism in Tibetan. As in the case of the Mongolians, in the eighteenth century the Chinese Qianlong emperor, whose dynasty was of Manchu origin, sponsored the translation of canonical texts into Manchu. Although these translations were made from Chinese recensions, the collection was then styled Bka' 'gyur after the Tibetan model. However, this enormous effort was primarily a political gesture and, unlike the Mongolian case, did not lead to Buddhist literary activity in Manchu.

South and Southeast Asia. Wherever Buddhism spread in South and Southeast Asia, its canonical literature was not transposed into the many vernaculars, but remained Indian. Depending on the background of the missionaries involved, it continued to be transmitted in either Pāli or Sanskrit. Although the canon of the Theravāda came to be written in many different scripts, such as Sinhalese, Burmese, Thai, and Khmer, its language until modern times was always Pāli, and Pāli remained the medium of Buddhist ritual and scholarship in Sri Lanka and in all the Theravāda countries of Southeast Asia. Individual texts of the canon, however, were translated into various vernaculars (Burmese, Khmer, Lanna Thai, Mon, Thai) from the eleventh century onward, and in these and several other vernaculars (Arakanese, Lao, Shan, Tai Khun, Tai Lue), rich indigenous Buddhist literatures were created. Sanskrit was used by other traditions of Buddhism, most of them following MAHĀYĀNA or even Tantrayāna doctrines, in Burma, Laos, and Cambodia before the arrival of Theravāda, and in Java and Bali.

Modern vernaculars

All this has changed dramatically during the last 150 years. In the West, scholarly studies of Buddhism began around the middle of the nineteenth century, when the first canonical texts were translated into Western languages. Somewhat later, scholars in countries throughout Asia started systematically to translate texts from their "church" languages into the modern vernaculars, especially when this entailed a shift between two different language families. As a result, one can hardly find a literary language in today's world, with the possible exception of Africa, that has not been used for translating Buddhist texts, and it would also be fair to say that English has now overtaken Chinese as the most frequently used medium for the spread of Buddhist ideas and literature.

See also: **Buddhist Studies; Canon; Chinese, Buddhist Influences on Vernacular Literature in; Gāndhārī, Buddhist Literature in; Language, Buddhist Philosophy of; Newari, Buddhist Literature in; Pāli, Buddhist Literature in; Sanskrit, Buddhist Literature in; Sinhala, Buddhist Literature in**

Bibliography

Bechert, Heinz, ed. *The Language of the Earliest Buddhist Tradition.* Göttingen, Germany: Vandenhoeck and Ruprecht, 1980.

Grönbold, Günter. *Der buddhistische Kanon: Eine Bibliographie.* Wiesbaden, Germany: Harrassowitz, 1984.

Hinüber, Oskar von. "Origin and Varieties of Buddhist Sanskrit." In *Dialectes dans les littératures Indo-Aryennes,* ed. Colette Caillat. Paris: Collège de France, 1989.

Jong, J. W. de. "Buddha's Word in China." *East Asian History* 11 (1996): 45–58.

Link, Arthur E. "The Earliest Chinese Account of the Compilation of the Tripiṭaka." *Journal of the American Oriental Society* 81 (1961): 87–103, 281–299 (esp. 283–292).

McDaniel, Justin. "The Curricular Canon in Northern Thailand and Laos." *Manusya: Journal of Humanities* 4 (2002): 20–59.

Meier, F. J. "Probleme der chinesischen Übersetzer des buddhistischen Kanons." *Oriens Extremus* 19 (1972): 41–46.

Nattier, Jan. "Church Language and Vernacular Language in Central Asian Buddhism." *Numen* 37 (1990): 195–219.

Norman, K. R. "The Languages of Early Buddhism." In *Premier Colloque Étienne Lamotte: Bruxelles et Liège 24–27 septembre 1989.* Louvain-la-Neuve, Belgium: Université catholique de Louvain, Institut orientaliste, 1993.

Röhrborn, Klaus, and Veenker, Wolfgang, eds. *Sprachen des Buddhismus in Zentralasien: Vorträge des Hamburger Symposions vom 2. Juli bis 5. Juli 1981.* Wiesbaden, Germany: Harrassowitz, 1983.

Ruegg, David Seyfort. "On Translating the Buddhist Canon." *Studies in Indo-Asian Art and Culture,* ed. Perala Ratnam. New Delhi: International Academy of Indian Culture, 1974.

JENS-UWE HARTMANN

LAṄKĀVATĀRA-SŪTRA

The *Laṅkāvatāra-sūtra* (*Discourse on the Descent into Laṅka*) is a text in the MAHĀYĀNA tradition, probably composed sometime around the fourth century C.E., that purports to be a teaching given by the Buddha on the island of Sri Lanka. The sūtra discusses a number of important Mahāyāna doctrines, including the nondifference of identity between SAṂSĀRA (or the cycle of REBIRTH) and NIRVĀṆA, and includes an entire chapter devoted to a denunciation of meat-eating. Its organization and presentation are haphazard, which has led a number of scholars to conclude that it is a compendium of heterogeneous materials that saw significant later interpolation. There are three extant Chinese (*Lengqie abadolo bao jing*) and two Tibetan (*Lang Kar gShegs pa'i mdo*) translations of the text, and one Sanskrit manuscript from Nepal, which was used by Bunyū Nanjio in 1923 to construct a critical edition.

The *Laṅkāvatāra-sūtra* is often associated with the Indian Yogācāra tradition because it discusses a number of basic doctrines associated with it, such as the storehouse consciousness (ĀLAYAVIJÑĀNA), the womb of the tathāgata (TATHĀGATAGARBHA), and mind-only (*cittamātra*). However, the *Laṅkāvatāra-sūtra* is not mentioned in the works of Yogācāra "founders" ASAṄGA (ca. 320–ca. 390) or VASUBANDHU (fourth century C.E.). It was far more influential in East Asia, and it played a prominent role in the development of the Chan tradition. Its importance in East Asia is attested by the fact that there are fifteen Chinese commentaries on it, the most important of which is by FAZANG (643–712). It is also one of the nine core Mahāyāna texts (Navagrantha) of Newari Buddhism in Nepal.

See also: **Chan School; Yogācāra School**

Bibliography

Sutton, Florin G. *Existence and Enlightenment in the Laṅkāvatāra-sūtra: A Study in the Ontology and Epistemology of the Yogācāra School of Mahāyāna Buddhism.* Albany: State University of New York Press, 1991.

Suzuki, Daisetz T., trans. *The Laṅkāvatāra-sūtra* (1932). Reprint, Boulder, CO: Prajñā Press, 1978.

JOHN POWERS

LAOS

The primary sources for the history of Buddhism in Laos are texts, such as palm leaf and mulberry leaf manuscripts, stone and metal inscriptions, traveler's reports, and printed materials. These sources, which are held in monastic, governmental, and royal archives, provide information on Lao Buddhism from only the fourteenth century and after, and many have yet to receive scholarly scrutiny. A survey of the information gleaned from these sources reveals the story of Buddhism in Laos to be a fragmented and contested history of royal patronage and governmental reform, as well as a creative engagement between local, indigenous beliefs and a translocal religion. As the various kingdoms of what became Laos emerged as regional centers of power and wealth, Buddhism helped construct Lao identity. In turn, royal reform, rituals, beliefs, aspirations, and vehicles of expression reconstituted Lao Buddhism.

Texts and inscriptions reflect the fragmented and, for lack of a better word, syncretic, nature of the early history of Lao Buddhism. Generally, the most common texts found in Laos before the twentieth century are *nithāns* (folktales such as *Thao Hung Thao Chuang, Sin Xai, Om Lom Dang Kieo*), *anisaṃsas* (blessings used in Buddhist ritual and magical ceremonies), *parittas* (incantations for protection), *xalongs* (ceremonial instructions for both lay and religious ceremonies), aprocryphal JĀTAKA (noncanonical birth stories of the Buddha), *nissayas* (creative glosses and commentaries of Pāli texts), and *tamnāns* (relic, image, and monastery histories). *Xalongs, anisaṃsas,* and *parittas* are used in everyday house, buffalo, monastery, and bodily blessings; they are also used when making love potions and protective tattoos. The *tamnāns* show the heavy Buddhist influence in the governmental, economic, and military history of Laos. *Nithāns* and apocryphal *jātakas* are intricate and entertaining stories of heroism, romance, and adventure that were (and are) often narrated at religious events or life-cycle rituals, such as funerals, and at the end of the rains retreat. *Nithāns* and apocryphal *jātakas* were also the basis for monastic education and public sermons. What should be emphasized is that Pāli canonical texts are often in the minority in these collections. Translocal Buddhist narratives and philosophical texts have been commented on and adapted by local Lao teachers, and these commentaries and adaptations are much more popular in Laos than their source texts from India and Sri Lanka.

Although they have yet to be fully surveyed, read, and catalogued, Lao Buddhist inscriptions, particularly votive inscriptions, generally provide evidence of royal or wealthy lay patronage of certain monasteries. They also reflect the great influence that Northern Thailand and, after 1560, Burma (Myanmar) had on the practice of Buddhism in Laos. One inscription from Dansai (formerly part of the Lao Kingdom of Lān Xāng, but part of Thailand since the mid-nineteenth century) tells of Buddhist monks accompanying the king to a political meeting with the king of AYUTTHAYA. Another inscription from Wiengjan (the present capital of Laos) suggests that there were many monks from Chiang Mai (Northern Thailand) in the region, which would account for similarities in Lao and Northern Thai Buddhist and secular literature composed between 1480 to 1620.

King Phōthisālarāt (r. 1520–1547) was probably the most active patron of Buddhism and Buddhist literature in Laos. It is Phōthisālarāt and his son Xētthāthirāt (r. 1548–1571) who were responsible for the creation of most of the extant sources of Lao Buddhist history. Phōthisālarāt actively tried to "purify" Lao Buddhism by banning magical practices and the worshipping of *phī* (ghosts) and *phrabhūm* (local deities of trees, rocks, waterfalls, etc.). However, modern rituals like the *riek kwan, phūk heuan,* and *bun bang fai* in various parts of Laos show the limited success of his reforms; all of these rituals combine the worship and propitiation of *phī* and *phrabhūm* by Buddhist monks with the chanting of Buddhist MANTRAS. The practice of drawing magical diagrams (*yantras*) by monks and lay experts has also been popular since at least the fifteenth century and involves the mixing of Buddhist prayers with aspirations to be lucky in love, finance, and the avoidance of attacks by knives, guns, and poison.

Laos did not have a printing press until the French colonial period (ca. 1893–1954) and only recently has there been a regular printing of religious books in Lao. These books cover a wide range of subjects, but generally resemble their palm and mulberry leaf manuscript predecessors. Still, whether it be printed books, inscriptions, or manuscripts, the textual sources resist easy classification and cannot be used to provide a clear, linear history of Buddhism in Laos. However, this should not suggest that Lao scholars from the fourteenth century to the present did not attempt to write (or perhaps preserve orally) historical chronicles. There are several extant royal and religious chronicles, the most famous being the *Nithān Khun Borom* (*The Story of Khun Borom*). These chronicles tell of the introduction of Buddhism into Laos under King Fā Ngum (r. 1353–1374) in the mid-fourteenth century; the growth and reform of Buddhism under King Xētthāthirāt in the late sixteenth century; the movement of monks, scribes, artisans, and so on from Chiang Mai to Laos after the Burmese invasion of the former in the 1560s; the patronage and building of numerous monasteries under King Surinyavong (r. 1638–1695); the burning of the Sisaket Monastery and the theft of the Emerald Buddha by the Siamese (Thai) in the late eighteenth century; the building of numerous monasteries and the reunification of the three kingdoms of Laos (Luang Pabang, Wiengjan, and Champasak) by King Ānuwong (r. 1804–1828) and the subsequent burning of the Wiengjan by the forces of Siam in 1827. Still, these chronicles, like Western and local modern historical reconstructions written in the twentieth century, generally sacrifice accuracy to clarity, covering over the variety of Buddhist beliefs and practices with a sheen of unity and linearity.

In the nineteenth and twentieth centuries, travelers' reports provide information about the history of Buddhist practice among the general population,

Monks circumambulate the Phra That Luang stūpa during an annual ceremony in Vientiane, Laos. © Nik Wheeler/Corbis. Reproduced by permission.

information that is lacking in royal chronicles, protective chants, and relic and monastery histories. Travelers' reports confirm the validity of some of the rituals described in folktales and epic poems. The multivolume collection by members of the Mission Pavie (1879–1895) and the work of Karl Izikowitz in the 1930s discuss how local animistic practices of the Hmong, Sedang, Moi, and other Lao hill tribes became mixed with Buddhist practices. These sources also describe how monks took on the roles of magicians, appeasers of local deities, doctors, and secular and religious teachers in Lao villages. Still, aside from these reports and many others, a comprehensive study of how Buddhism and indigenous Lao religions have interacted remains a desideratum.

After almost a century of war and foreign occupation, the independent People's Democratic Republic of Laos emerged in 1975. Its Marxist government has allowed the practice of Buddhism to flourish and has even enlisted Buddhist monks to serve as political advocates who hold up the communist ideals of generosity, community cooperation, and equality among the classes. The Lao government has encouraged greater involvement of monks in community development and secular education by sponsoring the Union of Lao Buddhists and other Buddhist/Communist organizations, while discouraging monks' practice of traditional healing rituals, exorcism, and prophecy, and discouraging them from using the monkhood to avoid military and government service. The Lao government has also attempted to limit lay donations (in order to gain merit for a favorable rebirth) to monasteries, even though this practice has been the foundation of lay/monk interaction for the entire history of Lao Buddhism. Still, like the efforts of King Phōthisālarāt and King Ānuvong to reform Buddhism, these government policies have mostly been quietly ignored, and although monks have played a greater role in secular education since 1975, the unique and syncretic practices of Lao Buddhists that the sources evince persist and even flourish among both the urban and rural populations.

See also: **Folk Religion, Southeast Asia; Southeast Asia, Buddhist Art in**

Bibliography

Archaimbault, Charles. "Religious Structures in Laos." *Journal of the Siam Society* 52, no. 1 (1964): 57–74.

Archaimbault, Charles. *Structures religieuses Lao (Rites et Mythes)*. Vientiane, Laos: Vithagna, 1973.

de Berval, René, ed. *Kingdom of Laos: The Land of the Million Elephants and of the White Parasol,* tr. Teissier du Cros and others. Saigon, Vietnam: France-Asie, 1959.

Bizot, François. *La pureté par les mots.* Paris: École Française d'Extrême-Orient, 1996.

Coedes, George. "Documents sur l'histoire politique et religieuse du Laos occidental." *Bulletin de l'École Français d'Extrême-Orient* 25, nos. 1–2 (1925): 1–202.

Finot, Louis. "Recherches sur la littérature Laotienne." *Bulletin de l'École Français d'Extrême-Orient* 17, no. 5 (1917): 1–218.

Lévy, Paul. "Les traces de l'introduction de Bouddhisme à Louang Prabang." *Bulletin de l'École Français d'Extrême-Orient* 40 (1940): 411–424.

Ngaosrivathana, Mayoury, and Breazeale, Kennon, eds. *Breaking New Ground in Lao History: Essays on the Seventh to Twentieth Centuries.* Chiang Mai, Thailand: Silkworm, 2002.

Nhouy, Abhay. *Aspects du Pays Lao.* Vientiane, Laos: Editions comite litteraire lao, 1956.

Pavie, Auguste. *Recherches sur l'histoire de Cambodge, du Laos, et du Siam.* Paris: E. Leroux, 1898.

Peltier, Anatole-Roge. "Les littératures Lao du Lan Na, du Lan Xang, de Keng Tung et Sip Song Panna." *Peninsule* 21 (1990): 29–44.

Reynolds, Frank. "Ritual and Social Hierarchy: An Aspect of Traditional Religion in Buddhist Laos." *History of Religions* 9 (1969): 78–89.

Saddhatissa, H. "Pāli Literature from Laos." In *Studies in Pāli and Buddhism: A Memorial Volume in Honor of Bhikkhu Jagdish Kashyap,* ed. A. K. Narain and Leonard Zwilling. Delhi: B. R. Pub. Corp., 1979.

Stuart-Fox, Martin. *A History of Laos.* Cambridge, UK: Cambridge University Press, 1997.

Stuart-Fox, Martin. *The Lao Kingdom of Lan Xang: Rise and Decline.* Bangkok, Thailand: White Lotus Press, 1998.

JUSTIN MCDANIEL

LAOS, BUDDHIST ART IN. *See* **Southeast Asia, Buddhist Art in**

LAW AND BUDDHISM

Comparative jurisprudence divides legal systems into families or types based on cultural and historical origins. Buddhist law is the most recent entrant into the category of religious legal systems, a category that includes Islamic law, biblical law, Hindu law, and Talmudic law. The development of Buddhist law as a disciplinary subject has been slow because of the lack of a single unifying religious language or script and Buddhism's wide cultural dispersal throughout Asia. Scholars have also presumed that Buddhism did not have an obvious relationship to secular legal systems because of its distinction between lay and monastic populations and its tolerant, as opposed to mutually exclusive, approach to local religions and politics. More recent studies, however, have demonstrated that the influence of Buddhism on law and political systems has been profound.

There are at least four ways in which Buddhism interacts with law. First, Buddhism itself incorporates a monastic law code, the VINAYA, and special disciplinary procedures for the monastic population. This code has been analyzed extensively and functions as a template for secular rules. Second, some regions have created Buddhist states following the example of AŚOKA, an early Buddhist political leader. Sri Lanka, Bhutan, and Thailand are current examples. Third, Buddhism has been a significant social force in shaping the cultural attitudes toward law and the legal system in many Asian countries that are not Buddhist states. The time period and the local context from which Buddhism was exported to the country, as well as the local context into which it has been adopted, are all important factors. Fourth, when the local population reasons through the lens of Buddhism, the legal system can be significantly affected. The form of reasoning and the backdrop of the vinaya rules, as well as the foundational principles of Buddhism, such as KARMA (ACTION), ANITYA (IMPERMANENCE), causation, factoral reasoning, and right action, can all strongly affect a legal system.

The origins of internal Buddhist monastic law are clear. After his enlightenment, Śākyamuni Buddha began to collect a group of disciples who followed his teachings. As part of the process of institutional definition, he made hundreds of casuistic determinations about the proper behavior, clothing, and speech of individuals, and he shaped the collective rituals of the SAṄGHA. The *Suttavihaṅga* section of the vinaya describes these early legal decisions. There are no similar legal decisions for the LAITY. In the vinaya, the most serious offenses (*pārājika*) for a monk—killing, stealing, having sex, or misrepresenting one's meditative powers—result in expulsion from the order. Nuns have an additional four *pārājika.* The PRĀTIMOKṢA, a list of over two hundred PRECEPTS for monks, and over three hundred for nuns, is recited twice a month by the members of every saṅgha to remind them of the guidelines for their society. The procedures and rules of the internal legal systems of monasteries and nunneries are based on the vinaya, with a formal meeting of the full saṅgha serving the authoritative decision-making body. Legal positivists argue that a religious entity is not a state authority and that ostracism from a group is not a true legal sanction, so the vinaya system cannot be considered a legal system. But this analysis is based on the misconception that law operates only in nation-state command systems and that the authority function in Buddhism is fulfilled by a divinity rather than the Buddha's designated successor, the saṅgha.

Several regions have followed the path of the third-century B.C.E. Magadhan emperor Aśoka by establishing Buddhist states based on received scripts, Buddhist scriptures, and the idea of the compassionate cakravartin (wheel-turning king). Such Buddhist-inspired law codes and jurisprudential cultures evolved in Sri Lanka, Burma (Myanmar), and Tibet. In Sri Lanka, for example, the arrival in the third century B.C.E. of Indian monks brought the oral tradition of the Pāli canon to the island. Combining the ideologies of race, religion, and region, Buddhist states governed much of the island until 1818, when the Kandyan monarchy was finally overthrown by the British.

Although Buddhism may have entered Southeast Asia as early as the time of Aśoka, King Anawrata was the first to unify Burma into a Buddhist state in the eleventh century. The king and monks of the capital city of Pagan combined the *Pāli Vinaya* with Hindu law and Buddhist treatises to create the *dhammasat* and *rājasat* secular law codes, which spread in the ensuing centuries across what is now Burma, Thailand, Cambodia, and Laos. In Tibet, the first king to be influenced by Buddhism was Srong bstan sgam po, who, in the seventh century C.E., sent his minister to Gandhāra to develop a written script and bring back Buddhist texts. Buddhism became the state religion in Tibet in the eight century and strongly influenced the local legal rules already in place from the period of the earliest kings. For example, the Ganden Phodrang law code of the Dalai Lamas, written in the seventeenth century, is a secular law code of customary practices filled with Buddhist reasoning, such as factoral analysis, consensus, uniqueness of cases, motivation, and veracity tests.

Buddhism has been a significant factor, although not usually the sole or even the central influence, in the legal structure of many Asian countries. Buddhism entered these regions at different historical points and through various sources. For example, Japan first received Buddhist monks, texts, and images from Korea, and although Prince SHŌTOKU promoted Buddhism as the state religion at the end of the sixth century, the Confucian and Daoist traditions of East Asia always accompanied and, some would argue, superseded, Buddhism's effect on the legal system of Japan. At the end of the Tokugawa period (1603–1868), Buddhism in Japan was also overshadowed by the indigenous Shintō religion and worship of the emperor. In Mongolia, Buddhism was adopted in the thirteenth century into a country that already had a strong legal administrative system based on the Zasag law code of Genghis Khan. Vietnam had state patronage of several different forms of MAHĀYĀNA and THERAVĀDA Buddhism competing with Hinduism from the tenth century, but after the fifteenth century, the state ideology of Confucianism led to a decline in Buddhism's influence on the legal system. The transplantation, waxing, and waning of Buddhist influence on law is a large area for further study.

Basic Buddhist principles, reasoning processes, and rules may influence law because they are employed by the population that use the legal system. Thus, a country may impose a strong socialist law code, such as the Russian-imported Mongolian codes in force between 1924 and 1992, upon a population whose culture reasons through Buddhist principles. This is true of the Tibetan population today, which, although it has been incorporated into the Chinese state, continues to employ Buddhist reasoning and principles in most of its decision making.

As Buddhism spread from India to China and Japan, Pagan, and Sumatra, it had extensive influence on secular legal systems. Modern scholars have begun to look more seriously at this influence, as well as the operation of legal procedures within Buddhist monasteries and nunneries. Scholars have also begun to study the overlay of exogenous legal systems and the transplantation of law codes from other countries onto Buddhist legal systems. Local-level influence of Buddhism is another interesting area of research. For example, in a 1970s study of litigation in Chiangmai, Thailand, interviews with litigants showed that the number of injury claims had steadily decreased over a ten-year period due to a stronger emphasis in the local community on reasoning through karmic causes and their consequences. Combining both BUDDHIST STUDIES and comparative law, Buddhist law is an emerging new disciplinary area.

Bibliography

Dutt, Sukumar. *Buddhist Monks and Monasteries of India: Their History and Their Contribution to Indian Culture.* London: Allen and Unwin, 1962.

French, Rebecca R. *The Golden Yoke: The Legal Cosmology of Buddhist Tibet.* Ithaca, NY: Cornell University Press, 1995.

Hinüber, Oskar von. "Buddhist Law According to the *Theravāda Vinaya*: A Survey of Theory and Practice." *Journal of the International Association of Buddhist Studies* 18 (1995): 7–45.

Holt, John C. *Discipline: The Canonical Buddhism of the Vinayapiṭaka.* Delhi: Motilal Banarsidass, 1981.

Horner, I. B., trans. *The Book of the Discipline* (*Vinaya-pitaka*), Vol. 1: *Suttavibhaṅga.* Oxford: Oxford University Press, 1938. Reprint, 1996.

Huxley, Andrew. "The Reception of Buddhist Law in Southeast Asia, 200 B.C.E.–1860 C.E." In *La réception des systèmes juridiques: implantation et destin,* ed. Michel Douchet and Jacques Vanderlinden. Brussels: Bruylant, 1994.

Tambiah, H. W. *Principles of Ceylon Law.* Colombo, Sri Lanka: H. W. Cave, 1972.

REBECCA FRENCH

LIBERATION. *See* Bodhi (Awakening); Nirvāṇa; Path

LINEAGE

Lineage formation permeates religious traditions. Lineages are commonly found outside of religious traditions as well, to note the roles played in the origin and development of various kinds of institutions. In Buddhism, lineage serves as an important organizational framework for connecting members of specific schools, factions, or institutions. It is the natural outcome of the recognition of authority, especially given the development of sectarian differences. In Buddhism, when individual sectarian groups compiled lineages, they did so retroactively in an attempt to shape past history in ways that would enhance group status. The most common practice was to link their teachings to past authorities and ultimately to the founder of Buddhism, Śākyamuni himself, thus legitimizing their own principles and practices and shielding them from accusations of unorthodoxy. In this way, lineage in the Buddhist context was associated with such notions as identity, legitimacy, and orthodoxy. As a result, the formation and promotion of sectarian lineages must be interpreted in accordance with the contemporary aims of the sponsoring groups; lineage formation was a means to sanction their cause, and not a literal account of the actual historical record.

Concern for lineage emerged early in Buddhism. According to Étienne Lamotte, the formation of Buddhist schools in India was due mainly to the geographical extension of the community over the entire Indian territory (*History of Indian Buddhism,* p. 519). Given this geographical dispersion, individual Buddhist communities developed unique interests and were confronted by particular problems. One of the results of geographical fragmentation was the rise of sectarian leaders representing the interests of particular communities. The authority of the sect was usually based on a professed doctrine linked to a well-known, but often fictitious, founder, whose doctrines were in turn traced to immediate DISCIPLES OF THE BUDDHA. In this way, the Sthavīras traced themselves to MAHĀKĀŚYAPA, and the MAHĀSĀṂGHIKAS traced themselves to Bāṣpa. The Sarvāstivādins (Kaśyapa, ĀNANDA, Madhyāntika, Śāṇavāsin, UPAGUPTA, Pūrṇa, Mecaka, Kātyāyanīputra) and Vātsīputrīyas (ŚĀRIPUTRA, RĀHULA, Vatsīputra) also developed lineages based on this premise (Lamotte, p. 521). As a result, lineage formation may be deemed a feature of Buddhist sectarianism from its outset in India, where it was a function of sectarian quests for authority and legitimacy.

Lineage was particularly important in East Asian Buddhism, where it served as the primary means of ascribing identity by linking and grouping individuals on the basis of their affiliations, whether as master-disciple, as patriarchs of a particular school, or as a succession of monastery abbots. As a mechanism for conferring legitimacy, lineages were frequently constructed to assert the claims of contemporary practitioners by assuming the authority or antiquity of presumed ANCESTORS. This practice had broad resonance throughout East Asian cultures, predicated on domestic reverence for ancestors and biological lineages. The formation of Buddhist sectarian-based dharma genealogies has structural parallels with this propensity for honoring ancestors and maintaining clan solidarity.

Lineage and ancestor veneration

The genesis of East Asian reverence for ancestors is revealed in the Chinese term *zong,* which informs the esteem placed on clan and lineage in both the broader cultural and specifically Buddhist contexts. The term *zong* is difficult to translate because it allows for a variety of connotations and nuances, depending on the context. Encyclopedic dictionaries of the Chinese language, such as the *Ci yuan* (*The Roots of Words*), provide several meanings for *zong,* including "ancestral hall" (*zu miao*), "ancestor" (*zuxian,* literally "patriarch-predecessor"), "clan" (*zongzu*), "origin" (*benyuan*), and "honor" or "respect" (*zunchong*). The character *zong* originally depicted an ancestral hall, where a clan's ancestor or ancestors were honored. The character is composed of two parts: The upper part depicts a roof, and the lower part depicts "a tablet for the deceased," indicating the term's original meaning of a hall where the tablets of ancestors are kept.

The term *zong* appears frequently in posthumous titles for Chinese emperors, as in Gaozong (High Ancestor) or Taizong (Great Ancestor), and one of the term's primary meanings in ancient China was as the progenitor of a specific clan. *Zong* eventually took on a concrete meaning as clan guardian or protector, a figure who was the object of ritual veneration by clan descendants. The living clan head was responsible for decisions affecting clan welfare and prosperity, for the preservation of clan identity, and for the perpetuation of its legacy. The authority of the clan head was symbolically linked to the clan progenitor. Chinese emperors naturally seized upon this symbolism, promoting themselves, as well as their own deceased ancestors, as protectors of the Chinese people, responsible for the welfare and prosperity of the country as a whole. In this sense, the imperial family represented the "grand clan" of the Chinese people, the focal point of collective as opposed to individual clan identity.

Following the Chinese predilection to ascribe individual identity on the basis of clan affiliation, Buddhists in China were officially removed from their natal clan and adopted into the "Buddhist" one using the clan name Shi. *Shi* is an abbreviation of the name Shijiamouni, the Chinese pronunciation of Śākyamuni, which is derived from the Buddha's clan name, Śākya, in India. Buddhist monks in China regarded their teachers as they would a father, and began to take great interest in genealogy. As in India, genealogy served as a means of validating claims, and lineage became the contested terrain of sectarian disputations. In the early fifth century, the Indian monk Buddhabhadra translated the *Damoduoluo chanjing* (*Dharmatrāta's Meditation Scripture*), with prefaces by HUIYUAN and Huiguan. The scripture highlights Buddhabhadra's Sārvastivādin lineage in an attempt to establish that the meditation teaching contained in the scripture was guaranteed by direct lineal succession from the Buddha. In addition, a vinaya work translated by Buddhabhadra and FAXIAN in 416 to 418 C.E. provided a similar lineage of succession from the Buddha to Buddhabhadra's teacher for a supposed vinaya lineage. Another indigenous Chinese work, the *Fu fazang yinyuan zhuan* (*Biographies of the Circumstances of Transmission of the Dharma Repository*), dated 472 C.E., provided a list of lineal heirs from the Buddha to Siṃha bhikṣu.

Lineage in Chinese Buddhism

The lineages of succession in these texts provided the bases for sectarian legitimation claims of leading Chinese Buddhist traditions, such as the TIANTAI SCHOOL and CHAN SCHOOL. Based on the *Fu fazang yinyuan zhuan*, the Tiantai school created a list of twenty-three patriarchs of the "sūtra-transmission," to which they added a series of three Tiantai meditation masters—Huiwen, Huisi, and ZHIYI (538–597)—to claim legitimate succession from the Buddha (see Table 1). According to Zhiyi's disciple Guanding (561–632), who created the lineage, Tiantai masters were connected because Huiwen adopted the meditation promoted in the *Da zhidu lun* (*Great Perfection of Wisdom Treatise*) attributed to the famed scholastic NĀGĀRJUNA (ca. second century C.E.), the thirteenth patriarch in the *Fu fazang yinyuan zhuan* list.

The notion of *zong* as clan ancestor connected to lineal descendants played a particularly important role in shaping identity in the Chan school. In Buddhist mythology, Śākyamuni Buddha was not the only Buddha, but the last in a line of seven BUDDHAS of antiquity—Vipaśyin, Śikhin, Viśvabhū, Krakucchanda, Kanakamuni, Kāśyapa, and Śākyamuni. According to Chan school traditions, the seven buddhas are believed to have transmitted a uniform dharma, or teaching, between them. This teaching is summarized in the four line refrain: "Shunning all evil; performing every good; purifying one's mind—this is the teaching of all buddhas." As the source of all Buddhist teaching, the various tenets of Buddhism are said to spring from these verses. In this way, Śākyamuni's message was conceived as a universal teaching transmitted to him through a line of predecessors, and handed down to his immediate disciples. Early Chan relied on the lineage supplied with Buddhabhadra's translations, eventually fusing it with Tiantai assertions based on the *Fu fazang yinyuan zhuan*, and supplanting it with their own innovations. Like the Tiantai list of lineage succession, the Chan list was composed of two parts: a list of Indian patriarchal transmission, coupled with a

TABLE 1

Tiantai lineage based on the *Fu fazang yinyuan zhuan (Biographies of the Circumstances of Transmission of the Dharma Repository)*

Śākyamuni	
1. Mahākāśyapa	14. Kāṇadeva
2. Ānanda	15. Rāhulata
3. Śaṇavāsa	16. Saṅghānandin
4. Upagupta	17. Gayaśāta
5. Dhṛtaka	18. Kumārata
6. Miccaka	19. Jayata
7. Buddhanandin	20. Vasubandhu
8. Buddhamitra	21. Manorhita
9. Pārśva	22. Haklenayaśas
10. Puṇyayaśas	23. Siṃha bhikṣu
11. Aśvaghoṣa	24. Huiwen
12. Kapimala	25. Huisi
13. Nāgārjuna	26. Zhiyi

SOURCE: Author.

TABLE 2

Chan lineage based on the *Baolin chuan (Transmission of the Treasure Grove)*

Śākyamuni

1. Mahākāśyapa	15. Kāṇadeva
2. Ānanda	16. Rāhulata
3. Śaṇavāsa	17. Saṅghānandin
4. Upagupta	18. Gayaśāta
5. Dhṛtaka	19. Kumārata
6. Miccaka	20. Jayata
7. Vasumitra	21. Vasubandhu
8. Buddhanandin	22. Manorhita
9. Buddhamitra	23. Haklenayaśas
10. Pārśva	24. Siṃha bhikṣu
11. Puṇyayaśas	25. Basiasita
12. Aśvaghoṣa	26. Puṇyamitra
13. Kapimala	27. Prajñātāra
14. Nāgārjuna	28. Bodhidharma

SOURCE: Author.

transmission among native Chinese masters. The Chan list of Indian patriarchs was conventionally fixed at twenty-eight in the *Baolin chuan* (*Transmission of the Treasure Grove*), completed in 801 (see Table 2).

Only two points separate Chan's assertion of lineage succession from the earlier Tiantai one. Vasumitra is inserted as seventh in the line of patriarchal succession, a claim based on the appearance of his name in the *Chanjing*, mentioned above. The addition of Vasumitra effectively expands the Tiantai list from twenty-three to twenty-four. More significantly, the Chan list maintains that the transmission was suspended with Siṃha bhikṣu, as the Tiantai list had supposed, but continued on and was eventually brought physically to China in the person of BODHIDHARMA (ca. early fifth century). This assertion was made to lend credence to the claim that Chan represented the unbroken succession of Buddhist teaching from Śākyamuni to a series of Chinese patriarchs, including the undisputed list of six masters from Bodhidharma to HUINENG (638–713) (see Table 3).

The assertion of a Chinese patriarchal tradition provoked a well-known dispute over correct lineal succession among rival Chan factions. The dispute began in 732 when a hitherto obscure monk named Shenhui (684–758) attacked the legitimacy of the imperially acknowledged representatives of Chan. In 701 or 702, an illustrious disciple of Hongren, Shenxiu (ca. 606–706), had been invited to court by Empress Wu, where he was received with great acclaim. Following Shenxiu's death, his disciples Puji (d. 739) and Yifu (d. 736) became the standard bearers of Chan at the imperial court. Until the arrival of Shenhui, Shenxiu was the undisputed sixth patriarch of Chan. Shenhui challenged that the true heir of Hongren's dharma had been his own master, Huineng, and that he himself was Huineng's heir. To substantiate his claim, Shenhui insisted Bodhidharma's robe, the symbol of legitimate transmission, had been passed by Hongren to Huineng, not Shenxiu. Shenhui branded Shenxiu's illegitimate Chan the "Northern school," in contrast to the legitimate "Southern school" teaching of his own master, Huineng. Over time, Shenhui's arguments gained favor and Huineng was officially accepted as the sixth patriarch in 816. All subsequent Chan factions traced their lineage through Huineng.

Chan and Tiantai lineage formation culminated in the Song dynasty (960–1279). While early Chan insisted on a single line of orthodox transmission through the sixth patriarch and accepted collateral lineages only with reluctance, the later tradition recognized multilineal branches. Fueled by the geographical spread of Chan throughout China, numerous groups sought legitimacy by tracing their lineage of patriarchs through Huineng. After Huineng, the principal or "trunk" lineage of Chan was presumed to bifurcate, and several branch lineages flourished. The bifurcation posited that all later Chan lineages were descended through two of Huineng's disciples, Nanyue Huairang (677–744) and Qingyuan Xingsi (d. 740). Huairang linked the flourishing movement of Mazu DAOYI (709–788) and his followers in the late eighth and early ninth centuries to the Chan tradition of Huineng, and it is clear that Huairang's record was tailored to legitimize these motivations. Xingsi's record was conceived

TABLE 3

Lineage of early Chinese Chan patriarchs and their connection to the "Five Houses"

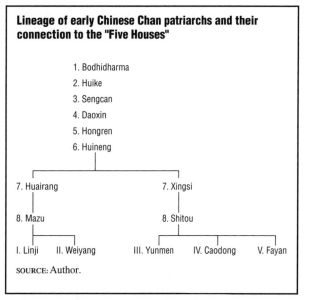

1. Bodhidharma
2. Huike
3. Sengcan
4. Daoxin
5. Hongren
6. Huineng
   - 7. Huairang
     - 8. Mazu
       - I. Linji
       - II. Weiyang
   - 7. Xingsi
     - 8. Shitou
       - III. Yunmen
       - IV. Caodong
       - V. Fayan

SOURCE: Author.

with similar aims, to legitimize the assertions of later lineages descended through Xingsi and Shitou Xiqian (700–790).

By acknowledging several branches, Chan was able to capitalize on its clan identity as an extended family. This framework served as the organizing principle for the classic works of Chan lineage formation compiled in the Song, the transmission histories, or lamp records (*denglu*): the *Zutang ji* (*Patriarch's Hall Anthology,* compiled 952); the *Jingde chuandeng lu* (*Jingde-Era Transmission of the Lamp Record,* compiled 1004); the *Tiansheng guangdeng lu* (*Tiansheng-Era Record of the Propagation of the Lamp,* compiled 1036); the *Jianzhong jingguo xudeng lu* (*Jianzhong jingguo-Era Supplementary Lamp Record,* compiled 1101); the *Zongmen liandeng huiyao* (*Combined Lamp Record of the Chan Lineage,* compiled 1183); the *Jiatai pudeng lu* (*Jiatai-Era Universal Lamp Record,* compiled 1202); and the *Wudeng huiyuan* (*Concise Compendium of the Five Lamp [Histories],* compiled 1252). The common metaphor employed throughout these works is the notion of transmitting the lamp or flame (*chuandeng* or *zhuandeng*), with the lamp representing the light of enlightenment or the teachings of Buddhism. In the Chan context, dharma transmission represents not just a particular teaching or principle, but the secret essence of the Buddha's awakening, referred to variously as "perfect wisdom," the "dharma-eye," the "mind-teaching," or the "mind-essence." The transmission of the dharma is likened to the passing of a flame from one lamp to another, representing the transmission of Buddha's enlightenment from one generation to the next.

As an organizing principle, these works share the belief in a common lineage of Chan ancestors, or patriarchs, extending from Śākyamuni and MAHĀKAŚYĀPA through the series of Indian patriarchs culminating with Bodhidharma, who brought the transmission to China, initiating the series of Chinese Chan patriarchs. These transmission records are principally concerned with documenting the profusion of Chan masters following the sixth patriarch, and organizing them according to lineage. The genesis of the so-called five houses or five clans (Weiyang, Linji, Caodong, Yunmen, and Fayan) of Chan Buddhism is found in these records. Organized in this fashion, the master–disciple relation serves as a surrogate father–son relationship, linking practitioners to the larger tradition of Chan ancestors and providing identity based on specific lineages. In this way Chan came to mirror the Chinese clan system, organized around common ancestors, patrilineal style relationships, factional branch lineages, and so on. The Chan clan came to represent a set of familial style relationships. Individual monks belonging to a lineage were related vertically as spiritual fathers, sons, grandfathers, grandsons, and so on. They were related to other Chan branch lineages horizontally as would be siblings, cousins, uncles, and nephews.

The last decades of the Song dynasty witnessed the production of two works, the *Shimen zhengtong* (*Orthodox Lineage of the Buddhist Tradition,* compiled in 1237) and the *Fozu tongji* (*Comprehensive History of the Buddhas and Patriarchs,* compiled between 1258 and 1269), which presented the universal history of Buddhism from the Tiantai perspective. These works held that the essence of Buddhism was embodied in Tiantai teaching and practice, which had been faithfully transmitted from Śākyamuni through the Indian patriarchs, to the Tiantai patriarchs in China. Like their Chan counterparts, the Tiantai records were structured around the principle of patriarchal succession. However, unlike Chan, they proposed that Tiantai patriarchs and their descendants occupied the central and dominant position of Buddhism in China. As in the case of Chan lineages, the essentially congruent Tiantai lineages presented in these works cannot be accepted uncritically, but should be regarded as products of a process aimed at securing prestige, patronage, and special privilege for Tiantai during the Song period (Shinohara, pp. 524–525).

By the Song dynasty, Dharma-transmission was formalized through the granting of a dharma-scroll conferred by a master on deserving disciples. The "dharma-scroll" contained a list of names through whom the transmission had passed, from Śākyamuni down through the current master. In effect, it constituted the dharma-lineage of the particular sect in question, and authorized the recipient to teach. According to Holmes Welch (*The Practice of Chinese Buddhism: 1900–1950,* p. 157), this system was still practiced in China in the twentieth century. In addition to dharma-lineages, individual monastery lineages listed the names of abbots who served at them.

The notion of lineage framed in the Chinese context had great impact on the development of Buddhism throughout East Asia. Lineage as a basis for sectarian identity was promoted in Japan and Korea, where native versions of Chinese Buddhist schools prospered, and native lineages were grafted onto their Chinese predecessors. Contemporary Zen priests in Japan continue to receive dharma-scrolls or dharma-certificates as authentication of their status in a Zen lineage. Mention should also be made of the use of lineage in Tibetan Buddhism, where incarnate lamas, leaders of the Buddhist community, are assumed to be successive embodiments of leading buddhas and bodhisattvas, following a notion introduced with the first KARMA PA Lama, Dus gsum mkhyen pa (Düsum Khyenpa; 1110–1193). This is the most distinctive of Tibetan hierarchical institutions, which identifies a future lama as the rebirth of his deceased predecessor. The most famous example of this is the DALAI LAMA, considered to be an incarnation of Tibet's patron bodhisattva, Avalokiteśvara, the bodhisattva of compassion.

Bibliography

Ebrey, Patricia Buckley. *Confucianism and Family Rituals in Imperial China: A Social History of Writing about Rites.* Princeton, NJ: Princeton University Press, 1991.

Faure, Bernard. *The Will to Orthodoxy: A Critical Genealogy of Northern Chan Buddhism,* tr. Phyllis Brooks. Stanford, CA: Stanford University Press, 1997.

Foulk, T. Griffith. "Myth, Ritual, and Monastic Practice in Sung Ch'an Buddhism." In *Religion and Society in T'ang and Sung China,* ed. Peter N. Gregory and Patricia Buckley Ebrey. Honolulu: University of Hawaii Press, 1993.

Foulk, T. Griffith. "Sung Controversies Concerning the 'Separate Transmission' of Ch'an." In *Buddhism in the Sung,* ed. Peter N. Gregory and Daniel A. Getz, Jr. Honolulu: University of Hawaii Press, 1999.

Foulk, T. Griffith, and Sharf, Robert H. "On the Ritual Use of Ch'an Portraiture in Medieval China." *Cahiers d' Extrême Asie* 7 (1993–1994): 149–219.

Jan, Yün-hua. "Tsung-mi: His Analysis of Ch'an Buddhism." *T'oung Pao* 58 (1972): 1–54.

Jorgensen, John. "The 'Imperial' Lineage of Ch'an Buddhism: The Role of Confucian Ritual and Ancestor Worship in Ch'an's Search for Legitimation in the Mid-T'ang Dynasty." *Papers on Far Eastern History* 35 (1987): 89–133.

Lamotte, Étienne. *History of Indian Buddhism: From the Origins to the Śaka Era,* tr. Sara Webb-Boin and Jean Dantinne. Louvain, Belgium: Université Catholique de Louvain Institute Orientaliste; Peters Press, 1988.

Shinohara, Koichi. "From Local History to Universal History: The Construction of the Sung T'ien-t'ai Lineage." In *Buddhism in the Sung,* ed. Peter N. Gregory and Daniel A. Getz, Jr. Honolulu: University of Hawaii Press, 1999.

Welch, Holmes. "Dharma-Scrolls and the Succession of Abbots in Chinese Monasteries." *T'oung Pao* 50 (1963): 93–149.

Welch, Holmes. *The Practice of Chinese Buddhism: 1900–1950.* Cambridge, MA: Harvard University Press, 1967.

Welter, Albert. "Mahākāśyapa's Smile: Silent Transmission and the Kung-an (*Kōan*) Tradition." In *The Kōan: Texts and Contexts in Zen Buddhism,* ed. Steven Heine and Dale S. Wright. Oxford: Oxford University Press, 2000.

Yampolsky, Philip B. *The Platform Sutra of the Sixth Patriarch.* New York and London: Columbia University Press, 1967.

ALBERT WELTER

LINJI SCHOOL. *See* **Chan School; Yixuan**

LITURGY. *See* **Chanting and Liturgy**

LOCAL DIVINITIES AND BUDDHISM

There is no single Buddhist term that covers the same semantic area as the English word DIVINITIES or its equivalents, such as deities, gods, and supernatural beings. In fact, Buddhist COSMOLOGY recognizes several kinds of divine or semidivine beings, all endowed with superhuman faculties: BUDDHAS and BODHISATTVAS; former disciples of the Buddha (*śrāvakas*); saints of various kinds (arhats in particular); angelic figures (*gandharva, kiṃnara*); "gods" proper (Sanskrit *devas*; Japanese *kami*; Burmese *nats*); anti-gods (asura); various kinds of ghosts; demonic and monsterlike figures (preta, yakṣa, *rākṣasa*); mythological animals (nāga, *garura, mahorāga*); and devils and other denizens of hell. Each of these classes has its own place in cosmology and its role in SOTERIOLOGY.

Buddhas, bodhisattvas, and Buddhist saints are not gods, but they are often worshiped as such. A major doctrinal distinction separates buddhas, bodhisattvas, and other saintly figures from all other superhuman entities in that the former are situated outside of the realm of transmigration. Gods, spirits, ghosts, and the like, in contrast, are still prisoners of the law of KARMA and will accordingly be reborn in the future in different shapes until they attain the supreme liberation. Even though Buddhist cosmology attributes a clear preeminence to the Buddha and other enlightened beings, local deities still play an important role in the life and the liturgy of Buddhists in many parts of the world.

Buddhism and local deities: approaches and problems

The role and status of divinities within the Buddhist tradition is complicated. Deities are often seen as something essentially different from "true" Buddhism (however defined). Negative views consider the worship of local gods as a deluded, superstitious practice. In general, however, divinities are treated as skillful means (UPĀYA), as a concession to popular beliefs that can be useful to guide the unenlightened toward salvation. Only in some cases are there specific attempts to give doctrinal legitimacy to local deities as full-fledged components of the Buddhist universe.

Despite the ambiguous doctrinal position of deities in the Buddhist system, it is important to emphasize that interaction with local divinities was a key factor in the diffusion of Buddhism, both inside and outside of India. Unfortunately, little information is available on the relationship between Buddhism and local deities in premodern times. Wherever Buddhism is the dominant or state religion, folkloric practices and traditions concerning local deities have often been downplayed as mere "superstition." Nativist movements in East Asia, in contrast, have tended to reduce the role of Buddhism in their countries and to emphasize instead the autochthonous tradition, with the result of often rendering invisible the connections between Buddhism and local divinities.

The difficulty of describing the relationship between Buddhism and local deities has also affected scholars. Buddhologists, on the one hand, tend to focus more on the translocal (orthodox doctrines and rituals), rather than on the local (actual Buddhism as it is practiced in specific historical and cultural contexts); as a consequence, they have paid little attention to local deities. Anthropologists, on the other hand, focus on contemporary cultural situations, without much emphasis on the history of the relationship between Buddhism and local cultures. Furthermore, the dominant tendency for many years among scholars of religious phenomena was that of privileging separate traditions, based on an emphasis on textualized doctrines and "faith," rather than on living religiosity, which often cannot be reduced to canonical, doctrinal scriptures.

Buddhist appropriation of local deities: motifs and models

From the beginning, Buddhism appears to have dealt with Indian deities in positive terms by incorporating them within its own system, rather than by ignoring or persecuting them. In fact, according to the Buddhist interpretation, the Indian gods need the appearance of a buddha among the humans before they can be taught the way to attain salvation; in this way, the Buddhists made deities into subordinates of the Buddha and, by extension, his emissaries.

Many stories about the establishment and the diffusion of Buddhism involve the conversion, subjugation, or control of local deities. Discreet but crucial interventions by the Indian gods accompany the spiritual career of Śākyamuni Buddha as told in classical narratives such as the BUDDHACARITA (*Acts of the Buddha*) or the JĀTAKA tales. The scriptures often present the Buddha as the teacher of gods. One of the earliest sūtras, the *Ekottarāgama* (*Numerically Ordered Collection*) describes a famous scene in which Buddha ascends to heaven and preaches to INDRA and the other gods of the classical Indian pantheon, who were gathered together with the Buddha's mother, Queen Māyā. In some cases, gods were reluctant to convert, which made recourse to violent methods necessary. Particularly famous is the subjugation of Maheśvara (Śiva), in which a bodhisattva entered the samādhi of adamantine anger and killed Maheśvara; the latter was then resuscitated as a buddha in a distant world system. On special occasions, the Buddha did not object to transforming himself into a frightening and powerful demon in order to subjugate other demons. Stories also recount the conversion of hostile local deities, which then turned into protectors of the dharma and its adepts. Early tales of interaction with divinities have set the standard for subsequent strategies employed by Buddhists to spread their teachings in foreign lands.

Buddhism was often propagated by monks traveling with traders. These monks addressed the political and economic elites of the new lands they visited. Their goal was to replace (or, at least, restructure) the preexisting cosmology and its related pantheon with the Buddhist worldview, with the Buddha on top. However, the spread of Buddhism among the commoners was to a large extent the work of saintlike figures who went around subjugating territorial guardian spirits, while at the same time establishing monasteries, schools, and other infrastructures, and preaching the Buddhadharma.

In an important sense, then, the diffusion of Buddhism in a country often began with the taming of local deities, usually described as hostile, violent, and dangerous. This practice started in India and was based on scriptural precedents. A number of local deities and spirits were thus included in the Buddhist pantheon as protectors of the dharma. The nāga (serpents/dragons), symbols of water and fertility, were worshiped by the original inhabitants of the Indian subcontinent prior to the Āryan invasions. Particularly well known are the conversion of the nāga Apalāla in northwestern India and the subjugation of the nāgas by MAHĀMAUDGALYĀYANA. The nāga cult also spread in Southeast and East Asia. YAKṢA and *yakṣinī,* evil spirits (ogres) of forests and uncultivated plains, were subjugated by the Buddha in Sri Lanka in order to spread the dharma there. Asura (anti-gods) are often a model for local deities, such as the *nats* in Myanmar and deified warriors in Japan. *Garuḍa,* mythical birds who were the enemies of the nāgas, turned into the flying vehicle of VIṢṆU before they were included in the Buddhist pantheon. *Rākṣasa,* cannibalistic evil spirits, became protectors of the LOTUS SŪTRA (SADDHARMAPUṆḌARĪKA-SŪTRA). Some of these deities, in spite of their intrinsic violent character, even became important foci of devotion, such as Mahākāla, the *yakṣinī* Hārītī, Kubera, and Hayagrīva. Still other divine beings became guardians of local images, stūpas, and monasteries.

In general, there were a few common strategies for the Buddhist conversion of local deities throughout Asia. Deities were first converted, sometimes violently (subjugation), either following their own request or after a confrontation. This step signaled the supremacy of Buddhism over local deities. Even when local spirits were not directly incorporated but marginalized (as happened in Tibet, where indigenous deities were subdued by erecting monasteries on specific parts of their bodies), there was still the need for propitiation, thus further emphasizing the fundamental evil nature of preexisting local deities and the importance of Buddhism to control them.

On a second stage, converted deities became protectors of the dharma, its adepts, and its facilities. In this way, deities were able to perform their usual, pre-Buddhist tutelary functions, but within a larger, translocal cosmology, and in a different soteriological framework. Later, we sometimes observe the formation of new, post-Buddhist local deities, distinct from but related to Buddhist divinities. Examples include HACHIMAN and Inari in Japan, BON deities in Tibet, and certain kinds of spirits in Thailand, such as the *winjan.* In some cases, local deities came to be envisioned as manifestations (*avatāra*) of translocal, usually Indian, gods. For example, the supreme *nat* spirit in Myanmar, Thagya Min nat, is identified with Inda (Indra). Japanese Shintō *kami* were also considered manifestations of Indian deities. In China certain local gods of a strong Daoist flavor are closely related to, if not completely identified with, Buddhist figures; such is the case of the goddess Mazu and her close relationship with the bodhisattva Guanyin (Avalokiteśvara).

By presenting local deities—and the social organization and power relations that support them—as manifestations of chaos and violence, these narratives emphasize the civilizing, ordering, and beneficial nature of Buddhism, its institutions, and its representatives. Even though the initial disruption was actually caused by Buddhist monks who questioned, altered, or destroyed local cultural practices represented by local deities, such an emphasis on order and peace was not simply groundless propaganda. In many cases, Buddhist missionaries came from more advanced cultures and brought with them new technologies, ideas, and representations that were structured in a translocal and more encompassing worldview. The inclusiveness of Buddhism, its capacity to integrate different and contrasting elements inside its own superior system was represented by the inclusion of previously anti-Buddhist forces and mutual enemies, such as Maheśvara and the asuras, or on a different level, nāgas and *garuḍas.*

Buddhism and local cults

Local deities in countries where Buddhism spread are usually regarded as manifestations of an animistic worldview. The term *animism,* however, cannot effectively represent the variety and complexity of cultures in which Buddhism penetrated. Local deities range from souls of individuals, spirits of the dead, ghosts, and other postmortem demonic entities, to local and tutelary deities of various kinds. These entities are envisioned as forces concerned with health, fertility, and prosperity (or lack thereof). The Buddhist intervention restructured all these multifarious forms into a system, more or less coherent, that was based (at least, to an extent) on Buddhist doctrines. For example, in present-day Myanmar a combination of Pāli Buddhism, nāga cults, and *nat* animism has been attested in the Pagan area since the tenth to eleventh centuries; analogous situations exist in Thailand and Laos. In premodern Japan, local deities were incorporated into the Buddhist cosmology and liturgy as manifestations of buddhas, bodhisattvas, and classical Indian gods. In other areas, such as China and Tibet, a division of labor arises between the Buddhist clergy and ritualists of other traditions (e.g., Daoists or Bon adepts, and traditional specialists).

While not directly related to the quest for ultimate liberation (be it configured as NIRVĀṆA or the attainment of Buddhahood), local divinities played an important role in merit-making and in securing protection, two areas, distinct but closely interrelated, that roughly correspond to karmic and apotropaic Buddhism as defined by Melford Spiro. Merit, often expressed as concrete, material benefits rather than in purely spiritual terms, could be conceived of as a form of protection from illness, evil spirits, and natural calamities often caused by supernatural entities. On the other hand, invoking protection from local divinities could result in benefits that were not much different in practice from those resulting from the performance of purely "orthodox" Buddhist devotions.

Buddhism dealt with local spirits in numerous ways, ranging from discursive structuring (definition of their status and attribution of a specific place within the Buddhist cosmology and soteriology), to ritual interaction, to mere noninterference. *Discursive structuring* seems to operate in general only on the main principles, but it does not work in detail. For example, in the case of Thai "village cosmology" the relationship is unclear between *thewada* (from the Sanskrit *devatā*), gods that are considered to be situated outside the cycle of rebirth (in itself a heterodox idea), and local spirits known as *phī*. *Ritual interaction* takes many forms, from the reading of Buddhist scriptures that took place in front of the Japanese *kami* until the anti-Buddhist persecutions of 1868, to the celebrations of festivals for the protectors of Thai monasteries (Chao Phau). In the case of *noninterference,* Buddhists leave certain issues concerning local spirits to traditional figures such as shamans, storytellers, diviners, and so forth. In fact, in most Buddhist cultures a number of such traditional specialists deal with local deities, spirits, and ghosts. In some cases, they form distinct and independent professional and social groups, such as *kami* priests in premodern Japan, Bon priests in Tibet, and certain shamanlike specialists in China and Southeast Asia. Most of the time, however, traditional specialists of local sacred affairs are not religious professionals, but perform their services as a side business in addition to their ordinary, secular professions.

Buddhist cosmology and popular religious practices concerning the afterlife

An area of religious life in which the interaction of Buddhism with local divinities is particularly intense is the one that deals with DEATH and the afterlife (funeral ceremonies, ancestor cults, and neutralization of evil ghosts). In particular, the Buddhist cosmology of HEAVENS and HELLS, together with its multiple PURE LANDS (Sukhāvatī, Potālaka, etc.) always involves theses kinds of issues. To most Buddhists, nirvāṇa is not an immediate goal; what matters most is REBIRTH into a higher state of being, from which the dead can bestow blessings onto the living who honor and worship them. This is the starting point of ancestor cults, which are associated with the idea that lack of proper ritual action toward the deceased will cause misfortune and disaster. In this way, memorialization brings together merit-making in the form of ritual exchanges with ANCESTORS and apotropaic beliefs and practices promising protection against evil ghosts. Memorialization also fuses Buddhist classic cosmology and local divinities (in the form of ancestors, tutelary deities, and spirits of various kinds). It is not by chance, then, that in most of Asia, Buddhist monks are directly involved in funerals, memorialization of the dead (who are turned into ancestors), and control of ghosts, often associated with evil deities of classical cosmology such as yakṣa and asura, the *nats* in Myanmar, and the *phī* in Thailand and Laos. Particularly interesting in this respect are East Asian Buddhist funerary practices and their underlying cosmology of hells. Chinese Buddhists applied the bureaucratic structure of their state to the afterlife, developing the cult of the Ten Kings of hell—judges who decide the destiny of the defunct in the afterlife. This cult combines Buddhist conceptions of hell, popular Indian ideas of rebirth, Indian gods such as Yāma, Daoist deities, and Chinese popular beliefs and practices (including Confucian bureaucracy). Another cult (known as *shi eguei gongyang* in China and *se gaki kuyō* in Japan) that developed in China dealt with the so-called hungry ghosts, an East Asian version of the Indian preta, which shows concerns and fear about the spirits of those who died a "bad" death or who were not properly memorialized by their families. These funerary cults spread all over the Sinicized world in East Asia and still constitute one of the most important and enduring contributions of Buddhism to East Asian cultures.

The problem of syncretism

The term *syncretism* has had a long history of negative connotations as indicating a random mixture of various religious elements dictated by ignorance, superstition, or even diabolic influences. The term presupposes the existence of a "pure" form of a given religious tradition, uncorrupted by blending with other religions. For these reasons, it is difficult to use *syncretism* as a neutral, descriptive term. The word was redefined, however, in *The Encyclopedia of Religion* (1987) as referring to "connections of a special kind between languages, cultures, or religions" (vol. 14, p. 218). In this form, however, it is too vague to be useful for analysis of specific cases of religious interactions. The essential problem is that religious and cultural interactions in general are not mere juxtapositions of distinct and independent elements. The case of the Buddhist impact on local divinities is particularly revealing. Certainly, some deities were abandoned and forgotten, and new ones were added. But what matters more is the systematic and pervasive restructuring of the cultural field of the sacred that the interaction with Buddhism generated. Local deities were given features of Indian gods and vice versa, thus generating new entities; but new deities were also created to deal with the new conceptual and ritual situation that had developed. Interestingly, some Buddhist deities (or some of their features) were rendered native by the phenomena of *relocalization,* a process that at times even obliterated their Buddhist origin. This is the case with *kami* such as Hachiman and Inari in contemporary Japan, of deities incorporated into the folk religions of China and Korea, and of the Bon tradition in Tibet (an independent establishment still clearly indebted to Buddhism). All these cases cannot simply be reduced to modes of juxtaposition, combination, or even connection. Various conceptual categories should be mobilized instead to describe the multifarious forms of Buddhist interaction with local divinities in shifting historical, cultural, social, and ideological contexts. In other words, rather than taking as a starting point an abstract and reified idea of Buddhism and analyzing how it deals with local deities, it appears to be more appropriate and fruitful to investigate the various roles that certain DIVINITIES play within specific Buddhist contexts. As examples, we can think of processes of state formation (with divinities protecting newly formed states and their regional divisions), social control (the symbolic order of families, clans, and local communities as represented by specific divinities and ritual interactions with them), labor and economic concerns, and semiotic practices guiding the combination of various deities (as based on formal, functional, structural, and semantic features).

See also: **Folk Religion: An Overview; Ghosts and Spirits; Kūkai; Merit and Merit-Making; Shintō (Honji Suijaku) and Buddhism; Syncretic Sects: Three Teachings**

Bibliography

Bechert, Heinz, ed. *Buddhism in Ceylon and Studies in Religious Syncretism in Buddhist Countries.* Göttingen, Germany: Vandenhoeck and Ruprecht, 1978.

Colpe, Carsten. "Syncretism," tr. Matthew J. O'Connell. In *The Encyclopedia of Religion,* Vol. 14, ed. Mircea Eliade. New York: Macmillan, 1987.

Gellner, David N. "For Syncretism: The Position of Buddhism in Nepal and Japan Compared." *Social Anthropology* 5, no. 3 (1997): 277–291.

Grapard, Allan G. *The Protocol of the Gods: A Study of the Kasuga Cult in Japanese History.* Berkeley, Los Angeles, and London: University of California Press, 1992.

Iyanaga Nobumi. *Daikokuten hensō* (Bukkyō shinwagaku 1). Kyoto: Hōzōkan, 2002.

Kamstra, Jacques H. *Encounter or Syncretism: The Initial Growth of Japanese Buddhism.* Leiden, Netherlands: Brill, 1967.

Kitagawa, Joseph M. *Religion in Japanese History.* New York: Columbia University Press, 1966.

Kvaerne, Per. *The Bön Religion of Tibet: The Iconography of a Living Tradition.* Boston and London: Shambhala, 1995.

Matsunaga, Alicia. *The Buddhist Philosophy of Assimilation: The Historical Development of the Honji-Suijaku Theory.* Rutland, VT, and Tokyo: Sophia University Press, 1969.

Murayama Shūichi. *Honji suijaku.* Tokyo: Yoshikawa Kōbunkan, 1974.

Sarkisyanz, Manuel (Emanuel). *Buddhist Backgrounds of the Burmese Revolution.* The Hague: M. Nijhoff, 1965.

Spiro, Melford E. *Buddhism and Society: A Great Tradition and Its Burmese Vicissitudes.* Berkeley, Los Angeles, and London: University of California Press, 1982.

Strong, John S. *The Experience of Buddhism: Sources and Interpretations.* Belmont, CA: Wadsworth, 1995.

Tambiah, Stanley J. *Buddhism and the Spirit Cults in North-East Thailand.* Cambridge, UK: Cambridge University Press, 1970.

Teeuwen, Mark, and Rambelli, Fabio, eds. *Buddhas and Kami in Japan: Honji Suijaku as a Combinatory Paradigm.* London and New York: RoutledgeCurzon, 2003.

Teiser, Stephen F. *The Ghost Festival in Medieval China.* Princeton, NJ: Princeton University Press, 1988.

Tucci, Giuseppe. *The Religions of Tibet,* tr. Geoffrey Samuel. Berkeley, Los Angeles, and London: University of California Press, 1980.

FABIO RAMBELLI

LOGIC

Indian thinkers of many traditions, including Buddhism, often maintain that reliable knowledge is the key to spiritual liberation. By the fourth century C.E., many such thinkers were engrossed in an ongoing conversation focused on two interrelated questions: What constitutes reliable knowledge? And what types of reliable knowledge are there? The answers to these questions led to intricate debates on the nature of perception, reason, and language. Buddhists participated prominently in this conversation, but their contribution does not constitute a separate "school" of thought. It is, instead, a style of Buddhist philosophy that eventually gained much sway among Buddhist thinkers in India; Tibetan traditions continue to employ it vigorously to this day. Since Buddhists have no indigenous term for this philosophical style, Western scholars invented the term *Buddhist logic* to describe especially the formulations initially presented by Dignāga (ca. 480–540 C.E.) and refined by Dharmakīrti (ca. 600–670 C.E.).

Dignāga gave the first systematic presentation of Buddhist logic, but Dharmakīrti and his followers provided the form that became widespread in India and Tibet. Concerning the types of reliable knowledge, Buddhist logic holds that there are just two kinds, each with a corresponding type of object: (1) perception, which cognizes particulars, and (2) inference, which cognizes universals. A particular is a completely unique, causally efficacious entity that exists for only a moment. We know that particulars are real because they are causally linked, directly or indirectly, to our cognitions of them. Universals, the objects of inference, are concepts that are meant to apply to many particulars. They are causally inert; hence, although we imagine them to be real, they cannot in fact be the causes of any cognition. For this reason, Buddhist logicians maintain that only particulars are truly real; universals may seem real, but they are actually mental fictions that we create through a process of excluding everything that is irrelevant to the context at hand.

To understand the difference between particulars and universals, suppose that this dot ● is a unique particular. It may seem to be the same as this other dot ●, but that sameness is created by associating two unique sensory experiences with a single universal, the concept *dot*. Each specific instance may also seem to last over time, but the apparent stability of particulars over time is also an illusion created by associating them with a single universal. Moreover, only the actual dot on the page can cause a cognition; the universal *dot* cannot do so (we can see ●; we cannot see our concept of it).

Buddhist logicians further argue that an instance of reliable knowledge must be an efficacious cognition—efficacious because it enables one to achieve one's goal. Strictly speaking, then, reliable knowledge can be partially defective. For example, a cognition might falsely attribute qualities to a thing but still remain effective: While correctly identifying something as fire, one might incorrectly believe that the observed fire is exactly identical to all other fires. Nevertheless, that cognition is still efficacious because those false attributions do not obstruct one from attaining one's goal: If you seek to warm your hands, then it does not matter whether you falsely believe that the fire in front of you is identical to all others.

Buddhist logicians must allow that reliable knowledge may be partially defective because they must make use of language without accepting some characteristics implied by universals. The concept *dot,* for example, makes us falsely believe that all dots are one; nevertheless, we can successfully use this concept to speak of the (actually unique) dots on this page. Likewise, the concept *person* falsely makes me believe that I am identical to the infant that I was; nevertheless, we can use *person* to speak of one who suffers and seeks liberation.

This critical approach to universals creates problems when Buddhist logicians present their theory of logic, which is in fact a detailed theory of inference. Here, the form of an inference is "S is P because E," where the terms are a subject (S), a predicate (P), and the evidence (E). An example would be, "Joe is mortal because of being human." An inference is well formed if three relations hold: the evidence entails the predicate (a human must be mortal); the negation of the predicate entails the negation of the evidence (a nonmortal must be nonhuman); and the evidence is a quality of the subject (Joe is indeed human). For Buddhists who employ this theory of inference, two notable problems persist. First, the inference's terms must be universals, and since universals are strictly speaking unreal, how does one account for relations among them? And second, if one uses an inference to prove that a purely imaginary entity does not exist, how can that purely imaginary entity be the subject of that inference? That is, if one wishes to prove that "an absolute Self is nonexistent," how can an imaginary entity (the absolute Self) bear any predicate? This latter question is particularly acute for Madhyamaka thinkers who employ the Buddhist logicians' theory of inference.

See also: **Madhyamaka School; Yogācāra School**

Bibliography

Dreyfus, Georges B. *Recognizing Reality: Dharmakīrti's Philosophy and Its Tibetan Interpretations.* Albany: State University of New York Press, 1997.

Stcherbatsky, Th. *Buddhist Logic,* 2 vols. Delhi: Motilal Banarsidass, 1992. Reprint of 1930–1932 edition.

Tillemans, Tom J. F. *Scripture, Logic, Language: Essays on Dharmakīrti and His Tibetan Successors.* Boston: Wisdom, 1999.

JOHN DUNNE

LONGMEN

The Longmen cave complex is located twelve kilometers south of Luoyang, Henan province, in China. From the end of the fifth century through the middle of the eighth century, CAVE SANCTUARIES were excavated out of the limestone hills on two sides of the Yi River. They were sponsored by Buddhist devotees from all sectors of the society—aristocrats and commoners, ethnic nomads and Chinese alike, attesting to the widespread support of Buddhism. The late Northern Wei and High Tang periods represent two periods of great activity, during which imperial patronage also played an important role. The central Binyang cave, begun in 505 and sponsored by the Northern Wei emperor Xuanwudi (r. 449–515), ushered in a new phase of Chinese Buddhist art that synthesized foreign and native Chinese art styles, combining a three-dimensional approach to form with minute attention to surface details and patterns. Fengxian Monastery, completed in 675, epitomized the imperial patronage of Emperor Gaozong (r. 649–683) and Empress Wu (r. 684–705) of the Tang dynasty. The colossal statue of Vairocana Buddha, accompanied by disciples, bodhisattvas, and guardian deities, is a powerful statement of the omniscience of the Buddha as the lord of the universe and as a protector of the state.

See also: **China, Buddhist Art in; Monastic Architecture**

Bibliography

Gong Dazhong. *Longmen shiku yishu (The Art of the Longmen Cave-Temples).* Shanghai: Renmin chubanshe, 1981.

Longmen Cultural Relics Conservation Institute and the Archaeological Institute of Beijing University. *Longmen shiku (Longmen Cave-Temples).* 2 vols. Beijing: Wenwu Press, 1991.

Mizuno Seiichi, Nagahiro Toshio, et al. *Ryūmon sekkutsu no kenkyū (A Study of the Longmen Cave-Temples).* Tokyo: Zayūho kankōkai, 1941.

DOROTHY WONG

LOTUS SŪTRA (SADDHARMAPUṆḌARĪKA-SŪTRA)

The *Lotus Sūtra* (Sanskrit, *Saddharmapuṇḍarīka-sūtra*) numbers among the most popular of MAHĀYĀNA scriptures. It is celebrated for its reconciliation of diverse teachings in the "one Buddha vehicle" (*ekayāna*) and for its promise that buddhahood can be achieved by all. Although it has not figured prominently in the Mahāyāna traditions of India or Tibet, the *Lotus Sūtra* has for centuries profoundly influenced Buddhist thought, art, and literature throughout East Asia. Its ideas have served as the basis for philosophical systems and meditative and ritual practice, while its parables and mythic imagery have inspired paintings, drama, and poetry. Since the late nineteenth century, the *Lotus* has also been read as supporting various forms of Buddhist social engagement.

Texts and translations

As with most Mahāyāna sūtras, little is known of the circumstances surrounding the composition of the *Lotus Sūtra.* There is only one extant full-length commentary that appears likely to have been composed in India: the *Fahua lun (Treatise on the Lotus)*, attributed to VASUBANDHU (ca. fourth century C.E.), which exists in Chinese translation. Scholars date the sūtra's compilation to roughly around the first two centuries of the common era. Six Chinese translations were made, of which three survive: *Zhengfa hua jing,* translated by DHARMARAKṢA in 286; *Miaofa lianhua jing,* translated by KUMĀRAJĪVA in 406; and *Tianben miaofa lianhua jing,* translated by Jñānagupta and Dharmagupta in 601 (this last is a revision of Kumārajīva's translation). Kumārajīva's translation has twenty-eight chapters; the material comprising its twelfth, "DEVADATTA," chapter is included at the end of chapter eleven in the other two translations, which have only twenty-seven chapters (subsequent chapter references in this entry are to Kumārajīva's twenty-eight chapter version). Whether Kumārajīva's translation originally contained the Devadatta chapter, or whether it was added later, has been a matter of some debate.

Of the three Chinese versions of the *Lotus Sūtra,* Kumārajīva's proved by far the most popular. A Tibetan translation, *Dam pa'i chos pad ma dkar po zhes bya ba theg pa chen po'i mdo,* was also made in the early ninth century by Surendrabodhi and Sna nam Ye shes sde. Since the nineteenth century, Sanskrit manuscripts and manuscript fragments of the *Lotus* have been discovered in Nepal, Kashmir, Tibet, and other parts of Central Asia. Critical comparison of these various versions has advanced scholarly understanding of the process of the sūtra's composition. As of the beginning of the twenty-first century, eight English translations have been published (all but one based on Kumārajīva's Chinese), along with translations into other modern languages.

Though the exact dating of individual chapters probably varies considerably, modern textual study suggests that the *Lotus Sūtra* may have been compiled, broadly speaking, in three stages. The first nine chapters, which focus on the themes of the "one vehicle" and "skillful means," represent an initial stage. Chapters ten through twenty-two, emphasizing BODHISATTVA conduct and the importance of revering, preaching, and transmitting the sūtra, constitute a second stage. This second stage corresponds, roughly, to that portion of the sūtra called the "assembly in open space," in which the jeweled STŪPA of the Buddha Prabhūtaratna appears from beneath the earth to testify to the *Lotus Sūtra*'s truth, and Śākyamuni Buddha, accepting Prabhūtaratna's offer of a seat beside him in the stūpa, uses his supramundane powers to lift the entire assembly into midair on a level with the two buddhas. The final chapters, dealing with devotion to specific bodhisattvas, appear to have been added still later. Traditionally, however, exegetes have divided the sūtra not by stages in its compilation but by interpretation of its content. ZHIYI (538–597), de facto founder of the TIANTAI SCHOOL, termed the first fourteen chapters the "trace teaching" (Chinese, *jimen;* Japanese, *shakumon*), preached by Śākyamuni in a provisionally manifested form as the historical Buddha, and the second fourteen chapters, the "origin teaching" (*benmen, honmon*), revealing Śākyamuni to be the original or primordial Buddha, awakened since the inconceivably distant past. This division of the sūtra into "trace" and "origin" sections formed the basis for numerous subsequent interpretations, especially in the Tiantai/Tendai and NICHIREN SCHOOLS.

In China, a practice began of grouping apparently related sūtras into threes. The "threefold *Lotus Sūtra*" consists of Kumārajīva's *Sūtra of the Lotus Blossom of the Wonderful Dharma* (Chinese, *Miaofa lianhua jing;* Japanese, *Myōhōrengekyō*) as the main sūtra; the *Sūtra of Immeasurable Meanings* (*Wuliang yi jing, Muryōgikyō*) as the introductory sūtra; and the *Sūtra on the Method of Contemplating Bodhisattva Samantabhadra* (*Guan Puxian pusa xingfa jing, Kan Fugen bosatsu gyōhōkyō*) as the concluding sūtra. No Sanskrit version is extant for either the introductory or the concluding sūtra, and the circumstances of their compilation remain unclear. According to the first chapter of the *Lotus Sūtra,* just before expounding the *Lotus* itself, the Buddha preached "a Mahāyāna sūtra called Immeasurable Meanings"; the *Sūtra of Immeasurable Meanings* was assumed to be that very sūtra. It also contains the statement: "In these forty years and more, I [Śākyamuni] have not yet revealed the truth." The "truth" here was taken to mean the *Lotus Sūtra,* and this passage was used as a proof text to support arguments according the *Lotus* a supreme position among the Buddha's lifetime teachings. The *Samantabhadra Sūtra* was clearly composed with reference to chapter twenty-eight of the *Lotus Sūtra,* which is also about Samantabhadra, and sets forth a detailed meditation on this bodhisattva that includes repentance for sins committed with the six sense faculties. Zhiyi incorporated this ritual of repentance into the *Lotus* samādhi, the third of the "four kinds of samādhi" taught in the Tiantai meditative system.

Central themes of the *Lotus Sūtra*

The one vehicle and skillful means. Mahāyāna polemics extol the ideal of the bodhisattva who strives for the liberation of all, over and against the goal of personal NIRVĀṆA sought by the Buddha's disciples (śrāvakas) and the privately enlightened (PRATYEKABUDDHAS), followers of the two so-called HĪNAYĀNA vehicles. Some Mahāyāna sūtras, such as the *Vimalakīrtinirdeśa,* condemn the way of the two vehicles as a spiritual dead end. The *Lotus Sūtra,* however, attempts to reconcile them with the Mahāyāna by asserting that the threefold division in the Buddha's teaching, into separate vehicles for śrāvakas, pratyekabuddhas, and bodhisattvas, is a skillful means (UPĀYA); in reality, there is only one buddha vehicle. That is, the Buddha taught these three separate vehicles as a pedagogical device, in accordance with his auditors' varying capacity for practice and understanding, but they are all designed to lead ultimately to the one buddha vehicle and thus spring from a unitary intent. These intertwined themes—the Buddha's teaching through skill in means and the ultimate resolution of the three disparate vehicles in the one vehicle—are presented discursively in chapter two and then illustrated in subsequent chapters through analogies and parables, such as the three carts and the burning house, the rich man and his poor son, medicinal herbs, the magically conjured city, the gem concealed in a robe, and so forth.

While the *Lotus Sūtra* repeatedly asserts the supremacy of the one vehicle, it never actually explains what it is. This has opened the way for diametrically opposed readings of the sūtra. One controversy among Chinese exegetes centered on whether the one vehicle is the same as, or different from, the bodhisattva vehicle (the so called "three carts or four" controversy). At stake was the question: Is the Mahāyāna the true, final teaching, and only the two vehicles provisional? Or is the Mahāyāna itself, like the two Hīnayāna vehicles, also ultimately a skillful means, leading to but transcended by a truth beyond expression? A related point of disagreement in the history of *Lotus* interpretation concerns whether the one vehicle should be read inclusively or exclusively. From an inclusive standpoint, since the one vehicle is all-encompassing, all practices and doctrinal formulations can be seen as provisional skillful means, which, while different in themselves, nonetheless all point toward the same realization. From an exclusive or hierarchical viewpoint, however, the one vehicle is equated with one specific teaching, the *Lotus,* which is thereby invested with absolute status, over and against all other teachings, which are then relegated to the lesser category of "provisional."

Universal buddhahood. A corollary to its claim that there is only one vehicle is the *Lotus Sūtra*'s assertion that buddhahood is the final goal of all. In the sūtra's words, "Among those who hear this dharma, there is not one who shall not attain buddhahood." This is illustrated by predictions of future buddhahood bestowed upon the Buddha's śrāvaka disciples, as they come to understand that the goal of personal NIRVĀṆA they had pursued was a skillful expedient, not a final destination in itself. The twelfth, Devadatta, chapter was widely interpreted as extending the promise of buddhahood to persons seen as having particular obstacles to liberation. The prediction of eventual buddhahood for Devadatta, the Buddha's wicked cousin, was read as illustrating the potential for enlightenment even in evil persons, and the instantaneous realization of buddhahood by the dragon king's daughter, described in the same chapter, as a promise of enlightenment for WOMEN. In keeping with traditional views that buddhahood must be achieved in a male body, the dragon princess changes into a male in the moment before her enlightenment. Modern readers seeking support in the Mahāyāna for a position of gender equality find this element in the narrative troubling. Historically, however, exegetes and devotees have not necessarily adhered to a literal reading, and the *Lotus* was in fact thought to hold particular relevance for women's attainment of buddhahood.

The primordial Buddha. The latter part of the *Lotus Sūtra,* especially the "origin teaching," presents a radically revised depiction of Śākyamuni, not as the historical Buddha who lived and taught in India, but as the original or primordial Buddha. In chapter eleven, before he opens the jeweled stūpa of Prabhūtaratna, Śākyamuni "recalls his emanations," and the buddhas who then gather from throughout the ten directions are shown to be his manifestations. Particularly in chapter sixteen, Śākyamuni reveals that he first achieved enlightenment, not under the bodhi tree in this lifetime as people think, but billions of kalpas ago, in the inconceivably remote past. Ever since then, he has been here in this world and also in others, preaching the dharma and converting living beings. Thus his birth, renunciation, practice, awakening, and entry into nirvāṇa are all revealed to be the skillful means by which he constantly teaches and liberates others.

The Buddha of the origin teaching is often spoken of as the "eternal Buddha," a term that, though easy to understand, flattens out a long and complex history of interpretation. Early Chinese exegetes disagreed over whether this Buddha's life span was finite or infinite, or whether he was a Buddha in the dharma-body (dharmakāya), the recompense-body (sambhogakāya), or the manifested-body (nirmāṇakāya) aspect. In a dynamic synthesis, Zhiyi interpreted the original Buddha of the *Lotus Sūtra* as embodying all three bodies in one: The dharma body is the truth that is realized; the recompense body is the wisdom that realizes it; and the manifested body, a compassionate expression of that wisdom as the human Buddha who appeared and taught in this world. In the Japanese Tendai tantric tradition (Taimitsu), the primordial Buddha of the *Lotus Sūtra* was identified with Vairocana or Mahāvairocana, the cosmic Buddha pervading everywhere, whose form is all things, whose voice is all sounds, and whose mind is all thoughts. In Tendai ORIGINAL ENLIGHTENMENT (HONGAKU) doctrine, the primordial Buddha is said to be the "triple body that is unproduced" (*musa sanjin*), that is, innate originally. Here, the Buddha's enlightenment in the remote past is taken as a metaphor for the original enlightenment that is the beginningless true aspect of all things.

NICHIREN (1222–1282), founder of the school that would eventually bear his name, regarded the Buddha of the origin teaching as the only true Buddha, of whom all other buddhas are but manifestations. The practitioner is identified with this Buddha in the act of embracing faith in the *Lotus Sūtra* and chanting its title or DAIMOKU, *Namu Myōhō-renge-kyō.*

The *Lotus Sūtra* and devotional practices

Following its introduction to China, numerous commentaries were written on the *Lotus Sūtra* by Buddhist scholars of many schools, stimulating doctrinal debate. The one vehicle doctrine played a key role in the Chinese scholastic project of establishing comprehensive classificatory systems (*panjiao*) that attempted to order the diverse Buddhist teachings transmitted from India and Central Asia into a coherent whole. Yet, while valued in elite circles, such doctrinal developments were probably less influential in the spread of faith in the *Lotus Sūtra* than were a range of devotional practices performed by both clerics and laypeople across social levels. These forms of *Lotus* practice transcended distinctions of school or sect and exerted a profound impact on the Buddhist ritual and devotional culture of East Asia.

Lotus Sūtra devotion in its Indic context belonged to a distinctive Mahāyāna "cult of the book," in which sūtras were enshrined and revered in a manner analogous to the worship of Buddha relics enshrined in stūpas. The sūtra itself exhorts its devotees to text-centered acts of reverence, such as the "five practices" of receiving and keeping, reading, reciting from memory, teaching, and transcribing the *Lotus Sūtra.* As with other Mahāyāna sūtras, *Lotus Sūtra* devotion in East Asia has often centered around copying, worshipping, and preaching the sūtra. Such devotional acts might be sponsored officially, by the court, or undertaken privately. The merit thought to result was dedicated toward a number of aims, including realization of enlightenment; birth in a buddha's pure land or other ideal realm; eradication of sins; the postmortem welfare of deceased relatives; and this-worldly benefits, including the peace and stability of the country, long life, recovery from illness, and prevention of calamity. Tales compiled in both China and Japan extol the wondrous blessings obtained by monks, nuns, ascetics, and ordinary lay people who carried out such practices.

Copying the *Lotus Sūtra* might be undertaken by an individual or by a religious association formed for the purpose, or a professional calligrapher might be commissioned. Sūtra copying was seen as a virtuous deed whose merit might be dedicated toward one's own salvation or that of deceased family members. In China, *Lotus Sūtra* copying flourished particularly in the Sui (589–618) and Tang (618–907) dynasties. In Japan, the *Lotus* was the sūtra most frequently copied in the Heian period (794–1185). Some transcriptions commissioned by wealthy patrons were copied on dark blue paper using gold or silver ink. Especially striking are surviving copies in which each of the *Lotus Sūtra*'s 69,384 characters has been drawn seated on a lotus pedestal or surrounded by a stūpa, thereby expressing the conviction that "each character of the *Lotus* is a living buddha." The *Lotus Sūtra* also numbered among those scriptures most often preserved in anticipation of the era of decline known as the Final Dharma age (Chinese, *mofa;* Japanese, *mappō*). In China, it was sometimes inscribed on stone slabs on hillsides, or in Japan, copied and buried in bronze cylinders to await the advent of MAITREYA, the next buddha. Vernacular sermons on the *Lotus,* sometimes with accompanying illustrations, made its message broadly accessible, as did popular songs, poems, and artistic representations. One of the most widespread visual images of *Lotus* is that of the jeweled stūpa, sometimes represented by the two buddhas, Śākyamuni and Prabhūtaratna, seated together. This scene is depicted in cave paintings, on steles, in MAṆḌALAS, and by small votive stūpas.

The *Lotus* has also been associated with devotion to, or emulation of, specific bodhisattvas described in its later chapters. Chapter twenty-three describes how a bodhisattva called "Beheld with Joy by all Living Beings" steeps his body in perfumed oils and then burns it in offering to the Buddha and the sūtra. This would become the textual basis for SELF-IMMOLATION, one of many forms of "discarding the body" undertaken by Buddhist ascetics. This controversial practice has been carried out as an act of renunciation, as an offering to the dharma, to achieve birth in a pure land, and as a form of protest when Buddhism has faced persecution. A broader influence on East Asian Buddhism as a whole stems from chapter twenty-five, which describes how the bodhisattva Avalokiteśvara (Guanyin, Kwan-ŭm, Kannon) will respond compassionately to those who call upon his aid. This chapter eventually circulated as an independent sūtra and helped promote devotion to Avalokiteśvara, which flourishes to this day. Descriptions in this chapter of the bodhisattva rescuing devotees from fire, flood, bandits, and other dangers were frequent subjects of *Lotus*-related painting.

An illuminated *Lotus Sūtra*. (Japanese, Heian period, 794–1185.) © Christie's Images/Corbis. Reproduced by permission.

The *Lotus Sūtra* and specific schools

While reverence for the *Lotus Sūtra* in East Asia has transcended all sectarian divisions, it has also come to be associated with two specific traditions: the Tiantai school, which spread in China, Korea, and Japan; and also the NICHIREN SCHOOL, which emerged in thirteenth-century Japan. The *Lotus*-related practices of these schools were influenced by, and in turn helped to shape, broader traditions of *Lotus* devotion.

The Tiantai/Tendai tradition. Zhiyi, the Tiantai founder, produced extensive and influential commentaries on the *Lotus*: the *Fahua xuanyi* (profound meaning of the *Lotus*), elucidating what he saw as the sūtra's underlying principles, and the *Fahua wenju* (words and phrases of the *Lotus*), a line-by-line exegesis. The *Lotus* also provided him with a textual foundation for his conceptual innovations. A passage in Kumārajīva's translation of chapter two sets forth the "ten suchlikes" (*shirushi;* Japanese, *jūnyoze*) as the "true aspect of the dharmas" (*zhufa shixiang;* Japanese, *shohō jissō*) that only buddhas can understand. By punctuating the passage in three different ways, Zhiyi derived the threefold truth of emptiness, conventional existence, and the middle, which informs the structure of his integrated system of doctrine and meditation. The same passage also provided him with a textual basis for "the single thought-moment being three thousand realms" (*yinian sanqian, ichinen sanzen*), his architectonic vision of the entire universe as an interpenetrating whole in which mind and concrete actualities are nondual and all dharmas are mutually inclusive. This is the "realm of the inconceivable," the first of ten modes of meditation set forth in his treatise on meditation, MOHE ZHIGUAN (*Great Calming and Contemplation*).

Though Zhiyi valued the *Lotus* as the "subtle" teaching that alone reveals the perfect interfusion of the three truths, he held that other sūtras also contain "subtle" elements; their particular admixtures of partial or provisional teachings were necessary responses to differences in human capacity and did not, in his view, reflect a rigid hierarchy of sūtras. However, the Tiantai systematizer and sixth patriarch ZHANRAN (711–782), who lived in a time of increased sectarian consciousness and rivalry with other schools, organized the sūtras into a hierarchy of "five periods and eight teachings," with the *Lotus Sūtra* at the apex. Zhanran's classification was instrumental in establishing the sūtra's reputation as supreme among the Buddha's teachings.

New approaches to the *Lotus Sūtra* developed in Japanese Tendai, differentiating it from the Tiantai of the Asian mainland. Most notable was the flowering of a distinctive Tendai system of tantric Buddhism, or Taimitsu. Taimitsu theoreticians such as ENNIN (794–864), Enchin (814–891), and Annen (841–?) reinterpreted the *Lotus Sūtra* as a tantric scripture and equated the Śākyamuni Buddha of the "origin teaching" with Vairocana or Mahāvairocana, the cosmic Buddha of the tantric teachings who is without beginning or end and who pervades everywhere. The *Lotus* also served as a basis for Taimitsu ritual, for example, in the "Lotus rite" (*Hokke hō*), performed to eradicate sin, build merit, and realize awakening. The MAṆḌALA used in this rite depicts Śākyamuni and Prabhūtaratna seated together in its central court, as they appeared in the jeweled stūpa, and may have influenced the form of Nichiren's maṇḍala. SAICHŌ (767–822), founder of Japanese Tendai, had already identified the *Lotus Sūtra* with the doctrine of "realizing buddhahood with this very body" (*sokushin jōbutsu*). Taimitsu thought and practice further promoted understandings of the *Lotus* as enabling the direct realization of enlightenment.

Another distinctive *Lotus*-based development of Japanese Tendai was the doctrine of original enlightenment, which dominated Tendai doctrinal studies from approximately the eleventh through seventeenth centuries. Though deeply colored by the assumptions of tantric Buddhism, original enlightenment doctrine was classified by its producers as "exoteric," in contrast to esoteric transmissions of tantric ritual. Original enlightenment thought might be seen as an attempt to reinterpret traditional Tiantai/Tendai doctrines and texts—including the works of Zhiyi and Zhanran, standard debate topics, and even the *Lotus Sūtra* itself—from the perspective that enlightenment is not "attained" but innate from the outset.

Largely through the medium of the Tiantai/Tendai tradition, both on the continent and in Japan, the *Lotus Sūtra* became associated with PURE LAND BUDDHISM. Zhiyi had incorporated Pure Land elements into the constantly walking samādhi, the second of the "four kinds of samādhi" in his system of meditation. Here the practitioner circumambulates an altar to AMITĀBHA Buddha while at the same time visualizing Amitābha's marks and qualities, eventually gaining insight into the nonduality of the visualized Buddha and the visualizing mind. During the Song dynasty (960–1279), Tiantai monks took the lead in promoting societies for Pure Land practice, including both monastics and LAITY. In Japan during the Heian period, an especially close connection existed between the *Lotus Sūtra* and Pure Land Buddhism, exemplified on Mount Hiei, the great Tendai monastic center, where monks performed the *Lotus* samādhi in the morning and chanted the *Amitābha Sūtra* in the evening. Mount Hiei was also the first site in Japan for practice of the "continuous *nenbutsu*," said to have been introduced from Mount Wutai in China by Saichō's disciple Ennin. This was a ritual form of contemplating Amitābha and intoning the *Amitābha Sūtra* with the aim of eradicating sin and achieving birth in Amitābha's Pure Land, which became incorporated into Tendai practices. *Lotus*-Pure Land associations flourished in the broader society as well, and many people recited and copied the *Lotus Sūtra* with the aspiration of achieving birth in Amitābha's paradise. Not until the Kamakura period (1185–1333), with the advent of teachers like HŌNEN (1133–1212) and Nichiren, would strongly exclusivist forms of both *Lotus* and Pure Land devotion emerge.

Nichiren and modern *Lotus*-based movements. Nichiren developed a strongly exclusivist reading of the *Lotus* as the only true teaching. He believed that the Buddha had intended this sūtra specifically for the Final Dharma age, in which he and his contemporaries believed they were living. Other, provisional sūtras, Nichiren insisted, could no longer lead to buddhahood in this benighted era. Accordingly, he stressed the practice of *shakubuku*, or teaching the dharma by directly rebuking attachment to provisional teachings. He saw his work of spreading faith in the *Lotus* as preparing the way for Bodhisattva Superior Conduct (*Viśiṣṭacāritra*; Japanese, *Jōgyō*), the leader of the bodhisattvas who are Śākyamuni's original disciples, taught by him since his enlightenment in the inconceivably distant past, as described in the origin teaching. In chapter fifteen, these bodhisattvas emerge from beneath the earth and vow to spread the *Lotus* after Śākyamuni's nirvāṇa. Much of the later Nichiren tradition would identify Nichiren as an actual manifestation of Bodhisattva Superior Conduct.

The *Lotus Sūtra* foretells grave trials that its devotees will face in upholding it in an evil age after the Buddha's nirvāṇa. Historically, these passages probably reflect opposition from the Buddhist establishment encountered by the particular Mahāyāna community that compiled the sūtra. Nichiren, however, saw these predictions as being borne out in the trials and persecutions he himself faced, and he read the *Lotus* as a work of prophecy being fulfilled by himself and his disciples. He termed this "reading with the body" (*shikidoku*), meaning to practice the *Lotus* not only by verbally reciting it and mentally believing in its teachings, but also by gladly undergoing in one's own person the harsh trials that the sūtra says its devotees in the latter age must endure.

By the spread of exclusive faith in the *Lotus,* Nichiren taught, the buddha land could be realized in this present world. Especially in the twentieth century, this goal inspired a number of modern and contemporary *Lotus*- or Nichiren-based movements, which have assimilated Nichiren's vision of transforming this world into a buddha land to a range of political and humanitarian agendas. These groups include the small ascetic monastic order Nipponzan Myōhōji, which is committed to the antinuclear movement and to absolute nonviolence, as well as the large lay movements Risshō Kōsei Kai and SŌKA GAKKAI, which engage in various local and international peace, educational, and relief projects.

See also: **Chanting and Liturgy; Folk Religion: An Overview; Gender; Scripture**

Bibliography

Bielefeldt, Carl. "The One Vehicle and the Three Jewels: On Japanese Sectarianism and Some Ecumenical Alternatives." *Buddhist-Christian Studies* 10 (1990): 5–16.

Davidson, J. Leroy. *The Lotus Sutra in Chinese Art: A Study in Buddhist Art to the Year 1000.* New Haven, CT: Yale University Press, 1954.

Dykstra, Yoshiko K. *Miraculous Tales of the Lotus Sutra from Ancient Japan: The* Dainihonkoku Hokekyōkenki *of Priest Chingen.* Osaka: Intercultural Research Institute, Kansai University of Foreign Studies, 1983.

Fujita, Kotatsu. "One Vehicle or Three?," tr. Leon Hurvitz. *Journal of Indian Philosophy* 3 (1975): 79–166.

Groner, Paul. *Saichō: The Establishment of the Japanese Tendai School* (1984). Reprint, Honolulu: University of Hawaii Press, 2000.

Groner, Paul. *Ryōgen and Mount Hiei: Japanese Tendai in the Tenth Century.* Honolulu: University of Hawaii Press, 2002.

Hubbard, Jamie. "Buddhist-Buddhist Dialogue? The *Lotus Sutra* and the Polemic of Accommodation." *Buddhist-Christian Studies* 15 (1995): 119–136.

Hurvitz, Leon. "The Lotus Sūtra in East Asia: A Review of *Hokke shisō.*" *Monumenta Serica* 29 (1970–1971): 697–762.

Hurvitz, Leon, trans. *Scripture of the Lotus Blossom of the Fine Dharma.* New York: Columbia University Press, 1976.

Pye, Michael. *Skilful Means: A Concept in Mahayana Buddhism.* London: Duckworth, 1978.

Reeves, Gene, ed. *A Buddhist Kaleidoscope: Essays on the Lotus Sutra.* Tokyo: Kosei, 2002.

Schopen, Gregory. "The Phrase *'sa pṛthivīpradeśaś caitabhūto bhavet'* in the *Vajracchedikā*: Notes on the Cult of the Book in Mahāyāna." *Indo-Iranian Journal* 17, nos. 3–4 (1975): 147–181.

Stevenson, Daniel B. "The Four Kinds of Samādhi in Early T'ien-t'ai Buddhism." In *Traditions of Meditation in Chinese Buddhism,* ed. Peter N. Gregory. Honolulu: University of Hawaii Press, 1986.

Stevenson, Daniel B. "Tales of the Lotus Sutra." In *Buddhism in Practice,* ed. Donald S. Lopez, Jr. Princeton, NJ: Princeton University Press, 1995.

Swanson, Paul L., ed. *Tendai Buddhism in Japan.* Special issue of *Japanese Journal of Religious Studies* 14, nos. 2–3 (1987).

Swanson, Paul L. *Foundations of T'ien-t'ai Philosophy: The Flowering of the Two Truths Theory in Chinese Buddhism.* Berkeley, CA: Asian Humanities Press, 1989.

Tamura, Yoshirō, and Kurata, Bunsaku, eds. *Art of the Lotus Sūtra: Japanese Masterpieces,* tr. Edna B. Crawford. Tokyo: Kosei, 1987.

Tanabe, George J., Jr., and Tanabe, Willa Jane, eds. *The Lotus Sutra in Japanese Culture.* Honolulu: University of Hawaii Press, 1988.

Tanabe, Willa J. *Paintings of the Lotus Sutra.* New York and Tokyo: Weatherhill, 1988.

Watson, Burton, trans. *The Lotus Sutra.* New York: Columbia University Press, 1993.

Yuyama, Akira. *A Bibliography of the Sanskrit Texts of the Saddharmapuṇḍarikasūtra.* Canberra: Centre of Oriental Studies and Australian National University Press, 1970.

Ziporyn, Brook. *Evil and/or/as the Good: Omnicentrism, Intersubjectivity, and Value Paradox in Tiantai Buddhist Thought.* Cambridge, MA: Harvard University Press, 2000.

JACQUELINE I. STONE